Texas

Nick Selby
Julie Fanselow
Ryan Ver Berkmoes

LONELY PLANET PUBLICATIONS
Melbourne · Oakland · London · Paris

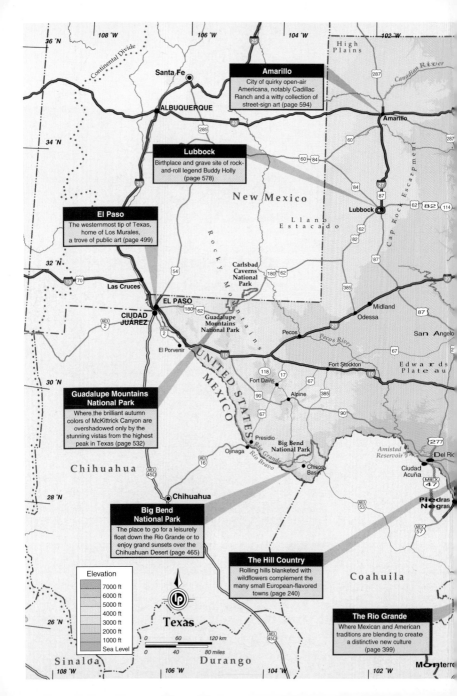

Amarillo
City of quirky open-air Americana, notably Cadillac Ranch and a witty collection of street-sign art (page 594)

Lubbock
Birthplace and grave site of rock-and-roll legend Buddy Holly (page 578)

El Paso
The westernmost tip of Texas, home of Los Murales, a trove of public art (page 499)

Guadalupe Mountains National Park
Where the brilliant autumn colors of McKittrick Canyon are overshadowed only by the stunning vistas from the highest peak in Texas (page 532)

Big Bend National Park
The place to go for a leisurely float down the Rio Grande or to enjoy grand sunsets over the Chihuahuan Desert (page 465)

The Hill Country
Rolling hills blanketed with wildflowers complement the many small European-flavored towns (page 240)

The Rio Grande
Where Mexican and American traditions are blending to create a distinctive new culture (page 399)

Elevation
7000 ft
6000 ft
5000 ft
4000 ft
3000 ft
2000 ft
1000 ft
Sea Level

Texas

0   60   120 km
0   40   80 miles

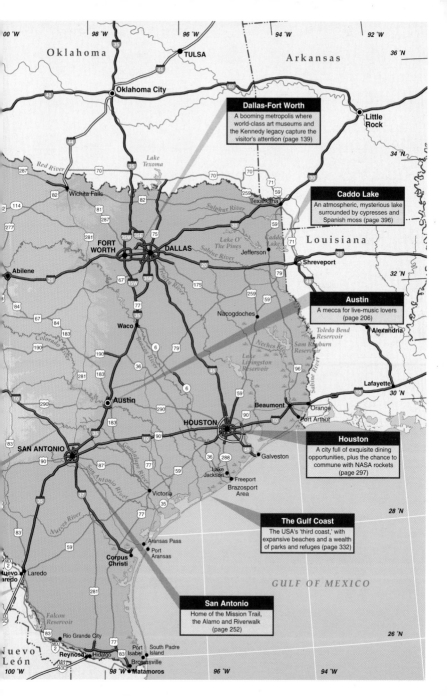

Dallas-Fort Worth

A booming metropolis where world-class art museums and the Kennedy legacy capture the visitor's attention (page 139)

Caddo Lake

An atmospheric, mysterious lake surrounded by cypresses and Spanish moss (page 396)

Austin

A mecca for live-music lovers (page 206)

Houston

A city full of exquisite dining opportunities, plus the chance to commune with NASA rockets (page 297)

The Gulf Coast

The USA's 'third coast,' with expansive beaches and a wealth of parks and refuges (page 332)

San Antonio

Home of the Mission Trail, the Alamo and Riverwalk (page 252)

Texas
1st edition – July 1999

Published by
Lonely Planet Publications Pty Ltd A.C.N. 005 607 983
192 Burwood Rd, Hawthorn, Victoria 3122, Australia

Lonely Planet Offices
Australia PO Box 617, Hawthorn, Victoria 3122
USA 150 Linden St, Oakland, CA 94607
UK 10a Spring Place, London NW5 3BH
France 1 rue du Dahomey, 75011 Paris

Photographs
John Elk III, Julie Fanselow, Laurence Parent, Nick Selby, Ryan Ver
Berkmoes, Tony Wheeler

The *Dallas Times Herald* headline on page 149 © *Dallas Morning News*
courtesy of the Sixth Floor Museum at Dealey Plaza

Some of the images in this guide are available for licensing from
Lonely Planet Images.
email: lpi@lonelyplanet.com.au

Front cover photograph
Texas longhorn (John Elk III)

ISBN 0 86442 571 6

text & maps © Lonely Planet 1999
photos © photographers as indicated 1999

Printed by The Bookmaker International Ltd
Printed in China

All rights reserved. No part of this publication may be reproduced,
stored in a retrieval system or transmitted in any form by any means,
electronic, mechanical, photocopying, recording or otherwise, except
brief extracts for the purpose of review, without the written permission of the publisher and copyright owner.

**Although the authors
and Lonely Planet try
to make the informa-
tion as accurate as
possible, we accept no
responsibility for any
loss, injury or incon-
venience sustained by
anyone using this
book.**

Contents – Text

GULF COAST   332

NORTHEAST TEXAS   384

RIO GRANDE   399

THE BIG BEND   465

WEST TEXAS   499

PANHANDLE PLAINS   555

LANGUAGE   611

TOLL-FREE NUMBERS   613

INDEX   632

Contents – Maps

TEXAS

DALLAS-FORT WORTH

SOUTH CENTRAL TEXAS

HOUSTON

GULF COAST

NORTHEAST TEXAS

RIO GRANDE

THE BIG BEND

WEST TEXAS

PANHANDLE PLAINS

MAP LEGEND

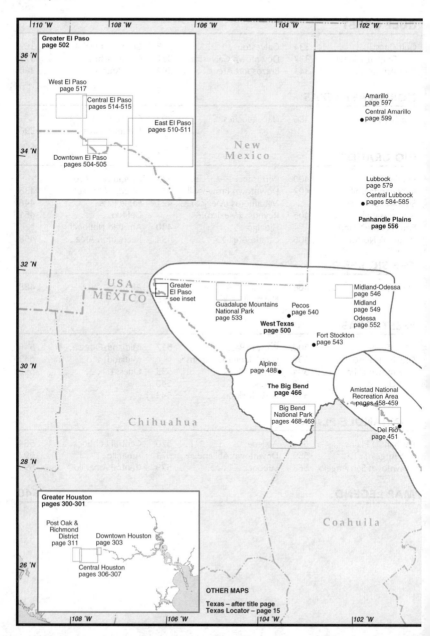

Greater El Paso
page 502

West El Paso
page 517

Central El Paso
pages 514-515

East El Paso
pages 510-511

Downtown El Paso
pages 504-505

New
Mexico

Amarillo
page 597

Central Amarillo
page 599

Lubbock
page 579

Central Lubbock
pages 584-585

Panhandle Plains
page 556

USA
MEXICO

Greater
El Paso
see inset

Guadalupe Mountains
National Park
page 533

Pecos
page 540

West Texas
page 500

Fort Stockton
page 543

Midland-Odessa
page 546

Midland
page 549

Odessa
page 552

Alpine
page 488

The Big Bend
page 466

Amistad National
Recreation Area
pages 458-459

Del Rio
page 451

Chihuahua

Big Bend
National Park
pages 468-469

Coahuila

Greater Houston
pages 300-301

Post Oak &
Richmond
District
page 311

Downtown Houston
page 303

Central Houston
pages 306-307

OTHER MAPS

Texas – after title page
Texas Locator – page 15

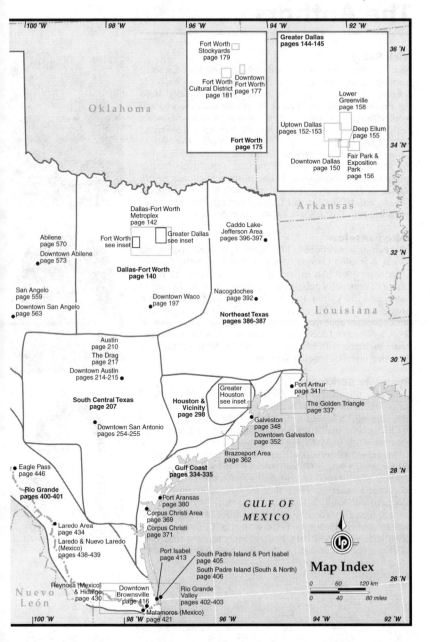

Fort Worth
Stockyards
page 179

Fort Worth
Cultural District
page 181

Downtown
Fort Worth
page 177

Fort Worth
page 175

Greater Dallas
pages 144-145

Lower
Greenville
page 158

Uptown Dallas
pages 152-153

Deep Ellum
page 155

Downtown Dallas
page 150

Fair Park &
Exposition
Park
page 156

Oklahoma

Dallas-Fort Worth
Metroplex
page 142

Fort Worth
see inset

Greater Dallas
see inset

Caddo Lake-
Jefferson Area
pages 396-397

Arkansas

Abilene
page 570

Downtown Abilene
page 573

Dallas-Fort Worth
page 140

San Angelo
page 559

Downtown San Angelo
page 563

Downtown Waco
page 197

Nacogdoches
page 392

Louisiana

Northeast Texas
pages 386-387

Austin
page 210

The Drag
page 217

Downtown Austin
pages 214-215

South Central Texas
page 207

Houston &
Vicinity
page 298

Greater
Houston
see inset

Port Arthur
page 341

The Golden Triangle
page 337

Galveston
page 348

Downtown Galveston
page 352

Downtown San Antonio
pages 254-255

Brazosport Area
page 362

Eagle Pass
page 446

Rio Grande
pages 400-401

Gulf Coast
pages 334-335

Port Aransas
page 380

Corpus Christi Area
page 369

Corpus Christi
page 371

GULF OF
MEXICO

Laredo Area
page 434

Laredo & Nuevo Laredo
(Mexico)
pages 438-439

Port Isabel
page 413

South Padre Island & Port Isabel
page 405

South Padre Island (South & North)
page 406

Map Index

0   60   120 km

0   40   80 miles

Reynosa (Mexico)
& Hidalgo
page 430

Downtown
Brownsville
page 416

Rio Grande
Valley
pages 402-403

Nuevo
León

Matamoros (Mexico)
page 421

The Authors

Nick Selby

Nick Selby was born and raised in New York City. Escaping from sound engineering (he recorded rap 'music' at Walker & Six Recording and Chung King in New York, connected *Mofo the Psychic Gorilla* for Penn & Teller's Broadway show, and worked 'mixing' 'music' on *As the World Turns* and *Guiding Light*, as well as sound for CBS Sports), Nick moved to Poland in 1990 and to Russia in 1991, where he wrote *The Visitor's Guide to the New St Petersburg*. Since then he has been traveling and working for Lonely Planet on a positively bizarre group of destinations, contributing to the guidebooks *Brazil*, *Russia*, *St Petersburg*, *Germany* and, with his wife, Corinna, *Florida* and *Miami*. He and Corinna recently left their enormous house in Tarifa, Spain, to live in Amsterdam.

Julie Fanselow

Julie Fanselow was born in Illinois, raised in Pennsylvania and educated at Ohio University, but she has lived in the Western USA since 1989. An experienced road warrior, she is the author of previously published guidebooks covering Idaho, the Lewis and Clark Trail and the Oregon Trail; this is her first project for Lonely Planet. Julie also writes for magazines, and her byline has appeared in *American Heritage*, *Entertainment Weekly*, *Sunset* and dozens of other publications. She makes her home in Idaho with her husband, Bruce Whiting, and their daughter, Natalie Fanselow Whiting.

Ryan Ver Berkmoes

Ryan grew up in Santa Cruz, California, which he left at age 17 for college in the Midwest because he was too young and naive to realize what a beautiful place Santa Cruz is. His first job was in Chicago at a small muckraking publication where he had the impressive title of Managing Editor because he was second on a two-person editorial staff and the first person was called Editor. After a year of 60-hour weeks, Ryan took his first trip to Europe, which lasted seven months and confirmed his long-suspected wanderlust. Since then his byline has appeared in scores of publications, and he has covered everything from wars to bars. He definitely prefers the latter. Among his projects for Lonely Planet, he is the author of *Chicago*, about a town with very good bars. He and his journalist wife, Sara Marley, reside in London, another town with very good bars.

FROM THE AUTHORS

Nick Selby Ryan and Julie – thanks for great stuff! A billion thanks to the folks in Texas whose help made my coverage possible, including Kim Baker at the TDED and tourist offices in Waco, Austin, San Antonio and the Hill Country. *Muchas gracias* Stephen Este, Mary Matese, Michael Bertin, Shannon Robertson, Amy Seagrove and Leslie Martine. Thanks especially to Pableaux Johnson, food critic extraordinaire, for his contributions on Texas food.

Thanks to Corinna for map and history help, Angela Wilson, Bernard Goldstein, Antony Sharman for computer miracles, and Lonely Planet authors John Noble and Susan Forsyth for invaluable assistance. Special thanks to Christina, Axel, Alex and Heinrich Guddas, and to Spijk, Butch and Olivia.

Julie Fanselow Thanks to coordinating author Nick Selby for the pep talks and sage advice, and to coauthor Ryan Ver Berkmoes for the Shiner Bocks in Houston. Thanks to Caroline Liou for hiring me on, and a special thanks to Tom Brosnahan for putting in a good word for me. From Lonely Planet Oakland, I'd also like to thank Kate Hoffman; editors Jacqueline Volin, Michele Posner, Laura Harger and Valerie Perry; fact-checker JoAnne Cabello; cartographers Alex Guilbert, Kimberly Moses, Eric Thomsen and Guphy; illustrator Hayden Foell; and designers Wendy Yanagihara and Emily Douglas.

Kimberley Baker from the Texas tourism office was a great help in paving the way. En route I received assistance and advice from countless people, but these folks stand out: Ana Maria Arizpe, Ted Aston, Mary Ellen Astudillo, Peggy Boone, David Cooper, Julie Driver, Elise Eustace, Kelly Fenstermaker, Buddy Garza, James Glendinning, Dan Heyman, John Hintz, Kay Irby, Gary and Susie Johnson, Janis Keasler, Mark Kimball, Susan Cottle Leonard, Shura Lindgren, Karen Marasco, Sondra Martinez, Jutta Matalka, Richard McCamant, Justin McGeath, Eric Miller, Ed Nemec, Joe Nephan, Brandy Owen, Kay Peck, Jeff Renfro, Diane Roque, Vince Scolaro, Greg Staley, Genora Young and Kacey Young.

Since 1st edition guidebook research doesn't mix well with parenting, Bruce and I relied on family and friends to keep Natalie happy and cared for in my absence. My father, Byron Fanselow, flew out from Pennsylvania to lend a hand; thanks also go to the staff of Kids' Club; to the LaMure, Barlow, Fothergill, Hom, Hall and Anderson-Adkins families; and to April Crnich. Special thanks to my friend Rebecca Hom and to Dr Tim Coiner, who helped literally keep body and soul together during this project.

To my rootin'-tootin' cowgirl, Natalie, I say thanks for hanging in there. And to my husband, Bruce, who was unsparing in his help, his encouragement and his timely hugs and back rubs, I say – once again – thanks for everything. I look forward to taking both of you down the Rio Grande, through the Caprock Canyons and to a Rangers game sometime.

Ryan Ver Berkmoes I first want to thank Nick Selby for somehow getting me involved in this project. Many thanks to Kim Baker, and to the following: Brian Carusella, Mark Fowler and JJ Watson at Half Price Books in Houston, who had a vigorous intellectual debate about Houston's best restaurants; Lauri and Scott Littlewood, D Day (the city's best DJ), Anita Clark and David Comerota, also all in Houston; and elsewhere in Texas, Cathy Henry of King Ranch, who told me where to step; Nancy Millar; Jeff Johnston; Cindy DuBois; and Carole Lawson. Francisco Tamez gave me a wonderful introduction to Los Dos Laredos that was hard to remember the next day. He was assisted in part by Memo Trevino. Thanks also to Faye Liss, a genius at putting Port Arthur and its amorous alligators on the map; Danny Sessum, who runs a damn good museum and who knows how to punch a mosquito; Jacqueline Volin, for allowing herself to be force-fed all that cheesecake; and Sandy Feet and Amazin' Walter, whose name says it all.

Finally, thanks and love to Sara Marley, who sent me emails reminding me I had a good place to go after Texas.

This Book

For this 1st edition of *Texas*, Nick Selby coordinated the project and wrote Facts about Texas; parts of Facts for the Visitor, Activities and Getting There & Away; Getting Around; Waco and Around Waco (in the Dallas-Fort Worth chapter); and South Central Texas. Julie Fanselow wrote parts of Facts for the Visitor, Activities and Getting There & Away; all of Dallas-Fort Worth (except Waco and Around Waco), the Big Bend, West Texas and Panhandle Plains; and the Rio Grande chapter from Eagle Pass on. Ryan Ver Berkmoes wrote parts of Activities; all of Houston, the Gulf Coast, and Northeast Texas; and the Rio Grande chapter from the Rio Grande Valley through Around Laredo.

FROM THE PUBLISHER

Texas is a product of Lonely Planet's US office. Jacqueline Volin, Michele Posner, Laura Harger and Valerie Perry edited it. Kate Hoffman stood by with sound advice and moral support, both much appreciated. JoAnne Cabello, Joslyn Leve, Paige Penland and Michele fact-checked the book, and Tara Duggan, Nancy Keller and Joslyn proofread it. Jacqueline indexed the book. Kimberly Moses, Eric Thomsen, Guphy, Margaret Livingston, Tracey Croom, Patrick Huerta, Andy Rebold, Chris Whinihan, Mary Hagemann, Colin Bishop, Monica Lepe, Dion Good and Bart Wright created the maps, under the auspices of Alex Guilbert and Amy Dennis. Hayden Foell, Wendy Yanagihara, Lara Sox Harrison, Hugh D'Andrade, Jim Swanson, John Fadeff and Mark Butler drew the illustrations. Wendy and Emily Douglas designed the book, with help from Scott Summers and Margaret Livingston. Rini Keagy designed the cover.

Foreword

ABOUT LONELY PLANET GUIDEBOOKS

The story begins with a classic travel adventure: Tony and Maureen Wheeler's 1972 journey across Europe and Asia to Australia. Useful information about the overland trail did not exist at that time, so Tony and Maureen published the first Lonely Planet guidebook to meet a growing need.

From a kitchen table, then from a tiny office in Melbourne (Australia), Lonely Planet has become the largest independent travel publisher in the world, an international company with offices in Melbourne, Oakland (USA), London (UK) and Paris (France).

Today Lonely Planet guidebooks cover the globe. There is an ever-growing list of books, and there's information in a variety of forms and media. Some things haven't changed. The main aim is still to help make it possible for adventurous travelers to get out there – to explore and better understand the world.

At Lonely Planet we believe travelers can make a positive contribution to the countries they visit – if they respect their host communities and spend their money wisely. Since 1986 a percentage of the income from each book has been donated to aid projects and human-rights campaigns.

Updates Lonely Planet thoroughly updates each guidebook as often as possible. This usually means there are around two years between editions, although for more unusual or more stable destinations the gap can be longer. Check the imprint page (following the color map at the beginning of the book) for publication dates.

Between editions, up-to-date information is available in two free newsletters – the paper *Planet Talk* and email *Comet* (to subscribe, contact any Lonely Planet office) – and on our website at www.lonelyplanet.com. The *Upgrades* section of the website covers a number of important and volatile destinations and is regularly updated by Lonely Planet authors. *Scoop* covers news and current affairs relevant to travelers. And, lastly, the *Thorn Tree* bulletin board and *Postcards* section of the site carry unverified, but fascinating, reports from travelers.

Correspondence The process of creating new editions begins with the letters, postcards and emails received from travelers. This correspondence often includes suggestions, criticisms and comments about the current editions. Interesting excerpts are immediately passed on via newsletters and the website, and everything goes to our authors to be verified when they're researching on the road. We're keen to get more feedback from organizations or individuals who represent communities visited by travelers.

Lonely Planet gathers information for everyone who's curious about the planet – and especially for those who explore it firsthand. Through guidebooks, phrasebooks, activity guides, maps, literature, newsletters, image library, TV series and website, we act as an information exchange for a worldwide community of travelers.

Research Authors aim to gather sufficient practical information to enable travelers to make informed choices and to make the mechanics of a journey run smoothly. They also research historical and cultural background to help enrich the travel experience and allow travelers to understand and respond appropriately to cultural and environmental issues.

Authors don't stay in every hotel because that would mean spending a couple of months in each medium-size city and, no, they don't eat at every restaurant because that would mean stretching belts beyond capacity. They do visit hotels and restaurants to check standards and prices, but feedback based on readers' direct experiences can be very helpful.

Many of our authors work undercover; others aren't so secretive. None of them accept freebies in exchange for positive write-ups. And none of our guidebooks contain any advertising.

Production Authors submit their raw manuscripts and maps to offices in Australia, the USA, the UK or France. Editors and cartographers – all experienced travelers themselves – then begin the process of assembling the pieces. When the book finally hits the shops, some things are already out of date, we start getting feedback from readers and the process begins again....

WARNING & REQUEST

Things change – prices go up, schedules change, good places go bad and bad places go bankrupt – nothing stays the same. So, if you find things better or worse, recently opened or long since closed, please tell us and help make the next edition even more accurate and useful. We genuinely value all the feedback we receive. Julie Young coordinates a well-traveled team that reads and acknowledges every letter, postcard and email and ensures that every morsel of information finds its way to the appropriate authors, editors and cartographers for verification.

Everyone who writes to us will find their name in the next edition of the appropriate guidebook. They will also receive the latest issue of *Planet Talk*, our quarterly printed newsletter, or *Comet*, our monthly email newsletter. Subscriptions to both newsletters are free. The very best contributions will be rewarded with a free guidebook.

Excerpts from your correspondence may appear in new editions of Lonely Planet guidebooks, the Lonely Planet website, *Planet Talk* or *Comet*, so please let us know if you *don't* want your letter published or your name acknowledged.

Send all correspondence to the Lonely Planet office closest to you:

Australia: PO Box 617, Hawthorn, Victoria 3122
USA: 150 Linden St, Oakland, CA 94607
UK: 10A Spring Place, London NW5 3BH
France: 1 rue du Dahomey, 75011 Paris

Or email us at: talk2us@lonelyplanet.com.au

For news, views and updates, see our website: www.lonelyplanet.com

HOW TO USE A LONELY PLANET GUIDEBOOK

The best way to use a Lonely Planet guidebook is any way you choose. At Lonely Planet, we believe the most memorable travel experiences are often those that are unexpected, and the finest discoveries are those you make yourself. Guidebooks are not intended to be used as if they provided a detailed set of infallible instructions!

Contents All Lonely Planet guidebooks follow the same format. The Facts about the Country chapters or sections give background information ranging from history to weather. Facts for the Visitor gives practical information on issues like visas and health. Getting There & Away gives a brief starting point for researching travel to and from the destination. Getting Around gives an overview of the transport options available when you arrive.

The peculiar demands of each destination determine how subsequent chapters are broken up, but some things remain constant. We always start with background, then proceed to sights, places to stay, places to eat, entertainment, getting there and away, and getting around information – in that order.

Heading Hierarchy Lonely Planet headings are used in a strict hierarchical structure that can be visualized as a set of Russian dolls. Each heading (and its following text) is encompassed by any preceding heading that is higher on the hierarchical ladder.

Entry Points We do not assume guidebooks will be read from beginning to end, but that people will dip into them. The traditional entry points are the list of contents and the index. In addition, however, some books have a complete list of maps and an index map illustrating map coverage.

There may also be a color map that shows highlights. These highlights are dealt with in greater detail later in the book, along with planning questions and suggested itineraries. Each chapter covering a geographical region usually begins with a locator map and another list of highlights. Once you find something of interest in a list of highlights, turn to the index.

Maps Maps play a crucial role in Lonely Planet guidebooks and include a huge amount of information. A legend is printed on the back page. We seek to have complete consistency between maps and text, and to have every important place in the text captured on a map. Map key numbers usually start in the top left corner.

Although inclusion in a guidebook usually implies a recommendation, we cannot list every good place. Exclusion does not necessarily imply criticism. In fact, there are a number of reasons why we might exclude a place – sometimes it is simply inappropriate to encourage an influx of travelers.

Introduction

Texas simultaneously epitomizes the greater USA and stands as an independent 'nation.' While much of the exported image of the American West comes from this immense state, Texas is far more complex than just cowboys and the open range. Even most Americans have an incorrect, incomplete or completely clichéd view of Texas, thinking of it as big, flat and mostly eventless – but punctuated by scattered pockets of riotous cowboys, saguaro cacti (which, actually, are found nowhere in Texas), gushing oil wells (which no longer exist) and enormous pickup trucks (100% accurate).

The reality is astoundingly different. From the blues bars of Austin to the restaurants of Houston to the natural splendor of the Big Bend region, Texas is full of surprises. It's a film capital and a mass-market music powerhouse. It's got rock climbing, kayaking, river running and backpacking opportunities, and there's even surfing off the mellow beaches of the Gulf Coast. And how many people realize that Texas is a wine-making region? (You read that right – some consider Texas wine, from producers such as Llano Estacado, some of the country's best). Texas' Celis beer is sold in Belgium – a place that doesn't exactly throw its doors open to newcomers when it comes to beer. And the food is just awesome.

Austin, the state capital, in addition to being the 'live-music capital of the USA,' is home to a literate, educated, computer-savvy and well-read populace. Texas' borders with Mexico have created an entire Tex-Mex subculture, which reflects the can-do attitude and creativity of the frontierspeople who

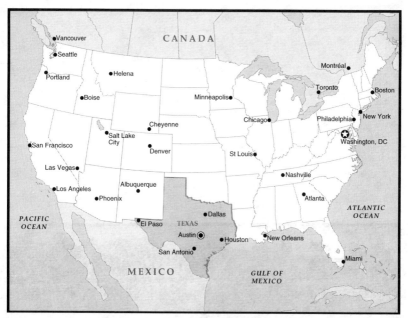

settled both sides of the border. Tejano music and Tex-Mex cuisine are unique regional hybrids that have spread northward from the border and can be enjoyed from Brownsville to San Angelo and beyond. Spanish is commonly spoken in many towns along the Rio Grande, and Mexican holidays such as Day of the Dead are celebrated throughout Texas with as much fanfare as the Fourth of July.

Unexpected, however, are the large groups of European settlers who have defined the flavor of central Texas. A drive through the Texas Hill Country reveals pockets of Czech bakeries, German breweries and French restaurants. *Wilkommen* appears on as many signs as 'Welcome' here.

Don't get alarmed. Texas *is* the big ol' place it's cracked up to be, and you can be sure you'll see the typical images you've come to expect from a state that reveres the Chevy Suburban, a vehicle more than 18 feet long, with a fuel tank that holds 41 gallons of gas. Big hair, big cars, big guys, big gals, big oil and really big cattle ranches really do abound; you *can* get on a high horse at a dude ranch and learn to lasso here. Just don't think that's all this state has to offer.

Facts about Texas

HISTORY
Early Inhabitants
Discounting beguiling theories of direct transpacific crossings from southeast Asia, it's now accepted that, barring a few Vikings in the north, the pre-Hispanic inhabitants of the Americas arrived from Siberia in waves of migrations between about 60,000 and 8000 BC, crossing land now submerged beneath the Bering Strait. The earliest known human traces in the US date from about 50,000 BC.

These tribes were highly mobile, and once they crossed into Alaska they moved south to warmer climates. The earliest evidence of human society in Texas, the Llano complex, lived on the Llano Estacado – staked plain – section of Texas and New Mexico, and hunted bison and a now extinct species of elephant. But because little written history exists of the various indigenous Texans or, indeed, of native peoples in the Americas, most information comes from the period after European settlement. But it seems clear that by the time the first Europeans arrived in the 16th century, several distinct groups of Indians had also settled in the region.

Native American tribes in Texas have been divided by anthropologists into four different cultural groups. The plains culture, which lived in the buffalo country of the West Texas plains, included Comanches, Kiowas, Lipan Apaches, Mescalero Apaches and Tonkawas; the Tampachoas, who lived in the vicinity of present-day El Paso, were called *Mansos* by the Spaniards. The southeastern culture, made up primarily of agrarian tribes that lived in the forests of eastern Texas, included the Caddo, Atakapa and Wichita communities. The western gulf culture centered around flat and gently rolling lands of the Gulf Coast and included Karankawas and Coahuiltecans. In far western and southwestern Texas, the Pueblo culture included the Jumanos and the Conchos. See the individual chapters for more information.

Spanish Exploration
In 1513, Juan Ponce de León, an explorer who sailed on Christopher Columbus' second voyage (1493) and took part in the Spanish siege of Puerto Rico (1506-7), sailed northwest from Spanish settlements in the Caribbean and ran smack into central Florida's Atlantic coastline, probably near present-day Cape Canaveral. Spanish development of Florida and battles with resident Calusa Indians raged on for several years. King Ferdinand V named Ponce de León governor of Florida in 1514, but he was unable to return there until 1521. Later that year he would die in Cuba as the result of a poison-arrow wound. De León's fate did not discourage the Spanish, who were convinced – based on experiences in South America and recent discoveries in Mexico – that the new land was one of untold mineral wealth.

In 1519 Alonzo Álvarez de Piñeda sailed along and mapped the coast of the Gulf of Mexico from Florida to Mexico, creating the first maps of present-day Texas. He stopped and camped at the mouth of the Rio Grande (which he called the 'river of palms'), and the following year Spain sent another expedition there under the command of Diego de Camargo. The Spanish planned a settlement along the Rio Grande, but in battles following disagreements between settlers and the Coahuiltecan Indians, 18 Spanish were killed; they withdrew and plans to settle Texas were postponed.

After Ponce de León's death in 1521, the Spanish made several other attempts to suss out just what the area encompassing much of the present-day southeastern USA had to offer.

Early Exploration
In 1528, the feckless Pánfilo de Narváez attempted to explore the region, bringing four ships, 400 men and 80 horses with him. Narváez' ships and men were separated, many among them killed. While exploring

inland, a large search party was lost. This group, which included Narváez's treasurer, Álvar Núñez Cabeza de Vaca, and his Moroccan-born slave, Estéban (most likely the first black person to explore the New World), built boats and attempted to sail across the Gulf of Mexico back to Florida or Cuba. They shipwrecked off modern-day Galveston Island, where they were seized by Karankawa Indians.

Cabeza de Vaca and a group of survivors lived among the Karankawas for more than seven years before gaining permission to leave; eventually they made it to the safety of Mexico City – see the Galveston section of the Gulf Coast chapter for more information. And although the Narváez expedition proved a disaster, Cabeza de Vaca did leave diaries documenting his experiences, providing crucial information about early exploration of the new continent (see Books in the Facts for the Visitor chapter for more information).

Coronado Visits Kansas

Stories told by Cabeza de Vaca and his men of the fierce Karankawas, their health and purported wealth led to another Spanish expedition to Texas in 1539, led by Franciscan friar Marcos de Niza (1495-1558) – Estéban attended as well. After Indian attacks wiped out half the expedition, including Estéban, the friar fled back to Mexico – after hastily claiming the ground he'd covered for Spain, of course.

In Mexico, Niza reported hearing of the fabulous golden 'Seven Cities of Cibolo' on his way. In 1540 he was chosen to act as guide to a new expedition, led by the wealthy 29-year-old Spanish explorer Francisco Vásquez de Coronado, which was to be the largest to date.

After defeating Zuñi Indians at the promised Seven Cities of Cibolo – actually gold-free Native American villages near present-day Zuni, New Mexico – it became clear to the explorers that they had been had. Ever optimistic, the expedition split into two groups; one, led by García López de Cárdenas, traveled west; the other, led by Coronado, traveled east.

Coronado's men ended up settling in the Rio Grande Valley in extreme southern Texas and, in typical Spanish-colonial fashion, enslaving the local Native Americans. One such slave, whom official Texas history books call 'El Turco,' told Coronado of another majestic golden city called 'Quivara.' And so goes the story of how total gullibility led to the first European exploration of the Texas interior: in 1541 Coronado scrambled, with all his remaining men and El Turco in tow, farther west and north into Texas, stumbling upon Palo Duro Canyon along the way, and eventually arriving at El Turco's famed 'Quivara' in modern-day Kansas.

Two years after setting out, after several wild goose chases and no discoveries of

---

Tasty Tidbits

Spanish accounts of the Karankawas, the Native Americans living on the Gulf Coast of Texas when the first Europeans arrived, describe frightening incidents.

The Karankawas painted their faces blue and yellow and pierced their nipples and lower lips with sharpened cane – an appearance made even more dramatic because they smeared themselves with mud and animal fats to repel mosquitoes.

Certainly – and as it turned out with good reason – they didn't extend the welcome mat to the various Spanish, French and British explorers and settlers.

Perhaps the most harrowing report came for the survivors of three Spanish galleons that ran aground on Padre Island in 1554. The Karankawas soon began attacking as the Spaniards tried to struggle south toward Mexico. In order to teach their enemies an unforgettable lesson, the Karankawas ate parts of the dead as well as parts of living prisoners. Only a few castaways lived to tell the tale.

Inevitably, the Karankawas were displaced from their ancestral lands and moved to West Texas, where they are thought to have died out.

massive gold reserves, Coronado and his surviving team made their way back to Mexico City.

The First Oil Discovery

While Coronado was busy walking, Hernando de Soto had been working in Florida since 1539. De Soto, the only member of this cast of characters to have actually discovered gold (though in Peru), began a long hunt for gold that would eventually take him on a 4000-mile journey through what is now Florida, Georgia, Alabama and Tennessee and along the Mississippi River, where he was killed in 1542.

Luis de Moscoso led de Soto's remaining men on a long exploration of present-day east Texas. He was frantically looking for gold – Indians would always tell him it was located somewhere else – but he never found any. What he and his men did notice was that the whole place was covered in this black stuff that was slimy, smelled bad and burned easily. They used the material to caulk ship seals and for other pedestrian applications, but apparently did not consider using it as fuel.

Spain Changes Tack

Busy with hauling treasures from Central and South America and the running of St Augustine and Pensacola, Florida, Spain lost interest in Texas almost completely for the next century or so. In 1601, Don Juan de Oñate, who had earlier led expeditions for gold and riches within New Mexico, sniffed around the region on his way to the area that was to become Kansas, but Indian battles and a decided lack of gold soon sent him packing for Mexico. With maps of east, west and south Texas and the Gulf Coast, Spain was happy to let the land sit for a while.

By 1600, Spain controlled Florida, all larger Caribbean islands (including Cuba), nearly all of present-day Mexico and Central America, and a strip of South America from present-day Venezuela to Argentina. Settlers in the new colonies sent hugely valuable cargoes of silver, gold and other riches back to Spain, where the crown was entitled to one-fifth of the bullion.

But Spanish policy toward the New World began to change in the late 16th and early 17th centuries. While the conquest of new lands was brutal, Spain's conquistadores considered it to have an economic, political and – more important (to hear them tell it) – moral objective: winning over new Christian souls.

By the mid-17th century, the Spaniards' tack was more 'please read this pamphlet' than 'take me to the gold.' The new order of the day was the construction of missions. Spanish missionaries established a series of missions and presidios (forts) throughout Florida and Texas and eventually clear across North America to California in an effort to convert the Native Americans to Christianity and, not incidentally, into Spanish subjects and taxpayers. More than 30 missions were constructed in Texas alone.

The missions at their best were fully self-reliant outposts in which missionaries taught local Native Americans Spanish, as well as European building and farming techniques. During the heyday of the missions, from 1745 to 1775, they became successful enough to attract the rather unpleasant attention of Apache and Comanche Indians – not big fans of Spanish settlements in their territory – who began a series of attacks that would eventually cripple the system.

The French Sniff Around

Meanwhile the French were also exploring North America. By 1682, René Robert Cavelier, Sieur de La Salle, became the first European to travel the Mississippi River from what is now Illinois to the Gulf of Mexico; he claimed this land for the French and called it Louisiana. Flushed with success, La Salle led another expedition in 1685, but was shipwrecked in Matagorda Bay on Texas' Gulf Coast. There he set up the ill-fated settlement of Fort St Louis (see the boxed text in the Gulf Coast chapter for a complete rundown on La Salle).

Despite the failure of Fort St Louis, the French laid claim to a piece of Texas, which hardly amused the Spanish. The Spanish immediately started planning a string of new missions to strengthen their position in Texas.

In 1690, construction of Spain's first mission in east Texas, Misión San Francisco de los Tejas, began. It was completed in 1691, failing only two years later – but not before the Spaniards had taken a corruption of the Caddo Indian word for friend, which they pronounced *tejas* ('TAY-has'), and found the name for the entire new territory.

Over the next 20 years, the Spanish continued to settle east Texas, but many of the missions fell to disease, incompetence, skirmishes with Indians and French troops, and other disasters. Nevertheless, they gave it the ol' college try with Misión Nuestro Padre San Francisco de los Tejas (1712), 12 miles east of the one built in 1690-91, and Misión Nuestra Señora de la Purísima Concepción, about 12 miles northeast of San Francisco de los Tejas, followed by several more over the next five years, all designed to fortify the east Texas border.

By 1717, the east Texas missions were quite well established, but Apache and Comanche raids of wagon trains caused serious supply problems. The nearest Spanish outpost was 500 miles to the southwest.

In 1718, the Spanish began building missions and presidios in south central Texas to reduce the distance crossed by supply trains. Presidio San Antonio de Béxar at San Pedro Springs was constructed, as well as the nearby Misión San Antonio de Valero. The latter was soon after moved to the banks of the San Antonio River and later became known as the Alamo (see the San Antonio section in the South Central Texas chapter for more information).

For the next quarter century, the mission system flourished. While the missionaries and Indians who lived within the system learned to defend themselves against physical attack, the failure of the Spanish colonial system itself was a major factor in the missions' eventual undoing. Under Mexican rule the missions were discontinued.

See the San Antonio section in the South Central Texas chapter for complete information and history of that area's missions, the Mission Trail National Park and the Alamo.

Superpower Shift

During the 17th century, the shape of the world superpowers was altered, with Spain losing control of many of its colonies and possessions, and Britain and France gaining power. While the British and French sent troops and explorers scurrying all over North America, the Spanish seemed perfectly content to maintain their far-flung Texas missions and itsy-bitsy settlements at St Augustine and Pensacola.

The British, who by the end of the 17th century had well-established colonies in the northeast of the present USA, continually pressed the Spanish on the southern boundaries of the British territory. In 1670, a demarcation line was established on what are roughly the present-day borders of Georgia and South Carolina, but the line was taken more as a suggestion than a rule, and the British repeatedly ran raids into the Spanish territory.

The French quickly established colonies along the Mississippi River in an attempt to link up the south with their new Canadian territories. Alliances between the colonial powers were formed as quickly as they were scrapped – and they were scrapped as soon as they were formed.

Throughout the 18th century the proximity of the British (in Georgia), the French (in Louisiana), and the Spanish (in Texas and Florida) raised tensions. By 1700 there were 12 British colonies, and the British definitely had their eyes on Spanish Florida. Spain continued to send settlers from various regions of its empire to central Texas, including in 1731 a large contingent from the Canary Islands.

In 1732, Englishman James Oglethorpe settled Savannah, Georgia, and after a trip to England for supplies and arms attacked Florida in 1740. While the Spanish held on, their position had become one under constant pressure from the British.

The French & Indian War

As pressure on Spain grew, so did the friction between England and France. As the two sought to expand west and east respectively, hostilities erupted between them in 1754.

It was the first war between European powers fought outside Europe. Known in the New World as the French and Indian War because of France's alliance with Native American groups against the British, in England it was considered part of the Seven Years' War, which lasted from 1756 to '63.

The Spanish jumped in on the side of France in 1761. In the First Treaty of Paris (1763), which ended the war, Spain gave Florida to the English in return for Louisiana.

Meanwhile, back in Texas, Spanish resources were poured into maintaining the mission system – Spanish presence had not been significantly affected by the outcome of the French and Indian War. Spain retook Florida at the end of the American Revolution, in 1776.

A Small Man with a Big Deal

For the Spanish, one happy result of the French and Indian War and the American Revolution was that Spain took control of the southern part of the enormous territory that was then Louisiana (much of what is the south central portion of the United States today); with all that land as part of New Spain, the threat from the east was gone, and the Spanish all but abandoned their Texas missions.

In 1800 Napoléon Bonaparte forced the Spanish to cede Louisiana to France. The eastern threat was back, but to make matters worse, three years later France turned around and sold, in the best real-estate deal since the Dutch bought Manhattan, the entire Louisiana Territory to the USA for $15 million.

Over the next three years, lots of posturing was made by the Spanish, now a fading colonial power, and the USA, an upstart, over who would actually control the region. In a face-saving deal, both sides agreed to call the territory 'neutral.'

This situation lasted until 1819, when the USA, eager to get its hands on Florida and looking toward westward expansion, cut the Adams-Onís Agreement – a deal with Spain establishing the Texas border at the Sabine River. The deal also stated that in exchange for Spanish control over Texas, the US

would control all territory east of it. The Spanish finally gave up control of Florida in 1821, and Texas became a state of newly independent Mexico.

Mexican Independence

Amid the superpower hubbub at the end of the 18th century, a growing movement in Mexico sought freedom from Spain. In 1810, Miguel Hidalgo y Costilla, parish priest of the town of Dolores, issued his now-famous call to rebellion, the *Grito de Dolores*, demanding 'death to bad government.'

Over the next month and a half the Mexican rebels captured Zacatecas, San Luis Potosí and Valladolid (now called Morelia). On October 30, the rebel army, numbering about 80,000, defeated loyalist forces at Las Cruces outside Mexico City, but hesitated to attack the capital. The rebels occupied Guadalajara but thereafter they were pushed northward by their opponents; their numbers shrank, and in 1811 their leaders were captured and executed.

José María Morelos y Pavón, also a parish priest, assumed the rebel leadership, blockading Mexico City for several months. Meanwhile he convened a congress at Chilpancingo, which adopted guiding principles for the independence movement. They included abolition of slavery and royal monopolies, universal male suffrage and popular sovereignty. Morelos was captured and executed in 1815, and his forces split into several guerrilla bands, the most successful of which was led by Vicente Guerrero in the state of Oaxaca.

Sporadic fighting continued until 1821, when the royalist general Agustín de Iturbide defected during an offensive against Guerrero and conspired with the rebels to declare independence from Spain. In 1821, Spain agreed to Mexican independence. Iturbide, who had command of the army, soon arranged his own nomination to the throne, to which he ascended as Emperor Agustín I in 1822.

The Mexican Republic

Iturbide was deposed in 1823 by a rebel army led by the opportunistic soldier Antonio

López de Santa Anna. A new constitution was drawn up in 1824, establishing a Mexican federal republic of 19 states and four territories. This administratively bunched Texas with the Mexican state of Coahuila, overseen by a legislature.

Guadalupe Victoria, a former independence fighter, became its first president. Mexico's southern boundary was the same as it is today, Central America having set up a separate federation in 1823. In the north, Mexico stretched as far as New Spain had, to include much of what is now the southwestern USA.

Vicente Guerrero stood as a liberal candidate in the 1828 presidential election and was defeated, but he was awarded the presidency eventually, after another Santa Anna-led revolt. Guerrero abolished slavery, but was deposed and executed by his conservative vice president, Anastasio Bustamante, in 1831. Bustamante didn't last long: Santa Anna, a national hero after defeating a small Spanish invasion force at Tampico in 1829, overthrew him and was elected president in 1833.

Americans Move In

By 1818, settlers moving to Texas from the US were mainly made up of resettled Native Americans, who had been 'removed' from newly acquired US territories in the southeast. The first large group of American settlers to wind their way into Texas were brought in under a deal brokered between 1819 and 1821 by Moses Austin (1767-1821), which made him Texas' first American *empresario* (colonial developer). Austin negotiated for the Spanish government to allow him and 300 families from the US to move into central Texas, but he died before the actual move could begin. His son, Stephen Fuller Austin (1793-1836), credited in Texas folklore as being the 'Father of Texas,' carried out his father's plans, and in 1821 settled along the Brazos River. Over the next several years, Austin's settlement attracted more than 5000 Americans and a bustling trade with Mexico.

Texas also attracted settlers from Mexico and the South because of Mexican government incentives in the form of cheap land. Empresarios were given title over vast regions, and by 1825 the word 'Texian' had been coined to describe residents of the region, who were beginning to form a state identity. In 1826, a short-lived attempt at an independent nation within Texas, the Republic of Fredonia, foreshadowed Texian demands for independence from Mexico.

This was not a new concept. By 1819 there had already been settlers in Texas calling for the region to be admitted to the US. But by 1830, with more than 30,000 settlers in the Texas territory, the situation was becoming, well, revolting.

In that year, a Mexican decree banning further American settlement and limiting the importation of slaves served to create a definite us-against-them atmosphere. By 1832, Texas was demanding that it be separated administratively from the adjoining Mexican state of Coahuila. By 1833, political unrest in Mexico had led Santa Anna to impose martial law on many Mexican territories, including, to a limited degree, Texas.

Texas War for Independence

By late 1835, war fever was in the air, and it was really a matter of when, rather than whether, a war would erupt. Stephen F Austin had, in 1833, traveled to Mexico City to plead the settlers' case to the Mexican government, but after being faced down by bureaucrats, he wrote to Texian settlers, telling them to forget about permission and go ahead and set up an independent government. Austin was arrested and detained until 1835.

Meanwhile, William B Travis led a group of hotheaded Texians who took up arms rather than allow Mexican troops to arrive in Texas to reinforce those already defending a customs office. This led to a direct confrontation with General Martín Perfecto de Cós, who would later be transferred to San Antonio.

Armed skirmishes throughout 1835 sparked the Texas War for Independence, which officially ran from September 30, 1835, to April 21, 1836.

In December 1835 at the outbreak of war, Texian troops (composed of Americans,

Mexicans, and a fair number of English, Irish, Scottish, Germans and other Europeans), captured San Antonio from General Cós. The Texians also occupied and further fortified the Alamo.

The Alamo & Goliad In January 1836, Mexican general Antonio López de Santa Anna and his troops stormed the Alamo in hope of taking it back. Although the Texians – among them Davy Crockett, James Bowie and William Travis – were outnumbered by more than 10 to one, they managed to hold back Santa Anna for about two weeks before succumbing to Mexican forces. The battle was bloody, and it's said all but one of the Alamo defenders were killed (Mexican losses were also quite devastating – estimated in the thousands). Those who died at the Alamo became heroes, and the battle itself is now considered a pivotal point in Texan – and American – history.

After the battle, Texian troops elsewhere gathered strength, taking advantage of the time wasted by Santa Anna on the Alamo. Colonel James Fannin and more than 400 volunteers in the Texas Independence Army had set out from Gonzales to assist, too late, at the Alamo, and had retreated in February toward Goliad (where the Declaration of Texas Independence had been signed on December 20, 1835).

Ten miles northeast of town they encountered Mexican troops under the command of Mexican brigadier general José de Urrea. After a daylong battle, the Texians surrendered and were taken to Goliad, which was occupied by the Mexican army. On March 27, Palm Sunday, Santa Anna ordered between 300 and 350 prisoners shot – a death toll about twice that suffered by defenders at the Alamo. The two events, instantly labeled 'massacres' by Texians, galvanized the troops, which continued fighting under the rallying cry 'Remember the Alamo! Remember Goliad!'

Perhaps because of losses suffered and supplies used at the Alamo and Goliad, Santa Anna's troops simply were not prepared when, on April 21, they ran into Texian troops under the command of Samuel Houston (1793-1863). Houston, a former congressman from Tennessee, major general in Tennessee's militia and 'Indian fighter' under US general Andrew Jackson, had come to Texas specifically to get involved in the fight against the Mexicans.

At the Battle of San Jacinto, Santa Anna's troops were routed, and Santa Anna was captured and briefly detained. While Texas declared itself an independent republic, neither the USA nor Mexico yet recognized it as such. See the South Central Texas chapter for a more detailed account of the Battle of the Alamo.

The Republic of Texas

Recognized or not, the major players in the Texas War for Independence – including Samuel Houston, Stephen Austin, Henry Smith and others – set the stage for elections as soon as September 1836. Houston, the best speaker of the three, was elected president of the Republic of Texas. Austin, who had been appointed secretary of state by President Houston, died in December of pneumonia.

The new republic's main business in its early years was maintaining its viability as a republic, forging trade and political ties with neighbors and trying very hard to establish a government-like capital city. In 1838, Texans elected Mirabeau B Lamar the second president of the republic, and if there was one thing Lamar was good at, it was spending money. In 1839, the central Texas village of Waterloo was renamed Austin, in honor of Stephen F, and the capital was established there. Lamar succeeded in raising (and spending) the funds to build one of the largest planned cities in North America, calling for the grid design of cities, such as that of New York, and wide thoroughfares to allow sweeping views up to the State Capitol Building, at the north end of Austin.

Also in 1839, the Republic of Texas' policy toward the Indians who lived within its borders changed drastically, and a ruthless campaign of Native American removal began. The Indians, understandably, were opposed to such a plan, and the turn of the decade was marred by attacks by Indians and harassment by Mexican troops from the south. By 1841, when Houston was elected for a second time, skirmishes with both groups were commonplace. Houston and the republic lobbied Washington for annexation as a territory in order to settle the border dispute with Mexico and gain assistance in ridding itself of Native Americans. After a state constitutional convention in 1845, Texas was annexed to the USA as a state.

The Mexican War

Texas' annexation by the United States led directly to the Mexican War, also known as the Mexican-American War (1846-48), a total rout in which US troops captured Mexico City from Santa Anna, who had lost and been restored to power several times since the Texas War for Independence. At the end of the war, by the Treaty of Guadalupe Hidalgo, Mexico ceded modern Texas, California, Utah, Colorado, and most of New Mexico and Arizona to the USA. Santa Anna's government sold the remaining bits of New Mexico and Arizona to the USA in 1853 for $10 million, in the Gadsden Purchase. This loss precipitated the Mexican liberal-led Revolution of Ayutla, which finally ousted Santa Anna for good in 1855.

European Settlers

Since the early 1840s, Europeans had been drawn to Texas' wide-open spaces and the relative political stability in the emerging nation. Traveling in groups arranged at home, the first German immigrants arrived in 1844 to settle land bought along the Guadalupe River in central Texas. Settling the city of New Braunfels, named in honor of Prince Karl of Solms-Braunfels, not only established a German base (prosperous to this day) that expanded throughout the Texas Hill Country, but according to locals it also introduced to the area something for which we can all be grateful: Texas barbecue. The method of smoke-curing meats for storage in such a way that it remained soft and tender has its origins, they say, in German shops here.

Baron Ottfried Hans Freiherr von Meusebach took over where Karl had left off,

sending out word that Texas was a very German-friendly location, and in keeping with the laid-back spirit of Texas, he changed his name to the breezier John O Meusebach.

The first French settlers, too, began arriving in 1844, soon to be followed by Czechs (Texas still has the largest population of Czechs outside of the Czech Republic), Italians, Dutch, Poles, Belgians, Norwegians and Jews from throughout Europe.

The Civil War

The US Civil War (1861-65) was brought on by a number of issues, but a few stand in the foreground, especially the profound moral and economic debate over slavery. In the 19th century, public opinion against it – and favoring 'free labor' – in the Northern states and England was quickly rising. Complicating the ethical questions raised by forced labor were crucial differences in the economic structures of the Northern and Southern states.

Northern states, while maintaining an agrarian base, were transforming rapidly to an economy based on manufacturing and industry. The South, instead, depended on selling raw materials, principally cotton, to manufacturing nations. The North, in order to protect its fledgling industry, was in favor of instituting trade tariffs; the South, to protect its thriving exports, was not.

Additionally, the introduction of new territories to the USA through westward expansion introduced a potential tilt in the balance of power between free and slave states within the US congress. California's admittance to the union in 1850 as a free state underscored this issue.

Though settlers poured into Texas from slave-owning states in the South, Governor Houston was firmly against the South-favored secession. Popular opinion and a referendum defeated him, and he was forced to resign as governor. Texas seceded from the USA and joined the Confederate States of America on March 16, 1861.

Aside from providing an estimated 80,000 troops to the Confederacy, Texas' role in the Civil War was mainly one of supplying the ever-growing food needs of the

Buffalo Soldiers

African American soldiers have served in the US military since the days of George Washington. Nearly a quarter-million blacks fought on the Union side in the Civil War, and 37,500 of them died. Not long after, Congress authorized the creation of several all-black cavalry and infantry regiments to go to the frontier to protect settlers. When the Plains Indians saw these men, many of them newly emancipated slaves, they called them 'buffalo soldiers' because their coarse hair and dark skin reminded Native Americans of the shaggy coats of bison. The black soldiers took this nickname as a compliment, because it meant the Indians viewed them with as much respect as they did the buffalo.

Buffalo soldiers proved to be the backbone of US forces on the Texas frontier – an irony of sorts, since they could probably relate more to the Indians' underdog perspective. But the troops did what was asked of them, and they did it well, paving the way for African American achievement in the military – a tradition that continues to this day. Retired US Army general Colin Powell, one of the most popular military men ever in the US, paid his debt to the buffalo soldiers in his autobiography, *My American Journey*, when he wrote of Lieutenant Henry O Flipper, a US military academy graduate who in 1877 was the first black man assigned to command a unit of buffalo soldiers, Troop A of the 10th Cavalry. Flipper was court-martialed on false charges of embezzling from commissary funds. Although he was found innocent, he was given a dishonorable discharge, which was not reversed until 1976, long after his death.

During the court-martial, Flipper's attorney had put the question squarely: '[Is] it … possible for a colored man to secure and hold a position as an officer of the army?' My own career and that of thousands of other black officers answered with a resounding yes. But we knew that the path through the underbrush of prejudice and discrimination had been cleared by the sacrifices of nameless blacks who had gone before us….To them, we owed everything.

Julie Fanselow

Confederate war machine. There were very few battles fought on Texas soil; notable battles included one at Sabine Pass, where a small fort was constructed to prevent the Union navy from gaining control of the coastal waterway – see the Gulf Coast chapter for more information.

Reconstruction

The Civil War was one of the bloodiest conflicts in the history of modern warfare, and wounds ran incredibly deep. From early on in the conflict until his assassination, President Abraham Lincoln (1809-65) put together a framework for reconstruction of the union known as the 10% Plan. Under the plan, the union would give federal recognition to states in which as few as 10% of the

populace had taken oaths of loyalty to the USA – a plan designed to grant political viability to dependable groups (in the Union's opinion) as quickly as possible.

But with Lincoln's assassination, all bets were off and a political void opened; Texas was ruled by martial law under Union troops. In the confusion that followed, dozens of factions struggled for power.

Under the terms of the Confederate surrender, all slaves would be freed immediately, and all governmental officials would have to petition the US government for a pardon before returning to government life. The Confederate states were responsible for any debts incurred during the Civil War.

As the federal government established and maintained order, the return to normal life progressed. Farmers scrambled to re-establish their businesses, and Texas blacks, though freed technically from slavery, found themselves working for the same plantations as before, now as hired hands. As business-people and former politicians struggled to re-create a state government, arguments arose at every level regarding the role of blacks in the state and the amount of free-dom and recognition they would receive. The discussions were not confined to Texas. Throughout the country, consensus on how to reestablish state and local government was proving far more difficult than had been expected.

President Andrew Johnson, a southerner and former slaveholder who succeeded Lincoln, devised a Reconstruction plan that struck a compromise between Lincoln's 10% Plan and more radical proposals filter-ing in from the South, such as one calling for the relocation of blacks to northern states under a 'one country, two systems' scheme. While his plan granted many concessions, it was absolutely firm that the states' constitu-tions ratify the 13th Amendment, abolishing slavery, before readmittance. The other major issue was black suffrage, something Southern states were loath to grant, but under the Reconstruction plan, martial law was eventually imposed to install it.

The Texas Constitution of 1866, hastily drawn up to assure readmittance to the union, granted blacks some measure of civil rights, such as the right to own property and to a jury trial. But it did not give them the right to vote or allow them to testify at trials involving whites, nor did it allow them to hold positions of government.

Hyperrestrictive Black Codes, later to be expanded to what became known as Jim Crow laws, were introduced, making it illegal for blacks to be unemployed, restrict-ing freedom of movement and changes of employment, and segregating much of Southern life into white and black camps.

The Ku Klux Klan, a secret organization designed to keep nonwhites (the definition of this term was very loose and was enlarged to include blacks, Jews, white Southern lib-erals and others) from gaining power or voting, emerged in Texas around this time. Riding in packs and disguising their identi-ties by wearing long white hoods and sheets, Klan members engaged in politics of terror, burning property and beating and brutaliz-ing nonwhites. But the movement to grant blacks the right to vote made significant progress nonetheless.

When Texas was readmitted to the Union in 1870, it had technically granted the vote to blacks, but the state's new constitution was carefully worded to ensure that it did not get a 'Negro government.' After federal troops left, Texas legislators imposed a poll tax to keep droves of black and poor white voters away from the voting booth.

Indian Wars

During the Civil War, soldiers that had pre-viously been used to deter and fight Native American attacks in the west were re-deployed to the fighting in the north, and Indian attacks increased, taking advantage of this weakness. After the war, as settlers pushed farther west, confrontations with Native Americans multiplied. Texas and US troops were deployed to combat the Indians and stave off 'Comanche raids.'

The US Cavalry began systematic raids of Comanche settlements in 1871. As the rail-roads expanded across the Texas Panhandle territories, the demand in the east for buffalo skins grew, and highly paid buffalo hunters began encroaching on Comanche territory as well, slaughtering tens of thou-sands of buffalo, an activity openly con-doned by the US government, as it deprived Indian tribes of a main food source.

By 1874, a new offensive was launched by Comanches, Kiowas and Cheyennes. Early in the fighting was the famed Battle of Adobe Walls, in which a lightly defended white settlement held out against Indian attack. US Cavalry troops hounded the Indians throughout the Panhandle and mas-sacred hundreds in a surprise attack at the Battle of Palo Duro Canyon.

With the removal of the Indian threat from West Texas, railroads were free to expand ever westward, bringing with them more settlers and troops.

On the Cattle Trail

During the Civil War, the Confederate forces' need for food had stepped up Texas cattle production, and after the war, railroads connecting much of the Midwest with the East had stepped up demand for beef. The demand for beef intensified in the East and Midwest as newly completed railroads connecting other states with Texas facilitated the transportation of cattle. While cattle in Texas was selling for $2 to $3 per head, it was selling for $30 to $35 a head in Missouri. Ranching in Texas became an enormous business, and cattle drives – the herding of up to 200,000 head of longhorn steers north from Texas to Missouri – were born (see The Cowboys).

Of the trails that ran through Texas, the temptingly named Goodnight-Loving Trail to Pueblo and Denver, Colorado, and Cheyenne, Wyoming, and the Sedalia Trail to Sedalia, Missouri, are most famous. But it was the Chisholm Trail to Abilene, Kansas, that really opened up the business of bringing

The Cowboys

Perhaps no other figure in literary or cinematic history has been so romanticized as the cowboy. The image has become a symbol of the freedom of the plains and the industrious and untamable nature of the American people themselves.

Normally reticent or even sneeringly anti-American visitors will drop all pretense of superiority and giggle delightedly given the chance to throw on spurs, chaps and gloves and take to the trail at a dude ranch. And the image of the American West – the one Hollywood exported through Western films – is engraved in the minds of people from Delhi to Denmark.

The origins of the American cowboy extend to 16th-century Spain and from there to Mexico. Cattle in those countries were allowed to graze freely over large tracts of land. Mexican vaqueros, or wranglers, brought their methods to Texas and passed them on to Texans, who mispronounced the Spanish and corrupted the word to 'buckaroo.'

With westward expansion and capture of new lands from Native Americans, cattle drives became common. Cowboys, under the direction of a foreman, would begin to herd together the thousands of cattle to be driven north. The cowboys caught calves, using a 'lariat' (from the Spanish *la reata)* and, using the heated-iron design that composed the owner's brand (such as one of those used on the trim of this box), imprinted them for identification.

During cattle drives, the pack was led by a scout and chuck wagon, which would prepare food in advance of the arrival of the herd. Cowboys would ride in packs at the front, sides and, if they were unlucky, the rear of the herd (eating dust the whole way). To filter the dust, cowboys used bandanna handkerchiefs tied over their noses and mouths.

While horses would be changed in relays along the trail, the cowboy always kept his own saddle. Masterfully crafted and as comfortable as possible to allow rides often of 24 hours or more, a cowboy's saddle was his most important tool, and the last thing he sold in hard times.

With the fencing of the range, the lives of the cowboys changed drastically. With smaller areas for grazing, the duties of a cowboy are far different today, though there are still cowboys throughout the western USA.

And the cowboy culture lives on even today. One particularly spectacular place to get an insight into the life of a cowboy on the cattle trail is the Cowboy Artists of America Museum in Kerrville, in the Texas Hill Country (see the section in the South Central Texas chapter). Staff members are available to explain many aspects of the life and customs of cowboys and ranching, and many of the works of the artists on display capture the true spirit of the life and times of cowboys in the American West.

Longhorn steer

Texas cattle to market. From Abilene, the western terminus of the Kansas Pacific Railroad, cattle could be shipped to packing houses in Chicago and Kansas City.

Throughout the late 19th century, cattle constituted Texas' main business, and ranching became a Texan way of life. As more people settled, the traditional Texas ranching method of using open fields to allow cattle to graze unchecked gave way to property lines and, with the invention of barbed wire, the fencing of the range.

With the exception of the discovery of oil, no single event has affected life in Texas as much as the invention of barbed wire in 1873 by Joseph F Glidden of DeKalb, Illinois. By the early 1880s, fences stretched across Texas, and a series of disputes over rights-of-way (ranchers were perfectly pleased to fence over access to watering holes) turned into an antifence campaign. Cowboys and ranchers would travel throughout the countryside cutting down fences, and shots were fired more and more frequently.

In 1883, Texas passed a law banning the cutting of fences, legislating a new way of life throughout the state. The Texas Rangers, who were established as border guards in 1835, called up for special services in the Civil War and for Indian fighting duties after it, were reinstated as a state police force to enforce the new law. This was, effectively, the end of what most of us think of as the cowboy era.

Discovery of Oil

Toward the end of the 19th century, cattle and other agricultural products, such as cotton, were the big news economically. Coal and wood were still the major fuel products being produced, but speculators bet that oil, found in sufficient supply, could replace coal as a source of heat. As early as 1866, oil wells were striking in Nacogdoches County, in east Texas, and in 1894, relatively large deposits were discovered near Corsicana, about 35 miles southeast of Dallas. At the time, oil was being put to a number of uses, including in the sealing of dirt roads.

But everything changed on January 10, 1901, when Patillo Higgins and Anthony Lucas' drilling site at Spindletop, east of Houston in Beaumont, pierced a salt dome, setting forth a gusher of oil so powerful that it took days to bring it under control, and hundreds of thousands of barrels' worth simply sunk back into the earth. After Spindletop began producing an estimated 80,000 barrels of oil per day, the price of oil plummeted. But as the automobile and railroads turned to the oil industry for fuel, an oil boom developed that financed the construction of much of modern east Texas.

The Mexican Revolution

The Mexican Revolution was no clear-cut struggle between oppression and liberty, but a 10-year period of shifting allegiances among a spectrum of leaders. Attempts to create stable governments were wrecked by outbreaks of devastating fighting. This instability south of the border led to militarization within Texas, and Mexico's constant chasing of outlaw and revolutionary hero Francisco 'Pancho' Villa (born Doroteo Arango) into US territory resulted in a US incursion into Mexican territory.

In 1910, Francisco Madero, a wealthy Mexican liberal from Coahuila, drafted the Plan de San Luis Potosí, which called for the Mexican nation to rise in revolution against its dictatorial government on November 20. When revolutionaries under Pancho Villa took Ciudad Juárez in May 1911, Mexican president Porfirio Díaz resigned. Madero was elected president in November 1911.

But Madero was unable to contain the factions fighting for power throughout Mexico. The basic divide that dogged the revolution was between moderately liberal reformers like Madero and more radical leaders, such as Emiliano Zapata from the state of Morelos, who fought for the transfer of land to the peasants with the cry *'¡Tierra y libertad!'* (Land and liberty!). Madero sent federal troops to Morelos to disband Zapata's forces, and in response the Zapatista movement was born.

In February 1913, two conservative leaders – Félix Díaz (the nephew of Porfirio) and Bernardo Reyes – were sprung from prison in Mexico City and commenced a counter-revolution that brought 10 days of fierce fighting to the capital. Thousands were killed or wounded, and many buildings were destroyed. The fighting ended only after the US ambassador to Mexico, Henry Lane Wilson (who saw many benefits for the USA in Mexican peace), negotiated for Madero's general, Victoriano Huerta, to switch to the rebel side and help depose Madero's government. Huerta himself became president; Madero and his vice president were executed. But Huerta only fomented greater strife.

In March 1913 three revolutionary leaders in the north united against Huerta under the Plan de Guadalupe: Venustiano Carranza, a Madero supporter, in Coahuila; Pancho Villa, in Chihuahua; and Álvaro Obregón, in Sonora. Terror reigned in the countryside as Huerta's troops fought, pillaged and plundered. Finally he was defeated and forced to resign in July 1914.

Carranza called the victorious factions to a conference but failed to unify them, and war broke out again. This time Obregón and the far-from-radical Carranza were pitted against the populist Villa and the radical Zapata.

Villa, at first the darling of the American media, portrayed as a dashing fellow fighting for freedom, turned ornery when the US recognized the Carranza government; he and his supporters began raiding Texas villages and settlements. The outcry in Texas was such that President Woodrow Wilson

sent federal troops and Texas' government sent Texas Rangers to catch Villa. They were all unsuccessful, though the Texas Rangers were accused of murdering dozens of Mexicans; after the incident their powers were significantly reduced. Villa was assassinated (by whom is still a mystery) in 1923.

WWI

During the brief Spanish-American War (1898) Texas had seen the development of a number of military bases. After the sinking by a German submarine of the passenger ship *Lusitania* in 1915, which held more than 100 Americans, the US entered WWI, and four major military bases were established in Texas for training – Camp Travis (San Antonio), Camp Logan (Houston), Camp MacArthur (Waco) and Camp Bowie (Fort Worth). More than 200,000 Texans served in the war, and although there were losses, the military bases brought many economic gains to the state.

The Roaring '20s

At the war's end, Texas' economic machine, as well as the nation's, was humming right along. The surge in private automobiles made for an enormous oil boom, and US industry grew and became more profitable than ever before. A boom economy, fueled by a robust stock market based on margin sales and quick profits, was bursting at the seams.

As radio and cinema became more popular in Texas, a new system of highways and ever-more vehicles brought products to market faster than ever before. The economy was soaring, Wall Street was everyone's darling and people were dancing the Charleston in the streets.

The Crash & the Dust Bowl

But trading practices on Wall Street at the time were a disaster waiting to happen. Overproduction was running unchecked, and investors were allowed to buy stocks on credit, which led to vastly inflated stock prices. This balloon was set to burst, and on Black Thursday, October 24, 1929, the New York Stock Exchange hiccuped, and the bottom began to fall out. Although panic followed, the real crash happened on Black Tuesday, October 29, 1929, when the market lost almost $30 billion in a single day. By the end of the year, business and industry losses in the USA exceeded $100 billion. The crash led the country and the world into the Great Depression. The northern section of Texas was in the southern region of what became known as the 'dust bowl,' an arid spot of land on which nothing would grow. Increased oil production (the government had tried to suggest production caps but producers couldn't come to terms with each other) caused a market glut that further depressed prices.

Texas was a major supporter of President Franklin Delano Roosevelt. In Roosevelt's 'First 100 Days' in 1933, he called an emergency session of congress, creating dozens of government agencies that had a profound effect on the state and the nation. As a part of Roosevelt's New Deal, the Works Progress Administration (WPA) and Civilian Conservation Corps (CCC) were created. The CCC worked to restore state and national parks, and the WPA sent armies of workers to construct buildings, roads, dams, trails and housing. Other federal programs created during this time included the Federal Communications Commission; Federal Deposit Insurance Corporation, which guarantees personal savings in US banks; National Housing Agency; and Social Security, which provides money to senior citizens, the disabled and others. It was the largest campaign of government-created jobs ever in the USA, and while critics at the time called it busywork, projects by both the WPA and CCC still stand today, many as national landmarks. For Texas, one of the most important contributions made by WPA workers was the restoration and renovation of the old Spanish missions, which had fallen into disrepair since Texas' independence from Mexico.

WWII
New Deal or not, some felt what the country really needed to break out of depression was a good war. And the Japanese attack on Pearl Harbor, Hawaii, on December 7, 1941, brought the US right into the fighting that had been going on throughout the world since 1939.

The Texas war machine was brought back up to full capacity, and with the activation of all its bases, the creation of more than a dozen new ones and more than 40 airfields, Texas became a major training ground for WWII soldiers – almost 1.5 million were trained in the state.

The Postwar Period
The economic prosperity in the US after WWII was unprecedented. The wartime economy had created a powerhouse, and when the fighting stopped in 1945, industry didn't really want to stop with it. For the next 15 years, the US economy surged, fueled by low consumer credit rates and a defense-based economy that plowed money into manufacturing military hardware.

The 1960s
Native son Lyndon Baines Johnson (1908-73) was born in Stonewall, east of Austin in south central Texas. The eldest of five children, Johnson, affectionately known as LBJ, had a well-deserved reputation for being a hard-nosed Southern Democrat. He was as stubborn as a barnful of mules, as dirty a political fighter as he needed to be, fiercely loyal to Texas in the fight for pork-barrel government contracts and dedicated to more socialistic Democratic Party programs and to racial integration – not because of personal beliefs, but because he sought to appease the huge numbers of his black, rural and poor constituents. As majority leader of the US Senate, Johnson was a contender for presidential nomination in 1960, but he accepted the vice-presidential nomination, seeing his chances of getting elected as being notably better if, as a Southerner, he helped balance the campaign of the charismatic New Englander John Fitzgerald Kennedy. Within three years, Johnson would become the country's leader for the rest of this tumultuous decade.

President Kennedy In televised debates leading up to the election, the dashing

Senator Kennedy so pummeled his visibly shifty opponent, Richard M Nixon, that there seemed to be simply no hope for 'Tricky Dick.' But Kennedy's election performance was far less impressive than his television performances – he narrowly eked out a victory. Kennedy took the White House by storm after his inauguration in 1961. His victory was greatly assisted by Johnson's tireless campaigning through the southern US – a good ol' boy speaking to the masses.

NASA One of the first things Johnson did upon election as vice president was to work on instituting well-funded federal programs back home in Texas. The most notable of these, of course, was the relocation of the National Aeronautics and Space Administration's (NASA) Mission Control from Florida to Texas. At the time, the Mercury space missions were just getting under way, and as the 'space race' between the USA and the USSR heated up, the forward-thinking vice president realized the enormous financial potential of the project. He lobbied congress mercilessly and in 1961 was victorious. Although launches continued to leave from Cape Canaveral, Mission Control and the astronaut training program were moved to the Manned Space Flight Center (now, cozily enough, the Johnson Space Center) near Houston.

JFK Assassination On November 22, 1963, Kennedy and Johnson rode in separate open limousines through downtown Dallas. At 12:30 pm, Kennedy was shot. Texas governor John M Connally, riding in the seat in front of the president, was also injured by gunfire. The president died at 1 pm; Connally (1917-93) survived. Later that day, as Kennedy's body was being transported to Washington, DC, Vice President Johnson took the oath of office aboard *Air Force One*, the presidential airplane, with Jacqueline Kennedy standing at his side.

JFK's assassination remains one of the most controversial events in US history, and the conspiracy theories surrounding it show no signs of abating. For more on the assassination, see the Dallas-Fort Worth chapter.

For conspiracy theories and stilted acting, see Oliver Stone's film *JFK*.

President Johnson LBJ defeated Barry Goldwater in the presidential election of 1964, and his administration oversaw some of the USA's most tumultuous events, from the troop buildup and invasion of North Vietnam to civil protest at home. The Johnson Administration also saw an unprecedented flurry of social legislation that changed the face of the country, including the creation of Medicare, the federal school-lunch program and civil rights legislation. For more information on LBJ, see the LBJ Presidential Library heading in the Austin section of the South Central Texas chapter.

The 1970s & '80s

The 1970s brought wealth – sheer, unadulterated, Sultan-of-Bruneian *wealth* – to Texas by way of the energy crisis. In 1973, Iran, Iraq, Kuwait, Saudi Arabia, and Venezuela, members of the Organization of Petroleum Exporting Countries (OPEC), imposed an oil embargo on – or, more specifically, a major reduction in oil sales to – the US and its allies to punish the US for its pro-Israel policy. Petroleum prices doubled and then tripled; gasoline prices tripled, then quadrupled; lines at gas stations stretched for blocks, then miles; in some states, gasoline rationing was imposed. Texans, finding themselves the biggest domestic suppliers of oil, laughed all the way to the bank.

The obscene wealth brought to Texas by the oil shortage created a class of nouveaux riches, who played the part as if they had been supplied by central casting. Newly rich Texans bought British titles outright from debt-ridden members of the British aristocracy, creating legions of Lady Jane Billy Bobs and Duke Zachary Jims. Ranches became practically passé in the move to bigger and better spreads for oil barons, who also built skyscrapers, hotels, casinos and pleasure domes. *Dallas*, the prime-time soap opera following the high jinks of that wacky, oil-rich Ewing clan, premiered in 1978 and showed off Texas excess for all the world, which lapped it up.

The boom ended for a number of reasons, not the least of which was the rather pathetic quality of US-made automobiles in the 1970s and 1980s. American carmakers grew fat and complacent, whereas Japanese auto manufacturers offered vastly superior technology and workmanship, not to mention markedly better fuel economy. As Americans stopped laughing at small, fuel-efficient cars and began driving them in droves, the USA's auto industry found itself looking at the business end of the shotgun of bankruptcy. The industry immediately set to producing cars and trucks with comparable gas mileage.

Industry, too, became more efficient, and for the first time, alternative fuel sources were examined closely on a macro scale.

By the close of the energy crisis, the country had developed new sources of oil (mainly in Texas and Central and South America, as well as in Alaska); new types of energy (nuclear, hydroelectric and others that had existed for years, but had yet to be put to large-scale use); and was even dabbling in wind and solar power. The result was an oil glut that by the mid-1980s devastated the world's and Texas' oil industry. This glut began in 1979, when Iran completely ceased sales to the US. Other OPEC countries had agreed on production quotas, but greed held the day, and none stuck to settled amounts. While OPEC nations argued, the price of oil halved; by 1986, the price was down to a paltry $10 a barrel, and Texas was hurting. Oil extraction and exploration became unprofitable. Downtown Houston, so recently rife with the newly rich, became little more than a ghost town, with unoccupied office towers filling the streets in what looked like a postapocalyptic nightmare (many argue it still looks that way, but more crowded). And since Kuwait wasn't exactly a model of democracy before the 1991 Persian Gulf War, some speculate about why former US president George Bush, whose adopted home is Texas, was so gung ho about leading the world into a war that, perhaps not incidentally, drove oil prices back up by several bucks a barrel. But that's another story.

Texas Today

After the oil bust Texas had to refocus its resources, mainly toward education and the space industry. In the early 1990s, an explosion of highly educated Texans got into the high-tech business, turning south central Texas, especially Austin, into a high-tech corridor that rivals California's Silicon Valley. Texas led all states in population growth in the 1990s (see Population & People). And the North American Free Trade Agreement (NAFTA – something you'll see referred to again and again in this book), which has since 1994 provided a degree of freedom of trade between the US, Mexico and Canada, was a huge economic shot in the arm for Texas. The entire Tex-Mex border hums with activity, mainly around maquiladoras, factories in Mexico that are staffed and run by Mexican workers who produce goods for American and Canadian corporations (and who earn lower wages with fewer safety regulations than their northern counterparts). Tax advantages of this arrangement are such that 'outsourcing' to maquiladoras has created tens of thousands of jobs for Mexicans – some say at an equal cost in American jobs north of the border.

But as Texas enjoys the very best of the general economic giddiness that has marked the closing years of 20th-century America, Texans themselves never let you forget that, as far as they're concerned, they got here all by themselves.

GEOGRAPHY

Texas, as everyone here will tell you, is big, but it's not the biggest. It's the second-largest state in the union, with an area of 268,601 sq miles. While that's less than half the size of Alaska, it's larger than all of Germany, the United Kingdom, the Republic of Ireland, Belgium and the Netherlands combined. The state resembles – if you really stretch your imagination – a top. The natural boundaries of the state are the Gulf of Mexico at the east and the Rio Grande at the west and south.

There are four major natural regions of Texas: the Gulf Coastal Plains, Great Plains, Interior Lowlands and the Basin and Range

Province. Within each region there is a remarkable range of terrain, most notably in the Piney Woods sections of east Texas, the Texas Hill Country (central Texas between Austin and San Antonio), the Llano Estacado (in the central north), and most dramatic of all, in the escarpments of the west. These, which include the Caprock in the north and Balcones in the southwest, create suddenly rising mountains.

In West Texas, the Trans-Pecos region of the Basin and Range Province is home to the Guadalupe Mountains, with elevations of more than 8000 feet, as well as to Chihuahuan desert lands.

South of the Guadalupe mountain range, the Big Bend region follows the Rio Grande through dramatic canyons and sheer mountain walls.

GEOLOGY

The most exciting geological aspect of Texas – to Texans, of course – is why there's oil underneath it. The black stuff sits beneath southern Mississippi and Alabama, and Louisiana; there are heaps of it under the Gulf of Mexico near all these states as well as the Mexican states of Tamaulipas, Veracruz and Tabasco – all areas that surround the huge sedimentary basin that forms the Gulf of Mexico. Evolving for more than 100 million years, the basin consists of a thick sequence of sedimentary rocks. As the sedimentary material makes its way deeper into the earth, it's subjected to a great deal of pressure and heat – enough to convert much of the organic debris (the remains of plants and animals that are always part of sedimentary material) into petroleum.

Petroleum flows freely under the earth, but it tends to collect into large masses that migrate into traps – so named because rocks or other impermeable materials trap the oil – where it forms pools. Pools are what oil explorers are after.

Under Texas, salt domes (which are just what they sound like – collections of crystallized salt that form domes) act as traps; when they're pierced, as was the case in Spindletop (see the Discovery of Oil section), oil that

has been trapped beneath gushes forth. Gushers, however, are rare these days, and oil exploration has become extremely sophisticated – see the boxed text There She Blows! in the Gulf Coast chapter for more information.

CLIMATE

Texas weather is the subject of most conversations outside big cities. Generally speaking, Texas enjoys a mild southern climate year-round, with statewide average temperatures of 50°F (11°C) in January and 85°F (30°C) in July. But weather varies throughout the large state (see chart). In much of the year, evenings in the mountainous regions of West Texas and the Texas Hill Country are cool enough for a jacket or even a coat in winter. And areas of east Texas and the Rio Grande Valley are among the hottest in the country, with summer daytime temperatures averaging 100°F (38°C).

Throughout the state, the weather is very changeable, and like much of the central part of the United States, susceptible to tornadoes – Texas leads the nation in tornadoes, with an average of almost 130 per year. And its proximity to the Gulf of Mexico makes Texas susceptible to hurricanes, though far less so than, say, Florida and Georgia. See the Dangers & Annoyances section in the Facts for the Visitor chapter for more information.

ECOLOGY & ENVIRONMENT

A growing level of awareness about ecology and the environment, plus the recognized value in 'green' tourism, means that many natural areas increasingly enjoy varying degrees of protection and management from local, state, federal or private government agencies. Since the 1970s, the various agencies have acquired lands for important environmental and recreational purposes, and the emission of hazardous wastes and air pollution have come under tighter control.

Greenbelts and greenways, areas of protected natural habitats within and around urban areas, are the focus of hot debates within the state, especially in Austin. There, as in other places, local and state government agencies are under intense pressure from developers to ease restrictions on development. So far the greenies have held out, but it would appear to be only a matter of time before money wins out over the earth in these valuable areas.

Oil drilling creates its own environmental challenges in Texas, and some highly publicized oil spills have occurred in the Gulf of Mexico, but economics dictate that oil companies are far, far more careful than ever before.

As well as providing opportunities for recreational activities, many public lands act as preserves for wildlife and offer interpretive activities and environmentally related educational programs. The Nature

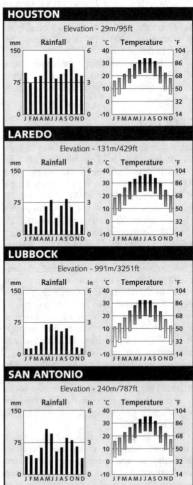

Conservancy (☎ 703-841-5300), 1815 N Lynn St, Arlington, VA 22209, is an international private nonprofit conservation organization that buys habitats to save them from threatened development or other destruction. It has branches in each state; contact the Texas branch at (☎ 512-263-8878), 11617 FM 2244, Austin, TX 78733.

FLORA & FAUNA

Texas' sheer size and environmental diversity mean that it's home to a startling array of flora and fauna; 5000 species of plants (including 2000 wildflowers), 550 species of birds and more than 140 species of animals call Texas home. The Texas Parks and Wildlife Press publishes several books on the subject; see Books in the Facts for the Visitor chapter for more information.

Flora

One native tree you'll find particularly interesting if you have any propensity whatsoever to allergies is the cedar, which grows throughout the state and turns Texas, especially central Texas, into the allergy capital of the USA.

Desert Plants The creosote bush is among the most prevalent species in Texas, with dark green leaves and a 30-foot taproot that searches for underground water. The ocotillo, sometimes called coachwhip, is a woody shrub with long, slender wands that produce scarlet flowers. Lechuguilla, a fibrous spined agave, is unique to the Chihuahuan desert and may grow 15 feet tall. Candelilla has long been used by the area's indigenous people to produce wax.

Prickly pear is the most common kind of cactus, with several varieties: Engelman, purple-tinged, brown-spine and blind, the last one so called because it looks like it has no thorns (but it does, so beware). Other cactus species include fishhook, cholla, claret cup, rainbow, eagle's claw and strawberry pitaya. One species you *won't* find is the saguaro cactus, which – although often used by New York City ad agencies as a symbol for West Texas – actually is found in the Sonoran Desert of Arizona.

Wildflowers To Texans, wildflowers are a way of life. Wildflower tourism is so entrenched in the state that the highway visitors' centers can help you plan entire trips around watching them bloom (call ☎ 800-452-9292 in spring for information). The best time to see Texas' wide range of wildflowers is from March to May, when roadsides and fields throughout central and West Texas and especially the Hill Country become explosions of color – blankets of wonderful reds, rusts, yellows and blue.

Plenty of people go to the Big Bend region specifically to see the wildflowers. The blooms peak in March and April in the lowlands and May to July in the Chisos, but it's possible to find flowers year-round; there's often a second bloom in late summer after the season's heavy rains. Big Bend bluebonnet, a relative of the Texas state flower, blooms from December through June in the lowlands. Other varieties you may see include prickly poppy, sweet william, snapdragon, cardinal flower, silverleaf, bracted paintbrush, rock-nettle and desert verbena.

For a whole lot more information on Texas wildflowers, see the National Wildflower Research Center in the South Central Texas chapter.

Fauna

To the eternal shame of early settlers, American bison, or buffalo, were hunted to the brink of extinction and today exist only in remnant populations. The two most famous Texas animals are the armadillo and longhorn steer, respectively the state's official small and large mammal (since you asked,

Armadillo

the state's official flying mammal is the Mexican free-tailed bat – see the Bats section later).

The nine-banded armadillo is a member of the order Xenarthra, which includes sloths, and has migrated to North America only relatively recently from South America. The armadillo, whose bony carapace is unique among mammals, resembles nothing less than an armored vehicle. As large as a small lap dog, the armadillo tends to seek arid land and avoid water; when forced to cross wide streams it can ingest air and inflate into its own personal flotation device. Its diet consists mainly of insects and other invertebrates and vegetable matter, but the armadillo is not above dining on carrion and its attendant maggots and larvae. Armadillos are found throughout the state, except in extreme West Texas.

Once the most common mammal found in West Texas, and another unofficial mascot of the state, is the black-tailed prairie dog – essentially a fat, friendly squirrel that lives off prairie grasses. Highly sociable, the prairie dog lives in large colonies called 'towns' and hibernates in winter. Natural and human-caused environmental changes have vastly reduced the prairie dog population over the years, but protected prairie dog towns can be found in West Texas.

Another fascinating plains animal is the pronghorn, also known as the pronghorn antelope. While no true antelope exists in North America, the scientific name for these astounding creatures is *Antilocapra*, literally 'goat-antelope.' Pronghorns are the fastest North American mammal, capable of short-burst speeds of up to 60mph and cruising for long distances at 30 to 40mph. Hunted to the brink of extinction by the mid-20th century, repopulation efforts were so successful that the state has, to the dismay of many people, permitted limited pronghorn hunting again. Pronghorn live in open prairies and on sagebrush plains and eat cacti, sagebrush and grasses.

Speaking of hunting, the most popular game in the state is the white-tailed deer, found primarily in the timbered sections of the state. Other deer include the Carmen Mountains white-tailed deer (see Big Bend) and the American elk, found in extreme West Texas.

Big Bend Fauna Seventy-five mammal species call the Big Bend region in West Texas home. Among them, the black bear – all but gone from the region by the mid-20th century – made an amazing comeback in the late 1980s and early 1990s. Nearly 600 sightings are now reported in a typical year, most in the Chisos Mountains.

Mountain lions (often called panthers) are seen more rarely, but about two dozen live in the Chisos Mountains. Another well-known Big Bend mammal, the collared peccary or javelina (pronounced hav-uh-LEEN-a), ranges all over the park, from the mountains to the desert. Javelina wander in bands of 10 to 25 and spend much of their time munching on prickly-pear cactus. Carmen Mountains white-tailed deer, a subspecies of the better-known white-tailed deer, are the second-smallest deer in the lower 48 United States (only Florida Key deer are smaller). These deer live only in

Pronghorn antelope

Big Bend and the surrounding mountain areas of the US and Mexico.

Jackrabbits, most often seen bounding across the desert, use their huge ears both as antennae to warn of approaching predators and – get this – radiators to transfer excess body heat to their surroundings. Other mammals you may see include raccoons, skunks, coyotes, desert mule deer and kangaroo rats.

Bats Thirty-two species of bats call Texas home. In Austin and throughout Texas you'll hear references to 'Mexican free-tailed bats'; this is a catchall for a migratory subspecies of Brazilian free-tailed bats *(Tadarida brasiliensis brasiliensis)* and, more important, the ones you'll see streaming out from underneath the Congress Ave Bridge in Austin or in Carlsbad Caverns just before dusk. For you bat nuts out there, *Tadarida brasiliensis cynocephala* is the nonmigratory subspecies of Brazilian free-tailed bats, which live primarily in the eastern US.

The endangered Mexican longnosed bat has its only US home in the Chisos Mountains, where it summers. Eighteen other bat species live at Big Bend, ranking it tops among national parks in bat diversity. Other bats in Texas include the big brown bat, evening bat, western red bat and, a personal favorite, the hoary bat.

Birds The official Texas state bird is the mockingbird. Of Texas' large bird population, more than 450 species are found in the Big Bend region. About 100 species nest within Big Bend National Park; the rest use it as a flyway during spring and fall migrations. Prime birding sites include Rio Grande Valley, the Sam Nail Ranch along the Ross Maxwell Scenic Drive, the Chisos Basin and Castolon near Santa Elena Canyon along the Rio Grande. Big Bend Birding Expeditions (☎ 915-371-2356) offers trips in and around the park and on the Rio Grande; see the Books section in the Facts for the Visitor chapter for some suggested birding guidebooks.

The Big Bend region may be best known for its peregrine falcons, which while still endangered have made a comeback as of late. A dozen known nests are found within or near the park, and in 1997, the region's falcons produced a record 17 offspring. Among other Big Bend bird celebrities, the Colima warbler has its only US nesting spot in the Chisos Mountains, where it lives from April through mid-September and may best be seen along the Boot Spring trail. The Chisos also are home to the endangered black-capped vireo. The vireo are having a tough time of it, since common (or brown-headed) cowbirds often lay their own eggs in vireo nests, tricking mama vireo into raising baby cowbirds while making it more difficult for the vireo offspring to survive. Other, more common, Big Bend species include golden eagles, cactus wrens, ravens, Mexican jays, roadrunners, acorn woodpeckers, canyon towhees, and a whole bunch of warblers and hummingbirds.

The 70,504-acre Aransas National Wildlife Refuge is the premier birding site on the Texas Gulf Coast – more than 500 species of birds migrate through here every year. The refuge is attractive mainly to birders trying to catch a glimpse of the endangered whooping crane, the tallest bird in North America – males approach 5 feet in height and have a 7-foot wingspan. Other birds commonly found in east Texas include various species of spoonbill, ibis, heron, egret, warbler and of course ducks and geese. See Bird Paradise for the finer details of avian enthusiasm in these areas.

The Texas Audubon Society (☎ 512-306-0225), 2525 Wallingwood Rd, No 301, Austin, TX 78746, has information about bird-watching areas throughout the state. With the popularity of bird-watching growing, almost every local tourist office in the main birding areas has information on local conditions.

Dolphins & Manatees Several species of dolphin call the Gulf of Mexico home, including rough-toothed, common, bottle-nosed, striped, pantropical, Atlantic spotted and Risso's dolphins.

The endangered West Indian manatee is found, exceedingly rarely, in rivers and bays, and only a tad less so in the Gulf of Mexico.

Bird Paradise

Possibly happier than the birds themselves are the bird-watchers who flock to south Texas every year. More than 400 bird species have been spotted at the many state and national parks that dot the area along the south Gulf Coast and the eastern Rio Grande Valley.

The best time for seeing birds is during the fall and spring, when migratory birds pass through on their journeys south and north. Winter is also popular because many species stay for the entire season, not bothering to head any farther south.

Information The Texas Parks and Wildlife Department (☎ 800-792-1112) has established the Great Texas Coastal Birding Trail, which stretches from Port Arthur south to the Rio Grande Valley. It has a wealth of free information available – write to 4200 Smith School Rd, Austin, TX 78744. Materials include excellent maps detailing hundreds of bird-watching locations, from major parks to minor town dumps popular with crows.

The Texas Audubon Society also has plenty of information on Texas birding (see Birds under Fauna in this chapter).

Birds The following are just a few of the birds that can be found in south Texas:

Buff-bellied hummingbird – This year-round resident of the Rio Grande Valley accents its dull chest with a shock of green on the throat. It's most often seen flitting between red-colored flowers.

Green kingfisher – Normally this 9-inch bird is well hidden in shrubs along waterways; it emerges to glide across water in search of fish.

Pileated woodpecker – This red-crested bird is shy, but it makes a big noise and is known to east Texans as the 'peckerwood.'

Prairie chicken – The buffalo of the bird world, this once prolific member of the grouse family was shot by the millions by hunters; it now survives in isolated groups.

Red-crowned parrot – Found in flocks of 15 or more in the Rio Grande Valley, this tree-dweller has bright red, green and yellow feathers.

Roseate spoonbill – This bird looks like a pink flamingo, only with a special beak to filter insects and other organisms out of the water.

Black-bellied whistling duck – Not your average quacker, this duck prefers sitting in trees to water; it has bright pink legs and feet and black and white wings.

White pelican – A common bird along the coast in the winter, this prodigious fish eater – up to three gallons in volume at a time – summers on lakes in north-central and western North America.

Locations There are hundreds of places in Texas popular with bird-watchers. See the Rio Grande chapter for information on: Laguna Atascosa National Wildlife Refuge, Sabal Palm Sanctuary, Boca Chica wetlands, Santa Ana National Wildlife Refuge and Bentsen Rio Grande Valley State Park.

Major locations for bird-watchers covered in the Gulf Coast chapter are Padre Island National Seashore and Aransas National Wildlife Refuge, which are south and north of Corpus Christi respectively.

Ryan Ver Berkmoes

Manatees have large, plump, grayish-brown bodies with two small forelimbs and a tail shaped like a beaver's. They have a large, flexible upper lip covered with small whiskers, range in size from about nine to 12 feet and weigh between 1000 and 2500lb. They are herbivores and consume 10% to 15% of their weight daily. After 13 months of pregnancy they give birth to only one calf every two to five years. They have no natural enemies except people.

Fish Game fish are common throughout the state, especially bass and trout, and sport fishing is very popular in the gulf; see the Gulf Coast chapter for more information. Most of the Big Bend region's native fish are tiny. One such species, the Big Bend mosquito fish, lives in only one pond inside Big Bend National Park and nowhere else in the world. At one time, the population had dwindled to two males and one female. Larger fish in the Rio Grande include catfish, gizzard shad, longnose gar, carp, sucker and freshwater drum.

Lizards & Arachnids The tarantula is fairly common in rural Texas, as are scorpions – 11 species of stinging scorpions live in the Big Bend region alone, including a whip scorpion, which uses pincers instead of a stinger to kill its prey. Poisonous spider bites are exceedingly rare, though – if you should see a scorpion (we came across one in a motel room on our first night in Texas – welcome, y'all), give it room or, if you're in a hotel, call someone to remove it. Lizards in the Big Bend region include the Big Bend gecko, collared lizard, whiptails and the Texas alligator lizard.

American Alligator The name 'alligator' derives from the Spanish *el lagarto*, 'the lizard,' and you'll find these reptiles in east Texas swamps and along the Gulf Coast. They are carnivorous: hatchlings eat insects, frogs, small fish, snails and the like. As they grow, they move on to bigger game, but they're never above small snacks like crickets or grasshoppers. An alligator's jaws close on reflex; the muscles that open its mouth

are far weaker than those that close it, and the closing mechanisms are triggered by anything touching the inside of the gator's mouth.

When that something is edible, the alligator clamps down on it, raises its head and gulps – swallowing prey small enough in one gobble and crushing and tearing larger prey repeatedly until swallowable. Stories of alligators dragging prey underwater to drown it are hooey.

Alligators indeed look like long, scary lizards. Male alligators grow to between nine and 12 feet, females six to eight feet.

Young alligators are black with cream-colored bellies and bright stripes and blotches of yellow on their backs. As they grow older they lose the stripes, but their stomachs remain light. It's said that Native Americans believed rubbing a gator's stomach would make it fall asleep – volunteers? Alligators have large corneas, which enhance their night vision; they can see under water, too: transparent, protective membranes cover their eyes when submerged. There's nothing external to distinguish male and female alligators to the casual observer.

They are usually (but not exclusively) found in fresh water – shallow lakes, marshes, swamps, rivers, creeks, ponds and human-made canals. They are warm-weather fans and will rarely feed when the temperature dips below 68°F. Their metabolism slows considerably in cold weather, but gators are cold-blooded and can die when the temperature is more than 100°F. To cool themselves, alligators sit on riverbanks or in the shade with their mouths wide open, which dissipates heat.

Alligators generally eat only when they're hungry, not as a punitive measure – unless they're feeling attacked. Things alligators like to eat: small animals or things that look similar, such as small children or people crouching down real small to snap a photo.

Snakes Of the more than 100 species of snakes in Texas, 16 are poisonous: the southern, broad-banded and Trans-Pecos copperheads; the Texas coral snake; the western cottonmouth; and 11 kinds of rattlesnake, of which the Mojave and very common western diamondback are most dangerous. The diamondback rattlesnake is the largest (and most dangerous) of the pit vipers; it injects venom that destroys the red blood cells and the walls of blood vessels. Diamondbacks can grow to be eight feet long and have a big, heavy, brownish body marked with dark (almost black) diamond shapes, set off by yellowish white borders. They usually rattle before they attack.

The coral snake, a relative of the cobra, is small and deadly: its poison is the most potent of any North American snake. It looks very pretty – its slim body has sections of black and red divided by thin orange-yellow stripes, and it can easily be mistaken for the harmless scarlet king snake. To tell them apart, remember this cheerful little rhyme: 'Red touch yellow, kill a fellow; red touch black, good for Jack.' Fortunately for us, the coral snake is very shy and generally nocturnal, and on the whole, it rarely bites people; when it does, it rarely, because of its size, injects enough venom to cause major damage.

In addition to the copperheads and four species of rattlesnakes, Big Bend has lots of nonpoisonous varieties, including the western coachwhip, bullsnake, Big Bend patchnose snake, black-hooded snake, Trans-Pecos blind snake and Mexican milk snake, among others.

See the Dangers & Annoyances section in the Facts for the Visitor chapter for information on treating snakebites (but the best way to treat a bite is to avoid it completely). When traveling in high-risk areas, such as Big Bend or anyplace where there are tall grasses or shrubs, you can reduce the risk of being bitten by practicing basic common sense.

- Wear high leather boots and long, preferably denim, pants.
- Don't gather firewood in the dark.
- Don't reach into holes.
- Stick to cleared paths as much as possible through grass, brush or rocky areas.
- Make noise as you walk; stomp, speak and generally make your presence known so snakes have time to get away from you lest they attack out of sheer panic.

- Always bring a flashlight and use extreme caution when you are leaving remote campsites at night – rattlers are nocturnal.
- If you hear a rattle, freeze – snakes are far more likely to attack a moving target, will probably move away from something as large as you, and in your haste to retreat you may step on the snake.
- Watch your hands; rolling over firewood or rocks may inadvertently uncover (and annoy) a snake – use a stick to be certain.

NATIONAL PARKS
There are about a dozen sites in the state of Texas operated by the National Park Service, such as the Amistad and other national recreation areas; national historic parks such as the missions of the Mission Trail in and around San Antonio; national seashores such as Padre Island; and a number of other subclassifications of national parks. Admission prices are generally less than $5 per vehicle; see Golden Opportunities for information on the various Golden passes. For more information on Texas national parks, head for the National Park Service website at www.nps.gov/parklists/tx.html.

NATIONAL FORESTS
National Forests are operated by the United States Forest Service (USFS), a division of the United States Department of Agriculture (USDA). They are less protected than national parks and are managed under the principle of 'multiple use,' which includes commercial exploitation in some areas such as timber cutting, grazing, watershed management (which theoretically ensures a balance between damage to the water table and development), wildlife management (which provides quotas for hunting, establishes hunting seasons and theoretically prosecutes poachers) and privately owned recreational facilities.

East Texas has four large national forests; see the Northeast Texas chapter for specific information on Texas national forests.

STATE PARKS
Texas maintains what some argue is the USA's finest network of state parks – more

Golden Opportunities

If you plan to visit a half-dozen or more National Park Service fee sites in 12 months, the Golden Eagle Passport is a good deal – even though its price recently doubled from $25 to $50. The passport admits its holder to any US national park site (parks, monuments and so on) that charges an entrance fee. It's good for a full year from the date of purchase, and it covers everyone in your vehicle.

Golden Age cards are available to all US residents over age 62. There's a one-time processing charge of $10, and then they're good for a lifetime – and they admit everyone in your family. Golden Access passports are free to any US citizen or permanent resident with a permanent disability; applicants simply need to sign an affidavit that they're eligible for federal benefits.

Once you're in the park, the Golden Eagle Passport doesn't reduce camping or other use fees. It's good only for entrance fees. But the Golden Age card provides a 50% discount on all federal-use fees: camping, parking, tours, boat launches and so on. It does not count toward special recreation permit fees or fees charged by park concessionaires.

The Golden Age and Golden Access cards must be obtained in person at any national park fee site. The Golden Eagle card can be obtained in person or by mail by sending a $50 check or money order to National Park Service, 1100 Ohio Drive SW, Room 138, Washington, DC 20242, Attention: Golden Eagle Passport.

than 120 areas of natural or historical value that are open to the public and maintained by the Texas Parks Department. They are in every region of the state and offer an incredibly diverse range of activities and programs, including swimming, climbing, excellent camping and some accommodations facilities (see Accommodations, later), horseback riding, biking and hiking trails, and some ranger-led programs. See each chapter for information on its state parks.

The Texas Parks Department maintains an excellent website at www.tpwd.state.tx.us/park/parks.htm. Park admission fees range from $1 to $5 per person or per carload. Texas residents who are older than 65 are entitled to discount entry fees, but nonresidents of any age pay the regular price.

The Gold Texas Conservation Passport ($50) is an annual vehicle pass that gives unlimited park entry to the holder and other passengers in the vehicle.

The Silver Texas Conservation Passport ($25) is a laminated receipt giving admission to the holder and other passengers in the vehicle to some wildlife management areas at certain times. For all pass information and order forms, write to Texas Parks and Wildlife, 4200 Smith School Rd, Austin, TX 78744.

GOVERNMENT & POLITICS

The United States has a federal system with a president and a bicameral congress, consisting of the 100-member Senate and the 435-member House of Representatives. Each of the 50 states has two senators and a number of congressional representatives in proportion to its population.

The president, whose term is for four years, is chosen by an electoral college consisting of a number of individual electors from each state equivalent to its number of senators and congressional representatives, who vote in accordance with the popular vote within their state. To be elected, the president must obtain a majority of 270 of the total 538 electoral votes (the District of Columbia, which has no voting representatives in Congress, nevertheless has three electoral votes). The president may serve only two terms of four years each.

The head of each state's government is the governor, who presides over a bicameral legislature consisting of a senate and a house delegation.

The hardworking Texas legislature meets for 140 days every two years (you read that right) to consider '… all bills and resolutions and other matters then pending,' according to the Texas Constitution (fun fact: Article VI, Section I of that document denies the vote to idiots and lunatics). It is made up of a house of representatives (with 150 members) and a senate (with 31 members). Bills are introduced by representatives and go through several subcommittees before being argued and amended on the floor of the house, which then passes it on to the senate, which sends it through several subcommittees and then argues and amends it further. The bills are then sent back to the house for even further amendment and, finally, to the governor, who can sign them into law or veto them. About half of all bills die in the process.

ECONOMY

Even though the US has the largest gross national product in the world, $7 trillion, the average Belgian, Norwegian or Kuwaiti has a higher per capita income.

US citizens pay taxes on a sliding scale, with the poorest paying around 15% of personal earnings. The richest fifth pay around 40%. Average Americans can expect to pay out 20% of their earnings.

The Texas economy is based these days on several breadwinners, and oil is rather surprisingly low on the list. Farming is a major industry in Texas, which has more farms, and more farmland area, than any other state. Texas produces the second-largest number of jobs per year in the United States, and despite cuts in defense spending that reduced the number of military jobs in the state, in 1996, Texans' personal incomes grew on average 2% more than those in any other state.

The service sector is still the largest employer in Texas; other economic powerhouses in the state are mining, energy, manufacturing, tourism, communications and, increasingly, high-tech industries.

Trade with Mexico since the passage of NAFTA has been booming. Mexico is the end market for more than one-third of Texas' exports; in 1996, this accounted for $27.5 billion in revenues – and Texas enjoys a trade surplus with Mexico, which exported $16 billion to Texas the same year. While NAFTA also includes freer trade with Canada, Canadian exports and imports barely affect the state.

POPULATION & PEOPLE

Texas added more people to its state population between 1990 and '96 than any other state in the union – according to census bureau estimates, up 2.1 million to 19 million statewide. Despite the notable absence of Native Americans (which is due to many factors, but chiefly because of mistreatment by American settlers), Texas' citizenry is a model of the 'melting pot' cliché, with a population of, in approximate order of percentage, white, Hispanic, African American and European immigrants. Of the latter, the standouts are German, Czech and French, now in their third and fourth generation in Texas – see the History section earlier for more information.

Hispanics have had perhaps a greater influence on Texas life than any other group save Native Americans, in terms of language, culture, architecture and food.

There are three formally recognized Indian tribes still living in Texas, though only two live on State of Texas-approved reservations. The best known is the Alabama-Coushatta Reservation (☎ 409-563-4391, 800-444-3567) in Livingston (see the Northeast Texas chapter), which is open to visitors.

In 1680 the Spanish forced the Tiguas (pronounced TEE-was) to relocate from their native lands near present-day New Mexico and proclaimed them extinct, much to their dismay. The premature announcement of their demise was echoed in the 1870s, when the town of Ysleta and all other Tigua lands in Texas, granted to the tribe by the king of Spain in 1682, were incorporated by the state and opened to white homesteading and settlement. This effectively confiscated all but three acres of Tigua land. To its disgrace, the Texas government didn't recognize the Tiguas as a tribe again until 1967. Their reservation is today again in Ysleta del Sur Pueblo near El Paso (see the West Texas chapter for more information).

In 1977, a Texas bill to recognize the traditional Kickapoo tribe of the Eagle Pass area passed the Texas legislature, but it was struck down by the state's attorney general as unconstitutional in 1979. In 1982 the Kickapoos sought and received federal recognition as an official subgroup of the Oklahoma Kickapoo Indian Tribe, enabling them to establish their own reservation, though this is under control of the Federal Bureau of Indian Affairs and not the State of Texas. The Kickapoo are migratory and spend only a fraction of each year on their reservation, near Eagle Pass; the rest of the year they spend in Mexico. An agreement between the US and Mexican governments permits them to move freely between the two countries.

EDUCATION

One of the stated reasons of Texas' desire for independence from Mexico was the lack of an effective system of public education, but the Republic of Texas never managed to establish one. The Texas public school system was set up in 1854 and today, despite grumbling from parents' groups, is one of the healthiest in the nation. State law requires the teaching of Texas history to all students and requires passage of a controversial standardized state test (TAAS, or Texas Assessment of Academic Skills test) before graduation – failure of any part of TAAS results in pupils being held back, regardless of their academic performance throughout their high school careers. Charges that the tests are weighted against Hispanic and black students were dismissed in 1997 by the governor, George W Bush III (yes, the son).

The US education system places children in classes (grades) based on age and performance from first to 12th grade. Generally speaking, pupils are placed in a grade number that is their age minus five: first grade begins at age six, 12th grade at age 17.

ARTS
Literature

There are hundreds of notable Texas writers, and more are coming up all the time, so this is not an exhaustive list, just one to familiarize you with some of the best that Texas has to offer. One very good way to get quickly into the swing of things is to pick up a copy of any edition of *Texas Bound* – see Books in the Facts for the Visitor chapter for more information.

Of all Texas' literary stars, a transplant seems to loom largest in the public imagination: Michigan-born James A Michener, who relocated to Texas after his work on a book of the same name. Michener wrote dozens of books on dozens of subjects, but he is best known for his fictionalized histories of regions and countries, including *Poland*, *Mexico*, *The Caribbean* and of course, *Texas*. He is also fondly remembered in the state as a philanthropist, having set up the Mari and James A Michener Collection of Twentieth-Century American Art in the Blanton Museum of Art in Austin, and the Texas Center for Writers at the University of Texas at Austin.

The best-known mass-market superstar of Texas literature is Larry McMurtry, the Wichita Falls-born writer whose books and screenplays have entered into classic territory in the USA; his works include *Lonesome Dove*, *The Last Picture Show* and *Terms of Endearment* and its sequel, *The Evening Star*.

Sandra Cisneros is one of the most important bicultural writers of the 20th century. In her novels, stories and poetry – such as the *House on Mango Street* (actually set in Chicago); its spin-off children's book, *Hairs/Pelitos*; *Woman Hollering Creek and Other Stories*; *My Wicked Wicked Ways* and the wonderfully sexy *Loose Woman* – Cisneros celebrates the bicultural spirit that travelers in Texas so often look right past.

More poetry with a bicultural theme, as well as books on the migrant workers of south Texas, comes from Tomás Rivera, in *The Searchers: Collected Poetry* and *Y no se lo tragó la tierra/And the Earth Did Not Devour Him*.

A communist sympathizer who was later called quasi-fascist and who became a political moderate even after that, Katherine Anne Porter (1890-1980) wrote many novellas and short stories. Some took place in and about Texas and Mexico; most are about people struggling to make sense of the world and include the classics *Ship of Fools*; *Pale Horse, Pale Rider: Three Short Novels*; and *Flowering Judas*, a collection of stories.

You absolutely must not miss El Paso-born Cormac McCarthy's Border trilogy, winner of national awards and acclaim, made up of brooding, dark and masterfully crafted coming-of-age stories involving young men from Texas who, for various reasons, head off to Mexico. McCarthy's use of odd punctuation – periods, commas, question marks and run-on sentences, but no quotation marks – enables the reader, after the first page, to seriously get into the speech rhythms of the characters. The trilogy consists of *All the Pretty Horses*, *The Crossing* and the latest, *Cities of the Plain*. *All the Pretty Horses* is to be released as a film by Billy Bob Thornton, starring Matt Damon.

Katherine Anne Porter

Austin-based Carol Dawson has produced three superbly received novels in recent years, all set in or including the mythical central Texas town of Bernice, and all told with blistering satire, an astounding attention to detail and magnificent plots. They are *The Waking Spell*, *Body of Knowledge* and her latest, *Meeting the Minotaur*, starring 22-year-old Taylor Troys. The last transplants the myth of Theseus and the Minotaur to Texas and then to Asia.

English-born Bastrop resident Michael Moorcock, whose books include the classic *Behold the Man* and scores of others (such as his best-selling Elric series) has a cult following of science fiction and fantasy fans.

Two very popular Texas romance writers are Adrienne De Wolfe *(Texas Wildcat)* and Lisa Kleypas *(Because You're Mine)*.

Suspense & Thriller Kinky Friedman, the cat-loving, cigar-chomping, lovable, on-again, off-again front man for the country-and-western group Kinky Friedman & the Texas Jewboys, currently sits in his Texas Hill Country ranch writing books that star himself as a cat-loving, cigar-smoking amateur private detective in such classics of the genre as *Armadillos and Old Lace*; *Elvis, Jesus & Coca-Cola*; *A Case of Lone Star* and *Greenwich Killing Time*, some set in the Hill Country, some in New York, all featuring his bizarre collection of friends and companions.

James Lee Burke's *Two for Texas* is a historical novel covering the Texas War for Independence and the events leading up to it. Burke began writing on Texas, then Louisiana and other areas of the South and is best known for his series of Dave Robicheaux mysteries. But Burke may be heading for a Texas-based series if *Cimarron Rose* gets where it probably will – into the hearts of Burke fans. The book, starring ex-Texas-Ranger-turned-attorney Billy Bob Holland and set in the Texas town of Deaf Smith, has all the trappings of a successful series.

Joe R Lansdale's books, such as *Bad Chili*, *Mucho Mojo* and *The Two-Bear Mambo*, star the east Texas field laborer Hap Collins and his decidedly dangerous friend Leonard Pine and include shitkickers, good ol' boys and enough folksy commentary to make Molly Ivins (see later) blush.

Lawyer-turned-shop-owner China Bayles runs an herb store in the mythical town of Pecan Springs, near Houston, in a long-running series by Susan Wittig Albert that includes *Thyme of Death*, *Witches' Bane*, *Rosemary Remembered* and *Hangman's Root*.

Mary Willis Walker's crime reporter Molly Cates is a Texas favorite, appearing in books including *Under the Beetle's Cellar* and the Edgar award-winning *Red Scream*.

If Rick Riordan can manage to make Tres 'I am Spanish. My name is Tres, it means three' Navarre, his San Antonio-based private eye, a bit less indestructible and smug about his Spanish-speaking and tai chi abilities, he'll have a real winner – the books are already very readable and the plots beautifully twisted; look for *Big Red Tequila* and *Widower's Two-Step*.

If someone is looking for a good serial-killer novel, the Austin bookstore Book People points them toward *Mercy*, by Austin-based David Lindsey.

And we can't forget Texas-born novelist Ann Rice, of vampire-tale fame.

Humor & Politics Nobody, but nobody, beats Molly Ivins on pure acerbic wit and the exposure of Texisms big and small. This nationally syndicated columnist for the *Fort Worth Star-Telegram* and contributor to publications including the *Nation*, the *Progressive* and the *New York Times Magazine* and the *New York Times Book Review* was born and raised in Texas and lives in Austin, where she reliably pens beautiful copy and the occasionally classic observation (she said, for example, that Kinky Friedman 'spreads more joy than Ross Perot's ears'). Her books include *Molly Ivins Can't Say That, Can She?*, *Nothin' But Good Times Ahead* and *You Gotta Dance with Them What Brung You: Politics in the Clinton Years*.

Two-term Texas agriculture commissioner Jim Hightower is another Texan critic of the Ivins spirit, if not of the same league, and a

Molly Ivins

lambaster of corporate culture in his book *There's Nothing in the Middle of the Road but Yellow Stripes and Dead Armadillos*.

Music
Texas musicians have had perhaps more influence on American music than those from any other state. From blues and country and western to western swing and rock and roll, Texas has produced and cultivated the trendsetters, the record-breakers and the kings (though not, unfortunately, the King). A great primer to Texas music is the three-CD series Texas Music (Rhino Records/Sony Music Special Projects), which contains a foreword from former governor Ann Richards. The CD volumes are *Postwar Blues Combos*, featuring such greats as T-Bone Walker, Big Walter and His Thunderbirds, Lester Williams and Freddie King; *Western Swing and Honky Tonk*, with cuts from Bob Wills and his Texas Playboys, Roy Newman and His Boys, the Blue Ridge Playboys, Al Dexter and His Troopers, and Asleep at the Wheel; and *Garage Bands and Psychedelia*, with 'Treat Her Right' from Roy Head and the Traits and cuts from the Steve Miller Band, the Ron-Dels and the Chessmen.

Classical There's not a whole lot of classical music in the state but what's there is darned good, notably with symphony orchestras in, as you'd expect, the larger cities: Dallas, Austin, Houston and San Antonio; see their chapters for specific information.

Van Cliburn Piano Competition In 1958, a Louisiana native named Van Cliburn became the first American to win the Tchaikovsky piano competition in Moscow. He was just 24 years old. Today, he lends his name to the Van Cliburn International Piano Competition, held every four years in Fort Worth to discover the world's top young pianists.

The Van Cliburn Foundation selects about 150 musicians to perform concerts in Milan, Moscow, Chicago, New York City, Utrecht and Fort Worth. From those recitals, 35 pianists are chosen for the final Fort Worth competition, which quadrennially draws aficionados, critics and classical-music talent scouts to Texas. Medalists gain immediate acclaim, with recording contracts, television specials and appearances with top orchestras worldwide.

The next competition, set for late May and early June 2001, will be the first at the Bass Performance Hall. If you're interested in tickets, call the Van Cliburn Foundation at ☎ 817-738-6536 to get on its mailing list, or for tickets call the central ticket office at ☎ 817-335-9000. Seats will be sold about six months in advance of the event.

Blues Discussing the blues is a dangerous subject, as everyone seems to have an opinion on it. We say that while blues music developed throughout the South, especially around the Mississippi Delta and in Memphis, Tennessee, Texas is definitely its home; what the world knows today as 'blues' is a direct legacy of Texas musicians. An evolution of field chants, the blues is as complex as it sounds simple – Texas blues musicians were the inspiration for so many modern rockers that Austin has dubbed itself America's live-music capital. It's also the site of one of rock music's most important annual showcases, South by Southwest

(see Special Events in the Facts for the Visitor chapter).

Blind Lemon Jefferson, who played clubs and brothels in Dallas, made the earliest known recordings of any Texas blues singer and went on to make more than 75 recordings of blues tunes in the four years between 1925 and his death in 1929. Other powerful early blues musicians included Aaron 'T-Bone' Walker, Lester Williams, Robert Johnson, WC Clark and, later, BB King and Albert Collins.

Rock & Roll There are those who say that Lubbock-born Buddy Holly (see the Panhandle Plains chapter) invented rock and roll – that's going a little batty, but it's true that Texan musicians have been at the forefront of rock since its inception. Among rock's ranks are Texan performers such as Holly, Roy Orbison, Roky Erickson of the 13th Floor Elevators, Janis Joplin, Stevie Ray Vaughan and Michelle Shocked, as well as bands such as ZZ Top, the Steve Miller Band, the Fabulous Thunderbirds and the Butthole Surfers. For more information on

Blind Lemon Jefferson

Texas rock and roll, see History in the Austin section of the South Central Texas chapter.

Country & Western Texas wasn't the birthplace of country and western – that twangy, slidey coagulation of styles that combines the Anglo-Irish folk influences of early settlers with cowboy music and fiddle playing – but many argue it's where it was perfected. Country-and-western music is played throughout the US, and some of its most successful stars have come from Texas, such as the original singing cowboy, Gene Autry, who starred in more than 100 movies; and the Big Two: Waylon Jennings and Willie Nelson. Other notable Texas contributors to the genre include Nanci Griffith, Roger Miller, Rosie Flores, Lyle Lovett, Barbara Mandrell, Kris Kristofferson, and the gambler himself, Kenny Rogers. Also, don't forget the contributions of Kinky Friedman, who along with his Texas Jewboys has given the world such classic tunes as *Ride 'Em Jewboy* and *Get Your Biscuits in the Oven and Your Buns in the Bed*.

Austin's Armadillo World Headquarters was a concert space in which the outlaw-country movement first drew wide attention, and *Austin City Limits*, a public television program, first brought country-and-western music a national audience – see the Austin section of the South Central Texas chapter for more information.

Western Swing While country and western can be traced to Anglo-Irish folk songs, Texas' most original contribution to modern music is western swing, a hodgepodge of styles, including ragtime, jazz, blues, mariachi, polka, country and western, Tejano and *conjunto* and everything else around when Bob Wills and His Texas Playboys began recording the genre in the 1920s. (For more on Wills, see the Quitaque & Turkey section in the Panhandle Plains chapter.)

Western swing continues to be popular in Texas; for a whole lot of information about it, get a copy of Duncan McClean's *Lone Star Swing* – see Books in the Facts for the Visitor chapter.

Gene Autry

Tejano Turn your radio on in south Texas and about all you'll hear is Tejano music, also known by many other names, including conjunto and Tex-Mex – an indigenous blend of European and local styles that is as cross-border in its popularity as is the region's culture.

Much of its origin dates to the mid-1800s, when central European immigrants brought their folk music to what is today Texas and Mexico. These waltzes, polkas and other forms soon mingled with Spanish influences. By the 1920s, a bilingual form of music had evolved. Songs with lyrics in Spanish and English drew on old thematic chestnuts such as love, broken hearts and beer drinking. The raucous and brassy sound was accented with a heavy dose of accordions and guitars. Tejano developed in clubs from Corpus Christi south to Brownsville and west to Laredo, spanning both sides of the border.

Beginning in the 1970s, groups such as La Familia and the Latin Breed adopted a more commercial sound that drew on rock, blues, country and even disco.

Another example of an artist who incorporates many traditional styles is San Antonio-born Tejana folk musician Tish Hinojosa. The migration of people from the border areas spread fans throughout the US. In the 1980s, a few groups signed with major record labels, and strong sales spurred the commercialization of the music. In the 1990s, Selena became the first Tejano superstar, a status that mushroomed after her murder in 1995 (see the Gulf Coast chapter for more information).

The folk traditions of Tejano are most apparent in the dances that accompany the music; many of them are derived directly from the group dances of the original immigrants. Tejano clubs large and small can be found throughout Texas. Spinning the radio dial in the areas of its greatest popularity will net its myriad of styles.

Cajun & Zydeco The exuberant cousin of traditional Cajun music is found in bayou towns south and east of Houston; it's a loud succession of two-step rhythms paced by a traditional 12-key Cajun accordion. Its roots are in the French Acadians who populated the swamps of Louisiana 200 years ago and spread into the geographically identical region of southeast Texas.

The origins of the name 'zydeco' – like many Cajun traditions – are somewhat lost in the bayou backwaters. It's known to be a vague adaptation of the first syllables of the French phrase *les haricots sont pas salés*, 'the snap beans aren't salted.' This is a traditional Cajun phrase describing hard times – for which zydeco in all its vibrancy is definitely the antidote.

Fiddles and various percussion instruments, many of them built from whatever their players found rusting in the swamp, are the main accompaniments to the accordions. The singers usually spend more time imploring the crowd to dance through shouts, whoops and sound effects than they do singing the heavily accented French lyrics that would confound any native French speaker.

Zydeco has gained a national following, and groups such as Buckwheat Zydeco have gained legions of fans through tours across the US.

Film

Given Texas' history, culture and mythology, it should be no surprise that the state has been both the setting and shooting location for scores of films. Besides the expected westerns, there are numerous dramas, comedies and other genres set in contemporary Texas.

What follows is a list of 25 of the most interesting movies – both good and bad – that were set and filmed in the state. All are widely available for rental and can serve as a good place to start building upon or busting your own Texas stereotypes.

The Alamo (1960) – At times this 151-minute movie seems longer than the siege in San Antonio. This was John Wayne's paean to Texas heroism. He directed and financed the production, which left him in debt for the rest of his life. Filmed on a huge set built in Brackettville that you can still visit today, the final battle scenes redeem much of the early speechifying, so you might want to hit the fast-forward button.

The Best Little Whorehouse in Texas (1982) – Burt Reynolds, Dom DeLuise and Jim Nabors tried to bring the hit Broadway musical to life and ended up a bit limp. Dolly Parton stars as the madam of the Chicken Ranch. Once in a while the music stops and somebody tries to get serious. They should keep singing.

Blood Simple (1984) – The first effort by offbeat moviemaking brothers Joel and Ethan Coen *(Fargo)*, this film shows all the little things that go wrong when a Texas roadhouse owner tries to off his wife. The characters are slimy, the gore intense and the complex script a pure delight.

Breast Men (1997) – This HBO movie is a hilarious yet cautionary tale of two Houston surgeons who developed the silicone breast implant in the 1960s. In a study of morality, one's career perks up while the other's sags.

Brewster McCloud (1970) – A strange but seemingly gentle boy named Brewster dreams of building a set of wings and flying in the Houston Astrodome. He's both helped and hindered by his wacko mom, played by Sally Kellerman. This early Robert Altman film is a prelude to some of his later and greater works.

Dazed and Confused (1993) – The mid-1970s return in all their polyester glory as we follow the exploits of a band of Texas high school seniors as they terrorize freshmen and engage in mind-numbed exploits. In this coming-of-age movie directed by Richard Linklater, the central characters achieve the mental age of three.

El Mariachi (1992) – Robert Rodriguez' little movie shot on the Texas-Mexican border for $7000 became an icon for film school students everywhere when it was shown across the US. It made Rodriguez a bundle and received much critical acclaim. Legends aside, it is a charming fable about an unlucky traveling mariachi.

Giant (1956) – At three hours and 21 minutes, this film is as sprawling as the King Ranch that was its inspiration. They never quite make that clear but writer Edna Ferber did spend several months there before penning her best-selling novel. Elizabeth Taylor, Rock Hudson, James Dean and many, many more are superb in this big-fun and big-ticket yarn tracing the life of an oil and ranching family. Facsimiles of the café where Hudson gets the tar beat out of him can still be found along some of the dustier Texas back roads.

Hellfighters (1968) – The screen doesn't exactly sizzle in this plodding drama with John Wayne as a Texas oil-well firefighter. The real infernos must be more exciting than this, although the film is a good chance to see the compelling details of oil exploration.

Hud (1963) – Everyone praises Paul Newman's performance in this excellent movie except Newman himself. He thinks he was *too* much of a stinker as the bad son of a crumbling Texas ranching family. The script is based on the Larry McMurtry novel *Horsemen, Pass By*.

The Last Picture Show (1971) – This engaging film is also based on the novel by Larry McMurtry, who cowrote the script with director Peter Bogdanovich. The seemingly simple, but actually complex, story traces the coming of age of two high school football players in a deader-than-dirt small Texas town in the 1950s. In 1990, Bogdanovich and many of the stars, such as Cybill Shepherd, Cloris Leachman and Jeff Bridges, reunited for the much less satisfying sequel, *Texasville*.

Lone Star (1996) – A compelling drama set against the unsettled racial atmosphere of a Texas border town. A sheriff (Chris Cooper) has to confront the misdeeds committed by his father (Matthew McConaughey) decades before. Besides working well as a mystery, the film does a

Texas Actors

We can't explain it, but it seems that Texas has produced a disproportionately large number of movie and television stars. One mind-blowing search on the Internet Film Database (us.imdb.com/search.html) for 'Actors born in Texas' produced page after bandwidth-hogging page of results. Yeah, most people know about Larry 'JR' Hagman, Tommy Lee Jones and Steve Martin, but the list just goes on and on (including two major *Star Trek: The Next Generation* characters as well as the show's creator).

Some of the names the search returned (including a couple of nonactors) were Debbie Allen, Tex Avery, Joe Don Baker, Robby Benson, Powers Boothe, spooky Gary Busey, Carol Burnett, tepid Indiana Jones sidekick Kate Capshaw, Cyd Charisse, the brilliantly dastardly Dabney Coleman, Joan Crawford, Wheat Thins pitchwoman Sandy Duncan, Shelley Duvall, former Oingo Boingo front man Danny Elfman, former journalist Linda Ellerbee, Farrah Fawcett, Michelle 'Ro Laren' Forbes, Ethan Hawke, Kris Kristofferson, Matthew McConaughey, Meat Loaf, musician and *Hee Haw* great Buck Owens, Robin Wright-Penn, H Ross Perot, Randy 'I play the drunk guy' Quaid, movie critic Rex Reed, Debbie Reynolds, Kevin Reynolds, *Star Trek* creator Gene Roddenberry, Ginger Rogers, Kenny Rogers, Roy Rogers, Aaron Spelling, Sissy Spacek, Brent Spiner, Patrick Swayze, Henry Thomas, Rip Torn, song-and-dance man Tommy Tune, Forest Whitaker, and JoBeth Williams.

good job of exploring the complex blend of cultures between the US and Mexico.

North Dallas Forty (1979) – Made when the Dallas Cowboys were at the zenith of their self-proclaimed tenure as 'America's Team,' this film is the best movie ever made about American football. Nick Nolte stars as a player on a fictional Dallas team who can barely get out to the field without a variety of drugs administered by team doctors. Needless to say, the National Football League hated it because of its uncompromising exposé of the sport. Think of it as *Network* with spikes.

Paris, Texas (1984) – Next to nothing in this movie is set in the title town. That clear, it should be said that this is a fascinating study of a man, Dean Stockwell, who finds his long-missing brother, Harry Dean Stanton, in Big Bend. The Sam Shepard script was directed by Wim Wenders.

Places in the Heart (1984) – Robert Benton wrote and directed this look at life in his hometown of Waxahacie. Set in the 1930s, the drama follows the struggle of a heroic farm woman to raise her kids and crops despite dust storms, drought and the Ku Klux Klan. Sally Field trumped her own Oscar-winning performance in the film with her famous speech at the awards ('You like me! You really like me!').

Red River (1948) – Director Howard Hawks was at his epic best in this battle of good and evil set on the Chisholm Trail in Texas. John Wayne stars as a hardheaded tyrant who drives cattle and drives off his charge a darkly handsome Montgomery Clift. The rolling plains of Texas never looked grander.

The Searchers (1956) – This moody and engrossing saga is just about the best western ever made and definitely John Wayne's finest role. A pioneer family is murdered by Indians on their Texas ranch, and their daughter Natalie Wood is kidnapped, setting off a decade-long search by her uncle, the Duke. The final shot may stay with you almost as long.

Selena (1997) – A straightforward retelling of the life of the Tejano music martyr that is better than one would expect given that it was produced by her father. See the boxed text in the Corpus Christi section of the Gulf Coast chapter for more details.

Slacker (1991) – Director and writer Richard Linklater got a bunch of his shiftless Austin friends together and made a wonderful little film about a bunch of shiftless people in Austin. Intricately interwoven, the film is a series of biting vignettes whose strength can be judged by the fact that you want to see more of everybody you meet.

The Texas Chainsaw Massacre (1974) – A backwoods Texas family runs a barbecue stand where they serve something even less palatable than roadkill. You've seen it all since, but this was one of the first films where a dorky boy goes into a house that he will later exit in pieces or a

where a girl screams a *lot* before the final blood-soaked slash. Sequels made since don't match the gory but appealing innocence of the original.

Tender Mercies (1983) – Robert Duvall won an Oscar for his superb and understated portrayal of a down-on-his-luck country-and-western singer who meets a woman and tries to redeem his life. It was filmed in Palmer.

Terms of Endearment (1983) – Winner of a slew of Oscars, including one for Best Picture, this movie has legions of fans and legions of those who flee screaming at the thought of listening to Shirley MacLaine and Debra Winger jabbering at each other in this typically yakky James L Brooks film. There is hope for the jaded, however, in Jack Nicholson's performance as a rogue ex-astronaut. The 1996 sequel, *The Evening Star*, which is also largely set in Houston, is widely regarded as unwatchable.

Thin Blue Line (1988) – Director Errol Morris' documentary is one of the most powerful films ever made. It tells the story of Randall Adams, who was given a life prison sentence for murdering a Dallas policeman but who, in fact, was innocent. The film got Adams released – no small feat – and captured the confession of the real killer. Not just a repetition of facts, the film is an engrossing investigation into the case and the characters involved.

Urban Cowboy (1980) – John Travolta followed up on his efforts promoting disco in *Saturday Night Fever* with this homage to macho cads that might as well be called *Saturday Night Bull*. Supposedly based on a bar called Gilley's in the petrochemical-laced Houston suburb of Pasadena, *Urban Cowboy* is centered on a competition to ride a mechanical bull. Amazingly, the film struck a note with other macho cads all over the United States, and for the next few years there were country-and-western bars in every major city filled with boot-clad white-collar yahoos mounting mechanical bulls (many of the bull joints had been converted from discos).

Viva Zapata! (1952) – John Steinbeck wrote the screenplay for this study of the Mexican revolutionary hero, who is played by a deadly serious Marlon Brando. Much of the filming was done in the tiny border town of Roma. Each day hundreds of Mexicans swam across the Rio Grande to work as extras on the film, this being a time before the border was lined with heavily armed guards. The story is dignified and enjoyable, although you'll probably agree that Brando went over the top in designing his own makeup.

SOCIETY & CONDUCT

On the whole, Texans are among the friendliest people on the planet and never hesitate to smile or laugh and wish you a nice day – and it's one of the only places where you get the sense that they mean it. It's common to engage in small talk with most everyone you meet.

There's a straightforward and conservative approach to life in much of the state – outward displays of emotion are looked upon as out of place. Texans are highly respectful in conversation, and 'Sir' and 'Ma'am' are used by almost everyone, so it's nice to get into the spirit of things by joining in. Women shouldn't be surprised by men or other women calling them 'honey,' 'doll' (yes, still!) or 'sugar-pie' – most people are just being friendly – see Women Travelers in the Facts for the Visitor chapter for more information.

Michael Hicks, in his excellent book *How to Be Texan* (see Books in the Facts for the Visitor chapter) has an entire section discussing 'How to Stay Alive in Texas,' including rule No 1, 'Never tell a Texan his dog is too skinny.' That's sound advice, and it can

be extended to most situations here: don't try to foist your opinions on Texans, who may have rather large opinions of their own.

Another fact of life in Texas is that, unless you're from southern Spain or another part of the US South, things are probably going to be quite a bit slower around here than you may be used to. Get into the rhythm of life here; slow down, smell the bluebonnets and enjoy yourself – you'll have a great time.

Sports

American sports developed separately from the rest of the world and consequently baseball (with its clone, softball), football and basketball dominate the sports scene, both for spectators and participants. The fact that football and basketball are sponsored by high schools and universities gives them a community foundation that reinforces their primacy. Basketball has the additional advantages of requiring limited space and equipment, making it a popular pastime among inner-city residents.

Baseball is so embedded in the American psyche that, despite complex rules and labor-management conflicts at professional levels, it continues to flourish. Many of the most meaningful metaphors in American language and political discourse come from the sport, such as 'play ball,' 'getting to first base' and the recently debased 'three strikes and you're out.'

Despite the success of the USA's hosting of the 1994 World Cup, soccer has made limited inroads, mostly among immigrants, but has failed as a spectator sport.

Car Culture

Foreign visitors will soon realize that, for better or worse, the automobile is more than just transportation – it's an extension of one's ego, a symbol of freedom and independence, a status symbol. It's impossible to overstate the impact of the automobile on American life, a topic that has become the subject of many books. For car culture at its best, tune in to National Public Radio's *Car Talk* on Sunday mornings. See also the boxed text on pickup trucks and Chevy Suburbans in the Getting Around chapter.

RELIGION

Texans are predominantly Christians; the largest single religious group is Roman Catholics, with almost 3.5 million, followed closely by the Protestant Southern Baptist Convention, with about 3.3 million. There are scores of other religious groups in Texas, including Greek Orthodox, Lutherans, Conservative Baptists and more than 100,000 Jewish people.

The US Constitution mandates separation between the powers of church and state, yet issues like prayer in public schools and the teaching of creationism versus evolution continue to be the subject of heated political discourse. Nominal allegiance is more widespread than church attendance, but many churchgoers are extremely devout – especially in Texas, which is considered to be the 'buckle in the Bible Belt' – the latter being a swath of states across the Southern and Midwestern US with large numbers of highly devout Christians.

Largely because of the immigrant nature of US society, travelers can find members of just about every religion, faith or sect in the major cities, and even smaller towns will have several smaller groups.

LANGUAGE

American English is the most common language spoken in Texas, though it's tinted with a variety of accents depending on where you are in the state. Don't try to impersonate any

High School Football

'Ref! You *suck*!' erupts an otherwise mild-mannered man, who could be an insurance salesman. Shouted several decibels above the already raucous crowd noise, it soars above the partisan cacophony near the end of the first half of a high school football play-off game between the Clear Brook Wolverines and the Worthing Colts.

Far from being admonished by those around him, the shouter – dressed in a custom-made, red-and-black jumpsuit emblazoned with Clear Brook's snarling logo – sees many heads nod in agreement, and a few other adults make much more profane judgments on the referees, their bloodlines and cognitive abilities.

All of these adults are surrounded by their young children, who join their parents in the vocal din.

That the official's call was accurate as seen by more neutral observers matters not a whit in this tiny snapshot of the world of Texas high school football, where passions run high. Before the game between these two Houston-area schools, the crowd of more than 1000 was admonished by a reedy voice over the public address system not to 'do anything to make these young people doubt their commitment to athletics.' And the manners lecture didn't end there; the reedy voice also implored people to show respect for the cheerleaders, band members and, yes, even the officials.

Texas high school football has taken on mythic proportions and meanings throughout the state. On autumn Friday nights fans gather to cheer their local teams at brightly lit stadiums in every town. At stake are local pride, reputations and other intangibles that fuel the mania. The focus of this raw emotion are teams of teenagers – many barely shaving – who do battle within the complex strictures that govern American football. The coaches at larger schools – who often make more money than the teachers – endeavor to train 16- and 17-year-olds to perform as facsimiles of the pros who play on Sunday afternoons.

How seriously these games are taken can be seen by the trappings that surround the game. The players are merely at the apex of a huge pyramid. There are legions of student assistants and trainers; handpicked varsity cheerleaders who ascend to these prima-donna

Texas drawls – unless you're Bob Hoskins or Kenneth Branagh it's about as embarrassing to Texan ears as it is when Americans try on their cockney – see Dick Van Dyke in *Mary Poppins* for more information.

Texan English contains some of the most colorful expressions in American English, a language not noted for its dryness. You'll notice that except in major cities, people speak a bit slower than you may be used to. See the boxed text for Texisms you might run across.

The accent is tricky. Contrary to public opinion, most Texans don't sound like JR, including, it seems, JR himself: Larry Hagman, despite his upbringing in Weatherford, had a rather neutral pre-*Dallas* accent (see the old television series *I Dream of Jeannie* for proof) and appears to have put on that ridiculous drawl specifically for his role as JR. In many Texas cities, people have a decidedly unflavored American accent that's hard to peg, even by other Americans. But the accent has affected pronunciations of town names on a statewide basis: 'PAY-cuss' for Pecos, 'green' for Greune, 'MAN-shack' for Manchaca, 'GWAD-uh-loop' for Guadalupe, 'no-AY-sis' for Nueces and 'san ja-SIN-to' for San Jacinto are a few that leap to mind. Note that 'Houston' is pronounced 'HYOU-stun,' not 'HOOS-ton' (while New Yorkers call the street with the same spelling in their city 'HOW-stun,' they all refer properly to the city in Texas as 'HYOU-stun').

spots through competitions as ruthless as those on the field; junior cheerleaders plotting their own rises; vast marching bands; dancing and drill teams; honor guards for the flags; and many, many more. All of these students are backed by the legions of parents who cheer, scream, raise money and more.

Watching the spectacle of a Texas high school football game, one wonders how any learning can take place at all during the season, what with all the football-related activities and preparations that occur. Concerned Texas school officials in the mid-1980s instituted regulations requiring players to meet minimal academic standards that at best would insure basic literacy and a vague grasp of mathematics. Even these standards were found outrageous in many schools, where it was feared that several minutes of homework a night might detract from a star quarterback's ability to complete a pass. School officials eventually backed off, but the issue of requiring student players to learn *something* in class remains a hot topic in the state. The state's 'no pass, no play' law requires a three-week suspension from school and competition in school sports for players who fail any course. While students under suspension can practice with the team, they may not participate in games. Of course, many teachers blanch at the thought of being responsible for keeping a star player out of a big game. For an inside view, see journalist HG Bissinger's *Friday Night Lights* (1991), an eye-opening look at the 1988 high school football season in a small West Texas town.

If you are in Texas on a Friday night from September to November, you should absolutely attend a high school football game. Nowhere will you have a better look at the local psyche as well as a chance to revel in the spectacle and watch the exploits on the field. Games are always covered in exhaustive detail in the sports sections of local newspapers, which discuss the forthcoming night's games every Friday.

The matches and hoopla last about three hours and are usually entertaining right down to the final ceremony, when the opposing teams line up for postgame handshakes – an event, incidentally, that has been banned in some counties to deter brawling.

Ryan Ver Berkmoes

As in most places, the stronger accents tend to come from the rural areas. But Texans love to drawl. Politicians especially have a way of cuddlin' up with the folks by stretchin' out the down-home country flavor of their words, which indeed endears them to the electorate – listen to the difference in a Southern senator's accent when speaking in Washington, DC, versus in Abilene.

Residents of the Texas Hill Country and some central Texas towns speak European languages, usually as a distant second language to English. Fredericksburg has a lot of German speakers, and Czech, Polish and French are spoken to lesser degrees.

'An' Ah Crush Mah Beer Cayans'

Regardless of accent, most Texans have the darndest way of speaking. Many sentences are peppered with folksy expressions, such as 'wise as a tree full o' owls,' and common horse-sense clichés like LBJ's gem, 'It's better to have your enemy inside the tent pissin' out than outside the tent pissin' in.'

On an episode of *Oprah*, taped in Amarillo during Oprah's trial (see the boxed text in the Amarillo section of the Panhandle Plains chapter), columnist Molly Ivins agreed that Texas talk isn't as much about accents as it is about inventing colorful similes and metaphors. While covering the Texas Legislature, Ivins said she learned that Texans have myriad ways of describing stupidity. Among her favorites: 'If dumb was dirt, he'd cover an acre.'

Two of the biggest Texisms you'll come across – affected as they may be – are 'I reckon…' and 'I'm fixin' to…' Some more collected along travels in the Lone Star State include:

Ahtellyawhut – 'I tell you what,' the start of many a sentence in Texas

awl – oil

big ol' – big, as in 'Dallas is a big ol' city.' Its antonym is 'itty bitty'

bob war – barbed wire

howdy; hidey – you'll still hear some people use this to say hello, but mainly it's a tourist thing

little bitty, itty bitty, bitty – small

Meskin – Mexican

sheeyit – shit, drawn out to as many syllables as possible: two is fine, three is better – 'shhh-eee-yit'

shucks – golly, gosh, as in 'aw, shucks, ma'am'

yassir – 'yes sir,' a catchall response

y'all – contraction of 'you all,' as in 'y'all come back now, ya hear?' though more and more frequently used as singular – 'where y'all goin'?' spoken to one person is not uncommon

On a trip in Mexico a few years back, I met a great Texan named Tim who said, in all seriousness, 'I'm pretty much yer avridge Texan, Nick. Ah don't eat quiche, Ah *don't* cross mah laygz an' Ah crush mah beer cayans.'

Facts for the Visitor

SUGGESTED ITINERARIES

During peak times, it's best to visit the larger cities on weekends and smaller towns and the countryside on weekdays in order to take advantage of the reverse commute.

One Week

With just a week in Texas, head for the juice and skip everything else. If you land in Dallas, spend a night there to burn off any jet lag and head for its Deep Ellum district. Then, head south for San Antonio and spend two nights there, taking in the Alamo, the Mission Trail and the Riverwalk. Then, head north and spend a night in the Hill Country, in Fredericksburg or Kerrville. The rest of your time, check out Austin's live-music scene, Barton Creek, the LBJ Library and Ranch and the lakes around town, and call it a trip.

Two Weeks

With a second week you could add the Rio Grande Valley, including South Padre Island and Los Dos Laredos, with side trips into some Tex-Mex border towns. Or, head west to the Big Bend region to witness some of the wonders of Big Bend National Park.

Three Weeks or More

With a bit more time you could add any number of trips farther afield, like a jaunt to the Panhandle Plains and the wine country around Lubbock or to the heavily forested east Texas region. You might also try your hand (or your stomach) at the 72oz steak at the Big Texan in Amarillo, or take in the theme parks around Arlington, San Antonio and Houston.

PLANNING
When to Go

Texas' mild climate makes it possible to visit year-round, but it's not exactly a tropical destination. In winter, temperatures can dip below freezing at night but usually stay rather moderate (see the Climate section in

Facts about Texas). But winter is definitely the off-season in Texas, and some of the larger theme parks, such as San Antonio's Sea World and Six Flags Fiesta Texas, close.

The best times to visit, aside from during special events (see Special Events later in this chapter) are from April to early June and

---

The Best and the Worst

We asked the authors for their choices of the very best that Texas has to offer.

The Best
1. Live music in Austin
2. San Antonio and the Texas Hill Country
3. Rafting the Rio Grande at Big Bend National Park
4. West Texas sunsets
5. The vibrant border culture of El Paso – murals, music and Tex-Mex
6. Autumn in Guadalupe Mountains National Park's McKittrick Canyon
7. The Sixth Floor Museum in Dallas
8. Rocket Park at NASA
9. South Padre Island and the Rio Grande Valley
10. Menil Collection, Houston

The Worst
1. Downtown Houston's confusing tunnel system
2. The sprawling Houston suburbs
3. Desolate Sunday nights in Amarillo
4. Rush-hour traffic in Dallas
5. People who drive on the shoulders of the roads in rural Texas
6. People who finish the 72oz steak at the Big Texan
7. Southeast Texas in August
8. Solicitations from cut-rate dentists in Laredo
9. Space Center Houston
10. Touristy Moody Gardens, Galveston

from September to November, when crowds are thinner, temperatures more moderate and most attractions haven't changed over to slow-season mode yet.

High summer – late June through August – can be stiflingly hot, but it's a dry heat, and there's air-conditioning almost everywhere. It's also when Texas is most crowded.

What Kind of Trip

What kind of trip you take depends on what you're after and how much time you have. If you're in Texas for a short time, your trip will probably center around either the Dallas-Fort Worth area, San Antonio or Austin (with day trips into the Hill Country). If you have time to explore, the most fascinating aspects of Texas – such as its multicultural personality and its surprising diversity of terrain and attractions – become more apparent. You'll be able to follow, say, trips out to the Big Bend area and along the Rio Grande, with occasional jaunts into Mexico, and make visits to the Gulf Barrier Islands, the forests of east Texas and the nightlife and live-music scene in Austin.

It's easily possible to plan thematic trips throughout the state; from winery tours and B&B holidays to hang-gliding or biking treks, the information and tourism infrastructure in Texas is highly developed and easy to navigate.

Travel, including solo travel, is generally safe and easygoing. Unlike in many states, there's a good public transportation network in Texas; all major cities and many smaller towns are served by public bus and train. It is always easier with a car or motorcycle, though, and Texas is a very good place to buy a used car (see Purchase under Car & Motorcycle in the Getting Around chapter).

Maps

Two good map companies to contact for all kinds of maps are MapLink (☎ 805-692-6777, fax 805-692-6787, custserv@maplink.com), 30 S La Patera Lane, Suite 5, Santa Barbara, CA 93117, and Omni Resources (☎ 336-227-8300, 800-742-2677, custserv@omnimap.com), 1004 S Mebane St, PO Box 2096, Burlington, NC 27216.

The Texas Department of Transportation (☎ 512-832-7000, 800-452-9292) produces the excellent *Texas Official Travel Map*, available free at visitors' centers and tourist offices. The American Automobile Association (AAA) produces the best city maps by far for major Texas cities. Other city map producers include Streetwise, HM Gousha and Rand McNally, all available in bookstores and gas stations.

The AAA issues the most comprehensive and dependable highway maps, free with AAA membership (see Useful Organizations later in this chapter) and for sale to nonmembers. These range from national, regional and state maps to detailed maps of cities, counties and even relatively small towns.

The US Geological Survey (USGS), an agency of the Department of the Interior, publishes detailed topographic maps of the entire country at scales up to 1:250,000. Maps at 1:62,500, or approximately 1 inch=1 mile, are ideal for backcountry hiking and backpacking. Many bookstores and outdoor-equipment specialists carry a wide selection of topographic maps.

Visitors spending any significant amount of time in the state may want to get the Texas volume of the DeLorme Mapping series of atlases and gazetteers, which contain detailed topographic and highway maps at a scale of 1:250,000. Available in some bookstores, these are especially useful off main highways and cost about $20. DeLorme also produces *Street Atlas USA* ($29), a CD-ROM that pinpoints addresses anywhere in the USA.

What to Bring

What to lug with you depends greatly on where and when you go. The rule of thumb is that the happiest travelers are those who can carry all their luggage onboard a plane, but that's often impractical.

If you're staying in cities and renting cars, then it doesn't really matter what you kind of luggage you use; a large sausage bag or suitcase generally works best. A travelpack is a combination of backpack and shoulder bag. Its straps zip away inside the pack when not needed, making it easy to handle in airports and on crowded public transportation. It also looks reasonably smart.

One of the best things about Texas is that clothing – and pretty much anything else you might need – is readily available and probably cheaper than it is at home, thanks to the enormous outlet malls in central Texas (see Shopping later in this chapter). But even in remote areas, anything you might forget is probably procurable.

Generally, if you come here in summer, you'll need light clothing, but be prepared for sudden downpours, Arctic air-conditioning and, in the northern sections of the state, wind. In winter, a medium-weight waterproof jacket, sweater and long pants are essential.

If traveling along the Gulf Coast, swimming, snorkeling and surfing gear; a rain poncho or umbrella (especially in summer); a day backpack for hiking trips or other excursions; solid walking shoes; and flip-flops or sandals (sometimes the sand on the beaches really heats up) will all make your trip more pleasant.

Texas is a very casual place, and jeans and T-shirts are widely accepted (though jeans and a button-up shirt or blouse buys a bit more credibility), but one set of dressy clothes isn't a bad idea for the odd night out in the chic symphony halls, cocktail bars or nightclubs of Austin, Dallas or San Antonio.

See the Activities chapter for the equipment you'll need to bring for hiking or backpacking in the wilderness.

TOURIST OFFICES
Local Tourist Offices
Larger cities and towns have tourist information centers run by local convention and visitors bureaus (CVBs). They're good sources of local information, offering details on local attractions and upcoming events and sometimes providing free trip-planner kits and reservations for hotels, tours and other activities. Many smaller towns don't have such tourist offices, but local chambers of commerce often perform the same functions. If you're stuck in a place and don't know what to do, try calling the local CVB or chamber of commerce and ask the staff to set up an

itinerary for you. Either can usually tailor the itinerary to your needs (travel with kids, ecotourism, organized tours, etc). The address and telephone number of each chamber of commerce and other visitors' centers are given in the Orientation & Information headings under each town.

If local visitors' centers don't turn up desired information, your next-best bet is the research desk at the main branch of the public library, which is usually able to point you to local organizations that specialize in whatever you're interested in. In this book, they're listed as often as possible.

State Tourist Offices
State tourist offices give out free maps and state vacation planners, and the free *Texas State Travel Guide* is rather good; it's a glossy magazine-style guidebook that lists information offices and major sights and attractions for almost every city and town in the state. It's available at all 12 Texas Travel Information Centers by calling ☎ 800-452-9292, which is what they prefer, or by writing the Texas Department of Transportation, Division of Travel and Information, PO Box 14248, Austin, TX 78714.

That same telephone number (☎ 800-452-9292) also gets you in touch with the main Texas Travel Information Center, which can give you statewide road conditions or the chance to order a variety of other tourist information. All Travel Information Centers are located on main highways throughout the state and are usually loaded with coupon booklets good for hotel and attraction discounts. These booklets, also available at highway convenience stores and fast-food restaurants, are sometimes the source of serious bargains and should be thumbed with care.

Following is a list of centers, open daily 8 am to 5 pm except New Year's Day, Easter Sunday, Thanksgiving Day, Christmas Eve and Christmas Day.

Amarillo
   (☎ 806-335-1441) I-40 E
Anthony
   (☎ 915-886-3468) I-10

Austin
  (☎ 512-463-8586) in the Capitol Complex

Denison
  (☎ 903-463-2860) US 75/69

Gainesville
  (☎ 940-665-2301) I-35 N

Langtry
  (☎ 915-291-3340) US 90, Loop 25

Laredo
  (☎ 956-722-8119) I-35 N

Orange
  (☎ 409-883-0416) I-10 E

Texarkana
  (☎ 903-794-2114) I-30

Valley
  (☎ 210-428-4477) US 77 at US 83

Waskom
  (☎ 903-687-2547) I-20 E

Wichita Falls
  (☎ 940-723-7931) I-44, exit C North

Tourist Offices Abroad

The USA currently has no government-affiliated tourist offices in other countries. Contact your travel agent for more information.

VISAS & DOCUMENTS

All foreign visitors (other than Canadians) must bring valid passports, and all visitors should bring any driver's licenses and health-insurance or travel-insurance cards.

Canadians must have proper proof of Canadian citizenship, such as citizenship cards with photo identification or passports. Most visitors also require US visas. See the Border section in the Getting There & Away chapter for information on leaving and entering Mexico while in the US.

You'll need a picture ID to show that you are older than 21 to buy alcohol or gain admission to bars and clubs (make sure your driver's license has a photo on it, or else get some other form of identification). It's a good idea to make a photocopy of your passport and international identification card to carry around instead of the original (though you can't use the photocopy to get into a bar). There's nothing worse than losing your identity on a trip.

Visas

Apart from Canadians and those entering under the Visa Waiver Pilot Program (see later), all foreign visitors need to obtain a visa from a US consulate or embassy. In most countries the process can be done by mail or through a travel agent.

Your passport should be valid for at least six months longer than your intended stay in the USA, and you'll need to submit a recent photo (37 x 37mm) with the application. Documents of financial stability and/or

HIV & Entering the USA

Any non-US citizen entering the USA is subject to the authority of the Immigration and Naturalization Service (INS), which can keep people from entering or staying in the USA by excluding or deporting them. Being HIV-positive is not grounds for deportation, but it is a grounds of exclusion, and the INS can refuse to admit HIV-positive visitors to the country.

Although the INS does not test people for HIV when they try to enter the USA, the form for the non-immigrant visa asks if you have 'ever been afflicted with a communicable disease of public health significance.' The INS will try to exclude anyone who answers 'yes' to this question.

If you do have HIV but can prove to the consular officials you are the spouse, parent or child of a US citizen or legal resident (green-card holder), you are exempt from the exclusionary rule.

For legal immigration information and referrals to immigration advocates, visitors may contact the National Immigration Project of the National Lawyers Guild (☎ 617-227-9727), 14 Beacon St, Suite 602, Boston, MA 02108; and the Immigrant HIV Assistance Project, Bar Association of San Francisco (☎ 415-782-8995), 465 California St, Suite 1100, San Francisco, CA 94104.

guarantees from a US resident are sometimes required, particularly for those from Third World, eastern European and former Soviet-bloc countries.

The most common visa is a Non-Immigrant Visitors Visa, B1 for business purposes, B2 for tourism or visiting friends and relatives. A visitor's visa is good for one or five years with multiple entries, and it specifically prohibits the visitor from taking paid employment in the USA. The validity period depends on your country of origin. The length of time you'll be allowed to stay in the USA is ultimately determined by US immigration authorities at the port of entry. If you're coming to the USA to work or study, you will probably need a different type of visa, and the company or institution to which you're going will probably make the arrangements. Allow six months in advance for processing the application.

Visa Waiver Pilot Program Citizens of certain countries may enter the USA without a US visa for stays of 90 days or fewer under the Visa Waiver Pilot Program. Currently these countries are Andorra, Argentina, Australia, Austria, Belgium, Brunei, Denmark, Finland, France, Germany, Iceland, Ireland, Italy, Japan, Liechtenstein, Luxembourg, Monaco, the Netherlands, New Zealand, Norway, San Marino, Spain, Sweden, Switzerland and the UK. You must have a nonrefundable roundtrip ticket, and you will not be allowed to extend your stay beyond 90 days. Check with the US embassy in your home country for any other requirements.

Visa Extensions & Reentry If you want, need or hope to stay in the USA longer than the date stamped on your passport, go to the local INS office (call ☎ 800-755-0777 or look in the local white pages telephone directory under US Government) *before* the stamped date to apply for an extension. Going anytime after that will usually lead to an unamusing conversation with an INS official who will assume you want to work illegally. If you find yourself in that situation, it's a good idea to bring a US citizen with you to vouch for your character. It's also a good idea to have verification that you have enough money to support yourself. Bring along a book, pack a lunch, and be prepared to wait.

Travel Insurance

No matter how you're traveling, make sure you take out travel insurance. This should cover you not only for medical expenses and luggage theft or loss, but also for cancellations or delays in your travel arrangements, and everyone should be covered for the worst possible scenario, such as an accident that requires hospital treatment and a flight home. Coverage depends on your insurance and type of ticket, so ask both your insurer and your ticket-issuing agency to explain the finer points. STA Travel and Council Travel offer travel insurance options at reasonable prices. Ticket loss is also covered by travel insurance. Make sure you have a separate record of all your ticket details – or better still, a photocopy of it. Also make a copy of your policy, in case the original is lost.

Buy travel insurance as early as possible. If you buy it the week before you fly, you may find, for instance, that you're not covered for delays to your flight caused by strikes or other industrial action that may have been in force before you took out the insurance.

Insurance may seem very expensive – but it's nowhere near the cost of a medical emergency in the USA.

International Driving Permit

An International Driving Permit is a useful accessory for foreign visitors in the USA. Local traffic police are more likely to accept it as valid identification than an unfamiliar document from another country. Your national automobile association can provide one for a small fee. They're usually valid for one year.

Hostel Card

Most hostels in the USA are members of Hostelling International-American Youth Hostel (HI-AYH), which is affiliated with the International Youth Hostel Federation (IYHF). You can purchase membership on the spot when checking in to a hostel, although it's probably advisable to purchase it

Embassies & Consulates

US Embassies & Consulates Abroad
US diplomatic offices abroad include the following:

Australia
(☎ 02-6270-5000)
21 Moonah Place
Yarralumla, ACT 2600

(☎ 02-9373-9200)
Level 59 MLC Center
19-29 Martin Place
Sydney, NSW 2000

(☎ 03-9526-5900)
553 St Kilda Rd
Melbourne, Victoria

Belgium
(☎ 02-512-22-10)
Blvd du Regent 27
B-1000, Brussels

Canada
(☎ 613-238-5335)
100 Wellington St
Ottawa, Ontario K1P 5T1

(☎ 604-685-4311,
fax 604-685-7175)
1095 W Pender St
Vancouver, BC V6E 2M6

(☎ 514-398-9695)
1155 rue St-Alexandre
Montreal, Quebec

France
(☎ 01.42.96.12.02)
2 rue Saint Florentin
75001 Paris

Germany
Deichmanns Aue 29
53179 Bonn
(☎ 02 28 339 1)

Ireland
(☎ 01-688-7122)
42 Elgin Rd
Ballsbridge, Dublin

Japan
(☎ 3-224-5000)
10-5 Akasaka 1 Chome
Minato-ku, Tokyo

Mexico
(☎ 5-211-0042)
Paseo de la Reforma 305
06500 Mexico City

New Zealand
(☎ 04-722-068)
29 Fitzherbert Terrace
Thorndon, Wellington

South Africa
(☎ 012-342-1048)
225 Pretorius St, Box 9536
Pretoria 0001

United Kingdom
(☎ 4471-4999000)
24 Grosvenor Square
London W1

(☎ 31-556-8315)
3 Regent Terrace
Edinburgh EH7 5BW

(☎ 44-71232-328-239)
Queens House
14 Queen St
Belfast BT1 6EQ

Your Own Embassy
As a tourist, it's important to realize what your own embassy – the embassy of the country of which you are a citizen – can and can't do.

Generally speaking, it won't be much help in emergencies if the trouble you're in is remotely your own fault. Remember that you are bound by the laws of the country you are in. Your embassy will not be sympathetic if you end up in jail after committing a crime locally, even if such actions are legal in your own country.

In genuine emergencies you might get some assistance, but only if other channels have been exhausted. For example, if you need to get home urgently, a free ticket home is exceedingly unlikely – the embassy would expect you to have insurance. If you have all your money and documents stolen, it might assist in getting a new passport, but a loan for onward travel is out of the question.

Embassies used to keep letters for travelers or have a small reading room with home newspapers, but these days the mail-holding service has been stopped and even newspapers tend to be out of date.

Foreign Consulates
Most nations maintain consulates in large US cities, like New York and San Francisco, and embassies in Washington, DC, the nation's capital. The easiest way to get the telephone number of your country's embassy is to call Washington, DC, information (☎ 202-555-1212).

There are many consulates in Dallas and Houston, and Mexican consulates are also peppered throughout border towns. Note that the German consulate in Dallas handles no visa inquiries; these must be made through the German consulate in Houston. Check the Yellow Pages for a complete listing of the consulates in the area in which are traveling. Foreign consulates in Texas include:

Australia
(☎ 713-629-9131)
1990 S Post Oak Blvd
Houston

Canada
(☎ 214-922-9806)
750 N St Paul, Suite 1700
Dallas

France
(☎ 512-480-5605)
515 Congress Ave
Austin

Honorary consulate
(☎ 214-855-5495)
750 N St Paul, Suite 220
Dallas

(☎ 713-572-2799)
777 Post Oak Blvd,
Suite 700
Houston

Germany
(☎ 972-239-0788)
5580 Peterson Lane,
Suite 160
Dallas

(☎ 713-627-7770)
1330 Post Oak Blvd,
Suite 1850
Houston

Japan
(☎ 713-652-2977)
1000 Louisiana St,
Suite 5300
Houston

Mexico
(☎ 512-478-2866)
200 E 6th St
Austin

(☎ 956-542-4431)
724 E Elizabeth St
Brownsville

(☎ 830-775-2352)
2398 Spur 239
Del Rio

(☎ 830-773-9255)
140 N Adams St
Eagle Pass

(☎ 915-533-3644)
910 E San Antonio Ave
El Paso

(☎ 214-630-7341)
8855 N Stemmons Fwy
Dallas

(☎ 713-339-4701)
10440 W Office Drive
Houston

(☎ 956-723-6360)
1612 Farragut St
Laredo

(☎ 956-686-0243)
600 S Broadway
McAllen

(☎ 210-227-9145)
127 Navarro St
San Antonio

New Zealand
(☎ 713-973-8680)
13006 Indian Creek
Houston

UK
(☎ 214-521-4090)
2911 Turtle Creek Blvd,
Suite 940
Dallas

(☎ 713-659-6270)
1000 Louisiana, Suite 1900
Houston

before you leave home. Most hostels allow nonmembers to stay but charge them a few dollars more.

Student & Youth Cards

If you're a student, get an international student identification card or bring along a school or university identification card to take advantage of the discounts that are available to students.

Seniors' Cards

All people older than the age of 65 get discounts throughout the USA. All you need is identification with proof of age should someone ask to see your card. There are organizations such as AARP (see Senior Travelers later in this chapter) that offer membership cards for further discounts and extend coverage to citizens of other countries.

Automobile Association Membership Cards

If you plan on doing a lot of driving in the US, it would be beneficial to join your national automobile association. See Useful Organizations later in this chapter for information.

CUSTOMS

See the Border section in the Getting There & Away chapter for information on crossing the border between Texas and Mexico.

US Customs allows each person older than the age of 21 to bring one liter of liquor and 200 cigarettes duty free into the USA. US citizens are allowed to import, duty free, $400 worth of gifts from abroad, while non-US citizens are allowed to bring in $100 worth.

Currency Regulations

US law permits you to bring in, or take out, as much as $10,000 in US or foreign currency, traveler's checks or letters of credit without formality. Larger amounts of any or all of the above – there are no limits – must be declared to customs.

MONEY
Currency

The US dollar is divided into 100 cents (¢). Coins come in denominations of 1¢ (penny),

5¢ (nickel), 10¢ (dime), 25¢ (quarter), and the seldom seen 50¢ (half dollar). Quarters are the most commonly used coins in vending machines and parking meters, so it's handy to have a stash of them. There is also a $1 coin that the government has tried unsuccessfully to bring into mass circulation; you may get them as change from ticket and stamp machines. Be aware that they look similar to quarters.

Bills (banknotes) come in $1, $2, $5, $10, $20, $50, and $100 denominations – $2 bills are rare, but perfectly legal. True to the American spirit of adventure, all the bills are the same size and color – make sure to check the denomination before handing someone a $100 for a pack of gum!

Exchange Rates

In Texas, some banks, like NationsBank, will exchange cash or traveler's checks in major foreign currencies, though banks in outlying areas don't do so very often, and it may take them some time if they do. Along the Mexican border exchange offices are more common. It's probably less of a hassle to exchange foreign currency in larger cities. Additionally, Thomas Cook, American Express and exchange windows in airports offer exchange services (although you'll get a better rate at a bank). At press time, exchange rates were:

country	unit		dollar
Australia	$1	=	$0.62
Canada	C$1	=	$0.66
EC	€1	=	$1.08
France	FF1	=	$0.16
Germany	DM1	=	$0.55
Hong Kong	HK$10	=	$1.29
Japan	¥100	=	$0.81
New Zealand	NZ$1	=	$0.53
United Kingdom	UK£1	=	$1.61

Exchanging Money

When you find a bank that will exchange foreign currency in Texas, the rate will probably be poor and commissions high, but still better than AmEx and Thomas Cook. You can (and should) negotiate the rate whenever possible – even banks will sometimes give you a better rate for the asking, especially if you're exchanging more than a couple hundred bucks.

Cash & Traveler's Checks Though carrying cash is more risky, it's still a good idea to travel with some for convenience; it's useful to help pay all those tips, and some smaller, more remote places may not accept credit cards or traveler's checks. Traveler's checks offer greater protection from theft or loss and in many places can be used as cash. American Express, Thomas Cook and Citibank traveler's checks are widely accepted and have efficient replacement policies. Barclay's checks are harder to cash; Westpac checks are difficult to cash anywhere except at certain banks.

Keeping a record of the check numbers and the checks you have used is vital when it comes to replacing lost traveler's checks. Keep this record separate from the checks themselves.

You'll save yourself trouble and expense if you buy traveler's checks in US dollars. The savings you *might* make on exchange rates by carrying traveler's checks in a foreign currency don't make up for the hassle of exchanging them at banks and other facilities. Restaurants, hotels and most stores accept US-dollar traveler's checks as if they were cash, so if you're carrying traveler's checks in US dollars, the odds are you'll rarely have to use a bank or pay an exchange fee.

Take most of the checks in large denominations. It's only toward the end of a stay that you may want to change a small check to make sure you aren't left with too much local currency. Following are toll-free numbers to call in the case of lost or stolen traveler's checks.

American Express	☎ 800-221-7282
MasterCard	☎ 800-223-9920
Thomas Cook	☎ 800-223-7373
Visa	☎ 800-227-6811

Automated Teller Machines ATMs, as they are called, are a convenient way of obtaining cash from a bank account back home (within the USA or from abroad). Even small-town banks have ATMs, and they are common in most shopping areas.

Most banks have these machines, usually available 24 hours a day. There are various ATM networks, and most banks are affiliated with several. Plus and Cirrus are the predominant networks. For a nominal service charge, you can withdraw cash from an ATM using a credit card or a charge card – but make certain to activate your credit card's personal identification number (PIN) before you leave home. Credit cards usually have a 2% fee with a $2 minimum, but using bank cards linked to your personal checking account is usually far cheaper. Check with your bank or credit card company for exact information.

Credit & Debit Cards Major credit cards are accepted at hotels, restaurants, gas stations, shops and car-rental agencies throughout the USA. In fact, you'll find it hard to perform certain transactions, such as renting a car or purchasing tickets to performances, without one.

Even if you loathe credit cards and prefer to rely on traveler's checks and ATMs, it's a good idea to carry one for emergencies. Some banks in Australia, New Zealand and the UK are now selling Visa Travel Money, a prepaid Visa card similar to a telephone card: your credit limit is equal to the amount you paid for the card, and although the card is unrechargeable, it's accepted like a regular Visa card. Those selling the card charge a 2% fee on the purchase price, so it's more expensive than traveler's checks, but also more accessible.

If you're planning to rely primarily on credit cards it would be wise to have a Visa or MasterCard in your deck, since other cards aren't as widely accepted.

Places that accept Visa and MasterCard are also likely to accept debit cards. Unlike a credit card, a debit card deducts payment directly from the user's checking account. Instead of an interest rate, users are charged a minimal fee for the transaction. Be sure to check with your bank to confirm that your debit card will be accepted in other states; debit cards from large commercial banks can often be used worldwide.

Carry copies of your credit-card numbers separately from the cards. If you lose your credit cards or they are stolen, contact the company immediately. Following are toll-free numbers for the main credit card companies. Contact your bank if you lose your ATM card.

American Express	☎ 800-528-4800
Diners Club	☎ 800-234-6377
Discover	☎ 800-347-2683
MasterCard	☎ 800-826-2181
Visa	☎ 800-336-8472

International Transfers You can instruct your bank back home to send you a draft. Specify the city, bank and branch to which you want your money directed, or ask your home bank to tell you of a suitable money-transfer location, and make sure you get the details right. The procedure is easier if you've authorized someone back home to access your account.

Money sent by telegraphic transfer should reach you within a week; by mail allow at least two weeks. When it arrives, it will most likely be converted into local currency – you can take it as cash or buy traveler's checks.

The most expensive, but often fastest and most convenient, way to transfer money is by American Express, Thomas Cook or Western Union, though the latter has fewer international offices.

Security

Be cautious, but not paranoid, about carrying money; in fact, put the money several places. If your hotel or hostel has a safe, keep your valuables and excess cash in it. It's best not to display large amounts of cash in public. A money belt worn under your clothes is a good place to carry excess currency when you're on the move or otherwise unable to stash it in a safe. Avoid carrying your wallet in a back pocket of your pants. This is a prime target for pickpockets, as are handbags and the outside pockets of day packs and fanny packs (bum bags). See Dangers & Annoyances later in this chapter.

Costs

Cost for accommodations vary seasonally, between the cities and the countryside, and between resorts and everywhere else. West Texas is, as a general rule, less expensive than the rest of the state, and San Antonio is less expensive than most other large cities except El Paso.

Generally rates are higher in summer, which is between Memorial Day (the last weekend in May) and Labor Day (the first Monday in September), and for special events like San Antonio's Fiesta Week or Austin's South by Southwest (see Special Events later in this chapter), when prices shoot through the roof in those cities. Large (meaning all) college football games or homecoming weekends also send prices heavenward.

The cheapest motel rates will usually be in the $20 to $30 range, and a few places have inexpensive hotels as well. Rustic camping is inexpensive, only about $5 or so per night, but costlier formal sites (around $10 to $20 per site) have amenities like hot showers.

Food is very reasonable. The occasional splurge at a first-rate restaurant will cost anywhere between $20 and $50 per person without wine depending on where you are, but good restaurant meals can be found for $10 – or even half that for some lunch specials. If you buy food at markets you may get by even more cheaply.

Intracity public transportation is relatively inexpensive; buses cost anywhere from free to 75¢ to $1.50 depending on distance and the system.

Owning or renting a car is much less expensive than in other parts of the world. In some areas a car is the only way of getting around; rentals are fairly inexpensive in large cities, and gasoline costs a fraction of what it does in Europe and most of the rest of the world. For more information on purchasing and operating a car, see the Getting Around chapter.

Tipping

Tipping is expected in restaurants and better hotels and by taxi drivers, hairdressers and baggage carriers. In restaurants, wait staff are paid minimal wages and rely on tips for their livelihoods. Tip 15% unless the service is terrible (in which case a complaint to the manager is warranted) or up to 20% if the service is great. Never tip in fast-food, takeout or buffet-style restaurants where you serve yourself.

Taxi drivers expect 10% and hairdressers get 15% if their service is satisfactory. Baggage carriers (skycaps in airports, attendants in hotels) get $1 for the first bag and 50¢ for each additional bag. In budget hotels (where there aren't attendants anyway) tips are not expected.

Taxes

Almost everything you pay for in the USA is taxed. Occasionally, the tax is included in the advertised price (eg, plane tickets, gas, drinks in a bar, and entrance tickets for museums or theaters). Restaurant meals and drinks, accommodations and most other purchases are taxed, and this is added to the advertised cost. Unless otherwise stated, the prices given in this book don't reflect local taxes. Neither, by the way, do prices in shops; the Texas sales tax of 8.25% will be added to the cost of the item at the cash register.

When inquiring about hotel or motel rates, be sure to ask whether taxes are included.

Special Deals

The USA is probably the most promotion-oriented society on earth. Though the bargaining common in many other countries is not generally accepted in the US, you can work angles to cut costs. For example, at hotels in the off-season, casually and respectfully mentioning a competitor's rate may prompt a manager to lower the quoted rate. Artisans may consider a negotiated price if you're making a large purchase. Discount coupons are widely available – check circulars in Sunday papers, at supermarkets, visitors' centers and chambers of commerce.

POST & COMMUNICATIONS
Postal Rates

Postage rates increase every few years and are expected to rise by about 10% by the time you read this, but hadn't been set as we went to press. Currently, rates for 1st-class mail within the USA are 33¢ for letters up to one ounce (22¢ for each additional ounce) and 20¢ for postcards.

International airmail rates (except to Canada and Mexico) are 60¢ for a half-ounce letter, $1 for a 1oz letter and 40¢ for each additional half ounce. International postcard rates are 50¢. Letters to Canada are 46¢ for a half-ounce letter, 52¢ for a 1oz letter and 40¢ for a postcard. Letters to Mexico are 40¢ for a half-ounce letter, 46¢ for 1oz letter and 35¢ for a postcard. Aerogrammes are 50¢.

The cost for parcels airmailed (called priority mail) anywhere within the USA is $3.20 for 2lb or fewer, increasing by $1 per lb up to $6 for 5lb. For heavier items, rates differ according to the distance mailed. Books, periodicals and computer disks can be sent by a cheaper 4th-class rate.

Sending Mail

If you have the correct postage, you can drop your mail into any blue mailbox. However, to send a package 16oz or larger, you must bring it to a post office. A visit to a post office is also necessary if you need to buy stamps or weigh your mail. The addresses of each town's main post office is given in that town's section. Larger towns may have branch post offices and post office centers in some supermarkets and drug stores as well. For the address of the nearest, call the main post office listed under 'Postal Service' in the US Government section in the white pages of the telephone directory, or try the United States Post Office's toll-free line, ☎ 800-275-8777.

Usually, post offices in main towns are open from 8 am to 5 pm, Monday to Friday and 8 am to 3 pm on Saturday, but it all depends on the branch.

Receiving Mail

You can have mail sent to you in care of (c/o) General Delivery at any post office that has its own zip (postal) code. Mail is usually held for 10 days before it's returned to sender; you might request your correspondents to write 'hold for arrival' on their letters. Mail should be addressed like this:

Lucy Chang
c/o General Delivery
Austin, TX 78701

Alternatively, have mail sent to the local representative of American Express or Thomas Cook, which provide mail service for their customers. Youth hostels will generally hold mail that is clearly marked with your date of arrival.

Telephone

All phone numbers within the USA consist of a three-digit area code followed by a seven-digit local number. If you are calling locally, just dial the seven-digit number. If you are calling long distance (except in certain areas, such as inside the Dallas-Fort Worth-Arlington Metroplex; see that chapter for details), dial 1 plus the three-digit area code + the seven-digit number. If you're calling from abroad, the international country code for the USA is 1.

For local directory assistance dial either ☎ 411, 1411 or 555-1212. For directory assistance outside your area code, dial ☎ 1 + the three-digit area code of the place you want to call + 555-1212. For example, to obtain directory assistance for a toll-free number, dial ☎ 1-800-555-1212.

Area codes for places outside the region are listed in telephone directories. Be aware that due to skyrocketing demand for phone numbers (for faxes, cellular phones, etc),

some metropolitan areas are being divided into multiple new area codes. Additionally, many Texas area codes have changed in the last couple of years, and these changes are not reflected in older phone books. When in doubt, ask the operator.

The 800, 888 and 877 area codes are designated for toll-free numbers within the USA and sometimes from Canada as well. These calls are free (unless you are dialing locally, in which case the toll-free number is often not available). It's common for organizations and businesses to change their 800 numbers, so if you try a number that's no longer in service or that has been picked up by another company, call ☎ 800-555-1212 and request the company's new number.

The 900 area code is designated for calls for which the caller pays a premium rate – phone sex, horoscopes, jokes, etc.

Local calls usually cost 35¢ at pay phones, although occasional private phones may charge more. Long-distance rates vary depending on the destination and which telephone company you use – call the operator (☎ 0) for rate information. Don't ask the operator to put your call through, however, because operator-assisted calls are much more expensive than direct-dial calls. Generally, nights (11 pm to 8 am), all day Saturday and from 8 am to 5 pm Sunday are the cheapest times to call (60% discount). Evenings (5 to 11 pm, Sunday to Friday) are midpriced (35% discount). Day calls (8 am to 5 pm, Monday to Friday) are full-price calls within the USA.

Many businesses use letters instead of numbers for their telephone numbers in an attempt to make them snappy and memorable. Sometimes that works, but sometimes it is difficult to read the letters on the keyboard. Here are the letters and their corresponding number keys:

International Calls To make an international call direct, dial ☎ 011, then the country code, followed by the area code and the phone number. You may need to wait as long as 45 seconds for the ringing to start. International rates vary depending on the time of day and the destination. Call the operator (☎ 0) for rates. The first minute is always more expensive than extra minutes.

Hotel Phones Many hotels (especially the more expensive ones) add a service charge of 50¢ to $1 for each local or even toll-free call made from a room phone, and they also have hefty surcharges for long-distance calls. Public pay phones, which can be found in most lobbies, are always cheaper. You can pump in quarters, use a phone credit card or make collect calls from pay phones.

Phone Debit Cards Phone debit cards allow purchasers to pay in advance, with access through a toll-free 800 number. In amounts of $5, $10, $20 and $50, these are available from Western Union, machines in some supermarkets and drugstores, and some other sources. Shop around for the best rates; you shouldn't ever pay more than 25¢ per minute on domestic long-distance calls, and some give a rate as low as 17¢ a minute, though some cards, like those offered by 7-Eleven convenience stores, can cost as much as 45¢ a minute. If a card merely says that you'll 'save up to 60%,' it's usually the sign of a deceptive deal, so move on.

When using phone credit cards, be cautious of people watching you punch in the numbers – thieves will memorize numbers and use your card to make phone calls to all corners of the earth.

Fax & Email

Fax machines are easy to find in the USA at shipping companies (like Mail Boxes Etc), photocopy centers (like Kinko's) and hotel business-service centers, but be prepared to pay high prices (more than $1 a page domestically, much more internationally). Telegraphs can be sent from Western Union (☎ 800-325-6000).

Email is quickly becoming a preferred method of communication; however, unless you have a laptop computer and modem that can be plugged into a telephone socket, it's sometimes difficult to get online – see Internet Resources later for some suggestions on how to stay connected on the road.

A great deal for staying in touch on the road is the free email accounts many of the larger search engines and other Internet resources provide. Companies such as Hotmail (www.hotmail.com), pobox (www.pobox.com) and Excite (www.mailexcite.com) will give you a free email account that you can access from any web browser, like ones at Internet cafés (see Internet Resources later) or libraries. To access your mail, point the browser at the provider's homepage, enter your user name and password and download your email. Remember to log off before you leave to avoid misuse of your account.

INTERNET RESOURCES

The World Wide Web is a rich resource for travelers. You can research your trip, hunt down bargain air fares, book hotels, check on weather conditions or chat with locals and other travelers about the best places to visit (or avoid!). There are Internet cafés in larger cities and even in smaller towns throughout the state where, for a wide range of fees, you can connect to the World Wide Web to surf the Internet or check your email. Public libraries often have computers and Internet connections available to anyone, sometimes free. Hotel business-service centers may provide connections, and many Kinko's locations now offer web access for about 20¢ a minute.

A good starting place for online resources about Texas and the USA in general is Lonely Planet Online, www.lonelyplanet.com. Here you'll find succinct summaries on traveling to most places on earth, postcards from other travelers and the Thorn Tree bulletin board, where you can ask questions before you go or dispense advice when you get back. You can also find travel news and updates to many of our most popular guidebooks, and the subWWWay section links you to the most useful travel resources elsewhere on the Web. You can also visit Lonely Planet Online on America OnLine (keyword: lp) or on the French Minitel system at 3615 lonelyplanet.

Although the nature of the Internet is transient, one of the most reliable starting spots for a virtual trip to Texas is the thoroughly excellent and incredibly comprehensive *Texas Monthly Ranch* (www .texasmonthly.com), which has articles, reviews and updated links to all things Texan.

BOOKS
Bookstores

Most books are published in different editions by different publishers in different countries. As a result, a book might be hardcover rarity in one country while it's readily available in paperback in another. Fortunately, bookstores and libraries can search by title or author, so your local bookstore or library is the best place to find out about the availability of the recommendations that follow.

Many larger towns and all cities in Texas have small, independent bookstores; to find them on the Internet, try heading to www .bookweb.org and search the member directory by state. The largest independent bookstore in the state is Austin's Book People. This book lists independent as well as larger chain stores as often as we can.

The big chains are here, of course. Barnes & Noble and Borders Books & Music have an absolutely phenomenal selection of books, CDs, calendars and, usually, enormous sections on 'Texana' – stuff pertaining to the state of Texas. Hastings is another book superstore that also sells CDs, videos and computer programs.

Half Price Books is a large regional chain that mixes new, used and publisher closeout books with CDs, videos and more. A book bought new here can later be sold back to the store. The travel section is well stocked and the staff members are all book lovers who can point you to that splendid, worthwhile work by someone you may have never heard of.

Travel

The *AAA Tour Book*, free to members (see American Automobile Association, later), is a startlingly good resource, listing almost every city and town in the state, providing attraction information, maps and even hotel prices and restaurant listings. University presses and the Texas Monthly Guidebook series publish some excellent regional and local guides to Texas. The latter publishes excellent guides to *San Antonio*, as well as the *Hill Country* that are in depth and comprehensive; check in any bookshop's Texana collection for more. *San Antonio On Foot*, by Diane Capito and Mark Willis (1993) is a delightful guide to walking through the city, with lots of maps and some great walk suggestions.

Along the Texas Forts Trail is a historical account and travel guide to the state using as references the series of forts constructed by the US Army after the Mexican War to defend against attacks by (and encroach upon the lands of) Native American groups in Texas.

Austin's Favorite Places Guide to restaurants, coffeehouses and microbreweries is pretty good. Even better, the Sierra Club's *Outdoors Austin* (1995) is a great resource to outdoor activities in and around Austin and into the Texas Hill Country.

Lonely Planet Lonely Planet's *Southwest*, *Deep South* and *Mexico* are good supplemental guides for travelers heading to North America's southern and western regions. If you're out to discover states farther flung, check out Lonely Planet's *USA*.

Spanish is widely spoken throughout Texas, especially in border towns, and of course, it's the native tongue in Mexico. Consult the Language appendix in this book and Lonely Planet's *Latin American Spanish phrasebook* for *ayuda*.

History

It's difficult to find books that contain a generalized history of the state of Texas; as the history has come in defined periods of fits and starts, books tend to focus on just those. If you can get hold of it in a used bookstore, *Texas, Our Texas* (1987) is a pretty good resource if you don't mind a healthy dose of propaganda with your history – it's used in many Texas high school history courses.

A good general history of Texas from European settlement to the 1920s is contained in the excellent *Texas Almanac* (see

General, in the Books section), another is found in a *Concise History of Texas*, by Mike Kingston (1998). An interesting look at the political history of the state is contained in the otherwise impenetrable *Texas Politics* (1990). For a history of Native American life, Angie Debo's wonderful *History of the Indians of the United States* (1970) and *The Indians of Texas – From Prehistoric to Modern Times* by WW Newcomb Jr (1995) are excellent choices.

Two very good histories of African American life in Texas come by way of Alwyn Barr's *Black Texans: A History of African Americans in Texas, 1528-1995* (1996) and *Bricks Without Straw: A Comprehensive History of African Americans in Texas*, edited by David A Williams (1997).

James L Haley's *Texas: From the Frontier to Spindletop* covers that period quite well. One of the most readable history books is Albert A Nofi's *The Alamo and the Texas War for Independence* (1994), crammed with sidebars on the heroes of that war; it's colorful enough to read like a novel, accurate on its facts and less reverential than most accounts, but still gushing enough to be sold in the Alamo gift shop by the Daughters of the Republic of Texas.

If you can find a copy of Maldwyn Allen Jones' *American Immigration* (1960) grab it – it's got a wonderful description of the patterns of immigration to the USA and to Texas and of the impact of immigrants on American life.

Along the Texas Forts Trail (1997) is part history, part travel guide – see Travel earlier. Another great read, though a bit stilted, is *Adventures into the Unknown Interior of America* by Álvar Núñez Cabeza de Vaca (see the History section in Facts about Texas), translated by Cyclone Cavey, which describes the doomed expedition of Pánfilo de Narváez, the first European to thoroughly explore the Southern USA.

Flora & Fauna

Mandatory guides for birders in Texas are the famous *Peterson Field Guides: Birds of Texas* (1988) and Edward A Kutac's excellent *Birder's Guide to Texas* (1998). Kutac also wrote *Birds and Other Wildlife of South Central Texas: A Handbook* (1994). For birders in the Big Bend region, *A Field Guide to Birds of the Big Bend* by Roland H Wauer and Nancy McGowan (1996) may help you build your list.

The Mammals of Texas (1994) is a dry but complete list put out by the University of Texas; the university press also publishes *Endangered & Threatened Animals of Texas*, by Linda Campbell, which lists threatened species, the factors that threaten them, and how to reduce the threats.

The most prolific publisher of guides to Texas flora and fauna is the Texas Monthly Field Guide Series, whose titles include *Field Guide to Texas Trees* (1989); the very popular *Field Guide to Wildflowers, Trees and Shrubs of Texas* (1991); the *Field Guide to Spiders and Scorpions of Texas* (1997); *A Field Guide to Butterflies of Texas* (1996); and *A Field Guide to Reptiles and Amphibians of Texas* (1988). Another good wildflower-watching resource is *A Field Guide to Southwestern and Texas Wildflowers* (1984).

For information on slithering Texans, pick up Alan Tennant's *Field Guide to Texas Snakes* (1990).

Good local nature guides are usually available in the area in which you're traveling. Particularly recommended is James Glendinning's *From Big Bend to Carlsbad: A Traveler's Guide* (1995), a natural history and guidebook of that region; also check out *Realms of Beauty: A Guide to the Wilderness Areas of East Texas* (1993), by Edward C Fritz, with photographs by Jess Alford.

Kids love it if you carry Darwin Spearing's *Roadside Geology of Texas* (1991) in the car; it's a beautifully and simply written geological guide to the state designed for car touring.

General

See Literature under Arts in the Facts about Texas chapter for a rundown on Texan authors and some recommended books about the state. A great general interest book on Texas is the *Texas Almanac* (Dallas Morning News, biennial), a compendium of just about every Texas fact there is, including facts about flora and fauna, history, an entire copy of the Texas state constitution, politics, culture, arts and much more. It's available at any larger bookstore in the state.

The excellent Texas Bound series (Southern Methodist University Press), Books I and II, contain stories by almost 50 Texas writers. Three companion audiocassette tapes contain stories written by Texas authors and read by Texas actors, including Tommy Lee Jones, Brent Spiner, Tess Harper, Norma Moore, Judith Ivey and others.

Michael Hicks' *How to Be Texan* (1981) is a scream – a must-read for visitors to Texas, who can learn about pronunciation, 'gimme' caps, belt buckles, state customs and traditions, and how to break in a new pair of boots the Texan way.

In his splendid book about Texas high school football, *Friday Night Lights* (1991), HG Bissinger notes that in schools he visited, trophies honoring athletic achievement were on prominent display, but that he could never find any honors for students who had excelled in their studies.

Duncan McLean's *Lone Star Swing* (1997) is a thrilling and glorious romp throughout the state in search of the roots of his hero, Bob Wills (see Music under Arts in the Facts about Texas chapter). It's a great read for a long bus ride.

NEWSPAPERS & MAGAZINES

The *Austin-American Statesman* is the capital city's paper of record, but throughout the state you can usually find copies of the *Dallas Morning News*, *Houston Chronicle* and *San Antonio Express-News*.

There is usually at least one place in every city, town or village that carries national papers like the *New York Times*, the *Wall Street Journal* and *USA Today* – if you can't find a newsstand that carries what you're looking for, try a supermarket or one of the larger hotels.

For excellent, unbiased and thoughtful coverage of international news, pick up a copy of the *Christian Science Monitor*.

Time and *Newsweek* magazines are also available in supermarkets, bookstores and newsstands.

In cities around Texas look for local tabloids, like *LareDOS* in Laredo, the *Current* in San Antonio and the *Austin Chronicle*, which have features, hard-hitting investigative journalism, comics and, of course, totally perverted and thoroughly enjoyable personal and classified advertisements.

RADIO & TV
Radio
All rental cars have car radios and travelers can choose from hundreds of stations. Most radio stations have a range less than 100 miles, and in and near major cities scores of stations crowd the airwaves with a wide variety of music and entertainment. Public radio stations carrying news-oriented National Public Radio (NPR) can usually be found in the lower numbers of the radio band.

Throughout most of Texas you'll also have the opportunity to listen to hate and political radio, featuring venal, fat blabbermouths, convicted felons and squeaky-voiced female radio therapists touting conservative political values. Christian radio is also big in Texas; you'll find at least one, usually more, Christian station in every Texas region. And local sports are covered here as nowhere else.

In Austin, community radio KOOP 91.7 FM is a hoot. Saturday mornings Jay Robillard cracks open his astounding collection of lounge music. KOOP also does everything from all movie-soundtrack shows to Latino and gay political forums. Another Texas radio phenomenon is KKDA 730 AM, out of the Dallas suburb of Grand Prairie. It's home to Cousin Linnie Henderson, part preacher, part politician. It's a gas listening to Henderson urge his mostly African American audience to take pride in themselves and their city. But as good as the gab is, it's the music that keeps you tuned in. The classic '60s and '70s soul is perfect stress relief on the frenetic Dallas freeways.

Just about every small-town radio station has a trading show, usually airing weekdays about 9 am. People call up and tell the host what they have for sale or what they need to buy. Garage-sale and church-supper notices sometimes go over the air on these programs, too.

Dead Zones There are areas in West Texas, especially in the Big Bend region, where radios all but go dead. Usually, the only stations you can pull in there are Spanish-language. Some boom from over the Mexican border, but quite a few originate in Texas, serving a Hispanic population, the majority in most West Texas towns.

Shortwave British news junkies or those who appreciate neatly clipped accents will appreciate broadcasts of the BBC news on shortwave. While there are news reports on the hour and half-hour throughout the day, pinning down exact frequencies or broadcast times is difficult – even the venerable Beeb can't give a totally straight answer.

The nature of shortwave is extremely unpredictable. The schedules, and some of the frequencies, change twice a year (in the beginning of April and end of October for the USA).

You can get a complete shortwave program guide from the BBC by writing to PO Box 76, Bush House, Strand, London WC2B 4PH, or calling ☎ 0171-257-8165, fax 0171-257-8252.

Television

Because of the popularity of American TV (a hodgepodge of talk shows, cop shows, dramas, melodramas, sitcoms, soap operas, game shows and commercials) around the world, you'll find few surprises on television. Despite pressure from Congress to clean up what it considers inappropriate subject matter on daytime talk shows, the genre is in no immediate danger; watching American TV can be an interesting way to spend an afternoon.

The five major broadcast television networks in the USA are ABC, CBS, Fox, NBC and PBS. Of them, Fox shows the most sensationalistic – but also the most groundbreaking – shows. It was Fox that first broadcast *The Simpsons, King of the Hill* (see the boxed text) and *The X-Files*. CBS, ABC and NBC all show a mix of quasi-current films, local news, news-magazine shows and sitcoms, as well as dramatic programming like *ER* and national news at 6:30 pm eastern standard time (EST).

PBS, the Public Broadcasting Service, shows mainly educational programs, music and theater presentations (including *Austin*

King of the Hill

King of the Hill is an animated TV series on the Fox network based on the life and times of Hank Hill, propane salesman, husband of Peggy and resident of the fictitious Texas suburb of Arlen. A slice of Americana, un-PC and unglamorous, it's the beer-swilling, huntin'-'n'-fishin' crowd going through the day and letting every wrinkle show. It's like *The Simpsons* on steroids.

All the characters in this wonderful program have histories out of the tabloid *National Enquirer*. Take, for instance, beauty-school student Luanne, Hank's niece, who has stayed with the Hills since her mother was jailed for stabbing her father. Or there's conspiracy theorist, exterminator and neighbor Dale Gribble, an avid believer in the storylines on *The X-Files* (another Fox show) and firm in his paranoia that every organization is out to get him except the Tobacco Institute.

The show is a screaming success both in Texas and throughout the country. When I was watching an episode with a roomful of Texans, they hooted throughout, saying that it showed Texans as they really are.

Not bad, considering that the show's executive producer and cocreator, Greg Daniels, is from New York City.

Nick Selby

City Limits, the longest-running country-and-western program on TV), foreign programs and films (usually uncensored) and excellent current affairs shows like *Newshour with Jim Lehrer*. Programming for PBS is mostly viewer supported – there are no standard commercial interruptions, but rather a list of corporate sponsors is read at the end or beginning of each program.

Cable TV is available at almost every hotel, which gives you access to, at the very least, ESPN (sports), CNN, CNN Headline News, the Weather Channel and Comedy Central. Some hotels offer premium channels like HBO and Showtime.

PHOTOGRAPHY & VIDEO
Film & Equipment

Print film is widely available at supermarkets and discount drugstores. Color print film has a greater latitude than color slide film; this means that print film can handle a wider range of light and shadow than slide film. However, slide film, particularly the slower speeds (lower than 100 ASA), has better resolution than print film. Like black-and-white film, slide film is rarely sold outside of major cities and when available is expensive.

Film can be damaged by excessive heat, so don't leave your camera and film in the car on a hot summer's day and avoid placing your camera on the dashboard while you are driving.

It's worth carrying a spare battery for your camera to avoid disappointment when your camera dies in the middle of nowhere. If you're buying a new camera for your trip, do so several weeks before you leave and practice using it.

Drugstores are a good place to get your film cheaply processed. If you drop it off by noon, you can usually pick it up the next day. Processing a roll of 100 ASA, 35 mm color film with 24 exposures will cost about $7.

If you want your pictures right away, you can find one-hour processing services in the Yellow Pages under 'Photo Processing.' The prices tend to creep up to the $15 scale, so be prepared to pay dearly. Many one-hour photofinishers operate in the larger cities, and a few can be found near tourist attractions.

Video

The USA uses the National Television System Committee (NTSC) color TV standard, which is not compatible with other standards (Phase Alternative Line or PAL; Système Electronique Couleur avec Memoire or SECAM) used in Africa, Europe, Asia and Australia unless converted.

Properly used, a video camera can give a fascinating record of your holiday. Often the most interesting things occur when you're actually intent on filming something else.

One good rule to follow for beginners is to try to film in long takes, and don't move the camera around too much. If your camera has a stabilizer, you can use it to obtain good footage while traveling on various means of transport, even on bumpy roads. Remember, you're traveling – don't let the video take over and turn your trip into a Cecil B DeMille production.

Remember to follow the same rules regarding people's sensitivities as for a still photography – having a video camera shoved in their face is probably even more annoying and offensive for locals than a still camera. Always ask permission first.

Airport Security

All passengers on flights have to pass their luggage through X-ray machines. Technology as it is today doesn't jeopardize lower-speed film, so you shouldn't have to worry about cameras going through the machine. If you are carrying high-speed (1600 ASA and higher) film, then you may want to carry film and cameras with you and ask the X-ray inspector to visually check your film.

TIME

Much of Texas is in central standard time, an hour behind New York (eastern standard time) and two hours ahead of Los Angeles. When it's noon in Austin, it's 6 pm in London, 7 pm in Paris, Berlin and Madrid, 9 pm in Moscow, 3 am/5 am in winter/summer Sydney. Parts of extreme West Texas are in the mountain standard time zone, one hour behind central standard time; when it's noon in Austin, it's 11 am in El Paso.

ELECTRICITY

In the USA voltage is 110V 60 Hz and the plugs have two (flat) or three (two flat, one round) pins. Plugs with three pins don't fit into a two hole socket, but adapters are easy to buy at hardware stores or drugstores. Most European appliances designed to work on 220V 50 Hz won't work, but some will.

WEIGHTS & MEASURES

Distances are in feet (ft), yards (yds) and miles (m). See the conversion chart at the back of this book. Three feet equal one yard (.914 meters); 1760 yards or 5280 feet are one mile. Dry weights are in ounces (oz), pounds (lb) and tons (16 ounces are one pound; 2000 pounds are one ton), but liquid measures differ from dry measures. One pint equals 16 fluid ounces; two pints equal one quart, a common measure for liquids like milk, which is also sold in half gallons (two quarts) and gallons (four quarts). Note, though, that soft drinks are usually sold in one- or two-liter bottles.

Gasoline is dispensed by the US gallon, which is about 20% less than the Imperial gallon. US pints and quarts are also 20% less than Imperial ones.

LAUNDRY

There are self-service, coin-operated laundry facilities in most towns of any size and in better campgrounds. Washing a load costs about $1 and drying it another $1. Some laundries have attendants who will wash, dry and fold your clothes for you for an additional charge. To find a laundry, look under 'Laundries' or 'Laundries – Self-Service' in the yellow pages of the telephone directory. Dry cleaners are also listed under 'Laundries' or 'Cleaners.'

TOILETS

Public toilets are rare, but Texans are rather accommodating when it comes to allowing strangers use of the facilities. Gas stations, fast-food joints and restaurants are the most common places where staff will hand you the key (rest rooms are often locked to prevent crime). Many restaurants in big cities will post signs saying that their toilets are for the use of their customers only, but they will often let you in if you ask very politely. Ask to use the 'rest room,' as it's more polite here than saying 'toilet.'

HEALTH

For most foreign visitors no immunizations are required for entry, though cholera and yellow fever vaccinations may be required of travelers from areas with a history of those diseases. There are no unexpected health dangers, excellent medical attention is readily available, and the only real health concern is that a collision with the medical system can cause severe injuries to your financial state. Hospitals, medical centers, walk-in clinics and referral services are easily found throughout the region.

In a serious emergency, call ☎ 911 for an ambulance to take you to the nearest hospital's emergency room (ER). But note that ER charges in the USA are incredibly expensive. It can cost you as much as $250 just to be *seen* by an ER doctor, and additional fees for X-rays, medication and wound covers can easily turn the cost of an entire visit into a bill for $800 to $1000. The price of health care in US hospitals and clinics is so outrageously high that most foreign visitors can't believe it, but there it is: aspirin can indeed cost $7 a tablet in a US hospital.

Predeparture Preparations

Make sure you're healthy before you start traveling. If you are embarking on a long trip, make sure your teeth are in good shape. If you wear glasses, take a spare pair and your prescription. You can get new spectacles made up quickly and competently for about $100, depending on the prescription and frame. If you require a particular medication, take an adequate supply and bring a prescription in case you lose your medication. Certain medications that don't require a prescription at home (such as Clarityne, called Claritin in the US, or aspirin or paracetemol with codeine) require one in the USA.

Health Insurance Taking out a travel insurance policy to cover theft, lost tickets and medical problems is a good idea, especially in the USA, where some privately run hospitals will refuse care without evidence of insurance (public hospitals must treat everyone, though standards are lower and, except in the most serious of cases, waits can last for hours).

There are a wide variety of policies, and your travel agent will have recommendations. International student-travel policies handled by STA Travel and other student-travel organizations are usually a good value. Some policies offer lower and higher medical expenses options, and the higher one is chiefly for countries like the USA with extremely high medical costs. Check the fine print.

Some policies specifically exclude 'dangerous activities' like scuba diving, motorcycling and even trekking. If these activities are on your agenda, avoid this sort of policy.

You may prefer a policy that pays doctors or hospitals directly, rather than your having to pay first and claim later. If you have to claim later, keep *all* documentation. Some policies ask you to call back (reverse charges) to a center in your home country for an immediate assessment of your problem.

Check whether the policy covers ambulance fees or an emergency flight home. If you have to stretch out, you will need two seats, and somebody has to pay for it!

Travel Health Guides There are a number of excellent travel health sites on the Internet. From the Lonely Planet home page there are links at (www.lonelyplanet.com.au/weblinks/wlprep.htm#heal) to the World Health Organization, the US Center for Diseases Control and Prevention and Stanford University Travel Medicine Service.

A number of books on travel health are available. Two are:

Staying Healthy in Asia, Africa & Latin America, Dirk Schroeder (1994): Though not specifically oriented toward North American travel, this is probably the best all-around guide, worth looking at if you'll be heading to Mexico. It's compact but very detailed and well organized.

Travelers' Health, Dr Richard Dawood (1994): This is comprehensive, easy to read, authoritative and highly recommended, but rather large to lug around.

Medical Kit If you're going off the beaten path, it's wise to take a small, straightforward medical kit. This should include

- Aspirin, acetaminophen or Panadol for pain or fever
- Antihistamine (such as Benadryl), which is useful as a decongestant for colds; to ease the itch from allergies, insect bites or stings; or to help prevent motion sickness
- Kaolin preparation (Pepto-Bismol), Immodium or Lomotil for stomach upsets
- Rehydration mixture to treat severe diarrhea, which is particularly important if you're traveling with children
- Antiseptic, mercurochrome and antibiotic powder or similar 'dry' spray for cuts and grazes
- Calamine lotion to ease irritation from bites or stings
- Bandages for minor injuries
- Scissors, tweezers and a thermometer (note that airlines prohibit mercury thermometers)
- Insect repellent, sunscreen lotion, lip balm and water purification tablets

Food & Water

Care in what you eat and drink is the most important health rule; stomach upsets are the most common travel health problem (between 30% and 50% of travelers experience this during a two-week stay), but the vast majority of these upsets will be relatively minor. American standards of cleanliness in places serving food and drink are very high.

Bottled drinking water, both carbonated and uncarbonated, is widely available in the USA. You can get a gallon of filtered drinking water (bring your own jug) from dispensers at supermarkets for 25¢. Tap water in Texas is usually fine to drink (though it tastes lousy); ask locally to make sure there aren't any major health concerns.

Everyday Health

Normal body temperature is 98.6°F or 37°C; more than 4°F or 2°C higher indicates a 'high' fever. The normal adult pulse rate is 60 to 80 per minute (children 80 to 100, babies 100 to 140). You should know how to take a temperature and a pulse rate.

Respiration (breathing) rate is also an indicator of illness. Count the number of breaths per minute: between 12 and 20 is normal for adults and older children (up to 30 for younger children, 40 for babies). People with a high fever or serious respiratory illness (like pneumonia) breathe more quickly than normal. More than 40 shallow breaths a minute usually means pneumonia.

Travel & Climate Problems

Motion Sickness Eating lightly before and during a trip will reduce the chances of motion sickness. If you are prone to motion sickness, try to secure a place that minimizes disturbance, for example, a seat one near the wing on aircraft or near the center on buses. Fresh air usually helps. Commercial anti-motion-sickness preparations, which can cause drowsiness, have to be taken before the trip commences; once you feel sick, it's too late. Ginger, a natural motion-sickness preventative, is available in capsule form from health-food stores.

Jet Lag Jet lag is experienced when a person travels by air across more than three time zones (each time zone usually represents a one-hour time difference). It occurs because many of the functions of the human body are regulated by internal 24-hour cycles called circadian rhythms. When we travel long distances rapidly, our bodies take time to adjust to the 'new time' of our destination, and we may experience fatigue, disorientation, insomnia, anxiety, impaired concentration and loss of appetite. These effects will usually be gone within three days of arrival, but there are ways of minimizing the impact of jet lag:

- Rest for a couple of days prior to departure; try to avoid late nights and last-minute dashes for traveler's checks or your passport.
- Try to select flight schedules that minimize sleep deprivation; arriving in the early evening means you can go to sleep soon after you arrive. For very long flights, try to organize a stopover.
- Avoid excessive eating (which bloats the stomach) and alcohol consumption (which causes dehydration) during the flight. Instead, drink plenty of uncarbonated, nonalcoholic drinks such as fruit juice or water.

- Make yourself comfortable by wearing loose clothing and perhaps bringing an eye mask and ear plugs to help you sleep.
- Avoid smoking, as this reduces the amount of oxygen in the airplane cabin even further and causes greater fatigue.

Sunburn Most doctors recommend sunscreen with a high protection factor for easily burned areas like your shoulders and, if you'll be on nude beaches or hanging at Hippie Hollow in Austin, areas not usually exposed to sun.

Heat Exhaustion Dehydration or salt deficiency can cause heat exhaustion. Take time to acclimatize to high temperatures and make sure that you drink enough liquids. Salt deficiency is characterized by fatigue, lethargy, headaches, giddiness and muscle cramps. Salt tablets may help. Vomiting or diarrhea can also deplete your liquid and salt levels. Anhydrotic heat exhaustion, caused by the inability to sweat, is quite rare, but unlike the other forms of heat exhaustion it is likely to strike people who have been in a hot climate for some time, rather than newcomers. Again, always carry – and use – a water bottle on long trips.

Heatstroke Long, continuous periods of exposure to high temperatures can leave you vulnerable to this serious, sometimes fatal, condition that occurs when the body's heat-regulating mechanism breaks down and body temperature rises to dangerous levels. Avoid excessive alcohol intake or strenuous activity when you first arrive in a hot climate.

Symptoms include feeling unwell, lack of perspiration and a high body temperature of 102°F to 105°F (39°C to 41°C). Hospitalization is essential for extreme cases, but meanwhile, get out of the sun, remove clothing, cover with a wet sheet or towel and fan continually.

Hypothermia Changeable weather at high altitudes can leave you vulnerable to exposure: after dark, temperatures in the mountains or desert can drop from balmy to below freezing, while a sudden soaking and high winds can lower your body temperature too rapidly. If possible, avoid traveling alone; partners are more likely to avoid hypothermia successfully. If you must travel alone, especially when hiking, be sure someone knows your route and when you expect to return.

Seek shelter when bad weather is unavoidable. Woolen clothing and synthetics, which retain warmth even when wet, are superior to cottons. A quality sleeping bag is a worthwhile investment, although goose down loses much of its insulating qualities when wet. Carry high-energy, easily digestible snacks like chocolate or dried fruit.

Get hypothermia victims out of the wind or rain, remove their clothing if it's wet and replace it with dry, warm clothing. Give them hot liquids – not alcohol – and high-calorie, easily digestible food. In advanced stages it may be necessary to place victims in warm sleeping bags and get in with them. Do not rub victims but place them near a fire or, if possible, in a warm (not hot) bath.

Fungal Infections Fungal infections, which occur with greater frequency in hot weather, are most likely to occur on the scalp, between the toes or fingers (athlete's foot), in the groin (jock itch) and on the body (ringworm). You get ringworm (which is a fungal infection, not a worm) from infected animals or by walking on damp areas, like shower floors.

To prevent fungal infections, wear loose, comfortable clothes, avoid artificial fibers, wash frequently and dry carefully. If you do get an infection, wash the infected area daily with a disinfectant or medicated soap and water, and rinse and dry well. Apply an antifungal powder and try to expose the infected area to air or sunlight as much as possible. Change underwear and towels frequently and wash them often in hot water.

Infectious Diseases

Diarrhea A change of water, food or climate can all cause the runs; diarrhea caused by contaminated food or water is more serious. It's an unlikely affliction in the United States, but common in Mexico.

Despite all your precautions you may still have a mild bout of traveler's diarrhea from exotic food or drink.

Dehydration is the main danger with any diarrhea, particularly for children, where dehydration can occur quite quickly. Fluid replacement remains the mainstay of management. Weak black tea with a little sugar, soda water or soft drinks diluted 50% with water are all good. With severe diarrhea a rehydrating solution is necessary to replace minerals and salts. Such solutions, like Pedialyte, are available at pharmacies.

Hepatitis Hepatitis is a general term for inflammation of the liver. There are many causes of this condition: poor sanitation, contact with infected blood products, drugs, alcohol and contact with an infected person are but a few. The symptoms are fever, chills, headache, fatigue, and feelings of weakness and aches and pains, followed by loss of appetite, nausea, vomiting, abdominal pain, dark urine, light-colored feces and jaundiced skin. The whites of the eyes may also turn yellow. Hepatitis A is the most common strain. You should seek medical advice, but there is not much you can do apart from resting, drinking lots of fluids, eating lightly and avoiding fatty foods. People who have had hepatitis should avoid alcohol for some time after the illness, as the liver needs time to recover. Viral hepatitis is an infection of the liver, which can have several unpleasant symptoms, or no symptoms at all, with the infected person not knowing that they have the disease.

HIV & AIDS HIV, the Human Immunodeficiency Virus, develops into AIDS, Acquired Immune Deficiency Syndrome, which is a fatal disease. Any exposure to blood, blood products or body fluids may put the individual at risk. The disease is often transmitted through sexual contact or dirty needles – vaccinations, acupuncture, tattooing and body piercing can be potentially as dangerous as intravenous drug use.

Fear of HIV infection should never preclude treatment for serious medical conditions. A good resource for help and information is the Centers for Disease Control AIDS hot line (☎ 800-342-2437, 800-344-7432 in Spanish). AIDS support groups are listed in the front of phone books.

Cuts, Bites & Stings

Cuts & Scratches Skin punctures can easily become infected in hot climates and can heal slowly. Treat any cut with an antiseptic such as Betadine. Whenever possible avoid using bandages and Band-Aids, which can keep wounds wet.

Bites & Stings Bee and wasp stings and nonpoisonous spider bites are usually painful rather than dangerous. Calamine lotion will give relief, and ice packs will reduce the pain and swelling. Bites are best avoided by not using bare hands to turn over rocks or large pieces of wood.

Ticks Ticks are a parasitic arachnid that may be present in brush, forest and grasslands, where hikers often get them on their legs or in their boots. Adult ticks suck blood from hosts by burying their head into skin, but they are often found unattached and can simply be brushed off. To remove an attached tick, use a pair of tweezers, grab it by the head and gently pull it straight out – do not twist it. (If no tweezers are available, use your fingers, but protect them from contamination with a piece of tissue or paper.) Do not touch the tick with a hot object such as a match or a cigarette – this can cause it to regurgitate noxious gut substances or saliva into the wound. And do not rub oil, alcohol or petroleum jelly on it. If you get sick in the next couple of weeks, consult a doctor.

WOMEN TRAVELERS

Women often face different situations when traveling than men do. If you are a woman traveler, especially a woman traveling alone, it's not a bad idea to get in the habit of traveling with a little extra awareness of your surroundings. Texas is part of the South, and women can expect to be called 'honey' and 'sweetheart' a lot. Some women might find this offensive, but many opt to accept it

graciously. Men aren't the only ones using these terms; women do too, to address both men and each other.

In general, you must exercise more vigilance in large cities than in rural areas. Try to avoid the 'bad' or unsafe neighborhoods or districts; if you must go into or through these areas, it's best to go in a private vehicle (such as a car or taxi). It's more dangerous at night, but in the worst areas crime can occur even in the daytime. If you are unsure which areas are considered unsafe, ask at your hotel or telephone the tourist office for advice. Tourist maps can sometimes be deceiving, compressing areas that are not tourist attractions and making the distances look shorter than they are.

While there is less to watch out for in rural areas, women may still may be harassed by men unaccustomed to seeing women traveling on their own. Try to avoid hiking or camping alone, especially in unfamiliar places. Hikers all over the world use the 'buddy system' (that is, never hiking alone, especially in the wilderness), not only for protection from other humans, but also for aid in case of unexpected falls or other injuries, or encounters with rattlesnakes, bears or other potentially dangerous wildlife.

Women must recognize the extra threat of rape, which is a problem not only in urban but also in rural areas, albeit to a lesser degree. See Drugging in the Dangers & Annoyances section later in this chapter for information on Rohypnol, a tasteless, odorless drug that can be slipped into a drink. Conducting yourself in a commonsense manner will help you to avoid most problems. For example, you're more vulnerable if you've been drinking or using drugs than if you're sober; you're more vulnerable alone than if you're with company; and you're more vulnerable in a high-crime urban area than in a 'better' district.

If you are assaulted, call the police (☎ 911). In some rural areas where 911 is not active, dial ☎ 0 for the operator. Cities and larger towns have rape crisis centers and women's shelters that provide help and support; they are listed in the telephone directory, or if not, the police should be able to refer you to them. In this book we list them where possible. Note you need not report a rape to the police to receive treatment at a rape crisis center.

Men sometimes interpret a woman drinking alone in a bar as a bid for male company, whether you intended it that way or not. If you don't want the company, most men will respect a firm but polite 'no thank you.'

Don't hitchhike alone, and don't pick up hitchhikers if driving alone. If you get stuck on a road and need help, it's a good idea to have a premade sign to signal for help. At night, avoid getting out of your car to flag down help; turn on your hazard lights and wait for the police to arrive. Be extra careful at night on public transit, and remember to check the times of the last bus or train before you go out at night.

To deal with potential dangers, many women protect themselves with a whistle, mace, cayenne-pepper spray or some karate training. If you decide to purchase a spray, contact a police station to find out about regulations and training classes. Laws regarding sprays vary from state to state, so be informed based on your destination. One law that doesn't vary is carrying sprays on airplanes – due to their combustible design, it is a federal felony to carry them on board.

Traveling in Mexico

Women traveling in the areas in Mexico and border towns can expect plenty of attention from Mexican men. Most are gracious, but some subject women to leers and catcalls. Women who'd rather not deal with this behavior can simply ignore it and may be able to reduce it by dressing modestly. That doesn't mean you need to wear several layers of clothing on a 95° Texas day, but halter tops and short shorts aren't the most recommended garb for women traveling alone on the border.

In Mexico, women traveling alone may be approached by men offering their services as 'guides.' Use extreme caution and exercise common sense, but don't automatically turn down such an offer. Julie wrote that in Ciudad Juárez,

I was approached by a middle-aged Mexican man who, after some small talk, offered to show me the history museum, and I accepted on a gut feeling the man would not harm me. After we visited the museum, he showed me a nearby marketplace infrequently seen by visitors, then walked me back to the trolley stop. As we parted, he asked me for a dollar. Money was probably his motive all along. I gave him a dollar. In return, in addition to his company, I got a parting kiss on my hand and a sweet memory of Mexico.

Organizations

Check the Yellow Pages phone directory under 'Women's Organizations and Services' for local resources. Women's bookstores, listed under 'Bookstores,' are good places to find out about gatherings, readings and meetings and often have bulletin boards with travel and short-term housing notices.

Here are two organizations with affiliates nationwide:

National Organization for Women (NOW)
    A good resource for any women-related information and can refer you to state and local chapters. 1000 16th St NW, Suite 700, Washington, DC 20036 (☎ 202-331-0066)

Planned Parenthood
    Can refer you to clinics throughout the country and offer advice on medical issues. 810 7th Ave, New York, NY 10019 (☎ 212-541-7800)

GAY & LESBIAN TRAVELERS

There are gay people everywhere in the USA, but by far the most visible communities are in the major cities. In cities and on both coasts it is easier for gay men and women to live their lives with a certain amount of openness. As you travel into the middle of the country it is much harder to be open. Gay travelers should be careful, *especially* in the rural areas where holding hands might get you bashed.

The larger cities in Texas, especially Austin, San Antonio, Houston and Dallas, are very gay friendly, and there are gay, lesbian, bisexual and transgender community centers in each that offer tips on everything from medical care and gay-owned businesses in the area to information on bars, clubs and accommodations.

Resources & Organizations

The Women's Traveller, with listings for lesbians, and *Damron's Address Book*, for men, are both published by Damron Company (☎ 415-255-0404, 800-462-6654), PO Box 422458, San Francisco, CA 94142-2458. *Ferrari's Places for Women* and *Places for Men* are also useful. These can be found at any good bookstore, as can guides to specific cities.

In Search of Gay America by Neil Miller (1989) is a good book about gay and lesbian life across the USA in the 1980s. It's a bit dated, but gives a good view of life outside of the major cities. For a pre-AIDS view there is Edmund White's *States of Desire* about gay men in the 1970s.

Another good resource is the Gay Yellow Pages (☎ 212-674-0120), PO Box 533, Village Station, NY 10014-0533, which has a national edition and also regional editions.

These national resource numbers may prove useful: National AIDS/HIV Hotline (☎ 800-342-2437), National Gay and Lesbian Task Force (☎ 202-332-6483 in Washington, DC) and Lambda Legal Defense Fund (☎ 212-809-8585 in New York City, 213-937-2728 in Los Angeles).

In Texas, publications like the *Texas Triangle* and *This Week in Texas* are good guides to the bar and club scene and also feature ads for gay hotels and B&Bs. The Austin and San Antonio Gay and Lesbian Yellow Pages is an excellent resource; order it by calling ☎ 512-891-0358 or 210-308-6636, or writing to PO Box 66045, Houston, TX 77266.

DISABLED TRAVELERS

Public buildings (including hotels, restaurants, theaters and museums) are required by the Americans with Disabilities Act (ADA) to be wheelchair accessible and have available rest room facilities. Public transportation services (buses, trains and taxis) must be made accessible to all, including those in wheelchairs, and telephone companies are required to provide relay operators for the hearing impaired. Many banks now provide ATM instructions in Braille and you will find audible crossing signals as well as dropped curbs at busier roadway intersections.

Larger private and chain hotels (see Places to Stay in each of the chapters for listings) have suites for disabled guests. Major car-rental agencies offer hand-controlled models at no extra charge. All major airlines, Greyhound buses and Amtrak trains allow service animals to accompany passengers and frequently sell two-for-one packages when seriously disabled passengers require attendants. Airlines will also provide assistance for connecting, boarding and deplaning the flight – ask for assistance when making your reservation (note: airlines must accept wheelchairs as checked baggage and have an onboard chair available, though some advance notice may be required on smaller aircraft). Of course, the more populous the area, the greater the likelihood of facilities for the disabled, so it's important to call ahead to see what is available.

Resources & Organizations

A number of organizations and tour providers specialize in the needs of disabled travelers:

Mobility International USA
   Advises disabled travelers on mobility issues; primarily runs an educational exchange program. PO Box 10767, Eugene, OR 97440 (☎ 541-343-1284, fax 541-343-6812, info@miusa.org)

Moss Rehabilitation Hospital's Travel Information Service
   1200 W Tabor Rd, Philadelphia, PA 19141-3099 (☎ 215-456-9600, TTY 456-9602, www.mossresourcenet.org)

SATH
   Society for the Advancement of Travel for the Handicapped, 347 Fifth Ave, No 610, New York, NY 10016 (☎ 212-447-7284, www.sath.org)

Travelin' Talk
   An international network of people providing assistance to disabled travelers. PO Box 3534, Clarksville, TN 37047 (☎ 931-552-6670, fax 913-552-1182, trvlntlk@aol.com)

Twin Peaks Press
   A quarterly newsletter; also publishes directories and access guides. PO Box 129, Vancouver, WA 98666 (☎ 360-694-2462, 800-637-2256)

Web pages
   A good website to check for resources for the disabled is www.access-able.com

SENIOR TRAVELERS

Though the age where the benefits begin varies with the attraction, travelers 50 years and older can expect to receive cut rates and benefits. Be sure to inquire about such rates at hotels, museums and restaurants.

Visitors to national parks and campgrounds can cut costs greatly by using the Golden Age Passport, a card that allows US citizens aged 62 and older (and those traveling in the same car) free admission nationwide and a 50% reduction on camping fees – see the Golden Opportunities boxed text under National Parks in the Facts about Texas chapter for more information. You can apply in person for any of these at any national park or regional office of the United States Forest Service or National Park Service.

Organizations

See Golden Opportunities under National Parks in the Facts about Texas chapter for more information on Golden Age Passports. Some national advocacy groups that can help in planning your travels include the following:

American Association of Retired Persons (AARP)
AARP (☎ 800-424-3410), 601 E St NW, Washington, DC 20049, is an advocacy group for Americans 50 years and older and is a good resource for travel bargains. US residents can get one- or three-year memberships for $8/20. Citizens of other countries can get the same memberships for $10/24.

Elderhostel
This organization (☎ 877-426-8056), 75 Federal St, Boston, MA 02110-1941, is a nonprofit organization that offers seniors the opportunity to attend academic college courses throughout the USA and Canada. The programs last one to three weeks, include meals and accommodations and are open to people 55 years and older and their companions.

Grand Circle Travel
This group offers escorted tours and travel information in a variety of formats and distributes a free useful booklet, 'Going Abroad: 101 Tips for Mature Travelers.' Contact Grand Circle at 347 Congress St, Boston, MA 02210 (☎ 617-350-7500 or 800-597-3644, fax 617-350-6206, www.gct.com).

National Council of Senior Citizens
Membership in this group (you needn't be a US citizen to apply) gives access to added Medicare insurance, a mail-order prescription service and a variety of discount information and travel-related advice. Fees are $13/30/150 for one year, three years or lifetime. The council is based at 8403 Colesville Rd, Suite 1200, Silver Spring, MD 20910-3314 (☎ 301-578-8800, 888-373-6467).

TEXAS FOR CHILDREN

Texas is very child-friendly – Texans love li'l cowpokes, and they'll usually get fussed over in restaurants and hotels. In this book we list as often as possible attractions that kids might like as well as the prices for children for admission to attractions. There's rarely an extra charge for kids in hotels; ask the hotel staff about baby-sitters.

Rental car companies will rent baby car seats for children under five for about $5 per day or $25 per week; AAA members (see Useful Organizations later) may be entitled to reimbursement for baby car seat rentals.

There are several theme parks in Texas, including Sea World in San Antonio and Six Flags parks in Arlington, San Antonio and Houston. Do try to take the kids away from the metro areas and into the boonies, where you'll see the Texas of your imagination: wide-open spaces, working cowboys, cool geology and unusual animals. Texas has one of the best state park systems anywhere, and there are usually several parks within easy reach.

Ideal destinations include Big Bend National Park, with its scenic beauty and cross-cultural feel, and Caprock Canyons State Park up in the eastern Panhandle, where you can do everything from going horseback riding and paddleboating to taking extended trips on the 64-mile Caprock Canyons Trailways.

See Lonely Planet's *Travel with Children*, by Maureen Wheeler, for more information on what to do when on the road with little ones. If you're stuck for ideas, contact the nearest convention and visitors bureau, which can help you work out an itinerary.

Remember, though, that Texas is a huge state. Don't try to do too much, and plan plenty of rest and recreation stops to keep the little ones happy.

Beaches

The open beaches of the barrier islands such as Padre Island are a delight for children and adults alike. However, be alert: the very hard-packed white sand that gives the beaches their allure also means that they are suitable for driving on. Except for limited areas around some park entrances, the beaches are wide open for cars and trucks. Most drivers stay back from the surf and use well-traveled routes along the shore, but there's always the occasional yahoo proving his or her toughness by driving a sport utility vehicle faster than the speed limit and right along the surf line where sand-castle builders may be caught unaware.

Playgrounds

Discovery Zone (☎ 800-282-4386) is a chain of indoor playgrounds that parents and younger kids absolutely adore – it's filled with ramps, rooms full of plastic balls, rope ladders, swings, tunnels, slides and trampolines. Admission to a Discovery Zone is about $6 per child (adults don't pay, but adults are not admitted without a child), and the playground is open daily. Discovery Zone has branches in Fort Worth, Houston, El Paso, Austin, San Antonio and Lubbock, among others.

Many McDonald's and some Burger King restaurants have children's play zones that do a good job of emulating the Discovery Zone, and a kids' meal at any of these fast-food places is usually enough to secure cheap admission to a good, safe playground. There are also public playgrounds in every city, especially along the beaches, and there are public toilets and water fountains at most of them as well.

Swimming Pools

Every sizable Texas city has a municipal swimming pool with organized programs and free swim periods. The Police Athletic League in many cities is a great source for weekend and after-school programs.

USEFUL ORGANIZATIONS

See also the organizations listed earlier for seniors and disabled travelers.

American Automobile Association

For its members, the American Automobile Association (AAA; www.aaa-texas.com/) provides great travel information, distributes free road maps and guide books, and sells American Express traveler's checks without commission. The AAA membership card will often get you discounts for accommodations, car rental and admission charges. If you plan to do a lot of driving – even in a rental car – it is usually worth joining the AAA. It costs $56 for the first year and $39 for subsequent years.

Members of other auto clubs, like the British and Australian AA, Canadian CAA and German ADAC, are entitled to the same services if they bring their membership cards and/or a letter of introduction.

AAA also provides emergency roadside service to members in the event of an accident, breakdown or locking your keys in the car. Service is free within a given radius of the nearest service center, and service providers will tow your car to a mechanic if they can't fix it. The nationwide toll-free roadside assistance number is ☎ 800-222-4357. All major cities and many smaller towns have an AAA office where you can start membership.

National Park Service & US Forest Service

The National Park Service (NPS), part of the Department of the Interior, administrates the use of parks. The US Forest Service (USFS) is under the Department of Agriculture and administrates the use of forests. National forests are less protected than parks, allowing commercial exploitation in some areas (usually logging or privately owned recreational facilities).

National parks most often surround spectacular natural features and cover hundreds of square miles. A full range of accommodations can be found in and around national parks. Contact individual parks for more specific information. National park campground and reservations information can be obtained at ☎ 800-365-2267 or by writing to National Park Service Public Inquiry,

Department of Interior, PO Box 37127, Washington, DC 20013-7127.

Current information about national forests can be obtained from ranger stations, which are also listed in the text. National forest campground and reservation information can be obtained by calling ☎ 800-280-2267. General information about federal lands is also available from the Fish and Wildlife Service and the Bureau of Land Management (see later).

Fish & Wildlife Service

Each state has a few regional Fish and Wildlife Service (FWS) offices that can provide information about viewing local wildlife. Their phone numbers appear in the blue section of the local White Pages directory under US Government, Interior Department, or you can call the Federal Information Center (☎ 800-688-9889).

Bureau of Land Management

The Bureau of Land Management, or the BLM, as it is commonly called, manages public use of federal lands. This is no-frills camping, often in untouched settings (most of BLM's holdings are in the desert Southwest). Each state has a regional office located in the state capital. Look in the blue section of the local White Pages directory under US Government, Interior Department, or call the Federal Information Center (☎ 800-688-9889).

DANGERS & ANNOYANCES
Personal Security & Theft

Although street crime is a serious issue in large urban areas, visitors need not be obsessed with security.

Always lock cars and put valuables out of sight, whether leaving the car for a few minutes or longer and whether you are in a town or in the remote backcountry. Rent a car with a lockable trunk. If your car is bumped from behind in a remote area, it's best to keep going to a well-lighted area or service station.

Be aware of your surroundings and who may be watching you. Avoid walking on dimly lighted streets at night, particularly when alone. Walk purposefully. Avoid unnecessary displays of money or jewelry. Divide money and credit cards to avoid losing everything. Aim to use ATMs in well-trafficked areas.

In hotels, don't leave valuables lying around your room. Use safety-deposit boxes or at least place valuables in a locked bag. Don't open your door to strangers – check through the peephole or call the front desk if unexpected guests try to enter.

Guns The USA has a widespread reputation, partly true but also propagated and exaggerated by the media, as a dangerous place because of the availability of firearms. And while the rifle rack is as much a Texas tradition as the pickup truck (see the National Vehicle of Texas boxed text in the Getting Around chapter), the main danger in the USA is from concealed handguns.

Texas has seen many gun-related disasters – the JFK assassination in Dallas, the shootings from the University of Texas Tower in Austin and the mass murder in Luby's in Killeen chief among them. On October 16, 1991, a madman opened fire on customers in a Luby's Cafeteria in Killeen, Texas. After the shooting, a survivor remarked that if only she'd been armed she could have stopped the carnage. This could have been the straw that broke the back of resistance to the passage of a state law granting a concealed weapons permit to any Texan never convicted of a felony and who passes a course in handgun use and safety. Among the victims at Luby's were the parents of Dr Suzanna Gratia; Gratia later became one of the most influential proponents of the concealed-weapons legislation. A version of the bill was vetoed by Democratic governor Ann Richards in 1993, but a new bill was passed by Republican governor George Bush Jr in 1995.

Vast numbers of Texans are now armed with concealed handguns, but the impact of the law is unclear – Texas hasn't seen an increase in random shootings, and it's likely you won't notice the situation at all. But some Texans have become more nervous. Some gun owners develop itchy trigger fingers on the assumption that if they don't shoot first the other person will.

Public offices and private businesses are permitted to ban the carrying of concealed weapons on their premises, which is why you'll see signs forbidding firearms in places like post offices, restaurants, movie theaters, theme parks and at the Alamo. But because the numbers of pistol-packin' people is unclear, you must take steps to avoid stepping into the line of fire. Never argue with or make rude gestures at other motorists. Actually, be nice to pretty much everyone. When pulled over by a police car, especially at night, keep both your hands in plain sight at *all times* (preferably atop the steering wheel) so the officer doesn't mistake your movements for a 'reach' (as in reaching for a weapon) and introduce you to the latest Colt Industries product.

Residents of more rural areas sometimes carry guns, but they most often target animals or isolated traffic signs, rather than humans. Be careful in the woods during the autumn hunting season, when unsuccessful or drunken hunters may be less selective in their targets than one might hope.

Most gun-owners are law-abiding citizens, and Texans are discovering that more often than not, an armed society is a polite society. But anyone with a gun can turn a situation deadly.

Street People The USA has a lamentable record in dealing with its most unfortunate citizens, who often roam the streets of large cities in the daytime and sleep by storefronts, under freeways or in alleyways and abandoned buildings.

This problem is less acute in Texas than in urban areas on both coasts, but it is certainly not absent. Street people and panhandlers may approach visitors in the larger cities and towns; nearly all of them are harmless. It's an individual judgment call whether it's appropriate to offer a street person money or anything else – you might want to just offer food if you have it in lieu of money. If you're truly concerned about the problem, consider donating time or money to an organization for the homeless – ask at visitors' centers or chambers of commerce for local contact numbers.

Drugging The tasteless, odorless drug called Rohypnol (generically Flunitrazepam), also known as 'rophies,' 'roofies' or 'the date-rape drug,' is sold legally in Mexico despite its ban in the USA and Europe. Rohypnol is dissolved into drinks (usually alcoholic ones) by predatory scumbags and given to victims, who are soon rendered unconscious. Sedation is so deep that rape victims have been known to have absolutely no memory of any wrongdoing. Effects, which can occur as fast as 15 minutes after ingestion, include dizziness, disorientation, extreme fatigue and memory loss. In 1997, Rohypnol manufacturer Hoffman-La Roche released a color-releasing tablet, which is harder to dissolve and turns light liquids blue and dark ones murky, but older tablets and generics remain in the market. Exercise *extreme* caution when you are offered cocktails, beer, wine and even soft drinks, cigarettes and sweets. If circumstances make you suspicious or uneasy, the offer can be tactfully refused by claiming stomach or other medical problems.

Hurricanes

A hurricane is a concentrated system of very strong thunderstorms with high circulation. The 74- to 160-mph winds created by a hurricane can extend for hundreds of miles around the eye (center) of a hurricane system. Floods and flash floods caused by the torrential rains it produces cause additional property damage, and perhaps most dangerous of all, hurricanes can cause a storm surge, forcing the level of the ocean to rise between 4 and 18 feet above normal. The storm surge caused in 1998 by Hurricane Mitch, a Category Four hurricane, destroyed major sections of Central America and killed thousands of people. The 9- to 12-foot surge caused by Hurricane Opal destroyed much of the coast of the Florida Panhandle in 1995.

The Saffir-Simpson scale breaks hurricanes into five levels of intensity, based on the speed of circular wind intensity. Storms circulate counterclockwise in the northern hemisphere. Some hurricane and storm terminology follows.

Tropical Depression Formative stage of a storm. This is an organized cloud system with winds of less than 39mph.

Tropical Storm Strengthened tropical depression. This is an organized system of powerful thunderstorms with high circulation and wind speeds between 39 and 73mph.

Category One Hurricane Winds between 74 and 95mph. This primarily effects plants, small piers and small crafts, and it can produce a storm surge of between 4 and 5 feet, flooding coastal roads. Note that a Category One hurricane is still a hurricane and not to be treated lightly.

Category Two Hurricane Winds between 96 and 110mph. This causes major damage to plants, and trees can be uprooted. Mobile homes, roofs, doors and windows are damaged or destroyed, and there is a 6- to 8-foot storm surge.

Category Three Hurricane Winds between 111 and 130mph. Large trees are uprooted and knocked over; mobile homes and small buildings near the coast and signs are destroyed; roofs, windows, doors and building structures damaged. Nine- to 12-foot storm surge cuts off coastal escape routes three to five hours before the storm.

Category Four Hurricane Winds between 131 and 155mph. Mobile homes, plants, trees and signs are ripped up and destroyed; roofs, windows and doors damaged; major structural damage to buildings. Thirteen- to 18-foot storm surge cuts off coastal escape routes three to five hours before the storm.

Category Five Hurricane Winds above 155mph. Destruction of buildings and roofs. Eighteen-foot storm surge cuts off coastal escape routes three to five hours before the storm.

Every year during hurricane season (June 1 to November 30) storms form over the Atlantic Ocean and the Gulf of Mexico and gather strength – and some roll right over Texas.

Hurricanes are deadly. They can throw cars and trucks. And as anyone can attest who saw the carnage left behind Hurricane Mitch, they can wipe out communities.

They're generally sighted well in advance and there's time to prepare. When a hurricane threatens, be sure to listen to radio and television news reports. Give credence only to forecasts attributed to the National Weather Service (shortwave radio listeners can tune to 162.55 MHz), and dismiss anything else as a rumor. You can also call the

National Hurricane Center (☎ 305-229-4470, option 1) for hurricane-tracking information. There are two distinct stages of alert: a hurricane watch, given when a hurricane *may* strike in the area within the next 36 to 48 hours; and a hurricane warning, given when a hurricane is likely to strike the area.

If a hurricane warning is issued during your stay, you may be placed under an evacuation order. Hotels generally follow these orders and ask guests to leave. The Red Cross operates hurricane shelters, but they're just that – shelters. They do not provide food. You must bring your own food, first-aid kit, blanket or sleeping bag and, hey, bring a book. Ask at your hotel or hostel for more information as to the logistics of evacuation.

If you're determined to sit out a hurricane warning – and we do *not* recommend you do, you will need at the very least the following:

• Flashlight
• As much fresh drinking water as possible (storms knock out water supply)
• Butane lighter and candles
• Canned food, peanut butter, powdered or UHT milk
• Cash (ATMs don't function)
• Portable, battery-powered radio

Stay in a closet or other windowless room. Cover yourself with a mattress to prevent injury from flying glass. Taping windows does not stop them from breaking, but it does reduce shatter.

Tornadoes

For a brief period after a hurricane – as if to add insult to injury – conditions become just ducky for a tornado. A tornado watch is generally issued as standard operating procedure after a hurricane, but twisters pop up in Texas annually. There's not much you can do about this except be aware of the situation and follow the instructions of local radio and television stations and police.

Floods

Low-lying southern and eastern Texas have a propensity to flood; in 1998, flooding was so severe that entire communities were evacuated and billions of dollars in damage occurred. Flash floods, like tornadoes, are inherently impossible to predict; follow the same advice you would for tornadoes: stay aware of changes in the weather and follow emergency instructions when provided.

Recreational Hazards

In wilderness areas the consequences of an accident can be very serious, so inform someone of your route and expected return.

Mosquitoes The swampy southern and coastal regions of Texas are perfect breeding grounds for a form of mosquito that deserves inclusion in the boast 'everything's bigger down here.' Seemingly immune to seasonal change, these bugs attack in swarms whether the temperature is in the 90s or down in the 50s. And they are especially resilient to physical abuse. One coastal biologist was observed repeatedly slamming one with his fist against a car window, only to have the bug resolutely return to his ripe and bare arm. Said the biologist, 'I socked him twice in the jaw and he came back for more.'

The best way to combat these bugs is by using an insect repellent that causes them to suck blood elsewhere. Look for those containing the chemical diethyltoluamide, called DEET. DEET can sometimes cause skin irritation, so start with formulas that have less than 10% DEET. You can move up in strength until you find something that sends the mosquitoes packing. Avon Skin-So-Soft is so effective that it's sometimes used by the US military. Commercial repellents such as Off! come in a variety of formulations.

Jellyfish Not very far up the evolutionary scale from the mosquito, but exponentially more pain-inflicting, jellyfish abound in the mild waters of the Gulf of Mexico. They're around throughout the year and often float in schools. Two varieties pack powerful stings: the Portuguese man-of-war, which is a translucent blue with long tentacles dangling from the center; and the sea nettle, which is also translucent but has tentacles attached to the edge of its bell-shaped central mass.

One good clue that jellyfish are in the area is if you find a dead one on the beach. But look, don't touch; the venom stings even after a jellyfish dies. If you are stung, treat the injured area with supermarket-bought unseasoned meat tenderizer containing a fruit enzyme called papain. This will relieve the severe stinging, but may make you that much more succulent to mosquitoes.

Wildlife As more people spend time in the backcountry or impinge on wildlife habitat, wildlife attacks on humans and pets are becoming more common. Bears and pumas (mountain lions) pose the most serious hazards, but seemingly placid and innocuous beasts such as bison and mule deer are equally capable of inflicting serious injury or even fatal wounds on unsuspecting tourists. Some carry rabies. You're unlikely to see a mountain lion, but if you do, take the following precautions: Hold your ground – don't run. Shout and wave your arms above your head. Stand close with the others in your group, and pick up small children. If the lion starts behaving aggressively, throw stones – not to hit it, but to scare it away. Keep your distance from all wild animals – even prairie dogs.

Anytime you're off paved trails, remember the first rule of the range as voiced by one cattle rancher is 'Look before you step' (the second rule is 'Leave every gate as you found it').

Snakebites See the Flora & Fauna section in the Facts about Texas chapter for information on the state's snakes. In the unlikely event of a bite by a poisonous snake, the main thing to do is stay calm – that's easy for us to say. If you can get to a telephone, call either the North Texas Poison Center in Dallas (☎ 800-764-7661) or the Southeast Texas Poison Center in Galveston (☎ 409-765-1420, 713-654-1701), which will connect you with the nearest Poison Information Center or hospital. If you can, find a ranger.

If you're alone, stave off panic with the knowledge that snakebites don't, no matter what you've seen in the movies, cause instantaneous death. But they are dangerous and you need to keep a good, clear head on your shoulders.

Wrap the limb tightly, as you would a sprained ankle, with a firm, Ace-type (rubberized) bandage over the bitten area, bandaging as much of the limb as possible, and splint. Get medical help as soon as possible, and if it's at all possible, bring along the dead snake for identification – but *do not* attempt to catch the snake if there's *any* chance of being bitten again. Sucking out the poison and attaching tourniquets has been widely discredited as treatment for snakebites, so do not apply ice, a tourniquet, elevate the limb or attempt to suck out the poison yourself. Instead, keep the affected area below the level of the heart and move it as little as possible. Coffee or tea is okay to give if you're feeling faint, but under no circumstances should you ingest alcohol or any drugs. Antivenoms are available in hospitals. If you're somehow bitten by a rare snake, your best bet is to telephone the nearest zoo, or contact the American Zoo and Aquarium Association in Wheeling, West Virginia (☎ 304-242-2160).

EMERGENCY

Throughout most of the USA dial ☎ 911 for emergency service of any sort; in large cities or areas with substantial Latino populations, Spanish-speaking emergency operators may be available, but other language speakers are less likely. This is a free call from any phone. A few rural phones might not have this service, in which case dial ☎ 0 for the operator and ask for emergency assistance – it's still free. Each state also maintains toll-free numbers for traffic information and emergencies.

Lost or Stolen Documents

Carry a photocopy of your passport separately from your passport. Copy the pages with your photo and personal details, passport number and US visa. If it is lost or stolen, this will make replacing it easier. In this event, you should call your embassy.

You can find your embassy's telephone number by dialing ☎ 202-555-1212 (directory inquiries for Washington, DC).

Similarly, carry copies of your traveler's-check numbers and credit-card numbers separately. If you lose your credit cards or they are stolen, contact the company immediately (see Credit & Debit Cards for company phone numbers.) Contact your bank if you lose your ATM card.

LEGAL MATTERS

If you are stopped by the police for any reason, bear in mind that there is no system of paying fines on the spot. For traffic offenses, the police officer will explain your options to you. Attempting to pay the fine to the officer is frowned upon at best and may compound your troubles by resulting in a charge of bribery. Should the officer decide that you should pay up front, he or she can exercise the authority to take you directly to the magistrate instead of allowing you the usual 30-day period to pay the fine.

If you are arrested for more serious offenses, you are allowed to remain silent. There is no legal reason to speak to a police officer if you don't wish, but never walk away from an officer until given permission. All persons who are arrested are legally allowed (and given) the right to make one telephone call. You're also given, as viewers of any cop show can tell you, the right to remain silent and to refuse to answer questions and the right to representation by an attorney, which will be appointed to you free if you request it from the office of the public defender. If you don't have a lawyer or family member to help you, call your embassy. The police will give you the number upon request. You are presumed innocent until proven guilty.

Driving & Drinking Laws

Each state has its own laws and what is legal in one state may be illegal in others. See Road Rules in the Getting Around chapter for more information.

Driving You must be at least 16 years old to drive in Texas. Speed limits are 70mph on interstates and freeways unless otherwise posted. You can drive 5mph over the limit without much likelihood of being pulled over, but if you're driving 10mph over the limit, you'll be caught sooner or later. In small towns, driving over the posted speed by any amount may attract attention. Speed limits on other highways are 55mph or lower, and in cities it can vary from 25 to 45mph. Watch for school zones, which can have strictly enforced speed limits as low as 15mph during school hours. Seat belts and motor-cycle helmets must be worn in most states.

Speeding tickets are expensive; going 10mph above the limit could land you a fine of more than $100.

Drinking & Driving The drinking age is 21 and you need an ID (identification with your photograph on it) to prove your age. Undercover agents from the Texas Alco-holic Beverage Commission pose as em-ployees or consumers in shops that sell alcohol trawling for underage buyers. You could incur stiff fines, jail time and penalties if caught driving under the influence of alcohol; statewide the blood-alcohol limit over which you are considered legally drunk is .10%, though if you're younger than 21 years old it is illegal to drive after you have consumed *any* alcohol – zero tolerance. As we go to press, a federal proposal to reduce the national blood alcohol level to .08% was being considered. During festive holidays and special events, roadblocks are some-times set up to deter drunk drivers.

For more information on car rental, insur-ance and other automobile-related con-cerns, see the Getting Around chapter.

BUSINESS HOURS & HOLIDAYS
Businesses usually stay open from 9 am to 5 pm, but there are certainly no hard-and-fast rules. In any large city, a few supermarkets, restaurants and the main post office are open 24 hours. Shops are usually open from 9 or 10 am to 5 or 6 pm (often until 9 pm in shop-ping malls), except Sundays when hours are noon to 5 pm (often later in malls). Post offices are open from 8 am to 4 or 5:30 pm, Monday to Friday, and some are open from 8 am to 3 pm on Saturday. Banks are usually open from either 9 or 10 am to 5 or 6 pm Monday to Friday. A few banks are open from 9 am to 2 or 4 pm on Saturdays. Hours are de-cided by individual branches, so if you need specifics, give the branch you want a call.

National public holidays are celebrated throughout the USA. Banks, schools and government offices (including post offices) are closed, and transportation, museums and other services run on a Sunday schedule. Holidays falling on a weekend are usually observed the following Monday.

New Year's Day
  January 1

Martin Luther King Jr Day
  Third Monday in January

Presidents' Day
  Third Monday in February

Easter
  A Sunday in late March or early April

Memorial Day
  Last Monday in May

Independence Day (also called the Fourth of July)
  July 4

Labor Day
  First Monday in September

Columbus Day
  Second Monday in October

Veterans' Day
  November 11

Thanksgiving Day
  Fourth Thursday in November

Christmas Day
  December 25

CULTURAL EVENTS
Besides the above holidays, the USA cele-brates a number of other events. Here are some of the most widely observed ones:

January
Chinese New Year begins the end of January or beginning of February and lasts two weeks. The first day is celebrated with parades, firecrackers, fireworks and lots of food.

February
Valentine's Day is on the 14th. No one knows why St Valentine is associated with romance in the USA, but this is the day to celebrate with your sweetie.

March

St Patrick's Day is the 17th. The patron saint of Ireland is honored by all those who feel the Irish in their blood and by those who want to feel Irish beer in their blood. Everyone wears green (or you can get pinched).

April

Passover is celebrated either in March or April, depending on the Jewish calendar. Jewish families get together to partake in the traditional seder dinner, which commemorates the exodus of Jews from slavery in Egypt.

May

Cinco de Mayo is the 5th. Commemoration of the day the Mexicans wiped out the French Army in 1862. Now it's the day all Americans get to eat lots of Mexican food and drink margaritas.

Mother's Day is the second Sunday of the month. Children send cards and flowers and call Mom. Restaurants are likely to be busy.

June

Father's Day is the third Sunday of the month. Same idea, different parent.

October

Halloween is the 31st. The evening sees kids and adults dressing in costumes. In safer neighborhoods children go 'trick-or-treating' for candy. Adults go to parties to act out their alter egos.

November

Day of the Dead is the 2nd. Observed in most of Texas and called Día de los Muertos in Spanish, this is a day for families to honor dead relatives and make breads and sweets resembling skeletons, skulls and such.

Election Day is the second Tuesday of the month.

December

Chanukah is usually in December (the date changes from year to year, as it's tied to the Hebrew calendar). This eight-day Jewish holiday commemorates the victory of the Maccabees over the armies of Syria and the rededication of their temple in Jerusalem.

Kwanzaa is from the 26 until the 31st. This African American holiday is a time to celebrate black culture, family, and future.

New Year's Eve is the last day of the year, the 31st. Celebrated with few traditions other than dressing up and drinking champagne or staying home and watching the festivities on TV. The following day people stay home to nurse their hangovers and watch college football.

SPECIAL EVENTS

This is by no means a complete list of Texas events – that would fill a small book of its own (you can search for Texas events at the Virtual Texan, www.virtualtexan.com). Throughout the book you'll find listed regional and local special events (including fuller descriptions of the ones listed here); following are events we think are worth planning a trip around.

January

Cotton Bowl is on New Year's Day, Dallas. Experience college-football nirvana in Dallas.

Southwestern Exposition Stock Show and Rodeo is the last week of January, Fort Worth. Between 800,000 and 1 million people attend the 17-day show and rodeo.

Janis Joplin Birthday Bash is on or near the 19th, Port Arthur. Celebrate the anniversary of Texas' '60s songwriter with live music.

February

Houston Livestock Show and Rodeo is in mid-February, Houston. Attend the nation's second largest rodeo and largest cattle show.

Annual Charro Days Celebration is in late February, Brownsville. This event celebrates the link between Brownsville and the Mexican border town of Matamoros.

Mardi Gras is 12 days before Ash Wednesday, Galveston. Texas has its own version of the parades, pageants, parties and puke.

March

South by Southwest is in mid-March, Austin. Get down at one of the nation's most important music festivals, held throughout the city; the festival also includes multimedia and film.

April

Hill Country Food and Wine Festival is the first week in April, Austin and the Highland Lakes. Sample freely at this wine and food celebration.

Fiesta San Antonio is in late April, San Antonio. If you missed Mardi Gras, this is a similar, incredible bash.

May

Kerrville Folk Festival is in late May, Kerrville. Enjoy this 18-day music and folk celebration.

June

Juneteenth is around the 19th, a multiday celebration of the emancipation of the slaves; special events are held throughout the state.

Luling Watermelon Thump is the last Thursday to Saturday of June, Luling. This needs no explanation, does it?

July

Independence Day is July 4th, throughout the US. Expect fireworks displays and classical concerts in all major cities.

West of the Pecos Rodeo is in early July, Pecos. This is the oldest rodeo in the US.

August

Texas Folklife Festival is in early August. San Antonio hosts the state's main arts and crafts fair.

Hotter'N Hell Hundred is in late August, Wichita Falls. This is the largest sanctioned century bicycle ride in the US.

September

Buddy Holly Birthday Celebration is around the 5th of September, Lubbock. Holly's hometown fetes its native son with a huge musical street festival in the Depot District.

National Cowboy Symposium is in mid-September, Lubbock. The symposium includes a festival and parade of horses, trail rides, rodeo events, dances and the national chuck-wagon cookoff championship.

October

Oktoberfest is the first weekend in October, throughout the state. There are many of these copies of the traditional German beer festival in central Texas and a huge one in Fredericksburg.

Texas State Fair is in late September and early October, Dallas. More than 3 million people attend, making it the largest state fair in the USA.

South Texas State Fair is in mid-October, Port Arthur. If you missed the statewide fair, there's this huge regional fair.

Cav-Oil-Cade Celebration is in mid-October, Port Arthur. It's a hoot at this weeklong celebration of the oil industry.

Halloween is October 31st, throughout the state. Expect costumes and parades galore, especially along E 6th St in Austin.

November

Chili Cookoffs is the first Saturday, Terlingua. Two cookoffs (each saying bad things about the other) boast the best chili in the world.

December

Christmas Lighting is throughout the month, Texas Hill Country. Indulge in light stringing and mulled-wine drinking throughout the Hill Country.

Christmas at Old Fort Concho is the first weekend in December, San Angelo. El Paseo de Santa Angela, a historic path linking the fort and town, is festooned with thousands of lights.

WORK

Seasonal work is possible in national parks and other tourist sites, especially ski areas; for information, contact park concessionaires or local chambers of commerce.

If you're not a US citizen, you'll need to apply for a work visa from the US embassy in your home country before you leave. The type of visa you'll need varies depending on how long you're staying and the kind of work you plan to do. Generally, you'll need either a J1 visa, which you can obtain by joining a visitor-exchange program, or a H2B visa, which you get when you are sponsored by a US employer. The latter is not easy to obtain (since the employer has to prove that no US citizen or permanent resident is available to do the job); the former is issued mostly to students for work in summer camps.

Music Work

Tens of thousands of musicians head for Austin and San Antonio every year to get work in the clubs there, and (though it's not legal and you risk deportation) even foreigners can get work without too much hassle with paperwork if the musician is good enough. To make things easier for musicians, the Texas government has put together a highly useful 'Indie Band Packet,' free for the asking, which is a listing, arranged by city, of clubs and dance halls specific to the type of music that you play as well as recording studios, radio stations, record stores, record distributors, music journalists and information on copyrights and trademarks and more. For a copy, write to the Texas Music Office, PO Box 13246, Austin, TX 78711, or head to www.governor.state.tx.us/music or send email to music@governor.texas.gov.

ACCOMMODATIONS

Camping

Camping is the cheapest, and in many ways the most enjoyable, approach to a vacation. Visitors with a car and a tent can take advantage of hundreds of private and public campgrounds and RV parks at prices of $10 per night or even less. Most Texas state park campgrounds and other park accommodations do not accept credit cards.

Public Campgrounds These are on public lands such as national forests, state and national parks and BLM lands (see Useful Organizations earlier in this chapter).

Free dispersed camping (meaning you can camp almost anywhere) is permitted in many public backcountry areas. Sometimes you can camp right from your car along a dirt road, especially in BLM and national forest areas. Obviously, in this situation there are no facilities. In other places, backpack your gear in to a cleared campsite. See the Activities chapter for minimum impact camping rules and suggestions of what you should bring for backcountry camping trips.

Information and detailed maps are available from many local ranger stations or BLM offices (addresses and telephone numbers are given in the text) and may be posted along the road. Sometimes, a free camping permit is required, particularly in national parks, less so in forests and BLM areas.

Developed areas usually have toilets, drinking water, fire pits (or charcoal grills) and picnic benches. Some don't have drinking water (this is mentioned in the text). At any rate, it is always a good idea to have a few gallons of water when venturing out to the boonies. These basic campgrounds usually cost about $5 to $7 a night.

More developed areas may have showers or RV hookups. These will cost several dollars more. On the whole, national forest and BLM campgrounds tend to be of the less-developed variety, while national park and state park campgrounds are more likely to have showers or RV hookups available. The less-developed sites are often on a 'first-come, first-served' basis, so plan on an early arrival, preferably during the week, as sites fill up fast on Fridays and weekends. More-developed areas may accept or require reservations; details are given in the text.

Costs given in the text for public campgrounds are per site. A site normally accommodates up to six people (or two vehicles). If there are more of you, you'll need two sites. Public campgrounds often have seven- or 14-night limits.

Private Campgrounds These are on private property and are usually close to or in a town. Most are designed with RVs in mind; tenters can camp but fees are several dollars higher than in public campgrounds. Fees given in the text are for two people per site. There is usually an extra person charge of $1 to $3 each. In addition, state and city taxes apply. However, there may be discounts for week or month stays.

Facilities can include hot showers, coin laundry, swimming pool, full RV hookup, games area, playground and convenience store. Kampgrounds of America (KOA) is a national network of private campgrounds with sites usually ranging from $12 to $15, depending on what kind of hookup you prefer, or if there are hookups at all. You can get the annual directory of KOA sites by calling or writing KOA (☎ 406-248-7444), PO Box 30558, Billings, MT 59114-0558.

Reservations To make a reservation, you must pay with Visa, MasterCard or Discover Card. For sites in national forests call ☎ 800-280-2267. For sites in national parks call Destinet at ☎ 800-365-2267.

Hostels

The US hostel network is less widespread than in the rest of the world, and the Texas hostel network is smaller than that in most states. Not all hostels are directly affiliated with Hostelling International-American Youth Hostels (HI-AYH). Those that are offer discounts to HI-AYH members and usually allow nonmembers to stay for a few dollars more. Dormitory beds cost about $10 to $12 a night. Rooms are $20 to $30 for one or two people, sometimes more.

There are staffed HI-AYH council offices in Austin, Houston and Dallas. Currently there are HI-AYH-affiliated hostels in Austin (the world's only hostel with waterbeds), San Antonio, El Paso and Houston. A new hostel in Dallas should be open by the time you read this.

HI-AYH hostels expect you to rent or carry a sheet or sleeping bag to keep the beds clean. Dormitories are segregated by sex. Kitchen and laundry privileges are usually available. There are information and advertising boards, TV rooms and lounge areas. Alcohol may be banned.

Reservations Reservations are accepted and advised during the high season, when there may be a limit of a three-night stay. You can call HI-AYH's national office (☎ 202-783-6161) to make reservations for any HI-AYH hostel, or use the code-based reservation service at ☎ 800-909-4776 (you need the access code for the hostels to use this service; they are available from any HI-AYH office or listed in its handbook).

Motels & Hotels

Motel and hotel prices vary tremendously in price from urban to rural areas (see Costs in the Money section earlier) and from season to season. Prices considered expensive in El Paso could be budget options in Austin, and a hotel charging $40 for a double in the high season may drop its rates to $25 in the low season and then raise them to $55 for a special event. Prices in this guide can only be an approximate guideline at best. Also, be prepared to add room tax to prices. Children are often allowed to stay free with their parents, but rules for this vary. Some hotels allow children younger than 18 to stay free with parents, while others draw the line at children younger than 12; others still may charge a few dollars per child. Call and inquire if you are traveling with a family.

Prices advertised by hotels are called 'rack rates' and are not written in stone. If you simply ask about any specials that might apply you can often save quite a bit of money. Booking through a travel agent also saves you money, and members of AARP or

AAA can qualify for a 'corporate' rate at several hotel chains.

Hotels hike up the price of local calls by almost 200%, and long-distance rates are gouged up from 100% to 200%! The best plan of action is to use a pay phone for all of your calls.

Special events and conventions can fill up a town's hotels quickly, so call ahead to find out what will be going on. The visitors' center is always a good resource.

Budget Motels with $20 rooms are found mostly in small towns on major highways and the motel strips of larger towns. However, what may be a budget motel in one town may pass for a mid-range hotel in another.

Rooms are usually small, and beds may be soft or saggy, but the sheets should be clean. A minimal level of cleanliness is maintained, but expect scuffed walls, atrocious decor, old furniture and strange noises from your shower. Even these places, however, normally have a private shower and toilet and a TV in each room. Most have air-conditioning and heat.

Even the cheapest motels may advertise kitchenettes. These may cost a few dollars more, but they do give you the chance to cook a simple meal for yourself if you're fed up with restaurants. Kitchenettes vary from a two-ring burner to a spiffy little mini-kitchen and may or may not include utensils. If you plan on doing a lot of kitchenette cooking, carry your own set.

Motel & Hotel Chains There are many motel and hotel chains in the USA. The level of quality and style tends to be repeated throughout the chain. If you plan to stay at hotels of the same chain, investigate the chain's frequent-guest program – discounts and guaranteed reservations are offered to faithful guests.

The cheapest national chain is Motel 6. Rooms start around $20 for a single in smaller towns, $30 in larger towns. They usually charge a flat $6 for each extra person.

Motel chains in the next price level start around $30 in smaller towns or around $40 in larger or more popular places. The main difference is the size of the room and the quality: firmer beds, cable TV, free coffee. If these sorts of things are worth an extra $10 or $15 a night, then you'll be happy with the Super 8 Motels, Days Inns or EconoLodges.

Stepping up to chains with rooms in the $45 to $80 range (depending on location) you'll find noticeably nicer rooms; cafés, restaurants or bars may be on the premises or adjacent to them; the swimming pool may be indoors; and there may be a spa or an exercise room also available. Less widespread but very good are the Comfort Inns and Sleep Inns.

Reservations The cheapest budget places may not accept reservations, but at least phone from the road to see what's available; even if the place doesn't take reservations it'll often hold a room for an hour or two.

Chain hotels all will take reservations days or months ahead of time. Normally, you have to give a credit-card number to hold the room. If you don't show up and don't call to cancel, you will be charged the first night's rental. Cancellation policies vary, so find out about them when you book.

Also make sure to let the hotel know if you plan on a late arrival – many motels will give your room away if you haven't arrived or called by 6 pm. Chains have toll-free numbers but their central reservation system might not be aware of local special discounts. Booking ahead, however, gives you the peace of mind of a guaranteed room when you arrive.

Telephone numbers for some of the best-known motel and hotel chains are listed in an appendix at the back of this book.

Lodges In national parks, accommodations are limited to either camping or park lodges operating as a concession. Lodges are often rustic looking but usually quite comfortable inside. Restaurants are on the premises and tour services are often available. National park lodges are not cheap, with most rooms going for close to $100 for a double during the high season, but they are your only option if you want to stay inside the park without camping. If you are coming during the high season, make a reservation months in advance.

Top End Full-service hotels, with bellhops and doormen, restaurants and bars, exercise rooms and saunas, room service and concierge, are found in major cities.

B&Bs

European visitors should be aware that North American B&Bs are much less the casual, inexpensive sort of accommodations found on the continent or in Britain. While they are usually family-run, many if not most B&Bs require advance reservations, though some will be happy to oblige the occasional drop-in.

A large majority of B&Bs prohibit smoking. All have substantial breakfasts included in their prices, but lighter continental breakfasts are not unheard of. The cheapest establishments, with rooms from $30 to $40, may have clean but unexciting rooms with a shared bathroom.

Pricier places have rooms with private baths and, perhaps, facilities like fireplaces, balconies and dining rooms with enticingly grand breakfasts and other meals. They may be in historical buildings, quaint country houses or luxurious urban townhouses. Most B&Bs fall in the $50 to $100 price range, but some go more than $100. The best are distinguished by a friendly attention to detail by hosts who can provide you with local information, contacts and other amenities.

Guest & Dude Ranches

Dude ranches and guest ranches are working ranches where guests pay to stay as well as to participate in ranching activities. You'll learn riding, some basic roping techniques and other hokey cowboy stuff. If that's the sort of thing you like, you'll like this sort of thing.

FOOD

Texas food kicks ass. One of the most pleasant surprises of our research trips was the diversity and high quality of food throughout the state. If you are expecting bland, starchy American food, think again: Texas has some of the best food in the USA.

The first thing that you might scratch your head over is the unbelievable quantity of food you are served at US restaurants. A plate of food in the States, especially in Texas, groans under its own weight. Two light eaters may do perfectly well to share one main course (it's called an entrée in the states; a starter is called an appetizer) – though some restaurants charge a 'sharing fee,' usually about $1 to $2.

Usually served between about 6 am and 10 am, a typical American breakfast is large and filling, often including eggs or an omelet, bacon (the type the British call 'smoked streaky bacon') or ham, home fries (fried potatoes, often mixed with onions, garlic and perhaps red or green peppers), toast with butter and jam, and coffee or tea. Some diners and restaurants offer a breakfast menu throughout the day. Many people opt for a bowl of cereal or coffee and a pastry. 'Continental breakfast' is a euphemism for anything from a donut and a cup of coffee to a European-like spread of cheese, bread, muffins and croissants, but usually no meats.

Texas Cookbooks

Two enormously popular cookbooks on Texas and Tex-Mex cuisines – *Matt Martinez's Culinary Frontier* and *Threadgill's: The Cookbook* – were crafted respectively by two Texas food celebrities: Matt Martinez Jr (along with Steve Pate) and Eddie Wilson (whose *Threadgill's* contains a foreword by country-and-western songwriter Jimmie Dale Gilmore). Martinez is owner of Matt's Rancho Martinez and Matt's No Place in Dallas and co-owner of the YO Ranch Restaurant in Dallas; Wilson is proprietor of the famed Austin music and food joint Threadgill's. Wilson says his book celebrates 'the Austin, Texas, landmark of Southern comfort food.' Fun fact: Renee O'Connors, who plays Xena's sidekick Gabrielle on the television program *Xena: Warrior Princess*, is Eddie's daughter.

Lunch, in terms of ritual, is traditionally the least important meal in the USA; many office workers have it at their desks, and most people simply grab something on the run – which is why the US has the best sandwiches in the world: it knows how to eat on the fly.

Sandwiches here are usually crammed with stuff, including fresh vegetables, meats (like roast beef, ham and turkey), cheeses and condiments, and except for cheese, everything on top – lettuce, tomato, onion, peppers, hot peppers, oil, vinegar, salt, pepper, mayonnaise, ketchup and mustard – is usually free.

Because of lunch is the neglected family member of meals, many fine restaurants (and some not-so-fine ones) offer drastically reduced prices at lunch time. You can get at lunch a meal for $5 that would cost $15 or more at dinner. Also in this category are early-bird dinners, offered from around 4 to 6 pm, which try to lure customers in for early trade by offering similar discounts.

Dinners, served between about 5 pm and 10 pm, are more expensive but often very reasonably priced; portions are usually large. Specials may also be available, but they will usually be more expensive than lunch specials. Some of the better restaurants require reservations.

Fast Food

Burger places like McDonald's, Burger King and Wendy's sell medium-size hamburgers, and toppings are usually free (at Wendy's you put them on yourself at a salad bar). Ketchup packets and other condiments are also free.

In big cities, check prices – sometimes fast food is more expensive than cheap local restaurants. But generally speaking, big fast-food places – primarily McDonald's, Burger King and Denny's – serve the cheapest breakfasts by far.

Other fast-food chains in Texas include Taco Cabana, with excellent and very cheap Mexican-style food; Popeye's, with awesome Cajun-style (peppered skin) fried chicken; KFC (Kentucky Fried Chicken); Luby's, a cafeteria chain that shoots toward downhome cuisine (see Farm Food Comes to Town); and more upscale entries like Denny's (open 24 hours), Shoney's, Bennigans and Cracker Barrel for bland American food. Chili's has Southwestern fare, Red Lobster has seafood.

Look in discount-coupon booklets for coupons to fast-food places – usually two-for-one deals or reduced-price combination meals – and remember that most fast-food places honor their competitor's coupons: a coupon for two Burger King Whoppers for the price of one will be happily accepted by McDonald's, which will give you two Big Macs. And it even extends to other kinds of fast-food places like KFC, where if you walk in with a coupon for a Whopper, fries and a drink, you can turn it into a three-piece chicken meal with fries and a drink. Poof!

Vegetarian

Vegetarianism is catching on in a big way in the US, and in the cities non-meat-eaters will have an easy time. In rural areas, though, it can be more difficult, with meat playing a key role in most Southern cooking. Ask twice if something contains meat – some people don't consider things like sausage seasoning, bacon bits or chicken to be meat! Salad bars are a good way to stave off hunger,

---

Farm Food Comes to Town: Home-Style Meals & Chicken-Fried Steak

When Texas food is slow-smoked, it's most likely served 'home-style' (also called 'down-home') in diners throughout the state. Typical noontime specials (a meal commonly called 'dinner' instead of 'lunch') feature huge pork chops or slow-cooked pot roast accompanied by huge servings of mashed potatoes, bacon-spiked green beans and crispy disks of fried okra. The typical meat-and-three setup (entrée and three vegetables) can be followed by a sweet slice of pie and a relaxing coffee.

Adapted from farmhouse meals common to the USA's Deep South, home-style foods worked their way from farms to small-town restaurants and into the Texas culinary repertoire. In the rural lunch counters of Texas, you can see the state's Southern roots in full, edible flower. These diners (and their counterparts in the cities) serve up variations on Deep-South farm foods with a decidedly Texas twist.

The most ubiquitous member of the home-style group, chicken-fried steak (CFS), ranks as hallmark of the Texas kitchen and holds a place of highest honor in the state's food pantheon. The flagship dish of cowboy cuisine, CFS unifies much of the state's mythos, both actual and imagined. From the northern Red River to the Rio Grande borderlands and from El Paso east to the Louisiana line, CFS stands alone in all its simple glory, representing a uniquely Texan culinary subculture.

Like most regionally revered dishes, the methods of preparing CFS are simple: a tough yet tasty cut of beef gets pounded within a quarter-inch of its life with any handy bludgeoning implement. After this high-impact tenderizing, the thin, pulverized cutlets are dipped in egg batter, double-dredged in seasoned flour and immediately placed in a cast-iron skillet filled with sizzling oil. In the next few minutes, the flour and batter turn into a crisp, delicate crust as the steak browns to perfection. After the steaks are done, a rich cream gravy is made by pouring off most of the frying grease and deglazing the pan with milk and adding a little flour for texture and pepper for seasoning. Done right, it's a recipe for righteousness.

Unfortunately, most of the time it's *not* done right, and the vast majority of CFS (even in the dish's Holy Land) borders on the inedible. Tough steaks are served entombed in a thick cast of starch, then topped with tasteless, gloopy gravy that closely resembles some variant of kindergarten paste (in other words, it's how most non-Texans would describe CFS).

and many restaurants serve large salads as main courses.

American

'Standard' American food is so influenced by the cuisines of other countries around the world that it's difficult to nail down other than the obvious: hamburgers. But modern American cooking can be summed up as combining American portions and home-grown foods with foreign sensibilities and techniques; there are many styles of American cooking that borrow heavily from French, Italian (which is probably the most popular foreign food in the USA), Asian and, to a lesser extent, Turkish and Greek.

Southern

Southern cuisine is heavy on fat and meats; typical specialties include biscuits – similar to but better than scones – and mashed potatoes, collard greens (served with hot-pepper-infused vinegar) and black-eyed peas, all of which are prepared with chunks of pork or ham in them. Main courses include fried chicken, roasted ham, pork in a variety of ways (including that favorite light snack, pickled pigs' feet) and gravies with

The key to locating a good CFS lies in asking a single, crucial question: 'Are your steaks hand-dipped?' If the answer is 'yes,' then order without fear. This simple query can save the adventurous (and hungry) traveler the culinary trauma of flash-frozen impostors listed as authentic CFS (variations on the above question – usually translated 'Do you make these here?' – should be employed when ordering onion rings or pies in diners throughout the country).

CFSs are usually only one option on deep menus of home-style favorites, which often include fried chicken, succulent pork roast, or any of a thousand substantial meat dishes and appropriate side vegetables. You're also likely to find fresh-baked cornbread or yeast rolls alongside your heaping plate and a sweet diner waitress offering you iced-tea refills at regular intervals.

Wait staff often ask their patrons to 'save room for dessert,' and savvy eaters should definitely pace themselves for a taste of the sweet stuff. Diner standbys include creamy-sweet banana pudding, a nearly infinite variety of pies, and seasonal cobblers (a dessert that can resemble either a deep-dish pie or hot-fruit compote dotted with sweet cake dough).

After paying your check, you're perfectly prepared for either a full afternoon of ranch work or a blissfully bloated midday nap. Our suggestion? Find a patch of shade and sleep it off. That's the way we'd do it at our homes.

Pableaux Johnson

corn bread, a dry, cakelike bread made from yellow cornmeal. If you're here on New Year's Day, have a plate of black-eyed peas for good luck in the coming year (every restaurant will be serving them); it's a Southern tradition.

Perhaps the biggest shock comes in the form of grits, a corn-derived white glop that's peculiar to the South (though similar to German *griesbrei*). Treat it as a hot cereal and add cream and sugar, or treat it as a side dish and add salt and pepper. It is served in lieu of potatoes at breakfast, and it's best when totally smooth and very hot.

Barbecue If you're even remotely carnivorous, Texas barbecue is heavenly, and when done well (as at Kreuz Market – see Around Austin in the South Central Texas chapter), stunningly, drool-makingly good. The great thing about barbecue is that it's relatively hard to screw up totally, so even the offerings of the state's chain barbecue places, like County Line, are pretty good. But seeking out the best is the lifelong hobby of many a Texan and the subject of countless newspaper and magazine articles. See the boxed text by Austin food critic Pableaux Johnson for information on barbecue.

Sauce There's huge debate over barbecue sauces: what kind, how much or whether you need it at all, and we'll leave it up to you to make up your mind. A typical barbecue sauce

Smoking the Sacred Cow: Texas Barbecue

Sometime during Texas' frontier history, slow-smoked barbecue crossed the line from simple eating pleasure to statewide obsession. Maybe it's the primal joy of gnawing tender, tasty meat directly from bone or the simplistic, sloppy appeal of the hands-on eating experience. Whatever the reason, dedicated barbecue eaters demonstrate nearly religious devotion by worshipping at the pits of Texas' renowned smokehouses. Vegetarian restrictions notwithstanding, travelers to Texas owe themselves at least one meal of this thoroughly spiritual regional specialty.

Developed to preserve meats before the advent of refrigeration, Texas barbecue owes as much to the state's German immigrants as it does to its mythical cowpunchers. Already well-schooled in the arts of slow smoking, German and Czech settlers in central Texas applied these skills to their new home's burgeoning cattle culture. Tougher cuts of meat would enter the smokehouse and emerge hours later – deeply flavorful and tender to the tooth. Some of central Texas' smaller towns – Lockhart and Elgin, to name only two – maintain regional reputations for their smokehouse cultures and routinely draw dedicated pilgrims from miles around.

Texas barbecue leans heavily toward beef – a logical outgrowth of the state's cattle industry – and most signature dishes come straight from the sacred cow. The most common is beef brisket, a cut most often seen as corned beef. With a combination of patience, experience and skill, a seasoned pit boss can transform this notoriously tough meat into a perfectly smoked, tender slab of heaven. Sliced thin and internally moistened by natural fat, a well-smoked brisket falls apart with the slightest touch and can rival more expensive cuts for butter-smooth consistency.

Carnivores seeking a more toothy challenge can indulge in beef ribs – huge meaty racks that would do Fred Flintstone proud – or relax with a saucy chopped beef sandwich. Word to the wise: If you're wearing a white shirt, think twice about the ribs, which tend to be a full-contact eating experience (even as part of a three-meat sampler plate).

is sweet and tangy with clovey overtones, but there are thousands of variations. Kreuz Market's stuff is served without any sauce at all, and it's so naturally juicy and tender you'll agree it's not necessary. But excellent sauce-heavy barbecue, like Sam's in Austin, is divine as well.

Mexican

While Californians may disagree, some say that Texas has the best Mexican food in the USA. At the very least it's darn good. And while both share many of the same staples, Mexican cuisine differs from its relative, Tex-Mex (see the Beyond Rice & Beans boxed text for a Tex-Mex primer). Mexican meals include one or more of three national staples: tortillas, chilis and frijoles. Tortillas are thin round patties of pressed corn- or wheat-flour dough cooked on griddles. Both can be wrapped around or served under any type of food. Always ask for homemade corn tortillas – if they've got 'em, get 'em; they're bound to be awesome.

Frijoles are beans, eaten boiled, fried or refried in soups, on tortillas, or with just about anything.

Chilis are spicy-hot chili peppers; they come in dozens of varieties and are consumed in hundreds of ways.

Breakfast Many Mexican restaurants offer combination breakfasts for about $1.50 to $4.50, typically composed of juice, coffee,

---

Lone Star cattle worship, however, stops short of excluding other meats from the pit. The noble pig makes appearances in the form of succulent pork ribs, thick buttery chops and perfect slices of loin so tender they melt on the tongue. Ground pork and beef combine with pungent spices to create the peppery sausage of regional renown – Texas hot links. In recent years, chicken has shown up on the menu boards, mainly to provide beginners with a non-hoofed barnyard option. Traditionalists, however, stick with the good stuff – red meat and plenty of it.

Though most barbecue restaurants serve their wares piled on Styrofoam plates, certain old-style joints still serve in traditional 'meat-market style' – wrapped in a generous swath of thick butcher paper. (The better to soak up the juices, my dear.) Restaurant-style side dishes usually include pinto beans, potato salad, and/or coleslaw, while markets usually opt for simpler accompaniments (onion slices, dill pickles, cheese slices, whole tomatoes). The universal bread course is usually either mushy white bread or a row of crispy saltine crackers.

Common wisdom about barbecue sauce varies widely from region to region and sometimes joint to joint. While some pit masters pour peppery tomato-based sauce bubbling within electric coffee pots, central Texas purists believe that unadorned meat should speak for itself. The most common sauce is a thin, vinegar-cayenne mix used for dipping or sloshing each forkful – spicy enough to add the right seasoning without drawing attention from the smoky nuances of perfectly prepared meat.

It's possible to find good 'cue in large cities, but the best examples of the art form usually come from the country. Small trailers reborn as makeshift smoking shacks dot Texas back roads, with handmade signs advertising 'Real BBQ Today.' These informal roadside gems, complete with fragrant, belching smokestack and outdoor picnic seating, represent the rural answer to franchise fast food and a lasting state obsession. Pull over and pay homage to Texas' tasty sacred cow.

Pableaux Johnson

and huevos (eggs), which are served in a variety of ways, including huevos fritos (con jamón o tocino) – fried eggs (with ham or bacon); huevos mexicanos – eggs scrambled with tomatoes, chilies and onions; or huevos rancheros – fried eggs on tortillas, covered in salsa. A new twist is breakfast burritos, usually eggs and either refried beans or bacon rolled in a soft tortilla.

Lunch La comida (lunch), the biggest meal of the day, is usually served between 1 and 3 or 4 pm. Most restaurants offer not only à la carte fare but also special fixed-price menus called *menú del día*. Prices typically range from $5 or cheaper at smaller places for a simple meal of soup, a meat dish, rice and coffee to $8 or $10 for elaborate repasts –

but typically you'll get four or five courses for $6.50 or so.

Staples Mexican staples you'll run into in Texas include the ubiquitous burrito – beans, cheese, meat, chicken or seafood seasoned with salsa or chili and wrapped in a wheat-flour tortilla; chile relleno; empanada, a small pastry with savory or sweet filling; enchilada, with ingredients similar to those used in burritos and tacos rolled up in a tor-tilla, dipped in sauce and then baked or partly fried; and gordita – fried corn dough filled with refried beans and topped with cream, cheese and lettuce.

All Mexican restaurants serve as appetiz-ers guacamole – mashed avocados mixed with onion, chilis, lemon, tomato and other

Beyond Rice & Beans: A Tex-Mex Primer

Most of what the world knows about Mexican food, it learned from Texas (or to be more precise, the former Mexican territory that's now part of present-day south Texas). Travelers will immediately recognize the signature dishes of Tex-Mex border cuisine (enchiladas, tacos, tamales) – most of which were universally adopted by restaurateurs and fast-food purveyors in the early part of this century. As a result, the now-cliché 'Mexican dinner' – a sampler of ground beef and bright-orange processed cheese – can be found in grocery freezers and chain restaurants from Seattle to Stockholm. As you make your way through Texas, forget every 'taco dinner' you've ever eaten and prepare to indulge in an entirely different experience.

Tex-Mex cuisine takes both its ingredients and cultural cues from its roots in the US-Mexican borderlands. Based largely on the classic beans-and-corn combination, Tex-Mex cuisine is dominated by hearty ingredients that can survive in the arid conditions of the greater Rio Grande Valley. Tomatoes, chili peppers, onions and garlic accent dishes made from just about every barnyard meat, with a special emphasis on plentiful Texas beef.

Native chilis add to most Tex-Mex food the characteristic spicy kick that can range from subtle to pleasurably painful. Jalapeños show up most often in Tex-Mex dishes, though recent years have seen a surge in the use of poblano, ancho and the deep-smoked chipotle peppers (just to be safe, diners with delicate palates or constitutions should ask about heat before ordering chili-based dishes).

The most common dish is, of course, the versatile and omnipresent taco. Nothing could be simpler to make – *anything* wrapped in a tortilla qualifies – and its simplicity makes the taco well adapted to everything from breakfast food to post-nightclub midnight snack. You'll rec-ognize the crispy (or hard shell) variety from previous Taco Bell experiences, but most Texas tacos include soft, bready tortillas made of corn or flour.

Enchiladas, rolled corn tortillas stuffed with meat or cheese, generally sit alongside the taco of your choice and the traditional side dishes – refried pinto beans, pimiento-flecked 'Spanish

ingredients; quesadilla, a flour tortilla topped or filled with cheese and occasionally other ingredients and then heated; and tacos – the numero uno Mexican snack: a soft corn tortilla wrapped or folded around the same fillings as a burrito.

Other popular Mexican offerings are tamales, corn dough stuffed with meat, beans, chilis or nothing at all, wrapped in corn husks or banana leaves and then steamed; torta, a Mexican-style sandwich in a roll; and tostada, a crisp-fried, thin tortilla that may be eaten as a nibble while you're waiting for the rest of a meal or that can be topped with meat, cheese, tomatoes, beans and lettuce. Many Mexican staples venture across the border into Tex-Mex cuisine, too (see the boxed text).

Seafood

The major cities in Texas have great seafood restaurants, but the prices can be high.

Lovers of fresh shrimp will be in heaven all along the Texas coast, where more than 80% of the commercial catch are shrimp. The ubiquitous sea critters come boiled, fried, sautéed, barbecued, in the shell and out and in all sizes. Platters heaping with shrimp prepared in a variety of ways are a common menu item and should put your cholesterol at a level that, if nothing else, will give the mosquitoes a good case of heart disease. Other locally caught seafood items widely found on menus include scallops, oysters and red snapper. In some of the smaller coastal towns, seafood haters are best advised to practice saying 'Big Mac.'

rice,' and a cooling guacamole salad, made from subtly spiced avocado paste. Other customary components include tamales (cornmeal and spiced pork steamed in a corn husk, then topped with meaty chili con carne) or chile relleno (a mild pepper stuffed with a ground beef mixture and then fried).

If you've had your fill of the usual suspects, there's always interesting house specialties to whet the imagination and appetite. A common soup course, caldo, includes chunks of cabbage, carrot and the meat of the day, usually chicken or beef. Nopalitos, the pads of the region's native cactus, are plucked clean, sliced thin and stuffed into tacos. (How could a curious vegetarian pass up cactus?)

Most Tex-Mex restaurants also serve menudo, the traditional Mexican hangover cure. A heady stew of jalapeños, hominy and tripe (beef stomach), menudo is reputed to be the only remedy for morning-after nausea and headaches. According to hard-drinking experts, one bowlful will make you think twice before pounding another 20 tequila shots.

The northward spread of the state's Hispanic population means that there's plenty of good Tex-Mex available throughout the state, and visitors would be well served to seek out smaller, family-run joints instead of glitzy chain restaurants. As a rule of thumb, the closer you can get to a family kitchen, the better you'll eat.

Tip: To cool off the inevitable pepper-burned tongue, reach past your water glass and dive straight for something starchy (a tortilla, some rice). It may seem logical to cool the burn with cold liquid, but the chili's heat comes from its natural oils, which don't wash away in water. In fact, deep swallows of water wash away other flavors and tend to make the burn more intense.

Pableaux Johnson

Supermarkets

US supermarkets are one-stop shopping extravaganzas that stock everything you'd ever need in every room of the house plus the garage, the garden and in many cases the office. It has everything from auto parts to garbage cans, electronics to full-fledged pharmacies, school supplies to contraceptives, and fresh produce, seafood, meats, wine and beer. Almost all supermarkets have bakeries, but you can also choose from more than 100 types of packaged breads. Some supermarkets also have full-service delicatessen counters, and fewer have full-service cafés or restaurants.

The biggest supermarket chain in Texas is HEB, but look out for specialized gourmet supermarkets like Whole Earth Foods and, in Austin, Central Market.

DRINKS
Nonalcoholic Drinks

The official soft drink of Texas is iced tea. It's served – unsweetened and with fresh lemon slices – in all restaurants and diners, in huge glasses that come with free refills.

Commercially available soft drinks in Texas are the same as everywhere in the world with two exceptions: Dr Pepper and Mr Pibb. Dr Pepper is a caffeine-heavy, sweet, fruity carbonated drink invented in Waco. Mr Pibb is an Americanized version of the Brazilian soft drink Guaraná; that is to say, it tastes like one of those tree-shaped car air fresheners.

Smoothies are drinks made from yogurt and fresh fruit blended like a milkshake. A milkshake, by the way, is fast-blended ice cream, milk and flavoring, usually chocolate, vanilla or strawberry. Cappuccino and espresso are readily available in more upscale restaurants and more and more in diners. Tea is likely to arrive as a cup of hot water and a tea bag on the saucer.

Alcoholic Drinks

The strictly enforced drinking age in Texas is 21. Carry a driver's license or passport as proof of age to enter a bar, order alcohol at a restaurant or buy alcohol. Servers have the right to ask to see your ID and may refuse service without it. Minors are not allowed in bars and pubs, even to order nonalcoholic beverages. Unfortunately, this means that most dance clubs are also off-limits to minors, although a few clubs have solved the underage problem with a segregated drinking area. Minors are, however, welcome in the dining areas of restaurants where alcohol is served.

Beer and wine are sold in supermarkets in Texas, while harder stuff is sold in liquor stores.

Beer Commercially available American 'beer,' for lack of a better term, is weaker in taste and alcohol content than its equivalent around the world. A bottle of beer can be either a 'pony' (8oz), a standard 12oz bottle, a 'long-neck' (also 12oz, but the neck of the bottle is longer) or a 32oz (1 quart) bottle. It's also available in 12oz and 16oz (1 pint) cans. Bottles and cans are generally sold in bundles of six (six-packs) or 12 or in cases of 24.

Possibly the two most popular brands are manufactured by Anheuser-Busch – Budweiser and Michelob – followed by Miller Genuine Draft and Miller Lite. A six-pack of any of these costs between $3 and $5 in supermarkets.

Texas, though, offers some excellent microbrewed beer – made by small breweries and sold in limited areas – and also produces two excellent commercially made beers, Shiner and Celis (see the Texas Breweries boxed text).

A high beer consciousness in Texas means that there's a ready availability of microbrews and specialty brews in larger cities, where pubs routinely have more than 50 beers on tap. Styles you'll likely encounter are Witbier or Weissbier, both wheat-based beers brewed in Belgian and southern-German styles, respectively; Kölsch, a slightly dry, fermented ale; brown porter ale, a sort of a weaker stout; stout, the most well known of which is Guinness; imperial stout, a stronger version; amber and red ales; lagers, including the clean, bitter pilsener and sweetish Helles Bier; and bock, a dark, strong beer.

Texas Breweries

There are about 20 small breweries operating in Texas that make beers sold in bottles and in bars. Here are three brands you shouldn't miss:

Celis Several flavors are brewed by Pierre Celis, an Austin brewmaster revered for his talents in his native Belgium. His Celis White is imported and widely sold throughout Belgium, a feat similar in significance to a California red wine being imported and enjoyed in Bordeaux. His Celis Raspberry packs more joy per sip than seems moral. This is one of the best brands of microbrewed beer in the US, and aficionados in other states have been known to hoard Celis' highly popular products.

Shiner Brewed in the city west of Houston of the same name, this is the people's beer – and the one you'll have the best chance of finding in stores or bars, where other choices are either Bud swill or Miller swill. Shiner Bock is widely available and packs a bit of a punch. Spoetzl Brewery, which brews Shiner beer, was established by German immigrants, and the beer is still made with German recipes and techniques.

Saint Arnold Since 1993, this Houston brand named for the patron saint of beer brews an excellent amber ale and the fine Kristall Weizen. The beer is distributed in stores statewide, but it's best served on tap, so look for it in those bars that have walls lined with spigots.

Note the silly Texas law that decrees microbreweries cannot sell beer to the general public at their breweries. Conversely, brew pubs can only sell their product on their own premises.

Ryan Ver Berkmoes

Hugely popular these days is 'ice beer,' a beer that's been frozen to concentrate its alcoholic content.

Wine Texas winemaking has come a long way, and those who scoff at wine being produced in Texas probably laugh at South African wine, too. When the Spanish settled in Texas, one of the first things they did – as they did in Florida and California – was set up wine production. Texas had the potential to become a wine-growing region of note, but at the beginning of the 20th century, only a handful of wineries were operating. Prohibition wiped out most of these, except for the few that managed to eke out a living producing sacramental wine or grape juice.

But since the 1970s, Texas wine production has boomed, making Texas the USA's fifth-largest wine producing region, and the general economic giddiness of the 1990s has resulted in a US wine boom that has also benefited Texan wine producers.

Most of the wine in Texas is produced using grapes grown in the West Texas plains around Lubbock, which is also home to the state's most celebrated wineries, including Llano Estacado vineyards. Although it has about 16 varieties that together have won more than 575 awards, Llano is probably best known for its cabernets and chardonnays. Nearby Llano's winery is another celebrated winemaker, CapRock Winery, which produces about a dozen varieties.

Most Texan wines, like most US wines, are varietals: made almost entirely from the type of grape listed on the bottle. Popular high-quality wines in Texas are cabernet sauvignon, merlot, chardonnay and pinot noir.

But while wine production is becoming more important and profitable, Texas wineries, for various reasons, are at a cost disadvantage compared to more traditional wine-producing states, such as California and New York. Texas wines are available throughout the state in better liquor stores, but the price for a Texas vintage will generally be a few dollars higher than a corresponding varietal from California, and perhaps not much better. Still, the better Texas wines are delicious, and for a couple of bucks you're helping to support a fledgling industry that's trying hard to compete with the big boys. For more information, contact the Texas Wine and Grape Growers Association, 701 S Main St, Grapevine, TX 76051.

Hard Liquor Bars in Texas are segregated by the types of alcohol they're licensed to serve, from beer and wine to cocktails. In most beer bars you can bring in a bottle of harder booze with which to sweeten your beer. The latest fad in US bars is the classic cocktail, with bars specializing in martinis, margaritas and others; Austin, San Antonio, Dallas and Houston are places where a request for a sidecar (brandy, Cointreau, lemon juice and ice) or Rob Roy (Scotch whisky, sweet vermouth, Angostura bitters, ice and a cherry) won't result in a quiz from the bartender.

Tequila, manufactured only in Mexico but available throughout the US, is something with which many travelers to this region may find themselves forced to contend. By Mexican law tequila can only be made from blue agave plants from the Mexican states of Jalisco, Guanajuato, Michoacan, Nayarit or Tamaulipas. Blue agave, a spiky succulent related to the lily, is split and cooked to produce the fermentable sugars from which tequila is made.

There are four types of tequila. Silver (plata) is bottled within 60 days of distillation; gold is unaged and has color and flavor added to it; reposado is aged from two months to one year; and añejo is aged for at least a year in oak barrels (by the way, the stuff that has a worm at the bottom of the bottle is mezcal, not tequila).

Tequila can be exquisitely expensive or extraordinarily cheap. Those same two words can be used to describe the condition your head will be in the morning after a tequila bout: exquisitely hungover or extraordinarily ill. The most popular tequila in the US is José Cuervo, though that doesn't say any-

Dry Counties

You can't let just anyone drink. Temperance movements, economic realities and other factors have led to a hodgepodge of drinking regulations in Texas, which works out to be a real annoyance if you're looking for a beer in Angelina County. Counties can ban sales of alcohol by the glass or set limits on the percentage of alcohol that's consumed within them as they please. And they do. So 'wet' and 'dry' counties exist throughout the state – 185 counties permit alcohol, but 53 ban it. To add to the fun, 11 counties only permit consumption of beer with less than 4% alcohol; 14 counties permit alcoholic drinks with less than 14% alcohol.

thing about its quality. To really taste fine tequila, ask for an excellent (and expensive) brand, such as El Tel Soro de Don Felipe, Patron Añejo or Sauza Hornitos. Them's sippin' tequilas and mightily worth the extra expense.

Margaritas, the most popular tequila cocktails, are made with tequila, lime juice and triple sec, either served on the rocks or whipped into a frozen slushy and served in a glass with a salted rim.

Tequila is best drunk in shots; it's said that Mexicans lick salt from their hands and squeeze lime into their mouths before the shot, but in actuality, most would never put up with so daggy a custom and prefer to throw down their shots and soothe the burn with a sip of beer.

ENTERTAINMENT

The main centers for classical music are discussed in the Arts section in the Facts about Texas chapter. Many smaller towns have their own local venues.

Bars

Bars in Texas range from down and dirty to as chic as one could expect, and prices range accordingly.

Bartenders in the US generally pour in a freehand manner that would make British publicans blanch. A 'shot,' ostensibly 1oz, is often larger than that. US custom says that you tip the bartender for each drink – generally $1 – and that (except in very crowded nightclubs) you place your cash on the bar and leave it there while you drink.

'Happy hours,' usually a lot longer than an hour – sometimes all day – are periods during which drink prices are reduced, sometimes substantially. Deals are usually two or even three for the price of one. 'Ladies' nights,' a ploy to lure horny, thirsty males by using a free-drinks-for-women gimmick, are usually held once a week in university areas.

Nightclubs

Nightclubs are found in all larger cities and come and go very quickly. In larger clubs, entry fees are between $5 and $10, while smaller ones charge less to try and draw people away from their huge competitors.

In many cities, bars turn into nightclubish places in the evenings, with contests or live music of some sort.

Gay and lesbian nightclubs often have live performances that may include drag shows, dating games, amateur nights or stripteases.

In Austin, music clubs are the norm; there could be 100 bands or more playing on an average summer Thursday. Other cities have large live-music scenes as well; Texans take their music seriously.

Cinema

Every major Texas city has at least one chain theater showing mainstream movies. American movie houses have taken the as-many-as-possible approach to cinemas, and the quaint one-movie cinema is practically extinct – look for five-, six-, nine-, 11- and even 18-plex cinemas.

The best place to look for a cinema is in the nearest shopping mall. Prices are usually from $2.50 to $3.25 in the afternoon before 4 pm and between $5 and $7 in the evening. Larger cities, especially Austin, have several independent film outlets that offer smaller budget, foreign or cult films, but outside of that, expect only mass-appeal Hollywood films with few exceptions.

SPECTATOR SPORTS

Sports in the USA developed separately from the rest of the world, and baseball (and its clone, softball), football and basketball dominate the sports scene, both for spectators and participants. Football and basketball, in particular, are huge. College and even high school sports are attended and followed to a degree that would make the average Manchester United football hooligan look like someone with just a passing interest in sport.

Not long ago, recreational, intercollegiate and professional sports were dominated by men, but in the last 25 years this has changed drastically, largely due to the passage of Title IX, a federal law prohibiting gender-based inequities in programs receiving federal funds. Each year more women and girls participate in sports. The fruits of this surge in interest were evident at the 1996 Olympics when the US women's basketball, softball, soccer and gymnastics teams brought home gold medals.

Professional Sports In professional basketball, the San Antonio Spurs and the Houston Rockets are both big crowd-pleasers, despite their records (the Spurs are the better team). NBA Basketball games are multimedia extravaganzas, with giant-screen TVs blaring forth images, statistics and, of course, commercials, in addition to crowd-pleasing chant leads.

The Dallas Cowboys, with their famous cheerleaders, are a consistently highly ranked football team, the Houston Oilers less so.

The Houston Astros and the Texas Rangers are professional baseball teams; the Rangers play at the Ballpark in Arlington, the Astros in the now rather quaint Astrodome.

College Sports What really gets the crowds going (some fans travel 10 hours or more to see it) is college football. The larger Texas colleges and universities are members of the Big 12 Conference, a league created when those schools merged with the Big Eight Conference; the Big 12 now consists of Baylor, University of Texas, Texas A&M, Texas Tech, Colorado, Iowa State, Kansas, Kansas State, Missouri, Nebraska, Oklahoma and Oklahoma State.

Big 12 Conference games held at any of the first four of the 12 schools are the cause of excitement equal to any seen at Brazilian World Cup qualification matches. The fans at these games let their competitive spirit flow forth by shouting tirades, painting their bodies or participating in intricately choreographed handheld sign productions.

High School Sports If college sports attract droves, high school sports, especially high school football, attracts enthusiastic parent supporters. See the High School Football boxed text in the Facts about Texas chapter for a complete description.

SHOPPING

Cowboy attire seems to be the biggest on the hit parade of things to buy in Texas. Boots, cowboy duds and, of course, Stetson hats are available at department stores and specialty shops throughout the state; see individual chapters for ones that offer particularly good values.

You may end up kicking yourself for the rest of your life if you visit Texas and don't spend at least an afternoon in a shopping spree at one of central Texas' outlet malls. These fantabulously enormous shopping malls are populated by stores that sell overstock or out-of-season merchandise from some of the largest manufacturers in the US. Typically, in these places you can buy clothing (including name-brand blue jeans and designer clothes) for 30% to 60% less than normal US retail price; books are next to nothing – figure on about $2 for paperbacks and $5 to $10 for hardcovers. Electronic appliances run about 20% cheaper in outlet malls than those for sale at full-price retail stores. In San Marcos, Sony has a shop that exclusively sells factory-reconditioned Sony products at about a 15% discount. Most electronics will work in other countries if you have the proper step-down converters.

Northeast Texas has numerous small towns, such as Jefferson and Gladewater, where the historic downtowns have been completely taken over by antiques stores. The goods that are most common include primitive items used by early settlers, such as rough furniture made from fence posts. Loads of late-19th-century oak items are also available at prices that would have bought an entire house when they were new.

Texans and tourists alike flock across the border to Mexico to buy leather goods, objects made from silver and liquors like tequila. Winter Texans in particular are drawn by prices on prescription items that can be less than half that on the US side of the border. Other health-bargain hunters patronize the scores of cut-rate storefront dentists drilling away near the entry point in most Texas border towns. See the Border section in the Getting There & Away chapter for details on crossing the US-Mexico border.

Activities

Texas is about the outdoors. The cowboy tradition of sleeping under the stars may not be as readily available as it was at the turn of the 20th century, but there are still plenty of ways to get out in the open. National and state park campgrounds are cheap and easy to find, and there are wonderful hiking and biking trails throughout the state.

Horseback riding is very popular in Texas, and there are many opportunities to get out on the trail for a day or longer. But Texas also offers much more; white-water rafting, kayaking, tennis, golf and, surprisingly, surfing, windsurfing and rock climbing are all easily arranged.

HIKING & BACKPACKING

There is perhaps no better way to appreciate the beauty of Texas than on foot and on the trail. Taking a few days' (or even a few hours') break from the highway to explore the great outdoors can refresh road-weary travelers and give them a heightened appreciation of the scenery that goes whizzing past day after day. Some travelers will experience one good hike and decide to plan the rest of their trip around wilderness or hiking areas.

Padre Island National Seashore, on the Gulf Coast, stretches for 80 of the 113 miles of Padre Island. The entire park is open to hikers; hardy souls favor the sparsely visited southern 60 miles, where the camping is as free as the inhibitions of those who make it that far. However, proper preparation is essential, since there is no shade and no fresh water available.

In south central Texas, the entire Austin Greenbelt is lined with hiking and biking trails, and the Texas Hill Country also offers some great opportunities for both.

In East Texas, dozens of miles of hiking trails wend through the Big Thicket National Preserve. Many of them pass through rural pockets of relatively unspoiled wilderness, but they also run close to logging operations, trailer parks and other human-made distractions that are prevalent throughout this less-than-preserved preserve.

National Parks

Unless you have a few days to get into the backcountry of a national park or are visiting during the off-season (between Memorial Day and Labor Day), expect hiking in national parks to be crowded.

Travelers with little hiking experience will appreciate the well-marked, well-maintained trails in national parks, which often have toilet facilities at either end and interpretive displays along the way. The trails give access to the parks' natural features and usually show up on Park Service maps as nature trails or self-guided interpretive trails. These hikes are usually no longer than 2 miles.

Most national parks require overnight hikers to carry backcountry permits. Available from visitors' centers or ranger stations, the permits require hikers to follow a specific itinerary and must be obtained 24 hours in advance. Although this system reduces the chance of people getting lost in the backcountry and limits the number of people using one area at any given time, it may detract from the sense of space and freedom that hiking can give. For more information, call the Park Service at ☎ 800-365-2267.

Treading Lightly

Backcountry areas are composed of fragile environments and cannot support an inundation of human activity, especially insensitive and careless activity. Treat the backcountry like you would your own backyard – minus the barbecue pit.

A new code of backcountry ethics is evolving to deal with the growing number of people in the wilderness. Most conservation organizations and hikers' manuals have their own set of backcountry codes, all of which outline the same important principles: minimizing the human impact on the land, leaving no trace and taking nothing but photographs and memories. Above all, stay on the main trail, stay on the main trail and, finally, even if it means walking through mud or crossing a patch of snow, *stay on the main trail*.

Wilderness Camping Camping in undeveloped areas is rewarding for its peacefulness, but it presents special concerns. Take care to ensure that the area you choose can comfortably support your presence, and leave the surroundings in better condition than they were on your arrival. The following list of guidelines should help.

- Bury human waste in cat holes dug 6 to 8 inches deep a good distance away from streams or lakes. Camouflage the cat hole when finished. The salt and minerals in urine attract deer, so use a tent-bottle (funnel attachments are available for women) if you are prone to middle-of-the-night calls by Mother Nature and don't want to venture outside.

- Use soaps and detergents sparingly or not at all, and never allow them to enter streams or lakes. When washing yourself (a backcountry luxury, not a necessity), lather up (with biodegradable soap) and rinse yourself with cans of water as far as possible away from your water source. Scatter dishwater after removing all food particles.

- It is recommended that you carry a lightweight stove for cooking and use a lantern for light, rather than building a campfire.

- If building a fire is allowed and appropriate, dig a hole and build it in there. On islands or beach areas, build fires below the high-tide line. Gather sticks no thicker than an adult's wrist from the ground. Use only dead and downed wood; do not twist branches off standing trees, whether they're living or dead. Pour wastewater from meals around the perimeter of the campfire to prevent the fire from spreading, and thoroughly douse it before leaving or going to sleep.

- Designate cooking clothes to leave in the food bag, away from your tent.

- Burn cans to get rid of their odor, then remove them from the ashes and pack them out.

- Pack out what you pack in, including all trash – yours *and* others'.

What to Bring

Equipment The following list is meant to be a general guideline for backpackers, not an 'if I have everything here I'll be fine'

guarantee. Know yourself and what special things you may need on the trail, and consider the area and climatic conditions you will be traveling in.

Boots – light to medium weight are recommended for day hikes; sturdy boots are necessary for extended trips with a heavy backpack. Most important, they should be well broken in and should have a good heel. Waterproof boots are preferable.

Alternative footwear – thongs, sandals or running shoes are ideal for wearing around camp; canvas sneakers or Tevas are good for crossing streams.

Socks – frequent sock changes during the day reduce the chance of blisters, but that's usually impractical.

Subdued colors – are usually recommended for clothing, but if you're hiking during hunting season, blazing orange is a necessity.

Shorts, light shirt – these are good for everyday wear; remember that heavy cotton takes a long time to dry and is very cold when wet.

Long-sleeve shirt – one made from light cotton, wool or polypropylene is best. One with a button-down front makes layering easy and can be left open when the weather is hot and your arms need protection from the sun.

Long pants – heavy denim jeans take forever to dry, and hey, this is the subtropics. Sturdy cotton or canvas pants are good for trekking through brush, and cotton or nylon sweats are comfortable to wear around camp.

Rain gear – light, breathable and waterproof is the ideal combination, but it doesn't exist, no matter what those catalogs say. We use Rainbird 2000 ponchos, which fold into their front pockets and crush down to very small sacks that make good pillows. If nothing else is available, you can use heavy-duty trash bags to cover yourself and your packs.

Hat – a cotton hat with a brim is good for sun protection.

Bandanna or handkerchief – either one is good for a runny nose, a dirty face, unmanageable hair, a picnic lunch or a flag (especially a red one).

Small towel – one that is indestructible and will dry quickly is ideal. Check in any sporting goods store for camping towels.

First-aid kit – this should include, at the least, self-adhesive bandages and adhesive tape, disinfectant, antibiotic salve or cream, gauze, small scissors and tweezers. An Ace-type bandage couldn't hurt, either.

Knife, fork, spoon and mug – a mug (a double-layer plastic mug with a lid is best) acts as eating and drinking receptacle, mixing bowl and wash basin, and the handle protects you from getting burned. Bring an extra cup if you like to eat and drink simultaneously.

Pots and pans – aluminum cook sets are best, but any sturdy one-quart pot would be sufficient. True gourmands who want more than pasta, soup and freeze-dried food will need a skillet or frying pan. A metal pot scrubber is helpful for removing stubborn oatmeal, especially when using cold water and no soap.

Stove – a lightweight and easy-to-operate stove is ideal. Most outdoor equipment stores rent propane or butane stoves. Test the stove before you head out – even cook a meal on it – to familiarize yourself with any quirks it may have.

Water purifier – this is optional but really nice to have; water can also be purified by boiling it for at least 10 minutes.

Matches or lighter – waterproof matches are good, and having several lighters on hand is smart.

Candle or lantern – candles are easy to operate but do not stay lit when they are dropped or wet and can be hazardous inside a tent. You can rent a lantern at an outdoors store; test it before you hit the trail.

Flashlight – each person should have his or her own flashlight and should be sure its batteries have plenty of life left in them. We like Petzl headlamps and MagLite flashlights, because they're both almost indestructible and have slots for spare bulbs.

Sleeping bag – goose-down bags are warm and lightweight, but worthless if they get wet; most outdoors stores rent synthetic bags.

Sleeping pad – this is strictly a personal preference, though on cold nights a pad helps you keep your heat. We hardly ever use them, but a friend swears by Therm-a-Rest pads, which fill up with air when unrolled and behave as a kind of air mattress. Use a sweater or sleeping-bag sack stuffed with clothes as a pillow.

Tent – make sure it is waterproof or has a waterproof cover and mosquito netting, and know how to put it up before you reach camp. Remember that your packs will be sharing the tent with you.

Camera and binoculars – don't forget extra film and waterproof film canisters (zip-lock plastic bags work well).

Compass, maps and GPS – each person should have his or her own, at least for the compass and maps (see the boxed text on GPS).

Eyeglasses – contact-lens wearers should always bring a backup set of glasses.

Sundries – biodegradable toilet paper, small zip-lock plastic bags, insect repellent, sunscreen, lip balm, unscented moisturizing cream, moleskin for foot blisters, dental floss (burnable and good when there is no water for brushing your teeth), sunglasses, deck of cards, pen or pencil and paper or notebook, books and nature guides are all worth considering.

Food Keeping your energy up is important, but so is keeping your pack light. Backpackers tend to eat a substantial breakfast and dinner and snack heavily in between. There is no need to be excessive. If you pack loads of food you'll probably use it, but if you have just enough you will probably not miss anything.

Some basic staples are packaged instant oatmeal, bread (the denser the better), rice or pasta, instant soup or ramen noodles, dehydrated meat (jerky), dried fruit, energy bars, chocolate, trail mix and peanut butter, honey or jam (in plastic jars or squeeze bottles). Don't forget the wet-wipes, but be sure to dispose of them properly or pack them out.

Freeze-dried food is available at larger sporting goods stores and at wilderness outfitters such as REI. If you have yet to sample it, you may be in for a shock: it actually tastes a lot better than you'd expect (but it's not, like, *great* or anything). Companies such as Natural High and Richmoore make a huge array of dishes. Some you dump into a pot of boiling water, and for some you add the water directly to the bag. For side dishes such as green beans or corn, expect to pay about $1.50 a bag. For breakfast items such as – get this – a cheese omelet, it's about $2.50, and for full a dinner including a main course and a side dish that's said to feed two but probably feeds only 1½, expect to pay from $5 (for beef stew or chicken teriyaki) to $6 (for more upscale stuff like honey-lime chicken and whole grain rice).

Books

There are quite a few good how-to and where-to books on the market, usually found in outdoors stores or the outdoors or sports and recreation sections of regular bookstores. Chris Camden's *Backpacker's Handbook* is a beefy collection of tips for the trail. *How to Shit in the Woods* is Kathleen Meyer's explicit, comic and useful manual on toilet training in the wilderness.

Maps

A good map is essential for any hiking trip. National Park Service and United States Forest Service ranger stations usually stock topographical maps that cost $2 to $6. In the absence of a ranger station, try the local stationery or hardware store.

Longer hikes require two types of maps: United States Geological Survey (USGS) Quadrangles and US Department of Agriculture Forest Service maps. To order a map index and price list, contact the USGS, PO Box 25046, Denver, CO 80225. For general

---

Global Positioning System

The Global Positioning System (GPS) was developed by the United States military. It involves 24 satellites that operate in six orbital planes at an altitude of 12,500 miles and put out coded signals to be received by small units on earth. With the magic of computer chips these instruments can simultaneously solve several sets of equations based on the signals and can determine their absolute location with surprising precision. In English, they can tell you:

- Where you are on earth (within about 55 to 109 yards, or 50 to 100 meters)
- Where you've been
- Where you're going (bearing, distance from any specific destination)
- How fast you're going
- When you'll get there
- What your altitude is above sea level
- And, of course, the time

As soon as I saw a GPS I began to invent various justifications for spending however much it would cost to buy one – I knew I *had* to have one. After some research into the different options, I finally went with the relatively inexpensive and very small Garmin GPS-40, which cost $329 at a Florida sporting goods store.

If you know where you want to be, you can enter the coordinates (latitude and longitude culled from, say, a good atlas or map), and the Garmin will show you an electronic 'road' (a graphical representation of a road stretching to the horizon; if the road bends left, you turn left at the same angle – the idea being that as long as you keep the electronic road on the screen pointing straight, you're going toward your destination. I've used it for practice in Germany, throughout Russia and in the Florida Everglades, where it is an invaluable piece of gear.

Annoying features of the units are that their coverage changes depending on where you are – city readings are not very accurate, nor are vertical readings: while in the Alps I once got a reading of 119 meters below sea level. And they're not as easy to understand as you'd hope – they have a terminology all their own, and it takes a good while to get the hang of it.

A GPS will come in handy for those traveling in remote areas without roads – if you're hiking, biking, canoeing, flying or parasailing. And if you'll be traveling anywhere off the beaten track, these gizmos are choice gear. Just don't depend on them as your *only* orienteering tool – unless you've spent a lot of money or had a lot of experience with them, bring along a good compass as well, for critical measurements.

Nick Selby

information on maps, see the Facts for the Visitor chapter; for information regarding maps of specific forests, wilderness areas or national parks, see the section on the area you wish to visit.

Safety

The major forces to be reckoned with while hiking and camping are the weather, which you can't control, and your own frame of mind, which you can – a positive attitude is helpful in any situation.

Carry a rain jacket at all times. Backpackers should have a pack-liner (heavy-duty garbage bags work well), a full set of rain gear and food that does not require cooking. If a hot shower, a comfortable mattress and clean clothes are essential to your well-being, don't head out into the wilderness for five days.

Those who follow the highest safety measures would suggest never hiking alone (see Women Travelers in Facts for the Visitor), but if you decide to try it, the important thing to remember is always let someone know where you are going and how long you plan to be gone. Use sign-in boards at trailheads or ranger stations. Travelers looking for hiking companions can inquire or post notices at ranger stations, outdoor equipment stores, campgrounds and youth hostels.

Fording rivers and streams is another potentially dangerous but often necessary part of being on the trail. In national parks and along maintained trails in national forests, bridges usually cross large bodies of water, but that is not the case in designated wilderness areas, where bridges are taboo. Upon reaching a river, unclip all of your pack straps – your pack is expendable, but you are not. Avoid crossing barefoot – you don't know where that bottom has been. Bring a pair of lightweight canvas sneakers or Teva-style sandals for crossings, to avoid sloshing around in wet boots for the rest of your hike.

Using a staff for balance is helpful, but don't rely on it to support all your weight. Don't enter water higher than mid-thigh – your body would give the current a large mass to work against. If you do get wet, wring your clothes out immediately, wipe off all the excess water on your body and hair and put on any dry clothes you (or your companion) might have.

People with little hiking or backpacking experience should not attempt to do too much too soon, or they might end up becoming nonhikers for the wrong reasons. Know your limitations, know the route you are going to take and pace yourself accordingly. Remember, there is absolutely nothing wrong with turning back or not going as far as you originally planned.

BICYCLING

Texas is bicycle friendly only in some places. Cities such as Austin have developed good bike trails, and bike clubs throughout the state run bicycle road trips for several hours or several days. See the Getting Around sections in the chapters for bicycle specific information. Note that in state parks, four bicyclists will pay more to enter than eight people in a car – generally admission for pedestrians and cyclists is $1 each.

Information

Members of the League of American Bicyclists (LAB; ☎ 202-822-1333, fax 202-822-1334, www.bikeleague.org/), 1612 K St NW Suite 401, Washington, DC 20006, may transport their bikes free on selected airlines and can obtain a list of hospitality homes in each state that offer simple accommodations to touring cyclists. The LAB's annual *Almanac* lists contacts in each state, along with information about bicycle routes and special events. Bicycle tourists will also want to get a copy of the *Cyclosource Catalog*, which lists books and maps, and the *Cyclist's Yellow Pages*, a trip-planning resource, both published by the Adventure Cycling Association (☎ 406-721-1776), 150 E Pine St, Missoula, MT 59801.

Laws & Regulations

Trail etiquette requires that cyclists yield to other users. Helmets should always be worn to reduce the risk of head injury, but they are not mandated by law. National parks require that all riders younger than 18 wear a helmet.

HORSEBACK RIDING

Few images are more Texan than riding horseback across the open plains. The state offers many opportunities for riding, with stables located everywhere – from big cities to state parks. Many are listed in this book; for others, check with local visitors' bureaus.

Stables typically offer a range of services, from one- to two-hour trail rides to extended pack trips. Riders will be given a horse matched to their level of riding experience, so don't be afraid to mention whether it's your first or 50th time on a horse.

It should be noted that while both of Texas' national parks – Big Bend and Guadalupe Mountains – have trails suitable for horseback riding, neither has horses available for rent. There are stables just outside Big Bend National Park, but none near Guadalupe Mountains National Park.

Dude Ranches

In his book *Dude Ranches and Ponies*, Lawrence B Smith defines the term 'dude' as 'an outsider, city person, or tenderfoot; one who came from another element of society; in short, a stranger as far as the American West and its ways are concerned.' Most people – men and women – who visit dude ranches today are 'dudes' in the truest sense, looking for an escape from a fast-paced, high-tech world.

Dude ranch history dates back to the late 19th century, when people from the eastern US took trains west and stayed on ranches for months at a time, pitching in with chores. When one such guest asked if he could pay room and board, the idea of the dude ranch as a business venture was born. Today dude ranches – often called guest ranches – may be working cattle ranches, or they may not. They are plentiful throughout Texas, and you can find everything from a working-ranch experience with rustic accommodations (smelly chores and 5 am wake-up calls included) to luxurious ranch retreats. Although the centerpiece of a ranch vacation is usually horseback riding, many ranches also feature swimming pools, mountain biking, tennis, golf, skeet-shooting and side trips to nearby attractions.

To learn more about ranch vacations, request the 'Texas Ranches' brochure from the tourism division of the Texas Department of Economic Development (☎ 800-452-9292; +1-512-462-9191 outside the US). This comprehensive directory includes information on all kinds of ranch-stay and day-visit opportunities.

BIRD-WATCHING

Texas has nearly 600 documented bird species – more than 75% of all species reported in the US – and bird-watching is one of the state's most popular activities. Hot spots include Big Bend National Park, the lower Rio Grande Valley, McFaddin and Aransas National Wildlife Refuges and the rest of the Gulf Coast. Birding is excellent throughout the year, but peak times are the migrations in spring (March through June) and fall (September through November).

Texas Parks and Wildlife, a state agency, offers a bird checklist and the *Birding Texas* booklet, which give plenty of information. For copies, call ☎ 800-792-1112 or 512-389-4800 or write to 4200 Smith School Rd, Austin, TX 78744. The national parks and wildlife refuges also have bird checklists for their specific areas; most can be obtained free or at low cost at the refuge or park office.

Birder's Guide to Texas, by Ed Kutac, is among several state-specific guidebooks available. The National Audubon Society has its Texas regional office (☎ 512-306-0225, fax 512-306-0235) at 2525 Wallingwood, Suite 301, Austin, TX 78746. Several Audubon chapters and independent birding clubs and nature organizations operate throughout the state. Look in the local white pages under National Audubon Society, or write the Texas regional office for a statewide list.

Birding festivals rank among the biggest special events in Texas. The Great Texas Birding Classic, for example, is sponsored by Texas Parks and Wildlife, and is held each April along the Gulf Coast; it is supposedly the biggest bird-watching tournament in the United States; call ☎ 800-792-1112 for information. Other festivals include Eagle Fest, in Emory (mid-January; ☎ 800-561-1182); the

Blue Bird Festival, at Wills Point (mid-April; ☎ 903-873-3111); the Migration Celebration in the Brazosport area (mid-April; ☎ 888-477-2505); the Hummer/Bird Celebration at Rockport and Fulton (mid-September; ☎ 512-729-9952); and the Rio Grande Valley Birding Festival at Harlingen (mid-November; ☎ 800-531-7346).

SURFING

For many, 'Texas surfing' is an oxymoron. But local aficionados will argue that it is not as bad in Texas as surfers elsewhere have heard. Long-board surfers, in fact, will have a fun time here on most days: the longer the board the more rideable the Gulf's mush. The key to riding the waves is timing, luck and patience.

For much of the year the Gulf of Mexico produces surf (for lack of a better term) along the Texas coast that averages an underwhelming 3 feet or lower. Conditions are better during the stormy season, which runs from September through February. Surf may be nonexistent one day, but reach 6 feet or higher the next. Hurricanes can be good news for surfers, who gleefully ride the storm-surge-driven waves until they are blown off their boards.

Although surfers patiently wait for the right conditions all along the coast, the best waves – when they occur – are found south of Galveston to the Mexican border. Mustang Island State Park, on Padre Island near Corpus Christi, is an especially popular spot. The best surfing is at South Padre Island, where there is the best chance of finding waves with good ground swell.

The larger towns along the Gulf Coast usually have one or more surf shops. They often specialize in windsurfing gear, but they have a selection of surfboards, wax and other critical items as well. Rentals average $40 a day.

Given the unreliability of Texas surf, few surfers will want to bring their boards to the coast. However, if the conditions are right, the long sandy beaches can make Texas surfing a pleasant experience, especially for those enthusiasts who are able to camp out and wait for the right conditions.

Surf Forecasts

The Oceanographic Office of the US Navy maintains a variety of sensors that monitor surf throughout the gulf, which it uses to prepare excellent color maps with wave height forecasts for the entire Texas coast. These are on the web at the following sites:

Current:
  128.160.23.54/products/MODELS/mex0.gif
One-day forecast:
  128.160.23.54/products/MODELS/mex4.gif
Two-day forecast:
  128.160.23.54/products/MODELS/mex8.gif

The 'Texas Wave Rider' website (www .orbitworld net/surftex/) has links to scores of additional sources for surf conditions and forecasts.

WINDSURFING

If Texas waves are unreliable, the wind is not. The constant coastal breezes, coupled with the large bodies of water sheltered by the barrier islands, make for great windsurfing.

Corpus Christi is an especially popular windsurfing spot, with national and international championships held there regularly. The Laguna Madre, the large body of water stretching from Corpus Christi south almost to the Mexican border, is good for windsurfing anywhere along its length. Corpus Christi Bay, some 10 miles across, is accessible to campers on beaches, day trippers in local parks and even downtown office workers,

Wetsuits

Water temperatures in the Gulf of Mexico range from a chilly January low of 55°F (12°C) to a sweltering August high of 80°F (27°C). In the winter, windsurfers can get away with a 3/2 wetsuit, but surfers will probably need a 4/3, because waves are few and far between, requiring long waits in the water for the next swell. Divers will want to wear a full 7mm wetsuit.

who are known to disappear from work a bit early on days when the conditions are especially good.

South Padre Island is also popular. Several shops and bars catering to windsurfers and their groupies line the lagoon side of the island; you can rent boards and gear for about $40 a day. Windsurfing stores are common in the larger towns and cities on the Gulf Coast.

If you have your own board, you can count on being able to windsurf anywhere along the Intracoastal Waterway, which runs along almost all the 624 miles of Texas coast.

DIVING & SNORKELING

Diving in the Gulf of Mexico is challenging and not recommended for beginners. The most interesting sites are located 40 or more miles offshore, where the water is very deep and divers are subjected to open-water waves and weather conditions. Basically, when the weather is good for surfing it's bad for diving – storms stir up sediment and make the water cloudy; if a long period goes by without storms, any time can be good.

The rewards of gulf diving can be many. The hundreds of offshore oil rigs are home to vast arrays of marine life, from barnacles to tropical fish. Every inch of metal, stretching for 100 feet or more from the bottom, is covered by marine life that thrives in the artificial reef environment. Close to shore, the best diving opportunities are at the many jetties stretching into the water all along the coast, which also act as artificial reefs, although visibility is often less than optimal.

Some 110 miles southeast of Galveston lie the Flower Gardens, a wild array of coral gardens growing atop underwater salt domes at the edge of the continental shelf. At a depth ranging from 50 to 80 feet, the coral heads form their own underwater metropolis, home to more than 500 species of fish and other sea creatures. The gardens are widely regarded as the premier dive spot in the Gulf of Mexico. Boats to the Flower Gardens typically leave Gulf Coast ports at night for the eight-hour journey. After a full-day of diving they then make a night journey back. For more information, check out the Dive Texas website: divetexas.com/ dtx04000.htm.

Muddy water and heavy plankton growth make the coastal areas of Texas no good for snorkeling, despite the shallow waters and calm conditions. The best areas are in the Laguna Madre south of Corpus Christi – the grass beds along the inner shore of Padre Island are home to blue crabs, flounder, redfish, sponges and stingrays. In July and August, millions of scallops line the bottom.

For complete details on Texas diving and snorkeling, pick up Lonely Planet's *Pisces Diving & Snorkeling Guide to Texas.*

KAYAKING & CANOEING
Off-Shore

The lagoons and canals of the long Intracoastal Waterway system are ideal for sea kayaking. Various estuaries, streams and rivers are ripe for exploration, and numerous parks make good bases from which to set off.

Popular places for kayaking include Galveston Island State Park and Goose Island State Park, which provides excellent access to the Aransas National Wildlife Refuge, north of Corpus Christi, and the entire length of the Padre Island National Seashore. For canoeing, Caddo Lake and Big Thicket Reserve are popular, and of course there's Big Bend National Park.

Rental is usually not a problem – if a place has good kayaking and canoeing conditions, there is usually some savvy entrepreneur around to rent you the gear. Prices tend to be around $15 a day for a canoe, $40 for a kayak. Where we don't list places, check with tourist information offices, as the providers of equipment seem to change frequently.

Inland

Caddo Lake, in northeast Texas on the border with Louisiana, is the largest natural lake in the state that wasn't created with the help of a dam. Often fog-shrouded, featuring Spanish moss hanging from every cypress tree, it is a moody and beautiful place that is perfectly explored in a kayak or a canoe. The waters weave in and out of islands, swamps and bayous.

There's also great kayaking in and around Austin.

The Rio Grande below Laredo to the gulf is heavily polluted by industrial wastes and sewage from the factories on the US-Mexican border. Although the river is pretty, locals strongly advise against dipping so much as a toe into its murky flow, and doctors regularly treat Mexicans who have gotten sick swimming across.

In the Houston area, SouthWest Paddle Sports (☎ 800-937-2335) caters to beginning kayakers and canoeists with a San Jacinto riverfront facility at 1101 Hamblen Road, Kingwood, TX 77339.

RIVER RUNNING

From the classic Rio Grande trips at Big Bend to canoeing on the Wichita River to lazy tubing on the Guadalupe River near New Braunfels, Texas offers plenty of wild and mild river adventure. Commercial outfitters provide white-water experiences ranging from short, moderately priced morning or afternoon trips to expeditions of a week or more. Outfitters on state or federal public lands operate with permits from the appropriate agency. If you plan to rent gear or float your own boat, you, too, should check on whether permits are necessary.

There is no real season for river running in Texas – you can go white-water rafting

or tubing year-round, weather and river conditions permitting.

Local visitors' bureaus are good sources of information on river running; others are the Texas Whitewater Association, PO Box 5429, Austin, TX 78763, and the Texas Water Safari organization, which annually stages a 260-mile river trip in East Texas. For more information, check the organization's bulletin board on the Internet (nac.tamu.edu/x075bb/safari/) or write to 9515 FM 1979, Martindale, TX 78655.

White-Water Rafting

White-water trips take place in either large rafts seating a dozen or more people or smaller rafts seating half a dozen; the latter are more interesting and exciting, because the ride over the rapids can be rougher and because everyone participates in rowing (or, sometimes, bailing water out of the boat). Most trips are suitable for novice rafters, but some may have age, weight or experience restrictions.

Safety Although white-water trips aren't without danger and it's not unusual for participants to fall out of the raft in high water, serious injuries and drownings are rare, and the huge majority of trips are without incident. It's important to keep your feet and arms inside the raft. For other safety concerns, outfitters usually give orientation and safety lectures before heading off, and trips will have at least one guide experienced in safety procedures and lifesaving techniques. You don't have to be able to swim to participate, but you must wear a US Coast Guard-approved life jacket and should be in reasonably good physical condition.

Tubing

Tubing is popular on smaller streams and rivers. Generally, you rent a 'tube' – the inner tube of a truck tire – which may or may not be outfitted with luxuries such as handles or seats. Then, much like white-water rafters, you 'put in' at a designated spot on the river and float downstream. Make sure you arrange shuttle service or a ride to pick you up at the other end – most places that rent tubes will do this for you at no extra fee.

BOATING

The same winds propelling windsurfers are also ready to fill canvas. Corpus Christi is the sailing center for the coast, and schools at the many marinas offer lessons and rentals.

Boating ramps for launching motorboats are common all along the Intracoastal Waterway, which is very popular with recreational boaters, who enjoy the sheltered waters. However, the various locks can slow down the journey on busy days, and there's always the huge barges to contend with. Most of the towns along the gulf have harbors where you can rent a slip by the night or longer.

Jet Skis

Jet Skis are quite popular, and you'll see lots of them zipping around the Gulf Coast waters and various inland lakes, but they exact a heavy toll on the environment. They can kill fish and other marine animals, rip sea plants and protected sea grass from the bottom, scare swimmers and disrupt a peaceful visit to the beach for all concerned. They also have resulted in several deaths – Gulf Coast waters in particular are shallow and tricky to navigate.

You will find Jet Skis available for rent around the state, but we encourage you to stay away from them and choose instead to help preserve the vitality of the state's lakes and coastal waters.

FISHING
Offshore

With the fortunes of the commercial fishing industry battered by reduced catches and stagnant prices, many fishing-boat owners have turned to offering charters and day trips for their livelihoods. Galveston, Freeport, Rockport, Port Aransas, Port Isabel, Port Arthur, Corpus Christi and South Padre Island each have dozens of boats offering trips to the rich fishing grounds in the gulf.

Far and away the most popular fish is red snapper, which are usually found 40 or more miles offshore. Charter trips for this prized deep-sea catch typically are gone for at least

12 hours, more typically 24. Costs begin at $40 per person and escalate rapidly. Check with charter operators first before planning a trip to catch snapper, because beginning in 1997, restrictions were placed on the fishing season because of the dwindling stock.

Closer in, the gulf yields huge marlin of the kind you used to see Kurt Gowdy battling on *The American Sportsman*. Huge creatures weighing 800lb or more have been caught, although after struggling to land one of these, the average vacationing angler may want to lie down on the dock next to the fish and die.

Other commonly caught fish are barracuda, pompano, sailfish and kingfish. As with diving, the best time for offshore fishing is when the waters are free of storm-related silt.

Onshore

From the scores of piers and jetties along the coast you can catch redfish, flounder and speckled and sand trout. Surf fishing from the beaches can yield the same fish, as well as the occasional hapless stingray or small shark. Although there is always some sort of fish in peak season throughout the year, autumn is best, because the most popular species for eating – including redfish, flounder and pompano – are more likely to land on your hook then. Seafood restaurants near concentrations of charter boats often will prepare the lucky vacationer's catch.

Licenses

A fishing license is required for all nonresident anglers older than 17. A five-day license costs $20, but for a mere $10 more you can make it good for the entire year. Special stamps that allow you to fish for trout or in salt water cost $7 each.

Licenses are sold at sporting goods stores, tackle shops and at some park offices and convenience stores. For more information, write or call the Texas Parks and Wildlife Department (☎ 800-792-1112, 512-389-4800), 4200 Smith School Rd, Austin, TX 78744.

TENNIS

There are municipal tennis courts in almost every Texas city; check in the blue pages of the telephone directory under Parks Department for local numbers. All resorts and many hotels have courts as well, and you may be able to get time on the courts at college or university campuses simply by asking.

GOLF

Golf courses can be found all over Texas, and though we have included some of the larger courses in this book, we are not altogether thrilled about it. Golf courses waste colossal amounts of water for irrigation, and runoff from the fertilizer and pesticides used on them poisons the environment; conservationists charge that the damage to local flora and fauna is unforgivable. Golf courses also take up huge tracts of land, and the development associated with them – condominium and resort development – adds to the damage.

There are many sources of information on golfing in Texas; practically every pamphlet handed out by convention and visitors' bureaus or chambers of commerce lists all the golf courses in the immediate area. You also can look in the Yellow Pages under Golf Courses.

HOT-AIR BALLOONING

Floating above the state in a wicker gondola has its attractions, given the scenery, but it's not cheap at the relatively few locations that offer it commercially (one-hour flights for two people typically cost $125 to $165). Most flights leave at dawn or at sunset and rise 1000 to 2000 feet above the ground. Generally speaking there's ballooning in every major city. The best place to check for balloonists in a given area is at the local convention and visitors' bureau or airport.

SKYDIVING

If jumping out of a plane and falling at a speed of 150 miles per hour before opening your parachute 3000 feet above the ground sounds fun to you, Texas won't disappoint. Skydiving companies have set up shop at airports around the state – just drive into any airport and ask at the information desk or tower.

For first-timers, lessons are easily arranged. The Texas A&M Skydiving Club (☎ 409-778-0245), No 674, Box 5688, College Station TX 77844-9081, offers a static line first-jump course for $145 (no free fall, just the kind of static line you see in old army movies, where a rope yanks the pin on your chute when you're clear of the plane), including ground school, flights and all equipment.

FLYING

Ultralights These are small aircraft that are regulated by the government but require no pilot's license to fly (the British call them microlights). Lessons cost about $75 an hour, and you'll need 10 to 12 hours of training before you can fly solo.

The United States Ultralight Association (USUA, ☎ 301-695-9100, fax 301-695-0763) is an advocacy group and information resource for ultralight and powered parachute pilots and clubs; contact them at PO Box 667, Frederick, MD 21705. In Texas, the Texas Powered Parachute Association (☎ 972-231-4127) can give information on powered parachute flying.

Single-Engine Planes If you've got a pilot's license, a current medical certificate and a satisfactory Biannual Flight Review in your log book, you can usually stop into any decent airport and rent a plane to give yourself an orientation of the area. The price for a single-engine plane such as a Cessna 152 or 172 runs between $50 and $80 an hour, including fuel. You'll usually have to go up with the owner for a check-ride, to show that you're capable of flying safely, which will give you the opportunity to ask about must-see attractions, local regulations and other information.

CLIMBING

Rock climbing and mountaineering are demanding activities requiring top physical condition. Technical climbing requires an understanding of the composition of various rock types and the hazards of the high country, as well as familiarity with equipment such as ropes, chocks, bolts, carabiners and harnesses.

In Texas, even the state's highest mountains can be summited without a technical climb, but plenty of opportunities exist for rock climbing, including indoor sites. Rock climbing is divided into two categories: bouldering, in which no ropes or other gear are needed, and technical climbing, which involves steep rock, great exposure, small holds, the obligatory use of ropes, and knowledge of knots and techniques such as belaying and rappelling.

Climbers rank routes using the Yosemite Decimal System, which categorizes climbs from Class 1 – essentially hiking, with no climbing required – to Class 6, where artificial aids such as bolts and pitons have been previously placed in the rock to support ropes and belayed climbing. Class 5 routes are the technical ascents sought by experienced climbers, with the leader placing protection en route up the rock. These routes are further categorized according to degree of difficulty: routes ranked 5.0 to 5.4 have good, obvious hand and foot holds; routes rated between 5.5 and 5.9 are more challenging, for intermediate-level climbers; and routes ranked 5.10 and up are the most advanced.

Sites

The best Texas rock climbing is at Hueco Tanks State Historical Park, near El Paso, although the park has started curbing access to preserve its prehistoric rock art. The Hill Country west of Austin is another popular area, especially Enchanted Rock State Park, north of Fredericksburg. Indoor climbing gyms are in most major Texas cities; they are a good place to learn the sport before attempting to climb real rock outdoors. For climbing gear, check with REI (☎ 512-343-5550, www.rei.com), in Austin at 9901 N Capitol.

Safety

Climbing is a potentially hazardous activity. Climbers should be aware of hazards that might prompt a fall, causing serious injury or death. Weather is always an important factor to consider, as rain makes rock slippery and lightning can strike an exposed climber. Hypothermia is an additional concern – be sure to dress appropriately for the conditions in which you'll be climbing. In dry weather, lack of water can lead to dehydration, so make certain you've got enough water with you.

Environmental Concerns

Many climbers follow guidelines similar to those established for hikers to preserve the resource on which their sport relies. They include concentrating one's impact in high-use areas by using established roads, trails and routes for access; dispersing one's use in areas infrequently used to avoid the creation of new routes; refraining from creating or enhancing handholds; and eschewing the placement of bolts whenever possible. Climbers should also take special care to respect archaeological and cultural resources such as rock art and refrain from climbing in such areas.

Instruction

Based in Austin, Mountain Madness (☎ 512-292-6624, www.mtmadness.com) is the oldest climbing school in Texas, offering classes, clinics and private lessons at top locations across the state. Texas Mountaineers (☎ 972-504-6766, www.texasmountaineers.org/) lists places to climb, climbing classes and more on its comprehensive website. Another good online resource is the Texas Climbing Guide at www.exploremag.com/ClimbTexas/core.htm.

Getting There & Away

No matter how you're traveling, make sure you take out travel insurance. This not only covers you for medical expenses and luggage theft or loss, but also for cancellation or delays in your travel arrangements (you might fall seriously ill two days before departure, for example), and everyone should be covered for the worst possible case, such as an accident that requires hospital treatment and a flight home. Coverage depends on your type of ticket and insurance, so ask both your insurer and your ticket-issuing agency to explain the finer points. Ticket loss is also covered by travel insurance. Make sure you have a separate record of all your ticket details – or better still, a photocopy of it. Also make a copy of your policy, in case the original is lost.

Buy your travel insurance as early as possible. If you buy it the week before you fly,

you may find, for instance, that you are not covered for delays to your flight caused by strikes or other industrial action that may have been in force before you took out the insurance.

If you're planning to travel a long time, the insurance may seem very expensive – but if you can't afford it, you certainly won't be able to afford a medical emergency in the United States.

AIR

US domestic air fares vary tremendously depending on the season you travel, the day of the week you fly, the length of your stay and the flexibility the ticket allows for flight changes and refunds. Still, nothing determines fares more than demand, and when things are slow, regardless of the season, airlines will lower their fares to fill empty seats. There's a lot of competition, and at any given time any one of the airlines could have the cheapest fare.

Airports & Airlines

Airports The main international gateways to Texas are, from Europe, Dallas-Fort Worth International Airport (DFW) and, from Latin America, Houston's George Bush Intercontinental Airport (IAH). Houston and Dallas are the major hubs as well for US domestic carriers, some of which also have direct flights into Austin's Robert Mueller Municipal Airport and San Antonio's San Antonio International Airport. San Antonio's airport also offers some flights to Mexico. See the Toll-Free Numbers appendix for a listing of major international and domestic airlines.

Buying Tickets

Rather than just walking into the nearest travel agent or airline office, it pays to do a bit of research and shop around. If buying tickets within the US, the *New York Times*, *Los Angeles Times*, *Chicago Tribune*, *San Francisco Examiner* and other major newspapers

Warning

The information in this chapter is particularly vulnerable to change: prices for international travel are volatile, routes are introduced and canceled, schedules change, special deals come and go, and rules and visa requirements are amended. Airlines and governments seem to take a perverse pleasure in making price structures and regulations as complicated as possible. Check directly with the airline or a travel agent to make sure you understand how a fare (and any ticket you may buy) works. In addition, the travel industry is highly competitive, and there are many lurks and perks.

Get opinions, quotes and advice from as many airlines and travel agents as possible before you part with your hard-earned cash. The details given in this chapter should be regarded as pointers and are not a substitute for your own careful, up-to-date research.

all produce weekly travel sections with numerous travel agents' ads. Council Travel (☎ 800-226-8624) and STA (☎ 800-781-4040) have offices in major cities nationwide. The magazine *Travel Unlimited*, PO Box 1058, Allston, MA 02134, publishes details of the cheapest air fares and courier possibilities.

For those coming from outside the US, you might start by perusing travel sections of magazines like *Time Out* and *TNT* in the UK, or the Saturday editions of newspapers like the *Sydney Morning Herald* and *The Age* in Australia. Ads in these publications often offer cheap fares, but don't be surprised if they happen to be sold out when you contact the agents: they're usually low-season fares on obscure airlines with conditions attached.

The plane ticket will probably be the single most expensive item in your budget, and buying it can be intimidating. It is always worth putting aside a few hours to research the current state of the market. Start shopping for a ticket early – some of the cheapest tickets must be bought months in advance, and some popular flights sell out early. Talk to other recent travelers – they may be able to stop you from making some of the same old mistakes. Look at the ads in newspapers and magazines, consult reference books and watch for special offers.

Note that high season in the USA is mid-June to mid-September (summer) and one week before and after Christmas. The best rates for travel to and within the USA are best from mid-September to mid-November and January through March.

Phone travel agents for bargains (airlines can supply information on routes and timetables; however, except at times of fare wars they do not supply the cheapest tickets). Airlines often have competitive low-season, student and senior citizens' fares. Find out the fare, the route, the duration of the journey and any restrictions on the ticket.

Cheap tickets are available in two distinct categories: official and unofficial. Official ones have a variety of names including advance-purchase fares, budget fares, Apex and super-Apex. Unofficial tickets are simply discounted tickets that the airlines release through selected travel agents (they aren't available through airline offices). The cheapest tickets are often nonrefundable and require an extra fee for changing your flight. Many insurance policies will cover this loss if you have to change your flight for emergency reasons.

And How Much Did *You* Pay?

The United States' airfare market is rather convoluted. With airlines, travel agents, discount travel agents, student travel services and consolidators – and now with Internet consolidation services that update by the second – all selling tickets, the odds that you're getting the absolute best deal are slim. When discount ticket agents buy their tickets, coach seat prices are slashed. But the real price wars begin when the consolidators get their hands on more tickets, and competition gets hot, nudging down prices in increments as low as 50¢.

For a cattle car full of coach travelers, then, the trick is to figure out who won the low-fare contest. Next time you fly, play a little game: ask the people sitting to the right and left of you how much they paid for their seats. Odds are you'll discover three prices for the three seats.

A friend of mine has a recurring fantasy. On a flight to Europe, she stands up after takeoff and announces, 'Ladies and gentlemen, starting from the front left-hand side of the coach section, please stand up and tell us how much you paid for your seat.'

And you thought armed air marshals were there in case of hijackers.

Nick Selby

Return (roundtrip) tickets usually work out cheaper than two one-way fares – often *much* cheaper.

Use the fares quoted in this book as a guide only. They are approximate and based on the rates advertised by travel agents and airlines at press time. Quoted airfares do not necessarily constitute a recommendation for the carrier.

If traveling from the UK, you will probably find that the cheapest flights are being advertised by obscure bucket shops whose names haven't yet reached the telephone directory. Many such firms are honest and solvent, but there are a few rogues who will take your money and disappear, to reopen elsewhere a month or two later under a new name. If you feel suspicious about a firm, don't pay all the money at once – leave a deposit of 20% or so and pay the balance on receiving the ticket. If they insist on cash in advance, go elsewhere. And once you have the ticket, telephone the airline to confirm that you are booked on the flight.

You may decide to pay more than the rock-bottom fare by opting for the safety of a better-known travel agent. Established firms like STA Travel, which has offices worldwide, Council Travel in the USA or Travel CUTS in Canada are valid alternatives and they offer good prices to most destinations.

Once you have your ticket, write down its number, together with the flight number and other details, and keep the information somewhere separate. If the ticket is lost or stolen, this will help you get a replacement.

Remember to buy travel insurance as early as possible (see the introduction to this chapter for more information).

Visit USA Passes Almost all domestic carriers offer Visit USA passes to non-US citizens. The passes are actually a book of coupons that you buy – each coupon equals a flight. You have to book these outside of the US and have a return flight out of the US. The following airlines are the most representative, but it's a good idea to ask your travel agent about other airlines that offer the service.

Continental Airlines' Visit USA pass can be purchased in countries on both the Atlantic and Pacific sides of the US. All travel must be completed within 60 days of the first flight into the United States or 81 days after arrival in the US by means other than airplane travel. You must have your trip planned out in order to purchase the coupons, because if you decide to change destinations once in the USA, you will be fined $50. High-season prices are $407 for three flight coupons (minimum purchase), $518 for five, and $1158 for 10 (maximum purchase). Off-season rates for the same are $333, $518 and $407.

Northwest Airlines offers a similar deal, but it lets you fly standby or reserve flights beforehand.

American Airlines uses the same coupon structure and also sells the passes on Atlantic and Pacific sides. You must know your whole route, reserve your first flight (subsequent flights can be booked a day in advance) and stick to that schedule or be penalized $75 per change. If a coupon only takes you halfway to your destination, you will have to buy the remaining ticket at full price. A packet of 10 coupons costs $839.

Delta has two different systems for travelers coming across the Atlantic. Visit USA gives travelers a discount, but you need to have your itinerary mapped out to take advantage of this. You will get the cheapest fare between two places but not a set ticket price. The other option is Discover America, in which a traveler buys coupons good for standby travel anywhere in the continental USA. One flight equals one coupon, and only two transcontinental flights are allowed. Three coupons (the minimum purchase) cost $419, four cost $519, five cost $619 and 10 cost $1249. Children's fares are about $40 cheaper per set of coupons (for example, it's $379 for three).

In order to purchase coupons, the transatlantic flight must be paid in advance. These passes can be cheaper in conjunction with a Delta International flight into the United States. For pass information for Delta in the UK, call ☏ 0800-414-767; elsewhere in Europe call ☏ 44-181-566-8262.

When flying standby, call the airline within a day or two of the flight and make a 'standby reservation.' This way you get priority over all the others who just appear and hope to get on the flight the same day.

Round-the-World Tickets Round-the-World (RTW) tickets have become very popular in the last few years. Airline RTW tickets are often real bargains and can work out to be no more expensive or even cheaper than an ordinary return ticket. Prices start at about UK£675, A$2000 or A$2500 (low or high season), or US$1500.

The official airline RTW tickets are usually put together by a combination of two airlines and permit you to fly to any destination on their route systems as long as you do not backtrack. Other restrictions are that you must usually book the first sector in advance and cancellation penalties apply. There may be restrictions on the number of stops permitted, and tickets are usually valid from 90 days up to a year. An alternative type of RTW ticket is one put together by a travel agent using a combination of discounted tickets.

Although most airlines restrict the number of sectors that can be flown within the USA and Canada to four, and some airlines black out a few heavily traveled routes (like Honolulu to Tokyo), stopovers are otherwise generally unlimited.

The majority of RTW tickets restrict you to just three airlines; from Australia you can usually get an RTW ticket called the Global Explorer, which allows you to a maximum of six flights and total of 28,000 miles for US$3100 or A$3192 (high season).

One of the best places to get an RTW ticket would seem to be Germany, where, for example, you could book an RTW routed Frankfurt-São Paulo or -Buenos Aires, then Lima-Miami-Frankfurt, for US$1258.

Canadian Airlines offers numerous RTW combinations ranging from C$3100 to $3600. Air Canada's base fare is C$3287. This is with two other carriers; as you add more, the price goes up.

Continental, TWA and Northwest also offer Round-the-World fares.

Getting Bumped

Airlines bump passengers off flights when they overbook them. If you are involuntarily 'bumped' you'll have to wait around for the next flight. Avoid this by reconfirming your flight and checking in early. If you aren't traveling on a tight schedule, though, try volunteering to be bumped and take advantage of the deals airlines give for compensation. Here's what you do if you're on a full flight: when you check in, ask if they will need volunteers and give your name if they do. Be sure to ask when they can get you on a flight to your destination, and try to confirm that flight so you aren't stuck in the airport for too long. If you have to spend the night, check whether the airline will provide a hotel room and money for meals.

Baggage & Other Restrictions

On most domestic and international flights you are limited to two checked bags, or three if you don't have a carry-on. There could be a charge if you bring more or if the size of the bags exceeds the airline's limits. It's best to check with the individual airline if you are worried about this. On some international flights the luggage allowance is based on weight, not numbers; again, check with the airline.

If your luggage is delayed upon arrival (which is rare), some airlines will give a cash advance to purchase necessities. If sporting equipment is misplaced, the airline may pay for rentals. Should the luggage be lost, it is important to submit a claim. The airline doesn't have to pay the full amount of the claim, rather they can estimate the value of your lost items. It may take them anywhere from six weeks to three months to process the claim and pay you.

Smoking Smoking is prohibited on all US domestic flights. Many international flights are following suit, so be sure to call and find out. Many airports in the USA also restrict smoking.

Illegal Items Items that are illegal to take onboard the plane, either checked or as carry-on, include aerosols of polishes, waxes, etc;

tear gas and pepper spray; camp stoves with fuel; and full divers' tanks.

Travelers with Special Needs

If you have special needs of any sort – a broken leg, dietary restrictions, dependence on a wheelchair, responsibility for a baby, fear of flying – you should let the airline know as soon as possible so that they can make arrangements accordingly. You should remind them when you reconfirm your booking (at least 72 hours before departure) and again when you check in at the airport. It may also be worth ringing round the airlines before you make your booking to find out how they can handle your particular needs.

Airports and airlines can be surprisingly helpful, but they do need advance warning. Most international airports can provide escorts from check-in desk to plane where needed, and there should be ramps, lifts, accessible toilets and reachable phones. Aircraft toilets, on the other hand, are likely to present a problem; travelers should discuss this with the airline at an early stage and, if necessary, with their doctor.

Guide dogs for the blind will often have to travel in a specially pressurized baggage compartment with other animals, away from their owner, though smaller guide dogs may be admitted to the cabin. Guide dogs are not subject to quarantine as long as they have proof of being vaccinated against rabies.

Deaf travelers can ask for airport and in-flight announcements to be written down for them.

Children younger than two years old travel for 10% of the standard fare (or free, on some airlines), as long as they don't occupy a seat (they don't get a baggage allowance either). 'Skycots' should be provided by the airline if requested in advance; these will take a child weighing up to about 22lb (10kg). Children between two and 12 years old can usually occupy a seat for half to two-thirds of the full fare and do get a baggage allowance. Strollers can often be taken on as hand luggage.

Departure Tax

Airport departure taxes are usually included in the cost of tickets bought in the USA, although tickets purchased abroad may not have this included. There's a $6 airport departure tax charged to all passengers bound for a foreign destination. However, this fee, as well as a $6.50 NAFTA tax charged to passengers entering the USA from a foreign country, are hidden taxes added to the purchase price of your airline ticket.

Within the USA

Many flights from Europe to Texas will be indirect and will stop in airline hubs like New York, Orlando, Chicago or Detroit. The main international gateway, and therefore likely the cheapest place to buy tickets to, is Dallas-Fort Worth (DFW). From within the USA, Dallas and Houston are the most likely gateways.

Sample discount low-season and high-season roundtrip fares available at press time to DFW included these:

Boston	$179/279
Chicago	$116/309
Los Angeles	$198/329
Miami	$252/509
New York	$179/279

Sample international airfares include:

high-season airfares (in US$)	
Amsterdam	$613
Auckland	$1225
Brussels	$695
Frankfurt	$701
Johannesburg	$1875
London	$590
Madrid	$689
Paris	$566
Rio de Janeiro	$1150
Sydney	$1317
Tokyo	$830
Toronto	$490
Vancouver	$575

Note: These are sample scheduled fares (not including tax). You will most likely be able to find discounted and special tickets that are much cheaper. For example, STA travel quoted us a summer student fare of just UK£199 from London.

Air Travel Glossary

Baggage Allowance This will be written on your ticket and usually includes one 44lb (20kg) item to go in the hold, plus one item of hand luggage.

Bucket Shops These are unbonded travel agencies specializing in discounted airline tickets.

Bumped Just because you have a confirmed seat doesn't mean you're going to get on the plane (see Overbooking).

Cancellation Penalties If you have to cancel or change a ticket you purchased at a discounted rate, there are often heavy penalties involved; insurance can sometimes be taken out against these penalties. Some airlines impose penalties on regular full-fare tickets as well, particularly against 'no-show' passengers.

Check-In Airlines ask you to check in a certain time ahead of the flight departure (usually one to two hours on international flights). If you fail to check in on time and the flight is over-booked, the airline can cancel your booking and give your seat to somebody else.

Confirmation Having a ticket written out with the flight and date you want doesn't mean you have a seat until the agent has checked with the airline that your status is 'OK' or confirmed. Meanwhile you could just be 'on request.'

Courier Fares Businesses often need to send urgent documents or freight securely and quickly. Courier companies hire people to accompany the package through customs and, in return, offer a discount ticket that is sometimes a phenomenal bargain. In effect, what the companies do is ship their freight as your luggage on regular commercial flights. This is a legitimate operation, but there are two shortcomings – the short turnaround time of the ticket (usually not longer than a month) and the limitation on your luggage allowance. You may have to surrender all your allowance and take only carry-on luggage.

ITX An ITX, or 'independent inclusive tour excursion,' is often available on tickets to popular holiday destinations. Officially it's a package deal combined with hotel accommodation, but many agents will sell you one of these for the flight only and give you phony hotel vouchers in the unlikely event that you're challenged at the airport.

Lost Tickets If you lose your airline ticket, an airline will usually treat it like a traveler's check and, after inquiries, issue you another one. Legally, however, an airline is entitled to treat it like cash; and if you lose it, then it's gone forever. Take good care of your tickets.

MCO An MCO, or 'miscellaneous charge order,' is a voucher that looks like an airline ticket but carries no destination or date. It can be exchanged through any International Association of Travel Agents (IATA) airline for a ticket on a specific flight. It's a useful alternative to an onward ticket in those countries that demand one, and is more flexible than an ordinary ticket if you're unsure of your route.

Air Travel Glossary

No-Shows No-shows are passengers who fail to show up for their flight. Full-fare passengers who fail to turn up are sometimes entitled to travel on a later flight. The rest are penalized (see Cancellation Penalties).

On Request This is an unconfirmed booking for a flight.

Onward Tickets An entry requirement for many countries is that you have a ticket out of the country. If you're unsure of what your next move may be, the easiest solution is to buy the cheapest onward ticket you can find to a neighboring country or a ticket from a reliable airline that can later be refunded if you do not use it.

Open Jaw Tickets These are return tickets on which you fly out to one place but return from another. If available, these can save you from backtracking to your arrival point.

Overbooking Airlines hate to fly with empty seats and since every flight has some passengers who fail to show up, airlines often book more passengers than they have seats. Usually excess passengers make up for the no-shows, but occasionally somebody gets bumped. Guess who it is most likely to be? The passengers who check in late.

Point-to-Point Tickets These are discount tickets that can be bought on some routes in return for passengers waiving their rights to a stopover.

Reconfirmation At least 72 hours prior to departure time of an onward or return flight, you must contact the airline and 'reconfirm' that you intend to be on the flight. If you don't do this, the airline can delete your name from the passenger list and you could lose your seat.

Restrictions Discounted tickets often have various restrictions on them – such as advance payment, minimum and maximum periods you must be away (eg, a minimum of two weeks or a maximum of one year), and penalties for changing the tickets.

Round-the-World Tickets RTW tickets give you a limited period (usually a year) in which to circumnavigate the globe. You can go anywhere the carrying airlines go, as long as you don't backtrack. The number of stopovers or total number of separate flights is decided before you set off, and they usually cost a bit more than a basic return flight.

Stand-By This is a discounted ticket on which you only fly if there is a seat free at the last moment. Stand-by fares are usually available only on domestic routes.

Travel Periods Ticket prices vary with the time of year. There is a low (off-peak) season and a high (peak) season, and often a low-shoulder season and a high-shoulder season as well. Usually the fare depends on your outward flight – if you depart in the high season and return in the low season, you pay the high-season fare.

Canada

Travel CUTS (www.travelcuts.com) has offices in all major cities, including Vancouver, Edmonton, Ottawa, Toronto, Montreal and Halifax. The Toronto *Globe & Mail* and *Vancouver Sun* carry travel agents' ads.

Australia & New Zealand

In Australia, STA Travel and Flight Centres International are major dealers in cheap air fares; check the travel agents' ads in the Yellow Pages and ring around. Qantas flies to Los Angeles from Sydney, Melbourne (via Sydney or Auckland) and Cairns. United Airlines flies to San Francisco from Sydney and Melbourne (via Sydney) and also flies to Los Angeles.

In New Zealand, STA Travel and Flight Centres International are also popular travel agents that often have discounted fares.

The cheapest tickets will have a 21-day advance-purchase requirement, a minimum stay of seven days and a maximum stay of 60 days. Flying with Air New Zealand is slightly cheaper, and both Qantas and Air New Zealand offer tickets with longer stays or stopovers, but you pay more.

The UK

Check the ads in magazines like *Time Out* plus the *Evening Standard* and *TNT*. Also check the free magazines widely available in London – start by looking outside the main railway stations.

Most British travel agents are registered with the ABTA (Association of British Travel Agents). If you have paid for your flight to an ABTA-registered agent who then goes out of business, ABTA will guarantee a refund or an alternative. Unregistered bucket shops are riskier but sometimes cheaper.

London is most likely the world's headquarters for bucket shops, which are well advertised and can usually beat published fares. Good, reliable agents for cheap tickets in the UK are Trailfinders (☎ 0171-9375400), 194 Kensington High St, London W8 7RG; Council Travel (☎ 0171-4377767), 28A Poland St, London, W1; and STA Travel (☎ 0171-9379971), 86 Old Brompton Rd, London SW7 3LQ. The Globetrotters Club (BCM

Roving, London WC1N 3XX) publishes a newsletter called *Globe* that covers obscure destinations and can help you find traveling companions.

Continental Europe

In Amsterdam, NBBS, the Dutch Student Travel Service, is a popular travel agent. Kilroy Travels (☎ 020-524-5100), Singel 413-415, in Amsterdam is also fine agency. Council Travel's outpost in France (☎ 01.44.55.55.65) is at 22 rue des Pyramides, Paris 75001. For great student fares, contact USIT Voyages (☎ 01.42.34.56.90) at 16 rue de Vaugirard, Paris 75006.

In Germany, an awesome travel discounter for students and nonstudents alike is Travel Overland, which has offices in several cities; for the nearest one, contact its Munich office (☎ 089 272 76 30 0), Barerstrasse 73, 80799 Munich.

Africa

STA (☎ 011-447-5551) has offices all over South Africa. Seriously helpful is the Johannesburg student union building branch at Wits University (☎ 011-716-3045).

Rennies Travel (☎ 27-11-407-3177, fax 27-11-403-2553, rennies.internet@travel.rennies .co.za, www.renniestravel.co.za) has a comprehensive network of travel agencies throughout South Africa. Its head office is in Johannesburg on the 10th floor of Safren House, 19 Ameshoff Street, Braamfontein, Johannesburg 2001.

Asia

Hong Kong is the discount plane ticket capital of the region, but its bucket shops can be unreliable. Ask other travelers for advice before buying a ticket. STA Travel, which is dependable, has branches in Hong Kong, Tokyo, Singapore, Bangkok and Kuala Lumpur. Many if not most flights to the USA go via Honolulu, Hawaii.

United Airlines has three flights a day to Honolulu from Tokyo with connections to West Coast cities, from where you can connect to Texas. Northwest and Japan Air Lines also have daily flights to the West Coast from Tokyo, and Northwest serves

DFW via Detroit; Japan Air Lines also flies to Honolulu from Osaka, Nagoya, Fukuoka and Sapporo.

Latin America

Most flights from Central and South America go via Miami, or direct to Houston. Most countries' international flag carriers (some of them, like Aerolíneas Argentinas and LANChile), as well as US airlines like United and American, serve these destinations, with onward connections. Continental has flights from about 20 cities in Mexico and Central America, including San José, São Paulo, Guatemala City, Cancún and Mérida. Mexicana Airlines also flies to San Antonio from Guadalajara, Mexico City and other Mexican cities in addition to offering flights from points within Mexico to Dallas-Fort Worth.

Arriving in the USA

Even if you are continuing immediately to another city, the first airport that you land in is where you must carry out immigration and customs formalities. Even if your luggage is checked from, say, London to Dallas, you will still have to take it through customs if you first land in New York.

If you have a non-US passport, with a visa, you must complete an Arrival/Departure Record (form I-94) before you front up to the immigration desk. It's usually handed out on the plane, along with the customs declaration. It's a rather badly designed form, and lots of people take more than one attempt to get it right. Some airlines suggest you start at the last question and work upward. Answers should be written *below* the questions. For question 12, 'Address While in the United States,' give the address of the location where you will spend the first night. Complete the Departure Record too (the lower part of the form), giving exactly the same answers for questions 14 through 17 as for questions one through four.

The staff of the Immigration & Naturalization Service (INS) can be less than welcoming. The office's main concern is to exclude those who are likely to work illegally or overstay, so visitors will be asked about their plans and perhaps about whether they have sufficient funds for their stay. If they think you're OK, a six-month entry is usually approved.

It's a good idea to be able to list an itinerary that will account for the period for which you ask to be admitted and to be able to show you have $300 or $400 for every week of your intended stay. These days, a few major credit cards will go a long way toward establishing 'sufficient funds.' Don't make too much of having friends, relatives or business contacts in the USA – the INS official may decide that this will make you more likely to overstay.

Finally, keep a civil tongue with INS agents, no matter how reprehensibly rude they may become. They are under no obligation to let you in, have a wide berth when it comes to their authority to exclude you, can delay you by sticking you in a room for hours on end, and, if they're very unhappy, put you on a plane home before you know what hit you. 'Yes, officer,' 'No, officer,' and 'Officer, I do not understand,' are the best three sentences you can say if you should unluckily come upon one who is in a bad mood as you try to enter the USA. Good luck!

LAND
The Border

For many visitors to Texas, a side journey across the Mexican border is a highlight of their trip. Crossing the Tex-Mex border is usually a low- or no-hassle affair, but you'll want to bear in mind these regulations and restrictions.

Where to Cross There are more than a dozen major crossings on the border. Locations and hours of operation include:

El Paso-Ciudad Juárez
Open 24 hours. Crossings include the Stanton-Santa Fe (Paso del Norte) bridges (☎ 915-872-5700); the Bridge of the Americas (☎ 915-872-5710); and the Zaragosa Bridge (☎ 915-872-3424)

Presidio-Ojinaga
Open 24 hours (☎ 915-229-3663)

Del Rio-Ciudad Acuña
Open 24 hours (☎ 830-775-2090)

Eagle Pass-Piedras Negras
Open 24 hours (☎ 830-773-2622)

Laredo-Nuevo Laredo
Open 24 hours. Crossings in this area include Bridge 1 (☎ 956-726-2360) and Bridge 2 (☎ 956-726-2387)

Falcon Reservoir-Ciudad Guerrero
Open 7 am to 8:45 pm (☎ 956-848-5221)

Roma-Ciudad Miguel Alemán
Open 24 hours (☎ 956-849-1678)

Rio Grande City-Carmago
Open daily 7 am to midnight (☎ 956-487-3498)

Los Ebanos-Díaz Ordaz (ferry)
Open daily 8 am to 4 pm; hours may vary with river conditions (☎ 956-485-1084)

McAllen-Reynosa
Open daily 24 hours. Crossings here include the Hidalgo Bridge (☎ 956-843-2471) and the Pharr-Reynosa International Bridge (☎ 956-781-1361); the Pharr Bridge is open daily 6 am to midnight

Progreso-Nuevo Progreso
Open daily 24 hours (☎ 956-565-6361)

Brownsville-Matamoros
Open daily 24 hours. Crossings include the B&M Bridge (☎ 956-548-2501) and the Gateway Bridge (☎ 956-546-1675)

For more information on border crossings, see the descriptions throughout this book or contact the local visitors' center at your anticipated crossing.

Regulations United States citizens should carry proof of citizenship – a passport, birth certificate or voter registration card plus a photo ID such as a driver's license – when crossing into Mexico. Canadians should carry

a passport or birth certificate. Other foreign nationals should have a passport and appropriate visas both before entering Mexico and returning to the US.

US and Canadian citizens who plan to enter Mexico past the border area, or who will be staying in Mexico longer than 72 hours, need a Mexican tourist card. The free cards are available from Mexican authorities at the border or from Mexican consulates or Mexican government tourist offices in the US. A birth certificate or passport is required.

When crossing into Mexico, if you have no merchandise to declare, you must go through the stop-and-go light checkpoint. A green light means proceed without inspection; the red light means stop for inspection. Visitors to Mexico can take in a wide range of recreational gear for personal use, but if you have expensive equipment with you (cameras, laptop computers, jewelry – especially goods made outside the US), it's smart to register it with US Customs before entering Mexico so you won't have to pay taxes on it when you return to the US. Each US citizen may bring back Mexican purchases valued to US$400 retail every 30 days. Check with customs before crossing the border for duty-free limits imposed on citizens of other nations. Certain items either may not be brought into the US from Mexico or are subject to quarantines. These include weapons, drugs, certain trademarked goods, most fruits, vegetables, plants, animals, birds and meats, and products made from the hides, shells, feathers or teeth of endangered species.

On returning to Texas from Mexico, a stop at US Customs is required. Be prepared to state your nationality and declare any purchases made in Mexico. Mexican citizens entering the US need to obtain a laser visa card from the US Embassy in Mexico City or its consulates in Mexico. The laser visa cards replace the old INS-issued Border Crossing Cards (usually called *micas* or *pasaportes locales*), which will not be accepted after September 30, 1999.

Driving into Mexico If you drive into Mexico, you'll need supplemental Mexican insurance for your vehicle. Policies cost

Visas to Mexico

Many travelers do not require a visa to enter Mexico as a tourist, including citizens of the USA, Canada, EC countries, Australia, New Zealand, Norway, Switzerland, Iceland, Israel, Japan and Argentina. Travelers from South Africa, Brazil and Eastern European nations all need visas.

Who Can Drive?

Whenever you drive into Mexico, perhaps the most important thing to remember is who can actually operate the car. Legally, the car must be driven only by the person whose name is on the title and by no one else. If, for example, if a married couple enters Mexico and only the wife's name is on the title, the husband may not drive – and if he does and is involved in an accident, the insurance company can refuse to pay.

If you're driving a car for which no one has the title – for example, a rental car, a company car or a car on which you're making payments (whether you own or lease the vehicle) – you must carry a notarized letter of permission from the rental company, business or bank holding title to the car.

about $7 to $12 for one day of full coverage, about half that if you buy only liability coverage. Policies are readily available in all border towns from such agencies as Sanborn's Insurance (☎ 800-222-0158, www.sanbornsinsurance.com), which has offices in most border communities, or AAA, with branches in the larger cities. Many rental-car companies do not allow their vehicles to enter Mexico, so check your agency's policy before reserving. If all of this sounds like an incredible hassle for a few hours over the border, take heart that many Tex-Mex towns offer cross-border public transportation, or – easiest and cheapest of all – you can simply hoof it across the bridge.

If you plan to drive beyond the border area, you'll also need to get an automobile permit, which may be obtained at the border after the tourist card is stamped by Mexican authorities. Auto permits are good for 180 days; they cost about $10 and must be paid for with a bank-issued credit card or by posting a bond. Permits are good for multiple entries into Mexico, but they must be surrendered before expiration.

The USA

Bus Greyhound (☎ 800-231-2222 for reservations), the only nationwide bus company, has reduced local services considerably, but still runs cross-country.

Because buses are so few, schedules are often inconvenient, fares are relatively high and bargain air fares can undercut buses on long-distance routes; in some cases, for shorter routes, it can be cheaper to rent a car than to ride the bus. However, very long distance bus trips are often available at bargain prices by purchasing or reserving tickets three days in advance.

Bus travel, of course, gives you the chance to see some of the countryside and to talk to some of the inhabitants that travelers by air or private car might miss. Then again, bus travel can subject you to conversation with some of the inhabitants that travelers by air or private car might miss – bus travel is a mixed blessing. Greyhound stations are generally sleazy places, and solo travelers may feel uncomfortable in them. Buses also provide a fine opportunity to meet those who have recently graduated from one of the USA's famous detention facilities; released prisoners are typically given a small amount of cash and a Greyhound bus ticket home.

For these reasons, traveling by car is recommended, if it's at all possible. Details of major bus routes will be given in the text if you have the time or inclination to see the Greyhound side of travel.

Meal stops are made on long trips; you pay for your own simple food in inexpensive and usually unexciting cafes. Buses have onboard lavatories. Seats recline, ostensibly for sleeping, but a couple of days in a Greyhound seat is quite a memorable experience. Smoking is not permitted aboard Greyhound buses.

In an effort to boost sagging ticket sales, Greyhound offers a series of incentive fares – like a $79 to-and-from-anywhere fare that pops up now and then – to a variety of locations around the country. These change frequently, so ask if there are any specials on when you book. Here are published one-way and roundtrip Greyhound fares between Dallas and some major US destinations. Travel times can vary dramatically depending on the time of day you leave, the route you take and other factors.

to/from	trip duration	one-way/ roundtrip
Atlanta	18 to 26 hours	$62/124
Chicago	21 hours	$103/185
Las Vegas	25 hours*	$92/169
Los Angeles	30½ hours	$84/164
New Orleans	12 hours	$72/118
New York	36 hours	$102/179
San Francisco	40 hours	$108/192
Washington, DC	35 hours	$102/204

*Some special tie-in prices apply if you're staying at a casino or hotel; ask when you book the ticket.

Train Amtrak (☎ 800-872-7245, which spells 800-USA-RAIL; www.amtrak.com) provides cross-country passenger service between Florida and Los Angeles and from the West Coast to Chicago; travelers from the East Coast must either head down to Florida or make connections in Chicago. Schedules usually get knocked off the published timetables the farther you are from your starting point.

Amtrak bases its fares on these routes based on a percentage of discounted tickets that are sold first and gradually fills seats with more and more expensive tickets, so the earlier you book the cheaper it is – you can book up to 11 months in advance.

Amtrak offers services through Texas aboard the *Sunset Limited*, which runs between Miami and Los Angeles, and the *Texas Eagle*, which runs between Texas and Chicago.

The *Sunset Limited* leaves Los Angeles on Sunday, Tuesday and Friday and arrives in San Antonio two days later on Tuesday, Thursday and Sunday at 4 am. It leaves from Orlando, Florida, on Tuesday, Thursday and Saturday, arriving in San Antonio Thursday, Saturday and Monday at 4:30 am. This train frequently runs anywhere from one to eight hours late in both directions, so it's important to call Amtrak to get an update before setting out for the train station. One-way fares aboard the *Sunset Limited* for between Miami and San Antonio range $258 to $462; from Los Angeles one-way fare is $149 to $223.

The *Texas Eagle* leaves San Antonio Sunday, Tuesday, Wednesday and Thursday at 8 am and arrives the following day in Chicago at 2:45 pm on Monday, Wednesday, Thursday and Friday. It leaves Chicago on Tuesday, Thursday and Saturday at 5:55 pm and arrives in San Antonio Thursday, Saturday and Monday at 11:30 am. One-way fares between San Antonio and Chicago are $139 to $207.

The best value overall is Amtrak's 'All Aboard America' fare. This costs $318 for adults in the off-season and $378 during peak times (between June 19 and August 23 and December 18 and January 3) and enables you to travel anywhere you want. There are limitations – travel must be completed in 45 days from the first date of travel, and you are allowed a maximum of three stopovers. Additional stopovers can be arranged at an extra cost. Your entire trip must be reserved in advance, and seats are limited, so book as far ahead as possible. These tickets are for reclining seats; sleeping cars cost extra. If you want to travel in just one region, the eastern, central or western parts of the country, 'All Aboard America' fares are $228 in high season, $198 in off-season; for two regions, fares run $318 and $258.

For non-US citizens, Amtrak offers a USA Rail Pass that comes in three types and must be purchased outside the US (check with your travel agent). A 15-day national pass runs $425 (high season) and $285 (off-season); one good for 30 days is $440 and $350. Regional passes vary: in the East and West Coasts, 15-day regional passes are $250 and $205. Sleeping accommodations are an extra charge. Advanced reservations are recommended, especially during high season.

Most small train stations don't sell tickets; they must be booked with Amtrak over the telephone or through its website. Some small stations have no porters or other facilities, and trains may stop there only if you have bought a ticket to that station in advance.

Car & Motorcycle

Drivers of cars and motorcycles will need to carry the vehicle's registration papers, liability insurance and an International Driving Permit (see the Visas & Documents section in the Facts for the Visitor chapter) in addition to a domestic license. Canadian and Mexican driver's licenses are accepted. Customs officials along the entry points between Canada and Montana can be strict and often wary of anything that doesn't look straitlaced. To avoid unnecessary conflicts, dress conservatively and be cordial for those few hours between countries.

For information on buying or renting a car, or using a drive-away (driving a car for someone else), see the Getting Around chapter.

ORGANIZED TOURS

Tours of the USA are so numerous that it is impossible to attempt any kind of comprehensive listing; for overseas visitors, the most reliable sources of information on the constantly changing offerings are major international travel agents, such as Thomas Cook and American Express. Probably those of most interest to the general traveler are coach tours that visit the national parks and make guest ranch excursions; for those with limited time, package tours can be an efficient and relatively inexpensive way to go.

Green Tortoise (☎ 415-956-7500, 800-867-8647, www.greentortoise.com), 494 Broadway, San Francisco, CA 94133, offers alternative bus transportation with stops at places like hot springs and national parks. Your meals are cooperatively cooked and you sleep on bunks on the bus or camp. This is not luxury travel, but it is fun. Its Mardi Gras package ($369 plus $81 for the food fund) runs from mid-February to early March and stops in El Paso, where you cross the border into Juárez for lunch, as well as stopping in Big Bend

National Park, before continuing to New Orleans via San Antonio and Houston.

Trek America (☎ 973-983-1144, 800-221-0596, fax 973-983-8551, www.trekamerica .com), PO Box 189, Rockaway, NJ 07866, offers roundtrip camping tours to different areas of the country. In England, it has an office at 4 Water Perry Court, Middleton Rd, Banbury, Oxon OX16 8QG (☎ 01295-256777, fax 01295-257399). In Australia contact Adventure World (☎ 9955-5000, fax 9954-5817), 75 Walker St, North Sydney, NSW 2060. These tours last from one to nine weeks and are designed for small, international groups (13 people maximum) of 18- to 38-year-olds. Tour prices vary with the season, with July to September having the highest prices. Tours cost about $606 for a 10-day tour to $2570 for a nine-week tour of the entire country. Some side trips and cultural events are included in the price, and participants help with cooking and camp chores.

Similar deals are available from Suntrek (☎ 707-523-1800, 800-786-8735, fax 707-523-1911), Sun Plaza, 77 W 3rd St, Santa Rosa, CA 95401. Suntrek also has offices in Germany (☎ 089-480 28 31, fax 089-480-24-11), Sedanstrasse 21, 81667 Munich; and Switzerland (☎ 01-13-87-7878, fax 01-13-87-7800), Bellerivestrasse 11, CH-8034 Zurich. Suntrek's tours are for the 'young at heart' and attract mostly young international travelers, although there is no age limit. Prices range from about $850 for the three-week trek to about $3200 for a 13-week trek around North America.

Road Runner USA/Canada (☎ 800-873-5872), 9741 Canoga Ave, Chastworth, CA 91311, organizes one- and two-week treks in conjunction with Hostelling International to different parts of the USA and across the country. It has offices in England (☎ 1892-512700), 64 Mt Pleasant Ave, Tunbridge Wells, Kent TN1 1QY. Prices run $449 for one week to $849 for two weeks. AmeriCan Adventures (☎ 800-864-0335) offers seven- to 21-day trips to different parts of the USA, usually following a theme like Route 66 or the Wild West. Prices range $450 for seven days to $1200 for 21 days.

Specialized Tours

Elderhostel (☎ 877-426-8056), 75 Federal St, Boston, MA 02110, is a nonprofit organization offering educational programs for those ages 55 and older and has programs throughout the US.

Bicycling, hiking and walking, running, cross-country skiing, kayaking and multisport tours are another possibility with companies such as Backroads (☎ 510-527-1555, 800-462-2848), 801 Cedar St, Berkeley, CA 94710.

Getting Around

Texas is big, but easy to get around. The easiest way is to rent a car, but you can get to most larger destinations by Greyhound bus. Flying is often a fine option as well if time is short, and with Southwest's special fares, it's sometimes even as cheap as the bus, so check before just assuming that flying is going to cost you an arm and a leg. There's also limited train service within Texas.

AIR
Regional Carriers
Most larger domestic airlines have connecting services to larger Texas cities through either Dallas or Houston as a Texas hub; you can fly within the state on these flights as well, but the price will probably be higher than with a regional carrier. See the individual chapters for small carriers that serve various destinations in Texas, but over the past several years the best deals have come consistently from Southwest, which serves Amarillo, Austin, Corpus Christi, Dallas (Love Field), El Paso, Harlingen-Rio Grande Valley, Houston (William P Hobby Airport), Lubbock and Midland-Odessa, offers a host of special fares, including at press time a $30 one-way fare from Austin to a string of destinations. Southwest also offers daily Internet special fares from its website at www.iflyswa.com/hotfares.

Whenever you're quoted airfares, remember that they may not include airport-assessed passenger facility charges (PFCs) of up to $12 roundtrip. The appendix at the back of this book lists toll-free telephone numbers for both major airlines and smaller commuter carriers.

BUS
Greyhound
Greyhound (☎ 800-231-2222), the main bus line for the region, has extensive fixed routes and its own terminal in most central cities, often in undesirable parts of town that attract unsavory types. Buses are generally comfortable, the company has an exceptional safety record and buses usually run on time. Where Greyhound doesn't travel, there are sometimes local bus companies that pick up the slack, like the Kerrville Bus Co (see the Bus section under Getting Around in South Central Texas), which runs buses in the Texas Hill Country.

Greyhound has reduced or eliminated services to smaller rural communities it once served efficiently. In many small towns Greyhound no longer maintains terminals, but merely stops at a given location, such as fast-food restaurants like McDonald's (which may be the only choice for meal stops – bring your own food if burgers and fries are unappealing). In these unlikely terminals, boarding passengers usually pay the driver with exact change.

Bus Passes Greyhound's Ameripass is potentially useful, depending on how much you plan to travel, but its relatively high prices may impel you to travel more than you normally would simply to get your money's worth. There are no restrictions regarding who can buy an Ameripass; it costs $199 for four days, $299 for 15 days, $409 for 30 days and $599 for 60 days of unlimited travel year-round. Children younger than 11 years old travel for half price. You can get on and off at any Greyhound stop or terminal. The Ameripass is available for purchase at every Greyhound terminal.

An International Ameripass can be purchased only by foreign tourists and foreign students and lecturers (with their families) staying in the US less than one year. Prices are $119 for a four-day pass for unlimited travel Monday to Thursday, $139 for five days, $179 for seven days, $229 for 10 days, $269 for 15 days and $369 for 30 days. Passes good for longer periods are available as well. The International Ameripass is usually bought abroad at travel agencies or can be purchased in the USA over the telephone through the Greyhound International depot in New York City (☎ 212-971-0492). The address is 625 8th Ave at the Port Authority subway level, North Wing building, open Monday to Thursday 8 am to 4 pm, Friday 8 am to 7 pm, Saturday 8 am to 3 pm. New York Greyhound International accepts MasterCard, Visa and American Express, traveler's checks and cash.

To contact Greyhound International to inquire about regular fares and routes, call ☎ 800-246-8572. Those buying an International Ameripass must complete an affidavit and present a passport or visa (or waiver) to the appropriate Greyhound officials.

There are also special passes for travel in Canada that can be bought only through the New York City office or abroad.

Costs It's hard to give an average per-mile rate; if there is a formula that Greyhound uses it's probably a corollary of Fermat's Last Theorem. From Dallas to Austin, the 196 miles you'll traverse cost $26, while you can ride the 317 miles between Laredo and Houston for $29. It's just like that. Tickets can be bought over the phone with a credit card (MasterCard, Visa or Discover) and mailed if purchased 10 days in advance or picked up at the terminal with proper identification. Greyhound terminals also accept American Express, traveler's checks and cash. All buses are nonsmoking, and reservations are made with ticket purchases only.

Greyhound will occasionally introduce a mileage-based discount fare program that can be a bargain, especially for traveling very long distances, but it's a good idea to check the regular fare anyway. As with regular fares, these promotional fares are subject to change.

TRAIN

Amtrak (☎ 800-872-7245) fares for travel within Texas vary greatly, depending on different promotional fares and destinations. Reservations (the sooner made, the better the fare) can be held under your surname only; tickets can be purchased by credit card over the phone, from a travel agent or at an Amtrak depot. Regional trains include the *Sunset Limited* to Miami and Los Angeles and the *Texas Chief* to Chicago. For more information, see the Getting There & Away chapter.

CAR & MOTORCYCLE

The US highway system is extensive, and since distances are great and buses can be infrequent, auto transport is worth considering despite the expense. Officially, you must have an International or Inter-American Driving Permit to supplement your national or state driver's license, but US police are more likely to want to see your national, provincial or state driver's license.

By far the most convenient and popular way to get around Texas is by car. Motorcycles are also very popular, and with the exception of the rain in the summer, conditions are perfect: good, flat roads and warm weather.

Unless you're coming here from Saudi Arabia or Indonesia, US gasoline prices are a gift from heaven – at press time about a dollar a gallon, or a little more than 30¢ per liter. But remember to always use the self-service islands at fuel stations, as full-service ones cost 25¢ to 50¢ more per gallon.

Road Rules

Americans drive on the right side of the road and pass on the left. A right turn on a red light is permitted after a full stop.

Speed limits in the city are between 15mph and 45mph. Be especially careful in school zones, which are limited to 15mph. Speeding tickets are outrageous: for example, if you're clocked at 50 in a 40mph zone, the fine is more than $125.

Roadside Hazards

In central Texas, especially around Del Rio and Eagle Pass, folks tend to drive on the shoulder of the road. I asked around and it seems some do it just because they plan to turn soon, even though 'soon' may be five miles down the road. Some drivers seem to do it out of courtesy to faster drivers. Whatever the reason, bicyclists and pedestrians traveling on smaller roads would do very well to stay aware and watch out for shoulder drivers.

Julie Fanselow

Accidents Do Happen

Accidents do happen – especially in such a car-dependent country as the USA. It's important that a visitor knows the appropriate protocol when involved in a 'fender-bender.'

- Don't try to drive away. Remain at the scene of the accident; otherwise you may spend some time in the local jail.
- Call the police (and an ambulance, if needed) immediately and give the operator as much specific information as possible (your location, if there are any injuries involved, etc). The emergency phone number is ☎ 911.
- Get the other driver's name, address, driver's license number, license plate number and insurance information. Be prepared to provide any documentation you have, such as your passport, international driver's license and insurance documents.
- Tell your story to the police carefully. Refrain from answering any questions until you feel comfortable doing so (with a lawyer present, if need be – see Legal Matters in the Facts for the Visitor chapter). That's your right under the law. The only insurance information that you need to reveal is the name of your insurance carrier and your policy number.
- Always comply with an alcohol Breathalyzer test. If you take the option not to, you'll almost certainly find yourself with an automatic suspension of your driving privileges.
- If you're driving a rental car, call the rental company promptly.

All passengers in a car must wear seat belts; all children younger than three years old must be in a child safety seat (rental-car companies will rent you one for about $5 a day). The fine for not wearing a seat belt can be as high as $150.

Safety

Seat belts are obligatory for the driver and all passengers in Texas. Texans are rather safe drivers, but you'll have to get used to being the smallest thing on the road – give way to vehicles larger than you, which is most of them (see The Pickup: The National Vehicle of Texas), and you'll be fine. Speed limits in smaller towns are strictly enforced, and Texans don't usually hurry, so if you're an agitated driver you should get used to driving a bit slower than usual.

Use of a crash helmet for motorcyclists is obligatory.

To avert theft, do not leave expensive items, such as purses, compact discs, cameras, leather bags or even sunglasses visibly lying about in the car. Tuck items under the seat, or even better, put items in the trunk and make sure your car does not have trunk entry through the back seat; if it does, make sure that is locked. Don't leave valuables in the car overnight.

Breakdown

If you break down in a privately owned vehicle, check in the Yellow Pages under 'Towing,' or if you're on the road without a phone book, get to a pay phone and call directory assistance (☎ 411) and ask an operator to call a towing company for you. If the operator says he or she can't, ask to speak to a supervisor and explain your situation; they'll usually look one up in the Yellow Pages for you. AAA members (see Useful Organizations in the Facts for the Visitor chapter) can call ☎ 800-222-4357, and a tow truck will be sent out but quick.

It may pay to rent or buy a cellular telephone, especially if you'll be traveling to remote areas. Most rental-car agencies rent phones for about $3 a day plus air time, which can be expensive (about $1.50 a minute).

Most rental cars are covered for breakdown; see your rental agreement for a toll-free number to call in case of breakdown. If the company can't get to you until the next day, ask if your motel costs can be covered. Even if they say no, keep the receipts for your motel and food expenses while you were waiting and take the matter up with a manager when you return the car – you may get reimbursed, or at the very least they'll give you a coupon for a free rental next time.

Car Rental

All major car-rental companies in the USA have offices throughout Texas. Rates go up and down like the stock market, and it's always worth phoning around to see what's available. Reserving ahead usually ensures the best rates – and reserving ahead can be from the pay phone in the rental office to the company's telephone reservation line (usually an 800 number). Sometimes the head office can get you a better price than the branch office, so always call ahead. If you're a member of a frequent-flyer club, be sure to check and see whether the rental company has a deal with your airline. Listed in the Toll-Free Numbers appendix are contact numbers for some of major rental companies in Texas.

Rates Typically a small car costs anywhere from $25 to $50 per day or $150 to $210 a week. On top of that there will be a 8.75% state sales tax and anywhere from $9 to $15 a day for each insurance option you take – plus local taxes.

Generally speaking, the best deals come on weekly or weekend rental periods. At the time of writing, the lowest rates consistently seemed to come from companies such as Alamo, Budget, Enterprise and Value, and the highest from Avis and Hertz, though there are always specials and the best bet is to shop around carefully. The same car can vary in price from operator to operator by as much as $20 a day or $75 a week. If you're planning on dropping off the car at a different location than the one where you originally rented it, check and make certain that there won't be any penalty.

Most car-rental companies here include unlimited mileage at no extra cost – be sure to check this point, because you can rack up hundreds of miles even just in the city, and at 25¢ per mile, this could lead to an unhappy surprise when you get the bill.

Age & Credit Requirements Most operators require that you be at least 25 years old and have a major credit card in your own name. Some will let you get away with the age thing by paying outrageous surcharges, but renting without a credit card – if you can even accomplish it – will require a large cash deposit, and you'll have to work things out well in advance with the company. It's hard to do, and even if they let you, you will be treated with great suspicion.

Insurance Note that in Texas, liability insurance is not included in rental costs. Some credit cards offer a Loss/Damage Waiver (LDW – sometimes also called CDW, or Collision/Damage Waiver), which means that you won't have to pay if you damage the car itself. Liability insurance means that you won't have to pay if you hit someone and he or she sues you. If you own a car and have insurance at home, your liability insurance may extend to coverage of rental cars, but be *absolutely* certain before driving on the roads in the litigious USA. Also, if you opt out of the LDW, be certain that your credit card really will cover you for it. If it doesn't, make sure you buy liability coverage when you rent, which costs from $10 to $25 a day in addition to the cost of the car, but is worth it.

Motorcycle Rental

It's difficult to rent motorcycles in the USA. You may find smaller companies in your journeys willing to rent motorcycles, but usually the insurance costs are too high to make them a popular offering. One exception is CruiseAmerica (see RV Rental for contact information), which rents Honda and Harley Davidson motorcycles for $69 to $109 per day including unlimited mileage. They do not rent helmets (and there's a helmet law in Texas), and renters must be older than 21 and have a valid motorcycle license and a major credit card. CDW and liability insurance are each $12 per day.

RV Rental

Renting a recreational vehicle (RV) makes sense if you meet one of two conditions: you're rich or there are several of you. An RV can be a great way to get out into Texas and is surprisingly roomy and flexible, and even the smaller ones can sleep four comfortably – as long as you're all close friends. If you're not, don't despair: many RV campsites are large enough to accommodate the RV and still leave room for a tent outside.

The downside is that you'll need transport when you get where you're going – at an average highway gas consumption of eight to 10 miles per gallon, RVs are not exactly a good method of city transport. You can, of course, get a bicycle rack or, if you also have a car, a tow-hitch to bring that along, but note that that makes your already dismal gas mileage even worse.

CruiseAmerica (☎ 800-327-7799) is the largest and best known of the nationwide RV rental firms. They have a huge variety of rentals available. The smallest are 22- to 24-foot vehicles with two double beds, a dinette that converts into a single bed, a bathroom with shower and a full kitchen. They cost $804 a week in the off-season (from April to June and from August to mid-December) and $1032 in high season, including insurance and an electrical generator. One thousand miles are included; after that you're billed at 29¢ a mile. The Recreational Vehicle Rental Association (☎ 703-591-7130, 800-336-0355) publishes *Who's Who in RV Rentals*, a directory of rental agencies around the USA, Canada and Europe, for $7.50, and *Rental Ventures*, which lists campgrounds that accommodate RVs ($3, or $2.50 when purchased with the directory). You can order by telephone or send a check payable to RVRA for the purchase price of the publications to RVRA, 3930 University Drive, Suite 100, Fairfax, VA 22030.

Car Purchase

If you're spending several months in the USA, buying a car is worth considering; a car is more flexible than public transport and likely to be cheaper than rentals, but buying one can be very complicated and requires plenty of research.

It's possible to buy a viable car in the USA for about $1500, but you can't expect to go too far before you'll need some repair work that could cost several hundred dollars or more. It doesn't hurt to spend more to get a quality vehicle. It's also worth spending $50 or so to have a mechanic check it for defects (some AAA offices have diagnostic centers where they can do this on the spot for its members and members of foreign affiliates). A used-car seller who won't let you take the car to a mechanic for a check is most likely hiding something – caveat emptor. You can check out the official valuation of a used car by looking it up in the *Kelly Blue Book*, a listing of cars by make, model and year issued and the average resale price. Local public libraries have copies of the *Kelley Blue Book* (it's also online at www.kbb.com), as well as back issues of *Consumer Reports*, a magazine that annually tallies the repair records of common makes of cars.

If you do want to buy a car, the first thing to do is contact AAA (☎ 800-477-1222) for some general information on ownership. Then, contact the Texas Department of Transportation (☎ 800-558-9368) to find out about registration fees and insurance, which can be very confusing and expensive. As an example, say you are a 30-year-old non-US citizen and you want to buy a 1984 Honda. If this is the first time you have registered a car in the USA, you'll have to fork over some $300 first and then about $100 to $200 more for general registration.

Inspect the title carefully before purchasing the car; the owner's name that appears on the title must match the identification of the person selling you the car. If you are a non-US resident, you may find it very useful to obtain a notarized document authorizing your use of the car, since the motor vehicle bureau in the state where you buy the car may take several weeks or more to process the change in title.

Insurance While car insurance is not obligatory in every state, all states have financial responsibility laws, and insurance is highly desirable; otherwise, a serious accident could leave you a pauper. In order to get insurance

The Pickup: The National Vehicle of Texas

Texans have a passion for the pickup truck that is unmatched perhaps anywhere else in the world. Chevrolet manufactures a Texas Edition of many of its trucks (essentially this means air-conditioning and a couple of extra options thrown in).

Born of necessity in the 1920s, early pickups were simple hauling vehicles used by farmers and ranchers. In Texas today, pickup trucks are status symbols driven by city folk as much as cowboys, and they can be decked out with as many options as the average Cadillac.

The popularity of these trucks (Texans bought 307,000 of them in 1997) can be attributed to several factors – that they're big couldn't hurt to start with (if you haven't noticed, Texans like big things). Low-priced gasoline makes them cheap to run, simple truck engines keep them easy and inexpensive to repair. They're hugely powerful and can be very comfortable (the Ford F-250 four-door has a cabin about as large as a passenger car).

But while more and more Texans get into trucks, even bigger vehicles are coming into vogue. Long the favorite ride of the US Secret Service and housewives who like to 'sit up hah,' the 18½-foot-long, 6-foot-high, 6½-foot-wide, 5293lb Chevrolet Suburban has become as common a sight in Texas cities as any pickup. The Suburban (the *Economist* joked that it's called that because you can fit a small European suburb inside) satisfies many needs that pickups just can't. It's perfect for soccer moms who drive the team around town, as it holds up to nine adult passengers, and it satisfies the USA's propensity toward gas guzzlers by coming with a standard 42-gallon (160-liter!) fuel tank. It gets an average of 12 miles to the gallon.

Perhaps the principal reason for the unbelievable numbers of these huge boats cruising along the roads is that they are distinctly American, and as far as most Texans are concerned, Texans are the quintessential Americans. While the pickup is also popular throughout Asia, where it's used as public transportation, it's still about as American as baseball, hot dogs and apple pie. And chances are, you would *never* catch any self-respecting Texan in a foreign-built pickup.

Nick Selby

some states request that you have a US driver's license and have been licensed for at least 18 months. If you meet those qualifications, you may still have to pay anywhere from $300 to $1200 a year for insurance, depending on where the car is registered and the state. Rates are generally lower if you register it at an address in the suburbs or in a rural area, rather than in a central city. Collision coverage has become very expensive, with high deductibles, and is generally not worthwhile unless the car is somewhat valuable. Regulations vary from state to state but are generally becoming stringent throughout the USA.

Obtaining insurance, however, is not as simple as walking into an agency, filling out a form and paying for it. Many agencies refuse to insure drivers who have no car insurance (a classic catch-22!); those who will do so often charge much higher rates because they presume a higher risk. Male drivers younger than 25 years old will pay astronomical rates. The minimum term for a policy is usually six months, but some insurance companies will refund the difference on a prorated basis if the car is sold and the policy voluntarily terminated. It is advisable to shop around.

Drive-Aways

A drive-away is a car that belongs to an owner who can't drive it to a specific destination, but who is willing to allow someone else to drive the car to the destination for them. For example, if somebody moves from Boston to Denver, they may elect to fly and leave the car with a drive-away agency. The agency will find a driver and take care of all necessary insurance and permits. If you happen to want to drive from Boston to Denver, have a valid driver's license and a clean driving record, you can apply to drive the car. Normally, you have to pay a small refundable deposit. You pay for the gas (though sometimes a gas allowance is given). You are allowed a set number of days to deliver the car – usually based on driving eight hours a day. You are also allowed a limited number of miles, based on the best route and allowing for reasonable side trips, so you can't just zigzag all over the country. However, this is a cheap way to get around if you like long-distance driving and meet eligibility requirements.

Drive-away companies often advertise in the classified sections of newspapers under 'Travel.' They are also listed in the yellow pages of telephone directories under 'Automobile Transporters & Drive-away Companies.' You need to be flexible about dates and destinations when you call. If you are going to a popular area, you may be able to leave within two days, or you may have to wait more than a week before a car becomes available. The routes most easily available are coast to coast, although intermediate trips are certainly possible.

BICYCLE

Cyclists should carry at least two full bottles of water and refill them at every opportunity. Spare parts are widely available and repair shops are numerous, but it's still important to be able to do basic mechanical work, like fixing a flat, yourself.

Bicycles can be transported by air. Your best bet is to disassemble or partially disassemble them and put them in a bike bag or box. You may have to remove the pedals and front tire so that it fits in your box or bag. Check all this with the airline well in advance, preferably before you pay for your ticket. Be aware that some airlines will welcome bicycles, while others will treat them as an undesirable nuisance and do everything possible to discourage them.

HITCHHIKING

Hitchhiking is never entirely safe in any country in the world, and we don't recommend it. Travelers who decide to hitchhike should understand that they are taking a small but serious risk. You may not be able to identify the local rapist, murderer, thief – or even a driver who has just had too much to drink – before you get into the vehicle. And in Texas, the chances are hitchhikers won't get picked up anyway – odds of catching a lift from someone here are next to nothing.

People who do choose to hitchhike will be safer if they travel in pairs and let someone know where they are planning to go.

Universities have ride-sharing programs, as well as bulletin boards that advertise ride-sharing possibilities, especially at the ends of semesters and during school holidays.

LOCAL TRANSPORT

Local bus service is available only in larger cities; generally bus fare is between 75¢ and $1.50, though in much of downtown Austin it's free (yup!). Transfers – slips of paper that allow you to change buses – are sometimes free, sometimes a few cents extra, but usually no more than 25¢ more than the regular adult fare. Pay as you board (always board through the front doors); exact change is usually required, though some buses accept $1 bills.

Passengers using wheelchairs should contact the local bus company to inquire about special transport services. Most local buses in Texas are wheelchair-accessible, though some bus companies offer individual transit services in addition to regular service for those with physical or mental disabilities. See the Facts for the Visitor chapter for information on organizations that assist with travel for the disabled. Operating hours differ from city to city, but in general, buses run from about 6 am to 10 pm.

Dallas-Fort Worth

Dallas and Fort Worth anchor a region of almost 5 million people – the most populous in Texas – and together constitute the most popular international gateway to the state. For almost all foreign visitors, Dallas is the first glimpse they have of Texas, and it lives up to the state's exported image: big, flashy and prosperous.

Although the cities are only 30 miles apart, closely linked by growth and geography, they offer two distinct takes on the Texas experience. Dallas is driven, a city endlessly occupied with growth and status. Fort Worth

Highlights

- The Sixth Floor Museum in Dallas, a moving tribute to the life and death of John F Kennedy
- Waco's peaceful Cameron Park and the stained-glass collection of the Armstrong Browning Library
- The Ballpark in Arlington and Legends of the Game, a baseball fan's dream
- World-class art museums in Dallas and Fort Worth
- The adventurous restaurants of Dallas
- Sundance Square, Fort Worth's after-hours playground

is going places too, but it doesn't seem so concerned with how its image plays outside the city limits. Between and around them are booming suburbs: Arlington, Plano, Mesquite, Irving, Garland, Grapevine and dozens more. If you're looking for JR Ewing's South Fork Ranch, Six Flags Over Texas, football's Dallas Cowboys or baseball's Texas Rangers, you're headed for the suburbs. None of these marquee attractions is in Dallas or Fort Worth proper, and that may be one reason why Texans refer to their biggest megalopolis simply as the Metroplex. Dallas-Fort Worth International Airport, midway between the two cities, is one of the world's busiest airports and an attraction in itself.

Dallas

Population 1,053,300

Dallas is Texas' most mythical city, with a past and present rich in the stuff of which American legends are made. The 'Big D' is famous for its contributions to popular culture – notably the Cowboys and their cheerleaders and *Dallas*, the television series that for a time was a symbol of the US to people worldwide. This is also a city known for its business acumen – especially in banking – its restaurants and its shopping. In the materially minded United States, Dallas stands tall as a paragon of conspicuous consumption. Its skyline lives large, with office towers and other temples of commerce sporting orbs, green argon tubing and daring angles.

That is the side of Dallas visitors are most apt to see. But the city has its surprises, and they are not difficult to find: a quiet, tiny sliver of downtown set aside to promote the ideal of gratitude, not greed; a stirring museum devoted to one of the greatest tragedies in United States history; acres of parks providing oases of relaxation and recreation.

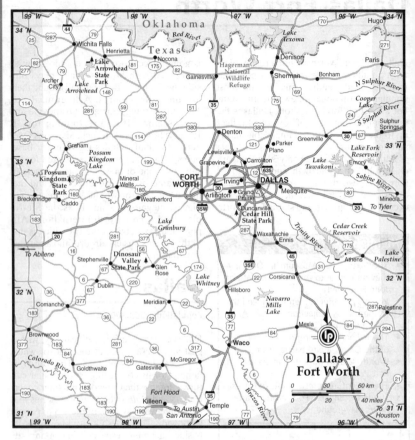

HISTORY

In 1839, John Neely Bryan, a Tennessee lawyer with a healthy case of wanderlust, stumbled onto the three forks of the Trinity River, a site he thought had the makings of a good trading post and maybe a town. Bryan returned to Tennessee for a time but came back in 1841, laid claim to 640 acres, built a cabin and sketched out a town. Dallas County was created in 1846, and both city and town were probably named for George Mifflin Dallas, a Pennsylvanian who served as US vice president under James K Polk, president from 1845 to '49; the two

were elected on a platform favoring Texas statehood.

Dallas grew slowly for 30 years, though from its start the city had a flair for self-promotion: Bryan saw to it that Dallas was placed on maps even before there was much of a town. One new arrival from Missouri, John Billingsley, wrote in his 1843 journal, 'We soon reached the place we had heard of so often; but the town, where was it? Two small cabins – this was the town of Dallas, and two families of 10 or 12 souls was its population.'

A group of French artists and intellectuals arrived in the 1850s to establish an artists' colony known as La Réunion just west of the fledgling city. The community did not last, but some of its members stayed, their presence giving Dallas a sophisticated edge on the frontier.

In the 1870s, at a Dallas legislator's suggestion, the state decided Dallas would be the junction of the north-south Missouri, Kansas and Texas Railroad and the east-west Texas and Pacific Railroad. The first train arrived in 1872, sparking a boom that ensured Dallas' preeminence as a trade center. Merchants from New York, Chicago, Boston and St Louis invested heavily in the city. In just one year (1873), 725 buildings valued at more than $1.37 million rose in Dallas.

Cotton caused another boom. In 1885, farmland sold for $15 an acre. By 1920, with cotton prices soaring, land values had risen to $300 an acre. And when the East Texas Oil Field was struck 100 miles east of town in 1930, Dallas became the financial center of the oil industry.

In the post-WWII era, Dallas continued to build on its reputation as a citadel of commerce. The 1950s were marked by the rise of pioneering high-tech company Texas Instruments, creators of many technical innovations, including the integrated circuit computer chip, the first single-chip microprocessor and the first electronic handheld calculator.

Dallas' image took a dive when President John F Kennedy was assassinated during a November 1963 visit to the city. This incident, coupled with the ensuing turmoil of the 1960s, badly battered Dallas' self-esteem. Gradually, however, the city reclaimed its Texas swagger with help from a few new chest-thumping sources of civic pride: the Dallas Cowboys won the first of five Super Bowl titles in 1972, and their success on the field – coupled with the popularity of the skimpily attired Dallas Cowboys cheerleaders – helped earn the Cowboys the unofficial title of 'America's Team.' DFW International Airport opened in 1973, and the city hosted the 1984 Republican National Convention. And then there was that little ol' TV show, the top-rated series in the US from 1980 to '82. Dallas was back, louder and prouder than ever.

ORIENTATION

Although not as sprawling as Los Angeles or even Houston, Dallas covers a lot of ground. I-30 is the major east-west thoroughfare and primary route to Arlington (where Six Flags and the Rangers' ballpark are) and Fort Worth, which are about 20 and 40 minutes away, respectively. I-20 is another east-west choice, traveling across the southern reaches of the Metroplex. Downtown Dallas is just east of the junction of I-30 and I-35 E (here called the Stemmons Freeway); the Commerce St exit off I-35 E is the easiest route to the heart of downtown. The central business district is logically laid out, with Commerce St running one way east toward Deep Ellum and Fair Park, Elm and Jackson Sts running one way west, and Main St allowing traffic in both directions (look for Elm St if you're trying to find your way back to I-30 or the Stemmons Freeway). East of downtown, I-30 is known as the RL Thornton Freeway; south of downtown I-35 E is called that as well.

Northwest of downtown, I-35 E travels past the Dallas Market Center trade-show complex and leads to the Dallas North Tollway (the area's only toll road, used mostly by commuters from the northern suburbs) and three major surface streets (Oak Lawn Ave, Inwood Rd and Mockingbird Lane) before splitting into two; I-35 E continues north, and the Carpenter Freeway – Hwy 183 – heads northwest and then west to Texas Stadium, Irving and DFW International Airport. (Allow 25 minutes to get to the airport in non-rush-hour traffic, twice that during rush hour, when anything can happen.)

Just north of downtown, the short Woodall Rodgers Freeway connects I-35 E with I-75 (the Central Expressway), which in turn leads to the northeast suburbs of Richardson, Plano and Parker. US 635, the Lyndon B Johnson Freeway, makes a wide arc from north of DFW International Airport at Grapevine across North Dallas and south past Garland and Mesquite before becoming I-20. There are about a dozen other freeways in Dallas, but these are the ones you'll need to know to find the city's top attractions.

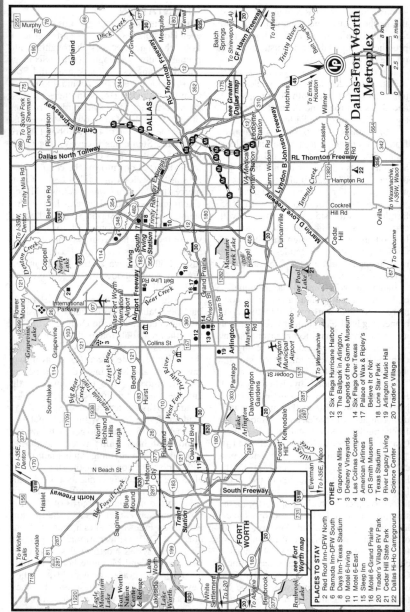

Dallas-Fort Worth Metroplex

PLACES TO STAY
2 Red Roof Inn-DFW North
6 Ramada Inn-DFW South
8 Days Inn-Texas Stadium
10 Motel 6-Irving
11 Motel 6-East
15 Sleep Inn
16 Motel 6-Grand Prairie
20 Trader's Village RV Park
21 Cedar Hill State Park
22 Dallas Hi-Ho Campground

OTHER
1 Grapevine Mills
3 Delaney Vineyards
4 Las Colinas Complex
5 American Airlines
   CR Smith Museum
7 Texas Stadium
9 River Legacy Living
   Science Center
12 Six Flags Hurricane Harbor
13 The Ballpark in Arlington;
   Legends of the Game Museum
14 Six Flags Over Texas
17 Palace of Wax & Ripley's
   Believe It or Not
18 Lone Star Park
19 Arlington Music Hall
20 Trader's Village

A note on Dallas addresses. Frequently, especially along the Stemmons Freeway and the Central Expressway, businesses add the directional 'North' to their address – but this practice is by no means universal. If you see a Stemmons Freeway or Central Expressway address including N, rest assured it's north of downtown on the appropriate route. There is no separate N Stemmons Freeway or N Central Expressway.

Maps

The AAA map is good, mainly because it indicates block numbers – a real help when you're trying to find an address on a miles-long street such as Mockingbird Lane, Inwood Rd or Lovers Lane. The *Illustrated Dallas Map*, by Travel Graphics International, is available free around town, and with its bird's-eye approach and numbered key to major attractions and buildings, it too is worthwhile. The ultimate Dallas maps come from Mapsco, which thoroughly updates its detailed Metroplex street atlases each year. They're not cheap, though; the 1999 set cost $64. For current prices and ordering information, call ☎ 214-521-2131 or write to 5308 Maple Ave, Dallas, TX 75235.

INFORMATION
Tourist Offices

The Dallas Convention and Visitors Bureau (CVB; ☎ 214-571-1000, fax 214-571-1008, www.dallascvb.com) has its Visitor Information Center in the Old Red Courthouse, 100 S Houston St. It's open Monday to Friday from 8 am to 7 pm and Saturday and Sunday from 10 am to 7 pm. The CVB also maintains an events hot line at ☎ 214-571-1301.

AAA (☎ 214-526-7911) has its central Dallas office at 4425 N Central Expressway between Oliver and Armstrong Aves, just south of Knox St on the southbound service road (see the Lower Greenville map). Open Monday to Friday 9 am to 6 pm, Saturday 9 am to 1 pm.

Gay & Lesbian

The Gay and Lesbian Community Center (☎ 214-528-9254), 2701 Reagan St two blocks northwest of Oak Lawn Ave, has lots of literature, including the *Lambda Pages* phone book of gay-friendly Metroplex businesses. Gays and lesbians can be open in the Oak Lawn area, Uptown. There's also a good-size gay enclave in Oak Cliff, southwest of downtown across the Trinity River; it's less expensive to live there, and it's an alcohol-free area.

Money

Thomas Cook has several offices at DFW International Airport, and at 2911 Turtle Creek Blvd (☎ 214-559-3564), in the same building as the British consulate. American Express has an office in the Galleria shopping center (☎ 972-233-9291), on the Dallas North Tollway at the LBJ Freeway. Most major downtown Dallas banks will exchange currency, including the main office of NationsBank (☎ 214-508-1383), 901 Main St, open Monday to Friday 7:30 am to 3:30 pm (incidentally, the 921-foot NationsBank Plaza is the tallest building in Dallas, illuminated each night by green argon tubing). Many tonier hotels will change currency, too. ATMs are just about anywhere you'd need one.

Post & Communications

The downtown post office (☎ 214-953-3045), 400 N Ervay St, is open Monday to Friday 8 am to 6 pm (closed Saturday and Sunday). Address poste restante mail to General Delivery, 400 N Ervay St, Dallas, TX 75221. In the Uptown area, a post office at 2825 Oak Lawn Ave (☎ 214-521-4000) is open Monday to Friday 8:30 am to 5 pm, Saturday 8:30 am to noon.

Phone The Dallas-Fort Worth area has been divvied up into three area codes – 214 (central Dallas), 972 (outer Dallas and suburbs) and 817 (Fort Worth and Tarrant County) – but if you're calling a Metroplex area code from within the Metroplex you don't need to dial 1 before the area code.

Internet Kinko's offers public Internet access for 20¢ a minute or $12 an hour. There's a 24-hour branch (☎ 214-522-7434) at 3905 Oak Lawn Ave, Suite 110. Another branch downtown (☎ 214-922-0403), 1305 Ross Ave,

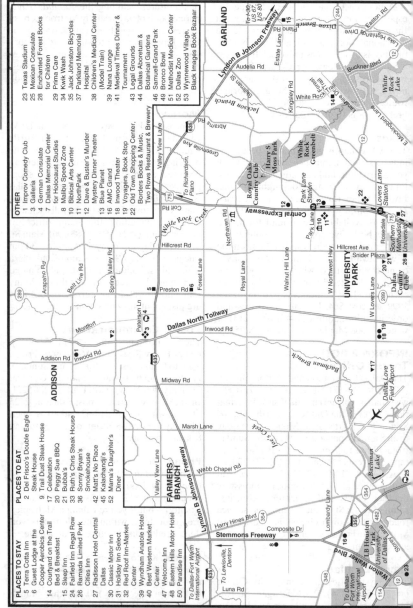

PLACES TO STAY

5 Terra Cotta Inn
6 Guest Lodge at the
   Cooper Aerobics Center
14 Courtyard on the Trail
   Bed & Breakfast
15 Sleep Inn
24 Fairfield Inn Regal Row
26 Ramada Limited Park
   Cities Inn
27 Radisson Hotel Central
   Dallas
30 Classic Motor Inn
31 Holiday Inn Select
32 Red Roof Inn-Market
   Center
39 Wyndham Anatole Hotel
40 Best Western Market
   Center
47 Welcome Inn
48 Eastern Hills Motor Hotel
50 Paradise Inn

PLACES TO EAT

2 Del Frisco's Double Eagle
   Steak House
9 Trail Dust Steak House
17 Celebration
20 Peggy Sue BBQ
21 Bubba's
33 Ruth's Chris Steak House
36 Sonny Bryan's
   Smokehouse
42 Matt's No Place
45 Kalachandji's
52 Mama's Daughter's
   Diner

OTHER

1 Improv Comedy Club
3 Galleria
4 German Consulate
7 Dallas Memorial Center
   for Holocaust Studies
10 Malibu Speed Zone
11 Biblical Arts Center
11 NorthPark
12 Dave & Buster's Murder
   Mystery Dinner Theatre
13 Blue Planet
16 AMC Grand
18 Inwood Theater
19 Voyagers, Book Stop
22 Old Town Shopping Center,
   Borders Books & Music,
   Two Rows Restaurant & Brewery
23 Texas Stadium
25 Mexican Consulate
28 Enchanted Forest Books
   for Children
29 Prima Care
34 Kwik Wash
35 Jack Johnston Bicycles
37 Parkland Memorial
   Hospital
38 Children's Medical Center
   (Model Train)
39 Nana Lounge
41 Medieval Times Dinner &
   Tournament
43 Legal Grounds
44 Dallas Arboretum &
   Botanical Gardens
46 Samuell-Grand Park
49 Bronco Bowl
51 Methodist Medical Center
52 Dallas Zoo
53 Wynnewood Village,
   Black Images Book Bazaar

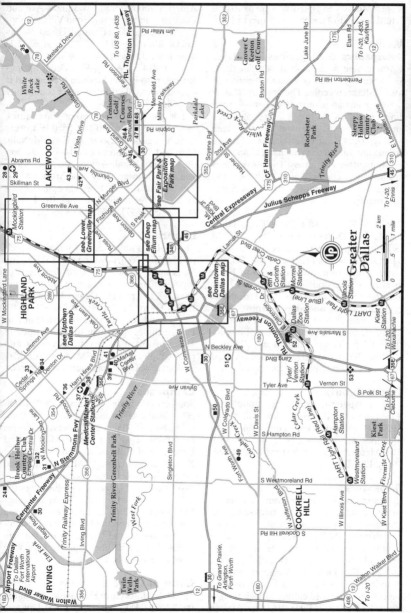

is open Monday to Thursday 6 am to 10 pm, Saturday 6 am to 7 pm, Sunday 10 am to 4 pm.

Media

Newspapers & Magazines The *Dallas Morning News* is the daily paper (50¢ daily, $1.50 Sundays) and is available online at www.dallasnews.com. The weekly *Dallas Observer* has an investigative bent, a good dining guide and thorough listings of what's on around town. *The Met*, another free weekly, focuses on entertainment, feature articles and subversive chitchat. *D Magazine* is the monthly city glossy. The *Advocate* is the local gay and lesbian weekly, and the *Dallas Weekly* serves the African American community.

Radio NPR is on 90.1 FM, KERA. For a real flavor of Dallas, tune in KKDA, 730 AM (Soul 73), especially on weekdays from 3 to 6 pm, when the politically charged 'Cousin' Linnie Henderson exhorts his mostly black listeners to take pride in their city and their lives. KRLD, 1080 AM, has the Metroplex's best talk show weekday mornings with Charlie Jones, a paragon of moderation and thoughtfulness. Other notable stations include 107.5 FM, with smooth jazz (the perfect tonic for crowded Dallas freeways), and 93.3 FM, the Zone, playing rock.

Travel Agents

Carlson-Wagonlit Travel has about two dozen offices in the Metroplex. Call ☎ 800-510-4703 to find the nearest one. Convenient locations are Uptown (☎ 214-720-1000), 3102 Maple Ave, and downtown (☎ 214-744-7600), 1201 Elm St.

Bookstores

Bookstore options range from huge megastores to small, specialized booksellers. In the latter category, check out the History Merchant (☎ 214-742-5487), Uptown at 2723 Routh St, specializing in rare and out-of-print volumes; Forbidden (☎ 214-821-9554), in Exposition Park at 835 Exposition Ave, described by its staff as 'a hodgepodge of subculture and weird culture'; Black Images Book Bazaar (☎ 214-943-0142), an African

American bookstore at W Illinois Ave and Zang Blvd in the Wynnewood Village shopping center; and Enchanted Forest Books for Children (☎ 214-827-2234), at 6333 E Mockingbird Lane. Crossroads Market Bookstore (☎ 214-521-8919), 3930 Cedar Springs Rd, caters to gay and lesbian readers and is a good source of information on community activities.

For guidebooks and other travel titles, Voyagers (☎ 214-654-0700), 5550 W Lovers Lane, is a good bet, as is the Rand McNally Map and Travel Store (☎ 214-987-9941) in the NorthPark mall. Among the superstores, you'll find Borders Books and Music (☎ 214-739-1166), in the Old Town Shopping Center at 5500 Greenville Ave, and Book Stop (☎ 214-357-2697), 5550 W Lovers Lane.

Libraries

The Dallas Public Library's main branch (☎ 214-670-1700), downtown at 1515 Young St, is open Monday to Thursday 9 am to 9 pm, Friday and Saturday 9 am to 5 pm, Sunday 1 to 5 pm. The Dealey Library at the Dallas Historical Society (☎ 214-421-4500), 3939 Grand Ave in the Hall of State at Fair Park, includes more than 10,000 volumes on Texas history, plus many rare maps and photographs. Hours are Monday to Friday 9:30 am to 4:30 pm (appointments preferred).

Campuses

Southern Methodist University (☎ 214-768-2000) is the city's main four-year school, with about 9500 students attending classes on a pretty campus north of Mockingbird Lane, east of Hillcrest Ave and west of the N Central Expressway. SMU is considered especially strong in business administration, psychology and theater. The other big area college is the University of Texas at Arlington, where 24,000 students are working toward degrees on the UT system's second-largest campus. The University of Dallas, in Irving, is a small liberal-arts school with ties to the Catholic Church.

Cultural Centers

The Dallas Institute of Humanities & Culture (☎ 214-871-2440), at 2719 Routh St Uptown, presents lectures and seminars exploring issues affecting US urban life; open Monday to Friday 9 am to 5 pm. The Mexican Cultural Center (☎ 214-824-9981), just north of Deep Ellum at 2917 Swiss Ave in the Dallas Visual Arts Center, sponsors local performances and exhibits and study tours to Mexico; open Monday to Friday 9 am to 5 pm.

Laundry
You won't have trouble finding a place to do laundry in Dallas. The Kwik Wash chain has about 25 locations, including 3131 Lemmon Ave E (☎ 214-526-6690), in the Uptown area, and 3008 Inwood Rd (☎ 214-352-7432), a block northwest of Harry Hines Blvd. Down a beer or two while doing wash at the angst-wrung Bar of Soap (☎ 214-823-6617), 3615 Parry Ave in the trendy Exposition Park neighborhood, opposite Fair Park.

Medical Services
Prima Care (☎ 214-828-0448), 6350 E Mockingbird Lane in the Lakewood area, treats walk-in patients with minor illnesses and injuries, charging a base rate of $70 per visit. It's open daily 8 am to 9 pm. Prima Care has about a dozen other Dallas-area locations; call ☎ 214-345-8345 for an automated list.

Emergency services are available at the following hospitals: Parkland Memorial Hospital (☎ 214-590-8000), 5201 Harry Hines Blvd (DART Rail Trinity Railway Express Medical-Market Center station); Baylor University Medical Center (☎ 214-820-0111), north of Deep Ellum at 3500 Gaston Ave (bus Nos 19 or 44); and Methodist Medical Center (☎ 214-947-8181), 1441 N Beckley Ave (bus Nos 1, 42 or 522). Baylor operates a physician referral line at ☎ 800-422-9567.

Emergency
The Sheriff's Department is at ☎ 214-749-8641, the Highway Patrol at ☎ 214-861-2000. The rape crisis and sexual abuse hot line is ☎ 214-590-0430. Suicide Prevention of Texas is at ☎ 214-828-1000.

Dangers & Annoyances
Like most cities, Dallas has a crime problem, consisting mostly of break-ins, thefts and muggings. Park in a well-lit, secured area and never leave valuables in sight. Better yet, take a cab to your destination and head home by about 1:30 am. Keep your wits – and maybe a few level-headed buddies – about you when you're out and about, especially in such party-hearty areas as Deep Ellum and Lower Greenville. For solo travelers, the West End Marketplace ranks among the city's safest areas after dark, with visible police patrols. Traffic jams rank high among the city's major annoyances; see the Getting Around section for more details.

DOWNTOWN DALLAS – THE KENNEDY LEGACY
Dallas will forever be known as the city where President John F Kennedy was shot, and the sites associated with his death are among Dallas' most visited attractions. Most travelers make sober pilgrimages to the museums and monuments; others congregate at Dealey Plaza, eager to swap conspiracy theories with other skeptics. All JFK sites are near the DART Rail West End station.

John F Kennedy

A Dark Day in November

In the early 1960s, the US was fascinated with its young president, his little children at play in the Oval Office and his regal wife. They seemed the perfect family, and the US – still awash in postwar prosperity – considered itself a place where justice and amity prevailed.

But beneath the glossy surface, the US was heading into its most divisive decade since the Civil War. By no means universally popular, Kennedy had won election over Richard Nixon by fewer than 120,000 votes from among 69 million cast. His 1961 Bay of Pigs invasion of Cuba was a foreign policy disaster, and he escalated the US presence in Vietnam from 5000 military 'advisors' to 17,000 troops (though before his death he'd announce a cutback to 1000 troops).

In the eyes of many, Kennedy redeemed his presidency in the fall of 1962, when he stood up to Soviet premier Nikita Khrushchev after US intelligence services discovered Soviet offensive missile sites in Cuba. Yet in the nine months prior to his November 1963 Dallas appearance, Kennedy had received more than 400 death threats, from critics on both the left, who felt him guilty of warmongering during the Cuban missile crisis, and the right, who charged he was soft on communism. The president's advisers were seriously concerned about the trip to Dallas, where right-wing groups including the John Birch Society and the Indignant White Citizens Council held powerful sway. But Kennedy remained wildly popular among the moderate masses, and nearly a quarter-million people lined the streets on November 23 to greet him.

What happened next has been endlessly debated and dissected by conspiracy theorists, but the events as officially recorded took place like this: Kennedy, his wife, Jacqueline, Texas governor John Connally and the rest of the motorcade left Love Field at 11:50 am and arrived downtown under sunny skies. Kennedy's open-air limousine made its way down Main St to Dealey Plaza, where three streets – Main in the middle, Commerce to the south and Elm to the north – converged under a railroad bridge known as the triple underpass. The limo made a one-block jog on Houston St, turning onto Elm St beneath the Texas School Book Depository building. Just as the limousine completed its turn at 12:30 pm, one shot rang out, then another. Both Kennedy and Connally appeared wounded, and then a third shot was heard,

The Sixth Floor Museum

If you have time to visit only one place in Dallas, make it this thoughtful, comprehensive tribute to the life, death and legacy of John F Kennedy (☎ 214-747-6660), 411 Elm St in the former Texas School Book Depository. The Sixth Floor Museum feels frozen in time, from the go-go days of 1960 when JFK proclaimed in his inaugural address, 'Let the word go forth . . . that the torch has been passed to a new generation' to the more tempestuous times that followed: the Cuban missile crisis, the dawning of the civil rights era and a deepening rift between the radical right and the far left.

With that background in place, the museum explains in minute-by-minute detail the events of November 22, 1963. Artifacts include the original layout for the front page of that afternoon's *Dallas Times Herald*, stills from the famous home movie by Abraham Zapruder, a Teletype machine endlessly reprinting United Press International's first report of the assassination and an FBI model of the assassination site. The most evocative exhibit is the corner window overlooking Dealey Plaza, the grassy knoll and the triple underpass. No one who was alive in November 1963 – and probably few born since – can fail to get choked up at the view: the same vista suspected sniper Lee Harvey Oswald had on that fateful day. Open daily except Christmas, 9 am to 6 pm; $4 for adults, $3 for seniors, $2 for kids, free

THE DALLAS TIMES HERALD FINAL EDITION

Books for Everyone On Your Gift List! Reviewed in the CHRISTMAS BOOK SECTION Coming Sunday

CONTINUOUSLY PUBLISHED FOR 87 YEARS   THE TIMES 1876   THE HERALD 1886   CONSOLIDATED 1888

87th Year—No. 292   ★ ★   DALLAS, TEXAS, FRIDAY EVENING, NOVEMBER 22, 1963   Telephones— 3 Parts   Price Five Cents

PRESIDENT DEAD

and part of the president's head exploded. Jacqueline Kennedy cradled her husband's body as the limo raced up the Stemmons Freeway toward Parkland Memorial Hospital. They arrived at 12:36 pm, but doctors could not save Kennedy, who had a bullet wound in his neck in addition to the massive head wound. He was pronounced dead at 1 pm.

Even before the announcement, Dallas and the nation were thrown into turmoil. Dallas police officer Marrion Baker, who had seen pigeons fly off the Book Depository roof as the shots were fired, entered the building and found a man in the employee lunchroom at 12:32 pm. Depository superintendent Roy Truly identified the suspect as Lee Harvey Oswald – an employee hired five weeks earlier – so Baker let him go. Soon after, police found the sniper's perch on the sixth floor, together with spent cartridges and finger and palm prints later identified as Oswald's. Meanwhile, Oswald was arrested at 1:50 pm in the Oak Cliff section of town, a suspect in the shooting of Dallas police officer JD Tippit. He was later charged with the murder of Kennedy, but the next morning – as Oswald was being transferred from the city to the county jail pending trail, denying both murders – Dallas nightclub owner Jack Ruby shot him in the basement of Dallas police headquarters. Kennedy was buried the following day at Arlington National Cemetery, outside Washington, DC.

for kids under six. The last ticket is sold one hour before closing. An audio tour, $2 extra, is available in English, Spanish, French, German, Italian, Japanese and Portuguese. A gift shop has an extensive selection of books and videos about the Kennedys and the assassination.

Dealey Plaza & the Grassy Knoll

Dealey Plaza was named in 1935 for George Bannerman Dealey, a longtime Dallas journalist, historian and philanthropist. The rectangular park south of the former Book Depository is now a National Historic Landmark. The grassy knoll is the hillock that rises from the north side of Elm St to the edge of the picket fence separating Dealey Plaza from the Missouri, Kansas and Texas railroad yards. Some witnesses to the assassination said shots came from this area, but investigators found only cigarette butts and footprints on the knoll after the shooting. The House Select Committee on Assassinations, investigating from 1976 to '78, concluded via acoustical analysis that a sniper did fire from behind the picket fence but missed. That bolstered the belief that Kennedy's assassination was part of a conspiracy, but the committee's findings were later disputed by a different government-sponsored panel. Differing opinions abound on who was behind the Kennedy assassination; the truth is, we may never know the truth.

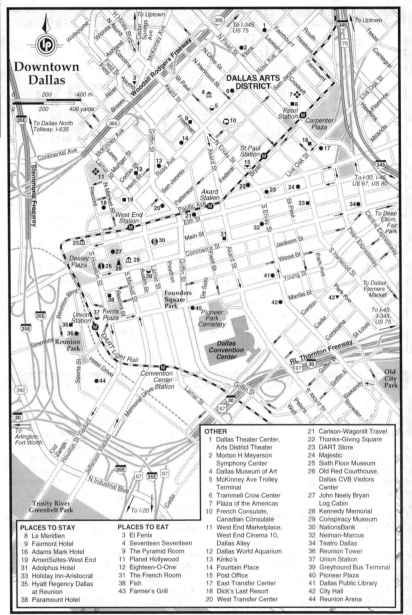

Downtown Dallas

OTHER

1 Dallas Theater Center, Arts District Theater
2 Morton H Meyerson Symphony Center
4 Dallas Museum of Art
5 McKinney Ave Trolley Terminal
6 Trammell Crow Center
7 Plaza of the Americas
10 French Consulate, Canadian Consulate
11 West End Marketplace, West End Cinema 10, Dallas Alley
12 Dallas World Aquarium
13 Kinko's
15 Post Office
17 East Transfer Center
18 Dick's Last Resort
20 West Transfer Center
21 Carlson-Wagonlit Travel
22 Thanks-Giving Square
23 DART Store
24 Majestic
25 Sixth Floor Museum
26 Old Red Courthouse, Dallas CVB Visitors Center
27 John Neely Bryan Log Cabin
28 Kennedy Memorial
29 Conspiracy Museum
30 NationsBank
32 Neiman-Marcus
34 Teatro Dallas
36 Reunion Tower
37 Union Station
39 Greyhound Bus Terminal
40 Pioneer Plaza
41 Dallas Public Library
42 City Hall
44 Reunion Arena

PLACES TO STAY

8 Le Meridien
9 Fairmont Hotel
16 Adams Mark Hotel
19 AmeriSuites-West End
33 Holiday Inn-Aristocrat
35 Hyatt Regency Dallas at Reunion
38 Paramount Hotel

PLACES TO EAT

3 El Fenix
4 Seventeen Seventeen
9 The Pyramid Room
11 Planet Hollywood
12 Eighteen-O-One
31 The French Room
38 Fish
43 Farmer's Grill

Kennedy Memorial
One block east of Dealey Plaza between Main and Commerce Sts, this plaza has as its centerpiece a cenotaph designed by noted US architect Philip Johnson. The monument's solid white walls nearly enclose a black slab of granite that bears only JFK's name.

John Neely Bryan Log Cabin
Across Main St from the Kennedy Memorial, this reconstruction of John Neely Bryan's cabin pays tribute to the city's founder. Nearby is a terrazzo map of early Dallas. The Old Red Courthouse, a handsome Romanesque building constructed in the early 1890s, stands just to the west at Main and S Houston Sts.

Conspiracy Museum
Polls have repeatedly shown that fewer than 15 percent of Americans believe Lee Harvey Oswald acted alone, which is why this maverick museum (☎ 214-741-3040), at 110 S Market St, stands as an intriguing companion to the Sixth Floor Museum. It posits that Kennedy's assassination was a coup d'état to shore up the military-industrial complex that had been gaining strength in the US since WWII, and that the same people and forces who killed Kennedy were later responsible for the deaths of Robert Kennedy, Martin Luther King Jr, Ted Kennedy's Chappaquiddick friend Mary Jo Kopechne (Kennedy himself was the real target) and, incredibly, the 269 people aboard Korean Airlines Flight 007, shot into the sea in 1983. The museum also delves into other assassinations from history, including those of Abraham Lincoln, James Garfield and William McKinley. Open daily 10 am to 6 pm; $7 for adults, $6 for seniors, $3 for children. Admission includes a 75-minute walking tour of the JFK assassination area Friday, Saturday, Sunday and by request on other days; the scheduled tours leave at 11 am, 1 pm and 3 pm.

ELSEWHERE DOWNTOWN
Reunion Tower
At 50 stories high with its three-level spherical top, Reunion Tower (☎ 214-651-1234) at the edge of Reunion Park off Reunion Blvd (DART Rail Union station), is among Dallas' most recognizable landmarks. The observation deck is open Sunday to Thursday 10 am to 10 pm, Friday and Saturday 9 am to midnight. Admission is $2 for adults, $1 for seniors and children.

West End Marketplace
Housed in the former Sunshine Biscuit Co factory in an area on downtown's northwest fringe called the West End, the West End Marketplace (☎ 214-748-4801), 603 Munger Ave at Market St (DART Rail West End station), includes specialty shops, a 10-screen movie theater, a food court, a miniature golf course, eight nightclubs (see Mega Clubs in the Entertainment section) and Planet Hollywood. It's all pretty standard stuff, although there are a few surprises, such as the Level IV Art Works, where visitors can watch artists at work. Open Monday through Thursday 11 am to 10 pm, Friday and Saturday 11 am to midnight, Sunday 11 am to 6 pm. Some businesses keep extended hours.

Dallas World Aquarium
We're not sure whether to call this aquarium (☎ 214-720-2224), 1801 N Griffin St (DART Rail West End station; the entrance is on Hord St), a rip-off or a revelation. On one hand, some of the world's most beautiful and unusual sea creatures are showcased here; this is among a handful of places outside their native habitats you can see such rarities as the moon jellyfish and leafy sea dragon. On the other, interpretation is minimal, and we left feeling more entertained than enlightened. The admission price – $11.85 for adults, $6.50 for seniors and children – might not seem wildly out of line until it's compared with admission at the unrelated Dallas Aquarium, at Fair Park. Open daily except Thanksgiving and Christmas 10 am to 5 pm.

Fountain Place
This parklike plaza, 1445 Ross Ave at Field St (DART Rail Akard station), features a half-million gallons of water flowing in streams and leaping from hundreds of fountains.

Architect IM Pei designed the angular Fountain Place 60-story office tower, above.

Dallas Museum of Art

This fine museum (☎ 214-922-1200), 1717 N Harwood St (DART Rail St Paul station), is divided into five sections: art of the Americas, of Africa, of Asia and the Pacific, and of Europe, and Contemporary Art. The collection's highlights include *Very Ugly*, by Frida Kahlo; *Sleepy Baby*, by Mary Cassat; *The Icebergs*, by Frederic Edwin Church; Monet's 1908 *Water Lilies* and more pieces by Piet Mondrian than any other US museum has. A special gallery re-creates the French Riviera villa of Wendy and Emery Reves, avid art patrons whose collection included works by van Gogh, Cézanne, Toulouse-Lautrec and Manet, as well as by Winston Churchill, a good friend of the couple; all are represented here. The villa was originally built in 1927 by the Duke of Westminster for Coco Chanel.

Free docent-led tours take place Tuesday to Friday at 1 pm, Saturday and Sunday at 2 pm. You'll find interactive Art Talk tours, live music and free admission to special exhibits Thursday evenings at 7 pm. The museum has a great gift shop and two restaurants. Open Tuesday, Wednesday and Friday 11 am to 4 pm, Thursday 11 am to 9 pm, Saturday and Sunday 11 am to 5 pm; closed New Year's Day, Thanksgiving and Christmas. Admission to special exhibits usually costs about $8 for adults, $6 for seniors and students; general museum admission is free.

Thanks-Giving Square

For all its din and drive, Dallas has a quieter side – a triangular piece of prime downtown real estate set aside for spiritual renewal and reflection. Surrounded by Bryan St, Pacific Ave and Ervay St, Thanks-Giving Square (☎ 214-651-1977; DART Rail Akard station) was established in the 1970s by the Thanks-Giving Foundation based on the idea that gratitude is a universal emotion. The ecumenical, nonprofit group describes Thanks-Giving Square as a 'place where people can use gratitude as a basis for dialogue, mutual understanding and healing.'

PLACES TO STAY
5 Days Inn Central
15 Melrose Hotel
22 Inn on Fairmount
23 Mansion on Turtle Creek
34 Stoneleigh Hotel
41 Hôtel St Germain
42 Hotel Crescent Court

PLACES TO EAT
1 Taj Express
4 Thai Taste
13 Eatzi's
18 Cosmic Cup
23 Mansion on Turtle Creek
26 Bread Winners
27 Primo's
31 Enigma
32 Dream Cafe, 8.0,
      Mediterraneo
37 Cedar Street
38 Hard Rock Cafe
39 Avanti
40 Old Warsaw
43 Sam's Cafe

BARS & CLUBS
3 Pegasus Pub
6 Moby Dick
7 Throckmorton Mining Co
8 JR's Bar & Grill
10 Village Station
11 Sue Ellen's
20 Jugs
21 Buddies II
33 Club Babalu
45 Velvet E

OTHER
2 Kinko's
9 Crossroads Market
      Bookstore
12 Java Jones
14 Dallas Theater Center,
      Kalita Humphreys Theater
16 Gay & Lesbian
      Community Center
17 Post Office
19 Kwik Wash
24 British Consulate,
      Thomas Cook
25 McKinney Ave Trolley
      Terminal
28 McKinney Avenue
      Contemporary
29 Infomart
30 Carlson-Wagonlit Travel
32 Quadrangle,
      Afterimage Gallery
35 The History Merchant
36 Dallas Institute of
      Humanities & Culture
44 Dollhouse Museum
      of the Southwest

Uptown Dallas

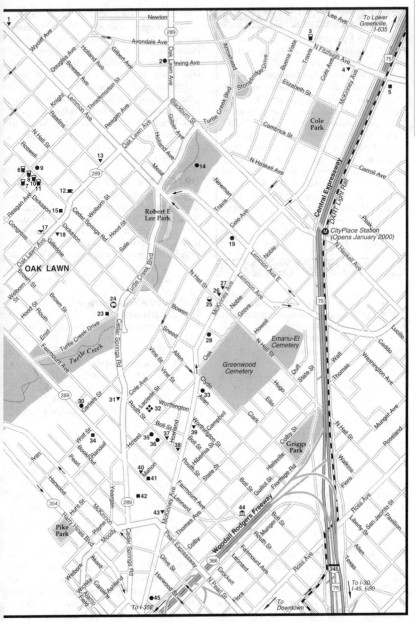

Dallas Arts District

The Dallas Museum of Art is one anchor of the Dallas Arts District, a 60-acre section of downtown dedicated to the fine and performing arts. Other landmarks include the dramatic IM Pei-designed Morton H Meyerson Symphony Center; the Trammell Crow Center, which has exhibition and performance spaces; and the Dallas Theater Center's Arts District Theater. Sometime early in the 21st century, the open space between the Dallas Museum of Art and the Meyerson Center will be transformed into a sculpture garden showcasing the world's greatest privately held sculpture collection, the Nasher Foundation collection; it will be the crowning touch on a district that puts Dallas in the big leagues among US art centers.

The center, designed by Philip Johnson, includes a meditation garden, an interdenominational Chapel of Thanksgiving topped by a 'Spiral of Life,' and a Hall of Thanksgiving – a kind of museum of gratitude. The buildings are open Monday to Friday 9 am to 5 pm, Saturday, Sunday and holidays 1 to 5 pm; admission is free, but donations are accepted.

Pioneer Plaza

At Young and Griffin Sts just north of the Dallas Convention Center, this plaza has as its showpiece a collection of bronze larger-than-life longhorns, amassed as if they were on a cattle drive. We're told by the visitors' bureau that they are the No 1 photo op in town and supposedly are the largest bronze monument in the world, but you don't need to go out of your way to find them.

Old City Park Museum

This museum of history and architecture on the western end of Old City Park (☎ 214-421-5141), 1717 Gano St on the south edge of downtown (bus Nos 2 or 3), shows what it was like to live in North Texas from about 1840 to 1910. The downtown skyline makes for a striking backdrop to the 37 buildings moved here from places around the state, including the 1886 Missouri, Kansas and Texas depot from Fate, a 1900 Queen Anne style home from Plano, a 1904 hotel from Carrollton and a circa 1890 doctor's office from the Oak Cliff section of Dallas. Volunteers demonstrate pioneer skills along the way. Open Tuesday to Saturday 10 am to 4 pm, Sunday noon to 4 pm; $6 for adults, $5 for seniors, $3 for children ages three to 12 (the family rate is $12).

UPTOWN DALLAS

Uptown, the catchall term for the neighborhoods immediately northeast of downtown, is a chic area that includes dozens of restaurants, shopping (mostly upscale) and opulent hotels. The McKinney Avenue Transit Authority serves Uptown with a trolley that travels regularly from downtown (see the Getting Around section).

Dollhouse Museum of the Southwest

In the Uptown area, this museum of historically authentic miniature houses (☎ 214-969-5502), 2208 Routh St (via the McKinney Ave trolley – see the Getting Around section), includes a 1900s New York City townhouse, a Texas farmhouse and a coastal Victorian home. Open Tuesday to Saturday 10 am to 4:30 pm, Sunday 1 to 4 pm; $4 for adults, $2 for seniors and children.

DEEP ELLUM

This renovated warehouse district just east of downtown and 'deep' up Elm St got its name from the Southern-drawl pronunciation of 'Elm.' It has long been Dallas' headquarters for live music – first the blues, now rock, jazz, alternative, Latin and country too. The district also has creative spots for dining and shopping. The Deep Ellum Association Visitor Center (☎ 214-748-4332, events line 214-747-3337, www.deepellumtx.com), 2932 Main St, has a helpful staff and stacks of brochures. Parking can be hard to find in the evenings – it's better to take a $2 or $3 cab ride from downtown. Bus Nos 3 and 29 serve

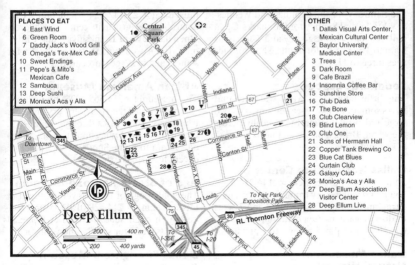

PLACES TO EAT
4 East Wind
6 Green Room
7 Daddy Jack's Wood Grill
8 Omega's Tex-Mex Cafe
10 Sweet Endings
11 Pepe's & Mito's Mexican Cafe
12 Sambuca
13 Deep Sushi
26 Monica's Aca y Alla

OTHER
1 Dallas Visual Arts Center, Mexican Cultural Center
2 Baylor University Medical Center
3 Trees
5 Dark Room
9 Cafe Brazil
14 Insomnia Coffee Bar
15 Sunshine Store
16 Club Dada
17 The Bone
18 Club Clearview
19 Blind Lemon
20 Club One
21 Sons of Hermann Hall
22 Copper Tank Brewing Co
23 Blue Cat Blues
24 Curtain Club
25 Galaxy Club
26 Monica's Aca y Alla
27 Deep Ellum Association Visitor Center
28 Deep Ellum Live

Deep Ellum, but they stop running before the clubs close. Catch either bus at the East Transfer Center, at Pearl and Live Oak Sts, or the Pearl DART Rail station.

FAIR PARK

Just east of Deep Ellum, Fair Park (☎ 214-670-8400), 1300 Robert B Cullum Blvd (bus Nos 11, 12 or 60 from the West Transfer Center, at Griffin St and Pacific Ave, or bus No 50 along Main St), was created in 1936, when Dallas hosted the Texas Centennial Exposition, a world's fair celebrating 100 years of the republic. The 277-acre park collects museums, open space and a few islands of green in a part of town that otherwise is rather unsavory. Fair Park is at its busiest during the annual three-week Texas State Fair, one of the largest in the US; it takes place in the park in September and October, and more than 3 million people attend. Fair Park is closed for two weeks before the fair starts.

Hall of State

Fair Park is full of superb 1930s art deco architecture, none of it quite as inspired as this tribute to all things Texan. The Hall of Heroes pays homage to such luminaries as

Stephen F Austin and Samuel Houston; the Great Hall of Texas features a great seal, 25 feet in diameter, and murals of Texas history from the 16th century on. Open Tuesday to Saturday 10 am to 5 pm, Sunday 1 to 5 pm; free except during special exhibits. The Dallas Historical Society (☎ 214-421-4500) has its offices and library here, too.

The Science Place

This hands-on museum (☎ 214-428-5555) bills itself as 'an amusement park for your brain.' Attractions include robotic dinosaurs, a medical gallery featuring a real brain and real beating heart, a planetarium and an IMAX theater. Museum hours are daily 9:30 am to 5:30 pm; call for the IMAX schedule. Admission is $6 for adults, $5 for seniors and kids ages three to 12.

Dallas Aquarium

Not as flashy as the Dallas World Aquarium downtown, this aquarium (☎ 214-670-8443) is a much better value for families and budget travelers. Get face-to-face with poison dart frogs, four-eyed fish, alligators, an electric eel and lots of other cool critters. Feeding time is 2:30 pm daily: Tuesday, Thursday and Saturday for the piranhas and Wednesday, Friday and Sunday for the sharks. Open daily except Thanksgiving and Christmas 9 am to 4:30 pm; $3 for adults, $1.50 for kids ages three to 11.

Leonhardt Lagoon
This little lake has a wavy walkway that looks something like a sea serpent, plus two large red orbs floating hypnotically across the water. Bring a picnic and nosh here between museums.

Dallas Horticulture Center
At the horticulture center (☎ 214-428-7476), you'll find a two-story tropical conservatory, a fragrance garden for the blind and 7 acres of display gardens. Open Tuesday to Saturday 10 am to 5 pm, Sunday 1 to 5 pm; free.

Dallas Museum of Natural History
In addition to the usual dioramas of natural habitats and cases of rocks and minerals, this museum (☎ 214-421-3466) includes City Safari, a hands-on activity center for children. Open daily except Thanksgiving and Christmas 10 am to 5 pm; $5 for adults, $3 for seniors and kids ages three to 18.

African American Museum
This museum (☎ 214-565-9026) has exhibits that richly detail the art and history of blacks from pre-slavery Africa through the present. Open Tuesday to Friday noon to 5 pm, Saturday 10 am to 5 pm, Sunday 1 to 5 pm; free except for special exhibits.

Age of Steam Railroad Museum
The golden age of train travel is relived at this museum (☎ 214-428-0101), open Wednesday through Sunday 10 am to 5 pm; $3 for adults, $1.50 for kids 12 and younger.

Dallas Firefighters Museum
Just outside the Fair Park gates, at 3801 Parry St, this museum (☎ 214-821-1500) displays a 1936 hook-and-ladder truck amid

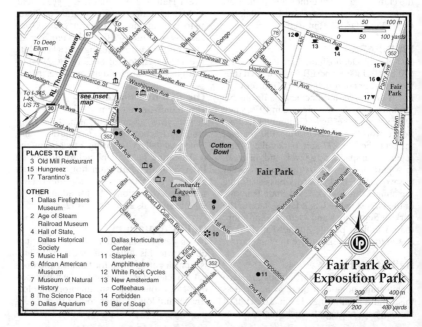

PLACES TO EAT
3 Old Mill Restaurant
15 Hungreez
17 Tarantino's

OTHER
1 Dallas Firefighters Museum
2 Age of Steam Railroad Museum
4 Hall of State, Dallas Historical Society
5 Music Hall
6 African American Museum
7 Museum of Natural History
8 The Science Place
9 Dallas Aquarium
10 Dallas Horticulture Center
11 Starplex Amphitheatre
12 White Rock Cycles
13 New Amsterdam Coffeehaus
14 Forbidden
16 Bar of Soap

Fair Park & Exposition Park

other vintage fire-fighting equipment. Open Wednesday to Saturday 9 am to 4 pm; free.

ELSEWHERE IN DALLAS
Dallas Arboretum & Botanical Gardens

On the shore of White Rock Lake, the arboretum (☎ 214-327-8263), 8617 Garland Rd (bus No 60), showcases more than 5000 varieties of plants. Many grow in theme gardens such as the Fern Dell, the Hidden Garden and the Woman's Garden. Admission includes entrance to the historic DeGolyer House, a gorgeous Spanish colonial revival mansion. Open daily 10 am to 6 pm from March to October, 10 am to 5 pm from November to February; closed New Year's Day, Thanksgiving and Christmas; $6 for adults, $5 for seniors, $3 for kids ages six to 12.

Dallas Zoo

It's not in the same league as the Fort Worth Zoo, but the Dallas Zoo (☎ 214-670-5656), 621 E Clarendon Drive 3 miles south of downtown off the I-35 Marsalis exit (DART Rail red line, Dallas Zoo station), is better than most. Highlights include the Wilds of Africa natural habitats, which can be seen from a nature trail or a 20-minute monorail ride ($1.50 extra); a children's zoo; rain forest aviary; and a reptile discovery center. Open daily except Christmas 9 am to 5 pm; $6 for adults, $4 for seniors, $3 for kids ages three to 11.

Biblical Arts Center

This nondenominational art museum (☎ 214-691-4661), 7500 Park Lane across from NorthPark shopping center (DART Rail red line, Park Lane Station), has as its centerpiece *Miracle at Pentecost*, a mural that depicts the birth of Christianity. More than 200 biblical characters nearly come to life during the light-and-sound show presented every half-hour. Open Tuesday to Saturday 10 am to 5 pm, Sunday 1 to 5 pm; closed New Year's Day, Thanksgiving, Christmas Eve and Christmas Day. Admission to the galleries is free; the *Miracle at Pentecost* presentation costs $4 for adults, $3 for seniors, $2 for children ages six to 12.

Dallas Memorial Center for Holocaust Studies

Photographs, artifacts, films and documents of the Holocaust are preserved on the lower level of the Jewish Community Center (☎ 214-750-4654), 7900 Northaven Rd (bus No 567). Open Monday to Friday 9:30 am to 4:30 pm (Thursday till 9 pm from September to May), Sunday noon to 4 pm; closed on Saturday, Jewish holidays and most national holidays; free.

Frontiers of Flight Museum

In the Love Field terminal, this museum (☎ 214-350-1651) traces the history of aviation from the Wright Brothers to the space shuttle. Artifacts include the radioman's chair from the ill-fated *Hindenburg*. Open Monday to Saturday 10 am to 5 pm, Sunday 1 to 5 pm; closed New Year's Day, Thanksgiving and Christmas; $2 for adults, $1 for children ages two to 12.

Children's Medical Center Model Train

The largest permanent model train exhibit in the US is in the lobby of Children's Medical Center (☎ 214-920-2000), 1935 Motor St near Parkland Hospital (DART Rail Trinity Railway Express Medical-Market Center station). Eight trains run over more than 1000 feet of track, winding past such US landmarks as Mount Rushmore, the Grand Canyon and the Dallas skyline. Free.

ACTIVITIES

Dallas has more than 50,000 acres of public parks. The biggest and most popular surrounds White Rock Lake, northeast of downtown. Other top recreational venues include Bachman Lake just northwest of Love Field and the greenbelt along Turtle Creek Blvd in the Uptown and Highland Park areas. For information, call Dallas Parks and Recreation at ☎ 214-670-4100.

Biking & Hiking

The longest trail in Dallas is the 11-mile circuit around White Rock Lake, which can be lengthened via the 7.5-mile path leading northwest along White Rock Creek. A 3-mile

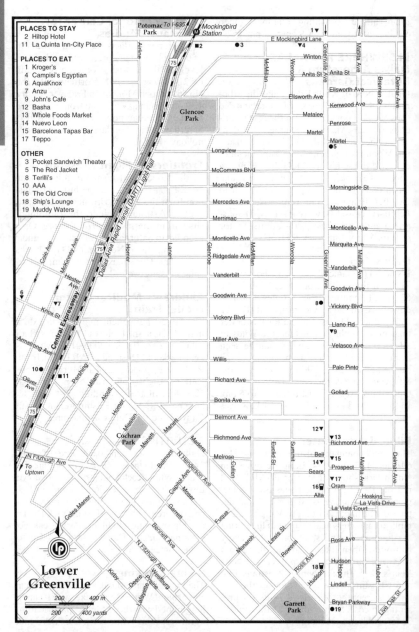

PLACES TO STAY
2 Hiltop Hotel
11 La Quinta Inn-City Place

PLACES TO EAT
1 Kroger's
4 Campisi's Egyptian
6 AquaKnox
7 Anzu
9 John's Cafe
12 Basha
13 Whole Foods Market
14 Nuevo Leon
15 Barcelona Tapas Bar
17 Teppo

OTHER
3 Pocket Sandwich Theater
5 The Red Jacket
8 Terilli's
10 AAA
16 The Old Crow
18 Ship's Lounge
19 Muddy Waters

Lower Greenville

0   200   400 m
0   200   400 yards

trail circles Bachman Lake. Jack Johnston Bicycles (☎ 214-328-5238), 9005 Garland Rd near White Rock Lake, rents bikes for $7 an hour, $25 a day and $73 a week.

In-Line Skating

Fair Park is a favorite in-line skating spot. Rent blades nearby at White Rock Cycles (☎ 214-824-5454), 731 Exposition Ave, for $6 an hour or $10 a day. It's open Monday, Thursday and Friday from 1 to 7 pm, Saturday and Sunday 2 to 7 pm, closed Tuesday and Wednesday.

Golf

Tenison Golf Courses (☎ 214-670-1402), 3501 Samuell Blvd at Samuell-Grand Park (bus No 60 or 11-Skyline), has two 18-hole links. Play one or both for $14 Monday to Friday, $17 Saturday and Sunday.

Drag Racing

At the Malibu Speed Zone (☎ 972-247-7223), 11130 Malibu Drive off the Stemmons Freeway, you'll find go-carts on steroids: 300-horsepower dragsters and built-to-scale Indy cars. OK, so you have to run them on rails, but at least you won't risk killing yourself.

ORGANIZED TOURS
Coach Tours

Kerrville Bus/Gray Line/Coach USA (☎ 214-630-1000) has tours visiting top Dallas and Fort Worth attractions; call for tour descriptions and information. Longhorn Tours (☎ 972-228-4571) also offers Dallas tours.

Offbeat Tours

The hour-long JFK Presidential Limo Tour (☎ 214-348-7777) leaves daily by reservation from in front of the Conspiracy Museum (or from anywhere else in downtown Dallas by prior arrangement). Founder and avid assassination maven Paul Crute takes passengers along the motorcade route used by President Kennedy in November 1963, complete with gunfire sounds and other audio effects. The tour costs $25 per person. The limo is also available for hire for nights on the town in Dallas.

PLACES TO STAY

One of the world's largest convention cities, Dallas has more than 43,000 hotel rooms – but just try to find one both in a prime location and less than $75 a night. The best areas to stay are downtown and Uptown, but they are also among the most expensive. The next best would be any area served by DART Rail. New stations are opening all the time, so when you make reservations, ask if your motel is near a DART Rail stop (see the Getting Around section for more information on DART).

Camping

The biggest area campground, *Cedar Hill State Park* (☎ 972-291-3900, reservations 512-389-8900), southwest of Dallas on FM 1382 (see the Metroplex map), has 355 campsites with water and electricity. The cost is $15 for a waterfront site on Joe Pool Lake, $12 for a site not on the lake, and a $5 park admission fee for each person age 13 or older. The park also has 20 primitive walk-in campsites priced at $7, but none are on the lake.

In the same area, the *Dallas Hi-Ho Campground* (☎ 972-223-4834), 200 W Bear Creek Rd in Glenn Heights, has full hookups for $20 and tent sites for $14.

Aside from a few residential mobile-home parks that occasionally take in travelers, folks with RVs need to head past the city limits. If you plan to visit Six Flags or Fort Worth, a good choice would be *Trader's Village RV Park* (☎ 972-647-8205), 2602 Mayfield Rd, Grand Prairie (see the Metroplex map), where full hookups cost $17 for back-in sites and $21 for pull-throughs.

Hostels

For many years, Dallas was the largest US city without an HI/AYH hostel. HI/AYH's North Texas Council hopes to eventually establish a local hostel. For an update on their progress, contact the HI North Texas Council (☎ 214-350-4294, hintex@juno.com).

Motels & Hotels

Budget It's close to impossible to get a clean, safe double in Dallas for less than $30. The *Eastern Hills Motor Hotel* (☎ 214-824-1633),

3422 Samuell Blvd, has run-down, ill-kept rooms for $33/35 a single/double. *Paradise Inn* (☎ 214-748-3939), 1736 Fort Worth Ave, is a better bet, with rates of $28/35 for acceptably clean rooms with TVs and phones. The *Welcome Inn* (☎ 214-826-3510), 3245 Merrifield Ave, has friendly management and no-frills rooms just off I-30 for $35/40.

There are 19 Motel 6 locations in the Metroplex. Rates at most are about $39/45 Memorial Day through Labor Day, $30/36 the rest of the year. Not exactly bargain-basement prices, but at least you'll know what you're getting. None is well located for exploring central Dallas, but *Motel 6-Grand Prairie* (☎ 972-642-9424, fax 972-262-3482), 406 E Safari Blvd, is a pretty good location between Dallas and Arlington. *Motel 6-Irving* (☎ 972-438-4227, fax 972-554-0048), at 510 S Loop 12, is reasonably convenient to either DFW or Love Field airports.

Most hotels with rooms for $40 to $60 are well out of central Dallas, but there is one exception: if you arrive on Greyhound, you can get a $49 room by showing your bus ticket at the *Paramount Hotel* (see the Mid-Range section), smack-dab downtown.

Days Inn, Sleep Inn and Red Roof Inn are all good budget bets. *Days Inn Central* (☎ 214-827-6080, fax 214-827-0208), Uptown at 4150 N Central Expressway, has rates starting at $50/60 a single/double. *Days Inn-Texas Stadium* (☎ 972-438-6666, fax 972-579-4902), 2200 E Airport Freeway (see the Metroplex map), is a good deal, with rooms at $38/45, although the rates go up on weekends when the Cowboys are in town and during other special events. *Sleep Inn* (☎ 214-341-0248), 10921 Estate Lane, is inconveniently located in northeast Dallas off the LBJ Freeway, but its rates of $45/50 are reasonable. The *Red Roof Inn-DFW North* (☎ 972-929-0020), 8150 Esters Blvd off the LBJ Freeway, has rooms for $46/60; the *Red Roof Inn-Market Center* (☎ 214-638-5151, fax 214-638-3920), 1550 Empire Central Drive, is closer to Love Field than to the Market Center; rooms are $50/58.

Classic Motor Inn (☎ 214-631-6633, 800-662-7437, fax 214-631-6616), 9229 Carpenter Freeway at Regal Row, is a mom-and-pop operation with rates of $45/55. The *Ramada Inn-DFW South* (☎ 972-399-2005, fax 972-986-7620), 4110 W Airport Freeway, has rooms for $68.

The *Hiltop Hotel* (☎ 214-826-9434), 5600 N Central Expressway (see the Lower Greenville map), is a former Hilton about a two-minute stroll from the Mockingbird DART Rail station. Rates are $50/60, although management will lower the rates in certain instances; for example, the day we dropped by the rate for a double had been knocked down to $49 because the phones weren't working.

Mid-Range Most choices in the $60 to $100 bracket are still a ways from downtown, with a few exceptions. *La Quinta Inn-City Place* (☎ 214-821-4220), 4440 N Central Expressway (see Lower Greenville map), has summer rates starting at $63, a bit lower the rest of the year. *Terra Cotta Inn* (☎ 972-387-2525, 800-533-3591, fax 972-387-3784), 6101 LBJ Freeway at Preston Rd in North Dallas, is like an overgrown bed-and-breakfast; rates are $65/75 a single/double. Rooms at the *Fairfield Inn Regal Row* (☎ 214-638-6100, fax 214-905-1963), 1575 Regal Row just off the Stemmons Freeway, are $69.

The hands-down champ in the mid-range category is the *Paramount Hotel* (☎ 214-761-9090, fax 214-761-0740), 302 S Houston St, within a few blocks of the JFK sites, Reunion Park and the West End Marketplace. Its comfortable, urbane rooms have good views, plenty of natural light and eclectic decor. The friendly staff seems perfectly suited to the hotel's well-traveled but value-conscious clientele. Best of all, the rates are downtown's most reasonable: Monday to Thursday they are $69/79 a single/double; Friday to Sunday they drop to $59/69. Junior suites, with a microwave, fridge, sitting area and two TVs, are available for $99/109 on weekdays, $79/89 on weekends.

Ramada Limited Park Cities Inn (☎ 214-521-0330, fax 214-521-0336), 6101 Hillcrest Ave, is across the street from Southern Methodist University in a lively neighborhood full of restaurants and shopping.

The Spiral of Life in the Chapel of Thanksgiving, Dallas

JOHN ELK III

Randy Duke at the Wichita Falls Railroad Museum

JULIE FANSELOW

Choosing chilis at the Dallas Farmers Market

JOHN ELK III

Misión San Antonio de Valero, better known as the Alamo

Butler Park, Austin

Festive wares at El Mercado in San Antonio

Spanish Governor's Palace, San Antonio

Downtown architecture, Austin

Cruising the San Antonio River while café patrons gaze from Riverwalk

Hikers at Brazos Bend State Park, outside Houston

Evening view of Houston's downtown skyline

Rooms start at $70, single or double. *Best Western Market Center* (☎ 214-741-9000, fax 214-741-6100), 2023 Market Center Blvd, is a moderately priced option – $79/89 – among upscale neighbors. *Radisson Hotel Central Dallas* (☎ 214-750-6060, fax 214-750-5959), 6060 N Central Expressway, is within walking distance of DART Rail's Mockingbird station; rooms cost $85. The huge *Adams Mark Hotel* (☎ 214-922-8000, fax 214-969-7650), 400 N Olive St at Live Oak St, has rooms for $99 on weekdays, $79 on weekends.

Holiday Inn Select (☎ 214-357-8500, fax 214-366-2670), 1241 W Mockingbird Lane, has rooms for $100, and its shuttle will take guests to Love Field or anywhere else within a 3-mile radius of the hotel, including the DART Rail Mockingbird station.

Top End Dallas has plenty of choices in the $100-plus category, some of them world class. As you'd expect, the high-end spots are concentrated downtown and Uptown. Rates during the week range from pricey to stratospheric, but special weekend rates put some places within reach of the mid-range budget.

Le Meridien (☎ 214-979-9000, fax 214-953-1931), 650 N Pearl St in the Plaza of the Americas shopping mall, has a lot going for it: a downtown location, large rooms and a fitness club (but no pool); rates start at $109 to $129 on weekdays, about $10 less on weekends. *AmeriSuites-West End* (☎ 214-999-0500, fax 214-999-0501), 1907 Lamar St in the West End, is the newest downtown hotel. Rooms run $139 to $159 on weekdays but can drop to about $99 on weekends. The *Holiday Inn-Aristocrat* (☎ 214-741-7700, fax 214-939-3639), 1933 Main St in the heart of downtown, is a historic hotel with a European charm that belies its chain affiliation; rates are $139 to $189 on weekdays, about $99 to $109 on weekends.

With 1620 rooms, the *Wyndham Anatole Hotel* (☎ 214-748-1200, fax 214-761-7520), 2201 Stemmons Freeway, is among the largest hotels in the US. It's a fabulous place, with shops and restaurants, peacocks strolling the grounds and guests playing croquet between trips to the trade shows. Rooms

start at $149 and climb into the $250 range on weekdays, but on weekends you can keep a straight face while asking for a $99 rate.

Fitness buffs may be interested in the *Guest Lodge at the Cooper Aerobics Center* (☎ 972-386-0306, 800-444-5187, fax 972-386-5415), 12230 Preston Rd. The self-described 'healthiest hotel in Dallas' caters to people participating in four, seven and 13-day live-in wellness programs developed by fitness guru Kenneth H Cooper, but anyone is welcome to stay here. Rooms are $125/135, and the rates include use of the tennis and racquetball courts, indoor and outdoor jogging tracks and plenty of fitness machines. An on-site restaurant specializes in healthful meals.

In the Uptown area, the restored historic *Stoneleigh Hotel* (☎ 214-871-7111, 800-255-9299, fax 214-871-9379), 2927 Maple Ave, supposedly has a big celebrity clientele. The rooms are spacious and charming, with old-style bath fixtures. They start at $170 on weekdays, but on weekends they can run as low as $109/119. There are several restaurants, including a sushi bar, on the premises.

The *Adolphus Hotel* (☎ 214-742-8200, 800-221-9083, fax 214-651-3588), 1321 Commerce St downtown, is rich and refined – the epitome of old Dallas. Rates here seem to change daily, depending on what conventions are in town: they can be anywhere from $135/185 to $245. The *Fairmont Hotel* (☎ 214-720-2020, fax 214-720-5269), 1717 N Akard St between the West End and the Arts District, is another grand old hotel that has been nicely updated over the years. Weekday rates are $189/209; weekend rates are about half that.

The *Hyatt Regency Dallas at Reunion* (☎ 214-651-1234, fax 214-742-8126), 300 Reunion Blvd, is a 939-room high-rise hotel next to Reunion Tower. Amenities include an outdoor pool and tennis and basketball courts; rates are $195/210 on weekdays, about $125 on weekends.

Uptown, the *Melrose Hotel* (☎ 214-521-5151, 800-635-7673, fax 214-521-2470), 3015 Oak Lawn Ave at Cedar Springs Rd, has oversize rooms, each with its own decor; rates start at $205 on weekdays, $119 on weekends. The ***Hotel Crescent Court*** (*☎ 214-871-3200, fax 214-871-3272)*, 400 Crescent Court between Cedar Springs Rd and McKinney Ave, is a newer hotel that is part of the upscale Crescent retail complex in the heart of Uptown. The least expensive rooms are $280 on weekdays, $195 on weekends.

And finally, we have Dallas' most renowned hotel, the ***Mansion on Turtle Creek*** (*☎ 214-559-2100, 800-527-5432, fax 214-528-4187)*, 2821 Turtle Creek Blvd at Gillespie Ave. The Mansion is usually ranked among the top 10 in the US, and its service is unimpeachable, with at least two staff members per guest. Ground-floor rooms open onto a private enclosed patio or the pool; rooms on the higher floors have balconies. Amenities in all rooms include a safe, fax machine, stereo with CD player and a generous selection of local and travel magazines. Standard room rates run from $320 to $425 on weekdays, $225 to $325 on weekends, according to availability. If money is truly no object, the suites cost $600 to $1750.

B&Bs

In the Uptown area, the ***Inn on Fairmount*** (*☎ 214-522-2800, fax 214-522-2898)*, 3701 Fairmount Ave, is a gay-owned but friendly-to-all B&B less than a block from the heart of the Oak Lawn district. Each of the seven rooms has a private bath, telephone and TV; plus, there's an outdoor deck with hot tub. Rooms range from $90 to $130, including a breakfast of juices, fruit and pastries.

Near White Rock Lake Park, the ***Courtyard on the Trail Bed & Breakfast*** (*☎ 214-553-9700, fax 214-553-9700)*, 8045 Forest Trail, is run by licensed massage therapist Alan Kagan. There are just three guest rooms, each with a private bath, and an outdoor pool. Rates are $105 to $160, including breakfast and other refreshments.

Although its name is ***Hôtel St Germain*** (*☎ 214-871-2516, fax 214-871-0740)*, 2516 Maple Ave, and it's often mentioned in the same breath as the Mansion on Turtle Creek, this European-style Uptown country inn has just seven rooms, each luxuriously furnished with a canopied feather bed, stereo, minibar, TV and VCR. A concierge is

on duty round the clock. Rates are $265 to $650, including a continental breakfast featuring freshly baked French pastries.

For other B&B accommodations, contact Bed & Breakfast Texas Style (*☎ 972-298-8596, fax 972-298-7118)*, a reservation service for 10 B&Bs in the Metroplex and 120 statewide. For a directory write to 4224 W Red Bird Lane, Dallas, TX 75237.

PLACES TO EAT

With about 5000 restaurants, Dallas has plenty for every taste and budget, from less-than-$5 barbecue sandwiches at Sonny Bryan's to take-out-a-home-equity-loan feasts at the French Room or the Mansion on Turtle Creek. The highest concentrations of sought-after restaurants are in the Lower Greenville area south of Mockingbird Lane, the Uptown area (especially along McKinney Ave) and in Deep Ellum.

American

John's Cafe (*☎ 214-827-4610)*, 2724 Greenville Ave in Lower Greenville, has basic food at hard-to-beat prices: $3.25 at breakfast for two eggs, meat, hash browns and toast or $6.25 at lunch for a rib-eye steak with potatoes, salad and Texas toast.

In the Uptown district, the ***Hard Rock Cafe*** (*☎ 214-855-0007)*, 2601 McKinney Ave, has meals from $6 to $13, including a Tennessee pulled-pork sandwich ($8). The other theme eatery, ***Planet Hollywood*** (*☎ 214-749-7827)*, 603 Munger Ave in the West End Marketplace, has a broad menu featuring such fun food as Cap'n Crunch-coated chicken strips ($6.50), burgers ($7.75 to $8.50), gourmet pizzas ($9.50 to $10.50) and for dessert, fruit fajitas ($7).

Asian

Thai Taste (*☎ 214-521-3513)*, 3101 N Fitzhugh Ave at McKinney Ave, is an Uptown favorite for its spicy treatments of such Texas favorites as catfish ($15). Farther north, at 4620 McKinney Ave (see the Lower Greenville map), ***Anzu*** (*☎ 214-526-7398)* has nouvelle 'Pacific Rim' cuisine such as red-curry shrimp stew or sake-simmered salmon (each $17).

In Deep Ellum, **Deep Sushi** (☎ 214-651-1177), 2624 Elm St, specializes in beautifully presented rolled sushi ($4 to $10). The Japanese Lunch Box combo features shrimp tempura, sushi, soba noodles and beef or chicken teriyaki for $12.50. Also in Deep Ellum, **East Wind** (☎ 214-745-5554), 2711 Elm St, serves well-prepared Vietnamese food amid a peaceful green decor (which momentarily led us to confuse it with the Green Room, two doors down; see the Eclectic section). Ask for a table facing Elm St.

Open daily for dinner and weekdays for lunch, with entrées ranging from $10 to $15, **Teppo** (☎ 214-826-8989), 2014 Greenville Ave, is getting raves for its blend of sushi and grilled yakitori dishes.

Bakeries & Delis
Bread Winners (☎ 214-754-4940), 3301 McKinney Ave Uptown, has one of the best Sunday brunches in town, along with a late-risers' breakfast menu served until 4 pm all week. Try the Normandy French toast, made from grilled sourdough bread stuffed with cream cheese and raspberry preserves ($7), or the San Antonio tacos, filled with cheddar, scrambled eggs and black beans, with salsa, sour cream and brunch potatoes on the side ($7). The extensive menu includes plenty of lunch and dinner goodies, too.

Hungreez (☎ 214-823-8677), 841 Exposition Ave, is a good place to grab a picnic for a day at Fair Park. Ample sandwiches cost $4 to $6, and they have a good selection of portable side dishes: fruit salad, cookies, chips and the like.

For late-night munchies on the weekends, look to **Sweet Endings** (☎ 214-747-8001), 2901 Elm St in Deep Ellum, where carrot cake ($4) is a favorite. Open till 1 am Friday and Saturday, till 10 pm Sunday through Thursday.

Barbecue
Sonny Bryan's Smokehouse now has locations all over the Metroplex, but real barbecue buffs make it a point to visit the original, 2202 Inwood Rd near Harry Hines Blvd (☎ 214-357-7120). It's open daily for lunch only. Indoors, two rows of school desks face each other; outdoor seating is available, too.

Beef on a bun costs $4; a full plate of beef, ham, ribs or sausage goes for $6.25.

Peggy Sue BBQ (☎ 214-987-9188), 6600 Snider Plaza near SMU, is one barbecue joint where you can either dig into a plate of ribs ($7.50 to $9.50) or opt for the salad bar ($3.25). The pulled-pork sandwiches ($5.25) are excellent.

Continental
For drop-dead opulence with prices to match, you can't beat the **French Room** (☎ 214-742-8200), 1321 Commerce St downtown in the Adolphus Hotel. Gilt-tinged arches, marble columns and ornately painted ceilings set the scene for the cuisine, which is updated traditional French. A chef's tasting menu is available. One evening it started with Long Island duck sausage with goat cheese polenta and sweet caramelized onions, moved on to Canadian pike fillet with crisp potato, capers and a French pistachio oil, then to a honey-orange and poppy-seed sorbet; next came Amish chicken breast with tomato preserves and a roasted portabella gayette with a thyme reduction, and for dessert there was flourless carrot cake with white-chocolate ice cream and spring berries. That particular meal was $65 per person; building your own meal from the full menu costs $45 for two courses, $55 for three and $65 for four, with wine additional.

The **Pyramid Room** (☎ 214-720-5249), 1717 N Akard St in the Fairmont Hotel, rivals the French Room for atmosphere, service and splendid French food, including a prix fixe dinner for $45, which when we were there included crab cakes with mango chutney, lobster bisque with brandy and breast of maple-leaf duck with kumquat sauce on walnut wild rice.

In business for nearly half a century, **Old Warsaw** (☎ 214-528-0032), 2610 Maple Ave Uptown, is another top-tier choice. Its specialties include chateaubriand and rack of lamb. Either of those costs $56 for two people; other entrées cost $21 to $27.

Italian & Mediterranean
Avanti (☎ 214-871-4955), Uptown at 2720 McKinney Ave, specializes in Northern

Italian veal and seafood for lunch ($7 to $10) and dinner ($11 to $23). Late-night revelers take note: Avanti serves a Moonlight Breakfast from midnight to 4 am on Thursday, Friday and Saturday.

It's not the best, but few Dallas restaurants are as famous as *Campisi's Egyptian* (☎ 214-827-0355), 5610 E Mockingbird Lane (see Lower Greenville map). One conspiracy theory maintains that Jack Ruby and Lee Harvey Oswald ate here together the night before Kennedy was killed. Square pizza is the big draw.

Basha (☎ 214-824-7794), 2217 Greenville Ave, features memorable Mediterranean fare in a serene atmosphere. Choose from the menu with main dishes starting at $10.50 or enjoy the prix fixe meals served in an indoor tent for $20 Wednesday and Thursday, $25 Friday and Saturday.

Mediterraneo (☎ 214-979-0002), 2800 Routh St in the Quadrangle retail-and-restaurants complex, is among the latest offerings from the same restaurateurs who brought Dallas the original Mediterraneo (on Preston Road), Toscano and Riviera – three of the city's most creative Italian restaurants. Among its signature dishes: halibut with horseradish-crabmeat crust ($21). *Sambuca* (☎ 214-744-0820), 2618 Elm St in Deep Ellum, has live jazz nightly and good Mediterranean food. Dinner selections include herbed gnocchi with forest mushrooms and pecorino Romano ($13) and fennel-crusted pork medallions ($17). Lunch entrées run from $7 to $14.

Down-Home & Southern

Celebration (☎ 214-351-5681), 4503 W Lovers Lane, is a favorite among Dallasites, with home-style meals that include vegetables, soup and even seconds on the main dish. Choices include meat loaf ($9), fried catfish ($10) and pot roast ($11.50); the prices are a few dollars lower at lunch. Finish your meal off with homemade cobbler ($1.75 for a small, $2.75 for a large). Similar but less expensive, *Mama's Daughters' Diner* (☎ 214-948-6200) has several locations, including the Wynnewood Village shopping center at W Illinois Ave and Zang Blvd southeast of

downtown. The lunch plate special ($6) includes meat and three vegetables.

When SMU students get homesick or heartbroken, they head for *Bubba's* (☎ 214-373-6527), 6617 Hillcrest Ave, where $6.50 buys a plate of fried chicken and veggies. The cobbler ($1.35) helps the hurt go away, too.

Old Mill Restaurant (☎ 214-426-4600), the only year-round restaurant within Fair Park, has lunch selections such as homemade tuna salad with seasonal fruit and mini muffins ($7) or meat loaf with applesauce, navy beans and okra ($6). They also serve dinner in summer when the musicals are on.

The *Farmer's Grill* (☎ 214-741-9361), 807 Park Ave a few blocks from the Dallas Farmers Market, is a longtime local favorite, with good, cheap food; try the homemade bean soup ($3). Service can be slow, so pick up a newspaper on your way in.

Eclectic

There's only one rule at the postmodern, come-as-you-are *Green Room* (☎ 214-748-7666), 2715 Elm St: everything's got to be great. Billing its fare as 'alternative cuisine,' this Deep Ellum restaurant offers a 'Feed Me' twist on the prix fixe dinner. For $36 ($58 with wine), chef Marc Cassel will prepare a four-course mystery meal drawing from the menu and the day's market specials. Beef tenderloin ringed with sun-dried tomato grits encircled by a black-eyed pea mole ($13). It was Nirvana – as was the music played in the dining room, along with Beck, Sarah McLachlan and occasional blasts of surf punk from the kitchen.

The aptly named *Enigma* (☎ 214-999-0666), Uptown at 3005 Routh St at Cedar Springs Rd, is perhaps the most unusual restaurant in Dallas. It has no sign, it does not advertise, and it seats only a few dozen people. Everyone gets a different menu, and everything is fresh. Most memorable, however, are the place settings – no two are alike, and all are works of art by such top names as Baccarat, Erte, Fabergé and Paloma Picasso. As for the food, bring your sense of adventure and your wallet. The menus change constantly, but you may see such rarities as

Scottish partridge ($35), alligator sirloin ($35) and buffalo tenderloin ($50).

An Austin transplant just northwest of the Hard Rock Cafe, *Cedar Street* (☎ *214-871-2232*), 2708 Routh St, is a gin joint with live jazz and blues, martinis and hand-rolled cigars, but the food is what will win you over. Entrées include steaks ($20 for the rib eye), build-your-own pastas ($8 to $10) and a seafood bar with such treats as Shiner Bock-poached clams ($10). For dessert, Cedar Street Blues ($7) is a tasty uptown twist on blueberry cobbler, with white and dark chocolate shavings, 'perle de brillet' cream and candied pecans.

Farther northwest on Routh St, the Quadrangle presents several more interesting options. *Dream Cafe* (☎ *214-954-0486*), is a family-friendly, indoor-outdoor spot popular with locals. The art-filled *8.0* (☎ *214-979-0880*) is a hip bar by night and a moody restaurant by day. Both places have moderate prices and two of the best Sunday brunches in town.

Eighteen-O-One (☎ *214-720-2224*) in the Dallas World Aquarium, 1801 N Griffin St, is a tiny, glass-walled restaurant serving food from the same locales represented in the aquarium's exhibits: Indonesian nasi goreng (fried rice) of the day ($8), Australian bacon and egg pie ($7), British Columbian grilled salmon ($11.50).

Seventeen Seventeen (☎ *214-880-0158*) in the Dallas Museum of Art, overlooks the museum's plaza entrance at Ross Ave and Harwood St, and it's a real find. The menu changes frequently but has included a Tecate black-bean soup ($5) and Tabasco-rubbed lamb chops with Cajun-skillet potatoes ($31). The Sunday brunch is grand (at $27.50, it had better be) and features many of the restaurant's signature dishes. One end of the dining room features the window panels Frank Lloyd Wright designed for the Francis Little House in Wayzata, Minnesota, in 1912.

Vegetarian & Indian

Cosmic Cup (☎ *214-521-6157*), Uptown at 2912 Oak Lawn Ave, has delicious, creative vegetarian fare at good prices; nothing on the menu tops $7. *Taj Express* (☎ *214-528-0200*), 4436 Lemmon Ave, is a great place for tasty, inexpensive Indian food.

Kalachandji's (☎ *214-821-1048*), 5430 Gurley Ave, serves buffet-style meals with Indian food and other international cuisines at lunch ($5 to $7) and dinner ($6 to $10). All meals include soup, homemade bread, dessert and tamarind tea.

Mexican, Tex-Mex & Southwestern

Our favorite Tex-Mex restaurant is *Omega's Tex-Mex Cafe* (☎ *214-744-6842*), a family-run spot tucked away in Deep Ellum at 212 N Crowdus Ave. By day Omega's serves quick, tasty fare to nearby Baylor Medical Center employees (killer shrimp and spinach quesadillas are $7), but at night the place transforms into a pre- or postclub noshing spot – and with the rooftop seating, a dead-on view of downtown and lovingly prepared food (most dinners cost $9.25 to $12), it's a must. Other good Deep Ellum choices are *Monica's Aca y Alla* (☎ *214-748-7140*), 2914 Main St, which has lunch and dinner daily except Monday, and *Pepe's & Mito's Mexican Cafe* (☎ *214-741-1901*), 2935 Elm St.

Nuevo Leon (☎ *214-887-8148*), 2013 Greenville Ave, is an upscale 'Mex-Mex' eatery with such choices as mole verde ($6 at lunch, $8 at dinner) and filete patrón, a beef fillet served with a sauce of wine-marinated guajillo peppers ($13.95).

Eat at *Primo's* (☎ *214-220-0510*), 3309 McKinney Ave Uptown, and you won't be hungry for the rest of the day. The botanas platter ($8.50) includes nachos, flautas, quesadillas, tacos, stuffed jalapeños, guacamole and sour cream. For a late breakfast (they're not open until 11 am), try migas ($6.50) – a mix of scrambled eggs, peppers, onions and cheese.

Dallas is the home of *Chili's Grill and Bar*, probably the most widespread southwestern sit-down chain in the US, with inexpensive fajitas, burgers and of course chili. The chain has about 20 Metroplex locations; the one at 3230 Knox St (☎ *214-520-1555*) is among the most convenient.

El Fenix, a Tex-Mex eatery best known for its Wednesday $4 enchilada specials, also has locations all over the Metroplex and beyond, including downtown at 1601 McKinney Ave at Field St (☎ *214-747-1121*).

Upscale Southwestern This may be the city's culinary strong suit; it's certainly Dallas' claim to fame. If you can get a table, the *Mansion on Turtle Creek* (☎ *214-526-2121*), 2821 Turtle Creek Blvd, will reward you with some of the most memorable food you'll find anywhere. At dinner, starters ($10 to $22) include quail mopped with barbecue sauce and chicken-fried rabbit with corn mashed potatoes, red-eye gravy and chopped salad topped with onion rings ($16). Main courses ($26 to $55) include hot smoked pecan red snapper placed on top of an artichoke-spinach casserole, with shrimp hush puppies and tomato chutney ($34), and ranch antelope with honey-malt glaze on roasted yellow tomato-pozole stew with barbecued venison fajitas ($40). There's also a fixed-price chef's tasting menu ($65 to $85, depending on the meal), a lunch menu with main courses for $15 to $22, and a wine list longer than some small-town Texas phone books.

Star Canyon (☎ *214-520-7827*), 3102 Oak Lawn Ave in the Centrum retail-office complex, has a more relaxed atmosphere than the Mansion, though reservations are suggested several weeks ahead, especially for Friday and Saturday. For starters, selections include spicy rock shrimp taquitos with mango-mustard barbecue sauce and avocado-tomatillo salsa ($10) or field greens with sherry-shallot vinaigrette and herbed Texas ricotta ($6). Main course choices range from pan-seared salmon with black bean and roast banana mash ($18) to a bone-in cowboy rib eye with pinto bean and wild mushroom ragout ($23). Desserts ($5 to $7) include a chocolate phyllo, espresso ice-cream sandwich with mocha sauce.

Sam's Cafe (☎ *214-855-2233*), 100 Crescent Court at McKinney and Maple Aves (in the same complex as the Crescent Court Hotel), is another Southwestern favorite. A Coyote Sampler of the restaurant's best starters, sized for sharing, goes for $13. Salads include a blackened salmon Caesar ($9), and main courses ($12 to $19) include

canyon carne asada with garlic batter for dipping ($14) and chipotle chicken ($13).

Tex-o-centric wild-game cuisine is the specialty at *Matt's No Place* (☎ *214-823-9077*), 6326 LaVista Drive, run by fourth-generation chef Matt Martinez. Starters include wild boar sausage ($6 to $8) and frog's legs ($8 to $9). Entrées include chicken-fried venison ($14) and elk chop ($30). Mexican vanilla-bean ice cream ($3) or Jack Daniel's black-bottom pecan pie ($5) will make a fine finish.

Seafood

Stephan Pyles, the same chef who wowed Dallas with Star Canyon (see the Upscale Southwestern section) has another hit with *AquaKnox* (☎ *214-219-2782*), 3214 Knox St (see the Lower Greenville map). Appetizers include a platter of assorted sushi and sashimi ($18) and a Gulf Coast crab tostada with pickled jicama and spicy corn sauce ($12). Main courses feature such creative fare as brown butter skate on crab-plantain hash with serrano-lime salpicón ($19) or hickory-grilled rack of lamb with a roast potato and goat cheese tamale, grilled asparagus and a charred tomato and wild mushroom sauce ($25). Desserts include frozen macadamia nut bombe with raspberry and vanilla custard sauces ($7) and a lace cookie cup with berries, cream and caramel ($8).

Fish (☎ *214-747-3474*), downtown at 302 S Houston St in the Paramount Hotel, is another good upscale catch. Dinner entrées ($20 to $33) include such fare as pan-roasted fillet of strawberry grouper served with roasted shallots, bacon, and a garlic and balsamic-vinegar demi-glace. Lunch selections (served Monday to Friday) include meat loaf with lobster mashed potatoes ($10). Cranberry crème brûlée ($6) is indicative of the creative dessert choices.

Daddy Jack's Wood Grill (☎ *214-653-3949*), in Deep Ellum at 2723 Elm St, is a good spot for moderately priced seafood. Start with a cup of lobster bisque ($3.50), crab cake ($5) or grilled portabella and asparagus ($6) before diving into pecan-breaded rainbow trout ($13) or red snapper with gulf shrimp and lobster brandy ($18).

Steak Houses

The heavy hitters are **Del Frisco's Double Eagle Steak House** (☎ 972-490-9000), 5251 Spring Valley Rd, and **Ruth's Chris Steak House** (☎ 214-902-8080), 5922 Cedar Springs Rd. Each has superb steaks in the $20 to $30 range, and both are favorites with Dallas' business class.

For something more down-to-earth, try the **Trail Dust Steak House**, with several locations, including 10841 Composite Drive off the Stemmons Freeway (☎ 214-357-3862). Dinners run from $8 to $23, with most entrées in the $10 to $15 range. Lunch costs $4 to $10. Don't wear a tie – they'll cut it off.

Tapas

The hot new entry is **Tarantino's** (☎ 214-821-2224), 3611 Parry Ave facing Fair Park. Selections include a warm dip of artichoke hearts, mushrooms and cheese served with pistachio pasta chips ($6) and stuffed European quail wrapped in smoked bacon ($10). Although the menu makes no mention of film director Quentin Tarantino (who does not own the joint), there are posters for *Reservoir Dogs* and *Pulp Fiction*, and we may have overheard a bar patron ask, 'Can I have a shot of adrenaline with that?'

Barcelona Tapas Bar (☎ 214-826-8600), 2100 Greenville Ave, is another good place for small, reasonably priced plates: garlic sautéed mushrooms ($3.25), New Zealand venison steak ($5) and chicken satay ($5) are among the many choices.

Fast Food & Markets

Quick bites are easy to find in Dallas, where inexpensive chain restaurants line every commercial area and every shopping mall has a food court. For some inspired fast food, try one of the following choices.

The **Dallas Farmers Market** (☎ 214-939-2808), 1010 S Pearl Expressway on the southeast fringe of downtown, has fresh-from-the-grower fruits, vegetables and flowers. It's open daily except Christmas and New Year's Day from 7 am to 6 pm. Rest rooms and an ATM are in the administration building.

Uptown at 3403 Oak Lawn Ave, *Eatzi's* (☎ 214-526-1515) is a certifiably Dallas phenomenon: it's got 8000 sq feet of sensory overload, from the opera music to the pungent aroma of spices swirling from the open kitchen to the visual and visceral appeal of the food (100 ready-to-eat meals for $5 or less, 35 kinds of bread, 122 types of cheese, and so on), which is ready for you to pick out, pay for and enjoy, either here or wherever you choose. If you're not in the mood to be so overwhelmed, try the big but pedestrian *Kroger's* (☎ 214-826-2901), 5665 E Mockingbird Lane.

Feeling a bit run-down by the Big D? Haul your carcass to the **Whole Foods Market** (☎ 214-826-7975), 2218 Greenville Ave. Not only can you refuel with a great meal from the salad, deli and juice bar, you also can get righteous groceries to go – and a massage on your way out the door. A 10-minute rubdown by a trained massage therapist costs $7.50.

ENTERTAINMENT

The weekly *Dallas Observer* is the city's best guide to what's on in all categories; Matt Weitz's *Street Beat* column gets the scoop on local music happenings in all genres.

Classical Music & Dance

The **Dallas Symphony Orchestra** (☎ 214-692-0203), the **Dallas Wind Symphony** (☎ 214-528-5576) and **Turtle Creek Chorale** men's chorus (☎ 214-526-3214) perform at the Morton H Meyerson Symphony Center (☎ 214-670-3600), 2301 Flora St in the Dallas Arts District. Music Hall at Fair Park is home to the **Dallas Opera** (☎ 214-443-1043) and Dallas performances of the **Fort Worth Dallas Ballet** (☎ 214-373-8000, 214-696-3932).

Live Music

Rock & Blues Most big-name concerts take place at the **Starplex Amphitheatre** (☎ 214-421-1111), in Fair Park; the **Bronco Bowl** (☎ 214-943-1777), 2600 Fort Worth Ave; or **Reunion Arena** (☎ 214- 939-2770), 777 Sports St near Reunion Park downtown. TicketMaster (☎ 214-373-8000 or 972-647-5700, www.ticketmaster.com) handles seats for the big gigs.

Deep Ellum Live (☎ 214-748-6222), 2727 Canton St, and the *Galaxy Club* (☎ 214-742-5299), 2820 Main St, are the hip district's biggest concert venues, with frequent shows by top-name alternative acts. Check with TicketMaster for tickets. Slightly less huge touring groups and top local talent can be seen at *Trees* (☎ 214-748-5009), 2709 Elm St, and the *Curtain Club* (☎ 214-742-2336), 2800 Main St.

Also in Deep Ellum, *Dark Room* (☎ 214-748-7666), 2713 Elm St, gets the award for most eclectic programming. Postmodern rock is a staple, but just about every other genre sneaks in. Local original rock and occasional cover bands also play at *Club Clearview* (☎ 214-939-0077), 2806 Elm St, and *Club Dada* (☎ 214-744-3232), 2720 Elm St. For blues, head to *The Bone* (☎ 214-744-2663), 2724 Elm St, or *Blue Cat Blues* (☎ 214-744-2287), 2617 Commerce St.

Muddy Waters (☎ 214-823-1518), 1518 Greenville Ave, is frequently cited among the best blues bars in Dallas. Uptown, the *Velvet E* (☎ 214-969-5568), 1906 McKinney Ave at St Paul St, began life as the Velvet Elvis until the King's estate sued. Aside from live music Friday and Saturday nights, there's good bar food and an array of martinis, single-malt Scotches and microbrews. *Dick's Last Resort* (☎ 214-747-0001), downtown at 1701 N Market St in the West End, has rock and R&B cover bands most evenings, and a gospel music brunch Sunday 11 am to 3 pm.

Country & Western Way down in Deepest Ellum, the *Sons of Hermann Hall* (☎ 214-747-4422), 3414 Elm St, is the place to hear authentic country music and other acoustic delights. It usually has an interesting crowd of true-blue fans and curious club-hoppers. If yodeler Don Walser is on the bill (also see Bars in the Austin section of the South Central Texas chapter), be there.

Jazz & Swing *Terilli's* (☎ 214-827-3993), 2815 Greenville Ave, has good jazz and fine Italian food. The *Red Jacket* (☎ 214-823-8333), 3606 Greenville Ave, bills itself as 'the Swing Palace of Dallas'; Fort Worth act

Johnny Reno & the Lounge Kings plays here every Thursday. Come early for free dance lessons.

Latin & Tejano Deep Ellum's *Monica's Aca y Alla* (☎ 214-748-7140), 2914 Main Street, is the place to be on Sunday nights, with great salsa music and a lot of really smooth dancers – even people with two left feet will have a good time there. The dancing starts at 9; there's live music Friday and Saturday nights, too. *Club Babalu* (☎ 214-953-0300), Uptown at 2912 McKinney Ave, is a good place as well.

Bars & Clubs

Classy atmosphere and a gorgeous view make the *Nana Lounge* (☎ 214-748-1200), 2201 Stemmons Freeway atop the Wyndham Anatole, a great choice for a date. For friendly neighborhood-style bars, find your way to Lower Greenville, where *Ship's Lounge* (☎ 214-823-0315), 1613 Greenville Ave, and the *Old Crow* (☎ 214-828-2769), 1911 Greenville Ave, have the knack for making out-of-towners feel at home.

Brew Pubs In the Old Town Shopping Center, *Two Rows Restaurant and Brewery* (☎ 214-696-2739), 5500 Greenville Ave, generally has a half-dozen handcrafted brews available, plus a good selection of eats. The cavernous *Copper Tank Brewing Co* (☎ 214-744-2739), 2600 Main St in Deep Ellum, has pool, darts and $1 pints every Wednesday night. Food isn't as big a draw here, but we hear the burgers are good.

Gay & Lesbian You've got to love that the top gay and lesbian bars in Dallas are named JR's and Sue Ellen's, respectively. They're owned by the same company, Caven Enterprises (☎ 214-559-0650), which runs four bars and has a pretty good lock on the Oak Lawn club scene.

Uptown, *JR's Bar and Grill*, 3923 Cedar Springs Rd, is open daily 11 am to 2 am and also serves lunch daily; at night it's a video bar. In the same area, *Village Station* (☎ 214-526-7171), 3911 Cedar Springs Rd, is a dance club open Wednesday through Sunday, and the leather-oriented **Throckmorton Mining Co** (☎ 214-521-4205), 3014 Throckmorton St, is open daily. Other popular gay bars include **Pegasus Pub** (☎ 214-559-4663), 3326 N Fitzhugh Ave, and **Moby Dick** (☎ 214-520-6629), 4011 Cedar Springs Rd.

Also Uptown, **Sue Ellen's**, 3903 Cedar Springs Rd, is open daily. Other lesbian bars include **Jugs** (☎ 214-521-3474), 4117 Maple Ave, and **Buddies II** (☎ 214-526-0887), 4025 Maple Ave.

Discos Most Dallas nightspots are off limits to people under 21, but **Club One** (☎ 214-741-1111), 3025 Main St, welcomes everyone 18 and older. **Blind Lemon** (☎ 214-939-0202), 2805 Main St, is another Deep Ellum favorite. **Blue Planet** (☎ 214-369-7009), 8796 N Central Expressway, is into disco.

Mega Clubs The trend in Texas seems to be to cram as many nightclubs as possible under one roof, charge one cover and let people wander among them. **Dallas Alley** (☎ 214-720-0170), at the West End Marketplace, includes a dueling piano sing-along bar, an upscale high-energy dance club, a retro dance club, a laser karaoke bar, a roadhouse country and Top 40 bar, a games arcade and a patio bar. It's easily the most deafening place in Dallas.

Coffeehouses

Get your caffeine fix and good food at **Cafe Brazil**, with several locations, including 2815 Elm St in Deep Ellum (☎ 214-747-2730); it's open 24 hours on Friday and Saturday. Also in Deep Ellum, the smoky **Insomnia Coffee Bar** (☎ 214-761-1556), 2640 Elm St, draws a young crowd.

New Amsterdam Coffeehaus (☎ 214-824-5301), 831 C Exposition Ave near Fair Park, is open till 2 am Friday and Saturday, but it's a cool afternoon hangout, too. Uptown, **Java Jones** (☎ 214-528-2099), 3211 Oak Lawn Ave, has a predominantly gay clientele and occasional live music.

But the most interesting java joint in town has to be **Legal Grounds** (☎ 214-823-7001), a combination coffee shop and law office at 2015 Abrams Rd near Gaston Ave.

Theater

The **Dallas Theater Center** (☎ 214-526-8210) has two venues: the Arts District Theater, downtown at 2401 Flora St, and the Kalita Humphreys Theater, Uptown at 3636 Turtle Creek Blvd. Performances range from dramas to musical comedies to cutting-edge new works.

Touring Broadway musicals with top-name talent perform at the **Majestic** (☎ 214-880-0137), 1925 Elm St downtown, and at Music Hall in Fair Park. The shows at Music Hall are presented by **Dallas Summer Musicals** (☎ 214-691-7200). Samuell-Grand Park is the setting for the summertime **Dallas Shakespeare Festival** (☎ 214-559-2778), a series of free performances.

McKinney Avenue Contemporary (MAC) (☎ 214-953-1212), Uptown at 3120 McKinney Ave, is a combination theater, art gallery and movie house. **Teatro Dallas** (☎ 214-741-1135), 2204 Commerce St downtown, presents classical and contemporary works by Latino playwrights.

For lighter fare, try the **Pocket Sandwich Theatre** (☎ 214-821-1860), 5400 E Mockingbird Lane (see the Lower Greenville map), which specializes in improvisational plays with high audience-participation quotients. Try to guess whodunit at **Dave & Buster's Murder Mystery Dinner Theater** (☎ 214-361-5553), 8021 Walnut Hill Lane. Or take in the **Medieval Times Dinner & Tournament** (☎ 214-761-1800), 2021 N Stemmons Freeway, a high-concept knights-and-charging-horses affair that's popular with convention groups.

Cinema

The biggest movie house in Dallas is the **AMC Grand** (☎ 972-724-8000), Northwest Hwy and Stemmons Freeway, with 24 screens and trams to shuttle moviegoers around the 13-acre parking lot. The **Inwood Theater** (☎ 214-352-6040), 5458 W Lovers Lane, ranks among the city's more adventurous multiplex cinemas, featuring foreign and independent films. The **Dallas Museum of Art** (☎ 214-922-1200 for schedule), at 1717 N Harwood St, runs a Sunday-afternoon art-film series at its Horchow Auditorium.

IMAX A 79-foot dome screen and 15,000-watt sound system set IMAX films apart from the pack. The Science Place, in Fair Park, typically has two films in rotation every day. Tickets cost $6 for adults and teens, $5 for seniors and children ages three to 12. Discount combination tickets allow admission to one or both IMAX features and the Science Place exhibits and planetarium. Call ☎ 214-428-5555 for information.

Comedy

National headlining comedians and live improvisational and sketch comedy are featured at the *Improv Comedy Club* (☎ 972-404-8501), 4980 Belt Line Rd in the north Dallas suburb of Addison. For other comedy clubs, check the listings in the *Dallas Observer*.

SPECTATOR SPORTS

Four major-league sports teams play within the Dallas city limits. The perennially disappointing Dallas Mavericks of the National Basketball Association (☎ 214-939-2800), the sharp-shooting Dallas Stars of the National Hockey League (☎ 214-467-8277) and the Dallas Sidekicks of the indoor Major Soccer League (☎ 214-939-2800) all play downtown at Reunion Arena for now, though Dallas voters have approved the construction of a new arena on the northwest fringe of downtown. The Dallas Burn soccer squad (☎ 214-979-0303) plays outdoor soccer at the Cotton Bowl, in Fair Park.

For information on the Texas Rangers, of Major League Baseball, see the Arlington section later in this chapter. For details on the Dallas Cowboys, of National Football League fame, see the Irving section.

SHOPPING
Neiman-Marcus

The flagship store of upscale department store chain Neiman-Marcus (☎ 214-741-6911), 1618 Main St at Ervay St downtown, has been thrilling shopaholics with top-tier goods and unflagging personal service since 1907. Open Monday to Saturday 10 am to 5:30 pm, with free parking in the Commerce St garage west of the store with ticket validation.

Shopping Malls

Dallas is reputed to have more shopping centers per capita than anyplace else in the US. Downtown, the Plaza of the Americas (☎ 214-720-8000) has 40 stores at 700 N Pearl St. NorthPark center (☎ 214-363-7441), west of the N Central Expressway at Northwest Hwy (DART Rail Park Lane station), has 160 stores, including Neiman-Marcus, FAO Schwartz, Ann Taylor and Dillard's. The Galleria (☎ 972-702-7100), on the Dallas North Tollway at the LBJ Freeway, has more than 200 stores, among them Macy's, Nordstrom, Tiffany & Co and Gianni Versace. To get there, take DART Rail's red line to Park Lane station, then transfer to bus 488, or take bus No 183 from downtown.

Art Galleries

Dallas' art galleries are concentrated in the Uptown area, especially along Routh and Fairmount Sts. Afterimage Gallery (☎ 214-871-9140), 2828 Routh St in the Quadrangle, features fine art photographs and works by top photojournalists. Prices range from $400 to $4000 for images by such lens masters as Robert Mapplethorpe, Sebastião Salgado, David Hume Kennerly and Berenice Abbott. In Deep Ellum, the *Dallas Visual Arts Center* (☎ 214-821-2522), 2917 Swiss Ave, serves as a clearinghouse for local visual arts information and has year-round exhibits featuring regional artists.

Miscellaneous

Techies will enjoy a stop at Infomart (☎ 214-800-8000), 1950 Stemmons Freeway (see Uptown map), the world's largest high-tech information center and the only part of the Dallas Market Center open to the public on a regular basis. Call for details of upcoming trade shows, classes and seminars. The Sunshine Store (☎ 214-748-4187), 2714-B Elm St in Deep Ellum, specializes in head gear for hippie holdouts.

GETTING THERE & AWAY
Air

DFW Dallas-Fort Worth International Airport (DFW; ☎ 972-574-4420, www.dfwairport .com) is 16 miles northwest of the city. From downtown, take I-35 E (the Stemmons Freeway) to Hwy 183 (the Carpenter Freeway) to Hwy 121 (International Parkway). The airport is served by taxis, public transportation and shuttles; see the Getting Around section for information.

DFW is one of the world's busiest airports, with more than 2000 scheduled flights arriving or departing daily from an airfield bigger than New York City's Manhattan Island. For a front-row seat to the action, visit the observation area on E Airfield Drive at Carbon Rd; it has binoculars, an audio feed from the control tower and picnic grounds.

DFW is served by Air Canada, Aeromexico, America West, American Airlines, American Eagle, Atlantic Southeast, British Airways, Canadian Airlines International, Continental, Delta, Korean Air, Lone Star/Aspen, Lufthansa, Midwest Express, Northwest Airlines, Sun Country, TWA, United, USAir, Vanguard and Western Pacific. There are four terminals, designated 2W, 2E, 3E and 4E; American Airlines, by far the largest carrier serving DFW, operates out of terminals 2E and 3E.

Parking in one of the five areas ranges from $5 to $12 a day. In addition to the general airport information number listed earlier, these numbers may help: parking, ☎ 972-574-6772; ground transportation, ☎ 972-574-2227; airport train, ☎ 972-574-6001. Flight information for American Airlines is broadcast near the airport on 1640 AM for departures and 1680 AM for arrivals.

Love Field For many years, Dallas' secondary airport, Love Field (DAL; ☎ 214-670-6080), was served by just one public carrier: Southwest Airlines. Congress recently eased – but did not erase – restrictions posed by the Wright Amendment, which limited travel to and from Love Field in part to give DFW a competitive advantage, and now American Airlines, Continental Express and Legend Air have all added service. Love Field's location, just off Mockingbird Lane at Cedar Springs Rd, is quite convenient, and more flights out of this airport should mean lower fares to and from DFW.

Bus

Greyhound (☎ 214-655-7727) operates out of the bus terminal at 205 S Lamar St. Travel times can vary wildly, depending on whether you hop an express bus or one making many stops. Check with the ticket agent for more information. Services include:

to/from	frequency (per day)	trip duration	one way/ roundtrip
Fort Worth	13	40 min to 1 hour	$7/13
San Antonio	16	4½ to 7 hours	$30/59
Austin	11	3½ to 6 hours	$27/50
Houston	10	5 to 6 hours	$28/53
El Paso	6	11 to 14 hours	$78/136

Train

Union Station, 401 S Houston St in the West End, is where Amtrak trains (☎ 214-653-1101) arrive and depart. The *Texas Eagle*, originating in Chicago, leaves Dallas on Wednesday, Friday, Saturday and Sunday at 4:01 pm and travels to Fort Worth, Austin and San Antonio; from San Antonio, the perennially delayed *Sunset Limited* heads west to Big Bend National Park, El Paso and Los Angeles. The northbound *Texas Eagle* leaves Dallas on Tuesday, Wednesday, Thursday and Sunday at 3:15 pm, arriving in Chicago early the next afternoon.

Car

Dallas is at the convergence of I-20, I-30, I-35, I-45, US 75 and US 80 – easy to access from all points of the compass. Houston is 244 miles south via I-45; Austin is 195 miles south, San Antonio 278, both via I-35.

GETTING AROUND
To/From the Airports

DART bus No 202 serves DFW from downtown via the Carpenter Freeway; the fare is $2. At DFW, catch the bus outside the lower level at any terminal. Downtown, the bus leaves from the West Transfer Center at Griffin St and Pacific Ave. Bus No 539 serves Love Field from the Mockingbird DART Rail station; the fare is $1.

Door-to-door shuttle services offering shared rides to and from DFW and Love

Field include Discount Shuttle (☎ 214-841-1900, 817-267-5150) and SuperShuttle (☎ 817-329-2000, 800-258-3826). The fare from DFW to downtown Dallas is $11; shuttles to downtown Fort Worth cost $12. From Love Field to downtown Dallas the fare is $8 to $9. No reservations are necessary to catch a shuttle from either airport, but they must be made for hotel or residence pickups. Some hotels offer complimentary shuttles to one or both airports. From DFW, the shuttles leave from outside the lower level of all terminals. At Love Field you can pick up shuttles outside in front of the airport.

A taxi to Central Dallas will cost between $35 and $45 from DFW. Taxis are available outside the upper level of each terminal. From Love Field, a taxi to downtown Dallas costs about $12.

Major car rental agencies at the airports include:

Advantage	☎ 972-257-1032
Alamo	☎ 972-621-0236
Avis	☎ 972-574-4130
Budget	☎ 817-329-2277
Dollar	☎ 972-484-0910
Enterprise	☎ 972-986-1890
Hertz	☎ 972-453-0370
National	☎ 972-574-3400
Thrifty	☎ 972-621-1234

Bus & Light Rail

DART (☎ 214-979-1111) is the Dallas region's public transportation system, with buses and light-rail trains serving downtown and the outlying areas. Trains run daily from 5:30 to 12:30 am; bus hours vary depending on route. Schedules and information are available downtown at the DART Store at the corner of Elm and Ervay Sts, and at the Akard DART Rail station, 1401 Pacific Ave; you also can get them at all area Albertson's and Minyard's grocery stores and at some downtown hotels. By 2000, DART's system should even reach DFW International Airport and Fort Worth via the Trinity Railway Express line. (This commuter route now reaches as far as Irving, running Monday through Saturday.)

Local bus and rail fares, including those for the Trinity Railway Express, are $1; some express and premium bus routes charge $2. Exact change is required for buses, but dollar bills are accepted. Rail passengers must buy their tickets from vending machines, which are on all station platforms. A variety of passes are available, including a $2 daily pass ($4 to include premium routes).

DART's downtown Trolley Bus circulator route covers many major downtown destinations. Loops A and B provide clockwise and counterclockwise service, respectively, between the East Transfer Center (at Pearl and Live Oak Sts) and the West (at Griffin St and Pacific Ave) via Main St and Ross Ave. Loop C provides service from 9 am to 3 pm between City Hall and the Arts District via Field and St Paul Sts and Ross Ave. The Trolley Bus fare is 50¢ per ride, free with a bus transfer slip or DART Rail ticket. Customers can transfer from a Trolley Bus to any DART local bus or train for a total fare of $1.

Car

If you're a masochist, you'll count rush-hour driving on Dallas' freeways among life's peak experiences. The rest of us need to just take public transportation whenever practical, and try to stay calm while driving.

If possible, stay off the busiest highways (Central Expressway, Stemmons Freeway, I-30) during the heaviest traffic times (7 to 9 am and 3:30 to 6 pm), and be ready for construction- or accident-related slowdowns.

For north-south travel in northwest Dallas, the Dallas North Tollway is a viable alternative to the Central Expressway, reaching from the Stemmons Freeway north of downtown up past Plano. The toll is $1.50 for the whole distance, or 30¢ to 50¢ for shorter trips.

There's little free parking in downtown Dallas. Meters are in effect well into the evening in many areas, so be sure to check when you park, or risk being towed. Many lots are self-pay, so carry plenty of $1 bills. Park in a secure, well-lit and preferably well-traveled area at night.

Trolley

Uptown and downtown Dallas are connected by the McKinney Avenue Transit Authority, which uses early-20th-century electric streetcars. The trolleys run between the Dallas Museum of Art (from the St Paul St side near Ross Ave) and Hall St, with frequent stops along the way and fun commentary from the drivers. Passengers are welcome to board at any of the frequent stops along the streetcar's McKinney Ave route. The cars operate Sunday to Thursday 10 am to 10 pm, Friday and Saturday 10 am to midnight; $1.50 for adults, 50¢ for seniors, $1 for children. At press time, MATA had plans to extend its line to the West End Marketplace. Call ☎ 214-855-0006 for updates.

Taxi

Cabs congregate at the airports, the Greyhound and Amtrak depots and many hotels. Rates are $1.50 flagfall and 30¢ for each additional quarter-mile, plus $1 each for extra passengers. Companies include:

Allied Taxi	☎ 214-819-9999
Checker Cab	☎ 214-841-0000
Republic Taxi	☎ 214-902-7077
Terminal Taxi	☎ 214-350-4445
Westend Cab Co	☎ 214-902-7000
Yellow and Checker Cab of Dallas	☎ 214-841-0000 214-426-6262

Fort Worth

Population 479,716

If Dallas is skyscrapers, Fort Worth is streetscapes: the Chisholm Trail mural at Sundance Square, the hitching posts of the Stockyards, old Camp Bowie Blvd west of the Cultural District, with its cobblestones, fine restaurants and funky shops. Fort Worth is proud of its nickname, Cowtown, but the livestock industry is just a small part of what's happening here. In fact, Fort Worth has done such a good job of preserving and yet transforming itself for the 21st century that even Dallas visionaries cite it as an example of how a city should work.

But the work is not done. Fort Worth has plans for more development in the new century, including several major museums, hotels, downtown lofts and a Mexican-style market complex. Dallas will likely always be the capital of the Metroplex, but Fort Worth is the unchallenged king of the burgeoning 'West-o-Plex,' as Fort Worth and surrounding Tarrant County have been dubbed by *FW Weekly*, the local alternative newsweekly.

HISTORY

Fort Worth got its start in 1849 as Camp Worth, one of a string of military forts on the Texas frontier. But the army had barely set up shop when settlers began arriving and opening their own businesses. By 1853 there wasn't much of an Indian threat left in the area, so the army withdrew and the townspeople took over the old fort buildings.

Fort Worth found fame during the great open-range cattle drives, which lasted from the 1860s to the 1880s. More than 10 million head of cattle trooped through the city on the Chisholm Trail. Most of the time, the herds moved on to the end of the trail in Kansas. But after the railroad arrived in 1873 and stockyards were established at Fort Worth, many drovers chose to end their trek here.

The late 19th century and early 20th century saw rampant lawlessness in Fort Worth. Robert LeRoy Parker and Harry Langbaugh – better known as Butch Cassidy

Butch Cassidy

The Sundance Kid

and the Sundance Kid – spent a lot of time hiding out in a part of downtown known as Hell's Half Acre, and depression-era holdup artists Bonnie Parker (no relation) and Clyde Barrow spent time in the city as well. Yet most of the mayhem in Fort Worth came not from celebrity ne'er-do-wells but from rank-and-file cowboys with too much pent-up energy from the trail. They were the ones who boozed and brawled their way down Exchange Ave, giving Fort Worth a far different image than that of Dallas. The cattle business remained the top industry in Fort Worth through the 1920s, even as major oil strikes in the Burkburnett and Ranger fields turned the city into an important operations center for oil.

Philanthropists wrote much of the mid- to late-20th-century history of Fort Worth. Amon Carter, an oilman and early publisher of the *Fort Worth Star-Telegram*, was the man most responsible for putting the city on the arts map, notably as founder of the museum bearing his name. The Bass family, among the world's richest, all live in Fort Worth, and collectively they've transformed the Sundance Square area into an urban showplace.

ORIENTATION

The three areas of Fort Worth most interesting to visitors form a lopsided triangle, with N Main St running between downtown and the Stockyards, Lancaster Ave connecting

downtown to the Cultural District, and University and Northside Drives connecting the Cultural District with North Main near the Stockyards. All these areas are north of and easily accessed from I-30, which cuts across the city east to west on its way from Dallas and Arlington. I-35 W intersects with I-30 just east of downtown Fort Worth, then heads north to Denton and south to Waco.

Unlike most cities in Texas, Fort Worth does not divide its streets into east-west and north-south from a central axis. Rather, the streets seem to pick up directional designations fairly randomly, although some make sense – Main becomes North Main north of the Tarrant County Courthouse, for example.

Greater Fort Worth is encircled by a loop route designated as I-820 on its west, north and east sides and as I-20 on the south. Along the way the loop is also referred to as the Northwest Loop, the Southeast Loop and so on, depending on where you are relative to downtown. From the northeast side, Hwy 183/121 and Hwy 10 both head east toward DFW International Airport; from the northwest, Hwy 199 (the Jacksboro Hwy) leads to Wichita Falls.

Maps

The Fort Worth Convention and Visitors Bureau's free maps lack detail for the entire city, but they are fine for finding your way to and around the major tourist areas. The *Dallas-Ft Worth Street Map & Visitor Guide*, also free and widely available at Metroplex attractions and visitors' centers, has a more detailed street map of central Fort Worth.

INFORMATION
Tourist Offices

The Fort Worth Convention and Visitors Bureau (☎ 817-336-8791, 800-433-5747, fax 817-336-3282, www.fortworth.com) has visitors' centers downtown at 415 Throckmorton St (with a few designated free parking spots in the lot across the street) and in the Stockyards at 130 E Exchange Ave. A third visitors' center is planned for the Cultural District. AAA (☎ 817-370-2503) is at 5431 S Hulen St in southwest Fort Worth.

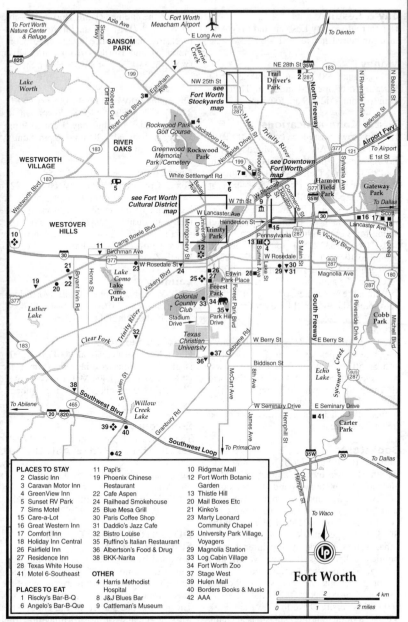

Fort Worth

PLACES TO STAY

2 Classic Inn
3 Caravan Motor Inn
4 GreenView Inn
5 Sunset RV Park
7 Sims Motel
15 Care-a-Lot
16 Great Western Inn
17 Comfort Inn
18 Holiday Inn Central
26 Fairfield Inn
27 Residence Inn
28 Texas White House
41 Motel 6-Southeast

PLACES TO EAT

1 Riscky's Bar-B-Q
6 Angelo's Bar-B-Que

11 Papi's
19 Phoenix Chinese
   Restaurant
22 Cafe Aspen
24 Railhead Smokehouse
25 Blue Mesa Grill
30 Paris Coffee Shop
31 Daddio's Jazz Cafe
32 Bistro Louise
35 Ruffino's Italian Restaurant
36 Albertson's Food & Drug
38 BKK-Narita

OTHER

4 Harris Methodist
   Hospital
8 J&J Blues Bar
9 Cattleman's Museum

10 Ridgmar Mall
12 Fort Worth Botanic
   Garden
13 Thistle Hill
20 Mail Boxes Etc
21 Kinko's
23 Marty Leonard
   Community Chapel
25 University Park Village,
   Voyagers
29 Magnolia Station
33 Log Cabin Village
34 Fort Worth Zoo
37 Stage West
39 Hulen Mall
40 Borders Books & Music
42 AAA

Gay & Lesbian

The Tarrant County Lesbian and Gay Alliance can be reached at ☎ 817-877-5544.

Money

NationsBank (☎ 817-390-6161), 500 W 7th St downtown, is open Monday to Thursday 9 am to 3 pm, Friday 9 am to 6 pm.

Post & Communications

The downtown post office (☎ 817-870-8102), 251 W Lancaster Ave, is open Monday to Friday 7:30 am to 7 pm. Address poste restante mail to General Delivery, Fort Worth, TX 76102. Mail Boxes Etc (☎ 817-735-8448) is at 6387-B Camp Bowie Blvd.

Many cities have Internet cafés; in Fort Worth they have cyber steak houses. Get online for $5 an hour at the Rodeo Steakhouse (☎ 817-332-1288), 1309 Calhoun St, open 4 to 10 pm. Kinko's (☎ 817-737-8021), 6020 Camp Bowie Blvd, offers Internet access for 20¢ a minute or $12 an hour.

Within the Metroplex, you need not dial 1 before the 817, 972 or 214 area codes.

Media

The *Fort Worth Star-Telegram* is the city's major newspaper, available for 50¢ daily and $1.50 Sunday or free online (www .star-telegram.com). *FW Weekly* is the local alternative paper, with investigative stories and good listings for dining and the arts. It comes out each Thursday and is distributed free all over the area.

Bookstores

Barber's Book Store (☎ 817-335-5469), 215 W 8th St downtown, is among the oldest and most complete independent bookstores in Texas. Unfortunately, it may have been sold by the time you read this. Books Etc (☎ 817-624-7766), 2402-A N Main St in the Stockyards, specializes in Western Americana, history, biography and international political collectibles. It's open Wednesday through Saturday in the afternoon.

For guidebooks and maps, Fort Worth's top choice is Voyagers (☎ 817-335-3100), at 1600 S University Drive in University Park Village, a branch of the Dallas-based chain.

Among the national chains, Barnes & Noble (☎ 817-332-7178) has an impressive two-level store on Sundance Square at 401 Commerce St and Borders Books and Music (☎ 817-370-9473) is at 4613 S Hulen St.

Libraries

The main Fort Worth Public Library (☎ 817-871-7700) is at 300 Taylor St downtown. It's open Monday to Thursday 9 am to 9 pm, Friday and Saturday 10 am to 6 pm, Sunday noon to 6 pm.

Campuses

Texas Christian University (☎ 817-921-7810), affiliated with the Disciples of Christ, has about 7000 students and strong departments in business, psychology, marketing and the arts. TCU's campus is off University Drive south of Forest Park and the Fort Worth Zoo.

Laundry

Kwik-Wash has about 10 Fort Worth locations, including 3410 W 7th St (☎ 817-332-7240), in the Cultural District.

Medical Services

Harris Methodist Hospital (☎ 817-882-3000) is at 1301 Pennsylvania Ave. PrimaCare (☎ 817-294-1651), 6404 McCart Ave at Alta Mesa Blvd, is a walk-in clinic for minor illnesses and injuries.

Emergency

The Sheriff's Department is at ☎ 817-884-1212, the Highway Patrol at ☎ 817-284-1490. The Women's Center of Tarrant County runs a rape crisis hot line at ☎ 817-927-2737; the Women's Haven shelter hot line is at ☎ 817-535-6464. Crisis Intervention handles suicide prevention at ☎ 817-927-5544.

DOWNTOWN FORT WORTH
Sundance Square

Bounded by Throckmorton St to the west, 2nd St to the north, Calhoun St to the east and 5th St to the south, this area is one of the most vibrant downtown districts in Texas. The renaissance started in the early 1980s with the opening of the Worthington Hotel

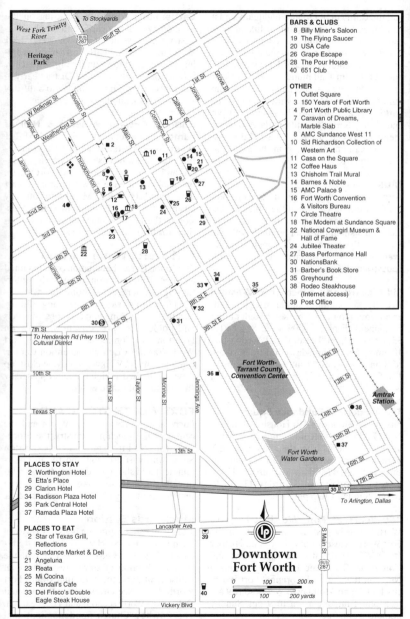

BARS & CLUBS
8 Billy Miner's Saloon
19 The Flying Saucer
20 USA Cafe
26 Grape Escape
28 The Pour House
40 651 Club

OTHER
1 Outlet Square
3 150 Years of Fort Worth
4 Fort Worth Public Library
7 Caravan of Dreams,
   Marble Slab
8 AMC Sundance West 11
10 Sid Richardson Collection of
   Western Art
11 Casa on the Square
12 Coffee Haus
13 Chisholm Trail Mural
14 Barnes & Noble
15 AMC Palace 9
16 Fort Worth Convention
   & Visitors Bureau
17 Circle Theatre
18 The Modern at Sundance Square
22 National Cowgirl Museum &
   Hall of Fame
24 Jubilee Theater
27 Bass Performance Hall
30 NationsBank
31 Barber's Book Store
35 Greyhound
38 Rodeo Steakhouse
   (Internet access)
39 Post Office

PLACES TO STAY
2 Worthington Hotel
6 Etta's Place
29 Clarion Hotel
34 Radisson Plaza Hotel
36 Park Central Hotel
37 Ramada Plaza Hotel

PLACES TO EAT
2 Star of Texas Grill,
   Reflections
5 Sundance Market & Deli
21 Angeluna
23 Reata
25 Mi Cocina
32 Randall's Cafe
33 Del Frisco's Double
   Eagle Steak House

Downtown
Fort Worth

0   100   200 m
0   100   200 yards

and the Caravan of Dreams nightclub, and it continues with a constant influx of new restaurants, shops and attractions. Colorful street-level architecture and plenty of public art – most notably Richard Haas' trompe l'oeil **Chisholm Trail mural** on the 400 block of Main St between 3rd and 4th Sts – help Sundance Square pulse with energy. Free parking is available weekdays after 6 pm and all day Saturday and Sunday. Look for the lots between 3rd and 4th Sts and Houston and Commerce Sts, or in the garage at Outlet Square.

Museums

Although Fort Worth's great museums are 2 miles from downtown in the Cultural District, the Sundance Square renaissance has included a small museum boom downtown. Some of the museums stay open into the evenings to take advantage of the after-work pedestrian traffic.

Sid Richardson Collection of Western Art Fifty-six paintings and bronzes by Frederic Remington and Charles Russell are on permanent display at 309 Main St (☎ 817-332-6554). Open Tuesday and Wednesday 10 am to 5 pm, Thursday and Friday 10 am to 8 pm, Saturday 11 am to 8 pm, Sunday 1 to 5 pm; closed major holidays. Admission is free.

The Modern at Sundance Square Exhibits at the Modern's 410 Houston St annex (☎ 817-335-9215) include temporary installations and pieces from the main museum's permanent collection. There's a great gift shop, too. Open Monday to Thursday 11 am to 6 pm, Friday and Saturday 11 am to 10 pm, Sunday 1 to 5 pm; free.

150 Years of Fort Worth Relive Fort Worth's rowdy past at this satellite of the Fort Worth Museum of Science and History (☎ 817-732-1631), at the corner of 2nd and Commerce Sts in the Former Fire Station No 1, on the site of the original Fort Worth city hall. Open Monday to Wednesday 9 am to 5 pm, Thursday 9 am to 9 pm, Sunday noon to 9 pm; free.

Cattleman's Museum Focusing on the development of the cattle and ranching industry, this museum (☎ 817-332-7064), 1301 West 7th St (see the Fort Worth map), is biding its time downtown until a big new facility is built for it in the Cultural District early in the new century. Open Monday to Saturday 10 am to 5 pm, Sunday 1 to 5 pm; free.

National Cowgirl Museum & Hall of Fame This museum (☎ 817-336-4475), 111 W 4th St, was established in 1975 in Hereford, Texas. It now has offices, preview exhibits and a gift shop in downtown Fort Worth, but it also will have new Cultural District digs around 2001. Open Monday to Saturday 10 am to 6 pm, Sunday noon to 5 pm; admission to the preview museum is free (donations for the new facility are accepted).

Fort Worth Water Gardens

The Amon Carter Foundation commissioned architect Philip Johnson to create this entertaining 5.4-acre playground for water – 19,000 gallons' worth – spraying, falling, trickling and rushing into cascades, channels and pools. The park, downtown between Houston and Commerce Sts near the Fort Worth-Tarrant County Convention Center, is lit up at night. Walkways provide close-up views of the hydro high jinks, but passersby should stay out of the water.

FORT WORTH STOCKYARDS

For years the heart of Fort Worth and the center of the ranching industry, the Stockyards (bus No 1 from 6th and Throckmorton Sts downtown) are now mostly an entertainment and shopping district, though a bit of cattle business still takes place. The area remains popular with visitors and residents.

Stockyards Station

The former sheep and hog pens of Cowtown are now home to Stockyards Station (☎ 817-625-9715, 972-988-6877), 130 E Exchange Ave, a collection of stores, restaurants, an amusement park, the Tarantula Train's Fort Worth depot (see Grapevine in the Around Dallas-Fort Worth section) and a beer garden. The **Cowboy Church** nondenominational

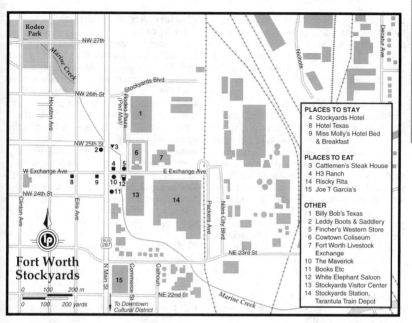

PLACES TO STAY
4 Stockyards Hotel
8 Hotel Texas
9 Miss Molly's Hotel Bed
  & Breakfast

PLACES TO EAT
3 Cattlemen's Steak House
4 H3 Ranch
14 Riscky Rita
15 Joe T Garcia's

OTHER
1 Billy Bob's Texas
2 Leddy Boots & Saddlery
5 Fincher's Western Store
6 Cowtown Coliseum
7 Fort Worth Livestock
  Exchange
10 The Maverick
11 Books Etc
12 White Elephant Saloon
13 Stockyards Visitor Center
14 Stockyards Station,
   Tarantula Train Depot

Fort Worth
Stockyards

0   100   200 m
0   100   200 yards

To Downtown
Cultural District

Christian fellowship (☎ 817-366-9675) meets here every Sunday at 2 pm. The small, Western-themed **Stockyards Park** has about a dozen rides, including a 1932 carousel. Open Friday 5 to 10 pm, Saturday 10 am to 10 pm, Sunday noon to 6 pm. Ride all you want for $9.95 or pay $1 to $1.50 per ride.

Fort Worth Livestock Exchange

Cattle are still traded at the Fort Worth Livestock Exchange, although the dealing now takes place via satellite and videotape. The Livestock Exchange, 131 E Exchange Ave, includes a museum of memorabilia and photos (☎ 817-625-5087) from the heyday of Fort Worth's cattle industry. Open Monday to Saturday 10 am to 5 pm; closed major holidays. Admission is free but donations are accepted.

Walking Tours

Ninety-minute tours cover all the major Stockyards sights, including the Fort Worth Livestock Exchange, the historic Cowtown Coliseum – which has hosted everything from Indian treaty talks to Elvis Presley concerts – and Billy Bob's Texas (see the Entertainment section). Tours meet at the Stockyards Visitor Center, 130 E Exchange Ave, Monday to Saturday at 10 am, noon, 2 pm and 4 pm, and Sunday at noon, 2 pm and 4 pm; $6 for adults, $4.50 for seniors, $4 for children ages three to 12.

FORT WORTH CULTURAL DISTRICT

The face of Fort Worth's Cultural District (bus No 2 from 6th and Throckmorton Sts) will change dramatically in the next few years. The new National Western Heritage Center will include the existing Will Rogers Memorial Center, the National Cowgirl Museum and Hall of Fame, the Texas and Southwestern Cattle Raisers Museum and a new Western-oriented wing of the Fort Worth Museum of Science and History, all set for completion by 2001. A few years after that, the Museum of Modern Art will open its new quarters, the first major building in the US designed by Japanese architect Tadao Ando – next to the Kimbell Art Museum. Watch for construction, but don't let sawhorses and road closures keep you away from one of the finest concentrations of museums in the US.

Amon Carter Museum

Visiting this museum (☎ 817-738-1933), 3501 Camp Bowie Blvd, is like taking a visual tour of the US – from Yosemite National Park with Albert Bierstadt to Taos, New Mexico, with Georgia O'Keeffe, from Pikes Peak in Colorado with George Caleb Bingham to Narragansett Bay in Rhode Island with Martin Johnson Heade. The museum also has an amazing collection of 350,000 photographs, including early masterworks by Mathew Brady, William Henry Jackson, Henri Cartier-Bresson and Laura Gilpin. The pieces are rotated regularly, and there is sure to be a lot of great stuff on view any time you visit. Open Tuesday to Saturday 10 am to 5 pm, Sunday noon to 5 pm; closed major holidays. Admission is free, and tours are given at 2 pm daily.

Kimbell Art Museum

The Kimbell (☎ 817-332-8451), 3333 Camp Bowie Blvd, is most famous for its building, a work by Louis Kahn with natural lighting that allows visitors to see paintings the way the artists originally intended. The art here ranges from antiquity through the Middle Ages and the Renaissance to the 20th century, with works by Fra Angelico, Caravaggio, Titian, Cézanne, Picasso and many other masters. It's a small collection, but a potent one, augmented by frequent major special exhibitions.

The Kimbell is open Tuesday, Wednesday, Thursday and Saturday 10 am to 5 pm, Friday noon to 8 pm, Sunday noon to 5 pm. Introductory art walks featuring the permanent collection are given at 3 pm Sunday, and special exhibition tours take place Tuesday through Friday and Sunday at 2 pm. Admission to the permanent collection is free; special exhibits are $8 for adults, $6 for students, $4 for children ages six to 11, free for children five and younger.

Modern Art Museum of Fort Worth

Never mind its name, the Modern (☎ 817-738-9215), 1309 Montgomery St, dates back to 1892, making it the oldest art museum in Texas. Its permanent collection includes works by Picasso, Warhol, Motherwell, Rauschenberg and Pollock, but the present quarters severely limit what can be shown at one time, which is why the new building, set to open early in the 21st century, will be so welcome. Open Tuesday to Friday 10 am to 5 pm, Saturday 11 am to 5 pm, Sunday noon to 5 pm; free. From February to April and October to December, the Tuesday Evenings at the Modern series features lectures by artists, art scholars and critics; the museum is open until 9 pm on those days.

Fort Worth Museum of Science & History

Everywhere you turn in this museum (☎ 817-732-1631), 1501 Montgomery St, you learn something: anatomy charts are posted in the rest rooms, and a sign above a pay phone explains how there are now more than 200 million phones in the US alone. At the outdoor Dino Dig, visitors can look for real fossils and replica bones in a sand pit. The Noble Planetarium has shows every half-hour from 11 am to 4:30 pm on Saturday, and from 12:30 pm on Sunday. The Omni Theatre has daily showings of IMAX films. The snack bar has ice cream, hot dogs, pizza and grilled chicken sandwiches, most priced at $3 or less.

Open Monday to Wednesday 9 am to 5 pm, Thursday to Saturday 9 am to 9 pm, Sunday noon to 9 pm; closed Thanksgiving, Christmas Eve and Christmas Day. Admission is $5 for adults, $4 for seniors, $3 for children ages three to 12, free for kids under three. Planetarium admission is $3; Omni Theatre tickets are $6 for adults, $4 for seniors and children under 12.

ELSEWHERE IN FORT WORTH
Fort Worth Zoo

Rated among the top zoos in the US by many publications, including *Family Life* and the *Los Angeles Times*, the Fort Worth

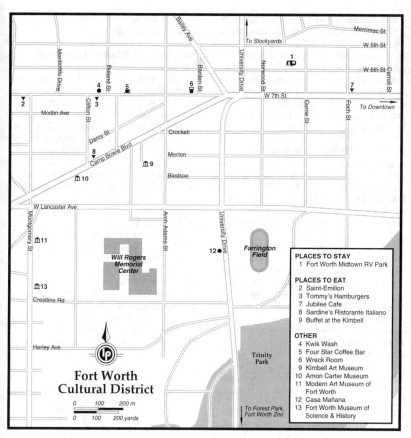

Fort Worth Cultural District

0   100   200 m
0   100   200 yards

PLACES TO STAY
1 Fort Worth Midtown RV Park

PLACES TO EAT
2 Saint-Emilion
3 Tommy's Hamburgers
7 Jubilee Cafe
8 Sardine's Ristorante Italiano
9 Buffet at the Kimbell

OTHER
4 Kwik Wash
5 Four Star Coffee Bar
6 Wreck Room
9 Kimbell Art Museum
10 Amon Carter Museum
11 Modern Art Museum of
    Fort Worth
12 Casa Mañana
13 Fort Worth Museum of
    Science & History

Zoo (☎ 817-871-7050, www.fortworthzoo .com) is in Forest Park off S University Drive, with nearly 5000 inhabitants representing 709 species, including 30 endangered species. Highlights include one of the nation's biggest reptile and amphibian collections, an 11-acre Texas area with native Texas species, and the Meerkat Mounds (parents: think Timon from *The Lion King*).

The zoo is open daily 10 am to 5 pm (till 6 pm April to October); Thanksgiving, Christmas and New Year's Day it's open noon to 5 pm. Admission is $7 for adults, $3 for seniors, $4.50 for children ages three to 12; on Wednesday admission is half-price and parking (usually $3) is free. Rental strollers ($3 to $5) are available just over the entry bridge at Safari Supplies. The indoor Zoo Creek Cafe is open year-round; other restaurants, food stands and picnic areas are open as weather permits. Bus No 7 serves University Drive, leaving downtown from 6th and Houston Sts, but plan on walking nearly a mile from the zoo bus stop to the gate.

Log Cabin Village
A living history museum in Forest Park (bus No 7 from 6th and Houston Sts), Log

Cabin Village (☎ 817-926-5881) re-creates 19th-century Texas pioneer life. Interpreters dressed in period clothing demonstrate spinning, blacksmithing, candle making, corn milling and other frontier skills. Open Tuesday to Friday 9 am to 5 pm, Saturday 10 am to 5 pm, Sunday 1 to 5 pm (no entry after 4:30 pm); $1.50 for adults, $1.25 for seniors and kids ages four to 17, free for kids four and under.

Fort Worth Botanic Garden

A European rose garden, a Japanese garden with a koi pond and a tropical conservatory are the highlights at the Fort Worth Botanic Garden (☎ 817-871-7686), in the southwestern section of Trinity Park (bus No 7 from 6th and Houston Sts). Open daily 9 am to 11 pm; free.

From April to October the garden's conservatory is open Monday to Friday 10 am to 9 pm, Saturday 10 am to 6 pm, Sunday 1 to 6 pm; from November to March it closes at 4 pm Saturday and Sunday. Admission $1 for adults, 50¢ for seniors and children ages four to 12.

Marty Leonard Community Chapel

Arkansas architect E Fay Jones, who apprenticed with Frank Lloyd Wright, is acclaimed for his striking Gothic-inspired buildings. This interfaith chapel (☎ 817-731-8681), at 4701 W Rosedale St on the grounds of a residential treatment center for troubled adolescents (take bus No 2 from 6th and Throckmorton Sts to Camp Bowie Blvd and S Hulen St, then transfer to bus No 25), features a 60-foot-high skylight and the repetitive cross beams that are a hallmark of Jones' style. Open Tuesday to Saturday 10 am to 4 pm; donations are accepted.

Thistle Hill

One of the Southwest's best-preserved Georgian-revival mansions, Thistle Hill (☎ 817-336-1212), 1509 Pennsylvania Ave (bus No 6 from 6th and Houston Sts), is open for hour-long guided tours Monday to Friday 11 am to 3 pm (last tour at 2 pm), Sunday 1 to 4 pm (last tour at 3 pm). Tours begin on the hour and cost $4 for adults, $2 for seniors and children under 12.

Fort Worth Nature Center & Refuge

Starting with the original 35-acre Greer Island Nature Center, this popular refuge (☎ 817-237-1111), 10 miles northwest of downtown on Hwy 199, has grown to 100 times that size, with 25 miles of hiking and nature trails and an interpretive center. Buffalo, white-tailed deer, prairie dogs and Texas wildflowers are the star attractions. Open Tuesday to Saturday 9 am to 5 pm, Sunday 12:30 to 5:30 pm; closed major holidays. Admission is free.

ACTIVITIES

Fort Worth has 195 parks, embracing nearly 10,000 acres. You'll find ample opportunity to hike, bike, canoe or kayak.

Heritage Park

On downtown's north side, this park borders the West Fork of the Trinity River and offers access to the Trinity Trails. The Heritage Park Boat and Recreation Center (☎ 817-238-9311), between the Tarrant County

Prairie dog

Courthouse and the river, rents canoes, kayaks, pedal boats, bicycles and in-line skates. It's open weekdays noon to dusk and weekends 9 am to dusk from March to October, and weekdays as weather permits and weekends 11 am to dusk from November to February.

Trinity Trails
This network of hiking, biking and equestrian trails covers 35 miles along the Trinity River, Sycamore Creek and Marine Creek. It can be accessed from most of Fort Worth's major parks. Check at the visitors' bureau for a current map and brochure.

Riverboat Excursions
The *Queen Maria* (☎ 817-238-9778) offers sight-seeing and dinner cruises on Lake Worth, northwest of downtown, off Hwy 199. Call for schedules and prices.

ORGANIZED TOURS
Walking Tours
Hell's Half Acre to Sundance Square (☎ 817-327-1178), a 2½-hour walking tour of downtown Fort Worth, leaves the Radisson Plaza Hotel lobby, 815 Main St, Friday and Saturday at 9:30 am; $10 per person.

Carriage Rides
Classic Carriages (☎ 817-336-0400) offers 16-minute moonlight horse-drawn-carriage tours of Sundance Square Wednesday to Saturday starting at 7:30 pm. Carriages leave from 2nd and Main Sts in front of the Worthington Hotel. Cost is $20 for up to four people, $5 for each additional person.

SPECIAL EVENTS
Between 800,000 and 1 million people attend the annual 17-day Southwestern Stock Show and Rodeo (☎ 817-877-2400), held from late January through early February at the Will Rogers Memorial Center, 1 Amon Carter Square in the Cultural District. The show marked its 100th anniversary in 1996. If you visit Fort Worth during the Stock Show, reserve a room at least two months in advance and expect to pay premium prices.

PLACES TO STAY
Fort Worth's budget motels are concentrated near highway interchanges and along the Jacksboro Hwy (Hwy 199), northwest of downtown via Henderson Rd. Moderately priced rooms are most abundant along S University Drive near the Cultural District. Prices everywhere climb sharply during special events.

Camping
Several Army Corps of Engineers campgrounds on Benbrook Lake, southwest of Fort Worth on US 377, have sites for tent campers and RVs; call ☎ 817-292-2400 for information.

The rates are high, but you can't beat the location of the *Fort Worth Midtown RV Park* (☎ 817-335-9330, 800-435-9330), 2906 W 6th St, just a few blocks from the Cultural District and about a mile from downtown. Full hookups cost $25, with showers and laundry on-site.

Sunset RV Park (☎ 817-738-0567, 800-738-0567), 5 miles west of downtown at 4921 White Settlement Rd, has full-hookup sites priced at $16 for one or two people ($2 per person for extra campers). There are no tent sites, but pop-up campers are allowed. Amenities include wheelchair-accessible rest room facilities, showers and a laundry.

Motels & Hotels
Budget *The Sims Motel* (☎ 817-335-3550), 901 N Henderson Rd north of downtown, has acceptably clean rooms for $27/20 a single/double, each with a TV, phone and Magic Fingers!

The *Great Western Inn* has several locations around town, including 1815 E Lancaster Ave (☎ 817-877-3500). The rooms are similar to those at Motel 6 and cost $35/40. The well-kept *GreenView Inn* (☎ 817-624-1698), 1816 Jacksboro Hwy across from the Fort Worth Municipal Golf Course, has king-size beds and rates of $35/40; rooms with kitchens are available for $45.

Fort Worth has a half-dozen or so outposts of Motel 6, including *Motel 6-Southeast* (☎ 817-921-4900), 4433 S I-35, which is 7 miles south of downtown, and

Motel 6-East (☎ 817-834-7361), 1236 Oakland Blvd, 3 miles east of downtown off I-30 (see the Metroplex map). Summer rates at both are about $36/42.

Classic Inn (☎ 817-624-3104, fax 817-624-3121), 2520 NE 28th St, has rooms for $36/48. The sprawling *Caravan Motor Inn* (☎ 817-626-1951), 2601 Jacksboro Hwy, has a pool and charges $38/48 in summer, a few dollars less in winter.

Mid-Range When we walked into the *Care-a-Lot Inn* (☎ 817-338-0215), at 1111 W Lancaster Ave on the fringe of downtown, we were surprised to see several tables full of senior citizens playing cards as if it were their home. Turns out it *is* – the hotel doubles as a retirement residence. Rooms start at $60; amenities include a laundry and covered parking.

Comfort Inn (☎ 817-535-2591, fax 817-531-1373), 2425 Scott Ave, is two miles east of downtown, has a pool and laundry facilities, and charges $52/60. *Fairfield Inn* (☎ 817-335-2000), 1505 S University Drive, 3 miles from downtown and a mile from the zoo, has an indoor pool and rooms for $63/73.

Park Central Hotel (☎ 817-336-2011, 800-848-7275), 1010 Houston St across from the convention center, has the least expensive rooms downtown ($65 single or double, $75 during conventions), plus a pool, guest laundry and free parking.

The *Hotel Texas* (☎ 817-624-2224, 800-866-6660, fax 817-624-7177), 2415 Ellis Ave, has an excellent Stockyards location and rooms starting at $49/59 on weeknights, $69/79 on weekends. Most guest rooms in this renovated 1939 hotel are on the small side, but a honeymoon room ($79 on weeknights, $109 on weekends) has a king-size bed and whirlpool tub, and the second-floor Bob Wills Suite ($250 on weeknights, $350 on weekends) has four rooms and a commanding view of the Stockyards district.

The 434-room *Ramada Plaza Hotel* (☎ 817-335-7000, 800-228-2828, fax 817-335-3333), 1701 Commerce St across from the Fort Worth Water Gardens, has rooms starting at $70/80, an indoor pool and an exercise center. The *Holiday Inn Central*

(☎ 817-534-4801, fax 817-534-3761), 2000 Beach St 2 miles from downtown, has singles and doubles starting at $83. It has a pool, exercise room and tennis court, but the fading guest rooms are overpriced. Rates at the *Clarion Hotel* (☎ 817-332-6900), 600 Commerce St downtown, start at $89/99.

Top End The all-suites *Residence Inn* (☎ 817-870-1011, fax 817-877-5500), at 1701 S University Drive, caters to business travelers on extended stays, with happy hours on weeknight evenings, a van shuttle service within a 10-mile radius and even a complimentary grocery-shopping service. Rooms are $110/120.

The *Stockyards Hotel* (☎ 817-625-6427, 800-423-8471, fax 817-624-2571), 109 E Exchange Ave, specializes in Western-style luxury, from the big leather sofas in the lobby to the Texas-size armoires in the guest rooms. Rates start at $105 on weekdays, $135 on weekends. Clyde Barrow (of Bonnie and Clyde fame) reportedly stayed in room 305, and memorabilia in the room includes one of Bonnie's Colt revolvers. The Celebrity Suite, the most romantic room in the house, is $260 on weeknights, $350 on the weekends. That will buy you a living area with fireplace, wet bar and stereo and a private patio with hot tub.

The *Radisson Plaza Hotel* (☎ 817-870-2100, fax 817-882-1300), 815 Main St, is an upscale downtown option with rates starting at $150/170. The newly renovated rooms have smart southwestern decor, and there's a rooftop pool and health club.

The top-tier choice in Fort Worth is the *Worthington Hotel* (☎ 817-870-1000, 800-433-5677, fax 817-338-9176), 200 Main St. This place is first-class, from the multitiered lobby fountains to the piano player on the mezzanine to the dark wood furniture and spacious feel of the guest rooms, which start at $205/225 on weekdays and $145 on weekends. Amenities include a pool, health club and two restaurants.

B&Bs

Etta's Place (☎ 817-654-0267), 200 W 3rd St downtown, is named for Etta Place, a friend to Butch Cassidy and the Sundance Kid who was by day a proper schoolteacher, by night a bon vivant. Rooms are $125 to $165. Each of the 10 guest rooms at this three-floor B&B has a private bath, TV and voice mail; the three suites have full kitchens, and the uppermost room, a split-level loft called Etta's Attic, has a kitchenette.

The *Texas White House* (☎ 817-923-3597, 800-279-6491, fax 817-923-0410), 1417 8th Ave, is a gracious historic home five minutes south of downtown. Each guest room has a private bath; rooms with TV or telephone are available on request. Rates run $105 for the first night, $85 for subsequent nights.

Miss Molly's Hotel Bed & Breakfast (☎ 817-626-1522, 800-996-6559), 109½ W Exchange Ave, is in the heart of the Stockyards, with eight rooms priced from $95 to $170. *Bed & Breakfast at the Ranch* (☎ 817-232-5522, 888-593-0352, fax 817-656-1330), 8275 Wagley Robertson Rd (via Hwy 287 and Boswell Rd), is north of the city on 15 acres. Its four rooms are priced from $95 to $159.

PLACES TO EAT
American
The *Star of Texas Grill* (☎ 817-882-1719), 200 Main St, is the more moderately priced of the two restaurants at the Worthington Hotel. They usually offer a three-course theatergoers' menu for $16.95. Other choices include smoked prime rib and black bean quesadilla ($4.95 as an appetizer, $7.95 as an entrée), herb-roasted ranch chicken ($9.95) or grilled swordfish ($16). At lunch, look for West Texas venison chili with pepper-jack cheese ($3.75) and sandwiches in the $6 range. Breakfasts run $5.50 to $10.95.

The Kimbell Art Museum's *Buffet at the Kimbell* (☎ 817-332-8451), 3333 Camp Bowie Blvd, serves upscale cafeteria fare for lunch Tuesday through Saturday. Pick a small plate ($4.50) or large ($6.50) and choose from among the salad and pasta selections, or opt for an entrée ($7.50), such as a quiche, quesadilla or gourmet sandwich. Soup is $3.50, desserts $2.50 to $3.50.

Paris Coffee Shop (☎ 817-335-2041), 700 W Magnolia Ave, ranks as a favorite among locals. The dining room is big and nondescript, with historical photos hung haphazardly on the walls, but nobody comes here for the ambience – they come for the food, which is actually pretty standard, but fast and filling. Breakfast includes all the usual choices, with most dishes costing $5 or so. For lunch there's a choice of fried catfish, grilled chicken livers in gravy, sliced beef brisket barbecue or grilled-chicken salad, served with hot rolls, corn bread and two vegetables ($5.45) or three ($6.25). If you have room, a slice of pie costs $1.75.

Tommy's Hamburgers, with several locations, including 3431 W 7th St in the Cultural District (☎ 817-332-1922), has some of the best burgers in town and live entertainment on weekend evenings. Burgers run about $5 to $7 and come with onion rings or fries. In the same neighborhood, the *Jubilee Cafe* (☎ 817-332-4568), 2736 W 7th St, has superb chicken-fried steak.

Asian
Named after airports in Bangkok and Tokyo, *BKK-Narita* (☎ 817-738-3175), 6060 Southwest Blvd, will transport you to Thailand, Japan or China for about $5 at lunch, $6 to $13 at dinner. *Phoenix Chinese Restaurant* (☎ 817-731-0561), 6500 Camp Bowie Blvd, is another good choice, with $4.25 lunch specials and dinners for about $7.

Barbecue
Fort Worth has several really good barbecue joints. The *Railhead Smokehouse* (☎ 817-738-9808), 2900 Montgomery St, has a delicious smoked chicken breast barbecue sandwich ($3.55). Dinners ($6.35 to $9.35) include ¾lb of your choice of pork, beef or chicken plus potatoes, salad and coleslaw. *Angelo's Bar-B-Que* (☎ 817-332-0357), 2533 White Settlement Rd, has been around for more than 40 years. Lunch is $2 to $5, dinner $3 to $9. You can't go wrong with *Riscky's Bar-B-Q*, with several locations, including 2314 Azle Ave at 28th St (☎ 817-624-8662) – the food is cheap, and the place has plenty of personality.

Continental
The Worthington Hotel's *Reflections* (☎ 817-882-1765), 200 Main St, has some of the most

memorable and pricey food in Fort Worth. Starters include lobster bisque ($5.25) or escargot sautéed with tree oyster mushrooms in a puff pastry with garlic cream sauce ($9.25). The main courses ($20 to $29) include roast breast of pheasant wrapped with grilled apple-wood-smoked bacon and puff pastry and served over caramelized pears ($27). Tuesday through Saturday, consider reserving a seat for the Chef's Table prix fixe dinner ($40 to $48 per person for four courses, not including wine) and watch the chef prepare your meal.

Saint-Emilion (☎ 817-737-2781), 3617 W 7th St, serves country French food in a charming Cultural District setting that is perfect for capping off a day at the museums. A fixed-price dinner ($32) includes appetizer, entrée and dessert; favorite choices include escargot pâté, fish flown in fresh from Boston and the raspberry tart. The wine list has about 220 selections.

French with a Mediterranean accent, *Bistro Louise* (☎ 817-922-9244), 2900 S Hulen St, serves such delicacies as macadamia-crusted shrimp ($8), tea-smoked duck ($20) and lamb loin ($25). Signature desserts include lemon coconut cake ($5) and Black Forest praline torte ($5.50).

Italian
Sardine's Ristorante Italiano (☎ 817-332-9937), 3410 Camp Bowie Blvd in the Cultural District, has just the atmosphere you'd expect – red-checkered tablecloths, flickering candles, jazz every night – and some you might not – check out the Bob Booth, with pictures of Bob Dylan and Bob Marley. Entrées ($10 to $18) include zuppa di pesce ($17), a seafood-filled soup with Italian spices and fresh tomato sauce, and costollette d'agnello ($15), broiled baby lamb chops. Open for dinner only.

Though Sardine's may be the hot date choice, many Fort Worthians say *Ruffino's Italian Restaurant* (☎ 817-923-0522), 2455 Forest Park Blvd, is even more romantic, and it's open for lunch ($8 to $11). Dinner selections include fettuccine delicate – fettuccine sautéed with portabella mushrooms, sun-dried tomatoes, spinach, onions and a touch

of goat cheese in a tasty white wine sauce ($12) – and Franco's famous grilled veal chop, served with a port wine demi-glace, slices of portabella mushrooms and chopped green onions ($22).

Mexican & Tex-Mex
The most famous restaurant in Fort Worth, *Joe T Garcia's* (☎ 817-626-4356), at 2201 N Commerce St near the Stockyards, started as a shack with maybe 20 seats. Four generations and five expansions later, it takes up a city block, with 2000 seats and extensive outdoor dining amid fountains and pools. This is the place to go for people who hate choices – there are only two possible meals: two enchiladas, two tacos and two nachos with all the trimmings ($9) or fajitas (beef, chicken or a combo; $10.25); children's plates cost $3.75. The food arrives maybe three minutes after you order it, and it's no better than average, but the atmosphere is lots of fun, and you may see a celebrity or two. Expect a half-hour wait on weekends, longer during special events. Mariachis play Friday, Saturday and Sunday nights. Credit cards not accepted.

Mi Cocina (☎ 817-877-3600), 509 Main St downtown, features fresh Tex-Mex combos and traditional Mexican fare priced from $6.25 to $15.75. There's outdoor dining in season. *Riscky Rita* (☎ 817-626-8700), 140 E Exchange St in Stockyards Station, has a taco and fajita buffet every day at lunch for about $5. Like the nearby steak house and seafood restaurants, Rita's is run by the same folks who operate the city's many Riscky's Bar-B-Q joints.

Southwestern
Perched on the 35th floor of the BankOne Building, at 500 Throckmorton St, *Reata* (☎ 817-336-1009) features upscale cowboy cuisine that will send your soul, if not your body, to wide-open West Texas. Fans say you haven't had chicken-fried steak until you've had it at Reata, with garlic mashed potatoes on the side ($10 at lunch, $13 at dinner). Other options at this restaurant include chicken chile relleno made with Mexican cheeses and roasted corn chowder ($8 at

lunch, $16 at dinner) or barbecued shrimp enchiladas ($15). Whatever you order, Reata is highly recommended.

Blue Mesa Grill (☎ 817-332-6372), 1600 S University Drive in University Park Village, has good Santa Fe-style eats. Starters include Painted Desert soup, a combination of black bean and corn chowder in one bowl ($3.25) and blue crab and shrimp cakes with cilantro cream and red bell pepper sauce ($6). Main courses range from Adobe Pie ($8), a twist on the traditional tamale, to a seafood mixed grill ($13). A spa menu features four entrée choices, each with no more than 610 calories and 8.6 grams of fat.

Steak Houses

The newly remodeled and much enlarged **H3 Ranch** (☎ 817-624-1246), 109 E Exchange Ave in the Stockyards Hotel, has dinners ranging from spit-roasted pig ($11) to a 16-ounce prime strip loin ($23). Lunch costs $6 to $9. Just north, at 2458 Main St, the **Cattlemen's Steak House** (☎ 817-624-3945) serves charcoal-grilled steaks for $14 to $27, including salad and baked potato. Downtown, the clubby **Del Frisco's Double Eagle Steak House** (☎ 817-877-3999), 812 Main St, has steaks from $16 to $30.

Eclectic

Across the street from the new Bass Performance Hall, **Angeluna** (☎ 817-334-0080), 215 E 4th St, is a see-and-be-seen hot spot featuring 'one-world cuisine.' Pizzas ($11 to $15) are a big hit, with such choices as Thai veggie or jerk chicken. For more of a splurge, the veal short ribs with white-truffle mashed potatoes goes for $20. Dessert choices include a warm green apple and dried cherry crisp with buttermilk black-pepper ice cream ($6).

Fort Worthians praise **Cafe Aspen** (☎ 817-738-0838), 6103 Camp Bowie Blvd, for its creativity and consistently good food, if not for its confused decor. For starters, try the french-fried sweet potato chips with pesto aioli ($2.25). Lunch entrées ($5 to $10) include vegetarian lasagna ($7.25) and rosemary-herbed orange roughy on lemon fettuccine with a minted Texas tomato sauce ($9.25). Dinners ($11 to $30) feature such

fare as chili-crusted tuna served over wild rice with an avocado-papaya sauce ($16.50). Dessert selections vary, but the strawberry rhubarb pie ($4) is a knockout.

Cheesecake is the specialty at **Randall's Cafe** (☎ 817-336-2253), 907 Houston St – and not just for dessert, but as an appetizer or even a light meal – would you believe Parmesan and smoked-salmon cheesecake? There are 60 varieties in all (though not all 60 are always available), priced from $5.50 to $10. Gourmet sandwiches and a fine wine list make this place a great choice.

Miscellaneous

Daddio's Jazz Cafe (☎ 817-926-7000), 715 W Magnolia Ave, features live music and good Greek food at terrific prices. A four-course chicken or lamb dinner (served Friday and Saturday) costs about $12; Sunday brunch averages $7, including champagne.

Papi's (☎ 817-763-8442), at 5336 Birchman Ave, has a wide variety of inexpensive Puerto Rican fare, with daily lunch and dinner specials.

If you're jonesin' for some good ice cream, head for **Marble Slab**, with several locations, including 312-A Houston St (☎ 817-335-5877), in Sundance Square in front of the Caravan of Dreams.

Markets

Sundance Market and Deli (☎ 817-335-3354), 353 Throckmorton St, has food to eat on the premises and a good selection of fresh produce, groceries, beer and wine to take with you, plus live music Friday and Saturday nights. **Albertson's Food and Drug** (☎ 817-922-9898), 3120 S University, is a good bet for more extensive grocery shopping.

ENTERTAINMENT
Classical Music & Dance

Fort Worth made big news in the arts world with the 1998 opening of the $65 million Bass Performance Hall, a Sundance Square venue that is now home to the **Fort Worth Symphony** (☎ 817-665-6000), the **Fort Worth Opera** (☎ 817-731-0200) and the **Fort Worth Dallas Ballet** (☎ 817-377-9988, 800-654-9545). Built on the southeast corner of 4th and Commerce Sts, its entrance flanked by 48-foot heralding angels, Bass Hall has been favorably compared to such top-flight venues as Carnegie Hall. Unlike most recent concert halls built back on a plaza, Bass Performance Hall sits hard against the sidewalk. The intimacy continues inside, where the 2100 seats are configured in traditional opera-house horseshoe style beneath a dome of painted sky.

Live Music

Fort Worth has two standout venues for live music: Billy Bob's Texas and the Caravan of Dreams. Both are worth a visit even if you can't catch a concert.

In the Stockyards at 2520 Rodeo Plaza, **Billy Bob's Texas** (☎ 817-624-7117, www.billybobstexas.com) features top-name country stars (with an occasional rock act) every Friday and Saturday night. The cover on Friday and Saturday is usually between $5 and $7 for general admission, $10 to $22 for reserved seats; otherwise, admission is $1 in the afternoon, $3 after 6 pm. Aside from concerts, Billy Bob's has live bull riding Friday and Saturday at 9 and 10 pm (an extra $2 admission), free dance lessons Thursday at 8 pm, and family line-dance classes Saturday at 2:30 pm ($3 per person). Kids are always welcome throughout the club with their parents. Billy Bob's opens at 11 am daily except December 24, when it's closed all day. The house restaurant, Coburn's Barbecue, serves meals priced from $3 for beef taquitos to $11 for a rib dinner.

For acoustics and atmosphere, the intimate **Caravan of Dreams** (☎ 817-429-4000), 312 Houston St on Sundance Square, is widely considered tops in the Metroplex. The Caravan typically hosts three concerts a week, with offerings all over the musical map. One month saw shows by the Spinners, Brave Combo, Ladysmith Black Mambazo, John Gorka and Joe Ely. When the concert hall is dark, the Caravan offers the open-air, grotto-style Rooftop Bar, with great downtown views and – we kid you not – a 32-foot-high, neon-lit geodesic dome housing a mini biosphere.

Billy Bob's Texas

The 100,000-sq foot building that is now Billy Bob's was once a barn for housing prize cattle during the Fort Worth Stock Show. The sloping floor that is now ideal for concert seating was originally constructed to allow easy runoff from the cattle pens. After the stock show moved to the Will Rogers Memorial Center, the barn became a department store so big that the stockkeepers wore roller skates.

Billy Bob's opened in 1981. It can hold more than 6000 people and has 40 bars to serve the thirsty masses. The most bottled beer sold in one night was 16,000 bottles, during a 1985 Hank Williams Jr concert. The runner-up was 13,000 bottles, during a 1989 Clint Black concert. There are tons of pool tables, slot machines and video games, but don't go looking for any of those silly mechanical bulls – Billy Bob's doesn't have 'em, and never did.

Bars & Clubs

Sundance Square *USA Cafe* (☎ 817-335-5400), 425 Commerce St, is an all-American party place and microbrewery carved out of the block-long downtown Barnes & Noble. Its facade sports a Statue of Liberty, and inside there's a mini Mt Rushmore. Downstairs is a sports bar on one side and a cocktail lounge on the other, with the usual bar menu (burgers, nachos, chicken wings and such) paired with brewed-on-the-spot Rushmore Bock, Old Glory Amber or one of several other specialty beers.

The *Flying Saucer* (☎ 817-336-7468), 111 E 4th St, has more than 76 beers on tap and 150 in bottles. The restaurant takes its name from the hundreds of commemorative plates on the walls. German bar eats include sausage and cheese plates ($6.25 to $13) and bratwurst sandwiches ($5.75). *Billy Miner's Saloon* (☎ 817-877-3301), 150 W 3rd St, is a downtown hot spot for after-work drinks. The *Pour House* (☎ 817-335-2575), at 209 W 5th St, is primarily a sports bar with occasional live rock.

The wine bar **Grape Escape** (☎ 817-336-9463), 500 Commerce St, offers tastings of wines from around the world.

Elsewhere About a million years ago, *Esquire* magazine named the **White Elephant Saloon** (☎ 817-624-1887), 106 E Exchange St, one of the 100 best bars in the US. It's as country as they come, with live music every night and lots of pool table action. The TV show *Walker, Texas Ranger* films its bar scenes here.

Other Fort Worth clubs have occasional brushes with the blues, but the **J&J Blues Bar** (☎ 817-870-2337), 937 Woodward Ave, is a down-and-dirty roadhouse where the blues are a way of life.

For the best jukebox in town (and occasional live music), head to the **Wreck Room** (☎ 817-870-4900), 3208 W 7th St.

Gay & Lesbian

Fort Worth's gay and lesbian scene is much smaller than the one in Dallas, but a few spots ensure that no one need drive 30 miles to Dallas for a good time. *FW Weekly* readers named **651 Club** (☎ 817-332-0745), 651 S Jennings Ave, the best place to meet someone of the same sex. **Magnolia Station** (☎ 817-877-4419), 600 Magnolia Ave, is a good dance club with a mixed gay-straight crowd. We couldn't find a lesbian bar in Fort Worth proper, but **Rumorhazzit** (☎ 817-649-7800), 2833 Galleria Drive in Arlington, draws a fun country-oriented lesbian crowd.

Theater

In 1936, Amon Carter brought New York producer Billy Rose to Fort Worth, paying him $1000 a day for 100 days to stage an extravaganza Rose called *Casa Mañana*. The show was such a hit that it continued annually for several years, drawing such top talents of the day as Eddie Cantor and Edgar Bergen. Today **Casa Mañana** (☎ 817-332-2272), 3101 W Lancaster Ave, is the name of a theater-in-the-round enclosed in a geodesic dome that hosts Broadway musicals, a drama series, a children's series and concerts. It also operates a downtown theater, **Casa on the Square** (☎ 817-332-3509), 109 E 3rd St.

Stage West (☎ 817-784-9378), at 3055 S University Drive, presents an eclectic mix of classics and newer, sometimes avant-garde works in a converted movie palace. Downtown, **Circle Theatre** (☎ 817-877-3040), 230 W 4th St, focuses on plays written by or about Texans. **Jubilee Theater** (☎ 817-338-4411), 506 Main St, specializes in works celebrating and exploring the African American experience.

Every summer, Trinity Park is the setting for an outdoor **Shakespeare in the Park** series (☎ 817-923-6698).

Wild West Show

The **Cowtown Coliseum** (☎ 817-654-1148), on E Exchange Ave in the Stockyards, is the setting for *Pawnee Bill's Wild West Show*, complete with trick shooters and ropers, singing cowboys, Indian ceremonial dancing and a stagecoach robbery. Performances take place Saturday at 2 and 4:30 pm from June to August; $7 for adults, $4 for children ages three to 12.

Cinemas

Between the **AMC Sundance West 11**, 304 Houston St, and the **AMC Palace 9**, on 3rd St between Commerce and Calhoun Sts (☎ 817-870-1111 for both), there isn't much need to leave downtown to see a movie – except perhaps to catch an IMAX show at the Fort Worth Museum of Science and History.

Coffeehouses

Coffee Haus (☎ 817-336-5282), 404 Houston St, is Sundance Square's top spot to catch a caffeine buzz. In the Cultural District, the **Four Star Coffee Bar** (☎ 817-336-5555), 3324 W 7th St, gets the locals' nod for the best coffee in town, and it serves light breakfasts and lunches, too.

SPECTATOR SPORTS

The humongous 150,061-seat Texas Motor Speedway (☎ 817-215-8500) is a National Association for Stock Car Auto Racing (NASCAR) track that hosts major auto-racing events from April through September. It's 15 miles north of downtown at the junction of I-35 and Hwy 114.

Fort Worth is, of course, a big rodeo town. The Stockyards Championship Rodeo takes place every Friday and Saturday at 8 pm in the Cowtown Coliseum (☎ 817-654-1148). Tickets are $8 for adults, $5 for children ages three to 12. There is also lots of rodeo action at the annual Southwestern Stock Show (see Special Events).

But who would have guessed that Fort Worth has not one but two minor league hockey teams? The Brahmas (☎ 817-335-7825) and the Fire (☎ 817-336-1992) play at both the Will Rogers Memorial Center and downtown at the Fort Worth-Tarrant County Convention Center (☎ 817-884-2222), 1111 Houston St.

SHOPPING

Factory outlet centers are big all over the US, but Fort Worth has one of the few such centers in a downtown area. Outlet Square (☎ 800-414-2817) in the Tandy Center, 150 Throckmorton St, has about 40 stores, a food court and an ice-skating rink. Look for the Fort Worth Store (☎ 817-415-8800), which carries goods from the Fort Worth Zoo and all the museum gift shops.

For Western gear, the Stockyards are ground zero. Country stars in town to play Billy Bob's sometimes shop for upscale apparel at the Maverick (☎ 817-626-1129), 100 E Exchange Ave, but the real cowboys are more likely to go for the down-to-earth duds across the street at Fincher's Western Store (☎ 817-624-7302), 115 E Exchange Ave. Leddy Boots and Saddlery (☎ 817-624-3149), 2455 N Main St, specializes in handmade goods.

The Ridgmar Mall (☎ 817-731-0856), 2060 Green Oaks Rd, has the only Neiman-Marcus in town. The Hulen Mall (☎ 817-294-1200), 4800 S Hulen St, is the city's largest, with about 120 stores. For good shopping closer to downtown, check out University Park Village (☎ 817-332-5700), 1612 S University Drive, and the stores on Camp Bowie Blvd west of the Cultural District.

GETTING THERE & AWAY
Air

Most visitors to Fort Worth arrive at DFW International Airport, 17 miles east of Fort Worth (see the Dallas Getting There & Away section). Fort Worth Meacham Airport no longer has any scheduled passenger service.

Bus

Greyhound Bus (☎ 817-332-4564) operates out of the bus terminal at 901 Commerce St opposite the Fort Worth-Tarrant County Convention Center. Services include:

to/from	frequency (per day)	trip duration	one way/ roundtrip
Dallas	13	40 min to 1 hour	$7/13
San Antonio	9	5 to 7 hours	$33/63
Houston	8	5 to 6 hours	$28/53

DART Rail

If you're traveling to or from Dallas, call DART (☎ 214-979-1111) for an update on the Trinity Railway Express, a light-rail line that is scheduled to reach Fort Worth sometime in 2000.

Train

Amtrak (☎ 817-332-2931) runs its *Texas Eagle* through the depot at 1501 Jones St downtown. Southbound trains for Austin and San Antonio depart Wednesday, Friday, Saturday and Sunday afternoons. Northbound trains for Chicago via Dallas and St Louis leave Fort Worth Tuesday, Wednesday, Thursday and Sunday afternoons.

Car

Fort Worth is 30 miles west of Dallas via I-30. Houston is 266 miles southeast via US 287 and I-45; Austin and San Antonio are 190 miles and 273 miles south, respectively, via I-35, and El Paso is 587 miles west via I-20 and I-10.

GETTING AROUND
To/From the Airports

In addition to the shuttle services listed in the Dallas Getting Around section, the T, Fort Worth's transit authority, offers Airporter shuttle service (☎ 817-334-0092) between DFW and four downtown hotels: the Worthington, Radisson Plaza, Clarion and Ramada Plaza. The fare is $8 for adults, $4 for seniors and disabled riders, free for kids 16 and younger who ride with a paying parent (one child per adult; beyond that, the fare for kids is $8 each). No reservations are necessary. A taxi from DFW to downtown Fort Worth costs about $30.

Bus

The T (☎ 817-215-8600) runs buses in Fort Worth weekdays from 6 am to midnight and weekends from 7 am to 7 pm. The fare is 80¢ for adults, 40¢ for seniors and children, with a free zone downtown.

Taxi

Fort Worth cab rates are $1.50 flagfall and 30¢ for each additional quarter-mile, plus $1 for each additional passenger. Cab companies include Yellow and Checker (☎ 817-534-5555 for both).

Around Dallas-Fort Worth

ARLINGTON
Population 294,816

Arlington is notable as one of the largest cities in the US without a public transportation system. It's a sprawling concrete suburb, but it does have a couple of world-class attractions. The Arlington Convention and Visitors' Bureau (☎ 817-461-3888 or 800-342-4305) is at 1905 E Randol Mill Rd.

Six Flags Over Texas

One of the oldest and biggest US amusement parks, Six Flags Over Texas can be either a lot of fun or a wretched drag – it all depends on whether or not the place is supercrowded when you go. If it is, you'll stand in hour-long lines all day. If it isn't, you'll have a ball and get more than your money's worth. Avoid weekends and arrive early in the day.

Orientation & Information Six Flags (☎ 817-530-6000, www.sixflags.com) is just south of I-30 off Exit 30, about a 20-minute drive from downtown Dallas or downtown

Fort Worth. From late May to late August it's open every day; from March to May and during September and October it's open weekends only. The park usually opens at 10 am and closes at 10 pm, but it can close as early as 8 pm on Sunday or stay open as late as 11 pm on Friday and Saturday. Six Flags also opens briefly in the winter, mostly on weekends in November and December, for Holiday in the Park, and most rides are in operation during that time. One-day tickets cost $38 for adults, $31 for seniors or children shorter than 4 feet tall. Two-day tickets are $45 for everyone, regardless of age. Parking is $7.

Guest Relations and lockers ($1) are in the entry mall just inside the park gate, as is a rental center for strollers ($6.50 per day), wagons ($8.75) and wheelchairs ($7). A kennel boards pets for $5 per day. ATMs are at the front gate, in Goodtimes Square and in the Mexico section. Changing tables are in all women's and most men's rest rooms, and a nursing and diapering area is inside the train caboose at the rear of Looney Tunes Land.

Highlights The park has six sections. **USA & Looney Tunes Land** has a small children's area, the Silver Star carousel, the Right Stuff Mach 1 ride (a jet flight simulator) and the free-falling G-Force ride. **Boomtown & Goodtimes Square** is home to the hot ride Mr Freeze – the tallest (242 feet) and fastest (70mph) roller coaster in Texas and the only one powered by linear induction motors; Flashback, a roller coaster that turns riders upside down six times; and Judge Roy Scream, a classic wooden coaster.

The **Tower** section includes Shock Wave – a roller coaster with back-to-back vertical loops – and the 300-foot Oil Derrick, featuring views of the Dallas and Fort Worth skylines. The 14-story Texas Giant roller coaster, often rated among the best by coaster aficionados, is the centerpiece of the **Texas** section, an area with several gentle rides, including the park railroad. **Old South & France** features the in-the-dark Runaway Mountain roller coaster and LaSalle's River Rapids, a white-water ride. Rides in **Spain & Mexico** include El Aserradero (a log flume ride) and La Vibora bobsleds. Aside from the rides, there are lots of shows – including big-name concerts, which cost a few dollars extra – and plenty of food choices.

Six Flags Hurricane Harbor Across I-30 from Six Flags Over Texas, this water park (☎ 817-265-3356) has lots of cool rides, including the 830-foot Sea Wolf raft slide; the Blue Raider, which shoots two-passenger inner tubes through a dark, flooded tunnel; and twin flume slides. Open daily from mid-May through mid-August and on weekends through mid-September; hours are 10 am to anywhere from 6 to 10 pm, depending on the month and day; $23 for people ages 10 to 59, $14 for seniors, $19 for children ages three to nine.

The Ballpark in Arlington
Baseball fans may be moved nearly to tears over the green sweep of sun-dappled grass at the Ballpark in Arlington. It's that beautiful. The park – easily accessed from I-30 via exits 28 or 30 – opened in 1994, an imposing neo-Romanesque structure designed by David Schwarz, the same architect responsible for much of Fort Worth's downtown glow. Stone carvings of longhorn steer and the Texas lone star emblem are everywhere. Inside, the design incorporates beloved elements from other parks, including replicas of the Fenway Park scoreboard from Boston and the right-field home-run porch from Tiger Stadium in Detroit.

The Texas Rangers (☎ 817-273-5100, 800-654-9545) play from April to October; tickets cost $4 to $30. When the Rangers are away, **stadium tours** (☎ 817-273-5099) are given Monday to Friday 9 am to 4 pm, Saturday 10 am to 4 pm, Sunday noon to 4 pm. When the Rangers are in town, tours take place Monday to Friday 9 am to noon, Saturday 10 am to noon. The tours are better on days when the Rangers are away, because then they can include the clubhouse, with its terrific collection of baseball movie posters, and a peek into the big-league ballplayers' inner sanctum, but they always include the dugout, batting cages and press box. Cost is

$5 for adults, $4 for seniors, $3 for children under 13.

Legends of the Game Museum From Babe Ruth's jersey to Willie Mays' shoes, this stellar museum (☎ 817-273-5600) includes the largest collection of memorabilia ever loaned by the National Baseball Hall of Fame Museum in Cooperstown, NY. Upstairs, a learning center puts a fun baseball spin on math, science, geography and more. From March to October, open Monday to Saturday 9 am to 7 pm, Sunday noon to 4 pm; from November to February, hours vary. Admission is $6 for adults, $5 for seniors, $4 for children ages six to 13. Combination tickets for the museum and ballpark tour (see above) cost $10 for adults, $8 for seniors, $6 for kids six to 13.

Other Attractions
Johnnie High's Country Music Revue (☎ 817-226-4400, 800-540-5127), a foot-stomping family show, takes place Saturday nights at the Arlington Music Hall, 224 N Center St about a half-block south of Hwy 180. The **River Legacy Living Science Center** (☎ 817-860-6752), 703 NW Green Oaks Blvd west of Collins St, offers environmentally minded exhibits, including a simulated raft ride down the Trinity River. The **American Airlines CR Smith Museum** (☎ 817-967-1560), Hwy 360 south of Hwy 183 at FAA Rd north of Arlington, details the workings of a major airline through an IMAX-like film and interactive exhibits.

Places to Stay & Eat
There's a *Sleep Inn* (☎ 817-649-1010) off I-30 right next to Six Flags; rooms start at $60/66 a single/double. The Ballpark in Arlington is home to *Friday's Front Row Sports Grill* (☎ 817-265-5191), run by the TGIF chain but with a baseball-themed menu. Meals are huge, even by Texas standards ($8 to $15 for dinner, a few dollars less for lunch). The restaurant is open daily for lunch and dinner, but special game-day packages include seats overlooking the ballpark action; call ☎ 817-273-5100 for details. For information on services in Arlington,

stop by the Convention and Visitors' Bureau (see above).

Getting There & Away
There is no public transportation to Arlington. The visitors' bureau runs a free trolley to Six Flags, Hurricane Harbor, the Ballpark in Arlington and area restaurants, but it's available only to guests of participating Arlington hotels, including the Sleep Inn.

GRAND PRAIRIE
Population 108,908
Grand Prairie's location astride I-30 just east of Arlington has helped it become a major tourist destination. Its information center is adjacent to the Palace of Wax and Ripley's Believe It or Not.

Palace of Wax & Ripley's Believe It or Not
This two-in-one attraction just north of I-30 at 601 E Safari Parkway (☎ 972-263-2391) features the usual array of lifelike celebrity tributes and oddities. Brad Pitt is a big draw at the Palace of Wax (though we guess he'll soon be upstaged by Leonardo DiCaprio, who hadn't been waxed last time we checked). Ripley's attractions include a Leaning Tower of Pisa made of matchsticks and a simulated Texas tornado. Open Monday to Thursday 10 am to 5 pm, Friday and Saturday 10 am to 4 pm, Sunday 10 am to 6 pm. Admission to either museum is $9.95 for adults, $6.95 for kids ages four to 12; combination tickets to both cost $12.95 for adults, $9.95 for kids.

Lone Star Park
Bet on the thoroughbreds at this racetrack (☎ 972-263-7223) on Belt Line Rd north of I-30. Live races take place from April to July and October to November. Year-round, the Post Time Pavilion (through Gate 1 on the right) has simulcast races from Churchill Downs, Del Mar and other top tracks.

Trader's Village
There's a huge flea market every Saturday and Sunday at this popular park (☎ 972-647-2331), 2602 Mayfield Rd off of Hwy 360.

From hubcaps to cowboy hats, it's all here, along with carnival rides and frequent special events. Admission is $2 per vehicle.

Getting There & Away
Grand Prairie is at Exit 34 off I-30 west of Dallas. Alas, you cannot get there via public transportation.

GRAPEVINE
Population 38,232
Although it's right next to DFW International Airport, Grapevine is as quaint a town as you'll find in the Metroplex. Much of its Main St is listed on the National Register of Historic Places. Pick up a walking tour brochure at the Grapevine Heritage Center, 701 S Main St.

Tarantula Railroad
This steam train (☎ 817-654-0898, 800-952-5717) makes daily trips between Grapevine and the Fort Worth Stockyards, a 75-minute ride one way. The roundtrip fare is $19.95 for adults, $9.95 for children ages three to 12. In Fort Worth, there's an optional cross-town train tour available for $10 for adults, $5.50 for children.

Grapevine Mills
Almost as big as Minnesota's Mall of America, the Grapevine Mills shopping center (☎ 972-724-4900, 888-645-5748) is 2 miles north of DFW International Airport on FM 2499 at Hwy 121. Huge sculptures of footballs, flags and Texas bluebonnets guard the entrances, and inside are more than 200 stores, a 30-screen movie theater and about two dozen restaurants.

Delaney Vineyards
With a name like Grapevine, there's got to be a few wineries in town. This lovely one (☎ 817-481-5668), 2000 Champagne Blvd off Hwy 121 at the Glade exit, is considered the best, and it's quite a sight, with its huge Douglas fir beams, cypress doors and grand barrel room. We were surprised they charge $12 for a combination tour and tasting session, but wine fanciers will probably find it worth the price. Tours ($5) are given

Tuesday to Saturday noon to 4 pm on the hour, with tastings ($7) every half-hour.

Tour 18

These links (☎ 817-430-2000, 800-946-5310), 8618 FM 1171 in Flower Mound (take the Lewisville exit off I-35 E and drive 10 miles west on FM 1171), replicate 18 holes from the best US golf courses, so if you've ever wanted to play Augusta's Amen Corner and Oakmont's No 3, here's your chance – *if* you've got the cash: it's $75 on weekdays, $85 on weekends.

Getting There & Away

Grapevine is northwest of DFW International Airport, off Hwy 114 or Hwy 121 north of Hwy 183. Other than the Tarantula Railroad to and from Fort Worth, you can't get there via public transportation.

IRVING

Population 176,993

Irving's big claim to fame is that it is home to the NFL's Dallas Cowboys. It's also the Metroplex's chief center for film and television production.

Texas Stadium

The Cowboys (☎ 972-579-5000) play from August to December at Texas Stadium, a behemoth of a stadium where the Carpenter/Airport Freeway (Hwy 183) meets Hwy 12, about 15 to 20 minutes from downtown Dallas. Stadium tours (☎ 972-554-1804) let visitors see the locker room, run a pass on the field and try to kick a field goal; they are offered Monday to Saturday every hour from 10 am to 3 pm, Sunday (except game days) 11 am to 3 pm, leaving from Gate 8. Cost is $5 for adults, $3 for children 12 and younger.

Many area hotels offer packages that include Cowboys tickets; for information, call the Irving Convention and Visitors Bureau at ☎ 800-247-8464.

Las Colinas Complex

Two miles northwest of Texas Stadium on Hwy 114, Las Colinas includes the Dallas Communications Complex, home of many entertainment and media companies. The **Studios at Las Colinas Tour** (☎ 972-869-3456) gives a behind-the-scenes look at a soundstage where numerous films and television shows have been made, including parts of *JFK*, *RoboCop* and *Leap of Faith*. There's also memorabilia from films made elsewhere – including a great collection of costumes from *Superman*, *Star Wars* and *The Wizard of Oz* – demonstrations of how special effects are created, and a museum of communications.

Tours take place daily at 10:30 am and 12:30, 2:30 and 4 pm (no 10:30 tour on Sunday). From mid-June to mid-August, tours are offered every hour from 12:30 to 6:30 pm. Admission is $12.95 for adults, $10.95 for seniors, $6.95 for children ages four to 12.

Other Las Colinas-area sights include the **Mustangs of Las Colinas**, nine larger-than-life bronze horses splashing dramatically through a stream, and the impressive **Las Colinas Flower Clock**, replanted with fresh flowers eight times a year. A Venetian-style water-taxi service (☎ 972-869-4321) plies the canals that meander through the complex, stopping at many shops and restaurants along the way.

Getting There & Away

Irving is served by DART Rail's Trinity Railway Express (☎ 214-979-1111) and by several DART bus routes, notably the No 202 express from downtown Dallas' West Transfer Center.

PARKER

Population 1200

Parker, set amid the rolling hills of North Dallas suburbia, is best known for South Fork Ranch – one of the most famous sites in US pop culture.

South Fork Ranch

Fans of the television show *Dallas* will enjoy a pilgrimage to the ranch where it was filmed (☎ 972-442-7800), 3700 Hogge Rd off FM 2551. For those who could not have cared less who shot JR, South Fork can easily be dropped from the agenda.

Built by JR Duncan in 1970, the ranch was a working spread for eight years, until helicopter-borne executives for Lorimar Productions spied it and landed in the front yard. The Duncans were reluctant to allow the show to film there; they finally agreed, but allowed only exterior shots to be filmed, and those only in the summer.

Lorimar built a 40,000-sq-foot set in California to depict the mansion's interior. Later, after the 'Who Shot JR?' craze of 1980, obsessed fans prowled the South Fork grounds night and day. The besieged Duncans decided to sell the property, and Lorimar began filming interior shots here, too. Today, South Fork is primarily a novelty spot for receptions and parties. Among the clients are the Dallas Cowboys Cheerleaders, who hold their annual slumber party on the ranch. ('Sorry guys, it's private,' the tour guides say.)

Open 9 am to 5 pm daily except Thanksgiving and Christmas. For day visitors, admission is $6.95 for adults, $5.50 for seniors, $4.50 for children ages four to 12; that buys entry to the *Dallas* museum, whose collection includes the prop gun used to shoot JR; a tram tour; and admission to the ranch house. To get to South Fork from Dallas, take Hwy 75 (N Central Expressway) to Exit 30. Go east 6½ miles on Parker Rd, then turn right on FM 2551. The ranch is immediately on the left.

Beyond the Metroplex

WAXAHACHIE
Population 18,200
Waxahachie, 35 miles south of Dallas via I-35 E, is a popular weekend destination best known for its Victorian, Greek Revival and Queen Anne architecture; 20 percent of all Texas buildings listed on the National Register of Historic Places are in Waxahachie. Each June, a Gingerbread Trail festival, which includes tours of several historic buildings, celebrates this heritage. Just west

of town, the Scarborough Faire Renaissance Festival takes place on weekends from late April to early June. For information on Waxahachie events, contact the Waxahachie Convention and Visitors Bureau (☎ 972-937-2390, 972-938-9827 from the Metroplex), 102 YMCA Drive, PO Box 187, Waxahachie, TX 75165.

GLEN ROSE
Population 2188
Like Waxahachie, Glen Rose is a favorite weekend destination for Metroplex residents looking for an escape. It makes a perfect day trip from either Dallas (75 miles away) or Fort Worth (58 miles away).

Fossil Rim Wildlife Center
The private 2700-acre Fossil Rim Wildlife Center (☎ 254-897-2960), which is 3 miles southwest of Glen Rose off US 67, specializes in the protection and breeding of exotic and endangered species from around the world. Thirty species roam free here, including cheetah, kudu, wildebeest and giraffe.

You can tour the center year-round from 9 am until two hours before sunset via a 9½-mile self-guided drive with audiotape rental ($12.95 for adults, $11.95 for seniors, $9.95 for children ages four to 11, free for kids 3 and younger) or on a guided tour ($25 for adults, $18 for children ages four to 11). Overnight accommodations include a lodge ($125 to $225) and deluxe safari-camp tents with private bathrooms ($150). Fossil Rim also offers mountain biking day trips ($30) and weekend workshops for beginning cyclists ($75).

Dinosaur Valley State Park
Some of the world's best-preserved dinosaur tracks are on view in this park (☎ 254-897-4588), 5 miles west of Glen Rose via US 67 and FM 205. The tracks are in the bed of the Paluxy River, which is usually dry or has no more than a few inches of water. Other activities include hiking, mountain biking and bird-watching. The campground has sites for $15 a night. Park admission is $5 per person ages 13 and older.

WACO
Population 103,000

Seventy miles south of Dallas-Fort Worth via I-35 is Waco, which has the misfortune of being known best for an event that didn't even take place here. In 1993, images of a standoff and shoot-out between federal agents and members of a religious cult called the Branch Davidians were beamed around the world, and viewers were told that what they were seeing was in Waco. It wasn't – it happened near Elk, Texas, about 15 miles out of town – but Waco is the name that stuck. And that's too bad. Waco is not the world's most exciting town, but it is a pleasant little city with a number of legitimate attractions, and it's a fun place for hiking or biking and a must for great, cheap Vietnamese food and barbecue. Waco is worth a stop, and anyone who says otherwise probably hasn't been here.

Orientation

Downtown Waco is south of the confluence of the Bosque ('BOS-kee') and Brazos Rivers; the Brazos cuts across the city from the northwest to the southeast. I-35 runs north-south at the east end of the city; its service road is called JH Kultgen Ave.

The downtown area is a grid oriented about 45° off true north. The pedestrian-only Waco Suspension Bridge over the Brazos River connects west and east Waco. New Mt Carmel, the site of the former Branch Davidian compound, is 14½ miles east of town.

Information

Tourist Offices The superb Waco Tourist Information Center (☎ 254-750-8696, 800-922-6386, fax 254-752-9233, www.wacocvb.com), is at the western end of Fort Fisher Park, which is off University Parks Drive. The friendly staff knows the area well, helps

---

Standoff

The Branch Davidians were an offshoot of a radical sect of Seventh Day Adventists. The original group, the Davidians, set up shop in Waco in 1935 but moved outside the city in 1959 to establish a new compound called New Mt Carmel, near the town of Elk. Fighting between internal factions led to splits and drama, and in 1987, Vernon Howell, who had joined the group in 1981, took control and changed his name to David Koresh.

Koresh's platform involved, among other things, arming the compound to defend it against the apocalyptic nightmare the world would become after the second coming of Christ. Believing that Koresh was buying, selling and storing illegal weapons, the federal Bureau of Alcohol, Tobacco and Firearms staged a shamefully understaffed, poorly planned raid to arrest Koresh on February 28, 1993. The agents were fired on; four ATF agents and five cult members were killed in the ensuing firefight. The resulting standoff lasted 51 days.

As local authorities and FBI hostage negotiators surrounded the compound with hundreds of police cars and even a tank, the international media had a field day; viewers around the world were treated to images of the dead ATF agents and the standoff, as well as interviews with officers from a host of government agencies. And because the compound was in the middle of nowhere, the press simply said it was in Waco – the nearest large city.

The standoff ended April 19, 1993, when officers fired tear-gas bombs into the compound. Within hours, the buildings were completely engulfed in flames fueled by the tear gas canisters' ignition. Nine cult members survived; of the dead, most were found to have been shot, probably by Branch Davidian members themselves. The government's handling of the incident is still the subject of controversy.

Nick Selby

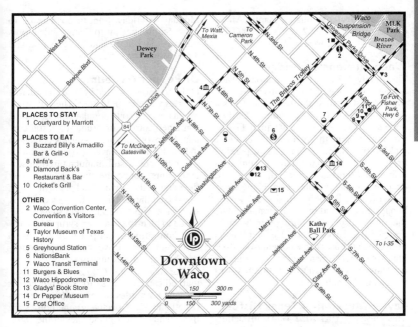

PLACES TO STAY
1 Courtyard by Marriott

PLACES TO EAT
3 Buzzard Billy's Armadillo
Bar & Grill-o
8 Ninfa's
9 Diamond Back's
Restaurant & Bar
10 Cricket's Grill

OTHER
2 Waco Convention Center,
Convention & Visitors
Bureau
4 Taylor Museum of Texas
History
5 Greyhound Station
6 NationsBank
7 Waco Transit Terminal
11 Burgers & Blues
12 Waco Hippodrome Theatre
13 Gladys' Book Store
14 Dr Pepper Museum
15 Post Office

**Downtown
Waco**

0   150   300 m

0   150   300 yards

with hotel reservations and sells Waco
Funfare tickets ($15 for adults, $6 for students), which give free or reduced admission
to many city attractions, including the ones
listed here. Open Monday to Saturday 8 am
to 5 pm, Sunday 9 am to 5 pm; closed major
holidays.

Money There's a large NationsBank at the
corner of Austin Ave and 6th St, with drive-
in tellers and ATMs.

Post & Communications The main post
office (☎ 254-754-4188) is at 800 Franklin
Ave. The area code for Waco is 254.

Bookstores & Libraries Gladys' Book
Store (☎ 254-754-7868), 710 Austin Ave, has
new and used books. There's a Barnes &
Noble (☎ 254-741-9495) at 4909 W Waco
Drive, between 49th and 50th Sts, southwest
of downtown. The main library (☎ 254-750-
5941) is at 1717 Austin Ave.

See the Armstrong Browning Library
section for information on Baylor University's
renowned manuscript collection.

Campuses Baylor University, the world's
largest Baptist-owned university, has 12,000
undergraduate and graduate students in a
wide array of fields, including law, business
and entrepreneurial studies. Its main campus is in Waco, south of the Brazos River
and east of I-35; it's home to the Armstrong
Browning Library and a large bear pit that
houses several of the university football
team's mascots.

McLennan Community College, west of
the confluence of the Bosque and Brazos
Rivers, is a two-year college with 6000 full-
time students and many more in continuing
education programs.

Laundry The most convenient coin laundry
is West Waco Drive Laundromat (☎ 254-
754-7038), 2424 W Waco Drive.

Medical Services Hillcrest Baptist Medical Center (☎ 254-202-2000) is at 3000 Herring Ave, 1½ miles west of downtown.

Waco Suspension Bridge

The stately 475-foot pedestrian-only Waco Suspension Bridge, built from 1868 to '70, was the first to cross the Brazos and was a key crossing along the Chisholm Trail. Two popular myths are associated with it. First, it was not, despite the plaque in the center making this claim, the longest suspension bridge of its time (that honor went to a bridge in Cincinnati). Second, it was not, despite an undeniable resemblance, the model for the Brooklyn Bridge. John Roebling, who invented the multistrand cabling that allowed such large bridges to be built, designed the Brooklyn Bridge, and Waco's bridge actually uses cable bought from Roebling's New Jersey wire factory. The bridge is off University Parks Drive between Washington and Franklin Aves.

Taylor Museum of Texas History

This museum (☎ 254-752-4774), 701 Jefferson Ave, has a good selection of just what the name implies, but it is outstanding for its exhibit on the history of the Davidian compound at New Mt Carmel and the infamous 51-day standoff between Davidians and federal agents that would so adversely affect the world's perception of the city of Waco (see Standoff). The exhibit includes a scale model of the compound, an objective history of the Davidian movement and details of the siege. Open Monday to Saturday 10 am to 4 pm, Sunday 1 to 4 pm (last admission 3 pm); $3 for adults, $2 for seniors, $1.25 for students and children.

Armstrong Browning Library

This museum (☎ 254-710-3566), on the campus of Baylor University, houses the world's largest collection of secular stained glass, as well as the largest collection of original manuscripts and personal effects of the English poets Robert and Elizabeth Barrett Browning. Glass highlights include the famous **Pied Piper of Hamlin** and the 'sunrise-sunset' windows in the **Foyer of Meditation**. Open

Monday to Friday 9 am to noon and 2 to 5 pm, Saturday 9 am to noon; guided tours run weekdays at 10 and 11 am and 2 and 3 pm. Admission is free.

Dr Pepper Museum

Dr Pepper was invented by Waco pharmacist Charles C Alderton in 1885. The soft drink, which never, despite popular American lore, contained cocaine or prune juice, still contains heaps of caffeine. It is hugely popular in the southern US and available in 17 countries.

Dr Pepper is still manufactured in several plants around the country, but only at the plant in the city of Dublin, northwest of Waco (see the Dublin section), is the drink still made with Imperial brand sugar, as opposed to high-fructose corn syrup. The Dublin plant ships its output only within 40 miles, and people drive there from throughout the state to pick up cases.

The Dublin stuff comes in specially marked cans (about $3 for six), but purists hold out for bottles. In 8oz and 10oz versions ($1.50 and $2, respectively), the bottles are the original issue – made back in the 1880s, when production on the drink started – and they roll off the assembly line only in Dublin. Once the stock of bottles is used up, they're gone forever, because they are no longer manufactured.

The Dr Pepper Museum (☎ 254-757-1024, www.drpeppermuseum.com), 300 S 5th St in Waco, has lots of Pepper paraphernalia, but the best part is the **soda fountain**, where the soda jerk behind the counter will shoot you a cold Dr Pepper (diet or regular, 60¢ to 90¢) or, even better, a Dr Pepper sundae ($1.75). Open Monday to Saturday 10 am to 4 pm, Sunday noon to 4 pm (till 5 pm daily from Memorial Day to Labor Day). Museum admission is $4 for adults, $3.50 for seniors, $2 for students; admission to the fountain is free.

Texas Ranger Hall of Fame & Museum

The headquarters of Texas Rangers Company F is housed within the Texas Ranger Hall of Fame and Museum (☎ 254-750-8631), in Fort Fisher Park. The museum is exactly

what it sounds like: a collection showing the history of the Rangers from their creation in the early 19th century through their days fighting cattle rustlers, Indians and Mexicans, through Bonnie and Clyde and the Rangers' present-day role as the most elite unit of state police officers in Texas. There are lots of guns, saddles, hats, colorful tales and slide shows. Open daily 9 am to 5 pm; $4 for adults, $2 for children.

Texas Sports Hall of Fame

This museum (☎ 254-756-1633), 1108 S University Parks Drive, is a festival of sports memorabilia, including photographs, interactive audio and video displays, old uniforms and equipment and – its pride and joy – the 1938 Heisman trophy awarded to TCU quarterback Davey O'Brien. Open Monday to Saturday 10 am to 5 pm, Sunday noon to 5 pm; $4 for adults, $3.50 for seniors, $2 for students.

Cameron Park & Zoo

At the western end of downtown, along both banks of the Brazos River and extending west along the Bosque, Cameron Park is a peaceful bit of green. Hills and limestone cliffs rise quickly, making the park a great place for hiking and mountain biking. The cliff-top Lovers' Leap affords sweeping views over the rivers. At the eastern end of the park is Pecan Bottoms, which is lined

with pecan and plum trees; you can keep whatever is on the ground (delicious!), but don't shake the trees.

Just south of Pecan Bottoms, the Cameron Park Zoo (☎ 254-750-8400), 1701 N 4th St, is a 430-acre zoo with 50 acres of natural habitat. It's a nice one, with a great collection of African animals, including elephants, rhinos and giraffes; Asian gibbons; a Texas section with about 30 native species, including Texas longhorns, armadillos, prairie dogs, snakes and spiders; the staggeringly beautiful and endangered Sumatran tiger; and the Herpetarium, the zoo's newest attraction, with reptiles large and small from around the world. Open Monday to Saturday 9 am to 5 pm, Sunday 11 am to 5 pm; $4 for adults, $2 for students.

Other Attractions

The **Art Center** (☎ 254-752-4371), 1300 College Drive on the campus of McLennan Community College, has rotating exhibits of works by artists from Waco and elsewhere in Texas. Outside, *The Waco Door*, a rusting sculpture by local artist Robert Wilson, is the focus of the lovely and wheelchair-accessible Sculpture Garden. Open Tuesday to Saturday 10 am to 5 pm, Sunday 1 to 5 pm; free (a donation of $2 per adult, $1 per student is suggested).

The stately antebellum **Earle-Harrison House** (☎ 254-753-2032), 1901 N 5th St, has five acres of beautifully manicured southern-style gardens, a pond and a double gazebo. Open Monday to Friday 9 am to 4:30 pm, Saturday and Sunday 1:30 to 5 pm; $2 for adults, free for children under 12.

Organized Tours

James S Wood (☎ 254-750-8696, 254-836-4845) runs tours of downtown Waco in a mule-drawn carriage, and by all accounts he's a hoot. The tours leave from the Texas Ranger Museum Monday to Friday every hour or so from 10 am to 3:30 pm; they last about 45 minutes and cost $6 per person.

Places to Stay

Everyplace down to a mouse hole is full during Baylor University special events, including their annual homecoming weekends in September.

Camping There's camping at *Fort Fisher Park* (☎ 254-750-8630, 800-922-6386), just east of I-35, where it's $10 to pitch a tent or $11 for an RV with water and electric hookups.

Motels & Hotels There's nothing terribly special in town. Motels and hotels line I-35; the cheaper options include a notably charmless and inhospitable *Motel 6* (☎ 254-662-4622), 3120 I-35, with singles/doubles for $34/38, and the *Super 8 Motel* (☎ 254-754-1023), 1320 I-35, with singles/doubles for $40/50.

A better choice is the very nice *Lexington Waco* (☎ 254-754-1266), 115 JH Kultgen Ave, with friendly staff and cheerful doubles starting at $62. Other mid-range options include the *Best Western Old Main Lodge* (☎ 254-753-0316), at I-35 and S 4th St, with singles or doubles starting at $62, and the *Waco Clarion Inn* (☎ 254-757-2000), 801 S 4th St opposite Baylor University, with two pools, a Jacuzzi and singles/doubles starting at $70.

The slickest place in town is the *Courtyard by Marriott* (☎ 254-752-8686), 101 Washington Ave, right across from the convention center, with large and comfortable rooms starting at $79.

B&Bs The pleasant *Judge Baylor House B&B* (☎ 254-756-0273), 908 Speight Ave, has comfortable, clean rooms starting at $70 on weekdays, $80 on weekends. Also nice is the *Brazos House* (☎ 254-754-3565, fax 754-3568), 1316 Washington Ave, a comfortable home with just four rooms, each with a phone and cable TV. The proprietors would be happy to give you a tour before you commit. The rooms start at $65. The *Colcord House Bed & Breakfast* (☎ 254-753-5537), 2211 Colcord Ave, has rooms inside the main house for $75 and in its nicer carriage house for $95.

Places to Eat

The usual bevy of fast food places lines I-35. Don't blow your chance for great Vietnamese food at the cubbyhole-size *Lee's Restaurant* (☎ 254-756-1294), 920 JH Kultgen Ave on the east side of I-35 at S 10th St, next to La Quinta Inn. Run by a Vietnamese family, the restaurant's Asian specialties are simply marvelous, and dirt cheap: delicious sandwiches cost $2 to $3; spicy chicken curry, spring rolls, spicy vermicelli with sliced beef and scallions or scrumptious barbecued marinated chicken and fried egg over rice are each $4.

There are two more holes-in-the-wall that serve up super, inexpensive stuff. *El Potosino Restaurant*, 324 David Drive two blocks west of Waco Drive, is open daily from 6:30 am to 1:30 pm (to 2 pm on Sunday). Try the chilaquiles, corn tortillas in a red chili sauce with queso blanco, onions and sour cream – it's about $3. And in East Waco, *Tony DeMaria Bar B Q* (☎ 254-755-8888), 1000 Elm St, is a serious Texas barbecue joint with terrific full barbecue plates from $3.19 to $5, including a bowl of grease . . . er, dipping sauce. Open Monday to Saturday 9:30 am to 2 pm.

Buzzard Billy's Armadillo Bar & Grill-o (☎ 254-753-2778), 208 S University Parks Drive, is a fun and locally famous Cajun place serving seafood and steaks; lunch costs $5 to $8, dinner $7 to $12. Look for the old cop cruiser outside.

On Mary Ave between 2nd and 3rd Sts, the River Center Square complex is home to some restaurants and live music venues. *Cricket's Grill* (☎ 254-754-4677), 211 Mary Ave, is much more of a beer hall than a restaurant, but they do make fine pizzas; 12-inch pies with pepperoni or sausage are $10. Their lunch specials are a great deal, with three daily choices of main course, side dish and soft drink for $5. Also in the complex, *Ninfa's* does Tex-Mex with fresh handmade flour tortillas for around $12 per entrée; try the spinach enchiladas or chiles rellenos. *Diamond Back's Restaurant and Bar* (☎ 254-757-2871), 217 Mary Ave, does southwestern food for lunch only.

Elsewhere in Waco, the *Elite Cafe* (☎ 254-754-4941), 2132 S Valley Mills at I-35, is famous for its typical diner food, but locals say it has gone downhill since its renovation. *George's Restaurant* (☎ 254-753-1421), 1925 Speight Ave, serves standard Texas fare and is locally famous for its 'Big O,' a beer served in a huge fishbowl glass.

Entertainment

Touring Broadway shows, ballet performances, and spiritual and other musical events take place at the historic **Waco Hippodrome Theatre** (☎ 254-752-9797), 724 Austin Ave. Ticket prices for shows in the Broadway series start at $22.

The **Waco Symphony Orchestra** (☎ 254-754-0851) performs from September to May at Waco Hall, on the Baylor campus.

There's often live music at the River Square Center complex, with Thursday to Saturday jazz at **Diamond Back's Restaurant & Bar** (☎ 254-757-2871), 217 Mary Ave, and blues at **Burgers & Blues** (☎ 254-752-5837), 217 Mary Ave, Wednesday and Friday. Also in River Square Center, **Cricket's Grill** (☎ 254-754-4677), 211 Mary Ave, has about 100 beers on tap, pool tables and a general frat-boy atmosphere. **Buzzard Billy's** (☎ 254-753-2778), 208 S University Parks Drive, has live Cajun music Friday and Saturday.

Gay & Lesbian There's no name or sign, but **David's**, (☎ 254-753-9189) 500 N 5th St (enter the limestone building at the corner of 5th St and Jefferson Ave), is a hopping gay place with drag shows at least twice a month. For a what's-on guide to the region, try the Gay and Lesbian Alliance of Central Texas (☎ 254-752-7727).

Getting There & Away

Bus There are at least five Greyhound buses a day ($13 one-way, $24 roundtrip, 1½ hours) between Dallas, Fort Worth and Waco. The Greyhound station (☎ 254-753-4534) is at 700 Columbus Ave.

Car Waco is on I-35, about halfway between the Dallas-Fort Worth Metroplex and Austin and about 1½ hours from both.

Getting Around

Bus Waco Transit (☎ 254-753-0113) buses cost 75¢. The main local bus transfer point is the Waco Transit Terminal, on 4th St between

Austin and Franklin Aves. From there to the Tourist Information Center, Sports Hall of Fame, Texas Ranger Museum and Baylor campus, take bus No 9-South Terrace. For the Cameron Park Zoo and the Art Center, take bus No 4-Park Lake.

Trolley The Brazos Trolley, a shuttle that stops at all major attractions in town, is run by Waco Transit daily from late May to late August, and on weekends only during the rest of the year. The cost is 50¢ per ride, or $1.50 per day; buy tickets on the trolley or at the Tourist Information Center. The trolley runs every 20 minutes or so.

Taxi Yellow Cab (☎ 254-756-1861) is the only game in town. Flagfall is $1.60, plus $1.20 per mile *plus* 75¢ per person over age 10.

AROUND WACO
New Mt Carmel

The site of the Branch Davidian compound – now called the Mt Carmel Center – at New Mt Carmel is closed to the public except for its one-room visitors' center (☎ 254-863-5985), but thousands of people make their way here each year. It's an interesting group: law-enforcement buffs, conspiracy theorists, the merely curious and antigovernment sympathizers – including convicted Oklahoma City bomber Timothy McVeigh – all find their way here on something of a pilgrimage. The only attraction here is the visitors' center and the holdout Branch Davidians who maintain it. They and other Branch Davidians (there are very few left) are in the midst of a dispute as to the direction of the cult, and you may be actively encouraged to join one or the other (albeit tiny) factions: as a friend of ours left after a visit, one Davidian insisted on presenting her with a copy of the *Decoded Message of the Seven Seals of the Book of Revelation*, by David Koresh.

From Waco, take University Parks Drive south to Hwy 6/Loop 340 north to FM 2491. Turn left onto FM 2491 and bear left at the fork. About 5 miles from Loop 340, just past the Double E Ranch Rd gates, is a paved road running off to the left. Take this road;

the compound is ahead on the right – though as the cops like to say, 'There's nothing to see here, folks. Keep moving.'

Dublin

Head to Dublin if you're in the area on a Tuesday morning and have a hankering to see the Dr Pepper Bottling Plant (☎ 254-445-3466) in operation. Though they bottle only on Tuesday mornings, the plant is open for tours Monday to Friday 9 am to 5 pm, Saturday 10 am to 5 pm, Sunday 1 to 5 pm; $1.50 for adults, 50¢ for kids.

From Waco, take Hwy 6 west to Dublin. At the light, turn left and the plant is one block down on your left – you can't miss it. There is a gift shop and soda fountain as well.

DENISON
Population 21,840

Denison, 75 miles north of Dallas on US 75, is best known as the hometown of former US president Dwight D Eisenhower, who was born at 208 E Day St on October 14, 1890. The state parks department has preserved the home and added a visitors' center (☎ 903-465-8908) with Eisenhower memorabilia. It's open Monday to Friday 10 am to 4 pm, Saturday 10 am to 5 pm, Sunday noon to 4 pm.

Dwight D Eisenhower's birthplace

Hagerman National Wildlife Refuge

Fishing and bird-watching are popular at this 11,300-acre preserve along the Big Mineral Arm of Lake Texoma, 13 miles west of Denison (☎ 903-786-2826). An auto-tour route hugs the shore, and the interpretive Crow Hill Trail is a nice short leg-stretcher along the way. For more ambitious trekking, the Cross Timbers hiking trails west of the refuge wind for 14 miles along and near Lake Texoma.

To get to the refuge from Denison, take Hwy 120 west to Hwy 1417. Drive 2 miles south, then 6 miles west on Refuge Rd. From Dallas, take US 75 north to Sherman, then take US 82 7½ miles west to Southmayd Rd, then drive 4 miles north.

WICHITA FALLS
Population 100,138

In 1886, just four years after Wichita Falls was founded, a flood washed away the little Wichita River cascade that gave the city its name. In 1986 the townspeople marked the anniversary by building a new waterfall. Plenty of towns might do such a thing mainly to attract tourism, but in Wichita Falls you get the sense that the waterfall was created by the local people just because they wanted to do it for themselves and their families, and if a few out-of-towners happened to show up, well, fine.

Wichita Falls is that kind of town – solid and steady, secure in its role as regional capital of what is known as 'Texoma,' so named because so many people in the region travel between Texas and Oklahoma for work and play. From here it's 112 miles southeast on US 287 to Fort Worth and 140 miles northeast on I-44 to Oklahoma City.

Orientation

In the downtown Wichita Falls area, US 281 and US 287 become the city's two main streets – Broad St, which is one-way north, and Holliday St, which is one-way south. US 82 is known within town as Kell Blvd. The city's main commercial core is south of Kell Blvd along Kemp Blvd and the Midwestern Parkway.

Information
Tourist Offices Wichita Falls has an official Texas Travel Information Center (☎ 940-723-7931) at 900 Central Freeway just off I-44 north of downtown. It's open daily except major holidays 8 am to 5 pm. The Wichita Falls Convention and Visitors Bureau office (☎ 940-716-5500, 800-799-6732, fax 940-716-5509) is in the Multi-Purpose Events Center, 1000 5th St. There's a vague but workable map in the bureau's visitors' pamphlet.

Money NationsBank (☎ 940-696-7700) is at 2733 Midwestern Parkway.

Post & Communications The main post office (☎ 940-766-4188) is downtown at 1000 Lamar St. Mail Boxes Etc (☎ 940-696-1142) is at 3916 Kemp Blvd in the Wichita Square shopping plaza. The same strip mall houses Kinko's (☎ 940-696-2679), where Internet access costs 20¢ per minute or $12 an hour.

Media The *Times Record News* sells for 50¢ ($1.50 on Sundays). Its Friday entertainment supplement, *What's Next*, is a good guide to local events.

Bookstores & Libraries There's a Hastings bookstore (☎ 940-691-4382) at 2801 Southwest Parkway. But the area's most interesting bookstore by far is 25 miles southwest, in Archer City: Booked Up (☎ 940-574-2511), 216 S Center, specializes in used, rare and antiquarian books – and it's owned by hometown boy Larry McMurtry, the author of such popular Texas classics as *Lonesome Dove* and *The Last Picture Show*. The Wichita Falls Public Library (☎ 940-761-8800) is downtown at 600 11th St.

Laundry The Econ-O-Wash Laundromat (☎ 940-322-6455), 1912 9th St, is just west of downtown.

Medical Services United Regional Health Care Systems (☎ 940-723-4111), 1600 11th St, has complete emergency services and a NowCare facility, which charges $55 per visit, no appointment needed. The NowCare entrance is on the hospital's 10th St side.

Emergency The Sheriff's Department is at ☎ 940-766-8170, the Highway Patrol at ☎ 940-855-6610.

The Falls & Lucy Park
The new Wichita Falls are 54 feet tall – about 10 times the height of the original drop. They were built not on but beside the Wichita River. Water is pumped from the river up a cliff and recirculated into the stream at the rate of 3,500 gallons of minute.

Although the falls are visible from I-44 heading south into town, many visitors get up close by taking the path east from Lucy Park (bus No 2 from Sikes Senter Mall or the Central Freeway), among the largest parks in Wichita Falls. Lucy park also has a duck pond, picnic areas and a great playground.

Natural Adventures
Wichita Falls' best-kept secret, Natural Adventures (☎ 940-781-0006), 400 Bridge St at Berends Landing (bus No 1 from Sikes Senter Mall comes close), rents canoes ($20) and rafts ($15) for floating the mild-but-scenic Wichita River; shuttle service ($6) is available to river put-in and take-out points. Natural Adventures also has the indoor Elevator Rock Climbing Gym ($8 for climbing, $3 for shoe rental). Open Monday to Saturday; call ahead for reservations.

Other Attractions
The **Wichita Falls Railroad Museum** (☎ 940-723-2661), 501 8th St (bus No 1 or 4 from the Sikes Senter Mall or Central Freeway) has the nation's largest collection of rolling stock from the Missouri-Kansas-Texas (Katy) Railroad. Open Saturday noon to 4 pm; free.

The **Kell House** (☎ 940-723-0623), 900 Bluff St (bus No 4), was the home of city founding father Frank Kell; it has been preserved with the original family furnishings. Tours are offered Tuesday, Wednesday and Sunday 2 to 4 pm; $3.

The **Wichita Falls Museum and Art Center** (☎ 940-692-0923), 2 Eureka Circle, is open Tuesday to Friday 9:30 am to 4:30 pm,

Saturday 10 am to 5 pm; $4. On Saturday this science and art museum puts on a planetarium show at 1 pm ($1.50) and a laser show at 3 pm ($3).

The **Wichita Falls Fire and Police Museum** (☎ 940-767-2412), Ave H at Giddings St (bus No 2), has more than 20,000 pieces of firefighting and police memorabilia. Open Saturday noon to 4 pm; free.

Special Events
Cyclists from nearly every state come to Wichita Falls late each August for the 100-mile Hotter'N Hell Hundred, the largest sanctioned century bicycle ride in the US. A major bike gear show takes place at the same time. Call ☎ 940-723-5800 for information. The Bike Stop (☎ 940-322-7301), 1922 10th St, is a good source of local cycling information.

Places to Stay
Camping Tent camping sites are available at *Lake Arrowhead State Park* (☎ 940-528-2211), 14 miles southeast of Wichita Falls via US 281 and FM 1954. Water-and-electric sites cost $10, and no-electric sites are $7; there's also a $2 park admission fee for all visitors ages 13 and up.

Wichita Falls RV Park (☎ 940-723-1532, 800-252-1532), 2944 Seymour Hwy, has showers, a laundry and full hookup sites ($19.50). *Wichita Bend RV Park* (☎ 940-761-7490), 300 Central Freeway, is a city park offering RV campsites with water, electricity and a dump station for $10.

Motels & Hotels The best deal in town is at the *Trade Winds Motor Hotel* (☎ 940-723-8008, 800-678-8885), 1212 Broad St, where rates start at $31. There's a pool, sauna and Jacuzzi, plus free passes to the nearby YMCA. The nicest place in town, the *Holiday Inn* (☎ 940-766-6000, fax 940-766-5942), 401 Broad St, has an indoor pool, whirlpool and exercise room. Singles/doubles are $75/85.

B&Bs *Harrison House Bed & Breakfast* (☎ 940-322-2299), 2014 11th St, has four bedrooms, each with private bath, for $75, and a three-room suite with an antique four-poster

bed, a balcony and private breakfast served in the room for $150.

Places to Eat
In a Best of Texoma poll, locals gave the *International House of Pancakes* (☎ 940-322-4555), 1004 Broad St, best breakfast in town and best coffee honors. It's open 24 hours and it's a hopping place, so plan on a short wait. The *Secret Garden Tea Room* (☎ 940-767-5570), 700 8th St, is a neat little downtown spot for lunch.

Uncle Lynn's Catfish (☎ 940-767-2345), 5½ miles south of downtown on US 287, gets rave reviews for its dinners ($5 to $14). It's closed Monday. Another local favorite, *McBride Land and Cattle Co* (☎ 940-322-2516), 501 Scott Ave, offers a deal called Steak & All: beef plus your choice of quail, trout, boiled or fried shrimp or frog legs, with all the trimmings, for $14. *El Gordo's Fine Mexican Food* (☎ 940-322-6251), 513 Scott Ave, has good fajitas for $7.50.

Entertainment
The *Wichita Falls Symphony* (☎ 940-322-4489) and the *Wichita Falls Ballet* (☎ 940-322-2552) perform at Memorial Auditorium, 1300 7th St downtown. *Graham Central Station* (☎ 940-691-7441), 4105 Maplewood Ave, is the largest nightspot in town, with five clubs under one roof.

Shopping
Sikes Senter Mall (☎ 940-692-5501), 3111 Midwestern Parkway, is the city's largest. Wichita Falls is a big antiques town, with prices far lower than those in the Metroplex. Most antiques shops are downtown or between Aves E and F.

Getting There & Away
Air Wichita Falls Municipal Airport (☎ 940-855-3621), 4000 Armstrong Drive north of the city, is served by American Eagle and America Southeast Airlines.

Bus The Texas New Mexico & Oklahoma (TNM&O) bus company (☎ 940-766-2223), 1406 14th St, has the following scheduled service on four major routes.

to/from	frequency (per day)	trip duration	one way/ roundtrip
Dallas	4	3 hours	$24/46
Fort Worth	4	2½ hours	$21/40
Lubbock	2	4 hours	$33/63
Oklahoma City	3	3½ hours	$29/55

Car Hertz (☎ 940-851-7900) has a rental desk at the airport. Elsewhere in town is Enterprise (☎ 940-767-0174).

Getting Around

To/From the Airport Cabs cost about $10 from the airport to downtown Wichita Falls.

Bus Wichita Falls Transit (☎ 940-761-7921) runs buses Monday through Friday from 5:30 am to 7:30 pm and on Saturday from 10:30 am to 5:30 pm. The fare is 75¢ for adults, 35¢ for senior citizens and children. Sikes Senter Mall serves as the city's main transit center.

Taxi Rates for taxis are $1.65 flagfall and $1.30 for each mile after that, plus $1 apiece for each additional passenger. Cab companies in Wichita Falls include All American Cab and Limousine Service (☎ 940-723-2678), Presidential Taxi (☎ 940-322-8294), and Falls Cab Co (☎ 940-691-0219).

South Central Texas

South Central Texas contains the state's largest tourist draws: San Antonio, Austin and the Texas Hill Country. It's also the area most significant to the development of the state; it was here that the Alamo was defended and lost, here that the Europeans settlers who would shape Texas' late 19th- and early 20th-century boom built their first communities. It's also perhaps Texas' most beautiful inland region. The rolling rises of the Hill Country give way to the Austin greenbelt at the north and to the beautifully restored Spanish missions of San Antonio at the south. If you've only got a short time in Texas, this is the place to head. Perhaps you've heard of the Heart of Texas? Well, here it is.

Highlights

- Austin, the live-music capital of the USA
- Kreuz Market in Lockhart, the best barbecue in the state
- Long drives through the Texas Hill Country
- The Alamo and the Mission Trail
- San Antonio's Riverwalk
- Sea World of Texas
- The King Ranch

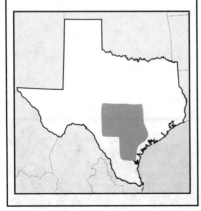

Austin

Population 567,000; metro area 1,075,000

Austin is one of the world's coolest capitals. Boasting status as the 'live-music capital of the USA,' Austin is perhaps better known for its 'slacker' mentality (lionized in the film of the same name by local filmmaker-turned-sensation Richard Linklater), its local ax men and its music clubs than for its politicians or attractions.

Filmmakers and the music industry have made Austin one of their darlings. South by Southwest (SXSW), the annual music industry love-in held here in March has become, according to the *New York Times*, 'domestic pop and rock industry's most important annual gathering,' and Linklater has teamed up with director Quentin Tarantino to host a biannual film festival here.

Austin has a lot less to offer in the way of developed tourist attractions than you'd expect, and that's its charm. While the State Capitol Building is impressive, as are several city museums, they're utterly outclassed by Austin's natural attractions, such as the magnificent natural pool at Barton Springs, Hamilton Pool, Hippie Hollow (where you can get your kit off) and the nightly flight of 1½ million Mexican free-tailed bats from beneath the Congress Ave Bridge. Austin is a city where you get outside and get busy, then get inside and get drinking, watching one of the hundred or so bands that play here nightly.

HISTORY

Austin began life as the village of Waterloo, which developed along the Colorado River. Legend has it that Republic of Texas vice president Mirabeau B Lamar came to the region in 1838 on a hunting trip with his

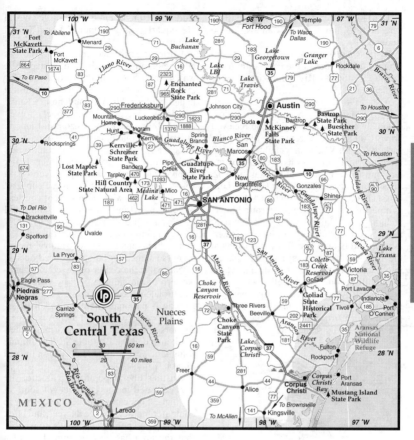

friend Jacob Harrell and fell in love with the place. In 1839, Sam Houston commissioned a city planner to begin the layout of the republic's new capital, which was renamed in honor of Stephen F Austin (see the History section in the Facts about Texas chapter for more information).

The capital was moved to Houston in 1842 after repeated attacks by Native Americans and Mexicans, but returned in 1845; construction on the first state capitol began in 1853.

The city began to boom after the arrival of the Houston and Texas Central Railroad in 1871, and Congress Ave was paved, its drain-

age ditches replaced by sewers. By 1884, with more than 15,000 residents, Austin built its first bridge over the Colorado River. By 1900, the city was as cosmopolitan as many in the East, with electricity, telephones, theaters, opera houses and the Moonlight Towers – 165-foot streetlights that illuminated the city by night. Seventeen towers still stand today and are designated historic landmarks.

The original capitol building burned in 1881, and the one that stands today was erected in 1888 – see the Capitol Complex later in this section for details.

The University of Texas was established here in 1883 and today has almost 50,000 students.

By 1938, a series of seven dams were constructed, which turned the constantly overflowing Colorado River into a series of artificial lakes.

Also in the '30s, Kenneth Threadgill opened a gas station-beer joint he called, originally enough, Threadgill's (he received Travis County Beer License No 01). By the early 1960s, his Wednesday-night hootenannies (informal jam sessions) were attracting local musicians from around Texas. In 1962, Janis Joplin, from Port Arthur (see the Gulf Coast chapter), began frequenting the place as a performer. Other venues around town, including the University of Texas student union, saw their fair share of live music acts as well, and people like Roky Erickson (of the 13th Floor Elevators) and Janis played into a growing national sound that would eventually become psychedelic rock.

Janis left Austin for California and fame (though she returned for her last Austin appearance in 1970), and the next big thing on the Austin music scene was in 1970, when

Willie Nelson

Eddie Wilson opened Armadillo World Headquarters in a former National Guard armory.

During the next decade, anyone who was anyone in music played at the Armadillo. It was ground zero for the outlaw cowboy movement of the '70s and was *the* musical hangout for acts like Waylon Jennings, Kinky Friedman, Asleep at the Wheel, Steven Fromholz and the Lost Gonzo Band, among others. The Armadillo opened its doors to all comers, hosting seminal rock and country acts such as the Clash, Bruce Springsteen, Frank Zappa, Van Morrison and BW Stevenson – a who's who of that time's music. People all over the US got wind of this talent courtesy of public television's *Austin City Limits*, still on the air at press time (call ☎ 512-475-9077 for taping information and free tickets).

The burgeoning 'outlaw country' movement (so named for being produced outside of Nashville, the center of the country-and-western music industry) led by Willie Nelson broadened country music's boundaries, gaining it national attention and listenership for years to come. Later Austin performers and bands that would make their mark included the Butthole Surfers, Jimmie Vaughan, and Stevie Ray Vaughan and Double Trouble.

Austin's liberal populace is one of the best educated in the USA; its got some of the highest per capita rates in the country in computer literacy, college degrees, and book and magazine purchasing. So it's no wonder that the area has become something of a high-tech mecca, attracting heaps of multinational and local computer hardware and software companies to outposts in Austin's suburbs. Austin today is one of the USA's most cosmopolitan cities.

You're going to love it.

ORIENTATION

The Austin area is ringed by highways to the north, east and west, and by the Colorado River to the south. At the east, I-35 runs north-south; US 183 runs north-south while in Austin, in the north veering east-west and connecting I-35 with the westernmost highway, the north-south Mo Pac Expressway (usually called simply 'Mo Pac,' it stands for Missouri-Pacific, as the highway was constructed along the trackbed of the old railroad lines).

The heart of downtown is an orderly grid system, though there's no rule about the direction of streets or avenues.

The main artery, which stretches from the southern part of the city across the Colorado River and continues to the steps of the State Capitol Building, is Congress Ave, which also serves as the east-west dividing line for addresses. Congress Ave becomes Speedway St north of Martin Luther King Jr Blvd, an important east-west thoroughfare north of the State Capitol Building.

Guadalupe (pronounced 'GWAD-ah-loop,' though some say 'gwad-ah-LOOP-ee') St runs three blocks west of Congress and becomes, near the University of Texas campus, the Drag.

The major east-to-west thoroughfare is 6th St. It's one-way, so if you're driving and need to reverse direction, 5th St, also a main street, will lead you back west to east.

The stretch of E 6th St between Congress and Sabine Sts, is the Strip, a dizzying collection of clubs, pubs and nightspots that's a tourist draw in its own right.

The Warehouse District, west of Congress Ave and south of W 6th St, is another entertainment district, catering to an older crowd as well as offering many gay and lesbian bars and clubs.

The University of Texas at Austin is in the northeastern downtown area.

Maps

The free AAA *Austin* map is detailed but, geez, it's unwieldy. Gousha makes a good map ($2.50) with a central Austin inset that's much better, and it's available in bookstores and gas stations, but note that the convention and visitor's bureau (see Information) hands out photocopies of the inset map for free.

INFORMATION
Tourist Offices

The Austin Convention and Visitor's Bureau (CVB; ☎ 512-404-4573, 800-926-2282, fax 512-404-4578, www.austintexas.org), at 201 E 2nd St, is a gold mine, and friendly staff members will do what they can to get you sorted. The walls are lined with good information. It's open Monday to Friday 8:30 am to 5 pm, Saturday 9 am to 5 pm, Sunday noon to 5 pm.

The Capitol Visitors' Center (☎ 512-463-8586), 112 E 11th St at the southeast corner of the capitol grounds on the corner of Brazos St, is a great source of information on the state of Texas. It's open Tuesday to Friday 9 am to 5 pm, Saturday from 10 am to 5 pm, closed Sunday and Monday.

The AAA has two inconvenient offices in town: south of downtown (☎ 512-444-4757), 3005 S Lamar Blvd, No D113; and north (☎ 512-335-5222), 13376 Research Blvd, No 124, at Balcones Club Drive. Both are open Monday to Friday 9 am to 5:30 pm, Saturday 9 am to 1 pm.

Gay & Lesbian Resources

Cornerstone (☎ 512-708-1515, cnrstone@io .com, www.cornerstonecenter.org), 1117 Red River St, is a gay and lesbian community center.

Money

NationsBank (☎ 512-397-2200), 501 Congress Ave, exchanges foreign currency and traveler's checks. There's an exchange booth at the airport, too. American Express has an office (☎ 512-452-8166) at 2943 W Anderson Lane, two blocks east of Mo Pac near the Northcross Mall (see Shopping). American Express traveler's checks in US dollars can be cashed commission free at Bank One (☎ 512-479-5400), 221 W 6th St at Colorado St.

Post & Communications

The central post office (☎ 512-494-2200), 510 Guadalupe St, is open Monday to Friday 7 am to 6:30 pm, Saturday 8 am to 3 pm, closed Sunday. Address poste restante to General Delivery, 510 Guadalupe St, Austin, TX 78701.

Mail Boxes Etc offers copy, communications and specialty mail services and has several locations within Austin: 815A Brazos St (☎ 512-476-5316), 613 W 13th St

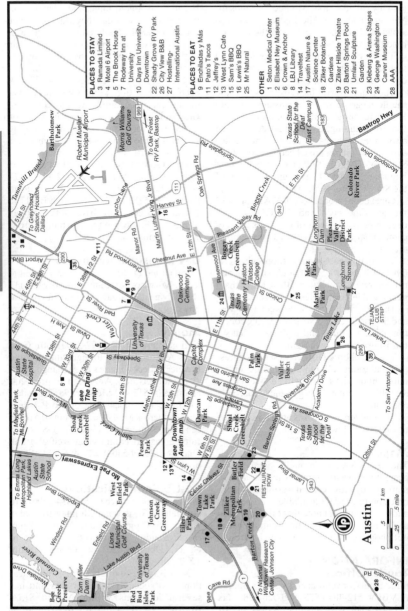

PLACES TO STAY
3   Ramada Limited
4   Motel 6 Airport
5   The Brook House
7   Rodeway Inn at
    University
10 Days Inn University-
    Downtown
22 Shady Grove RV Park
26 City View B&B
27 Hostelling-
    International Austin

PLACES TO EAT
9   Enchiladas y Más
11 Pato's Tacos
12 Jeffrey's
13 West Lynn Cafe
15 Sam's BBQ
16 Lewis's BBQ
25 Mr Natural

OTHER
1   Seton Medical Center
2   Elisabet Ney Museum
6   Crown & Anchor
8   LBJ Library
14 Travelfest
17 Austin Nature &
    Science Center
18 Zilker Botanical
    Gardens
19 Zilker Hillside Theatre
20 Barton Springs Pool
21 Umlauf Sculpture
    Garden
23 Kleberg & Arena Stages
24 George Washington
    Carver Museum
28 AAA

(☎ 512-478-2917), and near the University of Texas at 2002A Guadalupe St (☎ 512-478-2334). Kinko's copy and computer center (☎ 512-472-4448), 327 W Congress, is open daily 24 hours and rents computers for $12 per hour. Book People's computer terminals (see Bookstores) rent for $3 per half hour.

Austin has one of the most useful web presences around. Try some of the excellent Austin city information resources available on the web, like the *Austin Chronicle* (www.austinchronicle.com), *Austin360* (www.austin360.com) and City Search (www.austin.citysearch.com).

Media

Newspapers & Magazines The *Austin American-Statesman* (50¢) is the big daily in town. The best source for the music and club scene, independent coverage of local politics and personal advertising is the free *Austin Chronicle*, published Thursday and available at practically every bar, club and restaurant in town. The *Statesman* also on Thursday publishes *XL*, a free listings magazine that's another good what's-on guide. The *Texas Daily* is the University of Texas paper.

Radio National Public Radio is at 90.5 FM. Tune in to Austin community radio, KOOP 91.7 FM, Saturday morning from 10 am to noon, when Jay Robillard cracks open his astounding collection of lounge music and weird stuff – who else plays Telly Savalas' *Who Loves Ya, Baby*? KOOP also does everything from pan-Celtic, vintage jazz and movie-soundtrack shows to programs covering Latino and gay politics. At night on the same bandwidth as KOOP is KVRX, the University of Texas' student radio station. Both are excellent resources for local flavor.

Other FM stations include KMFA 89.5 (classical); KASE 100.7, KHLB 106.09 and KIKY 92.1 play country music; there's jazz on KAJZ 93.3; and alternative rock on KNNC 107.7.

Austin AM is heavily dominated by seething talk shows, but there's Mexican music on KELG 1440, gospel at KFIT 1060 and Spanish-language Christian music on KFON 1470 as well.

Travel Agencies

Council Travel (☎ 512-472-4931) has an office at 2000 Guadalupe St, open Monday and Wednesday to Friday 9 am to 6 pm, Tuesday 10 am to 6 pm, closed weekends. A good resource for cheap consolidated tickets is American Travel Services (☎ 512-477-5444), 800 Brazos St, suite 210, in downtown. They have supercheap fares to Europe and always find good deals. Travelfest (see Bookstores) has an excellent full-service travel agency in both of its shops.

Bookstores

Travelfest (www.travelfest.com) is a one-stop outlet for travel books and phrasebooks and also offers maps, atlases, travel gear and a full-service travel agency. Check when you're in town to see who's speaking for its weekly travel-destination series – see readings in Entertainment for information. There are two locations, one at West End Center (☎ 512-469-7906), 1214 W 6th St, and another at Gateway Square (☎ 512-418-1515), 9503 Research Blvd, both open Monday to Saturday 10 am to 8 pm, Sunday noon to 6 pm.

Bevo's Bookstore (☎ 512-476-7642), 2304 Guadalupe St, is the main University of Texas bookstore, with textbooks and university apparel. FringeWare (☎ 512-494-9273), 2716 Guadalupe St, is an independent place with great stuff frowned upon or banned by large chain shops. Book People (☎ 512-472-5050), 603 N Lamar Blvd, is a bookstore, music store and café teeming with excellent stuff and a good staff. Also excellent are the staff members at Congress Ave Booksellers (☎ 512-478-1157), 716 Congress Ave, which sells new and used books.

Half Price Books has three locations in town, the most convenient of which is at 3110 Guadalupe St (☎ 512-451-4463). Another good resource for travel books and travel gear is Whole Earth Provision Co, 2410 San Antonio St, near the University of Texas.

Book Market (☎ 512-499-8708), 2021 Guadalupe St in the Dobie Mall, has a great selection of used books. Other bookstores in Austin include Book Woman

(☎ 512-472-2785), 918 W 12th St, which specializes in feminist titles, and Toad Hall (☎ 512-323-2665), 1206 W 38th St, a children's bookstore.

The inescapable Barnes & Noble (☎ 512-457-0581) is at 2246 Guadalupe St. Borders Books, Music & Cafe (☎ 512-795-9553) is in the north of the city at 10225 Research Blvd at Great Hills Trail.

Libraries

John Henry Faulk Central Public Library (☎ 512-499-7300) is at 800 Guadalupe St. The Texas State Library and Archives (☎ 512-463-5514), 1201 Brazos St, is open Monday to Friday 8 am to 5 pm. The Center for American History at the University of Texas (☎ 512-495-4515), Richardson Hall, Unit 2, on the campus, focuses on the historical development of the USA. It's open Monday to Friday 9 am to 5 pm.

Campuses

The University of Texas at Austin (UT; ☎ 512-475-7440, www.utexas.edu) is the main campus of Texas' higher education system, which has 15 campuses throughout the state. Established in 1883, UT has almost 50,000 students in faculties that include architecture, business, communication, education, fine arts, law, liberal arts, nursing and public affairs.

Austin Community College (☎ 512-223-2022, 512-223-4730) is a two-year vocational college with campuses throughout the city.

Huston-Tillotson College ('hyou-ston'; ☎ 512-505-3027) was the first college west of the Mississippi River to accept black students. Today there are about 600 students in schools of teacher education, business and natural and social sciences.

Cultural Centers

German immigrants to the area established the German Free School building (☎ 512-482-0927), 507 E 10th St, in 1857 as a private school; it has evolved into a meeting place and cultural center promoting German-Texan connections. There are frequent special events, slide shows and guest lecturers; call for information.

Laundries

There are few coin laundries located in the downtown area; try First Street Laundry (☎ 512-476-3814), 1634 E Cesar Chavez St. But many hotels, motels and even the hostel have coin-laundry facilities. Clean & Lean (☎ 512-458-5326), 4225 Guadalupe St, is, yes, a laundry and a gym. There's a Kwik-Wash (☎ 512-448-7856) at 2100 S Lamar Blvd.

Medical Services

Brackenridge Hospital (☎ 512-476-6461), 601 E 15th St at Red River St, is the best emergency room around. Two excellent hospitals in town are St David's Hospital (☎ 512-476-7111), 919 E 32nd St at Red River St, and Seton Medical Center (☎ 512-324-1000), 1201 W 38th St at Guadalupe St.

Emergency

The Austin Police Department's non-emergency number is ☎ 512-480-5000. Two women's resources are the excellent Austin Rape Crisis Center (☎ 512-440-7273) and the Center for Battered Women (☎ 512-928-9070). Call these numbers and ask for directions.

Dangers & Annoyances

Common sense and awareness usually ensure problem-free travel here: if you're drunkenly counting your cash and appraising your jewelry in an alley at 2 am you're as likely to encounter interest here as anywhere else.

One major complaint visitors lodge is drunken college students letting it all hang out on the E 6th St Strip every Friday night. It's a party atmosphere, and if you're not into that, head for the Warehouse District instead.

Locals may tell you that anywhere east of I-35 is dangerous, and while there is some truth to that, overt or covert racism – this is a predominantly black and Hispanic part of town – may exaggerate claims of danger. Use common sense.

Austin natives claim they live in the allergy capital of America and indeed you'll likely sneeze and wheeze with the rest of them. If you're susceptible at all to hay fever, bring proper medication or get it locally.

There are allergy reports on television weather reports and on the web at www.austin360.com/weather/kvue/allergy/index.htm.

CAPITOL COMPLEX

The Capitol Complex is made up of more than two dozen state government offices including the capitol and surrounding buildings. Main attractions are the State Capitol Building and the governor's mansion, bound by Colorado St and San Jacinto Blvd on the west and east and 14th and 11th Sts on the north and south. The Capitol Visitors' Center (☎ 512-305-8400), 112 E 11th St in a German Romanesque-style building (the General Land Office from 1856 to 1857), has information on all offices in the complex and is an official Texas Travel Information Center. The staff offers free building tours Tuesday to Friday 9 am to 5 pm, Saturday 10 am to 5 pm, closed Sunday and Monday. Tours include a 23-minute film.

Excellent city walking tours run by the Austin CVB leave from the south steps of the capitol; see Organized Tours.

State Capitol Building

Appearing as a pink mirage in a sea of green in the center of the city, the Renaissance-Revival Texas State Capitol Building (1882-88; ☎ 512-463-0063) is certainly Austin's most distinctive landmark. Topped with a statue of the Goddess of Liberty, the building is constructed of Texas sunset-red limestone. Staff members constantly throw statistics out to impress visitors: it's the seventh-largest government building in the world, and someone actually went to the trouble of calculating that if you measure from the basement floor to the tippy top of the Liberty statue, the building's height of 311 feet makes it taller than the National Capitol in Washington DC. Well, gosh.

The building is the second state capitol in the area, built to replace the original (1852-53), which was destroyed by fire in 1881. Ruins of the former capitol can be seen at 11th St and Congress Ave.

Free guided tours of the building run Monday through Friday 8:30 am to 4:30 pm, and Saturday and Sunday 9:30 am to 4:30 pm. Guides are very informative and can fill notebooks with the minutiae of the building, its monuments, its construction and anything else you can think of.

The building's rotunda features terrazzo seals of the six nations whose flags have flown over Texas – Spain, France, Mexico, Republic of Texas, the Confederate States of America and the USA.

The second floor is a terrorist's wet dream. It includes the governor's public reception room, the chambers of the state senate and house of representatives, the Legislative Reference Library *and* the offices of the governor.

The third floor, housing the House of Representatives and Senate Chamber Galleries, is open to the public when congress is in session.

The State Capitol Building is open Monday to Friday 7 am to 10 pm, Saturday and Sunday 9 am to 5 pm.

Governor's Mansion

The lovely Greek Revival Governor's Mansion (1855-56; ☎ 512-463-5518) is the fourth-oldest building to be used as a governor's residence and sits nearby at 1010 Colorado St. It's open for tours Monday to Friday every 20 minutes from 10 to 11:40 am and closed during state holidays, official functions and whenever the governor wants.

BATS

That's right, bats. The reconstruction of the Congress Ave Bridge in 1980 created platforms and crevices underneath it. Somehow these caught the attention of some apparently homeless Mexican free-tailed bats (see the Flora & Fauna section in Facts about Texas for more information) that fly each spring from central Mexico to the southwestern US. They arrive in March, setting up shop in those attractive crevices and platforms under the bridge, and leave in early November. Every June, the females each give birth to one pup, and mom and kids set out each night in search of food.

It's a serious spectacle – up to 1½ million bats streaming out from beneath a bridge!

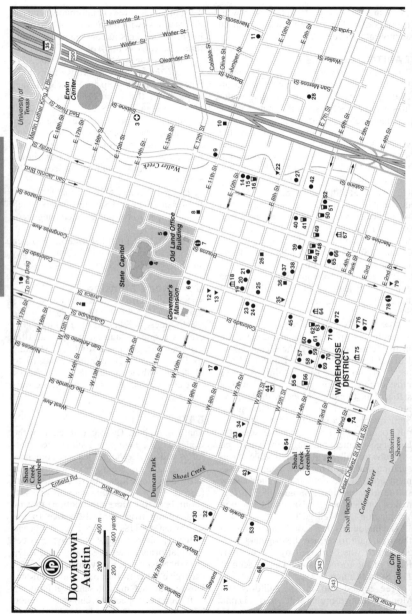

Downtown Austin

SOUTH CENTRAL TEXAS

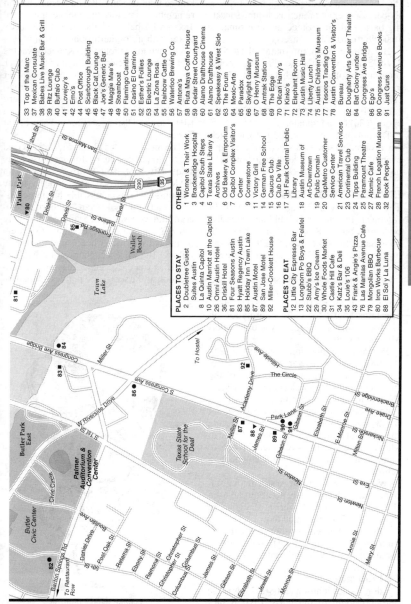

33 Top of the Marc
37 Mexican Consulate
38 Babes Live Music Bar & Grill
39 Ritz Lounge
40 Buffalo Club
41 Lovejoy's
42 Emo's
44 Post Office
45 Scarborough Building
46 Black Cat Lounge
47 Joe's Generic Bar
48 Maggie Mae's
49 Steamboat
50 Flamingo Cantina
51 Casino El Camino
52 Esther's Follies
53 Electric Lounge
54 La Zona Rosa
55 Rainbow Cattle Co
56 Waterloo Brewing Co
57 Antone's
58 Ruta Maya Coffee House
59 Cedar Street Courtyard
60 Alamo Drafthouse Cinema
61 Alamo Drafthouse
62 Speakeasy & West Side
63 The Forum
64 Mexic-Arte
65 Paradox
66 Skylight Gallery
67 O Henry Museum
68 Amtrak Station
69 The Edge
70 Olican Harry's
71 Kinko's
72 Elephant Room
73 Austin Music Hall
74 Liberty Lunch
75 Austin Children's Museum
77 Tesoros Trading Co
78 Austin Convention & Visitor's Bureau
82 Dougherty Arts Center Theatre
84 Bat Colony under Congress Ave Bridge
86 Ego's
90 Congress Avenue Books
91 Just Guns

PLACES TO STAY

2 Doubletree Guest Suites Austin
8 La Quinta Capitol
10 Austin Marriott at the Capitol
26 Omni Austin Hotel
36 Driskill Hotel
81 Four Seasons Austin
83 Hyatt Regency Austin
85 Holiday Inn Town Lake
87 Austin Motel
89 San Jose Motel
92 Miller-Crockett House

PLACES TO EAT

12 Little City Espresso Bar
13 Longhorn Po Boys & Felafel
22 Stubb's BBQ
29 Amy's Ice Cream
30 Whole Foods Market
31 Castle Hill Cafe
34 Katz's Bar & Deli
35 Louie's 106
43 Frank & Angie's Pizza
76 Las Manitas Avenue Cafe
80 Iron Works Barbecue
88 El Sol y La Luna

OTHER

1 Women & Their Work
3 Brackenridge Hospital
4 Capitol South Steps
5 Texas State Library & Archives
6 Old Bakery & Emporium
7 Capitol Complex Visitor's Center
9 Cornerstone
11 Victory Grill
14 German Free School
15 Caucus Club
16 Club De Ville
17 JH Faulk Central Public Library
18 Austin Museum of Art–Downtown
19 Public Domain
20 CapMetro Customer Service Center
21 American Travel Services
23 Continental Club
24 Tipps Building
25 Paramount Theatre
27 Atomic Cafe
28 French Legation Museum
32 Book People

It's become an Austin tradition to bring a six-pack of beer and watch as, around sunset, the bats head out to feed on an estimated 10,000lb to 30,000lb of insects.

Bat Conservation International (☎ 512-327-9721) has volunteers on hand and holds programs throughout the bat season. Check in the *Austin American-Statesman* for a bat calendar of events when you're in town, or call its Bat Hotline (☎ 512-416-5700, category 3636) for an update.

Do not pick up grounded bats or touch bat droppings; some bats carry rabies, and even if they don't, they don't need you picking them up, okay?

UNIVERSITY OF TEXAS

The University of Texas at Austin (UT) campus is the cluster of buildings bounded by Martin Luther King Jr Blvd at the south, Guadalupe St at the west, W 27th St at the north and roughly I-35 at the east. There are several notable buildings on campus, including **Memorial Stadium**, the site where long-time rivals UT and Texas A&M viciously duke it out every Thanksgiving Day (see Spectator Sports for more information on UT football), the LBJ Library and the Texas Memorial Museum.

Probably the most infamous structure in Austin is the **UT Tower**. In August 1966, Charles Whitman climbed the steps of the tower carrying a rucksack containing several rifles, handguns and ammunition, plus food, water, gasoline, deodorant and a roll of toilet paper, and opened fire on passersby. During the 99 minutes he was in the tower, Whitman killed 15 people and wounded 31 before being shot by three Austin policemen and a retired Air Force gunner.

Whitman lore is rife in Austin among students, who will cheerfully point out holes in the sidewalk and tell tourists that they're bullet holes from the fated day.

The tower is open to visitors (note the No Firearms sign); climb the east stone staircase for an excellent view of the city.

LBJ Library

Lyndon Baines Johnson (1908-1973) was the 36th president of the USA. LBJ, as he's known to practically all Americans who can remember him, was the menacingly jovial Texan who balanced the John F Kennedy ticket with a Southern political mainstay – not to mention a Protestant (Kennedy was the first Catholic elected president of the USA).

After JFK's assassination on November 22, 1963 (see the Dallas chapter for information), LBJ was sworn in as president aboard *Air Force One*. For more information on LBJ, see the History section in Facts about Texas.

The museum, (☎ 512-916-5137), 2313 Red River St, supported by former First Lady Lady Bird Johnson (born Claudia Alta Taylor), is a must-see attraction. By many accounts LBJ was an irascible, hardnose bastard of a traditional Texan Southern Democrat, and you won't see any of that here (absent, for example, is his quote, 'Grab 'em by the balls and their hearts and minds will follow'). But while it contains as much propaganda as you'd expect, it's also quite a candid look at the social and political climate of

Lyndon Baines Johnson

the era, with video clips of head-bashing cops, dope-smokin' hippies and a groovy soundtrack complementing solid exhibitions on the JFK presidency, the Bay of Pigs, the JFK assassination, Krushchev, segregation, the civil rights movement, the assassinations of Martin Luther King Jr and Robert Kennedy Jr, and the Vietnam War.

Upstairs, a new exhibit on Mexican Texans details pre-Republic of Texas life and that of Mexican Americans today.

The museum is free and open daily 9 am to 5 pm.

Texas Memorial Museum

The Texas Memorial Museum (☎ 512-471-1604), 2400 Trinity St, in a huge art-deco building on the UT campus, explores Texas' natural and social history, with exhibits on geology, paleontology, anthropology, natural history and dinosaur trackways taken from Glen Rose, Texas. It also has a display of a pterodactyl skeleton recovered at Big Bend in 1971. It's open from Monday to Friday 9 am to 5 pm, Saturday 10 am to 5 pm, Sunday 1 to 5 pm. Admission is free.

ART MUSEUMS
Jack S Blanton Museum of Art

The Jack S Blanton Museum of Art at UT (☎ 512-471-7024) is one museum in two buildings, the Harry Ransom Center (HRC), on the West Campus, and the Art Building, which is on the East Campus. The collection focuses on 20th-century US art, 20th-century Latin American art and prints and drawings from the 15th century until the present.

The main permanent exhibition is in the HRC. It includes on the first floor 18th- and 19th-century American paintings, art of the American West and the big banana, the Mari and James A Michener Collection of 20th-Century American Art. Most major figures in 20th-century American art are represented, including Ellsworth Kelly, Leon Golub, Philip Guston, Joan Mitchel, Thomas Hart Benton, Peter Saul and Robert Henri.

Also on the first floor is the museum's prized Gutenberg Bible.

The second floor contains Latin American works that range from the early 20th

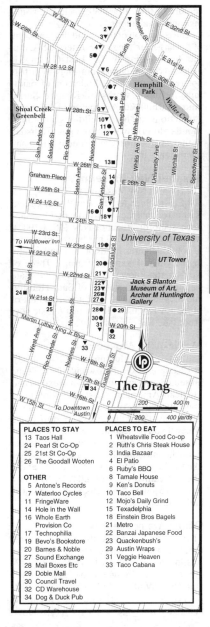

SOUTH CENTRAL TEXAS

PLACES TO STAY
13 Taos Hall
24 Pearl St Co-op
25 21st St Co-Op
26 The Goodall Wooten

OTHER
5   Antone's Records
7   Waterloo Cycles
11 FringeWare
14 Hole in the Wall
16 Whole Earth
    Provision Co
17 Technophilia
19 Bevo's Bookstore
20 Barnes & Noble
27 Sound Exchange
28 Mail Boxes Etc
29 Dobie Mall
30 Council Travel
32 CD Warehouse
34 Dog & Duck Pub

PLACES TO EAT
1   Wheatsville Food Co-op
2   Ruth's Chris Steak House
3   India Bazaar
4   El Patio
6   Ruby's BBQ
8   Tamale House
9   Ken's Donuts
10 Taco Bell
12 Mojo's Daily Grind
15 Texadelphia
18 Einstein Bros Bagels
21 Metro
22 Banzai Japanese Food
23 Quackenbush's
29 Austin Wraps
31 Veggie Heaven
33 Taco Cabana

century to the early 1980s, including paintings and installations.

The collection of prints and drawings, one of the largest in the southwestern USA, is in the Art Building on the East Campus. It includes contemporary drawings by artists not represented in the collection of paintings, including works by Richard Serra, Andy Warhol, Vito Acconci and Ed Ruscha. Collections in both buildings are open Monday to Friday 9 am to 5 pm (Thursday until 9 pm), Saturday and Sunday 1 to 5 pm; admission is free.

Elisabet Ney Museum

The Elisabet Ney Museum (☎ 512-458-2255), 304 E 44th St at Ave H near Waller Creek, is the reconstructed studio of German-born sculptor Elisabet Ney (1833-1907), with more than 100 of her busts and statues of political figures, heads of state and royalty in the USA, Texas and Europe. Three of Ney's better-known works are in the State Capitol Building: statues of Sam Houston and Stephen F Austin and a marble bust of Miriam A Ferguson, Texas' first female governor (she was elected in 1924).

Mexic-Arte Museum

The Mexic-Arte Museum (☎ 512-480-9373), 419 Congress Ave, is a wonderful, eclectic museum featuring works from Mexican and Mexican-American artists in exhibitions that rotate every two months. The gift shop is intense, with killer Mexican stuff that's pricey if you're heading south of the border but not if you're not. It's got a great selection. The museum also hosts special events, like the Latino Film Festival; call for details. The museum is open Monday to Saturday 10 am to 6 am; $3 for adults, $1.50 for seniors and children.

Other Art Museums

There are rotating exhibitions at several other downtown museums, including the **Austin Museum of Art-Downtown** (☎ 512-495-9224), 823 Congress Ave, and **Women and Their Work** (☎ 512-477-1064), at 1710 Lavaca St, with works that are predominantly, but no longer exclusively, by women.

OTHER MUSEUMS
George Washington Carver Museum

Located at 1165 Angelina St in Austin's first public library building, this is Texas' first museum (☎ 512-472-4809) dedicated to African American culture. There are photographs, videos and an extensive document archive of the life of African Americans in the state. There are also very good rotating exhibitions throughout the year. It's open Tuesday to Thursday 10 am to 6 pm, Friday and Saturday noon to 5 pm, closed Sunday and Monday; admission is free.

O Henry Museum

Austin resident and writer, lyricist, punster and convicted embezzler William Sydney Porter (O Henry) lived in this cottage (☎ 512-472-1903), 409 E 5th St, now open as a museum to his work and life. It was in Austin that O Henry began publishing the weekly newspaper *The Rolling Stone*, one of the first to take political satire seriously. The museum is also the site of the annual Pun-Off, a pun-making contest that attracts thousands of potential punsters vying for Punniest of Show. The museum is open Wednesday to Sunday noon to 5 pm; admission is free.

Austin Children's Museum

The Austin Children's Museum (☎ 512-472-2499) was closed and getting ready to move to new and larger downtown digs at 201 Colorado St, one block west of Congress Ave, as we researched, but is now open. The new location should expand on the already excellent exhibits of the old one, which had a real ambulance, a child-sized grocery store and a playground. The museum is open Tuesday through Saturday 10 am to 5 pm (Wednesday until 8 pm), Sunday noon to 5 pm; admission is $3.50, free Wednesday 5 to 8 pm.

French Legation Museum

France was one of the few countries to recognize the Republic of Texas, and the French Legation Museum (☎ 512-472-8180, www.french-legation.mus.tx.us), 802 San Marcos St (take bus No 8-Old Pecan St 'Dillo), up the little hill just east of I-35, was built in

1840-41 to house the French chargé d'affaires. It's been restored and also contains a meticulous reconstruction of the first truly Creole kitchen in Texas. It's open Tuesday to Sunday 1 to 5 pm, closed Sunday.

PARKS & GARDENS

See Around Austin for information about Travis Lake.

Zilker Metropolitan Park

If there's an epicenter to outdoor recreation in Austin, it's Zilker Park (☎ 512-478-0905), just south of the Colorado River about a mile west of I-35 (bus No 30-Barton Creek). The park itself is only a very nice 8-acre slot of green, lined with hiking and biking trails and home to a nature center, botanical and sculpture gardens, and a museum. But Zilker is also the place to gain access to the famed Barton Springs natural swimming pool and Barton Creek Greenbelt area. It also provides access to the 60-acre Zilker Nature Preserve at its western end.

The park is open daily 5 am to 10 pm and it's free.

Barton Springs Pool (☎ 512-476-9044), 2201 Barton Springs Rd, is a 1000-foot long and truly wonderful natural spring pool that's simply the bee's knees when it comes to year-round swimming fun. Every Austin native and student holds this place dear in their hearts, and after one visit you'll see why.

The Edwards Aquifer pumps 32 million gallons of very cold but very clear water into the pool, which is a constant 68°F year-round. The area around the pool is a social scene in itself, and the place is packed on a hot summer day. A museum of the aquifer is said to be opening soon.

Until developers get their way and pave it over for a parking lot (the debate over Barton Creek and the pool has raged on for years, see below) the pool is open year-round daily 5 am to 10 pm except Thursday, when it's open 5 to 9 am and 7 to 10 pm. It's best to call ahead though, as these hours sometimes vary. Admission is free from November to March 15; the rest of the year it's $2.50 for adults on weekdays, $2.75 on weekends, 75¢ for students and 50¢ for children.

Canoeing & Kayaking Kayaking or canoeing along the 8 miles of waterways in the Barton Springs Greenbelt – an environmentally sensitive area constantly under pressure from developers who firmly believe in the need for Austin to have more condos and golf courses – is one of the highlights of a trip to the city.

There's access to the waterways at several spots along the creek, and you can get information and maps from Zilker Park Boat Rentals (☎ 512-478-3852) or the City of Austin Parks and Recreation Department (☎ 512-499-6700); or, check out the *Austin Chronicle*'s Barton Creek Guide at www .auschron.com/guides/bartoncreek.

Commonly spotted birds along the creek include green and little blue heron, belted kingfisher and wood duck, and it's just amazing how quickly you can be immersed in nature in what's essentially the center of the city.

Zilker Park Boat Rentals, just below Barton Springs pool, rents 17-foot canoes and a whole variety of ocean kayaks. The price is $6 per hour or $25 per day including paddles and life jackets. They also have maps and will tell you the best routes and how long they take. They're open in spring and summer Monday to Friday from 11 am to dark, Saturday and Sunday from 9 am. In fall and winter, they're open weather-permitting weekends only 11 am to dark.

KMart and Wal-Mart auto centers sell inflatable boats (anywhere from $30 to $60 or even higher) and pumps for them ($15 to $20).

Zilker Botanical Gardens The Zilker Botanical Gardens (☎ 512-477-8672), 2220 Barton Springs Rd, is another lovely free area packed with flowers, ponds, trees and shrubs. It's open daily 8:30 am to 6 pm.

Austin Nature & Science Center In the northwestern area of the park, the Austin Nature & Science Center (☎ 512-327-8181), has exhibitions of native mammals, birds, reptiles, amphibians and arthropods that have been injured and nursed back to health here at the center. The center also has outdoor nature trails lined with native plants, where you'll see bats, butterflies and birds. There's a hands-on discovery center inside the visitor center. The nature center is open Monday to Saturday 9 am to 5 pm, Sunday noon to 5 pm; admission is free but donations are requested.

Umlauf Sculpture Garden This open-air and enclosed museum (☎ 512-445-5582), 605 Robert E Lee Rd, in Zilker Park shows 130 mythological bronze works by 20th-century American sculptor Charles Umlauf, who was an art professor at UT for 40 years before retiring in 1981. It's open Wednesday to Friday 10 am to 4:30 pm, Saturday and Sunday 1 to 4:30 pm; admission is $3 for adults, $2 for students and kids younger than 6 are free.

Zilker Nature Preserve The 60-acre Zilker Nature Preserve, at the west end of Zilker Park, has footpaths that lead through a wilderness made up of meadow, streams and a high cliff with caves. There is a good view of downtown Austin from the rock-walled ramada. Access is from the intersection of Barton Springs Rd at the Loop 1 bridge, about 2½ miles west of Riverside Drive.

Shoal Creek Greenbelt

The Shoal Creek Greenbelt is complete with a very cool Frisbee (okay, flying disk) course, which runs from Pease Park around Enfield Road, north and parallel to the west side of Lamar St through the greenbelt to just past 24th St. On any warm day, dozens of beer-toting slackers can be seen maneuvering the course, using a variety of disks, in hopes of ultimately landing their 'putting disks' into metal cages. There's biking and hiking here as well.

Town Lake

Town Lake is actually a dammed-off section of the Colorado River just south of downtown, lined with hiking and biking trails. It's a very nice area – as you know if you're staying in the Hostelling International-

Austin, whose windows overlook it (see Places to Stay later). You can rent kayaks at the hostel, from Zilker Park Rentals (see Zilker Park later) or from Austin Canoe and Kayak (☎ 512-719-4386).

Mayfield Park and Preserve

Northwest of the city on a bluff over the Colorado River sits Mayfield Park and Preserve (☎ 512-474-9692), 3505 W 35th St, bus No 9-Enfield to 35th and Pecos). Allison Mayfield, Texas' secretary of state and railroad commissioner, settled in this idyllic spot at the turn of the 20th century. Over the next 50 years he and his wife built up their estate's formal gardens, and the whole kit and caboodle is now run by the city's parks department. The gardens, featuring lily ponds, a gazebo overlooking the Colorado and a flower garden, are very peaceful and far less crowded than the overlook at Mt Bonnell (see later). There's free parking, but don't leave any valuables in your car.

Down the road from the park in another charming patch of green overlooking the Colorado River is the **Austin Museum of Art at Laguna Gloria** (☎ 512-458-8191), 3809 W 35th St. On display are works from local contemporary artists that change every two months or so. Open Tuesday to Saturday 10 am to 5 pm (Thursday until 9 pm), Sunday 1 to 5 pm; admission is $2 for adults, $1 for students, $1 for everyone on Thursday.

Mt Bonnell

Farther west from Mayfield Park is the tostada *grande* of Austin overlooks, the much-heralded Mt Bonnell, one of the highest points in the city (785 feet above sea level), offering a panoramic view of the Colorado River and all the way back to downtown. Climb the 99 steps to the observation level; it's best to go around sunset, though that's when it's most crowded, too. It's open daily from dawn to dusk. It's not accessible via bus.

National Wildflower Research Center

Anyone with an interest in flora and fauna should make the 20-minute journey to this wonderful center (☎ 512-292-4200) south of downtown Austin. The center, founded in 1982 with the assistance of Lady Bird Johnson, has a display garden featuring every type of wildflower and plant that grows in Texas, separated by geographical region. Signs tell of range, bloom season, family and other important statistics. Note the aqueducts and cistern system are part of the largest rainwater harvesting system in North America.

The best time to come is in spring and summer, but there's something in bloom all year. There's a small quarter-mile nature trail, rock gardens and a really awesome playhouse for the kids, with frequent programs to keep them busy. Every Saturday from 1 to 4 pm is the open house for children, with programs where they make arts projects and listen to stories.

The center also runs an enormous interactive database of plants and wildflowers for all regions of the USA – if you want to know if a certain plant will grow in your area, tap it in and all the particulars pop out.

The center is open Tuesday to Sunday 9 am to 5:30 pm; admission is $4 for adults, $2.50 for students and seniors, preschool-age children are free. By car, take Mo Pac straight south about half a mile past Slaughter Lane and follow the signs; there's no bus service from Austin.

The pleasant *Wildflower Cafe* here does a very nice lunch special with salad and sandwich or soup for $6.

Texas State Cemetery

East of downtown, the Texas State Cemetery (☎ 512-478-0098; bus No 4-Montopolis or No 88-Old Pecan St 'Dillo) is just what it sounds like – the final resting place of key figures in the history of Texas. Interred here are luminaries such as Stephen F Austin, Alamo survivor Susanna Dickinson, state flag designer Joanna Troutman and Declaration of Independence signer Robert Potter, along with soldiers who died in the Civil War and more than 100 leaders of the Republic of Texas who were exhumed from other sites and reburied here. It's open Monday to Saturday 8 am to 5 pm, Sunday and holidays 9 am to 6 pm. The main entrance is on Comal St, just north of 7th St.

BREWERIES & WINERIES

There are several microbrewers in town; see Bars in Entertainment for more information. Also, see the Shiner section in Around San Antonio for information on the Spoetzl Brewery, which makes Shiner beer.

Celis Brewery

The Celis Brewery (☎ 512-719-7141), 2431 Forbes Drive (from I-35, take US 290 east 3 miles, turn left on Forbes into the Walnut Creek Business Park; no public transport), was established in 1992 by Pierre Celis with his daughter Christine and son-in-law Peter Camps. Thank goodness they did. For Celis is from Hoegaarden, Belgium, and he's brought his beermaking skills and recipes with him. The brewery's success has been extraordinary; it has gained avidly loyal customers (like the authors of this book) in Texas and the USA, but the real proof-in-the-pudding is that their excellent beers are exported to Belgium – not exactly a place devoid of superb beers on its own.

The brews include Celis White, with curaçao orange peel and cilantro; Celis Pale Bock, a pale ale; Celis Raspberry, a tart fruit beer; Grand Cru (special vintage) made with pale malt, curaçao orange peel and Saaz and Cascade hops; and Celis Golden, a pilsener.

You can take a free tour of the brewery, followed by a free tasting session (which, face it, is why you'd come), Tuesday through Saturday at 2 and 4 pm.

Wineries

The area's finest wineries are outside the city; see the Highland Lakes section in Around Austin for more information. Hill Country Cellars Winery and Vineyard (☎ 512-259-2000), 1700 N Bell Blvd, in Cedar Park just off US 183 north of the city, holds tastings every weekday and gives tours daily of the 200-year-old vineyard.

ORGANIZED TOURS
Walking Tours

One of the best deals around is the free walking tour of downtown Austin, which leaves from the south steps of the State Capitol Building Thursday to Saturday at

SOUTH CENTRAL TEXAS

9 am and Sunday at 2 pm. The tour, led by very informative and sometimes funny guides, takes in the major sights around the Capitol Complex and then heads south down N Congress Ave; it includes explanations and histories of Austin landmarks including the **Old Bakery and Emporium**, the art deco **City Building**, the Romanesque-style columns and arches of the **Tipps Building**, the **Scarborough** and **Posner buildings**, the **Mexican Consulate** (see the Facts for the Visitor chapter for details on the consulate) and the **Driskill Hotel**. The tour lasts about 1½ hours and is wheelchair accessible.

Self-guided walking tours are possible through a delightful series of free pamphlets put out by the city and available at the CVB. The remarkably detailed pamphlets include Congress Ave and E 6th St, the West Austin and Hyde Park neighborhoods and others.

Train Tours

The Texas Steam Train Association (☎ 512-477-8468), 116 E 6th St at the west end of the Driskill Hotel, runs half-day trips aboard the *Hill Country Flyer* steam train along Austin and Texas Central Railroad lines into and around the Texas Hill Country. There are also 90-minute jaunts aboard the *River City Flyer* through historic neighborhoods in Austin. Short tours are $15 for adults, $10 for children; four-hour trips are $38 for adults, $10 for kids.

SPECIAL EVENTS

There are large and small special events throughout the year, contact the CVB for a complete list, including the December Christmas rush of activities. Here are some special events worth planning a trip around.

January

The Red-Eye Regatta

At the Austin Yacht Club at Lake Travis, this regatta (☎ 512-266-1336) is the annual New Year's Day race of 50 first-class keel boats.

March

South by Southwest

March is the biggest month for events in Austin, because of what's now touted as the biggest event in the American music industry – South by Southwest (SXSW; ☎ 512-467-7979), the middle of March at the Convention Center, Palmer Auditorium and in dozens of Austin nightclubs. They get packed with record company execs, gaggles of critics and wannabe critics, producers and, usually more than 600 bands. The town goes absolutely barking, the locals both get rich off it and hate it (often calling it South by So What), and if you're around you can't miss it. It's been expanding in recent times to include multimedia and film as well.

Jerry Jeff Walker's Birthday Celebration

The outlaw-country icon's birthday celebration (☎ 512-477-0036), held the 27th to 30th, includes a golf tournament, dances and a Saturday night concert by Jerry Jeff at the Paramount Theatre (☎ 512-472-5470) at 713 N Congress Ave.

Capitol 10,000 Road Race

Held at the end of the month, this huge race starts at 15th St and N Congress Ave.

April

Wildflower Days

In the middle of the month this annual flower show (☎ 512-292-4200) takes place at the National Wildflower Research Center.

May

Cinco de Mayo Festival

This festival (☎ 512-499-6720) on, yes, the fifth, ostensibly celebrates the Mexican cavalry victory at the Battle of Puebla in 1862, but it's an excuse to drink lots of tequila and dance to the music.

The Fiesta Laguna Gloria

Held at the Austin Museum of Art at Laguna Gloria, this festival (☎ 512-458-6073) is an enormous food and art fair near the museum's beautiful parkside setting.

Spamarama

Held on May 1st at Auditorium Shores, this festival (☎ 512-834-1960) celebrates, yes, the luncheon meat, along with live music. It's a trip, but skip the Spamburger.

July

Austin Symphony Concert and Fireworks

During this event (☎ 512-476-6064), the city's 4th of July celebration, about 40,000 people come to watch the symphony perform a free two-hour concert followed by a fireworks, music and laser show at Auditorium Shores.

Bastille Day
Alliance Française d'Austin celebrates Bastille Day at the French Legation Museum (☎ 512-451-1704) with lots of French food and music.

October

Halloween on 6th St
This is about as rowdy as Halloween can get, with a costumed parade and party along E 6th St into the wee hours.

November

Día de los Muertos
The first two days of the month celebrate this Mexican holiday – Day of the Dead – with lots of fanfare, parades and special exhibitions at the Mexic-Arte.

Thanksgiving Day
The Thanksgiving Day football game between UT and Texas A&M is a major annual event.

PLACES TO STAY

There's no shortage of rooms in Austin until major events, such as the Thanksgiving Day football game between UT and Texas A&M and especially during SXSW, during which you should just forget about it. At all these peak times, prices skyrocket and rooms are booked up months in advance. Note that there's more camping outside of town, near Lake Travis – see the Around Austin section for more information.

Hotel prices are higher in Austin than in San Antonio, and the offerings are almost entirely blah chain places with little variation in the cookie-cutter mold of prefabricated hotels. The cheap motels that line S Congress Ave south of the Continental Club are seedy places notorious for prostitution and drug use, so steer clear. Most of the cheaper places in town are on the northern side of the city, convenient to the airport or Greyhound station.

Camping

There are campgrounds right near Austin and also around Lake Travis – see Around Austin for the latter.

Cheapest and most pleasant is *Emma Long Metropolitan Park* (☎ 512-346-1831), 6½ miles north of downtown off Rural Route 2222, with tent sites for $6 and RV sites for $10, both plus your first entrance ($3 per carload Monday to Thursday, $5 weekends). There's no public transport; take Mo Pac north to RR 2222, turn west. Past the intersection of US 360, take a left at the first light, which is City Park Rd, and follow this (it's windy but just keep going) until it dead ends into the park.

Another great bet is the tent camping inside *McKinney Falls State Park* (☎ 512-243-1643), 5808 McKinney Falls Parkway, just southeast of the city. It's got primitive, walk-in sites (pack your stuff in and out) that are set apart from the rest of the sites for $7 per person and sites with electricity for $12 plus $2 per person older than 13 per night for the park admission.

The *Austin Lone Star RV Resort* (☎ 512-444-6322), 7009 S I-35, south of downtown near W Cannon Drive, has tent and RV sites for $32; from downtown Austin take bus No 13-S Congress to the last stop, which is a couple of blocks north of the campsite.

Very pleasant RV sites are available right near Zilker Park from the *Pecan Grove RV Park* (☎ 512-472-1067), 1518 Barton Springs Rd, and the nearby *Shady Grove RV Park* (☎ 512-499-8432), 1600 Barton Springs Rd, both with RV sites for $20 per day with full hookups.

The friendly folks at *Oak Forest RV Park* (☎ 512-926-8984, 800-478-7275), 8207 Canoga Ave, have sites for $20 a day, $120 a week and $250 per month.

Hostels

The very cool *Hostelling International-Austin* (☎ 512-444-2294, 800-725-2331), 2200 S Lakeshore Blvd, is a really cheerful, clean hostel with a great common area whose windows overlook Town Lake. Dorm rooms are $13/16 for members/nonmembers, private double rooms are $32 for members, $35 for one member and one nonmember and $38 for two nonmembers. And oh, yes, it may be the only hostel in the world that has waterbeds in some of the rooms.

The hostel rents kayaks ($6 per hour) and bicycles ($10 per day) with a $100 deposit. It also offers a kitchen and a library with a computer terminal.

From the Amtrak station, take bus No 22 to 5th St and Congress Ave and change for a southbound bus No 26 or No 27 to Burton and Riverside Drive, then walk three blocks north. From the Greyhound station, take bus No 7-Duval south to Burton Drive and Riverside Drive. From the airport, take bus No 20-Manor Rd to the State Capitol Building and then a southbound bus No 26-Riverside or 27-Dove Springs. By car, take I-35 to exit 233, Riverside Drive, turn east three blocks, turn left on S Lake Shore Blvd and it's a quarter-mile down on the left on the south shore of Town Lake.

Dormitories

Three UT student houses participate in the UT hostelling program that runs annually from June 1 to August 15th. This allows students traveling in the US to stay, on an as-available basis (no reservations accepted), in either *Taos Hall*, 2612 Guadalupe St, the *21st St Co-Op*, 707 W 21st St, or the *Pearl St Co-Op*, 2000 Pearl St, for a maximum of two weeks. Rates range from $15 to $18, and its rooms fill up fast, so show up early in the day. In summer the *Goodall Wooten* (☎ 512-472-1343), another dorm at 2112 Guadalupe St, rents beds and private rooms on a nightly basis only as they become available and at the discretion of the night manager, who also sets prices. Call the Goodall Wooten for information on all UT dormitory accommodations.

Motels & Hotels

Budget We barely recommend the *San Jose Motel* (☎ 512-444-7322), 1316 S Congress Ave, but the price is good, it's convenient to the Continental Club and El Sol y La Luna, and a sign absolutely prohibits alcohol, fighting and guns, so here goes: singles/doubles are $30/38 on weekdays, $35/43 on weekends.

Motel 6 has three outposts in the Austin area. The first (☎ 512-444-5882, fax 512-442-3759), 2707 S I-35, and second (☎ 512-339-6161, fax 512-339-7852), 9420 N I-35, both have singles/doubles for around $39/45. The third, at the airport (☎ 512-467-9111, fax 512-206-0573), 5330 N I-35 just past 51st St, has singles/doubles for $42/48.

The classic digs are at the inimitable *Austin Motel* (☎ 512-441-1157), 1220 S Congress Ave, family run for 60 years. It's like sleeping in a Graceland postcard. Small singles are $49.57, large ones $56.53, good doubles $56, better doubles $61 all the way up to $106. Very friendly service.

Back on the pedestrian-offerings side, *Rodeway Inn at University* (☎ 512-477-6395, fax 512-477-1830), at 2900 N I-35, has singles from $50 to $58 and doubles for $55 to $63. Across the street is the *Days Inn University-Downtown* (☎ 512-478-1631), at 3105 N I-35, a decent, locally owned place with singles from $64 to $95 and doubles from $69 to $99.

There's a perfectly reasonable *Ramada Limited* (☎ 512-451-7001, fax 512-451-3028), 5526 N I-35 up near the airport, with singles from $39 to $59 and doubles from $49 to $69.

Even farther north, the *Travelodge Suites Austin North* (☎ 512-835-5050, fax 512-835-0347), 8300 N I-35, is a good deal with rooms from $44 to $54.

Mid-Range A very good option if you're staying a month or more is out at *Balcones Woods Luxury Suites* (☎ 512-343-0584, fax 512-345-1718), 11215 Research Blvd, which rents apartments (it calls them suites) on monthly terms. The apartments are fully stocked with everything you'll need except, oddly, towels. You can get a one-bedroom, one-bathroom flat for $1400 per month ($46.66 per day). There are also two-bedroom, two-bath flats for $1600.

There's a delightfully retro *EconoLodge* (☎ 512-458-4759), 6201 E US 290 at exit 238B from I-35, which has an entrance that looks like the American Airlines terminal at JFK Airport in New York, plus a decent pool and continental breakfast included in the price; singles are $48 to $58, doubles $52 to $62.

The *Days Inn Austin North* (☎ 512-835-4311, fax 512-835-1740), 820 E Anderson Lane, is nicely located north of the airport and quiet even though it's right at a highway exit; rooms here run $60 to $69.

We stayed at the *Super 8 Motel* (☎ 512-467-8163, fax 512-452-8728), 6000 Middle Fiskville Rd, which is a block and a half from the Greyhound station and managed by the Hilton that's right next door. Good breakfast and coffee all day is included in the single rate of $49 to $59 and double rate of $54 to $64.

Several more mid-range chain places are around Austin and all offer almost identical accommodations. The **Best Western Seville Plaza Inn** (☎ *512-447-5511, fax 512-443-8055)*, 4323 S I-35, has rooms for $55/60; and the **Days Inn South** (☎ *512-441-9242, fax 512-441-9247)*, 4220 S I-35, has rooms from $54 to $69.

The cheerful and well-located **Clarion Inn South** (☎ *512-444-0561, fax 512-444-7254)*, 2200 S I-35, has fine singles from $60 to $65 and doubles for $69 to $75.

There are two Fairfield Inn hotels in town, the **Fairfield Inn South** (☎ *512-707-8899, fax 512-441-5704)*, 4525 S I-35, with singles/doubles for $69/75, and at the airport, **Fairfield Inn Austin Airport** (☎ *512-302-5550, fax 512-454-8270)*, 959 Reinli St; it has a free shuttle service and slightly cheaper rooms at $79 to $89.

The Drury Inn chain has two entries in Austin as well; the **Drury Inn Austin Highland Mall** (☎ *512-512-454-1144)*, at 919 E Koenig Lane, has rooms from $64 to $80; and way north the **Drury Inn North** (☎*/fax 512-467-9500)*, 6711 N I-35, has singles/doubles for $73/83.

A very nice option downtown – one of the best values in this price range – is the **La Quinta Capitol** (☎ *512-476-1166, fax 512-476-6044)*, 300 E 11th St right near the capitol; it has clean and comfortable doubles for $79 to $99.

Top End The more expensive places in town tend to be more expensive just because they cater to the expense-account market of lobbyists and others in the capital on business, but there are a couple of gems.

Of the top-end chain places, the best bets for convenience and services are the **Omni Austin Hotel** (☎ *512-476-3700, fax 512-320-5882)*, 700 San Jacinto Blvd, with rooms from $119 to $159; the perfectly located **Austin Marriott at the Capitol** (☎ *512-478-1111, fax 512-478-3700)*, 701 E 11th St, $105

to $165; and the very nice **Doubletree Guest Suites Austin** (☎ *512-478-7000, fax 512-478-5103)*, 303 W 15th St, which offers excellent service and suites from $109 all the way up to $245.

Flanking Town Lake are two other decent options, the **Hyatt Regency Austin** (☎ *512-477-1234, fax 512-480-2069)*, 208 Barton Springs Rd (at the bottom of the curvy driveway), with rooms from $109 to $169; and the **Holiday Inn Town Lake** (☎ *512-472-8211, fax 512-472-4636)*, 20 N I-35, off of exit 2333 Riverside-Town Lake, with singles/doubles starting at $100/120.

One gem is the famous **Driskill Hotel** (☎ *512-474-5911, fax 512-474-2214)*, 604 Brazos St, an absolutely wonderful place with a colorful history (built by a braggart cattleman) and rooms for $155 to $185. Lady Bird Johnson herself designed the LBJ suite ($350 to $500, no balcony), and other suites here run from $340 for a junior to $2500 for the Cattle Baron. It's nice to walk in, even if you're not staying; nab some of the free hard candies or sample the nightly peanut-butter-and-jelly buffet.

Top of the pops here is the **Four Seasons Austin** (☎ *512-478-4500, fax 478-3117)*, 98 San Jacinto Blvd, where service is sublime, food is awesome and most rooms have lake views. They don't come cheap; the rate for an executive suite, the cheapest, starts at $220; rooms with and without balconies overlooking the lake are $250/290, and suites run from $550 to $1350.

B&Bs

The **Brook House** (☎ *512-459-0534)*, at 609 W 33rd St, very close to the UT campus, is a stately old place (1922) with six very nice rooms, all with private bath, for $75 to $99. Breakfast is served on the veranda in nice weather.

The **Miller-Crockett House** (☎ *512-441-1600)*, 112 Academy Drive south of Town Lake, is a New Orleans Victorian-style house (1888), with awesome views of downtown Austin. It has rooms from $89 to $139 and private bungalows that sleep three – call for rates on those. A big continental breakfast is served daily.

If you'd like to mix a little Texas history with a stay in a beautiful colonial house, head for the *Wildflower Inn* (☎ 512-477-9639, fax 512-474-4188), 1200 W 22½ St, which is run by Kay Jackson, a direct descendant of David G Burnet, temporary president of the Republic of Texas (from March to October 1836). It serves nice breakfasts, and rooms are $79 and $89 with shared bath and $94 with private bath.

Friends in Austin recommended what they called the 'expensive-retro' *City View B&B* (☎ 512-441-2606), 1317 E Riverside Drive near the hostel, featuring '50s Danish-modern decor.

PLACES TO EAT
Snacks & Fast Food
The *Tamale House* (☎ 512-472-0487), 2825 Guadalupe St, is a totally no-frills Mexican take-out place with excellent, cheap stuff to go.

The best of the chain fast food Tex-Mex joints is *Taco Cabana* (☎ 512-478-0875), 517 W Martin Luther King Jr Blvd, with a drive-thru, open 24 hours a day.

It looks innocuous enough, but the *Austin Wraps* stand in the food court at the Dobie Mall, 21st St at Guadalupe St, is great; for $3.50 feast on a burrito big enough to kill a man with and spicy sauces.

Up on the Drag, *Texadelphia* (☎ 512-480-0107), 2422 Guadalupe St, does good cheesesteak sandwiches with salsa and chips for $4. Nearby, *Banzai Japanese Food* (☎ 512-320-0657), 2120 Guadalupe St, has swell daily lunch specials and sushi specials for $5. How they survive next door to the all-encompassing and frighteningly popular *Quackenbush's* (☎ 512-472-4477), 2120 Guadalupe St, is a miracle; throbbing with UT students all the time, with great daily lunch specials for $4 and awesome espresso shakes, the place had an instant of fame as a backdrop in *Slacker*. In the back there's a cigar stand and smoking area as well as a reading room with free newspapers.

Also on the Drag is *Veggie Heaven* (☎ 512-457-1013), 1914A Guadalupe St, with Asian vegetarian food like lo mein, pasta or California rolls for $5. There's also a food court upstairs in the Dobie Mall, at 21st and Guadalupe Sts.

Another UT fave and also loved by late-night revelers is *Ken's Donuts* (☎ 512-320-8484), 2820 Guadalupe St, with good, cheap donuts and coffee 24 hours a day. Also up here is an *Einstein Bros Bagels* (☎ 512-457-8722), 2404 Guadalupe St.

Downtown, *Longhorn Po Boys & Felafel* (☎ 512-476-7735), 906 N Congress Ave, does good po'boys, sandwiches and felafel from $3.35.

Coffee Bars
In the UT area, there's a feely-dealy would-be Marxist scene at the very deep *Mojo's Daily Grind* (☎ 512-477-6656), 2714 Guadalupe St, open Monday to Saturday 24 hours and to midnight Sunday, reopening at 8 am on Monday. You'll also find poetry readings ('I Am The Rainforest/Nurture Me') and a poetry board, live folk music, chessboards and very good coffee.

Another 24-hour place is the industrially chic *Metro* (☎ 512-474-5730), 2222 Guadalupe St, which also offers cakes, pies and sandwiches.

Downtown, *Little City Espresso Bar* (☎ 512-476-2489), at 916 N Congress Ave, is aptly named – a little stand in a big building, but the espresso and coffee are cheap and fine.

Barbecue
See the boxed text for Austin's best barbecue. *Stubb's BBQ* (☎ 512-480-8341), at 801 Red River St, is the Austin branch of the Lubbock chain famous for its role in bringing live Texas music to the restaurant (see Blues & Barbecue in the Lubbock chapter). It's a nice place in an old brick house but the food is overpriced; chicken is $6.50, brisket $6, both served with two side dishes. The bar's also overpriced but good as well.

Ruby's BBQ (☎ 512-477-1651), at 512 W 29th St, serves hormone-free, USDA-choice meats, and the brisket is good though erratic. While the restaurant has an antiseptic environment, it does offer live music and is an Austin tradition.

Iron Works Barbecue (☎ 512-478-4855), 100 Red River St, on Waller Creek opposite

Austin's Best Barbecue

Barbecue is a highly subjective subject, and there are lots of opinions on the matter, so we went around with some Austin natives, transplants and a Louisiana-born food writer from the *Chronicle*, so if you disagree with our opinion, your opinion's wrong, bubba.

Head immediately for the east side of Austin to the ramshackle restaurant that consistently serves up the finest beef, pork, sausage and gamy mutton at Austin's best: *Sam's Barbecue* (☎ 512-478-0378), 2000 E 12th St. The best barbecue in the region, however, is *Kreuz Market* (☎ 512-398-2361), which is in Lockhart – see Around Austin.

Sam's walls are covered with photos and notes from grateful clients, who form a long line at lunch and dinner. It's so beloved that when the place burned down a few years back, local contractor clients chipped in and rebuilt it.

Delicious mixed plates (two meats, beans, bread, onions, pickles and potato salad) are $6.

the Convention Center, has very dependable smoked pork loin and huge beef ribs. Nearby, kids love the buffet and decor at *Mongolian BBQ* (☎ 512-476-3938), 117 San Jacinto Blvd across the street from the CVB, where you pick from 17 veggies and three types of meat, which the staff stir fries in front on the giant Mongolian grill. You'll pay less than $5 for lunch weekdays 11am to 3pm, and it's open for dinner, too.

For gargantuan portions of pork ribs, head for *Lewis's BBQ* (☎ 512-473-2225), 1814 Harvey St at E Martin Luther King Jr Blvd.

Tourists head for the pedestrian options at the *County Line on the Hill* (☎ 512-327-1742), 6500 W Bee Cave Rd, the first in what's now a regional chain of barbecue places. It's definitely fine but heading pretty darn mainstream. Its second location in town, the

County Line on the Lake (☎ 512-346-3664), 5204 FM 2222, does about the same, and the decor is as imaginative as the local Shoney's decorated by Bennigan's. The earlier you show up, the better.

Speaking of touristy food, down on the restaurant row south of the river, *Green Mesquite BBQ & More* (☎ 512-479-0485), 1400 Barton Springs Rd, is one of the new tourist faves. It's fine and all, but it's mentioned here mainly because it's so mainstream and in all the tourist pamphlets. While we're at it, we have to mention that *Chuy's* (☎ 512-474-4452), at 1728 Barton Springs Rd, has touristy Mexican.

The *Broken Spoke* (☎ 512-442-6189), 3201 S Lamar Blvd, is better known as a live-music venue (see Entertainment) but it also serves respectable steaks, chicken-fried steaks, barbecue and hamburgers.

Mexican & Tex-Mex

This is huge in Austin, and there are places throughout the city to grab a bite of something. Ask if the restaurant you're in has homemade corn tortillas – if they're made on the premises they're a taste treat; otherwise, get flour. See Fast Food & Snacks earlier for more listings.

Two UT traditions are *El Patio* (☎ 512-476-5955), 2938 Guadalupe St, which has been around for more than 40 years, doing very good and very cheap Tex-Mex (served up with saltines and salsa); and *Enchiladas y Más* (☎ 512-478-9222), 2804 N I-35 at 26th St, with about the same offerings a bit farther east.

A great eastside Tex-Mex place is *Nuevo Leon Restaurant* (☎ 512-479-0097), at 1209 E 7th St, a consistent place with basic but great food. Fun (if bright pink) atmosphere, and the family-run place has great service.

A really popular place downtown is *Las Manitas Avenue Cafe* (☎ 512-472-9357), 211 N Congress Ave, with salads from $4, quasi-vegetarian offerings, such as tofu chorizo with eggs and vegetables for $5, and the awesome house special, the garlicky migas especiales con hongos. There's a patio out back.

One of the best breakfasts in Austin and an always reliable spot for good Mexican food is *El Sol y La Luna* (☎ 512-444-7770), 1224 S Congress Ave, a really funky family-run place whose proprietors have bizarre taste in wall furnishings but who serve thoroughly excellent breakfasts from $3.50 to $5 – don't miss the huevos rancheros. It's right next door to the Austin Motel (see Places to Stay).

Get seriously off the beaten path at *Pato's Tacos* (☎ 512-476-4247), 1400½ E 38½ St, behind the Big Fiesta supermarket. This place is a hoot – a slapped-together shack that has three rooms, two pool tables, live music on Friday and Saturday nights and humongous plates of great Mexican fare. Full meals are around $5; skip the crab-stuffed jalapeños in favor of draft Bass ale. When the train goes by it's something straight out of the *Blues Brothers*.

Soul Food

And then there's *Dot's Place* (☎ 512-255-7288), 13805 Orchid Lane, about 5 miles north of town near the town of Wells Branch. Call it soul food. Call it home cooking. Whatever, but if you find yourself north during lunch, be sure to hit this incomparable stop. Dot herself starts cooking around 4 am to prepare for the daily lines of blue-collar folks who show up around noon for her fried catfish, meat loaf and chicken and dumplings. Add a side of stewed okra or collard greens. Save room for the blackberry cobbler or the sweet-potato pie, the latter of which can bring about world peace. Take the Howard Lane exit off I-35 and head west, or go east from Mo Pac from Wells Branch and look for the sparkly sign; open 11 am to 2 pm, closed on weekends.

Pizza

Frank and Angie's Pizzeria (☎ 512-472-3534), 508 West Ave, serves up pretty darn good New York-style pie. A huge slice and a salad will run just less than $5. It also serves up some mean sandwiches, pastas and calzoni and has a couple of vegan options.

A fine budget choice is *CiCi's Pizza* (☎ 512-453-4488), at 5365 N I-35 in the Capitol Plaza Shopping Center, which does a daily lunch buffet with anywhere from 10 to 15 types of pizza for $3 including salad bar and 'dessert pizza.'

Asian

For Vietnamese food worth driving for you absolutely must not miss *Pho Cong Ly* (☎ 512-832-5595), 8557 Research Blvd next to the Target north of town, where scrumptious Vietnamese classics are served in a room jam-packed full of Vietnamese and Asian food-loving Austinites. Lunch will run about $6 per person, and the portions are huge.

Almost as good and more convenient is the fantastic *Fortune Pho 75* (☎ 512-458-1792), at 5501 N Lamar Blvd just south of Koenig Lane, with stunningly good bún from $4, wonderful soups from $1 and Vietnamese specials like stir-fried chicken in hot chili and lemongrass with soup or egg roll for $4 at lunch and $6 at dinner. The shrimp dishes are divine.

Another very popular pho place is *Kim Phung* (☎ 512-451-2464), 7601 N Lamar Ave.

Vegetarian

Mother's Cafe (☎ 512-451-3994), 4215 Duval St opposite Julio's, is a vegetarian mecca. Daily specials run the gamut from fresh salads to curried lentil soup, and it has an extensive regular menu. There's also a nice, covered fern-heavy patio when the weather's warm. Lunch will run you $5 to $7. Them Mother's folks also operate the more upscale *West Lynn Cafe* (☎ 512-482-0950), at 1110 W Lynn, which serves up slightly upscale (well, from $8 to $10) fresh vegetarian fare featuring a lot of freshly picked herbs in a swanky steel-and-glass building.

Mr Natural (☎ 512-477-5228), at 1901 E Cesar Chavez east of I-35 near Chicon St – not the most overly salubrious of neighborhoods to traverse at night – is a vegan-veggie place (in that order) that has a juice bar, supermarket and awesome veggie Tex-Mex food; it's open from 7 am to 6 pm.

There are vegan and veggie options at many area restaurants – even *Threadgill's* (see American) does a three-vegetable plate for $6 and a Chef's Choice (a nine-hot-veggie orgy) for $7. *Frank and Angie's Pizza* (see Pizza) also has options good for vegetarians.

American

Jeffrey's (☎ 512-477-5584), 1204 W Lynn, is a highly respected American place with dinner for $15 to $26; it's open Monday to Thursday 6 to 10 pm, Friday and Saturday 5:30 to 10:30 pm, closed Sunday.

The now-historic *Threadgill's Restaurant* (☎ 512-451-5440), at 6416 N Lamar, the re-incarnation of Threadgill's gas station-beer joint opened by Eddie Wilson of Armadillo World Headquarters fame, is open for lunch and dinner. Good chicken-fried steak, meat loaf and down-home diner food (good enough to have spawned a cookbook; see the boxed text in the Facts for the Visitor chapter) run from $5 to $15. It's open Monday to Saturday 11 am to 10 pm, Sunday 11 am to 9 pm, and there's live music on some nights. Work-week lunch specials are a good deal – main course and side dish for $5.50, served Monday to Saturday 11 am to 3 pm.

Castle Hill Cafe (☎ 512-476-0728), 1101 W 5th St, is an Austin favorite, with good southwestern spicy stuff and some Asian American dishes as well, all in the $9-to-$14 range. The *Café at the Four Seasons Hotel* (☎ 512-478-4500), 98 San Jacinto St, is a pricier and excellent American entry, and the Sunday brunch is awesome, too – see Sunday Brunch.

For steaks, the *Ruth's Chris Steakhouse* (☎ 512-477-7884), 3010 Guadalupe St, is as good here as it is anywhere else in the country, and just as pricey.

To call *Katz's Bar and Deli* (☎ 512-472-2037), 618 W 6th St, 'American' is a stretch – it has Jewish deli offerings like roast beef sandwiches and knishes – but its fare is certainly New York-style (it's not affiliated with the superior deli of the same name in New York City), and it's open 24 hours.

Sunday Brunch

Every Sunday the brunch at *La Zona Rosa* (☎ 512-472-2293), 612 W 4th St, has the Asylum Street Spankers, featuring Guy Forsyth and bunch of guys with saws and bizarre instruments who play a variety of styles, including gospel, blues and anything they feel like. It's not to be missed.

The *Café at the Four Seasons Hotel* (see American), has a fabulous all-you-can-eat Sunday brunch buffet from 10:30 am to 2:30 pm (not enough time, really) for $35 for adults and $18 for children (those five and younger are free).

There's a fabulous gospel brunch at *Stubb's BBQ* (see Barbecue earlier), with seatings at 11 am and 1 pm, for $12. The *West Lynn Cafe* (see Vegetarian earlier), has vegan options and a Saturday and Sunday brunch from 11 am to 3 pm.

Mediterranean

Louie's 106 (☎ 512-476-1997), 106 E 6th St, is perhaps the best restaurant in town, and it's certainly a flashy place to bring a date. The food is Spanish, Provençal and Italian, and there's a Mediterranean grill and tapas bar. It's *muy caro*, but it's worth it.

Ice Cream

With spades a-flyin', the keen staff at one of the five branches of *Amy's Ice Cream* bash and flatten huge portions of solidly frozen, delicious, full-fat ice cream, then mush in toppings before grinding it into a cup, cone or bowl. If you ask nicely, one counterperson will walk across the street and, with the flamboyance of a prestidigitator and the macabre studiousness of Penn and Teller, have a second counterperson toss your scoop high over the traffic to be caught in a bowl by the first. Just for the hell of it. Excellent Mexican vanilla, key-lime cheesecake and Belgian and dark chocolate flavors just scratch the surface. Scoops are $1.50 to $3 depending on the size. Our favorite branch (☎ 512-480-0673) is opposite Whole Foods (see Markets) at 1012B W 6th St.

Markets

The big news in town are the two big health-food supermarkets, which both carry a huge line of gourmet and organic foods. The winner is the simply unbelievable *Central Market* (☎ 512-206-1000), which is on

Free Lunch

Want a free lunch? Or snack? Head for Central Market (see Markets) any time of the day and walk the aisles, and it won't be too long before you're approached by someone handing out something great. Fruits, fish, pasta, guacamole and chips, desserts – you name it. You're actually *encouraged* to take samples from the salad and olive bars, and there is even free coffee.

It's one of Austin's best deals, so don't miss it.

Lamar Ave between 38th and 45th Sts. With aisle after aisle of mind-bogglingly good fresh and packaged foods, you can stock up for cooking at the hostel, or buy the wonderful take-away foods (super sushi and hand rolls for $6, sandwiches from $2 to $5, hot meals a bit more) plus bulk nuts, dried fruits and trail mixes, a billion types of olives, bulk guacamole, salsa, salads and probably the best wine selection in town – with specials for less than $10 and wines from around the world. Central Market Cooking School does regular 2½-hour classes from $35 to $50.

Second best (and still pretty darn good) is the pricier **Whole Foods** (☎ *512-476-1206*), 601 N Lamar, which has the same sort of stuff and is certainly more central. Upstairs, the expensive **Fresh Planet Cafe** has wine by the glass, bowls of noodles for $5, burgers (fish, veggie or meat) from $6.50 to 7.50, and soups from $3.50.

India Bazaar (☎ *512-494-1200*), 3004 Guadalupe St, does Indian groceries and specialties. (Speaking of Indian, there's said to be a good Indian lunch buffet at **Star of India** (☎ *512-452-8199*), 2900 W Anderson Lane, for about $6 per person.

Wheatsville Food Co-op (☎ *512-478-2667*), 3101 Guadalupe St, is open to non-members and offers organic and imported foods and coffees.

ENTERTAINMENT

A free monthly pamphlet, *Austin Arts*, is available at many downtown entertainment venues and contains listings for readings, gallery openings and other arts-related happenings around town. The best sources for entertainment information are the *Chronicle*, the *Austin American-Statesman* and their websites (see Media earlier in this chapter).

Theater

The **Paramount Theatre** is the main theatrical venue in the city; see Classical Music & Opera for more information.

Zilker Hillside Theatre (☎ *512-397-1463*), 1110 Barton Springs Rd in Zilker Park opposite Barton Springs Pool, is a 2500-seat outdoor theater – you sit on blankets on the grass – with a wonderful summertime array of performances. Admission is free; show up two hours before show time to ensure you get a spot – space is given out on a first-come first-served basis. By car, take Riverside Drive west to Barton Springs Rd, turn left (left), and it's a little more than a mile; there's parking on the left. Or you can take bus No 30-Barton Creek from downtown.

The **Zachary Scott Theatre Center** (☎ *512-476-0594*) runs musicals, comedies and dramas year-round at two locations – the Arena Stage, 1510 Toomey Rd, and the Kleberg Stage, 1421 W Riverside Drive. The **Public Domain** (☎ *512-474-6202*), at 807 N Congress Ave, is an alternative playhouse.

The teeny (150-seat) **Dougherty Arts Center Theatre** (☎ *512-397-1471*), 1110 Barton Springs Rd, runs a wide range of performances throughout the year.

Cinema

Malls have the usual offerings for multiplex cinemas. God bless **Discount Cinema 8** (☎ *512-244-6622*), at 3407 Wells Branch, with first-run films that cost $1.50 until 6 pm and $2 after that.

The **Alamo Drafthouse Cinema** (☎ *512-867-1839*), 409 Colorado St, has excellent specials (Monday $1 admission, Tuesday $2 pints of beer, Wednesday $5 pizzas and midnight movies with $2 pints and $5 pizzas).

Every Monday is Funhouse Cinema night at the *Ritz Lounge* (see Bars and Live Music), with underground film and video for $4 for two shows at 8 and 10:30 pm.

The *Dobie Cinema* (☎ 512-472-3456), in the Dobie Mall at 21st and Guadalupe Sts, is probably the biggest venue in town for independent films; there's free parking in the garage at Whitis and 20th Sts, just behind the mall.

Film Festival The Austin Film Festival (☎ 512-478-4795), 1600 Nueces St, is held every October at area cinemas. It's dedicated to showcasing local filmmakers as well as calling itself the first festival to pay attention to the writers, and choices reflect that. Tickets to individual screenings are usually $6.50; passes to the entire festival are $275 if booked before December 31, with rates going up by at least $100 afterward.

Classical Music & Opera

The 1300-seat *Paramount Theatre* (1915; ☎ 512-472-5470), 713 N Congress Ave, is Austin's premier venue for classical concerts, ballet, children's theater and touring road shows. The gorgeous, former-vaudeville stage has been completely renovated. Tickets can be bought at the box office from Monday to Saturday noon to 5:30 pm, or by calling ☎ 512-469-7469.

The *Austin Symphony* (☎ 512-476-6064, 888-462-3787) performs throughout the year at a number of venues throughout the city; get information at the box office in Symphony Square at 11th and Red River Sts or in the *Chronicle*.

There are also concerts and theater performances at Bass Concert Hall, the B Iden Payne Theatre and Bates Recital Hall (☎ 512-471-1444), all in the performing arts complex on the UT campus.

Live Music

Austin's contention that it's the 'Live-Music Capital of the World' may very well be true. It's the town's leading nighttime attraction, and musicians come from all over the world to try their hand at playing the blues or any other style of music. Music is serious business here, and not just on weekends. On a

SOUTH CENTRAL TEXAS

Films in Austin

Austin has a more illustrious film career than you might imagine, and recently Hollywood has been doing a whole lot of shooting around here. In 1991, Austin writer-director Richard Linklater's *Slacker* unexpectedly brought the world's attention to a group of overeducated college-aged kids; the low-budget film was picked up by Orion for distribution, which launched Linklater's career. Linklater followed that up with the very successful *Dazed & Confused* (see Films in Facts about Texas). Most recently Linklater has directed *SubUrbia*, written by Eric Bogosian, and *The Newton Boys*, starring Matthew McConaughey, Ethan Hawke and Julianna Margulies. A former waiter in the 6th St Strip in Austin, McConaughey, now a hot property with an annoying accent, got his start making commercials for a local car dealer.

Other major films shot in and around Austin include Steven Soderbergh's *The Underneath*; *Michael*, starring John Travolta as an angel; the bizarre suburban nightmare of *What's Eating Gilbert Grape* with Johnny Depp and what's-his-name; *Nadine*, in which Jeff Bridges pursues a goofy yet dangerous Kim Basinger; *The Return of the Texas Chainsaw Massacre, Part 4* (versions one through three show, as you'd expect, some of the finer points of Texas scenery), with Matthew McConaughey; *DOA* with Dennis Quaid and Meg Ryan; and in the '70s, the first big-budget Hollywood feature shot in Austin, *Outlaw Blues*, starring Peter Fonda and Susan St James.

given Friday night there are probably more than 200 bands playing in the town's 150 or so venues, and on an average, low-season Monday night about 26 bars and clubs in town will have live music.

Cover charges to shows cost anywhere from $3 to $15. It's usually $3 for local bands; touring bands are $15 or more. Emo's (see later) always charges $2.

Generally there are two to three bands per venue. Most places have a happy hour with reduced-price drinks daily from around 4 to 7 pm, but sometimes to as late as 10 pm. Music shows usually start late, with the head-liner getting on anywhere from 10:30 pm to midnight. Bars serve liquor until 2 am; dance clubs stay open until 4 am.

Music Clubs In the documentary *The History of Rock and Roll*, Jimmy Page wore a T-shirt from *Antone's* (☎ 512-474-5314), 213 W 5th St, the 'Home of the Blues,' safely ensconced in new downtown digs. Every-body, but everybody, plays Antone's, and if they can't play here, they'll come in to get cool credibility – as did U2 (even Bruce Willis *tried*). There's something on every night, the bar has great service and excel-lent tequila, and the shoe-shine guy's been at it for more than 20 years. For a seedier scene, complete with biker ambience, try *Joe's Generic Bar*, (☎ 512-480-0171), at 315 E 6th St.

Another major venue in town is the *Con-tinental Club* (☎ 512-441-2444), at 1315 S Congress Ave south of the river, a smaller but very important Austin venue. There's a lot of '50s-worshiping – and a lot of love for Buck Owens – but it's got a good mix of blues, rockabilly, country and pretty much anything else. If you can catch Junior Brown when you're in town, you're in for a standing-room-only treat.

Almost as famous is *Liberty Lunch* (☎ 512-477-0461), 405 W 2nd St, which hosts midsize touring acts from John Hiatt to Keanu Reeves and his Dogstar boys.

Stubb's BBQ (☎ 512-480-8341), 801 Red River St, has live music nightly, showcasing alot of the newer insurgent country acts as well as blues and lots more, and it's got a

good jazz brunch on Sunday – see Sunday Brunch in Places to Eat earlier.

There's also a wide variety of music at *La Zona Rosa* (☎ 512-472-2293), 612 W 4th St. Everybody from Ladysmith Black Mam-bazo to David Byrne has played La Zona Rosa. If no touring band is on the marquee, there's usually still local music to be had here any night of the week.

World Beat & Reggae World beat and reggae are featured at the *Flamingo Cantina* (☎ 512-494-9336), 515 E 6th St.

Folk & Acoustic The *Cactus Cafe* (☎ 512-475-6515), in the Texas Union, hosts people like Graham Parker and Steve Forbert in a tiny room right on the UT campus. Expect to find a postcollegiate, preprofessional, tree-hugger crowd.

Ian McLaglan, the keyboard player from the Faces (see a pre-1975 rock magazine for more information) plays every Tuesday night when he's in town at the *Saxon Pub* (☎ 512-448-2552), 1320 S Lamar Blvd.

Country & Western The *Broken Spoke* (☎ 512-442-6189), 3201 S Lamar Blvd, is country-and-western nirvana – a smallish but nonetheless totally authentic (down to the pitchers of Pearl) Texas dance hall. It offers live music Tuesday through Saturday. Try to line dance there though, and you may discover how real cowboys like to bar brawl. There's also country and western at *Thread-gill's* (see American under Places to Eat).

The Continental Club and Stubb's BBQ also have a fair amount of alternative-country bands.

Smaller Bands If alternative hadn't be-come mainstream, it would still be played at *Emo's* (☎ 512-477-3667), 603 Red River St, a Sub-Pop kind of place where a bunch of degenerate punks play nightly.

One step up from this is the highly smoky *Electric Lounge* (☎ 512-476-3873), at 302 Bowie St – it requires (or creates) a tobacco addiction, but has great shows, with acts from Jonathan Richman to Medicine to '50s surf-guitar innovator Link Wray. Big independent bands or small-label bands play here or at places like the Continental Club.

Larger Bands Everyone from Tom Jones and Bob Dylan to Aerosmith and Luciano Pavarotti play at the town's two huge venues, the *Austin Music Hall* (☎ 512-263-4146), 208 Nueces St, and the *Erwin Center* (☎ 512-471-7744), 1701 Red River St, on the UT campus.

Austin Bands While local bands will play at Antone's, Continental Club, the Electric Lounge and Stubb's, there are a couple of places that practically specialize in Austin bands. *Steamboat* (☎ 512-478-2912), at 403 E 6th St, offers pretty straightforward rock and roll, and the *Hole in the Wall* (☎ 512-472-5599), 2538 Guadalupe St, is just what it sounds like, with live local bands nightly and an Elvis shrine above the stage. 'Cheap' describes both the beer and the crowd here. Every Sunday is the Sunday Night Rock and Roll Free For All – four or five bands and no cover. There are usually pretty good local bands playing new lounge stuff like Ta Mere and the Recliners (playing lounge versions of AC/DC and Nirvana) upstairs at the *Ritz Lounge* (☎ 512-474-2270), 320 E 6th St.

Jazz The best-known places in the city for jazz are the *Cedar Street Courtyard* (☎ 512-495-9669), 208A W 4th St, a hip jazz bar way ahead of the curve on the martini craze (and one that has happily cashed in on it, too); it still caters to a slightly upscale crowd. The *Caucus Club* (☎ 512-472-2873), 912 Red River St; the *Elephant Room* (☎ 512-473-2279), 315 Congress Ave; and, about six blocks west of the Strip and attracting an older crowd, the *Top of the Marc* (☎ 512-472-9849), 618 W 6th St, all usually support good jazz. The slightly more adventurous head over to the east side to the *Victory Grill* (☎ 512-474-4494), 1104 E 11th St, which is what a really cool jazz room would have been in St Louis during the '20s and '30s. Don't go much further east, though.

Metal The *Back Room* (☎ 512-441-4677), 2015 E Riverside Drive, has cheap beer and heavy-metal stuff throughout the week. The place shelters an interesting crowd and more pinball machines and video games than you can shake a stick at.

Tejano Once you cross I-35 on Riverside going east, every strip mall on the right-hand side of the road for the next half mile will have a Tejano bar inside it, and the places get packed. It's a very Latin scene – the flavor is Country Music Television-meets-Univision.

Clubs along this stretch include *Club Latino* (☎ 512-441-2999), 1907 E Riverside Drive, *Club Kao* at No 2003, *Club Carnival* at No 2237 and *Club La Noche* (☎ 512-326-2965) at No 2120.

Industrial Gothic and industrial bands from around the country flock to the *Atomic Cafe* (☎ 512-457-0644), 705 Red River St, a medium-size place with a couple of pool tables and a whole lot of people in black. There's currently a fetish night every Tuesday, with S&M and bondage demonstrations on the stage.

Bars

There are bejillions of bars in Austin, and the Strip along 6th St is the major college crowd-tourist strip place to head. Don't get us wrong, there are some very fun places and you'll have a great time, but there are so many that what follows is a selected list.

6th St The first two of these places plus Emo's (see Live Music) form 'the black triangle': *Casino El Camino* (☎ 512-469-9330), 517 E 6th St, has a great jukebox and great burgers. Films, like subtitled Hong Kong films or sometimes softcore pornography are shown regularly on the television sets, but the volume isn't always on. *Lovejoy's* (☎ 512-477-1268), at 604 Neches St, is very cool – try drinking on top of the coffin. There's a pool table, and it bills itself as Texas' smallest microbrewery – they made about six pints last year. The homebrew is very good; their Helmut Kölsch is dark and heavy, but not thick like a stout. All the beers made on the premises are always $2 a pint and $7.50 a pitcher.

There are two distinct areas in the *Ritz Lounge* (☎ 512-474-2270), 320 E 6th St in a converted cinema. Upstairs there's live music (see earlier); downstairs it's cheap beer (maybe the cheapest on 6th St), no cover, cheap pool and air hockey, and lots of slackers.

Maggie Mae's (☎ 512-478-8541), 323-325 E 6th St, is the tourist trap – it's cover-band hell, but there's an enormous wall of taps for about a hundred different beers in what's called the old side of the bar. Similarly cheesy and huge with college students is *Bob Popular* (☎ 512-478-3352), at 402 E 6th St.

Joe's Generic Bar (☎ 512-480-0171), 315 E 6th St, and *Black Cat Lounge*, 309 E 6th St, are two of the seedier entries on 6th St, usually notable for the Harley-Davidsons parked out front.

Other Downtown Bars *Waterloo Brewing Company* (☎ 512-477-1836), at Guadalupe and 4th Sts (never to be confused with *Waterloo Ice House* (☎ 512-472-5400), at 600 N Lamar Blvd), loves to claim that it's Texas' oldest brew pub. True enough, but it dates to 1993. It has a really nice wheat beer in the summer, and it's a fun hangout.

Copper Tank Brewing Company (☎ 512-478-8444), 504 Trinity St at E 5th St, is a microbrew pub that's also a frat-boy hangout and boomingly loud sports bar. It's also a blast if that's the sort of thing you're after, and it has killer happy hours, with pints for $2 and shot specials daily from 3 to 8 pm. Beers include River City Raspberry, Big Dog Brown Ale, Firehouse Stout and White Tail Pale Ale.

The *Elephant Room* (☎ 512-473-2279), 315 Congress Ave, is a well-established yuppie kind of hangout downstairs in a long room that also has live jazz.

Ego's (☎ 512-474-7091), 510 S Congress Ave, is pretty much the Regal Beagle. Oh, all right, there's lounge music and a weird crowd. It's in the apartment complex just south of the river.

When you graduate from the Crown & Anchor (see Neighborhood Bars) you start hitting the *Dog & Duck Pub* (☎ 512-479-0598), 406 W 17th St, a Britishy place with English draft beers and pub grub.

Don Walser, the rotund, callipygian, actual cowboy yodeler and guitar player plays every Monday night at *Babes Live Music Bar & Grill*, (☎ 512-473-2262), 208 E 6th St, from now to the end of time. Always a sight to see, always great, the music more than makes up for the lack of atmosphere, which should keep you away from the place from Tuesday to Sunday.

Speakeasy (☎ 512-476-8017), at 412D N Congress Ave, and its next-door neighbor *West Side* seem to attract large numbers of silicone-enhanced bodies, those who would be attracted to such folks and other hangers-on. That's also somewhat the case at *Cedar Street* – see Jazz earlier.

Club de Ville (☎ 512-457-0900), located at 900 Red River St, is a great place to go out to get a drink before going out to get drinks. Pathologically dark inside, it's a very low-key, unobtrusive, not-very-smoke-filled bar with an outside patio – note the tree-bound chandelier.

Neighborhood Bars Gotta love the *Crown & Anchor* (☎ 512-322-9168), 2911 San Jacinto Blvd, a low-key pub with cheap beer (Shiner pitchers are $6) and good, dirt-cheap hamburgers.

Right down the hill from the Crown & Anchor is *Posse East* (☎ 512-477-2111), 2900 Duval St. Inside it's as run down as the Crown, but there's a more upmarket crowd here, and there are picnic tables outside.

There's nothing like the *Carousel Lounge* (☎ 512-452-6790), 1110 E 52nd St in the middle of nowhere, north of the airport. It's a favorite Austin hangout – director Richard Linklater stops in now and then. The usual crowd is a whimsical mixture of rednecks; college kids learning ballroom, swing and lindy hop; Elk and Moose lodge members; and slackers, all of whom dance happily to the cheesy sounds of Mr Jay Clarke, who plays the Wurlitzer organ. The decor is plastic elephants and other circus-carousel paraphernalia. It serves beer only, but you can bring your own hooch. Local flavor? You bet.

Dance Clubs

Dance clubs in Austin are for those 18 and older. They're also serious pick-up joints; most play more house and techno music than anything else. The dance-club scene isn't as developed as you'd think, probably because all the potential clientele are out at live-music shows. And there's incredibly high turnover in dance clubs – don't be surprised if some of these are gone or replaced with new ones when you visit.

But the gay clubs in town are great fun and pretty welcoming to all sexual orientations. They're mostly located in the Warehouse District just southwest of N Congress Ave and W 6th St.

Paradox (☎ 512-469-7615), 311 E 5th St, is probably the largest and most popular dance club in Austin. The *Buffalo Club* (☎ 512-476-8828), 405 E 7th St, has a small dance floor and people gyrating on it – it's a good pick-up spot for drunk singles and doesn't even get started until after 1 am. *Abratto's* (☎ 512-477-1641), 318 E 5th St, is another longtime player in town, and there's also *Eden 2000* (☎ 512-499-8700), 614 E 6th St.

Gay & Lesbian Most of the gay clubs in town are a mixture of gay and lesbian, usually about 55% men to 35% women, and 10% straight folks, though there are exceptions. On the whole, there's a very good mixed crowd in most places on most nights and a fun atmosphere.

Yee-haw! The *Rainbow Cattle Company* (☎ 512-472-5288), 305 W 5th St, has country and western, shirtless bartenders, lots of cowboy hats and an enormous dance floor.

The *Edge* (☎ 512-480-8686), 213 W 4th St, is never very crowded, despite the cool dance floor at the back, square bar and pool and Foosball tables. There are more women than men on weekends.

It's much more fun next door at *Oilcan Harry's* (☎ 512-320-8823), 211 W 4th St, where it's often so crowded that you can't move – more of a mosh pit, but there's a great patio area out back.

The *Forum* (☎ 512-476-2900), 408 Congress St, has an all-male, Speedo-clad crowd with occasional strippers and an outdoor patio.

Dance Classes Really fun classes in swing and lindy hop are run in several places around town each week by Four on the Floor (☎ 512-453-3889) for $6 per person. Swing classes are held each Monday at the Carousel Lounge (see Neighborhood Bars), Wednesday at the Caucus Club (see Jazz under Live Music) and Thursday at the *Skylight Gallery* (☎ 512-474-9005), 307 E 5th St between San Jacinto Blvd and Trinity St.

Readings

The Destinations series at TravelFest (see Bookstores earlier) is a total winner with travelers, staff and guidebook authors giving one- to two-hour talks. They cover destinations as well as basic trip preparation, packing and general budget travel topics. They're free and not to be missed.

There are lots of readings at Book People (see Bookstores earlier) with big names – anyone from Deepak Chopra to Jimmy Carter could be on the bill.

There are regular poetry readings at *Quackenbush's* (see Places to Eat earlier) and at the *Ruta Maya Coffee House* (☎ 512-472-9638), 218 W 4th St.

Comedy Clubs

Capitol City Comedy Club (☎ 512-467-2333), 8120 Research Blvd, has local and some national comics Tuesday to Sunday at 8 pm and Friday and Saturday at 8 and 10:30 pm.

The ComedySportz Players have been performing improvisational comedy for more than 10 years at the *ComedySportz Playhouse* (☎ 512-266-3397), 2525 W Anderson Lane, which also serves decent food and lots of drinks.

Everyone in town says *Esther's Follies* (☎ 512-320-0553) at Esther's Pool, 525 E 6th St, is funny and worth seeing – it's mainly a satire of current events, movies and the like.

The *Velveeta Room* (☎ 512-469-9116), 521 E 6th St, has a range of different performances throughout the week.

SPECTATOR SPORTS

The UT Longhorns play football from September to November. They encourage fans to come early and be loud, and fans oblige. Every game is pandemonium, but you don't even want to come *close* to the stands during a game involving the Big 12 Conference (see Spectator Sports in the Facts for the Visitor chapter). Tickets in the 1998 season ranged from $28 to $40; for ticket and seating information call ☎ 512-471-3333, 800-982-2386.

SHOPPING

Music is top on the list of things to buy in Austin, and record-shop staff are on the whole more knowledgeable than most you'll find in other cities. Many bands you'll see performing in town sell their own CDs or cassettes. The Big Kahuna of record stores in town is Antone's Records (☎ 512-322-0660), 2928 Guadalupe St, which has a great selection of Austin, Texas and American music, plus a bulletin board for musicians.

There are a few used-CD places on the Drag that can offer phenomenal buys – Technophilia (☎ 512-477-1812), 2418 Guadalupe St, has used CDs for around $8, plus rare stuff for more. Other used CDs can be had at the CD Warehouse (☎ 512-477-3475), 2001B Guadalupe St; Sound Exchange (☎ 512-476-2274), 2100 Guadalupe St, with independent rock, magazines and both CDs and records; and Disc Go Round (☎ 512-479-7779), 2021 Guadalupe St on the 2nd floor of the Dobie Mall, which has a good world music selection.

There's also a very good new selection at Borders Books, Music & Cafe – see Bookstores earlier.

The gift shop at the Mexic-Arte Museum (see Art Museums) is a must stop-off for kitschy Mexican stuff, but the mother lode of kitsch and iconographic crap-a-roonie is Tesoros Trading Co (☎ 512-479-8377), 209 N Congress Ave, which offers books, candles, candlesticks, nun finger puppets and Latin American and Haitian items. Great fun for the whole family.

Also in the Dobie Mall, Service Menswear (☎ 512-476-1672) has vintage and new hipster wear, cocktail shakers, lighters, dice cufflinks, Elvis mouse pads, and Mexican wrestler souvenirs.

The Radio Ranch (☎ 512-459-6855), 1610 W 35th St (bus No 19-Bull Creek), is a testosterone-packed gizmotronics warehouse, run by Neil, a guy's guy who'll point at some impossible-looking contraption and say 'Oh, that's a 5000-watt halogen photo coagulator.' Prices are astronomical, but where else will you find a Ritter dental setup, complete with spit sink, in primo condition – Kmart?

Celebration (☎ 512-453-6207), 108 W 43rd St, the new-age witch store, has jewelry, books, cards, runes, tribal drums and a huge selection of beads and stones.

Get pro-handgun bumper stickers to amaze your friends and family back home (actual example: Practice Gun Control – Shoot Daily) at Just Guns (☎ 512-447-4555), 1325 S Congress Ave very near the Continental Club. No, they don't sell knives. Just guns. And there's a 10% restocking fee if you fail to pass the Brady background check.

Malls

The biggies in town are the Arboretum (☎ 512-338-4437), 10000 Research Blvd, served by the Leander Express bus from downtown ($1); the Northcross Mall (☎ 512-451-7466), 2525 W Anderson Lane at Burnet Rd (bus No 3-Burnet from downtown) and Crossroads Mall, 9070 Research Blvd (bus Nos 3-Burnet, 5-Woodrow or 19-Bull Creek from downtown).

GETTING THERE & AWAY
Air

While Austin plans a new airport at the former Bergstrom Air Force Base, currently the only choice is Robert Mueller Municipal Airport (☎ 512-472-5439), about a 20-minute drive northeast of the city. It's served by America West, American, Aspen Mountain Air-Lone Star Airlines (☎ 800-877-3932), Austin Express (☎ 888-325-2879), Continental, Delta, Northwest, Southwest and United. AeroLitoral Airlines' service to Mexico was suspended as we went to press, but intends to restart.

Bus

The main Greyhound station (☎ 512-458-4463), as well as the Kerrville Bus Co station

(☎ 512-458 3823), is at 916 E Koenig Lane, at the north end of the city off I-35 and convenient to nothing but itself, a couple of hotels and the Highland Mall. From the Greyhound station, take bus No 7-Duval to downtown. Buses leave from here to everywhere frequently, though service to Hill Country destinations is limited to one bus a day at 6:30 pm; to Kerrville (2½ hours) it costs $21/40 one way/roundtrip, and to Fredericksburg (1¾ hours) it costs $17/33.

to/from	frequency (per day)	trip duration	one way/ roundtrip
Dallas	15	3½ to 5 hours	$22/44
El Paso	8	12¼ to 14 hours	$99/198
Houston	7	2¼ to 3½ hours	$17/33
Laredo	9	4¾ to 5½ hours	$24/48
Lubbock	4	9¼ to 16½ hours	$55/110
New Orleans	4	10½ to 12½ hours	$89/178
San Antonio	12	1½ to 1¾ hours	$12/24
Waco	8	2 to 3¼ hours	$10/20

Train
The Amtrak station (☎ 512-476-5684) is at 250 N Lamar Blvd. Austin is served by both the Texas Eagle and Sunset Limited trains; see the Getting There & Away chapter for more information.

Car
To the Dallas-Fort Worth Metroplex and Waco, take N I-35; to San Antonio, take S I-35. I-10 heads east to Houston and west to El Paso.

GETTING AROUND
To/From the Airport
Bus No 20-Manor Rd runs between 6th St and Congress Ave and Robert Mueller Municipal Airport every 20 minutes and takes about 20 minutes in light traffic. A taxi between the airport and downtown runs $7 to $9.

Bus
Austin's public transit rocks. It's run by Capital Metro (CapMetro; ☎ 512-474-1200), which is happy to help everyone out as much as it can. Call for directions to anywhere or

stop into the Customer Service Information Center at 106 E 8th St.

The happiest transportation news in Austin after the Yellow Bikes (see Bicycle) is the 'Dillo service, a free shuttle bus run by CapMetro. Bus No 86-Congress Ave 'Dillo offers free circular service through downtown Austin, to the UT Campus and the State Capitol Building. Other 'Dillo services in town are bus No 87-ACC-Lavaca 'Dillo, running along Lavaca St and to Austin Community College, and bus No 88-Old Pecan St 'Dillo.

City buses other than the 'Dillo cost 50¢.

Car
Parking downtown is difficult; look for garages, as officers will ticket you instantly.

Taxi
The rate at flagfall is $1.50, and it's $1.50 for each additional mile. Companies include:

American Yellow Checker Cab	☎ 512-452-9999
Austin Cab	☎ 512-478-2222
Roy's Taxi	☎ 512-482-0000

Bicycle
Bikes not Bombs (☎ 512-916-3553) runs Austin's free Yellow Bike Program, which repairs old bicycles, paints them yellow and makes them available free for public use. When you see a yellow bike you can pick it up, ride were you're going and leave it standing against a wall or lamppost for the next rider. There are about 150 yellow bikes at present and more to come.

Rent bikes from Waterloo Cycles (☎ 512-472-9253), 2815 Furth St just off Guadalupe St south of 29th St, from $10 per day for a single-speed cruiser to up to $75 per day for a shit-kickin' front-suspension whatchamacallit. Waterloo is the place to inquire about local biking groups, such as the Austin Ridge Riders (☎ 512-453-1955), and a good spot to pick up copies of *Austin Cycling News* (free) or Austin Bicycle Maps ($3.50).

There are bicycle racks (where you can hitch your bike for free) on the front of almost all CapMetro buses.

SOUTH CENTRAL TEXAS

AROUND AUSTIN
The Highland Lakes

The Lower Colorado River Authority, or LCRA (☎ 512-473-4083, 800-776-5272), is a conservation district stretching from central Texas to the Gulf of Mexico. The LCRA supports itself through electricity and water sales and, happily, manages the fabulous string of parks to the northwest of Austin that make getting out of the city such an appealing prospect. These parks front the 'lakes' created by the series of dams along the Colorado River in the 1930s.

The main recreation area northwest of Austin is along Lake Travis and Lake Austin, which are divided by Mansfield Dam. Some of the parks are owned by the LCRA but managed by Travis County. Further northwest, Lake Buchanan is a bit more serene, as it's just that much further from the crowds that descend on Lake Travis every summer weekend.

Many of the parks have camping opportunities, either primitive or developed. And let's not forget Hippie Hollow (officially known as McGregor Park), Texas' only clothing-optional beach.

Lake Travis The most popular destination in the Highland Lakes, Lake Travis offers heaps of opportunities for swimming, sailing and camping.

Perhaps the area's most prestigious winery, and certainly the one with the nicest location, is Lake Travis' **Slaughter Leftwich Vineyards** (☎ 512-266-3331), 4209 Eck Lane, on Lake Travis about a 20-minute drive east of Austin. The winery – which moved here from Lubbock – makes a number of award-winning wines, including Texas chardonnay, Texas cabernet sauvignon, Texas sauvignon blanc, Austin blush, Austin rouge and Austin blanc, the last a blend of chenin blanc and muscat.

The winery is one mile south of the Mansfield Dam; take the Eck Lane exit from RR 620. It's open for tasting and sales Thursday to Sunday 1 to 5 pm; free tours are given Thursday and Friday at 3 pm and Saturday and Sunday at 1:30 and 3:30 pm. The hours seem to change quite a bit, so call ahead.

You've got to be at least 18 to enter **Hippie Hollow** park, Texas' only clothing optional beach. Aside from the views of the people, there are excellent views of the lake, opportunities for swimming and wonderful primitive hiking trails through the hills. From the intersection of RR 620 and FM 2222, take RR 620 south 1⅓ miles to Comanche Trail; turn right and the entrance is 2 miles ahead on the left.

Pace Bend park (☎ 512-264-1482), with swimming-only coves, boat launches and hiking and biking trails, is looped with a 7-mile roadway connecting piers, campsites and swimming beaches. The interior of the park is a wildlife preserve and can be reached only by hiking, biking or horseback. Isolated primitive tent sites with picnic tables, barbecues and fire rings cost $10 per car and are assigned on a first-come, first-served basis. On the east side of the park above Levi Cove are improved campsites with full hookups for $15 per car. You are also allowed to camp on the beach for free.

Camp Chautauqua is a recreation area (☎ 512-264-1752) near Pace Bend and offers a fishing pier, swimming, playground and volleyball courts.

Lake Buchanan Thirty miles long and 5 miles wide, Lake Buchanan is a reservoir that provides central Texas with hydro-electricity.

Fall Creek Vineyards (☎ 512-476-4477) in Tow, on the northwest shore of Lake Buchanan, lies about 25 minutes northeast of Austin. It's open for tasting and tours Monday to Friday 11 am to 3 pm and Saturday noon to 5 pm. In summer it's also open for tasting and sales on Sunday noon to 4 pm. Fall Creek's wines include the award-winning Texas chardonnay and sauvignon blanc and the 1996 Texas Sweet Jo, a dessert wine similar to a sweet Johannesburg. Take US 183 north to Hwy 29 going west past Buchanan Dam; turn north on Hwy 261 and the winery is 2 miles north of the Tow post office on the right.

Black Rock Park is a rather serene little park with 30 campsites, each with a table and grill.

Lake LBJ This lake, between Lakes Travis and Buchanan, is popular with waterskiing yahoos and other motorsports fanatics.

Camping Areas There are more than three dozen Highland Lakes-area campsites; the LCRA (☎ 800-776-5272) can send you a copy of its free Park Pack, which lists all LCRA parks, admission fees, camping fees and facilities. The following sites – among others – are included in the pack:

Arkansas Bend (LCRA), near Lago Vista off Lohman's Ford

Cypress Creek (LCRA), at the intersection of FM 2769 and Old Anderson Mill Rd

Mansfield Dam Park (LCRA), FM 620 at the Mansfield Dam

Pace Bend Park (LCRA), FM 2322, 4½ miles east of US 71

Sandy Creek Park (LCRA), on Lime Creek Rd near FM 1431 and FM 620

Bastrop
Population 5000
Bastrop (named for Philip Hendrick Nering-Bogel, a buddy of Stephen F Austin, who falsely claimed to be the Dutch Baron de Bastrop) is a sleepy little town 40 miles east of Austin. It's got a couple of nice parks, a charming little historic district and some nice barbecue that make it a pleasant day trip from Austin. The Bastrop Chamber of Commerce (☎ 512-321-2419), 927 Main St, has brochures and lists of B&Bs and hotels.

State Parks A mile east of town, the lovely **Bastrop State Park** (☎ 512-321-2101) has hiking trails through pine forests and primitive tent camping sites for $4 per person, with water $9, with water and electricity $12. Day admission to the park is $3. Just southeast is **Buescher State Park** (☎ 512-237-2241), home to birds, deer and the endangered Houston toad. Primitive campsites go for just about the same rates as Bastrop State Park. Sites with water are $7, with water and electric $10.

Places to Stay & Eat Most people make it a day trip or camp in the parks. When you're in town, don't miss a meal at *Cartwright's*

BBQ (☎ 512-321-7719), 490A US 71, with awesome open-pit barbecue (everything's less than $6 per plate) and peach pie.

Getting There & Away Unfortunately, taking public transit means you have to spend the night. Kerrville Bus Co buses (see Bus under Getting There & Away in the Austin section of this chapter) run from Austin at 1:15 pm daily (45 minutes, $7 one way, $13.30 roundtrip), returning at 11:15 the next morning. By car, take US 71 east from Austin.

Lockhart
Population 9300
The reason to come to this little town, about a 20-minute drive south of Austin on US 183, is to indulge – this is the barbecue capital of the world. We don't mean to eat, we mean to stuff yourself silly.

In 1895, Charles Kreuz established a meat market and grocery store here; in 1900 it was bought by the Schmidt family, who have run it ever since as *Kreuz Market* (☎ 512-398-2361), 208 S Commerce St. As you walk in, you approach the 14-foot-wide indoor open pit, where immense oak branches are slowly smoking and heating succulent pork chops ($7 a pound), brisket ($7) or prime rib ($10). Our mouths are watering just typing this listing – try one of the unbelievably, fantastically, overwhelmingly good pork chops here or maybe some of the brisket, served on butcher paper with mushy white bread and sides of cheddar, pickles and onions. Words can't describe how wonderful this is, but it's so moist and tender there's no sauce accompaniment. Let the meat speak for itself; it's been voted the Best Barbecue in Texas by dozens of publications – including this one. It's open Monday to Saturday 7 am to 6:30 pm, closed Sunday.

Also in Lockhart is *Black's BBQ* (☎ 512-398-2712), 215 N Main St, with sausage so good Lyndon Johnson had the establishment cater a party at the nation's capitol. We were less enthused, and the sauce was too clovey, but there's no denying it's damn good. *Chisholm Trail Bar-BQ*, 1323 S Colorado St, serves up a darn respectable selection of ribs, brisket, chicken and sausage and on Monday, Wednesday and Friday, fried catfish.

Getting There & Away Greyhound has service from Austin (see Bus under Getting There & Away in the Austin section of this chapter) daily at 11:45 am (30 minutes; $6 one way $12 roundtrip). By car, take US 183 south and you'll run right into town.

The Hill Country

The Hill Country is rightfully one of the state's biggest tourist draws, sitting pretty much in the heart of Texas and between Austin and San Antonio. It's an area of gently rolling hills and valleys freckled with cacti and cattle ranches, lined with rivers and dotted with peaceful, picturesque little towns. The Hill Country is formed by the Balcones escarpment and the limestone ledges and hills of the Edwards Plateau upon which the area sits. It was in this area that many of the original German and Czech settlers in Texas set down roots (see History in the Facts about Texas chapter), and there's still a large population of their descendants here. As attractive as the Hill Country is though, the fake *fachwerk* and sundry German flavor of places like Fredericksburg can get a little twee.

The best parts of the Hill Country are those in between the big towns ('big' here is a relative term; the biggest towns, Kerrville and Fredericksburg, are both pretty small) in the parks, along the rivers and even in the dude ranches.

You can spend an entire vacation in the Hill Country and not really see it all. If you've got time to spend, a good investment is Texas Monthly's *Hill Country* (1997), a 600-page guide to the area that covers each and every hamlet, from Buda and Bee Cave to Stringtown and Welfare.

Orientation

Highway I-35 runs north-south along the easternmost edge of the Hill Country, which makes up most of the area between Austin and San Antonio and extends all the way west to US 83. Ask 10 people the boundaries of the Hill Country and you'll get 11 different answers, but for traveling purposes this is close enough. The main capitals of activity are Fredericksburg and Kerrville; most people make their base in one of these towns and make day trips from there. For information about San Marcos and New Braunfels (often considered part of the Hill Country), see the Around San Antonio section later in this chapter.

One of the best times to visit is in the month of December, when the Hill Country's Regional Christmas Lighting Tour (☎ 830-997-8515) goes around the whole place stringing up lights and making everything look incredibly romantic.

Roads

Major Hill Country roads include US 290 (west from just south of Austin through Johnson City and Fredericksburg); Hwy 16 (between Fredericksburg and Kerrville, it becomes the scenic route to Bandera then winds slowly down to San Antonio); I-10 (runs southeast to northwest from San Antonio through Boerne, Comfort, Kerrville and Mountain Home); and Hwy 173 (between Kerrville and Bandera).

FREDERICKSBURG
Population 7800

If there's a center to the Hill Country, Fredericksburg is it, and the town knows it. Pushing the line between quaint and grating, it celebrates its German heritage along with group tourists; shops called 'Der' this and 'Das' something-or-other; and – credit is due – great beer, heavenly breads and pastries and good food. While it's heavily over-touristed, Fredericksburg is a fine Hill Country base, though note that – holding with German tradition – many businesses and even some restaurants slam shut their doors at the stroke of 5 pm, except in the height of summer or during the city's Oktoberfest.

While some motels line US 290 to the east and west of the city, most people stay in B&Bs, reserved mainly through a little cartel of booking agencies.

Established in 1846 by Baron Ottfried Hans Freiherr von Meusebach (see History in the Facts about Texas chapter), the town is the birthplace of Admiral Chester Nimitz, and the WWII museum here is definitely worth a stop.

Orientation

From Austin, US 290 becomes Main St; Hwy 16, which runs between Fredericksburg and Kerrville, becomes S Adams St, which divides Fredericksburg addresses into east and west. The town's grid is actually oriented about 45° off true compass bearings, but locals say anything northeast of Main St is north, southwest of it is south. The center of town is at the intersection of Llano and Main Sts.

Information

The Fredericksburg Convention and Visitor's Bureau (☎ 830-997-6523, fax 830-997-8588, dgwhitw@ktc.com) has an information center at 106 N Adams St open Monday to Friday 8:30 am to 5 pm, Saturday 9 am to noon and 1 to 5 pm, and Sunday 1 to 5 pm. On the northwest side of Crockett and W Main Sts, Broadway Bank has an ATM that accepts Pulse, MC-Cirrus and Visa; opposite it is Security State Bank and Trust, which also has an ATM. The post office is at 122 W Main St.

The Main Bookshop (☎ 830-997-2375) has a decent collection of Texana and some Texas guidebooks.

Things to See & Do

Admiral Nimitz Museum This state historical park and museum (☎ 830-997-4379), 328 E Main St, in the former Nimitz Hotel, has detail on the history of the city and the life and times of its favorite son, WWII fleet admiral Chester Nimitz. His family ran the hotel, and the list of luminaries who stayed there is interesting reading. There are three floors of exhibits on the War in the Pacific, including a big Pearl Harbor display, war photos and, best of all, the recording of Franklin D Roosevelt's famous 'day that will live in infamy' radio address (drive the staff batty by playing it). In back is the serene **Japanese Peace Garden**, a gift from

the Japanese government. The **Walk of the Pacific War** is a 3-acre exhibit of fascinating WWII relics: a TBM Avenger torpedo bomber, an LVT landing craft, tanks, anti-aircraft guns and more. The **George Bush Gallery of the Pacific War** will contain dioramas of Guadalcanal and other battle sites; the **Plaza of the Presidents** is a monument to the past 10 US leaders.

The museum is open daily 8 am to 5 pm; admission is $3 for adults and $1.50 for students.

Vereinskirche The city's Vereinskirche (Society Church), in Marktplatz just off of W Main St, was the original town church, meeting hall and school; rebuilt in 1935-36, the compound now houses exhibitions from the Gillespie County Historical Society.

Pioneer Museum The Gillespie County Historical Pioneer Museum (☎ 830-997-2835), 309 W Main St, but taking up much of the south side of W Main St between Orange and Milam Sts, has its center at the preserved Kammlah family house and store (1849), with furnished rooms and a wine cellar. There are several other houses and a blacksmith shop. The museum is open Monday to Saturday 10 am to 5 pm, Sunday 1 to 5 pm; admission is $3 for adults, free for kids younger than 12.

Organized Tours

Fredericksburg Tours (☎ 830-990-0155) runs walking tours Thursday to Saturday at 10 am, Saturday at 2 pm and Sunday at 11 am (other times by appointment) for $10; meet in front of George's Old German Bakery (☎ 830-997-9084) at 905 E Main St. The Fredericksburg Carriage Co (☎ 830-997-2211) does horse-drawn buggy tours through the historic district for $45 for two people for an hour. And there's a little tourist choo-choo that does one-hour tours daily at 11 am and 1, 3, 5 and 7 pm for $5 for adults, $3 for kids; it leaves from 406 E Main St.

Special Events

The mid-June Peach JAMboree and Rodeo (☎ 830-644-2735) is held at the apex of the peach-pickin' season, which runs from May to September (though the best picking is in June and July). Hallford Orchards (☎ 830-997-3064), a mile east of downtown, has pick-your-own peaches, the Peach Basket (☎ 830-997-4533), 334 W Main St, sells fresh peaches and jams, and most every restaurant in town sells peach-based desserts. The jamboree has bake-offs and a rodeo.

The main special event in town is the annual Oktoberfest (☎ 830-997-4810). It's held the first weekend in October and is a copy of the traditional German celebration – lots of beer, sausage and oompah bands. Hotels and B&Bs sell out months in advance, so book early. Admission is $6 per day. There's a second, simultaneous Oktoberfest at the grounds of Fort Martin Scott, 2 miles east of downtown, which has lots of historical demonstrations and more beer.

In the last week of October, the city presents its annual Fredericksburg Food and Wine Fest (☎ 830-997-8515), with wine tastings and special meals at many of the city's restaurants; admission is $15.

Places to Stay

Camping The cheapest camping ($7 per site or $15 with full hookups) is just south of town at *Lady Bird Johnson Municipal Park* (☎ 830-997-4202), on the Pedernales River. Cheerful staff remind you not to pick the pecans – they're city property.

KOA Fredericksburg (☎ 830-997-4796, 800-562-0796), 5 miles east of Fredericksburg Junction at US 290 and FM 1376, has tent sites for $17.75, RV sites with hookups for $20.50, and one-room Kamping Kabins for $32 – though prices go up around special events.

Hill Country RV Park (☎ 830-997-5365) has very simple tent areas (no fire rings) for $5 per tent or with hookups for $13; it's a couple of miles east of town on US 290 between the Wal-Mart and the Law Enforcement Center.

There's RV camping only at both the *Frontier Inn RV Park* (☎ 830-997-4389; sites are $13) – from the center head west on Main St until the road forks, follow US 290 (to the left) and it's an eighth of a mile

ahead. The cheery *Oakwood RV Park* (☎ 830-997-9817), with sites from $21 to $23 – from the intersection of Main and Adams Sts head south on Hwy 16 (Adams) for 2 miles and turn right on Tivydale Rd.

Motels & Hotels *Dietzel Motel* (☎ 830-997-3330), at the junction of US 290 and Hwy 87 at the west end of town, has phoneless singles/doubles for $37/39 on weekdays and $44/46 on weekends, higher during special events, lower when it's really cold out. There's free coffee and the place is antiseptically clean – a good deal.

Frederick Motel (☎ 830-997-6050), 1308 E Main St, is owned by a pleasant young couple and has singles from $25 to $45 and doubles for $45 to $60.

Deluxe Inn Budget Host Hotel (☎ 830-997-3344), 901 E Main St, sports wonderfully friendly people and a nice continental breakfast. Prices are $34/40 for standard singles/doubles here and in the *Miller Inn* across the street (also owned by the Deluxe Inn), but the Deluxe also has rooms with queen-size beds ($36/55) and kings ($45/60), too.

The *Best Western Sunday House Inn* (☎ 830-997-4484), 501 E Main St, has comfortable singles/doubles that run $55/60 Sunday to Wednesday from September to February and $65/70 all other times; breakfast ($6) is next door at the Sunday House Restaurant.

Bed & Brew at the Fredericksburg Brewing Company (☎ 830-997-1646), 245 E Main St, is for adults only (no kids, no pets, no smoking); rooms are $79 to $89, all with private bathroom and queen-size bed.

B&Bs There are 10 million B&Bs in Fredericksburg, or if not, it seems like it. Also popular in town are guesthouses, where there's no breakfast or hosts, but which usually come with kitchens – there's a huge supermarket just south of town on Hwy 16. Almost everyone uses one of the city's booking services to find a place, and they're reliable and efficient. Rooms generally run from $50 to $110 for double occupancy. Following are some reservation services.

Bed & Breakfast of Fredericksburg
(☎ 830-997-4712)

Gästehaus Schmidt
(☎ 830-997-5612, fax 830-997-8282)

Hill Country Lodging & Reservation Service
(☎ 830-990-8455, 800-745-3591)

Main St Bed & Breakfast
(☎ 830-997-0153)

Places to Eat

The winner is the *Dietz Bakery* (☎ 830-997-3250), 218 E Main St. This third-generation family bakery kicks out the best breads and pastries outside Germany; cinnamon rolls for 35¢, donuts for 30¢, fruit rolls for 45¢, sinful danish pastry for 65¢ and exquisite loaves of pumpernickel, whole wheat or rye bread for $1. Yippee!

Almost as good (and with a better variety) is the *Fredericksburg Bakery* (☎ 830-997-3254), 141 E Main St, a lovely place to sit for coffee and pastry. Feast on three types of cinnamon rolls, really good pies and lots more.

Also nice for coffee and cake is the *Clear River Pecan Company* (☎ 830-997-8490), 103 S Llano, which has great brownies, cookies and cakes. Opposite, the *Dog Haus*, on the southwest corner of Llano and Main Sts, does hot dogs and German sausage.

The Best of Texas

The Best of Texas (☎ 830-997-0123), 217A E Main St in Fredericksburg, is a marvelous deli that sells just what its name implies – the best foodstuffs produced in the state. There's an unrivaled selection of Texas wine at the front of the store, and tastings are always free (California and imported wines are kept in the back, but you can taste them as well), with heaps of hot sauces and barbecue sauces, beers, pecans, fruits and other treats. It's open Monday to Friday 10:30 am to 5:30 pm, Saturday 10:30 am to 6:30 pm, Sunday noon to 5:30 pm.

Old German Bakery (☎ 830-997-9084), 225 W Main St, is pretty authentic, with sauerbraten for $8, good soups for $3, and lots of schnitzel from $7 to $9.

The *Fredericksburg Brewing Company* (next to the Bed & Brew; see Places to Stay) at 245 E Main St is a really fun place with starters averaging $3. It serves good old American and German American food like meatloaf ($8), grilled pork chops ($8), a German sausage sampler with German potato salad ($8) and a wild game plate for $19. Daily specials at lunch go for $7 to $8. Beers, made on the premises, include the excellent Not So Dumb Blonde Pale Ale, a pilsener and a dunkles. There are beds upstairs if you do too much sampling.

The *Gallery Restaurant* (☎ 830-997-8777), 3230 E Main St, is much cozier than it looks at first, especially when the fire's going in winter. The staff is friendly, and main courses run $5 to $8 at lunch, a bit higher at dinner. Downstairs is a wine bar that sometimes doubles as a sports bar.

Altdorf Restaurant & Beer Garten (☎ 830-997-7865), 301 W Main St, is the big German place in town, with lots of big mugs of beer, oompah-pah bands and typical Bavarian specialties for around $9 to $13.

Navajo Grill (☎ 830-990-8289), 209 E Main St, is a more upmarket entry, with a nice patio; at lunch, grilled, free-range chicken sandwiches are $8, grilled salmon salad is $11, and green salads are $5 – prices shoot skyward at dinner.

Friedhelm's Bavärian Inn & Bar (☎ 830-997-6300), at 905 W Main St, is said to have good German food, but since they misspell 'Bavarian'…

Entertainment

There is live music at several spots in town on weekends, including at the Altdorf Restaurant and the Fredericksburg Brewing Company.

Getting There & Away

See Roads in Orientation earlier for driving information.

Bus There is a Kerrville Bus Co bus (see Bus under Getting There & Away in the

SOUTH CENTRAL TEXAS

Austin section) from Austin daily at 6:35 pm ($17 one way, $32.30 roundtrip, 1½ hours), returning from Fredericksburg at 9 am.

Getting Around

Rent bicycles at the *fahrradverleih stadtrundfahrten* (bike rental and city tours office), 406 E Main St, for $5 per day, adult trikes are $8 per day, tandems are $5 per hour.

AROUND FREDERICKSBURG
Enchanted Rock
State Natural Area

Enchanted Rock State Natural Area, 16710 Ranch Rd 965, about 18 miles north of Fredericksburg off RR 965 south of Llano, is, in addition to being the best place in Texas to look at granite, a wonderful area of hiking trails and rock-climbing opportunities, and there's camping here as well.

It's a hugely popular park, especially during peak periods such as weekends, spring break and holidays, and park staff may close the park when it reaches its maximum occupancy (and they won't say how many people that is). When it's closed, you can only get into the park if you've made a reservation – call the ranger's office (☎ 915-247-3903) to make one.

The park is open daily 8 am to 10 pm; entry is $5 per adult (children younger than 13 are free).

Things to See & Do The rock itself, which rises 425 feet and covers 640 acres, is the second-largest batholith (underground rock formation) in the USA. The granite exposed is of the Town Mountain granite suite from the Proterozoic era.

Tonkawa Indians, hearing crackling and snapping noises from the rock at night, believed that ghost fires were burning – the park says that as the granite cools at night, it crackles.

There are 7 miles of hiking trails, including the easy 4-mile loop that wraps around the granite and the three-fifths-of-a-mile **Summit Trail**, a 425-foot elevation-gain hike to the top of the rock.

Rock climbers head for the 1000-foot **Enchanted Rock Fissure**, one of the world's largest granite caves; a list of climbing routes is available at the ranger office. Scott Harris-Crump's *Climber's Guide to Enchanted Rock* (1996) is a complete guide to climbing in the park (rock climbers must check in at headquarters, where route maps and climbing rules are available).

The park has open oak woodlands, mesquite grasslands, floodplains and a granite rock community, and there are both rock and fox squirrels, rabbits, white-tailed deer, armadillos and turkeys in the park as well.

Camping The park permits walk-in tent camping only – no vehicles or RVs allowed. Reservations are required; to make them, call ☎ 512-389-8900. Standard sites with toilets, showers, fire rings and picnic tables cost $9 per site plus the entrance fees. There are three primitive campsites as well, with no services for $7 per site plus admission fees with a four-person maximum per site.

Luckenbach
Population fewer than 10

In 1977, Waylon Jennings told the world that in 'Luckenbach, Texas, ain't nobody feeling no pain,' and this tiny Hill Country community has been a pilgrimage zone for zealous country-music fans ever since. In reality, there aren't many reasons to drop by, but if you're in the neighborhood and ready for a change, that's certainly reason enough. It is closed Wednesdays. That's right. The town. Closed.

Things to See & Do Luckenbach's downtown area consists of its 120-year-old **general store** (☎ 830-997-3224), which also serves as the local post office, **dance hall**, **saloon** and **community center**. Its walls are decorated with the hand-scrawled howdies of pilgrims and devotees, its floor with six generations of scuff marks.

The dance hall periodically hosts weekend **musical performances**, but about the only times you can count on a crowd are during the Labor Day and 4th of July **weekend concerts**.

Native Texans Jennings and Willie Nelson are the prime draws, but dozens of country music's finest also fill out the bills.

Special Events The annual Cowboy Christmas Ball, on the 26th of December in the dance hall, is pretty much a cowboy-style *Christkindlmarkt* – carols by the fire, mulled wine and dancing. Admission is between $5 and $10.

Getting There & Away Your only option is to arrive by car. From Fredericksburg, take US 290 east and turn south on FM 1376 for about 3 miles. From San Antonio, take I-10 north to FM 1376 north and follow it for about 25 miles.

Johnson City
Population 1000

Named for the Hill Country's hometown-boy-made-good, the working LBJ Ranch and Johnson's boyhood home are now open as state and national historical sites. There are two distinct sites – the boyhood home and settlement in Johnson City and the ranch area about 14 miles west on US 290. Admission to both is free, and they're open daily except Christmas from at least 8 am to 4:30 pm. Free 1½-hour bus tours of the ranch run from 10 am to 4 pm; board at the state park visitor center.

The *Feed Mill* (☎ 830-868-7771), at 101 Main St, is a bizarre combination of antique shop, restaurant and community theater. Upstairs in the restaurant is a hall of fame of sorts, featuring exhibits on lots of country-and-western stars; downstairs, the restaurant has an all-you-can-eat buffet for $5.50 at lunchtime and main courses at dinner for $6 to $13.

Getting There & Away The bus between Austin (see Fredericksburg earlier in this chapter) and Fredericksburg stops in Johnson City; from Austin it's $9 one way, $17.10 roundtrip. By car, it's between Austin and Fredericksburg along US 290.

KERRVILLE
Population 18,250

Kerrville's not the most jumping of towns, but it's central, very friendly and home to the best museum of cowboy life in the world. Kerrville's a pleasant place to use as a base, with lots of accommodations options and good Mexican food, and it's got its visitor information infrastructure down pat – the excellent tourist office has everything you'll need to get out and about in the Hill Country.

Just south of I-10, Sidney Baker St runs straight south into Main St and over the Guadalupe River.

Information
Tourist Offices Kerrville Convention and Visitors Bureau's Visitor Information Center (☎ 830-792-3535, 800-221-7958, kerrcvb@ktc.com, www.ktc.net/kerrcvb), 1700 Sidney Baker St, Suite 200, is open Monday to Friday 8:30 am to 5 pm, Saturday and Sunday 10 am to 3 pm. It's got heaps of brochures and very helpful staff.

Money Change money (and get free coffee) at the NationsBank Kerrville (☎ 830-896-3111), 741 Water St.

Bookstores & Libraries The Main Bookshop (☎ 830-257-5777), at 709 Water St, has a huge Texas history and travel section and a good Texas fiction section – not to mention Alex, the shop's loud bird and mascot. Next door, Pampell's Antique Books & Records (☎ 830-257-8484), 701 Water St, has heaps of Western novels plus postcards and records. Hastings Books, Music & Video (☎ 830-896-8233) has a branch at 501 Main St.

The Butt-Holdsworth Memorial Library (☎ 830-257-8422) is in the round building at 505 Water St.

Medical Services Kerrville State Hospital (☎ 830-896-2211) is at 721 Thompson Drive.

Cowboy Artists of America Museum

The Cowboy Artists of America Museum (☎ 830-896-2553), 1550 Bandera Hwy, is a nonprofit showcase of the works of – you guessed it – the Cowboy Artists of America (CAA). In 1965 in Sedona, Arizona, a group of cowboys by day and illustrators of, among other things, Western novels by night, got together to form the Cowboy Artists of America. The quality and detail of the works, paintings and bronzes mostly, is astounding; all depict scenes of cowboy life, the Western landscape or vignettes of Native American life. The works themselves are very moving and incredibly detailed, and the museum has permanent displays of two of the artists' studios, the equipment of cowboy life (where kids can climb on saddles, feel a lasso and play with spurs) and a research library available to anyone interested in the frontier way of life. Staff is very knowledgeable about both the art and about cowboy life in general. The building itself is pretty fabulous, with handmade mesquite parquet and unique *bóveda* (vaulted) domes overhead.

The museum is open Monday to Saturday 9 am to 5 pm, Sunday 1 to 5 pm; admission is $3 for adults, $2.50 for seniors and $1 for kids. From downtown, take Hwy 16 south to Hwy 173 (Bandera Hwy), turn left and it's a half-mile ahead on the right.

Hill Country Museum

The former residence of Charles Schreiner – see YO Ranch in Mountain View later in this chapter – has been restored and opened as a

NICK SELBY

An Honest Day's Work, by Fred Fellows
Cowboy Artists of America Museum

museum of Hill Country history (☎ 830-896-8633), 622 Earl Garrett St. The space features period costumes and furniture. It's as interesting for the architecture as the exhibits, which are a little ho-hum. It's open Monday to Saturday 10:30 am to 4:30 pm (excluding a short staff lunch break every day but Thursday), closed Sunday; admission is $3 for adults, $1.50 for students.

Kerrville-Schreiner State Park

This lovely state park (☎ 830-257-5392, 512-389-8900 for reservations) is a cycling area (rent bikes in town at Bicycle Works, ☎ 830-896-6864, 1412 Broadway) and lots of fun for walking, swimming, canoeing, tubing and camping. The concession stand rents tubes for $4 per day for lazy floats along the Guadalupe River; four-person canoes are $7 per hour or $18 for four hours. Every year on the Thursday before Easter, the Hill Country Bicycle Tour starts here. See Places to Stay for information on camping and especially for the four-person cabin – whadda deal.

The park is open daily 8 am to 5 pm. Admission is $3 for adults. From the Cowboy Artists of America Museum, continue south on Hwy 173, and the entrance is on the right-hand side of the road.

Other Parks

At the south end of downtown, the Riverside Nature Center (☎ 830-257-4837), 150 Francisco Lemos St near the river, has walking trails, a wildflower meadow and river access. It's free and open daily dawn to dusk.

Swim on weekends from 7:30 am to 11 pm at Louise Hays City Park (☎ 830-257-7300), Thompson Drive west of Sidney Baker St S. Park admission is free.

Canoeing

The Rio Raft Co (☎ 830-964-3613) runs two-hour canoe trips along Guadalupe River from Kerrville-Schreiner State Park to Center Point. The trips cost $28 at lunchtime and $35 at dinner, both including food.

Horseback Riding

There's horseback riding by the hour at the Lazy Hills Guest Ranch, Mo-Ranch and the

YO Ranch; see Ingram, Hunt and Mountain View in Around Kerrville for more information.

Special Events

The Kerrville Folk Festival (☎ 830-257-3600) is an 18-day music festival at the Quiet Valley Ranch, 9 miles south of town on Hwy 16. It begins the Thursday before Memorial Day, and there is music from national and local acts, great food and lots of fun. You can camp at the Ranch during the festival. Advance-purchase one-day tickets cost from $10 to $22; at the gate, day tickets run from $12 to $22. You can also purchase in advance consecutive-day tickets good for three ($45), five ($65), eight ($95), 11 ($115) and 18 ($195) days. Camping at Quiet Valley during the festival is free if you have tickets for three or more consecutive days; otherwise it's $5 per person and $7 per vehicle.

The Kerrville Wine and Music Festival is a three-day version of the folk festival held on Labor Day weekend.

The Easter Hill Country Bike Tour and Chili Cook-Off (☎ 830-792-3535) are held around Easter Weekend. They're both huge. Weekend rodeos are held at various venues throughout the summer.

Places to Stay

Camping Campsites at the *Kerrville-Schreiner State Park* (see previous section) are $9 per site with water only, plus admission fees, or $15 plus admission with full hookups. Screened-in shelters are $16 per person; each holds up to eight people. The seventh night is free from December to February. See later in the Places to Stay section for information on the cabin.

The *Kerrville KOA* (☎ 830-895-1665, 800-562-1665), 2950 Goat Creek Rd west of town, has tent sites for $15, RV sites for $19 with full hookups and one-room Kamping Kabins for $26, plus a pool, playground and coin laundry. From town, head west on Hwy 27, north on Hwy 1338, and it's on the right.

The *Guadalupe River RV Resort* (☎ 830-367-5676), 2605 Junction Hwy, is a full-fledged RV resort, popular with an older crowd; pull-through sites are $21.

Motels & Hotels The *Budget Inn Motel* (☎ 830-896-8200, 800-219-8158), 1804 Sidney Baker St, has clean and simple singles/doubles for $30/35 in the winter, $43/47 in the summer. The motel restaurant has cheap breakfasts.

The spanking new *Motel 6* (☎ 830-257-1500), 1810 Sidney Baker St, has rooms for $36/40 in winter and $44/49 in summer, but it's cheaper if you stay longer.

The *Days Inn* (☎ 830-896-1000), 2000 Sidney Baker St, is very friendly, gives you a free continental breakfast and has discounts for everyone on standard prices of $49/59 for full-size beds, $59/69 for king-size.

Four Jacks and a Jill have moved from the Kansas City Ramada Inn to the lounge at the *Best Western Sunday House Inn* (☎ 830-896-1313), 2124 Sidney Baker St; absolutely white-bread singles/doubles are $55/60 in winter, $65/70 in summer; ask for the corporate rate – rooms are often up to $10 cheaper.

The *Sands Motel* (☎ 830-896-5000), 1145 Junction Hwy west of town is a clean and perfectly pleasant place though a bit worn at the seams; rooms are $39/49 year-round, with kitchenettes (minimum four-day stay) are $45.

The staff-built *cabin* at Kerrville-Schreiner State Park (see earlier) is a steal – a spotless place in the middle of the wilderness with four bunk beds, a full kitchen, satellite television, a VCR and your own campfire and barbecue pit for $75 a night. Reserve early – it goes fast.

The *Inn of the Hills Resort* (☎ 830-895-5000, 800-292-5690, fax 830-895-6091), 1001 Junction Hwy, has an Olympic-size pool, sauna, river access and tons of amenities, with rooms from $59 in winter and $89 in summer; cabanas are $65/89. Everything's big, clean, and the place is a good value.

The biggest – in the Texas sense of the word – place in town is the *Holiday Inn YO Ranch Resort* (☎ 830-257-4440, 800-531-2800 in Texas only) at 2033 Sidney Baker St. It is enormous and has branding-iron chandeliers in the lobby; tennis, basketball and volleyball courts; a walking track and a kids' playground. Singles/doubles are $89/99 in winter, $109/119 in summer, with one- and two-bedroom suites for $168/257.

Places to Eat

Right downtown, **Taco To Go** (☎ 830-896-8226), at 428 Sidney Baker St, looks like a dump, but has terrific breakfasts for $3.50 and soft tacos at lunch and dinner from $1 to $1.35; 1lb fajitas are $10.

Pampell's Old Soda Fountain (☎ 830-257-8454), 701 Water St, is a soda fountain and antique shop right downtown. Awesome shakes (three scoops of ice cream and milk mixed in an old Hamilton Beach blender) or real malted milks are $3. It's open Monday to Saturday 9 am to 5:30 pm, closed Sunday.

Choo Choo's Bar-B-Q (☎ 830-896-4414), in the old train depot at 615 Schreiner St, has good pecan-smoked meat. Better, west of town, head for **Bill's Bar-B-Que** (☎ 830-895-5733), 1909 Junction Hwy, which serves lunch plates with one meat for $5 and two for $6.25 (including potato salad, beans, pickles, onions and bread). It also serves succulent beef ($8.50 per lb), sausage ($6.50) and chicken breast ($2.75). Bill's is closed Sunday and Monday.

Terrific all-you-can-eat Chinese food is $5 and more than 35 entrées await you south of the Guadalupe River at **China Town** (☎ 830-896-6688), 735 Hill Country Drive.

Cypress Grill (☎ 830-896-5577), at 433 Water St near the library, looks like a very romantic place to bring a date; it offers game, beef and some vegetarian options in the $13 to $18 range.

The **Sam Houston Dining Room** at the Holiday Inn YO Ranch Resort (see Places to Stay earlier) does great burgers from $5.50 to $6.25, steaks from $13 to $17 and all-you-can eat barbecue for $10.

The **River View Restaurant** (☎ 830-895-6016), behind the Inn of the Hills River Resort (see Places to Stay earlier) is the flashiest place in town, with excellent seafood, such as Guadalupe paupiette (baked red fish with a vegetable julienne) at $14. It's open for dinner only. Also in the Inn of the Hills is the fun **Annemarie's Alpine Lodge Restaurant**, a buffet place with theme nights, such as 'pasta Wednesdays' ($8 per person)

and 'prime rib Sundays' ($13). At lunch daily it's all you can eat for $8, including dessert.

Getting There & Away

The Kerrville Bus Co (☎ 830-257-7454) has its office and station at 701 Sidney Baker St. There's daily bus service to Austin at 8:30 am (2½ hours, $18) and service to San Antonio (five to six per day, 1½ hours, $12), San Angelo (8:30 am, 4½ hours, $26) and Fredericksburg (8:30 am, 30 minutes, $5).

If you're coming by car from Austin, take US 290 going west to Fredericksburg, turning south onto Hwy 16, which hits Kerrville south of I-10. From San Antonio, take I-10 north to Hwy 16 and head south.

AROUND KERRVILLE
Ingram
Population 1408

There's not a whole lot here, but what there is can be readily explained by the West Kerr County Chamber of Commerce (☎ 830-367-4322), 3 Retama Center on the north side of Hwy 27, just west of the town line, open Monday to Friday 9 am to noon and 1 to 3 pm. There are a few craft shops along the **Old Ingram Loop**, an area that may be worth visiting just to grab a frosty Schlitz beer at the delightfully dilapidated **Miss Kitty's Social Club** (☎ 830-367-5783), at 208 Old Ingram Loop.

Hill Country Arts Foundation This theater and fine-arts complex (☎ 830-367-5121), Hwy 39 at Johnson Creek, is the main reason people come to Ingram, and it's packed in summer. The Point Theatre, a riverside outdoor complex, and the indoor pavilion are both respected community-theater stages (Tommy Tune himself worked here), and classics and musicals are performed on them in summer.

Its 1700-square-foot exhibition space is host to three national shows annually; the smaller Duncan-McAshan Gallery holds about 10 shows a year. The foundation also runs children's classes and, in summer, classes in sculpture, photography and other crafts, taught by professionals in the field. The complex, 2 miles west of downtown, is open

Monday to Friday 9 am to 5 pm, the theater during performances; call for information.

Ingram Dam There's free swimming at this nice little park, a couple of miles west of downtown Ingram.

Lazy Hills This friendly guest ranch (☎ 830-367-5600, 800-880-0632) has a pretty magnificent spread about 10 miles west of Kerrville. Ride (Western only) on dozens of trails on one-hour guided tours that cost $25 per person (kids must be at least six years old). Or, stay over for the full-blown dude-ranch experience. The cost for single/double accommodations in summer is $103/156, including the room and three meals daily (three-night minimum); from October to February there's no minimum stay, and the rooms cost $75/134.

Murals There are murals of the Texas pioneer days painted on the side of the TJ Moore Lumber Co at the junction of Hwys 27 and 39 just west of the downtown Ingram traffic light.

Places to Stay & Eat Other than the Lazy Hills Guest Ranch, the **Hunter House Motor Inn** (☎ 830-367-2377, 800-655-2377), at 310 Hwy 39, has clean and nice singles/doubles for $45/49. Attached to it is the **River Road Cafe** (☎ 830-367-3383), which has breakfast for $3.25 to $5.25, lunch plates from $4 to $6, and nice-looking steaks for $9. Just down the road is the amazing **Maggie and Hector's Fast Taco Stand** (☎ 830-367-2298), with awesome breakfast tacos for $1 and enormous burritos and fajitas for $1.40; it's open Wednesday to Sunday 6:30 am to 1:30 pm.

Getting There & Away Ingram is about 5 miles west of Kerrville on Hwy 27; Hwy 27 cuts north just west of the center of town, and Hwy 39 continues west to Hunt.

Hunt
It's definitely worth a drive 2 miles north of the hamlet of Hunt, 6 miles west of Ingram, to view Stonehenge II, a 60%-scale model of the ancient megalithic structure found near

Salisbury, England. Two locals built the thing – and threw in some Easter Island statues for good measure – and it's now open to the public for free. The reason for the construction of the replica is as enigmatic as the construction of the original, but hell, there's free parking, so why not? At the entrance to the tiny town of Hunt, turn north on FM 1340 and follow it for 2 miles; the monument's on the left. Watch out for fire ants if you lie down in the grass.

Mo-Ranch There's horseback riding ($15 per 30 minutes, $25 per hour) at the North Fork Riding Stables at Mo-Ranch (☎ 830-238-4455), which is about 10 miles west of Stonehenge II; keep going west on FM 1340 and you'll hit it. There are rides at 9:30 and 11 am and at 2, 3:30 and 5 pm; it's closed on Sundays.

Mountain Home
For all intents and purposes, the town of Mountain Home *is* the **YO Ranch** (☎ 830-640-3222, 800-967-2624), founded by Texas Ranger captain Charles Armand Schreiner in 1880. Today, it's a 40,000-acre cattle ranch and home to imported exotic animals, including zebra, giraffe, oryx and eland. The ranch is open to the public for horseback riding and overnight stays. On a more controversial note, the ranch is also open year-round for hunting. According to the staff, the people who come to hunt do so mainly in November and December (which are traditional hunting-season months), and hunting areas don't overlap with areas used for other ranch activities. The ranch allows the hunting of animals (both imported and domestic) that shed their antlers annually. You can stay at the ranch for $95 per night (for those younger than 12 years old, it's $50), including all meals, or $120 with an hour of horseback riding; or, just come for a ride along the trail for $24.50 for the first hour, $18.50 each additional hour. There's an Old-Western bar here, too, and a wonderful fireplace in the lodge.

Getting There & Away From Kerrville, follow Hwy 27, and bear right in Ingram, staying on Hwy 27 all the way for about half an hour. Turn into the ranch road and follow it to the padlocked gate; the padlock combination is 1880 – *always* close the gate behind you – and from there it's 7 miles to the chuck wagon.

Lost Maples State Park
The foliage spectacle in November at the Lost Maples State Park (☎ 830-966-3413), near Vanderpool, gives the one in New England a run for its money. Big-tooth maple trees here turn shocking golds, reds, yellows and oranges in autumn. There's tent camping, primitive camping and an interpretive center. From Kerrville, take Hwy 39 west to Hwy 187 south and follow the signs.

BANDERA
Population 1175
Bandera has the look and feel of an old Western movie set, and that's just the effect the locals want – they claim the town as the cowboy capital of Texas. There are lots of dude ranches around town, and you can drink beer in a working forge, but the best reason to come here is to get outfitted for a day of kayaking or tubing down the Medina River. Nearby, Lake Medina and the Hill Country State Natural Area are very pleasant diversions.

Orientation & Information
Main St runs roughly north-south through the center of town. At the south end of downtown, Cypress St goes roughly east-west; heading east it's the continuation of Hwy 16. East of Main St about 500 yards in the little minimall on the right is the Bandera County Convention and Visitor's Bureau (☎ 830-796-3045, 800-364-3833), at 1808 S Hwy 16.

Things to See & Do
There are several historic buildings, including the St Stanislaus Catholic Church and adjacent Convent Cemetery and the First Bandera Jail. The Frontier Times Museum (☎ 830-796-3864) has exhibits on the history of Bandera County; on display are guns, branding irons and cowboy gear, and there are rotating exhibitions as well. It's open

Monday to Saturday 10 am to 4:30 pm and Sunday 1 to 4:30 pm; admission is $2.

Medina River Company at Fred Collins' Workshop (☎ 830-796-3553), a mile north of downtown on Hwy 16 on the left-hand side of the road, rents tubes for **tubing** ($5 per day) and sit-on-top **kayaks** ($25 all day for up to two people). The shuttle service ($2 with tube; $8 minimum with kayak) will drive you down to Medina with your vessel of choice, and you can tube or kayak back to town along the river – it's usually pretty tame, but when it runs, it runs fast; count on six hours to kayak the 18 miles between Medina and the Bandera landing.

Nearby, the Bandera Beach Club, at the corner of Main and Cottonwood Sts, rents tubes for the same price. You can also rent canoes and tubes at the town's two camping options – see Places to Stay.

The CVB has a list of about ten places in and around town were you can go **horseback riding** for about $20 per hour. There is also riding at all the area's dude ranches – see Places to Stay.

Organized Tours
Laura Jean Parker runs the Bandera Carriage Service (☎ 830-634-7886), which gives city tours in her horse-drawn carriage for up to four people for $20 per person for a short ride, $40 for a long ride.

Places to Stay
Camping The *Bandera Beverage Barn, RV and Recreational Park* (☎ 830-796-8153), 1503 Main St, is bizarre – a drive-in liquor store and RV campsite with sites for $10. It also has a nice park right on the river, barbecue pits and coin laundry.

Yogi Bear's Jellystone Park (☎ 830-796-3751), just south of the river at Hwy 173 and Maple St, has good sites for $17 per day without hookups, $19 with hookups.

There's also camping nearby in the Hill Country State Natural Area – see Around Bandera later.

Motels & Hotels On the river at the south end of town, the very friendly *River Front Motel* (☎ 830-460-3690) is the best bet, a

U-shaped ring of bungalows with singles/ doubles $44/49 from Sunday to Thursday and $54/59 Friday and Saturday.

The *River Oak Inn* (☎ *830-796-7751*), at 1105 Hwy 16, has friendly management and clean, nice rooms for $39 to $69 on weekdays and $59 to $99 on weekends, all with microwave and fridge.

Dude Ranches There are more than a dozen dude ranches in the area, all with hundreds of acres, enormous ranch houses, resort features and heaps of riding opportunities. All cost about the same – about $80 a night per person in low season and $85 per person in high season (June to September), sometimes including meals and horseback riding.

Most of them also offer horseback riding to nonguests, usually around $20 per hour, $80 for a half day with lunch and $180 for overnight rides including meals.

The big players are the *Dixie Dude Ranch* (☎ *830-796-4481*), about 8 miles west of town on FM 1077, and the *Yellow Rose Ranch* (☎ *830-562-3456*), 22 miles northwest in Tarpley. Near the Hill Country State Natural Area (see Around Bandera) are the *Silver Spur* (☎ *830-796-3037*) and *Running-R Ranch* (☎ *830-796-3984*). *LH7 Ranch* (☎ *830-796-4314*) is about 3½ miles northwest of town. The Bandera Convention and Visitor's Bureau makes reservations and has brochures on all of the above.

B&Bs The very nice people at the *Hackberry Lodge* (☎ *830-460-7134*), 1005 Hackberry St, have several rooms, all with kitchenettes, from $58 to $110 in winter and $75 to $145 in summer. Janice tries to bake on weekends, and there's always a big continental breakfast.

Places to Eat

You can get stellar pie from *Granny's Pie*, 403 Main St, for $2.25 to $3.50 per slice. A wonderful place to sit, more like New England than Bandera, is the *Full Moon Cafe* (☎ *830-460-8434*), 204 Main St, with real cappuccino and caffè latte from $2.25 to $3.25 and huge Sunday breakfasts for $5.50.

The *Indian Wolf Cafe* (☎ *830-796-7611*), 706 Main St, is run by a wonderful New Jersey transplant and has terrific buffalo nuggets ($2.50), breakfast biscuits for $1.39 and the best burgers in the county for $3.50.

The supernaturally friendly *Billy Gene's Restaurant* (☎ *830-460-3200*), behind the River Oak Inn, serves up good chicken-fried chicken with mashed potatoes and two veggies for $6. At dinnertime, skip the bland offerings at the OST (the Old Spanish Trail restaurant) and Harvey's Old Bank Steakhouse in favor of the more proletarian, but far superior, offerings of *Busbee's BBQ and Catering* (☎ *830-796-3153*), 319 Main St, with one-meat plates for $6, sandwiches for $4, scrumptious brisket for $7.40 per pound, great smoked chicken and decent burgers. It's open Sunday to Thursday 10:30 am to 8 pm (until 9 pm on Friday and Saturday).

It's hard to believe, but the Chinese food at the *Dragon Garden* (☎ *830-796-7972*), next to the CVB, is darn good; lunch specials go for $4, such as pork with garlic sauce or vegetarian delite, and dinner entrées are $6.25 to $7.25 – good vegetarian selection, too.

Entertainment

There are *rodeos* once or twice a week from June to mid-August at Mansfield Park, on Hwy 16 heading toward Medina, and a Saturday-night rodeo in summer at Twin Elm Guest Ranch. The *11th St Cowboy Bar*, 301 N 11th St just north of Cypress St, is a tiny little hole in the wall (two tables) with a fun crowd and occasional guitar playing.

Arkey Blue's *Silver Dollar Bar* (☎ *830-796-8826*), 308 Main St, and the *Cabaret* (☎ *830-796-8166*), 801 Main St, are both dance halls where you can root, toot and cotton-eyed-Joe with the best of them. Right next door to the Cabaret, the *Bandera Forge* (☎ *830-796-7184*), 807 Main St, is a working iron forge that also sells $2 beers and has live music.

Getting There & Away

From Kerrville, the most direct route is Hwy 173, the Bandera Hwy. The far more pleasant and scenic way – through hill and dale and past Medina – is to take Hwy 16 south.

AROUND BANDERA
Hill Country State Natural Area

The Hill Country State Natural Area (☎ 830-796-4413), which is 10½ miles southwest of town (RR 1077 runs right into the main entrance), is a protected wilderness area lined with 32 miles of trails that are open for hiking, bicycling and horseback riding from Thursday to Monday and camping from Thursday to Sunday.

There are no services – not even water – in the park, so you'll have to bring in your own. For riding information, contact the Silver Spur or Running-R Ranch (see Dude Ranches).

There are eight primitive campsites; park maps can be obtained at the Bandera County CVB. Bury human waste in cat holes and pack out anything you've brought in – this is the most litter-free park in Texas. Camping is free to hikers, bicyclists and equestrians; cars and RVs pay $4.

Pipe Creek

In the little town of Pipe Creek, which is 10 miles southeast of Bandera, **Brighter Days Horse Refuge** (☎ 830-510-6607) is a center dedicated to nursing abused and injured horses back to health. It's now home to more than 50 horses and ponies. You can visit Tuesday, Thursday and Saturday from 10 am to 3 pm; admission is a bag of either carrots or apples, and donations are appreciated. From Hwy 16, the entrance is 1.8 miles south of the intersection of Hwy 46.

Medina Lake

Water activities abound on Medina Lake, which sits 22 miles south of Bandera. The result of a privately funded dam (1910), the lake includes a natural rock spillway. Unfortunately, noisy jet skiing and waterskiing are among the lake's offerings, but there are quieter areas and several good places to swim. The towns of Mico and Lakehills are the main sources of services. From the lake's north banks you can catch the Medina River back up to Bandera if you're boating. Several campgrounds around the lake have campsites for around $12.

Medina calls itself the apple capital of Texas, and **Love Creek Orchards Cider Mill** and Country Store (☎ 830-589-2588) sells apple everything (pies, cakes, cookies, ice cream, cider – everything).

Getting There & Away From Bandera, take Hwy 16 south to Pipe Creek, then Hwy 1283 south; staying on it through Mico brings you past a scenic overlook and eventually to the dam itself; turning left on Hwy 37 brings you to Lakehills parking and the state boat launch.

San Antonio

Population 1.1 million

San Antonio has the be-all and end-all of butch monuments to American courage, the Alamo. It was here in San Antonio that John Wayne – sorry, Davy Crockett, Jim Bowie and about 190 Texas revolutionaries stood firm and held out against all odds and thousands of Mexican troops. The story of the Battle of the Alamo is one of the USA's most enduring legends.

One of Texas' most walkable downtowns graces San Antonio, and the city's Texian roots and Spanish origins are still readily apparent. The Riverwalk, touristy as it may be, is still a pleasant strolling ground, and no matter how hard-boiled you are, you'll probably still enjoy a river cruise along it. See the boxed text for more on Riverwalk.

San Antonio is the only city in the USA that still has five original Spanish colonial missions within city limits; the missions' churches still function, and their aqueducts still carry water to local farmers. The downtown is laid out in the sort of discombobulated grid system one associates with cow paths laid out during a more colonial era.

San Antonio is a major melting pot of American and Mexican residents and cultures, and there's an awful lot of Spanish spoken here.

Locals joke about San Antonio's laid-back feel – everyone's on San Antonio Standard Time here, and 'mañana syndrome' is considered rife. But don't be fooled by the 'jes' folks' breeziness. San Antonio, or SA, as

Films in San Antonio

San Antonio is shown off splendidly in 1972's *The Getaway*, an exciting thief-on-the-run movie starring Steve McQueen and Ali McGraw – who fell in love during the shooting. San Antonio is less busy than Austin for films, though it always looks good – even in the 1983 film *Cloak and Dagger*, which featured Henry Thomas blasting evil bad guys along the Riverwalk and purse-snatching in the Alamo. More recently, the city was featured in the classic *Ace Ventura: When Nature Calls*.

locals call it, is the nation's 10th largest city. And San Antonio's quaintness neatly distracts attention from the fact that it's a major export zone, a biotechnology and technology sector, and a town with a whole lot of firepower – five military bases call the region their home. Bean counters from the country's theme parks were among the first to cash in on the powerhouse economy, and Sea World and Six Flags Fiesta Park are both big draws.

San Antonio is also a big college town (11 colleges and universities reside here), and you can stay and eat relatively cheaply for such a large city. And the food – Tex-Mex at its finest – may be worth the trip on its own, including possibly the best chicken-fried steak in the state.

HISTORY

San Antonio was established as a Spanish military garrison in 1718, but Europeans had been sniffing around the area and probing the local Coahuiltecan tribes since 1691. The original settlement, along San Pedro Creek, was eventually moved to what's now downtown San Antonio in 1724 as the Misión San Antonio de Valero, later to be renamed the Alamo. Spanish troops established a presidio, or fort, at the mission.

In 1731, the settlement of Villa de Bexar was established by Spanish colonists imported from the Canary Islands (a Spanish-controlled island group about 100 nautical miles west of the southwest Moroccan coast), and a civil government was established in the area. By the time the missions were secularized in 1791, the area was attracting Mexican and American settlers as well.

During the seven months of the Texas War for Independence (1835-36), the Battle of the Alamo was fought here (see the Alamo later). After Texas won independence, San Antonio, at the southern end of the Chisholm Trail, boomed as a cattle town. European settlers, including vast numbers of Germans and Czechs, moved to the area, and the Germans built the city's King William area, named for Kaiser Wilhelm I of Prussia. In 1879, Fort Sam Houston was established by the US Army.

San Antonio's 20th-century growth was largely due to military presence; Fort Sam Houston was joined by Kelly Air Force Base, the nation's oldest air force base, in 1917, followed by Lackland, Randolph and Brooks Air Force bases. Today, the city is the state's biggest tourism draw; major industries include beer, petroleum and livestock, and there is an emerging biotechnology and high-tech community.

ORIENTATION

Downtown San Antonio is surrounded by two concentric rings of highways. The ring closest to downtown is formed by I-35 in the west and north, Hwys 87 and 90 and I-10 in the south and west (they run along I-35 for awhile), and I-37 and US 281 in the east. All these roads feed out to I-410, locally called Loop 410, which circles the city.

Downtown San Antonio is a mishmash of grid systems at odd angles to each other that's initially confusing. The San Antonio River runs from south to north through the center of downtown. The Riverwalk is a developed canal loop off the San Antonio River right in the heart of downtown, extending east from the river, like the curvy part of a lowercase 'b.'

The intersection of Commerce St and Losoya Ave is the very heart of both downtown and the Riverwalk. The Alamo is

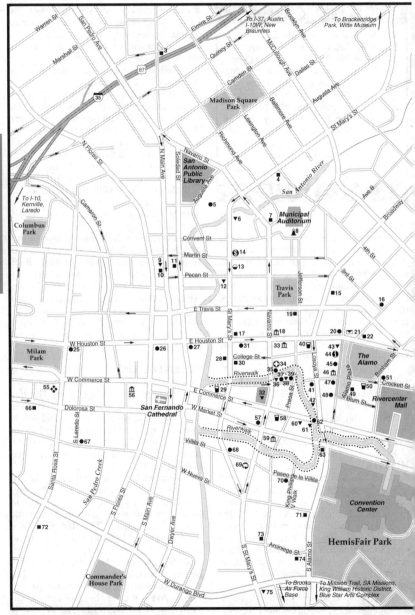

SOUTH CENTRAL TEXAS

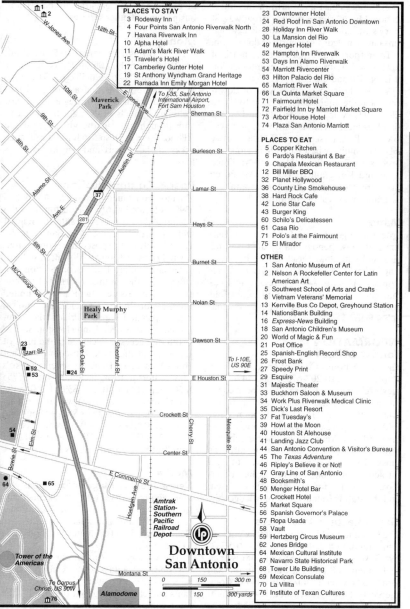

SOUTH CENTRAL TEXAS

PLACES TO STAY
3 Rodeway Inn
4 Four Points San Antonio Riverwalk North
7 Havana Riverwalk Inn
10 Alpha Hotel
11 Adam's Mark River Walk
15 Traveler's Hotel
17 Camberley Gunter Hotel
19 St Anthony Wyndham Grand Heritage
22 Ramada Inn Emily Morgan Hotel
23 Downtowner Hotel
24 Red Roof Inn San Antonio Downtown
28 Holiday Inn River Walk
30 La Mansion del Rio
49 Menger Hotel
52 Hampton Inn Riverwalk
53 Days Inn Alamo Riverwalk
54 Marriott Rivercenter
63 Hilton Palacio del Rio
65 Marriott River Walk
66 La Quinta Market Square
71 Fairmount Hotel
72 Fairfield Inn by Marriott Market Square
73 Arbor House Hotel
74 Plaza San Antonio Marriott

PLACES TO EAT
5 Copper Kitchen
6 Pardo's Restaurant & Bar
9 Chapala Mexican Restaurant
12 Bill Miller BBQ
32 Planet Hollywood
36 County Line Smokehouse
38 Hard Rock Cafe
42 Lone Star Cafe
43 Burger King
60 Schilo's Delicatessen
61 Casa Rio
71 Polo's at the Fairmount
75 El Mirador

OTHER
1 San Antonio Museum of Art
2 Nelson A Rockefeller Center for Latin American Art
5 Southwest School of Arts and Crafts
8 Vietnam Veterans' Memorial
13 Kerrville Bus Co Depot, Greyhound Station
14 NationsBank Building
16 *Express-News* Building
18 San Antonio Children's Museum
20 World of Magic & Fun
21 Post Office
25 Spanish-English Record Shop
26 Frost Bank
27 Speedy Print
29 Esquire
31 Majestic Theater
33 Buckhorn Saloon & Museum
34 Work Plus Riverwalk Medical Clinic
35 Dick's Last Resort
37 Fat Tuesday's
39 Howl at the Moon
40 Houston St Alehouse
41 Landing Jazz Club
44 San Antonio Convention & Visitor's Bureau
45 The *Texas Adventure*
46 Ripley's Believe it or Not!
47 Gray Line of San Antonio
48 Booksmith's
50 Menger Hotel Bar
51 Crockett Hotel
55 Market Square
56 Spanish Governor's Palace
57 Ropa Usada
58 Vault
59 Hertzberg Circus Museum
62 Jones Bridge
64 Mexican Cultural Institute
67 Navarro State Historical Park
68 Tower Life Building
69 Mexican Consulate
74 La Villita
76 Institute of Texan Cultures

Downtown San Antonio

0   150   300 m
0   150   300 yards

several blocks east and north of this intersection. Major arteries include Broadway, St Mary's St, and Fredericksburg Rd, which runs into San Pedro Ave north of downtown.

The airport is a 15-minute drive north of downtown SA, just north of the intersection of Loop 410 and US 281.

Sea World is 25 minutes west of downtown near the intersection of Loop 1604 and US 151 (Hwy 151 is accessible via US 90). Six Flags Fiesta Texas is northwest of downtown at the intersection of I-10 and Hwy 1604. The military bases, Fort Sam Houston, Brooks Air Force Base, Randolph Air Force Base and Kelly and Lackland Air Force bases are, respectively, northeast, southeast, east and southwest of downtown.

Maps

Procuring a good map of the city is a challenge, as those handed out by the CVB are distorted and almost useless. The best free map is the AAA's *San Antonio Texas*. *Streetwise San Antonio* ($4.95) is relatively accurate and very easy to carry in its fivefold laminated pocket-size edition; it's available at bookstores.

INFORMATION
Tourist Offices

The San Antonio Convention and Visitors Bureau (☎ 210-207-6700, 800-447-3372, sacvb@ci.sat.tx.us, www.sanantoniocvb.com), has a well-stocked visitors' center at 317 Alamo Plaza at Houston St, open daily 8:30 am to 6 pm except Thanksgiving, Christmas and New Year's Day. It also stocks the brochure stands at the San Antonio airport's kiosks. The office doesn't sell tickets to local attractions or book hotel rooms, but it does have brochures for everything in the area, and the staff is friendly and knowledgeable.

Gay & Lesbian Resources

The Gay and Lesbian Community Center of San Antonio (☎ 210-732-4300, fax 210-733-6949), 3126 N St Mary's St, suite 400, is open daily noon to 8 pm. They also run the San Antonio Gay and Lesbian Chamber of Commerce (GLCCSA@stic.net, www.stic.net/users/glccsa/chamber), which provides lists

of gay-owned and gay-friendly bars, clubs, businesses and other services.

Money

Change foreign currency at Frost Bank (☎ 210-220-5651), 100 W Houston St, or NationsBank (☎ 210-270-5555), 300 Convent St. There are ATMs that accept most network and credit cards throughout the city, including in malls, both major theme parks and, thoughtfully, in the gift shop at the Alamo. There are also two foreign-exchange desks at the airport and one in Six Flags Fiesta Texas.

Post & Communications

The most convenient post office (☎ 210-227-3399) is located at 615 E Houston St at the Alamo. Address poste restante to General Delivery, 615 E Houston St, San Antonio, TX 78205-9998. The post office is open Monday to Friday 8:30 am to 5:30 pm, closed Saturday and Sunday. The Arsenal Station Post Office is on the northeast corner of Laredo and S Alamo Sts near the Ramada Limited and Comfort Inn Suites hotels. Downtown, make copies at the Speedy Print, at the southeast corner of Soledad and Houston Sts.

Internet access is included in the price of admission at the Witte Museum (see Children's Museums). There are several Kinko's copy centers in town, including one at 5755 NW Loop 410 (☎ 210-521-8395; I-410 to the Leon Valley-Bandera exit), with Internet access for 20¢ per minute or $12 per hour, and one at 3740 NW Loop 410 at Fredericksburg Rd (☎ 210-731-4400), with access for $12 per hour. Both are open 24 hours.

Media

Newspapers & Magazines The *San Antonio Express-News'* (50¢) Weekender and food sections (on Friday and Wednesday, respectively) are good what's-on guides. Jim Beal's 'Night Lights' column is a good guide to live music.

The *San Antonio Current* is a free weekly covering local politics and the club and entertainment scene; it's available in bars, restaurants and clubs throughout the city. It's the most comprehensive what's-on source for live music and arts. Less useful are the glossy pages of *Rio Magazine* and *Fiesta Magazine*, widely available free monthlies.

La Prensa is a Spanish-language weekly, and the *San Antonio Observer* covers SA's African American community. The *San Antonio Marquise* is a free monthly gay and lesbian magazine.

Radio National Public Radio (NPR) is at KSTX 89.1 FM. Other local stations include country at KCYY 100 FM; jazz on KCJZ 106.7 FM; gospel and Christian at KCHG 810 AM; Tejano on KEDA 1540 AM and KRIO 94.1 FM; and classical at KPAC 88.3 FM. There are more standard rock and contemporary offerings throughout the dial.

Travel Agents
Champagne Travel (☎ 210-344-6231) has seven offices in San Antonio – call them for the nearest office. They specialize in cheap travel to Mexico.

Bookstores
Brentano's (☎ 210-223-3938) has a shop in the Rivercenter Mall. Booksmith's (☎ 210-271-9177), 209 Alamo Plaza with another entrance on Losoya St, has a fair selection of books as well.

Otherwise, you're heading out to mall land for Borders Books, Music & Cafe (☎ 210-561-0022), in the Huebner Oaks Center, 11745 W I-10 between Huebner Rd and Woodstone Drive. There is another branch (☎ 210-828-9496) at 255 E Basse Rd in Quarry Market on the corner of Basse Rd and US 281. Black Voices (☎ 210-222-0567), 2242 E Commerce St near New Braunfels Ave, specializes in books on African American culture.

For used books, head north of downtown to the Antiquarian Book Mart (☎ 210-828-4885), 3127 Broadway at Eleanor. Right behind it is the Book Mart Annex (☎ 210-828-4885), which has a stock of out-of-print editions. Another spot for used and out-of-print titles is Cheever Books (☎ 210-824-2665), 140 Carnahan Rd, opposite the Witte Museum.

Other bookstores in SA include Viva Books (☎ 210-826-1143), 8407 Broadway,

selling books on religion and philosophy, and the Twig Bookshop (☎ 210-826-6411), 5005 Broadway.

Gay & Lesbian Gay and lesbian bookstores in town include the Q Bookstore (☎ 210-734-4299), 2803 N St Mary's St; and Textures Books and Gifts (210-805-8398), a women's bookstore at 5309 McCullough.

Libraries
The new central San Antonio Public Library (☎ 210-207-2500), 600 Soledad St, opened to the public in 1995. It's a massive building that is painted a red so distinctive a local contest was held to name the shade. The winning entry stuck, and everyone in town now refers to the library as being 'enchilada red.' It's a first-rate multimedia facility with a very helpful staff, with regularly scheduled programs for children, teens and adults. The library is open Monday to Thursday 9 am to 9 pm, Friday and Saturday 9 am to 5 pm, and Sunday 11 am to 5 pm. Parking at the library garage is free if you get a librarian to validate your ticket. The library is just north of downtown in the grid that is bounded by Soledad St to the west, Navarro St to the north, Augusta Ave to the east and Giraud St to the south.

Campuses
The University of Texas at San Antonio (UTSA; ☎ 210-567-7000) is the city's main public university. About 17,500 students are enrolled in bachelor's, master's or doctoral degree programs here. UTSA's main campus is northwest of the city center. Its planned expansion of its downtown campus, which will be just west of I-35 at Buena Vista, is scheduled to open in 1999; the Cypress Tower campus north of downtown functions today.

Trinity University (☎ 210-736-7011) is a smaller (2500 students), private university offering liberal arts, sciences, engineering, business and communication degrees. The campus is just north of downtown off US 281.

There are two Catholic universities, University of the Incarnate Word (UIW; ☎ 210-829-6000), 4301 Broadway, and St Mary's

University (☎ 210-436-3011), 1 Camino Santa Maria. UIW has about 3500 students, and St Mary's is the oldest university in San Antonio. St Mary's also operates the only law school in the city.

Other universities and colleges in town include San Antonio College (☎ 210-733-2000), Our Lady of the Lake University (☎ 210-434-6711) and St Philip's College (☎ 210-531-3200).

Cultural Centers

The Mexican Cultural Institute (☎ 210-227-0123), 600 HemisFair Park (see Parks & Gardens later), the cultural wing of the Mexican consulate, offers concerts, art exhibits, food days, dance and choral performances and other cultural events throughout the year.

The Institute of Texan Cultures is more of a museum than a cultural center, so see that listing under Museums.

Laundry

San Antonio is not a place to bring dirties, as finding a coin laundry can be an all-day affair. Most larger hotels have laundry facilities for their guests only. In a tiny room at 218½ N Broadway, attached to the Traveler's Hotel (see Places to Stay), is a rather grim, but open to the public, coin laundry.

Medical Services

For a doctor, call the Physician's Referral Service at ☎ 210-734-6691. Work Plus River Walk Medical Clinic (☎ 210-271-1841), at 408 Navarro St, is a walk-in clinic just north of the river.

The most central hospitals are Baptist Medical Center (☎ 210-297-7000), at 111 Dallas St just east of Navarro and Soledad Sts, and Santa Rosa Health Care (☎ 210-704-2011), 519 W Houston St between Santa Rosa and San Saba Sts just east of I-10.

Emergency

The sheriff's department is at ☎ 210-270-6000, and the highway patrol is at ☎ 210-533-9171. The San Antonio Rape Crisis Center (☎ 210-349-7273; call for directions) runs a 24-hour hot line for rape victims.

Dangers & Annoyances

The swarming-with-cops downtown is considered safe. Poorer areas to the south of the city are considered dangerous, though we didn't experience any difficulties.

The San Antonio River is not a toy – there are several drownings a year. Be especially careful in areas near Riverwalk that don't have fences along the river – this is less don't-run-with-scissors advice than an advisory to watch out for drunk college kids who might inadvertently or intentionally push you in.

WALKING TOUR

A one-hour downtown orientation tour runs from the southern part of downtown to the Southwest School of Arts and Crafts at the northern end of Riverwalk; it doesn't cover the King William Historic District (see that section later).

Start near the main entrance to **HemisFair Park**, at the corner of S Alamo and Arciniega Sts, and head north on S Alamo. Behind to your left is the **Plaza San Antonio Hotel**, and HemisFair Park is to the right, with the **Tower of the Americas** looming over the city. Head a block north on S Alamo and turn left onto Nueva St; immediately on the right is **La Villita**, the tourist-thronged art studio collection. Either walk through this to the north along lovely little **King Phillip V Walk**, or save it for later and continue to the intersection of S St Mary's, Navarro and Nueva Sts.

Turn right (north) on Navarro St, and immediately ahead on the left is the **Mexican Consulate**, a building with the still stolid appearance it was given in its former life as one of the USA's Federal Reserve banks – see the Facts for the Visitor chapter for details on the consulate.

Turn left at the corner onto Villita St and you're looking at one of the kings of the SA skyline, the soaring and octagonal art-deco **Tower Life Building** (1929). Inside the lobby (enter from the Villita St side), there's a little museum devoted to the construction and history of the building.

Back heading northward on S St Mary's St, walk up a block and you will come to the **Paseo del Rio**, more commonly referred to as **Riverwalk** (see the boxed text). Walk down the little staircase and, if you stay on the south side of the bank (though note the old **public library** building on the northwest side), you can gain access to the walk itself. Follow the Riverwalk as it meanders beneath the **Villita Assembly Hall** and the **Hertzberg Circus Museum** (in the former Carnegie Library, the city's first totally free library, built in 1903) and cuts north next to the **Hilton Palacio del Rio** (see Brezhnev Fans Unite! later in this chapter).

Riverwalk

In 1921, floods destroyed downtown San Antonio, as water 10 feet deep from the overflowing San Antonio River gushed through the center of the city, obliterating homes and businesses and drowning as many as 50 people. As a result, the Olmos Dam was constructed to handle overflow and route the extra water around the downtown area through a canal called the Oxbow.

The fix was meant to be temporary and was intended later to be submerged and turned into an enormous storm drain beneath the city. Before this was able to happen though, some locals formed the San Antonio Conservation Society and dedicated themselves to preserving and developing the canal into an attraction.

In an example of how some say the stock-market crash of 1929 was actually good for San Antonio, the Works Progress Administration (WPA) in 1938 assumed control of the canal's fate. Workers for the WPA executed a plan to develop a central business district of shops and restaurants along a cobbled walk – a plan introduced almost a decade earlier by an astute local businessman, Robert Hugman. More than 1000 jobs were created during the construction of Riverwalk, and the project is definitely among the top ten most beautiful results of the WPA effort.

Riverwalk (like London's Docklands) didn't take off like a rocket. Most of the occupants of the buildings lining the river used it for the same romantic purpose as their Venetian counterparts – that is, they dumped their trash into it. The first commercial entry right on the water was the Casa Rio Mexican Restaurant; in 1946, a quick-witted man named Beyer began renting boats and canoes right in front of the Casa Rio. Beyer reckoned that after an hour or so of paddling in the summer heat, boaters might want to cool down with a nice drink and maybe a little food – which would be convenient for him as he owned the land on which both the Casa Rio and its next-door neighbor, Schilo's Delicatessen, sat.

The idea worked, but the Riverwalk itself had only limited success. Over the next 15 years, it stagnated and became a dangerous, sleazy section of town. What saved it and turned it into the money-minter it is today was HemisFair. In 1968, an extension of the Riverwalk was constructed, running about a half-mile east parallel to Market St. Lighting and improved staircases (and a whole lot of cops) were added, and the area never looked back.

Today Riverwalk is one of the most successful restaurant rows of its kind – and if it looks familiar, it's because you've seen it in dozens of films.

The restaurants along it try to be chic, trendy and expensive while still catering to the hordes, and generally speaking, the food's merely average. But there is absolutely nothing like sitting along the bank, cool margarita in hand, watching the boats go by as the sun goes down.

San Antonio's Mud Festival, held every January, is when citizens drain the canal, lug out all the garbage, fix up the pumps and refill it with water that stays – until February, anyway – clean and sparkling fresh.

SOUTH CENTRAL TEXAS

Walk a block further north along River-walk and use the staircase on the other side of the **Jones Bridge** to climb up to the corner of E Commerce and Losoya Sts. If you're thirsty, head just southwest to **Schilo's Deli-catessen** (pronounced 'SHEE-lows') for two glasses of some serious homemade root beer (85¢). Cut northeast and you'll find yourself walking north up Alamo Plaza. Continuing north, on the east side, as soon as the street widens, is the **Menger Hotel** and, just east of that, the **Crockett Hotel**. Just north of these two landmarks is *the* landmark itself, the **Alamo**. Continue past the Alamo (get maps and pamphlets as you pass the **visitor information center** on your left), and if you stand on the corner of Houston St and Alamo Plaza and look 45° to your right, you'll get a good view of the **post office** and, a block farther, the art-deco *Express-News* **Building** on the corner of 3rd St and Ave E.

Head west on Houston St, noting for future reference the **Houston St Alehouse** between College and Houston Sts on Losoya St and past the **Children's Museum**. Stand looking west on the corner of Navarro and E Houston Sts and, on the far left-hand side of the street you'll see the splendid **Majestic Theater** (1928-29), a beautifully renovated, atmospheric theater that's currently home to the San Antonio Symphony.

Now decide whether you're up for touristy eating and drinking (if so, turn south on Navarro and head for Crockett, on which you'll rejoin the Riverwalk, near several restaurants), or turn north on Navarro and head past **Travis Park** (a lovely little patch of green), the **Municipal Auditorium** and nearby **Vietnam Veterans' Memorial**, and, on the right as the road bends, the **Havana River-walk Inn**, one of the city's loveliest hotels.

Crossing the river, turn back south onto N St Mary's St; on the west side is the **Southwest School of Arts and Crafts**. While you're up there, grab a good and surprisingly cheap lunch special from **Pardo's**, which is right across the street from the art school.

MISSION TRAIL

See the Facts about Texas chapter for information on the Spanish colonial mission system. Five missions in the San Antonio area were constructed in a flurry of building in the early 18th century. These, combined with others constructed in the late 17th century in east Texas, were an effort to provide way-stations and staging areas for Spanish colonial expansion to the north and maintain tight supply lines as French forces began encroachments from Louisiana. The relatively peaceful locals, the Coahuiltecans, showed a willingness to be colonized (or at least to stick around to learn about new technologies and farming techniques).

The first and most impressive mission in the area was constructed in present-day downtown San Antonio, San Antonio de Valero, later renamed Misión del Alamo del Parras, since shortened to the Alamo.

With the destruction by war or disease of many east Texan missions, the Spanish built four more missions in the San Antonio area, San José, Concepción, San Juan and Espada.

They also built an extensive *acequia* (aqueduct) system throughout the region around this time. The largest section of this was the Espada Dam, which diverted water from the San Antonio River through an elaborate, arched aqueduct that still functions – you can follow the waterway (unfortunately, you can't swim in the aqueduct even though it looks so inviting) from the dam in Espada Park south to the Mission Espada.

Today the Mission Trail, a marked path traversing roads and fields between the Alamo and Mission Espada, is maintained by the National Park Service as part of the San Antonio Missions National Historical Park (www.nps.gov/saan). While the Daughters of the Republic of Texas (see the Alamo) maintain control and police duties at the Alamo, park rangers run the rest of the show.

The main visitors' centers are in San José and Concepción, both of which have interpretive displays and slide shows covering the history of the missions. All except the Alamo (which sets its own hours) are open daily 9 am to 5 pm except major holidays. The National Park Service visitor information guide is chock full of interesting data on architectural highlights of each of the missions as well as mission life in general.

Church services are still held in the mission churches at San José, San Juan and Espada, and the mariachi mass at noon on Sunday is a San Antonio tradition.

Park rangers run fascinating and free interpretive walks and other programs at San José daily. Other missions have irregularly held programs as well – pick up a schedule of the week's programs from the visitors' center at each mission.

There are picnic tables at San José, San Juan, Espada Park and Acequia Park, and general information about the missions (except the Alamo – see the next section) can be obtained at ☎ 210-932-1001.

The Alamo

The Alamo (☎ 210-225-1391) is a former Spanish presidio that is currently a shrine to those who died defending it in the Texas War for Independence. It's managed by the rather persnickety Daughters of the Republic of Texas (DRT), a group of women who can document its lineage directly to the Texas Republican period (1836-45). The DRT insists that all visitors to the shrine behave in a manner due such a monument – keep a respectful tongue in your head, wear a shirt and shoes at all times and don't make any jokes and you should get along just fine.

The surprising things about the Alamo are its size (it's much smaller than many people think) and its beauty. An ornately decorated portal leads to a typical Spanish colonial church that has a distinctly Moorish flavor – Muslims ruled Spain from the 8th to the 15th centuries and had a great influence over Spanish architecture.

The Alamo was originally constructed in 1724 in this location as the Misión San Antonio de Valero, though the Valero mission had had two unsuccessful starts in other locations, along San Pedro Creek in 1718 and on the banks of the San Antonio River. After the destruction by storms of both, construction on the present compound began.

Throughout the 18th century, the mission was operated much along the same lines as the others along San Antonio's Mission Trail, as a relatively self-supporting home for Spanish missionaries and Native American converts who worked the fields and studied Christianity.

The missions were secularized in 1793, but at the turn of the 19th century, Spanish colonial troops reoccupied the mission, expanded on its buildings, added defenses and renamed it Misión del Alamo del Parras, after the troops' hometown (some sources say it was in honor of the cottonwood trees that grow in San Antonio – but in Spanish, *álamo* means poplar).

It's hard to accurately tell the story of the Battle of the Alamo – there is hot debate about almost every fact. It's even difficult to get solid numbers on the defenders, the Mexican troops, their losses and many other aspects. It's a volatile issue because Americans – like anyone, really – are touchy about people challenging the legends of their national heroes. So getting an objective view of the Battle of the Alamo is almost impossible. Consider, for example, how the Alamo defenders are described in text reprinted in dozens of city-produced manuals and histories: '[They fought] against Santa Anna's intolerable decrees. Other [defenders] were Volunteers such as Davy Crockett and his "Tennessee Boys" who owned nothing in Texas and owed nothing to it. Theirs was a fight against tyranny wherever it might be.'

It is, however, generally agreed that on February 23, 1836, Mexican general Antonio López de Santa Anna led anywhere from 2500 to 5000 Mexican troops in an attack against the Alamo. The 160 or so men inside the fortress, as almost every American will tell you, included James Bowie (of knife fame), who was in command of the Alamo until pneumonia rendered him too sick; William B Travis, who took command of the troops after Bowie's incapacity; and perhaps most famous of all, David Crockett, called 'Davy' by everyone. Crockett, a two-time Tennessee state senator with interesting taste in headgear, gained fame as a frontiersman and later for his public arguments with General Andrew Jackson over the latter's murderous campaigns of Indian 'removal' in the southeastern USA. Less well known is that Bowie's and Travis' black slaves fought alongside their masters during the battle and survived.

Davy Crockett

The Alamo's defenders repelled continual Mexican advances.

Travis dispatched a now-famous letter to other revolutionaries pleading for reinforcements, saying that his men would not stand down under any circumstances – his call was for 'Victory or Death.' Because of slow communications, the only reinforcements that arrived in time were a group of about 30 men from Gonzales, Texas, bringing the total number of Alamo defenders up to 189, according to literature from the Daughters of the Republic of Texas, which lists the names of all but one, an unidentified black man.

Santa Anna's troops pounded the Alamo for 13 days before retaking it. Mexican losses were devastating; estimates run as low as 1000 and as high as 2000. When the Alamo was finally recaptured, the advancing troops executed almost all of the surviving defenders. The few who were spared were interrogated and released.

The Battle of the Alamo was pivotal in the war because during the two weeks Santa Anna's army was distracted in San Antonio, Texas troops were gathering strength and advancing, fueled by what they called the wholesale slaughter of their brothers in arms, under the battle cry 'Remember the Alamo!' The Battle of San Jacinto was won, some say, due to the reduction by Alamo defenders of Santa Anna's troops into almost a ragtag state.

Visiting the Alamo Today, the former fort and mission is one of the premier tourist attractions in the entire state and occupies the entire area between Houston St at the north, Bonham St at the east, Crockett St at the south and Alamo Plaza at the west. The main entrance sits on Alamo Plaza.

Admission is free, though donations are encouraged. The DRT has been in charge of the Alamo since 1905, and it runs all areas of the monument, including the gift shop, museum and its (armed) police force, and the organization is the beneficiary of the donations. It produces a number of informative free brochures describing the Alamo and the battle in a number of languages, available from the desk to the right in the center as you enter.

The Alamo is open daily except December 24 and 25. In winter, it's open Monday to Saturday 9 am to 5:30 pm, Sunday 10 am to 5:30 pm; in summer Monday to Saturday 9 am to 6:30 pm, Sunday 10 am to 6:30 pm.

In the main chapel building is the shrine, with an exhibit on the battle and the defenders of the Alamo. Frequent free talks given by docents give the DRT's history of the battle and a highly colorful description of pre-revolutionary life in San Antonio.

As you exit the shrine, to your right is the museum gift shop; to your left is the convent garden and wishing well. Farther on is the Long Barrack Museum. In the convent garden itself is an excellent timeline history that covers the Spanish missionary period to the present day.

The Long Barrack, or Long Hall, served as residence for the Spanish priests and later a hospital for Mexican and Texan troops. The museum has displays on the history of the Republic of Texas.

The museum gift shop is also a museum and contains a fine collection of guns, coonskin caps (the preferred headgear of Davy Crockett), a nice diorama of the battle, a very good book selection and some fun crapola, like Alamo Crackers and bottles of Alamo sand. And there's a cash machine, too.

Finally, the Texas Historical Library of the DRT Library is a research library covering the four centuries of Texas history since European settlement.

Alamo-Related Attractions See Theme Parks and Entertainment later for information on the *Texas Adventure*, a multimedia show on the Texas War for Independence and the *Alamo Adventure*, an IMAX film showing in the IMAX cinema in nearby Rivercenter Mall.

Concepción

The Misión Nuestra Señora de la Concepción de Acuña was established in east Texas in 1716 to try to serve as a buffer against French invasion. That it was moved to San Antonio in 1731 tells you how successful it was in its first incarnation. It contains a spectacular Spanish colonial church (which was completed in 1755), and the southern-Spanish and Moorish influences in the architecture remind one of Seville more than San Antonio. The mission served as the center of the colonists' religious universe, housing the Father President of the local church.

The visitors' center here has a very good bookstore as well as a brochure explaining the wall art.

San José

In 1720, Franciscan missionary Antonio Margil de Jesús founded Misión San José y San Miguel de Aguayo. It's certainly the largest and possibly the most beautiful of all on the trail, and in its time it was known as the Queen of the Missions. By the time the entire mission – stone walls, granary, church and bastions – was finished in 1782, it had become quite a place, and the local Native Americans were not slow to pick up on this fact. The mission was attacked repeatedly and often looted quite successfully until the converted Indians and missionaries could figure out how to defend themselves.

While the place was allowed to deteriorate terribly since the 19th century, the reconstruction was spectacular, and today it's one of the busiest on the trail. Ranger-led tours, which leave the visitors' center at 10 and 11 am and 2 and 3 pm, cover life in the mission and show up close the magnificent church and its famous rose window, a stunningly carved masterpiece attached to the sacristy. The best time to visit is on Sunday during church services, when a locally famous mariachi band plays at noon. More serene services are held in Spanish at 7:45 am, in English at 9 and 10:30 am.

San Juan

The most somber of the missions, Misión San Juan Capistrano was moved to the middle of what's now Espada Park in 1731. There were attempts to enlarge it in 1757, but the large church was never finished. The National Park Service plans to return water to the San Juan Acequia in an attempt to recreate a model farm. Today the surviving church is open, as is the good bookstore at the visitors' center.

Espada

The southernmost in the mission chain, Misión San Francisco de la Espada was built in its current location between 1745 and 1756 as a training ground for artisans studying weaving, blacksmithing and other skills. Today, Mission Espada has nice displays on weaving cotton and the Spanish colonists along with a slide show in the visitors' center on the mission system.

Espada Water System The main irrigation system for the mission is still in use. It was part of a 15-mile network that began at the **Espada Dam** (1740), which diverted water from the San Antonio River into the Espada Aqueduct. It's the only functioning aqueduct in the USA from the Spanish colonial period, and it still carries water over Piedras Creek to the mission.

Espada Park The entire area between the Espada Mission and the Espada Dam is set aside as park land, and the marked paths through it allow access by foot, bicycle or car. There are picnic tables and barbecue pits at various places.

SOUTH CENTRAL TEXAS

SOUTH CENTRAL TEXAS

Getting There & Away

From downtown, bus No 42 goes to San José, otherwise you must have a car or bicycle. From downtown, take S St Mary's St south until it becomes Mission Rd; this leads to all the missions.

ART MUSEUMS
McNay Art Museum

This museum (☎ 210-824-5368), 6000 N New Braunfels Ave (bus No 11 from downtown), is in a spectacular Mediterranean-style mansion (1927-29) that was the private residence of Marion Koogler McNay. After her death in 1950, McNay left her impressive collection of European and American modern art to the city, which has been supplemented since by other Texas family collectors. Today the collection is perhaps the best in the Southwest. It includes works by van Gogh, Toulouse-Lautrec, Gauguin, Chagall, Cézanne, Hopper, Pissarro and Dalí, and there is an entire room dedicated to Matisse. Works in the Matisse gallery include many etchings, a bronze *(Small Torso)* and *The Red Blouse*, an oil painting featuring a small self-portrait of the artist appearing over the main subject's left shoulder.

Smaller exhibitions, including rotating shows and the Oppenheimer galleries of medieval and Renaissance art, are located upstairs. In the courtyard, wonderful tiles tell the story of Don Quixote. Downstairs, the research library is open to the public.

The museum is open Tuesday to Saturday 10 am to 5 pm, Sunday noon to 5 pm, closed Mondays and major holidays. The library is open for research Tuesday to Friday 10 am to 4:45 pm. Docent-led tours run Sunday at 2 pm. Admission and parking for the library and the museum are free.

San Antonio Museum of Art

Housed in the original Lone Star Brewery (1884), the San Antonio Museum of Art (SAMA; ☎ 210-978-8100, www.sa-ma .org; bus No 11 from downtown), 200 W Jones Ave, houses exciting rotating exhibitions in addition to a permanent collection of Asian, Egyptian and ancient art. It also hosts regular poetry readings, concerts, films and other events. The east wing's four floors are the place to start; the ground floor houses a terrific collection of Egyptian art (boggle at the *Seated Statue of a God)*, serving trays and ancient glassworks, as well as a fine series of Greco-Roman sculpture. The 3rd floor houses Chinese porcelain from the Ming and Qing dynasties, including bowls, vases, urns and tomb figures of horses and warriors. On the 2nd floor, the Asian collection has more items from China (including a sensational canopy bed and yoke-back armchair), plus Thai pottery, Vietnamese dishes, Korean bronze works, Japanese folding screens and a cool *norimono,* a single-passenger vehicle carried on the shoulders of bearers.

It's open Tuesday to Saturday 10 am to 5 pm (until 9 pm on Tuesday) and Sunday noon to 5 pm. Free parking is available. Admission is $4 for adults, $2 for seniors and students, $1.75 for kids four to 11 years old.

Rockefeller Center for Latin American Art

Right next door to (and part of) the San Antonio Museum of Art complex, the Nelson A Rockefeller Center for Latin American Art makes up SAMA's new east wing. It's an expansion and consolidation of SAMA's impressive trove of Spanish-colonial, Mexican, pre-Columbian, folk, modern and contemporary works from Latin America that was originally combined with other exhibits in the main SAMA building. The facility opened in October 1998 also features interactive computer displays.

CHILDREN'S MUSEUMS
Witte Museum

The Witte Museum (pronounced 'witty'; ☎ 210-357-1900), 3801 Broadway, north of downtown along the east edge of Brackenridge Park (bus Nos 7, 9 or 14 from downtown), is a great place to spend the day with kids; the Science Treehouse, a high-tech activity center in back of the museum building, is a marvelous diversion. Kids begin downstairs with lots of cool physical-property displays designed to tire out the little darlings before getting to the more cerebral displays upstairs, which include music makers, a video-light microscope and an Internet room with about a dozen terminals. Outside the treehouse, a deck overlooks the San Antonio River; there's a real treehouse as well.

Inside the main museum are excellent permanent exhibits on Texas natural history and the people of the Lower Pecos region, including a replica of their cave dwellings. Downstairs is Texas Wild, which covers the flora and fauna of all Texas ecological regions.

The museum is open from Monday to Saturday 10 am to 5 pm (Tuesday until 9 pm) and Sunday noon to 5 pm. There's free parking with admission at the River Bend garage across the street. Admission is $5.95 for adults, $4.95 for seniors older than 65 and $3.95 for children; it's free on Tuesdays from 3 to 9 pm.

San Antonio Children's Museum

Set in a former dime store, the San Antonio Children's Museum (☎ 210-212-4453), at 305 E Houston St, is one of the state's best kids' museums. It has two floors of exhibits – included among them are the News Room, where kids put together a newspaper, a compost room (where about a billion worms are helping to make our world a better place) and interactive computers. Local volunteers come in for special projects, such as when employees from the local Home Depot stopped in to help kids build a house. It's open from Tuesday to Friday 9 am to 5 pm (until 6 pm on Saturday) and Sunday from noon to 4 pm; admission is $4, kids younger than two are free. The museum staff will validate your parking.

MILITARY MUSEUMS

With all the firepower in the area, the city is teeming with military museums. But note that access to all the bases is restricted, and you'll need to get visitor's passes (obtainable through the front gate) for all (except Fort Sam Houston), so bring identification.

Fort Sam Houston

The Fifth Army headquarters and home of Brooke Army Medical Center, Fort Sam Houston (☎ 210-221-1886), just northeast of

downtown (bus No 15 or 11 from downtown), is a working collection of historic buildings upon whose grounds designated museums are open to the public.

The **Quadrangle** (☎ 210-221-1886), just off New Braunfels St north of I-35, was built in 1876. The base briefly held prisoner Apache chief Geronimo. Today, the Quadrangle is open as a museum of the history of the fort, and it leads through to sort of a petting zoo – deer have been kept here for more than 100 years, and rabbits, ducks and chickens abound. Pick up the free, self-guided tour pamphlet at the Quadrangle. The Quadrangle is open Wednesday to Sunday 10 am to 4 pm (hours depend on the army's schedule); the gift shop's hours are Friday to Tuesday 8 am to 4 pm.

Medical Museum The US Army Medical Department Museum (☎ 210-221-6358), in the northeast section of the fort's grounds, has a display of army medical gear from the US and several other countries, including Germany, the former Soviet Union, Vietnam and China and a cool collection of restored ambulances. But what makes the free admission really worth the price is the collection of Civil War surgical gear. Note the saws, ladies and gentlemen. The museum is open Tuesday to Sunday 10 am to 4 pm, closed Monday and federal holidays.

Air Force History Museum

The Air Force History and Traditions Museum (☎ 210-671-3055) at Lackland Air Force Base, 12 miles southwest of downtown off US 90 at SW Military Drive (from downtown, take bus No 76 to Military Drive and US 90 and then change for bus No 614 or No 551 east), was established in 1956 to teach Air Force recruits something of the development of the Air Force. Now open to the public, it's got amazing vintage historical aircraft on display, including a Curtiss JN-4D Jenny, an F-15, an A-10 and an SR-71 Blackbird surveillance plane as well as a research library. It's a must for flight buffs. The museum is open Monday to Friday from 8 am to 4:45 pm, closed Saturday, Sunday and federal holidays. Admission is free.

Hangar 9

Getting a bit more esoteric, Hangar 9 – the Edward H White Museum at Brooks Air Force Base (☎ 210-536-2203), 7 miles southeast of downtown (bus No 34 or No 36 from downtown), is a museum dedicated to the oldest aircraft hangar in the air force. Displays concern early manned flight and the evolution of aerospace medicine. Another exhibit is dedicated to flight nurses. The museum is open Monday to Friday 8 am to 4 pm, and admission is free.

OTHER MUSEUMS
Hertzberg Circus Museum

The Hertzberg Circus Museum (☎ 210-207-7819), 210 W Market St, houses an amazing variety of circus paraphernalia collected by Harry Hertzberg. Located in the former San Antonio Public Library building, the Hertzberg contains about 20,000 items and rivals the collection at the Ringling estate in Sarasota, Florida. Featured items include a splendid model of a 1920s-era big top, posters and stuff relating to Tom Thumb, the midget star of PT Barnum's circus (including Thumb's carriage and his signed temperance pledge).

Kids go nuts over the hands-on Magic of Faces exhibit that lets them distort their faces with mirrors and interactive PCs, and they love the face painting and mask-making workshops (additional $1 each) too. It's open Monday to Saturday 10 am to 5 pm (open the same hours on Sunday from June to August). Admission is $2.50 for adults, $2 for seniors and $1 for children. The museum validates parking.

Southwest School of Arts & Crafts

Set in the former Academy Building (1851) of the Ursuline Academy, San Antonio's first all-girls school, the Southwest School of Arts and Crafts (☎ 210-224-1848), 300 Augusta Ave at the north bank of the San Antonio River, should be a required stopping point. The center offers the largest art curriculum in south Texas, with free workshops, classes and lectures on work in many media, including ceramics, photography, painting and sculpture. Visiting artists make installations, and regularly scheduled workshops invite the public into the real studios, including the recently opened Tire Store, between the main complex and the central library. It houses, among other things, the Picante Paper Studio, a working papermaking facility.

A popular open-house event at the school is the Saturday Morning Discovery, a free Saturday-morning program from September to May, designed for kids between the ages of eight and eighteen. Programs last a month and include workshops in batik, drawing, painting and other art techniques.

There are several galleries, most open Monday to Saturday from 10 am to 5 pm. The Ursuline Sales Gallery exhibits and sells works by the school's artists and visiting artists as well. The Emily Edwards Gallery holds six exhibitions per year for works by local, regional and national artists. The Amy Shelton McNutt Garden Room (next to the Edwards Gallery) houses volunteer tour guides who ply visitors with lemonade. That there is probably to make you feel like the heel you are if you don't make a donation to this wonderful place, whose admission is otherwise free.

Buckhorn Saloon & Museum

The Buckhorn Saloon and Museum (☎ 210-270-9467, www.BuckhornMuseum.com), at 318 E Houston St, is one of the best kitsch values around. Halls of mounted stuffed animals from around the world are as disgusting as any of these collections, and one features such oddities as a two-headed cow and a nine-legged goat. But the reason to come is the cheezoid Americana – there are maps of Texas made from rattlesnake rattlers, a wonderful collection of Lone Star Beer paraphernalia (such as a guitar made from pull-tabs) and the pièce de résistance, the wax museum, which was clearly assembled by buying wax figures from other wax museums and changing the costumes. In one diorama, Teddy Roosevelt consults with what's gotta be Alan Ladd, and in another, it's Tom Selleck as Magnum PI as General Robert E Lee.

The museum is open daily 10 am to 5pm; admission is $9.95 for adults, $7.95 for kids six to 11.

Texas Pioneer & Ranger Museum

Right next door to the Witte Museum (see earlier under Children's Museums) in Brackenridge Park, the Texas Pioneer, Trail Driver and Texas Rangers Museum (☎ 210-822-9011), 2805 Broadway, is exactly what it sounds like, housed in a rather impressive WPA building (1936) specifically designed for it. Staff and volunteers (mainly former Rangers) are very interesting guides. The museum is open daily, from May to August 10 am to 5 pm, and from September to April it's open 11 am to 4 pm. Admission is $2 for adults, $1 for seniors and active military, 50¢ for children.

Spanish Governor's Palace

Built at the turn of the 18th century, the Spanish Governor's Palace (☎ 210-224-0601), 105 Plaza de Armas (behind city hall between Commerce and Dolorosa Sts), was originally the quarters for the commander of the area's Spanish colonial troops. In 1722 it became the seat of Texas' colonial government – it was from bureaucrats in this palace that Moses Austin sought permission to import American settlers to the area. After Texan independence, the house saw a variety of uses (including as a saloon), but it was bought and refurbished by the city in 1928.

Today, it's a museum filled with period furniture that provides a charming foreground against the backdrop of the palace's adobe walls, brick ovens and fireplaces.

It's open Monday to Saturday 9 am to 5 pm, Sunday 10 am to 5 pm. Admission is $1 for adults, 50¢ for children younger than 14 years old and free for children seven years old and younger.

Institute of Texan Cultures

One of the most rewarding museums in San Antonio is the Institute of Texan Cultures (☎ 210-458-2330, www.texancultures.utsa.edu), 801 S Bowie St. Run by the University of Texas at San Antonio, the institute explores the diverse nature of the settlers of Texas. Originally slated for a six-month run during HemisFair, the institute is now a permanent museum and the state of Texas' official center for the interpretation of its history.

The main exhibit, spread out over an enormous single-floor space, has sections devoted to 27 ethnic and national groups of settlers in Texas; the groups include Anglo-Americans, Mexicans, Germans, Irish, Belgians, Dutch, Polish, African Americans and Jews, among others. There's a puppet theater where interpretive shows are held daily (check at the desk for schedules), a real chuck wagon, displays on fibers and fabrics and a post office.

The Back 40 Area, behind the main exhibition, has reconstructed buildings such as a fort, schoolhouse, log cabin and a windmill.

The institute is open Tuesday to Sunday 9 am to 5 pm, closed Monday, Thanksgiving and Christmas. Admission is $4 for adults, $2 for seniors and for children from three to 12 years old.

Cowboy Museum

If you can't get to the Cowboy Artists of America Museum in Kerrville (see the Hill Country earlier in this chapter), the Cowboy Museum (☎ 210-229-1257), 209 Alamo Plaza, is definitely worth the admission ($3 for adults, $2 for kids ten to 14 years old). It's a collection of cowboy paraphernalia, including guns (lots o' guns), spurs, lassos, hats and cowboy costumes. Staff members explain much of the cowboy life immortalized to the world in Western movies. It's open daily 10 am to 7 pm.

OTHER THINGS TO SEE
San Fernando Cathedral

The nation's oldest surviving chapel, the San Fernando Cathedral (1731-50), 115 Main Plaza, on N Main Ave just south of E Commerce St, was established by settlers from the Canary Islands. Today it's the parish church of the Archbishop of San Antonio. The original dome collapsed in 1872, and the center of the replacement dome is considered the geographical center of the city. During the Battle of the Alamo, Santa Anna used the church as an observation post.

Remains uncovered in 1936, purported to be those of Davy Crockett, William Travis and James Bowie, are now kept in a marble casket at the rear of the church. Bowie, by the way, was married here. The church also features impressive stained-glass windows and a pipe organ dating to 1884.

There are services in English and Spanish Saturday at 5:30 pm, Sunday at 6:15 am and 5 pm, and a televised Spanish-language mass at 9 am Sunday. There's also a 10:30 am Sunday service in Latin, English and Spanish, a 12:15 pm service in Spanish, and a 2 pm service in English.

Navarro State Historical Park

José Antonio Navarro (1795-1871), a mayor of San Antonio under the Mexican government as well as a state legislator, was a lawyer and rancher who became one of two native Texans to sign the Texas Declaration of Independence. The wealthy Texan built a large residence and office in downtown San Antonio, which is now open to the public as a state historical park (☎ 210-226-4801), 228 S Laredo St. The park consists of three separate adobe and limestone buildings that were his home, office and kitchen. Guided tours and demonstrations of equipment and household gadgets run from August to January, Wednesday to Sunday 10 am to 4 pm, and from February to July daily 10 am to 4 pm. Admission is $2 for adults and $1 for children between six and 12 years old.

King William Historic District

This charming neighborhood in southwest downtown was built by wealthy German settlers at the end of the 19th century. The architecture here is mostly Victorian, though there are fine examples of Italianate, colonial-revival, beaux-arts, and even art-moderne styles. Most of the district's houses have been renovated and are privately owned or run as B&Bs. It's a very pleasant area for a long stroll, and the visitors' center and the San Antonio Conservation Society (☎ 210-224-6163), 107 King William St, hand out a very helpful walking tour map of the district. VIA streetcars (Blue Line) pass throughout the area – see Getting Around later for streetcar details.

Guenther House Museum German immigrant Carl Hilmar Guenther founded the Pioneer Flour Mill in Fredericksburg in 1851, moving it to San Antonio in 1859 and building his family house right next to the mills in 1860. The house, at 205 E Guenther St, has been restored and today is one of the biggest draws in the district, open as a pioneer museum and restaurant (☎ 210-227-1061).

The museum is open Monday to Saturday 9 am to 5 pm, Sunday 8 am to 2 pm; admission is free.

Steves Homestead Volunteer docents from the San Antonio Conservation Society run guided tours through this Victorian and Second Empire-style home (1876; ☎ 210-225-5924) at 509 King William St. Formerly the home of Edward Steves, a wealthy merchant, the house has been restored to demonstrate the life of the affluent at the end of the 19th century. On the property is San Antonio's first indoor swimming pool. The museum is open daily 10 am to 4:15 pm; admission is $2 for adults, free for kids younger than 12.

Market Square

Market Square (☎ 210-207-8600), at 514 W Commerce St, is a recreation of a Mexican marketplace by, it would seem, Disney engineers. That's not to say it's bad – it's actually a good deal of fun, even if it does feel a whole lot like a tourist trap, which it is. But as far as tourist traps go, you could do worse than three discrete sections with about 100 merchants selling fabrics, bags, rugs, craftwork, clothing and reasonable Mexican food at decent prices. The market is just east of I-35, about a 15-minute walk (or five-minute streetcar ride) west of the Alamo, open January to August 10 am to 8 pm, September to May 10 am to 6 pm.

The Alamodome

Paid for by what could be called a local sports-team extortion tax, the Alamodome (☎ 210-207-3600), 100 Montana St just east of I-37, near the southeast corner of HemisFair Park, is a rather extraordinary 65,000-seat stadium and is home to the city's NBA basketball team, the San Antonio Spurs. One of the most flexible stadiums in the world, the seating system can be configured to hold as many as 72,000 people and is the largest of its kind. The building's dome roof stands, at its highest point, at about 170 feet, and the JumboTron monitor – which thoughtfully provides ads during breaks in the action – weighs in at an amazing 30 tons.

The building looks like a dead armadillo, but no matter, a tour of the place is absolutely fascinating – see Spectator Sports later for more information on Spurs games and other activities held here.

Southern Pacific Railroad Depot
The Southern Pacific Railroad Depot, still in use as the city's Amtrak station, is just north of the Alamodome and just west of I-10 (bus No 24 from downtown). It's still in the process of being restored and promises to be spectacular when completed, with features such as stained-glass windows and a wild interior. The terminal building is open to the public and free. See Getting There & Away for information on the Amtrak *Sunset Limited* and *Texas Eagle* services.

Union Stockyards
For wholesome fun for the whole family, head on over to the Union Stockyards (☎ 210-223-6331), southwest of downtown at 1716 S San Marcos St at Pendleton Ave (bus No 54 from downtown), to watch a beef auction, hosted by auctioneers who speak at such a frenetic pace it's just about as easy for the uninitiated to follow as NASDAQ traders' hand signals. And the meat – well, let's just say we're eating a lot less after seeing it. The auction is highly recommended and runs Monday and Wednesday from 9 am; admission is free. Get a good burger across the street at the Exchange Building café.

ART GALLERIES
Blue Star Arts Complex
This art complex (☎ 210-227-6960), at 1400-1414 S Alamo St near Probandt St in the south end of the King William Historic District (bus No 44 or the blue-route streetcar from downtown), is another working arts center, with seven galleries and more than 30 art studios. It's more commercially minded than the Southwest School of Arts

and Crafts, but it's still very much the real McCoy and is also one of the city's cultural hubs, with regular openings and shows. The Blue Star Brewing Company, a chichi restaurant, is part of the complex – it does a mean Sunday brunch and great dinners. There are five other spaces associated with the complex, including San Angel Folk Art (☎ 210-226-6688), 110 Blue Star, which offers Mexican folk crafts and Talavera pottery, and the Blue Star Art Space (☎ 210-227-6960), 116 Blue Star, which is a series of contemporary art studios.

La Villita
La Villita, 'the little village,' was a settlement of Mexicans and Europeans founded in the 1850s that developed downtown at Riverwalk's southern end. Today it's a legitimate national historic landmark district charmingly restored as a tourist trap.

Its **Little Church** is open for services Sunday and Thursday at 11 am. The San Antonio Conservation Society (see King William District) sponsors frequent exhibits on the history of the area at the **La Villita Exhibit**, in the center of the area just off King Phillip V Walk, and performances are held throughout the year at the **Arneson River Theatre**. General Martín Perfecto de Cós (see the Alamo earlier) surrendered to Texas revolutionaries in the **Cós House** at the northeast corner of King Phillip V Walk and Villita St.

The village went into decline around the beginning of the 20th century and was renovated by the city in the late 1930s, giving birth to **La Villita complex** (☎ 210-207-8610), 418 Villita St, a heavily touristed and touristy collection of commercial art and craft shops where you can watch artists creating the stuff they hope you buy. It's fun – certainly no more hokey than others of the same ilk – and the architecture and grounds make it a lovely place to walk through.

PARKS, GARDENS & ZOO
HemisFair Park
Site of the 1968 World's Fair, HemisFair Park is at the center of the city and has provided it with one of its landmark structures, the

750-foot **Tower of the Americas** (☎ 210-207-8615). The observation deck at 579 feet offers huge views of the city. It's open daily 9 am to 10 pm; admission is $3 for adults, $3 for seniors, $1 for kids. If heights aren't making you queasy yet, there's always the revolving *Tower Restaurant* up there, too.

The 15-acre park fell on bad times in the 1950s and was quite a scoundrel magnet until a renovation that was completed in 1988. Today, it's home to waterfalls and fountains (set to be turned on after expansion of the convention center is completed), playgrounds and the Universidad de México and Mexican Cultural Institute.

Brackenridge Park

A couple of miles north of downtown (bus No 8 from downtown), Brackenridge Park is a favorite San Antonian getaway spot, lovers' lane and gentle amusement park, with serene offerings including boat rentals, a Japanese garden, a little putt-putt railroad and an old-fashioned carousel. Its main attraction – other than its lovely green setting – is that it's the headspring for the San Antonio River. The miniature railroad ($2.17 for adults, $1.62 for children younger than 12), in the center of the park, and the carousel and skyride (a Swiss-made cable car that grants so-so views of the city) are open Monday to Friday 9:30 am to 5 pm, to 5:30 pm weekends.

Stables Brackenridge Stables (☎ 210-732-8881), 840 E Mulberry St, rents horses for individual riding through the park ($23 per hour per person) and runs guided tours on horseback ($15 for 30 minutes, $20 for 45 minutes) as well as pony rides ($6 for 15 minutes, $11 for 30 minutes). The staff explains the trails and the paths. Hours vary by season, but the stables are always open from at least 9 am to 3 pm.

Japanese Tea Gardens At the park's northwestern end, an ugly quarry was transformed into a wonderful Japanese formal garden with stone bridges, floral displays and a 60-foot waterfall. The whole place was under renovation when we visited. The gardens are open 8 am to dusk; admission is free.

JOHN ELK III

Tower of the Americas at HemisFair Park

San Antonio Zoo Established in 1914, the San Antonio Zoological Gardens & Aquarium (☎ 210-734-7183) is famous for its animal breeding programs that have given it one of the largest endangered-animal collections in the country. There are more than 3500 animals here, and the exhibits are well signed and easy to get around. Other things to see include enormous free-flight aviaries, a very cute camel and a petting zoo and playground. The newest addition is the Pad – 17 naturalistic environments in which amphibians are shown off – including aquatic and yellow-striped caecilians and European fire, Texas blind and tiger salamanders. Also check out some neat frogs, such as poison dart and Madagascar tomato frogs.

The zoo is open May 14 through Labor Day 9 am to 8 pm, until 6 pm the rest of the year. Zoo admission is $6 for adults, $4 for seniors and children from three to 11; kids younger than three are free.

San Antonio Botanical Gardens

What a place for a date – the San Antonio Botanical Gardens (☎ 210-207-3250, www.sabot.org), 555 Funston Place northeast of downtown (bus No 11 from downtown), is a 33-acre garden that re-creates all native Texas flora. There's also a fragrance garden and a wonderful conservatory, with tropical and desert plants and a large indoor pond. The gardens and conservatory are open Tuesday to Sunday 9 am to 6 pm, closed Monday, Christmas and New Year's Day. Admission is $4 for adults, $2 for seniors, $1 for children from four to 13 years old, children younger than four are free.

THEME PARKS & ATTRACTIONS
Ripley's Believe It or Not!
Offerings at the Ripley's Believe It or Not! museum (☎ 210-224-9299), 301 Alamo Plaza opposite the Alamo, are pretty much what you'll find in the other Ripley's museums across the country. Items in this one include the *Lord's Prayer* written on a grain of rice, an iron maiden torture device and the man with four pupils – the believe-it-or-not part is up to you. Even if the answer is 'not,' it still may be worth the admission price ($12.95 for adults and students older than 13, $11.95 for seniors, $9.95 for children four to 12 years old, those younger than four are free). Included in that admission price is entrance to the Plaza Theatre of Wax, which sports a Hollywood-and-horror theme with figures of such luminaries as Brad Pitt, Whoopi Goldberg, Frankenstein, Michael Jackson, Charlton Heston, Godzilla and Dracula. Also included are figures from Texas history, including, of course, Davy Crockett.

The Texas Adventure
The Texas Adventure (☎ 210-227-0388), 307 Alamo Plaza opposite the Alamo, is a multimedia show based on the Texas War for Independence and focuses on the Battle of the Alamo. The show is pretty amazing and an exciting (if dramatic) depiction of the battle. Just so you won't forget it too soon, there's an unbelievably huge gift shop right outside. Admission is $7.50 for adults, $4.50 for children three to 11.

Sea World
Sea World of Texas in San Antonio is one in a chain of 10 such parks owned by brewery giant Anheuser-Busch, perhaps to redeem itself to the world for bringing it Budweiser beer. The park claims to give aid to real scientific research and conservation efforts and contribute to education throughout the country. It's also got a kick-ass roller coaster, marine-life displays that'll have the kids in awe, and if you're in the mood for a theme park, it's probably your best bet in the area.

Orientation & Information Sea World (☎ 210-523-3611, www.seaworld.com, or for teachers, the educational www.seaworld.org), at 10500 Sea World Drive, is at the western edge of town, near the intersection of Loop 1604 and Hwy 151 (also called Westside Parkway). Guest services and the lost-and-found center are right at the main entrance. Get park maps as you pick up your ticket. The park is open March through October with varying operating hours, from at least 10 am to at least 6 pm, later in high season.

The admission for a single day pass is $31.95 for adults (there's a 10% discount for seniors), $21.95 for children from three to 11 years old. Two-day passes are a better buy, with tickets at $35.95 for adults and $25.95 for kids. Parking is $5 for cars, $7 for vans and buses. Sea World accepts Visa, MasterCard and Discover, but not American Express. ATMs are available near the main entrance and near the Great White coaster, where there are also pay lockers (50¢). All attractions are wheelchair accessible. Stroller and wheelchair rentals are $5; double strollers are $10; electric wheelchairs are $25.

Toilets are well signed and clean. There are diaper-changing areas adjacent to most toilets. Kennels are available free, but you need to bring your own food and come back to walk your animal throughout the day.

Rides Other than playing a recording of David Hasselhoff singing *Fallin' in Love* as part of the *Baywatch at Sea World* show, Sea World hadn't been in the terror side of the entertainment business until 1997, when the rides were opened. Sea World has possibly the USA's most terrifying roller coaster, the Great White (if you ride it, check your flip-flops in the lockers near the entrance if you want to wear them home). Tamer rides include the Rio Loco and Texas Splashdown water rides.

Rides are included in the price of admission, and lines for them get to be very long in summer – there's often an hourlong wait for the Great White. The earlier you show up, the better.

The **Great White** is an inverted steel roller coaster, which means as you streak down 2500 feet of looping, twisting track at 50 mph, you're hanging under the track, your legs dangling beneath (or flopping above) you. You're upside-down five times during the ride, which begins with an 80-foot drop and gets scarier. There's a minimum height requirement of 54 inches (130cm), and we're serious about stashing your stuff in the lockers.

The **Rio Loco** is a white-water raft ride right next to the Great White. Its height requirement is 42 inches (107cm). During the course of the ride, you'll be sprayed by people who have paid to fire water cannons at you. **Texas Splashdown** is a water-flume ride with two plunges, including one spanning five stories.

The children's ride section features remote-control cars and merry-go-rounds.

Other Attractions Sea World's excellent whale and dolphin shows unfold in the **White Whale Stadium**. Beluga whales and Pacific white-sided dolphins boogie to Caribbean music and perform synchronized leaps from the water as foxy trainers ride on their backs.

People movers carried us past penguin tanks with manufactured snow in the **Penguin Encounter**, the sounds of penguin calls barely audible over the hilarious and somehow appropriate oompah-pah music. There's a learning center there as well.

Take children to see the *Pirates of Pinniped* at the **Sea Lion Stadium**, which stars 'comedians' in the form of sea lions, otters and Pacific walruses. The kids at least find it screamingly funny.

Get very close to the sharks, rays, barracudas, lion fish and skates in the fascinating **Sharks-Coral Reef** exhibit, which also includes smaller tanks on venomous fish.

A wonderful kids' recreation area (all ages) with probably the best climbing nets on earth is **Shamu's Happy Harbor**, which also features an air-bounce for kids who are up to 48 inches tall (122cm), water slides for kids shorter than 42 inches (107cm) and a great sandbox.

Killer whales perform stunts – some choreographed to rock music – and splash the crowd at the **Shamu Stadium**.

The **Water Ski Stadium** fronting the lake was home to the *Baywatch at Sea World* show, which is every bit as exciting as the television series, but there's talk of revamping the show. If the show is still running, you'll see some great water-ski and jet-ski stunts. The first 15 rows are splash zones, and there are some explosions during the show. If you hate bangs, sit in the back.

Getting There & Away The Shamu Shuttle (☎ 210-212-5395) runs between the Alamo visitors' center and Sea World and costs $30.95 roundtrip, including the adult admission, $8 without admission to the park. Schedules change annually, so call for information.

By car from downtown San Antonio, take I-37 south to US 90 west, and take that to the Hwy 151 W exit. Turn left at Westover Hills Blvd, which takes you right to the front entrance.

Six Flags Fiesta Texas

The city's other major theme park is something of a disappointment. There are great roller coasters, swimming pools, water rides and kiddie rides; the setting – against a limestone quarry that looks similar to the Arizona desert – is dramatic; and there's plenty of music and shows. But at the end of the day, Six Flags Fiesta Texas is a theme park without a theme.

The park is broken into several sections, and there is a semblance of a theme celebrating the diversity of Texas and the Southwest – with Batman and Bugs Bunny thrown in. The park is owned by Time Warner Inc, which explains why a guy dressed as the Green Lantern can be seen in a Hispanic-theme area.

Orientation & Information The park (☎ 210-697-5000, 800-473-4378) is at the northwestern end of the city, just off I-10 and north of Loop 1604. Inside the park, areas include Crackaxle Canyon, where all the big rides are; the Ol' Waterin' Hole, a water park with kiddie and swimming pools; Los Festivales, a Hispanic-theme area; Spassburg, a German-theme area (where the tastefully named revue of German traditional music is entitled the *Sauerkrauts*); and Rockville, which is set to resemble the 1950s. The Fiesta Bay Boardwalk is home to several more rides.

One-day tickets cost $33 for adults and $23.50 for seniors, children and disabled visitors. Two day tickets are $37 and $27.

Guest relations, lockers, stroller rental ($6 per day), wheelchair rental ($7 per day), a kennel and an ATM are right at the main gate. There's another ATM in Spassburg and a foreign exchange office in Los Festivales. Rest rooms are spotless, and Mother's House in Spassburg has a changing and nursing area. Lockers are available for $5 per day in the water park areas and 50¢ per use in other areas of the park.

Rides Giving Sea World's Great White a serious run for the scariest coaster category, the **Joker's Revenge** is an absolutely devastating ride with double-loop inversions, two corkscrews and a spiral curve. When you think you've been there and done that, the thing does the entire circuit again backwards. Riders must be a minimum of 48 inches (122cm) tall.

The **Rattler** is a traditional wooden roller coaster that gets its PQ (puke quotient) from sheer speed (73 mph) and steepness (a 61° slope). The park claims it's the fastest wooden coaster in the world, and it's hard to argue with it – it's a little like riding a runaway mine car, which is exactly what it's supposed to be.

The recently added **Road Runner Express** promises that guests will 'interact with Wile E Coyote in a number of unsuccessful, zany antics.' This means that as you whiz around turns and dip and lunge through the three spiral curves – including a section that actually meshes with the track of the Rattler – you're hounded by cartoons, sound effects and compressed-air-operated animatronic figures. It's a mild, fun ride for kids or those too scared to get on the other two.

Variety Shows A number of high-quality variety shows take the park's stages daily, including *DC Comics Super Heroes Live*, *Reunion at Rockville High*, *What's Up Rock?!* and the *Lonestar Spectacular*, which is an evening showstopper on the history of Texas with fireworks and laser beams.

Getting There & Away San Antonio's public transit department, VIA (☎ 210-362-2020), runs a public bus year-round from downtown San Antonio and from the Crossroads Mall (see Shopping), to the main entrance. See Getting Around for details on using VIA buses. By car from downtown, take I-10 west to the La Cantera-Fiesta Texas exit and follow the signs.

BREWERIES

A few microbreweries in town offer tours, and some are also live-music venues. Frio Brewing Company (☎ 210-225-8222), at 1905 N St Mary's St, open Monday to Friday 8:30 am to 6 pm, brews Frio Lager and Frio Honey Wheat, and tours are available on request. The N St Mary's Brewing Co (☎ 210-737-6255), 2734 N St Mary's St, is a bar and microbrewery that has lots of live music – see Entertainment.

Sadly, major breweries that once offered tours do so no longer; Lone Star packed up its operations here, and Pearl Brewing Company (☎ 210-226-0231), 312 Pearl Parkway – maker of Pabst Blue Ribbon, Olde English 800, Pearl and Hooch – no longer offers tours.

LANGUAGE CLASSES

Spanish-language instruction at all levels is offered throughout the year at the Universidad Nacional Autonoma de México's San Antonio campus (☎ 210-222-8626), at 600 HemisFair Plaza.

ORGANIZED TOURS

There are several good options for tours of the city.

Streetcar Tours

Lone Star Trolley Tours (☎ 210-222-9090) run one-hour streetcar tours through downtown San Antonio. Boarding is at Ripley's Believe it or Not! (see earlier), where you can also buy tickets ($9.50).

Coach Tours

Gray Line of San Antonio (☎ 210-226-1706, 800-472-9546), 217 Alamo Plaza, runs coach tours ranging from simple city orientation to more elaborate full-day programs, including admission to Sea World or Six Flags Fiesta Texas; contact Gray Line for more information.

San Antonio City Tours (☎ 210-212-5395, 800-868-7707), 217 Alamo Plaza, next to the visitors' center opposite the Alamo, run 3½-hour walking and coach tours of the city ($24). Also offered is a tour including admission to the IMAX cinema and a riverboat cruise (see later) for $39.75. It runs Hill Country Magic tours as well, which last eight hours and visit Hill Country areas, such as Fredericksburg, Stonewall and the LBJ Ranch.

River Tours

Yanaguana Cruises (☎ 210-244-5700), at 315 E Commerce St, suite 202, offer 40-minute narrated tours along the Riverwalk in kitschy boats. Tickets are $5.25 for adults, $1 for kids five years old and younger. If you're with a group, the boats make a nice charter option ($90 for the first hour before 5 pm and $45 for each additional 30 minutes), and almost every restaurant along Riverwalk will book you onto the boats for dinner – it's romantic and fun, but the food's no better on the water than on land.

Alamodome Tours

Organized tours of the Alamodome run Tuesday to Saturday at 11 am and 1 pm. For tour information, call ☎ 210-207-3652; tours cost $3 for adults, $1.50 for seniors and children from four to 12 years old.

Tours Off the Beaten Path

The Alamo City Paranormal Club (☎ 210-436-5417) runs tours on many evenings (call to see if one is scheduled). The tours usually leave from the defender's monument in front of the Alamo and visit what are purported to be downtown San Antonio's most haunted addresses. The 1½-hour walking tour costs $10 for adults, $5 for children younger than 17.

SPECIAL EVENTS

San Antonio is a city with a full calendar of festivals and events; visitors are bound to run into at least one.

January

San Antonio Mud Festival
Held the first Saturday in January, this celebration fetes the draining of the San Antonio River and features live music and the annual crowning of the Mud King and Queen.

February

San Antonio Livestock Show and Rodeo
In mid-February, two weeks' worth of buckin' broncos and other Western stuff come to the Freeman Coliseum (☎ 210-224-1374), at 3201 E Houston St.

Carnaval del Rio
Five days before Ash Wednesday, the riverfront fills up with all manner of local musicians from adagio to zydeco, including all the Texan twang most folks can take.

March

St Patrick's Day
On the weekend closest to the 17th, the city dyes the river green and celebrates the feat by tossing back downright Irish quantities of beer.

April

Fiesta San Antonio
Late in the month, a 10-day series of events (☎ 210-227-5191, www.fiesta-sa.org) makes the city's biggest celebration, with general mayhem, fairs, feeds, rodeos, races and a whole lot of music and dancing. Hundreds of thousands throng the streets – it's the high point of the SA year.

May

Cinco de Mayo
Similar activities to those of Fiesta San Antonio on the 5th celebrate Mexico's defeat of French troops at the 1862 Battle of Puebla.

Tejano Conjunto Festival
Enjoy five days in late May of the world's best conjunto musicianship and Tex-Mex cooking (☎ 210-271-3151).

Fiesta Noche del Rio
Every Thursday, Friday and Saturday night from Memorial Day (May 30) through Labor Day (the first Monday in September), the Fiesta Noche del Rio brings Latino music to the Arneson River Theater in a series of concerts and dance performances.

June
Ballet Folklórico de San Antonio
Also at the Arneson River Theater, this dance festival runs every Sunday through August.

August
Texas Folklife Festival
Early in the month, this main arts and crafts fair is held at the Institute of Texan Cultures.

September
Mexican Independence Day
Held on the weekend closest to the 16th, this festival is celebrated all across the city with food, music and theater.

December
Feast of the Virgen de Guadalupe
On the 12th, this is a festive, Mexican traditional gathering.

Las Luminarias and Las Posadas
These colorful, Mexican celebrations follow up the feast of the Virgen de Guadalupe on the two weekends preceding Christmas.

PLACES TO STAY
San Antonio has loads of places to stay that become booked solid during major NCAA games, city festivals like Fiesta San Antonio and large conventions. There aren't many really cheap hotels in town that are recommended; the heaps of reasonably priced motels downtown, out by the airport and along the interstates are most travelers' best bets. Many are new or have been remodeled, and lots have perks like morning coffee, continental breakfast, newspapers and shuttle services. Most of the better motels have laundry services or coin-operated machines.

Prices skyrocket during special events and conventions – see the listings for price ranges per category.

The Lodging Line of San Antonio (☎ 800-858-4303) and Texas Accommodations Incorporated (☎ 210-523-7070) are free reservations

services. Check with the visitors' center to see if there are coupons – many times you can get a discounted price just by asking.

Hostel
The *HI San Antonio International Hostel* (☎ 210-223-9426, fax 210-299-1479), at 621 Pierce St, is a large colonial ranch-style building north of downtown with a swimming pool and day-only common area. Dorm beds are $12.85 for HI members, $15.85 for nonmembers (breakfast $4 extra), and private rooms (singles or doubles) are $35.10/39.10 for members/nonmembers not including breakfast, or $43/47 including breakfast. There's a $10 key deposit. The office is open 7:30 am to 11 pm daily. There's a kitchen, but no laundry facilities.

The hostel is 2 miles north of downtown off I-35 exit 159A; if you're coming from downtown, turn left, go through three lights to Grayson St, turn left again, go two blocks down Grayson St to the corner of Pierce St and there it is. By bus from Navarro St in downtown, take bus No 11 or No 15 heading north and let the driver know you're heading for the hostel. From the Amtrak station, take bus No 516 along Hackberry St to Grayson St.

Camping
Tents & RVs The friendly and isolated *Dixie Campground* (☎ 210-337-6501, 800-759-5267), is about 3½ miles northeast of downtown San Antonio. It has tent sites without electricity for $12, with electricity for $14, and RV spots with full hookups for $18. It's about as flashy as the average KOA and cheaper, too. By car, take I-35 north to exit 159B (Coliseum), turn right (south) at the lights onto Coliseum Rd. Turn left (east) onto Gembler Drive; the campground is about three-quarters of a mile ahead on the left. By bus from downtown, take bus No 24 right to the driveway.

A bit closer in and also served by bus No 24 from downtown is the cheery-as-usual *San Antonio KOA Campground* (☎ 210-224-9296), 602 Gembler Rd, which has tent sites for $14.95 with water and electric hookups and RV sites for $18 with water and electric or $20 with full hookups. By car, take I-35 north to exit 159B, turn right onto Coliseum Rd, left on Gembler and it's on the right – follow the signs for the KOA, which you'll reach before Dixie Campground.

McAllister Park (☎ 210-207-3000) has lots of tent-camping sites; they're $5 per day from Monday to Saturday, but to stay from Saturday to Sunday the price goes up to $10. From downtown by car, take US 281 north to the Bitters Rd exit, turn right and continue to Jones Maltsberger Rd; then, turn left, follow Jones Maltsberger Rd for about 1½ miles, and the park is on the right. From downtown, take bus No 3, No 4 or No 5 to the North Star Mall, then change for bus No 502.

RVs Only *Greentree Village North RV Park* (☎ 210-655-3331), 12015 O'Connor Rd about 12 miles northeast of the city, charges RVs $18 per day or $108 per week with full hookups. Take I-35 to exit 169, and turn left (west) and head west for a quarter of a mile; the campground is on the left.

Closer to downtown and convenient to Sea World is the *Admiralty RV Resort* (☎ 210-647-7878, 800-999-7872), 1485 N Ellison Drive, with RV sites for $23 per day with full hookups. From downtown by car, take US 90 west to Hwy 151 to Potranco Rd; turn left, stay on Potranco for about a mile, and turn right when you see the Diamond Shamrock filling station on the right. That's N Ellison Drive, and the campground is about a half mile on the left. There's no public transport from downtown, but Sea World (see Theme Parks earlier) runs a free shuttle service between the campground and Sea World in summer.

Hotels & Motels
Budget Most cheap hotels are located disconcertingly near pawn shops and in marginal parts of town. But there are two that would do quite nicely in a pinch; both are clean and run by friendly (if sometimes suspicious of those walking through) management and are safe.

The shootout scene between Steve McQueen and the bad guys in *The Getaway* could easily have been filmed in the *Traveler's Hotel* (☎ 210-226-4381), 220 N Broadway,

which is between Pecan and Travis Sts, where cleanish singles and doubles without bath run from $22.94/34.44, with bath $29.90/36.80, plus a $2 key deposit. (If Sally Struthers tries to get into your room, block the door.) It accepts all major credit cards, and the establishment is a member of the Better Business Bureau of all things.

Marginally nicer is the *Alpha Hotel* (☎ 210-223-7644), 325 N Main Ave, which at first looks like a dive with ratty hallways festooned with armchairs. But the management is very friendly and the rooms – singles/doubles are $30.75/35.75 year-round – are clean and comfortable, if very worn.

Motels are the best bet when staying in San Antonio, and there are a fair number of good deals to be had right downtown. In greater San Antonio, budget places run from about $35 to $60 per night; downtown places run higher.

There are several Super 8 Motels in the city, all of which are clean, comfortable and relatively cheap, with free coffee and donuts in the morning. The downtown *Super 8 Motel* (☎ 210-222-8833, fax 210-354-2882), 1614 N St Mary's St, has singles and doubles for $49 to $59 and $54 to $69. There are two northern SA entries; the *Super 8 Motel* (☎ 210-227-8888, fax 210-224-2092), at 3617 N I-35, has rooms for $41, and the *Super 8 Motel* (☎ /fax 210-637-1033), 11027 N I-35, has singles and doubles for $35 to $47 and $39 to $50. Slightly flashier than the norm, the *Super 8 Motel Sea World* (☎ 210-520-0888, fax 210-520-8852), 5336 Wurzbach Rd, offers singles/doubles for $46/52, and the *Super 8 Motel Six Flags Fiesta Texas* (☎ 210-696-6916, fax 210-696-4321), at 5319 Casa Bella at W I-10, has singles and doubles from $40 to $45 and $44 to $49.

A great deal that's just east of downtown is the *Red Roof Inn San Antonio Downtown* (☎ 210-229-9973, fax 210-229-9975), at 1011 E Houston St just east of I-37, which is brand-spanking new, totally spotless and has huge standard singles/doubles for $56/61 or king-size singles/doubles for $60/65. There's an itty-bitty pool in front.

Nearby, the *Downtowner Hotel* (☎ 210-227-6233, fax 210-228-0901), on Starr St just where it shoots northeast from Houston St west of I-37, is owned and managed by the Days Inn across the street (see Places to Stay – Mid-Range). It's a better deal than the Days Inn, with clean rooms for $59, $79 during special events.

Silver Dollar Motel (☎ 210-826-3859, fax 210-826-3859), 1125 Austin Hwy near Broadway, has singles/doubles for $26/34.

Gay & Lesbian The *Villager Lodge Downtown* (☎ 210-222-9463, 800-584-0800), 1126 E Elmira St, has rooms for $34. It welcomes all and is a predominantly gay, lesbian and transgender establishment. The place turns into party central during Fiesta week (see Special Events earlier), when it becomes what seems to be the world headquarters for drag queens. Management donates rooms to HIV-positive people waiting for housing or treatment elsewhere.

Mid-Range San Antonio's mid-range options are essentially better-end motels and lower-end hotels, and often the former is more appealing than the latter. Mid-range offerings in the city run from around $60 to $100 per night.

There are several Ramada Inns in the city, the best of which is probably the *Ramada Emily Morgan Hotel* (☎ 210-225-8486, fax 210-225-7227), 705 E Houston right behind the Alamo, with clean and pretty large singles and doubles from $95 to $125 and $105 to $135. Other Ramada offerings include the *Ramada Inn Six Flags* (☎ 210-558-9070, fax 210-558-4604), 9447 W I-10, with singles and doubles for $59 to $69 and $69 to $89, and the *Ramada Limited* (☎ 210-229-1133, fax 210-229-1023), 1122 S Laredo St, with singles and doubles for $65 to $75 and $69 to $85.

The *Days Inn Alamo Riverwalk* (☎ 210-227-6233, fax 210-228-0901), 902 E Houston St, also runs the Downtowner Motel across the street (see Places to Stay – Budget); it has clean, cheerful rooms for $69, $89 during special events.

A decent place away from the lunacy of the exact center but within walking distance of all you need is the *Fairfield Inn by Marriott Market Square* (☎ 210-299-1000, 800-228-2800, fax 210-299-1030), 620 S Santa Rosa St, with rooms from $79. As nice but a little more expensive in the same area is the *La Quinta Market Square* (☎ 210-271-0001, fax 210-228-0663), 900 Dolorosa St, with singles and doubles from $92 to $97 and $92 to $107.

Two other good downtown options are the *Hampton Inn Riverwalk* (☎ 210-225-8500, fax 210-225-8526), 414 Bowie St, with rooms from $85 to $95, and the slightly overpriced-for-what-you-get *Rodeway Inn* (☎ 210-223-2951, fax 210-223-9064), at 900 N Main Ave, with rooms from $93 to $99.

Top End One of the flashiest places to stay, and perhaps the one with the best location (in the shadow of the Alamo), is the *Menger Hotel* (☎ 210-223-4361, 800-345-9285, fax 210-228-0022), 204 Alamo Plaza. Service is appropriately hushed, and the place is quite aware of its historical importance while managing not to be snooty. Built in 1859, it has long been the luxury standard-setter in town; Teddy Roosevelt hung out in the bar at the end of the 19th century (see Entertainment later for details). Rates are a lot less than they could be – singles start at $132, doubles at $142. Rooms are not as lavish as they could be but they're nice, spotless and homey, and there's a pool and gym. Ask for a room with a view.

The *Camberley Gunter Hotel* (☎ 210-227-3241, fax 210-227-9305), 205 E Houston St, is another fine old dame of a place with some deals that make it definitely worth checking out, like a regular $105-per-room deal when you can get it – they only have a couple at that price; singles are usually $110 to $130, doubles are $120 to $140.

The *St Anthony Wyndham Grand Heritage* (☎ 210-227-4392, 800-996-3426, fax 210-227-0915), 300 E Travis St, has that understated elegant look, tucked discreetly between Jefferson and Navarro Sts. Singles/doubles here run from $135/155.

Marriott River Walk (☎ 210-224-4555, 800-648-4462, fax 210-224-2754), 889 E Market, is a fine top-end option with rooms from $142 to $162.

Looking like an architect's rendering, the fantastically huge *Marriott Rivercenter*

(☎ 210-223-1000, fax 210-223-6239), 101 Bowie St, is a 1000-room superhotel opposite the convention center and the Rivercenter Mall. It's a small city of its own, with shops, restaurants, bars and cafés and rooms from $189 to $209.

Holiday Inn River Walk (☎ 210-224-2500, fax 210-223-1302), 217 N St Mary's St, is one of the best bets if you're going to stay along Riverwalk, with rooms from $126 to $150.

The *Four Points San Antonio Riverwalk North (☎ 210-223-9461, 800-288-3927, fax 210-223-9267)*, 110 Lexington Ave, is the latest incarnation of a hotel that's been up and down and now, under Sheraton management, is decidedly up again after a thorough renovation. Rooms here run from $139 to $149.

A perennial favorite in the center of the action is the posh *Adam's Mark River Walk (☎ 210-354-2800, 800-444-2326, fax 210-354-2700)*, 425 Soledad St, where plush rooms run from $175 to $200. There's a very nice bar here as well.

To say the luxurious *Havana Riverwalk Inn (☎ 210-222-2008, fax 210-222-2717)*, 1015 Navarro St, is fabulous is an understatement. It's a completely renovated hotel in a national historic landmark building dating to 1914. It aims to evoke 1920s San Antonio, and the rooms are furnished with what the owners term 'United Nations garage-sale chic' – antiques and bric-a-brac from a century of good flea markets. Rooms here (ask for one with a river view) average from $145 to $160 but go as high as $600, and the Club Cohiba is a big draw if you enjoy a good cigar – see Entertainment later.

Things are highly exclusive in the 30 or so rooms at the *Fairmount Hotel (☎ 210-224-8800, 800-996-3426, fax 210-475-0082)*, at 401 S Alamo St opposite HemisFair Park, and service is wonderful. There's a great bar and restaurant downstairs, Polo's (see Places to Eat and Entertainment); singles and doubles here run from $195 to $550 and $215 to $550.

La Mansion del Rio (☎ 210-225-2581, 800-292-7300, fax 210-226-0389), 112 College St, is another fabulous downtown property, with rooms running from $210 to $305.

The *Plaza San Antonio Marriott (☎ 210-229-1000, 800-727-3239, fax 210-223-6650)*, 555 S Alamo St, is a glitzy place at the south end of downtown just off of HemisFair Park. It's nice and all, but the rooms aren't quite up to their starting price of $209 – a nice bet in the same neighborhood is the Arbor House (see B&Bs), for a lot less money and a lot more personal service.

B&Bs The city has its fair share of B&Bs, and generally speaking they are good values, in fine old homes in the more historic areas of the city, especially the King William Historic District.

A very good deal if you're staying for a while is to do *Bed & Breakfast by the Month (☎ 210-271-9016, 800-209-7171)*, 320 Madison St, where clean and comfortable singles and doubles run from $495 to $579 and $569 to $789 per month. That works out to as little as $15.50 to $19 per day. Credit cards are not accepted.

We went back and forth about whether to list the *Arbor House Hotel (☎ 210-472-2005, 888-272-6700, fax 210-472-2007)*, 339 Presa St, as a hotel or a B&B, because it's got so much of the latter's character but the former's amenities. It's a charming, small hotel run by very friendly owners, and each room (there are three buildings, each with two or so rooms in the complex) is individually decorated and has a kitchenette. It's a really nice place, and the atmosphere is very laid back. Rooms run from $105 to $225.

Other B&Bs in town include the *A Classic Charm Bed & Breakfast (☎ 210-271-7171, 800-209-7171)*, 302 King William St, with rooms from $59 to $125, cheaper midweek and by the week; *A Victorian Lady Inn Bed & Breakfast (☎ 210-224-2524, 800-879-7116, fax 210-224-5123)*, 421 Howard St, with rooms from $79 to $135; and *Bed & Breakfast on the River (☎ 210-225-6333, 800-730-0019, fax 210-271-3992)*, at 129 Woodward Place, with rooms for $99 to $175.

Gay & Lesbian Most of the city's B&Bs are gay-friendly. The very charming *A Classic Charm Bed & Breakfast* and the *Arbor House Hotel* (see earlier) are all-welcoming and especially gay-friendly. The chic, woman-owned and predominantly lesbian (though all are welcome) *Painted Lady Guesthouse*

Brezhnev Fans Unite!

The *Hilton Palacio del Rio* (☎ 210-222-1400, fax 210-270-0761), at 200 S Alamo St, is the triumph of prefabricated, prefurnished design west of the Berlin Wall. The hotel was assembled in 1968 of 500 prefab cubes lifted into place by crane in a record 202 working days. Each 35-ton, 33-by-30-foot room unit was hoisted into place completely decorated – from the beds and curtains down to the ashtrays and bottle openers.

The building is as appealing as the average power plant in Severomorsk, Russia, but although it's easy today to scoff and look down one's nose, it's more fun to be amazed at just how groovy this place really is. And hell, most things that were really boss in the '60s – martinis, bare midriffs, velvet suits and lounge music – make comebacks sooner or later. And in the '60s, kids, this place was *boss*. Imagine the complexity – each steel-reinforced concrete unit was equipped with a Sikorsky helicopter tail unit (complete with stabilizing propeller and magnetic compass) that nudged and cajoled the unit to stay in place as the room was being lifted by the 350-horsepower crane.

Looking at the blight it creates on San Antonio's otherwise marvelous architectural backdrop, it's still hard not to crack jokes or make comparisons with other tasteless, American, mass-produced, prefabricated offerings (McSingles and McDoubles here run $196 to $244 and $217 to $265). But the hotel's interior has been recently and gloriously renovated, and Hilton is justifiably proud of its ugly duckling. The Stetson restaurant (see Places to Eat) doesn't mess around – service is definitely five-star, and there's a pool, sauna, health club and spa. It's well worth a visit.

(☎ 210-220-1092), 620 Broadway, has rooms from $79 to $189. Its upstairs balcony looks out onto Broadway and right out over the madness of Fiesta San Antonio (see Special Events earlier).

PLACES TO EAT

San Antonio is moving right up there with places to eat and has several claims to fame, including excellent Southern and American food and the best onion rings on the planet.

Fast Food

The *Pig Stand*, part of the chain that invented the drive-in restaurant in 1921, has three locations in town. All are open 24 hours, and the signature pig sandwich – barbecued pork and relish on a bun – is $3.65, or $4.75 with fries and a Coke; sandwiches run $2.50 to $4.50, burgers from $4.50 to $6.50 and steaks for less than $10. The coolest Pig Stand, which holds drive-in antique car shows every weekend, is at 1508 Broadway

(☎ 210-222-2794); others are at 801 S Presa St south of Durango St (☎ 210-225-1321) and 3054 Rigsby St (☎ 210-333-8231). All serve breakfast 24 hours, including breakfast tacos from $1, huge three-egg omelets from $4.25 to $5 and totally awesome cinnamon rolls.

A local family created the *Taco Cabana* chain, and its several locations around town, including an entry at 3310 San Pedro Ave at Hildebrand Ave north of downtown (☎ 210-733-9332), offer the best Mexican fast food you'll ever taste on either side of the border and make places such as Taco Bell look incredibly foolish. Tacos run from $1 to $1.50, quesadillas from $4.30 to $5.30, and the super Tex-Mex combo – more food than you can shake a stick at – is $5. It offers vegetarian versions of most offerings and also does breakfast from $2 to $4.

There's an upstairs dining room in the *Burger King* directly opposite the Alamo, where a window table provides a spectacular view of the Alamo.

Diners & Delis

Some of the best chicken-fried steak and onion rings in the known universe are at *De Wese's Tip Top Cafe* (☎ 210-732-0191), which has been at 2814 Fredericksburg Rd northwest of downtown off I-10 since 1938. The decor and the cooking haven't changed much at all, and customers almost always come back (even after they banned smoking). The colossal chicken-fried steak ($6) is enough to make you weep – not just for the tender beef or preternaturally crunchy coating, but also for the cream gravy on which it sits. The heaving plates of crunchy and enormous onion rings ($1.50) are just spectacular, as are most menu items, especially the chili enchiladas. Those and other lunch specials are around $5.50. There's more – freshly baked yeast rolls (only available after 3 pm) are heavenly, and pies (chocolate or banana meringue, chocolate, coconut or egg custard or apple) are good enough to fight over. It's all made here from scratch, and hey, don't sweat the cholesterol: take some solace in the fact that the rolls come with margarine, not butter (butter available on request). Keep children's hands and feet clear of your mouth.

A stop at *Schilo's Delicatessen* (☎ 210-223-6692), 428 E Commerce St, is a grand old tradition; it's one of the few truly great options along Riverwalk that has kept its traditional atmosphere – it's been there for 80 years. Specialties include wonderful split-pea soup ($2), but stuffed croissant sandwiches are terrific too, all about $4 (including a vegetarian option). Skip most dinner plates other than the wienerschnitzel or jaegerschnitzel, but if you're there when beef stew ($6 with fresh pumpernickel bread) is the daily special, stop what you're doing to eat it – it's extraordinary. It's also famous for its homemade root beer (85¢ for a frosted mugful and a refill) and for desserts. Get a strudel and a cheesecake and share both of them for a delicious treat.

The *Copper Kitchen* (☎ 210-224-0123), 300 Augusta St in the Southwest School of Arts and Crafts (see Other Museums earlier in the San Antonio section) does soups, salads and sandwiches and has daily lunch specials for less than $6.

Riverwalk Restaurants

Generally speaking, you go to Riverwalk for the atmosphere, not the food. All of the restaurants along the walk set up tables outside most of the year, and the view is truly lovely. The vast majority of the food has a Mexican or at least Tex-Mex theme, and all establishments serve large, multicolored and frozen cocktails. Our advice is to stick to those and appetizers, practicing the Tourist Trap Theory of Perpetual Motion – one drink and maybe a little something to nibble per stop. Most of the places, except Boudro's, do main courses from about $8 to $14, appetizers from about $4 to $9, beers are about $3 and frozen drinks are about $5.

Offerings along the walk include *Casa Rio* (☎ 210-225-6718), 430 Commerce St, SA's oldest Mexican restaurant; *Cafe Olé!* (☎ 210-223-2939), 521 Riverwalk; the upscale *Boudro's on Riverwalk* (☎ 210-224-8484), 421 E Commerce, which is hugely popular even with locals and pricier than the rest (main courses from $12 to $22 and appetizers from $4 to $9) – it's usually packed on weekends. Avoid at all costs the chili at the *Lone Star Cafe* (☎ 210-223-9374), 237 Losoya St, which is diabolical, though mashed potatoes are good and burgers are okay. The chili across the river at *Rio Rio Cantina* (☎ 210-226-8462), 421 E Commerce St is…well, at least it tries. It does far better on straight Mexican offerings, such as spinach and onion quesadillas.

The *Bayous* (☎ 210-223-6403), 517 N Presa St, is a decent seafood place offering several daily $4 lunch specials in addition to Cajun-leaning menu, which has main courses from $12 to $18. The major chains are all here too, including the *Hard Rock Cafe* (☎ 210-224-7625), at 111 W Crockett St, which sports a 23-foot-long Cadillac hearse hanging from the ceiling and surprisingly good burgers, BLTs and other sandwiches from $8 to $9 and chicken fajitas for $11. Not to be outdone, a gaggle of action figures opened *Planet Hollywood* (☎ 210-212-7827), right across the street at 245 E Commerce St – it's got the same stuff, but here it's served in a setting punctuated with photos of buff actors and movie paraphernalia such as the duster

Kevin Costner wore in the unforgettable classic, *Wyatt Earp*. Both the Hard Rock and Planet Hollywood are relentlessly crowded.

Right next to the Hard Rock Cafe is the *County Line Smokehouse* (☎ 210-229-1941), 111 W Crockett St, with pretty good barbecued ribs and brisket and a hugely tumultuous (and on weekends, meat-market) ambience. Steaks run $17, and a mixed barbecue platter with beef ribs, brisket and sausage is $11.

American

What could be finer than two superb American places – *Josephine Street* (☎ 210-224-6169), 400 E Josephine St, and *Liberty Bar* (☎ 210-227-1187), 328 E Josephine St (bus No 516 from downtown) – right next to each other? The two, in creaking Victorian houses (Liberty Bar's walls are so crooked it seems as if the place is sliding downhill), offer tremendous bang for the buck. Josephine Street serves up an incredible 12oz blackened sirloin steak ($10), or steak and grilled shrimp for the same price, and on Tuesday all dishes more than $7.50 are discounted by $2. Liberty Bar consistently has super everything in addition to lots of vegetarian options, and most main courses are less than $10, though the glorious crabcakes are $13.50. Try the geranium cream cheese: rich, sweetened Creole cream cheese mixed with edible geraniums, drizzled with raspberry-lemon sauce and served with homemade shortbread cookies. Josephine St is off US 281, north of downtown just a few blocks north of where I-35 and Hwy 35 meet US 281.

A reliably good hot spot of the moment is *Blue Star Brewing Company* (☎ 210-212-5506), inside the Blue Star Art Complex at 1414 S Alamo St; see that listing under Art Galleries.

One of the most justifiably praised restaurants in town is *Restaurant Biga* (☎ 210-225-0722), in a Victorian house at 206 E Locust St north of downtown off McCullough Ave, run by Bruce Auden, formerly the chef at Polo's at the Fairmount (see later). The menu is a wonderful mix of European, Tex-Mex, American and Asian influences that probably don't cost as much as they should (certainly not what they could). Starters

include Biga smoked-salmon nachos with chipotle cheese; escabeche (pickled) veggies and capers for $9; black-bean and white-cheddar soup with pumpkin, cilantro and crème fraîche for $5; and Texas escargot in garlic-port sauce for $8. Main courses run $15 to $25 and include oak-smoked pheasant on sherried wild rice ($19), south Texas fallow deer rubbed with 11 spices, and quail on white-cheddar grits with huckleberry-rosemary sauce ($25).

Polo's at the Fairmount (☎ 210-224-8800), in the Fairmount Hotel at 401 S Alamo St, offers a great cigar-friendly bar, and the elegant atmosphere and shushed (and good) service reveals that the place is as expensive as you think, with main courses (like pan-seared Colorado trout with sautéed scallops in tequila butter for $23) running from $23 to $45. It's a good deal less expensive at lunch, when it also serves gourmet pizzas from $10.

Mexican

El Milagrito (☎ 210-734-8964), 521 Woodlawn Ave north of downtown, has cheap and consistently great food, the lardiest beans in the world and truly great soft tacos. Fill up at breakfast for $2.10, which would include a taco loco with extra bacon and an egg and bean tortilla; full plates with side dishes are about $5, and all are good. Bus No 8 from downtown stops right there.

El Mirador (☎ 210-225-9444), located at 722 S St Mary's St, does so-so breakfasts but dependably good lunches and dinners. The main reason for you to come here and why so many others do, is Sopa Azteca Saturday, when from 6 am it serves up portions of justifiably famous Sopa Azteca, a heavenly chicken-and-vegetable soup ($6). People line up out the door for it.

Three doors north of the Alpha Hotel (see Places to Stay) is the *Chapala Mexican Restaurant*, a little dive of a place that has good, cheap breakfasts, such as chorizo and eggs for 65¢, bacon and one egg for $1, and lunch specials from $3.75 including iced tea.

Market Square has a food court that's not half bad, with lots of kiosks selling Mexican snacks and food for pretty cheap, and if you think music's good for the digestion, you're in luck: mariachi bands and Mexican guitar players constantly make the rounds. *La Margarita* (☎ 210-227-7140), at 120 Produce Row, is a serviceable Mexican place in Market Square with a bar and an oyster bar; it features main courses from $8 to $15, or you could order the prix-fixe parrillada estilo la Margarita, with chicken, beef fajitas, ribs, sausage and cheese for $25 for two people and $45 for four.

Southern, Tex-Mex & Steak Houses

A good weekday lunchtime deal is the $5 buffet at the restaurant inside the *Ramada Inn Emily Morgan Hotel* (☎ 210-225-8486), 705 E Houston St, which changes its cuisine daily, from Mexican to barbecue to Cajun to Tex-Mex.

The *Guenther House* (☎ 210-227-1061), 205 E Guenther St (see the listing in the King William Historic District earlier), does dependable southern and Tex-Mex specialties for breakfast and lunch. It's open Monday to Saturday 7 am to 3 pm, Sunday 8 am to 2 pm, and it serves breakfast all day: the Guenther's favorite is two biscuits with country sausage or homemade preserves, fresh fruit and bacon and eggs for $6.75, or $5.50 without the eggs. At lunchtime daily specials are $6.50, and the fave, champagne chicken enchiladas with salad and fruit, is $6.75.

The *Barn Door* (☎ 210-824-0116), at 8400 N New Braunfels near Loop 410 north of downtown, is a popular local steak house in a cavernous barn of a place with good service, steaks and appetizers. Steaks run from $10, appetizers are $4 to $10.

Right downtown, almost on Riverwalk, is the *Little Rhein Steak House* (☎ 210-225-2111), in the small stone building at 231 S Alamo St with a really nice outdoor sitting area. This place is very popular and for a carnage fest of flesh, you could do a lot worse – it serves solidly dependable steaks, lamb and pork from $17 to $28.

And for insatiable carnivores with deep pockets, there's always the local *Ruth's Chris Steak House* (☎ 210-821-5051), Concord Plaza, 7720 Jones Maltsberger Rd at US 281

near Loop 410, inconveniently located but serving respectably great steaks and shrimp; appetizers (try the barbecued shrimp) run from $8 to $9, steaks from $24 for a standard filet to $55 for porterhouse for two. There's a free shuttle service from downtown – call ahead and it'll pick you up.

Barbecue

There aren't that many exceptional barbecue places in San Antonio, but there are a lot of barbecue places. The easiest places are the *County Line Smokehouse* (☎ 210-229-1941), 111 W Crockett St, which has standard fare for the chain place, or one of the several *Bill Miller BBQ* outlets in SA, including one that is diagonally opposite the Greyhound bus station at 501 St Mary's St (☎ 210-212-4343) – a good thing while you're waiting.

Bob's Smokehouse (☎ 210-344-8401), 1219 S St Mary's St south of downtown, a converted gas station that someone spent about $12 converting into a south Texas barbecue joint, has greasy lamb ribs and good brisket, all on paper plates. *Carranza's* (☎ 210-223-0903), 701 Austin St north of downtown off Cherry St, gets consistent recommendations from locals.

European

Almost next door to El Milagrito (see Mexican) north of downtown is *Cafe Camille* (☎ 210-735-2307), 517 E Woodlawn Ave, a lovely, Mediterranean-looking place with a sweet courtyard – perfect for a date. It has upmarket French-inspired and American offerings, with dinner's main courses running $9 to $15; there's live music on Friday evening.

Pardo's Restaurant & Bar (☎ 210-228-9999) 700 N St Mary's St, is an exceptionally good value at lunch, despite the Russian-airport ambience. It has nice service and fine food, like portabella mushrooms marinated in red wine and grilled with orzo, onions and garlic and served over wild rice ($6); pecan-crusted chicken breast with magnificent grilled veggies ($6.75) and tequila shrimp with linguine ($7). At dinner the main courses get a bit more elaborate, as do the prices, from $12 to $17, except when it's free – see the boxed text.

Free Dinner

One Wednesday per month, Pardo's Restaurant & Bar decides to give away food. It works like this: go in and order and eat as you normally would; no one will tell you until you've asked for the bill. If you're lucky enough to have picked the right Wednesday, the check will arrive charging you only for fish of the day, steaks or alcohol – everything else is free.

Asian

Gin's (☎ 210-684-7008), 5337 Glen Ridge Mall, No 105, northwest of town, would do much better if it were more convenient – you need a car. If you've got one, take Loop 410 to the Evers St exit, turn right on Evers St and right again into the mall; look for the Chinese restaurant out of central casting: red walls, golden dragons and snappy service. Eat lunch for $3.50 (pepper steak, chicken with broccoli or other special dishes). Prices are just a bit higher at dinnertime. Wonderful appetizers like crab Rangoon (cream cheese, crab and spices in deep-fried bow noodles; six for $2.50) or amazing potsticker pork dumplings (steamed then pan-fried dumplings served with a rice vinegar, soy and ginger sauce) that are sold in batches of 20 (yes, 20) for $6 or 25 for $7.50.

Across the street from De Wese's Tip Top Cafe (see earlier) is **Lan's Indochine Restaurant** (☎ 210-734-4017), 2901 Fredericksburg Rd, whose Thai owner cooks up good Thai and okay Vietnamese food. The lunch specials (including vegetarian or beef lemongrass with rice and a spring roll) run from $4 to $5; dinners are from $5 to $9.

Thai Taste (☎ 210-520-6800), at 5520 NW Evers Rd in northwest San Antonio has an enormous menu of Thai and Chinese dishes from $5 to $11, and if you want the kitchen to, it'll do your meal *really* spicy.

ENTERTAINMENT

There's a lively entertainment scene in San Antonio, and although the live-music scene

in the city isn't quite as jumping as in Austin, it ain't like in Kansas, either. Check the *Current* or Jim Beal's 'Night Lights' column in the Weekender section of the *Express-News* for upcoming concerts. Both the *Current* and the *Express-News* also have comprehensive listings of art exhibitions and openings, visiting road shows, theater, classical music and cinema. For gay and lesbian activities, check the *Texas Triangle*, a free statewide monthly available at gay bars, restaurants and gay- and lesbian-friendly businesses.

Theater

The **San Pedro Playhouse** (☎ 210-733-7258), in San Pedro Park at Ashby south of downtown (bus No 3 or No 4 from downtown), is the performance venue for the nonprofit San Antonio Little Theatre, which stages several shows a year, usually classics, with seats at $16 and $20. It's also home to the SALT Cellar Theatre, a 60-seat venue that holds scaled-down and experimental works.

The **Alamo Street Theatre** (☎ 210-271-7791), 1150 S Alamo St in a restored former church, has two playhouses. Performances here focus on works by Texas playwrights; some are dinner theater ($25 to $28) while others hold the food ($12 and $15). Special events throughout the year, such as holiday buffet brunches and a New Year's Eve ball, also happen here.

Classical Music

The **San Antonio Symphony** (☎ 210-554-1010, www.sasymphony.org), 222 E Houston St, performs a wide range of classical concerts, operas and ballets at the spectacular Majestic Theater (☎ 210-226-3333), 226 Houston St, which is also host to performances by visiting groups and artists throughout the year. Tickets (which range wildly but start at about $12) can be bought from the symphony, the Majestic box office or from Ticketmaster outlets (there's one at 1 HemisFair Plaza Way, ☎ 210-224-9600). The San Antonio Symphony also performs at Trinity University's **Laurie Auditorium** (☎ 210-736-7011).

The **Alamo City Men's Chorale** (☎ 210-495-7464) is a group of about 60 gay singers who perform a large repertoire of classics, pops, spirituals and new works, sometimes alongside the San Antonio Symphony and more often on its own at various venues.

Rock & Blues

The Strip North of downtown along N St Mary's St, the Strip is a very vibrant music and bar scene that's at the center of the university student's universe. The live-music venues here feature lots of local bands, and they're good places to start the search for live music in San Antonio. Venues along the Strip include *Salute* (☎ 210-732-5307), 2801 N St Mary's St; *N St Mary's Brewing Co* (☎ 210-737-6255), at 2734 N St Mary's St; *Joey's 2417* (☎ 210-733-9573), at 2417 N St Mary's St; and *Tycoon Flats* (☎ 210-737-1929), 2926 N St Mary's St.

Downtown There's regularly scheduled live rock and blues at a number of downtown venues, including the 111 W Crockett St group on the south bank of Riverwalk – the *Hard Rock Cafe* (☎ 210-224-7625) has occasional live bands; there are dueling pianos at *Howl At The Moon*; the *County Line Smokehouse* (☎ 210-229-1941) also has occasional music; and *Fat Tuesday's* (☎ 210-212-7886) is also located here. Another live-music venue downtown is *Acapulco Sam's* (☎ 210-212-7367), 212 College St, on the 2nd and 3rd floors.

Live blues and rock acts play Friday night at the *Houston St Alehouse* (☎ 210-354-4694), 420 E Houston St, with no cover charge. The place is a pretty good local bar, hangout and cigar bar as well, open daily from noon to 2 am.

Tequila Mockingbird (☎ 210-226-2473), 245 E Commerce St underneath Planet Hollywood, has a tequila-laden bar with live blues, rock and rockabilly every weekend in a frat-boy-goes-upmarket atmosphere.

Greater San Antonio There's a surprising amount of rock, blues and acoustic music on weekends at the cafes in the two local *Borders Books, Music & Cafe*; see Bookstores in the Information section for information. *Wings* (☎ 210-366-9464), 4904 West Ave, has local blues bands, as do the *Laboratory Brewing*

Company (see Swing); the *San Antonio Infirmary* (☎ 210-342-1796), 1711 Babcock Rd northwest of downtown near Loop 410 (bus No 90 or No 522 from downtown); and the *Grill On the Hill* (☎ 210-614-8855), 7920 Fredericksburg Rd also northwest of downtown (bus No 91 from downtown). N San Pedro Ave runs into Fredericksburg Rd.

Out of town, there's live music in the city of Gruene (pronounced 'green'; see Around San Antonio).

Tejano & Conjunto

The *Cibolo Creek Country Club* (☎ 210-651-6652), 8640 E Evans Rd (no bus service), is a rather bizarre dance hall way northeast of downtown SA, past Loop 1604 near the intersection of E Evans Rd and FM 2252 (Nagocdoches Rd). Every month it plays host to a wonderfully eclectic music calendar of Tejano, rock, disco, zydeco, blues and pretty much anything else you can think of in addition to special events, live radio broadcasts and the occasional formal ball.

There are two well-known spots in town for conjunto music, *Lerma's Night Club* (☎ 210-732-0477), 1602 N Zarzamora St north of downtown and west of I-10 off Culebra Rd, and the *Royal Palace Ballroom* (☎ 210-924-5651), 3506 SW Military Drive southwest of downtown off I-35. Others include *Hacienda Salas Party House* (☎ 210-923-1879), 3127 Mission Rd near E White Ave a bit north of the San José mission; *Casas Night Club* (☎ 210-433-4101), 3239 W Commerce St; and the *Fiesta Club* (☎ 210-923-0151), 1112 Pleasanton Rd, which hits Flores Rd south of downtown.

Jazz

A San Antonio tradition is jazz at the *Landing Jazz Club* (☎ 210-223-7266), on the Riverwalk level at the Hyatt Regency Hotel. The seven-piece Jim Cullum Jazz Band plays Monday to Saturday at 8:30 pm, and local jazz group Small World plays on Sunday night on the outside patio. Live duos play daily on the outdoor riverside patio noon to 1 am. About two dozen Cullum performances per year are broadcast live on Public Radio International and rebroadcast locally on KSTX 89.1 FM. Tickets are free, but reserve them way in advance.

There's music blaring away nightly at *Dick's Last Resort* (☎ 210-224-0026), at 406 Navarro St, with a whole range of offerings, from Dixieland jazz to soul, blues and rock.

Right downtown at the corner of Commerce and Presa Sts is the *Vault* (☎ 210-475-0031), 314 E Commerce St, a slick cigar and martini bar with a nightly happy hour from 4 to 9 pm.

Other venues include the club in the *Adam's River Walk* (☎ 210-354-2800), at 425 Soledad St; the occasional tinkling piano in *Swig Martini Bar* (☎ 210-476-0005), at 111 W Crockett St; and the constant tinkling piano in *Polo's at the Fairmount* (☎ 210-224-8800), 401 S Alamo St.

Swing Swing has made a comeback in the SA area, and there's usually some swing or swing-inspired live music happening at the *Laboratory Brewing Company* (☎ 210-824-1997), 7310 Jones Maltsberger Rd north of downtown off US 281. It also hosts a mix of other shows that is not quite as eclectic as the lineup at Cibolo Creek (see earlier), but it's getting up there. Can't dance to swing? No sweat – Four on the Floor (☎ 210-828-5304) holds beginner and more advanced swing-dance classes Sunday at 6 and 7 pm at the Laboratory and also teaches the lindy hop at 2 pm on the fourth Saturday of the month at the *Treehouse Dance Studio*, 304 Norwood Rd; call Four on the Floor for prices and directions to the studio.

Bars

A classic San Antonio favorite is the *Esquire* (☎ 210-222-2521), 155 E Commerce St, with what's billed as the longest bar in Texas (and the most odiferous toilets on earth). It's a gas and a blast, with a Tejano and college-student crowd all taking advantage of really cheap cocktails and beer and comfortable booths. There's waiter service in the booths – if he gets around to it. A stop here is highly recommended.

The bar at the *Menger Hotel* (see Places to Stay) is a great summer- or rainy-day bar – dark, woody, serious but laid-back. It's

modeled on the British House of Lords and was a hangout of Teddy Roosevelt back in his Rough Rider days.

The cigar-friendly bar at *Polo's at the Fairmount* (see Top End in Places to Stay) is a very chic place to have a martini or a good whiskey, with live piano music and attentive service.

Dance Clubs

These things change as often as you'd expect; check with the usual sources when you come for the flavor of the week. A relatively long-term tenant has been the *Bonham Exchange* (☎ 210-271-3811), 411 Bonham St right behind the Alamo, which has a mixed, predominantly gay crowd (except on 'straight' Wednesday nights) as SA's largest dance club. It's in a Victorian mansion with five bars, three huge dance floors and laser and light shows – it's definitely a scene. A fun young straight and gay crowd mixes at the renovated *Cameo Theatre* (☎ 210-226-7055), at 1123 E Commerce St, which has 17-and-older nights held on the first Wednesday of each month. There's a decent Latin scene at *Tejano Junction* (☎ 210-737-2344), 1818 N Main Ave north of downtown near San Antonio College.

Gay & Lesbian The *Eagle Mountain Saloon* (☎ 210-733-1516), at 1902 McCollough Ave near San Antonio College, is exclusively gay and rather upmarket, with an enormously long bar. A trendy lesbian bar is *Petticoat Junction* (☎ 210-737-2344), at 1818 N Main Ave.

Comedy

There's nightly comedy featuring major headliners and up-and-coming local comedians at the *Rivercenter Comedy Club* (☎ 210-229-1420), on the third level of the Rivercenter Mall. Saturday at 3:30 pm is the local amateur hour, when there's no cover charge. There are also comedy performances from visiting headliners at venues like the Majestic Theater and Laurie Auditorium on the Trinity campus; check in the *Current* or the *Express-News*' Weekender section for more information.

SOUTH CENTRAL TEXAS

If you get a traffic ticket (an easy thing to do with the speed traps at the city's entrances – see the boxed text) and need to go to defensive driving school to have it quashed from your record, try the *Comedy Defensive Driving School* (☎ 210-223-8669), at 2267 NW Military Drive in the Winston Hills Shopping Center, which runs classes daily.

Readings

Cabeza de Piedra Art Studio (☎ 210-271-3777), 527 El Paso St southwest of downtown near the intersection of I-10 and Guadalupe, has poetry readings on occasion; call for information. There are also regular poetry readings at Borders Books, Music & Cafe and Barnes & Noble – see Bookstores under Information.

Cinema

There are plenty of googolplex cinemas in San Antonio, including a convenient one right in the Rivercenter Mall, where first-run films are $7 for adults and $4.50 for children. Check in the Weekend section of the *Express-News* for cinemas and showtimes.

IMAX *San Antonio IMAX At Rivercenter* (☎ 210-225-4629), 217 Alamo Plaza in the Rivercenter Mall, plays several movies in the IMAX (IMage MAXimum) format – if you've never seen a film on a 6-story-high screen in 6-track surround sound, it's worth the admission price ($7.25 for adults, $4.75 for children three to 11 years old) just for the experience. Films shown here include the 45-minute film *Alamo: the Price of Freedom*, about guess what, as well as *Mystery of the Maya* and *Everest*.

Gay & Lesbian *Out of the Closet: Cinema!* is held every Friday evening at the *Gay and Lesbian Community Center of San Antonio* (☎ 210-732-4300), 3126 N St Mary's St near Brackenridge Park. It screens a wide range of films.

SPECTATOR SPORTS

The big news in town is the San Antonio Spurs (☎ 210-554-7773, 210-554-7787), who play professional basketball at the Alamodome.

Regardless of the Spurs' performance, San Antonians are simply psychotic in their support of the team, and games are exciting, action-packed spectacles. Tickets can be bought at the box office on the southwest corner of the Alamodome Monday to Friday 8:30 am to 5:30 pm. Prices range from $10 to $24, depending on where you sit, and there is more expensive box seating as well.

There's pari-mutuel horse racing at Retama Park (☎ 210-651-7000), in northeast San Antonio, north of Loop 1604 on I-35 exit 174A. Admission to races, which are held daily year-round, is $2.50.

SHOPPING

Don't overlook the museum gift shops; some of them – especially the one at the San Antonio Museum of Art – are exceptional.

Clothing

Ropa Usada on Navarro St, just north of Market St, is a great used-clothing store, with lots of stuff for cheap. To get fashionably macabre, head for Selena Etc (☎ 210-826-2796), 3703 Broadway north of downtown (bus No 9 from downtown), a memorial to the murdered Tejana singer (see the boxed text in the Gulf Coast chapter) that also sells T-shirts and other clothing and has a hairdressing salon on the premises.

The two top sellers of Western gear in town are musts for those on a serious quest to get rigged out cowboy-style. Lucchese (☎ 210-828-9419), 255 E Basse St, hand-makes cowboy boots shaped specifically for your feet – a better fit is hard to find. It has ready-made items, jewelry and accessories, too. If you'd just as soon not drop $550 on a pair of boots though, head for Sheplers (☎ 210-681-8230), 6201 NW Loop 410, next to the Ingram Park Mall (see Malls), a Western-wear chain.

Paris Hatters (☎ 210-223-3453), 119 Broadway, like Lucchese, has been around a long, long time, and is one of the best places in the state to get a Stetson (or any other brand of cowboy hat).

If you're just desperate and forgot to get gifts, there are two opportunities at the airport to get Texas stuff; in Terminal One is a Texas Flowers and Wines shop, and in Terminal Two, the Texas Products Store, with wine, overpriced clothes and cowboy hats and other Texan items. See Getting There & Away later for airport details.

Botanicas
Papa Jim's Botanica (☎ 210-922-6665), 5630 S Flores St (bus No 44 from downtown), is a religious and Santeria superstore, selling items like Door-Evil stopper; Court-Case and Do-As-I-Say floor wash; Law: Stay Away candles; and Stop-Gossip soap, all for less than $3.50 per piece. Papa Jim also has books, incense, good-luck charms, other Santeria-related items and a card reader ($10 per reading). It's open Monday to Friday 9 am to 6 pm, until 5 pm on Saturday.

Infinito Botanica (☎ 210-224-5350), 1526 S Flores St downtown, is a much more commercial place with folk art as well as potions.

Mexican Stuff
Market Square (see earlier in the San Antonio section under Other Things to See) really does have a good selection of authentic Mexican goods at reasonable prices for the USA. Mexican records and CDs are available at the Spanish-English Record Shop on the south side of Houston St just east of Laredo St.

Malls
Rivercenter Mall (☎ 210-225-0000), the easiest mall to access in town, isn't bad at all, and because of the cinemas, IMAX theater, comedy club, restaurants and dozens of shops, you'll probably end up here at some point in your stay. It's at 849 E Commerce St at Bowie St.

The chic North Star Mall (☎ 210-340-6627), Loop 410 at San Pedro Ave, is north of downtown (bus No 3, No 4 or No 5 from downtown), houses the usual places, such as Saks Fifth Avenue, the Sharper Image, Macy's and the Disney Store.

Two other major shopping malls in the city are the Crossroads of San Antonio (☎ 210-735-9107), 4522 Fredericksburg Rd, and the Ingram Park Mall (☎ 210-684-9571), northwest of town at Loop 410 and Ingram Rd.

Magic
Why magic is so big in SA is beyond us, but there are two great magic-supply stores in town that sell a combination of legitimate magic tricks, novelties, practical jokes and other junk. The most convenient is World of Magic & Fun (☎ 210-475-9309), at 105 N Alamo St, Suite 511, opposite the post office on the 5th floor of the Gibbs Building. The well-stocked but profoundly depressing Fun 'n' Magic Co (☎ 210-226-0690) is at 520 Broadway.

GETTING THERE & AWAY
Air
San Antonio International Airport (☎ 210-821-3450) is about 10 miles north of downtown, just north of the intersection of Loop 410 and US 281. It's served by taxis, public transportation and shuttles; see Getting Around for more information.

USA San Antonio offers frequent flights to destinations in Texas and the USA from the following airlines. Some connecting services from AeroLitoral (see next section) connect San Antonio with Phoenix, Arizona.

American	☎ 800-433-7300
America West	☎ 800-235-9292
Delta	☎ 800-221-1212
Northwest-KLM	☎ 800-225-2525
Southwest	☎ 800-435-9792
United	☎ 800-241-6522

Mexico AeroLitoral (☎ 800-237-6639), runs daily flights between San Antonio and Monterrey, with connecting flights from there throughout Mexico. There is also direct or connecting service to Mexico with Continental (☎ 800-525-0280), Aeromar (☎ 210-829-7482), American and AmericaWest.

Train
Amtrak *Sunset Limited* and *Texas Eagle* trains arrive at the beautiful Southern Pacific Railroad depot (☎ 210-223-3226), 224 Hoefgen St. Prices vary wildly; call Amtrak on ☎ 800-872-7245, or visit www.amtrak .com, for more information.

Speed Traps

There are speed traps and cops waiting for you at the outer city limits on every interstate heading into San Antonio. This is particularly nasty because at the outer city limits the speed limit drops from 70mph to 55mph to 50mph, and tickets are quite expensive – as in they start at more than $100 and can get pricey soon after. Obey the signs and slow it down!

Car

San Antonio radiates from the convergences of I-35, I-10 and I-37. The transcontinental interstate for the southern USA is I-10, and it runs from Florida through Louisiana to California, passing through much of Texas. I-35 runs from the north and Dallas-Fort Worth through Waco and Austin and south to Laredo, where you can cross into Mexico and pick up Mexican Hwy 85 south to Monterrey or Mexican Hwy 2 running northwest to Piedras Negras – though if that's your destination you're better off taking I-35 south to Hwy 57 west to Eagle Pass.

I-37 runs between San Antonio and Corpus Christi on the Gulf of Mexico. For the Texas Hill Country, the best route is US 281, which is the northbound continuation of I-37 from San Antonio.

Bus

Greyhound (☎ 210-270-5824), and Kerrville Bus Co (☎ 210-227-5669), share a terminal at 500 N St Mary's St between Martin and Pecan Sts, a five minute walk from the heart of downtown. Greyhound services from San Antonio include:

to/from	frequency (per day)	trip duration	one way/ roundtrip
Austin	14	1½ hours	$12/24
Dallas	16	5 to 9 hours	$34/63
Galveston	4	5½ to 8 hours	$47/93
Houston	10	3¼ hours	$19/38
New Orleans	8	11 to 15 hours	$53/102

GETTING AROUND
To/From the Airport

Airport shuttles (75¢) run about every 45 minutes at peak times, less frequently at other times (check with the ground-transportation desk), between the airport and downtown. Star Shuttle Services (☎ 210-341-6000) also run shuttle buses to downtown for $6 per person, for more to other destinations. Many of the larger downtown hotels have free shuttle buses, so be sure to check. A taxi ride to downtown costs between $13 and $18 for up to four people.

Car-rental agencies in the airport include Advantage, Alamo, Avis, Budget, Dollar, Hertz and National. See the introductory Getting There & Away chapter for more information on major rental outlets.

Bus

VIA Metropolitan Transit (☎ 210-362-2000; route information ☎ 210-227-2020) is San Antonio's public bus network, which operates more than 100 regular bus routes, plus five San Antonio downtown streetcar routes that circle the downtown area. Its downtown information center, 112 Soledad St (between Houston and Commerce Sts), is open Monday to Friday 7 am to 7 pm and Saturday 9 am to 2 pm. VIA passes and bus schedules are available there. The visitor information center opposite the Alamo also carries VIA schedules.

Local bus fares are 75¢ (5¢ for a transfer), and exact change is required. Express buses, which use interstate highways and include buses to theme parks, are $1.50. You can buy a $2 Day Tripper Pass for unlimited rides for one day on all VIA buses or streetcars.

VIA also operates year-round express routes from the downtown area to Sea World and Six Flags Fiesta Texas.

Streetcar

The VIA Historic Streetcar (☎ 210-362-2020), with a downtown information center at 112 Soledad St, operates four streetcar routes throughout downtown daily. The fare is 50¢ for adults (discounts available for children and seniors) or $5 for the month. Streetcars run to and from Market Square, HemisFair Park, Cattleman Square, and the King William Historic District. There are stops throughout downtown and at several hotels including the Plaza San Antonio, Camberly Gunter, Red Roof, Ramada Emily Morgan and Crockett Hotels.

Car

San Antonio is a nightmare for drivers, and parking is no treat either. While driving, pay close attention to the street and highway signs, especially when they indicate a left-hand exit – miss an exit in San Antonio and you're in for the nickel tour of the surrounding suburbs.

Loop 410, the outer loop road, is your fallback position; although in itself not very user-friendly, it will always bring you back to where you were when you started, even if it's an hour later.

I-10, which usually runs east-west, runs north-south in most of San Antonio; directions to take I-10 west from downtown to Six Flags Fiesta Texas (which is almost due north of downtown) are accurate. Watch out for the confluence of I-37, I-10, US 281 and US 90 – US 90 and I-37 end at that point.

With similar jocularity, downtown has a complex system of one-way streets, as well as streets that change direction at will and at once. There are public parking lots throughout downtown and at most of the major hotels. Use these lots or face the relentless ticketing agents who will ticket and tow in the time it takes to suck down a chili dog. Or better yet, park at the southern end of downtown, or leave the car somewhere else – like Waco.

Taxi

Taxi stands are at most major downtown hotels, the Greyhound and Amtrak stations and the airport. In all other circumstances you'll need to telephone for one. Taxi rates are $2.90 at flagfall, $1.30 for each additional mile. Companies include Checker Cab (☎ 210-222-2151), Yellow Cab (☎ 210-226-4242), Alamo City (☎ 210-475-9828), Downtown (☎ 210-523-0600) and Fiesta (☎ 210-666-6666).

Bicycle

The friendly folks at Mission Trail Bike Rentals (☎ 210-805-8937) rent mountain bikes, including maps, helmets and locks, for $19.50 per day and will deliver bikes free to any address in San Antonio. With the bicycle also come maps and information about local bike trails, including a self-guided tour along the Mission Trail.

AROUND SAN ANTONIO

The area directly north of San Antonio is known primarily as a haven for shoppers who stream in by the hundreds of thousands to the unbelievably cheap factory-outlet malls that line I-35 in the cities of San Marcos and New Braunfels. The shopping is definitely something every traveler should put on their itinerary, especially if you're coming from Europe – prices are extraordinary.

East of the city, the towns of Luling and Shiner are both interesting day trips.

Natural Bridge Caverns

One of the state's largest underground formations, this national landmark cave (☎ 210-651-6101) is about halfway between San Antonio and New Braunfels on Hwy 3009, west of I-35.

Its name comes from the 60-foot natural limestone bridge that spans the entrance, but inside (where it's always 70°F) are simply phenomenal formations, including the **Watchtower**, a 50-foot pedestal that looks like a crystallized flower. You can only see the caverns as part of guided tours, which leave every half hour from 9 am to 6 pm in summer, until 4 pm at other times. The caverns are open daily except Thanksgiving, Christmas and New Year's Day. Admission is $9 for adults, $6 for children. Attached is the Natural Caverns Wildlife Park, a small zoo with rare animals.

New Braunfels

Population 33,906

This little town has a couple of fine attractions, including a water park and a good museum, and it's worth stopping in town if you're around for the annual Wurstfest (sausage festival) on November 1 and 2.

Perhaps the best part of a visit here is rafting or tubing down the icy Guadalupe River.

Hummel Museum It's too bad the porcelain figurines fashioned after the works of Sister Maria Innocentia Hummel (1909-1946) are the only impression many get of her work. As cheesy as the figures are, the paintings on which they're based are quite marvelous. The museum (☎ 830-625-5636), 199 Main Plaza, is packed with the nun's works, many depicting angelic children. It also includes the disturbing *Stations of the Cross* series of 14 sketches. The museum is open Monday to Saturday 10 am to 5 pm, Sunday noon to 5 pm; admission is $5 for adults, $4.50 for seniors and $3 for students.

Alamo Classic Car Museum This newly enlarged museum (☎ 830-620-4387), just south of town off I-35 between exits 180 and 182, houses a private car collection of more than 150 cars and trucks. It's open weekdays 9 am to 5 pm, and admission is $5 for men, $4 for women.

Landa Park At Garden Street and Union Avenue, Landa Park gives access to the headwaters of the teeny but very fun **Comal River**, which merges with the Guadalupe River nearby. It's a favorite tubing spot, and the **Chute** in Prince Solms Park lets you fly down rapids into the Comal.

The Rockin' 'R' River Rides (☎ 830-629-9999, 800-553-5628) in Gruene (see later) rents tubes for $9.50 without bottoms and $10.50 with them and provides a shuttle service for trips upriver (north toward Canyon Lake) or downriver. From New Braunfels, take Hwy 46 west for 2.3 miles from I-35, turn right onto Gruene Rd, and it's about a mile ahead on the right-hand side of the road.

Schlitterbahn The Schlitterbahn (☎ 830-625-2351) is Texas' largest water park, with about 30 different slides and water pools all using water from the Comal – it's great fun. Adult all-day passes are $23.45, kids three to 11 years old pay $19.25. The admission includes parking, inner tubes and life vests.

You can bring your own food, but no glass or alcohol.

From I-35 going north, take exit 189 to Loop 337; turn west on 337, left on Common St and then right on Liberty St and look for the huge castle.

The park is open daily 10 am to either 6 pm or 8 pm from May to September, with weekend hours only in April.

Factory Stores The New Braunfels Factory Stores (☎ 830-620-6806), off I-35, is one of the area's factory outlet malls, open Monday to Saturday 9 am to 8 pm, until 6 pm on Sunday.

Gruene

Pronounced 'green,' this historic little shopping center...er, town, just four miles northeast of New Braunfels is choc-a-bloc with antiques and crafts shops (Old Gruene Market Day is held the third weekend of every month), but it's best known for Texas' oldest dance hall, *Gruene Hall* (☎ 830-606-1281), 1281 Gruene Rd. There's no air-con, but it's got cold beer and great bands. It's so packed every Friday and Saturday, with live music on other nights, too, that it's considered a local San Antonio club.

San Marcos
Population 38,700

While practically every one of the tens of thousands who come through here daily are heading to the factory outlet malls (maybe the best around), San Marcos also is home to Southwest Texas State University's Aquarena Center; Wonder World, Texas' most visited cave; and some charming historic districts. The San Marcos Convention and Visitor's Bureau (☎ 512-396-2495) has lots of brochures and information on the city's burgeoning B&B industry.

Factory Outlets There are more than 100 name-brand outlets (American Tourister to Calvin Klein, Coach to Eddie Bauer and Gap Outlet to Waterford, Wedgwood and a Sony superstore, to name a very few) within the unbelievably large **Prime Outlet at San Marcos** complex (☎ 512-396-2200, 800-628-9465), exit 200 off I-35. The complex is open year-round Monday to Saturday 10 am to 9 pm, Sunday 11 am to 6 pm. Nearby, the similarly gargantuan **Tanger Outlet Center** (☎ 800-408-8424) has about the same offerings. Both places' shops offer at least 30% off retail prices, sometimes up to as much as 70% off – new jeans for $15 is commonplace.

Aquarena Center This historic park (☎ 512-245-7575), owned by Southwest Texas State University, is home to exhibitions on Spanish missions, pioneer houses and archaeology and offers glass-bottom boat tours of San Marcos Springs. It's open daily 9:30 am to 6:30 pm; admission is free to the grounds, buildings and aquarium. As we went to press the park was closed for renovation to fix flood damage. When it's open, hourlong glass-bottom boat tours start at 10 am (last tour at 5:30 pm) and cost $5 for adults, $4 for seniors and $3 for kids four to 15 years old.

Wonder World A minitheme park built around the USA's largest earthquake-created cave, Wonder World (☎ 512-392-3760, 800-782-7653) is the most visited cave in Texas. Take a tour through the **Balcones Fault Line Cave**, where you can look at the Edwards aquifer up close and personal; outside, in the 110-foot **Tejas Observation Tower**, you can actually make out the fault line. Other attractions include a petting park filled with Texas animals, a train ride around the park and the bizarre **Anti-Gravity House**. We don't recommend a visit if you have a hangover.

Guided tours lasting 1½ hours leave every 15 minutes in summertime and every 30 minutes in wintertime; combination tickets are $14 for adults, $12 for seniors and $10 for children four to 11 years old (children younger than four are free). Tickets to the cave only are $10 for adults and $7.50 for children; for the train ride through the wildlife park all tickets are $5. Tickets for the Tejas Observation Tower and the Anti-Gravity House are each $3. There is free parking and a picnic area on the grounds. From I-35, exit at Wonder World Drive and follow the signs.

Guadalupe River State Park

This exceptionally beautiful state park (☎ 830-438-2656) in Spring Branch, 30 miles north of San Antonio, straddles a 9-mile stretch of the sparkling clear, bald cypress tree-lined Guadalupe River and is great for canoeing and tubing. There are also 3 miles of hiking trails through the park's almost 2000 acres.

Two-hour guided tours of the geology, flora and fauna of the nearby Honey Creek State Natural Area are included in the price of admission. Tours leave from the Guadalupe ranger station Saturdays at 9 am. There are picnic areas along the river. Admission is $4 per person, $2 for children 12 and younger.

Tent sites with water only are $12, and RV sites with water and electricity are $15 with an additional $3 admission fee per person.

By car from San Antonio, take US 281 north to Hwy 46, and turn west (left) for 8 miles.

Luling
Population 5000

Luling trumpets that it's the 'crossroads to everywhere.' When you consider that it's home to the famous annual Luling Watermelon Thump (covered in *People* magazine and the *New York Times)* and twice-holder of the world watermelon seed-spitting championship as documented in the *Guinness*

Book of World Records, the town may have a claim indeed. The Thump, a fruit-growing contest complete with a queen, takes place the last Thursday to Saturday of June.

Luling was founded as the western end of the Sunset branch of the Southern Pacific Railroad in 1874, and in 1922 oil was discovered beneath it. Pretty much the only reason to stop here these days as you whiz through on the way to Shiner is to see the **Central Texas Oil Patch Museum**, which is a keeping-house for Luling's history and heritage in the Walker Bldg at 421 E Davis St. Patrons to the museum are designated Oil Baron, Wildcatter, Driller, Roughneck and Roustabout, depending on the size of the donation. For information on the museum (open by appointment) or the city's antiques shops, stop into the friendly Luling Area Chamber of Commerce (☎ 830-875-3214), in the same building.

Getting There & Away Greyhound buses leave San Antonio three times per day, at 7:45 and 11:30 am and 4:15 pm. The trip lasts 1¼ hours and costs $12 one-way, $24 round-trip. Greyhound also sends buses to Luling from Austin at 11:45 am – the trip takes 45 minutes, and is $9 one-way, $18 roundtrip. Luling is on US 183 where it meets Hwy 80, just north of I-10.

Shiner
Population 2075
The self-proclaimed 'cleanest little city in Texas,' Shiner was founded as a trade center for German and Czech settlers. Today the town is best known as the home of the Spoetzl Brewery (pronounced 'SHPET-zul'), manufacturers of Texas' best-selling bock beer, Shiner Bock. It makes a nice day trip from San Antonio – or even from Austin.

Spoetzl Brewery The highlight of any trip to Shiner is a free, 45-minute tour of the brewery (☎ 512-594-3383), 603 E Brewery St, which run Monday to Friday at 11 am and 1:30 pm, with extra tours at 10:30 am and 2:30 pm in summer. The Czech and German founders of the brewery began making beer under brewmaster Kosmos Spoetzl, and

today they produce several types using the same methods, including blonde, bock, honey wheat and Kosmos Reserve. You can sample the beers free after the tour in the little bar. There's a cool gift shop opposite the bar, too.

Other Things to See & Do Don't miss the historic **Sts Cyril & Methodius Church** (☎ 512-594-3836), 306 S Ave F (1891), which has very impressive stained-glass windows with Czech and German inscriptions and the Holy Water Cooler. Services are held Saturday at 5 pm, Sunday at 6:30, 8 and 10 am. The **Kaspar Wire Works** (☎ 512-594-3327), N US 95, is the largest employer in town – they make the wire racks for *USA Today* stands. Tours are by appointment only.

Places to Stay & Eat *The Old Kaspar House B&B (☎ 512-594-4336)*, 219 Ave C at 3rd St, has three properties: the Victorian House, with rooms from $49 to $79; the Honeymoon Cottage, a newly renovated place with a Jacuzzi and king-size canopy bed for $99; and Marenka's Cottage, as country as you can stand it with singles/doubles at $65/85. All include a full breakfast.

Don't miss **Werner's** *(☎ 512-594-2928)*, 317 N Ave E, with great decor – note the stuffed moose – and lunch specials from $8 and a salad bar for $5.

Getting There & Away There's Greyhound service from San Antonio once a day at 11:30 am (two hours; $18 one-way, $36 roundtrip), returning at 4:30 pm. There's a bus from Austin daily at 11:45 am (1¼ hours; $15 one-way, $30 roundtrip), also returning at 4:30 pm. By car from San Antonio, take I-10 to US 95 and go south right to the very doors of Spoetzl Brewery. From Austin, take US 183 south through Luling to Gonzales, then turn east on US 90A, which brings you right into the center of town. Cross the railroad tracks and make a left turn on US 95.

VICTORIA
Population 56,000
Victoria has more than 100 historic homes near its downtown. Many have been restored by owners drawn to deeply shaded,

oak-lined streets. Pick up the self-guiding brochure 'A Tour of Old Victoria' from the Victoria Convention and Visitors Bureau (☎ 512-573-5277), 700 Main St. The office has quite a bit of information, including a cheerful free regional map with the motto 'Happy to help you find your way around!' It's open Monday to Friday 8:30 am to 5 pm. The granite and limestone Old Victoria County Courthouse, 101 N Bridge St at Constitution, dates from 1892, when towns took pride in such places. The interior, including a carefully restored courtroom, is open Monday to Friday 8 am to 5 pm.

The town is at the junction of US 77 and US 59 and is 120 miles south of Houston and 100 miles north of Corpus Christi. It is a good place to spend the night while exploring the historical parks in Goliad, 25 miles to the south on US 59.

The *American Inn* (☎ 512-575-8244), just north of downtown at 204 E Rio Grande Ave (Business US 59), has very basic accommodations; singles/doubles are $30/35. *Fairfield Inn by Marriott* (☎ 512-582-0660), at 7502 N Navarro St (US 77) at Loop 463, is close to shopping and has basic rooms for $57/63. Nearby, the *La Quinta Victoria* (☎ 512-572-3585), 7603 N Navarro St, has comfortable rooms for $65 to $75. Close to downtown, the *Friendly Oaks Bed and Breakfast* (☎ 512-575-0000), 210 E Juan Linn St, is a 1915 wooden home. Owners Bill and CeeBee McLeod will give you touring advice for other historic homes in the neighborhood. Rooms cost from $55 to $75.

Every kind of franchised fast-food eatery imaginable lines N Navarro St (US 77) from downtown past Loop 463. Local choices include *Jimmy John's Cajun Cookhouse* (☎ 512-573-1552), 13861 N US 77, about 8 miles north of downtown, a fun seafood joint ($7 to $10 a person) unless you're a crawfish. *Tejas Cafe & Bar* (☎ 512-572-9433), at 2902 N Navarro St, has spicy Mexican food for around $5 and a good selection of beer.

GOLIAD
Population 1900
'Remember the Alamo!' is the verbal icon of the Texas revolution, but it should also be

'Remember Goliad!' where, on Palm Sunday, March 27, 1836, Mexican general Antonio López de Santa Anna ordered 350 Texian prisoners shot. The death toll was double that at the Alamo and helped inspire the Texians in their victory over Santa Anna at San Jacinto the following month (see the Alamo in the San Antonio section earlier in this chapter for more information).

Goliad is home to other historical sights and makes for a good daylong excursion into Texas history. The Goliad Chamber of Commerce (☎ 512-645-3563), at the corner of Market and Franklin Sts on Courthouse Square, has information and a walking tour brochure for the town. It's open from Monday to Friday 9 am to noon and 1 to 5 pm and some weekend days. Call first or try stopping by. In the same building, the chamber of commerce operates the small Market House Museum, which has the same hours and contains a few artifacts not snatched up by the area's major sights.

The town and its sights are 25 miles off of US 77, which is the major highway along the coast. Take US 59 coming from the east and US 183 coming from the south.

Presidio La Bahia
Built in 1749 by the Spanish to deter the French who were sniffing around the eastern edges of their empire, the presidio played a role in six revolutions and wars. It even played a role in the American Revolution, when soldiers garrisoned here were sent to assist the British.

Texas revolutionaries seized the fort in October 1835. The following year, Colonel Fannin and his men were held by the Mexican forces inside the walls for two weeks before their execution. A plaque mounted outside the chapel doors reads 'Here fell the men in martyred death to gain the freedom and independence of Texas; and here for centuries generations of men will gather in reverence and appreciation of La Bahia's glorious past.'

Ironically, despite the bluster of the sign, it was a woman's reverence that is responsible for the fort being kept in its excellent condition. Kathryn O'Connor funded the presidio's restoration in the 1960s and laid the groundwork for the private society of primarily women that operate it today.

The presidio is considered one of the best-preserved Spanish colonial forts in the world. Its walls enclose a large parade ground as well as officers' quarters and a chapel where services are held in the simple interior at 5 pm on Sunday. The museum is staffed by volunteers, who may at times be a bit addled, but they are very charming nonetheless. The museum is open daily from 9 am to 4:45 pm. Admission is $3 for adults and $1 for children. It is 1 mile south of US 59 on US 183. You can retrace the last walk of the doomed Texians by driving 1 mile further south to a memorial site where they are buried.

Goliad State Historic Park

Established in 1749, the Misión Santo de Zuñiga has a less bloody history than the presidio just down the road. It now stands as the focal point of this state park (☎ 512-645-3405) which has quiet hiking trails, a petting zoo with well-fed goats and a pool that's open in summer.

The mission buildings have been restored, and there is a good museum in the old school and workshop building that shows what life was like in the mission during the 110 years it functioned. Displays in the museum show how the Indians who lived here made pottery, fabrics and other items of day-to-day life. A highlight of the large church is the Door of Death, which is complete with skull and crossbones.

The park office is open 8 am to 5 pm daily. Entrance fees are $2 per person. There are several camping areas, including several along the Antonio River. Fees are $4 for tent sites, $8 for sites with electricity and $12 for RV sites with full hookups. The park is a quarter-mile south of US 59 on US 183.

Historic Goliad

Courthouse Square, in the center of Goliad has – surprise! – a grand old 1894 courthouse. Among the many stately oaks on the square is one labeled the 'Hanging Tree,' for self-explanatory reasons. A historical marker recalls the Regulators, who were the 50 vigilantes who during 1868 to 1870 'pursued criminals with vigor and often with cruelty.' One of the most violent incidents in Goliad's history occurred as recently as 1976, when 100 longhorn steers taking part in a Bicentennial parade stampeded. The event has become an excuse for an annual party each June.

Places to Stay & Eat

The *Antlers Inn* (☎ 512-645-8215), at 1013 W Pearl Ave (US 59), has basic singles/doubles for $35/40. The *Dial House* (☎ 512-645-3366), 306 W Oak St, is a charming B&B with gourmet breakfasts and rooms for $65. On the square, *Empresario Restaurant* (☎ 512-645-2347), 141 S Courthouse Square, is the classic sort of lunch place you would expect on a square like this – right down to the homemade pie.

CHOKE CANYON STATE PARK

This is a state park divided into two sections – the South Shore Unit (☎ 512-786-3538) and the Calliham Unit (☎ 512-786-3868), both on 26,000-acre Choke Canyon Reservoir. Access to the North Shore Area is for groups of eight or more only; get permits at the South Shore Unit office.

Both units have camping, boating, a total of almost 4 miles of hiking trails and, in the Calliham Unit, a lake beach and summer swimming pool, gym, dining hall and screened shelters.

The 1700-acre North Shore Area has 18 miles of hiking and equestrian trails as well as developed and primitive campsites and boat ramps.

There are almost 200 bird species found in the park; ranger-led birding tours on a huge golf cart leave regularly. The park is open daily 5 am to 10 pm for day use. Admission is $3 per person, children 12 and younger are free.

Places to Stay

Primitive camping tent sites are $5 per night, $10 with water and electricity. Shelters are $14 plus the admission fee and can be reserved by calling ☎ 512-389-8900.

Getting There & Away

The South Shore Unit (☎ 512-786-3538) is 3½ miles west, and the Calliham Unit (☎ 512-786-3868) is 12 miles west of Three Rivers on US 72. Three Rivers is 55 miles west of Goliad and 60 miles south of San Antonio.

KINGSVILLE
Population 26,000

King is the name of the game in this company town that is the direct result of the fabled 825,000-acre King Ranch, the largest of its kind in the world. Former riverboat captain Richard King established the ranch in 1853 on land that others saw as a scrub-covered semidesert. King instead saw the area as scrub-covered semidesert that had the only natural springs north of Brownsville. Today the ranch is bigger than Rhode Island, a state that the ranch's fences would reach if they were laid end to end.

The town has a surprisingly vibrant downtown that has actually continued to function without having to be stuffed with antiques shops like so many other Texas towns. Local residents still do their daily shopping downtown, and when supermarket giant HEB wanted to build a new superstore on the edge of town, the residents persuaded the chain to locate it downtown.

Kingsville's big attractions are mostly ranch-related, except for the **John E Conner Museum** (☎ 512-593-2819), on the campus of Texas A&M University-Kingsville, at Santa Gertrudis and Armstrong Sts. Local history back to the dinosaurs is brought to the present with displays that concentrate on the multicultural heritage of the area. It's open Monday to Saturday 9 am to 5 pm; admission is free.

Kingsville is on US 77 and makes a good stop on a drive between Corpus Christi and the Rio Grande Valley.

King Ranch

Because of its size, much of the King Ranch (☎ 512-592-8055) is not open to the public. However, daily tours visit parts of the working ranch, which fully lives up to every stereotypical image of a large Texas ranch. There

are working cowboys on horseback, bulls lazily grazing in the huge pastures and the lavish main buildings, some still with guard towers built in the 1800s, when raids from Mexico were common.

A large visitors' center is open Monday to Saturday 9 am to 4 pm and Sunday noon to 5 pm. Tours in air-con buses depart whenever there is a full load, but one always departs one hour after the center opens. Guides for the 90-minute tours are either retired employees or relatives of the more than 500 people who work on the ranch. The tours cost $7 for adults, $2.50 for children. Tours are suspended for two weeks every May, when the 100 King family descendants return from their homes around the world for an annual meeting to discuss business.

Housed in a renovated ice-storage house downtown, the **King Ranch Museum** covers the history of the ranch. Among the highlights are the specially designed 1949 Buick hunting car complete with bar and a series of photos by Toni Frissell showing life on the ranch in the 1940s. It's open Monday to Saturday 10 am to 4 pm and Sunday 1 to 5 pm. Admission is $4 for adults, $2.50 for children with discounts for packages that include ranch tours. The visitors' center is just inside the rather modest entrance to the ranch on the west side of Kingsville on Santa Gertrudis St.

The **King Ranch Saddle Shop** (☎ 800-282-5464), 201 E Kleberg Ave, is in a 1906 brick building and has everything from custom-made saddles ($1250 and up) and luggage ($195 and up) to golf shirts ($28). All come with the distinctive King Ranch logo that looks like a squiggly snake.

Places to Eat

The *Wild Olive* (named for the husband of a King daughter; ☎ 512-595-4992), in the Sellers Market at 205 E Kleberg Ave, is famous for its millionaire's pie, made with several fruits. It's open for lunch Wednesday to Friday. The name says *Young's Pizza* (☎ 512-592-9179), 625 Santa Gertrudis St, but sandwiches are king. The Texicali ($5 for a 'large') is huge and dripping with grilled steak, mushrooms, onions and jalapeño

Look Before You Step

Among the facts you'll learn on a tour of the King Ranch are the following:

- The first rule of the range is: look before you step. That's not just because of all the cows around but also because you might anger a poisonous snake.

- When a prize horse dies, breeders usually just bury the head and the heart, to save on digging. Only especially prized animals get the full-body treatment.

- Young thoroughbreds are stabled with donkeys whose stoicism and stubbornness calm the skittish horses.

- Those bovine Texas icons – longhorn cattle – were bred to be tough beasts that could make thousand-mile drives to market in the time before railroads. In modern ranching, their very toughness makes them a tough chew for consumers.

- The first beef breed ever produced in the US was the Santa Gertrudis at the King Ranch. It combines Brahman cattle from India with British shorthorns.

- A special fence wire on the ranch was developed to replace barbed wire, which caused cuts and wounds vulnerable to attacks from the dreaded screwworm.

- Many of the cowboys are the sixth-generation descendants of Mexicans who moved to the ranch in the 1850s. King bought cattle from a drought-stricken village, and realizing the people were starving, offered to move them to his new ranch.

- Nobody knows the origins of the famous logo – the Running W – it may have been a used brand the captain picked up cheap.

Ryan Ver Berkmoes

peppers (ask for extra). The legendary *King's Inn* (☎ 512-297-5265), 24 miles southeast of Kingsville, regularly wins polls as one of the most popular restaurants in the state. Vast platters of fresh seafood are served family-style; delicacies include fried shrimp ($19) and fried oysters ($10). Get the onion rings and avocado salad and make no plans for a few hours. It's open Tuesday to Sunday 11 am to 10 pm. Take US 77 15 miles south from Kingsville, then go east 9 miles on FM 628 until you reach Loyola Beach and the restaurant. Be sure to make reservations in advance for dinner.

Houston

Population 1.7 million

Although Houston surpassed Philadelphia in the 1990 census to claim the title of the fourth-largest city in the US, the numbers are deceiving. When metropolitan regions – the groups of cities that form one urban area – are ranked, Houston and its surrounding towns fall to 10th place overall, behind such places with relatively small core cities as San Francisco, Boston and (horrors!) Dallas.

Houston dominates its region thanks to a historic commitment to growth unfettered by zoning and other planning restrictions. The result is that there are several 'downtown' areas in addition to the traditional center. The city's third-tallest building, the 64-story Transco Tower, is 6 miles west of downtown in the Galleria Mall area.

Visitors and residents alike find Houston to be a confusing sprawl. However, most of the areas of interest lie in the 6 miles between the Galleria Mall and downtown. Seeing the sights won't take more than a day or two, and many people make Houston a day-trip from one of the pleasant Gulf Coast cities. However, if you stay in the city longer you'll be able to sample the scores of restaurants, bars and clubs enjoyed by Houston's generally young and ebullient population.

HISTORY

The most important two words in Houston's history are not 'oil' and 'cattle' – although they have been extremely important. Rather, the two words critical to the city's spectacular growth are 'air' and 'conditioning.'

In his 1979 book *The Right Stuff*, about the early days of the US space program, Tom Wolfe describes Houston as 'an unbelievably torrid effluvial swamp with a mass of mushy asphalt, known as Downtown, set in the middle.' And it was. And it still is.

Until the 1930s, Houston was a sleepy regional center with a population barely edging toward 100,000. Office workers grumpily plugged away at their desks in sweatshop conditions; laborers desperately sought out the shade. In July, when the *average* daytime temperature is a sweltering 94°F (34°C), work simply melted away as Houstonians fled north or to the Gulf Coast in search of mild breezes. For those too poor to travel, relief was as fleeting as an ice cube on a hot day.

But in the 1930s air-conditioning became available on a widespread basis. It was the breath of life Houston had been waiting for. Offices, stores, theaters, restaurants and other public spaces were quick to embrace

Highlights

- Hanging out in University Village and the Montrose and Upper Kirby districts

- Emerging into daylight from the mind-numbing downtown pedestrian tunnel system

- Relaxing at one of the scores of friendly outdoor bars

- Gazing at the *Saturn 5* rocket at the main NASA entrance

- Wandering Armand Bayou Nature Center in Pasadena

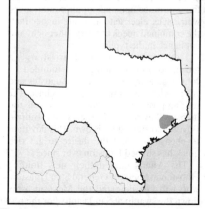

HOUSTON

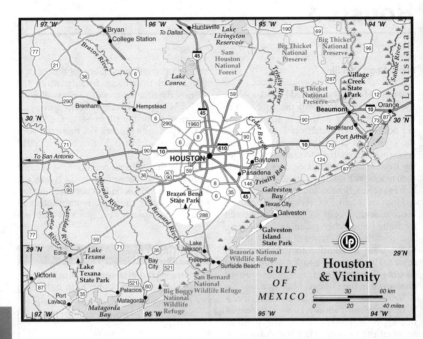

Houston & Vicinity

HOUSTON

the cool breezes. Homeowners weren't far behind, and today even the poorest shack sports one or more window air conditioners. By 1950 Houston's population had jumped to 600,000. By 1960 it had reached nearly 1,000,000 and has never looked back. Power-plant construction has barely kept pace with the enormous demands of air conditioners, which suck electricity at a rate higher than the combined needs of every other light and appliance in the typical home.

Houston started as Harrisburg, a mosquito-ridden trading post founded by John Harris in 1824. In 1836 Augustus and John Allen attempted to purchase the trading post but decided the price was too high, so they moved farther up the Buffalo Bayou and started their own. This devotion to cheap land and the desire to get rich quick has shaped Houston ever since.

The Allens named their new holding Houston in honor of General Sam Houston, who had just defeated the Mexican army down the swamp at San Jacinto. For the rest

of the century the city grew slowly, fed by the profits from cotton and the cattle trade. In 1901 the discovery of oil – the ultimate get-rich-quick scheme – in nearby Spindletop set the tone for Houston's future. By the 1970s oil was the foundation of the economy. Hundreds of firms involved in exploring, refining and selling the 'black gold' brought wealth to Houston. When oil reached $40 a barrel in 1981, Houston was awash in money as scores of happy Texans got rich quick. Four years later, the price of oil plummeted to single digits and Houstonians got poor quick in droves. Glitzy high-rises stood empty, their insides filled with cardboard walls so the sun wouldn't shine through the vacant floors.

In the 1990s Houston's economy diversified a bit into medical services and high-tech as the city rode the general economic boom that swept the country. Many Houston residents hail from the northern US, having moved to the area in the 1980s during the huge shift of jobs to the Sunbelt. They – like other Houstonians and probably you as well – can be glimpsed darting from their air-conditioned cars to their air-conditioned homes and offices and stores and everything else, unless of course they avail themselves of one of the many air-conditioned parking lots.

The bulk of the city's population is white. Hispanics and African Americans each make up about 25% of the population, and the Hispanic population is growing rapidly. In 1997, Houston elected its first black mayor, Lee Brown.

ORIENTATION

Houston's sprawl radiates from downtown in all directions. Much of the recent development is along the corridors of highways, including US 59 (the Southwest Freeway), I-45, I-10 and US 290. Within the city, the streets are laid out in a grid pattern that is fairly predictable. However, since most long-range city planning has been eschewed, you can be driving on a major thoroughfare that suddenly dead-ends in a subdivision.

Given Houston's size and lack of geographic definition – it's flat, flat, flat – a map is the best way to keep track of where you are. In fact, you may want to have a compass as well. Since office towers aren't just downtown, eyeballing a skyscraper won't help much. The closest thing the city has to an interesting landscape is along the Buffalo Bayou, west of downtown, where roads such as Memorial Drive follow the creek's sinuous path and the banks are a relatively stunning 20 feet high in places.

Houston's street names can be very confusing. Many have no official suffix such as St, Rd, Ave, Drive, etc. As a city planning official told us: 'You can call them what you want – we do.' Furthermore, there is no official boundary between north and south or east and west designations on streets, though people sometimes include those designations in addresses in reference to downtown. Thus you will see references to N Main St, Main St, S Main St, N Main, Main and S Main, and all are correct and are often used interchangeably. We have tried to use the street name favored by individual businesses in our listings.

General Sam Houston

Neighborhoods

Although Houston's development in recent years has favored faceless suburbs with generic names that always seem to include the word 'oak' and strip malls with vast parking lots, there are some older neighborhoods in the city with distinctive and interesting characteristics.

Downtown The original business center in Houston, the downtown area is a thicket of high-rises interspersed with parking lots. During the day the streets can seem surprisingly empty, with nary a pedestrian to be found braving the hot and shimmering sidewalks. But the people are there. In a variation on the postapocalyptic nightmare theme, most downtown buildings are linked by air-conditioned underground pedestrian tunnels with shops and restaurants. After dark, the area is sparsely populated above or below ground, although some life can be found around the major cultural centers. The nicest area is Sam Houston Park, with its collection of historic homes.

Montrose Centered at the intersection of Montrose and Westheimer Rd (see the Central Houston map), this area has a funky mix of shops, restaurants, galleries and tattoo parlors. It is the center of Houston's gay scene but not exclusively so.

HOUSTON

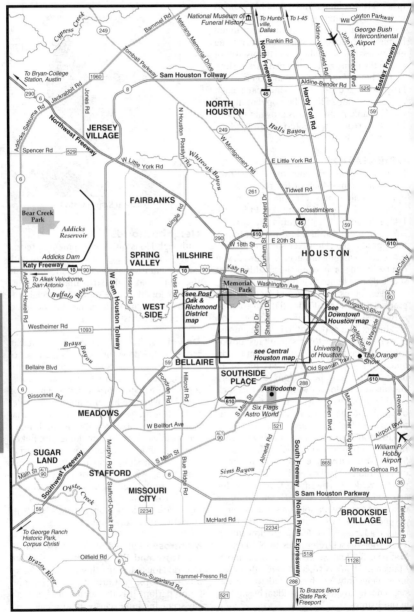

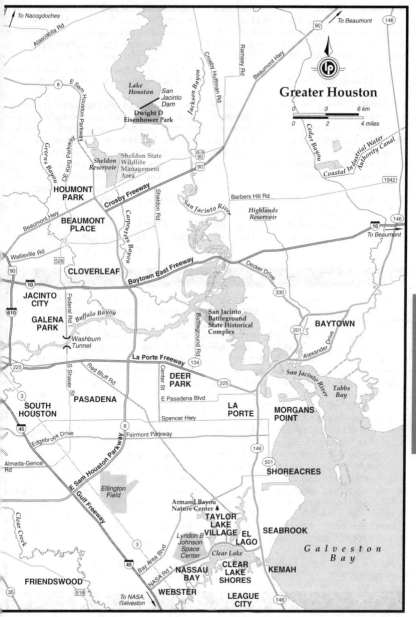

Greater Houston

Museum District The blocks northeast of Hermann Park are home to Houston's major museums. Old trees overhang the streets, and some of the city's grandest old homes are sheltered in the deep shade of the draping Spanish moss. Many restaurants and cafés line the streets.

University Village Several square blocks with more than 300 shops and nightspots west of Rice University are home to many locally owned businesses. One of the few parts of town best explored on foot, the 'Village' (also called Rice Village) can easily occupy an afternoon or evening.

Texas Medical Center The Texas Medical Center covers numerous square blocks just south of Rice University and Hermann Park (see the Central Houston map). The huge hospitals, clinics and other buildings are unattractive even by the usually low standards of medical architecture. Unless you or a loved one are seeking medical treatment, you'll be happier and healthier by avoiding this part of town, which is arrayed along Main St heading southwest of downtown.

Astrodome Not just a stadium but a neighborhood, the Astrodome and the surrounding malls and developments were the boom area of Houston in the 1960s (see the Greater Houston map). Sadly, the original developers spared no effort in cutting corners, and now, more than three decades later, development has moved elsewhere and the entire area is verging on the seedy.

River Oaks Home to Houston's old money (which means the folks have been in it for

Dome Alone

When completed in 1965, the Astrodome (☎ 713-799-9852) was proclaimed in typically modest Houston fashion 'the eighth wonder of the world.' Indeed the 66,000-seat, air-conditioned stadium was a marvel. If nothing else, it was a credit to developer Judge Roy Hofheinz, who got rich quick by using taxpayer money to finance much of the cost.

Originally the roof was translucent so grass would grow inside, but the glare proved blinding. So the dome was made opaque, and Astroturf – artificial grass – was invented, to the eternal delight of patio builders everywhere and the eternal lament of athletes, who are far more prone to injury when playing on bristly plastic stuff with a concrete base.

Houston's baseball Astros and football Oilers made the dome home for the next 25 years. Then, in the 1990s, trouble struck: the Oilers decamped to Tennessee and the Astros announced they would be moving to a new high-tech stadium downtown with real grass. Shorn of its two major tenants, the Astrodome now must make do with the annual Houston Livestock Show and Rodeo and events such as tractor pulls and demolition derbies.

Since the Astrodome was completed, much larger domes have been built in cities such as Seattle, New Orleans and Detroit. Like Houston, these cities are now trying to figure out what to do with these sterile structures, as professional teams opt for greener pastures elsewhere.

Critical opinion about the dome and its adjoining exhibition halls, motels and theme park has always been mixed. In 1974 an Italian writer had this to say about this latter-day coliseum: 'The whole thing far surpasses all current definitions of kitsch, obscenity and bad taste.' Conversely, the always upbeat Reverend Billy Graham said it signified 'the boundless imagination of man transformed into reality.'

The Astrodome is at Kirby Drive and I-610. Tours of the building depart Tuesday to Saturday at 11 am, 1 and 3 pm unless something big like the rodeo is on; $4 for adults, $3 for seniors and kids.

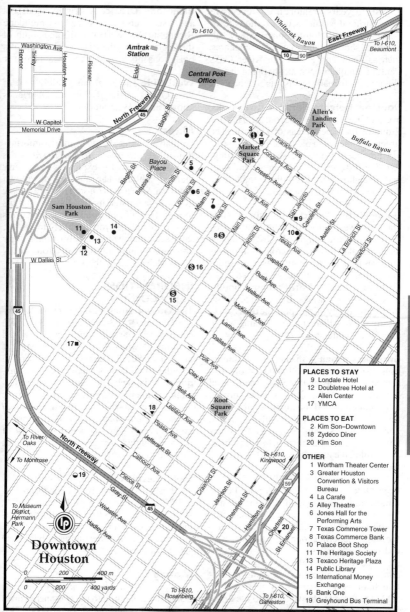

PLACES TO STAY
9 Londale Hotel
12 Doubletree Hotel at
   Allen Center
17 YMCA

PLACES TO EAT
2 Kim Son–Downtown
18 Zydeco Diner
20 Kim Son

OTHER
1 Wortham Theater Center
3 Greater Houston
   Convention & Visitors
   Bureau
4 La Carafe
5 Alley Theatre
6 Jones Hall for the
   Performing Arts
7 Texas Commerce Tower
8 Texas Commerce Bank
10 Palace Boot Shop
11 The Heritage Society
13 Texaco Heritage Plaza
14 Public Library
15 International Money
   Exchange
16 Bank One
19 Greyhound Bus Terminal

Downtown
Houston

0   200   400 m
0   200   400 yards

almost 20 years or more), this exclusive neighborhood is 3 miles west of downtown (see the Central Houston map). Many galleries and shops line the major thoroughfares, such as Gray and Kirby. The River Oaks Center is an older open-air shopping district that is home to many nightspots and theaters.

Houston Heights North of River Oaks, overlooking the Buffalo Bayou, the 'Heights' is one of the oldest areas of Houston. The streets are lined with old oaks, hundred-year-old homes and antique shops. The long-standing ordinance forbidding alcohol sales in this neighborhood keeps the Heights from developing much of a nightlife.

Upper Kirby District Just south of River Oaks and west of the Museum District (see the Central Houston map), 'UK,' as it calls itself, has taken inspiration from its initials as the basis for a British motif in its many shops and galleries. The theme is carried right down to the old red British phone booths that dot the sidewalks. Besides the retail, there are many nightspots here as well, mostly on Westheimer and Alabama where those streets intersect Kirby.

Greenway Plaza A thicket of 1980s high-rises just north of US 59 and east of I-610 composes Greenway Plaza (see the Central Houston map), home to various hotels, office buildings and the Summit – the arena for the Houston Rockets of the NBA. Unless you're staying at one of the many hotels, there is little reason to come here. Many think it could someday go the route of the Astrodome.

Post Oak The center for high-priced chain hotels, high-priced chain restaurants and high-priced chain stores, the Post Oak area is epitomized by – and often known for – the huge Galleria shopping mall. Just west of I-610 and 6 miles west of downtown, the area is so centered on the car – even for traveling between adjoining shopping malls – that hapless pedestrians trying to use an ATM are forced to brave traffic to use drive-through lanes.

Richmond District A strip of nightspots and restaurants strung along busy, multilane Richmond Ave west of I-610 and south of the Galleria Mall, the Richmond District is a boisterous mix of chains and local favorites.

West Side The area immediately west of Post Oak and the Richmond District is known as the West Side.

Maps

Available free at the main tourist information office, *Above & Below Downtown* is an essential tool for exploring the poorly marked subterranean maze of downtown Houston. *Streetwise Houston* ($5) is a widely available laminated map of the city that fits in a pocket. It has a good index and covers most of the places you are likely to go. The same sales racks will probably contain larger and more complete maps of Houston by Rand McNally and others.

INFORMATION
Tourist Offices

The Greater Houston Convention & Visitors Bureau (☎ 713-227-3100, 800-365-7575) has a brochure-stuffed office in a restored building downtown across from Market Square at 801 Congress Ave. It is open Monday to Friday 8:30 am to 5 pm. Information desks in the baggage areas of all the terminals at the two airports have more erratic hours. The quarterly magazine *Official Guide to Houston* is packed with information, although you'll notice that the list of 'Recommended Restaurants' corresponds to those that advertise.

Gay & Lesbian The Greater Houston Gay and Lesbian Chamber of Commerce (☎ 713-523-7576, www.ghglcc.org), PO Box 66129, Houston, TX 77266, has a wealth of information on gay and lesbian life in Houston. Another good resource on the web is http://gay-houston.com.

Money

Houston's myriad banks are open at least from 9 am to 4 pm, with many branches open later in the evening and on Saturdays. ATMs can be found in bank lobbies and drive-throughs, shopping centers, gas stations, convenience stores and many nightspots. Most are connected to ATM networks such as American Express, Cirrus, Discover, Master-Card, Plus and Visa. Beware of high access fees, which by law have to be disclosed before you get your cash.

Foreign-exchange brokers are more common in Houston than in other parts of the US owing to the large amount of international trade. Among them:

American Express
(☎ 713-626-5740) Galleria Mall,
5085 Westheimer Rd
(☎ 713-796-8200) Texas Medical Center,
6560 Fannin
Bank One
(☎ 713-751-6100) 910 Travis downtown
Barri Giros A Mexico
(☎ 713-981-7671) 8000 Bissonnet
International Money Exchange
(☎ 713-654-1900) 1130 Travis downtown
Texas Commerce Bank
(☎ 713-216-4865) 712 Main St downtown
Thomas Cook Currency Services
(☎ 713-782-8092) West Side near
Sam Houston Parkway, 10777 Westheimer Rd

Airport currency exchanges include:
George Bush Intercontinental Airport
(☎ 281-233-3864) International Arrivals Building
(☎ 281-233-3873) Terminal C
Hobby Airport
(☎ 713-641-2785) Concourse B

Post & Communications

Much of central Houston still uses the 713 area code. The outer areas, including George Bush Intercontinental Airport (IAH), have switched to 281. Additional area codes are expected to be added as the number of telecommunications devices proliferates.

Post The central post office (☎ 713-226-3066) is at the north edge of downtown near the Amtrak station at 401 Franklin. More handy branches include River Oaks (☎ 713-528-3366), 1900 W Gray; Galleria (☎ 713-622-0764), 5015 Westheimer Rd; and Greenbriar (☎ 713-528-2283), 3740 Greenbriar.

Internet Copy.com (☎ 713-528-1201), in the heart of the Montrose District at 1201 Westheimer Rd, has an Internet bar with ISDN connections where you can quaff your choice of joe while checking your email. It's open weekdays 7 am to midnight, Saturday 10 am to 10 pm, Sunday noon to 9 pm. They also have complete desktop publishing and copy services in case you feel compelled to get to work on the memoirs of your Texas vacation.

Media

Newspapers & Magazines The daily *Houston Chronicle* (50¢) is as sprawling and bland as its namesake city. Whole forests are consumed by its daily press run, with scores of sections and inserts. It does deserve credit for carrying possibly every syndicated comic strip in the universe. The *Houston Press* is the mainstream entertainment weekly, chock full of the futon store ads, coffeehouse come-ons and singles pleas you expect of the genre; it's free and available all over. *Public News* is also a free weekly, but it has a much sharper edge and the pages are dominated by ads for tattoo shops and the like.

Radio & TV The television stations are of the usual network lot found anywhere in the US, and the local news shows sadly have the same interchangeable Cindys and Rods that populate anchor desks everywhere. No Texas accents are heard on the news here.

Radio has a few bright spots. KPFT, 90.1 FM, has an unabashedly liberal slant to its news and talk that is almost unheard of – literally – on American radio. KUHF, 88.7 FM, carries the bare minimum of NPR programming (fans of *Fresh Air* are out of luck). KKHT, 106.9 FM, is hard-core evangelical Christian, with a string of talk shows aimed at hopeless sinners *just like you*! KTRH, 740 AM, has frequent news updates, traffic, weather and lots of home-improvement shows, during which people phone in with the kinds of horrifying pest infestations common to swampy areas.

Photography & Video

Film and videotapes are sold at pharmacies such as Walgreens and at most supermarkets.

HOUSTON

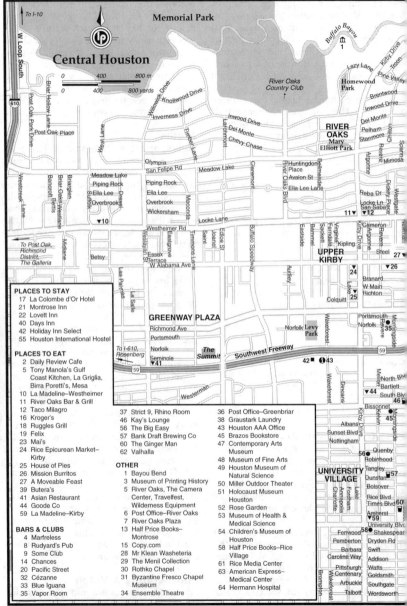

Central Houston

Memorial Park

To I-10

W Loop South

610

Buffalo Bayou

Kirby Drive

River Oaks
Country Club

Homewood
Park

RIVER
OAKS
Mary
Elliott Park

UPPER
KIRBY

GREENWAY PLAZA

The Summit

Southwest Freeway

UNIVERSITY
VILLAGE

PLACES TO STAY
17 La Colombe d'Or Hotel
21 Montrose Inn
22 Lovett Inn
40 Days Inn
42 Holiday Inn Select
55 Houston International Hostel

PLACES TO EAT
2   Daily Review Cafe
5   Tony Manola's Gulf
    Coast Kitchen, La Griglia,
    Birra Poretti's, Mesa
10 La Madeline–Westheimer
11 River Oaks Bar & Grill
12 Taco Milagro
16 Kroger's
18 Ruggles Grill
19 Felix
23 Mai's
24 Rice Epicurean Market–
    Kirby
25 House of Pies
26 Mission Burritos
27 A Moveable Feast
39 Butera's
41 Asian Restaurant
44 Goode Co
59 La Madeline–Kirby

BARS & CLUBS
4   Marfreless
8   Rudyard's Pub
9   Some Club
20 Chances
32 Pacific Street
32 Cézanne
33 Blue Iguana
35 Vapor Room

37 Strict 9, Rhino Room
46 Kay's Lounge
56 The Big Easy
57 Bank Draft Brewing Co
60 The Ginger Man
62 Valhalla

OTHER
1   Bayou Bend
3   Museum of Printing History
5   River Oaks, The Camera
    Center, Travelfest,
    Wilderness Equipment
6   Post Office–River Oaks
7   River Oaks Plaza
13 Half Price Books–
    Montrose
15 Copy.com
28 Mr Klean Washeteria
29 The Menil Collection
30 Rothko Chapel
31 Byzantine Fresco Chapel
    Museum
34 Ensemble Theatre

36 Post Office–Greenbriar
38 Graustark Laundry
43 Houston AAA Office
45 Brazos Bookstore
47 Contemporary Arts
    Museum
48 Museum of Fine Arts
49 Houston Museum of
    Natural Science
50 Miller Outdoor Theater
51 Holocaust Museum
    Houston
52 Rose Garden
53 Museum of Health &
    Medical Science
54 Children's Museum of
    Houston
58 Half Price Books–Rice
    Village
61 Rice Media Center
63 American Express–
    Medical Center
64 Hermann Hospital

HOUSTON

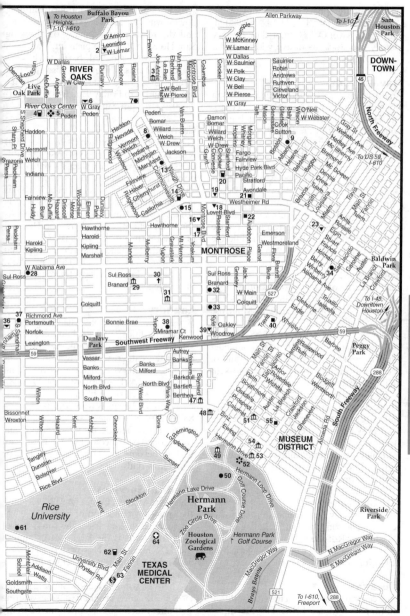

Serious photographers will be happy at the Camera Center (☎ 713-523-1422), 1980 W Gray in the River Oaks Center; they are very friendly and stock about every kind of film you can imagine.

Travel Agents

American Express has large travel offices in Houston (see the previous Money section). The Hostelling International Bluebonnet Council/AYH (☎ 713-661-2050) has budget travel services at its office at 2656 S Loop West, Suite 510, near Rice Village; it's open weekdays 2 to 5:30 pm (Thursday 2 to 7 pm). Travelfest (☎ 713-522-2828) is in the River Oaks Center at 1953 W Gray (see Bookstores). The main Houston AAA office (☎ 713-524-1851), 3000 Southwest Freeway on the south side of the road near Rice Village, has a full travel agency in addition to the usual maps and other AAA services.

Bookstores

Half Price Books has two locations: 2537 University Blvd in Rice Village (☎ 713-524-6635), and 2410 Waugh Drive in Montrose (☎ 713-520-1084).

The Brazos Bookstore (☎ 713-523-0701), 2421 Bissonnet near Rice Village, is an independent bookseller with strong selections of fiction and art books; the store also sells major international newspapers.

Travelfest (☎ 713-522-2828), the chain whose concept marries travel books, luggage and travel agents in one store, has a location at 1953 W Gray in the River Oaks Center. Besides a full selection of travel guides, they have literature littering almost every surface in the store, inviting you to invest in the phenomenon.

Crossroads Market (☎ 713-942-0147) is at 1111 Westheimer Blvd.

The Barnes & Noble superstore chain has several outlets in Houston, including two on Westheimer Rd: one at No 5000 (☎ 713-629-8828) and one across from the Galleria Mall at No 7626 (☎ 713-783-6016).

Libraries

The central branch of Houston's Public Library (☎ 713-236-1313), 500 McKinney Ave, is in a bright and modern building downtown. The staff is especially helpful, and the reading areas, many overlooking Sam Houston Park, are pleasant. The travel section is well stocked, particularly with books on Texas. The library also has free Internet access and other online services. It's open Monday to Friday 9 am to 9 pm, Saturday 9 am to 6 pm, Sunday 2 to 6 pm.

Campuses

The University of Houston (☎ 281-283-7600) is the major local university, with several utilitarian campuses that reflect its status as a primarily commuter school serving 31,000 students. Rice University (☎ 713-527-4803) is the tony private school that self-consciously affixes to itself the label favored by self-conscious schools everywhere: 'the Harvard of [blank]' (in this case Texas). More than 4,000 students attend classes on the large and pretty campus just west of Hermann Park. Some of the biggest oaks in the region grow in its rarefied confines.

Laundry

Budget accommodations usually have coin laundry facilities. There are hundreds of self-service laundries listed in the Yellow Pages under the category sensibly titled 'Laundries – Self Service.' Two, however, stand out: Graustark Laundry (☎ 713-529-9028), 4506 Graustark three blocks west of Montrose, and Mr Klean Washeteria (☎ 713-529-8871), 3103 S Shepherd at Alabama in the Upper Kirby District. Both facilities are air-conditioned, a vital consideration unless you wish to become as hot and steamy as your laundering duds.

Medical Services

The Texas Medical Center (☎ 713-790-1136), the sprawling collection of hospitals, teaching facilities and clinics at the south end of Hermann Park, is the largest of its kind in the US; Hermann Hospital (☎ 713-704-3627), 6411 Fannin, is the center for emergency care.

There's a string of Kelsey-Seybold Clinics (☎ 800-215-3573) around Houston, offering outpatient care without appointment. In the

West Side and Galleria area, the clinic (☎ 713-780-1661) is at 1111 Augusta Drive; near George Bush Intercontinental Airport, the clinic (☎ 281-443-2260) is at 8484 Will Clayton Parkway (the access road between the airport and US 59).

Emergency
Important telephone numbers include Travelers' Aid (☎ 713-526-8300), the HIV-AIDS Hotline (☎ 800-342-2437), the Houston police (nonurgent; ☎ 713-222-3131), and the Rape Crisis Hotline (☎ 713-528-7273).

Dangers & Annoyances
The usual advice for American big cities applies in Houston. Lock your car, keep valuables out of sight, beware of dark and lonely streets and if an area looks dangerous, it probably is. Areas to the east and southeast of downtown Houston can be dangerous at any time, but that description is by no means universal.

Heat is probably the biggest danger you will have to contend with. In July the average daytime high is 94° F; coupled with extreme humidity it can quickly exhaust all but the most acclimated people. Stay in the shade and in cool places, drink plenty of water, and watch out for the seats in your car, which can fry an egg or a thigh if they've been exposed to the sun.

The other problem when it's hot is the cold – inside, that is. As if to prove that their air-conditioning is better than anyone else's, Houstonians crank the air-con levels to the max. Entering many malls or offices you'll encounter a wall of Arctic air.

No matter what the temperature, Houston air is not for the faint of lung. The air quality is the second-worst in the US and may soon surpass that of Los Angeles to attain the crown of the nation's worst. High ozone counts have sparked what the *Houston Chronicle* calls a 'near epidemic of asthma and respiratory disorders.'

Finally, for people who like to brag about size, Houstonians are mum when it comes to the one area where they truly have bragging rights: mosquito size. See the Dangers & Annoyances section in the introductory

Facts for the Visitor chapter for advice on dealing with these devils.

DOWNTOWN
The downtown Houston skyline is best seen at night, when many of the buildings have special lighting. The tallest building is the Texas Commerce Tower, at Travis and Texas, completed in 1981 at the height of the building boom that was fueled by the huge increase in oil prices in the 1970s. Exactly 1002 feet tall, it has an observation deck on the 60th floor (☎ 713-223-0441) open weekdays 8 am to 5 pm (free). The 53-story Texaco Heritage Plaza, at Bagby and Lamar, has a postmodern top inspired by a Mayan temple.

The oldest parts of downtown are evident in a few surviving buildings from the mid-19th century around Market Square Park and Allen's Landing Park. Efforts are under way to restore the latter, where the Allen brothers got rich quick in 1836.

Sam Houston Park
The Heritage Society (☎ 713-655-1912) has relocated eight of Houston's oldest buildings to Sam Houston Park, amid the roar of traffic. Among the houses, assembled in the park over a period of many years, are the **Yates House** (1870), the former home of a prominent black preacher; the **Old Place** (1823), a log cabin; and the **Pillot House** (1868), home to the Pillot family for 96 years. Three museums and galleries display 19th-century furniture and other items and give details on the buildings themselves. Guided tours of the houses leave daily every

HOUSTON

The pesky mosquito

hour. Open Monday to Saturday 10 am to 4 pm, Sunday 1 to 4 pm (last tour leaves at 3 pm daily). Admission to the galleries is free; tours cost $6 for adults, $4 for children. Start at the office, at 1100 Bagby. There is a somewhat hidden free parking lot off Clay St west of Bagby.

MUSEUM DISTRICT
Museum of Fine Arts
Founded in 1900, this museum (☎ 713-639-7300), 1001 Bissonnet, is the oldest art museum in the short history of Texas. The large collection is heavy on the 19th century, including impressionism, postimpressionism and works by Texan and other US artists. Across the street is a sculpture garden with works by Rodin and others. Open Tuesday to Saturday 10 am to 5 pm (Thursday till 9 pm), Sunday 12:15 to 6 pm; $3 for adults, $1.50 for kids.

Contemporary Arts Museum
Nothing is ever the same inside the stainless-steel walls of the Contemporary Arts Museum (☎ 713-526-3129), 5216 Montrose. With no permanent collection, it presents 10 or more temporary shows a year. Open Tuesday to Saturday 10 am to 5 pm (Thursday till 9 pm), Sunday noon to 5 pm; free.

Children's Museum of Houston
Kids run through the doors of this crayon-colored playground for the mind (☎ 713-522-1138), 1500 Binz, and don't look back. Adults can find some fun too, especially watching the tots milk the mechanical cow. Open Tuesday to Saturday 9 am to 5 pm (Thursday till 8 pm), Sunday noon to 5 pm; $5 per person till 3 pm, $3 per person after 3 pm, free for kids under two (free for everyone Thursday from 5 to 8 pm).

Holocaust Museum Houston
'Our destination was extermination,' says Houstonian holocaust survivor Siegi Izakson on one of the many videos shown at this excellent museum and memorial (☎ 713-942-8000), 5401 Caroline, which opened in 1996. The permanent exhibition, housed in a black cylinder meant to evoke the ghastly image of a smokestack, traces the lives of European Jews from before WWII, through the Holocaust and after the war as the survivors tried to rebuild their lives. There is a well-stocked reading room, a good bookstore and a memorial room. Open Monday to Friday 9 am to 5 pm (Thursday till 9 pm), Saturday and Sunday noon to 5 pm; free.

Houston Museum of Natural Science
A huge granite globe rotates in a fountain near the west entrance to this vast museum (☎ 713-639-4629), One Hermann Circle, and that's just the start of the fun. The **Cockrell Butterfly Center** is a large three-story dome where you can wander in the company of 2000 live butterflies. Get your ticket first ($3 for adults, $1.50 for kids), then explore the rest of the museum, which has all the usual features of a natural history museum, right down to the dinosaurs and the IMAX theater. The atrium picnic area is catered by McDonald's – consider yourself warned. Open Monday to Saturday 9 am to 6 pm, Sunday 11 am to 6 pm; $4 for adults, $2 for children (IMAX films cost extra).

Museum of Health & Medical Science
That enlarged liver you see isn't due to last night's debauchery, it's just one of the many huge organs on display in this museum (☎ 713-521-1515), 1515 Hermann, which lets you have your own fantastic voyage through the human body. Open Tuesday to Saturday 9 am to 5 pm (Thursday till 7 pm), Sunday noon to 5 pm; $4 for adults, $3 for children, free on Thursday after 4 pm.

HERMANN PARK
A huge statue of noted drunk and Texas pioneer Samuel Houston commands the entrance to this 407-acre wooded park, which is south of the Museum District. There is a large rose garden east of the Museum of Natural Science.

Houston Zoological Gardens
Gorillas, tropical birds, lions, bats and a menagerie of other critters make their home

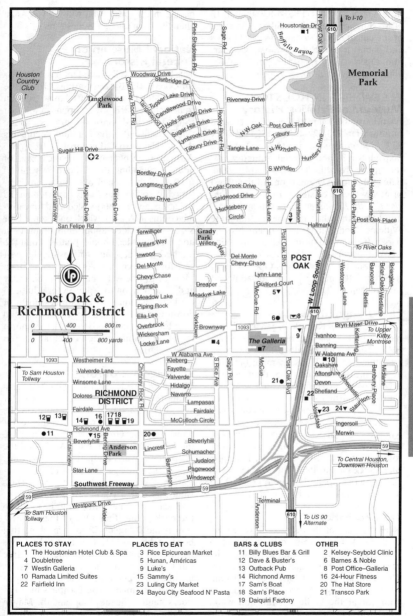

HOUSTON

PLACES TO STAY
1 The Houstonian Hotel Club & Spa
4 Doubletree
7 Westin Galleria
10 Ramada Limited Suites
22 Fairfield Inn

PLACES TO EAT
3 Rice Epicurean Market
5 Hunan, Américas
9 Luke's
15 Sammy's
23 Luling City Market
24 Bayou City Seafood N' Pasta

BARS & CLUBS
11 Billy Blues Bar & Grill
12 Dave & Buster's
13 Outback Pub
14 Richmond Arms
17 Sam's Boat
18 Sam's Place
19 Daiquiri Factory

OTHER
2 Kelsey-Seybold Clinic
6 Barnes & Noble
8 Post Office–Galleria
16 24-Hour Fitness
20 The Hat Store
21 Transco Park

in this large zoo (☎ 713-284-8300), at 1513 N MacGregor Way, which takes advantage of the climate to grow many tropical plants and palms. It also has an adjoining aquarium. Open daily 10 am to 6 pm; $2.50 for adults, 50¢ for children.

ELSEWHERE IN HOUSTON
Museum of Printing History

An often-missed gem, this carefully curated museum (☎ 713-522-4652), 1324 W Clay west of Montrose (see the Central Houston map), has rare and unusual printed works that range from the Dharani Scroll, which dates from 764 AD and is one of the oldest printed works in existence, to the *San Francisco Daily Examiner* from March 4, 1887, heralding the day newspaper magnate William Randolph Hearst bought his first paper. If the word 'font' means something to you, you'll enjoy the vast displays of typography through the ages. Open Tuesday to Sunday 10 am to 5 pm; $2 for adults, $1 for children.

The Orange Show

In 1954, Jeff McKissack began building a monument to honor the orange (☎ 713-926-6368), 2401 Munger southeast of downtown (see the Greater Houston map; take the Telephone Rd exit off I-45, then use the access road on the south side to reach Munger). Starting with a simple house, he added sculptures, wishing wells, plaques with folksy bromides, observation decks, and wheels – lots of wheels. Everything is of course painted orange. Some call the work folk art, others dub it madness. It's both. McKissack died in 1987, but volunteers still run the show. Open Monday to Friday 9 am to 5 pm; a $1 donation is requested.

Transco Park

Near the base of the Transco Tower in the Galleria Mall area, Transco Park features a 64-foot horizontal U-shaped water wall. The cascading fountain makes for great photos. The park is near the corner of Post Oak Blvd and Hidalgo. You may have to park your car at the Galleria Mall and walk, which will get you suspicious stares from the

people in the tower, who will see you as an alien life form called a 'pedestrian.'

National Museum of Funeral History

This huge and well-funded museum (☎ 281-876-3063), 415 Barren Springs Drive (see the Greater Houston map), has to be seen to be believed. Run by an organization that trains funeral directors – courses include 'Merchandising' – the museum documents the vast industry that profits from the American way of death. There are dozens of hearses, including the ill-fated bus model from 1916 that tipped over on a San Francisco hill, spilling the dearly departed on the mourners, and an antique sled used for carrying coffins in Alaska, which once rented for $5. A sterile video about embalming (you don't see any dead bodies) intones that the methods are designed to 'ensure the best care for the deceased.' As if they care. Open Monday to Friday 10 am to 4 pm, Saturday and Sunday noon to 4 pm; $5 for adults, $3 for kids. The museum is 15 miles north of downtown on I-45; take the Airtex exit, head west for half a mile to Ella Blvd, then north to the museum on the corner at Barren Springs Drive.

Six Flags AstroWorld

More than 40 rides are among the highlights of this theme park and the adjoining Water World (☎ 713-799-8404 for both), on the south side of I-610 across from the Astrodome (see the Greater Houston map; use the Kirby Drive exit). AstroWorld and the Astrodome were built at the same time. Under the tutelage of the Six Flags organization, the parks are now home to Bugs Bunny and other Warner Bros characters.

Each year a new thrill ride is added to the park's collection. One of the most recent is the **Dungeon Drop**, a machine that hoists riders up 227 feet and then drops them (and maybe their lunches) in a free fall back to earth. The 10 roller coasters include the **Viper**, which does a 360° loop in the dark; **Batman – The Escape**, which has riders stand while they loop; and the **Mayan Mindbender**, on which riders hurtle around inside a fanciful pyramid that would have been imaginable to a real Mayan only if he or she were messed up on peyote. The themed areas, such as the generic **European Village**, the hokey **Americana Square** and the stir-fried **Oriental Village**, exist primarily to differentiate the fast food and novelties that are sold.

The park's schedule may have been devised by Daffy Duck. For much of the year it is open on weekends, except for seemingly random stretches when it closes for weeks at a time. From roughly mid-May to mid-August the park is open daily. *When* it's open, AstroWorld has six different sets of hours, which change daily. Obviously, you'll want to call to confirm times in advance. Admission is $37 for adults, $24 for those shorter than 48 inches tall, $15 for seniors 54 and older. (Smart parents will tell

Artful Women & Their Legacies

Not all of Houston's get-rich-quick money has gone into conspicuous consumption. A large portion has financed the major cultural institutions in town, and two women in particular are responsible for much of Houston's cultural heritage today.

The unfortunately named Ima Hogg was the only daughter of James S Hogg, a Texas governor and oil millionaire. She gave generously to the arts, medicine and historical preservation during her long life (1882-1975). **Bayou Bend** (☎ 713-639-7750), in the River Oaks district at 1 Westcott, along the Buffalo Bayou, was her home and is now the site of an impressive collection of decorative arts. Some 4800 pieces trace American style from colonial times until the mid-19th century. Outside her soft-pink stucco home, which was one of the first homes in River Oaks, are 18 acres of immaculate gardens. The museum and gardens have a complex seasonal schedule that varies by the day (they are always closed Monday); it includes guided and self-guided tours. Admission varies greatly as well, but for a self-guided tour of the museum the cost is $10 for adults, $5 for children; for the gardens it's $3 for everyone older than 10. Reservations may be required on some days, so call first.

Before her death in 1997 at age 89, Dominique de Menil not only funded one of the finest small art museums in the nation, she also used her influence to push for desegregation in Houston and highlight human-rights abuses worldwide. In 1986 she established the Carter-Menil Human Rights Foundation with former president Jimmy Carter. The **Menil Collection** (☎ 713-525-9400), 1515 Sul Ross Drive northeast of the Museum District, embraces a lifetime of acquisitions by Menil and her husband, John. It is housed in an architecturally magnificent building that is a work of art itself. The huge old oak just east of the main gallery may be the finest tree of its kind in Houston. A variety of artistic media and periods are represented in the collection. Several rooms are devoted to the surrealists, notably René Magritte. An annex houses a permanent collection of the works of American painter Cy Twombly, known for his formless yet graceful works. Open Wednesday to Sunday 11 am to 7 pm; free. Free parking is a short walk away, at 1515 W Alabama Blvd.

One block east of the Menil Collection are two of Menil's other legacies to Houston. The **Rothko Chapel** (☎ 713-521-3990), 3900 Yupon St, looks like a nuclear bunker, which is appropriate, because you'd probably want to be praying in one of those as well. Designed by Philip Johnson, it has 14 large paintings by American abstract expressionist Mark Rothko. Open daily 10 am to 6 pm; free. The **Byzantine Fresco Chapel Museum** (☎ 713-521-3990), 4011 Yupon St, contains stunning 13th-century frescoes that came to Houston from their home in Cyprus early in the 20th century in a manner not unlike the travels of the Maltese Falcon. The full story is inside the modest structure, which re-creates the original home of the frescoes. Open Wednesday to Sunday 11 am to 6 pm; free.

the tykes to look real old – maybe smoke cigars.) Look in hotel and motel lobbies for the AstroWorld brochures, which have coupons good for $4 off admission.

WaterWorld Adjoining AstroWorld, this park (☎ 713-799-8404) makes the most of the torrid weather by providing a plethora of slides, pools, beaches and watery pleasures. There's even a splashy inner-tube ride. The business hours are as mixed up as the ones next door, but generally the park is open during the daylight hours from May to September; call for details. Admission is $18.35 for adults, $15.10 for those shorter than 48 inches or older than 54 (parents: no need for cigars). A combined ticket to both worlds costs $31 per person, regardless of age, height and smoking preference.

ACTIVITIES

Memorial Park and Hermann Park are the two main areas in the city for walking and running. If your heat tolerance is less than that of a lizard, head out to Main St where it runs past Rice University. The huge oak trees provide deep shade over the wide sidewalks. For nature hikes, see the parks listed in the Around Houston section later in the chapter.

Cycling

Built in 1986 for training of the US Olympic bicycle team, the open-air Alkek Velodrome (☎ 281-578-0693), 19008 Saums Rd in Cullen Park, features a regulation 33° banked, 333m track. You can rent racing bikes and take classes. If you bring your own bike it costs $2 to ride; if you rent one there, total cost is $5.

Golf

The golf courses at Hermann Park (☎ 713-526-0077), 6201 Golf Course Drive, and Memorial Park (☎ 713-862-4033), 1001 Memorial Loop Drive, are open to the public. Hours generally reflect those of the sun. If you can wrangle an invite, a visit to the River Oaks Country Club (☎ 713-529-4321), 1600 River Oaks Blvd, will yield a glimpse of Houston's elite at play.

Ice Skating

There are thrills and spills at the ground-floor skating rink in the Galleria Mall (☎ 713-621-1500), 5015 Westheimer Blvd, where folks raised in a subtropical environment take to the ice. The rink is open to the public Monday and Wednesday 9 am to 4 pm and 8 to 10 pm, Tuesday and Thursday 9 am to 5 pm and 8 to 10 pm, Friday 9 am to 11 pm, Saturday 12:30 to 11 pm, Sunday noon to 6 pm; entry is $5.50, skate rental $2.50.

Health Clubs & Gyms

Most expensive hotels have their own health clubs or arrangements with ones nearby. Less luxurious hostelries can often recommend facilities or arrange discount admissions. Regular health clubs usually offer some sort of visitor pass for the day. In the heart of the Richmond District, 24-Hour Fitness (☎ 713-783-8448), 5800 Richmond Ave, has day passes for $10.

SPECIAL EVENTS

Highlights of the Houston calendar include the following:

February
Houston Livestock Show and Rodeo
This is the nation's second-largest rodeo and largest cattle show (☎ 713-791-9000). For 17 days beginning in mid-February and extending into March, big-name cowboys perform in the rodeo in the Astrodome, big name country music acts perform afterward, and next door in the exhibit halls big-name bulls perform their own special magic. This event is well worth seeking out if you want to step right into Texas culture; admission is $12.

April
Home and Garden Tours
Six or more historic homes in the Heights are open for tours during this early-April event (☎ 713-861-4002).

Houston International Festival
This multicultural celebration of food, art and music lasts for 10 days beginning the third week of the month. Events are held all over the city and include the Houston International Film Festival (☎ 713-965-9955).

Westheimer Colony Arts Festival
This festival (☎ 713-521-0133) is the Montrose District at its flamboyant best, with blocks of

booths selling arts, antiques, food and items that defy classification. There's usually a parade or two. The dates vary, and the event repeats itself in October.

Art Car Parade
A local favorite that's highly appropriate in this car-dependent town, this parade has residents dress up their autos in costumes and show them off on a course that winds through downtown.

June
Juneteenth
This celebration lasts for several days around June 19, the day in 1865 when word reached Texas that the slaves had been emancipated. Events include gospel and blues festivals and other celebrations of African American culture. Call the Convention & Visitors Bureau for more information.

September
Fiestas Patrias
This September 16 festival (☎ 713-926-2636) features a parade, ball and music in celebration of Mexican Independence Day.

November
Thanksgiving Day Parade
Why go to New York for Macy's version when Houston has one of its own?

PLACES TO STAY
The accommodations listed here are divided into categories by price. Within the listings you will find places near both airports, and although they would be convenient if you have a late flight in or an early flight out, they are situated in pretty generic suburban areas. Try to stay near one of the interesting neighborhoods, which can be a challenge, given that most of the lodgings are in modern office areas. Almost all the hotels offer free parking and a swimming pool. Where weekend rates are noted, they are usually good for Friday and Saturday nights.

Places to Stay – Budget
Camping None of the campgrounds is easily accessible by public transportation. *All Star RV Resort* (☎ 713-981-6814), 10650 Southwest Freeway (US 59) near the Sam Houston Parkway, is geared for RVs, with full hookups and cable. Rates average $25 a night. *KOA Houston Central* (☎ 713-455-4040), 1620

Peachleaf a half-mile south of the Sam Houston Parkway off Aldine-Westfield Rd, is 12 miles north of downtown. Rates begin at $18 for tent sites and $24 for RVs.

Hostels In a moth-eaten old house in the Museum District, the *Houston International Hostel* (☎ 713-523-1009), 5302 Crawford, is very well located. HI members pay $11.39 a night (everyone else pays $14.39) for a bunk in one of the four rooms. From downtown or the Greyhound station, take bus No 8, 15 or 65 southwest on Main or No 1, 2 or 4 on Fannin. Get off at Southmore and walk five or six blocks east to Crawford; the hostel is one block south.

Motels & Hotels Right downtown, the *Londale Hotel* (☎ 713-237-8830), 419 San Jacinto at Prairie, has spartan rooms in a 1920s building that go for $25/31 a single/double. They will pay $3 of your $4 cab fare from the Greyhound station. At the *YMCA* (☎ 713-659-8501), 1600 Louisiana downtown, the simple rooms are clean and range from $20 to $30.

The best of the faded string of 1960s motels that line Main St near the Astrodome, the *Grant Motor Inn* (☎ 713-668-8000), 8200 S Main St, offers big rooms and free doughnuts. Rates start at $45/50.

Places to Stay – Mid-Range
Motels & Hotels You might think you're home at the roomy *Doubletree* (☎ 713-961-9000), 6353 Westheimer Rd near the Galleria Mall. The $109 rooms really are full suites that can sleep up to four easily. For $144 you get a two-bedroom number big enough for a van-full.

In a converted apartment house, the *Ramada Limited Suites* (☎ 713-621-2797), 4723 W Alabama, is just across I-610 and a 10-minute walk from the Galleria Mall. The units have full kitchens and are a great value, since four or more can sleep in the two separate rooms, which run $99 weekdays and $79 weekends.

Be sure to get a room that doesn't face the highway at the otherwise comfy *Fairfield Inn* (☎ 713-961-1690), 3131 W Loop

HOUSTON

South, just on the east side of I-610 from the Galleria Mall. The fairly new rooms cost $59/64 a single/double on weekdays, $49/54 on weekends.

If you need to stay near the Astrodome, your best bet is *La Quinta Inn-Astrodome* (☎ 713-668-8092), 9911 Buffalo Speedway, off I-610 at the exit of the same name. The rooms have big televisions, big desks and big bathrooms, but not big prices: $70 to $79 with a $5 discount on weekends.

It's not much to look at, but the *Days Inn* (☎ 713-523-3777), 4640 S Main St, is one of the few motels near Montrose and the Museum District. Rooms are a simple $64 year-round.

Convenient to Upper Kirby and University Village, the *Holiday Inn Select* (☎ 713-523-8448), 2712 Southwest Freeway just north of US 59, is a modest place with singles and doubles for $130 on weekdays and $80 on weekends.

Airports The *Sleep Inn* (☎ 281-442-7770), 15675 JFK Blvd, is the cheapest lodging close to George Bush Intercontinental Airport (IAH). The newish rooms are designed for little more than what the joint's name implies and cost $69/65 a single/double.

The *Houston Airport Marriott* (☎ 281-443-2310), 18700 JFK Blvd, couldn't be closer to IAH because it's *in* IAH, right between Terminals B and C. It even boasts its own stop on the airport's silly little train. The rooms are a comparatively good value, with a weekday corporate rate of $145 (available to anyone who asks). On weekends it falls to $79. You can listen to the roar of the jets while splashing in the pool or bubbling in the whirlpool.

Away from the jets, the *Hotel Sofitel* (☎ 281-445-9000), at 425 N Beltway about 10 minutes from IAH, is run by French proprietors who leave little touches everywhere, such as free baguettes for guests. Large rooms run $189 weekdays and $109 weekends, with frequent specials whose rates are much lower.

Right across the street from the Hobby Airport terminal, the *Howard Johnson Lodge* (☎ 713-644-1261), 7777 Airport Rd, is a simple place with a pool and a rarely used volleyball court. The rates of $51/56 a single/double drop by $10 on weekends.

Don't be misled by the name *Sumner Suites* (☎ 713-943-1713), 7922 Mosley next to I-45 at Hobby, because each room is really just a large space with a small divider, although each features a couch and a microwave. Included in the room rates of $109 on weekdays, $69 on weekends is a free drink with the cheery employees in the lobby bar-cum-breakfast room.

A bustling sports bar may be the best place to escape the otherwise basic *Radisson Hotel* (☎ 713-943-7979), 9200 Gulf Freeway next to I-45 at Hobby. The rooms are large and the staff is very friendly, but the place is almost generic in most respects. Rates are $109 during the week, $69 on the weekend.

B&Bs The Bed & Breakfast Reservation Service of Texas (☎ 713-523-1114) has a listing of almost 75 places, many of which are in some of the more interesting parts of town. Rooms start at about $50 for a single and escalate rapidly.

Built in 1891, *Sara's Bed & Breakfast* (☎ 713-868-1130), 941 Heights Blvd in the historic Houston Heights neighborhood, has 12 well-equipped rooms, with VCRs, in a range of shapes and sizes with and without baths for $55 to $150.

It's exclusively gay men at the *Montrose Inn* (☎ 713-520-0206), 408 Avondale just north of Westheimer Rd. This B&B is known for its late-night snacks and late-morning breakfast. Rooms start at $50.

The *Lovett Inn* (☎ 713-522-5224), 501 Lovett, three blocks east of Montrose, is popular with couples of all persuasions. The former home of a mayor, it also has a pool. Rooms start at $75.

Places to Stay – Top End

You can probably skip the rest of Houston if you stay at the *Houstonian Hotel Club & Spa* (☎ 713-680-2626), 111 N Post Oak Lane west of I-610 and north of Woodway. This resort has three pools, several spas, a health club, racquetball and tennis courts and a bunch of other facilities that may not leave you time to try out the climbing wall. Weekdays, rooms on the 18 wooded acres are $239; weekends they go for a relative bargain at $109.

Hopelessly addicted mall shoppers will love the *Westin Galleria* (☎ 713-960-8100), 5060 W Alabama in the Galleria Mall. The swank rooms are a mere elevator-ride away from the stores of the mall. Weekdays rooms run $150 to $175, weekends $99.

Out west by the Sam Houston Parkway, the *Adam's Mark Houston* (☎ 713-978-7400), 2900 Briarpark off the 10000 block of Westheimer Rd, offers free shuttle service to the Galleria Mall area and the Richmond District. Rooms average $165 weekdays and almost half that on weekends. Ask about specials.

Live high on the hog at *La Colombe d'Or Hotel* (☎ 713-524-7999), 3410 Montrose, two blocks south of Westheimer Rd. There are six suites in this opulent old mansion filled with antiques. The rates run $195 to $575. The restaurant wins praise too for its French classics.

If you get lost in the 7 miles of tunnels downtown, seek refuge at the *Doubletree Hotel at Allen Center* (☎ 713-759-0202), 400 Dallas at Bagby. Although you may need the aroma of cheese to find them in the downtown maze, rooms run $215 weekdays and $119 weekends.

PLACES TO EAT

In researching this book we asked scores of Houstonians what they liked best about the city. More often than not there would be a troubled pause, followed by something along the lines of 'Well, I don't know, but you sure can eat well.' And indeed you can. Houston's variety and quality of eateries is deliciously good. The restaurants listed here are categorized by cuisine, but Cajun and Tex/Mex elements are found on menus as diverse as Italian and Asian.

American

Pastrami and other deli standards are piled high at *Butera's* (☎ 713-523-0722), 4621 Montrose Blvd near the Montrose District.

A long list of beers rounds out the simple pleasures of this inexpensive and popular sidewalk café.

The best burgers in the Galleria area are grilled at the cheesy old building that's home to *Luke's* (☎ 713-627-8545), 2626 W Loop South right between the highway and the mall. Open 24 hours, Luke's piles its burgers with fresh stuff, and they still cost less than $3.

After a tough morning prowling among the priceless old objects of the Heights antiques shops, spend lunch with the priceless old residents of *Houston Heights Tower* (☎ 713-864-3322), 330 19th right across from the main shops, a retirement home with a cafeteria. The lunch specials ($3.45) are popular with locals of all ages, and you can enjoy the music of Charlotte the piano player.

With equally high scores for food and romance, *Ruggles Grill* (☎ 713-524-3839), 903 Westheimer Rd in Montrose, is a local sensation. Carnivores and vegetarians alike will thrill to its generous, imaginative, moderately priced creations, and all will get a bit giddy at the fantastic desserts. Consider the following description of the chocolate cheesecake from LP editor Jacqueline Volin, a careful woman not normally prone to wild spurts of embellishment: 'a big, fat, melt-in-your-mouth savory slice.' She went on, but decorum prevents us from quoting further.

Bogart and Sinatra gaze stoically from a wall mural at diners tucked into the retro booths at *River Oaks Bar & Grill* (☎ 713-520-1738), 2630 Westheimer Rd at Kirby. Superb steaks with prices to match assuage the hunger of the status-conscious, while others return the doleful stares of Bogie and Frank from behind perfectly poured martinis.

Asian

Nationally renowned *Kim Son* (☎ 713-222-2790), 300 Milam St at Congress Ave downtown, and (☎ 713-222-2461) 2001 Jefferson near I-59, has become a local legend since it was opened in 1993 by the La family, who escaped in a boat from Vietnam in 1979. The 280-item menu ranges from rice-noodle soup to jellyfish to lotus root. Among the

HOUSTON

most popular items are the 'Vietnamese fajitas': lemon-grass-marinated beef with a range of fresh condiments and rice-paper wrappers ($9.50). Lunch specials average $5.

Anything would taste good in the lime, garlic and jalapeño dip at *Mai's* (☎ 713-520-7684), 3403 Milam St, two blocks from Main St in Montrose. But the moderately priced Vietnamese specials here taste good even before they gain a new level of tastiness in the wondrous dip. Open daily until 3 am.

The fellow deftly handling the chopsticks at the corner table at *Hunan* (☎ 713-965-0808), 1800 Post Oak Blvd near the Galleria, should know what he's doing: he was once the US ambassador to China. Of course, most people remember regular patron George Bush for his later résumé entries. He and Barbara are big fans of the spicy, low-fat, moderately priced entrées at this surprisingly casual Chinese restaurant.

Barbecue

Houston's favorite barbecue place, *Goode Co* (☎ 713-522-2530), 5109 Kirby two blocks south of Hwy 59, serves up the beef with a bit of élan, but the prices are nevertheless cheap. No white bread here; you get specially baked jalapeño-cheese bread with every order. The pecan pie is tops, and the outdoor picnic tables under the overhang inspire lingering over the typically gallon-sized iced teas.

A friendly, relaxed place in a sea of pretension, *Luling City Market* (☎ 713-871-1903), 4726 Richmond Ave, serves up fine barbecue for fine prices. A spicy-chopped beef sandwich with tangy potato salad runs $5.

Cajun

If you see people dancing in the street in this otherwise dull-as-dirt neighborhood near downtown, it's because *Zydeco Diner* (☎ 713-759-2001), 1119 Pease, is having one of its frequent after-work crawfish boils, complete with live zydeco music. These outdoor events draw huge crowds that party into the night. By day, huge crowds are drawn to the oyster po'boys ($5.50) and plates dripping with jambalaya, red beans and rice and other New Orleans classics.

A mere $8 will get you far at *Bayou City Seafood N' Pasta* (☎ 713-621-6602), 4730 Richmond Ave in the Richmond District, where the shrimp and oysters are fresh from the gulf and priced to travel quickly to your mouth. The staff is as relaxed as should be expected at a 'Big Easy'-inspired café.

Shrimp, oysters and other denizens of the gulf meet their fate with a Cajun flourish at *Tony Manola's Gulf Coast Kitchen* (☎ 713-528-3474), 1962 W Gray in the River Oaks Center. Try the shrimp and crab quesadillas ($7.25) or the signature blackened snapper in lime butter ($19.25).

Diners

Long a haunt of red-eyed poets and other night owls, the 24-hour *House of Pies* (☎ 713-528-3816), 3112 Kirby in Upper Kirby, dishes up its namesake specialty in a range or flavors, plus burgers, omelets and other foods that strike just the right harmonious, affordable cadence with your comfort-food cravings.

Simple dishes your mother would have made if she were Julia Child are the norm at *Daily Review Cafe* (☎ 713-520-9217), 3412 W Lamar at Dunlavy in River Oaks. The fresh bread served with your meal is often something like cinnamon-raisin; the potato soup ($5) comes garnished with apple-smoked bacon. There's a restful patio at this moderately priced café as well.

Italian

Bright tile and mosaics set the cheery tone at *La Griglia* (☎ 713-526-4700), 2002 Gray in the River Oaks Center. The high ceilings help absorb the roar of the stylish crowd of patrons, who spend more time mouthing solicitations across the bustling room than mouthing their food. Classics such as linguine alle vongole ($12) and veal Milanese ($15) are joined by a 'Spa' menu that lists the calorie counts of its light entrées.

Gourmet pizzas pour from the stone oven at *Birra Poretti's* (☎ 713-529-9191), 1997 Gray in the River Oaks Center. Prices range from $8 for dinky to $14 for large, and the toppings include grilled chicken and sun-dried tomatoes. Many regulars skimp on their orders to save room for the tiramisu ice-cream sundae ($6), a giant creation that leaves many sighing with joy. On Sundays there's a jazz brunch.

Mexican

Build your own burrito at **Mission Burritos** (☎ 713-529-0535), 2245 W Alabama in Upper Kirby. For $4 you choose from a long list of fresh ingredients to create a meal in the shape of a log. The monster-size $9 version would make a good foundation for a cabin. The fruit-flavored all-you-can-drink iced tea ($1) is a bargain. There are great seats under the big oak out front.

Irma Galvan herself welcomes you to her café, **Irma's** (☎ 713-222-0767), at 22 N Chenevert near Ruiz east of downtown, where the waiters are her sons and the menu is inexpensive and ever changing. The lineup reflects what's in season but usually includes enchiladas oozing cheese and mole or tomatillo sauce. Open weekdays for lunch only.

If you find yourself lodging out by Hobby Airport, skip the franchised strips that shine like a neon-lit gastronomic Hades and drive 10 minutes west to **Taqueria Jesus Maria** (☎ 713-943-8822), 1106 Spencer Hwy in South Houston. From the marinated carrots on every table, you know that these people care about good food, even if the decor could, with the addition of a few washing machines, pass as a Laundromat. Prices are as inexpensive as the food is tasty.

You serve yourself at **Taco Milagro** (☎ 713-522-1999), 2555 Kirby at Westheimer Rd, a plebeian chore that takes a turn for the royal when you get to the salsa bar, a carnival of colorful salsas freshly made every day. Standard Mexican fare attains new heights in order to provide suitable underpinnings for the salsas. The chicken enchiladas in poblano sauce ($7) are among the many treats. On pleasant days nab your margarita and head out to the terrace, complete with burbling fountain.

. A cool refuge from the hot streets of the Montrose District, **Felix** (☎ 713-529-3949), 904 Westheimer Rd, has been dishing up classics such as chile rellenos ($7.25) since 1948.

Ignore the pretenders all over town; the original **Ninfa's** (☎ 713-228-1175), at 2704 S Navigation east of Hwy 59, rocks to the beat of people pounding margaritas. The beef fajitas ($11) are the best around, and the tortillas are homemade by the seemingly soberest person in the place.

Middle Eastern

Snapshots of regulars and artwork from the owner's kids vie for wall space at **Sammy's** (☎ 713-780-0065), 5825 Richmond Ave in the Richmond District. The staff raises 'friendly' to a new level and serves up classics such as shish kebabs ($13) and vegetarian dishes such as falafel with hummus ($6.50).

Miscellaneous

La Madeline is a French-inspired chain of inexpensive bakeries and self-serve cafés that got its start right in University Village. The croissants are of course perfectly flaky, and the soups, such as tomato basil, and salads, such as the zesty Caesar, are *très magnifique*. Among the many neighborhood locations are the original at 6205 Kirby (☎ 713-942-7081) and one east of the Galleria Mall at 4002 Westheimer Rd (☎ 713-623-0645).

One of Houston's finest and most innovative temples to fine dining, **Américas** (☎ 713-961-1492), 1800 Post Oak Blvd north of the Galleria Mall, draws its inspiration from South America. The beef tenderloin in chimichurri sauce ($25) might make you want to move into the upscale condos across the street so you can return at will.

Southwestern

The smell of chilis permeates everything at **Mesa** (☎ 713-520-8900), 1971 Gray in the River Oaks Center. The decor is slick and arty, and you can enjoy adobe pie, which is like a tamale in pie form ($8), around a large tree outside.

Relive the campfire scene from *Blazing Saddles* at **Rio Ranch** (☎ 713-952-5000), 9999 Westheimer Rd near the Sam Houston Parkway. Beans, beans, beans and more wagon-train chow is served at moderate prices in a vast dining room meant to evoke the old frontier.

HOUSTON

Vegetarian

The daily 'macro' plate tells you all you need to know about the serious but tasty vegetarian fare at *A Moveable Feast* (☎ 713-528-3585), 2202 W Alabama at Greenbriar. Order at the counter and enjoy the fine selection of alternative papers while you await delivery of your greens.

Asian Restaurant (☎ 713-629-7805), 3701 Weslayan north of US 59 in Greenway Plaza, claims to serve the 'best macrobiotic food in town.' Even if the competition is a bit sparse, the moderately priced, grain-heavy dishes are hearty and the homemade garlic and soy sauces are a dream.

Markets

The 24-hour *Kroger's* (☎ 713-526-7865), 3300 Montrose a block south of Westheimer Rd, has lots of ready-to-eat foods good for picnics. The *Rice Epicurean Markets* are a chain of upscale stores with excellent salad bars. Two locations worth noting are 3102 Kirby at Alabama in Upper Kirby (☎ 713-526-8961) and 5016 San Felipe at Post Oak near the Galleria Mall (☎ 713-621-0422).

ENTERTAINMENT

The mainstream heart of Houston entertainment is the downtown theater district, around the intersection of Smith St and Prairie Ave. In 1997 it was bolstered by the creation of Bayou Place, a former convention hall on Texas between Bagby and Smith that now has movies, restaurants and music. Clubs and bars can be found throughout the University Village, Montrose, Upper Kirby and River Oaks areas and in the west parts of the Heights. Country and western music is not as prevalent as you might think.

During the summer, outdoor concerts are held on Thursday evenings at Jones Plaza, in front of Jones Hall for the Performing Arts downtown, and the *Miller Outdoor Theater* (☎ 713-284-8350), 2020 Hermann Loop Drive in Hermann Park, presents a full schedule of music, dance and theater.

The weekly *Houston Press* is the best source for entertainment listings; it has a hip attitude lacking in the flaccid Friday entertainment section of the *Houston Chronicle*.

For major events or concerts, you may have to get your tickets through the Ticketmaster monopoly (☎ 713-629-3700).

Theater

The local theater scene is not huge, but the *Alley Theatre* (☎ 713-228-8421), 615 Texas Ave downtown, is well funded and well regarded. Winner of a Tony Award for outstanding regional theater in 1996, the Alley's resident company presents classic, modern and musical works.

Theatre Under the Stars (☎ 713-558-8887) is actually inside and fully air-conditioned. A nonprofit group, TUTS produces more than 150 performances a year of new and moldy-oldie musicals on the stages of the major venues downtown.

In 1997 renovations were completed on the home of the *Ensemble Theatre* (☎ 713-520-0055), 3535 Fannin near the Montrose District. The oldest and largest professional African American theater in Texas performs well-known and brand-new works.

Dance & Opera

The *Houston Ballet* (☎ 713-227-2787) performs at its own space in the Wortham Theater Center, downtown at 550 Prairie. The schedule mixes classics with contemporary works.

In the same bombastic facility, which looks like one of those bad futuristic cities they'd conjure up on the old *Star Trek*, the *Houston Grand Opera* (☎ 713-546-0200) stages seven productions from October to May.

Cinema

The *Houston Chronicle* has listings every day for what's playing at the myriad first-run movie houses. More unusual choices are usually being screened at the *River Oaks Plaza* (☎ 713-524-8781), 1450 W Gray at Waugh, and the *River Oaks* (☎ 713-524-2175), a fine old theater at 2009 W Gray in the River Oaks Center. Really offbeat stuff is shown at the *Rice Media Center* (☎ 713-527-4853) on the campus near University Blvd. The *Angelika Film Center and Cafe* (☎ 713-225-5232), 510 Texas Ave at Smith in Bayou Place, has eight screens and the most

The grand Ashton Villa along gracious Broadway Ave in Galveston

Mansion in Sam Houston Park, Houston

Fulton Mansion, Rockport

Bait stand, Rockport

RYAN VER BERKMOES

Texas bluebonnets along the Gulf Coast

JOHN ELK III

Horseback riding on the beach at Padre Island National Seashore

JOHN ELK III

Shrimp boats in Corpus Christi's harbor

JOHN ELK III

The Strand, Galveston

LAURENCE PARENT

Boardwalk trails at Big Thicket National Preserve

Canoers savoring the ambience on Sawmill Pond at Caddo Lake State Park

comfortable seats in town. You can discuss what you've seen in the café until midnight weekdays and 2 am weekends.

Music

Houston's music scene is as varied as its population. This variety extends to many clubs, which feature a different type of music each night. The big news downtown has been the opening of the *Aerial Theater* (☎ 713-230-1600), 520 Texas Ave at Bayou Place, which is a major venue for rock, jazz, salsa, and country and western.

At the other end of the hype scale, *Dan Electro's Guitar Bar* (☎ 713-862-8707), 1031 E 24th near N Main St in Houston Heights, is a down-home neighborhood kind of joint that hosts local blues, country and western, rock, and various garage bands still searching for a style.

The motto at the *Fabulous Satellite Lounge* (☎ 713-869-2665), 3616 Washington Blvd at Heights, is 'One small step for man, one cold beer for mankind.' The music can be anything from folk to bluegrass to pop to just about anything else that you'd never hear on an elevator.

Classical The *Houston Symphony* (☎ 713-224-4240) plays in town at least 18 weekends a year amid its busy touring schedule. The 90-plus members perform in the Jones Hall for the Performing Arts, 615 Louisiana, which is part of the downtown theater district.

Jazz & Blues Above a small restaurant, *Cézanne* (☎ 713-522-9621), 4100 Montrose near Richmond Ave, mixes some of the best Texas jazz with a very cool piano bar.

It looks hokey as hell with its 63-foot-tall saxophone built out of scraps, and the place itself is way too slick, but *Billy Blues Bar & Grill* (☎ 713-266-9294), 6025 Richmond Ave in the Richmond District, is one of Houston's most popular full-time venues for hearing live blues.

Rock The *Blue Iguana* (☎ 713-523-2583), 903 Richmond Ave at Montrose, books some of the best local rock bands in its no-nonsense setting. Farther north, *Rudyard's*

Pub (☎ 713-521-0521), 2010 Waugh two blocks west of Montrose, is a local institution for booking good local rock and alternative acts, with the occasional blues band tossed in.

Other The *Big Easy* (☎ 713-523-9999), 5731 Kirby in University Village, honors Houston's New Orleans connection with live blues and zydeco, the music brought by immigrants from the Louisiana bayous, who flocked to Houston beginning in the early 1960s.

For a real local original, find your way northeast of downtown to the *Last Concert Cafe* (☎ 713-226-8563), 1403 Nance. After you knock on the red door, you can hang out drinking cheap suds at the bar or head out back for some cheap Mexican grub and live music (it varies a lot) on the verrrrry laid-back patio.

Dance Clubs

The *Vapor Room* (☎ 713-942-7666), 2407 Norfolk near Kirby, is a high-concept dance place that's open late and has New York club aspirations. Cut your teeth on a much sharper edge at *Some Club* (☎ 713-529-3956), 2700 Albany near the Montrose district, where techno and alternative beats boom till dawn.

Two DJ dance places nearly adjoin in trendy Shepherd Plaza, at the corner of Richmond Ave and Shepherd west of Montrose: *Strict 9* has safe water despite the name, and *Rhino Room* is like a neighborhood bar with good music.

Heading out of town, the stylish *Crystal Nite Club* (☎ 713-784-7743), 6680 Southwest Freeway, off Hwy 59 about 3 miles west of I-610, plays every Latin rhythm, from Tejano to salsa.

Bars

Houston's subtropical climate is best enjoyed after dark in one of the many bars that dot the city. Most are insubstantial affairs that open to the night air on all sides and have vast and often raucous patios.

The *Ginger Man* (☎ 713-526-2770), 5607 Morningside, is a beer-lover's dream in University Village with nearly 70 brews on tap and 100 more in bottles. Nearby on the Rice

HOUSTON

University campus, **Valhalla** (☎ 713-527-8101), 6100 Main, is open to the public, and you can join the students quaffing Pearl beer for an absurdly low 60¢ a draft.

The friendliest of Houston's many brew pubs is the **Bank Draft Brewing Co** (☎ 713-522-6258), 2424 Dunstan in the Village, where Lauri and Scott Littlewood have forsaken the perils of white-collar employment for the world of hops. The beers are tasty, including the Bad Czech Ale which is anything but. If you luck out and meet local radio super jock D-Day, your conversational needs are met for the night.

For an escape from all pretension, try **Kay's Lounge** (☎ 713-528-9858), 2324 Bissonnet east of Kirby, where you can enjoy pizza, submarine sandwiches, cheap beer and pool in a time warp back to the early days of air-conditioning in Houston.

Should romance strike, or should you just want to consummate an affair of the heart, **Marfreless** (☎ 713-528-0083), 2006 Peden around the building from the River Oaks cinema (look for the unmarked blue door under the fire escape), is ready to turn a blind eye. The lighting is very dark, the customers are groping more than their drinks and the waiters look the other way as they take your order.

Ask a Houstonian what his or her favorite bar is and don't be surprised when you hear 'La Carafe.' Located in a downtown building dating from 1860 (that's prehistoric in Houston), **La Carafe** (☎ 713-229-9399), 813 Congress Ave at Travis, has the town's best jukebox, 30 wines by the glass and an ancient wooden bar lit by huge, wax-dripping candles.

Gay & Lesbian Houston has one of the most lively gay scenes in Texas. The many bars and clubs are centered in the Montrose District. Pacific St, two blocks north of Westheimer east of Montrose, has several places, including the locationally named **Pacific Street** (☎ 713-523-0213), 710 you know what, which is very laid back and has a good balcony for scoping the action. **Chances** (☎ 713-523-7217), 1100 Westheimer Rd, is a popular, mainly lesbian bar with dancing until 2 am.

Richmond Strip

You may need to be driving a red Camaro and living in a swinging apartment complex to fully enjoy Houston's most popular entertainment district, but if a rowdy weekend scene is enough to sate you, you'll find plenty of satisfaction on the Richmond Strip. The bars and clubs stretch from Chimney Rock 1½ miles west to Hilcroft. Following are some of them.

Daiquiri Factory (☎ 713-789-1303), 5706 Richmond Ave, has a mangy thatched motif, loud rock and dirt-cheap versions of its namesake drink.

Sam's Place (☎ 713-781-1605), 5710 Richmond Ave, has more of that mangy thatch, but you won't notice after a few 99¢ margaritas. **Sam's Boat** (☎ 713-781-2628), 5720 Richmond Ave, is easily the wackiest joint on the strip and is built around a boat right out of *Gilligan's Island*. Sunday parking-lot parties spill over to the sibling bar next door.

Richmond Arms (☎ 713-784-7722), 5920 Richmond Ave, is all Houston on the outside and somewhat British on the inside, especially the patrons. The 85 beers on tap include Newcastle.

Outback Pub (☎ 713-780-2392), 3100 Fountain View, should not be confused with the bargain steak chain. This simple place is simply lit by neon beer signs and features lots of live and simply loud rock.

Dave & Buster's (☎ 713-952-2233), 6010 Richmond Ave, may best be experienced after several rounds at one of the previously mentioned places. 'Fine' dining, arcade games and several bars compete for the attention of swells who work overtime trying to think of someone to call on their cell phone.

SPECTATOR SPORTS
Baseball

The Houston Astros (☎ 713-799-9555) are chomping at the bit to flee their namesake dome for a new stadium that will be built downtown at Texas and Crawford Sts. The new facility will feature a retractable dome that will open to the sky on days when the temperature falls below 80. Tickets cost $15 to $40.

Basketball

The Houston Rockets of the NBA (☎ 713-627-3865) play at the Summit, a modern auditorium at Greenway Plaza just off the Southwest Freeway (US 59). Tickets cost $25 to $75.

Football

Local football fans are still cursing the day when the NFL's Oilers were lured from the Astrodome to Tennessee. The college teams of Rice University (☎ 713-527-4803) and the University of Houston (☎ 281-283-7600) haven't had much success in recent seasons.

SHOPPING

For browsing in a wide variety of stores that aren't affiliated with chains, the best places are the River Oaks Center on Gray between Shepherd and Woodhead; in the Upper Kirby District on Kirby, Westheimer Rd and Alabama Ave; and University Village west of Rice University. Stores that are more unusual, selling things you can pierce your body with, can be found in the Montrose area.

Antiques

In Houston Heights, West 19th St between Ashland and Yale boasts a string of stores. The Heights Antique Co-Op (☎ 713-864-7237), 321 W 19th St, has merchandise from 15 dealers on two floors. Much of what is for sale are the same items laboriously brought to the region by settlers through the 1920s. American oak and other Victorian furniture are prevalent.

Outdoor Gear

If your pack is kaput or you need to augment your rain gear, visit Wilderness Equipment (☎ 713-522-4453), in the River Oaks Center at 1977 W Gray. They also have information on regional hiking trails and wilderness campgrounds.

Galleria Mall

When one of the authors appeared on a Houston radio station and asked listeners to suggest their favorite places in town, the first caller was an earnest woman who said, 'The Galleria.' When the skeptical author demurred, saying that he didn't find anything unique about its collection of franchise and chain stores found in malls nationwide, the woman said, 'Well yes, but it has the Purple Store, where everything's purple.' We leave the decision up to you.

The Galleria Mall (☎ 713-622-0663), 5015 Westheimer Blvd, attracts attention far in excess of its appeal. Unless you have never been to the Gap, you'll find few surprises here. The department stores Macy's, Lord & Taylor, Saks Fifth Avenue and Neiman Marcus are joined by 200 other stores on three levels. Perhaps the worst thing that can be said about the Galleria Mall is that if you close your eyes for a moment and open them, you can imagine you're in Dallas.

The blocks surrounding the Galleria Mall are littered with various strip malls sucking off the popularity of the mother mall.

Western Wear

You may be disappointed at first at the dearth of cowboy hats you'll see being worn. But that's no reason you can't do your own best to rectify the situation. The Hat Store (☎ 713-780-2480), 5587 Richmond Ave at Chimney Rock, has everything from budget specials for broke cowpokes to dolled-up custom numbers for well-heeled dudes. When you're ready to strap on your spurs, Palace Boot Shop (☎ 713-224-1411), 1212 Prairie at Caroline downtown, has been readying folks for the range for more than 70 years.

GETTING THERE & AWAY
Air

Houston has two airports: George Bush Intercontinental Airport (IAH; ☎ 281-230-3100), 22 miles north of the city center, served by major domestic and international airlines, and William P Hobby Airport (HOU; ☎ 713-640-3000), 11 miles southeast of the center, primarily served by discount carrier Southwest Airlines.

The following airlines serve Houston (the airports served are listed, as well as addresses if the airline has a city ticket office; see the Toll-Free Numbers appendix for more information):

Aeromexico (IAH)
(☎ 713-939-0077) 13405 Northwest Freeway

Air Canada (IAH)

Air France (IAH)

American Airlines (IAH)
JW Marriott Hotel, 5150 Westheimer Rd

America West Airlines (IAH)

Aviateca Airlines (IAH)
(☎ 713-665-2883) 5821 Southwest Freeway

British Airways (IAH)
10700 North Freeway, Suite 900

Cayman Airways (IAH)
(☎ 800-422-9626)

Continental Airlines (IAH)
1100 Louisiana, Suite 175

Delta Air Lines (IAH, HOU)
JW Marriott Hotel, 5150 Westheimer Rd

KLM (IAH)

Lufthansa (IAH)
5000 Westheimer Rd

Northwest Airlines (HOU)

Southwest Airlines (IAH, HOU)
(☎ 281-922-1221)

TACA (IAH)
(☎ 800-535-8780)

TWA (HOU)

United Airlines (IAH)
5000 Westheimer Rd, Suite 158

US Airways (IAH)

George Bush Intercontinental Airport Renamed for ex-president Bush in 1997, Houston's primary airport is a sprawling place that – like airports worldwide – is continually under construction. Continental Airlines has a major hub here and offers service to more than 30 cities in the United States from Terminal C. The other domestic airlines operate out of Terminals A and B. Combined, the airlines serve more than 60 destinations in the United States. All three terminal complexes have their parking garages *above* the terminals, since they couldn't be dug down into Houston's swampy ground.

International flights call at the Mickey Leland International Airlines Building, a modern and airy structure that usually boasts quick immigration and customs processing. To the chagrin of Houston boosters, no Asian airlines fly to Houston, opting to take their passengers to rival Dallas instead. However, United Airlines has connecting service to its myriad Asian flights from San Francisco.

Nonstop service to Europe from a variety of airlines includes flights to Amsterdam, London and Paris. Continental flies to eight cities in Mexico and seven Central American nations, plus Ecuador and Colombia. Air Canada flies to Calgary and Toronto.

The four terminals are linked by a comical little electric train that runs back and forth in a basement corridor. The small cars hold very few passengers, and the train rarely runs on its much touted three-minute intervals. If you have to change terminals, you'll get there quicker and do your heart a favor by walking the rather long distances between each of them. Fortunately, part of the construction encircling the airport terminals is for a much larger and more capable transit system, which is set to open in 2000.

Amenities in the terminals are surprisingly few. Food service is of an especially low order, with stale muffins, well-aged pizza slices and high-priced weenies that have made more revolutions on their little cookers than the blades in your plane's jet engines.

If you want a sit-down meal, your best bet is to head over to the Houston Airport Marriott Hotel (☎ 281-443-2310), 18700 John F Kennedy Blvd between Terminals B and C. One of the two restaurants there revolves on the rooftop, although even if you linger over your food, your revolution count will never come close to that of those snack-bar weenies.

Although the airport has posted almost no maps showing where anything is situated, ATMs and newsstands are scattered throughout all four terminals. Large signs in each terminal's luggage area list lodgings near the airport and have free direct phone lines.

William P Hobby Airport A much smaller and therefore much calmer airport than Bush, Hobby is a good choice if your onward travels will take you south or east of the city. The modern terminal is easily navigated, and the food options and other amenities – while not worth a special trip – offer more variety than Hobby's larger counterpart.

Discount carrier Southwest Airlines has a major hub at Hobby, with nonstop service to more than 10 US cities outside Texas, including New Orleans and Phoenix. In-state destinations include Harlingen, Corpus Christi, San Antonio, Austin, El Paso and Dallas, which is served at least every half-hour through the day.

Bus

Houston has a modern bus terminal at 2121 Main, between downtown and the Museum District. Greyhound (☎ 713-759-6565) is the major carrier, offering a web of services in all directions, some of which are operated by a contractor named Valley Transit. Among the destinations with several departures a day are:

to/from	trip duration	one way/ roundtrip
Brownsville	8 to 9 hours	$28/56
Corpus Christi	4 to 5 hours	$21/42
Dallas	4 to 6 hours	$28/56
New Orleans	7 to 8 hours	$40/80
San Antonio	3 hours	$20/40

Train

Service on Amtrak (☎ 713-224-1577), 902 Washington, is limited. The chronically late *Sunset Limited* wanders through town three times a week in each direction on its runs between Los Angeles (34 hours, $155 to $215), New Orleans (10 hours, $57 to $85) and Orlando, FL. The spartan station is in a typically scruffy area at the western edge of downtown.

Car & Motorcycle

As a city built around the car, Houston has highways radiating in all directions. The major routes, destinations and mileage are as follows:

I-45 North	Dallas	243
I-45 South	Galveston	49
I-10 East	Beaumont/New Orleans	83/347
I-10 West	San Antonio/El Paso	199/751
Hwy 290	Austin	163
US 59	Corpus Christi/Brownsville	220/384

If you're just passing through Houston during daylight hours, take the Sam Houston Parkway north and around the city. What you'll pay in tolls will more than offset the psychological toll from traffic aggravation on other roads.

GETTING AROUND
To/From the Airport

Public Transit Metro (see the Bus section) has limited bus service to IAH. Bus No 102 runs to and from the Greyhound Bus Terminal downtown Monday to Friday 6 am to 7 pm; there's no weekend service. The fare is $1.50 ($1 from 10 am to 3 pm), and the ride can take an hour or longer.

Service to Hobby in the southeast is more reliable. Bus No 88 connects downtown to the airport every 30 minutes every day from 5 am to midnight. The fare is always $1 and the trip can take 30 minutes or longer.

Shuttle Airport Express (☎ 713-523-8888) offers van service from both airports to several clusters of hotels in the Houston area. The vans run every day from about 5:30 am to 11 pm and leave from outside the baggage areas at all terminals at both airports. Routes and fares include the following (if you buy a roundtrip ticket at the airports, you save $4):

IAH to downtown	$16
IAH to the Galleria	$17
IAH to the Astrodome	$17
IAH to West Side	$21
IAH to Hobby	$17
Hobby to downtown	$11
Hobby to the Galleria	$12
Hobby to the Astrodome	$12

HOUSTON

Taxi Cabs are readily available at both airports. Some sample fares (not including tip) are:

IAH to downtown	$32
IAH to the Galleria	$41
IAH to the Astrodome	$44
IAH to West Side	$47
Hobby to downtown	$17
Hobby to the Galleria	$34
Hobby to the Astrodome	$20

Public Transit

The Houston area is served by Metro (☎ 713-635-4000), a network of 124 bus lines that cover the Houston area from north of IAH south all the way to Clear Lake. Much of the system is geared toward weekday commuters to the downtown area, which means that you may not find service to where you want to go.

Buses are divided into three types: locals putter along major thoroughfares, stopping at most intersections; limiteds have 'Ltd' on their destination signs and make fewer stops along major roads; commuters run primarily on weekdays and use special lanes built into the freeways for a significant part of their journey. Most of the lines reach the downtown area at one end of their routes. Dedicated bus riders will spend a lot of time wandering the streets downtown, transferring from one bus to another. Even journeys between major areas such as the Galleria and the Museum District require a time-consuming change of buses downtown.

A Metro map, found at the tourist information office downtown (☎ 713-227-3100), 801 Congress Ave, is a vital resource for your public-transit planning, but deciphering its spaghetti-like maze of multicolored bus lines can consume hours of time otherwise spent in such pursuits as sightseeing or shopping.

Fares are quite cheap. An unlimited day pass, good for 24 hours of riding Metro buses, costs only $2. Single rides on the locals and the limiteds cost $1 and include a free transfer good for three hours. Fares for the commuter buses range from $1 to $3.50, depending on the distance covered and the time of day. You can use dollar bills to pay for your fare, but you must pay the exact amount, because the buses do not give change. Detailed route and schedule information is available on the Metro website: www.hou-metro.harris.tx.us.

Car & Motorcycle

By far the best way to get around Houston is by car. Parking is plentiful and usually free, and the various concentrations of sights in clusters mean that you can ditch your wheels and walk around a bit when you wish. Other sights and attractions are so scattered that driving is the only viable way to reach them.

Traffic on Houston's streets can be dense throughout the day, which means that you will have plenty of time to fully appreciate the city's sprawling streetscape – for better or worse. The most direct route from the popular west side to central Houston would seem to be US 59, but it is often as clogged as the arteries of dedicated barbecue eaters. Three streets – Westheimer Rd, Alabama and Richmond Ave – span west Houston and pass through several interesting neighborhoods. Traffic, while often slow, moves steadily.

Highways If you're going to travel the freeways passing through central Houston, plot your course in advance, because signage is among the worst we've encountered in the US. It's very easy to miss an exit, and if you do you'll have to travel miles to backtrack. If traffic is backed up, Hardy Toll Rd offers the fastest route from the city to IAH. The Sam Houston Tollway from US 59 in the south to I-45 in the north is usually clear of traffic jams. However, road signs are almost non-existent, the worst example being at the frequent toll plazas, where most of the lanes are designated 'Automatic' but no information is posted regarding what the toll will be. In 1998, most toll booths charged $1, but that could change; if you're in doubt you'll have to opt for the slow lanes with attendants, on the far right side.

The E Sam Houston Parkway is best avoided, as construction is set to continue well past 2000 and several stop lights can cause traffic backups for miles. Concerning construction, you'll find it on almost every highway radiating out from Houston as the suburban sprawl continues unchecked.

Car Rental Rental cars are readily available at both Houston airports. The volume of business helps keep prices down, making Houston a good place to rent a car for a Texas visit. Rates vary widely, with numerous specials usually on offer. The Travelocity website (www.travelocity.com) is a good place to compare rates. In early 1998, one of the authors had no problem finding a compact car for $150 a week with unlimited mileage. But don't forget the 25% in taxes, plus another $2 per day in special charges.

The companies listed here operate shuttle buses that will pick you up at the baggage claim areas of the terminals at both airports. Most also have additional offices at hotels around town, but the best rates are often restricted to cars picked up at the huge airport locations.

Alamo	☎ 281-590-5100
Avis	☎ 281-443-5800
Budget	☎ 713-988-7300
Dollar	☎ 713-227-7368
Enterprise	☎ 713-645-7222
Hertz	☎ 281-443-0800
National	☎ 281-443-8850
Thrifty	☎ 281-442-5000

Taxi
Cab rates are $3 flagfall and $1.50 for each additional mile. Given Houston's sprawl, your cab tab can quickly surpass car rental rates. However, cabs are an excellent way to get out at night when no one is ready to take on the responsibility of being the designated (read: nondrinking) driver. You can't hail cabs, but most hotels, restaurants, bars and clubs will call one for you.

Among the largest cab companies are:

Fiesta Cab
    ☎ 713-236-9400, 713-225-2666
United Cab
    ☎ 713-699-0000, 713-699-8040
Yellow Cab
    ☎ 713-236-1111, 713-224-4445

Around Houston

As you drive the freeways out of Houston, in particular south on I-45 or US 59, you will see how Houston's sprawl continues snake-like along these corridors. As you pass mile after mile of barn-size new homes crammed into treeless walled subdivisions with improbable names such as 'Bridlewood,' you'll notice that many of the developments bear signs touting the low taxes of the development. This message is meant to draw in buyers from the legions of Americans who are rabidly tax averse.

What happens next is the very paradox that is responsible for the unsightly, land-wasting suburbs that are nowhere more pronounced than around Houston. Once the new arrivals buy their barn-size houses in this low-tax paradise, they start demanding services such as police, fire protection and schools, all of which were unnecessary when the land was used for growing cotton or grazing cattle. As local governments raise taxes to pay for the demanded services, people yell about taxes and promptly move to a new development of barn-size houses in a treeless walled subdivision. And so it goes.

The following sites are within a one-hour drive of downtown Houston.

GEORGE RANCH HISTORIC PARK
You can experience four generations of Texas ranches in one place at this 23,000-acre working cattle ranch (☎ 281-545-9212). The 480 acres that are open to the public include an 1830s pioneer cabin, an 1890s Victorian home, a 1930s mansion and parts of the contemporary ranch. The visitors' center explains the development of ranching from the early days, when cattle grazed the range freely, through the introduction of barbed wire and cowboys. On weekends and some weekdays, guides in various period costumes demonstrate chores and how people lived in each era; you also can take yourself around the grounds without joining a tour. March through December open daily 10 am to 6 pm; $6 for adults, $5 for seniors, $3 for kids. The ranch is 25 miles southwest

of downtown Houston off US 59. Take the Crab River Rd exit and drive south, first on FM 2759, then on FM 762, for about 8 miles.

BRAZOS BEND STATE PARK

One of the most popular state parks in Texas (☎ 409-553-5101), Brazos Bend comprises nearly 5000 acres of coastal prairie; hardwood forest with oaks, pecans and black walnuts; and aquatic areas with swamps, lakes and creeks. Despite the popularity of the park, most of it has been left in its natural state. Stop by the office at the entrance for maps and information about the many nature and hiking trails.

Spring is a good time for alligator watching: the cold-blooded reptiles bask in the springtime sun, trying to bake away their winter somnolence. In the summer they're in the shade, like everyone else.

Camping at the large campground costs $12 to $18, depending on the level of services. Reserve well in advance for weekends (☎ 512-389-8900). Gates are open daily 7 am to 10 pm. Admission is $3 for those older than 12. Take Hwy 288 28 miles south from downtown Houston, then turn west on FM 1462 and go about 14 miles before turning north to the park (a sign points the way).

SAN JACINTO BATTLEGROUND

It was late afternoon on April 21, 1836, and the Mexican army of General Antonio López de Santa Anna was taking a break in the shade of some scruffy oaks. Suddenly, Sam Houston and his ragtag army appeared in a surprise attack. The Mexicans surrendered after only 18 minutes, but the killing continued for two hours as Houston's men 'remembered the Alamo.' The final tally was 630 Mexicans dead and hundreds more injured, as opposed to only nine Texan casualties. The victory was total: Santa Anna retreated to Mexico, and Texas had won its independence.

More than 1,000 acres of the battleground are now preserved as the San Jacinto Battleground State Historical Complex (☎ 281-479-2431). Away from the monument and the museum, the land is pretty much as it was. A walk on one of the trails on a hot day is a good introduction to the conditions endured by early settlers of all stripes.

The park is 22 miles east of downtown Houston. Take Hwy 225 east to Hwy 134, then north to the park. Open daily 9 am to 9 pm (till 7 pm November 1 to February 29); free.

Monument & Museum

The 570-foot San Jacinto Monument (☎ 281-479-2421) was built between 1936 and '39 to commemorate the battle. Both the inside and the outside are clad in limestone naturally studded with shells contributed by marine creatures through the aeons. During the elevator ride to the observation deck at the 489-foot level, the operator will inform you in typical Texas fashion that the monument is '15 feet higher than the Washington Monument.' There's an excellent view of the surrounding park and the sobering sight of petrochemical plants stretching in all directions just beyond. On many days you can admire the Houston skyline through the clouds of gaseous emissions.

San Jacinto Monument

The museum at the base of the monument has a collection of historical Texas artifacts. An adjoining theater has the inevitable multimedia show, *Texas Forever!! The Battle of San Jacinto*. The 35-minute spectacle is narrated by actor and National Rifle Association shill Charlton Heston, who does plenty of tut-tutting about the exploits of the Texans.

The museum and tower are open daily 10 am to 6 pm. Admission to the museum is free; for the observation deck it's $3 for adults, $2 for kids, and for *Texas Forever!!* (shown on the hour from 10 am through 5 pm) it's $3.50 for adults, $2.50 for kids. Parts of the monument will be surrounded by scaffolding through 2000.

Battleship *Texas*
Commissioned in 1914, the USS *Texas* (☎ 281-479-2411) is the only preserved American naval vessel that saw service in both world wars. Obsolete for front-line combat by World War II, the *Texas* still made itself useful for bombarding the invasion beaches at Normandy, Iwo Jima and Okinawa. Retired in 1948, the ship is now undergoing long-term restoration; about 20 of its more than 500 compartments are finished. Volunteers greatly improve the tours with tales of life aboard the ship. It's right near the monument, open daily 10 am to 5 pm, except during periodic restoration-related closures (call first). $5 for adults, $3 for seniors, $2.50 for kids.

ARMAND BAYOU NATURE CENTER
More than 350 species of birds and animals are at this 2500-acre preserve (☎ 281-474-2551), reached by taking the Bay Area Blvd exit off I-45 south, then driving about 7 miles east to FM 8500, in petrochemical-dominated Pasadena. Privately operated, the nature center is named for its late founder, Armand Yramategui, whose Basque name means 'to see great beauty.' Hiking trails traverse three ecosystems: bayou, forest and prairie. A wooden walkway stretches over the swamp. Besides birds, you might see armadillos, swamp rabbits, turtles and various poisonous snakes. A museum and interpretive building help explain the sights and species. This is an excellent place to escape the urban sprawl. Open Wednesday to Saturday 10 am to 5 pm, Sunday noon to dusk; $2.50 for adults, $1 for kids. On many weekends they have free guided tours.

NASA & Clear Lake

The Lyndon B Johnson Space Center, 25 miles southeast of downtown Houston, is one of the most popular tourist destinations in Texas. Neighboring Clear Lake is the most popular weekend destination for Houstonians. Both are well worth a visit.

NASA
The Manned Spacecraft Center (MSC) opened in 1963. It was the brightest star ever placed in Houston's orbit. To see how that was accomplished, note how a bit of Houston proper juts down like an appendix through Harris County – the city limits were extended in the 1960s to incorporate MSC. For a highly amusing account of how the city 'welcomed' the original seven astronauts to town, check out chapter 13 of Tom Wolfe's book *The Right Stuff*.

Thanks to the US push to reach the moon in the 1960s, MSC was one of the most exciting places on the planet for scientists and engineers interested in space. Although the high-profile launches of missions such as the Apollo series and the space shuttles have been from the Kennedy Space Center in Florida, the planning and most of the training for the astronauts is accomplished at MSC. The center's activity has waxed and waned since Apollo, linked to the levels of congressional funding for the space shuttles, the international space station still under development and a possible future mission to land astronauts on Mars.

Space Center Houston
One would expect the US to take pride in the many accomplishments of its space program. Certainly that is the case in Washington, DC, where the Smithsonian's National Air and

HOUSTON

Space Museum does an excellent job of documenting the nation's achievements in space. But it is not so at MSC, where, in what foreign visitors must consider a perfect example of American commercialism, the entire manned spaceflight program has been turned into a theme park, and a not very good one at that. Tours of MSC used to be straightforward and informative affairs highlighting the functions and accomplishments of the place; now, Space Center Houston (SCH; ☎ 281-244-2100, 800-972-0369) substitutes a carnival for the science, a sideshow for the legacies of the US space program and two ludicrous cartoon characters for the astronauts. All of that is a result of the decision during the Bush administration in the early 1990s that people should not profit from NASA's exploits, but the government should profit from peoples' interest in NASA (the government gets a cut of the money SCH draws in).

The fun begins with the $3 charge to park at SCH, which is separate from the Johnson Space Center. When we visited, the entrance to the building was dominated by several Saturn automobiles. Inside, the first display we encountered was a huge one touting the 'space-age plastic' in SCH sponsor Saturn's cars. The next huge exhibit also celebrated plastic, in this case Lego, which sponsored a large exhibit of the nifty rockets one can build with their blocks (available in the gift store). Even the poorly designed guide given to each visitor had several commercial sponsors.

Once past the entrance advertising displays, there's more. You can visit the 'IMAX Theater Sponsored by Coca-Cola,' or you can try to learn about current NASA missions at the 'Mission Status Center Sponsored by Southwestern Bell.' If you look behind all the hype, you can find some actual evidence that the space program once had a function beyond serving as a marketing tool. But we'd understand it if, while you look at a photo of Neil Armstrong's first footstep on the moon, you wonder whether the same footstep today would leave the impression of the Nike swoosh.

Past the Starship Gallery you can find an area simply called Artifacts (evidently the sponsors were tapped out). Here is where the real stories are. Among them: *Faith 7* (1963), the Mercury capsule used to orbit the earth during a flawless mission lasting 34 hours and 20 minutes; *Gemini 5* (1965), used by Gordon Cooper and Pete Conrad to orbit the earth for eight days (think about sitting in that tiny space for that long); *Apollo 17* (1972), the spacecraft used for the last trip by humans to the moon; and finally, a trove of actual moon rocks, including one you can touch.

Tours The chance to see the actual MSC is why most people come to Space Center Houston, and admission covers guided tram tours of the center. You can see Mission Control, the space shuttle training mock-up and other training facilities, zero-gravity labs and more. To see them all, you have to take more than one of the 90-minute tours, which follow several different routes. Add the complexities of the tour schedules to the inevitable waiting in line for the trams and you'll soon determine that it will take most of the day to see the MSC. That, of course, leaves plenty of time for the Zero-G Diner, which is appropriately named, given the effect it will have on your wallet. Or you can visit the well-stocked gift shop . . .

Space Center Houston is open Monday to Friday 10 am to 5 pm, Saturday and Sunday 10 am to 7 pm (Memorial Day to Labor Day it's open 9 am to 7 pm). Admission is $13 for adults, $12 for seniors, $9 for kids. Take the NASA Rd 1 exit off I-45 south and drive east until you see the huge signs for the Space Center.

Rocket Park

This display of discarded NASA hardware can be visited free. The SCH trams all stop at Rocket Park, but you'll be using your time more wisely if you stay on the trams and visit the park later.

The display is dominated by *Saturn 5*, a rocket that looks like a huge fallen tree. It's a fitting metaphor, because this particular rocket was built for Apollo 18, one of three missions to the moon eliminated by budget cutters. Even though all the expensive hardware had been bought and the astronauts trained, the government declined to actually pay for the missions, so that the tax money could be used for other activities, such as the war in Vietnam.

To get an idea of what was accomplished with the Apollo program, compare the *Saturn 5* with the nearby *Redstone Rocket*. A mere firecracker by comparison, the *Redstone* had been state of the art in 1961, just eight years before the *Saturn 5* took the first humans to the moon.

To get to Rocket Park, turn north off NASA Rd 1 at the Johnson Space Center sign just past Space Center Houston. Drive 200 yards and turn east into the NASA employee entrance. The guard at the gate will direct you to a visitor parking lot from which the park is a two-minute walk.

CLEAR LAKE

The lake really doesn't look clear, but it's the home of one of the largest concentrations of recreational boats in the US. Continue east of NASA on NASA Rd 1 and you'll find beaches, harbors, jetties and scores of delightful, laid-back waterfront joints that attract fun-seekers in droves.

Oasis (☎ 281-326-1475), 3905 NASA Rd 1, Nassau Bay, is typical of the many restaurants lining the lake side of the road. They have seafood, volleyball nets, lots of tables on the lawn by the water and a playground for kids. Farther east, ***Lance's Turtle Club*** *(281-326-7613)*, 2613½ NASA Rd 1 at the intersection of Lake Side Drive in Seabrook, is a rowdy floating bar surrounded by boats belonging to its patrons. There's live rock Thursday through Sunday.

HOUSTON

Gulf Coast

Three out of four migrating waterbirds in North America drop by the wetlands lining the Gulf of Mexico, and the Texas coast is an especially popular stop. These birds are clearly using their brains, and you should, too. The Gulf Coast is one of the most interesting places in Texas. Many of the towns have long histories going back to the Spanish days.

America's 'Third Coast,' as it likes to call itself, is a mostly relaxed place. Its major coastal city, Corpus Christi, bears little resemblance to someplace like Miami Beach. Most of the year, the streets are quiet by 9 pm. Galveston has scores of old buildings and a feel that is more Louisiana than Texas. Much smaller towns line the coast, which wends its way around coves, bayous, rivers and bays. You'll find places that seem un-changed in decades, or at least since the last hurricane blew through.

Perhaps the Gulf Coast's greatest attraction is the hundreds of miles of almost untouched beaches. If your idea of heaven is a stretch of beach far from any other person, then you can spend a pleasant eternity wandering these sands.

Golden Triangle

The cities of Beaumont, Port Arthur and Orange make up the corners of the Golden Triangle, the southeasternmost corner of the state, which is home to more than 350,000 people. First settled by French and Spanish trappers in the early 19th century, the area has more in common culturally with neighboring Louisiana than it does with the rest of Texas. A large and freewheeling Cajun community and the state's largest African American population by percentage (33%) combine to give the Triangle a culture that is as rich and spicy as the ubiquitous gumbo. This is not a part of Texas that subscribes to the abstemious notions in force elsewhere in the state.

Prior to 1901, the subsistence lives of the local trappers meant that the area could have been legitimately called the Beaver Triangle. Then oil was discovered south of Beaumont on a site called Spindletop, and the Triangle turned golden with cash. It was then the richest discovery made in the USA, and it sparked the creation of the entire US petroleum industry. Companies that later transmogrified into giants, such as Chevron, Texaco, Mobil and Exxon, got their starts here. Some of the largest petrochemical works in the world are found near Port Arthur and Beaumont.

Although oil has brought wealth and growth to the swampy region, it has also left a legacy of environmental damage and pollution. Much of the money has gone west to Houston, where the oil companies

GULF COAST

Highlights

- Exploring old Galveston
- Stalking whooping cranes at Aransas National Wildlife Refuge
- Pounding the endless sand at Padre Island National Seashore

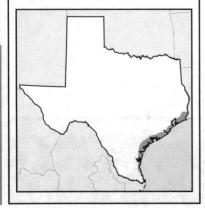

moved, leaving generations of Cajun and black workers to tend the oil fields and the refineries. All is not golden today in the Triangle, with its stagnant population growth and its economy pegged to fluctuations in the global price of oil.

Taken separately, the cities of Beaumont, Port Arthur and Orange are not compelling tourist destinations, but together they warrant a few days of exploration. They bristle with small museums as well as fascinating sights related to the oil industry. The towns are each roughly 20 miles apart and well connected by roads, meaning that it makes most sense for a visitor to treat them as one. Port Arthur's proximity to the coast makes it the most convenient place to stay for visits to the beach.

South of the Golden Triangle, the Texas Gulf Coast begins. The stretch curving southwest to Galveston is quiet most of the year and boasts attractive beaches and grass-covered dunes.

BEAUMONT
Population 111,000
Lumber culled from the vast forests of the Big Thicket to the north was the economic engine driving Beaumont's growth in the 19th century. Rice cultivation and the profitable beavers rounded out the economy. On January 10, 1901, a heretofore dry exploratory well leased by Anthony Lucas started to rumble and then blew out a fountain of warm, sticky, smelly oil. More than 100,000 barrels of oil a day gushed from the hole, and close to a million barrels had spilled over the land by the time the well was capped. Soon hundreds of wildcat oil explorers were doing their best to relieve the pressure by drilling their own wells. Pictures from the era show oil rigs crowded together like pine trees in a forest. The Spindletop field dried up within 10 years, but the oil industry was in the Golden Triangle to stay.

Besides the petrochemical industry, Beaumont has developed a busy port on the Neches River and a shipbuilding and repair industry that has grown to include lucrative work on the offshore oil-drilling platforms. To the north and west are lush green

Oil derricks

rice fields interspersed with the ubiquitous oil wells.

Orientation
Beaumont is linked to Houston, 83 miles to the west, by I-10, which continues east into Louisiana. Orange is 23 miles east on I-10. Port Arthur is 17 miles south on the combined US 69/96/287; the parallel Hwy 347 is a slower but more interesting road. The fairly compact downtown area is right on a bend in the Neches River.

For a panoramic view of the Golden Triangle, venture up to the 8th floor of the Mary and John Grey Library at Lamar University (☎ 409-880-8118), 211 Redbird Lane. You can see all the way to Port Arthur and the gulf on a clear day, and you can appreciate the vast spread of petrochemical plants. Hours vary widely through the academic year, so call first.

Information
Tourist Offices A state-operated Texas Travel Information Center (☎ 409-883-9416)

GULF COAST

is at 1708 I-10 E in Orange. It is open daily 8 am to 5 pm and has information on the region and the entire state.

The Beaumont Convention & Visitors Bureau (☎ 409-880-3749, 800-392-4401), downtown at 801 Main St, is open weekdays 8 am to 5 pm. You can get information on weekends by calling ☎ 409-833-4622. It has vast volumes of information, including a useful and complete *Visitor's Guide*. The front desk at the conveniently located Babe Didrikson Zaharias Memorial Museum (☎ 409-833-4622) has regional information; see the section on the museum, below.

Post The main post office (☎ 409-842-7200) is at 5815 Walden Rd at I-10. It's open weekdays 8 am to 5:30 pm and Saturday 8:30 am to 1 pm.

Libraries Beaumont has a surprising number of libraries. The main public library (☎ 409-838-6606) is downtown at 801 Pearl St

and is open weekdays from 9 am to 7 pm and Saturday 10 am to 4 pm. The Malcolm X Community Library (☎ 409-833-5575), at 1469 I-10 E on the access road, focuses on African American fiction and culture. It's open weekdays 1 to 5 pm. The Tyrrell Historical Library (☎ 409-833-2759), downtown at 695 Pearl St, has genealogy records, archives and a large Texas history collection. Housed in a 1903 landmark building, it is open Wednesday to Saturday 8:30 am to 5:30 pm and Tuesday 8:30 am to 8 pm.

Media The *Beaumont Enterprise* (50¢) is the local daily. KVLU, 91.3 FM, is the National Public Radio affiliate.

Medical Services The Convenient Care Center at Baptist Hospital (☎ 409-654-5472) is part of the vast medical complex at College and 11th Sts, just east of I-10. As the name implies, it is set up for people without appointments.

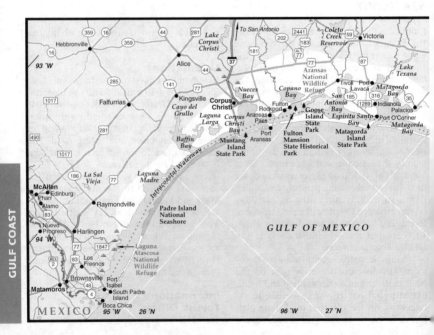

Dangers & Annoyances 'Mosquito Triangle' has been an appropriate nickname for this area since long before the arrival of humans, and no doubt will be appropriate long after we're gone. These remarkably tough little buggers are in season 12 months of the year and attack in swarms. Wear a good repellent if you go to parks, beaches or swampy areas.

Texas Energy Museum

This excellent museum (☎ 409-833-5100), on Main St, covers the Spindletop discovery and the subsequent growth of the Texas oil industry, and it's worth at least an hour or two. A series of scenes use life-size mannequins and film to give lively and often delightfully campy narrations about the oil boom. An old coot talking about the early days and the hazards inherent to eating beans and falling off a drilling rig is especially delightful. Open Tuesday to Saturday 9 am to 5 pm, Sunday 1 to 5 pm; $2 for adults, $1 for children. The museum shares a free parking lot with the Art Museum of Southeast Texas, next door.

Art Museum of Southeast Texas

This small museum (☎ 409-832-3432) is housed in a distinctive, architecturally significant building right downtown. Its ever changing exhibits are drawn from the permanent collection and visiting shows and focus on regional and American artists. The shows are very well curated, and a special effort is made to present companion exhibits giving information about the artworks and their styles, to appeal to kids and make the art more interesting. (Adults might enjoy these displays as well.) Open Monday to Saturday 9 am to 5 pm, Sunday noon to 5 pm; free (contributions are welcome). Overlooking a sculpture garden, the museum's Cafe Arts is open for lunch weekdays 11 am to 2 pm and has creative sandwiches and salads that average $5.

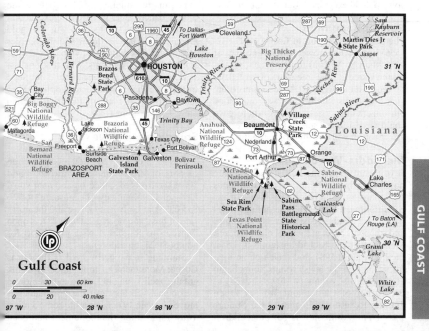

Gulf Coast

Fire Museum of Texas

Fans of old fire engines will enjoy this small museum (☎ 409-880-3927), in the fire department's headquarters downtown at 400 Walnut St. In addition to the fire engines, some hair-raising displays tell children about the hazards posed by electricity. Although the exhibits are drawn from the entire state, the most moving display is local: the graves of the Beaumont Fire Department's official dogs, marked simply 'Bob,' 'Spot' and 'Major.' Open weekdays 8 am to 4:30 pm; free.

Edison Plaza Museum

A holdover from the days of cheap-power shill Ready Kilowatt (a moronic cartoon character who encouraged power use), the museum (☎ 409-839-3089), 350 Pine St, tells those kids who haven't been permanently scared off electricity by the fire museum about the inventions of Thomas Alva Edison and the future of power generation. Open weekdays 1 to 3:30 pm; call for reservations if you would like a guided tour at another time.

Port of Beaumont

The fourth-busiest port in Texas (☎ 409-832-1546) is right downtown, with its entrance at 1255 Main St. Various tourist brochures extol the virtues of the free tours offered daily by request, but when we tried, a gun-toting guard said, essentially, that we could stick our fingers in an electrical socket before we could have a tour. Call ahead and reserve a group tour if you'd really like to see the port.

McFaddin-Ward House

If you want to see the kind of riches made possible by the oil boom, visit this fabulous 1907 mansion. Built before the advent of air-conditioning, it makes full use of huge overhangs and shade trees as well as awnings and transoms to let in the cool night breezes. Members of the McFaddin family lived in the house until 1984, and their rich antique furnishings fill the lavish rooms. Tours begin at the visitors' center (☎ 409-832-2134) at the corner of Calder and 3rd Sts. Open Tuesday to Saturday 10 am to 4 pm, Sunday 1 to 4 pm. Admission is $3, but children

under age eight have to remain outside, where they can ponder any recently learned facts about electricity.

John Jay French Museum

A survivor of Beaumont's early economy, the John Jay French House was built in 1845 and now houses a museum (☎ 409-898-0348), at 3025 French Rd east of US 69/96/287. The building was the area's first home made with lumber rather than logs. Displays document life in the mid-19th century, long before the time of electricity and its dubious benefits. Open Tuesday to Saturday 10 am to 4 pm; $3 for adults, $1 for children.

Babe Didrikson Zaharias Memorial Museum

Known simply as 'the Babe,' one of the world's greatest female athletes and Beaumont native Babe Didrikson is remembered at this affectionate museum (☎ 409-833-4622), just north of I-10 at exit 854, the Martin Luther King Parkway, which recalls her many, many athletic triumphs before she died of cancer at 45 in 1956. She excelled at basketball early, went on to win two gold medals in the javelin throw and the hurdles at the 1932 Los Angeles Olympics, and later won 82 golf tournaments. With this, our last sight in Beaumont, we probably don't need to mention that the Babe accomplished her feats without the aid of electricity. Open daily 9 am to 5 pm; free.

Spindletop Gladys City Boomtown Museum

This is an altogether too tidy reconstruction of part of the original boomtown – add 800,000 barrels of spilled oil and *then* you'd have some authenticity. The museum (☎ 409-835-0823), at University Drive and the north side of busy and noisy US 69/96/287, is open Tuesday to Sunday 1 to 5 pm; $2.50 for adults, $1.25 for children.

Standing in a nearby field is the **Lucas Gusher Monument**, an imposing 58-foot pink granite obelisk built in 1941 to commemorate the original well. However, the monument was moved here in 1978 from a site some 3 miles away – a location the monument had been

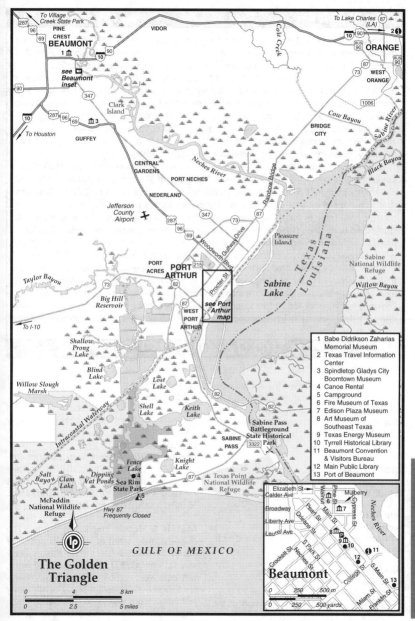

To Village Creek State Park

To Lake Charles (LA)

PINE CREST BEAUMONT

VIDOR

Cole Creek

ORANGE

see Beaumont inset

WEST ORANGE

Clark Island

Cow Bayou

BRIDGE CITY

To Houston

GUFFEY

Neches River

Rainbow Bridge

Sabine River

CENTRAL GARDENS

PORT NECHES

NEDERLAND

Black Bayou

Jefferson County Airport

Woodworth Blvd

Gulfway Drive

Pleasure Island

Texas Louisiana

Sabine National Wildlife Refuge

Taylor Bayou

PORT ACRES

PORT ARTHUR

Sabine Lake

Willow Bayou

Big Hill Reservoir

WEST PORT ARTHUR

see Port Arthur map

Proter St

To I-10

Shallow Prong Lake

Blind Lake

Lost Lake

Willow Slough Marsh

Shell Lake

Keith Lake

Sabine Pass Battleground State Historical Park

SABINE PASS

1 Babe Didrikson Zaharias Memorial Museum
2 Texas Travel Information Center
3 Spindletop Gladys City Boomtown Museum
4 Canoe Rental
5 Campground
6 Fire Museum of Texas
7 Edison Plaza Museum
8 Art Museum of Southeast Texas
9 Texas Energy Museum
10 Tyrrell Historical Library
11 Beaumont Convention & Visitors Bureau
12 Main Public Library
13 Port of Beaumont

Salt Bayou

Clam Lake

Dipping Vat Ponds

Fence Lake

Sea Rim State Park

Knight Lake

Texas Point National Wildlife Refuge

McFaddin National Wildlife Refuge

Hwy 87 Frequently Closed

GULF OF MEXICO

The Golden Triangle

0   4   8 km
0   2.5   5 miles

Elizabeth St

Calder Ave

Broadway

Liberty Ave

Laurel Ave

Mulberry

Pine St

Cypress St

Main St

Walnut

Pearl St

Orleans St

Crockett St

S Neches St

S Park St

College Ave

Milam St

Franklin St

S Main St

Neches River

Beaumont

0   250   500 m
0   250   500 yards

There She Blows!

First, we need to dispel the number-one false notion about oil drilling. When a crew strikes a deposit, there is no longer a deep rumbling in the ground followed by a geyser of oil that shoots far into the air, sending equipment flying and workers running for cover.

'It just makes too big a mess,' says Rod Moore, a drilling foreman with Spirit Energy, a division of Unocal, a huge oil company. Rather than fountains of oil – which do provide a dramatic climax to the long and uncertain drilling process – a reading on a computer screen in an air-conditioned office is most likely to tell today's oil explorers that they've struck oil. A variety of equipment prevents blowouts, as they are called. Various environmental considerations and laws, as well as the fact that there are fewer wide-open spaces where you can let the oil fly, mean that gushers are part of the petroleum industry's past.

But oil drilling remains a very messy business. Much of the process of drilling a hole thousands of feet into the ground involves mud. Not the stuff you get when you mix water and dirt – although there's plenty of that at any drilling site after it rains – but rather the fluid used to lubricate the shaft as it drills the hole. The brown stuff is pumped down the hole under pressure, which forces out the cuttings created by the drill bit. This 'mud' is really high-tech stuff mixed under the guidance of the mud engineer. The ever-varying water-based concoction can include thinners, thickeners, lubricants and a substance called weighting agent, which increases the density of the mud so it can keep water from aquifers out of the hole.

At the drilling rig we visited north of Port Arthur, computer readouts in an air-conditioned trailer were relayed to the mud engineer, who used the information to determine what ingredients to toss into the swirling vats of mud. Meanwhile, the drill tower roared away as workers known as 'roughnecks' fed 20-foot lengths of drilling pipe into the hole. The site, like most, was noisy and dirty. Several trailers surrounded the central drilling tower, and the workers' pickups

moved to in the 1950s when the actual, original site of the gusher collapsed due to subsidence and became a swamp. No doubt when it comes time to move the monument again, they will harness the amazing powers of electricity to do so.

Special Events

Highlights of the Beaumont calendar include the following:

Late April
Neches River Festival
Parades, dances, concerts, boat races and more celebrate the river downtown.

Mid-June
Juneteenth
Held on the weekend closest to June 19, these festivities celebrate the day that news of the Emancipation Proclamation reached Texas.

Mid-October
South Texas State Fair
A huge regional fair features comely 4-H critters, entertainment, a carnival and more.

Places to Stay

Camping *Village Creek State Park* (☎ 409-755-7322), 1101 Alma Drive, 10 miles north of Beaumont on US 96 in Lumberton, has tent ($6) and RV sites ($10). *Sea Rim State Park*, 30 miles south, is covered later in this chapter.

Motels & Hotels Plagued by moths? The overwhelming smell of mothballs at the *JJ Motel* (☎ 409-892-4241), 6675 Eastex Freeway (US 69/96/287), 4 miles north of town, will cure your problem. Very basic rooms are $26/35 for singles/doubles. The adjoining restaurant has a very good coffee shop and a remarkable work of folk art depicting 'the

stood in rows to one side. Typically, a crew lives on the site for 14 days at a time, working in 12-hour shifts before they swap with another crew and get 14 days off. 'It gets in your blood,' says Moore, who lives in Oklahoma, 'because you'd have to be crazy to do this otherwise.'

Besides the dramatic gusher, another aspect of oil exploration that is rapidly disappearing is the dry hole. By the time a crew starts drilling, geologists have used tools that include satellite images and computer modeling to determine the odds that oil is present. More than 50% of holes drilled today strike oil, which is an order of magnitude better than just a few decades ago, when people drilled by intuition or whim. It wasn't unusual for wildcat drillers, as they were called, to go years without making a discovery. Gushers such as the one at Spindletop set off frenzies of drilling because that was the closest one could get to a sure thing at that time.

Another big change is the ability of drill bits to alter their course. Holes are rarely straight these days; instead, they arc out up to a mile or more in any direction. This saves money because multiple holes can be drilled from one site, and the camp does not need to be moved each time a new hole is drilled. Given that it costs $15,000 to $30,000 a day to drill on land – $200,000 a day or more at sea – exploration companies are always looking for ways to save time.

Given the mess inherent to a drilling site and the constant roar of the generators and machinery, foremen such as Rod Moore have to be ready to appease neighbors unhappy with the new arrival in the neighborhood. 'We pay them off,' he says simply. For some, however, the payoff is just the beginning. Oil companies usually own only the mineral rights to the land they drill on. These are purchased from the landowners over the area the drill bit will traverse. If oil is found on your land, you can expect to receive $100,000 a month or more in royalties. Not a bad deal – as Moore says, 'People whose land we've drilled under have brought us cookies.'

---

history of the world' in miniature that was created by the present owner's great-uncle in the 1940s. **Scottish Inn** (☎ 409-899-3152), 2640 I-10 E at exit 855A, has basic rooms for $28/31. **Super 8 Motel** (☎ 409-899-3040), 2850 I-10 E, is almost as cheap but slightly nicer for $37/43.

The **Best Western Beaumont Inn** (☎ 409-898-8150), 2155 N 11th St at I-10 exit 853B, has average rooms for $47/49. Next door, **Holiday Inn Midtown** (☎ 409-892-2222), 2095 N 11th St, is a classic example of that chain and has rooms for $80.

Places to Eat

Budget **Novrozsky's Hamburgers Etc** (☎ 409-898-8688), 4230 Calder St, is the original, and some say best, location of Beaumont's best restaurant for burgers ($4). Wash the spicy hand-cut fries down with one of several draft beers. Just up the road, **Three Amigos** (☎ 409-832-4701), 1716 Calder St, is a fine family-owned Mexican place that excels at the classics ($5 to $7). **L&T** (☎ 409-835-7170), 1705 College St, has a good $5 Chinese lunch buffet, but to really sample the kitchen's art, order from the Vietnamese menu available at dinner.

Painted the color of a canned green bean, the **Green Beanery Cafe** (☎ 409-833-5913), 2921 McFaddin St at 6th St, is a charming little lunch place with crepes, salads and soups for about $4. It's two blocks from the McFaddin-Ward House.

Mid-Range Barbecued crabs are found on menus all over the Triangle, but **Sartin's Seafood** (☎ 409-892-6771), 6725 Eastex Freeway (US 69/96/287) 4 miles north of town, claims to have invented them. Actually, the crabs

GULF COAST

are seasoned and then deep-fried whole, but they are excellent. All-you-can-eat seafood platters served during a period of two hours are $16 each. **Willy Ray's Bar-B-Q and Co** (☎ 409-832-7770), 145 I-10 N at Laurel St, will grill just about anything, but the pork creations are both special and succulent. Those that somehow have extra room can dive into the house key lime-margarita cheesecake. Dinner runs about $10 per person.

Entertainment

Cutters (☎ 409-842-0500), 4120 College St, has been the birthplace of many a country musician's career, including those of Tracy Byrd and local favorite Mark Chestnut. It's open Thursday to Saturday. **Rocky Octanes** (☎ 409-860-9969), 1170 Montrose St, is a huge club that schedules everything from oldies to country to rock on different nights. Call to check the schedule. **Copa** (☎ 409-832-4206), 304 Orleans St, is a gay dance club popular with men and women.

Getting There & Away

Air Jefferson County Airport (BPT, ☎ 409-722-0251), US 69/96/287 at Nederland Ave, is 12 miles south of Beaumont and just north of Port Arthur. American Eagle (☎ 800-433-7300) and Continental Express (☎ 800-525-0280) have service to their respective hubs in Dallas-Fort Worth and Houston.

Bus Greyhound (☎ 409-832-2557), just north of downtown at 650 Magnolia St, has nine buses daily to Houston ($13). There are three buses daily to Orange ($7) and one daily to Port Arthur ($7).

Train Amtrak's oft-maligned *Sunset Limited* creeps through Beaumont three times a week in each direction on its runs linking Los Angeles and Orlando, FL, stopping at the station at 2555 W Cedar St. Usually hours late, the train can be a delightful experience if you are not in a hurry. Check with Amtrak (☎ 800-872-7245) for the current schedule. The train, whenever it arrives, is scheduled for a leisurely two-hour, 20-minute run to Houston. To New Orleans, it takes a sedentary 7½ hours.

Getting Around

You'll definitely need a car here to get around. All major car rental firms have offices at Jefferson County Airport.

Although there is one Greyhound bus a day in each direction between Beaumont and Port Arthur, local service useful to visitors is nonexistent. Yellow Cab (☎ 409-833-6404) is the major local taxi company.

ORANGE
Population 20,000

The smallest of the Triangle cities, Orange may have been named for citrus trees that once grew here or for some Dutch settlers. No one is certain. The widely scattered Cajun population lives along secluded bayous and tributaries of the Sabine River, which forms the border with Louisiana. You can take tours of these remote and fascinating areas – see the Swamp Tours section. Orange makes a good side trip from a visit to Beaumont or Port Arthur.

Orange's compact downtown is 3 miles south of I-10 on a bend in the Sabine River. The Orange Convention & Visitors Bureau (☎ 409-883-3536), downtown at 1012 Green Ave (Business US 90), has area information. It is open weekdays 8:30 am to 5 pm (Friday till 4 pm).

Stark Museum of Art

This good regional museum (☎ 409-883-6661), 700 W Green, is named for the family that funded it, not for the first adjective that comes to mind when you see its spare exterior. The collections focus on artworks depicting native wildlife such as birds, including works by John J Audubon. One gallery is devoted to craftworks by Native Americans from the Great Plains and the Southwest. The museum is open Wednesday to Saturday 10 am to 5 pm and Sunday 1 to 5 pm; admission is free.

Across the street from the museum, the **WH Stark House** (☎ 409-883-0871), 610 W Main, shows how families that can build whole museums live. The 1894 Victorian home is filled with ornate and heavy furnishings that must have felt oppressively hot during the long Texas summers. Open for

GULF COAST

guided tours Tuesday to Saturday 10 am to 3 pm (reservations recommended); $2. Children under 14 are banished to wait outside the fence.

Swamp Tours

A quick ride into the bayous will transport you far from civilization. The only way to get into these fascinating places is by airboat, one of those flat-bottomed racers that have a huge aircraft engine and propeller mounted on the rear. Besides the usual profusion of bird species, there are alligators, raccoons and turtles in the bayous. You'll also see nutria, the endlessly hungry South American rodents that were foolishly introduced into the USA and are now munching their way across the South when they're not busy breeding.

Super Gator Tours (☎ 409-883-7725), 106 E Lutcher St at Lutcher Lake off I-10 exit 878, has one-hour daytime tours and special night tours (when the number of red eyes you'll see in the dark may remind you of the morning after a bad bachelor party). Tours cost $20 for adults, $10 for children. Seniors save 25%, and there are $1-off coupons at every tourist information kiosk.

PORT ARTHUR

Population 59,000

The history of Port Arthur is a classic tale of Texan boom and bust. Railroad tycoon Arthur Stillwell established the town in the late 1890s as the southern terminus of his grandly named Kansas City, Pittsburgh and Gulf Coast Railroad. He happily named the town after himself, which makes one wish he'd been named Fred or Egbert. Stillwell, who was quite the character, cheerfully told people that he had designed the town based on the advice of 'Brownies' – small people who came to him in his sleep.

Unfortunately, the Brownies' business advice was somewhat lacking and Stillwell soon found himself in financial trouble. Shrewd dealer John Gates offered to bail him out, and before Stillwell knew what hit him, Gates had taken over the town.

Shortly thereafter, the Spindletop oil well blew in and Port Arthur became a major

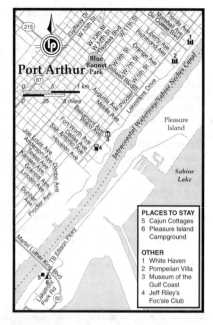

PLACES TO STAY
5 Cajun Cottages
6 Pleasure Island Campground

OTHER
1 White Haven
2 Pompeiian Villa
3 Museum of the Gulf Coast
4 Jeff Riley's Foc'sle Club

oil transit point. Gates reaped a fortune, and Stillwell was left to seek consolation from the Brownies.

For the first half of the 20th century, Port Arthur prospered, growing around one of the prettiest downtowns in the South. But the combination of unsightly strip-mall development out by the highways and oil price fluctuations drained the life out of the downtown. Today, it is merely a melancholy shadow of its former self.

The Port Arthur economy is on display in many interesting ways all over town. Downtown, the Sabine Neches Canal, on the busy Intracoastal Waterway, runs through the center behind high dikes, which protect parts of the city that are 4 feet below sea level. On foggy nights, the sight of the ghostly superstructures of ships gliding silently behind the high walls can be both unnerving and highly evocative. Hwy 82 passes through two of the largest petrochemical plants in the world. Flames from exhaust towers, spewing gases and a constellation of

GULF COAST

multicolored lights, make these places an arresting vision, especially at dusk. Closer to the gulf, huge deep-sea drilling rigs beached at the maintenance yards tower over the landscape.

Port Arthur has an excellent museum and is close to interesting historical sights and parks at Sabine Pass and on the Gulf Coast. It lies directly across Sabine Lake from an appendage of Louisiana.

Orientation

Coming from the west, exit I-10 onto Hwy 73 to enter town. From the east, exit I-10 at Orange and use Hwy 73/87, which passes over the graceful arc of the Rainbow Bridge, the tallest bridge in the South, which was built to allow access on the Neches River to the Beaumont port. Beaumont is 17 miles north along speedy US 69/96/287 or interesting Hwy 347. From Port Arthur, Hwy 82 is linked to Louisiana Hwy 82 by a bridge over Sabine Pass.

Information

The Port Arthur Convention and Visitors Bureau (☎ 409-985-7822, 800-235-7822) is right off Hwy 73 and 9th Ave, in a large modern building on Cultural Center Lane. It is easily one of the most inventive operations of its kind in the state, going so far as to stage weddings between people dressed up as alligators to entertain people visiting on locally lucrative bus tours. Open weekdays 8 am to 5 pm, it has a wealth of local information. Be sure to get a copy of the *Easy Driving Tour* brochure.

The main post office (☎ 409-971-2500), 4550 Jimmy Johnson Blvd, is open weekdays 8:30 am to 5 pm.

You can scrub your duds at the Fabric Care Center (☎ 409-983-7104), 2925 25th St.

Petty crime is a problem in Port Arthur, so keep your car doors locked. At the very cheapest accommodations, don't be surprised if prostitutes knock on your door late at night. They solicit business from the oil

The Big Ditch

Stretching in an arc more than 1300 miles long, from Florida around the Gulf of Mexico to Brownsville on the Mexican border, the Gulf Intracoastal Waterway (or simply Intracoastal Waterway, as it's called in Texas) is a major link in the US transportation chain. To some people, it's simply known as 'the Big Ditch,' which is an apt description given its minimum depth of 12 feet, width of 125 feet and length (along the Texas coast) of 432 miles.

The waterway protects its traffic from the vagaries of the coastal gulf waters by its linked series of canals, channels and protected lagoons formed by barrier islands. It's the aquatic superhighway of choice for shrimp boats, yachts and barges – lots of barges. Shoved along by powerful push-boats, one of these barges can carry more than 1.2 million gallons of jet fuel, soybean oil or chemicals of every type, and some even carry rockets for NASA. About 75 million tons of materials are moved along the Big Ditch every year.

The canal was begun in 1905, but the last leg, from Corpus Christi to Brownsville, wasn't finished until 1949. It's maintained by the US Army Corps of Engineers, which is responsible for inland waterways in the USA. About 8 million cubic yards of muck, silt and sand have to be dredged out of the waterway every year to keep it clear. Although the water generally teems with sea life, there is concern that all the dredging clouds the water and kills things such as sea grass, which in turn is used for shelter by smaller forms of marine life. Few people want to contemplate the environmental repercussions if any of the many barges filled with toxic substances were to collide or otherwise come to grief, but to date the waterway has had a good safety record.

industry contract workers who stay in the area for months at a time. The odds of this happening to you are directly proportional to the number of pickup trucks in the parking lot.

The usual Gulf Coast mosquito warnings are doubled here.

Museum of the Gulf Coast
This is a splendid museum (☎ 409-982-7000), 700 Procter St, that covers the natural, geological and cultural history of the region 'from Jurassic to Joplin.' It's well worth a visit if you are anywhere near the Golden Triangle.

Allow a couple of hours to explore the two floors of exhibits in an old bank building downtown. A vast and colorful mural tracing the geologic development of the area from the time of the dinosaurs dominates the main display room. Upstairs, the lives of local-born celebrities such as helmet-haired football coach Jimmy Johnson are detailed.

Several musicians hail from Port Arthur, including Jiles Perry Richardson Jr, otherwise known as 'the Big Bopper,' who was best known for the song 'Chantilly Lace.' A large area is devoted to Janis Joplin, who remained loyal to her hometown right up until her death from a heroin overdose in 1970. Compare the photos from her final days to her high school yearbook photo, complete with bouffant hairdo. Open Monday to Saturday 9 am to 5 pm, Sunday 1 to 5 pm; $3.50 for adults, $1.50 for children.

Pompeiian Villa
Constructed in 1900 by barbed-wire baron Isaac Ellwood, this pink one-story house (☎ 409-983-5977), at 1953 Lakeshore Drive, is modeled after a villa uncovered in Pompeii, Italy. Despite its many charms, Ellwood soon sold the house to matchstick mogul James Hopkins, who got very lucky thanks to his delicate wife. When she came down from St Louis to see her new house, she pondered the heat, the mosquitoes and muddy roads for at least one minute and then went back to St Louis, never to return. A sad Hopkins traded the house to George Craig for $10,000

in shares in a new oil company called the Texas Co, which later became Texaco. Hopkins' shares were later valued at $3 billion. Open weekdays 10 am to 2 pm; $2 for adults, $1 for children.

White Haven
One of the surviving mansions along Lakeshore Drive, imposing White Haven (☎ 409-982-3068), 2545 Lakeshore Drive, is painted a brilliant white, although it is actually named for the White family, which lived there until 1985. Dating from 1915, it has been carefully restored and is furnished with antiques. Tours are given Monday, Wednesday and Friday 10 am to 1 pm and by appointment. The cost is $2.

To really get a feel for the place, you can stay in one of its three bedrooms for $96 to $141. Before going to your room and falling asleep to the soft rumble of ships passing along the canal outside, read through the binders downstairs, filled with decades of correspondence between the family and a supercilious Lyndon Johnson.

Queen of Peace Shrine & Gardens
A huge statue of the Virgin Mary is set among picturesque Asian gardens in this shrine, 801 9th Ave, which was built in the 1980s by Catholics who were among the 8000 Vietnamese people relocated to Port Arthur after they fled their homeland following the Vietnam War. Although things are much more peaceful now, in the late 1970s violent disputes flared between the new arrivals and local boat owners, who saw their already precarious livelihoods threatened by the newly arrived Vietnamese fishermen. The shrine is free and always open.

Fishing
Water, water everywhere, and you can fish in all of it. Anglers can fish on Sabine Lake, the Gulf of Mexico, the Intracoastal Waterway and other places. There are many boat ramps, and many guides and boat charters are available, including B&L Charter (☎ 409-983-5617) and Sabine Lake Guide Service (☎ 409-736-3023).

GULF COAST

Fishing Seasons

Fishing is easily the most popular activity in Port Arthur. Here are some of the major fish caught and the best seasons for catching them.

Sabine Lake

Drum	December to April
Flounder	November to March
Redfish	Year-round
Speckled trout	Year-round

Gulf of Mexico

Amberjack	May to August
Barracuda	June to August
Grouper	December to April
Kingfish	June to August
Ling	April, May, September, October
Mackerel	May, September
Marlin	July to September
Pompano	April, October
Red snapper	March, October
Sailfish	July to September

Special Events

For details and exact dates of the following, call ☎ 800-235-7822.

January

Janis Joplin Birthday Bash

On or near the 19th, this celebration of the rich musical heritage of Port Arthur includes tributes to Harry James, Tex Ritter, Bobby Kimball and 'Moon' Mullican.

October

Cav-Oil-Cade Celebration

This weeklong celebration of local industry is more fun than its name suggests.

Places to Stay

Camping *Pleasure Island* has a pleasant and simple public tent campground on Martin Luther King Blvd at Hwy 82. It is open year-round and is free. There's no office at the campsite; call the Pleasure Island Com-

mission at ☎ 409-982-4675 for information. The *Sabine Pass* and *Sea Rim* state parks, south of town on Hwy 87, have campgrounds and are detailed below.

Motels & Hotels The *Sea Gull Motel* (☎ 409-962-4437), 6828 Gulfway Drive, has a bright-turquoise exterior and new interiors. Rooms are $25/28 for singles/doubles. *The Driftwood* (☎ 409-985-8411), 3700 Memorial Blvd, has basic rooms for $29/33. *Comfort Inn* (☎ 409-729-3434), 8040 Memorial Blvd, has large rooms for $65/75 that are usually $5 less on weekends. Should the mood strike, you can splurge for the waterbed/hot tub suite. *Holiday Inn Park Central* (☎ 409-724-5000), 2929 Jimmy Johnson Blvd, has rooms overlooking the coach's street for $84 Sunday to Thursday and $72 Friday and Saturday.

The *Cajun Cottages* (☎ 409-982-6050, 800-554-3169), 1900 TB Ellison Parkway, are a delightful motor court of little one-bedroom units with kitchens on Pleasure Island overlooking the channel. They rent for about $60.

Places to Eat

Shrimp cooked every possible way are the staple of local cuisine, and they're supplied by the more than 400 shrimp boats that call Port Arthur home. *Larry's Cajun Cafeteria* may be the most delightful place you'll ever dine; see the listing under Entertainment, below. *Golden Gate* (☎ 409-982-3100), 3444 Gulfway Drive, serves crowd-pleasing Chinese fare cooked by a local Vietnamese family, who sneak some of their native cuisine onto the menu as well. The entrées – many with shrimp! – average $4. Lavish seafood dishes start at $8 at *Esther's Seafood and Oyster Bar* (☎ 409-962-6268), 7237 Rainbow Lane at the base of Rainbow Bridge on the Port Arthur side. Crabs join shrimp in many of the spicy dishes.

Just north in Nederland, *The Schooner* (☎ 409-722-2323), 1507 Hwy 69 at Hwy 365, is a delightful family-run supper club with classic seafood dishes that start at $8. South of Port Arthur in Sabine Pass, the *Channel Inn Seafood Restaurant* (☎ 409-971-2400) has a lunch buffet ($8) that's hugely popular with oil workers and cops. The tables are covered with plastic and boast rolls of paper towels and jumbo bottles of Tabasco sauce that come in handy for the $17-per-person family-style seafood feasts, which only end when you surrender.

Entertainment

Larry's Cajun Cafeteria (☎ 409-962-3381), 3701 Atlantic Hwy in neighboring Groves, is part Cajun supermarket, part tasty Cajun restaurant ($5 average) and part Cajun dance hall. On Wednesday and Saturday nights, a Cajun band with a fiddler, accordion player, guitarist and a guy hitting something called a 'ding-a-ling' play backcountry dance tunes for diners ages two to 92 (one woman really was 92; she showed us her ID). The place is owned by a family that includes AJ Judice, a charming bloke who was declared the state's 'Official Cajun' a few years back.

Jeff Riley's Foc'sle Club (☎ 409-983-5050) is a bright-green spot of Ireland downtown at 416 Procter St. The late Riley was proud of his native land and his career in the merchant marine. Memorabilia from both line the walls of this very friendly and convivial place, which has a great jukebox.

Live zydeco and Cajun music are the main events at the *Boudin Hut* (☎ 409-962-5079), 5714 Gulfway Drive (Hwy 87), a lively place with a mural of Kenny Rogers. As one local said, 'It's a friendly place where you're not likely to get clobbered.'

Getting There & Around

Jefferson County Airport is just north of Port Arthur; see the Beaumont section for details. Greyhound (☎ 409-985-4356), 3825 Golfway Drive at 10th Ave, has five buses daily to Houston ($23) and four daily to Orange ($7) and on to Louisiana. Four buses go daily to Beaumont ($7).

Without your own car, motorcycle or bike, you won't get around at all.

NEDERLAND

A small town north of Port Arthur that really feels like an extension of it, Nederland has one both notable and incongruous sight.

The **Dutch Windmill & Tex Ritter Museum** (☎ 409-723-1545), 1500 Boston Ave near 17th St, neatly combines a realistic windmill, which honors early settlers from Holland, with an interior museum, which honors Tex Ritter, the famed country-and-western singer and film star. Ritter gave up his law studies in the 1920s after he found out he could sing. It's open Thursday to Sunday 1 to 5 pm, with possible longer hours during the summer (call to check); admission is free.

SABINE PASS AREA

Driving 12 miles south from Port Arthur to Sabine Pass and beyond, along Hwy 87, offers a fascinating look at the area's historic past, its economy today, and the natural areas that are being preserved for the future.

Going south, you pass through the town's major local petrochemical plants, which are owned by Texaco, Chevron, Clark and Fina. As you go over the bridge across the Intracoastal Waterway, look to the south. The huge, bargelike metal structure you see is a vast floating dry dock that was used by the US Navy in the Philippines during WWII to lift battle-damaged ships out of the water for repairs. Now, more than 50 years later, it is used by TDI-Halter Inc to lift offshore drilling rigs out of the water for repairs.

You may or may not see tall and massive offshore rigs docked along the Sabine Pass channel. When the price of oil is more than $20 a barrel, it's economically feasible for oil companies to drill exploratory wells in the gulf. When the price is under $20, companies can't make money, and you'll see dozens of their huge rigs stored along the waterway.

South of Sea Rim State Park, Hwy 87 theoretically continues for 50 scenic miles south to the ferry to Galveston Island, but the road is usually closed because of wave damage. If that is the case, you'll have to take the long way around via Hwys 73 and 124.

Sabine Pass Battleground State Historical Park

During the Civil War, it was vital to the Confederacy that it continue its lucrative cotton trade with England and France. Weapons,

GULF COAST

RYAN VER BERKMOES

Idle offshore oil rig

supplies, medicine and more were bought with the cotton. The Union responded with a fairly effective blockade of Southern ports along the Atlantic and Gulf of Mexico coasts, from Virginia all the way to the Mexican border near Brownsville.

At Sabine Pass, a small fort was built to prevent the Union Navy from gaining control of the waterway. On September 8, 1863, a lone guard saw four Union gunboats approaching. He ran 2 miles into town and summoned 46 additional troops – mostly Irish mercenaries – who were drunk in a bar. Hastening back to the fort and seeing the attacking boats loaded with 4000 Union troops proved sobering. The men used the fort's six cannons to force two of the gunboats aground, and ran off the others. It was a major victory for the Confederacy, and in 1936 the state of Texas built the park to commemorate it.

The site of the fort is now offshore, but detailed outdoor displays recall the battle. The park (☎ 409-971-2451) offers great views of passing ships and has several amenities, such as shaded picnic tables and a boat ramp. There are no entrance fees, but there is an honor box for the campsites, which have water and electricity but no showers and cost $10. To reach the park, take FM 3322 1½ miles south from the junction with Hwy 87 in Sabine Pass.

Texas Point National Wildlife Refuge

This almost 9000-acre preserve (☎ 409-971-2909) lies between Sabine Pass and Sea Rim State Park on the gulf side of Hwy 87. The refuge's facilities are sparse except for two rough trails. Dozens of wildlife species and hordes of birds thrive in this difficult-to-visit preserve.

Sea Rim State Park

More than 15,000 acres in size, the park (☎ 409-971-2559) includes vast marshlands north of Hwy 87 and 5.2 miles of beaches south of the road. The wetlands are very popular with birders, who can use blinds that have been built at key points. The beach areas are popular on summer weekends but are almost deserted at other times of the year. Only a short walk is required to reach pristine sand, where the only sounds you'll hear are seagulls and the usually meager waves lapping along the shore. In both areas, alligators soak up the sun and signs needlessly warn all but the thickest of park visitors not to 'annoy' the sharp-toothed reptiles.

There is an information center at the main parking lot off Hwy 87, and there are also seasonal 'hosts,' retired people who distribute information and answer questions in return for the park's permission to camp all winter for free. The entrance fee is $1.

Activities Canoes can be rented on the marshland side of the park for $10 for four hours or $15 for the entire day. They are an excellent way of exploring the estuaries, which teem with life, much of it far more benign than the alligators. You can also take one-hour tours of the marshes on airboats for $13.50 for adults, $8.50 for children. Call the park to reserve canoes or to check on the airboat schedule. There are boardwalks and an interpretive nature trail near the main parking area on the beach side.

GULF COAST

Places to Stay Primitive camping ($4) is allowed throughout the park on the beaches and marshlands. Developed tent sites ($8) and RV sites ($12) are near the information center, and they have water, electricity and access to bathrooms and showers.

McFaddin National Wildlife Refuge

Covering more than 41,000 acres of beaches, marshlands and coastal prairie, this refuge is given an extra measure of protection by the fact that Hwy 87, which traverses its length, is usually closed. There are concentrations of alligators along with minks, foxes and many other mammals. Deep in the marshes you can find the slow-moving and elegant roseate spoonbill, among dozens of other bird species. A few trails wind through the park, and you can primitive-camp on the beach for free, but access can be a problem. Check conditions with the office (☎ 409-971-2909). Be aware that the primary users of the refuge are duck hunters, so you should also determine the dates of hunting season before you set out.

Galveston Area

GALVESTON
Population 60,000

A mixture of failed dreams and high hopes for the future, its history overshadowed by tragedy, sultry Galveston is as close as you will get to the Deep South in Texas. Along block after oleander-scented block, people in tar-paper houses one step above shacks live cheek by powdered jowl with the mansions of the moneyed. The latter have their own closed society, and if you're not a BOI – 'born on island' – you don't quite fit in, no matter how many decades you've lived in the 30 sq miles that comprise the heart of town.

In Galveston, nostalgia for the town's past mingles with memories of what was lost. In the 19th century, the island was home to both the greatest port and the greatest city of the great state of Texas. Had a hurricane not blown in 1900 – in the era before hurricanes had names – Houston surely would now be a backwater to the great Galveston.

But it wasn't to be. The winds and waves took 6000 lives, the worst natural disaster ever in the USA, and they took the island's future. Business and commerce moved north, and rather than trade on its greatness, Galveston had to trade on its pleasures, which for much of the 20th century were of the flesh.

But now, a century after the cataclysm, Galveston is learning to build on its past. For many visitors, it's just a beach town with some history. But there are better beaches elsewhere, and what makes Galveston irresistible is that it's actually a historic town with some beaches. Visitors can revel in the town's heritage even as the BOIs and island latecomers are rediscovering it.

History

Galveston Island is thought to have been first inhabited by Akokisa Indians. By the 16th century, they had been replaced by the Karankawas, who made a spectacular discovery in 1528: Spanish explorer Álvar Núñez Cabeza de Vaca washed ashore with some of his men, thus becoming the first of many Europeans to end up shipwrecked near Galveston. Cabeza de Vaca was alternately treated like a slave and honored as a medicine man. Eventually he managed to take his leave and reached Mexico City, his original destination, in 1536.

Other Europeans didn't arrive until 1786, when José de Evia, a midlevel Spanish explorer, charted the entire coast. In what was no doubt a wise move under colonial politics, he named the island for his boss, Bernardo de Gálvez, the governor of Louisiana, who never actually saw his namesake island.

The pirate Jean Lafitte set up shop in 1817 and made the island into the biggest slave market in the New World. For nonslaves, the setup was one big bacchanal. Tales still survive of whiskey-soaked orgies and other debauchery. Lafitte stayed neutral during the Mexican Revolution, but when he attacked an American ship in 1821, US troops were sent in and the party ended. Needless to say, all sorts of stories are still told about buried

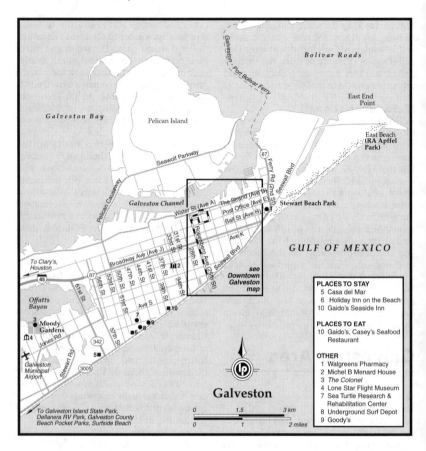

Galveston

PLACES TO STAY
5 Casa del Mar
6 Holiday Inn on the Beach
10 Gaido's Seaside Inn

PLACES TO EAT
10 Gaido's, Casey's Seafood Restaurant

OTHER
1 Walgreens Pharmacy
2 Michel B Menard House
3 The Colonel
4 Lone Star Flight Museum
7 Sea Turtle Research & Rehabilitation Center
8 Underground Surf Depot
9 Goody's

treasure on the island. The Karankawas, meanwhile, had been dispatched to west Texas, where they died out.

Lafitte's little town continued without him. By this time, its name had been Anglicized to 'Galveston.' Developers arrived in the mid-1830s, and the island's golden age began. Galveston boasts a long list of Texas firsts from this era: the first private bank (1854), first opera house (1870), first electric lights (1883), first country club (1898) and many more. By the turn of the 20th century, Galveston was the leading city in Texas and had the nation's third-busiest port.

All that changed on September 8, 1900, when the nation's deadliest natural disaster struck. A hurricane with winds of 120mph drove a storm surge that submerged much of the island under 20 feet of water. Where Galveston Island had been, there were now only the waters of the Gulf of Mexico.

Of the town's 37,000 people, at least 6000 died, but no one will ever know for sure. Survivor and rescuer accounts from the days after the water receded all mention the same word: stench. Bodies couldn't be buried in the waterlogged sandy soil, so they were taken out to sea by the hundreds and sunk.

But in a further ghoulish nightmare, the gulf washed them back ashore. Finally, huge funeral pyres were built, which witnesses refused to ever talk about again.

Galveston never recovered. The port business moved to Houston along with most of the banks, the stock exchange and much of the commerce. The huge seawall was built, eventually extending for 10 miles, and much of the town was raised 20 feet or more, but the mood was that of a battered population just going through the motions.

From the 1920s through the '50s, Galveston was best known for moral turpitude on a scale that would have pleased Lafitte. Gambling, prostitution and anything money can buy could be bought on its streets. Many of the piers that still survive between 10th and 61st Sts – the one holding the Flagship Hotel being the most appalling example – date from this era. When authorities on one of their occasional show raids entered the hotel's front door, all evidence of criminal activity could be tossed overboard before it was discovered.

Bottom for the island came in the 1960s, when even the illicit trade moved elsewhere. The port, which had carved out a lucrative niche for itself handling specialty products such as bananas, lost business to huge container ports elsewhere. Old mansions, buildings that had weathered the hurricane, and even the Strand, which had once been 'the Wall Street of the Southwest,' fell into ruin.

However, a preservation movement began just in the nick of time, and to date it has restored hundreds of buildings and entire neighborhoods. In the 1970s, the beaches found favor with a new generation of sun seekers, and since then the island has worked hard at trading on its sun-drenched historic charms.

Orientation

Nothing more than a sandy barrier island, Galveston stretches 30 miles in length and is no more than 3 miles wide. The city itself is 100 blocks long, from the ferry dock in the east to the newest developments west of the airport. I-45 from the mainland becomes Broadway Ave, which runs through the heart of town. Seawall Blvd is just that, and it follows the gulf shore for more than 10 miles. A beach runs along the base of the seawall, and a long, wide sidewalk runs along the boulevard. On the north side of the boulevard are restaurants, motels and shops selling various stuff; they're much less tacky than you might expect in a beach town.

Navigation is generally a breeze: north-south streets are numbered and correspond to the house numbers of the east-west streets. Thus an address of 2700 Seawall Blvd is at the corner of 27th St. The Strand historic district and the center of much of Galveston's life are on the bay side between 19th and 25th Sts. There are good views of passing ships from East End Point, at the end of Seawall Blvd.

Galveston's simple layout means that you shouldn't need more than the maps in this book or the many free ones that are widely available.

Information

Tourist Offices The Galveston Convention & Visitors Bureau (☎ 409-763-4311, 800-351-4236, www.galvestontourism.com), 2106 Seawall Blvd in the Moody Civic Center, is open daily 8:30 am to 5 pm and has tons of information on the island and the surrounding region. The office may move in 1999, so call ahead to confirm its address.

The Galveston Historical Foundation operates the Strand Visitors Center (☎ 409-765-7834), 2016 the Strand, daily 9:30 am to 5 pm (until 6 pm June to August). Its information focuses on historical sites and museums. Tickets for many of these attractions are sold in a bewildering variety of packages that may or may not really save you money. It also operates tours of several historic homes. Perhaps its most useful service is its clean rest rooms.

Money NationsBank (☎ 409-765-2420), 2200 Market St, is a large, full-service bank open weekdays 9 am to 5:30 pm. ATMs can be found at gas stations, convenience stores and bank branches all over the island.

Post The main post office (☎ 409-763-1527), 601 25th St, is open weekdays 8:30 am to 5 pm and Saturday 9 am to noon.

Bookstores Novel Ideas (☎ 409-763-3844), 1816 Market St, is an absolutely splendid independent bookstore. Owner Larry Beebe sells new and used books, music, magazines and more in an old building that he has converted into his idea of the perfect bookstore, featuring lots of comfy couches for in-depth browsing. The store also has a vegetarian-friendly café; see its listing under Places to Eat.

The Galveston Bookshop (☎ 409-765-6919), 317 23rd St, has a good selection of used and rare books right near the Strand.

Libraries The Rosenberg Library (☎ 409-763-8854), 2310 Sealy Ave, is the main public library and is open Monday to Thursday 9 am to 9 pm and Friday and Saturday 9 am to 6 pm. September to May, it is also open Sunday 1 to 5 pm. The library has a huge section on Galveston history, including genealogy records from the ships loaded with European immigrants that arrived in the city in the years before the 1900 hurricane.

Media The *Daily News* (50¢) is the main Galveston newspaper. Other major Texas and national newspapers are widely available. Many Houston radio stations also reach Galveston.

Campuses The University of Texas Medical Branch at Galveston (UTMB, ☎ 409-747-0008) is the main state medical school in Texas, with 2800 students. The Ashbel Smith Building, the school's first building, was built in 1890, and its handsome red sandstone construction survived the hurricane. It can be found amid the surrounding squalid medical architecture at 916 the Strand.

Laundry W&D Washeteria (☎ 409-763-8916), 2301 Broadway Ave, is big, clean and air-conditioned.

Medical Services UTMB (☎ 409-770-0492) has a large clinic open daily 7 am to 11 pm. It is within the vast UTMB facility on University Blvd (also known as 6th St) between Market and Post Office Sts. A Walgreens pharmacy (☎ 409-763-3588) is at 308 Seawall Blvd.

Emergency The US Coast Guard Search & Rescue is at ☎ 409-766-5623. The Women's Crisis Center of Galveston County is at ☎ 409-765-7233.

Dangers & Annoyances Galveston is not all restored mansions and fun-filled tourist attractions. It has a bad drug problem and neighborhoods as decrepit as any you'll find in the USA. Use your own judgment in determining a neighborhood's safety. The Strand and Seawall Blvd are usually okay, but be especially wary west of 25th St.

Although the worst hurricane struck Galveston in 1900, many others have caused damage, including Alicia in 1983. But fear not – there's usually plenty of warning of a hurricane's approach, so you'll have plenty of time to head for high ground.

Moody Gardens

A vast array of attractions, Moody Gardens (☎ 409-744-4673) is at 1 Hope Blvd. This complex – which combines botanical exhibits, IMAX theaters and other goodies – is Galveston's number-one tourist attraction. But that said, we didn't like it at all.

The complex has an unusual history. It was started in 1986 as a therapy center for people with head injuries and emotional disabilities, and it continues that excellent work today. But Moody Gardens has branched out into areas unrelated to its original mission. In 1993, the first of several attractions aimed at tourists opened under the banner name 'The Pyramids of Moody Gardens.' They are separated from the medical facility and are detailed below. A convention center and an adjoining hotel are set for completion in 1999.

March to October, Moody Gardens is open Sunday to Thursday 10 am to 9 pm, Friday and Saturday 10 am to 10 pm. The rest of the year, it is open Sunday to Thursday 10 am to 6 pm, Friday and Saturday 10 am to 9 pm. Admission to one attraction is $6, two

GULF COAST

$11 and the whole place $16. To reach the complex, take 81st St from Seawall Blvd to Jones Rd.

Rainforest Pyramid A 10-story glass pyramid covers a lush tropical forest, which is a good place to see your house plants in their native settings. You can pass time here at a pool waiting for the resident archerfish to spit at a passing bug.

IMAX 3-D Theater The ubiquitous tourist-attraction megasize theater literally takes on an extra dimension here, thanks to special glasses. The quality of the experience depends on what movie is shown.

IMAX Ridefilm Theater This ride combines a large screen (not IMAX, however) with chairs that jump about (they don't go anywhere, though). After a long wait, you'll be ushered into a little room and strapped into a seat. We saw a silly story about a hunt for a rare gem in a sort of futuristic-cum-Egyptian underground empire. The experience lasted only about 10 minutes, which was merciful not just because of the insipid storyline, but because the ride was similar to the one a can of paint gets at the store when they put it on the shaker. A teenage girl in front of us took on a green pallor and made straight for the bathroom.

Discovery Pyramid When we visited, an elderly woman was wandering around looking at the meager space-related exhibits here and complaining, 'Is this all there is? What a rip-off!' A teenage employee with a sort of 'check-is-in-the-mail' sincerity tried to placate her with, 'We're adding more next year...' But neither the lady nor we were convinced.

Other Attractions The Aquarium Pyramid, a '2-million-gallon tribute to the world's oceans,' is set to open in 1999. Palm Beach is an artificial beach that seems somewhat superfluous, given that Galveston already has 32 miles of real beaches. *The Colonel* is a replica paddle wheeler (see the Organized Tours section for details).

The Strand

The center of activity on the island, this historic district can be covered on foot. Checking out the many attractions, shops, restaurants and bars can easily take a day or more. Informative historical markers identify buildings and sights all over the district. Walking around, you'll soon appreciate the work of the preservationists who prevented this fascinating area from being demolished in the 1960s and '70s.

Pier 19 is an area of shops and museums north of Water St that has been converted from an old dock area.

Galveston County Historical Museum

This small, well-funded and well-designed museum (☎ 409-766-2340), 2219 Market St, is in the proud and solid 1919 City National Bank Building. The barrel ceilings and architectural details are the perfect backdrop for

---

Are You Moody?

After a short time in Galveston, you'll start to wonder if everybody on the island is Moody (the family, not the state of emotional fluctuations).

William L Moody was a Virginia lawyer who moved to Galveston in 1866 and got rich trading cotton, selling insurance and running banks. His son, William L Moody Jr, took over the family empire in the 1890s. After the 1900 hurricane, many of the island's richest families and largest employers moved to the mainland. However, the Moodys decided to stick with Galveston, and their fortune grew. When William L Moody Jr died in 1954, he left much of the empire to his daughter, Mary Moody Northern, who spent the rest of her days until 1986 funding charitable causes.

Moody money has funded projects all over Galveston, many of which bear the family name.

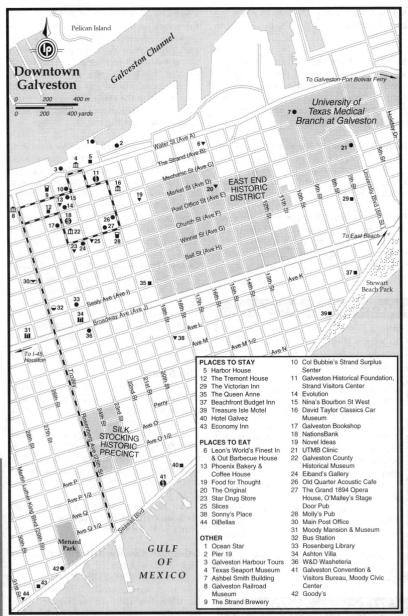

Downtown Galveston

Pelican Island

Galveston Channel

To Galveston-Port Bolivar Ferry

University of Texas Medical Branch at Galveston

EAST END HISTORIC DISTRICT

To East Beach

Stewart Beach Park

To I-45, Houston

SILK STOCKING HISTORIC PRECINCT

Menard Park

GULF OF MEXICO

Seawall Blvd

GULF COAST

PLACES TO STAY
5 Harbor House
12 The Tremont House
29 The Victorian Inn
35 The Queen Anne
37 Beachfront Budget Inn
39 Treasure Isle Motel
40 Hotel Galvez
43 Economy Inn

PLACES TO EAT
6 Leon's World's Finest In & Out Barbecue House
13 Phoenix Bakery & Coffee House
19 Food for Thought
20 The Original
23 Star Drug Store
25 Slices
38 Sonny's Place
44 DiBellas

OTHER
1 Ocean Star
2 Pier 19
3 Galveston Harbour Tours
4 Texas Seaport Museum
7 Ashbel Smith Building
8 Galveston Railroad Museum
9 The Strand Brewery
10 Col Bubbie's Strand Surplus Senter
11 Galveston Historical Foundation, Strand Visitors Center
14 Evolution
15 Nina's Bourbon St West
16 David Taylor Classics Car Museum
17 Galveston Bookshop
18 NationsBank
19 Novel Ideas
21 UTMB Clinic
22 Galveston County Historical Museum
24 Eiband's Gallery
26 Old Quarter Acoustic Cafe
27 The Grand 1894 Opera House, O'Malley's Stage Door Pub
28 Molly's Pub
30 Main Post Office
31 Moody Mansion & Museum
32 Bus Station
33 Rosenberg Library
34 Ashton Villa
36 W&D Washeteria
41 Galveston Convention & Visitors Bureau, Moody Civic Center
42 Goody's

the displays, which include a sobering look at the 1900 hurricane. The displays explain, among other things, that slate shingles carried by the winds acted as horizontal guillotines, and that the wreckage of houses destroyed by the surf acted as battering rams upon their neighbors. Open Monday to Saturday 10 am to 4 pm, Sunday noon to 4 pm; free.

The Great Storm This 30-minute multimedia documentary, presented in the theater in the Pier 19 complex at the end of 21st St, avoids the maudlin as it recounts the 1900 hurricane through photos, eyewitness accounts and various special effects. Even the most jaded in the crowd will get a good idea of the horror that Galveston residents experienced as the hurricane submerged much of the island. The presentation begins Sunday to Thursday 11 am to 6 pm at the top of every hour, and Friday and Saturday 11 am to 8 pm; $3.50 for adults, $2.50 for children.

Texas Seaport Museum This vast and interesting museum (☎ 409-763-1877), on Water St at the end of 22nd St, explains life around Galveston's port during its heyday in the 19th century. One of the best displays shows how gunpowder was smuggled through the port during the Texas Revolution. Follow the little lights on the elaborate model, which traces the route of the illicit kegs from schooner to rowboat to warehouse to saloon (where they probably wished the kegs were filled with something else) to pawnshop and onward.

Outside, the *Elissa*, a sailing ship built in Scotland in 1877, has been carefully restored and is a good example of the typical boat that called on Galveston harbor in the late 19th century. Open daily 10 am to 5 pm; $5 for adults, $4 for children.

Ocean Star From 1969 to 1984, this offshore drilling rig explored for oil in up to 173 feet of water out in the gulf. Now moored in the Pier 19 area at the end of 20th St, it has been converted into a three-level exhibit that explains offshore oil exploration. If this sort of stuff sounds interesting, you'll enjoy

it. Otherwise, you might get bogged down in the minutiae of drill-bit technology. However, the views from the drilling platform are pretty spectacular. Open daily 10 am to 4 pm (June to August till 5 pm); $5 for adults, $4 for children.

Galveston Railroad Museum On April 11, 1967, the last train to Houston pulled out of this pretty station, which has now been converted into a museum (☎ 409-765-5700), at 123 Rosenberg Ave (25th St). The coolest part is the open, high-ceilinged waiting room with plaster models of representative passengers. At a row of vintage telephone booths, you can hear recreated conversations with famous locals such as John Henry Clouser, who was a local champion of school desegregation. Outside are dusty rows of old railroad cars and locomotives. A model train layout depicting the Galveston docks features 'Billy,' the unintentionally funny narrator who talks about wanting to work on the banana docks. Open daily 10 am to 4 pm; $5 for adults, $2.50 for children.

David Taylor Classics Car Museum Gearheads and car nuts will love this museum (☎ 409-765-6590), 1918 Mechanic St, with more than 55 vintage cars from the 1920s to the '60s. Among the highlights: a 1937 Cord with hidden headlights, a 1936 Fleetwood Cadillac convertible with a V-12 engine (no word on whether it came with its own oil well), and actress Carole Lombard's 1940 Mercury, which was a gift from her hubby, Clark Gable. Open daily 10 am to 5 pm; $5 for adults, $4 for children.

Lone Star Flight Museum

A great place for historic airplane lovers, this museum (☎ 409-740-7722) is housed in twin hangars at Galveston Municipal Airport. Most of the planes have been fully restored, although others are in various stages of restoration, which is itself interesting. War planes used by the US Navy in WWII are well represented in the collection, which includes the SBD Dauntless, PBY Catalina, TBM Avenger and F4U Corsair, as well as the B-17, P-38 and more than

30 others. Open daily 10 am to 5 pm; $6 for adults, $4 for children.

Sea Turtle Research & Rehabilitation Center

The National Oceanic and Atmospheric Administration has an often-ignored facility (☎ 409-766-3523) on the island at 4700 Ave U, which is devoted to saving the highly endangered Kemp's ridley sea turtle. Injured adults are treated and young turtles are raised for release in the gulf. Free tours are given Tuesday, Thursday and Saturday at 10 and 11 am and 1 and 2 pm.

Historic Homes

The **East End Historic District** is filled with pretty old buildings and is bounded by 11th, 19th and Mechanic Sts and Broadway Ave. A good driving and walking-tour guide and map can usually be found with other brochures on information racks all over town. It has details on 105 buildings, many of which have been restored.

The **Silk Stocking Historic Precinct** runs along 23rd, 24th and 25th Sts between Aves N and P. It is home to some of the grandest mansions and some of the lushest oleander bushes and gardens.

Many historic homes in Galveston have been beautifully restored and are open at various times for tours. They include the following:

Ashton Villa This gracious three-story brick Italianate mansion (☎ 409-762-3933), 2328 Broadway Ave, was built in 1859. The 45-minute tours leave on the hour Monday to Saturday 10 am to 4 pm, Sunday noon to 4 pm; $6 for adults, $3 for children.

Michel B Menard House Built in 1838, this wood house (☎ 409-762-3933), 1605 33rd St, with its imposing white pillars, is set among gracious gardens. The 30-minute tours leave every half-hour Friday to Sunday noon to 4 pm; $6 for adults, $3 for children.

Moody Mansion & Museum The grandest mansion on the island (☎ 409-762-7668), 2618 Broadway Ave, dates from 1895 and is completely restored to its original splendor. Open Monday to Saturday 10 am to 4 pm, Sunday 1 to 4:30 pm (closed Monday from January through March); $6 for adults, $3 for children.

Beaches

There are beaches all along Seawall Blvd. Usually. Storms can take the sand away, leaving little to enjoy. However, Galveston has valiantly fought back with 'beach nourishment' projects, a remarkable euphemism for the complex process of pumping sand from the gulf onto the shore. The result: instant beach.

Of course, beachgoers here have to contend with the aesthetic problems posed by the 17-foot-tall concrete seawalls. However, the situation is greatly ameliorated by the addition of an almost 3-mile-long mural from 27th to 61st Sts called the *SEE-Wall*, which features some rather clever images of cavorting fish. Despite this, you'll probably find the beaches listed here more to your liking.

East Beach Also called RA Apffel Park, this vast expanse of hard-packed sand is at the very eastern end of the island. On summer weekends, it has live concerts and an outdoor bar. This is definitely the party beach; the city makes a point of letting you know that you *can* drink on this beach. We were there on a quiet day when the only other person around

Beach Flags

From Memorial Day to Labor Day, Galveston beaches have lifeguards from East Beach all the way west to 61st St. They use a colored flag system to advise swimmers about water conditions. An absence of flags does not guarantee safe conditions. Here's what the colors mean.

yellow normal water conditions

red unusually strong winds, currents or surf; bathers should only go in to their hips

blue large numbers of dangerous marine life, such as jellyfish or stingrays, are in the area

was a woman with a metal detector. When we asked her what she finds, she smiled and said, 'You'd be surprised.' Her car was parked nearby, and it was a new Cadillac. Admission is $5 per car, so if you walk in, it's free.

Stewart Beach Park The Park Board sponsors all sorts of family activities on Galveston's original beach during the summer, such as sand castle contests and volleyball competitions. There is a playground and amusements including Amaze'N Texas, a human-size maze, and miniature golf. You can drink anything you want here as long as it's nonalcoholic. Admission is $5 per car. The beach begins at the south end of 6th St and Seawall Blvd.

Galveston County Pocket Parks The crescent-shaped beaches run by the county (☎ 409-737-1222) are found southwest of town off Seawall Blvd (FM 3005) at three roads with names taken right off an odometer: 7½ Mile Rd, 9½ Mile Rd and 11 Mile Rd. All have bathrooms and showers, and the first two have concession stands.

Galveston Island State Park Aimed more at nature lovers than fun-seekers, this park is 10 miles southwest of town on the island. Full details are given in the Around Galveston section, later in this chapter.

Activities

Biking During the summer and on warm weekends, stores along Seawall Blvd rent bicycles, as well as in-line skates and other gear. Goody's, a convenience store with two locations – 2828 Seawall Blvd (☎ 409-763-2304) and 4400 Seawall Blvd (☎ 409-765-6221) – rents throughout the year. Simple bikes or 'blades go for $5 an hour or $10 for three hours.

Fishing Red snapper is the fish most prized by people fishing offshore from Galveston. But because there's been too much success, you're not allowed to catch any during certain periods. Several charter boats leave from the Pier 19 area for trips of varying lengths, from four hours up to 25 hours. The

prices depend on the length of the trip, starting around $15 and going as high as $150 or more. To find out what's biting and what you're allowed to catch, check with Galveston Party Boats (☎ 409-763-5423) or Texsun II (☎ 409-762-8808).

Diving There's little to see near Galveston. The tides, for one, scour the bottom clean. However, offshore oil rigs give marine life something to cling to, and rich and varied communities of fish and plant life develop around the rigs' massive legs. At press time, however, the one dive shop operating in the area had closed. Ask at the Galveston Convention & Visitors Bureau if they know of any shops that have opened.

Surfing One of the authors of this book (his initials are NS) derides surfing in Texas at every opportunity, and he is right. But if you have no other opportunity, then give it your best shot. In Galveston, the best time for waves is October to February, although there are plenty of days when the gulf could be mistaken for Lake Placid. For supplies and board rentals, you can patronize the Underground Surf Depot (☎ 409-763-4036), 4700 Seawall Blvd, but note that its owners were unfriendly during our visit. However, if you need some wax or you have a firm desire for a T-shirt that reads 'If it swells, ride it,' then this is the place to go. Boards rent for $30 a day, but the shop doesn't rent wetsuits – which you'll need in winter. See the Surfing section in the introductory Activities chapter for more information.

Organized Tours

The Colonel (☎ 409-740-7797) leaves from Moody Gardens on one-hour tours of Offats Bayou, an inlet on the north side of the island. Voyages depart daily at 2 and 3 pm (April to Labor Day 2 and 4 pm). Tickets cost $6; tours are free for kids under three.

Galveston Harbour Tours (☎ 409-765-1700) has a name that makes further description unnecessary. The 1½-hour tours on a modern, open boat depart every hour during the summer, less frequently the rest of the year. Departures are from Pier 22, west of the

Texas Seaport Museum. Call for schedules. Tickets are $10 for adults, $6 for children.

The Galveston Sightseeing Train (☎ 409-765-9564) is one of those tractor-pulled fake affairs where the riders look slightly embarrassed. But it really is better to be on the inside looking out, because these tours cover 17 miles of the island over 1½ hours and are a good introduction to the Galveston area. The narrated tours depart from the Moody Civic Center at Seawall Blvd and 21st St at 9 and 11 am and 1:30, 3:30 and 5:30 pm from June to August; $5.50 for adults, $3 for kids. There is a reduced schedule the rest of the year.

Special Events

Because tourism is the island's number-one source of revenue, Galveston schedules a succession of special events. The following are the most notable; call to check exact dates:

February

Mardi Gras
For 12 days before Ash Wednesday and the onset of Lent, Galveston does its best to outdo New Orleans with parades, pageants, parties and more (☎ 888-425-4753 for information). Make lodging reservations well in advance.

May

Historic Homes Tour
The city's star historic homes are joined by privately owned mansions that can only be toured during this event (☎ 409-765-7834).

June

Sand Castle Competition
More than 60 teams compete on East Beach during this competition (☎ 409-762-3278).

December

Dickens on the Strand
During this event (☎ 409-765-7834), held the first weekend in December, the Galveston Historical Foundation goes all out to create its own version of Victorian London. Street vendors serve food, and there are scores of performances and readings. Watch out for mimes.

Places to Stay

You can find bargains only during the off-season (basically, during the cooler months), when some of the nice places work to fill rooms at any price. But don't count on it, because the growing meeting trade and increasing number of special events in what used to be the off-season mean that rates aren't always what you'd expect: often they are higher during the previously 'off' season.

Camping *Galveston Island State Park* has excellent camping facilities. See the listing under Around Galveston, later in this chapter. The city operates *Dellanera RV Park* (☎ 409-740-0390) at 10901 San Luis Pass, west of Seawall Blvd (FM 3005) and Six Mile Rd. It has full hookups, a laundry, grocery store and other amenities. Rates range from $15 to $18.

Motels & Hotels Galveston's budget motels and hotels are not an impressive lot. They don't have to be, since they can easily fill up throughout the peak season. *Beachfront Budget Inn* (☎ 409-765-8386), 800 Seawall Blvd, has cell-like rooms off a central alley that can boast of being near Stewart Beach. The rates of $25/31 a single/double don't include meals shoved under the door. *Economy Inn* (☎ 409-762-0664), 3008 Seawall Blvd, is a slightly ramshackle wooden building with rooms that start at $27 and can reach nonbudget levels of $89 in peak periods. Equally austere, *Treasure Isle Motel* (☎ 409-763-8561), 1002 Seawall Blvd, has basic rooms for $29/35 ($10 higher in peak season).

Gaido's Seaside Inn (☎ 409-762-9626, 800-525-0064), 3828 Seawall Blvd, is part of the famous restaurant (see its listing in Places to Eat). The motel-style lodge is very well maintained, with rooms that go for a very good $49 in the low season to $59 in the high. Each of the lodge's two suites costs $115.

Holiday Inn on the Beach (☎ 409-740-3581), 5002 Seawall Blvd, is a well-equipped high-rise where all the rooms have a view of the gulf. Rooms range from $79 to $99 Sunday to Thursday all year and go as high as $179 on summer weekends. *Casa del Mar* (☎ 409-740-2431, 800-392-1205), 6102 Seawall Blvd, has condo-style units with good kitchens, living rooms with views, balconies and accommodations for six for a very good rate of $69 Sunday to Thursday and $109 weekends from September to March. Weekday rates are $119 and weekends are $159 the rest of the year.

Near the Strand in the Pier 19 complex, *Harbor House* (☎ *409-763-3321, 800-874-3721*), No 28 Pier 21, has luxurious rooms with good views of the harbor for $89/99 Sunday to Thursday and $135 weekends. It also has its own boat slips, useful if you're arriving by sea.

The premier hotel on the island is the *Tremont House* (☎ *409-763-0300, 800-874-2300*), downtown at 2300 Mechanic St. In 1984, no expense was spared in turning an 1870s dry-goods store into a luxury hotel. The interior courtyard stays naturally cool without air-con thanks to the massive brick construction. The rooms are a mix of new and old and have high Victorian windows that let in lots of light. The best feature, however, is the rooftop open-air bar with views of sunsets and passing ships. Rooms run from $99 to $434, depending on size and season.

Hotel Galvez (☎ *409-765-7721*), 2024 Seawall Blvd, was originally built as a grand hotel in 1911. Its fortunes followed the island's, and by the 1970s it was decidedly tawdry. Restoration began in 1993, and the hotel has been returned to its former glories, with a huge new pool. Rooms begin at $109 and rapidly rise to $229, depending on size, season and view.

B&Bs It seems that half the old renovated homes on the island have rooms available for B&B. Of course, given renovation costs, that shouldn't come as a surprise.

The *Queen Anne* (☎ *409-763-7088*), 1915 Sealy Ave, is a late Victorian house built in 1905 that is close to the Strand. Rooms cost from $85 to $145. The *Victorian Inn* (☎ *409-762-3235*), 511 7th St, is a massive Italianate villa built for a lucky cement contractor who later got the contract for the seawall. Rooms cost from $100 to $175.

Condos There are a lot of condominium developments on Galveston Island, especially as you go southwest, away from

town. Most are low-rise, compared with the hulking high-rise monstrosities found in other beach resorts. Numerous realtors handle bookings in all price ranges. Here are a few:

All on Beach Rentals
  ☎ 800-227-5883

Gary Greene Better Homes and Gardens
  ☎ 409-737-5200, 800-880-9697

Sand N' Sea Properties
  ☎ 409-737-2556, 800-880-2554

Places to Eat

Budget Worth a visit even if you're not in the mood for a $3 egg salad sandwich, the *Star Drug Store*, 510 23rd St, bills itself as 'The Oldest Drug Store in Texas.' The drugs are gone, but the menu, the interior and the friendly help are totally authentic. The store dates from the 1890s, but the lunch counter dates from the 1950s; as a waitress explains, 'Yep, they all used to be marble, but somebody ripped that out in the '50s for the latest and greatest – Formica.' The chocolate malts ($2.75) are made with real ice cream and are thick as tar. At press time we received word that a fire had slightly damaged the building and the store had temporarily closed, but plans were to reopen the business soon.

The Original (☎ *409-762-6001*), 1401 Market St, is just that. It began serving Mexican food in 1916 and hasn't stopped since. Its charming old building has been spiffed up a bit lately to accentuate its history, but the food remains cheap and classic. Tamale and enchilada combos go for $5.

Food for Thought (☎ *409-763-4694*), in the Novel Ideas bookstore at 1816 Market St, has an 'Avocado Mountain' sandwich for the down-to-earth price of $5. Burgers come in both veggie and meaty for $4 and $5, respectively. It also has fresh bagels and muffins for $1 and a variety of coffees.

Three blocks south of the Strand, *Slices* (☎ *409-766-1779*), 2113 Post Office St, serves small individual whole pizzas ($5.50) rather than slices, but it's doubtful that a place named Small Individual Whole Pizzas would have the same panache, right? It also has

GULF COAST

handfuls of hoagies ($4.50) and other bar chow that you can wash down with beer in a real laid-back sports bar kind of setting.

The ***Phoenix Bakery & Coffee House*** *(☎ 409-763-3764)*, on 23rd St between Mechanic St and the Strand, has gorgeous baked goods, pastries and a long breakfast menu that stars strawberry waffles ($4.75), which usually cause diners to modestly exclaim, 'Oh my!' before they dive in.

Follow your nose to the chopped beef sandwich at ***Leon's World's Finest In & Out Barbecue House*** *(☎ 409-744-0070)*, 101 14th St. It has really good potato salad as well, and you'll have a hard time getting in and out for more than $5.

Sonny's Place *(☎ 409-763-9602)*, 1206 19th St, looks like a local hangout left over from the '50s, and it is. But what keeps locals hanging out year after year are the New Orleans-style muffulettas (spicy meats, olives and seasonings on Italian flat bread) for $5. It also has the juiciest, greasiest and therefore best cheeseburgers on the island. But don't lose control with joy: 'Behave or Be Gone' is written everywhere.

Mid-Range & Top End *Gaido's* *(☎ 409-762-9625)*, 3800 Seawall Blvd, has been run by the same family since 1911. Easily the best-known and best-loved restaurant in Galveston, it serves vast platters of no-compromise seafood at no-compromise prices. Entrées can easily top $20, but you definitely get what you pay for. The tragedy is that few diners have room for the crustless pecan pie – those who think they do, explode. The same owners also run *Casey's Seafood Restaurant* *(☎ 409-762-9625)*, next door at 3828 Seawall Blvd. The standards are just as high, but everything is more casual, including the prices.

Clary's *(☎ 409-740-0771)*, 8509 Teichman Rd by the I-45 causeway, has elegant old-style seafood dishes such as lump crabmeat baked with cheese, bacon and green onions ($15). BOIs come here for special occasions.

DiBellas *(☎ 409-763-9036)*, 1902 31st St, is where BOIs go when they want a family feast of the kind of tasty Italian food your grandmother might have cooked had she

a) been Italian, and b) been a really good cook. Pastas with sausage, meatballs and the like are the staples of the moderately priced menu.

Entertainment

Opera House The beautifully restored ***Grand 1894 Opera House*** *(☎ 409-765-1894, 800-821-1894)*, 2020 Post Office St, gives you an idea of the pre-hurricane culture and wealth that were found in Galveston. Saved from demolition in the mid-1970s, the Opera House is used for musical and theatrical performances throughout the year. The box office is open Monday to Saturday 9 am to 5 pm and Sunday noon to 5 pm. During these hours you can tour the ornate interior for $2.

Bars & Clubs All of the places in this section are around the Strand, so you can bar-hop until you fall over. ***O'Malley's Stage Door Pub*** *(☎ 409-763-1731)*, 2022 Post Office St, right next to the Opera House, is home to some very friendly young and eccentric locals who lounge about on the mismatched furniture. ***Molly's Pub*** *(☎ 409-763-4466)*, 2013 Post Office St, has a whopping 63 beers on tap from all over the USA and the world. The regulars are happy to give tart-tongued commentary on the merits of some of the more unusual brews. If Ed's there, ask him about the Belgian Trappist ale.

Two places with live music both lack phones, so you'll just have to drop by to see who's playing: ***Old Quarter Acoustic Cafe***, 413 20th St, features mostly female acoustic guitar and fiddle players. ***Nina's Bourbon St West***, 215 22nd St, has live blues many nights and 30 beers on tap every night.

Look for the black awning to find ***Evolution*** *(☎ 409-763-4212)*, 2214 Mechanic St. It's a dance place that's very popular with gay men and lesbians. On Friday and Saturday, it closes at 4 am.

An old meat-packing plant now packs people in for microbrewed beer at ***The Strand Brewery*** *(☎ 409-763-4500)*, 101 23rd St. It usually has four house brews on tap that rotate with the seasons. (The hoppy amber lager Karankawa Gold is the most popular.)

It has a scenic rooftop beer garden and live music on weekends. The most popular item on the menu is the roasted garlic pizza ($7.50).

Finally, a vestige of Galveston's port survives south of the Strand on 22nd St, where there is a row of tough and tawdry seamen's bars.

Shopping

People allergic to cute froufrous and touristy knick-knacks had best avoid the stretch of the Strand between 21st and 22nd Sts (here also known as Moody and Kempner Sts). On the other hand, if your trip will only be complete if you can buy a limited-edition plate bearing the likeness of an adorable kitten, then you're in luck!

Antique stores abound around the Strand. Judging from the volume of antiques for sale, it's evident that much of the merchandise did not originate on the island. Typical of the many large stores, Eiband's Gallery (☎ 409-763-5495), 2201 Post Office St, has a 13,000-sq-foot showroom in a building dating from 1870. Several more shops can be found in a one-block radius.

Local legend Meyer Reiswerg is better known as Colonel Bubbie, of Col Bubbie's Strand Surplus Senter (☎ 409-762-7397), 2202 the Strand. A military surplus store, it features mountains of stuff cast off by the world's militaries, such as really comfortable olive drab cotton socks for $2. Ask the colonel about the saga of Colonel Bubbie's Earth Shoes, a triumph of adaptive marketing.

Getting There & Away

Air Galveston is one to 1½ hours by car from Houston's William Hobby Airport (HOU) and George Bush Intercontinental Airport (IAH).

Bus The Kerrville Bus Company (☎ 409-765-7731), 714 25th St, has four buses a day to/from the Greyhound bus station in Houston. Trips take about one hour and cost $13.

Car Galveston is 49 miles from Houston on I-45. There is little point in trying for scenery on the parallel Hwy 3. It passes the same strip malls and scrubland, and it has lots of stoplights. Traveling to/from the south, if you are hugging the coast, you can connect to Surfside Beach via a bridge between Galveston Island and Follets Island. Inland, avoid Houston by taking Hwy 6, which links US 59 with I-45.

If you're traveling to or from the north, the Galveston-Port Bolivar Ferry is an attraction in itself (see listing below under Around Galveston). It links to Hwy 87, which – except during one of the many road closures – links with Hwy 124 to I-10 and Hwy 73 to Port Arthur.

Getting Around

To/From the Airport Galveston Limousine Service (☎ 409-765-5288, 800-640-4826) has service to/from HOU (one hour, $21) and IAH (two hours, $25). Call in advance to arrange pick-ups from either end.

Bus Island Transit (☎ 409-762-2903) operates buses on six routes from the central stop at 20th and Market Sts. Fares are 60¢ for adults, 30¢ for children, and you can transfer between the bus and trolley systems for free. The six routes are designed for carless residents in the neighborhoods, and service is centered on Broadway Ave. There is no service to the outlying beaches or parks.

Trolley Galveston Island Rail Trolley (☎ 409-762-2903) is an unusual hybrid. Replica trolley cars run on rails, but they are powered by diesel engines rather than electricity. The service is handy, because it links the Strand with Seawall Blvd via 25th St. Trips from one end to the other take about 30 minutes and cost the same as the bus. The daily service has a widely varying schedule; check the signs at stops or call for details. A 15-minute loop around the Strand is free, though open only in summer.

AROUND GALVESTON
Bolivar Peninsula

The drive north along this windswept peninsula is the antidote to civilization. The gulf side is lined with vacation homes that seem to be always uninhabited. It's interesting to note that they were originally built on stilts to accommodate storm surges, which can send the tide sweeping across the sandy landscape. But note how many people haven't been able to resist the temptation to put up a few walls at ground level, ruining the protective qualities of the stilts.

There are few real towns or attractions over the 50-mile length of the peninsula. On stormy days, turn up any of the rough paths leading to the beach for wonderfully moody scenes of surging surf and barren sands.

Galveston-Port Bolivar Ferry The link between Galveston Island and the Bolivar Peninsula, this is one of many connecting ferries that the state runs along the barrier islands. The boats (☎ 409-763-2386) run around the clock daily and are free. On summer weekends the waits at either end can easily be one hour or longer. The 15-minute ride is an attraction in itself. You'll see a big shipwreck, passing freighters from all over the world, and dolphins, which frolic alongside the ferries.

Anahuac National Wildlife Refuge Of the three national wildlife refuges along the Gulf Coast from Galveston to Louisiana, Anahuac has the best access and is therefore the most popular. In practical terms, this means that on some days you'll actually see other people! A 3-mile road leads to the visitors' center, which is really just the park office (☎ 409-267-3337); you are asked to register here when it is open. Admission is always free and the gates are always open. There are bathrooms at the office and free camping is allowed on the shore of Galveston Bay, about 6 miles from the entrance.

Several miles of gravel and dirt roads have been cut through the refuge, which includes deep marsh, ponds, prairie and bayous. A visit to the refuge is really for serious nature lovers because of the primitive roads and the lack of facilities. Bird-watchers with good bird guides and binoculars will enjoy themselves the most. During the winter, 50,000 or more large Canadian snow geese gather at one time, a truly spectacular sight.

The refuge's access road is off FM 1985, 10 miles west of FM 1985's juncture with Hwy 124. The FM 1985 turnoff is slightly less than 10 miles north of Hwy 87.

Galveston Island State Park

Sort of a seafood platter of a park (there's a little bit of everything), these 1950 acres link the gulf and bay sides of Galveston Island. The park (☎ 409-737-3400), 6 miles southwest of Galveston on Seawall Blvd (FM 3005), has 4 miles of nature trails through the coastal dunes, salt marshes, bayous and mud flats. Swimmers will find a beach, birdwatchers will find observation platforms and blinds, kayakers will find pleasant twists and turns and theatergoers will find drama.

That's right, every summer five musical productions are presented in the Mary Moody Northern Amphitheater (☎ 409-737-1744). Look for crowd-pleasers such as *South Pacific* as well as perennial favorite *The Lone Star*, still another celebration of the birth of Texas. Actors love the place, but what they don't realize is that half of what they think is clapping is really the slapping of mosquitoes. Performances are held Monday to Saturday from June to August; tickets average $25 for adults, $13 for children.

The park's campsites are suitable for tents and/or vehicles and come with water and electricity. The cost is $12, plus $3 per adult Sunday to Thursday and $14 weekends. Sites with screened shelters cost from $3 to $5 more. They're very popular in the summer, so reserve well in advance.

Brazosport Area & the Coastal Bend

The name 'Coastal Bend' rather amorphously applies to communities from Galveston to South Padre Island. But its heart is the rural stretch running from the Brazosport area south to Corpus Christi. Here small towns, many forgotten by time, lie next to the water at the end of long and quiet roads. Many shelter on the profusion of inlets and bays, protected by more than 100 miles of uninhabited barrier islands. The only visitors to the islands are birds, which flock here by the millions.

The region just south of Galveston, around the Brazos River, Lake Jackson and Freeport, doesn't get much respect despite the clever marketing moniker that has been dreamed up for it: 'Brazosport.' Or maybe that's because of it. Anyway, this collection of towns and waterways offers more texture to visitors than do the glitzier resorts to the north and south. The area is not brimming with formal attractions, but discovering your own can be worthwhile in itself.

You can make the drive from Houston to Corpus Christi in a little more than three hours if you hammer the gas pedal, and if that's all the time you have, let 'er rip. But taking a day or more to wander this stretch of the Gulf Coast can yield some memorable discoveries.

BRAZOSPORT AREA
Population 190,000
The towns of Lake Jackson, Clute, Freeport, Quintana and Surfside Beach are part of a confused hodgepodge crisscrossed by railroads, highways, creeks, lakes and channels and surrounded by chemical plants collectively known as Brazosport. In fact, it soon becomes obvious that Dow Chemical is the major landowner in the region, since it seems that every fence bears its diamond-shape red logo. Many of the streets have very unbucolic names, such as Chlorine Rd.

But despite the obvious aesthetic cost of such a high concentration of industrial activity, that very industry has served to shield interesting towns, such as Freeport and Surfside Beach, from massive development.

Orientation
Set a three-year-old loose with crayons, and what he or she produces will look very much like a map of the Brazosport area. To simplify things, here are the main roads you'll need to know about:

Hwy 288 The main road to/from Houston. It curves past all the shopping areas of Lake Jackson and ends just west of the historic part of Freeport.

Hwy 332 Joins with Hwy 288 in Lake Jackson and Clute. On the east end, it reaches Surfside Beach and Bluewater Hwy/FM 3005 to Galveston. On the west end, it connects with Hwy 36, 5 miles east of Lake Jackson. From there, you can take Hwy 36 8 miles north to Hwy 35, which is the road to use for exploring the coast to the south.

Information
The Brazosport Chamber of Commerce (☎ 409-265-2505, 888-477-2505), 420 Hwy 288/332 in Clute, has a lot of information and a good map of the area, and if you should decide to move here, well, the staff will do everything but pay for your house. It's open weekdays 9 am to 5 pm.

Lake Jackson
This is a planned community built after WWII. The shopping-area streets off Hwy 288/332 are a treat in themselves, with names such as This Way, That Way and Parking Way, but, sadly, no No Way.

Sea Center Texas, a lavish nature center and fish hatchery, is the town's major attraction. It opened in 1996 and is funded by government agencies and Dow. The complex (☎ 409-292-0100) is at 300 Medical Drive, 1 mile south of Hwy 288/332 (look for the Albertson's supermarket) off Plantation Drive. It's worth a couple of hours and is an excellent place to learn about salt marshes, the surf zone, coastal bays and individual features such as jetties. There are numerous large aquatic tanks filled with local marine life, and out back are 35 acres of fish hatcheries. It's open Tuesday to Friday 9 am to 4 pm, Saturday 10 am to 5 pm and Sunday 1 to 4 pm; admission is free.

Clute
In the Center on the campus of Brazosport College, the small **Brazosport Museum of Natural Science** (☎ 409-265-7831), 400 College Drive just south of Business Route 288, has a fascinating collection of seashells from all over the world, but especially from the Brazosport area. Among the local favorites are the tulip mussel shell, which looks just like a tulip bud, and the lightning whelk, a huge shell that can sell for $15. Members of the Sea Shell Searchers, a group of mostly retired men and women who do just that, are often hanging around, and they will

GULF COAST

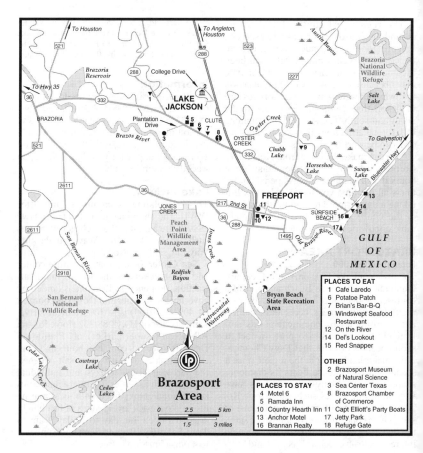

Brazosport Area

PLACES TO EAT
1 Cafe Laredo
6 Potatoe Patch
7 Brian's Bar-B-Q
9 Windswept Seafood Restaurant
12 On the River
14 Del's Lookout
15 Red Snapper

OTHER
2 Brazosport Museum of Natural Science
3 Sea Center Texas
8 Brazosport Chamber of Commerce
11 Capt Elliott's Party Boats
17 Jetty Park
18 Refuge Gate

PLACES TO STAY
4 Motel 6
5 Ramada Inn
10 Country Hearth Inn
13 Anchor Motel
16 Brannan Realty

regale you with many good stories from the beaches. It's open Tuesday to Saturday 10 am to 5 pm and Sunday 2 to 5 pm; admission is free.

Freeport

The old town of Freeport is almost hidden south of the dikes on the Old Brazos River, east of the Brazos River. Working shrimp boats line the harbor along the old river (which now is a channel to the gulf), and the owners are not just happy, but flattered to talk about their hard work. W 2nd St is lined with homes from the 19th century.

Surfside Beach

This completely unadorned beach town features long white beaches. Development thins out quickly if you head north to Galveston on Bluewater Hwy/FM 3005. **Jetty Park**, at the south end of town, has a – get ready – jetty that extends a half mile into the gulf and offers good views. Just north of the park is one of the ugliest houses you will see anywhere. But given that it is built 100 feet closer to the surf than any other house, a good storm should fix things. Jetty Park is also the spot favored by local surfers.

GULF COAST

National Wildlife Refuges

The Brazoria and San Bernard National Wildlife Refuges (☎ 409-849-6062 for both) are very remote areas that are northeast and southwest, respectively, of Brazosport. San Bernard National Wildlife Refuge is the easier of the two to visit. Although it has no developed facilities, trails run through its variety of watery habitats, which include salt marshes and ponds. The San Bernard gate is open every day; to reach it, drive 10 miles west from Freeport on Hwy 36, turn south onto FM 2611, drive 5 miles until FM 2918 branches off to the southeast, and proceed to the refuge gate.

Brazoria is quite swampy, and the best access is by boat from the Intracoastal Waterway. Vehicle access is limited to 4WD vehicles the first full weekend of each month, but the US Fish and Wildlife Service says you should call first for information and directions.

Fishing

Capt Elliott's Party Boats (☎ 409-233-1811), in Freeport, has a fleet of boats that go on a variety of trips for all sorts of fish. Prices are as varied as the catch, but one of its most popular trips is a 45-hour adventure far out into the gulf to catch the big tuna, which costs $250. More modest 12-hour trips for red snapper start at $55. The pier is just east of the intersection of FM 523 and Hwy 36.

Special Events

Highlights of the Brazosport calendar include the following:

Mid-April
Migration Celebration
This four-day birding festival features field trips, seminars and other events. For information, call the Brazosport Chamber of Commerce (see Information).

July
The Great Texas Mosquito Festival
This event (☎ 409-265-8392) is held on the last weekend of the month in Clute – and you have to give these people lots of credit for making the best of a bad situation. Dances, contests, a carnival and a truly hideous mascot named Willie Manchew are among the highlights.

Places to Stay

Lake Jackson & Clute Several motel chains have properties along Hwy 288/332. *Motel 6* (☎ *409-265-4764*), 1000 Hwy 332, has the usual cheap rooms for $32. *Ramada Inn* (☎ *409-297-1161*), 925 Hwy 332, has nicer rooms for $55/60 a single/double.

Freeport *Country Hearth Inn* (☎ *888-325-7818*), 1015 W 2nd St, has nice rooms in a pleasant part of town for $49.

Surfside Beach *Anchor Motel* (☎ *409-239-3543*), 1302 Bluewater Hwy, has very basic accommodations for $35 September to May and $45 during the summer. Brannan Realty (☎ 409-233-1812), 246 Bluewater Hwy, offers an excellent color booklet showing the scores of oceanfront condos that it rents; weekend rates run from $345 in winter to more than $500 summer.

Places to Eat

Lake Jackson & Clute *Cafe Laredo* (☎ *409-297-0696*), 403 This Way, is a hopping local Mexican restaurant in Lake Jackson that has all the standards for $4 to $6. Food flies at the *Potatoe Patch* (☎ *409-265-4285*), 1415 Hwy 332 in Clute, where the waitresses toss your hot biscuits across the restaurant to you. When you're not grabbing for buns, you can tuck into home cooking, such as fried chicken for about $5. The food is excellent at *Brian's Bar-B-Q* (☎ *409-265-1232*), 151 Commerce St, one block behind the Brazosport Chamber of Commerce. Check out the pictures of Brian's regulars wearing his T-shirts in locations around the world.

Freeport & Oyster Creek *On the River* (☎ *409-233-1352*), 919 W 2nd St in Freeport, is a very busy old seafood place with dinners from $11 to $13.

Windswept Seafood Restaurant (☎ *409-233-1951*), 105 Burch Circle in Oyster Creek, is a simple supper club surrounded by a collection of mobile homes. The good shrimp and fresh fish entrées average $8 and come straight from the Freeport fleet, 4 miles south. To get here, take FM 523 north from

Hwy 332 and follow the numerous directional signs.

Surfside Beach The *Red Snapper* (☎ *409-239-3226)*, 402 Bluewater Hwy, is near the beach in Surfside Beach and has seafood entrées for about $11. *Del's Lookout* (☎ *409-239-2666)*, 106 Yucca St on the beach just east of Bluewater Hwy, is a tremendous blues club with live music on Saturday and Sunday.

Getting There & Around
To see the Brazosport area and the little towns south to Corpus Christi, you will need a car.

SOUTH OF BRAZOSPORT
Hwy 35 is the main road through the coastal towns between Brazosport and Corpus Christi. For an even more rural drive, take FM 521 south from Brazoria. The land is gently rolling, with a succession of farms and homesteads. There are scores of small towns along the way that seem to have changed little in decades; many of them are on bays and inlets that try to shelter themselves behind the barrier islands.

Being on sort of a corner of the gulf seems to put this area at the wrong end of a hurricane funnel. Woeful stories of the toll the huge storms have taken can be heard in almost every town. Indianola, a mere hamlet on Lavaca Bay, was once a thriving port, but hurricanes in 1866 and 1886 literally wiped out its future. Port Lavaca was battered in 1945. Just up the road in Palacios, people still talk about the big ones in 1935 and 1961. And those are just a few of the larger hurricanes. Certainly the memories of these storms must in some way restrain development of what is otherwise a very pretty area.

Matagorda
This crossroads is one of the few links to a barrier island between Brazosport and Corpus Christi. Hwy 60 runs almost due south to the coast. About 5 miles past Wadsworth, where the highway crosses FM 521, huge silver orbs suddenly appear amid the scrub. A blimp manufacturer has a factory seem-

ingly in the middle of nowhere, and the helium-filled blimps are a visual surprise.

Matagorda consists of just a few stores. A drawbridge over the busy Intracoastal Waterway is frequently raised to allow ships to pass. It's a good excuse to stop the car, stretch the legs and get a good look at the barges.

After the drawbridge, the road becomes FM 2031, which makes a beeline across the white sandy soil to the nearly endless beaches of the barrier island that forms part of the Matagorda Peninsula. There is a fishing jetty out into the gulf that helps to protect the entrance to the ship channel, which is maintained by the Army Corps of Engineers. You can spot those areas that are the Corps' responsibility – they are the ones covered with trash. A short walk on the beach from the parking area and you are completely removed from any sign of development.

Palacios
At a pleasant bend in Hwy 35, this tiny town overlooks an inlet off Matagorda Bay. Besides the nice view, the best feature of town is the *Luther Hotel* (☎ *512-972-2312)*, 408 S Bay Blvd, one block south of Hwy 35. The huge place was first built in 1903 as a resort, and now it is the full-time avocation of the Luther family. Just maintaining the place is an endless chore, as the neglected motel-style units on one side of the crescent drive suggest. Stepping inside the main building is like stepping back 70 years. The only phone allows people to call in with reservations. And a TV that once graced the lobby has been permanently tuned out. Everything is charming in a delightfully natural way – don't look for fussy bowls of potpourri or other B&B nonsense here. Rooms cost $50 except during the summer, when they can go as high as $150.

Port O'Conner
The Intracoastal Waterway goes right past this tiny port town at the end of Hwy 185 and FM 1289, and you can relax at an outdoor café while huge boats surge past a few feet away. The best place to eat in town is *Clark's Marina* (☎ *512-983-4388)*, on 7th St. It serves

Lost at Sea

Sometimes you need to quit when you're ahead. In 1682, French explorer René Robert Cavelier, Sieur de La Salle, ensured that his name would be placed among the great explorers of history when he became the first European to travel the Mississippi River from what's now Illinois to the Gulf of Mexico.

In 1685, he returned from France with three ships filled with supplies and colonists. He wanted to establish a colony for France at the mouth of the Mississippi. Instead, unable to calculate his longitude (the technology did not yet exist), he missed his mark by 400 miles and ended up in Matagorda Bay. Accounts show that although La Salle had many heroic qualities, which made him a good explorer, he also had a few bad ones, not the least of which was a long streak of stubbornness. Even as it became clear that he wasn't anywhere near the Mississippi, he insisted on forging ahead with a colony. The local Karankawa Indians did not extend the welcome mat, having sensibly surmised that nothing good was going to come from the arrival of the Europeans.

One of La Salle's boats, the *Aimable*, soon ran aground in the bay and was lost with much of the colony's supplies. Before long, some prescient colonists returned to France in a second ship, leaving 180 behind with La Salle. Conditions, however, did not improve. The water was brackish, the land hot and dry, the bugs worse and the Karankawas unfriendly. The final blow came in 1686 when the last ship, *La Belle*, was lost offshore during a storm. With the ship went the colonists' remaining supplies and their last hopes.

In 1687, La Salle and a few others set out to walk to Illinois to arrange a rescue. Some of the men decided they'd had enough of their leader and killed him near what today is Bryan, Texas. The Karankawas slaughtered the colonists who had remained behind at what was called Fort St Louis, near today's town of La Salle, Texas. Although the colony was a disaster, it had lasting effects on Texas history. When the Spanish learned of the French interest in the region, they began their colonization of Texas.

Archaeologists searched for *La Belle* for decades. In 1995, it was found in Matagorda Bay. A huge cofferdam was built around its resting place in 12 feet of water so that the remains could be excavated in dry conditions. What's been found has been called the most important shipwreck discovery in North America; the Matagorda Bay mud protected and preserved *La Belle* and its cargo to a high degree. An exhibit of some of the thousands of recovered items tours Texas museums, and plans are under way to establish a permanent museum. The Texas Historical Commission (☎ 512-463-6096) has exhibition schedules. It also has an excellent website filled with information and news from the archaeologists (www.thc.state.tx.us/belle).

sandwiches, salads and more at modest prices in its bright dining area or outside along the waterway. It also has a dock, a bait and tackle shop, boat ramp and market.

Matagorda Island State Park
To completely escape civilization, you can't do much better than this desert island. Matagorda Island has no bridge connection to the mainland, and it has no water. It does have 80 miles of white beaches along its 38-mile length, plus almost limitless hiking possibilities. More than 300 species of birds drop by throughout the year; deer, coyotes, raccoons, rabbits, alligators and more call it home.

Primitive camping ($4) is allowed by the dock area and along a 2-mile segment of beach. A bunkhouse that recalls the barracks left over from a small WWII airbase sleeps 14 each in boot-camp conditions ($12 per person). There are cold-water showers, but the water is not fit for drinking. Visitors must bring enough water for their intended period of stay, plus food and other essentials, such as bug spray and sunscreen.

The park operates a small boat between park headquarters (☎ 512-983-2215) in Port O'Conner and Matagorda Island. However, the boat only runs for sure Thursday to Sunday and on holidays. At other times, you'll have to check with the park. Rangers may also be able to recommend local boat owners who might take you over for a price (usually more than $100).

The park boat journeys for 11 miles and costs $10 for adults, $5 for children, roundtrip. That cost includes a ride on a shuttle truck between the island dock and gulf beaches 2 miles away. People coming by private boat pay $2 to use the shuttle. Park headquarters in Port O'Conner, which has fenced parking, is well marked and right off Hwy 185 on 16th St just before town.

Aransas National Wildlife Refuge

For bird-watchers, the 70,504-acre Aransas National Wildlife Refuge is the premier site on the Texas coast. Even people who don't carry binoculars and ornithological checklists can get caught up in the bird-spotting frenzy that peaks here every March and November but is great throughout the year.

The scenery alone is spectacular – the blue Aransas Bay waters are speckled with green islets ringed with white sand. Native dune grasses blow gently in the breezes while songbirds provide choral background music from the stands of trees.

On the ground, you may well see some of the refuge's wild boars, alligators, armadillos, white-tailed deer and many more species. Everywhere you will see some of the close to 400 bird species that have been documented at Aransas. None are more famous, more followed or more watched than the whooping cranes.

Some of the rarest creatures in North America, the few survivors of the species summer in Canada and spend November to March in the refuge. Spotters and scientists come from all over the world to study the 5-foot-tall birds, which are the tallest in North America. Their dramatic size is heightened by their snow-white bodies, black-tipped wings and red-and-black heads atop sinuous necks.

Huge efforts have been made to protect the surviving birds, and they seem to be paying off. In the 1954 season, only 21 whooping cranes spent the winter in Aransas. By 1980 the number had climbed to 78, and in 1997-98, a total of 181 cranes were counted, including a record 29 chicks. One of the biggest obstacles to increasing whooping crane numbers is that typically a pair will only raise one chick a year.

Besides the whooping cranes, some of the other popular birds at the refuge and when they are typically present are as follows:

Ducks/geese	October to March
Herons/egrets	Year-round
Spoonbills/ibises	Year-round
Warblers	March to May, September to November

Orientation & Information Aransas is 35 miles northeast of Rockport; take FM 774 off Hwy 35 and follow the signs. From the north, take Hwy 239 south off Hwy 35, just past Tivoli. The land outside the refuge is as flat as a frozen pond. Corn grows on the local farms, and there are few areas you can visit that look more like the place where the crop duster tried to mow down Cary Grant in *North by Northwest*.

The refuge (☎ 512-286-3559) is open daily dawn to dusk. Admission is $3 per person or $5 per carload.

An interpretive visitors' center is near the entrance. It's open daily 8:30 am to 4:30 pm. It should be your first stop, because it has various interesting exhibits about the refuge and the volunteers will be happy to load you down with information, including the decent free map. A 40-foot observation tower overlooks much of the refuge and should be your next stop. It is an excellent place to get an overview of the site, and it has free telescopes.

The auto loop covers 16 miles, and the free map is a good guide. There are 6 more miles of trails; the 1.4-mile Heron Flats trail is the one to take if your time is limited. The trail touches on many of the different areas of the refuge and starts near the visitors' center.

Bikes are allowed in the refuge and are an excellent way to cover the many miles of roads and trails outside of a car. There is no camping anywhere in the park, but there is a picnic area. You can camp in Goose Island State Park; see the next section.

Organized Tours Several boats tour the estuaries from November to March spotting whooping cranes. The tours usually leave in the mornings and afternoons for three- to four-hour tours and cost from $25 to $35. The following companies all leave from various harbors in Rockport:

Captain John Howell
  ☎ 512-729-7525, 800-245-9324

Captain Ted's Whooping Crane Tours
  ☎ 512-729-9589, 800-338-4551

Wharf Cat
  ☎ 512-729-4855, 800-782-2473

Goose Island State Park

The closest camping to Aransas National Wildlife Refuge is in this small park (☎ 512-729-2858), right on Aransas Bay and popular with kayakers. The namesake marshy island is a mere 140 acres, linked to another 174 acres on the mainland. Somehow this area has fared better during hurricanes than neighboring areas, and as a result the mainland area is heavily wooded with old-growth oaks. In fact, the oldest tree on the coast is a 1000-year-old oak that has a trunk 35 feet in circumference. It is in a special protected area near the park.

The entrance to the park is on Park Rd 13, which is east of Hwy 35, just north of the bridge over Copano Bay. The park is open daily. The busiest times are during the summer and whooping crane season. The en-

trance fee is $2 a person; ask for directions to the old oak.

Island campsites with water are $8, mainland sites with partial hookups are $11 and bay-front sites with hookups are $13. A word of caution: The phrase 'bring insect repellent' appears more frequently in this park's official brochure than in any other.

Rockport & Fulton
Population 7000

These two adjoining port towns remain separate municipalities, but they have grown together to such an extent that the casual visitor will think of them as one entity.

The side streets between Hwy 35 and Aransas Bay are dotted with numerous art galleries. Rockport and Fulton together claim to be home to the state's highest percentage of artists. There are quite a few, but it's doubtful that anyone will undertake the census required to actually prove the claim.

The towns have more of a cosmopolitan feel compared to the sleepy burgs to the north. The streets are quiet, however, and they make for a relaxing stop on your way to or from the bright lights of Corpus Christi, 40 miles south. The Rockport-Fulton Area Chamber of Commerce (☎ 512-729-9952), 404 Broadway St in Rockport, has area information and can help you find out what's going on in the ever-changing local art scene. It's open Monday to Saturday 9 am to 5 pm (Friday till 2 pm).

GULF COAST

Rockport and Fulton host the Hummer/ Bird Celebration each September and the Seafair, celebrating local fisherfolk, in October; call the chamber of commerce for more information.

Rockport Harbor Crescent-shaped Rockport Harbor is one of the prettiest on the Gulf Coast. It is lined with shrimp boats, fishing charter boats, whooping crane tour boats, pleasure craft, and a series of rustic peel-and-eat shrimp joints and bait shops. In Fulton, the ***Boiling Pot*** (☎ 512-729-6972), on Palmetto St and Fulton Beach Rd, is a rustic classic: mountains of shellfish are dumped in a pot full of spicy boiling water; when they're done, they're dumped on your paper-covered table and you dive in. The average cost is under $10 a person, laundry expenses not included.

Texas Maritime Museum Everything from fishing boats to offshore oil rigs to the story of the short-lived Texas Navy is covered at this fun little museum (☎ 512-729-1271), on Rockport Harbor at 1202 Navigation Circle. The displays emphasize the human aspects of the Texas seacoast and focus on the lives of the people who have made their living off the Gulf of Mexico and the oceans beyond it. Several old boats that were used to rescue people caught in storms are displayed outside. Open Tuesday to Saturday 10 am to 4 pm, Sunday 1 to 4 pm; $4 for adults, $2 for children.

Fulton Mansion State Historical Park This 1870s mansion (☎ 512-729-0386), at Henderson St and Fulton Beach Rd in Fulton, dominates the shoreline in the Rockport and Fulton area. It was built by George Fulton, an entrepreneur who made his fortune in a variety of professions, such as engineering, publishing and construction. That he was no dummy is evident in the construction techniques he employed in his mansion. On the outside, it looks like an imposing French Second Empire creation, right down to the mansard roofs. Inside those walls, however, are concrete foundations and walls more than 5 inches thick.

Although other contemporary buildings have been blown away, the mansion has withstood several hurricanes. It has been fully restored and is open for guided tours Wednesday to Sunday 9 am to 4 pm; $4 for adults, $2 for children.

Corpus Christi Area

The bright lights of Corpus Christi are at the center of the region around Corpus Christi Bay. Scores of museums, tourist attractions, restaurants and clubs are here. Beyond the calm bay waters, the sandy charms of Padre Island and its seemingly endless beaches have their own allure, and Port Aransas is easily the most charming beach town in Texas.

CORPUS CHRISTI
Population 285,000

Let's get this out of the way quickly: everybody who lives in Corpus Christi calls it simply Corpus. Saving on the space needed for the extra seven letters will surely save at least one tree branch over the life of this book.

More and more people are also calling Corpus home. Its growth rate has been close to 3% a year during the 1990s. Although it was once known as a grimy port town with a strip of raunchy beach clubs filled with bands of drunken sailors and naval pilots, it is now a glittering seaside city with an economy fueled by tourism and conventioneers.

This would please Colonel Henry Kinney, a promoter right out of Texas central casting in every classic sense. In 1839, he established a trading post on what was then still a disputed border area between Texas and Mexico. Kinney flacked the area and its charms incessantly, although the only really receptive audience he found was smugglers, who exploited the region's political confusion.

When a post office was established in 1846, the town changed its name from 'Kinney's Trading Post' to Corpus Christi. Spaniards named the bay after the Roman Catholic holy day in 1519, when Alonzo Álvarez de Piñeda discovered its calm waters.

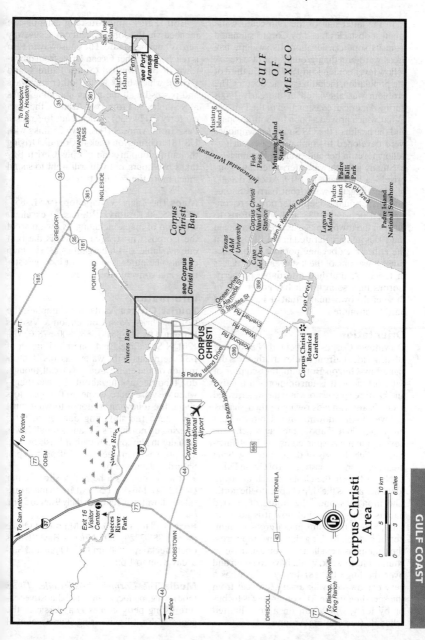

Corpus Christi Area

In the latter half of the 19th century, the greatest obstacles faced by Corpus stemmed from its southern location. Its swampy bay areas were breeding grounds for diseases. A yellow fever epidemic in 1867 killed a third of the population, including all the doctors. The problem was alleviated in the early 1900s during American construction of the Panama Canal, which proved a boon for both shipping and the health of the US South, as techniques were developed to combat diseases such as yellow fever in hot and swampy Panama.

Steady growth was interrupted by – surprise! – a hurricane in 1919. After a decade of wrangling, the waterfront barrier, Shoreline Drive and the deepwater port were constructed between 1933 and '41. Efforts to burnish the town's image as a resort began in the 1960s and accelerated in the 1980s, when the entire area became popular, in part because it was one of the last oceanfront places in the USA that had affordable property. Corpus may soon find it has grown out of the beach-town image that it has worked hard to promote.

Orientation

Downtown Corpus lies behind N Shoreline Blvd, a wide seafront boulevard that was designed by Gutzon Borglum, the sculptor of Mt Rushmore. It is uncommonly attractive and has three projections into the water, called T-heads and L-heads owing to their shapes.

Overlooking downtown is Uptown, built on an area 40 feet above the bay. Much of its development was spurred by the 1919 hurricane, which did lots of damage to low-lying areas and sparked construction of Ocean Drive.

North Beach, the closest beach to downtown, lies across the ship channel to the north. The area was once the home of storied haunts of ill repute, but now it is home to sand, hotels, museums and a growing number of condos. Making the short hop across the channel is a challenge – you can drive, of course, but to walk, you'll have to go up and over the huge US 181 bridge, which has a very narrow sidewalk a very few feet from the speeding traffic. The other way is by bus or by ferry, which run on a very limited schedule (see Getting Around).

Both Padre and Mustang Islands are reached via the John F Kennedy Causeway across Laguna Madre. The causeway in turn is reached by either Ocean Drive from downtown or by Hwy 358 (South Padre Island Drive), which links to the other highways and passes by all the major shopping malls at S Staples St. From Port Aransas, there's a car ferry to Hwy 361, which leads to Aransas Pass; from Aransas Pass, Hwy 35 links with US 181 to bring you back to Corpus. Driving the entire loop around Corpus Christi Bay takes two hours, but you will want to spend much more time on the trip.

Maps The Zdansky Map Store (☎ 512-855-9226), 5230 Kostoryz Rd, has an excellent selection of maps, including its own map of the Corpus Christi area, which is the best one available. It is a bargain at $3. The map can also be purchased at most local gas stations and convenience stores.

Information

Tourist Offices As its name implies, the Corpus Christi Area Convention & Visitors Bureau (☎ 512-881-1888, 800-678-6232), 1201 N Shoreline Blvd, one block north of I-37's terminus at the water, has lots of information on the entire area. If you call, though, don't bother asking about the weather – when we were there, we heard the operators giving the following response to what must have been the shivering queries of folks freezing up north: 'It's 74° and sunny!' It was actually in the low 60s with a brisk breeze. The office is open weekdays 8:30 am to 5 pm, Saturday 9 am to 3 pm.

It also operates a helpful Visitor Center (☎ 512-241-1464) at I-37 exit 16, 16 miles outside of downtown. It's open daily 9 am to 5 pm.

Post The Hector P Garcia Main Post Office (☎ 512-886-2226), 809 Nueces Bay Blvd, is open weekdays 7:30 am to 5:30 pm and Saturday 8 am to 1 pm.

Media The *Corpus Christi Caller Times* (50¢) is a good local daily. Its exhaustive feature listing petty crimes is a classic of the genre. We're still snickering at an account of

GULF COAST

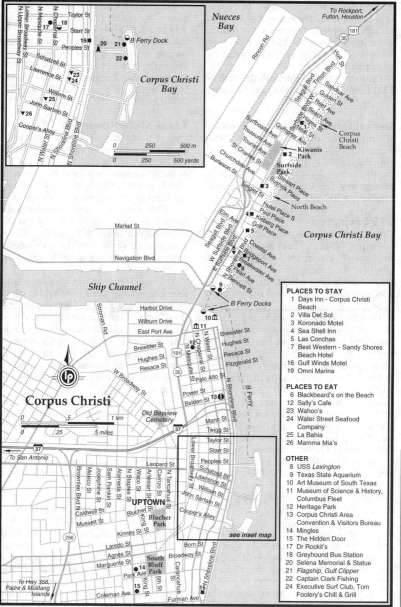

Corpus Christi

To Rockport,
Fulton, Houston

Nueces Bay

Corpus Christi Bay

■ Kiwanis Park
Corpus Christi Beach

Surfside Park
North Beach

Corpus Christi Bay

Market St

Navigation Blvd

Ship Channel

Harbor Drive
Wilburn Drive
East Port Ave

B Ferry Docks

Corpus Christi

Old Bayview Cemetery

To San Antonio

UPTOWN

Blucher Park

South Bluff Park

To Hwy 358,
Padre & Mustang Islands

see inset map

PLACES TO STAY
1 Days Inn - Corpus Christi Beach
2 Villa Del Sol
3 Koronado Motel
4 Sea Shell Inn
5 Las Conchas
7 Best Western - Sandy Shores Beach Hotel
16 Gulf Winds Motel
19 Omni Marina

PLACES TO EAT
6 Blackbeard's on the Beach
12 Sally's Cafe
23 Wahoo's
24 Water Street Seafood Company
25 La Bahia
26 Mamma Mia's

OTHER
8 USS *Lexington*
9 Texas State Aquarium
10 Art Museum of South Texas
11 Museum of Science & History, Columbus Fleet
13 Corpus Christi Area Convention & Visitors Bureau
14 Mingles
15 The Hidden Door
17 Dr Rockit's
18 Greyhound Bus Station
20 Selena Memorial & Statue
21 Flagship, Gulf Clipper
22 Captain Clark Fishing
24 Executive Surf Club, Tom Foolery's Chill & Grill

GULF COAST

the theft of statues depicting the Three Wise Men from a lawn. On Friday, it publishes a weekend section listing area entertainment and cultural events. You can get free copies of this useful guide all week long at the visitors' centers.

The local National Public Radio outlet is KEDT, 90.3 FM. Most of the rest of the radio stations play Tejano music.

Medical Services Primary Care Physicians of Corpus Christi (☎ 512-852-0600), 4626 Weber Rd at South Padre Island Drive (Hwy 358), is open weekdays 8 am to 5 pm.

Emergency The Coast Guard emergency number is ☎ 512-937-1898.

USS *Lexington*

The second sight you are likely to notice in Corpus (after the bay) is this 900-foot-long aircraft carrier (☎ 512-888-4873) sitting near the beach just north of the ship channel. Since 1992, it has been open for visitors, who can explore at will over many of its decks.

The fifth US Navy ship to bear the name, the *Lexington* replaced another aircraft carrier of the same name that was sunk in the Battle of the Coral Sea in 1942. The Essex-class carrier served in the Pacific during WWII and was later modernized and continued on active duty until 1962, when the navy converted it into a training ship. For the next 29 years, the *Lexington* steamed out of Pensacola, Florida, and navy pilots practiced takeoffs and landings on it out in the gulf. The city of Corpus Christi bought the ship when it was retired in 1991, and it will continue to serve indefinitely as a tourist attraction.

The most interesting part of a visit to the *Lexington* is just wandering some of the decks and thinking about what it would have been like to serve with 3000 men in the engine room, bridge, hangar deck, flight deck and elsewhere. Unfortunately, the sweep of the hangar deck is ruined by lots of little displays and exhibits that have eaten into the space. Rather than letting the ship speak for itself, plans are afoot for various arcade-style amusements.

The ship is open daily 9 am to 5 pm except during the summer, when it is open until 6:30 pm. Admission is $9 for adults, $4 for children. You shouldn't have any problem finding the ship; it's the big thing in the water. The entrance to the pier is at 2914 N Shoreline Blvd. During the evening, the ship is eerily lit with blue lights that recall its WWII nickname, 'the Blue Ghost.'

Texas State Aquarium

One of those 'destination aquariums' that have been popping up in tourist areas, this one (☎ 512-881-1200), right on the bay at 2710 N Shoreline Blvd, is a good place to learn about marine life along the Gulf Coast and has many interesting live creatures in its exhibits. The main exhibits, on a circular course, include an area with live shorebirds that shows what happens at the gulf's edge and a huge tank replicating the environment around offshore oil rigs, complete with sharks, grouper and red snapper.

The biggest problem with the aquarium is its size: small. Just as we were writing 'This is an excellent aquarium and the visit should be good,' we realized that we were back at our starting point. Outside are a few more displays, including the 'Touch of Adventure,' a pool that you can stick your hand into to annoy – er, touch – small sharks and rays. A viewing platform has good views of the *Lexington* and the bay.

The aquarium is open Monday to Saturday 9 am to 5 pm, Sunday 10 am to 5 pm. During the summer, it is open until 6 pm. Admission is $8 for adults, $4.50 for children. Note that both the aquarium and the *Lexington* give you poorly designed 'guides' that are mostly advertising and almost useless for your visit. Complain.

Museum of Science & History

This fairly large museum (☎ 512-883-2862), 1900 N Chaparral St, right on the south side of the ship channel, gets more interesting the deeper you probe. The exhibits are all well done and do a good job of explaining complex subjects. One area shows how archaeologists find shipwrecks on Padre Island and explains what they've learned. Be sure

Selena

Selena Quintanilla Perez was easily the most famous person Corpus Christi has produced. She almost single-handedly was responsible for the crossover of Tejano music, hugely popular with Hispanics in the USA, to mainstream charts. She had an energetic and charismatic stage presence that connected with legions of fans. Since her murder in 1995, she has assumed martyr status with many, who cling to an idealized image of a woman who started singing when she was nine.

Selena was 23 when Yolanda Saldivar, the president of her fan club, shot her in the parking lot of the Days Inn near the Corpus Christi airport. At the trial later that year, prosecutors successfully argued that Saldivar shot the singing star because Selena had discovered that she was stealing Selena's money. The jury in the case gave Saldivar life in prison.

In death, Selena is even a bigger star than when she was alive. In 1997, her albums still sold at a rate that put her fourth on the charts for Latino performers in the USA. Her story has been embraced by many fans because it is one with which they can empathize. Selena's parents tried and failed at running a Mexican restaurant in Corpus, and it fell to their plucky daughter and her crowd-pleasing talents to save the family from ruin. Along the way, she ran afoul of her father, Abraham Quintanilla, an authoritarian who objected to her revealing stage clothes. She also married her lead guitarist, Chris Perez, in a secret ceremony.

It all sounds like a script for a movie. It was. In 1997, *Selena* did pretty good business, even if its portrayal of the pop star was the most reverential treatment of a young woman since that given to a mere saint in *The Song of Bernadette*. Selena's father was the film's executive producer, which definitely ensured that the movie reflected the family's view of things.

Definitely not in the film were details from a book by Maria Celeste Arraras, *Selena's Secret: The Revealing Story Behind Her Tragic Death*, which detailed Selena's growing affection for a rich Mexican doctor and the unraveling of her marriage at the time of her death.

In Corpus Christi, a memorial and statue of Selena have been constructed at the entrance to the Peoples St T-head on N Shoreline Blvd. It has numerous platitudes cast in bronze, but a more revealing look at the affection of her fans lies in the scribbled poetry and verse that adorn the site.

'Our flower, our rose, our blossom that didn't open,' reads one poem.

GULF COAST

to read the diary entries of one hapless passenger who found himself aboard a foundering boat with an inept crew. A large exhibit called 'Seeds of Change' shows the cultural impact on the Americas of corn, potatoes, sugar, disease and horses. One good map shows how corn and potato cultivation spread from South America and are now grown in more places than are wheat and rice. Open Monday to Saturday 10 am to 6 pm, Sunday noon to 6 pm; $8 for adults, $4 for children, 50¢ for people in a military uniform (so join today).

Columbus Fleet There is palpable local shame over the status of this attraction (☎ 512-883-4118). In 1992, the government of Spain built replicas of Columbus' ships, the *Niña*, the *Pinta* and the *Santa María*. After sailing them around the Atlantic, Spain agreed to lease them to the city of Corpus Christi for 50 years. Shortly after they arrived to huge fanfare in 1993, a rogue barge went out of control on the ship channel and rammed all three, causing huge damage. The *Niña* stayed afloat and is usually moored someplace in town. The other two are now sitting in a concrete courtyard behind the museum, looking quite the worse for wear and rather forlorn. A multiyear effort is under way to repair the ships and return them to the water in a *protected* dock.

Art Museum of South Texas
Rotating exhibits of contemporary art are the main feature at this dramatic museum (☎ 512-884-3844), at 1902 N Shoreline Blvd across a plaza from the Museum of Science & History. It was designed by Philip Johnson, and its entrance is dominated by *East Rim Passage*, a large painting by Dennis Blaos depicting South Texas as a settler would have found it. The museum is open Tuesday to Saturday 10 am to 5 pm (Thursday till 9 pm), Sunday 1 to 5 pm; $3 for adults, $1 for children except on Tuesday, when it is free.

Heritage Park
Originally a neighborhood of old homes, Heritage Park is steadily growing into a theme park of old homes. Nine Corpus

houses dating back as far as 1851 have been moved to this area, bounded by Mesquite, N Chaparral and Hughes Sts. Many are home to nonprofit groups. The NAACP is in the Littles-Martin House, which was home to an early African American family in Corpus.

Tours of the restored houses are given Wednesday and Thursday at 10:30 am and Friday and Saturday at 10:30 am and 12:45 pm; $3 for adults, $1 for children. They depart from the Galvan House, a 1908 house with huge porches that serves as the park's information center (☎ 512-883-0639). There is a good café in the Merriman-Bobys House; see the Places to Eat section for details.

Corpus Christi Botanical Gardens
These unusual gardens (☎ 512-852-2100), 8545 S Staples St, feature greenhouses filled with more than 2100 types of flowering orchids. Outside, nature trails wander through mesquite forest and surrounding wetlands. Restoration efforts are under way on the banks of neighboring Oso Creek. Open Tuesday to Sunday 9 am to 5 pm; $2 for adults, $1 for children.

Old Bayview Cemetery
An almost forgotten place just west of US 181 and downtown, this quiet spot on a hill is where some of the first Europeans in Corpus were buried. Many of the tombstones are too weathered to read, but the ancient, scraggly oaks and constant bay breezes make it an evocative location. Look for the cemetery at the corner of Padre and Ramirez Sts.

Activities
Boating The alphabetically shaped T and L docks downtown (one sort of wishes they'd gone for G or Q) are home to large marinas. The city maintains slips for visiting boaters. Call ☎ 512-882-7333 for reservations and fee information.

The International School of Sailing (☎ 512-881-8503) offers a variety of sailing lessons that start at $30 for three hours on a small Sunfish and go as high as $825 for bareboat certification, a five-day course during which you live aboard a sailboat and learn the skills necessary to charter 30- to 48-foot sailboats anywhere in the world.

The surviving member of the replica Columbus trio, the *Niña*, is home to courses in the ancient (quite literally) arts of sailing, including navigation. Although why you'd want to learn how to set off for India and find America is beyond us. The Columbus Fleet Association Sail Training Program (☎ 512-883-4118) has details on these intensive courses.

Fishing Many of the skippers who charter boats are based in Rockport or Port Aransas because it puts them closer to the gulf. In Corpus, the visitors' centers have lists of local charters. Downtown, Capt Clark Fishing (☎ 512-884-4369) offers four-hour trips aimed at people driven more by whim than by serious intent. The boat has lots of railings to prevent landlubbers from joining their quarry in the water, and the ever patient crew is adept at demonstrating the complexities of baiting. Trips usually leave during the summer at 7:30 am and 2 and 8 pm. Call to confirm and to check off-season schedules. The cost ($15 for adults, $10 for children) is quite affordable, even if the person next to you ends up with hooks in both thumbs. The boat departs from the Peoples St T-head dock.

Windsurfing Corpus Christi Bay and Laguna Madre, inside Padre Island, are prized windsurfing locations thanks to the unusually calm waters and the nearly constant breezes. Many competitions and championships are held throughout the year. Wind & Wave Watersports (☎ 512-937-9283), 10721 S Padre Island Drive (Hwy 358), is a good place to get information on local conditions. It rents windsurfing boards, boogie boards, surfboards for the terminally optimistic, and kayaks.

You can check local wind conditions by calling ☎ 512-992-9463. Beach and surf conditions are reported at ☎ 512-949-8175.

Organized Tours
The *Flagship*, a 400-person faux paddle wheeler, and the 250-person *Gulf Clipper*

(☎ 512-884-1693 for both) depart on regular bay cruises year-round. From September to May, one of the boats sails daily except Tuesday at 3 pm. During the summer their schedule is much more frequent, with daily trips at 11 am and 1 and 3 pm, augmented by various sunset and evening cruises. Tickets are $7 for adults, $4 for children; the boats leave from the Peoples St T-head.

Special Events
Corpus Christi is home to several large festivals, which attract many happy people from around the region.

Late April
Buccaneer Days
   This is a celebration of Corpus Christi Bay's discovery Spanish Buccaneers, with citywide festivals, concerts and other events.

Late July
Texas Jazz Festival
   Several stages feature live music near the Art Museum of South Texas.

Late September
Bayfest
   Boat races, parades and fireworks are featured along N Shoreline Blvd.

Places to Stay
Camping The cheapest place to stay in the Corpus area is the free camping at *Nueces River Park*, which is next to the parking lot at the visitors' center at I-37 exit 16. Of course, you get what you pay for: little shade, no showers and no public transit to cover the 16 miles into town.

The parks on Padre and Mustang Islands all have various camping facilities that are detailed under those sections, below.

Motels & Hotels There are three budget motels on Corpus Christi beach that also offer access to the local attractions. All offer basic and convenient accommodations. *Koronado Motel* (☎ *512-883-4411*), 3615 Timon Blvd, has rooms for $35/50 for singles/doubles; they're $10 more March to September. *Las Conchas* (☎ 512-887-1010), 3101 E Surfside Blvd, has rooms for $38/48. *Sea Shell Inn*

(☎ 512-888-5391), 202 Kleberg Place, has rooms for $45/52, which are $25 more May to September.

Downtown, *Gulf Winds Motel* (☎ 512-884-2485), 801 N Shoreline Blvd, has very simple rooms, which are a breeze to find, for $35/45; prices rise by $20 May to September.

There are several chain hotels along I-37 by the airport, but there is little reason to stay in this charmless quarter when you can stay close to the bay. However, should you for some reason want to stay out here, *Days Inn* (☎ 512-888-8599), 901 Navigation Blvd at I-37 exit 3A, is notable only because it is where Tejano music star Selena (see boxed text) was killed by the president of her fan club. Rooms are $75/80, rising by $5 May to September.

You can't get any closer to the USS *Lexington* than the *Best Western – Sandy Shores Beach Hotel* (☎ 512-883-7456), 3200 Surfside Blvd (the building itself is on N Shoreline Blvd), a sprawling property with a huge pool, whirlpool and shops, including one selling kites that has a small attached kite museum. Rooms range from $69 to $119 except from May to September, when they can cost $10 more. North along the shore, *Days Inn – Corpus Christi Beach* (☎ 512-882-3297), 4302 Surfside Blvd W, has average rooms that are as low as $39 in the off-season if you take one facing the highway, or as high as $89 facing the water during the summer. *Villa Del Sol* (☎ 512-883-9748), 3938 E Surfside Blvd, is a condo-style motel with large units with kitchens. Off-season rates average $80. June to September, they climb to an average of $125.

Omni Marina (☎ 512-882-1700), at 707 N Shoreline Blvd, is the nicer of two high-rise Omni hotels on the waterfront downtown. It has indoor and outdoor pools and good views of the boats at the marinas. Rates for single/double rooms are $139/149.

B&Bs Sand Dollar Hospitality (☎ 512-853-1222, 800-528-7782) is a booking agency for B&Bs around the Corpus area. It represents rooms in private homes close to downtown, the beaches and Padre Island. Rates range from $65 to $125.

Places to Eat

Budget *La Bahia* (☎ 512-888-6555), at 224 N Chaparral St, is popular with downtown workers for breakfast and lunch. The food and the decor are unadorned Mexican, but the prices are low and the quality great. *Sally's Cafe* (☎ 512-887-9043), at Heritage Park in the Merriman-Bobys House, serves soups, salads and sandwiches for lunch on vintage china. 'The Verdi,' a sandwich that hits the right note with avocado, black beans and cheese, is $4.75. Diners are treated to free homemade chocolate-chip cookies.

One of the biggest fans of *B&Js Pizza* (☎ 512-992-6671), 6335 S Padre Island Drive (Hwy 358), describes it as a 'hole in the wall.' It is, but it has great cheap pizza and a huge selection of beer. And after dinner, you can work off the extra toppings with a fast game of pool. Finally, *Whattaburger*, the ubiquitous local fast-food chain with the tired '70s logo, is based in Corpus. But the food is just the same.

Mid-Range Several restaurants crowd around N Water St downtown. Although they could be tourist traps, they aren't, and they're very popular with locals. *Wahoo's* (☎ 512-888-8522), 415 N Water St, has good Cajun specialties that verge on the chi-chi. Entrée prices average $11. *Water Street Seafood Company* (☎ 512-882-8684), at 309 N Water St, is busy even early in the week. It has a huge and changing daily selection of fresh seafood, much of it *not*, we repeat *not*, deep-fried. Entrées are a comparative bargain at $9 to $15.

You can't help but smile at *Mamma Mia's* (☎ 512-883-3773), 128 N Mesquite St, where owner Marino Delzotto gives as much joy to his patrons as his chefs put garlic in the food. Women get roses and everybody gets to watch the action in the big, open kitchen. Every table has jugs of decent wine, and you're charged by how much you chug or sip delicately. Entrées all cost about $12, and the specialties include rigatoni and eggplant and linguine with clams. This is a fun place.

North of the ship channel, *Blackbeard's on the Beach* (☎ 512-884-1030), at 3117

E Surfside Blvd, is a few cuts above the average seashore joint. The food is imaginative versions of Mexican and American, and the homemade salsa will have you scheming to swipe some. Meals range from $7 to $12, and there's live music from gregarious guitarists.

Entertainment

The N Water St area downtown is home to several hopping bars and clubs. None is more hopping than the *Executive Surf Club* (☎ 512-884-7873), 309 N Water St. The huge indoor and outdoor club has live rock on the patio many nights and is mobbed with locals of all ages and stripes. It has bar food and a great selection of Texas microbrews.

Tom Foolery's Chill & Grill (☎ 512-887-0029), 301 N Chaparral St in the same complex as the Executive Surf Club, has music that's more serious than the name implies. Alternative live rock is featured many nights. *Dr Rockit's* (☎ 512-884-7634), 709 N Chaparral St, is an old, classy '50s bar that's found new life as a live music venue. It features blues, reggae and touring rock bands. The cover averages from $5 to $8.

Close to downtown, *Mingles* (☎ 512-884-0711), 512 S Staples St, is a gay bar with dancing that's popular with women. Three blocks south, the boys enjoy the *Hidden Door* (☎ 512-882-0183), 802 S Staples St, which draws a big leather crowd.

Getting There & Away

Air Corpus Christi International Airport (CRP, ☎ 512-289-2679) is 6 miles west of downtown at International Drive and Hwy 44. Delta Connection (☎ 800-221-1212) and American Eagle (☎ 800-433-7300) have commuter plane service to Dallas-Fort Worth. Continental Express (☎ 512-883-3554) has commuter service to its Houston hub. Southwest (☎ 800-221-0016) also flies to Houston.

Bus Greyhound (☎ 512-882-2516) and its affiliate Valley Transit use the bus station at 702 N Chaparral St. They have six buses daily to Houston ($21) and six daily to Brownsville ($21), in the opposite direction.

Car I-37 runs from San Antonio, 141 miles away. It also hooks up with Hwy 77, the major road running 225 miles north to Houston and 164 miles south to Brownsville.

Getting Around

To/From the Airport Coastal Breeze Transportation (☎ 512-937-7079, 800-838-5577) has two vans daily between the Corpus area and San Antonio International Airport. Rates and schedules vary; call for details.

Bus 'The B' is the jaunty marketing name for the city buses run by the Regional Transportation Authority in Corpus (☎ 512-289-2600). Fares are cheap: 50¢ on weekdays, 25¢ on Saturday. The biggest drawbacks to the system are that it doesn't run on Sunday and it doesn't go out to the islands. Buses on most routes run about 6:30 am to 6:30 pm.

Useful routes for travelers are the No 79, Downtown Shuttle, which covers the downtown area, including N Water St, on a circular route (this service is free) and the No 78, CC Beach Connector, which makes the jump over the ship channel via US 181 and links the downtown area with the aquarium, the *Lexington* and the beach.

In addition, the B operates a waterfront fake trolley, dubbed 'The Harbor Trail,' along Shoreline Blvd, and a ferry boat between the Peoples St T-head and North Beach. They operate on Saturday and Sunday from March to May and September and October, and daily during the summer. The trolley is free and the ferry costs $1.

Car All the major car rental firms are represented at the airport.

Taxi Star Cab (☎ 512-884-9451) is the largest cab company, charging $1.50 flagfall and another $1.50 per mile.

AROUND CORPUS CHRISTI

The natural attractions of the Corpus area are out on the barrier islands. Mustang and Padre Islands have suffered some development, but both have many parks and natural areas, especially Padre Island. The two islands have grown together, and plans are afoot to separate them again with a channel to benefit recreational boaters.

Plans are also afoot to raise the entire causeway a whopping 16 inches, at a cost of millions of dollars. This scheme has been pushed by affluent condo owners on the island since high tides closed the causeway in 1997. The proposal is just as vigorously opposed by taxpayers on the mainland.

Padre Island
This small but growing beach community, at the end of the John F Kennedy Causeway from Corpus, is a good place to stop for supplies on your way to the beaches. South Padre Island Drive between the causeway and Hwy 361, the road north to Port Aransas, is lined with convenience stores, gas stations and banks.

See the Rio Grande chapter for information on South Padre Island.

Beaches
The gulf side of Mustang and Padre Islands is one 131-mile-long beach. The notable parks, Mustang Island State Park and Padre Island National Seashore, are covered in their own separate sections below. The rest of the beach is administered by Nueces County. You can drive on the beaches, but you have to buy a sticker from any of the area convenience stores for $5.38 for a month or $10.78 for a year.

There are beach access roads every few miles, and most have a parking area; parts of the beach are blocked off so that yahoos in sport utility vehicles can't mow you down. Camping is permitted anywhere, but you are limited to three days in any one location. Sand dunes back most of the beach area, and only since the 1970s have developer-driven insurance policies allowed the construction of a few monstrous condo developments on Mustang Island south of Port Aransas.

The most developed county beach area is Padre Balli Park, just south of Padre Island, the town. Its Bob Hall Pier extends 200 yards into the gulf and has an RV camping area that's rather stark.

Mustang Island State Park
This well-equipped park (☎ 512-749-5246) covers 3703 acres and has 5½ miles of beach. It also has excellent beach camping facilities that stretch for more than 1 mile. Every 1000 feet, this area has portable rest rooms, showers and water supplies. This is some of the most convenient beach camping on the Gulf Coast for people who want to hike along the beach to a remote area, but don't want to have to forgo toilets or drinking water. Fees are $7 a night with a $2-per-person entrance fee.

At the main entrance, about 6 miles north of the causeway, is a more formal campground offering sites with electric and water hookups and shaded shelters. The nightly fee here is $12.

This park is popular with surfers, but given the normally calm nature of the gulf, you may have to wait for storms to see any surfable waves.

PADRE ISLAND NATIONAL SEASHORE
One of the longest stretches of undeveloped seashore in the USA, this part of Padre Island is administered by the National Park Service. Its main feature is 70 miles of white sand and shell beaches, backed by grassy dunes and the very salty Laguna Madre.

The island is home to all the coastal wildlife found elsewhere along the coast and then some. There are numerous coyotes, white-tailed deer and other fairly large mammals here. *Not* here are cows, the last of which was moved off the island in 1971 when the park was first established. The bovines had denuded the dunes of grass, and the whole island was suffering. Completely recovered now, it offers a delightful day's outing for anyone who wants to try a little natural beauty, or a major adventure for anyone who wants to escape civilization.

Orientation
The first 6 miles of road into the park are paved. After that are 5 miles of beach to the south, which has very hard-packed sand suitable for driving most cars. After milepost 5 on the beach, the sand becomes filled with

shells and only 4WD vehicles can continue the trip. Sixty miles south of where the beach driving begins, the park ends at Mansfield Channel, a waterway cut through Padre Island that isolates the park from South Padre Island (see the Rio Grande Valley chapter). Short of swimming or kayaking, there is no way to bridge the channel.

The typically excellent color Park Service map is free at the entrance and at the visitors' center (see below). Besides showing the island in great detail, it has good information about flora, fauna and various activities such as fishing and beachcombing.

Information

Sadly, the US Congress has mandated that the National Park Service charge ever-escalating fees to its facilities. Entrance to the park costs a stiff $10 per vehicle, although this is good for seven days.

The visitors' center (☎ 512-937-2621) is on the beach just before the end of the paved road. It is open every day but December 25 and January 1 and has showers, rest rooms and picnic facilities. A small grocery store, open 9 am to 5 pm, has little in the way of fresh food but plenty in the way of convenience foods. It also has no shortage of drinking water, which is unavailable anywhere to the south. There are good displays showing how the island has made a comeback since cows were banished.

There is very little past the visitors' center except beautiful beaches and dunes where the only sounds you'll hear are the wind and water, punctuated by the occasional bird's cry.

Camping & Hiking

Camping in the Malaquite Campground, which is near the entrance and has rest rooms and showers, costs $8 a night. Camping near the visitors' center and on the beaches is free. Reservations are not accepted for any of the facilities.

There is a developed camping area near the visitors' center with parking for RVs; however, it doesn't have any hookups. Many people park their RVs and trailers along the first 5 miles of beach, where driving is both allowed and fairly easy.

At milepost 15, there is a very primitive camping area called Yarborough Pass on the Laguna Madre side. Its amenities are limited to a few tables. At low tide, just south of milepost 50, you can see the top of the smokestack of the *Nicaragua*, a steamer that ran aground in 1912. To give you an idea of how transitory barrier islands are, note that when it was wrecked, the *Nicaragua* was high up the beach, but as the island has migrated west the wreck has been left farther out in the water.

The rangers are very careful to advise campers and hikers of the common sense needed for a trek south on the island. They recommend bringing at least 1 gallon of water per person per day, along with sunscreen, insect repellents, good shady hats and other sensible attire. Shore fishing is permitted with a Texas state fishing license.

PORT ARANSAS
Population 2500

Port Aransas is in many ways the most pleasant beach town on the Texas Gulf Coast. It is small enough that you can ride a bike or walk anywhere. It is large enough that it has several good restaurants and other services that make a stay more enjoyable. The pace is very relaxed, and activities are dominated by hanging out on the beach, fishing and doing nothing.

The development of large condo complexes south of town is reason for some concern for the future, but Port Aransas may take several years to wake up and discover them. July weekends are the busiest days of the year.

Information

The Port Aransas/Mustang Island Chamber of Commerce/Tourist & Convention Center (☎ 512-749-5919, 800-452-6278) is much more relaxed than its endless name implies. In a small cottage at 421 Cotter Ave, it's open weekdays 9 am to 5 pm and Saturday 9 am to 3 pm. It has stacks of brochures, maps and information. Pick up a copy of the exhaustive and free *Visitor's Guide* newspaper, which lists every place in the area that charges sales tax.

Beaches

Port A, as it is commonly called, has several miles of beaches on the gulf side. With a $6.50 permit (available from most stores), you can drive and park on the beaches. The main access point is via a paved road that runs all the way east from the town center and brings you to Nueces County Park. The park has rest rooms, showers, a fishing pier and seasonal concessions. A camping area charges $4 for tents and $12 for RVs, for which water and electric hookups are provided. Away from the campground, beach camping is free. As you head south, away from the condos, the sand gets more pristine with each step.

University of Texas Marine Science Institute

The school's visitors' center (☎ 512-749-6729) is on the small campus at 750 Channelview Drive. It is pretty thin going, with eight small aquariums holding some sluggish fish. The best display shows sand from around the world (it's at least a bit more interesting than its description implies). Signs suggest that you walk to an adjoining building to see more displays. Those taking the bait are

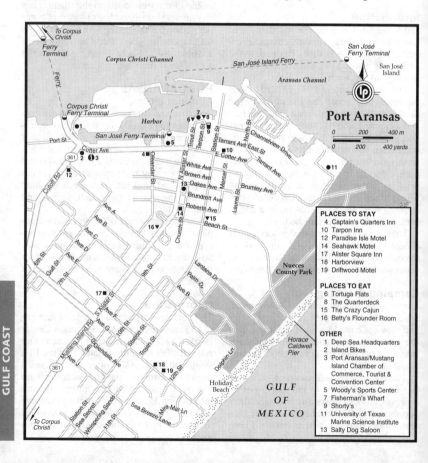

Port Aransas

0   200   400 m
0   200   400 yards

PLACES TO STAY
4 Captain's Quarters Inn
10 Tarpon Inn
12 Paradise Isle Motel
14 Seahawk Motel
17 Alister Square Inn
18 Harborview
19 Driftwood Motel

PLACES TO EAT
6 Tortuga Flats
8 The Quarterdeck
15 The Crazy Cajun
16 Betty's Flounder Room

OTHER
1 Deep Sea Headquarters
2 Island Bikes
3 Port Aransas/Mustang Island Chamber of Commerce, Tourist & Convention Center
5 Woody's Sports Center
7 Fisherman's Wharf
9 Shorty's
11 University of Texas Marine Science Institute
13 Salty Dog Saloon

rewarded with scientific displays on the walls, many of which seem to involve lurid photos of diseased fish and all of which are voluminously written in the kind of windy verbiage filled with biglongwords that only a scientist could love.

The center is open weekdays 8 am to 5 pm; admission is free.

San José Island

A privately owned island, known as St Jo to locals, is just across the ship channel from Port Aransas. The island has a dock, and that's it. It's popular for fishing and beachcombing, although users are advised to bring over virtually everything they will require, including water. The ferry runs many times daily from 6:30 am to 6 pm; the dock is off Cotter Ave behind Woody's Sports Center. The roundtrip fare is $8.95 for adults, $4.95 for children. You can camp on the beach, but it has no facilities.

Fishing

There are more than 100 charter boats for fishing in Port Aransas. The chamber of commerce (see Information) has listings. You can also visit one of the large harbor stores, which represent several boats. There are a net-full of charter rates, depending on whether you're going to the bay or gulf, the length of the trip and what exactly you're trying to catch.

Woody's Sports Center (☎ 512-881-9903), 136 Cotter Ave, reps several boats and has a large store and friendly employees filled with fishing information. Four-hour bay fishing trips cost $23 and include all equipment and bait. They also organize dolphin watches and nature tours.

Deep Sea Headquarters (☎ 512-749-5597) has a name that says it all, and it is right at the ferry landing.

Fisherman's Wharf (☎ 512-749-5448, 800-605-5448), 900 N Tarpon St, represents a fleet of boats. It is also home to the picturesquely named *Scat Cat* and *Wharf Cat* catamarans, which travel quickly to and from the fishing sites to shorten the journey times. Bottom-

Fishing boats at rest

fishing trips last 12 hours and cost $70 for adults, $44 for children; nine-hour bottom-fishing trips cost $55. Rates are $5 higher from June to August.

Places to Stay

A large proportion of the lodging around Port A is in condos.

Camping You can camp at *Mustang Island State Park* or *Nueces County Park*, both of which are described above.

Motels & Hotels For friendly and simple, you can't beat the *Seahawk Motel* (☎ 512-749-5572), 105 N Alister St. It is within walking distance from most places and it has a nice big pool. Single/double rooms are $50/60, and $5 more in the summer. *Driftwood Motel* (☎ 512-749-6427), 300 W Ave G, is at the south end of town, near the beach. Rooms are $45/48, and $10 more in the summer. *Paradise Isle Motel* (☎ 512-749-6993), 314 Cutoff Rd, is another clean and basic place with a pool. Rooms are $49/55, and $10 more in the summer.

Tarpon Inn (☎ 512-749-5555), 200 E Cotter Ave, dates from 1900 but has been rebuilt several times after hurricanes, most extensively after the 1919 big blow. The lobby has more than 7000 of the huge silver scales that come from tarpon, the 6-foot-long namesake

RYAN VER BERKMOES

GULF COAST

fish. Each has been autographed by the guest who caught it while staying at the inn; one was signed by Franklin Delano Roosevelt, who fished here in 1937. The newly redecorated rooms have patios or balconies but no phones or TVs and cost $56/78 for most of the year.

The fairly new **Captain's Quarters Inn** (☎ 512-749-6005, 888-272-6727), 235 W Cotter Ave, has comfortable rooms and is right across the street from the harbor. Room rates are complex, ranging from $54/59 in the off-season to $69/74 on summer weekends. **Alister Square Inn** (☎ 512-749-3000, 888-749-3003), 122 S Alister St, has modern, comfortable rooms and a pool inspired by a Rorschach test. Room rates are again complex but range from a winter low of $49/54 to a summer weekend high of $82/88.

B&Bs **Harborview** (☎ 512-749-4294, 800-561-8180), 502 E Ave G, has rooms in a modern and airy house with sweeping views. Rates throughout the year range from $70 to $125, depending on the date and the number of guests.

Condos Port A is home to a lot of condo buildings. They range from simple units in town and away from the water to imposing high-rises on the beach. When making reservations to rent a condo, ask a lot of questions. Many developments are south of town, beyond walking distance. Some of the large projects are also aesthetically challenged (read: ugly).

A few agencies represent many condos in the area. Through Wes-Tex Management Co (☎ 512-749-6113, 800-221-1447) the average price for a condo on a summer weekend is $135 a night. Through Coastline Adventures (☎ 512-749-7635, 800-656-5692) it's $165, and through the Rental Management Company (☎ 512-749-7070, 800-580-7070) it's $110 to $350.

Places to Eat

Budget Sit among the boats at **The Quarterdeck** (☎ 512-749-4449), 914 Tarpon St, which has a dining room built over the water amid the docks. The onion rings ($5) are the

product of several onions and should not be attempted by less than four people. They make a great start for the burgers and sandwiches.

Mid-Range Good views are the norm at **Tortuga Flats** (☎ 512-749-5255), 821 Trout St at the water. The popcorn shrimp are spicy and there are many good beers on tap, which combine for good sunset-watching. Prices for the many seafood entrées range from $7 to $12. The **Crazy Cajun** (☎ 512-749-5069), at the corner of Beach and Station Sts, has a short but delightfully authentic menu, with a full dinner of spicy Cajun treats for $10 a person. **Betty's Flounder Room** (☎ 512-749-4869), 129 N Alister St, is a large and traditional seafood place with a long menu highlighted by several daily fresh flounder specialties that average $16. One of the most popular restaurants in Port Aransas, it will prepare fish you've caught any way you want.

Entertainment

Port A gets quiet early – folks need to get to bed so they can go fishing at dawn – but there are a few friendly local joints where you can meet a seaman. **Salty Dog Saloon** (☎ 512-749-4912), 230 N Alister St, has live blues, country and oldies. **Shorty's** (☎ 512-749-8077), off Tarpon St behind the Coast Guard station, is a real hole in the wall filled with real local seadogs and characters. It has real darts and pool tables.

Getting There & Away

To reach Port A, you'll probably have to drive. The Flexi-B (☎ 512-749-4111) is a van operated by the city that makes trips to and from Corpus Christi for a mere $1. It may even pick you up at the airport, but you'll have to call to check when it is running.

From the south, you drive north on Mustang Island along Hwy 361. From the west, you get to take a free ferry operated by the state between Hwy 361 and the center of Port Aransas near the docks. The trip takes about 10 minutes, and you should plan on waits of one hour or more on summer weekends.

Getting Around

The Port A Shuttle (☎ 512-289-2600) covers the entire town and runs daily 10 am to 5:30 pm. The faux trolley runs every 50 minutes and is free. It stops anywhere along its route.

In the traditional center of Port A, you can easily walk or ride a bike. Island Bikes (☎ 512-749-6566), 520 Cutoff Rd, rents a variety of bikes for an hour, a day, a month, longer or any variation thereof.

Northeast Texas

Lacking any 'must-see' sights, northeast Texas still has many interesting areas, including several natural and historical parks such as those at Caddo Lake and the Big Thicket. There are scores of pretty small towns that follow the classic pattern of a central square surrounded by stately brick buildings. Only a few, such as Nacogdoches and Jefferson, have begun to exploit their tourism potential.

The region, which encompasses the area east of Dallas to Louisiana and south from Oklahoma to an imaginary line running roughly 50 miles north of Houston and Beaumont, is fairly homogenous. Baptist is the dominant religion and much of the area is 'dry,' meaning you just can't walk into a bar and buy a beer. The thirsty populace has devised numerous dodges around this rule in order to enjoy a drink, although frequently they have to buy a silly 'temporary membership' to a private club to do so.

Should you fall in love with the region, you'll be happy to know that land here is among the most affordable in the US. It's not uncommon to find a large home on several acres of land priced under $100,000.

Getting There & Away

If you're flying into the area, Houston is the most convenient major airport for locales south of Lufkin, and Dallas is most convenient for places north. Bus service is not extensive, primarily sticking to routes serving the medium-size cities along the interstates.

Much of northeastern Texas gently rolls, with few real hills and little of the endless vistas found farther west. Four interstates traverse the region – I-45, I-30, I-20 and I-10. Your trip will be much more scenic and enjoyable, though, if you try taking some of the secondary roads, such as US 80, US 79, US 59 and US 96.

BRYAN-COLLEGE STATION
Population 55,000

The permanent population of the Bryan area is deceptively small; most of the year the

Highlights

- A hike in the Big Thicket National Preserve
- Early-morning mist on Caddo Lake

number is doubled thanks to the 50,000 undergraduate students at Texas A&M University (☎ 409-845-5851), Texas' oldest school and one of the nation's largest.

The 'Aggie' campus sprawls over several square miles of College Station, which in feel and is actually part of Bryan. While not especially picturesque, the university is steeped in student tradition, and catching an Aggies game can be an unforgettable experience of 'maroon madness.' On Thanksgiving Day each year, the school lights a huge bonfire in anticipation of its match the following day against its hated rival, the University of Texas. Many of the students shave their heads, all scream their lungs out and the fire burns for days.

The Bryan-College Station Convention and Visitors Bureau (☎ 409-260-9898, 800-777-8292), 715 University Drive E off of Hwy 6, has excellent free maps and enthusiastic recommendations of the area's many good, locally owned restaurants.

George Bush Presidential Library & Museum

Continuing the trend of ever-bigger presidential libraries (one wonders what the likes of Millard Fillmore or Calvin Coolidge would have made of this phenomenon), Texas A&M has built a massive facility to honor the one-term 41st US president, George Herbert Walker Bush.

The complex (☎ 409-260-9552), at 1000 George Bush Drive W, is at the end of a seemingly endless road that begins off FM 2818. The museum is fascinating as much for how the material on Bush's life is presented as for the actual collections. An impressive section documents his heroism in WWII, when he flew – fittingly enough – off the aircraft carrier USS *San Jacinto*. There's an amusing exchange of letters during the Watergate scandal between Bush and a disheartened campaign donor who bemoans the fact that then-President Nixon was acting like 'an apprehended pickpocket.' His surprising loss to Bill Clinton in the 1992 election is obfuscated this way: 'As the presidential campaign heated up, his opponents exploited the theme that America was stalled. President Bush disagreed and predicted the economy would resume major growth very soon. He was correct.' There is a large area devoted to Millie, the Bushes' dog while he was president. In fact (and perhaps fittingly), the pooch receives about 10 times the coverage as Bush's vice president, Dan Quayle.

The museum is open Monday to Saturday 9:30 am to 5 pm and Sunday noon to 5 pm; $3 for adults, $2.50 for seniors and students and free for those younger than 16.

Places to Stay & Eat

La Quinta Inn (☎ 409-696-7777), across from the campus at 607 Texas Ave east of University Drive, is well located and has comfortable rooms for $55 to $119. More places line both sides of Texas Ave, which is the business route of Hwy 6. The *Texan* (☎ 409-822-3588), 3204 S College Ave in Bryan, looks like the old drive-in that it was, but now the food is worth a much longer stop. Steaks and seafood are the main event, and the house dessert is a creation called 'flaming guavas.' A string of

lively college bars line University Drive between Boyett and Tauber Sts. The most infamous is *Dixie Chicken* (☎ 409-846-2332), 307 University Drive.

HUNTSVILLE
Population 27,900

About an hour north of Houston on I-45, Huntsville is in the news every time Texas puts one of its condemned prisoners to death, which is pretty often. Death row and the execution room are downtown at 'the Walls' (☎ 409-295-6371), the vast old brick prison at 815 12th St.

The **Texas Prison Museum** (☎ 409-295-2155), 1113 12th St, is a no-nonsense place complete with videotaped interviews with convicted murderers and the families of the victims. The electric chair, used before lethal injections became the preferred means of dispatching the condemned, is displayed. Its nickname: Old Sparky. The museum is open Tuesday to Sunday noon to 5 pm. On Saturday it opens at 9 am; admission is $2 for adults, $1 for children.

The Huntsville-Walker County Chamber of Commerce (☎ 409-295-8113, 800-289-0389), downtown at 1327 11th St, has information on non-prison sights.

Sam Houston Memorial Museum Complex

Sam Houston spent much of his life in Huntsville. The 'world's largest statue of an American hero,' a 67-foot version of Sam, looms near the visitors' center at 7600 Hwy 75, off I-45 at exit 109. Several Houston-related buildings (☎ 409-295-7824) stand on a 15-acre compound that once belonged to him; it's at 1836 Sam Houston Ave, half a mile west of downtown. 'Woodland,' his longtime home, and 'Steamboat,' the house where he died in 1863, are open Tuesday to Sunday 9 am to 4:30 pm; admission is free.

New Zion Missionary Baptist Church

Well sure, you can worship God here, but most people come to worship the incredibly good and cheap barbecue cooked in a smoky shack (☎ 409-295-7394) next to the church.

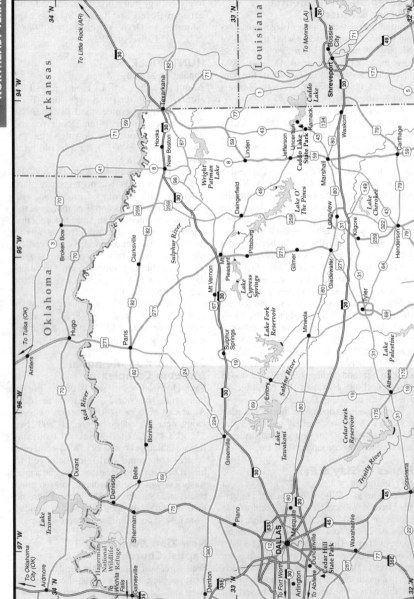

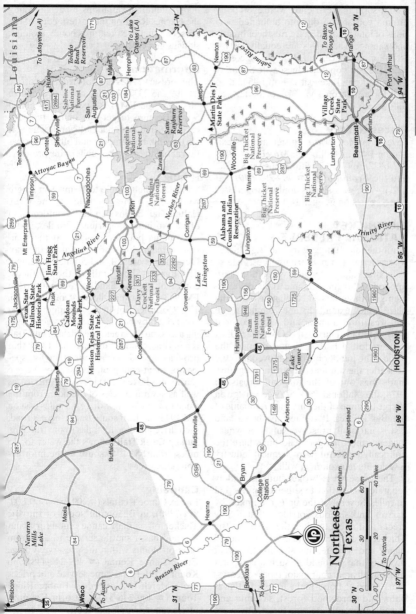

You'll soon make friends with everybody around you as you dig into unlimited portions of long-smoked spare ribs, beef brisket and sausage. The prices are equally tasty – $8.50 for all you can eat. A sandwich costs a mere $2.50. It's open Wednesday to Saturday 11 am to 7 pm. Take exit 114 off I-45 and go east for a mile on FM 1374, or better yet, follow your nose.

Places to Stay

Several budget motels cluster around exit 116 on I-45, including the *Motel 6* (☎ *409-291-6927*), 1607 I-45, with rooms for $36/40, and the *EconoLodge* (☎ *409-295-6401*), at 112 I-45 N, with singles/doubles for $43/48 plus $2 extra on weekends.

BIG THICKET NATIONAL PRESERVE

Until the mid-19th century, the Big Thicket was a dense and mysterious forest, whose mile after mile of tangled vegetation were impervious to humans and their developments. Both settlers and Indians avoided the place, which extended some 70 miles north and west of Beaumont and which covered 5469 sq miles. During the Civil War, draft dodgers found perfect shelter deep in the woods. The lumber business moved into the area after the war and over the next century made logs out of the ancient forests. In 1974, the National Park Service was given charge of some of the surviving remnants of the Big Thicket. It created the first – and last – national preserve, an area where loggers can no longer tread but where the politically powerful petrochemical industry is welcome to explore at will.

The preserve is broken into 15 widely separated units that together comprise 132 sq miles. Several of the units are linked by narrow and sinuous corridors that follow creeks and rivers through the area. The Big Thicket is unique, not just for its unusual plants and wildlife, but also for the great diversity that is found in such a comparatively small area. Four major types of ecosystems coexist: flood-plain forest, flatlands palm and hardwood forest, savanna and mixed hardwood, and pine forest. There are many additional variations, especially along the Neches River on the eastern edge of the preserve; that area features ponds, swamps, sloughs and creeks.

Information

The preserve has an information office (☎ 409-246-2337) 7 miles north of Kountze off US 69 on FM 420, open daily 9 am to 5 pm. Be sure to get one of the typically excellent, free National Park Service maps. It also has hiking, camping and other information about the scattered units of the preserve.

Hiking

Trails from half a mile to 18 miles in length wind through the Big Thicket. The **Kirby Nature Trail** begins behind the information office. An inner loop runs 1.7 miles, and a self-guiding booklet available at the trailhead explains flora and fauna along the way. Outer loops are 2.4 and 5 miles in length. The **Beaver Slide Trail**, in the southeast corner of the Big Sandy Creek unit, is on FM 943, a quarter-mile west of FM 1276. The 1½-mile loop winds around several ponds built by beavers and offers good fishing access on the creek. The **Pitcher Plant Trail** is a fully accessible half-mile boardwalk that provides a good look at four of the five species of meat-eating plants (see the Veggie Carnivores boxed text) in North America, as well as several species of orchids. From the small town of Warren, drive 4.3 miles east on FM 1943 and turn south on the access road; then drive another 1.9 miles to the trail. The **Turkey Creek Trail** follows the water for 15 miles, from FM 1943 south to the information office.

Canoeing

Eastex Canoe Rentals (☎ 409-385-4700, 800-814-7390), in Beaumont south of the Big Thicket, offers daily canoe rental for about $20 and has a shuttle service to and from drop-off points within the preserve. Village Creek Canoe Rental (☎ 409-246-4481), in Kountze, offers the same service and prices. From March to November, Timber Ridge Tours (☎ 409-246-3107), also in Kountze, offers canoe rentals and tours.

Places to Stay & Eat

There are no developed campgrounds in the preserve units; however, backcountry camping is possible in some areas with a permit from the information office. The **Turkey Creek Unit** is popular with campers who hike in and those who use canoes along the creek. **Martin Dies Jr State Park** (☎ 409-384-5231), off US 190, 20 miles east of Woodville, has two developed camping areas on a reservoir about 2 miles from Beech Creek Unit. Tent sites are $9; sites with electricity and water are $12. Screened shelters, in which you pitch your tent inside while the mosquitoes look on from outside, are $17. Prices drop about $2 in winter. The **Alabama & Coushatta Indian Reservation** has a large campground and adjoins the Big Sandy Creek Unit – see the next section for information.

Beaumont, about 30 miles south of the information center, has numerous motels – see the Golden Triangle section in the Gulf Coast chapter for details. Woodville, which is 24 miles north of the information center,

has the pleasant and simple **Woodville Inn** (☎ 409-283-3741), at 201 N Magnolia St. Rooms average $50. The small towns of Kountze and Warren are closest to the Big Thicket units and have groceries and small cafés where your cheeseburger is likely to come wrapped in waxed paper.

ALABAMA & COUSHATTA INDIAN RESERVATION

In the 1840s, Sam Houston gave the Alabama and Coushatta tribes several large tracts of land in the Big Thicket. The two tribes had come to east Texas during the 18th century, when they were pushed off their lands by European settlers in the eastern US. For the next 90 years, the tribes waged a successful and peaceful legal battle to keep their new land from being swiped by various forestry and government interests that thought that everyone would be much happier if the tribes moved from their valuable land to the deserts out west.

In the latter half of the 20th century, the Alabamas and Coushattas – who elect a

---

Veggie Carnivores

As if they were some space alien plopped down on earth, pitcher plants lead lives radically different than those of their root-bound, nitrogen-sucking fellow flora. For one, they look weird: big green flowers with red and purple veins called 'pitchers' perch atop the plants, emitting a perfume highly attractive to insects. Their unusual appearance is appropriate given that they don't just wait around manufacturing pollen, hoping some bee will wander along and pick some up. Rather, pitcher plants hope to make a lunch out of that bee or any other bug who takes their bait. Hapless insects in search of the sweet-smelling nectar plunge into a pool of digestive juices inside the pitcher. Large, downward-pointing spiked tendrils prevent escape.

The plants thrive in the swampy and bug-infested lowlands of east Texas and can be seen in many parts of the Big Thicket. Sadly for the intrepid hiker, the human neck still seems to give off a scent even more attractive to mosquitoes than that of the pitcher plant.

common chief – have largely integrated with the surrounding communities. They have also built a successful and profitable tourist attraction (☎ 409-563-4391, 800-444-3507) based on their culture.

They dress in traditional costumes, perform ceremonial dances, sell crafts made from pine needles and operate a small train that runs through a re-creation of an Indian village. They also operate excellent nature tours of the Big Thicket that explain how their ancestors lived off the land. On the first weekend in June, they host a large powwow where dancers from Indian tribes in several states compete.

The village is 17 miles east of Livingston on US 190. June to August, it's open Monday to Saturday 9 am to 6 pm and Sunday 12:30 to 6 pm. It's open Saturday 10 am to 5 pm and Sunday 12:30 to 5 pm March to May and September to November; during these months, tribal dances are performed only on the weekends. The admission price of $12 adults, $10 children covers all of the tours and performances. A *restaurant* in the village serves Tex-Mex and Indian foods.

Places to Stay

The Alabama-Coushatta tribe *campground* (☎ 409-563-4391, 800-444-3507) surrounds a lake and is adjacent to the village and the Big Sandy Creek Unit of the Big Thicket National Preserve. It's open all year; tent sites are $10, and RV sites are $15.

NATIONAL FORESTS

East Texas has four large national forests. Comprising more than 1016 sq miles of piney woods, they have a wealth of recreational facilities, but visitors should remember that the primary purpose of the US Forest Service (which administers these areas) is forestry, so recreation takes a backseat to commerce. In preserved areas, you can see otters, beavers, bald eagles and scores more species as well as more than 300 kinds of trees.

Detailed maps of each forest and its recreational areas are available for $4 each from the US Forest Service office (☎ 409-639-8501), 701 N 1st St, Lufkin, TX 75901.

The individual ranger offices in each forest are listed here.

You can wilderness camp virtually anywhere in the national forests without a permit. There are scores of designated camping areas ranging from ones with simple fire rings to well-equipped areas complete with grocery stores. Ratcliff Lake in Davy Crockett and Red Hills Lake in Sabine (see those sections) have the most fully equipped campgrounds, including electrical hookups. Campsites are available on a first-come, first-served basis. Rates at the developed sites are $4 to $10 per night.

Various hamlets and lumber camps are scattered throughout the forests. You can be on what seems like a remote trail only to round a corner and find yourself among several mangy mobile homes. Locals advise visitors to lock their cars and keep valuables out of sight because car break-ins at the remote parking lots are a problem. People are strongly discouraged from hiking or wilderness camping during hunting season each year, which typically runs from November to December (call ☎ 409-639-8501 for the exact dates). In one incident, a hunter offered this explanation for shooting a camper: 'I thought he was a turkey.'

Angelina National Forest

The smallest of the forests at 239 sq miles, Angelina has the **Sawmill Hiking Trail**, a 5½-mile-long gem along the Neches River that connects with Boykin Springs and Boykin Lake, a remote pool deep in the forest. Boykin Springs has a *campground* 14 miles southeast of Zavalla, off Hwy 63 on USFS 313. The huge **Sam Rayburn Reservoir** is popular for boating and fishing. There are several boat ramps, including one at Caney Creek, 14 miles southeast of Zavalla, off Hwy 63 and Hwy 147 on FM 2390.

The ranger office (☎ 409-544-2046) is at 701 N 1st St, Lufkin, TX 75901. Its staff offers information on camping and the campground.

Davy Crockett National Forest

With 251 sq miles, Crockett is one of the less-developed forests. **Ratcliff Lake Recreation Area**, on USFS 520 between Ratcliff and

Kennard, is well equipped, offers canoeing possibilities and has a long pier that provides a good vantage point for viewing wildlife. The **Four C National Recreation Trail** covers 20 miles from Ratcliff Lake to a 40-foot bluff overlooking the Neches River. Walnut Creek, midway on the trail, has pretty rural *campsites*. The **Big Slough Canoe Trail** is part of a 3000-acre wilderness area that is a flood plain for the Neches River. The trailhead is 2 miles north of Ratcliff via FM 227, and then east 5 miles on USFS 314.

Crockett's ranger office (☎ 409-544-2046) is at Route 1, Box 55FS, Kennard, TX 75847. Inquire here for information on camping, canoe rental and hiking.

Sabine National Forest

This 251-sq-mile forest lines the west bank of the Toledo Bend Reservoir, which spans the Texas-Louisiana border. There is a string of developed recreational, boating and camping sites along the water, including **Indian Mounds Recreation Site and Wilderness Area**, which has several hiking trails and is 5 miles east of Hemphill on FM 83 and then 7 miles southeast on USFS 115 and 115A. **Red Hills Lake Recreation Area** surrounds a small natural lake where powerboats are banned. It's 3 miles north of Milam on Hwy 87.

The ranger office (☎ 409-787-3870) is at 201 S Palm St, Hemphill, TX 75948.

Sam Houston National Forest

The largest of the forests of this cluster has 255 sq miles and is 50 miles north of Houston. It has facilities for every kind of recreation, including 55 miles of off-road vehicle tracks – meaning Suburban drivers abound – and 15 miles of mountain-bike trails. The 126-mile **Lone Star Hiking Trail** traverses the park, beginning west of Lake Conroe off FM 149 and ending at FM 1725. Among the many highlights are magnificent flowering magnolia trees. The trail is maintained by the Houston Sierra Club (☎ 713-895-9309) and has many sources of drinking water at developed campgrounds along its length. **Double Lake Recreation Area** has swimming, canoeing and hiking and is 4 miles south of Coldspring off Hwy 150 and FM 2025.

You can write to the ranger office (☎ 409-344-6205), at 394 FM 1375 W, New Waverly, TX 77358, for maps and information.

NACOGDOCHES

Population 31,000

Whether Nacogdoches is the oldest town in Texas (as it claims) is open for debate. But it definitely is old, dating from 1716, when a mission was established as a remote outpost in the Spanish empire. The town and the surrounding area have the greatest concentration of historical sites and attractions in east Texas. Nacogdoches is also in the center of some rich farming and ranching land. The

---

Drinking Clubs

Nacogdoches County, like 162 other counties in Texas, has local restrictions on alcohol consumption. In practice this means that people can get a drink, but they have to jump through a few legalistic hoops first.

In Nacogdoches, alcohol may be served only in private clubs that sell annual memberships. For hapless visitors just passing through, this means they must buy a 'temporary membership' to partake in alcohol consumption. Usually costing $2 to $5, the memberships allow one to be a 'member' of the restaurant or bar for the evening. For town residents who like to go out, this means they probably have to buy bigger wallets or purses to accommodate all their membership cards. 'All the kids have a stack of cards,' explained a student at Stephen F Austin State University. 'They advertised something called the unicard that was supposed to be accepted everywhere, but only one place took it. I guess that's what they meant by "uni."'

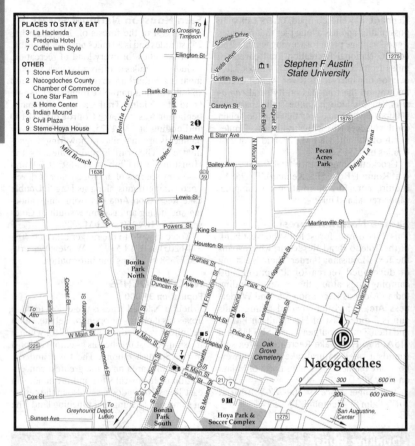

PLACES TO STAY & EAT
3 La Hacienda
5 Fredonia Hotel
7 Coffee with Style

OTHER
1 Stone Fort Museum
2 Nacogdoches County
   Chamber of Commerce
4 Lone Star Farm
   & Home Center
6 Indian Mound
8 Civil Plaza
9 Sterne-Hoya House

Lone Star Farm & Home Center (☎ 409-560-8377), 608 W Main St, is a delightful place to glimpse the local lifestyle. You can buy everything from a stump remover and a $110 Stetson hat to $18 Wrangler jeans and 'Chew Stop,' a sort of paint that keeps your horses from snacking on fence posts. Many more stores line North St (Business Route US 59), north of downtown. Lone Star Farm & Home Center is open Monday to Saturday 7 am to 7 pm.

A weeklong Heritage Festival is held early every June. It includes shows, food, barn dances and an antiques show.

Information

The Nacogdoches County Chamber of Commerce (☎ 409-564-7351), 1513 North St, Nacogdoches, TX 75963, has a wealth of information on the town and region, including an excellent walking-tour map of the historic center. It's open Monday to Friday 8 am to 5 pm.

Historical Sites

Much of historic Nacogdoches can be explored on foot, and most sites have free admission. The **Civil Plaza**, at Main St and N Fredonia St downtown, is the first of 15 sights on the town's historic walking tour. It dates to 1779, when Spain gave Nacogdoches official status. The **Sterne-Hoya House** (☎ 409-560-5426), at 211 S Lanana St at Pillar St, was built in 1828 and is notable for being the site of Sam Houston's baptism (sites visited by Sam Houston are the Texas equivalent of the old saw back East, 'George Washington slept here'). The house is open Monday to Saturday 9 am to 11:30 am and 2 to 4:30 pm. The **Indian Mound**, 516 N Mound St, is significant evidence that a thriving society of Caddo Indians lived in the area long before the arrival of Europeans. It is thought to date from about 1250.

The **Stone Fort Museum** (☎ 409-468-2408) is a replica of a 1779 house that belonged to one of the founders of Nacogdoches. The original stood at Main and Fredonia Sts. The replica is near the corner of Clark and Griffith Blvds, on the campus of Stephen F Austin State University, a 2000-student state school. The museum covers the history of eastern Texas and is open Tuesday to Saturday 9 am to 5 pm and Sunday 1 to 5 pm.

Millard's Crossing (☎ 409-564-6631), north of town at 6020 North St, is a collection of 12 old buildings dating from 1820 to 1905, including an old schoolhouse and a log cabin. Millard's Crossing is open Monday to Saturday 9 am to 4 pm and Sunday 1 to 4 pm; admission is $3 for adults, $2 for children.

Places to Stay

The *Continental Inn* (☎ 409-564-3726), close to the university at 2728 North St, has rooms for $36. The *Stratford House Inn* (☎ 409-560-6038), 3612 North St, is a modern motel with whirlpools in the bathrooms of rooms that cost $41. The *Fredonia Hotel* (☎ 409-564-1234) is a restored 1955 hotel right downtown at 200 N Fredonia St. There's a nice curved row of rooms surrounding a pool and cabana. Single and double rooms are $64 and $74. The chamber of conference has a list of B&Bs.

Places to Eat

The most popular restaurant in town is *La Hacienda* (☎ 409-564-6450), 1411 North St, in an old mansion, which serves tasty and somewhat upscale Mexican food for an average of

$7 a person. Downtown at 316 E Main St, *Coffee with Style* (☎ 409-564-6410) has coffees, iced teas and desserts Monday to Saturday 10 am to 5 pm.

Getting There & Away

Nacogdoches is at the confluence of US 59 and Hwy 21. Greyhound (☎ 409-564-4631), 2803 South St, serves Nacogdoches with a bus line that runs from Houston (three hours, $24 one way) and Shreveport, Louisiana (three hours, $24.50 one way), four times a day in each direction.

AROUND NACOGDOCHES

West of Nacogdoches, Hwy 21 travels through a pretty region of hills and farms to the comely little town of Alto. Here the road joins the historic El Camino Real (the King's Highway), which was a well-traveled trail during the Spanish colonial era and later was used by waves of settlers from the east. Lovers of historical markers can spend a day hitting the brakes on the 34 miles of Hwy 21 between Alto and Crockett. There is a granite or metal marker every few hundred yards. Typical is one remembering a Daniel McClean, who built a cabin on the marker's site in 1813 and was killed by Indians in 1837.

Caddoan Mounds State Historical Park

This grassy site is the southwesternmost known ceremonial center of the mound-building culture that lived in much of the eastern US from 1000 BC to AD 1500. The Caddo Indians lived on the site in AD 800, taking advantage of the good soil for agriculture and the Neches River for water. Archaeologists generally agree that the Caddoan Mounds were the home of a ruling class of Indians until they were abandoned in the 13th century. Many think that the scattered Caddoan tribes became independent, which put the elite out of work.

The exact purpose of the mounds continues to elude archaeologists, although it is thought they had religious and ceremonial uses. Within the park (☎ 409-858-3218) are three mounds, one of which was used for burials. There is also a reconstruction of one of the domed wood-and-straw structures that were the Caddo people's homes. An interpretive center explains what is known about the culture and the mounds. The park is open Thursday to Monday 9 am to 5 pm; admission is $2 for adults, $1 for children. The park is 6 miles southwest of Alto on Hwy 21.

Mission Tejas State Historical Park

Six miles southwest of the Caddoan Mounds on Hwy 21 is the birthplace of 'Texas' – the name of the state, that is. In 1689, Spanish captain Alonso de León led an expedition through the area and discovered the Nabedache Indians, the successors to the Caddos. These agrarian people were successful farmers, growing corn, melons, beans and more. The Spaniards called the tribe the Tejas, which was the native word for 'friends' or 'allies,' and they called the area 'Land of the Tejas,' which was later shortened and modified to 'Texas.'

The park (☎ 409-687-2394) is on the site of the Spanish mission San Francisco de los Tejas (1690). Although none of the mission buildings survive, there is a commemorative log structure, built in the 1930s, and a log cabin built by settlers in 1828. The 163-acre park has a small pond, hiking trails and a *campground*. Sites cost from $6 to $10 depending on their amenities. Entrance to the park costs $2 for adults.

Texas State Railroad State Historical Park

Near the Rusk-Palestine State Park, the Texas State Railroad State Historical Park (☎ 903-683-2561, 800-442-8951) contains a small branch rail line that was acquired by the state in 1969. Trains powered by old steam engines take passengers on rides to and from Palestine, 26 miles west. The excursions pass through pine and hardwood forests while traversing 30 bridges.

The park has a lake with paddleboats, nature trails, a playground, tennis courts and other features that make it a fun place to stay. The *campground* has tents and RV sites with full hookups – it's a good idea to reserve ahead of time if you're planning to camp.

Prices are $6 to $12, and the park is open daily. Trains operate weekends late March to late October; in addition, they run on Thursday and Friday from late May to late July, departing from each end of the line at 11 am and returning at 3 pm. One-way fares are $10 for adults, $6 for children; roundtrip fares are $15 and $9. The park is 3 miles west of Rusk on US 84. The Palestine depot is 4 miles east of the town of the same name, also on US 84.

TYLER
Population 81,000

Named for John Tyler, the US president who signed the resolution admitting Texas to the US in 1845, Tyler is the largest town in the region and draws people to its large shopping malls. There are two annual festivals tied to flowers here – the Azalea and Spring Flower Trail in late March and the Rose Festival in mid-October.

The Tyler Convention and Visitors Bureau (☎ 903-592-1661, 800-235-5712), in the slightly gentrified old downtown at 407 N Broadway, has mountains of material to delight and inform visitors. It's open Monday to Saturday 9 am to 5 pm and Sunday 1 pm to 5 pm.

Municipal Rose Garden

Tyler supplies 20% of the rose plants sold in the US. The storied flower is celebrated at this free 14-acre garden (☎ 903-531-1212), 2 miles west of downtown at W Front St and Rose Park Drive. The best time to visit is mid-May to early October, when the blooms and the fragrance are overwhelming. The adjoining Tyler Rose Museum is eminently missable, especially given that it charges $3.50 for adults and $2 for children to see old gowns worn by past Rose Festival queens.

Caldwell Zoo

Founded by the Caldwell family in the backyard of their preschool in 1937, this 50-acre zoo (☎ 903-593-0121), one block east of US 69 at 2203 Martin Luther King Jr Blvd, has become one of the most honored and professionally run small zoos in the US. Animals from Africa, South America and the US are displayed in large and naturalistic settings, and there is a successful breeding program of the severely endangered black rhinoceros. The zoo is open October to March daily 9:30 am to 4:30 pm, from April to September daily 9:30 am to 6 pm. Best of all, it's free.

Places to Stay & Eat
The *Rodeway Inn* (☎ 903-531-9513), 4 miles north of downtown at 2729 W Northwest Loop 323, just west of US 69, has basic rooms for $42/48. The *Holiday Inn* (☎ 903-593-3600), 3310 Troup Hwy just north of E Loop 323, has rooms for $75. *La Quinta Inn* (☎ 903-561-2223), a mile west of US 69 at 1601 W Loop 323, has comfortable singles/doubles for $79/89. Chain restaurants of every description line Loop 323 and cluster around the motels.

Getting There & Away
Tyler is about 10 miles southeast of the junction of I-20 and US 69. Seven Greyhound buses (☎ 903-597-7441) per day stop in each direction between Dallas ($17 one way) and Shreveport, Louisiana ($26 one way). The Tyler station is downtown at 303 N Bois D'Arc Ave. Note the bulletin board visible behind the ticket counter covered with 'stupid rider quotes,' including this one: 'The sign on the bus says Dallas – does that mean it goes to Shreveport?'

AROUND TYLER
Leaving town on US 271, a half-mile northeast of Loop 323, the road passes a small park on the right that was the site of **Camp Ford**, a Confederate prison that held 48,000 captured Union troops in miserable conditions during the Civil War. Two miles farther, on the left, are rows of warehouses that were part of **Camp Fannin**, a WWII camp that each month trained 10,000 'replacements,' a military euphemism for troops used to replace those killed in battle. **Gladewater**, 20 miles northeast of Tyler at the junction US 271 and US 80, is a little town with a long, dignified central square surrounded by antiques shops.

KILGORE
Population 11,000
This town is 2 miles south of the intersection of Hwy 31 and I-20. It has two notable sights

right next to each other on the campus of Kilgore College. The **East Texas Oil Museum** (☎ 903-983-8295), at Henderson Blvd (US 259) and Ross St, documents how sleepy Kilgore became a boomtown in the 1930s when oil was discovered. More than 1000 drilling rigs were jammed into just a few acres, and the downtown was filled with lavish new art-deco buildings. The displays are elaborate, well done and a delightful commentary on human nature and greed. The museum is open Tuesday to Saturday 9 am to 4 pm (until 5 pm April to September) and Sunday 2 to 5 pm; admission is $4 for adults, $2 for children.

The college's **Rangerette Showcase Museum** (☎ 903-983-8265), a block west of Henderson Blvd on Ross St, honors Kilgore College's famous all-female dance-and-drill team, a uniquely Texas institution that features dozens of young women performing routines as rigid as their smiles. It's open Monday to Friday 9 am to 4 pm and Saturday 10 am to 4 pm; admission is free.

LONGVIEW
Population 70,300
Industries supplying the oil industry dominate the Longview economy. Short on sights itself, the town is a good base for exploring the surrounding region, which is dotted with lakes. It is the only wet county from Louisiana to Dallas – which means you can walk into a store and buy a beer. In July, the sky is filled with color from hundreds of hot-air balloons floating overhead during the Great Texas Balloon Race. The Longview Convention and Visitors Bureau (☎ 903-753-3281) stands ready to help at 410 N Center St.

One of the region's best independent bookstores, Barron's Books (☎ 903-663-2060), in the Albertson's strip mall at McCann Rd and Loop 281, has a wide selection of regional fiction and a large travel section. It also has a good café, a music shop and an assortment of regional food items. The staff is top-notch as well – one chased an LP author halfway across the parking lot to return a dropped $5 bill. Barron's is open from Monday to Saturday 9 am to 9 pm and Sunday 1 to 6 pm.

NORTHEAST TEXAS

Places to Stay

Out by I-20, the *Days Inn* (☎ *903-758-1113*), 3103 Estes Parkway, has basic rooms for $45/60. The name is the only thing generic about the *Guest Inn* (☎ *903-757-0500*), at 417 Spur 63, a half mile north of US 80. Owner Rose Strong scurries about, making sure her guests are happy. Rooms are several notches above the usual motel standard and cost $49/64 for singles/doubles.

Places to Eat

People drive for hours to *Johnny Cace's Seafood & Steak House* (☎ *903-753-7691*),

at 1500 E Marshall Ave (US 80). The menu features Creole seafood and the motto 'The oysters you eat here today slept in their shells last night.' The prices are high – $20 per person or more (although some items start at a lower price) – but the quality is higher. At the opposite end of the culinary scale in every department except taste, *Bodacious Barbecue* (☎ *903-753-8409*), at 227 S Mobberly St, has plates for $6.

CADDO LAKE AREA

Featuring myriad inlets and bayous deeply shaded by bald cypress trees strung with

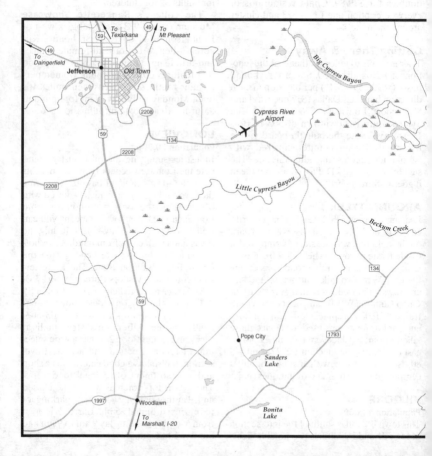

Spanish moss, Caddo Lake is one of the most evocative places in Texas, and when the steam rises off the water in the early morning, it is one of the most mysterious as well.

Caddo Lake State Park

On the western edge of the lake, the park (☎ 903-679-3351), on FM 2198 off Hwy 43, 4 miles west of Uncertain (see next section) has *cabins* for rent for $40/50/60 for two, four or six people. RV sites are $12, and tent sites close to the water (popular with kayakers) are $8. A three-quarter mile nature trail explains the unique combina-

tion of plants and wildlife around the lake. A tour boat (☎ 903-679-3743) explores the lake daily except Wednesday from March to December. The 75-minute trips cost $8 for adults, $6 for children. Canoes can be rented for $6 per hour and $20 per day. Park admission for people between 13 and 67 years old is $2.

Uncertain

Really a long stretch of lakeside buildings strung along Cypress Drive off FM 2198, Uncertain certainly profits from its proximity to Caddo Lake. At any business, pick up a

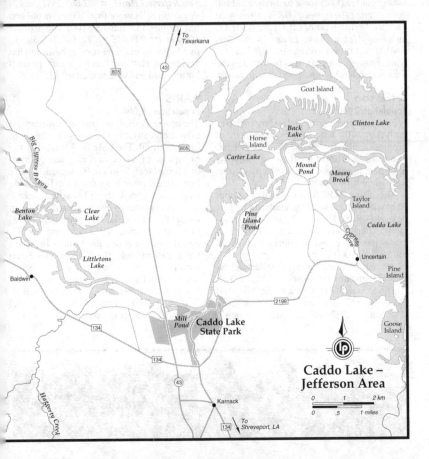

Caddo Lake – Jefferson Area

free copy of the *Uncertain News*, which is filled with maps and area information. **Caddo Lake Steamboat Co** (☎ 903-789-3978) uses a little steam-powered paddle wheeler for 90-minute tours of the lake. Adults pay $15, seniors $12 and children $6 on weekends, slightly less on weekdays; call for a departure schedule. The steamboat leaves from Bois D'Arc Lane off Cypress Drive.

Shady Glade (☎ 903-789-3295), at 449 Cypress Drive, is a one-stop shop on the lake with a restaurant (local fried catfish, $5), motel (rooms are $50), boat launch ($2), lake tours ($15 per person, $40 minimum) and fishing guides ($125 for a half day, $200 full day). Among the scores of B&Bs are several on tiny Taylor Island, off Cypress Drive, including *Mossy Brake Lodge* (☎ 903-789-3440). B&B rooms average from $65 to $95. Numerous galleries can also be found in the area, which has become popular with artists.

Jefferson
Population 2500
A busy steamboat port on the Cypress River until the 1870s, Jefferson was passed by as progress and river traffic went elsewhere. The town slumbered for the next 100 years until people realized that its sleepy charms were ideal for tourism.

The historic Old Town comprises about 30 blocks, with most of the retail action on or near N Polk St. Despite the town's increasing popularity with visitors, prices are moderate and the count of tourist-trap shops selling fudge is still low.

Among the many sights, the **Jefferson Historical Museum** (☎ 903-665-2775), 223 W Austin St, is in the 1890 Federal Building and has good exhibits on early life in east Texas. It's open daily 9:30 am to 5 pm; admission is

$2 for adults, 50¢ for children. Be sure to pick up a copy of the 'Historic Jefferson Walks' brochure, widely available in shops or from the Marion County Chamber of Commerce (☎ 903-665-2672), 116 W Austin St.

Jefferson is located 15 miles north of I-20 on US 59 and 14 miles west of Lake Caddo via scenic FM 134.

Places to Stay & Eat There are many historic inns and B&Bs including the 1850 *Excelsior House* (☎ 903-665-2513), at 211 W Austin St, owned and operated by the local garden club. Rooms range $65 to $75. The *Jefferson Hotel* (☎ 903-665-2631), at 124 W Austin St, is more than 100 years old and has rooms for $65 to $100. The *Corner Market* (☎ 903-665-6122), 101 N Polk St, overlooks the old river-turning basin and has vegetarian chili for $3 and a rare peanut-butter-and-banana sandwich for $2.

PARIS
Population 25,000
The movie *Paris, Texas* put this town on the map. Ironically, the film doesn't take place in Paris at all. The only tie is that it is the birthplace of the central character, played by Harry Dean Stanton. We include it here because every time we told non-Texans we were doing a book about Texas, they asked, 'Are you going to Paris, Texas?' We can report that it is a pleasant place near Oklahoma at the junction of US 82 and US 271, and that there is one photo op – the giant **soup can** outside the Campbell's Soup factory in town – but it doesn't merit a special trip. However, if you go, the Lamar County Chamber of Commerce (☎ 903-784-2501), 1651 Clarksville St, has a passel of brochures to guide you.

Rio Grande

The Rio Grande (Big River; the Mexicans call it the Río Bravo, or Brave River) flows from its source in Colorado's San Juan Mountains almost 2000 miles to the Gulf of Mexico. On its way it forms the natural border between Texas and Mexico. This lively border region blends two cultures: slick Americana meets traditional Mexican, producing an enticing mixture of both.

US immigration officers patrol the border in their perpetual battle against illegal immigration. US Fish & Wildlife Service officers patrol the region on the lookout for smuggled animals, mainly 'exotic' creatures such as birds, alligators and caimans poached from forest regions throughout Latin America – hyacinth macaws from Brazil reportedly sell for between $6000 and $12,000 in the USA.

And yet the atmosphere is relaxed. Border crossings are mundane, everyday affairs, and formalities for travelers are minimal. But delays for motorists have also become commonplace, to the dismay of the ever increasing commercial traffic crossing back and forth between the highways of the USA and the maquiladoras on the Mexican side. One result of that has been the expansion of existing border crossings and the construction of new ones.

The contrasts and similarities between Mexico and the USA are exemplified by the barely separated centers of Laredo and Nuevo Laredo, which are the area's prime attraction. Locally, the two are known as 'Los Dos Laredos' – the Two Laredos.

Any of the border crossings in this chapter are fine options for travelers heading farther into Mexico; see the Border section in the Getting There & Away chapter for information on procedures and formalities. For much more information about all regions of Mexico, see Lonely Planet's *Mexico*.

HISTORY

The Laredo border area was sparsely populated with nomadic Indian groups until Don Tomás Sánchez, a captain in the Spanish royal army, was given a grant of land here in 1775. The first non-Indian settlers were ranchers, and missionaries passed through the area, heading into the interior of Texas.

The 1836 Texas secession from Mexico inspired the Rio Grande Valley, and much of what is now northeastern Mexico, to declare itself a separate republic – the

Highlights

- Crossing into Mexico at Piedras Negras and Ciudad Acuña
- Walking along San Felipe Creek in Del Rio
- Viewing rock art at Seminole Canyon State Historical Park
- Watching cross-border traffic crowding the bridges in Los Dos Laredos
- A raucous evening at the El Dorado Bar & Grill in Nuevo Laredo
- Partying with 130,000 of your best friends during spring break on South Padre Island
- Penetrating the jungle at Sabal Palm Sanctuary near Brownsville

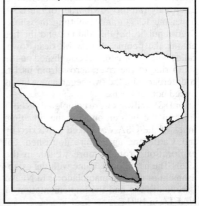

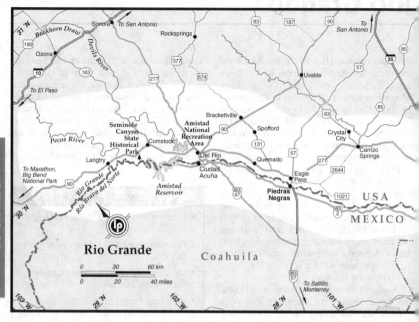

Republic of the Rio Grande – in 1840. With its capital at Laredo, the republic lasted just 283 days, until the Mexican Army regained control.

The Treaty of Guadalupe Hidalgo, which ended the Mexican War, also ended any hopes of a new Republic of the Rio Grande. The treaty ran the new border of the USA down the Rio Grande, splitting the short-lived republic, but that did not end the ties among the people. A new Mexican town, called Nuevo Laredo, was established on the south side of the river, across from its US counterpart, and the two began a new life as linked border towns.

In 1881, railways were completed on both sides of the border, and for the first time much of the USA was linked to Mexico by rail. Cattle and agriculture flourished. Oil exploration brought more wealth in the 1920s. The next booms came with the establishment of the first maquiladoras in Nuevo Laredo in 1965 and the implementation of NAFTA in 1994.

Rio Grande Valley

The semitropical southern border area of Texas is much wetter than the arid west, thanks to the moisture-laden winds off the Gulf of Mexico. This lush environment is perfect for farming; much of the winter produce sold in the USA comes from Texas. Among the products you'll see are bushes studded with multicolored peppers, spiky aloe plants and groves of citrus. Don't be surprised to see road vendors selling huge bags of grapefruit for absurdly low prices, such as $1.

The temperate winter climate attracts hordes of migratory creatures. A breed known as 'Winter Texans' – retirees from the US Midwest – arrives in flocks, as do the sand-seeking, licentious mobs otherwise known as college students on spring break. Oh, and more than 300 species of birds pass through as well, making the area a bird-watcher's paradise.

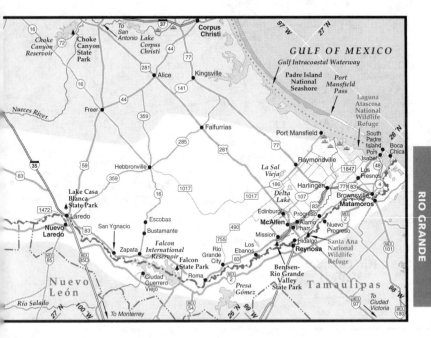

The valley begins at the mouth of the Rio Grande, which meets the gulf in vast palm-studded wetlands, lagoons and remote beaches. To the north, long, skinny Padre Island (see the Gulf Coast chapter) is separated by a channel from South Padre Island.

Farther west in the valley, most of the land is given over to farming. Along the river is a series of parks and nature preserves. Past McAllen, the gulf winds diminish and the land becomes more arid. The area around Rio Grande City and Roma still has the feel of the frontier and the landscape has changed little for centuries.

NAFTA is bringing much more traffic to the valley, and towns such as Nuevo Progreso, in Mexico 30 miles west of Brownsville, have economies based entirely on cross-border traffic. Illegal trade is thriving as well, and people living near the Rio Grande have learned not to notice things that go bump in the night.

The temptations of the enormously profitable drug trade are irresistible for some, and hardly a month goes by that federal prosecutors don't indict some local official for narcotics-related activities.

Orientation

US 77 is the main southbound route into the eastern end of the valley. South of the town of Kingsville, the highway passes through 70 miles of desolate ranchlands and little else. The only break in the drive is an Immigration and Naturalization Service (INS) inspection station 50 miles north of Harlingen.

The main east-west corridor through the valley is US 83, which is a busy freeway at Brownsville but gradually thins in rough proportion to the rainfall and population, so that it is a quiet two-laner west of Rio Grande City. US 281 takes a scenic course through the riverside farmlands east of McAllen.

Maps All the tourist offices listed for the towns in this section (and those offices listed

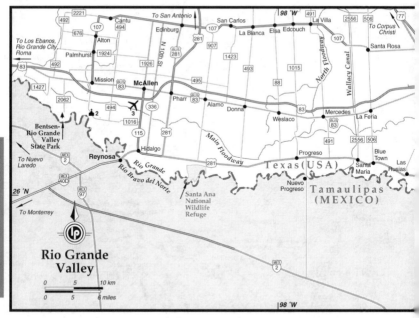

Rio Grande Valley

0   5   10 km

0   5   6 miles

under Information) have free copies of the very good *Rio Grande Valley of Texas* map. It shows local streets for almost all the cities and towns and also provides a regional overview. The map is colorfully printed on coated paper that rapidly falls apart with use, so get two.

Information

Most of the valley towns have their own energetic tourist information operations. In addition, the state has a Texas Travel Information Center (☎ 956-428-4477) on the western edge of Harlingen at 2021 W Harrison St, at the junction of US 77 and US 83. The center has maps, brochures and other information about the Rio Grande Valley and the entire state. It is open daily 8 am to 5 pm.

The Rio Grande Valley Chamber of Commerce (☎ 956-968-3141), 417 S International Blvd, off US 83 at the FM 1015 exit just east of Weslaco, has area information and oodles of information about activities aimed at Winter Texans.

SOUTH PADRE ISLAND
Population 2100 (permanent)

Comprising the bottom 5 miles of South Padre Island, the town of South Padre Island (SPI) works hard to exploit its sunny climate and beaches. The water is warm for much of the year, the beaches are clean, and the locals are ready to welcome each and every tourist who crosses the 2½-mile Queen Isabella Causeway from the mainland (the permanent population of 2100 is augmented by 10,000 or more visitors at any given time).

Certainly much of civic life on the island is devoted to attracting free-spending visitors. What passes for political debate was exemplified in 1997 when the mayor declared SPI a 'tie-free zone,' whereupon the head of the city council chopped off his tie. Slogans include 'Let's Padre' and 'It's sunconventional.' Dubious marketing efforts aside, SPI is not as highly developed as some beach resorts – despite a few '60s high-rise nightmares that will make the uncharitable

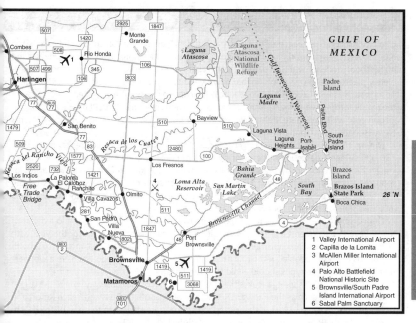

1 Valley International Airport
2 Capilla de la Lomita
3 McAllen Miller International Airport
4 Palo Alto Battlefield National Historic Site
5 Brownsville/South Padre Island International Airport
6 Sabal Palm Sanctuary

long for a hurricane. The people are laid-back, and to the north are miles of unspoiled beaches and parks.

Until 1962, there was no South Padre Island. There was only the 147-mile Padre Island, a barrier island that was the longest of its kind in the world. However, the pleas of Port Mansfield for more direct access to the gulf shipping lanes were finally heeded, and a channel was cut through the island, creating 34-mile South Padre Island.

The island's lower 5 miles were developed with the wooden-shack construction typical of old beach towns, mixed with large concrete monstrosities. The latter buildings are a result of state legislation requiring insurance companies to extend hurricane insurance to barrier islands, which are highly storm-prone. Developers, given this promise that their mainland policyholders would be forced to cover their barrier-island losses, are now building large projects.

January and February, when the weather can be either balmy or a bit chilly, are the cheapest months to visit SPI, because prices are lowered to attract budget-conscious Winter Texans. The summer is the most expensive period, when the moderating gulf breezes make the shore more tolerable than the sweltering inland areas.

Orientation

South Padre Island is only a half mile wide at its widest point. Laguna Madre, the shallow inland waterway between the island and the mainland, is ideally suited for windsurfing (see Water Sports & Windsurfing, below). The developed area is good for walking, and the beaches are packed hard with fine, white sand.

SPI's spine, Padre Blvd, extends 10 miles into the undeveloped part of the island. Past the remote central part of the island, the beaches at the north end are popular with nudists, anglers, bird-watchers and other outdoorsy types. However, the future of this natural beauty is by no means assured; a map given out by an SPI Realtor

A Party for 130,000

Like other second-tier beach resorts, such as Florida's Panama City Beach, South Padre Island has discovered gold in spring break, the period in March when hordes of college students (and high school students with lax parents) congregate at beaches for a week or more of completely pleasurable excess that's limited only by the capacity of their livers, loins and billfolds. Resorts such as Fort Lauderdale, Florida, now turn up their noses at spring break, even though their early fortunes were made from crowds of libidinous students, but SPI does everything in its power to welcome them, right down to creating a special website loaded with enticements (www.sopadre.com/springbreak).

During March, when various US colleges and universities have their breaks, more than 130,000 students descend on the island for days of drinking, swimming, sunbathing, frolicking and more, followed by nights of drinking, skinny-dipping, frolicking and more. Major sponsors, such as beer and soda companies, stage all sorts of concerts and games on the beaches. The large resorts and condos literally rock as far more guests than the designers intended squeeze into the rooms.

During spring break, it's hard to escape the mobs of students cruising the developed part of town. Several bars open their doors wide and attempt to make their profit for the year with huge beer-soaked bashes. Basically, if the idea of spending a week at a beach party with thousands of young people on their first real bender appeals to you, you will have a wonderful time. More sedate types should avoid the island for the month.

Ground zero for SPI's spring break is the area near the end of the causeway, where the largest condos and hotels, such as the Radisson Resort, Sheraton South Padre Island Beach Resort and Holiday Inn, are located. Most of the games and concerts are staged on this part of the beach.

Major clubs catering to the spring-break crowds include the following:

> *Charlie's Paradise Bar & Country Club* – Out of season, the chain-link fences and battered metal sheds that comprise Charlie's (☎ 956-761-4995), 90 South Padre Rd, suggest a holding area for illegal immigrants, but during spring break, 5000 to 7000 people a night ignore the aesthetics and turn the place into the largest spring-break bar on the planet, with 24 bars and 11 dance floors. A free shuttle bus runs all night, culling the streets for customers, who can later romp across the dunes to the beach.

> *Louie's Backyard* – This lagoon-side club (☎ 956-761-6406), 2305 Laguna Blvd, serves a mere 3000 to 4000 every spring-break night. Amenities include bungee-jumping, dancing, cheap food and free buses to shuttle you back and forth to Charlie's.

> *Parrot Eyes Water Sports* – The walls of this wide-open joint on the lagoon (☎ 956-761-9457), 6101 Padre Blvd, are covered with a collage of rotten palm fronds and beer posters. You can rent water-sports equipment during the day, and there are lots of tables scattered about the sand that you can collapse on all night.

The best accommodations – meaning those closest to the action – usually book up six months or more before March.

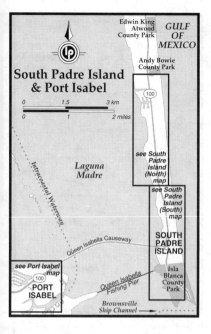

South Padre Island & Port Isabel

Edwin King Atwood County Park

GULF OF MEXICO

Andy Bowie County Park

Laguna Madre

see South Padre Island (North) map

see South Padre Island (South) map

SOUTH PADRE ISLAND

Intracoastal Waterway

Queen Isabella Causeway

see Port Isabel map

PORT ISABEL

Queen Isabella Fishing Pier

Isla Blanca County Park

Brownsville Ship Channel

shows future development planned for the island's entire length.

There is no ferry or bridge across Port Mansfield Pass. To cross this narrow channel to the south end of Padre Island, you must either have your own boat or make the 250-mile drive all the way around through the mainland.

Information

Tourist Offices The South Padre Island Convention & Visitors Bureau (☎ 956-761-3063, 800-767-2373) has an information center near the end of the Queen Isabella Causeway at 600 Padre Blvd. It has a very wide range of accommodations, restaurant and entertainment information, plus a good free map that shows virtually every business on the island. It's open weekdays 9 am to 6 pm (8 am to 5 pm in winter) and weekends 9 am to 5 pm.

Money Numerous banks line Padre Blvd, and the many convenience stores all have ATMs available around the clock.

Post The island's modern and storm-proof post office (☎ 956-761-4252), 4705 Padre Blvd, is open weekdays 8 am to 4 pm and Saturday 10 am to noon.

Media The major Rio Grande Valley daily newspapers all circulate on SPI. The *Coastal Current Weekly* is one of the many free ad-stuffed papers found near the doors of most businesses.

Photography Photographer Richard Stockton (☎ 956-761-1355) sells professional films, camera batteries and other shutterbug accessories from his office at 1004 Padre Blvd, Suite B.

Bookstores Island Traders Espresso and Books (☎ 956-761-5231), 104 W Pompano St, is a funky place selling a good mix of locally oriented books and various coffee drinks. On Thursday, Friday and Saturday nights, local folk bands, self-described poets and others provide live entertainment.

Laundry The Island Washateria (☎ 956-761-9031), at 2500 Padre Blvd, is open daily from 8 am to 10 pm.

Medical Services The major medical centers are on the mainland. The largest is Columbia Valley Regional Medical Center (☎ 956-350-7000), 100A Alton Gloor Blvd in Brownsville. It operates Valley Regional Island Clinic (☎ 956-761-4524), on the island at 3000 Padre Blvd, which is open Monday to Wednesday 9 am to 5 pm and Thursday to Saturday 9 am to 2 pm.

Emergency The US Coast Guard station can be reached at ☎ 956-761-2668.

Isla Blanca County Park

Just south of the causeway, this large Cameron County park (☎ 956-761-5493) has beaches, fishing, biking, a marina, and vast RV and tent camping areas. The gate, at the end of Padre Blvd, is like a busy toll plaza. The various pavilions and concessions draw beachgoers who want plenty of amenities. Admission is $4 per vehicle per day or

RIO GRANDE

RIO GRANDE

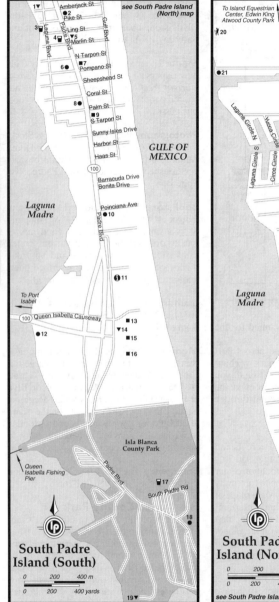

Amberjack St
1▼
Pike St
●2
Ling St
3●
Laguna Blvd
Padre Blvd
4▪️ ▼5
Marlin St
Gulf Blvd
N Tarpon St
Pompano St
●6 ▪️7
Sheepshead St
Coral St
●8
Palm St
▪️9
S Tarpon St
Sunny Isles Drive
Harbor St
Haas St
100
GULF
OF
MEXICO
Barracuda Drive
Bonita Drive
Laguna
Madre
Poinciana Ave
●10
Padre Blvd
To Port
Isabel
ℹ️11
100 Queen Isabella Causeway
●12
▪️13
▼14
▪️15
▪️16
Isla Blanca
County Park
Queen
Isabella Fishing
Pier
Padre Blvd
📷17
South Padre Rd
●18

South Padre
Island (South)

0   200   400 m
0   200   400 yards

19▼

To Island Equestrian
Center, Edwin King
Atwood County Park
Andy Bowie County Park
GULF
OF
MEXICO
✈20

●21
▪️22
▪️23
Laguna Circle N
Yucca Circle
Circe Circle
Sunset Drive
100
Palmetto Drive
24●
Parade Drive
Coronado Drive
Morningside Drive
📷25
Cora Lee Drive
26●
Carolyn Drive
▼27
Georgia Ruth Drive
Verna Jean Drive
Polaris Drive
Aries Drive
28
▼
30
📷
▪️29
Capricorn Drive
●31
Constellation Drive
Laguna
Madre
Mars Lane
32
▪️
Jupiter Lane
Venus Lane
Laguna Blvd
Padre Blvd
▼33
Saturn Lane
Esperanza St
34▪️
Hibiscus St
Gardenia St
35▪️
Oleander St
Lantana St
Huisache St
Mesquite St
Retama St
Atol St
📷36
Bahama St
Gulf Blvd
Campeche St
▼37
Acapulco St
Kingfish St
✚39
Dolphin St
●38
Red Snapper St
▼40
Swordfish St
▼42
Whiting St
43▪️
Amberjack St

South Padre
Island (North)

0   200   400 m
0   200   400 yards

●41

see South Padre Island (South) map

SOUTH PADRE ISLAND (SOUTH & NORTH)

PLACES TO STAY
7 Service 24
9 Island Services
13 Radisson Resort South
   Padre Island
15 Sheraton South Padre Island
   Beach Resort
   Holiday Inn-Sun Spree Resort
   Tiki Apartment Hotel
23 Bahia Mar Beach Resort
29 Brown Pelican Inn
32 Sea Grape Motel
   Ramada Limited
35 Days Inn
   Surf Motel

PLACES TO EAT
1 Amberjack's Bayside Bar &
   Grill
5 Tacos Al Pastor
14 Blue Rays Diner

19 Dolphin Cove Oyster Bar
27 Rovans Bakery & Restaurant
28 Scampi's
33 Blackbeard's
37 Naturally's Veggie Cafe
40 Manuel's Restaurant
42 Blue Marlin Supermarket

ENTERTAINMENT
3 Louie's Backyard
4 Black Marlin
10 Island Cinema
17 Charlie's Paradise Bar &
   Country Club
21 Parrot Eyes Water Sports
25 Kelly's Irish Pub
31 Island Cinema North
36 Padre Island Brewing
   Company
43 Boomerang Billy's Beach Bar &
   Grill

OTHER
2 Island Washateria
6 Island Traders Espresso &
   Books
8 American Diving
10 Richard Stockton
11 South Padre Island Convention
   & Visitors Bureau
12 Sea Ranch Fishing Pier
18 University of Texas –
   Pan American Coastal Studies
   Laboratory
20 Laguna Madre Nature Trail
21 Parrot Eyes Water Sports
24 Sea Turtle, Inc
26 Windsurf, Inc
30 Post Office
38 Windsurf the Boatyard
39 Valley Regional Island Clinic
41 Jim's Pier

$12.50 for a 90-day pass good at all the county beaches on SPI.

In the park, the **University of Texas-Pan American Coastal Studies Laboratory** (☎ 956-761-2644) is a working lab open for self-guided tours of its fish tanks and various wall displays. If you can get past its meager utilitarian charms, you'll find quite a bit of information about local marine life. An 824lb blue marlin caught in 1984 dominates one wall. Grapefruit-size conch show you how the popular fritters look while still in the water. It's open Sunday to Friday 1:30 to 4:30 pm; admission is free.

Other Parks
Across from the South Padre Island Convention Centre, **Andy Bowie County Park** (☎ 956-761-2639), at the north end of town on Park Rd 100, has picnic areas, and you can drive on the beach. Entrance to the park costs $4 a car, or you can buy a $12.50 pass good for 90 days.

Two miles north, **Edwin King Atwood County Park** is a new facility with towering sand dunes backing the beach, which extends 28 miles north to Port Mansfield Pass. If you return a full bag of litter to the hut at the entrance, the staff will give you 50¢.

At the convention center, **Laguna Madre Nature Trail** has boardwalks over 4 acres of wetlands and mudflats. Screened shelters provide a minor respite from the bugs.

Activities
Diving An artificial underwater reef 7 miles offshore from SPI provides some interest in the otherwise desertlike bottom of the gulf. American Diving (☎ 956-761-2030), 1807 Padre Blvd, takes divers out to any of 40 locations for $75 to $125. It also rents equipment.

Fishing Besides the public piers in Isla Blanca County Park, Sea Ranch Fishing Pier (☎ 956-761-4665), immediately south of the causeway on the lagoon side, is open Friday and Saturday 24 hours and Sunday to Thursday 6:30 am to midnight. It sells licenses, bait, snacks and more, and it rents gear. Admission is $2 to $4.

More than 50 fishing boats leave from the piers on the lagoon. Many, such as Jim's Pier (☎ 956-761-2865), 209 Whiting St, offer four-hour trips onto the bay ($15); bait is included, but equipment must be rented. Other charters make more extensive journeys for trout, red snapper and shark. Rates for several people begin at $200 for half a day near shore and escalate depending on the trip's duration and distance. Most charters supply bait, tackle and gear.

Golf The Rio Grande Valley boasts more than a dozen major golf courses. The closest to SPI is the South Padre Island Golf Club (☎ 956-943-5678), on Golf House Rd in Laguna Vista off Hwy 510, 8 miles west of the island. Green fees are $50 weekdays and $55 weekends.

Horseback Riding Island Equestrian Center (☎ 956-761-4677), about 1 mile north of the convention center, rents horses for all levels of riders and leads tours of the beaches. One-hour rides cost $25 to $35, and longer rides cost more. The center is open Thursday to Monday year-round.

Water Sports & Windsurfing The lagoon is ideal for windsurfing and the gulf is normally calm enough for anything that doesn't require a wave, so water sports are very popular on SPI. On the lagoon side, Parrot Eyes Water Sports (☎ 956-761-9457), 6101 Padre Blvd, has Wave Runners ($90 per hour, $100 for two people) and parasailing ($45 a flight). Those wanting to parasail during the off-season (after Labor Day) need to make a reservation at least one day in advance.

Though the gulf is usually quite calm, South Padre Island is popular with surfers; they just have to wait for storms to see any surfable waves.

Two stores dominate the booming SPI windsurfing business: Windsurf the Boatyard (☎ 956-761-5061), 212 Dolphin St, rents equipment for $15 an hour and $45 for all day. Windsurf, Inc (☎ 956-761-1434), at 224 W Carolyn Drive, rents gear for $20 an hour and $55 for all day. Both offer lessons.

Special Events

To keep visitors coming, SPI schedules events continuously throughout the year. In

The Shell Dame

Sea turtles don't have many friends. After they've hatched on gulf beaches, they have to run a gauntlet of seagulls, coyotes and other predators as they crawl to the water. Thousands become snacks. In the water, things aren't much better, with fish from sharks to barracuda waiting for a quick meal. Even when they get older and can fend for themselves, they are in danger from humans, who accidentally snare them in fishing nets, destroy their egg-laying beaches for condominiums and not only dig up their eggs before birth but also turn adults into soup.

In 1978, these terribly endangered creatures got the best friend they could hope for when longtime South Padre Island resident Ila Loestcher decided to devote her considerable talents to their survival. She raised money to help prevent the extinction of the sea turtle, especially the Kemp's ridley, the smallest of the world's seven species of nesting sea turtles. Once common on the Texas coast, the few ridleys that survive nest on a remote stretch of the Mexican coast to the south.

Loestcher took the cause of turtles to the media, and she started giving talks about them from her home on SPI. Other volunteers came aboard, and today Sea Turtle, Inc, benefits from the talents of many people devoted to these gentle and intelligent creatures. Loestcher has retired from day-to-day operations of the nonprofit organization, but her former home (near the northern end of Gulf Blvd) is still the site of Sea Turtle, Inc's presentations, which feature sea turtles of several species that were found injured and are being nursed back to health in large tanks. The presentations (☎ 956-761-1720) are given Tuesday and Saturday at 10 am. Just seeing these graceful reptiles swimming in the water is worth the admission, which is $2 for adults and $1 for children.

addition to spring break in March, some of the major events and their usual dates include the following (call the SPI Convention & Visitors Bureau for information):

May

Windsurfing Blowout
First weekend of the month

July

Texas International Fishing Tournament
Toward the end of the month

October

Sand Castle Days
Mid-month

November

Kite Festival
Early in the month

Places to Stay

Camping *Edwin King Atwood County Park*, 2 miles north of the convention center, offers camping on 28 miles of beach and has bathrooms and showers at the entrance. There are no camping fees, just day-use fees, which are $4 per person. You can come and go at will for 90 days with the $12.50 unlimited pass.

Far more popular, because of its proximity to the action, is *Isla Blanca County Park* (☎ 956-761-5493), at the south end of SPI, with a variety of camping facilities. Tent sites are $12; sites with electricity and water, as well as full-hookup RV sites are $16; and 'superslab' sites with a beach view are $30. Various long-term rates are available. Reservations may only be made for stays of seven or more days. During spring break, overflow sites are available for tents, although they may not impress those whom you ask, 'Want to come back to my tent?' The park's mailing address is PO Box 2106, South Padre Island, TX 78597.

Motels & Hotels The *Surf Motel* (☎ 956-761-2831), 2612 Gulf Blvd, is a simple, older place right on the beach with low-season/peak-season rates of $29/79. *Sea Grape Motel* (☎ 956-761-2471), 120 E Jupiter Lane, two minutes from the beach, has rooms with

kitchens for $45/85 a single/double. *Ramada Limited* (☎ 956-761-4097), 4109 Padre Blvd, is a new place with average rooms for $45/95. *Days Inn* (☎ 956-761-7831), 3913 Padre Blvd, has basic rooms for $49 to $59 a single, $59 to $89 a double.

The *Tiki Apartment Hotel* (☎ 956-761-2694), 6608 Padre Blvd, has faux-Polynesian-style units for $79/125 single/double. *Bahia Mar Beach Resort* (☎ 956-761-1343), 6300 Padre Blvd, is a vast beachside place that is quite unattractive from the outside. But if you're inside, you can't see it, right? Rates range from $85 to $145 year-round.

The following three hotels are the center of spring-break activities during March, when rates can be much higher than in the peak season. *Radisson Resort South Padre Island* (☎ 956-761-6511), 500 Padre Blvd, is a huge complex on the beach with pools, tennis and other diversions, including a '70s lounge where you'd expect to hear groups with names such as the Dacrons. Basic rooms are $95/170. The best rooms, with large balconies on the beach, are double these rates. *Holiday Inn – Sun Spree Resort* (☎ 956-761-5401), near the beach at 100 Padre Blvd, has a pool and standard accommodations for $95/195. *Sheraton South Padre Island Beach Resort* (☎ 956-761-6551), 310 Padre Blvd, is a high-rise with a good beach. Rooms are $109/175.

B&Bs The *Brown Pelican Inn* (☎ 956-761-2722), 207 W Aries St on the lagoon, is in a modern Victorian-style building with a huge porch good for bird-watching over the wetlands. Room rates begin at $69/105.

Condos More than 4000 apartments are available for rent on SPI. They are in myriad locations: inland, beachside and lagoonside high-rises and low-rises. They're both ugly – notable examples are the Saida Towers and the Bridgepoint – and nice. They come with one, two or three bedrooms and always have kitchens. Most of the larger complexes have pools and other facilities such as tennis courts and whirlpools.

Rates run the gamut. Some places offer daily rentals; others require a week minimum. Monthly rates are sharply discounted.

Generally, beach-view two-bedroom units average $800 to $1200 a week for units that sleep at least four. For the peak summer season, reservations are recommended three months in advance. During the winter, you can often bargain for substantial discounts.

Among the scores of condominium rental agents are the following:

Island Services
(☎ 956-761-2649, 800-425-6530),
1700 Padre Blvd, South Padre Island, TX 78597

Service 24
(☎ 956-761-1487, 800-828-4287),
2100 Padre Blvd, South Padre Island, TX 78597

Places to Eat

Except for the very peak periods, South Padre Island closes early. Unless noted below, plan on sitting down for dinner by 9 pm most nights.

If you're coming for a while, stock up on things such as groceries and laundry soap on the mainland. The *HEB* (☎ 956-943-1171), 1679 W Hwy 100 at Hwy 48 in Port Isabel, is a huge supermarket open daily 6 am to midnight. On SPI, *Blue Marlin Supermarket* (☎ 956-761-4966), 2912 Padre Blvd, is a small supermarket with big prices; it's open daily 7:30 am to 10 pm.

Budget *Tacos Al Pastor* (☎ 956-761-6787), at 2216 Padre Blvd, has cheap and spicy Mexican fare for about $5 a person. The Mexican tortas are authentic and come with a choice of seven homemade sauces. *Blue Rays Diner* (☎ 956-761-7297), 410 Padre Blvd, is a faux-'50s place with excellent burgers ($6). It also has a long list of salads ($5 to $7). *Manuel's Restaurant* (☎ 956-761-9563), 100 E Swordfish St, is renowned for its huge breakfast tacos on homemade tortillas, including one with potato, egg and cheese ($3.50). *Naturally's Veggie Cafe* (☎ 956-761-5332), 3112A Padre Blvd, has a café, juice bar and health-food store.

Two places are worth special mention. *Dolphin Cove Oyster Bar* (☎ 956-761-2850), in Isla Blanca County Park, has oysters on the half shell, fresh shrimp and gumbo. This simple place is a popular spot for watching

the sun set. *Rovans Bakery & Restaurant* (☎ 956-761-6972), 5300 Padre Blvd, has a vast menu of homemade food, including mesquite-smoked barbecue, Mexican dishes and breakfasts with muffins from its bakery. A model train bearing signs listing the day's specials circles tracks suspended from the ceiling. It has early dinner buffets ($6) that are served until closing time at 9 pm. The top-selling take-out bakery items are the luscious cream horns ($1.25).

Mid-Range *Blackbeard's* (☎ 956-761-2962), 103 E Saturn Lane, is a top choice for locals, who like the mahimahi and steaks (both $14). The large, elevated restaurant is busy most nights, so reservations are a good idea. *Amberjack's Bayside Bar & Grill* (☎ 956-761-6500), 209 W Amberjack St, has a popular bar and good views of the lagoon. Food ranges from steaks to seafood to Italian. *Scampi's* (☎ 956-761-1755), 206 W Aries Drive, has a bright and open dining room and an extensive wine list. The food leans toward complex seafood creations such as peanut-butter shrimp ($14). Other specials depend on what's been caught in the lagoon and gulf.

Entertainment

The rowdiest bars are listed in the boxed text A Party for 130,000, earlier in this chapter.

Boomerang Billy's Beach Bar & Grill (☎ 956-761-2420), at 2612 Gulf Blvd, behind the Surf Motel, is right on the beach, and the atmosphere is about as laid-back as you can get. The *Black Marlin* (☎ 956-761-1997), 2301 Padre Blvd, has pool tables and live rock. *Kelly's Irish Pub* (☎ 956-761-7571), 101 E Morningside Drive, is a friendly spot with pool tables and dartboards. This is a good spot to hear locals recount their favorite 'stupid tourist' stories.

On an island where the national breweries sponsor constant promotions that emphasize quantity over quality, *Padre Island Brewing Company* (☎ 956-761-9585), 3400 Padre Blvd, serves the best beer because they brew it themselves. Burgers and other bar food are also available.

Two theaters show first-run films: *Island Cinema* (☎ 956-761-6600), 1004 Padre Blvd at Sunchase Mall, and *Island Cinema North* (☎ *956-761-7828*), 4700 Padre Blvd.

Getting There & Away

Reaching SPI from the nearest airports and the rest of Texas is not easy or cheap. You might want to consider renting a car, which also will allow for side trips.

Air SPI is served by the airports in both Harlingen and Brownsville; see those sections, later in this chapter, for details on locations and service.

Bus Service is limited to four buses daily in each direction between Port Isabel and the Greyhound station in Brownsville ($5). The

Sand Castles

If you've always dreamed of having your own castle, you can build one on South Padre Island – out of sand. And not just some humdrum, upended-bucket-and-garnished-with-a-seagull-feather affair either, but an honest-to-goodness *castle*, standing about 8 feet tall, with towers, moats, a keep and anything else your heart desires.

Of course, such a creation doesn't come easy. That's where Sandy Feet comes in – the person, not what you walk on. Feet is a longtime resident of SPI who has carved out a lucrative life teaching people how to build vast creations that live only until the

next dawn – or whenever the tide comes in. With her partner, Amazin' Walter (hey, these are professional sand-castle builders; what kind of names do you think they'd have? Dick and Jane?), Sandy has won countless contests and traveled the world building fantasies out of sand with a shovel, a bucket and a few household tools.

The pair often practice in her backyard near the beach, where she has an experimental sand-castle lab. The day we visited, we picked up a little dirt on the controversies that rage among professional sand-castle builders. 'We're trying to use molds,' she said. 'Normally we hate them, but they let you build faster, and others use them a lot.' With a sniff, Walter added, 'Yeah, the art is to carve it yourself, but some people always want to take shortcuts.'

Their favorite beach location is in front of Boomerang Billy's Beach Bar & Grill (☎ 956-761-2420), 2612 Gulf Blvd, because, says Walter, 'they have beer.' Sandy and Walter offer lessons in their art – sans molds – for $50 an hour (call ☎ 956-761-6222). They also do custom creations, such as the one for the guy who wanted a sculpture that asked his beach-loving girlfriend, 'Will you marry me?' She accepted.

Before Sandy and Walter will give lessons to anyone, students have to take a sacred vow:

    I promise to have fun
    I promise to help others have fun
    I promise to un-litter [which means to remove more trash than you bring]

At SPI's annual Sand Castle Days in mid-October, you won't find Sandy and Walter competing for prizes (totaling $3000) in the professional category, because they've permanently placed out. Instead, they build a giant new creation each year. As for a carefully considered strategy and design, Walter says, 'We wing it.'

service is operated by Valley Transit; the stop in Port Isabel is at the Circle Drive-Inn (☎ 956-943-1961), 319 Hwy 100. To get to SPI from the Port Isabel stop, walk six blocks east to the lighthouse at Hwy 100 and Tarnava St and catch the Wave (see Getting Around).

Car To reach SPI from the north on US 77, take the Hwy 100 exit, 10 miles south of Harlingen, and drive 25 miles east to SPI. From Brownsville, drive 17 miles east on Hwy 48.

Getting Around

If you can get out to SPI, you won't necessarily need a car. The developed area is fairly compact and easy for walking or biking.

To/From the Airports Gray Line (☎ 956-761-4343) runs an airport shuttle charging $45 per person, or $17 per person if there are three or more in your party, to or from Valley International Airport in Harlingen or Brownsville/South Padre Island International Airport. Surtran (☎ 956-761-1641, 800-962-8497) has shuttles serving both airports for rates that begin at $40 for one person but decrease if there are more people or if you want roundtrip tickets. Make arrangements in advance with both companies.

Bus Income from tourism isn't just lining people's pockets; it also pays for the Wave (☎ 956-761-1025), a free shuttle service that uses buses made to look kind of like trolleys. The service runs every day of the year, 7 am to 7 pm, and plies Padre Blvd from the convention center all the way south to Isla Blanca County Park and over the causeway to the lighthouse in Port Isabel. During special events such as spring break, hours are extended into the evening.

Car Car rentals are available at the Harlingen and Brownsville airports; see those cities' sections, later in this chapter, for details.

Taxi There's BB's Taxi (☎ 956-761-7433) and Island Cabs (☎ 956-761-2222). Cab fares to the airports are $30 to $45.

PORT ISABEL
Population 4500

In the days before inexpensive hurricane insurance made South Padre Island viable as a town, Port Isabel was the focus of life near the southern end of Texas. Records show that Spaniards and pirates both made frequent landfalls here in the 16th, 17th and 18th centuries. In 1853, the US government completed a lighthouse that guided ship traffic for the next 50 years. A large fishing and shrimp-trawling fleet continues to call the port home, and many of the residents' livelihoods are tied to the sea.

The town has the nontouristy shopping that SPI lacks. It also has budget motel accommodations that are usually cheaper than those across the Queen Isabella Causeway. You can make day trips to the island beaches by using the free Wave trolley bus operated by SPI (see above). It stops at the lighthouse.

For information on Port Isabel and the many charter fishing boats that are docked here, contact the Port Isabel Chamber of Commerce (☎ 956-943-2262), 421 Queen Isabella Causeway, in the old keeper's house at Lighthouse Square.

Things to See

The almost 150-year-old **Port Isabel Lighthouse State Historic Structure** (☎ 956-943-2262), by the causeway at Hwy 100 and Tarnava St, was restored and opened to the public in 1970. A climb up its 70 steps yields a great view of the surrounding area, SPI and the gulf. Note that the lighthouse was closed for another reconstruction in 1998; it was scheduled to reopen in summer 1999. When it is open, you can visit Wednesday to Sunday 2 to 4 pm; $2 for adults, $1 for children.

Built sturdily of bricks to resist storms, the 1899 home of the **Port Isabel Historical Museum**, a block off Hwy 100 near the lighthouse, was once the town's post office and general store. Inside are many good photos and artifacts from the early days of development of the area, when it was the new home of hundreds of immigrant Italian and Portuguese fishermen and their families. It's

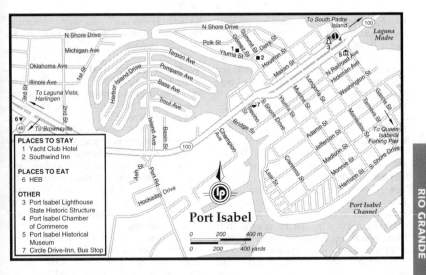

PLACES TO STAY
1 Yacht Club Hotel
2 Southwind Inn

PLACES TO EAT
6 HEB

OTHER
3 Port Isabel Lighthouse
  State Historic Structure
4 Port Isabel Chamber
  of Commerce
5 Port Isabel Historical
  Museum
7 Circle Drive-Inn, Bus Stop

Port Isabel

RIO GRANDE

open weekdays from 10 am to 4 pm and Sunday 1 to 4 pm; donations requested.

Famous pirate Jean Laffite was one of the first developers of this part of Texas. In about 1800, he dug the first **well** in what's now Laguna Vista, 3 miles west of Port Isabel. To reach the well and historical marker, turn north on FM 510 off Hwy 100, go to Fernandez St, turn south and drive three blocks.

Places to Stay & Eat
The *Southwind Inn* (☎ 956-943-3392), 600 Davis St, is popular with people who will be leaving on fishing charters from the nearby docks. Simple rooms cost from $35 to $50. The *Yacht Club Hotel* (☎ 956-943-1301), 700 Yturria St, is a restored 1920s lodge with a pretty outdoor pool and a highly regarded and expensive seafood restaurant (try 'Ron's Shrimp'). During the low/high season, rooms cost $42/82.

LAGUNA ATASCOSA NATIONAL WILDLIFE REFUGE
From the moment you step out of your car at this 70-sq-mile federal preserve (☎ 956-748-3607), northwest of Port Isabel, you are surrounded by the calls of birds. You may think you've stepped into the Hitchcock movie or are trapped in a hellish version of the old Woolworth's parakeet department, but you haven't. The calls blend into a melange of melodies that cause you to stop and just listen.

Laguna Atascosa holds the record for most bird species spotted: 393 as of late 1997. (See the introductory Facts about Texas chapter for more information on local birds, and the Facts for the Visitor chapter for birding guidebooks.) The land is a veritable avian playground; wetlands, thorn brush, trees and grasses offer something for everything with feathers. The refuge is also home to many land animals, including the very rare ocelot, a relative of the jaguar.

The only two-legged creatures allowed to camp in the park are birds, but there are hiking and driving trails and occasional tours. The gates are open every day, dawn to dusk. The visitors' center, near the park entrance, is open daily 10 am to 4 pm October to April, and the same hours on weekends only May to July 4. It's closed July 5 to September 30. When the center is closed, self-guiding tour brochures are left near the entrance. Admission is $2 per vehicle.

The roads to the refuge, like many in Texas, are not well marked. From Harlingen, take FM 106 east 18 miles until it dead-ends, then turn left and drive 3 miles to the entrance of the refuge. If you're coming from the east, take Hwy 100 to Laguna Vista, turn onto FM 510 and drive 7.7 miles until you see a small road on the right marked only 'Airport.' Take this road about 8 miles north to the refuge.

HARLINGEN
Population 49,000

Harlingen just isn't what it used to be, and that's a good thing. In 1910 it was called Six-Shooter Junction because of the explosive stew of lawless bands, Mexican raiders, Texas Rangers and US National Guardsmen that prowled its streets. Today, most permanent residents are more occupied with agriculture than lawlessness. Look for fields of large, spiky aloe plants, which produce the soothing substance used in lotions, shampoos and ointments.

Harlingen markets itself as the hub of the Rio Grande Valley. And indeed, you are bound to pass through it, whether you're traveling through its airport or driving the major highways that meet here. Like many hub cities, Harlingen has a few diversions that are worth a look, but they shouldn't needlessly delay you on your way to your next stop.

The Harlingen Chamber of Commerce (☎ 956-423-5440, 800-531-7346), 311 E Tyler St, has area information.

Rio Grande Valley Museum

This well-funded facility (☎ 956-430-8500), at the corner of Boxwood and Raintree Sts near the airport, is a Mission-style complex that combines several museums in one. An 1870s stagecoach inn recalls the hot, dusty conditions of the old trail, where the only friend you were likely to make at the end of a long day was a bedbug. The region's colorful and violent past are extensively documented, as is the conversion of guns to butter by agriculture visionary Lon C Hill. Hill introduced many of the crops now grown in the area, thus helping diversify the economy away from the smuggling and other nefarious activities that had dominated it. Hours are Wednesday to Saturday 10 am to 4 pm and Sunday 1 to 4 pm; $2 adults, $1 children.

Iwo Jima Memorial

The photograph of US marines struggling to raise the American flag atop Mt Suribachi at the height of the battle for the Japanese-controlled island of Iwo Jima has become an icon of WWII. A bronze sculpture modeled upon the photo now stands at Arlington National Cemetery in Washington, DC. The working model used for *that* sculpture now stands in Harlingen on the campus of the Marine Military Academy, a $16,000-a-year private high school for boys that's known for its boot-camp atmosphere and tough academic standards.

The figures depicted in the Iwo Jima Memorial, which stands in an open park, are 32 feet high. The marine at the base of the flagpole is Corporal Harlon Block, who was from the valley and was later killed in battle.

The school also operates a small museum (☎ 956-412-2207), close to the memorial at 320 Iwo Jima Blvd near the airport, that shows the battle's cost to the people of Iwo Jima; it is quite good. Fought from February 19 to March 16, 1945, it was one of the most furious battles of the war. Veterans are often on hand to answer questions. The museum is open Monday to Saturday 10 am to 4 pm and Sunday noon to 4 pm; admission to both the museum and memorial is free.

Texas Air Museum

Winter Texans, many of them veteran aviators, make this museum (☎ 956-748-2112), 7 miles east of Harlingen off FM 106, hum with activity during the nonsummer months as they work to restore the planes in its collection of military and civilian aircraft. Most are more than happy to tell you far more about the planes than any sign ever could. Among the major displays are two German FW-190s and the bridge structure removed from the US aircraft carrier *Iwo Jima*. The museum is open daily 9 am to 4 pm; $4 adults, $2 children.

Special Events
The Rio Grande Valley Birding Festival takes place in mid-November; call the chamber of commerce (see above) for details.

Places to Stay
The appropriately named *Save Inn* (☎ 956-425-1212), 1800 W Harrison St, near the junction of US 77 and US 83, has simple rooms for $30/42 a single/double. Summer rates are $5 more. *Best Western Harlingen Inn* (☎ 956-425-7070), 6779 W Expressway 83, at the Stuart Place Rd exit off US 83, has rooms with coffeemakers; rates range from $55 to $62. *Ramada Limited* (☎ 956-425-1333), 4401 S Expressway 83, at the Ed Carrey exit off US 83, has average rooms that are especially well fitted with mirrors. Rates are $58/67.

Places to Eat
Platters of barbecue are the specialty at *Lone Star* (☎ 956-423-8002), west of town at 4201 W Business Route 83, which is known for its smoked pork. Platters start at $8. *JJ's Restaurant and Bar* (☎ 956-423-2225), 409 E Harrison St, downtown, has the best burgers in the valley ($7), served with wedge-cut fries. The bar has live music Thursday to Saturday. Fajitas are the draw at *Los Asados* (☎ 956-421-3074), 210 N 77 Sunshine Strip. It also has vast platters of other standards ($6 to $12).

Getting There & Around
Air Valley International Airport (HRL, ☎ 956-430-8600), on Hwy 499, 3 miles east of downtown next to the Lockheed-Martin missile plant, is the main airport for the Rio Grande Valley. It is served by American Eagle (☎ 800-433-7300), with five flights daily to and from Dallas-Fort Worth; Continental Express (☎ 800-525-0280), with four flights to and from Houston; and Southwest (☎ 800-435-9792), with 10 flights to and from Houston and seven to and from San Antonio.

Car The major firms are all represented at the airport. Advantage Rent-A-Car (☎ 956-430-8677, 800-777-5500) is a small regional company that has about the least expensive rates in the valley, although all the majors

frequently offer specials, so shop around. The weekly rate for an economy car is $169 with unlimited mileage; it's a bit higher during the summer and spring break.

BROWNSVILLE
Population 135,000
Matamoros, Brownsville's Mexican counterpart across the Rio Grande, grew to prominence in the 1820s as the Mexican port closest to then-booming New Orleans. After the Mexican War (1846-48), American merchants and traders thought it wise to cross the Rio Grande to Texas, where they established Brownsville. The town was named for Major Jacob Brown, the US commander of Fort Taylor (later renamed Fort Brown), who died during a Mexican raid.

During the rest of the 19th century, the fast-growing town was filled with ornate brick structures that drew their architectural inspiration from Mexico and New Orleans. Many survive today.

Since the passage of NAFTA, trade again has become paramount for Brownsville. The railroad bridge over the river throbs with traffic day and night. Truckers queue for hours to pass through the border-inspection facilities in both countries. The deep-water port is the last stop on the busy 1300-mile-long Gulf Intracoastal Waterway, which stretches from Florida all the way around the Gulf Coast (see the boxed text in the Gulf Coast chapter). Brownsville is the third-fastest-growing city in Texas, with an annual growth rate of 4%.

Orientation
Brownsville lies at the southern end of US 77, the road that connects the valley to San Antonio (305 miles away), Houston (388 miles away) and points north. South Padre Island is 17 miles east on Hwy 48, which parallels the port waterway for a good part of its length. The quickest way to McAllen (67 miles west) is to take US 77 to its junction with US 83 in Harlingen, and then take US 83 west. Taking US 281 to McAllen is a slightly slower but more interesting journey through farmlands, including huge fields of sugar cane. Laredo is 209 miles northwest on

RIO GRANDE

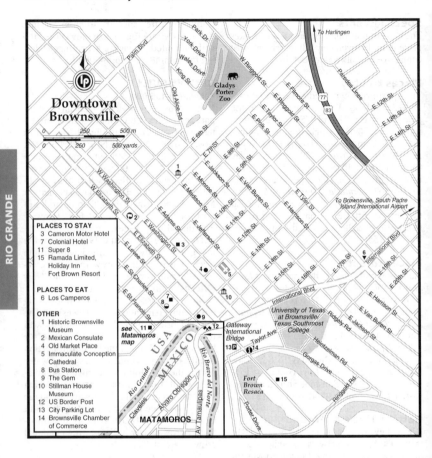

Downtown Brownsville

0   250   500 m
0   250   500 yards

To Harlingen

Gladys Porter Zoo

To Brownsville, South Padre Island International Airport

PLACES TO STAY
3 Cameron Motor Hotel
7 Colonial Hotel
11 Super 8
15 Ramada Limited,
     Holiday Inn
     Fort Brown Resort

PLACES TO EAT
6 Los Camperos

OTHER
1 Historic Brownsville
    Museum
2 Mexican Consulate
4 Old Market Place
5 Immaculate Conception
    Cathedral
8 Bus Station
9 The Gem
10 Stillman House
    Museum
12 US Border Post
13 City Parking Lot
14 Brownsville Chamber
    of Commerce

see Matamoros map

Gateway International Bridge

University of Texas at Brownsville/ Texas Southmost College

Fort Brown Resaca

MATAMOROS

US 83. Matamoros, Mexico, is just across the Rio Grande; use the international bridge right downtown at International Blvd and E Levee St.

The original town planners devised a fiendish street system. Named streets downtown are designated East and West and run northwest to southeast; Palm Blvd is the dividing line between east and west. Numbered streets are all twins: 1st St W is the first street west of parallel Palm Blvd, 1st St E is the first street east, and so on. Just to add a bit more confusion, the numbered streets actually run southwest to northeast.

The downtown area, near the international bridge and E Elizabeth St, is a busy place, its streets lined with the sort of shops catering to everyday needs that were common elsewhere in the USA until the advent of malls. Groups of men with makeshift carts stand ready to help Mexican shoppers who are laden with purchases get back across the border.

Information

Tourist Offices The Brownsville Convention & Visitors Bureau (☎ 956-546-3721), 650 FM 802, on the west side of US 77/83 at the FM 802 exit, is an excellent source of information on the entire area. Among its stacks of literature is the excellent *Guide to Historic Brownsville*, a lavish and free publication detailing the area's heritage. It has a superb walking tour of downtown. The office is open Monday to Saturday 8 am to 5 pm, Sunday 9 am to 4 pm.

The Brownsville Chamber of Commerce (☎ 956-542-4341), at 1600 E Elizabeth St, about 200 yards east of the international bridge, can also provide information if you are downtown. It's open weekdays 8 am to 5 pm.

There's a Mexican consulate in town; see the Facts for the Visitor chapter.

Money Places to change dollars into pesos and vice versa line International Blvd near the bridge. ATMs can be found at convenience stores, gas stations and, yes, even at the many banks downtown and along the highways.

Post The main post office (☎ 956-546-2411) is off US 77/83 at 1535 E Los Ebanos Blvd. It's open weekdays 8 am to 5 pm and Saturday 8 am to noon.

Media The daily *Brownsville Herald* (50¢) has good coverage of local events and news. KMBH, 88.9 FM, carries National Public Radio.

Travel Agencies Several agencies are adept at travel plans for Mexico. Among them are the Aldana Travel Agency (☎ 956-541-5444), downtown at 409 E 13th St, and Sanborn's International Travel Service (☎ 956-682-3401), 2011 S 10th St.

Campuses The University of Texas at Brownsville and Texas Southmost College share a campus (☎ 956-544-8200) at 80 Fort Brown, downtown. Together they have an enrollment of 8000.

Laundry The coin laundry closest to the border is Handy Laundry Systems (☎ 956-541-2662), 3002 E 14th St at Southmost Ave. It's open daily 8 am to 8 pm.

Medical Services The Brownsville Medical Center (☎ 956-544-1400) is close to downtown at 1040 W Jefferson St. The Columbia Valley Regional Medical Center (☎ 956-350-7000) is at 100A Alton Gloor Blvd.

Emergency The crisis intervention line for personal problems is ☎ 956-544-7273.

Historic Brownsville

Downtown Among the scores of structures downtown is one of the oldest city halls in continuous use in the USA, the **Old Market Place** (☎ 956-548-6000), on Market Square between E Adams and E Washington Sts. It was built in 1850. **The Gem**, 400 E 13th St at E Levee St, is the city's oldest building, dating from 1848. Its projecting balconies once sheltered a saloon.

The **Immaculate Conception Cathedral**, 1218 E Jefferson St at E 12th St, is a late-19th-century Gothic-style example of the artistry of local brickmasons.

A **marker** across from the international bridge at the northeast corner of E Elizabeth St and International Blvd shows the spot where the storied Chisholm Trail began in the 1860s and 1870s. More than 10 million head of cattle journeyed the trail to railroads in Abilene and Dodge City, Kansas. Locally they sold for $2 a head, but in Chicago they fetched $40.

Historic Brownsville Museum Housed in the grand Spanish-Colonial-style 1928 Southern Pacific Railroad Depot, this small Brownsville museum (☎ 956-548-1313), 641 E Madison St, houses historical artifacts. The highlights are an 1872 steam locomotive once used for the 22-mile run to Port Isabel and a pointed display of the many kinds of barbed wire used on the Texas range. It's open weekdays 10 am to 4:30 pm, Saturday 10 am to 1 pm; $2 for adults, 50¢ for children.

Stillman House Museum The 1850 home of Brownsville founder Charles Stillman houses a small museum on his life (☎ 956-542-3929), 1305 E Washington St. It's open weekdays 10 am to noon and 2 to 5 pm, and Sunday 3 to 5 pm; $2 for adults, 50¢ for children.

Fort Brown A hurricane swept the original fort away in 1867; what survives today was built in 1868. The buildings have been incorporated into the joint campus of the University of Texas at Brownsville and Texas Southmost College (☎ 956-544-8200), downtown at May St and Gorgas Drive, south of International Blvd. The Post Hospital is now called Gorgas Hall, and the Cavalry Building is now used for classrooms and offices.

Palo Alto Battlefield National Historical Site

General Zachary Taylor defeated a Mexican army on this site on May 8, 1846. It's now a large field covered with thorny shrubs, but the National Park Service is planning a major park here. A school of historical markers congregates at the intersection of FM 1847 and FM 511, 5½ miles north of town (see the Rio Grande Valley map).

Gladys Porter Zoo

Get a color map at the entrance gate to guide yourself around this 31-acre zoo (☎ 956-546-2177), 500 W Ringgold St at E 6th St. The 1500 animals are displayed in large areas that replicate their natural habitats. One of the most popular displays is a flock of flamingos near the entrance. You can walk right up to the slow-moving, stick-limbed pink beauties.

Some of the rarest species at the zoo include the following:

Guar These are the world's largest wild cattle. They grow to more than 1 ton apiece and are native to India.

Double-wattled cassowary These foul-tempered, flightless, 125lb birds from northern Australia and New Guinea will attack humans with their sharp claws.

Malaysian sun bears The world's smallest bears, they grow to only 2 feet in height.

The zoo is open weekdays 9 am to 5 pm, weekends 9 am to 5:30 pm; $6 for adults, $4.75 for seniors, $3 for children.

Rio Grande Valley Wing Flying Museum

The local branch (☎ 956-541-8585) of the Confederate Air Force, the large Texas-based historical aircraft preservation group, has a few planes in two hangars in this museum at the Brownsville/South Padre Island International Airport, at 955 S Minnesota Ave. The WWII artifacts are well displayed. It's open Monday to Saturday 9 am to 4 pm; $5 for adults, $4 for seniors, $3 for kids.

Sabal Palm Sanctuary

The only palm tree native to Texas grows at this 527-acre sanctuary operated by the National Audubon Society. Sabal palms reach 20 to 48 feet in height and have feathery crowns and thick, bristly trunks. They once lined the Rio Grande, covering an area of nearly 63 sq miles. In the past 150 years, most have been cut down, first by early settlers who needed lumber and later by those clearing land for agriculture. In the sanctuary, the palms are primarily found in a lush 32-acre section that is one of the largest remaining groves of its kind in the valley.

The preserve has two half-mile trails, which explore the sabal palm grove as well as the surrounding area of wetlands, clay dunes and abandoned farms. The visitors' center (☎ 956-541-8034) has trail guides you can borrow that cover the plants native to the sanctuary, including its many endangered species. It also has guides to resident animals such as armadillos and rabbits and the scores of bird species. Insect repellent is necessary year-round.

The visitors' center is open Tuesday to Sunday 9 am to 5 pm from October to May, and weekends only from June to September. The gates are open daily, sunrise to sunset; $4 for adults, $2 for children.

To reach the preserve, drive east on FM 1419 (also called Southmost Rd), which intersects International Blvd 1 mile northeast of downtown Brownsville. Continue for 6 miles until you see an access road to the sanctuary on the south side. This 1-mile road, which can get very muddy after rains, leads to the refuge.

Brazos Island State Park

You can enjoy the raw surf at the meeting of the Rio Grande and the Gulf of Mexico at this park, some 22 miles east of Brownsville on Hwy 4. Mexico is south across the churning brown water, and far to the north, over the Boca Chica wetlands, are the hotel towers of South Padre Island. Brazos Island State Park is not much more than a concept, with a place to turn your car around and a forlorn trash can. The beach is small and there are absolutely no services. However, bird lovers ignore these minor details for the splendid bird-watching opportunities on the Boca Chica wetlands, which are home to as good a selection of species as can be found in this bird-rich part of the state.

Organized Tours

The Brownsville Convention & Visitors Bureau operates three trolley bus tours (☎ 956-546-3721) that cover historic Brownsville, the port and historic churches. They depart from the bureau, 650 FM 802, on the west side of US 77/83 at the FM 802 exit, Monday to Saturday at 10 am and 1 pm. The lineup rotates each day. Tickets are $7 for adults, $3.50 for seniors and children.

Several companies offer tours of the valley and neighboring Mexico. The three-hour Matamoros tours led by David Burlingame (☎ 956-233-1900) are highly recommended because, as he says, 'We don't just take you to all the tourist traps.' He visits historic areas, middle-class suburbs and slums. The cost is $35 for two people or $15 each for three or more.

Other tour operators with extensive schedules covering the area include SurfTran (☎ 956-421-2252, 800-338-0560) and Go... with Jo! (☎ 956-831-2976, 800-999-1446).

Special Events

Many special events throughout the valley are timed for the months when Winter Texans swell the population.

Late February
Annual Charro Days Celebration
This celebration linking Brownsville and Matamoros, beginning the last Thursday of the month, includes parades, carnivals, dances, concerts and more.

Early March
Confederate Air Force Air Fiesta
Held the first weekend in March, this event includes numerous vintage WWII aircraft and aerial acrobatics.

International Art Show
Works by artists from the USA and Mexico are featured.

Places to Stay

Lodgings in Brownsville are divided between places near the border that are convenient to Mexico and the sights downtown, and places on US 77/83 that are convenient for getting out of town.

Border Area The *Cameron Motor Hotel* (☎ *956-542-3551*), 912 E Washington St, has basic accommodations for $37/42 single/ double. The equally simple *Colonial Hotel* (☎ *956-541-9176*), 1147 E Levee St, has rooms for $40. *Super 8* (☎ *956-546-0381*), 55 Sam Perl Blvd (E 12th St), adds a pool to the equation and charges $46/52.

In a parklike setting east of the border crossing, the *Ramada Limited* (☎ *956-541-2921*), 1900 E Elizabeth St, is an amenity-filled place with rooms for $55/61. Right next door, the *Holiday Inn Fort Brown Resort* (☎ *956-546-2201*), 1900 E Elizabeth St, is the best place downtown and has extensive gardens set on a lake. Rooms are $75/83, and there are frequent specials.

US 77/83 We never promised you a *Best Western Rose Garden Inn* (☎ *956-546-5501*), 845 N Expressway 77/83, at the Price Rd exit, but you may want to stay here anyway for $52/58. *Red Roof Inn* (☎ *956-504-2300*), 2377 N Expressway 83, at the FM 802 exit, has nice rooms for $57/72. Next door to the Best Western, *Comfort Inn* (☎ *956-504-3331*), 825 N Expressway 77/83, has large rooms for $70/85.

Places to Eat

If you're not in the mood for Mexican food, you may want to leave town, because almost every place serves it. *Los Camperos* (☎ *956-546-8172*), 1442 International Blvd, is locally famous for its charcoal-broiled chicken with zesty salsas and fresh corn tortillas. It has live music on Friday and Saturday and, like most other Mexican restaurants in town, strolling mariachis the rest of the week. *Los Brasas* (☎ *956-542-9372*), 2040 Central Blvd, has a breakfast menu that begins 'Flour tortillas with...' During the rest of the day, it specializes in vast mixed platters of Mexican specialties that average $5 to $7 a person.

They'll love you almost to death at *Antonio's* (☎ *956-542-6504*), 1800 N Expressway 77/83, north of the Price Rd exit. Between the time the last bite of the best fajitas you'll ever have ($9) leaves your plate and reaches your mouth, one person takes your plate away while another refills your iced tea. The guacamole is pretty darn good as well.

If you want a break from tortillas, *New York Deli* (☎ *956-542-7484*), 2245 Central Blvd, is a good place for lunch and specializes in huge and creative sandwiches ($3 to $6).

Getting There & Away

Air Brownsville/South Padre Island International Airport (BRO, ☎ 956-542-4373), 4 miles east of downtown at 700 S Minnesota Ave, hosts four flights a day to and from Houston, operated by Continental Express (☎ 956-504-5864, 800-525-0280).

Bus The bus station is downtown at 1134 E St Charles St, three blocks west of the border crossing. Greyhound (☎ 956-546-7171) and its affiliate Valley Transit have 10 daily buses to Corpus Christi ($22) and 12 to Houston ($28). From 5 am to 11 pm, there's hourly service west to McAllen ($10); the ride takes an hour. Two buses a day continue to Laredo ($25).

Direct service to Mexico includes buses to Mexico City ($50) that take 14 hours. Frequent buses to and from the Matamoros bus station cost $5, but for a simple town visit, it takes less time to walk across the bridge and grab a taxi.

Getting Around

Bus The Brownsville Urban System (BUS – you don't find this kind of clever acronym in places like Pittsburgh) operates a limited service Monday to Saturday during daylight hours. Primarily geared toward linking residential neighborhoods with the downtown, it charges 75¢. For schedule and route information, call ☎ 956-548-6050.

Car Three car-rental companies have offices at the Brownsville airport:

Avis	☎ 956-541-9271
Budget	☎ 956-546-5563
Hertz	☎ 956-542-7466

MATAMOROS (MEXICO)
Population 600,000
☎ 88 within Mexico, 011-52-88 from Texas

First settled during the Spanish colonization of Tamaulipas in 1686 and given the name Los Esteros Hermosos (Beautiful Estuaries), this town was renamed in 1793 after Father Mariano Matamoros. In 1846, Matamoros was the first Mexican city taken by US forces in the Mexican War, and Zachary Taylor then used it as a base for his attack on Monterrey.

During the US Civil War, when sea routes to the Confederacy were blockaded, Matamoros was a transshipment point for cotton from Confederate Texas, as well as incoming supplies and war material. A major player in this trade was Richard King, of King Ranch fame.

Today, Matamoros is no historical monument, but there is more evidence of the past here than in most border towns, and the town center, with its church and plaza, looks typically Mexican. South of the central area is a broad circle of newer industrial zones. Apart from its maquiladoras, Matamoros is a commercial center for a large agricultural hinterland – tanneries, cotton mills and distilleries are among its main industries.

Orientation

Matamoros lies across the Rio Grande from Brownsville. The river, which forms the international boundary, is spanned by a bridge with US border controls at the north

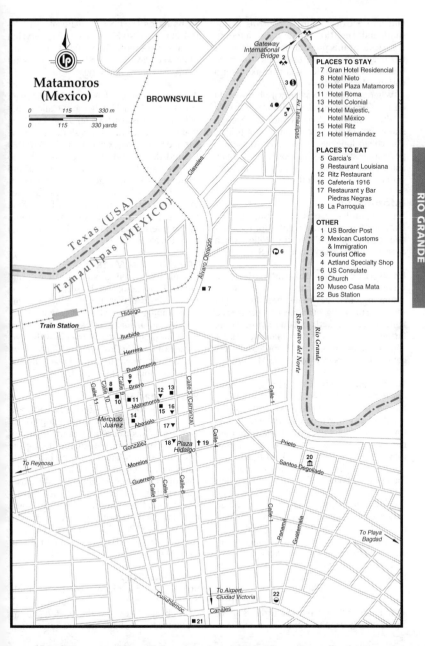

Matamoros (Mexico)

BROWNSVILLE

0   115   330 m
0   115   330 yards

Texas (USA)
Tamaulipas (MEXICO)

Gateway International Bridge

Av Tamaulipas

Claveles

Alvaro Obregón

Río Bravo del Norte

Río Grande

PLACES TO STAY
7   Gran Hotel Residencial
8   Hotel Nieto
10 Hotel Plaza Matamoros
11 Hotel Roma
13 Hotel Colonial
14 Hotel Majestic,
    Hotel México
15 Hotel Ritz
21 Hotel Hernández

PLACES TO EAT
5   Garcia's
9   Restaurant Louisiana
12 Ritz Restaurant
16 Cafetería 1916
17 Restaurant y Bar
    Piedras Negras
18 La Parroquia

OTHER
1   US Border Post
2   Mexican Customs
    & Immigration
3   Tourist Office
4   Aztland Specialty Shop
6   US Consulate
19 Church
20 Museo Casa Mata
22 Bus Station

RIO GRANDE

Train Station

Hidalgo
Iturbide
Herrera
Bustamente
Bravo
Matamoros
Abasolo

Calle 11
Calle 9
Calle 5 (Carranza)

Mercado
Juárez

González
Morelos
Guerrero

Calle 7
Calle 8

Calle 6
Calle 4
Calle 1

Plaza
Hidalgo

Prieto
Santos Degollado

Panamá
Guatemala

To Reynosa

Cuauhtémoc
Canales

To Airport,
Ciudad Victoria

To Playa
Bagdad

end and Mexican border controls at the south end. The Rio Grande is a disappointing trickle at this point, as most of its water has been siphoned off upstream for irrigation. On the US side, its dirt banks swarm with border patrols.

Whereas downtown Brownsville is right on the border, central Matamoros is 1 mile to the southwest along Álvaro Obregón, a major thoroughfare beginning at the bridge. The cheap lodgings are around Abasolo, a pedestrian street a block north of the main plaza, Plaza Hidalgo. Nearby are two markets with tourist-oriented crafts.

Information

See the Border section in the introductory Getting There & Away chapter for the rules and regulations you'll need to follow when crossing into Mexico from the USA.

Immigration The Mexican border post waves most pedestrians through on the assumption that they're just here for a day's shopping or eating, but some cars get the red light to be checked. If you're proceeding farther south into Mexico than the border zone, get a tourist card at the border post and get it stamped before you leave Matamoros.

Tourist Offices Just past the bridge, an informal tourist office (☎ 88-12-36-30) is in a hut on the right-hand (west) side of Álvaro Obregón. What it lacks in written material it makes up for with the helpfulness of its staff, who are mostly bilingual taxi drivers. Needless to say, they offer transport and guided tours for a price, but they're happy to answer questions for nothing. Someone's usually there daily, 8 am to noon and 2 to 5 pm. If you need maps, brochures and printed giveaways, you will do better at the Brownsville Chamber of Commerce (☎ 956-542-4341), 1600 E Elizabeth St, about 200 yards east of the bridge; open weekdays 8 am to 5 pm, closed weekends.

The Brownsville Convention & Visitors Bureau (☎ 956-546-3721), on the west side of US 77/83 at the FM 802 exit, is an excellent source of information on the entire area. It's open Monday to Saturday 8 am to 5 pm, Sunday 9 am to 4 pm.

Consulates The US Consulate (☎ 88-12-44-02), at Calle 1 No 232, can issue US visas but usually takes more than a day to do so. It's open weekdays 8 am to 5 pm, but it does not issue visas on Wednesday.

Money Matamoros has several banks (with ATMs) on Plaza Hidalgo and Calle 6 that will change cash or traveler's checks. Often you get a better rate for cash dollars in the casas de cambio (exchange houses) dotted around the central area. Casa de Cambio Astorga, on Calle 7 between Bravo and Matamoros, will change traveler's checks.

In Brownsville, there are several currency exchanges on International Blvd, the road running straight ahead from the north end of the international bridge. Many are open 24 hours a day.

Museo Casa Mata

This old fort, on the corner of Guatemala and Santos Degollado, was the scene of fighting in the Mexican War. It now contains some memorabilia of the Mexican Revolution, a few Indian artifacts and some ill-assorted miscellany. Entry is free. From Plaza Hidalgo, head east on Morelos as far as Calle 1, turn right, go two blocks to Santos Degollado and then two more blocks to the left.

Playa Bagdad

Matamoros' beach was formerly known as Playa Lauro Villar, but it has adopted the name *Bagdad*, after a town at the mouth of the Rio Grande that prospered during the US Civil War but later succumbed to floods, hurricanes and military attacks. It's 23 miles east of Matamoros on Hwy 2, and it has a wide stretch of clean sand and a few beachside seafood restaurants. There are some mid-range motels along the road approaching the beach. 'Playa' buses go here from the corner of Abasolo and Calle 11 in downtown Matamoros.

Places to Stay

Staying in Matamoros can be a viable budget alternative to Brownsville, which lacks cheap places near the border, and the Matamoros street life is more interesting.

Many budget hotels are on or near Abasolo near the center of town. Budget rooms are basic, but cheap enough at around US$7 a double. Mid-range lodging, with air-con and parking, starts at around US$25 and there's not much between these levels.

One of the better deals in town is *Hotel Hernández* (☎ 88-13-35-58), on Calle 6, 50 yards south of Canales. The hotel is five short blocks from the bus station, twice that to the main plaza. The popular Hernández is a four-story hotel set around a narrow courtyard with palm trees. The rooms are clean and have new air-con units and firm beds. Singles/doubles go for US$18/20.

Hotel Colonial (☎ 88-14-64-18), one block north of Abasolo, on the corner of Matamoros and Calle 6, is friendly and has lots of cleanish rooms with minimum comforts for US$5/7. Check the room before you decide – some need maintenance and others are noisy, but it's not a bad place to stay.

Hotel México (☎ 88-12-08-56), at Abasolo 87 between Calles 8 and 9, charges US$5.50/11 for cleanish rooms with bathrooms and ceiling fans. Nearby, *Hotel Majestic* (☎ 88-13-36-80), Abasolo 89, is not quite as clean but has more character and some classic 1950s furnishings. It's a family-run place that charges US$6.50/8 for rooms with private baths. Both are often filled, and neither is as pleasant as the Hernández.

Moving up the scale, *Hotel Nieto* (☎ 88-13-08-57), at Calle 10 No 1508, is like stepping back in time. It's an ordinary-looking 1960s-style hotel, with original wall paneling, carpets and paintings, and air-con, TVs and parking, charging US$25. Its rooms are worn but spacious and quite tolerable. *Hotel Roma* (☎ 88-16-05-73), on Calle 9 between Matamoros and Bravo, is central, modern, clean and friendly. It charges US$30 for smallish rooms with cable TVs, telephones and carpeting. *Hotel Ritz* (☎ 88-12-11-90), on Matamoros between Calles 6 and 7, is a lot classier, with bigger rooms and fax and laundry services; its rooms cost US$50.

Top places include *Hotel Plaza Matamoros* (☎ 88-16-16-96), on the corner of Calle 9 and Bravo, which is tasteful and comfortable, with rooms for US$46. For more money, a better bargain is probably the *Gran Hotel Residencial* (☎ 88-13-94-40), Álvaro Obregón 249, with large and pleasant gardens and a swimming pool. The 120 air-con rooms with cable TVs go for US$75.

Places to Eat

Near the plaza, the clean, classy and cool *La Parroquia*, on González between Calles 6 and 7, is popular from morning to evening, with a wide selection of breakfasts (US$1.30 to US$2.50) and dinners (US$2 to US$4); its chicken mole (US$3) is delicious. In the same price range is the *Ritz Restaurant*, opposite the Hotel Ritz. Popular meals at this tasteful and stylish restaurant, with cozy booths and lots of scrubbed tile, include grilled chicken (US$3) and filet mignon (US$4.50).

Cafetería 1916, on Calle 6 between Matamoros and Abasolo, is slightly less atmospheric but quite popular with local residents. It's a tad pricier than the restaurants listed above, with antojitos starting at US$2.50, but it's still very reasonable.

Farther up the scale is *Restaurant y Bar Piedras Negras*, at Calle 6 No 175, half a block north of the main square, which is favored by better-off Mexicans and a few gringos. A meal at this restaurant – perhaps the best in town – could well set you back US$8 or more. *Restaurant Louisiana*, on Bravo between Calles 8 and 9, has a somewhat elegant atmosphere and offers meals ranging from US$4.50 to US$9. These include Louisiana frog legs (US$8), rib-eye steak with mushrooms (US$9) and shish kebab (US$9).

Garcia's (☎ 88-12-39-29) is at Álvaro Obregón 82, right at the end of the border-crossing bridge. Chateaubriand ($20 for two) is the specialty, and the service is very attentive. It also has a large store of duty-free booze.

Shopping

The 'new market,' or Mercado Juárez, is the larger of Matamoros' two markets, occupying a block between Abasolo, Matamoros, and Calles 9 and 10. A lot of the stuff is second-rate, but there's plenty of variety, including blankets, hats, pottery, leather and glass, so you may find something appealing. Prices are 20% to 30% higher than those at the cheapest markets farther south, but you can bargain them down a bit.

The second market, called Pasaje Juárez, is in an arcade with entrances on Bravo and Calle 9. Its range of goods is more limited, and it has a slightly more aggressive sales style. There are a few interesting but expensive folk-art shops along Álvaro Obregón.

Getting There & Away

Air Matamoros has an airport (☎ 88-12-00-01) 10 miles south of town on the road to Ciudad Victoria. There are direct daily Aeroméxico flights to/from Mexico City. The Aeroméxico office (☎ 88-12-51-60) is in the Matamoros airport. Aero California (☎ 88-12-19-43), on Calle 5 between Abasolo and Matamoros, offers service to Matamoros from Los Angeles and Tucson.

Bus You can get frequent buses from the Brownsville bus station (☎ 956-546-7171), 1134 E St Charles St at E 12th St, to its Matamoros counterpart, on Canales near the corner of Guatemala, for US$5.

There's also direct bus service from the Brownsville station to several cities deeper inside Mexico, but fares from Brownsville are higher than those from Matamoros, and the buses may take up to two hours to cross the international bridge and pass through customs and immigration. If you're heading deeper into Mexico, it's quicker to walk across the bridge and take a maxi-taxi (see Getting Around, below) to the Matamoros bus station. Going into the USA, it's quicker to get local transport to the bridge and walk across it.

Both 1st- and 2nd-class buses into Mexico run from the Matamoros bus station, which has public telephones, currency exchange and a 24-hour restaurant. It also has a left-luggage service (US20¢ per hour). A number of big companies provide 1st-class bus service to/from Matamoros. There's daily service from Matamoros to destinations including Mexico City, Monterrey and Reynosa, plus service all the way along the border to Tijuana.

Train One train a day runs in each direction between Matamoros and Monterrey, via Reynosa. Though cheap, it's neither quick nor reliable. The 9:20 am train from Matamoros is scheduled to take about two hours to Reynosa and seven hours to Monterrey, but may take longer (*primera clase* fare to Monterrey is US$8). Making the run from Matamoros to Reynosa can, however, be an entertaining way to see the Mexican border area along the Rio Grande. You can then return to your starting point in the United States via a bus.

Car Driving the Gateway International Bridge to/from Brownsville costs US$1.40. But day-trippers here, as in most Mexican border towns, are better off parking their cars on the US side and walking across the bridge. The city of Brownsville operates a guarded lot behind the Jacob Brown Auditorium at May St and Taylor Ave, one block from the Gateway International Bridge. It costs US50¢ an hour.

The main routes into Mexico from Matamoros are Hwy 180 south to Tampico and the Gulf Coast, and Hwy 101 southwest to Ciudad Victoria and into the Bajío region. These are both two-lane roads, not very busy, in fair condition and free of heavy tolls. Officials at various checkpoints will want to see your tourist card and vehicle permit; if your papers are not in order, you will be sent back to Matamoros.

Getting Around

Bus Matamoros is served by small buses called maxi-taxis, which charge US70¢ to anywhere in town. You can stop them on almost any street corner. Their destinations are usually painted on the front windscreens: the town center is 'Centro'; the bus station is 'Central de Autobuses'; and the international bridge is 'Puente Internacional.' From the Gateway International Bridge, walk south until you see a row of yellow maxi-taxis; read their windscreens to find one going to the town center or bus station.

You can also take a free shuttle bus run by the Aztland Specialty Shop (☎ 88-16-29-47), Álvaro Obregón 75, one block south of the bridge, which shuttles between the shop and the Mercado Juárez in the town center. Look for the white school bus in front of the shop. The shop owners are very friendly about the service and don't make you buy anything, although they will happily sell you duty-free liquor on your return trip. Owner Yolanda Castañeda is fluent in English and is a storehouse of local knowledge.

Taxi Taxis from the border to the town center or the bus station cost about US$5.

NUEVO PROGRESO (MEXICO)
Population 10,000

This small town has completely devoted itself to day-tripping Americans. In fact, on the US side of the approach to the border bridge, the town has erected a sign that says, 'Bienvenidos, Winter Texans. We love ya.' A short strip of restaurants and shops begins right at the end of the bridge over the Rio Grande. The overall feel is close to an American strip mall. As one tour operator told us, 'We drop 'em off the bus at the bridge and they walk over. It's clean, it's simple, they can buy souvenirs, come back in one hour and we're gone, and they can say they've been to Mexico.' A parking lot on the US side charges $1 for the entire day.

The most interesting aspect of the 1-mile drive south to the border crossing (which is on FM 1015, reached from US 281, 20 miles east of McAllen) are the stands selling perfectly ripe and very cheap produce grown on the surrounding farms. See the Getting There & Away chapter for information on crossing the Mexican border.

SANTA ANA NATIONAL WILDLIFE REFUGE

Another birder's heaven, this 2000-acre sanctuary, southeast of McAllen off US 281, is one of the most beautiful spots in the valley. Lakes, wetlands, thorny bushes and palms combine for a bucolic setting where the only noises come from birds. Besides serving as the seasonal home to more than 300 bird species, Santa Ana is also a favorite among the silk-spinning set – butterflies. Hundreds of butterfly species have been

spotted flitting about the many flowering plants and shrubs.

The refuge has a 7-mile nature drive, but to really experience the place, you have to ditch the car and hit some of the 12 miles of trails. Loop A is a good introduction to the many features of the site and is only a half mile long. Spanish moss-draped ash, cedar and elm trees shade the trail, which has full wheelchair access and several sheltered seating areas where you can watch the action on Willow Lake.

Camping is not allowed in the refuge, which is run by the US Fish & Wildlife Service and is open daily, dawn to dusk. The visitors' center (☎ 956-787-3079) has good displays and is the starting point for guided tours, scheduled in winter, that are led by plant and wildlife experts. It is open Sunday to Thursday 8:30 am to 4 pm; admission is free.

McALLEN & AROUND
Population 101,000

McAllen is not just near the Mexican border; it is also near a natural border. To the east are the lush and green lands of the Rio Grande Valley, with its farms, palm trees and fast-growing population. To the west is the beginning of the Chihuahuan Desert. As you head west toward Laredo, the land becomes more barren due to the increasingly arid climate. Population growth in this sparsely populated region is negligible, and towns such as Rio Grande City feel as if they've changed little in decades.

McAllen is the center of the Texas citrus industry. Grapefruit trees grow by the thousands, their shiny green leaves set off by their huge globes of bright-yellow fruit. Each year the industry ships 10 million 40lb boxes filled with the tangy citrus to the rest of the USA and abroad. During the long harvest season, from September to May, the air is often redolent with the fragrant smell of citrus.

Several small towns near McAllen – such as nearby Pharr – have interesting sights, and Reynosa, a bustling Mexican border town, is just 6 miles south. Although McAllen may be short on its own attractions, its

Driving South for the Winter

Every fall, 100,000 creatures begin their annual migration to the Rio Grande Valley from points throughout the USA and Canadian Midwest. But they aren't wildlife. Not even close. They're retired folks drawn to the south end of Texas by the bone-warming climate and the low prices.

Affectionately dubbed 'Winter Texans' by grateful civic boosters, they add at least $250 million to the local economies during the prime season from October to March. They come in huge rumbling RVs, or they drive their cars and stay in thousands of mobile homes. There are scores of senior-citizen parks from Brownsville to McAllen, and they usually have accommodations for both RVs and mobile homes.

Most Winter Texans return to the same parks every year, where they are part of a close and friendly seasonal society. The communities bustle with activity, including square dancing, bike riding, water sports, bingo, craft classes and much, much more. While many folks engage in sedate matches of shuffleboard, others indulge in rougher pursuits, such as water polo.

Many make regular treks to Mexico, where they can obtain economical medical and dental care as well as cheap pharmaceuticals. Most restaurants do a big dinner business from 4 to 6 pm, which is the traditional suppertime on the Midwestern farms that are home to many of these retirees.

The valley's many museums, parks and attractions benefit from the Winter Texans who volunteer in droves to staff information desks in visitors' centers. They are invariably very well informed and anxious to not only help but to chat for a while. Residents and tourists also benefit from the value-conscious Winter Texans, who know a good deal when they see it and know how to stretch fixed incomes. Prices are generally low everywhere.

Come spring, when the snow-blanketed lands they hail from begin to thaw, the Winter Texans head north for the summer.

many hotels and restaurants and central location make it a good base for exploring the surrounding area. It also is the center of a range of Winter Texan activities, of which square-dancing is only the most prominent.

Orientation

McAllen is 236 miles south of San Antonio via US 281, a desolate road for the 70 miles north of the city. Laredo is 142 miles west on US 83, Brownsville is 67 miles east on the same highway. The town is removed from the Reynosa border area, 6 miles south at Hidalgo. Shopping is strung along 10th St north and south of the center.

Information

Tourist Offices The McAllen Convention & Visitors Bureau (☎ 956-682-2871, 800-250-2591), 10 N Broadway at Business US 83, has extensive information on the city and the surrounding towns. During Winter Texan season, it offers free juice and details on the many events that are scheduled all winter long. It's open weekdays 8 am to 5 pm. There's a Mexican consulate in town; see the Facts for the Visitor chapter.

Post The post office (☎ 956-971-1700), 620 E Pecan St, is open weekdays 8:30 am to 5:30 pm, Saturday 8 am to noon.

Travel Agencies Gray Line/Tourimex (☎ 956-994-8824), 1704 N Jackson St, can arrange trips and tours throughout Texas and Mexico. Express Travel (☎ 956-630-1002), 1001 S 10th St, Suite P, is a full-service agency.

Medical Services McAllen Medical Center (☎ 956-632-4000), 301 W Expressway 83, is a large full-service hospital.

McAllen International Museum

This museum (☎ 956-682-1564), 1900 Nolana Ave, hosts rotating exhibitions devoted to the arts and sciences. Occasional shows are mounted from the permanent collection of Mexican folk art and textiles. It's open Tuesday to Saturday 9 am to 5 pm and Sunday 1 to 5 pm; admission is usually $2 for adults, $1 for children.

Pharr

You can keep time – either musically or chronologically – at two museums in this town of 33,000, which abuts the east side of McAllen. **Smitty's Jukebox Museum** (☎ 956-787-0131), in a storefront at 116 W State St, has 50 lovingly maintained beauties from the time when songs cost a nickel and records were played with a needle. It's open weekdays 9 am to 5 pm; admission is free.

When the big hand hits 12, the **Old Clock Museum** (☎ 956-787-1923), 929 E Preston St, becomes a cacophonous place as more than 2000 European and American clocks strike the hour. It's open weekdays 1 to 5 pm; a $1 donation to charity is requested.

Alamo

They don't water much at **Sunderland's Cactus Gardens** (☎ 956-787-2040), where more than 2000 plants are on display. Owners Harry and Viola Sunderland will cheerfully explain the finer points of growing these denizens of the desert. October to April, the gardens are open weekdays 9 am to 5 pm and Sunday 2 to 5 pm; May to September, hours are Tuesday to Friday 9 am to 5 pm.

They're closed in August. Admission is free. The gardens are at the corner of FM 495 and FM 907, 1 mile north of US 83 and 7 miles east of McAllen.

Edinburg

The **Hidalgo County Historical Museum** (☎ 956-383-6911), 121 E McIntyre St, about 9 miles northeast of McAllen, has artifacts and displays covering the life of Indians in the area from precolonial times through the arrival of the Spaniards to the Mexican and American land battles. The gift shop has an excellent selection of regional books. Open Tuesday to Friday 9 am to 5 pm, Saturday 10 am to 5 pm and Sunday 1 to 5 pm; $2 for adults, $1.50 for seniors, 50¢ for children.

Every Saturday night, the **Sheriff's Posse Rodeo** (☎ 956-686-7038) demonstrates all sorts of stuff you can do with bulls and calves if you are a cowpoke. The action begins at 5 pm and lasts until midnight. The arena is on Wisconsin Rd, 2 miles south of town and just off US 281.

Mission

Poinsettias aren't the only red things grown here. Mission is also a center of ruby red grapefruit production. You can pick your own at **3 Palms Citrus** (☎ 956-585-2463), 2906 N Shary Rd off US 83. It's open daily 8 am to 6 pm November through May; call for costs.

The **Capilla de la Lomita** (Chapel of the Little Hill, ☎ 956-580-8760) was once a rest stop for traveling *padres*. The reconstructed version dates from 1889 and is a good example of the construction techniques used at that time. On 7 acres of land with picnic facilities and nature trails, the chapel is open daily, dawn to dusk. It's on FM 1016, 3 miles south of US 83 and 9 miles from McAllen.

Special Events

McAllen is the center of many of the largest festivals in the valley.

Late January
Texas Citrus Fiesta
  This valley-wide festival centered in Mission features parades, dances, cooking contests and more. (☎ 956-585-9724)

Early February

Texas Square Dance Jamboree
More than 2000 dancers gather in McAllen for several days of contests and shows. (☎ 956-682-2871)

Mid-April

Texas Tropics Nature Festival
Seminars on topics such as nature photography, reptiles and even moths are offered, as well as field trips throughout the region. (☎ 800-250-2591)

Early December

Candlelight Posada
This bicultural celebration of Christmas is held in McAllen. (☎ 956-682-2871)

Places to Stay

Camping *Bentsen-Rio Grande Valley State Park* (☎ 956-585-1107), 15 miles southwest of McAllen, has numerous camping facilities that are fully detailed in the section on the park later in this chapter. *RV parks* are almost as common as grapefruit in the valley. The various tourist-information offices have book-size listings of the parks, which fill up with Winter Texans beginning in October. Rates can be quite cheap: $150 for a month or $500 for the season.

Motels & Hotels Several older motels congregate on the old S 10th St strip, offering faded but clean accommodations for rates that average about $35 for a double. Among them: *El Matador Motor Inn* (☎ 956-682-6171), 501 S 10th St; *Imperial Motor Inn* (☎ 956-686-0281), 601 S 10th St; and *Paradise Motel* (☎ 956-682-2453), 313 S 10th St.

The *Microtel* (☎ 956-630-2727), at 801 E Expressway 83 at the Jackson Ave exit, is a new budget place with large rooms, but unlike almost all the other accommodations in the valley, it has no coin laundry. Rooms are $46/51 single/double. *La Quinta – McAllen* (☎ 956-687-1101), 1100 S 10th St at US 83, offers the chain's usually well-appointed rooms for $60/65.

The swankiest place in town is *Embassy Suites* (☎ 956-686-3000), 1800 S 2nd St at US 83. Staff will cheerfully show off the suite where President Bill Clinton stayed for a night in 1998. Suites, which easily sleep four

in two rooms, range from $125 to $140. Check for discounts.

Places to Eat

Mexican *El Pocito* (☎ 956-686-1188), downtown at 203 S 17th St, serves up gorditas (crispy fried buns) with a variety of meat fillings for $1.75. Other good standards at this simple '50s café average $4. *Maria Bonita* (☎ 956-687-7181), 1621 N 11th St, has all the classics for about $6, and a popular guitar trio performs at night.

Local favorite *Koko's* (956-630-5656) is at 119 S Broadway. Stylish interiors set off the tasty food, which includes a spectacular 'Botana' sampler for two or more ($12) that visits most of the menu for its ingredients. *El Patio* (☎ 956-519-8575), 2003 N Conway in Mission, serves updated Mexican classics in a bright and lively setting. Expect to pay about $8 each for dinner at this vibrant place.

Other Cuisines The veteran waitresses are as much fun as the food at *Ferrell's Pit* (☎ 956-585-2381), at Business US 83 and Shary Rd in Mission. Between piles of long-smoked barbecue, you'll hear about their latest romantic exploits among the Winter Texan crowd. The real prize, however, is the fresh grapefruit pie ($3), which uses sugar-sweet ripe local fruit. Don't balk, just try it.

House of China (☎ 956-631-0188), 4008 N 10th St, is hugely popular, which makes the buffet ($7) a good option because its fresh and tasty items turn over quickly. The *Mill Restaurant* (☎ 956-686-6847), 4105 N 10th St, has popular salads and stuffed baked potatoes for about $5. *Pepe's River Fiesta Bar & Grill* (☎ 956-519-2444) is just that: a river fiesta. This rustic, open-air place on the Rio Grande has live music, and people dance on the tables between bites of the tasty burgers ($5). It's 4 miles south of Mission on FM 1016.

Entertainment

Square Dancing McAllen has dubbed itself 'the square dance capital of the world,' and that may be true – during the winter, people are grabbing their partners and doing unspellable things such as dosey-doeing every night at locations throughout the city. On a typical Tuesday, for instance, 28 weekly events are scheduled at dance halls and activity centers.

The best source of information on all this twirling is the McAllen Convention & Visitors Bureau (☎ 956-682-2871, 800-250-2591), 10 N Broadway at Business US 83, which maintains comprehensive listings of dances, lessons and callers, many of whom have their own following and groupies. In fact, some Winter Texans pick their RV or mobile-home park based on who the resident caller will be.

Bars & Clubs *Simon Sez (☎ 956-686-9688)*, 2007 Orchid St, has live rock and blues most nights; call for the schedule. No points if you guess the kind of music at *Hillbilly's (☎ 956-687-1106)*, 6000 N 10th St, which has a jammed dance floor.

South Dalls, 500 Hackberry, mixes country with Tejano. *Austin St Inn*, 1110 Austin St, has DJ dancing and is popular with gay men and women.

Getting There & Around
Air McAllen's airport must be the closest one in the United States to an indoor shopping mall. McAllen Miller International Airport (MFE, ☎ 956-682-9101) is right across Wichita St from La Plaza Mall. Both are reached on S Main St south of US 83. The airport is served by Continental Airlines (☎ 956-383-8101) and American Airlines (☎ 956-632-5900), which have jet service to their respective Houston and Dallas-Fort Worth hubs.

Bus Greyhound (☎ 956-682-5513) and its affiliate Valley Transit have hourly service to Harlingen and Brownsville from the bus station at 120 S 16th St. Two buses a day make the 3½ hour trip to and from Laredo, to the west ($15). Valley Transit runs buses south to Hidalgo and Reynosa ($2.50).

Car The major car-rental firms are all represented at the airport.

REYNOSA (MEXICO)
Population 350,000
☎ 89 within Mexico, 011-52-89 from Texas

Reynosa was founded in 1749 as Villa de Nuestra Señora de Guadalupe de Reynosa, 12 miles from its present location. Flooding forced the move to the present site in 1802. Reynosa was one of the first towns to rise up in the independence movement of 1810, but there is little of historical interest here today.

Today, Reynosa is one of northeast Mexico's most important industrial towns, with oil refineries, petrochemical plants, cotton mills, distilleries and maquiladoras. Pipelines from Reynosa carry natural gas to Monterrey and into the USA. It's also the center of a big agricultural area, where cattle, cotton, sugar cane and maize are grown.

Reynosa is 6 miles south of McAllen and just across the border from the small town of Hidalgo. As a commercial border crossing, Reynosa is busier than Matamoros but less important than Nuevo Laredo. It has good road connections into Mexico and Texas, but most travelers heading farther into Mexico will probably find one of the other crossings more direct and convenient.

Reynosa's tourist trade is geared to short-term Texan visitors, with restaurants, night-clubs, bars and even bawdier diversions. Some handicrafts are available in the tourist markets, but the quality is generally low, although the prices are not.

Orientation
Reynosa's central streets are laid out on a grid pattern between the Rio Grande and the Anzalduas Canal. The Plaza Principal, on a rise a few blocks southwest of the international bridge, has a modern church, a town hall, banks and hotels. Between the bridge and the main plaza lies the Zona Rosa, with restaurants, bars and nightclubs. Reynosa's industries have expanded so much on the south side of town that the 'central' area has more or less become the town's northern edge.

If you're driving into town from Mexico, follow the signs to the Puente Internacional and then go to the town center if you want.

RIO GRANDE

RIO GRANDE

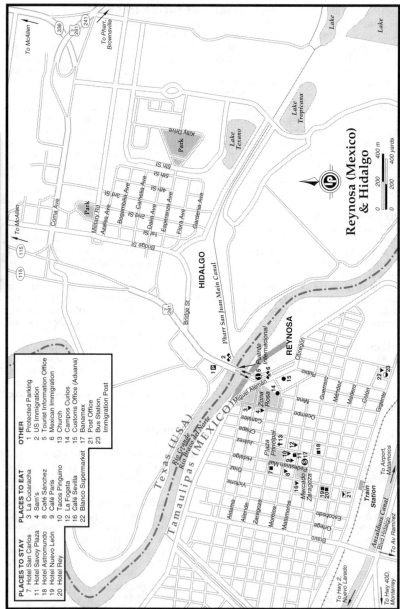

PLACES TO STAY
7   Hotel San Carlos
11 Hotel Savoy Plaza
18 Hotel Astromundo
19 Hotel Nuevo León
20 Hotel Rey

PLACES TO EAT
3   La Cucaracha
4   Sam's
8   Café Sánchez
9   Café Paris
10 Tacos Pinguino
12 La Fogata
16 Café Sevilla
22 Blanco Supermarket

OTHER
1   Protected Parking
2   US Immigration
5   Tourist Information Office
6   Mexican Immigration
13 Church
14 Campos Curios
15 Customs Office (Aduana)
17 Banamex
21 Post Office
    Bus Station,
23 Immigration Post

Reynosa (Mexico) & Hidalgo

0   200   400 m
0   200   400 yards

Avoid the maze of streets in the industrial zone south of the canal.

Information

See the Border section in the Getting There & Away chapter for details on crossing the Mexican border.

Immigration US immigration is at the north end of the international bridge. Mexican immigration is at the south end, and there's another immigration post in the Reynosa bus station. Get a tourist card stamped at either Mexican post if you're proceeding beyond Reynosa and deeper into Mexico.

Tourist Offices There's a so-called tourist information office at the south end of the bridge, opposite the immigration office, but its staff are unhelpful and the office doesn't even have a sign indicating what it is. However, the owner and staff of Campos Curios (☎ 89-22-44-20), a store just around the corner from the immigration office, speak English and enjoy assisting tourists. Campos Curios is open Monday to Saturday 9 am to 7 pm and Sunday until 5 pm.

Money The customs building, on Avenida Miguel Alemán just down the street from Mexican Immigration, has a Bancomer that changes traveler's checks. You can also change traveler's checks at Banamex, on Guerrero between Hidalgo and Juárez. The main banks have ATMs, some of which dispense US dollars as well as pesos, and there are several casas de cambio. Some shops also change money.

Things to See & Do

The central **Plaza Principal** is lined with benches and shade trees. At night, it is popular with families and courting couples. Take a stroll down **Hidalgo**, a pedestrian shopping strip on the west side of the square, to the touristy crafts market, **Mercado Zaragoza**.

The **Zona Rosa** has a slew of restaurants, bars and nightclubs, but it only comes to life on the nights when the young Texan crowd visits. Much sleazier entertainment – exotic

dancing and prostitution – is the rule at **'boys' town,'** a few miles to the west, just beyond where Aldama becomes a dirt road.

Special Events

Reynosa's major festival is that of Nuestra Señora de Guadalupe, on December 12. Pilgrims start processions a week early, and there are afternoon dance performances in front of the church.

Places to Stay

There are two particularly good budget hotels on Díaz, a few minutes' walk from the Plaza Principal. The cheaper of the two, *Hotel Nuevo León* (☎ 89-22-13-10), between Méndez and Madero, has sizable, clean singles/doubles with fans and private bathrooms for US$11; some rooms are much better than others. The popular *Hotel Rey* (☎ 89-22-29-80), two doors down, has clean, bright rooms with air-con and TVs for US$20. It may not have a vacant room if you arrive late.

Just south of the plaza, at Juárez 860, the pleasant *Hotel Savoy Plaza* (☎ 89-22-00-67) has air-con rooms for US$36. *Hotel San Carlos* (☎ 89-22-12-80), on Hidalgo between Zaragoza and Morelos, is a step toward the luxury bracket, with clean, bright, air-con rooms with phones and TVs for US$37. It has its own restaurant and parking.

The top downtown place is *Hotel Astromundo* (☎ 89-22-56-25), on Juárez between Guerrero and Méndez. It has clean, spacious rooms with TVs, plus a swimming pool, parking facilities and a restaurant. Rooms are US$43.

Places to Eat

There are a number of good, centrally located places to eat in Reynosa. The most popular is *Café Paris*, on Hidalgo near Morelos, which offers tasty Mexican lunches and dinners from US$2 to US$4 and breakfasts for up to US$2.50. It also stocks a wide selection of pastries.

Sam's, at Allende and Ocampo, has been serving cheap classics ($4) to generations of tourists since 1932. The clean and tidy *Café Sánchez*, Morelos 575, half a block from the

RIO GRANDE

main square, is popular with locals and has pretty good food; main courses range from US$3 to US$5. *Café Sevilla*, on the corner of Matamoros and Díaz, offers a filling comida corrida for US$4. For tacos, try *Tacos Pinguino*, on Morelos near Juárez.

The brunch ($5) at *La Cucaracha* (☎ *89-22-01-74*), at the corner of Ocampo and Aldama, one block west of the bridge, is popular with locals from Texas. It has live music at night.

You can feel the heat through the windows overlooking the kitchen at *La Fogata* (☎ *89-22-47-72*), Matamoros 750 near Juárez. Young goat *(cabracita)* is splayed out over the grill, and tortillas are produced in endless quantities. The impressive entrance is adobe mission-style with wrought-iron details and lush plants. Dinners are $7 or more.

Getting There & Away

Air Reynosa's airport is 8km east of town, off the Matamoros road. There are daily direct Aeroméxico flights to Mexico City, and also flights to/from Guadalajara via Saltillo. The Aeroméxico office (☎ 89-22-11-15) is at the airport.

Bus Valley Transit (☎ 956-686-5479) runs buses both ways between the McAllen station (120 S 16th St) and the stations in Reynosa, Gigante and Rubio. Buses leave every 30 minutes between 5 am and 7:30 pm (US$2.50 one way). There are three later services; the last leaves the Reynosa station at 10:05 pm. Reynosa's bus station (the Central de Autobuses) is on the southeastern corner of the central grid, next to the Blanco supermarket.

If you're coming from McAllen and don't want to go all the way to the Reynosa bus station, you can get off at the Greyhound office on the US side of the bridge and then walk over the bridge into Reynosa. Leaving Mexico, you can walk over the bridge and pick up the bus at the same Greyhound office.

Both 1st- and 2nd-class buses run from Reynosa to almost anywhere you'd want to go in Mexico, but avoid 2nd-class buses on long trips because they're very slow. First-class lines serving Reynosa are Transportes del Norte, ADO, Ómnibus de México, Tres Estrellas de Oro, Futura, Transportes Frontera and Blanca. There's daily service from Reynosa to Mexico City, Matamoros and Monterrey, among other destinations.

Train The Reynosa train station is at the southern end of Hidalgo, six blocks from the main square. There's one slow train daily to Matamoros (scheduled departure time is 2:40 pm) and one to Monterrey (scheduled departure time is 11:25 am). Journey time is about 2½ hours to Matamoros and 5½ hours to Monterrey. First-class fare to Monterrey is US$6.

Car Hwy 336 from McAllen and US 281 from Pharr converge in Hidalgo, the small town on the US side of the border. Hidalgo has several guarded parking lots near the bridge that cost $2 a day. Because cars returning to the USA must wait, on average, for more than 40 minutes to clear inspection, it's a very good idea to leave your car in one of these lots and walk across the bridge.

In Reynosa, there's an *aduana* (customs) office on Avenida Miguel Alemán that can issue temporary car-import permits; to get there, simply turn left after clearing immigration and look for the office on the south side of the street half a block away.

Going west to Monterrey (225km), the toll Hwy 40 D is excellent; the tolls total US$15. Hwy 2, which follows the Rio Grande upstream to Nuevo Laredo and downstream to Matamoros, is not in bad shape, but it is quicker and safer to travel on the US side.

Getting Around

Battered yellow microbuses rattle around Reynosa, providing cheap but jarring transport. From the international bridge to the bus station, catch a Valley Transit coach coming from McAllen with 'Reynosa' on its front; the service is free. You can also catch the '17 Obrera' bus from Madero, which travels Canales, Aldama, Bravo and Colón; it's a slower, less comfortable way to go, and it costs US50¢. From the bus station to the center, turn right out of the main entrance, walk to the end of the block, turn right again, and catch a '17 Obrera' on the next corner (Colón at Rubio).

BENTSEN-RIO GRANDE VALLEY STATE PARK

Named in honor of longtime Texas senator and US treasury secretary Lloyd Bentsen, Dan Quayle's nemesis in the 1988 vice-presidential debates, this 587-acre park (☎ 956-585-1107) has several good trails and camping facilities. Much of the park surrounds several *resecas* – water-filled and crescent-shaped former river channels that support lush foliage.

The visitors' center at the gate has excellent trail guides to the 1½-mile Singing Chaparral Trail and the 2-mile Rio Grande Hiking Trail. There's the usual proliferation of birds, along with coyotes, tortoises and other animals. Both trail guides do a good job of pointing out the vast variety of flora. The free guide *Critters of the Bentsen-Rio Grande Valley State Park* is aimed at children, but it's filled with fun information for kids of all ages. Did you know that Mr Skunk doesn't get along with Mr Dog? So keep Fido tied up.

The park's widely spaced tent **campsites** are surrounded by thorny brush, shaded by trees, come with water faucets and cost $8 a night. **RV sites** with pull-through access for trailers and the all-important dump station cost $14 a night.

The park is open daily. The entrance fee is $2 a person. To get here, take the FM 2062 exit off Business US 83, 3 miles west of Mission. Drive south 5 miles to the park.

LOS EBANOS FERRY

This small barge (☎ 956-485-2855), the only hand-pulled ferry across the Rio Grande, carries people over an isolated section of the river west of McAllen. The ferry can carry three cars and several people on each five-minute journey.

Privately operated since 1742, the ferry doesn't really serve as a vital transportation link on this part of the Rio Grande. Most of its patrons are drawn by novelty, and as the ferry's fame has spread, it is in danger of becoming a tourist trap. The operators have erected some especially hokey 'Old West' stores near the ferry's entrance.

Still, the overlook on the bank at the entrance offers good views of the ferry, which travels as fast as the passengers can tug, and of the surrounding unspoiled countryside. You'll probably see quite a few wet clothes lying on the riverbanks. These were discarded by people who swam across illegally and then changed into dry clothes that they carried in a plastic bag. Wet clothes are a dead giveaway to border police.

The ferry operates every day 8 am to 4 pm, unless water levels are too high. Call to check. Pedestrians pay 25¢ to ride the ferry or just use the overlook, and drivers pay $1.25 plus 25¢ for each extra person. The wait on weekends for cars is usually one hour.

The tiny hamlet of Los Ebanos is 6 miles south of US 83 on FM 886. All three roads in town lead to the ferry.

Central Rio Grande

Dominated by the binational cities of Laredo and Nuevo Laredo, much of the central Rio Grande Valley away from this metropolis is arid and desolate. On little-traveled roads it's easy to feel the same sense of desolation surely felt by succeeding generations or immigrants.

LAREDO
Population 170,000

'I'd like a quarter pounder *con queso, por favor.*' This exchange, heard at a Laredo McDonald's, neatly illustrates the intermingling of American and Mexican cultures in this fast-growing city on the Rio Grande.

More than anywhere else, the effects of NAFTA can be seen in Laredo and its Mexican counterpart, Nuevo Laredo. The pair are separated by the river, but their economies are inseparable. Thousands of people commute across the border every day. Trucks bearing goods and merchandise wait in long lines to cross the bridge at the end of I-35. The sound of air horns protesting the

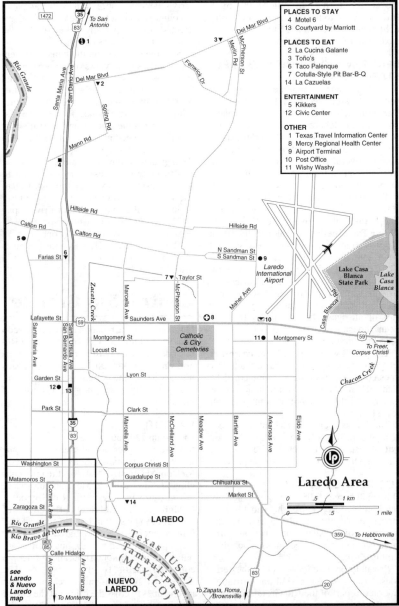

PLACES TO STAY
4 Motel 6
13 Courtyard by Marriott

PLACES TO EAT
2 La Cucina Galante
3 Toño's
6 Taco Palenque
7 Cotulla-Style Pit Bar-B-Q
14 La Cazuelas

ENTERTAINMENT
5 Kikkers
12 Civic Center

OTHER
1 Texas Travel Information Center
8 Mercy Regional Health Center
9 Airport Terminal
10 Post Office
11 Wishy Washy

delays reverberates through both cities day and night.

More than 90% of Laredo's population is of Hispanic origin, and most are bilingual. 'Spanglish,' as the linguistic mixture of Spanish and English is commonly known, is the common tongue. 'We are in danger of becoming a third culture, not Spanish, not American,' laments a local business owner who worries that Laredo and Nuevo Laredo will become an island unto themselves. But that hardly seems a concern to many. Since 1990, Laredo has been the second-fastest-growing city in Texas, with population growth of close to 7% a year. In 1996, Laredo had the highest birth rate in the United States, with 29 babies born per 1000 people, as opposed to the national average of 16 per 1000.

As you approach the center of most US cities, you pass through chronological rings of development, dating from each decade back to WWII and beyond. As you approach Laredo on I-35, you pass through this year's development, last year's development, the 1990 development and the 1980 development, and then you're in the historic downtown.

Orientation

Historic Laredo is centered in a compact area on the north bank of the Rio Grande, at International Bridges Nos 1 and 2. This is the area that is most interesting to visitors. Just west of downtown, the Rio Grande makes a sharp turn north that hems in the western edge of Laredo. The area's surging growth can be readily seen north along I-35 and east along US 59.

San Antonio is 150 miles north, Corpus Christi 140 miles east. There is very little between either of those places and Laredo.

RIO GRANDE

Laredo's Ranchers

If you talk to a Texas landowner, you'll soon realize the deep bond that many of them have with their land. This bond is exemplified by María Eugenia Guerra, who owns 1000 acres 40 miles west of Laredo. The land has been in her family for more than 200 years. Despite her work in the city – she publishes the monthly newspaper *LareDOS* – she makes the drive home every night, because she couldn't imagine living anywhere else.

'My family's history is tied to the area,' she says. 'My great-grandparents held onto the land during the revolutions, and it would be painful and excruciating to sell it off.' Guerra has seen the pain other families experienced when they sold their land. 'For many, it is the glue that holds the family together.' However, she notes that it is very difficult to make a profit from the local ranches, which are typically 1000 to 2000 acres.

'To make money from cattle, you need a much larger operation for the economy of scale,' she says, noting that she has cattle on her land mostly for tradition's sake. 'Most people have to work a cash job in town.'

Many ranchers make a substantial part of their livelihood by allowing deer hunters onto their lands for a hefty price. Others have resorted to subdividing their lands for housing. 'There's nothing sadder than to see somebody have to sell chunks of their land for mobile homes,' says Guerra. Worse, she says, are the ranchers who build *colonias*, the barely legal slums for immigrants that are hidden in the hills around Laredo.

Guerra is familiar with every square yard on her ranch, she says, having walked it her entire life. For her, one of the greatest pleasures she gets from ranch life is also the simplest: 'At night you can't hear a thing. The absolute and total silence is majestic.

'People who haven't experienced it, can't understand it.'

Information

Immigration US border posts are at the north ends of International Bridges Nos 1 and 2.

Tourist Offices The Laredo Convention & Visitors Bureau (☎ 956-795-2200, 800-361-3360), 501 San Augustín Ave at Lincoln St, is very friendly and has information for both sides of the border. The office is open weekdays 8 am to 5 pm and Saturday 9 am to 5 pm.

The state has a Texas Travel Information Center (☎ 956-722-8119) along I-35, 6 miles north of the border. It has a huge amount of information on regional and statewide attractions. It's open daily 8 am to 5 pm.

There's a Mexican consulate in town; see the Facts for the Visitor chapter.

Post The main branch of the post office (☎ 956-723-2043) is at 2700 Saunders Ave (US 59). Counters are open weekdays from 7:30 am to 6 pm and Saturday from 8:30 am to 1:30 pm.

Media The *Laredo Morning Times* (50¢) is a sleepy small-town newspaper that hasn't kept pace with the area's growth. Regional papers from large Texas cities and national papers are available. *LareDOS* (free) is a feisty independent monthly newspaper that concentrates on Laredo politics and culture. *Alarma!* (75¢) is a wildly popular Spanish-language supermarket weekly sold throughout Texas and Mexico. Its stories and photos are a lurid mix of true crime and the peccadilloes of the famous.

Laundry The coin laundry closest to downtown is Wishy Washy (☎ 956-728-0844), 3504 Arkansas Ave at Montgomery St, two blocks south of Saunders Ave (US 59). Its machines will decisively clean your clothes for $2 a load, including drying. Open daily 8 am to 7 pm.

Medical Services Mercy Regional Health Center (☎ 956-718-6222) opened a huge new facility in March 1999 at 1700 Saunders Ave (US 59) and Meadow Ave. The center has a 24-hour emergency room and several outpatient clinics.

Dangers & Annoyances Most of your health worries in the Laredo area should concern water. In Mexico, don't drink it. On the border, don't swim in it. The Rio Grande is horribly polluted (Immigration and Naturalization Service police are even forbidden to pursue people into the water). In Laredo, drink plenty of it, because of the heat: the average high temperature in August is 100°F. Away from Laredo, carry plenty of it. This last warning also goes for gas – fill up before you leave. All the roads leading away from town travel through desolate territory for 50 miles or more in each direction.

The region's fast-growing population includes a few people who see petty crime as a means of survival. Follow all the usual precautions – keep valuables hidden and purses and wallets guarded on both sides of the border. In Nuevo Laredo at night, be wary of walking down dark streets away from the tourist area.

San Augustín Plaza

Parts of this plaza, the oldest in town, date from 1767. The streets surrounding it are cobblestoned and lined with ancient oaks where you can escape the sun. Pick up a copy of the brochure *Heritage Walking Tour of Historic Laredo* at the Convention & Visitors Bureau or at area hotels for details about buildings throughout the downtown.

San Augustín Church This is the third church that has stood on this site at the east end of the plaza. Vaguely Gothic-revival, the thick whitewashed walls were erected in 1872. The decoration inside and out is very simple. It hops with large traditional weddings all weekend long.

Republic of the Rio Grande Museum Housed in the 1840 home of the short-lived Republic of the Rio Grande, the museum (☎ 956-727-0977), 1003 Zaragoza St, has an excellent collection of items from the period. It's open Tuesday to Saturday 9 am to 4 pm and Sunday 1 to 4 pm; admission is free.

The museum also operates **Heritage Trolley Tours**, which are narrated two-hour tours of the historic center of Laredo on an air-conditioned bus made to look like a trolley. This is a great way to learn about the city's long history. The actual ages of many of the buildings on the tour have only recently been determined. Tours leave from the museum during its opening hours; $8 adults, $4 children.

Downtown Area
Laredo has scores of stores within a few blocks of International Bridge No 1. A busy trade shuttles back and forth between these places and their counterparts in Nuevo Laredo, depending on where the price for a particular item is cheapest at the moment. One week, cooking oil is cheaper on the Mexican side; the next, it's cheaper in the USA. In an effort to avoid customs charges, many people strip the boxes off their purchases, feeding a small cottage industry of box recyclers.

The **River Drive Mall** (☎ 956-724-8241), 1600 Water St, two blocks west of Convent Ave and International Bridge No 1, has dozens of independent and chain stores, including a JC Penney department store. It is very popular with Mexican families, who shop in their best clothes on Sunday. It's open daily 9 am to 9 pm.

The view from **International Bridge No 1** is an attraction in itself. To the west, trains creep across one of the busiest railroad bridges in the USA, and to the east, trucks creep across International Bridge No 2. Below you can see the dubious waters of the Rio Grande. Right along its US bank is the American authorities' main inspection point. Watching the drug-sniffing dogs set loose upon an ancient pickup filled with piñatas is a show in itself.

Special Events
Held in mid-February, George Washington's Birthday Celebration (☎ 956-722-9895, 800-361-3360) is a huge cross-border series of festivals and parties that lasts for 10 days around Washington's birthday. Although old George never heard of Los Dos Laredos, he might

have approved of the pageants, parades, outdoor concerts, dances and many other events. Anyone can compete for the title of 'King Chili' in the jalapeño-eating contest.

Places to Stay
Camping *Lake Casa Blanca State Park* (☎ 956-725-3826) is a large lake and park on the north side of US 59, just past the airport. There are some trees for shade and a bit of a beach, but the real attraction here is the swimming pool. Tent sites are $8; those with electricity are $12. Entrance to the park is $2 each for those older than 12.

Motels & Hotels Most of Laredo's lodgings are along I-35, an inconvenient distance from downtown. A *Motel 6* (☎ 956-722-8133), 5920 San Bernardo Ave, at I-35 exit 4, has rooms that are better than the chain's usual standard for $48/51 single/double. Two miles north of downtown, the fairly new *Courtyard by Marriott* (☎ 956-725-5555), 2410 Santa Ursula Ave, at I-35 exit 3, has several amenities such as a health club and whirlpool (after a day touring in 100°F weather, there's nothing like relaxing in a vat of boiling water). Rooms cost $89 on weekdays, $69 on weekends, although they may have specials. Ask.

Far and away the best choice in Laredo, if your budget allows, is *La Posada Hotel & Suites* (☎ 956-722-1701), 1000 Zaragoza St on San Augustín Plaza. The hacienda-style hotel is in a complex of buildings built in 1916 that were originally a high school. The comfy rooms now surround large pools and flowering plants. The deeply shaded verandahs are a world away from the city bustle just outside. Some rooms have patios overlooking the action of the river and border area. Rates range from $99 to $169, depending on the size of the room and its location in the hotel. There are frequent specials, however, when the rates may be as low as $69. This is one of the nicest independent hotels in southern Texas.

Places to Eat
During the day, numerous street vendors ply the streets of Laredo, offering tacos, ice cream

RIO GRANDE

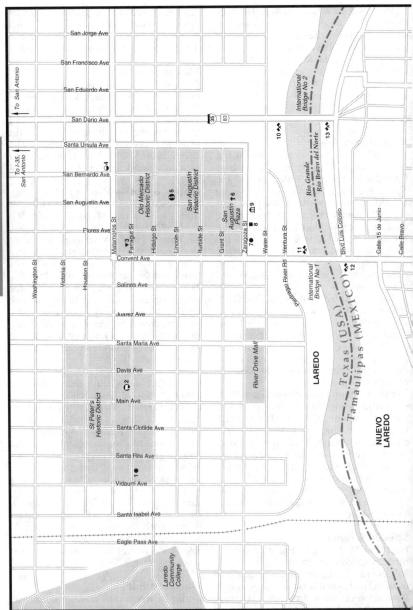

RIO GRANDE

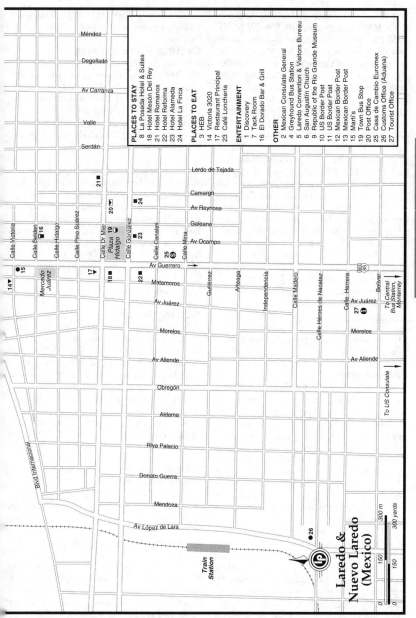

PLACES TO STAY
8   La Posada Hotel & Suites
18 Hotel Mesón Del Rey
21 Hotel Romanos
22 Hotel Reforma
23 Hotel Alameda
24 Hotel La Finca

PLACES TO EAT
3   HEB
14 Victoria 3020
17 Restaurant Principal
23 Café Lonchería

ENTERTAINMENT
1   Discovery
7   Tack Room
16 El Dorado Bar & Grill

OTHER
2   Mexican Consulate General
4   Greyhound Bus Station
5   Laredo Convention & Visitors Bureau
6   San Augustin Church
9   Republic of the Rio Grande Museum
10 US Border Post
11 US Border Post
12 Mexican Border Post
13 Mexican Border Post
15 Marti's
19 Town Bus Stop
20 Post Office
25 Casa de Cambio Euromex
26 Customs Office (Aduana)
27 Tourist Office

Laredo &
Nuevo Laredo (Mexico)

and other cart-distributed treats. A downtown *HEB* supermarket (☎ 956-791-3571), 1002 Farragut St, is packed morning, noon and night and is one of the busiest in the entire chain. *Las Cazuelas* (☎ 956-723-3693), 303 Market St, serves breakfast and lunch until 2 pm daily. Try the avocado taco ($2) or one of the fresh soups. A Laredo institution, the pepper-filled 'Mariachi' breakfast taco ($3), is said to have originated here.

Cotulla-Style Pit Bar-B-Q (☎ 956-724-5747), 4502 McPherson St between US 59 and Calton Rd, has extra-spicy smoked meats and some winning fajitas ($5). You can get your Mariachis two dozen different ways. It's open for breakfast and lunch. *Taco Palenque* (☎ 956-725-9898), 4515 San Bernardo Ave, one block west of I-35, is open 24 hours a day, which leaves you to determine when it's early enough to order a Mariachi.

The kind of Mexican food you've never had but may have dreamed about is standard fare at *Toño's* (☎ 956-717-4999), 1202 E Del Mar Blvd, 2 miles east of I-35. Antonio Savignon combines classic ingredients such as cilantro and tomatillos into surprising creations that average $8 to $12. The marinated filet may be the finest steak you'll ever have.

Entertainment

Tejano music is big in Laredo; you'll have a hard time finding much else on the radio. Several clubs feature Tejano bands. *Kikkers* (☎ 956-791-7019), 5100 Santa Maria Ave, has both live Tejano and country and western on Friday and Saturday. Laredo's *Civic Center* (☎ 956-722-8143), 2400 San Bernardo Ave, has frequent live appearances by some of the better regional bands. *Discovery* (☎ 956-722-9032), 2019 Farragut St, is a mixed gay bar and dance club that also plays plenty of Tejano.

Although it is owned by La Posada Hotel & Suites, the *Tack Room* (☎ 956-722-1701) is in a separate building just west of the main entrance at 1000 Zaragoza St. The building was the town's turn-of-the-20th-century telephone exchange. Its classy old bar is staffed by bartenders who remember the drink preferences of the local movers and shakers who gather after work. The warm and spicy peanuts are a treat.

Getting There & Away

Air Laredo International Airport (☎ 956-795-2000) has commuter service from American Eagle (☎ 800-712-9431) and Continental Express (☎ 956-723-3402) to and from their respective hubs at Dallas-Fort Worth and Houston. The airport's new terminal can be reached by taking Calton Rd from I-35 and Maher Ave from US 59.

Bus Greyhound (☎ 956-723-4324) has a convenient station downtown at 801 San Bernardo Ave. There is hourly service to San Antonio (three hours) for $15 and 15 trips a day to Houston (seven hours) for $29. Greyhound and its affiliate Valley Transit each make one trip a day down the Rio Grande Valley to Brownsville (six hours) for $24. You can get buses to Mexico from the station as well, but it is both cheaper and quicker to leave from Nuevo Laredo (see below).

Getting Around

All the major car-rental firms are represented at the airport, including Avis (☎ 956-722-1533), Hertz (☎ 956-791-8732) and National (☎ 956-722-2561). However, most rental-car contracts specifically forbid you to take the car into Mexico.

Taxis from the airport to downtown and from downtown to Nuevo Laredo can run $15. Numerous companies dispatch cabs, including ABC Taxi (☎ 956-722-7479) and Yellow Cab (☎ 956-723-8285).

NUEVO LAREDO (MEXICO)
Population 450,000
☎ 87 within Mexico, 011-52-87 from Texas

Nuevo Laredo now collects more in tariffs and customs revenue than any other Mexican port of entry. It also has more than 60 maquiladoras producing goods for the US market.

More foreign tourists enter Mexico through Nuevo Laredo than any other town on the northeast border. The town has a charming urban character, and it is very close to Laredo; just a pair of bridges over the Rio Grande separate the two. A visit to Nuevo Laredo should be at the top of your list of things to do in the area.

Nuevo Laredo has many restaurants, bars and souvenir shops catering to day-trippers from the USA – most accept US currency and quote prices in dollars. Many Mexican travelers pass through, too. The town has a fair selection of budget places to stay and eat, and numerous dental offices cater to cavity-prone Americans looking for a cheap filling. One of the most disreputable touts we encountered sidled up to us and made the following eminently refusable offer: 'Hey, mister, need a dentist?'

Two international bridges cross the Rio Grande to Laredo, Texas. From that city, I-35 goes north to San Antonio. A third crosses the border 20km to the northwest, enabling motorists in a hurry to bypass Laredo and Nuevo Laredo altogether. An excellent road runs south to Monterrey, which has good connections with central Mexico and the east and west coasts.

Orientation

Walking is the best way to reach Nuevo Laredo from the USA (see Getting There & Away, for details). Two international bridges carry vehicles and pedestrians between the two Laredos. International Bridge (Puente Internacional) No 1 is the one to use if you're heading into Mexico. You can get a tourist card at the immigration office at its southern end, but you have to go to the *aduana* (customs) office in town, on Avenida López de Lara, to get a vehicle permit. This bridge brings you into Mexico at the north end of Avenida Guerrero, Nuevo Laredo's main street, which stretches for 2km (one-way going south). If you're heading north, look for the signs directing traffic around the western side of the city, via Avenida López de Lara, to International Bridge No 1.

International Bridge No 2 is for those who don't need a tourist card, and it is often used by heavy vehicles. It is at the very end of I-35, which begins 1588 miles north in Duluth, Minnesota.

The city's center spreads out along both sides of Avenida Guerrero for the first mile

south of International Bridge No 1. The main plaza, with a kiosk in its middle, the Palacio de Gobierno on its east side, and a few hotels and restaurants surrounding it, is on Avenida Guerrero seven blocks south of the bridge.

Street addresses on Avenida Guerrero indicate how far they are from the bridge: No 109 is in the block nearest the bridge, No 509 is in the fifth block south and so on. Addresses on other north-south streets, which are parallel to Avenida Guerrero, are numbered in the same way.

Nuevo Laredo's Central Camionera, the arrival and departure point for long-distance buses, is a long way away, on the southern side of town. Local buses run between the bus station, the town center and the international bridges.

Information

See the Getting There & Away chapter for detailed information about crossing into Mexico from the USA.

Tourist Offices A tourist office (☎ 87-12-01-04) at the corner of Calle Herrera and Avenida Juárez is open daily 8 am to 8 pm. Its staff are friendly and have brochures, but few employees speak English. The Laredo Convention & Visitors Bureau (see the Laredo section, above) has a lot of material about restaurants, shopping and sights in Nuevo Laredo.

Consulates A US Consulate (☎ 87-14-05-12) is at Avenida Allende 3330, near the corner of Calle Nayarit, on the south side of town. It doesn't issue US visas. It's open weekdays 8 am to 12:30 pm and 1:30 to 5 pm, but US citizens needing after-hours emergency assistance can call a Laredo number (dial ☎ 1-95 for international access from Mexico, then ☎ 210-727-9661).

Money There's a Casa de Cambio Euromex on Guerrero between Canales and Mina. Most casas de cambio do not change traveler's checks, but most businesses accept them if you want to make a purchase, and the main Mexican banks should change them. Most businesses within a few miles of the border crossing accept dollars, but the exchange rate can be low. Many tourist-frequented places also accept credit cards. Be sure you get your carbon and that the charge slip doesn't list improper charges – note especially that the symbols for American and Mexican currency are the same ($), so be certain that all prices are labeled US$, not just $.

Special Events

Nuevo Laredo holds EXPOMEX, an agricultural, livestock, industrial and cultural fair, during the second week of September. It even includes a circus.

Places to Stay

Hotel Romanos (☎ 87-12-23-91), at Calle Dr Mier 2434, just east of the plaza, is the least expensive decent place in town, with clean, air-con rooms at US$12/14 single/double; TV costs extra. Slightly cleaner and more comfortable air-con rooms are available at *Hotel La Finca* (☎ 87-12-88-83), at the corner of Calle González and Avenida Reynosa, for US$14/16.

There are no standouts among the mid-range hotels, but as the quality of rooms within each hotel varies, it's wise to ask to see at least two rooms before registering. *Hotel Mesón Del Rey* (☎ 87-12-63-60), Avenida Guerrero 718 on the main plaza, has all the amenities and is comfortable and quite a good value at US$21/23. *Hotel Reforma* (☎ 87-12-62-50), on Avenida Guerrero a half block north of Calle Canales, has bright, clean, air-con rooms with color TVs, phones and firm mattresses for US$22/26. *Hotel Alameda* (☎ 87-12-50-50), at Calle González 2715, has similar rooms (though softer beds) for the same price.

There are nicer, pricier motels on the highway heading south, but if you want this sort of lodging, you'd do better in Laredo, on the US side.

Places to Eat

There are lots of eating possibilities, though the places lining the first few blocks of Avenida Guerrero south of the bridge are filled with tourists eating at high tourist prices. The side streets have cheaper restaurants less geared to the tourist trade, and the tourist eateries offer better value as you go farther south.

One of the first attractive-looking places is *Restaurant Principal*, Avenida Guerrero 624, with a substantial Mexican menu with antojitos around US$4 and meat dishes from US$3.50; cabrito (roast young goat) costs about US$7.

Victoria 3020 (☎ 87-13-30-20) is one of the nicest restaurants on this side of the border and specializes in elegantly prepared regional Mexican cuisine for about US$10 per person. It is at the corner of Calles Matamoros and Victoria, two blocks south and one block west of International Bridge No 1.

On the south side of the plaza, on the corner of Avenida Ocampo and Calle González, is a small, cozy, family-run place, fairly clean and not too expensive. It is the *Café Lonchería*, and the menu includes fish (US$3 to US$5) and soups and breakfasts (about US$2.50). It's open 7 am to midnight.

Two places very popular with locals lie a half mile or so down Avenida Guerrero from the international bridge. At Avenida Guerrero 2114, between Calles Venezuela and Lincoln, *El Rancho* is a not-so-poor person's taco-and-beer hall, offering a long list of different types of tacos. *Río Mar*, Avenida Guerrero 2403, is packed at night with people gobbling mouth-watering seafood dishes starting at around US$4.

Entertainment

On and around Avenida Guerrero, bars happy to pour tequila drinks for visitors from the USA are as common as cheap tacos. A decent margarita should not cost more than about $2.

If you want to plunge into the swirling cross-border social scene, visit the famous *El Dorado Bar & Grill* (☎ 87-12-00-15), at the corner of Calle Belden and Avenida Ocampo. It has enclosed parking, but you shouldn't drive after an evening here. To reach it, go three blocks south of International Bridge No 1 on Avenida Guerrero, and then left one block on Calle Belden. On weekend nights, the place is jammed with young professionals from both Mexico and the USA, and at any given table half the people live on one side of the border and half on the other. Spanish is the language of choice. This is an excellent place to see the area's unique cross-border culture at its raucous best. The house drink is the Ramos gin fizz (US$3), but most people have beer and margaritas.

Spectator Sports

The city's horse and greyhound racing venue, the *Hipódromo-Galgódromo*, is closed and doesn't appear likely to reopen. However, gamblers can place off-track bets and watch US and Mexican sports on satellite TV at the *Turf Club*, at the intersection of Calle Bravo and Avenida Ocampo.

Two or three bullfights are held each month at the *Plaza de Toros*, Avenida Monterrey 4101 near Calle Anáhuac. Admission ranges from US$6 to US$8. For dates and times, call ☎ 87-12-71-92 in Mexico or ☎ 888-240-8460 in the USA.

Shopping

If you're just setting out, the less you buy the better. But if you're on your way home, it's worth browsing around some of the shops and markets for the odd souvenir.

There's a crafts market on the east side of Avenida Guerrero, half a block north of the main plaza. El Mercado, on the west side of Avenida Guerrero, half a block south of Calle Hidalgo, is a large two-story market where you can buy everything from pastries to blankets to saddles. At the small Mercado Juárez, on the west side of Avenida Guerrero, between Calles Hidalgo and Belden, lots of handicrafts are mixed in with a lot of stuff best described as cheap junk. At all of these places, prices are a bit higher than in places farther south, but not outrageously so, and with a bit of bargaining and cash payment, you may get 10% to 20% off the asking price.

Marti's (☎ 87-12-31-37), at Avenida Guerrero and Calle Victoria, is the high-class department store of the street. It is rich with things for the rich, including tapestries, silk, antiques and crystal.

Getting There & Away

Walking is the best way to reach Nuevo Laredo from the USA. International Bridge No 1 begins right at the end of Convent Ave, two blocks from San Augustín Plaza. Pedestrians pay US35¢ going to Mexico and US25¢ returning to the USA. The walk takes about five minutes, and you arrive right at Avenida Guerrero. You can park your car in Laredo in a free city lot below the bridge at Salinas Ave and Water St. International Bridge No 2 is only open to vehicles.

Bus Buses from the Laredo Greyhound station (☎ 956-723-4324), 801 San Bernardo Ave, run directly to cities in Mexico, including San Luis Potosí, Querétaro and Mexico City, but these are more expensive than services from Nuevo Laredo. You can sometimes use these buses to go between the Laredo and Nuevo Laredo bus stations, but you have to ask the driver – it's easier to just walk over the international bridge.

Nuevo Laredo's bus station, the Central Camionera, is 2 miles from International Bridge No 1, on Avenida Ocampo between Calles 15 de Septiembre and Anáhuac on the south side of town. It has a left-luggage section and restaurant. First- and 2nd-class buses serve every city in the northern half of Mexico. The main companies providing 1st-class services here are Futura and Ómnibus de México. For longer trips, 2nd-class buses are slow and not recommended.

Car Drivers can cross on both International Bridges No 1 and No 2. To Mexico, the bridge toll is US$1. To the USA, the toll is US$1.40. Parking may be difficult once across the border because the streets are very crowded.

For a vehicle permit, you have to go to the customs office. To get there, drive about 14 blocks south on Avenida Guerrero, turn right at Calle Héroes de Nacataz and then go about eight blocks west to the corner of Avenida López de Lara, where you'll see the agency on the right. The office is always open and should issue a permit without hassle if your papers are in order. To avoid a fine, don't forget to cancel the permit when you leave Mexico.

RIO GRANDE

The route via Monterrey is the most direct way to central Mexico, the Pacific Coast and/or the Gulf Coast. An excellent toll road, Hwy 85D, goes south to Monterrey. It's fast but expensive (tolls total US$15). The alternative free road is longer, rougher and slower. Hwy 2 is a rural road that follows the Rio Grande to Reynosa and Matamoros.

Getting Around

Frequent city buses (US40¢) make getting around Nuevo Laredo simple enough. The easiest place to catch them is on the east side of the plaza, where all the buses seem to pass. Bus No 51 goes from the plaza to the bus station, but you may be able to catch a bus from a point closer to the bridge. From the bus station, local buses run into town. A taxi from the bus station to the bridge will cost about US$2.75. There are lines of taxis at International Bridge No 1. Agree on a price before you get in.

AROUND LAREDO

The miles of semiarid scrub that surround Laredo have a certain desolate beauty. **San Ygnacio**, 30 miles southeast on US 83, was founded as a ranching outpost in 1830. Time stands still on its oak-shaded central square, dominated by Our Lady of Refuge Church (1875). In town, La Paz Museum (☎ 956-765-4483), at the corner of Morales and Matamoros Sts, is in a 200-year-old house and has photos of Zapata (the revolutionary) and bits of old ranch gear. It is open only by appointment.

Zapata

Named for Emiliano Zapata, land reformer and freedom fighter during the Mexican Revolution (1911-17), this town is a quiet place mostly of interest to people in need of gasoline. Its best sight is the view of the Rio Grande Valley from a scenic overlook on US 83, 6 miles west of town. The view is of an archetypal Western landscape, complete with mesas on the horizon.

Zapata capitalizes on its proximity to Falcon International Reservoir, as the following two listings attest. The **Bass Lake**

Sundome Motel (☎ 956-765-4352), 2 miles southeast of Zapata, just off US 83 at the bridge over the reservoir inlet, would do Buckminster Fuller proud with its unusual domed units that rent for $30/35 single/double. It also has RV sites for $15. **Best Western Inn by the Lake** (☎ 956-765-8403), a half mile southeast of town on US 83, has a small pool and modest rooms for $54.

Falcon International Reservoir

Stretching from north of Zapata to Falcon Heights, this 136-sq-mile lake was formed by the Falcon Dam (1953) on the Rio Grande. The 500-acre **Falcon State Park** (☎ 956-848-5327), 3 miles west of US 83 off FM 2098, lines the US side of the lake, which is very popular for fishing. The land is mostly covered by cactus and shrubs, so there are shaded shelters and picnic areas. The lack of any swimming facilities should tell you what the authorities think of the lake's water quality.

There is a fully equipped *campground*. Rates are $6 for basic tent sites, $12 for those with water and electricity, and $14 for full hookups.

If you have a 4WD vehicle, you can cross the dam into Mexico and follow Hwy 2 north 30 miles to a rough dirt road that leads to the evocative ruins of **Ciudad Guerrero Viejo**. The once-beautiful town of 4000, dating to 1750, was destroyed during the reservoir construction. As you drive to the town, you'll pass through several private ranches, and gates blocking the dirt road are locked daily at 6 pm. The Texas Historical Commission (☎ 512-463-6100) in Austin has information on the town and is part of a binational effort to preserve its remains.

Roma
Population 8,438

Unlike neighboring Rio Grande City, Roma has actively preserved its heritage. Now somebody just has to pay a visit. The downtown, one block south of US 83, was designated a National Historic Landmark and is such a perfect representation of an early-1900s border town that the 1952 movie *Viva Zapata* was filmed here.

Many of the finely crafted brick buildings are the work of Heinrich Portscheller, a German-born mason who established a brickyard in Roma in 1883. His artistically molded brick survives today in buildings such as the 1884 **Manuel Guerra Store**, a dignified two-story building at Convent and Portscheller Sts. The 1853 **Noah Cox House**, one block south of Portscheller St on Convent St, has a charming cupola.

Several state agencies have been quietly paying for the restoration of historic Roma, and the results are well worth the cost. Displays in a city permit office at the southeast corner of Convent and Hidalgo Sts, open weekdays 8:30 am to 4 pm, document the careful work being performed. The Roma Historical Museum (☎ 956-849-1555), at Estrella and Lincoln Sts, is usually closed, but a call may coax someone to open the doors for you. Staff at the Roma Restoration Project (☎ 956-849-9092) answer the phone sporadically because they are busy doing the work their name implies. But craftspeople often can be found working on one building or another near Convent St, and they enjoy talking to people.

What's most interesting about Roma is that its remote location on the border has kept it almost tourist-free. The streets and the buildings in the six blocks around Convent, Lincoln and Hidalgo Sts are very quiet and almost business-free. An overlook provides a good view of the Rio Grande and Ciudad Miguel Alemán, a scruffy Mexican border town festooned with radio towers. Take a quick listen to the AM band on your car radio – it's jammed with Mexican stations.

Rio Grande City
Population 5000

A small town 52 miles west of McAllen in arid Starr County, Rio Grande City regularly makes the area news because the surrounding desolate territory is often used by drug smugglers and there are frequent raids by law enforcement agencies. Next to the courthouse at 2nd and Britton Sts stands the incongruous **Our Lady of Lourdes Grotto**, built in 1928 by a German

priest, a replica of the real thing in France. Unlike the original, however, this grotto is decorated with cactus plants. It has been a shrine for local pilgrims.

The town was once a busy trading center, and several brick buildings dating from the 19th century rot in the sun around town. One of the few that have been restored is *La Borde House* (☎ 956-487-5101), 601 E Main St, a restored 1893 villa that was designed by a French architect. It has a very pleasant and shady courtyard and a small restaurant serving Mexican food. Rooms filled with period furniture cost $60. Just off the courtyard, the Starr County Industrial Foundation (☎ 956-487-2709) has an excellent illustrated map on the county's historic buildings. The foundation keeps erratic hours, but you can get a copy of the map inside the hotel.

EAGLE PASS
Population 27,600

Eagle Pass may be the most Mexican town in the USA. About 97% of its residents are of Mexican origin, and Spanish is spoken far more often than English. In fact, the main reason most travelers come to Eagle Pass is to get to its sister city – Piedras Negras in Mexico – and beyond. By a slim 10-mile margin over Laredo, Eagle Pass is the closest Mexican border crossing to San Antonio.

No road parallels the Rio Grande between Laredo and Eagle Pass, so travelers must make the 124-mile journey via US 83 and US 277. From Eagle Pass, Del Rio is another 55 miles north on US 277, and San Antonio is 142 miles away via US 57 to I-35. Eagle Pass is 265 miles from Saltillo, capital of the Mexican state of Coahuila.

Orientation

Eagle Pass is a small city and easy to get around. US 277 and US 57 become Main St in town. Garrison St and the bridge to Piedras Negras are two blocks south of Main St. From the downtown area, US 277 swings north along Ceylon St (an area of beautiful homes), 2nd St and Del Rio Blvd. Highway Blvd, which is also known as the

RIO GRANDE

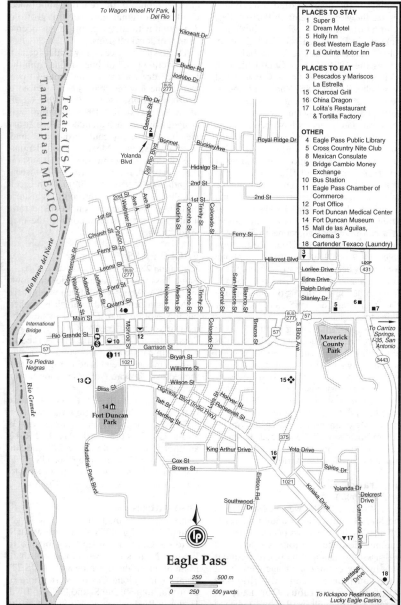

To Wagon Wheel RV Park,
Del Rio

Killowatt Dr

Texas (USA)

Tamaulipas (MEXICO)

Rio Bravo del Norte

Butler Rd

Jodobo Dr

Rio Dr

George Blvd

BUS 277

Bonnet

Yolanda Blvd

Buckley Ave

Royal Ridge Dr

Hidalgo St

2nd St

2nd St

2nd St

1st St

Medina St

Concho St

Trinity St

Colorado St

Ferry St

Del Rio Blvd

2nd St

Webster St

Ave A

Ave B

1st St

Church St

Ceylon St

Ferry St

Leona St

BUS 277

San Marcos St

Blanco St

Hillcrest Blvd

3

LOOP 431

Lorilee Drive

Edna Drive

Ralph Drive

Stanley Dr

5   6   7

Commerce St

Washington St

Adams St

Jefferson St

Ford St

Quarry St

4

Nueces St

Medina St

Concho St

Trinity St

Comal St

Colorado St

Brazos St

BUS 277

57

57

S Bibb Ave

Maverick County Park

To Carrizo Springs, I-35, San Antonio

3443

International Bridge

57

Main St

Rio Grande St

8

10

12

Monroe St

Garrison St

9

11

1021

Bryan St

Williams St

Wilson St

Highway Blvd (Indio Hwy)

Hoover St

S Roosevelt St

15

To Piedras Negras

Rio Grande

13

Bliss St

14

Fort Duncan Park

Taft St

Harding St

Industrial Park Blvd

375

King Arthur Drive

Cox St

Brown St

16

Yota Drive

Spies Dr

Eidson Rd

1021

Southwood Dr

Kirasa Drive

Yolanda Dr

Delcrest Drive

Camarinos Drive

17

Eagle Pass

18

Heritage Drive

To Kickapoo Reservation,
Lucky Eagle Casino

0   250   500 m
0   250   500 yards

PLACES TO STAY
1 Super 8
2 Dream Motel
5 Holly Inn
6 Best Western Eagle Pass
7 La Quinta Motor Inn

PLACES TO EAT
3 Pescados y Mariscos
   La Estrella
15 Charcoal Grill
16 China Dragon
17 Lolita's Restaurant
   & Tortilla Factory

OTHER
4 Eagle Pass Public Library
5 Cross Country Nite Club
8 Mexican Consulate
9 Bridge Cambio Money
   Exchange
10 Bus Station
11 Eagle Pass Chamber of
   Commerce
12 Post Office
13 Fort Duncan Medical Center
14 Fort Duncan Museum
15 Mall de las Aguilas,
   Cinema 3
18 Cartender Texaco (Laundry)

Indio Hwy or FM 1021, runs southeast toward the Kickapoo reservation.

Information
Tourist Offices The Eagle Pass Chamber of Commerce (☎ 830-773-3224), 400 Garrison St, has information on both its own city and Piedras Negras. Ask for a copy of its map, which includes both cities.

There's a Mexican consulate in town; see the Facts for the Visitor chapter.

Money There is no need to change United States currency into Mexican pesos or vice versa, because both are accepted on both sides of the border. But if you need to convert cash for trips farther afield in Mexico, several currency exchanges operating near both sides of the international bridge will fit the bill, including Bridge Cambio Money Exchange (☎ 830-773-1225), 124 N Adams St. It's open Monday to Saturday 8 am to 6 pm and Sunday 10 am to 4 pm. Locals say exchange rates are similar on either side of the border.

Post The post office (☎ 830-773-3210) is at 757 E Rio Grande St.

Media *Zocalo*, a daily out of Piedras Negras, is available for 50¢ on Eagle Pass newsstands. Three weekly newspapers serve Eagle Pass itself: the *News Gram*, *Southwest Times* and the *News-Guide*. For regional entertainment and lifestyle news, pick up a copy of the *Interviewer*.

Tejano rules the airwaves here; popular stations include KEPS (1270 AM) and Radio La Rancherita (580 AM). For country, tune to KINL (93 FM).

Bookstores Waldenbooks (☎ 830-757-0131), in the Mall de las Aguilas, across from the airport at 455 S Bibb Ave, is the only general bookstore in town.

Libraries The Eagle Pass Public Library (☎ 830-773-2516) is at 589 Main St.

Laundry The Cartender Texaco service station (☎ 830-757-6996), 1989 FM 3443, has one of the nicest self-service laundries in town, open daily 7 am to 11 pm.

Medical Services Fort Duncan Medical Center (☎ 830-773-5321), 350 S Adams St, is the hospital in Eagle Pass.

Fort Duncan Museum
For centuries, the favored crossing of the Rio Grande in this area was 30 miles south of present-day Eagle Pass at Guerrero, Coahuila – a route used by everyone from 17th-century Spanish explorers to Antonio López de Santa Anna as he led his troops to the Alamo. After the Texas Revolution, the Mexican government prohibited direct trade with Texans, but Mexican villagers near the Rio Grande continued to use a clandestine road that ran north of the old San Antonio Rd, crossing the river near what was called Paso del Águila (Eagle Pass) for the many eagles' nests perched in the nearby pecan trees. The US Army established Fort Duncan at the Paso del Águila in 1849 to protect emigrants heading west in the California gold rush, as well as the flow of trade from Mexico.

Lone Star

One of Eagle Pass' most prominent claims to fame is that it was the stand-in for the fictional town of Frontera in *Lone Star*, which made many film critics' Top 10 lists in 1996. Directed by John Sayles and starring Chris Cooper, Kris Kristofferson, Elizabeth Peña and Matthew McConaughey, *Lone Star* has currents of mystery and romance, but it is also a fascinating study of how cultural lines have blurred along the Tex-Mex border. In fact, if you're looking for a primer on how Anglos and Mexicans have made lives together along the Rio Grande, this movie fits the bill. Much of it was filmed in and around Eagle Pass; locations included the Maverick County Courthouse lawn and Big O's, a roadhouse bar out on the Indio Hwy.

The Fort Duncan Museum (☎ 830-773-1714), housed in the old fort headquarters building, has exhibits and artifacts from the Spanish colonial period through the early 20th century. It's open Monday to Saturday 1 to 5 pm; there is no admission fee, but donations are accepted. The museum is in Fort Duncan Park, which also has a nine-hole golf course, playground and picnic areas. It's just south of downtown along Bliss St.

Maverick County Park

On the southeast side of town, this park (☎ 830-773-3824) has a lake stocked with catfish, along with picnic areas and a new playground. This is also the site of Eagle Pass' annual Fourth of July celebration.

Lucky Eagle Casino

Operated by the Kickapoo Traditional Tribe of Texas, Lucky Eagle Casino (☎ 830-758-1936, 888-255-8259) is a rather spare operation that began in 1996. Attractions include a poker room, video gaming machines and bingo. The casino is open Wednesday and Thursday 1 pm to 4 am, and continuously between Friday at 1 pm and Monday at 4 am. Bingo sessions take place Wednesday to Sunday at 7:30 pm, with extra sessions Saturday and Sunday at 4:30 pm. The small Kickapoo Kafé serves a limited menu, mostly sandwiches ($2 to $5). To reach the casino from Eagle Pass, take FM 1021 (the Indio Hwy) to Rosita Valley Rd. Turn west (right) and follow the signs. It's about 4 miles from the Eagle Pass city limits.

Special Events

Eagle Pass and Piedras Negras team up for an International Friendship Festival the last weekend in March. A Nachos Festival happens in mid-October in Piedras Negras, which claims to be the birthplace of the popular cheese-topped tortilla-chip snack.

Places to Stay

Camping There's no official campground at **Maverick County Park** (see above), but self-contained RVs can pull in and camp free for the night. North of Eagle Pass, **Wagon Wheel RV Park** (☎ 830-758-1973) has $12 hookup sites and a restaurant on the west side of US 277, a half mile south of FM 1588.

Motels The **Dream Motel** (☎ 830-773-6990), 1395 Del Rio Blvd, has rooms for $30/40 single/double. The **Holly Inn** (☎ 830-773-9261, 800-424-8125), 2421 E Main St, has singles/doubles for $38/54 ($32/47 for seniors). A pool, restaurant and the Cross Country Nite Club are on the premises. **Super 8** (☎ 830-773-9531, 800-272-9786, fax 830-773-9535), 2150 Del Rio Blvd, has rooms for $50/54.

La Quinta Motor Inn (☎ 830-773-7000, 800-531-5900, fax 830-773-8852), 2525 Main St, has rooms for $60/70 a single/double. **Best Western Eagle Pass** (☎ 830-758-1234, 800-272-9786, fax 830-758-1235), 1923 Loop 431, has rates of $62/68, along with a pleasant outdoor pool area. There's a small fridge and microwave in each room, and rates also include a breakfast with the usual continental fare, plus tacos and sweets in the evening.

Places to Eat

The most popular restaurant in Eagle Pass may well be the **Charcoal Grill** (☎ 830-773-8023), in the Mall de las Aguilas. It's huge and sort of dark, but the food is good and its 200 or so seats fill up many days at lunch. The burgers here are especially renowned, at $5 for three-quarters of a pound of beef and $4 for the 'Babyburger,' which includes fries. The wide menu also includes about a half-dozen steak choices plus a steak-and-shrimp combo for $17, along with Mexican dishes, catfish, chicken and pasta.

For authentic, cheap Mexican fare, try **Lolita's Restaurant & Tortilla Factory** (☎ 830-773-7862), 2653 Indio Hwy. Breakfast choices include tacos ($1) and huevos rancheros ($3), and lunches run about $5 for various taco-burrito-enchilada combos.

Another local favorite, **Pescados y Mariscos La Estrella** (☎ 830-757-2995), 800 N Bibb Ave, specializes in seafood prepared Mexican-coastal style, heavy on the garlic. Try the catfish-and-shrimp special ($7). **China Dragon** (☎ 830-757-8439), 771 S Bibb Ave, sells a lot of its broccoli chicken ($6).

Entertainment
The liveliest nightlife is over in Piedras Negras (see below). In Eagle Pass, *Impressions Nite Club* (☎ 830-773-9765), 3116 Del Rio Hwy, draws a country-and-western, Tejano and pop-dance crowd, and *Cross Country Nite Club* (☎ 830-773-9621), 2421 E Main St, presents live rock on some weekends. Big-name Tejano concerts sometimes take place in Eagle Pass at the *Texas Ballroom* (☎ 830-773-9944), on E Hwy 277 just east of where US 57 leaves Hwy 277 for San Antonio, and in Carrizo Springs, 43 miles southeast of town on US 277, at *Bear's Tejano Country*. First-run movies are screened at *Cinema 3* (☎ 830-773-1035), in the Mall de las Aguilas.

Getting There & Around
Air Maverick County Memorial International Airport (☎ 830-773-9636) is 12 miles north of Eagle Pass along US 277. As of early 1999, there was no scheduled air service to the area. There are plans to get a commercial carrier in, but nothing was definite at press time.

Bus Kerrville (☎ 830-773-9574) and Greyhound (☎ 830-773-9575) bus lines share the terminal at 164 Jefferson St. Kerrville specializes in travel to other Texas towns, and Greyhound handles more out-of-state routes. Sample Kerrville fares (one-way/roundtrip) and approximate minimum one-way travel times are: San Antonio, $19/32 (2½ hours); Austin, $34/65 (4 hours).

Car Enterprise Rent-a-Car (☎ 830-773-3931, 800-736-8222) has vehicles available at 1930 S Loop 431.

PIEDRAS NEGRAS (MEXICO)
Population 230,000
☎ 878 within Mexico, 011-52-878 from Texas
Piedras Negras' population dwarfs that of its Texas sister. The city's population has boomed in the past decade because of the presence of more than 40 maquiladoras. Historically the area has been a major coal producer, but we're told there isn't much of that going on now. Piedras Negras isn't a major tourist destination, but it has plenty to keep visitors happily occupied.

Information
For information on crossing into Mexico, see the Border section of the Getting There & Away chapter.

As soon as you enter Piedras Negras, you'll see, at the corner of Calle Abasolo and Calle Hidalgo, a tourist information building topped with an orange triangle. Stop in there to get the helpful *Turismo Mapa Region Norte*, which includes a Piedras Negras city map.

Things to See & Do
Attractions in Piedras Negras include the **Plaza Principal**, where musicians sometimes play in the gazebo, and the **Iglesia de Santa Maria de Guadalupe**, on the plaza's east side. There's a public **market** area on Avenida Allende between Calle Hidalgo and Calle Zaragoza.

At the **Plaza de Toros Monumental Arizpe**, on Avenida López Mateos, bullfights typically take place once a month from June to September. Dates are irregular, but the Eagle Pass Chamber of Commerce (☎ 830-773-3224) usually knows fight dates about a month in advance.

Places to Stay
Lodgings include *Motel California* (☎ 878-2-77-69, fax 878-2-54-66), Avenida Emilio Carranza 1006, where rooms are about $25/37 single/double, and the *Holiday Inn* (☎ 878-3-06-46, 800-465-4329 in the US, fax 878-3-00-50), Carretera 57 at Avenida Las Brisas, with rooms for $44/49.

Places to Eat
According to local legend, *Moderno Restaurant* (☎ 878-2-06-84), Allende 407, is the place where nachos were invented. Whether or not that's true, the Moderno is always a good choice in Piedras Negras, with a wide menu featuring fajitas, steak and seafood.

Other popular eateries include *El Rancho Steak Grill* (☎ 878-2-20-00), adjacent to Plaza de Toros Monumental Arizpe; quaint *La Casita* (☎ 878-2-51-00), Avenida Emilio

Carranza 1400; and *Casa Grande* (☎ *878-3-64-41*), Calle Roman Cepeda 311.

Entertainment

People come to Piedras Negras to party. *Kokomo* (☎ *878-2-37-68*), Avenida López Mateos 801-A, and *El Capote* (☎ *878-2-86-99*), near the Plaza de Toros Monumental Arizpe, appear to be perennial favorites among younger revelers, and older adults often patronize the bars at the *Moderno* and *Casa Grande* restaurants.

Getting There & Away

Walking is popular – it's just four short blocks from downtown Eagle Pass to downtown Piedras Negras on the main international bridge. We thought US officials at the return crossing from Piedras Negras seemed a bit more wary than those upriver at Ciudad Acuña, but the delay was minimal. A second international bridge is due to open between Eagle Pass and Piedras Negras sometime in mid-1999. It will be south of the bridge between the two downtowns; access will be from Industrial Park Blvd in Eagle Pass.

Bus An international bus runs between Eagle Pass and Piedras Negras daily 9 am to 5 pm, picking up passengers about every half hour at Main and Jefferson Sts and Commercial and Rio Grande Sts in Eagle Pass. The fare is US$1 to Piedras Negras and US75¢ for the return trip. In Piedras Negras, bus stops include Farmacia Benavides on the Plaza Principal and the Soriana shopping center on Avenida Lázaro Cárdenas, among others.

Car Tolls on the international bridge run US$1.50 for vehicles and US10¢ for pedestrians going into Piedras Negras, and US$1.35 for vehicles and US25¢ for pedestrians coming back to Eagle Pass.

If you plan to drive into Mexico, be sure your vehicle is insured. For a supplemental Mexican insurance policy, see two companies in Eagle Pass: Barrera Insurance Services (☎ 830-773-0927), 1036 Del Rio Blvd, or Capitol Insurance Services (☎ 830-773-2341), 1115 Main St.

DEL RIO
Population 34,500

If you have time to visit only one Tex-Mex border community, Del Rio (and its Mexican counterpart, Ciudad Acuña) is a good choice. Del Rio is big enough to offer a selection of sophisticated restaurants and lodgings, but small enough that its ambience is relaxed. Its location is a plus, too, with recreation aplenty at nearby Amistad National Recreation Area and Seminole Canyon State Historical Park.

Laughlin Air Force Base, 6 miles east of town, is a major presence, as are growing numbers of Winter Texans, who migrate to the area from November to March for the mild weather.

We got the feeling that Del Rio is an ideal, if a bit far-flung, weekend getaway for Texas urbanites. For out-of-state travelers, it's probably most logical as an intermediate stop – overnight, if time permits – between San Antonio (154 miles east via US 90) and Big Bend National Park (243 miles west via Marathon).

US 277/377 heads north from here, hitting I-10 at Sonora (91 miles); to the south, it's 56 miles to Eagle Pass via US 277 and 179 miles to Laredo via US 83.

Orientation

In Del Rio, US 90/277/377 becomes Ave F, the main north-south street through town. US 90 then heads east as E Gibbs St. Southwest of downtown, Garfield St becomes Las Vacas St and then Spur 277 as it approaches the international bridge into Mexico. Another crossing is found west of town, over Lake Amistad.

The best map is the free foldout one available at the chamber of commerce. It includes insets for Ciudad Acuña and Laughlin Air Force Base, along with a map of Amistad National Recreation Area on the flip side, and it also points out the locations of more than a dozen Pulse ATMs around town.

Information

Tourist Offices The Del Rio Chamber of Commerce (☎ 830-775-3551, 800-889-8149,

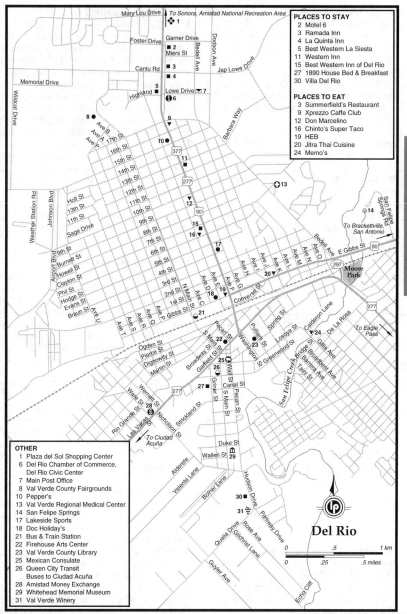

PLACES TO STAY
2 Motel 6
3 Ramada Inn
4 La Quinta Inn
5 Best Western La Siesta
11 Western Inn
15 Best Western Inn of Del Rio
27 1890 House Bed & Breakfast
30 Villa Del Rio

PLACES TO EAT
3 Summerfield's Restaurant
9 Xprezzo Caffe Club
12 Don Marcelino
16 Chinto's Super Taco
19 HEB
20 Jitra Thai Cuisine
24 Memo's

OTHER
1 Plaza del Sol Shopping Center
6 Del Rio Chamber of Commerce,
   Del Rio Civic Center
7 Main Post Office
8 Val Verde County Fairgrounds
10 Pepper's
13 Val Verde Regional Medical Center
14 San Felipe Springs
17 Lakeside Sports
18 Doc Holiday's
21 Bus & Train Station
22 Firehouse Arts Center
23 Val Verde County Library
25 Mexican Consulate
26 Queen City Transit
   Buses to Ciudad Acuña
28 Amistad Money Exchange
29 Whitehead Memorial Museum
31 Val Verde Winery

Del Rio

0   .5   1 km
0   .25   .5 miles

fax 830-774-1813, www.chamber.delrio.com/) is at 1915 Ave F.

There's a Mexican consulate in town; see the Facts for the Visitor chapter.

Money US currency is readily accepted in Ciudad Acuña, but currency exchange is available on both sides of the border. Try Amistad Money Exchange (☎ 830-774-6602), 707 Las Vacas St.

Post The main post office (☎ 830-775-3571) is at 2001 Bedell Ave.

Media The *Del Rio News-Herald* daily is available on newsstands for 50¢ Monday to Saturday and $1.25 Sunday. It includes a daily Spanish-language section. Area radio stations include KTDR (rock, 96.3 FM), KDLK (country, 1230 AM/94.3 FM) and KWMC (oldies, 1490 AM).

Bookstores Waldenbooks (☎ 830-775-7551) is in the Plaza del Sol shopping center, 2203 Ave F.

Libraries The Val Verde County Library (☎ 830-774-7595) is at 300 Spring St. Hours are Monday, Wednesday and Friday 9 am to 6 pm, Tuesday 1 to 8 pm, Thursday 9 am to 7 pm and weekends 1 to 5 pm.

Laundry Pepper's (☎ 830-774-4280), 1602 Ave F, is a combination convenience store, gas station, car wash and laundry open 24 hours daily.

Medical Services The local hospital, Val Verde Regional Medical Center (☎ 830-775-8566), is at 801 Bedell Ave.

Emergency The Amistad Family Violence & Rape Crisis Center is at ☎ 830-774-2744; out of town, call ☎ 888-774-2744.

Walking & Driving Tour

Ask the chamber of commerce or your motel for *A Guide to Historic Del Rio*, a free pamphlet that outlines an eight-point walking tour of the Val Verde County Courthouse Square area and a driving tour of the rest of town.

San Felipe Springs

Even though *del río* means 'of the river' in Spanish, the missionaries who named the area in the 17th century weren't referring to the Rio Grande but to San Felipe Springs, which gushes at the rate of 90 million gallons a day. Early settlers used the springs, the third-largest in Texas, to create an irrigation system still in use today. Although the springs can be viewed by taking San Felipe Springs Rd off US 90, just east of the San Felipe Country Club, they're really not much to see. Instead, stroll along San Felipe Creek in town, especially **Moore Park** between Garfield St and S Bedell Ave. Swans, ducks and splashing kids make the scene on warm days, and the creek's rising mist creates a pretty picture in cooler weather. Moore Park also has a swimming pool complete with water slide.

Val Verde Winery

Breathe deeply when you enter Val Verde Winery (☎ 830-775-9714), 100 Qualia Drive. This family-owned winery was established in 1883, making it the oldest continually operating vintner in the state, and the heavily scented air is thick with a century's worth of winemaking. (The winery rode out Prohibition by making sacramental wine for church communion use.)

Val Verde is best known for its tawny port, but it's not a widely available label; most of the winery's output is sold on the premises. Free tours and tastings are available Monday to Saturday 9 am to 4:30 pm. Fall is the best time to visit, since that's when bottling takes place and the most varieties are available.

Whitehead Memorial Museum

A cut above the average local museum, Whitehead Memorial Museum (☎ 830-774-7568) sprawls across a city block at 1308 S Main St. Judge Roy Bean, the 'Law West of the Pecos,' is buried here along with his son, Sam. Other interesting exhibits include a small Spanish-style cathedral, a room devoted to border radio (legendary '50s DJ Wolfman Jack got his start here in the late 1940s) and a 1287-item nativity-scene collection amassed by the late Beatriz Cadena. The museum is open Tuesday to Saturday 9 am to 4:30 pm and Sunday 1 to 5 pm; $3 for adults, $2 for seniors and teens, and $1 for children ages six to 12. Picnic tables are available.

Firehouse Arts Center

Headquarters for the Del Rio Council for the Arts (☎ 830-775-0888), 120 E Garfield St, the Firehouse includes a visual-arts gallery and a great little gift shop featuring some of the same stuff you'd see at the Dallas

---

Del Rio's Old Goat

Texas has seen its share of characters, but few were as audacious as Dr John Richard Brinkley, the infamous goat-gland surgeon of Del Rio. Brinkley never earned a medical degree, but that didn't stop him from practicing medicine.

His notoriety began in the late 1920s in Milford, Kansas, when a fatigued farmer told Brinkley he wished he still felt as frisky as his goats. As a Whitehead Memorial Museum leaflet tells it, 'An idea exploded like a bomb behind Brinkley's ambitious eyes, and he replied, "You could, with a minor operation."' Inspired, Brinkley began a prostate operation that implanted goat glands in men, a procedure he claimed would restore physical vigor and cure impotence. Before long, he was making $25,000 a week on the $750 operation, and he hired seven assistants to keep up with the demand.

Los Angeles Times publisher Harry Chandler invited Brinkley to California to perform the surgery on several assistants. It was great publicity, but it began Brinkley's downfall, too. The visit attracted the attention of the California attorney general, who soon asked Kansas officials to extradite Brinkley. Kansas refused, calling Brinkley a 'public benefactor.' But when newspapers in Kansas learned the good doctor had no medical degree, the state's medical board revoked his license.

Brinkley headed for the Tex-Mex border with the idea of starting a radio station and advertising his services on the air. His Ciudad Acuña station, XERA, supposedly used a 500,000-watt transmitter and an antenna that boosted the station's signal to a million watts. The station brought Brinkley fame and riches. People poured into Del Rio for the goat-gland operation, which Brinkley and his staff performed in the Roswell Hotel. They also flocked to nearby San Juan, Coahuila, where a Brinkley-run clinic treated rectal problems. 'Remember,' Brinkley would say in his radio ads, 'San Juan for rectal troubles and Del Rio for the old prostate.'

Brinkley lived in a Spanish-style mansion at what is now 512 Qualia Drive, with fountains that shot colored water 30 feet into the air and a private zoo with penguins, flamingos and Galápagos Islands tortoises. But the good times didn't last. In 1934, Brinkley said he'd replaced the goat-gland procedure with a new and improved rejuvenation surgery. Not long afterward, Mexican authorities canceled his radio license, ostensibly because of claims that the new operation was a fraud, but possibly because the Mexican government resented XERA's power. The American Medical Association sued Brinkley, as did many of his former patients, and he wound up owing $1.5 million in court judgments. The federal government added a mail-fraud charge in 1941. Brinkley died bankrupt a year later in San Antonio.

Despite everything, Brinkley is remembered fondly in Del Rio. He employed 300 people and contributed lavishly to charities and government services on both sides of the border, helping Del Rio ride out the depression with ease. His grand mansion still stands, and much of the rest of his property is now a subdivision called Brinkley Estates. Certainly, the goat-gland prostate surgeon is recalled as being among the most colorful people in the annals of Del Rio history.

Museum of Art store. Open weekdays 8 am to 5:30 pm, Saturday noon to 5 pm.

The arts council is also the presenter for the Firehouse Fantastics, a performing-arts series at the Paul Poag Theatre, 746 S Main St. If you like the looks of what this vibrant small arts council is doing, drop by the Del Rio Civic Center, 1915 Ave F, where bingo games held every Monday, Tuesday and Wednesday at 7 pm benefit the council's efforts.

Special Events

Locally, everyone just calls it the Super Bull, but the George Paul Memorial Bull Riding Competition (☎ 830-775-3551, 830-775-9595) is the full official name of a big ol' rodeo that takes place the last weekend of each April at the Val Verde County Fairgrounds, which sit along N Main St.

Fishing tournaments are another big draw almost year-round; the biggest, the Texas Travis Open in early August, lures nearly 1200 entrants each year. Contact the Del Rio Chamber of Commerce for exact dates and details.

Places to Stay

Motels The best budget buy is the *Western Inn* (☎ 830-774-4661, fax 830-774-3194), 1203 Ave F, where clean, basic rooms go for $21 to $23 a single and $28 to $34 a double. *Motel 6* (☎ 830-774-2115), 2115 Ave F, has rooms for $36/40 a single/double. See Amistad National Recreation Area, later in this chapter, for good budget choices at the lake.

Days Inn & Suites (☎ 830-775-0585, fax 830-775-1981), 3808 Ave F, has singles for $43 to $55 and doubles for $51 to $75. *La Quinta Inn* (☎ 830-775-7591, fax 830-774-0809), 2005 Ave F, has rooms for $55/62 a single/double, including continental breakfast.

There are two identically priced ($55/64) Best Western properties in town: *Best Western La Siesta* (☎ 830-775-6323, 800-336-3537), 2000 Ave F, and *Best Western Inn of Del Rio* (☎ 830-775-7511, fax 830-774-2194), 810 Ave F.

The business-oriented *Ramada Inn* (☎ 830-775-1511, 800-272-6232), 2101 Ave F, is probably the most plush motel in town; it has rates of $67/72 and a private jogging track.

B&Bs Del Rio has several excellent B&Bs. We were impressed by *Villa Del Rio* (☎ 830-768-1100), 123 Hudson Drive. Surrounded by stately palms and magnolias, the 1887 home has an elegant yet updated feel. The top-end room is the Peacock Suite ($135), featuring a private porch; three other rooms go for $85 a night. The inn is just around the corner from Val Verde Winery and some fine country roads for strolling.

The Southern plantation lives on at the *1890 House Bed & Breakfast* (☎ 830-775-8061, 800-282-1360, fax 830-775-4667), downtown at 609 Griner St. This inn has three rooms and two suites, all with four-poster beds and either a Jacuzzi or oversize bathtub. Rates are $89 to $125.

Places to Eat

Don Marcelino (☎ 830-775-6242), 1110 Ave F, and *Chinto's Super Taco* (☎ 830-774-1592), 400 E 6th St, both sell fast, cheap and authentic Mexican fare popular with Anglos and Latinos alike. For a sit-down meal, try *Memo's* (☎ 830-775-8104), 804 E Losoya St, a Del Rio institution overlooking San Felipe Creek. The 'Memo's Special' includes a cheese enchilada, beef taco, loaded chalupa, rice and beans for $6.

Jitra Thai Cuisine (☎ 830-775-7553), 800 E Gibbs St, serves Chinese and Japanese food as well as Thai. *Xprezzo Caffe Club* (☎ 830-774-7003), 1811 Ave F, specializes in build-your-own pasta plates ($5 and up, depending on toppings chosen), about 30 kinds of sandwiches (mostly in the $4 to $5 range) and New York-style cheesecakes. *Summerfield's Restaurant* (☎ 830-775-1511), in the Ramada Inn, features a 'Texas Breakfast and Lunch Buffet' every day – $9 buys your fill of chicken and beef fajitas, pork spareribs and fried catfish. On Sunday from 11 am to 3 pm, any child who's under 49 inches tall eats for free when an accompanying adult buys the $9 brunch.

For groceries, head to the mammoth *HEB* supermarket (☎ 830-774-5666), 200 Ave F, open 24 hours a day. And if you're heading back to town from a day at Amistad National Recreation Area, consider a dinner stop at *Cripple Creek*. (See the Amistad NRA section for details.)

Entertainment

Del Rio is home to hip country songsmith Radney Foster and to 'Blondie' Calderón, who for years has played piano for singer Ray Price. Any Tuesday or Thursday when he's not on the road, you might catch Calderón stretching his jazz legs at his family's restaurant, *Memo's* (see Places to Eat). Among the local dance clubs, *Doc Holiday's* (☎ *830-775-6040*), 202 E Gibbs St, features Tejano and country music.

Shopping

Whether you want to rent a kayak or select a stogie, Lakeside Sports (☎ 830-774-5288), 601 Ave F, is the place to stop. This nifty shop is the best source in town for outdoor information and gear.

The Plaza del Sol shopping center (☎ 830-774-3634) has 45 stores and an eight-screen cineplex at 2205 Ave F.

Getting There & Away

Air There is currently no scheduled air service to Del Rio. For updated information, call Frontera Aviation at ☎ 830-768-4842.

Bus Kerrville and Greyhound bus lines (☎ 830-775-7515) operate from the station at 1 N Main St. Sample fares (one-way/roundtrip) and approximate minimum one-way travel times are: Dallas, $56/107 (7 to 8 hours); San Antonio, $17/32 (3 hours).

Train The Amtrak station (☎ 800-872-7245) is at 1 N Main St. Westbound trains leave Sunday, Monday, Thursday and Saturday at 8:30 am; eastbound trains leave Sunday, Tuesday and Thursday at 12:25 am. Plan on a nine-hour one-way trip ($97) to either El Paso to the west or Houston to the east.

Getting Around

Trolley Queen City Transit (☎ 830-774-0580) runs a trolley route in Del Rio. Pick-up points include the Plaza del Sol shopping center on Ave F. Fares are $1 for adults, 80¢ for seniors 55 and up and children three to 11.

Car Enterprise (☎ 830-774-2527) rents cars at 2104 US 90 W.

Taxi Taxi rates are $1.50 flagfall and $1.20 a mile. Cab companies include City Taxi (830-775-6344) and Del Rio Taxi Service (☎ 830-775-4448).

CIUDAD ACUÑA (MEXICO)
Population 120,000
☎ 877 within Mexico, 011-52-877 from Texas

Teeming with life but without the menacing undercurrent that characterizes larger border cities such as Ciudad Juárez and Nuevo Laredo, Acuña is a vibrant place. Like other border towns, Acuña is growing fast: its population has roughly doubled over the past decade. Yet we got the sense that people in Acuña and Del Rio have a great affinity for one another, and culture and commerce flow freely between their communities. The two cities team up for lots of projects, including an annual Fiesta de Amistad each October, but this is not yet a major tourist center.

The international bridge from Texas feeds right onto Calle Hidalgo, which is the main shopping street. It's one-way westbound; the next street south, Calle Madero, is one-way eastbound, leading back to the bridge. The other main street in central Acuña is the north-south Blvd Guerrero, lined with more shops and hotels and the main city plaza.

See the Border section in the Getting There & Away chapter for information on crossing into Mexico; check with the Del Rio Chamber of Commerce for tips on visiting Acuña.

Places to Stay

There are no chain lodgings in Acuña. Locals recommend *Hotel San Antonio* (☎ *877-2-51-53*), at Calles Hidalgo and Lerdo, with air-conditioned rooms for US$30 to US$40. If it's full, try the comparably priced *Motel Los Alpes* (☎ *877-2-61-38*), Blvd Guerrero 2975. *Hotel San Jorge*

(☎ 877-2-50-70), Calle Hidalgo 165, is a bit funkier but cheaper, too, with rooms at about US$25/30 single/double.

Places to Eat

Acuña restaurants are great values. *Landos* (☎ 877-2-39-82), Calle Hidalgo 280, has sirloin steak, chicken mole or fajitas for US$5 at lunch and a wide range of dinner specialties, including beef shish kebab (US$14) and red snapper filet (US$12). *Crosby's* (☎ 877-2-20-20), Calle Hidalgo 195, has been a favorite among folks from both sides of the border since 1930. Specialties include enchiladas with rice (US$4), fish from Lake Amistad (US$6 to US$8) and filet mignon topped with mushrooms (US$10). There's live music Thursday to Saturday. A bit more downscale, *Los Tacos Grill* (☎ 877-2-40-41), Blvd Guerrero 1490 Sur, is popular for its Mexican home cooking and thatched-roof atmosphere.

Entertainment

Panchos Bar (☎ 877-2-53-66), Calle Hidalgo 249, is one of the premier party spots in Acuña. Friday and Saturday nights, it stays open until 4 or 5 am. *La Fiesta Disco* (☎ 877-5-13-59), huge and impossible to miss on Calle Hidalgo not far from the bridge, is another hot new dance club.

Getting There & Away

It's 4 miles between Del Río's and Acuña's downtowns, so most people take the bus, drive or call a taxi.

Bus An international bus runs between Del Rio and Acuña every 30 minutes from 7:50 am to 6:30 pm. (The last bus leaves Acuña for Del Rio at 7 pm.) The fare for everyone age five and up is US95¢ one-way or US$1.40 roundtrip from Queen City Transit, 110 N Greenwood St in Del Rio. In Acuña , the bus stop is right over the border at the international bridge.

Car Supplemental Mexico insurance for travelers driving their own vehicles is available in Del Rio through Arreola's Insurance (☎ 830-775-3252), 1002 E Gibbs St, and Big

Rio Insurance Agency (☎ 830-774-3003), 600 Bedell Ave.

Taxi A taxi ride from an Ave F hotel in Del Rio to central Acuña costs about US$13.

AMISTAD NATIONAL RECREATION AREA

'Amistad' means friendship in Spanish, and Mexican-US cooperation was the spirit in which a dam and reservoir transformed this area of the Rio Grande in the late 1960s. The other word often used to describe Amistad is 'big': The reservoir covers 105 sq miles spanning two nations, with 851 miles of shoreline – 547 in the USA and 304 in Mexico. Amistad Dam itself is 6 miles long, with about two-thirds of its length in Mexico. From the dam, the Gulf of Mexico is 587 river miles away down the Rio Grande, and El Paso is 683 miles upriver. The reservoir also runs 25 miles up the Devils River and 14 miles up the Pecos River. (The Pecos, which begins in New Mexico, reaches the end of its 926-mile course here at the Rio Grande.)

Amistad NRA has two major recreational access points, **Diablo East** and **Rough Canyon**. Diablo East is 10 miles northwest of Del Rio on US 90; facilities include a marina, boat ramp, beach, handicapped-accessible fishing dock, scuba diving access, picnic areas and a nature trail, and close by are plenty of privately run services. Nearby Governors Landing has a campground, beach and picnic area.

Rough Canyon is 23 miles north of Del Rio via US 277/377 and Recreation Rd 2. Known for its multicolored 150-foot cliffs, which are only visible from the water, Rough Canyon has a marina, boat ramp, beach and picnic area.

Additional access points around the lake include the following:

Pecos River – boat ramp, picnicking, trail and ranger station

Spur 406 – boat ramp and camping

Box Canyon and Amistad Acres – boat ramps

Playa Tlaloc – in Mexico near the west side of Amistad Dam; picnicking and a monument to the rain god Tlaloc

US Air Force – boat ramps
Black Brush Point – boat ramp and picnicking
Spur 454 – boat ramp
San Pedro – camping and picnicking
277 South – boat ramp and picnicking
277 North – boat ramp and camping
Rock Quarry – group camping

Information

The National Park Service Lake Amistad headquarters (☎ 830-775-7491, fax 830-775-7299, www.nps.gov/amis) is just north of Del Rio on US 90 W at Quail Rd, just past the US 90 W and US 277/377 split. Its mailing address is PO Box 420367, Del Rio, TX 78842. Hours are weekdays 8 am to 5 pm and weekends 9 am to 5 pm. This is a worthwhile stop for general information on Lake Amistad, water levels, visitor services and interpretive programs, which are sometimes held at the Governors Landing amphitheater and at various campgrounds in the NRA.

The cinderblock visitors' center out on the dam was pretty lame the last time we checked, but it's supposed to be gussied up by the time you read this. Among the new exhibits will be one on how the natural world doesn't recognize political boundaries, and the ways in which the USA and Mexico must work together to protect scarce water resources. The center is open daily 10 am to 6 pm.

Drinking water is available at the park headquarters on US 90 W, and dump stations can be found on the Diablo East entrance road and in Del Rio at the Civic Center. There is no admission fee for land day use at Amistad, but camping and boating fees and permits apply.

Dangers & Annoyances Remember, Amistad is surrounded by desert. Drink plenty of water, especially in summer, and keep an eye out for local wildlife. Poisonous snakes include the broadbanded and trans-Pecos copperheads; the banded rock, western diamondback, and black-tailed rattlesnakes; and the Texas coral snake. Javelinas, scorpions, wasps, black widows, tarantulas and brown recluse spiders must

be left alone, too. Watch out for thorny plants; when hiking around Amistad, it's best to wear long pants, long sleeves and high-top leather boots for protection.

Rock Art

Indians who lived 3500 to 4500 years ago were drawn to what is now Lake Amistad by the convergence of the Rio Grande and the Devils and Pecos Rivers. They left behind a wealth of rock art, fashioned in what archaeologists call the Lower Pecos River style (see the boxed text Pecos River Style, later in this chapter).

The best pictograph sites are along the Rio Grande just downriver from the Pecos confluence. Visitors must boat to the **Panther Cave** dock and then climb a steep stairway to the cave. The cave's highlight is a 9-foot-long drawing of a mountain lion, along with many other animal and human figures. **Parida Cave** is also best reached by boat, but when the water is low it can be accessed via a moderately strenuous 3-mile roundtrip hike through tall brush.

Activities

Boating You need a permit to boat on Lake Amistad. A permit costs $4 a day (good for 24 hours from purchase) or $40 a year. Holders of Golden Age and Golden Access passports pay half price. Permits may be bought at park headquarters or from machines at Diablo East and Rough Canyon. The machines accept MasterCard, Visa and cash.

RIO GRANDE

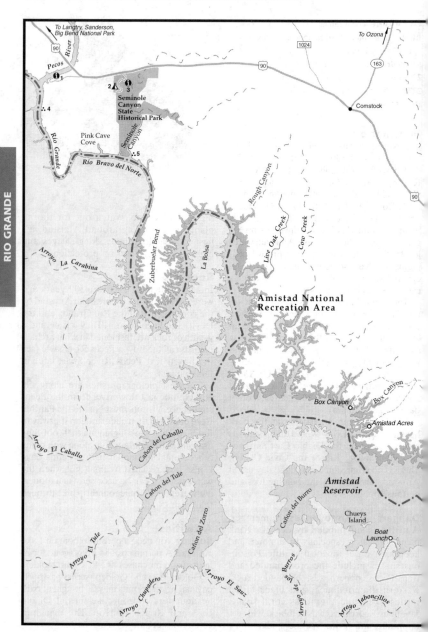

RIO GRANDE

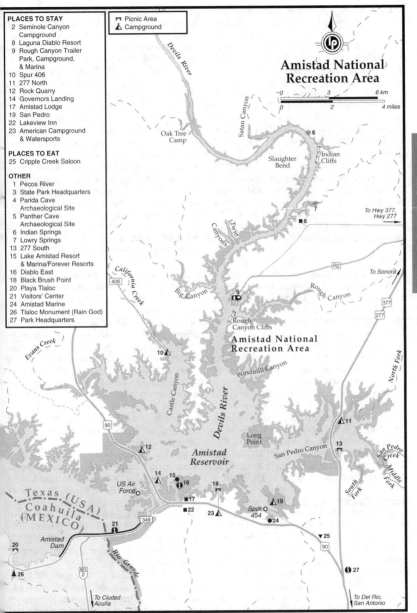

PLACES TO STAY
2   Seminole Canyon
    Campground
8   Laguna Diablo Resort
9   Rough Canyon Trailer
    Park, Campground,
    & Marina
10 Spur 406
11 277 North
12 Rock Quarry
14 Governors Landing
17 Amistad Lodge
19 San Pedro
22 Lakeview Inn
23 American Campground
    & Watersports

PLACES TO EAT
25 Cripple Creek Saloon

OTHER
1   Pecos River
3   State Park Headquarters
4   Parida Cave
    Archaeological Site
5   Panther Cave
    Archaeological Site
6   Indian Springs
7   Lowry Springs
13 277 South
15 Lake Amistad Resort
    & Marina/Forever Resorts
16 Diablo East
18 Black Brush Point
20 Playa Tlaloc
21 Visitors' Center
24 Amistad Marine
26 Tlaloc Monument (Rain God)
27 Park Headquarters

⚲ Picnic Area
⛺ Campground

**Amistad National
Recreation Area**

0   3   6 km
0   2   4 miles

Devils River

Satan Canyon

Oak Tree
Camp

Slaughter
Bend

● 6

Indian
Cliffs

● 7

To Hwy 377,
Hwy 277

■ 8

Twin
Canyons

To Sonora

R2

Rough Canyon

377

277

California Creek

406

Big Canyon

⚲ 9

Rough
Canyon Cliffs

**Amistad National
Recreation Area**

Evans Creek

Castle Canyon

10 ⛺

Windmill Canyon

Devils River

North Fork

⛺ 11

13

San Pedro Creek

Middle Fork

⛺ 12

Amistad
Reservoir

Long
Point

San Pedro Canyon

14
⛺   15
    ● 16

US Air
Force

18

⛺ 19

Spur
454

South Fork

Texas (USA)
Coahuila (MEXICO)

21

■ 17

■ 22

23 ⛺

● 24

349

▼ 25

90

20

Amistad
Dam

26 ⛺

MEX
2

Rio Grande

To Ciudad
Acuña

● 27

To Del Rio,
San Antonio

Lake Amistad Resort & Marina/Forever Resorts (☎ 830-774-4157, 800-255-5561), at Diablo East, rents a variety of boats, from 16-foot fishing boats ($50 a day) on up to houseboats. High season for houseboats is June through August, when a 50-foot rig costs $845 and a 56-foot boat costs $1550 for three nights. The marina's mailing address is PO Box 420635, Del Rio, TX 78842. Similar boats and rates are available at Rough Canyon Marina (☎ 830-775-8779), PO Box 420845, Del Rio, TX 78842. The NRA boat permit is included in the cost of rental.

The boat ramps farther from Amistad Dam are sometimes left high and dry by fluctuating water levels, so call ahead to park headquarters or inquire locally to check water levels before picking a launch site. The Diablo East and Rough Canyon ramps are almost always accessible.

Fishing Lake Amistad is one of the top fishing areas in Texas. Its approximately 30 species include a half-dozen kinds each of bass and sunfish, five kinds of catfish, and assorted crappie, perch, pike, walleye and gar. A Texas fishing license is required on the Texas side, and a Mexican permit is needed over the border. See the Activities chapter for information on obtaining a Texas license; Mexican licenses are available at many Texan businesses near the reservoir.

A complete list of fishing guides is available through the Park Service office or its website. Two representative guides include Jim Nolder Guide Service (☎ 915-292-4581), HCR 3, Box 220, Box Canyon, Del Rio, TX 78840, which specializes in catfishing, or Lake Amistad Guide Service (☎ 830-774-3484), PO Box 421072, Del Rio, TX 78840.

Scuba Diving Amistad's clear water and varied depths make it a favorite among divers. Air is available at Amistad Marine (☎ 830-775-0878), 7410 US 90 W, which also rents gear: wetsuits are $15, tanks are $10, and masks, snorkels, a pair of fins and tank refills are $5 apiece. The complete outfit is $35.

November to April, surface water temperature is about 50°F, with 25 to 30 feet visibility; May to October, surface temperatures

can reach the mid-80s, but visibility declines to 10 feet or less. Since Amistad's fishing popularity means lots of discarded fishing line and hooks, divers should always carry a good-quality diver's knife.

The scuba cove at Diablo East is buoyed to keep out boats; it's the only Amistad site where you can dive without displaying a dive flag. Depths here range to 100 feet, with two boat wrecks to explore. Other good dive areas include Castle Canyon, waters surrounding the US 90 bridge, and Indian Springs (6½ miles up the Devils River from Rough Canyon). Ask at Park Service headquarters (see Information, above) for *Dive Amistad Safely*, a leaflet offering more information on precautions and possible sites.

Places to Stay

Camping All four Amistad NRA *campgrounds* operate on a first-come, first-served basis. A fifth campground, Rock Quarry, is available to groups by reservation. Cost is $4, or $2 for Golden Age and Golden Access passport holders. There is no drinking water, or showers or hookups. Each designated campsite has a ramada (a Southwest-style shelter to shield campers from the elements), picnic table and grill. Ground fires are not allowed, but you can use the grills provided at each designated site or bring your own stove. Firewood collection is OK, but since wood is pretty scarce, pick up a bundle before you arrive. Boaters may camp free of charge along the shoreline at dispersed areas away from developed areas.

Private campground options include *American Campground & Watersports* (☎ 830-775-6484, 800-525-3386), on US 90 W opposite the Black Brush Point boat ramp turnoff. It has tent sites for $12 for two people and full hookups for $16.75 for two; each extra person is charged $3. The mailing address is HCR 3, Box 44, San Angelo, TX 78840. *Rough Canyon Trailer Park & Campground* (☎ 830-775-8779), 7 miles west of US 277/377 on Recreation Rd 2, has primitive campsites for $4 for two people and $1 per extra person, which includes water. RV sites cost $11 for two people and

$1 per extra person, which includes all hookups except TV, which is available for $2.50 extra per day. Also available are metal cabanas with electricity, which sleep up to four people for $12.

Motels & Hotels *Lakeview Inn* (☎ 830-775-9521, fax 830-775-9521), just across US 90 W from the Diablo East area access road, has bargain rooms that run $27/35 a single/double. The mailing address is HCR 3, Box 38, Del Rio, TX 78840. Nearby and still very reasonable, *Amistad Lodge* (☎ 830-775-8591, 800-775-8591, fax 830-775-8697) bills itself as 'closest to the lake,' with rates of $38/50, and $60 for rooms with kitchenettes. The mailing address is HCR 3, Box 29, Del Rio, TX 78840. Both motels have pools.

In the Rough Canyon area, *Laguna Diablo Resort* (☎ 830-774-2422) has one- and two-bedroom lakeview apartments for $79 to $99 per night. Its postal address is HCR 1, Box 4RC, Del Rio, TX 78840. The road to Laguna Diablo heads west from US 277/377 not far north of R2.

Places to Eat

Both the *Lakeview Inn* and *Amistad Lodge* (see Places to Stay) have restaurants. There are no restaurants in the Rough Canyon area, but groceries are available at the *Rough Canyon Marina*. En route back to Del Rio, *Cripple Creek Saloon* (☎ 830-775-0153), on US 90 W, is a local favorite for prime rib ($10 to $17), available daily after 6 pm (except Sunday, when the restaurant is closed).

BRACKETTVILLE
Population 1700

Thirty-one miles east of Del Rio, Brackettville is famous for its Alamo replica movie set and for Fort Clark Springs, a frontier post turned retirement village.

Fort Clark Springs

Although Fort Clark was established in 1852, it is best known as the base for the Seminole-Negro Indian Scouts, who served here in the 1870s. It was also a major training grounds and even a German prisoner-of-war camp in WWII. Now it's a vacation and retirement community.

Fort Clark Springs (☎ 830-563-2493, 800-937-1590), right on US 90 in the heart of Brackettville, sells memberships for its facilities, but travelers passing through can get a full-hookup RV site for $15 per night or a motel room for $48. (Tent sites are not available to nonmembers.) Rates include use of the spring-fed swimming pool, one of the largest in Texas. The pool is open year-round but closes each Thursday for cleaning. There are also two restaurants and an 18-hole golf course on the grounds. Non-members can golf for $16 Monday to Thursday and $18 Friday to Sunday. The mailing address is PO Box 345, Brackettville, TX 78832.

Alamo Village

Two dozen movies, a mess of TV shows and who knows how many commercials have been filmed at this movie set (☎ 830-563-2580), 7 miles north of Brackettville on FM 674. It is among the largest sets ever built outside Hollywood. The set went up in the late 1950s for *The Alamo*, starring John Wayne; since then, it's also served as a staging area for such screen gems as *Lonesome Dove* and *Bandolero!* According to the Shahan family, on whose ranch the set resides, more than a million adobe bricks, 12 miles of water pipe and 30,000 sq feet of imported Spanish roofing tile were used to construct the exact replica of the Alamo and a surrounding village that aims to recreate San Antonio in the early 19th century. Anything anyone could ever want when filming a Western is here – stagecoaches, a saloon, a deserted Mexican village, even a herd of Texas longhorns.

It's open daily except December 21 to 26 from 9 am to 5 pm. Memorial Day to Labor Day, the $6 admission ($3 for children ages six to 11, free for kids five and under) includes live Western-style entertainment. The rest of the year, admission is $5 for adults and $2.50 for children. FM 674 is considered one of the prettiest scenic drives on the southwest fringe of the Hill Country.

RIO GRANDE

SEMINOLE CANYON STATE HISTORICAL PARK

The best art galleries in south central Texas are right here along the Rio Grande, and their works of rock art have been on view for at least 4000 years.

At Seminole Canyon State Historical Park (☎ 915-292-4464), off US 90, 9 miles west of Comstock, park rangers lead visitors on a fascinating hike to **Fate Bell Shelter**, a natural canvas of ancient rock art. If the art here was merely decorative, it would be magnificent. But the pictographs are more than drawings: they're windows into their creators' daily routines, dreams, hopes and fears. Some of the art is slowly disappearing. That's to be expected after 4000 years; humidity, oxidation and acid rain all take their toll on the pictographs. However, other pictographs, also thousands of years old, are just now emerging after centuries of fine sandblasting by the elements.

Guided tours to the pictograph sites take place Wednesday to Sunday at 10 am and 3 pm, weather permitting. Cost is $3, plus the park's $2 per-person admission fee. (Children 12 and under get into the park free and pay $1 for the tour.) The tour takes about an hour and includes some stairs, but it's a slow, easy hike. Before or after the trek, stop by the visitors' center to see exhibits on the area's human history from prehistoric times to more recent railroading and ranching days. A day-use picnic area sits outside park headquarters.

Fit travelers with a keen interest in rock art may want to plan their trip to coincide with one of Seminole Canyon's **Presa Canyon** tours, typically held several times between October and March each fall and

Pecos River Style

Although humans visited the Rio Grande region 12,000 years ago, they were wanderers, hunting the mammoth and bison that once lived here in abundance. By 7000 years ago, the climate had changed into the arid desert it is today, and a new culture appeared. Although these people lived amid harsh conditions, they possessed a creative spark and produced a distinctive style of art seen only along the Lower Pecos River, Devils River and Rio Grande. It has come to be known as the Pecos River Style.

The defining characteristic of Pecos River Style art is a towering shaman who usually holds an *atlatl*, or ancient spear, in his hand. According to rock-art expert Solveig Turpin, 'The figure may be headless or crowned with antlers, feline ears, radiant hair or horns. The body is rectangular, often tapering to stubby legs...the shaman can be surrounded by miniature replicas of itself, sometimes inverted as if falling from the sky, or herds of deer, often pierced by spears.'

The shaman is sometimes surrounded by undulating lines, interpreted as snakes or water. Some scholars believe the Pecos River artists may have been inspired by eating the buttonlike tops of mescal, a cactus, which produce a dreamlike state (along with a bunch of other nasty side effects, such as cramping and nausea – we're not suggesting you try this).

Visitors to Fate Bell Shelter and similar sites often must crane their necks to view the rock art, which raises a question: were the Pecos River people really that tall? In fact, the ledges on which modern-day hikers stand are far lower than those the artists used. Flooding has washed away much of the rock in Seminole Canyon; one 1954 torrent sent an 84-foot wall of water washing down the gorge. The artists probably also used stalks of native plants – lechuguilla or river cane, perhaps – to extend their reach. For a good synopsis of Pecos River Style and its origins, see the website members.aol.com/rockart01/Turpin.html.

winter. These eight-hour hiking tours take participants to more remote rock-art sites that are seldom seen by visitors. The hikes are limited to 24 people age 12 or older in good physical condition. The park also offers occasional two-hour boat tours to area pictograph sites. Call the park for more information and reservations for the Presa Canyon tours or the boat tours.

Also adjacent to Seminole Canyon, the **Galloway White Shaman Preserve** is a private rock-art site managed by the San Antonio-based Rock Art Foundation (☎ 888-525-9907). The foundation offers four separate tours in the Lower Pecos region on the first weekend of each month. On Saturday, a tour goes to the Galloway White Shaman Preserve and White Shaman Shelter, plus Seminole Canyon; another visits the Lewis Canyon petroglyph site, for which a high-clearance vehicle is a must. On Sunday, a tour covers pictographs in the Devils River area; another includes Devils River plus Cedar Springs and Mystic Shelter. Tours cost $20 per person per day, with a maximum of $50 per day for an immediate family. Advance reservations are required in order to schedule a guide for the day.

Hiking & Mountain Biking

A short path, the **Windmill Nature Trail**, makes a loop two-thirds of a mile long from the headquarters parking lot past native plants and the remains of two windmills. Another trailhead, near the campground, gives access to 8 miles of trails for hiking and mountain biking. One 6-mile roundtrip loop leads to the Rio Grande across from Panther Cave. A spur that takes off from the main trail leads to another reach of Seminole Canyon for a total of 4 miles roundtrip from the main trailhead.

Places to Stay

A 31-site *campground* with showers and a dump station makes a good base for exploring the Seminole Canyon area overnight or in longer stays. Rates are $8 for tent campers and $11 for electric hookup sites, plus the $2 park admission fee. The campground itself is on a hill and surrounded by beautiful desert vegetation. Campers often look to the nearby purple sagebrush as a weather barometer; its fragrant flowers bloom before rain and after a downpour. Reservations are a good idea, especially in spring and near Thanksgiving and Christmas, among the park's most popular times. Call Texas Parks & Wildlife's reservations office in Austin at ☎ 512-389-8900.

Comstock has limited visitor services along US 90. From Comstock, it's 36 miles southeast to Del Rio and 91 miles west to Sanderson, where there's another good selection of services.

Desert Hills RV Park (☎ 915-292-4451) has full RV hookups for $12, but no tent sites or rest rooms. The *Comstock Hotel* (☎ 915-292-4431), on Hwy 90 west, is the only hotel in Comstock, with no-frills rooms running about $28 to 35.

Places to Eat

Locals recommend *El Matador* (☎ 915-292-4521), on US 90 in Comstock, for Mexican food and steaks in the $3 to $6 range; it's open for lunch and dinner daily except Sunday and Wednesday. If it's closed, try the hamburgers at *Emilio's* (☎ 915-292-4597), also on US 90.

LANGTRY
Population 30

Langtry is a long way from anywhere, but it has managed to parlay its principal claim to fame into a major tourist attraction on US 90: the newly renovated Judge Roy Bean Visitor Center (☎ 915-291-3340), where you can load up on maps and brochures for destinations all over Texas and learn about the life of a legendary Lone Star lawman. Exhibits on view at the visitors' center include Judge Bean's handcuffs and the .41-caliber Smith & Wesson revolver he used as his gavel. Six listening-station dioramas highlight Bean's reign. The center grounds also include an impressive cactus garden and the Opera House, where Bean lived. The center is open daily 8 am to 5 pm, except Easter Sunday, Thanksgiving, Christmas Eve, Christmas Day and New Year's Day; admission is free.

Places to Stay & Eat

Langtry's small population means that visitor amenities are few. Just a stroll from the visitors' center, **Wagon Wheel RV Park** (☎ 915-291-3230) has full-hookup sites for $8, along with a small restaurant serving burgers and barbecue in the $3 to $4 range. No tent facilities are available. Check out the barrel marked 'Baby Rattlers' on the porch. That's exactly what's inside; stop and see.

The Law West of the Pecos

Judge Roy Bean has been called the West's most colorful justice of the peace. He called himself the 'Law West of the Pecos,' and he ruled the frontier from his combination court-house, saloon and pool hall. Bean was named the local JP in August 1882 to help bring order to the towns and tent camps that had sprung up in the wake of the Southern Pacific's new Sunset Route. There was no other legal authority within 100 miles, so Bean did things his own way, holding court at his bar or on the front porch in good weather. His punishments were unusual and good for business: he'd often order a defendant to pay $30 or $45 and buy a round of drinks.

Bean was a promoter, too, staging prizefights on the banks of the Rio Grande and telling anyone who would listen that the great English actress Lillie Langtry would someday come to town to perform. He wrote her many letters to tell her he'd named his business and even the town for her. (Historians say, however, that the town was actually named for a railroad construction foreman; meanwhile, Bean's sign painter misspelled the actress' name, forever after making her 'The Jersey Lilly.') Langtry did finally come to visit in 1904, but she was too late: the heartbroken judge had died a few months before, and Bean's daughter wound up giving the actress a welcoming speech, along with the judge's favorite pistol.

For a look at the life and times of Judge Roy Bean, you can stop by the visitors' center or rent the movie of the same name. The 1972 John Huston-directed film starred Paul Newman as the judge and Ava Gardner as Lillie Langtry.

The Big Bend

Texas is defined by sheer sweep; its much-ballyhooed bigness may be the characteristic most apparent to visitors. But almost all of this sprawling state – some 98% of its 268,601 sq miles – is privately owned. Despite its frontier mentality, much of Texas has a big 'No Trespassing' sign prominently posted on it. You can't simply get out of your pickup and start hiking, as you can across much of the US West in places such as Nevada, Idaho and Wyoming.

The Big Bend country of southwest Texas provides an exception to this rule. Together, Big Bend National Park, Big Bend Ranch State Park and Black Gap Wildlife Management Area total 1844 sq miles of public land. There are still plenty of regulations and fees, and even the Big Bend country can fill up with people during prime vacation season; Big Bend is a major spring break destination. Still, more than any other region of Texas, the Big Bend country provides ample opportunity to get off the pavement and into an environment that is among both the most serene and most unforgiving in North America.

Actually, given the area's wide vistas and spacious skies, even the pavement isn't bad. You can see plenty from your car window, which is why Big Bend is such a popular 'drive-through' park. But be sure to abandon your vehicle at least long enough to take a day float on the Rio Grande and sample a few of the area's superb hiking trails. Once those wilderness explorations are done, more good times await in towns such as Terlingua, Alpine, Marathon and Fort Davis – small communities blessed with the unbeatable blend of laid-back attitudes and sophisticated amenities.

Big Bend National Park

With its 1252 sq miles – making it one of the biggest preserves in the lower 48 states – Big Bend National Park is a land of incredible diversity, vast enough to allow a lifetime of discovery, yet laced with enough well-placed roads and trails to permit short-term visitors to see a lot in two to three days.

Like many popular US parks, Big Bend has one area – the Chisos Basin – that absorbs the overwhelming crunch of traffic. The Chisos Mountains are beautiful, and no trip

> ### Highlights
>
> - Floating the Rio Grande, perhaps in the company of a noted musician or a top Texas chef
>
> - Crossing the river for lunch in Mexico
>
> - Sunsets – and moonrises – over the Chihuahuan Desert
>
> - Driving FM 170, El Camino del Rio, west of Big Bend National Park
>
> - Western Civilization 101 at the Big Bend's best hotels and restaurants: the Gage Hotel in Marathon, the Reata in Alpine, the Hotel Limpia in Fort Davis, Cibolo Creek Ranch south of Marfa
>
> - Star parties at the McDonald Observatory near Fort Davis

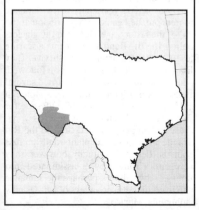

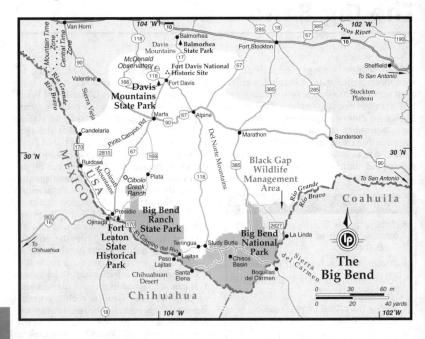

here would be complete without an excursion into the high country. But any visit to Big Bend National Park should also include time in the Chihuahuan Desert, home to curious creatures and adaptable plants, and the Rio Grande, an international border zone that is blurrier and more permeable than anywhere else along the US-Mexico line. See the boxed text for sample itineraries covering one- and two-day visits.

Big Bend National Park is about 400 miles west of San Antonio. The shortest route to the park is US 90 west to Marathon, then US 385 south to the Persimmon Gap entrance at the park's northern edge. From El Paso, plan on a trip of about 325 miles via I-10 east to Van Horn, US 90 to Alpine, and Hwy 118 south to the park's west entrance at Study Butte.

From Midland-Odessa, it's a 235-mile trip via US 385. There is no public transportation to or within Big Bend National Park. See the Getting There & Away section for public

transportation options to and from Alpine, which is the park's largest gateway community.

HISTORY
Early History

Settlement of the Big Bend country began 10,000 to 12,000 years ago, when nomadic hunters pursued game into the region at the end of the last ice age. But once the glaciers melted, the Big Bend area became a searing desert that few animals could survive. They disappeared, and the hunters soon followed. When humans and animals returned several thousand years later, conditions – although still harsh – allowed a bountiful lifestyle for those who understood the desert's ways. These Indian peoples lived close to the Rio Grande and harvested plants and animals from the desert. Eventually, however, they were either routed by or assimilated into other nearby cultures, perhaps the Jumanos who lived in the river valleys of what is now Chihuahua, Mexico.

Spanish & Anglo Settlement

The Spaniards were on the scene by the early 16th century, but they usually paid little attention to the Big Bend region, focusing their energies instead on El Paso and points west. Meanwhile, the Jumanos had established a village near what is now Presidio, and a Mexican band of Indians known as Chisos came north each summer to live in the mountains that now carry their name.

The Chisos fended off the Spaniards' early-17th-century efforts to take them into slavery, but they were soon joined by the Mescalero Apaches, who had emigrated down the Rio Grande from New Mexico. Here, they became known as Chisos Apaches. The Apaches dominated the region for most of the 18th century, yet the Chisos stayed too. The Comanches were very much a presence as well; every fall, the Big Bend country shook with the thundering hooves of horses carrying Comanche war parties on their autumn raids into Mexico.

The desert environment and Indian presence long discouraged Anglo Americans from settling in the Big Bend. In the 1850s, after the Mexican War (1846-48) had established the Rio Grande as the southern border of the USA, federal survey crews came to have a look – and US troops followed soon afterward, ordered to move the Indians toward reservations. It took the soldiers a quarter century to force the Mescalero Apaches from the land, for the Indians knew this country far better than their pursuers. For their part, the Chisos were offered asylum in Mexico, but once there, they were killed or shipped into slavery – tricked by the very Mexicans who had offered them refuge.

20th Century

By the end of the 19th century, Anglos had begun sheep and cattle ranches throughout the Big Bend. The economy diversified in a hurry when the settlers discovered cinnabar. This substance, which the region's Indians had long used for war paint and rock art, was also the principal ore from which mercury was extracted. Before long, some 2000 people lived in the boomtowns of Terlingua and Study Butte, and the Chisos Mining Company – second-largest in the world at the time – produced 100,000 flasks of mercury between 1900 and 1940. But when the cinnabar veins played out, the boom ended with a thud, leaving ghost towns that have only recently and partially been reclaimed by recreation-oriented businesses.

In the 1930s, civic leaders in Alpine proposed an international park on the Rio Grande. The US Congress authorized Big Bend National Park in 1935, but it took another nine years for the state of Texas to wrangle the proposed parklands out of the hands of private landowners. Establishing the adjacent parks in Mexico took another half century. In 1994, Mexican President Carlos Salinas de Gortari finally proclaimed that not one but two parks had been officially designated – the 1070-sq-mile Cañon de Santa Elena preserve in the state of Chihuahua and the 804-sq-mile Maderas del Carmen protected area in Coahuila. The two nations are now contemplating a 'sister park' or 'binational park' arrangement, under which the two nations would manage their own park areas but work together to preserve the shared ecosystem, which knows no border.

GEOLOGY

According to Indian legend, after the Great Spirit finished creating the rest of the earth, he dumped the leftover rocks in a pile at Big Bend. Big Bend's geology, from the Chisos Mountains to fantastic desert rock formations, often appears random, but geologists have pinned down the following facts.

For millions of years, Big Bend lay at the bottom of the sea, part of a trough that extended into what is now Arkansas and Oklahoma. Over time, the sea became shallower and eventually disappeared, leaving a wondrous fossil record of marine life and beds of limestone both thick (the Sierra del Carmen and Santa Elena formations) and thin (the Boquillas formation). Once the sea was gone, the dinosaurs took over; Big Bend was especially favored by pterodactyls, the largest flying creatures ever, with a wingspan of 35 feet or more. Bones from a pterodactyl skeleton recovered at Big Bend in

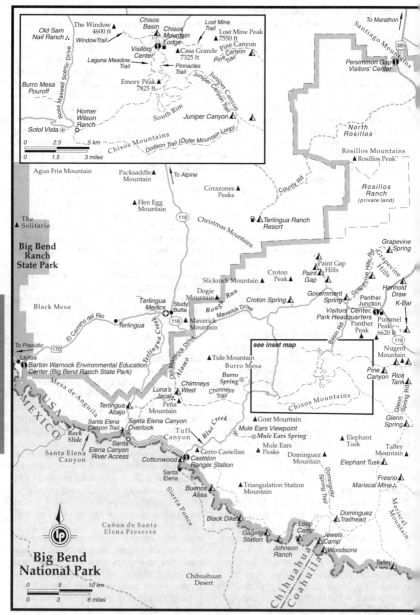

--- Unpaved Road	▲ Campsite
--- Primitive Road	∴ Ruins
— Trail	⛽ Gas Station
>> Rapids	⛱ Picnic Area

1971 can be seen at the Texas Memorial Museum at the University of Texas at Austin – see the South Central Texas chapter for more information.

Starting about 65 million years ago, the 'mountain building' Cenozoic era began, and tectonic forces produced the Rocky Mountains and the Sierra Madre. Volcanic activity followed, spreading ash and lava over thousands of square miles in the region. Increased tensions in the earth's crust created faulting, dropping the central portion of the park between the Santiago Mountains (near the Persimmon Gap entrance) and the Mesa de Anguila (in the park's western reach near Lajitas) and creating what geologists call the Sunken Block, while further elevating the Chisos Mountains. Meanwhile, the Rio Grande – perhaps working in tandem with the Rio Conchos from Mexico – carved the great canyons that define the river today. Erosion has left its mark all over the landscape in such unusual forms as the Grapevine Hills, Elephant Tusk and Mule Ears peaks.

FLORA & FAUNA
Because Big Bend has so many different environments, from riparian to desert to mountain, there's an amazing variety of critters and plants: 450 bird species (more than any other US national park), 1000 types of plants, 70 mammals, 115 types of butterflies and 56 reptiles and amphibians. See Flora & Fauna in the introductory Facts about Texas chapter for more information.

WHEN TO GO
Most travelers consider spring and fall the best times of year to visit Big Bend National Park. Summer (June through August) is very hot, with typical daytime temperatures around 100°F; late summer can be rainy, too. Spring means moderate temperatures and lots of wildflowers (and lots of people), and fall is also quite pleasant, especially for river running.

Some park fanciers believe winter is the best time of all to come; it's usually relatively mild, although temperatures in the Chisos can fall below freezing and Basin Rd typically closes two or three times each winter, sometimes for several days. But the

THE BIG BEND

snow is never deep enough to preclude hiking, and the touch of frost makes the trees and cacti a beautiful sight. At all times of the year, it's wise to layer your clothes in the morning and peel off the top layers if you get too warm.

ORIENTATION

Park headquarters and the main visitors' center are at Panther Junction, which is on the main park road 29 miles from the Persimmon Gap entrance and 22 miles from the Maverick entrance near Study Butte. The visitors' center is open daily 8 am to 6 pm; it may be closed on Christmas Day and New Year's Day. A Chevron service station is nearby, offering fuel, repairs and a small stock of snacks and beverages.

From Panther Junction, another major road leads 20 miles southeast to Rio Grande Village. Two other principal roads, the 7-mile Basin Rd and 30-mile Ross Maxwell Scenic Drive, take off from the main park road west of Panther Junction. Sharp curves and steep grades make Basin Rd unsuitable for RVs longer than 24 feet and trailers longer than 20 feet.

Maps

The free National Park Service *Big Bend* map, available at the entrances and visitors' centers, is adequate for most visitors to the park. More detailed topographic maps, recommended for backcountry travel, can be purchased at the visitors' centers.

INFORMATION
Visitors' Centers & Fees

Get information in advance of your visit by writing the Superintendent, PO Box 129, Big Bend National Park, TX 79834; by calling ☎ 915-477-2251; or accessing the park website at www.nps.gov/bibe.

In addition to Panther Junction, visitors' centers are found in the Basin, at Persimmon Gap and at Rio Grande Village. Castolon has a ranger station. There's a lost-and-found at Panther Junction.

Big Bend charges a $10 fee per passenger vehicle; bicyclists, motorcyclists and walk-in visitors are charged $5. A $20 annual pass is

good for one calendar year from the date of purchase. The park also sells and honors the Golden Eagle, Golden Age and Golden Access passports (see National Parks in the Facts about Texas chapter for details).

Check the bulletin boards at any of the visitors' centers or at park campgrounds for a list of upcoming interpretive activities, which are held daily November through April, less often the rest of the year. Some programs are geared especially for children ages seven to 11, who can also take part in the Big Bend Junior Ranger program. Junior Ranger activity books are available for $1 at visitors' centers; kids who complete them can earn stickers, badges and other prizes.

The park offers a variety of free leaflets on special-interest topics, including biological diversity, border towns, hiking and backpacking, Glenn Springs, geology, archaeology, history, and dinosaurs, pterosaurs and crocodiles. All are available at park visitors' centers. Park information is available in Spanish and German as well as English.

Another good source of information is the Big Bend Natural History Association (☎ 915-477-2236), PO Box 196, Big Bend National Park, TX 79834, an educational organization that publishes *The Big Bend Paisano*, a park newspaper, and several informative booklets about Big Bend trails and attractions. Each year, the association leads about two dozen seminars on many aspects of life in Big Bend country. Most are in spring or fall, last one to three days and cost $50 a day. Past topics include bird-watching, bats, geology, desert tracking and area history. The association also holds seminars at Amistad National Recreation Area and at the McDonald Observatory, near Fort Davis (see later in this chapter). Call or write for a current brochure.

On the Internet, the Terlingua-based outfitter Desert Sports posts a daily report on weather and river conditions at Big Bend. See www.desertsportstx.com/DS/BBdaily.html.

Money

Just when you thought there was nowhere in the USA without an ATM, you've found that place at Big Bend. The closest money machine is in Study Butte, 24 miles west of Panther Junction.

Media
No regular newspapers or radio or TV stations serve the Big Bend area; some motels get TV via satellite or cable, and you can pick up regional newspapers at the Chisos Mountain Lodge. For car tunes, your best bet is to bring along a bunch of cassettes. Try anything by Aaron Copland or Steve Earle.

Books
Although it's decades old and was out of print at press time, Ross Maxwell's *Big Bend of the Rio Grande* remains the definitive look at the area's geology and history. Check Big Bend-area used bookstores for a copy. Also interesting is *Big Bend: A Homesteader's Story* ($11.95, University of Texas Press), a reprint of the memoir penned by JO Langford, who settled in the park's Hot Springs area early in the 20th century.

Medical Services
Big Bend National Park is no place to get seriously injured or gravely ill. The closest hospital is in Alpine, 108 miles from Panther Junction. The nonprofit Terlingua Medics (☎ 915-371-2222 for emergencies, 915-371-2536 otherwise) have a first-aid station that's 26 miles west of Panther Junction, where trained paramedics can offer some assistance. Since there are no medical services in the park, it's smart to play it safe and be prepared for minor problems. Carry a good basic first-aid kit, and be positive it includes tweezers (for removing spines and thorns).

Short Stays in Big Bend

Considering how far Big Bend is from everywhere else and how hard it is to reach, you'd think people would stay put awhile once they get here. But the Park Service says a quarter of all Big Bend visitors spend only one day in the park. Here are a few suggestions on how to do Big Bend if time is short:

If you have only one day, get an early start! Take Ross Maxwell Scenic Drive to its end at the Santa Elena Canyon Overlook. Walk the 1.7-mile roundtrip trail to see Big Bend's most famous canyon. Backtrack 8 miles on Ross Maxwell Drive to the spur road just before Castolon. Park your vehicle in the designated area and make the short walk to the Rio Grande. Hail the rowboat ferry and cross to the Mexican village of Santa Elena for lunch. (See the boxed text later in this chapter for information and warnings on unofficial crossings into Mexico from Big Bend.)

Return to the main park road via Ross Maxwell Scenic Drive and then take Basin Rd into the Chisos Mountains. Hike a trail or two – the Windows Trail and Lost Mine Trail are good hikes of moderate length and difficulty. Next, depending on the time of year and available daylight, enjoy a sunset from the Chisos Mountain Lodge Restaurant (open only until 8 pm, closing even earlier in winter; see later in this chapter) or from the short Window View Trail.

If you have two days, spend your first day making the classic Rio Grande float through Santa Elena Canyon (see River Trips, later in this chapter, for details). On day two, take either Ross Maxwell Scenic Drive or Rio Grande Village Drive and plan a late-morning arrival at either of the park's two crossings into Mexico: Santa Elena, near Castolon (off Ross Maxwell Scenic Drive), or Boquillas del Carmen, near Rio Grande Village. Have lunch in Mexico and then return to the USA. Drive to Chisos Basin and spend the afternoon hiking the high country.

THE BIG BEND

Emergency

To report an emergency in the park, call the main park number (☎ 915-477-2251). After the automated telephone system answers, press 9. If there's no answer, hang up and dial ☎ 911.

Dangers & Annoyances

Big Bend is one of the most remote spots in North America, set amid wild country with all kinds of potential hazards. This doesn't mean it's an inherently dangerous place, but this does mean that safety and common sense should be your constant travel companions.

Driving Most Big Bend deaths happen in car accidents, usually involving motorists who were either driving too fast or were too tired. Drunken driving is a problem, too, since the best places to scare up some nighttime fun in Big Bend country are a long way from where people bunk down.

The park's maximum speed limit is 45mph, but there are plenty of places, such as the harrowing final descent into Chisos Basin, where slower speeds are posted and must be observed. Watch for animals on or alongside the roadway, especially at night. And if you plan to drink alcohol, choose a designated driver, stay in the close-in park gateways, or stay in Terlingua, Study Butte or Lajitas, where nightspots are within walking distance from accommodations.

Heat & Hiking Safety This is the desert, after all. The Park Service recommends that hikers carry and drink at least 1 gallon of water per person per day during the hottest months and only slightly less in winter. Although there are occasional springs, they are unreliable and the animals need them, too. Wear a hat, sunscreen, long pants and a long-sleeved shirt. And take a cue from the animals: Do your hiking early in the morning or in the evening, not at midday when the unrelenting sun turns Big Bend into one big Easy-Bake Oven.

Plan hikes according to your ability. There are plenty of well-marked, well-trod trails in the park, and these are best for casual hikers. More ambitious trekkers should carry and use a compass and map. People heading out overnight should register with the park for its free backcountry use permit (see Backpacking, later in this chapter). If you do get lost or hurt, stay in one place to conserve your energy, and signal for help. Distress signals include three blasts on a whistle or a large 'X' marked on the ground with rocks or any other material visible from the air. Let a friend or relative know your whereabouts and return date, so they can call park rangers if you're not back when expected.

Spines & Thorns Of all the myriad natural hazards at Big Bend, plants may be the worst. We're talking spines, thorns, daggers and more, all within inches of the park's desert trails. Walk carefully, watch where you sit, and dress smart: Sturdy boots or shoes are a must, and rugged clothing is a good idea. Carry a pair of tweezers in case you need to extract any sharpies. Finally, watch what you eat: the Park Service says visitors have gotten mouthfuls of delicate but debilitating spines while trying to eat the fruit from some species of prickly pear cactus.

Wild Animals There's a slim chance you might encounter a black bear at Big Bend. If you do, keep a safe distance and do not feed, follow or approach it. If a bear approaches you, scare it away by shouting, waving your arms or throwing objects. If you see cubs, back away slowly so the mother won't fear an attack.

Rangers are trying to keep Big Bend's bears from getting habituated to people. Store all food, coolers, cooking utensils and toiletries in a hard-sided vehicle or hard-sided cooler, preferably the trunk of your car, or in the special bear-proof lockers available throughout the Chisos Basin area. Don't use Styrofoam coolers, which are susceptible to raids by wild animals. Discard trash in the bear-proof rubbish containers provided, and report all bear sightings to a park ranger. In bear country, you should not store water in your tent if the water bottle has your scent on it.

Mountain lions are here, too, but you probably won't see them. Children are more vulnerable than adults to mountain lion attack, so adults should not allow children to hike by themselves or far apart from the group. The park posts signs on trails where mountain lion activity has been reported; if you're hiking with small children, you might consider choosing another trail. The visitors' centers have lists of recent bear and mountain lion sightings.

Other critters at Big Bend may seem harmless, but javelinas, skunks, coyotes and raccoons are wild, too. Don't feed them. Leave them alone. This means you.

Venomous Animals Big Bend's five poisonous snake species won't attack unless provoked. Local lore has it that snakebite victims are nearly always drunken males who decided to tease a snake. But even sober park visitors must avoid reaching or stepping into spots where snakes might be resting or hiding. Most snakes keep a low profile in daylight, when you're unlikely to see them. Night hikers should stay on the trail and carry a flashlight.

Tarantulas inhabit the park, but they, too, will not attack you unless you deliberately annoy them. Big Bend's scorpions are not deadly, but you should still get prompt attention if you're stung.

Automotive Services

Inside the park, gas is available only at Panther Junction and Rio Grande Village. The Panther Junction Chevron station (☎ 915-477-2294), open daily 7 am to 7 pm year-round, also has a tow truck and garage for minor repairs. More extensive repairs can be performed in the gateway towns.

HIKING

Big Bend has 150 miles of trails amid the largest area of roadless public land in Texas. The slim booklet *Hiker's Guide to Trails of Big Bend National Park* ($1.25 at all park visitors' centers) gives short descriptions of three dozen trails ranging from easy walks to primitive backpacking routes. The book is fine for casual visitors; repeat trekkers may want to spring for *Hiking Big Bend National Park*, by Laurence Parent ($12.95, Falcon

The curious javelina

Press). Pets are not allowed on park trails, nor are they permitted in the backcountry.

See Dangers & Annoyances, earlier in the chapter, for some good advice about planning your hike.

Chisos Mountains

The Chisos have the park's densest concentration of trails, including several of the park's most popular. Look for a copy of the *Chisos Mountains Trails Map* (50¢) to help plan your treks. Following are a few of the most popular trails.

The short **Window View Trail**, just a third of a mile roundtrip from the Basin convenience store, is especially popular at sunset. Time it right, and you may see the sun go down right through the Window, a low point in the Basin through which you can see back onto the desert.

For a bit more of a stretch, take the **Chisos Basin Loop Trail**, an easy 1.6-mile roundtrip hike from the Basin Trailhead along the Laguna Meadow Trail, and then turn off on a left fork toward a promontory overlooking the upper basin. From there, return via the Boot Springs section of the Pinnacles Trail.

This 4- to 5½-mile roundtrip trek on the **Window Trail** is unusual – it's downhill one-way, with a gradual climb back. The shorter route takes off from the Chisos Basin Campground; the longer one starts at Basin

THE BIG BEND

Trailhead. Birders will enjoy this trail, and bears sometimes show up, too.

The **Lost Mine Trail** takes off from a roadside parking lot at Panther Pass. Starting at 5600 feet, it winds up the northern flank of Casa Grande to a promontory on the ridge separating Pine and Juniper Canyons. Although the trail is 4.8 miles roundtrip, it can easily be shortened to about 2 miles roundtrip by turning around at the Juniper Canyon Overlook. A self-guiding booklet is available at the trailhead.

Sturdy hikers can bag the highest peak at Big Bend, **Emory Peak**, on the 9-mile portion of the Pinnacles Trail complex. The 1-mile spur trail to the 7825-foot peak leaves the main trail after Pinnacles Pass, 3½ miles from the Basin Trailhead. It ends with a short scramble up a sheer rock wall. Although the mountaintop is dominated by communications equipment, that doesn't detract much from the wide-angle views.

Many serious hikers say the **South Rim** is their favorite Big Bend trek, mainly because of the payoff view at the end: from the South Rim at the southwestern edge of the High Chisos, the vista includes Santa Elena Canyon and the Sierra del Carmen. On clear days, it's even possible to see mountains up to 80 miles away in Mexico. This is a 13- to 14½-mile roundtrip hike, depending on the route taken, so plan on either a very long day or an overnight outing. The shortest route from the Basin Trailhead is 6½ miles via Laguna Meadow; either hike back out the same way or take the loop approach via the Boot Spring Trail.

Desert & Riverside Hikes

These hikes range from short introductions to the Chihuahua Desert to trails leading to the Rio Grande. Don't forget to drink plenty of water, and wear a hat and sunscreen.

Take a crash course in desert ecology on the **Chihuahuan Desert Nature Trail**, an easy half-mile roundtrip interpretive trail off Rio Grande Village Drive, at the Dugout Wells picnic area about 6 miles east of Panther Junction.

Beginning at campsite 18 at the main Rio Grande campground (not the RV park), the three-quarter-mile **Rio Grande Village Nature Trail** passes through dense riparian vegetation before emerging in the desert for a view of the Rio Grande. This is a good short trail for birding and photography.

Although it's only 1.4 miles roundtrip, the **Boquillas Canyon Trail** is rated as moderately difficult because of a short climb at the start followed by a descent to the Rio Grande. Leave time to play on the sand slide and enjoy the sunlight dancing on the canyon walls. The trail begins at the end of the Boquillas Canyon spur road, east of Rio Grande Village.

A hike on **Santa Elena Canyon Trail** is a must if you don't have time to float the Rio Grande. The 1.7-mile roundtrip trek from the end of Ross Maxwell Scenic Drive takes hikers upriver into the amazingly steep, narrow Santa Elena Canyon. The trail crosses Terlingua Creek near its start, so pack along some old shoes in case you need to wade.

The 2-mile roundtrip **Hot Springs Historic Walk** offers an easy stroll into the past. JO Langford homesteaded here in 1909 and built a small health resort centered on the hot springs nearby. ('The fountain that Ponce de León failed to find,' one of Langford's ads proclaimed.) The site includes remains of the town, along with a 105°F spring still in use today. Soakers will find a stone bathtub at river's edge. Swimming in the Rio Grande itself can be dangerous due to strong currents and submerged debris. The trailhead is at the end of a 2-mile dirt road leading south from Rio Grande Village Drive, not far west of the village.

If Boquillas Canyon is the sandbox of giants, the boulders of **Grapevine Hills** are their building blocks. The 2.2-mile roundtrip trek off Grapevine Hills Rd (6 miles from Maverick Drive) leads through a sandy wash rimmed by huge hunks of granite. One famous sight, another Big Bend window – this one of boulders – can be seen by following the trail 100 yards along a ridge to the right of the low pass at the south end of the wash.

BACKPACKING

Big Bend's primitive backpacking routes range from well-traveled desert washes to the truly challenging limestone uplifts of Mesa de Anguila and the Deadhorse Mountains. Rangers say that because of the constantly changing trail and spring conditions, it's pretty much impossible to plan an extended backpacking trip before you actually get to the park. What you can do instead is figure out how much time you have and the distance you'd like to cover; based on that information, park staff will help you plot a trip. Many trails require use of topographical maps and a compass.

Free backcountry use permits are necessary for overnight backpacking. They must be picked up in person no earlier than 24 hours before you hit the trail. People backpacking alone are also asked to fill out a 'Solo Hiker Form.' Backcountry use permits are available at all visitors' centers, but hikers considering a trail in the Chisos Mountains should make arrangements at the Basin visitors' center since staff there are the most familiar with that popular area.

SCENIC DRIVES

Big Bend National Park has 110 miles of paved road and 150 miles of dirt road, and scenic driving is easily the park's most popular activity. The booklet *Road Guide to Paved and Improved Dirt Roads of Big Bend National Park* is an excellent guide to the park's most popular drives. A similar booklet, *Road Guide to Backcountry Dirt Roads of Big Bend National Park*, offers advice on major secondary routes. The booklets cost $1.25 apiece, and they're available at visitors' centers. (See the boxed text El Camino del Rio for a scenic drive just outside the park.)

Maverick Drive

If you enter Big Bend National Park from the west, this is the road you'll be on. It's 22 miles from the west entrance to park headquarters at Panther Junction; the Ross Maxwell and Basin Scenic Drives take off along the way. Maverick Drive is notable for its desert scenery. You're likely to see coyotes, javelinas and mule deer along the way. Just west of Basin Junction, a side trip on Grapevine Hills Rd leads to fields of weirdly shaped, highly eroded boulders.

Ross Maxwell Scenic Drive

This 30-mile route leaves Maverick Drive, the main park road, midway between the west entrance and Panther Junction headquarters. The Chisos Mountains provide a grand panorama along the way; other landmarks include Old Sam Nail Ranch, Sotol Vista, Tuff Canyon, the Mule Ears peaks and Castolon. This drive's big payoff comes near the end: the view of Santa Elena Canyon and its 1500-foot sheer rock walls.

On the return trip, as an alternative to backtracking on Ross Maxwell Scenic Drive, consider taking the 14-mile improved dirt Old Maverick Drive from Santa Elena Canyon back to the main park road. Old Maverick Drive leads past **Luna's Jacal**, a primitive homestead built smack-dab along Alamo Wash, the old Comanche War Trail. Gilberto Luna not only lived peaceably amid the Indians; he managed to successfully farm the dry wash *and* he supposedly had about 50 children. He died in 1947 at age 108.

Basin Rd

This 7-mile drive climbs from the main park road to Chisos Basin. Sights include Panther Peak; Pulliam Ridge; Lost Mine Peak; Green

Coyote

THE BIG BEND

Gulch, the canyon between the desert lowlands and the mountains; and Panther Pass, at 5679 feet the highest point on the road. Finally it reaches the Basin itself, with the park's most famous landmarks: Casa Grande, Emory Peak (highest in the park at 7825 feet) and the Window.

Rio Grande Village Drive
This 20-mile drive leads from park headquarters at Panther Junction toward the Sierra del Carmen range, running through the park southeast into Mexico. Highlights along the way include the Glenn Spring gravel road, which leads to a former ranching and wax-industry settlement; Dugout Wells, once the site of a pioneer schoolhouse; Langford Hot Springs; Old Ore Rd, another primitive route for high-clearance vehicles; the international crossing to the scenic Mexican village of Boquillas del Carmen; and the Boquillas Canyon Overlook.

Persimmon Gap Drive
This 29-mile drive from park headquarters to the northern park entrance has several interesting detours. A fossil bones exhibit may be seen down a short side road near the north side of the Tornillo Creek bridge. Another side road, this one 7½ miles long, leads to Dagger Flat, a stand of giant dagger yuccas that grow more than 15 feet tall.

RIVER TRIPS
Originating in southern Colorado, the Rio Grande is an insignificant trickle by the time it enters Texas. It would be unfloatable if not for the Rio Conchos, a Mexican river that flows into the Rio Grande near Presidio, giving it new life and power for its 118-mile run along the southern border of Big Bend National Park.

A federally designated wild and scenic river in the park and positioned downstream to the Terrell-Val Verde county line, the Rio Grande has earned its place among the top North American river trips for both rafting and canoeing. Rapids ranging up to Class IV alternate with calm stretches that are perfect for wildlife viewing, photography and just plain relaxation.

Trips on the river can range from several hours to several days:

Santa Elena Canyon is a classic float featuring the Class IV Rockslide rapid and lasts at least 11 to 12 hours (overnight is better).

Mariscal Canyon is noted for its beauty and isolation and lasts two to three days.

Boquillas Canyon is the longest and most tranquil of the park's three canyons and is best for intermediate to advanced boaters and canoeists with camping skills; it lasts three to four days.

Lower Canyons is downriver from the park; unescorted rafters and canoeists should have wilderness skills; the trip lasts a week to 10 days.

Just upriver from the park, Colorado Canyon has lots of whitewater. It's a popular day-trip option, especially if water levels at Santa Elena aren't favorable for floating. Colorado Canyon is also a good run for experienced canoeists.

Guided floats cost about $100 to $125 per person per day, including all meals and gear (except a sleeping bag for overnighters, and your personal effects). Three companies offer guided river rafting trips in and around Big Bend:

Big Bend River Tours
  (☎ 915-424-3219, 800-545-4240)
  PO Box 317, Terlingua, TX 79852

Far Flung Adventures
  (☎ 915-371-2489, 800-359-4138, fax 915-371-2325,
  miked@farflung.com, www.farflung.com)
  PO Box 377, Terlingua, TX 79852

Texas River Expeditions
  (☎ 915-371-2633, 800-839-7238, fax 915-371-2633)
  PO Box 583, Terlingua, TX 79852, with its office
  in Study Butte

All three have been in business a long time and have solid reputations, yet Far Flung Adventures generally gets the best reviews, for both its highly experienced, personable staff and its creative trip offerings. Several times each year, chef François Maeder of Crumpets Restaurant in San Antonio joins Far Flung on special gourmet floats, which run three days and two nights and cost about $650 per person. Other specialty trips feature prominent Texas musicians such as Darden Smith, Jimmie Dale Gilmore and Butch

Hancock. Sometimes (as on the annual New Year's float) the troubadours simply come along to play; other times, they lead song-writing workshops. Cost varies depending on trip length.

Desert Sports (☎ 915-371-2727, 888-989-6900), PO Box 448, Terlingua, TX 79852, offers guided canoe trips throughout the Big Bend region. Although the Rio Grande is better known for rafting, travelers looking for a more active adventure should consider canoeing, a more hands-on experience.

Gear Rental & Permits

Rafts and other river gear can be rented from Rio Grande Adventures (☎ 915-371-2567, 800-343-1640) and Desert Sports (see previous section), both in Terlingua. Desert Sports also rents canoes, and Rio Grande Adventures runs a shuttle service.

Floaters boating on their own must obtain a free permit at Panther Junction within 24 hours before putting in. Permits for the Lower Canyons of the Rio Grande are available at the Persimmon Gap visitors' center and the Stillwell Store, on FM 2627. A self-permitting station for Santa Elena Canyon can be found at the Barton Warnock Environmental Education Center, just west of Lajitas. But the park encourages river runners to get permits in the park to obtain the latest information on conditions, which change rapidly.

HORSEBACK RIDING

Although horses are permitted on many trails at Big Bend, no animals can be rented inside the park. If you bring your own, get the required stock use permit, available free at any visitors' center. Government Spring, a primitive campsite near Panther Junction, caters to parties with between four and eight horses. It can be reserved up to 10 weeks in advance by calling ☎ 915-477-2251 ext 158. Several stables outside the park offer guided trail rides in the Big Bend region; see the Terlingua, Lajitas and Fort Davis & Davis Mountains sections later in this chapter.

PLACES TO STAY & EAT
Camping

Big Bend has three main campgrounds: **Rio Grande Village**, **Chisos Basin** and **Cottonwood** (near the Castolon area). Sites are first-come, first-served and cost $7 a night. Rio Grande Village is the only area that provides hookups, camper showers and a coin laundry.

Rio Grande Village also has a concessionaire-operated *RV park* (☎ 915-477-2293). Rigs using these 25 full-hookup sites ($14.50 for two people, $1 additional for each extra person age 12 or older) must have water and 20- or 30-amp electrical hookups as well as a 3-inch sewer connection. An adjacent 100-site campground is geared to 'dry' RV camping and tenting, with water and flush toilets but no hookups. Generators may only be used from 7 am to 9 pm; mercifully, a no-generator zone is also available. June through February, the village store is open 9 am to 6 pm, with laundry until 5 pm and showers until 5:30 pm. March to May, the store is open 9 am to 8 pm, with laundry until 7 pm

and showers (75¢ for five minutes) until 7:30 pm.

The 65-site Chisos Basin and 31-site Cottonwood campgrounds have small sites that are best suited to tents and small RVs. Neither campground is recommended for vehicles towing trailers longer than 20 feet, nor for RVs longer than 24 feet, mainly because of the steep and winding access roads.

Tent camping is also permitted at primitive sites throughout the Big Bend backcountry. These sites are free, but a backcountry use permit must be obtained at a park visitors' center. All park camping areas typically fill up during spring break in March and April, and over the Thanksgiving and Christmas holidays. During peak periods, plan to be at the campground by about 1 pm to try for any sites that might open up. When all of the campgrounds are full, rangers direct tent

Crossing into Mexico

There are no official border crossings in or around Big Bend National Park, and it sometimes seems there's no border here at all. People wade horses across the Rio Grande. Pickups are driven through in low water. And no one pays much mind to such trips, perhaps because anyone crossing illegally would face a long trek across the Chihuahuan Desert to get anywhere they might want to go.

Visitors shouldn't miss the chance to make one or two of these casual border crossings. But despite the laid-back atmosphere, it's a good idea for visitors – particularly people of color or anyone who isn't a US citizen – to bring along a passport or visa, just in case you're hassled by a park ranger or Customs official. You'll need to go to the nearest official border crossing – at Presidio – if you have anything to declare to Customs when returning to the USA. Also, see the Border section of this book's Getting There & Away chapter, which details the official technicalities of crossings to and from Mexico.

From the park, people can cross to Boquillas del Carmen, Coahuila, and to Santa Elena, Chihuahua, via ferry during daylight hours. Each town has about 250 residents. Simply hail a rowboat, pay the nominal fee (about $2 roundtrip) and walk into a different world.

We chose **Santa Elena** for a lunch crossing. From the Mexican riverbank, it was a short walk up the hill to town; our destination, *Restaurant de Maria Elena*, was just to the right. Inside a screened porch we enjoyed a plate of enchiladas, with sopapillas for dessert, while watching Maria Elena's young granddaughter play. We paid our $5 bill and moved on.

Just down the dirt road, a new arts-and-crafts shop was selling an array of handmade goods from all over Mexico, which owner Lydia Garcia receives in shipments from her daughter, who lives in the city of Chihuahua. We found pottery, blankets, dolls and drums, with prices marked in US dollars, and noted that bargaining doesn't seem to be as prevalent a practice here as in the large border towns.

campers into available backcountry. There's also an overflow RV area at Rio Grande, which opens only when every other RV space in the park is taken. When it's full, RVers must take their chances in the park's gateway cities.

Chisos Mountain Lodge

This concessionaire-operated complex (☎ 915-477-2291) in the Basin gets good, if not great, marks for accommodations and passing grades for food. You can do better on both counts if you stay outside the park, but the scenery here is a lot better.

The choice accommodations are the stone cottages, which rent for $78 for up to three people. (Extra people are charged $10 each; the cottages each have three double beds, so you could sleep six people semicomfortably.) But there are only four of these cottages, so

they're hard to come by. ('No 103 has the best view in the state of Texas, but we'd prefer you don't print that,' we were told. Shhhhh. You didn't hear it here, OK?)

Next nicest are rooms in the Casa Grande Motor Lodge, which have balconies and good views of the Basin and surrounding mountains, not to mention the javelinas wandering around in search of a handout (obey the signs and turn 'em down). Rates for all rooms run about $65 to $75. Most have two double beds; a few have one double and one single. Children younger than 12 stay free. Guest rooms don't have TVs or telephones, but a pay phone and TV are in the lobby.

Reservations are a must, but management says there are often cancellations. Go ahead and check, but do it before you get to the park. To get a reservations form or more information, call the above number or write

---

Another block or so down the street, we came to the school, where a sign on the side door read, 'Welcome to our small but interesting museum,' a promise that proved true on both counts. Inside, we perused exhibits of fossils, rocks, arrowheads, stone cookware and photos of the schoolchildren's field trip to La Perla, a much bigger town about 93 miles (150km) to the south. That excursion was funded by donations to the museum, so we dropped another dollar in the box on the way out.

The **Boquillas del Carmen** crossing, near Rio Grande Village, leads to a landing 1 mile from the Mexican town. From here, visitors can walk, rent a burro or take a pickup-truck taxi to the village, which has a restaurant, a cantina and a few stores selling crafts and limited groceries. (Horses can be rented in both Boquillas and Santa Elena; ask your boat driver for directions to the stables.) Boquillas is probably the most-used crossing, because of its location near the Rio Grande park campgrounds; consequently, the town has become considerably more commercial than Santa Elena.

Unofficial crossings can be found outside the park, too. West of the park, the farming village of **Paso Lajitas**, accessible via a rowboat ferry from Lajitas, stands in stark contrast to the bustling US resort across the river. Paso Lajitas is the jumping-off spot for San Carlos Excursions (☎ 915-424-3221), which offers small-group day trips along the scenic 20-mile dirt road to **San Carlos**, Chihuahua, a spring-fed town with waterfalls and terraced rock gardens. The cost is $65 per person for two or three people, or $50 per person for four or more, including lunch. Participants have the option of staying overnight at modern *La Gloria Bed & Breakfast* in San Carlos for $40 per person, including dinner and breakfast.

East of the park, FM 2627 leads to **La Linda**, Coahuila. The bridge here – the only one in the region – was closed to vehicular traffic several years ago, but people still walk across, and vehicles sometimes ford the river at low water.

Chisos Mountains Lodge, Big Bend National Park, TX 79834.

Oops. We almost forgot to talk about food – that's understandable because the fare in the lodge is quite forgettable. Breakfast ($4 to $6) features French toast, eggs, pancakes and the like. At dinner, you'll find such choices as grilled breast of chicken ($8.50) or pork chops and applesauce ($8) on the menu, with homemade cobblers for dessert. Ho hum. Try to get a window table, since the sublime Basin view is the best thing about this place. And if you're a devoted foodie, be sure to bookend your Big Bend visit with a stop in Alpine, Fort Davis or Marathon, where there are truly memorable restaurants.

GETTING THERE & AWAY

There is no public transportation to or from the park. The closest buses and trains run through Alpine, 108 miles northwest of Panther Junction. The nearest major airports are in Midland (230 miles northeast, with shuttle service available to Alpine) and El Paso (325 miles northwest). Smaller airports in Lajitas and Alpine cater to charter and private aircraft. See Alpine (in this chapter) and El Paso and Midland (in the West Texas chapter) for more information.

There is no public transportation within the park. Mountain-bike rentals are available at Desert Sports in Terlingua (see the River Trips section), but you'll need to get to Terlingua by private transportation.

West of Big Bend National Park

The three tiny communities of Study Butte, Terlingua and Lajitas – with a total population of a few hundred at most – are the outfitting headquarters for Big Bend National Park. Together, they also offer a good selection of visitor services; interestingly, despite the tens of thousands of people who pass through here annually, this is one of a very few places in the USA without chain motels or restaurants – at least so far. If you'd like

to stay here during peak periods, it's wise to book months in advance. Keep in mind that there is no public transportation to these three towns.

See the River Trips section earlier in this chapter to get information on Rio Grande floats within and outside the park. Other activities are listed later in the chapter under the outfitters' respective towns.

STUDY BUTTE
Population 120

Pronounced 'stoody byoot,' this former mining boomtown sits at the junction of Hwy 118 and FM 170; it's often considered inseparable from Terlingua, although the latter is officially a few miles west.

Information

Look for the 24-hour ATM at the Quicksilver Branch of the First National Bank (☎ 915-371-2211). There's a post office (☎ 915-371-2269) at the crossroads; you can address poste restante mail to General Delivery, Terlingua, TX 79852. Use the same zip code when writing any of the businesses listed in the Study Butte, Terlingua and Lajitas sections.

Places to Stay

Terlingua Oasis RV Park (☎ 915-371-2218, 800-848-2363), right at the Hwy 118-FM 170 intersection, charges $15 for full-hookup sites and $8 for up to two people in a tent campsite; extra people are charged $2 apiece. Reservations are accepted, making this a good bet during peak periods such as spring break. *Big Bend Motor Inn/Mission Lodge* (☎ 915-371-2218, 800-848-2363), also at the Hwy 118-FM 170 junction, has rooms ranging from $70 to $80; expect to pay the higher rate during peak periods. The *Chisos Mining Co Motel* (☎ 915-371-2430), three-quarters of a mile west on FM 170, has rooms for $42 to $50 and cabins with full kitchenettes starting at $60. This place is also sometimes called the Easter Egg Motel.

Seventeen miles north of Study Butte, a 16-mile dirt road leads east off Hwy 118 to the remote *Terlingua Ranch Resort* (☎ 915-371-2416); see the Big Bend National Park map. The 313-sq-mile ranch is primarily used

Socorro Mission, a highlight along the Mission Trail south of El Paso

Misión San Antonio de los Tiguas in Ysleta del Sur Pueblo, El Paso

JOHN ELK III

JOHN ELK III

Hot springs along the Rio Grande in Big Bend National Park

Along the Chisos Mountains' South Rim trail

Hot Springs ghost town in Big Bend

View of Boquillas Canyon from Rio Grande Village

Rafters paddling through Santa Elena Canyon

Prickly pear cacti in Big Bend National Park

The well-known boulder window in the Grapevine Hills, Big Bend National Park

Living the rock climber's dream at Hueco Tanks State Historical Park

McKittrick Canyon, Guadalupe Mountains NP

The ocotillo, a common Chihuahuan Desert sight

by people who own property here, but it's also open to guests, with tent spaces for $3, RV hookups for $9 and cabins for $38. There are no phones or TVs, but there's a pool, restaurant, barbecue pits and gasoline, plus lots of room for hiking, birding and mountain biking.

Places to Eat
Roadrunner Deli (☎ *915-371-2364*), in the Study Butte Mall, east of the Hwy 118-FM 170 intersection, specializes in packing tasty picnics for the Big Bend-bound. Breakfast, lunch and the area's best coffee are available all seven days of the week. Next door, the **Study Butte Store** (☎ *915-371-2231*) has groceries, gas, ice and a lending library.

TERLINGUA
Population 25
Terlingua seems more a state of mind than an actual place. Even its precise location is elusive, though when most people say 'Terlingua,' they mean the so-called ghost town about 4 miles west of the junction of Hwy 118 and FM 170. Several businesses make their homes in and around the ghost town; nearby, the old adobes – some without electricity – have been reclaimed by river guides, artists and others who relish life in the outback.

Information
The bulletin board outside the post office at the Hwy 118-FM 170 junction is a prime source for news about local goings-on. Also look for the *Terlingua Moon*, circulation 45, a photocopied news sheet posted around the area. Wryly written, the *Moon* features a blend of news and gossip. One item describing *Brides Magazine*'s photo shoot at Ernst Tinaja, an impressive desert cliffs area in Big Bend National Park, suggested a possible caption: 'Tammy is holding a bouquet of prickly pear, catclaw and jimsonweed and is wearing snake-proof shin guards and SPF 50.'

Activities
Terlingua sits amid prime mountain-biking territory. Desert Sports (☎ 915-371-2727,

888-989-6900, info@desertsportstx.com, www .desertsportstx.com) provides rental bikes and guided tours of all types, along with advice on the best places to ride. For horseback riding, call Big Bend Stables (☎ 915-371-2212, 800-887-4331), where rates run $22 for one hour, $33 for two hours and $44 for three hours. Big Bend Touring Society (☎ 915-371-2548) is another local guide service handling a variety of activity trips.

Special Events
Terlingua is best known to the rest of Texas as home of the Chili Cook-Off, but there are actually two cookoffs, held the first Saturday of November: the Chili Appreciation Society International (CASI) event and the Frank X Tolbert-Wick Fowler Memorial Championship Chili Cook-Off. The feud between the two events boiled over in the

THE BIG BEND

El Camino del Rio (The River Road)

Lists of the most scenic roads in the USA nearly always include FM 170 west of Big Bend National Park, and you won't hear any argument from us. This eye-popping, gear-dropping route is a memorable adventure, one experienced by relatively few Big Bend visitors, even though it can be driven in any vehicle with good brakes. You have the Rio Grande on one side, fanciful geological formations all around and grades as steep as 15%. Strap in and hold on!

A milepost guide to FM 170 is available for $4 at area booksellers. Highlights along the way include the Big Hill, Colorado Canyon views, an old movie set, the Teepees picnic area and the southern reaches of Big Bend Ranch State Park. The only commercial establishment between Lajitas and Presidio, the **Redford Convenience Store** (☎ 915-384-2327), is open daily with snacks, a pay phone, post office and restrooms, but no gas.

FM 170 winds 67 miles from Study Butte to Presidio, which is as far as most people take it, but it continues another 48 miles upriver through more splendid desert landscapes and the tiny blips of Ruidosa and Candelaria. From Ruidosa, the Pinto Canyon Rd takes off for a wild and scenic drive that winds up in Marfa (see the Presidio County Outback section at the end of this chapter).

early 1980s. These days, CASI is a lot bigger and is strict about entrants' qualifications (competitors must have already qualified in one of the local cookoffs held around Texas and beyond); the Tolbert-Fowler event is less competitive and more of a big party. About 10,000 people invade Terlingua on cookoff weekend each year.

Terlingua also hosts the Chihuahuan Desert Challenge in mid-February, perhaps the biggest midwinter mountain-bike meet in the USA, featuring races and fun rides for all ages and abilities. For more information, see the folks at Desert Sports.

Places to Stay

Big Bend Travel Park (☎ 915-371-2250) is a pleasantly shaded campground on FM 170 between Terlingua and Study Butte. Tenters can camp for $2.50 per person per night; full hookups are $12 per night and $70 per week. This is on the same grounds as La Kiva, a locally popular bar and restaurant (see the next section). There's a laundry and showers, but the bathrooms could be cleaner. The nearby **BJ RV Park** (☎ 915-371-2259) is little more than a parking lot, but it's suitable for RVs. Nightly fees are $11, and showers are available.

Places to Eat

Every night's a party at the **Starlight Theater** (☎ 915-371-2326), in the Terlingua ghost town. This former movie theater had fallen into roofless disrepair (thus the 'starlight' name), but Angie Dean converted it into one of the area's favorite restaurants. Dinners are mostly in the $8 to $9 range, with frequent specials including tortilla soup ($3.50) on Sunday and pork chop chipotle ($8.75) on Saturday. The creative decor includes suspended cattle skulls, a mirror ball and a mural where the movie screen once hung. There's live music nearly every night in spring and fall. All in all, this is the best place to take the pulse of Terlingua.

The next three restaurants are all along on FM 170 between the Terlingua ghost town and Study Butte. **La Kiva** (☎ 915-371-2250), open evenings only, is an unusual underground restaurant attached to an outdoor courtyard. Barbecue is the specialty here: the Terlingua Trio of beef, pork and chicken goes for $12. Other offerings include El Diablo chili pie ($6.25) and Fiesta chicken topped with jack cheese and bacon ($7). The decor blends bulbous wood and exposed rock with a bit of bawdiness; check out the *Penisaurus erectus* set of bones donated to the restaurant by the Anthropological Society of Houston. If things get too smoky inside, the airy patio is a breath of fresh air. There's frequent live music, including an open-mike night every Wednesday 8 pm to midnight.

Desert Opry (☎ *915-371-2265*) is highly recommended by Big Bend vegetarians. It's run by Jack and Alice Knight, who also work as artists and musicians. The Knights closed down for several years while their son attended high school in San Antonio (there wasn't a high school in Terlingua until recently), but now the restaurant is open again, serving meals daily 8 am to 8 pm (at least fall through spring; in summer they're often on the craft-fair circuit). The menu includes veggie pizza pita ($3.75) and tofu burgers ($3.50), and an organic juice bar serves a variety of healthy concoctions, most less than $3. The live music here is usually 'on request,' with regular matinees scheduled about 2 pm in springtime. 'If no one is here, it turns into a rehearsal,' Jack explains.

We couldn't catch it open, but the *Hungry Javelina* might be worth a try for quick snacks. The eatery is housed in a tiny, multicolored trailer, and its sign promises tacos, burgers and chili.

Shopping

Terlingua Trading Co (☎ 915-371-2234), in the ghost town, has great gifts, everything from hot sauces and wines to an impressive selection of books. Check out the cool map on the wall, showing Terlingua in its mining heyday.

LAJITAS

Lajitas on the Rio Grande (☎ 915-424-3471, 800-944-9907) is a self-contained resort town with lodging, food, recreation and shops. It seems to attract mostly middle-age and older vacationers from Texas' urban areas, along with a fair number of young honeymooners. It's a comfortable and convenient base for anyone exploring the area, but if you stay here, be sure to get away from the resort for a while to ensure a true Big Bend experience.

Activities

The scenic nine-hole Lajitas golf course (☎ 915-424-3211) is a favorite among West Texans. Greens fees are $12 weekdays and $16 on weekends and holidays. Carts are $15 extra. The resort also has a pool and lighted tennis courts.

Lajitas Stables (☎ 915-424-3238) offers horseback trail rides ranging from a $22 hourlong trip to an $90 by-reservation day trip (including lunch) to overnight trips. Both Lajitas Stables and Glass Mountain Enterprises (☎ 915-426-3013), out of Fort Davis, offer extended horseback trips into Mexico, too.

Places to Stay & Eat

The resort's *RV park* (☎ *915-424-3467*) charges $10 for tents and $18 for full hookups. RVers can reserve a space, but tenters must take their chances.

Indoor resort accommodations range from motel rooms to condos to bunkhouses. Motel rooms range in price from $45 to $65 for one person up to $85 to $90 for four people. Among the nicest guest rooms are those in the high-ceilinged Officers' Quarters, a complex modeled after the original at Fort Davis. To reserve accommodations, call the central resort number listed above.

The resort's spacious *Badlands Restaurant* (☎ *915-424-3471*) has a wide, basic menu with moderate prices. Breakfast dishes range from 'Texas breakfast toast' to tasty chili 'n' eggs to omelets and fresh-baked cinnamon rolls. At lunch and dinner, you'll find a 'Lajitas Burger' (cheeseburger with scrambled egg and jalapeño), salads, fajitas, barbecue brisket, steaks and catfish. The food is good and hearty, but the atmosphere is noisy and service can be inattentive. A drugstore soda fountain and bakery are nearby for light meals and snacks.

Shopping

For years, the Lajitas Trading Post (☎ 915-424-3234) has doubled as home to Lajitas mayor Clay Henry Jr, who is famous for his beer-drinking prowess. It never bothered Clay when folks called him an old goat, because that's what he is. Visitors used to ply him with brewskis, but the trading post's new owner has put the mayor on the wagon – probably not a bad idea. The store is open daily 8 am to 8 pm, and it has a little bit of everything, including film, hardware, fishing tackle, groceries and beverages.

BIG BEND RANCH STATE PARK

At 433 sq miles, Big Bend Ranch State Park is more than 11 times larger than Texas' next-biggest state park, Franklin Mountains near El Paso. Taking up almost all the desert between Lajitas and Presidio, Big Bend Ranch reaches north from the Rio Grande into some of the wildest country in North America. It is full of notable features, most prominently the Solitario, formed 36 million years ago in a volcanic explosion. The resulting caldera measures 8 miles east to west and 9 miles north to south.

Information

You can reach the park's main office in Presidio at ☎ 915-229-3416. Aside from the well-traveled areas along FM 170, access to the park is limited and by permit or group bus tour only. Visitors planning to hike or drive into the park's interior must obtain permits and instructions from either the Barton Warnock Environmental Education Center (☎ 915-424-3327), 1 mile east of Lajitas, or Fort Leaton State Historical Park (☎ 915-229-3613), a half mile east of Presidio. The park entrance fee is $6 per day per person (free to Texas Conservation Passport holders and children 12 and under); an additional $3 per-person, per-day activity fee is charged.

Activities

Colorado Canyon lies within the park; see River Trips under Big Bend National Park, earlier in this chapter, for information on outfitters and permitting. Hiking is a popular pastime here, with trails ranging from Closed Canyon, a 1.4-mile roundtrip trek, to the 19-mile Rancherias Loop Trail, for serious backpackers. About 14 miles of trails are designated for mountain biking.

Organized Tours

The interior of Big Bend Ranch State Park is so big that it helps to have a guide along with you. Texas Parks and Wildlife runs twice-monthly bus tours from Presidio on the first Saturday of the month and from Lajitas on the third Saturday. Cost is $65 per person, which includes lunch; Texas Conservation Passport holders get a $5 discount. To reserve a space, call ☎ 512-389-8900. For more information, call the main park office, which also has a list of guides who can help if you're unable to travel to the park on a tour date.

Places to Stay & Eat

Camping areas are found along FM 170 at **Madera (Monilla) Canyon** and **Grassy Banks River Access**. These sites have self-composting toilets but no hookups or water. Ten designated primitive campsites in the backcountry are accessible only to high-clearance vehicles; RVs and trailers aren't recommended. Camping is included under the activity fee.

Up to eight people can rent the comfortable **Big House**, deep within the park's interior at the Sauceda complex. Cost is $40 per person per night, and reservations must be made by calling the main park office. A kitchen is available, but you'll have to bring your own food – unless a group is staying in the nearby **Sauceda Lodge**, a dorm-style facility that can accommodate up to 30 people and costs $15 per person per night. If that's the case, meals will be available with advance notice. Prices are $4 for breakfast, $7 for lunch and $9 for dinner, plus tax (cash only).

PRESIDIO

Population 4000

Presidio is best known as the hottest town in Texas; it was about 90°F when we visited in November, and summer temperatures climb well above 100°F. Presidio and its Mexican sister, Ojinaga (OJ to the locals), are sleepy communities rooted in agriculture. This is also the site of the only official border crossing in the 450-mile stretch between El Paso and Del Rio.

Information

The Presidio Chamber of Commerce (☎ 915-229-3199), PO Box 2497, Presidio, TX 79845, has a small office on US 67 near the north edge of town. Be sure to get a copy of the fun brochure *Presidio?! You don't want to go there!*

Fort Leaton State Historical Park

Established in 1848 by former Indian bounty hunter Benjamin Leaton, this restored adobe fortress (☎ 915-229-3613) now serves as the western staging area for trips into Big Bend Ranch State Park and as an interesting monument to the area's pioneer days. Exhibits describe the region's natural history and culture; a short slide show, 'Harvesting the Desert,' is especially good. On weekends, Presidio High School students sometimes drop by to help with living-history programs. Fort Leaton is open daily (except December 25) 8 am to 5 pm. Admission is $2; children ages six to 12 pay $1. Picnic grounds are available. Fort Leaton is 3 miles south of Presidio along FM 170.

Places to Stay & Eat

Since rooms are scarce in Presidio, it's good to book ahead. Small and inexpensive *La Siesta* (☎ 915-229-3611), on US 67, has a pool and is a good budget option, with rates ranging from $23 to $28. *Three Palms Inn* (☎ 915-229-3211), on Old US 67 N, has a pool and rooms for about $30 to $45.

Next to the Three Palms, *Cafe Rose's* (☎ 915-229-3998) is a locally popular restaurant with Mexican and American food priced in the $5 to $9 range, plus ice cream and frozen yogurt.

OJINAGA (MEXICO)
Population 35,000

Maps of Ojinaga are available at the Presidio Chamber of Commerce. Monday through Saturday from about 10 am to 2 pm, the Ruta Presidio-OJ shuttle runs between the two towns for about $2. Catch it outside MB's Supermarket, which is on the south side of Presidio's main drag. Once you reach OJ, make sure you know where and when to re-board the shuttle. If it stops running before you're ready to return, either hail a cab (about $5) or hike back over the bridge. The border crossing is at the end of US 67, and it's open 24 hours daily.

Ojinaga, site of a major battle fought by Pancho Villa in 1913, is among the least touristy of Mexico's border towns. Its main modern attraction may well be *Panaderia*

La Francesca, a bakery on Calle Zaragoza near the town plaza that sells more than 4000 loaves of bread each day. People line up to get the bread, sweet rolls and other goodies fresh and hot from the ovens. There's also a small museum at the corner of Independence and Hidalgo.

OJ is a jumping-off spot for bus trips to Chihuahua and tours into Mexico's famous Copper Canyon country. For information on guided tours, contact the Stella D McKeel Agency (☎ 915-229-3221, 888-883-6910, fax 915-229-3279), PO Box 2886, Presidio, TX 79845, or Tours of La Junta (☎ 915-229-4621, 800-847-8305), PO Box 743, Presidio, TX 79845. La Junta also sells insurance for motorists driving their own vehicles into Mexico.

North of Big Bend National Park

The country north of Big Bend National Park is sprawling and scenic, with the Santiago and Del Norte mountain ranges rising between Hwy 118 and US 385. Marathon and Alpine, two interesting outposts in the region, serve mainly as gateways to Big Bend. Farther north, Fort Davis and the nearby Davis Mountains are popular destinations in their own right.

BLACK GAP WILDLIFE MANAGEMENT AREA

This 159-sq-mile preserve (☎ 915-376-2216) is the biggest of its kind in Texas, popular for deer and javelina hunting, birding and fishing. It's east of Big Bend along FM 2627, which itself diverges from US 385 just north of Persimmon Gap. See the Big Bend National Park map. There is no public transportation down FM 2627, so you'll need to get here on your own.

Stillwell Ranch

Camp, relax and get a heaping helping of Big Bend history at this outpost (☎ 915-376-2244), 6 miles east of US 385 on FM 2627. Before her death in 1997, Hallie Stillwell was one of the best-known women in Texas – at various times a teacher, ranch wife, author, storyteller and justice of the peace. **Hallie's Hall of Fame Museum** pays tribute to her in fine fashion, keeping alive tales such as this one: After she graduated from Alpine High School in 1916, Hallie got a job teaching school in Presidio. Before she left for the job, her father handed her a .38 Colt revolver, saying, 'Take this gun and protect yourself. You may need it.'

The Stillwells run morning jeep tours to nearby **Maravillas Canyon**. Highlights include evidence of prehistoric Indian settlements and lots of information on Chihuahuan Desert flora and fauna. Tours cost $30 per adult, $15 per child. Participants should pack a lunch and water and arrive early since tours leave at 8:30 am to beat the midday desert heat.

The ranch's **RV park** charges $14 for full hookups, $12 for just electricity and water. Tenters can camp for $4 per person; kids ages seven to 12 pay $2, and those under seven stay free. Showers for noncampers cost $2, or $3 if you need a towel.

The **Stillwell Store** has gasoline, groceries, snacks, videos for rent and a seasonal café (it's not open in summer). People often gather in the museum at night for sing-alongs or to watch videos.

Heath Canyon

Off the beaten path, on the Rio Grande and at the end of the FM 2627 pavement, **Heath Canyon Ranch Inn** (☎ 915-376-2235) provides accommodations and meals to adventurous souls. This is an excellent staging area for river trips in Big Bend's Lower Canyons.

The 622-acre ranch was formerly owned by DuPont, which mined fluorspar in the area. Today, geologist Andy Kurie welcomes river runners, rock hounds, hunters and people in need of simple peace and quiet. Lodgings range from beds in a bunkhouse ($25) to two- and three-bedroom quarters with kitchen ($70 and $100, respectively). Campers can tent on the beach for $3 per person, and two RV spaces go for $12 apiece a night. No credit cards are accepted.

The ranch's **Open Sky Cafe** serves fare such as burritos (two for $4) and burgers ($3.50 to $4.50). A breakfast menu is served all day. Horse corrals and an airstrip are available on the ranch.

MARATHON
Population 800

Marathon (usually pronounced 'Mar-a-thun' hereabouts) began in 1882 when the Southern Pacific laid railroad tracks through the area. Albion Shepard, a surveyor for the railroad, thought the West Texas countryside resembled the plains near Marathon, Greece. Today, most travelers stopping here do so to eat or stay at the Gage Hotel, a true Texas treasure.

Information

Call or write the Marathon Chamber of Commerce (☎ 915-386-4516), PO Box 163, Marathon, TX 79842. The chamber is located within Front Street Books at 105 US 90 W.

Things to See & Do

On hot days, Marathoners head for the **Post**, the ruins of Fort Peña Colorado, 4 miles south of town on an unnumbered county road west of US 385, where people can swim, picnic and watch the abundant wildlife. **Pope Ranch** (☎ 915-376-2200), 35 miles south of Marathon on US 385, offers horseback riding, bird-watching tours and bunkhouse-style accommodations.

Places to Stay & Eat

The **Gage Hotel** (☎ 915-386-4205, 800-884-4243), at 102 US 90 W, is among the best-known small-town inns in Texas, and it's earned its rich reputation. Every room has a horseshoe hanging over the door, but the similarities end there; inside, each is decorated differently, and most memorably. Each room also comes with a written description of its furnishings and their origins, such as this: 'Bob's Room, No 23, is named after the pair of batwing chaps that hang on the wall. We know that they were Bob's chaps because he put his name on them.'

Rooms in the main hotel cost $85 with a private bath, $65 with a bath down the hall. Rooms in the newer Los Portales annex run $100 and up. A beautiful courtyard at Los

Portales features fountains and a lovely pool. This is easily one of Texas' most noteworthy lodgings. The mailing address is PO Box 46, Marathon, TX 79842.

The Gage also manages *Captain Shepard's Inn*, the large adobe home built by an old railroad man in 1899, now a B&B with five rooms priced from $85 to $120. An adjacent carriage house, complete with two bedrooms, a porch, kitchenette and living area with fireplace, rents for $120 for up to four people, $15 for each additional person.

Café Cenizo (☎ 915-386-4205), the restaurant at the Gage, has the same kind of upscale Western comforts as the hotel. For breakfast, try 'Badland' burritos or cinnamon-raisin French toast ($5 each). Lunch choices include chicken-fried steak ($8) and hamburgers ($6). For dinner, appetizers such as smoked cabrito (goat, a favorite dish throughout the Big Bend and West Texas; $6) might be followed by a 14oz rib eye ($18) or quail in a mild apricot-Chardonnay sauce ($20). Saturdays, the café serves a 'West Texas Bar-B-Que Buffet' ($16 for adults, $10 for senior citizens, $6 for kids).

Shopping
Marathon is evolving into a small arts-and-crafts center, with several galleries and interesting shops. The James H Evan Gallery (☎ 915-386-4366), at 21 S 1st St, has unusual photo lamp shades and a good selection of fine-art photographs, books and note cards. The Chisos Gallery (☎ 915-386-4200), at 106 US 90 E, sells Southwestern-themed art; it also sells a framable poster map of the Big Bend-Davis Mountains region for $10.

Getting There & Away
There is no public transportation to Marathon. Amtrak serves Alpine, 32 miles west on US 90.

ALPINE
Population 6200
Alpine may seem an unlikely name for a Texas town, but it's no misnomer. This town, at 4481 feet, is the capital of the Big Bend region in many ways. It's the only city of more than 5000 people, and it also has the

area's sole four-year college and its lone hospital. It's where South Brewster County outlanders come when they need to do some serious shopping or when they just want a weekend in town.

Here in Alpine, you'll find one of West Texas' best restaurants, a hot Austin-style music club, a good selection of accommodations and a growing arts community. (Alpine was named one of 'The 100 Best Small Art Towns in America' in the book of the same name by John Villani.) And when you're ready to get outta Big Bend country altogether, Amtrak will be around (sooner or later) to sweep you away.

Orientation
Alpine is positioned at the junction of US 90 and Hwy 118, 26 miles east of Marfa, 31 miles west of Marathon, 26 miles southeast of Fort Davis and 78 miles north of Study Butte. In town, US 90 breaks up into two one-way streets: Ave E, which travels southwest toward Marfa, and Holland Ave, which heads northeast toward Marathon. If you're Big Bend-bound, follow E Holland Ave to S Cockrell St, which takes a one-block jog to become S Walker St (and Hwy 118) as it heads out of town.

The best map in town, produced by and available at the Art & Craft Mall of the Big Bend (☎ 915-837-7486), 101 W Holland Ave, shows points of interest and many major businesses.

Information
Tourist Offices The Alpine Chamber of Commerce (☎ 915-837-2326) is at 106 N 3rd St. Alpine's Main Street organization has put together a *Historic Walking & Windshield Tour* brochure featuring 39 stops in the downtown area plus a few notable spots farther out. Get a copy of the brochure at the chamber office or many local businesses.

Money An ATM is available at the First National Bank (☎ 915-837-3375, 800-250-8880 in Texas only), 101 East Ave E.

Post & Communications Alpine's post office (☎ 915-837-2524) is at 107 West Ave E.

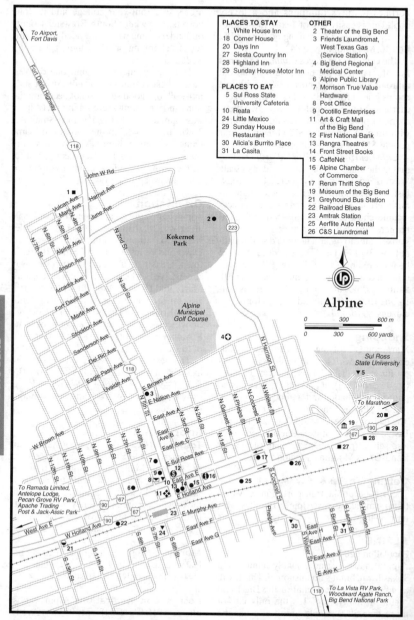

Alpine

0   300   600 m
0   300   600 yards

THE BIG BEND

To Airport,
Fort Davis

Fort Davis Highway

118

John W Rd

Vulcan Ave
Mars Ave
Harriet Ave
June Ave
N 8th St
N 7th St
Alpine Ave
Anson Ave
Arcadia Ave
Fort Davis Ave
Marfa Ave
Stockton Ave
Sanderson Ave
Del Rio Ave
Eagle Pass Ave
Uvalde Ave
N 3rd St
N 2nd St

Kokernot
Park

Alpine
Municipal
Golf Course

118

E Brown Ave
E Nation Ave
East Ave A
East
Ave B
East Ave C
W Brown Ave
N 11th St
N 10th St
N 8th St
N 7th St
N 6th St
N 5th St
N 12th St
E Sul Ross Ave
E Ave E
E Holland Ave
E Murphy Ave

N Garnett Ave
N Phelps St
N Cockrell St
N 1st St
N 2nd St
N 3rd St
N Harrison St
N Walker St

Sul Ross
State University

To Marathon

223

Kokernot
Park

Sul Ross
State University

To Ramada Limited,
Antelope Lodge,
Pecan Grove RV Park,
Apache Trading
Post & Jack-Assic Park

West Ave E

W Holland Ave
S 7th St
S 8th St
S 9th St
S 11th St
S 13th St

East Ave F
East Ave G

S Cockrell St

Phelps Ave

East
Ave H
East Ave I
East Ave J

East Ave K

S Bird St
S Lecky St
S Harrison St

67   90
90   67

118

To La Vista RV Park,
Woodward Agate Ranch,
Big Bend National Park

Address poste restante to General Delivery, Alpine, TX 79830. Internet access is available at CaffeNet (☎ 915-837-7255), 201 E Holland Ave. Cost is $3 for 15 minutes, $5 for a half hour and $8 for an hour.

Bookstores The best bookstore in town, Front Street Books (☎ 915-837-3360), at 121 E Holland Ave, is open daily with a smart selection of new, used and out-of-print titles – and the *New York Times* and *Wall Street Journal*, rare commodities out this way. Ocotillo Enterprises (☎ 915-837-5353), 205 N 5th St, and the Apache Trading Post (☎ 915-837-5506), on the edge of town via US 90, also have well-stocked bookshelves.

Libraries The Alpine Public Library (☎ 915-837-2621) is at 203 N 7th St. The Bryan Wildenthal Library (☎ 915-837-8123), at Sul Ross State University, is open to the public, too.

Media The *Alpine Avalanche* is published every Thursday and costs 50¢. The *Desert Candle*, a regional quarterly, also is headquartered in Alpine.

Campuses About 3200 students attend Sul Ross State University, taking courses toward 32 bachelor's degree programs and 14 master's degree disciplines. The campus sits on the east side of town, its 'brand' decorating the nearby hillside.

Laundry Alpine has two places to do wash: the C&S Laundromat, 902 E Holland Ave (open 9 am to 11 pm), and Friends Laundromat (☎ 915-837-7147), at the West Texas Gas service station, 708 N 5th St (open daily 7 am to 10 pm).

Medical Services Big Bend Regional Medical Center (☎ 915-837-3447), at 801 E Brown Ave, offers basic care. When matters get serious, people tend to leave town for hospitals in Midland.

Emergency The Family Crisis Center of the Big Bend (☎ 915-837-2242, 800-834-0654) has a regionwide 24-hour hot line for victims of family violence and sexual assaults.

Museum of the Big Bend
Once housed in the former Sul Ross State bowling alley, this fine little museum (☎ 915-837-8143) has new digs in Lawrence Hall, the closest campus building to US 90 E. The major exhibit depicts more than 10,000 years of life in Texas, including a replica of a camp used to make *candelilla* wax and ranching, mining and military artifacts. There's also a children's corner and a Chihuahuan Desert cactus garden. The museum is open Tuesday to Saturday 9 am to 5 pm and Sunday 1 to 5 pm; admission is free, but donations are accepted.

Woodward Agate Ranch
Eighteen miles south of town on Hwy 118, this cattle ranch (☎ 915-364-2271) has 3000 acres open to rock hounds. Hunt for red plume and pom-pom Texas agate, jasper, labradorite feldspar, calcite, opal and other minerals. A lapidary shop and guide service are available. It doesn't cost anything to look, but agate costs 50¢ a pound and opal costs $1 a gram. The ranch also has cheap camping and cabin accommodations.

Activities
The swimming pool at Sul Ross State University is open to the public late afternoons when classes are in session. Hours are typically weekdays 4 to 8 pm and weekends from 2 to 6 pm; you can double-check by calling ☎ 915-837-8236. Admission is $1. There's also an outdoor city swimming pool at Kokernot Park. The hill behind the Sul Ross State campus is the best place in Alpine to catch a sunset.

Special Events
The Cowboy Poetry Gathering, held the first weekend in March, is a down-home event that takes over most of town, from university classrooms to Kokernot Park. The Sul Ross National Intercollegiate Rodeo Association Rodeo happens the first weekend each October.

Places to Stay
La Vista RV Park (☎ 915-364-2293), 6 miles south of the city on Hwy 118, borders a

THE BIG BEND

working ranch. Full hookups are $11 per night. A few tent spaces rent for $3 per night, but no showers are available. *Pecan Grove RV Park* (☎ 915-837-7175), 1902 US 90 W, has full hookups for $14 to $15.50 and tent spaces for $9, including use of the showers and coin laundry.

Woodward Agate Ranch (☎ 915-364-2271), 18 miles south of Alpine on Hwy 118, has primitive tent camping for $5, full-hookup sites for $10 and a cabin with electricity and a refrigerator that will sleep up to 12 people for $15 per person. Bathroom and shower facilities are available at the ranch house for no extra charge.

Alpine has lots of motels, most located at the east and west entrances to town on US 90 (Holland Ave). *Antelope Lodge* (☎ 915-837-2451, 800-880-8106, fax 915-837-3881), at 2310 US 90 W, has cottage-style rooms costing $31/42 singles/doubles. Also on the west side, *Ramada Limited* (☎ 915-837-1100, 800-272-6232, fax 915-837-7032), has rooms for $60.

On the east side of town, the following four motels have rooms that cost between $45 and $55 for singles, $50 and $60 for doubles: *Days Inn*, 2000 US 90 E (☎ 915-837-3417, fax 915-837-5909); *Highland Inn*, at 1404 US 90 E (☎ 915-837-5811, fax 915-837-5215); *Siesta Country Inn*, 1200 US 90 E (☎ 915-837-2503, fax 915-837-3454); and *Sunday House Motor Inn*, 1440 US 90 E (☎ 915-837-3363, fax 915-837-7493, 800-510-3363).

In addition to the Corner House (see boxed text), Alpine is home to the *White House Inn* (☎ 915-837-1401, fax 915-837-2133), 2003 Fort Davis Hwy, where two rooms with phones and TVs are available for $80 to $105.

Places to Eat

If you eat only one meal in Alpine, make sure it's at the original *Reata* (☎ 915-837-9232), 203 N 5th St. This place is worth going out of your way – especially if you won't be visiting Fort Worth, where another Reata now perches atop a skyscraper. Try to come on Sunday, when lunch is served family-style; the meal features chicken, catfish, ribs, cornbread and peach cobbler for $9 ($7 for kids under 12). For lunch ($4 to $13), try a bowl of jalapeño and cilantro soup served with tortilla strips ($4.75) or a chicken chile relleno with goat cheese and roasted corn chowder ($8). Dinner begins with such tempting appetizers as bacon-wrapped shrimp with three-onion marmalade and polenta

---

The Best Little Guest House in Texas

Texas has lots of charming B&B inns, but we think the *Corner House* (☎ 915-837-7161), at 801 East Ave E in Alpine, is tops for footloose global travelers. Innkeeper James Glendinning – a guidebook author and world traveler, with maps of most of the 110 nations he has visited on his walls – is a gracious, informative host. He has seen a lot of places, but he loves Alpine, and he's eager to share it with visitors.

Although the Corner House isn't lavish, it is comfortable. Grab a magazine from the eclectic selection on the living room table (or a Lonely Planet guidebook from Glendinning's home library) and spend some time in the porch hammock. Get some suggestions from Glendinning on where to go and what to do in West Texas. Or simply get a good night's sleep before setting out for Big Bend National Park.

Glendinning offers three hostel-type bunks at $15 per person, $20 with breakfast. (Guests sign up for breakfast the night before; Glendinning will even gather a morning meal for you to grab on your way out the door if you're heading south for an early date on the Rio Grande.) Rates for the other five guest quarters, most with private bathrooms, range from $28 for the Little Room, suitable for one person, to $45/65 single/double for the Tree House Room.

stars or Bock-battered quail with chimi-churri (both are $9). Entrées range from Reata chicken-fried steak ($11) to pan-seared, pepper-crusted tenderloin with port wine glaze ($25).

If you hit town at an odd time, try the *Sunday House Restaurant (☎ 915-837-2817)*, on US 90 E at the motel of the same name. It's open 24 hours with a wide menu. Mexican food and its Tex-Mex hybrid are staples of the Alpine dining scene. *La Casita (☎ 915-837-2842)*, 1104 East Ave H, is probably the most popular Mexican eatery in town, with meals priced at about $4 to $8. *Little Mexico (☎ 915-837-2855)*, 204 W Murphy Ave, gets good marks from locals, too. Good, inexpensive Mexican and American food is the rule at *Alicia's Burrito Place (☎ 915-837-2802)*, 708 East Ave G.

The *Sul Ross State University cafeteria (☎ 915-837-8287)* is open to the public. Prices range from about $4 at breakfast to $5.50 at dinner. The cafeteria was slated to move from the Mountainside Residence Hall to the new student center at the end of 1999.

Entertainment

Railroad Blues (☎ 915-837-3103), at 504 W Holland Ave, is the place to go in Alpine for live music. The club frequently draws Austin-based musicians who are heading west on tour. The *Rangra Theatres (☎ 915-837-5111)*, 109 E Holland Ave, get first-run movies a month or two after the big cities. Admission is $4, with a $2 bargain night on Thursday.

In summertime, consider an evening at the *Theater of the Big Bend*, a Sul Ross State-sponsored outdoor theater series at Kokernot Park. Performances begin around the Fourth of July and continue through early August, with show times Thursday to Sunday at 9 pm. Tickets are about $4; call ☎ 915-837-8218 for more information.

Shopping

Morrison True Value Hardware (☎ 915-837-2061), 301 N 5th St, has a decent selection of camping and outdoors gear for the Big Bend-bound. Good buys for a good cause can be found at the Rerun Thrift Shop (☎ 915-837-1522), at 611 East Ave E, whose

proceeds benefit the Family Crisis Center of the Big Bend.

Apache Trading Post and Jack-Assic Park (☎ 915-837-5506), 3 miles west of downtown on US 90, has a good selection of topographic and raised-relief maps, plus a lot of jewelry, rugs, pottery and so on. When you're done browsing, have your picture taken with one of the store's six live burros. The trading post also screens a short video on the Marfa Lights (see the Marfa section later in this chapter).

Getting There & Around

Air Alpine had no scheduled air service at press time, but it has in the past and may well in the future. Check with the chamber of commerce (see Information) to find out. Alpine's airport, north of town along Hwy 118, can accommodate charter flights.

Aerflite Auto Rental (☎ 915-837-3463, www.aerflite.com), 504 E Holland Ave, runs shuttle service several times weekly from Midland International Airport to Alpine and Fort Davis. Cost is $99 per person roundtrip. More information, current schedules and reservations are available on Aerflite's website.

Bus Alpine is served by Greyhound. The bus station (☎ 915-837-5302), 804 W Holland Ave, has the following scheduled service:

to/from	trip duration	one way/ roundtrip
Midland Airport	3 to 4 hours	$23/44
El Paso	4 hours	$38/76
San Antonio	9 hours	$53/105

Train The Amtrak station (☎ 800-872-7245, www.amtrak.com for general information, prices and reservations) is on the south side of W Holland Ave at N 6th St. The eastbound *Sunset Limited* comes through Monday, Wednesday and Saturday at 7:55 pm, reaching San Antonio at about 4 am the next day. The westbound train stops Monday, Thursday and Saturday at 1:10 pm, arriving in El Paso at about 4 pm, then traveling on to Los Angeles by 6 am the next morning. This train frequently runs anywhere from one to eight hours late in both directions, so it's important to call Amtrak to get an update before setting out for the train station.

Car Rental cars are available in Alpine from Aerflite Auto Rental (☎ 915-837-3463), at 504 E Holland Ave, and Big Bend Aero Auto Rental (☎ 915-837-2744, 915-837-3009), at the Alpine airport.

FORT DAVIS & DAVIS MOUNTAINS
Population 900

People in Fort Davis are fond of saying that from here, the rest of Texas is all downhill. That's not just hyperbole; Fort Davis, at an elevation of 5050 feet, really is the state's highest town.

People from all over West Texas like to come here in summer, when Fort Davis and the nearby Davis Mountains offer a cool respite from the searing desert heat. So despite its small size and the lack of some key amenities (no public transportation to town, for one), Fort Davis definitely caters to visitors. There's a lot to do in and around Fort Davis, or you can do nothing at all.

Fort Davis is 39 scenic miles south of I-10 via Balmorhea. From here, Alpine is 26 miles southeast via Hwy 118 and Marfa is 21 miles southwest via Hwy 17.

Information

The Fort Davis Chamber of Commerce (☎ 915-426-3015, 800-524-3015) is open Tuesday to Friday 9 am to 5 pm and Saturday 9 am to 1 pm. It's on the Town Square catercorner to the Hotel Limpia; its mailing address is PO Box 378, Fort Davis, TX 79734. The *Fort Davis Visitor's Guide* newspaper has a helpful (if somewhat dated) map and a guide to the 75-mile Davis Mountains scenic loop drive.

The Fort Davis Bank (☎ 915-426-3211), on the town square, has a 24-hour ATM. Have mail held at the Fort Davis post office (☎ 915-426-3914) by addressing it to General Delivery, Fort Davis, TX 79734.

The town library is housed in the former county jail between the town square and the courthouse. Laundry facilities are available at the Overland Trail Campground.

Fort Davis National Historic Site

Fort Davis (☎ 915-426-3224), north of town along Hwy 17, was the first military post to guard the San Antonio-El Paso pioneer route across West Texas, yet it remains one of the best preserved. This is an especially good stop June through August, when interpreters dressed in period clothing are on hand to describe life at the fort. There's also a museum full of military and Indian artifacts.

Fort Davis visitors may hear a series of bugle calls. The calls are played regularly to simulate the orders buglers made during days on the frontier. The visitors' center has a leaflet describing what each call meant.

Memorial Day (late May) through Labor Day (early September), Fort Davis is open daily 8 am to 6 pm; the rest of the year, hours are 8 am to 5 pm. The fort is closed Christmas Day. Admission is $2 per person, with anyone 16 or younger admitted free.

History Fort Davis was established in 1854. At that time, the San Antonio-El Paso road was full of pioneers and gold seekers moving west, but the travelers were frequently attacked by Comanche and Apache war parties. Military authorities in San Antonio decided a fort was necessary. Major General Persifor F Smith personally selected this site on Limpia Creek and dispatched six companies of the 8th US Infantry to build the fort. Over the next seven years, the troops spent most of their time escorting wagon trains through the area, but they made little headway against the Indian raids.

Although Confederate troops occupied Fort Davis for a time during the Civil War, the post – heavily damaged by the Apaches – was deserted between 1862 and 1867. When federal troops returned, they began building a new fort, which eventually included 50 stone and adobe buildings. This era also was marked by the presence of the buffalo soldiers, the African American regiments who patrolled the Texas frontier after the Civil War (see the boxed text in the Facts about Texas chapter). In 1885, the Fort Davis Buffalo Soldiers were reassigned to the Arizona Territory. There they fought against Geronimo, whose 1886 surrender finally brought the Apache Wars to an end. Troops served at Fort Davis until 1891, and Congress authorized the post as a national historic site in 1961.

Hiking Fort Davis National Historic Site serves as trailhead for several hikes, ranging from the 1-mile Tall Grass Loop nature trail to more ambitious treks to Davis Mountain State Park. Ask in the fort's visitors' center for a trail map.

McDonald Observatory

You may have heard the song: 'The stars at night are big and bright/deep in the heart of Texas.' Whoever wrote that old tune could have been standing atop Mt Locke, at 6791 feet the highest point on any Texas highway, with some of the clearest and darkest skies in North America. This is the site of the University of Texas' McDonald Observatory (☎ 915-426-3640, www.as.utexas.edu), where visitors can see some of the world's biggest telescopes and learn stargazing from the pros. It's 19 miles northwest of Fort Davis via Hwy 118 and Spur 78. Allow a half hour to drive from town.

The observatory offers guided tours daily at 11:30 am and 2 pm. In March, June, July and August, there's an additional tour daily at 9:30 am. Tours feature both the 107-inch Harlan J Smith Telescope, which can see objects 10 billion light years away at 50,000 times their actual brightness, and the new 430-inch Hobby-Eberly Telescope, the largest optical telescope in North America and third-largest in the world (see the boxed text). Tickets are available at the visitors' center (open daily 9 am to 5 pm) and cost $3 for adults, $2 for kids six to 12, free for kids five and under, and $8 for a family. Arrive about a half hour early since tours often fill up. Self-guiding tours also are possible; pick up a copy of the 50¢ walking-tour map at the visitors' center.

Visitors on guided tours don't get to look through the telescopes, but there are opportunities for stargazing. One night a month – the Wednesday nearest the full moon – the observatory holds a public viewing night. This is your chance to peek through the

Harlan J Smith scope to view nebulae, star clusters, galaxies and so on. It's even possible to see stars that have stopped giving off light, which look something like bubbles or disks in the sky. Each public viewing is led by a professional astronomer who discusses his or her research and takes questions. Space is limited and reservations are necessary; call for upcoming dates and times.

The observatory has free solar viewings daily at 11 am and 3:30 pm. Using a 16-inch

---

To Infinity & Beyond!

Stargazers everywhere are abuzz over the opening of the new Hobby-Eberly telescope at McDonald Observatory. The HET (as it's nicknamed) went into full operation early in 1998 as the third-largest telescope in the world and the largest publicly accessible on regularly scheduled tours. It was built by a consortium of five universities – three from the USA, two from Germany – at a cost of $13.5 million. The telescope features a 430-inch primary mirror made up of 91 hexagonal mirrors, each 1m across, and an 85-ton telescope structure that can rotate horizontally to cover 70% of the sky. It's all housed in a striking building that echoes the mirror's hexagonal design.

The HET's main purpose is spectroscopy, or the study of light emitted and absorbed by celestial objects. A spectroscope breaks light emitted from an object into the colors of the spectral rainbow: red, orange, yellow, green, blue, indigo and violet. Through spectroscopy, astronomers can track stars' motions and identify materials present in stars and their atmospheres. The HET's enormous primary mirror helps it to detect very faint objects. With it, astronomers plan to study the composition and evolution of stars in our galaxy, search for planets around other stars, study the makeup of the gas clouds that serve as stellar nurseries, and much more.

telescope with a hydrogen-alpha filter, visitors can see a tiny portion of our sun; some viewers have even seen solar flares in progress. In addition, star parties are held every Tuesday, Friday and Saturday night. Times vary, but they generally begin about an hour after sunset. Participants take a tour of the night sky and look through several telescopes with mirrors up to 24 inches. Admission is $3 for adults, $2 for children six to 12. No reservations are necessary. The parties are held outdoors, so dress warmly.

Of course, the visitors' center has a gift shop, and it's a good one, full of cool science stuff. Kids 12 and under can ask at the reception desk for paper and crayons, draw a picture of something they've learned at the observatory, and get a prize (many of the drawings are later posted in the shop and on the observatory's website). Check the parking lot bulletin boards on your way out, too; you'll find lots of timely stargazing tips.

Davis Mountains State Park
Set amid the most extensive mountain range in Texas, this 2708-acre state park (☎ 915-426-3337) is 4 miles from Fort Davis on Hwy 118. Camping, bird-watching and sightseeing are the big attractions here. Park admission is $3 per person for day use; campers pay $2 per person plus camping fees. **Indian Lodge State Park**, a park-within-the-park, features a 39-room hotel built in the 1930s by the Civilian Conservation Corps.

Other Attractions
The **Neill Doll Museum** (☎ 915-426-3969), seven blocks west of the Davis County Courthouse, features a collection of antique toys and dolls. Hours are Tuesday to Saturday 10 am to noon and 1:30 to 5 pm and Sunday 1:30 pm to 5 pm; $3 for adults, $1 for children. The **Overland Trail Museum** (☎ 915-426-3904) preserves the home of early settler Nick Mersfelter; to get there, turn toward Sleeping Lion Mountain at the Stone Village Motel on Main St and walk two blocks.

Four miles south of town on Hwy 118, the **Chihuahuan Desert Research Institute and Visitor Center** (☎ 915-364-2499) exhibits the region's flora in gardens and on trails. Hours

are weekdays 9 am to 5 pm year-round; April 1 to Labor Day, it's also open weekends 9 am to 6 pm. It's closed Thanksgiving, Christmas and New Year's Day. Suggested admission is $2 per car.

Activities
Bicycling Fort Davis is one of Texas' best areas for road cycling. There's some nice, gentle terrain just outside of town for casual cyclists, and then there is the gut-busting 75-mile Davis Mountains loop via Hwys 118 and 166 – a route recently named by *Outside* magazine as the top bike ride in Texas.

Unfortunately, there's no local spot to rent bikes; the closest specialty bike shops are in Terlingua (108 miles south) and Midland-Odessa (160 miles northeast). Perhaps an enterprising cyclist will set up a sales and rental shop in Fort Davis sometime in the next few years. Meanwhile, the town has a Cycle Fest and Race every year in mid-September. Call the chamber of commerce (see Information) for details.

Horseback Riding Davis Mountain Horseback Tours (☎ 915-426-3022) offers small-group rides ranging from a one-hour trot around town to sunrise or sunset rides to the top of Barry Scobbee Mountain. Call ahead for prices and reservations.

Places to Stay
Fort Davis is chock-full of accommodations, including two historic hotels and West Texas' highest concentration of B&B inns. Best of all, prices are reasonable, especially for such a major vacation area.

Camping In town, *Overland Trail Campground* (☎ 915-426-2250), on Main St, has full hookups for $13 and tent sites for $7. (Rates are for two campers; add $1.50 apiece for additional campers.) Noncampers can take showers here for $1.50. The showers and laundry are open 24 hours. The campground's mailing address is PO Box 788, Fort Davis, TX 79734.

Davis Mountains State Park (☎ 915-426-3337), north of town on Hwy 118, charges $8 for tent sites and $13 for full hookups.

Backcountry camping is available in the park's Limpia Canyon Primitive Area. *Prude Ranch* (see Ranches) charges $8.50 for pop-up campers and $12.50 a night for hookups.

Cabins *Davis Mountains Community Headquarters* (☎ 915-426-3918, 915-426-3872), 20 miles west of town in the Upper Limpia Basin, has four cabins available for $30 to $50. Each cabin has a full kitchen and is furnished with linens and towels. Campers are welcome, too; tent spaces are $5 and full hookups run $10. Showers and a laundry are available, and there's a small seasonal store with groceries, fresh eggs and produce plus gasoline and camping items. The mailing address is HCR 74 Box 120A, Fort Davis, TX 79734.

Motels & Hotels The least expensive rooms in Fort Davis are at *Stone Village Motel* (☎ 915-426-3941, 800-649-8487), on Main St north of downtown. Rates here run $35 to $55. *Old Texas Inn* (☎ 915-426-3118, 800-328-4768), downtown on Main St, has Old West-themed rooms for $45 and up. *Fort Davis Motor Inn* (☎ 915-426-2112, 800-803-2847), just north of town on Hwy 17 near the fort, has standard motel rooms for $50 to $80.

The historic *Indian Lodge* (☎ 915-426-3254), at Davis Mountains State Park, is a handsome inn with 18-inch-thick adobe walls, hand-carved cedar furniture and ceilings of pine viga and latilla that give it the look of a Southwestern pueblo village – albeit one with a swimming pool and restaurant! The comfortable guest rooms are a steal at $55 to $85. Reservations are a must, and they can be hard to come by. The mailing address is PO Box 1458, Fort Davis, TX 79734.

Butterfield Inn (☎ 915-426-3252), along Main St, has four country cottage rooms for $75 apiece. Each has a wood-burning fireplace, reclining chairs, cable TV and a jetted tub in the bathroom. The mailing address is PO Box 345, Fort Davis, TX 79734.

The *Hotel Limpia* (☎ 915-426-3237, fax 915-426-3983, 800-662-5517, www.hotellimpia.com), on Main St (Hwy 17) on the town square, spreads out over five buildings

erected between 1912 and the 1940s. All have been restored, and the rooms and suites here ($89 to $150) are as tasteful as they come, making this another great value. Many have kitchens, walk-in closets and private porches; all have gracious touches such as old-fashioned light fixtures and baskets of potpourri. The mailing address is PO Box 1341, Fort Davis, TX 79734.

B&Bs Fort Davis has about 10 B&Bs and guest houses, but one stands out: *Boynton House* (☎ 915-426-3123, 800-358-5929), a Spanish hacienda-type lodge atop Dolores Mountain, just south of town. Rooms run $55 to $95 a night; the common areas include two libraries, a music room, an exercise room and porches with panoramic views. The mailing address is PO Box 916, Fort Davis, TX 79734.

Veranda Country Inn Carriage House (☎ 915-426-2233, 888-383-2847, veranda@overland.net), one block west of the courthouse, is another good choice, with eight rooms and rates starting at $55/68 single/double. This is the former Lempert Hotel, built in 1883 and used as a guest house ever since. Its mailing address is PO Box 1238, Fort Davis, TX 79734.

Ranches One of Texas' best known guest ranches, the *Prude Ranch* (☎ 915-426-3202, 800-458-6232, fax 915-426-3502) is just a short 6-mile drive north of town on Hwy 118. The mailing address is PO Box 1431, Fort Davis, TX 79734.

The Prude family settled here in 1897 and started taking in dudes in 1921. Currently, four generations of Prudes live and work on the ranch. There's plenty to do here, from trail rides and swimming in the Olympic-size pool to stargazing and campfire sing-alongs. John Robert Prude has even been known to shuttle guests up to McDonald Observatory or to see the Marfa Mystery Lights; he also leads bird-watching treks, both locally and in Mexico. Call for a current brochure.

Unlike many guest ranches, visitors aren't tied to a five-day or weeklong stay. There's a variety of rooms, including lodge-style quarters ($65/75 single/double) and family bunk rooms with one double bed and sets of bunk beds (starting at $58). Meals ($5 to $8 for adults; half price for children ages three to 10) are served buffet style, with lots of choices. The Prude Ranch also holds senior symposiums each year, some designed for grandparents and their grandchildren.

Places to Eat

The **Hotel Limpia Dining Room** (☎ 915-426-3241) has the best food in town. The burgundy-marinated roast beef ($10) is the restaurant's top seller, but the catfish ($10) and rib eye ($16) get good reviews, too. Entrées are served with cream-cheese potatoes or wild rice and some of the best biscuits we've had anywhere. A half-dozen items are available as children's portions for $6. The Limpia's lone drawback is a creaky ceiling that doubles as a floor to the private club upstairs. Ask for a table away from the low-ceilinged restaurant entrance so the squeaks won't detract from an otherwise fine dining experience. The Limpia is open Tuesday to Sunday for lunch and dinner. Reservations are advised.

Get good Mexican food at **Cueva de Leon** (☎ 915-426-3801), on Main St, or **Poco Mexico** (☎ 915-426-3939), on Hwy 17 near the Fort Davis Motor Inn. Meals at both run in the $4 to $7 range. **Drug Store Restaurant** (☎ 915-426-3118), on Main St below the Old Texas Inn, features sandwiches, a soda fountain, a $5.55 sirloin steak special and a breakfast many folks rate as the best in town.

Shopping

If you're in the market for a medicine ball, put the Lineaus Athletic Company (☎ 915-426-3475, 800-426-3224) on your itinerary. Former Austin accountant Lineaus Lorette makes the large leather exercise balls for a clientele that includes college and professional sports teams. Prices start at about $250. Call for an appointment.

Getting There & Around

No regularly scheduled public transportation serves Fort Davis or the Davis Mountains. Shuttle service from Midland International Airport (about 160 miles away) is available via Aerflite Auto Rental. See the Alpine Getting There & Around section.

MARFA
Population 2500

Marfa sees fewer Big Bend-bound travelers than do Alpine, Fort Davis and Marathon, but anyone who passes through here will be intrigued. The epic movie *Giant*, starring James Dean, Rock Hudson and Elizabeth Taylor, was filmed here, and now the town is known as the site of the Marfa Mystery Lights – an unexplained phenomenon that can be seen east of town. Marfa also is home to Texas' highest golf course.

Information

The Marfa Chamber of Commerce (☎ 915-729-4942, fax 915-729-4956) has its office on US 90 W; its mailing address is PO Box 635, Marfa, TX 79843. Ask for the walking-tour leaflet, which describes interesting West Texas architecture such as the 1886 Presidio County Courthouse, the 1927 El Paisano Hotel and several beautiful churches.

Chinati Foundation

Unlikely as it may seem, Marfa is home to one of the world's largest permanent installations of modern art. In the 1970s, artist Donald Judd created the Chinati Foundation (☎ 915-729-4362, fax 915-729-4597) on the grounds of Fort DA Russell, a former army post a half mile south of town on US 67. Here, on 400 acres and in more than a dozen scattered buildings, he installed his own art as well as works by Claes Oldenburg, John Chamberlain and Ilya Kabakov. Changing exhibits feature the work of other artists, too. The foundation is open Thursday to Saturday 1 to 5 pm or by appointment made at least two days in advance; admission is $10.

Marfa Lights

In an age when *The X-Files* is a top TV show and alien images adorn T-shirts and backpacks everywhere, it's no mystery why the Marfa Lights are one of West Texas' top tourist attractions. No one knows what these orb-like white lights really are or why they dance across the skyline beneath the Chinati Mountains. Local folks say they can usually be seen two out of every three nights, and that fall is the best time for viewing. Cloud cover doesn't matter, since the lights are fairly low to the ground, but fog, haze or rain may dim the lights.

No one is certain about what causes the lights, although a variety of explanations are offered. Apache Indians believe the lights are the spirit of their Chief Alaste, who was killed by Mexican insurrectionists in the 1860s. Others believe the lights are UFOs, static electricity, reflections or swamp gas. 'My theory is I'm glad they're a mystery,' says John Robert Prude of the Prude Ranch near Fort Davis, who shuttles visitors to the viewing site. 'I don't really want to find the answer.'

The designated viewing area is about 8 miles east of Marfa on US 90/67 (the land on which the lights are seen is privately owned, so this is the closest you can get). Look for the signs and pull over onto the south shoulder. Picnic tables are available; you might want to pack a meal and arrive just before dusk to get oriented and enjoy the sunset. To find the lights, first locate the tower with the red light, then look just to the left or right of it. The Marfa Lights appear and disappear, sometimes splitting apart. If the lights you see are constant, they're probably car headlights, not the mystery orbs.

We wouldn't plan a vacation around the Marfa Lights. We wouldn't even recommend you drive more than an hour out of your way to see them. But if you're in the area, it's worth stopping by. Even if the lights don't show, you'll probably have a good time chatting with the Marfa locals, many of whom return on a regular basis just to hang out.

Places to Stay
The jointly managed *Holiday Capri Inn* (☎ 915-729-4326) and *Thunderbird Motel* (☎ 915-729-4391) together offer about 50 rooms on US 90 near Marfa's center. Singles run about $40; doubles go for about $50.

The Henry Trost-designed *El Paisano Hotel* (☎ 915-729-3145) sits at 207 N Highland Ave. Rooms and suites now rent for $80

to $150. Check out the collection of movie memorabilia from *Giant* in the lobby.

Places to Eat
Marfa has no destination restaurant, but several eateries serve basic, reliable food. *Mike's Place* (☎ 915-729-8146), at 120 E El Paso St, is locally popular for its burgers and chili.

Getting There & Away
Marfa is served by Greyhound. The bus station (☎ 915-729-8174) is at the Jimenez Chevron Station, at 3988 US 90 W, with the following scheduled service:

to/from	trip duration	one way/ roundtrip
El Paso	4 hours	$34/68
Midland Airport	4 to 5 hours	$38/76
San Antonio	9 to 11 hours	$76/146

PRESIDIO COUNTY OUTBACK
Presidio County may have two good-size towns in Marfa and Presidio, but the vast space between the two of them ranks among Texas' most sparsely populated areas. Rugged beauty and solitude are the hallmarks of this country.

Cibolo Creek Ranch
In the mid-19th century, frontiersman Milton Faver ranched and farmed at the base of the Chinati Mountains, protecting his empire with a series of private forts. The restored outposts are now collectively known as Cibolo Creek Ranch (☎ 915-229-3737, fax 915-229-3653, www.cibolocreekranch.com), south of Marfa off US 67, a handsome, pricey retreat that's a favorite among wealthy Texans and celebrities. What the Mansion on Turtle Creek is to Dallas, 25,000-acre Cibolo Creek is to the Big Bend.

The main fort, El Cibolo, has 11 guest quarters that can be rented together (for $3000 a day) or separately, with most priced at $290 per double. El Cibolo has a pool, Jacuzzi, multimedia room, stocked reservoir – even its own museum. La Cienega has four guest rooms plus common areas and a pool. It rents for $1300 a night, with individual rooms sometimes available at $350 apiece. La Morita, the most remote fort, rents for $350 a night. All rates include a wide range of activities and memorable meals by Culinary Institute of America-trained chef Lisa Ahier. Ranch staff will pick you up in Alpine for free, but many guests touch down on the private airstrip.

The mailing address is PO Box 44, Shafter, TX 79850.

Pinto Canyon Rd

FM 2810 southwest of Marfa is also known as Pinto Canyon Rd. It's a way-off-the-beaten-path route of about 50 miles that winds all the way to FM 170 at Ruidosa. The pavement ends 32 miles before the steep descent into Pinto Canyon; here, the road is best suited for high-clearance, 4WD vehicles, though sturdy normal vehicles may be able to make it. Be sure to have a usable spare tire, and carry plenty of water here and elsewhere in the West Texas backcountry. A side road between the canyon and Ruidosa leads to **Chinati Hot Springs** (☎ 915-229-4165), where travelers can enjoy a bathhouse and several adobe cabins. A one-hour soak costs $10 for one or two people and the cabins go for $40 to $50. Because this place is so remote, visitors need to call ahead to let the caretakers know they're coming. Everything is closed on Tuesday and Wednesday.

West Texas

West Texas spans 300 miles and two time zones – but so far, only one telephone code. It includes the world's largest binational metropolis, El Paso-Juárez with 2.4 million people, but it also takes in Loving County – the most sparsely populated county in the US. To many people, West Texas is a wasteland – so much so that the area has been proposed as a major nuclear dump. But to those who live here and those who have come to cherish West Texas, the region has charms unlike any other: spacious, sunny skies; a little-known national park showcasing the state's highest mountain; small towns full of frontier lore; and El Paso, heart of a growing binational, bistate metropolis where multiculturalism isn't some academic buzzword but a way of life.

EL PASO
Population 599,865

San Antonio has the Alamo and the Riverwalk, Houston the space program, Dallas the state fair and all three cities have theme parks and big-time sports. But El Paso – fourth largest city in Texas and 17th largest in the US, with an 80% Hispanic population – has none of these lures, nothing to tell the world, 'This is who we are.' The city's identity crisis is compounded by the presence of neighboring Ciudad Juárez, a Mexican city whose population is three times that of El Paso, and by the fact that El Paso is so far removed from the rest of Texas – and most everywhere else. It's 790 miles to Los Angeles, three states away. It's 795 miles to Texarkana; Dallas (633 miles) and Houston (753 miles) aren't a lot closer. El Paso and the rest of far west Texas, including Guadalupe Mountains National Park, are in the mountain time zone, one hour behind the rest of the state.

Politically, El Paso is an orphan, too. Election turnouts are abysmally low, and people half-jokingly talk about seceding to become part of New Mexico – Santa Fe is only 325 miles away, compared to Austin (573 miles), and El Paso has a far stronger Southwestern

feel than the rest of Texas. Apathy is so entrenched that relatively few El Pasoans have become involved in efforts against the proposed nuclear waste dump less than 100 miles away at Sierra Blanca, TX.

Fiscally, El Paso is in limbo, too, as most labor-intensive manufacturing flows toward Juárez. The Mexican city has 330 maquiladoras employing about 200,000 people, more than any other border community, but

Highlights

- Multicolored sunsets that go on and on
- El Paso's missions and murals
- Scrambling on the boulders at Hueco Tanks State Historical Park
- Guadalupe Mountains National Park, especially beautiful in fall
- West of the Pecos Museum in Pecos – the region's best small-town museum
- Sarah's Cafe in Fort Stockton – friendly service and tasty Mexican food
- Bull riding, bands and great Tex-Mex at Dos Amigos in Odessa
- Sunday brunch at the Wall Street Bar & Grill in Midland

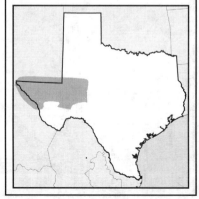

WEST TEXAS

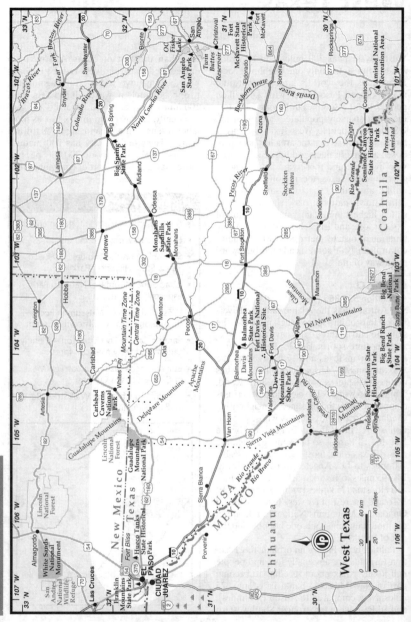

Juárez's cheap labor pool keeps wages in El Paso low, too. El Paso's per capita income is $13,100, compared to $23,000 for the US as a whole.

El Paso is still trying to figure itself out – a process that may continue indefinitely amid social and economic change. But when El Paso looks backward to its rich past – and upward to the Franklin Mountains, southernmost point in the Rockies and largest urban park in the US – the city seems to make a lot of sense. There may be no Six Flags amusement park or major league sports team in El Paso, but the city's beauty runs deep: in the murals of the barrio, the blooms of the outlying desert and the spirit of people for whom the American dream transcends state, national and tribal boundaries.

History

Although Indians of the Tampachoa tradition lived in the El Paso area a thousand or more years ago, Europeans first found El Paso del Norte (The Pass of the North) in the 16th century – either in the 1530s when Álvar Núñez Cabeza de Vaca traveled from the Gulf Coast at present-day Galveston to the Pacific Coast of Mexico or during the 1581 Rodriguez-Chamuscado party.

In 1598, while blazing El Camino Real from Mexico to Santa Fe with an eye toward settling the Southwest, Don Juan de Oñate led 500 followers to the banks of the Rio Grande at what is now San Elizario, Texas. There, the Spanish colonists met Native Americans for what many El Pasoans say was the real first Thanksgiving, 23 years before the Pilgrims feasted at Plymouth Rock in Massachusetts.

The first El Paso del Norte was built at what is now Juárez in 1659; the Mexican city kept that name until 1888, when the new name was given to honor Mexican president Benito Juárez. In 1680, a Pueblo Indian revolt in New Mexico launched a wave of refugees – some Tigua, some Spaniards and some of uncertain origin – southeast along the Rio Grande. In their new home of Ysleta del Sur and in nearby Socorro, the refugees established what are now the oldest permanent settlements in Texas.

The town now known as El Paso started in 1827; early on, it was named Franklin, after a prominent Anglo settler. A US Army post, the first Fort Bliss, was established in 1849 to protect US interests after the end of the Mexican War. Franklin voted to join Texas in 1850, and the city incorporated as El Paso in 1873. The last 20 years of the 19th century proved to be El Paso's Wild West era, as gunfighters followed the railroads to town. John Wesley Hardin, among the most famous, lived and died here.

Juárez was the scene of one of the first major battles of the Mexican Revolution, an event of major importance on both sides of the border. Mexicans fled to safety in El Paso, and even Pancho Villa briefly took refuge here before turning against the US government for its support of his foe, Venustiano Carranza. In 1916, US President Woodrow Wilson dispatched an expedition led by General John J 'Black Jack' Pershing to search for Villa. The mission proved unsuccessful, but it strengthened Fort Bliss' position as a major military post – a role it still has today.

The mid-20th century was marked by the resolution of a controversy that had been simmering ever since the Mexican War: fixing the US-Mexico border by channeling the Rio Grande into a concrete ditch between El Paso and Juárez. (See Chamizal National Monument, below.) But even with the border demarcated and separate allegiances, El Paso and Juárez remain tightly connected – a closeness sure to set the tone for the 21st century and beyond.

Orientation

The Franklin Mountains divide El Paso into a west side and an east side, with downtown sitting due south of the mountains and I-10 serving as the primary through route. I-10 is paralleled on the city's heavily commercial east side by two one-way frontage highways: Gateway Blvd W to the north and Gateway Blvd E to the south. US 54 (the Patriot Freeway), running north-south down the city's near east side, also has parallel frontage roads, Gateway Blvd N and Gateway Blvd S. The intersection where I-10 and US 54 come

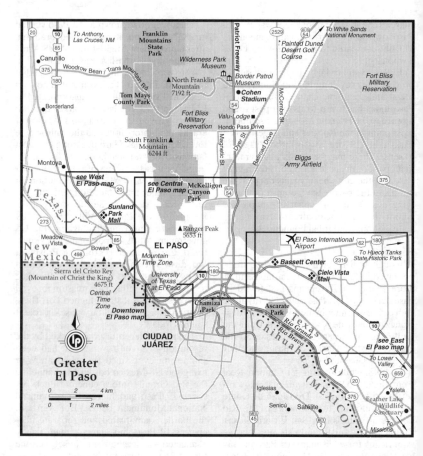

Franklin Mountains State Park

Wilderness Park Museum

▲ North Franklin Mountain 7192 ft

● Cohen Stadium

Valu-Lodge

Hondo Pass Drive

To Anthony, Las Cruces, NM

Canutillo

Woodrow Bean / Trans Mountain Rd

Borderland

Tom Mays County Park

Fort Bliss Military Reservation

South Franklin ▲ Mountain 6244 ft

Montoya

see West El Paso map

Sunland Park Mall

Meadow Vista

Bowen

Sierra del Cristo Rey (Mountain of Christ the King) 4675 ft

Central Time Zone

see Downtown El Paso map

CIUDAD JUÁREZ

Greater El Paso

0   2   4 km
0   1   2 miles

Patriot Freeway

Painted Dunes Desert Golf Course

Border Patrol Museum

McCombs St.

To White Sands National Monument

Fort Bliss Military Reservation

Magnetic St.

Dyer St.

Patriot Drive

Biggs Army Airfield

see Central El Paso map

McKelligon Canyon Park

▲ Ranger Peak 5653 ft

EL PASO

Mountain Time Zone

University of Texas at El Paso

Chamizal Park

✈ El Paso International Airport

❖ Bassett Center

❖ Cielo Vista Mall

To Hueco Tanks State Historic Park

Ascarate Park

Rio Grande

Rio Bravo

see East El Paso map

To Lower Valley

Texas (USA)

Chihuahua (MEXICO)

Iglesias

Senicú   Satélite

Ysleta

Feather Lake Wildlife Sanctuary

To Missions

together is known around El Paso as the Spaghetti Bowl.

The northern reach of Loop 375, El Paso's outer belt route, is also called the Woodrow Bean/Trans Mountain Rd, an attraction in itself as it crosses the Franklin Mountains through Texas' second-largest state park. (East of downtown, the loop becomes first the Avenue of the Americas, then the Border Highway as it runs along the Rio Grande with Juárez just yards away.) Major surface streets include Mesa St, which runs from downtown past the UTEP campus back to I-10 on the far west side; Montana Ave,

which travels from the northern edge of downtown east to the airport then east out of town as US 62/180; and Yarbrough Drive and Lee Trevino Drive, both principal commercial east-side thoroughfares. Airway Blvd, exit 25 off of I-10, is the fastest way to El Paso International Airport.

Maps AAA's El Paso city map, available only to members, is good, although its downtown inset is out of date. (Downtown maps became obsolete after several streets were vacated for the new El Paso Museum of Art. New maps should be available locally by the time you read this.) The widely circulated *Citi-Guide Map of El Paso* lacks detail, but it's good for finding major attractions and many businesses. It's distributed free at motels and merchants.

Information

Tourist Offices The Civic Center Plaza downtown is the best one-stop source for visitor information. On the plaza level, the El Paso-Juárez Trolley Co (☎ 915-544-0061, 800-259-6284), One Civic Center Plaza, is well stocked with brochures and other literature. Downstairs, you'll find the offices of the El Paso Civic, Convention & Tourism Department (☎ 915-534-0696, 800-351-6024, fax 915-534-0686) and the El Paso Council for International Visitors (☎ 915-534-0520). The latter is mainly concerned with people in El Paso for business or educational reasons, but it's still a good resource point for foreign vacationers. AAA (☎ 915-778-9521) is near the airport at 1201 Airway Blvd, Suite A-1, in East El Paso. A Texas Travel Information Center is on I-10 near Anthony at the Texas-New Mexico line.

Gay & Lesbian Adelante, a bilingual gay and lesbian information line, is at ☎ 915-533-9875. Its options include a calendar of events, bars and organizations. There is no community center in El Paso.

Money Currency exchange is available at NationsBank (☎ 915-747-2922), 416 N Stanton St downtown. NationsBank also has branches in many area Albertson's and Smith's grocery stores. Outside of banking hours, go to Valuta (☎ 915-544-1152), 307 E Paisano Drive at Mesa St, open 24 hours.

Post & Communications The downtown post office (☎ 915-532-2652), 219 E Mills Ave, is open Monday to Friday 8:30 am to 5 pm and Saturday 8:30 am to noon. Poste Restante must be retrieved at the new main post office (☎ 915-780-7500), 8401 Boeing Drive, open Monday to Friday 8:30 am to 5 pm. Address mail to General Delivery, El Paso, TX 79910. Mail Boxes Etc (☎ 915-545-2626) is at 2626 N Mesa St.

In addition to its close ties with Juárez, El Paso does big business with neighboring New Mexico. It's not necessary to dial a 1 before New Mexico's 505 area code.

Internet access is available at Kinko's (☎ 915-532-7970), 4190 N Mesa St at Executive Center Blvd. Cost is 20¢ a minute or $12 an hour.

Media The *El Paso Times*, 50¢ daily and $1.50 Sunday, is the city's major newspaper. Many people read *Diario de Juárez*, which sells on El Paso newsstands for 65¢ daily and 80¢ Sunday. Another Spanish-language newspaper, *Norte*, sells for 50¢.

El Paso Scene is a monthly publication oriented to the arts. *El Paso Inc*, a weekly, focuses on business and lifestyle news. The gay-and-lesbian statewide monthly *Texas Triangle* rarely includes El Paso in its coverage. Instead, try the local monthly *El Callejon*, available at local gay and lesbian bars.

Radio The local NPR station, KTEP (88.5 FM), plays jazz much of the day. Other happening stations include KBNA (97.5 FM) with its 'Qué Buena' blend of Latino music, KLAQ (95.5 FM) for rock and KHEY (96 FM) for country and talk radio. KROD (600 AM) is mainly a sports talk radio station, but weekdays from 6 to 10 am it airs an interesting local general interest talk show hosted by Paul Strezlin.

Travel Agents Sun Travel (☎ 915-532-8900), 3100 N Mesa St, is one of El Paso's largest travel agencies. AAA (see above under Tourist Offices) provides travel assistance, too.

Bookstores El Paso doesn't have much in the way of general-interest independent bookstores, but the Bookery (☎ 915-859-4066), 10167 Socorro Rd on the Mission Trail, is an interesting small shop specializing in Hispanic literature and books for children. Barnes & Noble has two locations; the West El Paso store at 705 Sunland Park Drive (☎ 915-581-5353) is popular with the local literati, with a packed calendar of author signings and special events.

WEST TEXAS

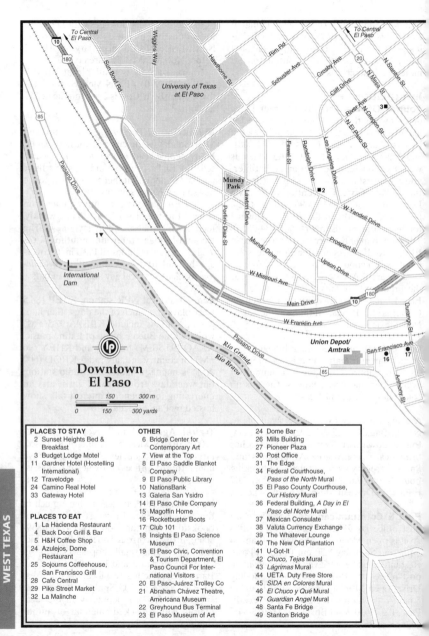

Downtown El Paso

| 0 | 150 | 300 m |
| 0 | 150 | 300 yards |

PLACES TO STAY
2 Sunset Heights Bed & Breakfast
3 Budget Lodge Motel
11 Gardner Hotel (Hostelling International)
12 Travelodge
24 Camino Real Hotel
33 Gateway Hotel

PLACES TO EAT
1 La Hacienda Restaurant
4 Back Door Grill & Bar
5 H&H Coffee Shop
24 Azulejos, Dome Restaurant
25 Sojourns Coffeehouse, San Francisco Grill
28 Cafe Central
29 Pike Street Market
32 La Malinche

OTHER
6 Bridge Center for Contemporary Art
7 View at the Top
8 El Paso Saddle Blanket Company
9 El Paso Public Library
10 NationsBank
13 Galeria San Ysidro
14 El Paso Chile Company
15 Magoffin Home
16 Rocketbuster Boots
17 Club 101
18 Insights El Paso Science Museum
19 El Paso Civic, Convention & Tourism Department, El Paso Council For International Visitors
20 El Paso-Juárez Trolley Co
21 Abraham Chávez Theatre, Americana Museum
22 Greyhound Bus Terminal
23 El Paso Museum of Art

24 Dome Bar
26 Mills Building
27 Pioneer Plaza
30 Post Office
31 The Edge
34 Federal Courthouse, Pass of the North Mural
35 El Paso County Courthouse, Our History Mural
36 Federal Building, A Day in El Paso del Norte Mural
37 Mexican Consulate
38 Valuta Currency Exchange
39 The Whatever Lounge
40 The New Old Plantation
41 U-Got-It
42 Chuco, Tejas Mural
43 Lágrimas Mural
44 UETA Duty Free Store
45 SIDA en Colores Mural
46 El Chuco y Qué Mural
47 Guardian Angel Mural
48 Santa Fe Bridge
49 Stanton Bridge

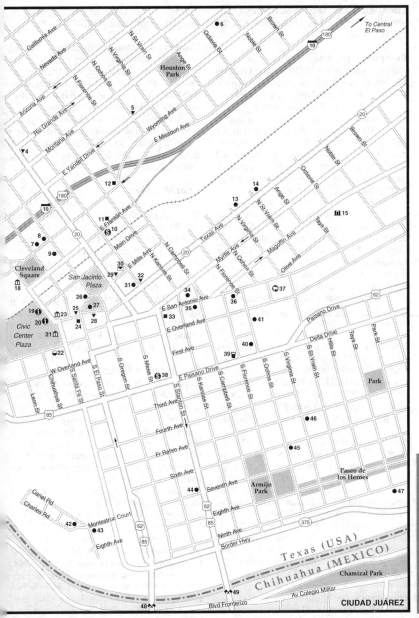

Libraries The El Paso Public Library's main branch (☎ 915-543-5433) is downtown at 501 N Oregon St.

Campuses The University of Texas at El Paso was established in 1914 in the Franklin Mountain foothills north of downtown. UTEP is the largest Hispanic-majority university in the United States; about 65% of its 16,000-student enrollment is Hispanic, and 8% of all students are Mexican nationals. Six colleges and the graduate school offer 60 bachelor's degrees, 53 master's degrees and six doctoral programs, with strengths in geology, engineering, metallurgy, psychology and business administration.

UTEP is also notable for its campus, much of which was constructed using the same architecture seen in the Himalayan kingdom of Bhutan. UTEP's buildings – with their red-tiled roofs, frescoes and archways – recall the Lhasa palace of the Dalai Lama, and they're the only examples of the Bhutanese style in the Western Hemisphere. Looming over all is the Sun Bowl football stadium, home of the major post-season game of the same name. The campus is served by bus Nos 10 and 17.

Laundry Amigo Laundry & Cleaners (☎ 915-532-2937), 301 Cincinnati Ave, is convenient to downtown, UTEP and the great restaurants of Old Kern Place. Señor Bubbles (☎ 915-544-1015), 1930 Olive Ave, is walking distance from a half-dozen of El Paso's beautiful murals (see the boxed text Los Murales).

Medical Services The Company Doctor (☎ 915-592-1444), at 1865 N Lee Trevino Drive, provides no-appointment care for minor illnesses and injuries. Fees start at $47. Conveniently, there's a 24-hour Walgreens (☎ 915-594-1129) across the street in the Vista Hills Shopping Center at 1840 N Lee Trevino Drive. El Paso's major hospitals include Sierra Providence Memorial Hospital (☎ 915-577-6011), 2001 N Oregon St, and Sierra Medical Center (☎ 915-747-4000), 1625 Medical Center St.

Emergency The Sheriff's Department is at ☎ 915-546-2217, and the Highway Patrol is at ☎ 915-855-2105. The local suicide prevention and rape crisis line is ☎ 915-779-1800.

Dangers & Annoyances El Paso is among the safest cities of its size in the US. This is due in part to Operation Hold the Line, an effort to crack down on illegal immigration into El Paso. Green-and-white Border Patrol vehicles are highly visible all along the El Paso side of the Rio Grande, and the police presence has had the side effect of quelling crime on both sides of the border. Still, common sense should apply, as it would in any large city.

Scenic Drive

Popular with joggers and strollers, Scenic Drive offers great views of El Paso, Juárez and the surrounding mountains. Access it via Rim Rd off Mesa St just east of the southern part of UTEP, or via Richmond Ave off Alabama St on the near east side. En route, keep an eye out for little **Murchison Park** – at 4222 feet, a fine spot for sunrises.

The **Star on the Mountain** has overlooked El Paso since 1940. Once just lit during the Christmas season, it's now illuminated year-round from 6 pm until midnight. It can be seen from 100 air miles away.

San Jacinto Plaza

Bordered by Main Drive, Mesa St, Oregon St and Mills Ave, San Jacinto Plaza is the historic heart of El Paso. People hang out here on sunny days, which is most days in El Paso, and you'll see vendors and the occasional busker or two. Spanish is spoken far more than English here and throughout much of El Paso, though nearly everyone serving the tourist trade is bilingual.

The fountain at the center of the plaza has an interesting story. It used to hold several live alligators that were hauled out nightly in burlap bags and placed in someone's bathtub to keep warm, then brought back to the plaza every morning. This went on for the better part of a century, until the late 1960s, when some people started to abuse the reptiles. The gators were taken to the zoo, but they've been memorialized in a sculpture, *Los Lagartos*, by Luis A Jiménez.

The Mills Building, on S Oregon St across from the plaza, is among the most historic in town. It was designed by Henry Trost, West Texas' most famous early-20th-century architect, and it was among the first in the US to use reinforced concrete in its structure. The windows of Ruly's Barber Shop on the Mills Ave side are a veritable El Paso capsule history, with tales and photos of Pancho Villa, John Wesley Hardin and other colorful characters from the city's past.

Pioneer Plaza

The little triangular park where El Paso St meets Mills Ave was the site of El Paso's first mass media: the Newspaper Tree. Before the city had a newspaper of its own, folks used to post their news and notices on a big cottonwood tree that stood at this site. The *El Paso Times* still hangs its daily edition in a glass case here.

The statue on the plaza is of Fray García de San Francisco, who was among the men who founded the first El Paso de Norte – now Juárez – in 1659. This is the first of a planned series of XII Travelers statues to commemorate the area's founders.

El Paso Museum of Art

This new museum (☎ 915-532-1707), 1 Arts Festival Plaza, is the most exciting thing to happen downtown in many years. When it opened in 1998, the new facility allowed the museum four to five times the gallery space of its old digs on Montana Ave. With the striking swoop-roofed Abraham Chávez Theatre close by and the surrounding plaza filled with shade trees, a water wall, reflecting pool and performance spaces, El Paso finally has a true arts district.

Inside, the 104,000-sq-foot museum includes permanent collections of European, Mexican and American art plus about 15 changing exhibits a year. Bilingual docent tours are available, and the museum is also a setting for children's activities, lectures, concerts and a film series. Tuesday to Saturday, the museum is open 9 am to 6 pm (except Thursday, when it stays open until 9 pm). Sunday hours are noon to 5 pm. Admission is free.

Insights El Paso Science Museum

'Please touch' is the motto at this hands-on museum (☎ 915-542-2990), 505 N Santa Fe St. In addition to more than 100 interactive exhibits, it has frequent special shows; for example, it was one of 12 museums to host the Smithsonian Institute's Christopher Columbus exhibition during the 500th anniversary of the explorer's 1492 voyage. Open Tuesday to Saturday 9 am to 5 pm, Sunday noon to 5 pm. Admission is generally $5 for adults, $4 for students ages six to college age and $3 for children ages three to five, but rates can vary when a special show is on. No tickets are sold in the last 45 minutes each day.

Americana Museum

The major attraction at this downtown museum (☎ 915-542-0394), 5 Civic Center Plaza, is **Art & Legacy of a Vanished People**, a display of prehistoric artifacts and pottery from the Southwest. Changing art exhibits feature noted local and regional artists. The museum is located street level at the corner of Santa Fe St and San Antonio Ave. It's open Tuesday to Friday 10 am to 5 pm; free.

El Paso Centennial Museum

This museum (☎ 915-747-5565) at University Ave and Wiggins Way on the UTEP campus (bus No 10) specializes in the human and natural history of the El Paso region. It includes pottery, stone tools and shell jewelry from prehistoric Mexico, mineral and rock collections, dinosaur bones, fossils and other artifacts from the Ice Age. Open Tuesday to Saturday 10 am to 5 pm, except major holidays. Admission is by donation.

El Paso Holocaust Museum & Study Center

You might not expect to see a facility like this in El Paso, which seems far removed from the heart of American Judaism. But the **El Paso Holocaust Museum and Study Center** (☎ 915-833-5656), 401 Wallenberg Drive on the west side (bus No 14 to Festival Drive), is a moving tribute to the 6 million Jews killed by the Nazis. Galleries exhibit many artifacts from the ghettos and death

WEST TEXAS

camps; there's also an outdoor Garden of the Righteous that memorializes the many non-Jews who risked death trying to save Jews from persecution. Open Tuesday to Thursday and Sunday 1 to 4 pm. Admission is by donation.

Magoffin Home

Now a Texas State Parks site, this El Paso landmark (☎ 915-533-5147), 1120 Magoffin Ave (bus Nos 21, 22, 31, 55, 62 or the East-West Trolley), was built in 1875 for Joseph Magoffin, an early El Paso politician and businessman. With 4-foot-thick adobe walls and many of its original furnishings, the home is a fine example of the Southwest Territorial style of architecture prevalent during the late 19th century. Guided tours are given Wednesday to Sunday 9 am to 4 pm. Admission is $2 per person, $1 for students or seniors with ID.

Concordia Cemetery

Just west of the busy I-10/US 54 interchange in Central El Paso, Concordia Cemetery (☎ 915-542-1591) (bus Nos 1, 2, 42, 51, 52, 53 or 59) is the oldest, biggest and most historic graveyard in El Paso. Outlaw John Wesley Hardin and other notable El Pasoans are buried here. The cemetery is bounded north and south by Yandell Drive and Gateway Blvd W.

Chamizal National Monument

Located along the Rio Grande on the US-Mexican border, Chamizal National Monu-

---

Los Murales

They're not always mentioned in guidebooks – perhaps because they're primarily in the poorest areas of town – but 'Los Murales,' the murals of El Paso, are perhaps the city's preeminent cultural treasure. Of the more than 100 murals in the city, the greatest concentrations are south of downtown between Paisano Drive and the Border Hwy and north of Paisano Drive near Douglass Elementary School. The Junior League of El Paso, which has long supported the murals and even funded the creation of some, has published two good mural guides; copies can usually be found at the El Paso Civic, Convention & Tourism Department. *Los Murales Guide and Maps to the Murals of El Paso* locates murals throughout the city, while *An Art of Conscience: A Guide to Selected El Paso Murals* focuses on barrio-area art, including several murals that have been destroyed.

In the introduction to *An Art of Conscience*, major El Paso muralist Carlos Callejo had this to say:

These murals have made a very real contribution. There was a time when there was no interest to help in our parts of town. Many felt those places were off limits, or wanted nothing to do with them. Now, even though the paintings have dark elements, even though there still are people who do not understand all of our symbols, they, too, take pride in the paintings. Now these places are a part of us all.

Here's a sampling of some of the more memorable examples:

North of Paisano Drive Painted in 1983 and restored in 1991, *Virgen de Guadalupe con Juan Diego* (Cypress Ave west of Eucalyptus St) depicts the story of Mexico's patron saint and her 1531 appearance to Juan Diego.

South of Paisano Drive *Guardian Angel* (Ninth Ave at Tays St) is visible all the way up and down Tays St. It is intended to be a positive image for the neighborhood's young

ment (☎ 915-532-7273) (bus Nos 23, 24 or 65) pays tribute to the 1963 settlement of a longtime dispute between the two nations over land isolated by the shifting river channel. Chamizal is a major gathering place for El Paso, with performing arts spaces and parklands complemented by a museum and art gallery. A companion park sits on the Mexican side of the border just over the Cordova Bridge.

History In his book *Border: The US-Mexico Line*, El Paso-based historian Leon C Metz wrote: 'Rivers are never absolutely permanent. They evaporate, flood, change channels, shrink, expand and even disappear.' The Rio Grande was fixed as the US-Mexico border following the Mexican War, but it soon

became clear this boundary might not last. A tract of farmland between El Paso and Juárez was bordered on the south by the Rio Grande, whose course was gradually shifting southward. Mexico laid claim to the area in 1895, prompting US counter-claims. Matters were complicated by the presence of adjoining Cordova Island, a detached part of Mexico on the north side of the Rio Grande.

The dispute simmered for most of the following century. By the 1960s, with both cities' planning efforts stymied by the standoff, the US and Mexico agreed to build a concrete-lined channel to control the Rio Grande's flow and bisect the Chamizal and Cordova Island. The compromise was worked out by US president John F Kennedy and Mexican president Adolfo López Mateos in 1962.

people. The mural, painted in 1988, depicts an angel shepherding two small children across a rickety bridge.

The title of *El Chuco y Qué* (S Virginia St at Fr Rahm Ave) is slang for 'El Paso, So What.' It depicts a huge Anglo cowboy leaning on a border-symbolic fence on which several Chicano people are teetering, trying to find their roles on the international frontier. The mural (1991) seems to say that although El Paso is not stereotypically Texan, Anglo influence looms large.

SIDA en Colores (Sixth Ave at S Ochoa St) is a stark warning against the risky behaviors that can lead to AIDS. The mural (1988) was created by Callejo, then a social worker from the nearby Clínica La Fe, together with two dozen area youth.

West of Santa Fe St Painted in 1975, *Chuco, Tejas* (Canal Rd and Seventh Ave) shows Aztec imagery that links it to an effort to build community pride in the Chiuhuahuita (Little Chihuahua) barrio. The artists have said the design is symbolic of friendship and looking out for one another.

Although untitled, the faded 1977 mural at Montestruc Court at Canal Rd is frequently called *Lágrimas*, or the tears shed by barrio dwellers who tried to stop the Texas Highway Department from redirecting the Border Hwy through their neighborhood.

Downtown El Paso has three major murals that can be seen in their respective buildings during business hours. Tom Lea's *Pass of the North*, completed in 1938, depicts early explorers of the Southwest. It's on view inside the Federal Courthouse, 511 E San Antonio Ave. Past and present blend in *A Day in El Paso del Norte* by John Valadez, a 1994 photo-realistic work in the Federal Building, 700 E San Antonio Ave. Carlos Callejo's 1995 *Our History* spans three walls of the third-floor atrium of the El Paso County Courthouse, 500 E San Antonio Ave, with images including an array of major and minor players from El Paso's past.

WEST TEXAS

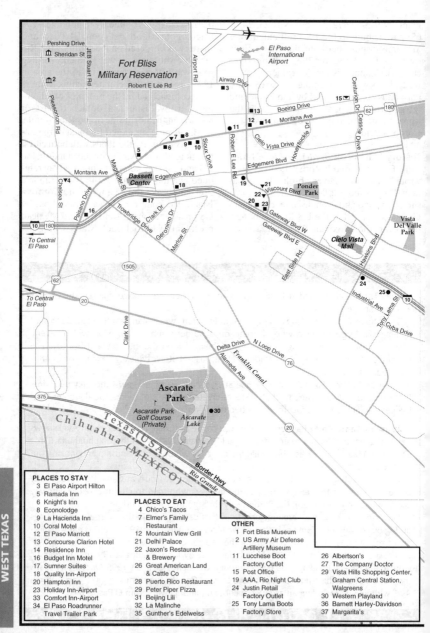

PLACES TO STAY
3 El Paso Airport Hilton
5 Ramada Inn
6 Knight's Inn
8 Econolodge
9 La Hacienda Inn
10 Coral Motel
12 El Paso Marriott
13 Concourse Clarion Hotel
14 Residence Inn
16 Budget Inn Motel
17 Sumner Suites
18 Quality Inn-Airport
20 Hampton Inn
23 Holiday Inn-Airport
33 Comfort Inn-Airport
34 El Paso Roadrunner
    Travel Trailer Park

PLACES TO EAT
4 Chico's Tacos
7 Elmer's Family
   Restaurant
12 Mountain View Grill
21 Delhi Palace
22 Jaxon's Restaurant
    & Brewery
26 Great American Land
    & Cattle Co
28 Puerto Rico Restaurant
29 Peter Piper Pizza
31 Beijing Lili
32 La Malinche
35 Gunther's Edelweiss

OTHER
1 Fort Bliss Museum
2 US Army Air Defense
   Artillery Museum
11 Lucchese Boot
    Factory Outlet
15 Post Office
19 AAA, Rio Night Club
24 Justin Retail
    Factory Outlet
25 Tony Lama Boots
    Factory Store
26 Albertson's
27 The Company Doctor
29 Vista Hills Shopping Center,
    Graham Central Station,
    Walgreens
30 Western Playland
36 Barnett Harley-Davidson
37 Margarita's

WEST TEXAS

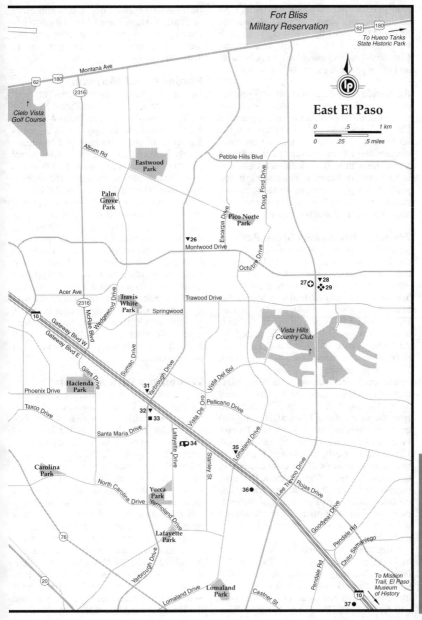

But since Kennedy was killed before he could sign the treaty, Lyndon B Johnson finalized the effort the following year. Both nations agreed to use their side of the Chamizal-Cordova parcel for schools, parks and other public uses.

Activities The Chamizal visitors' center screens a video on the origins and resolution of the Chamizal dispute. Outside, a mural by Carlos Flores depicts the key players in the settlement and cultural themes from both nations. The 1.9-mile Cordova Island Trail is a favorite with walkers, joggers, cyclists and in-line skaters. Picnic tables and barbecue grills dot the grounds, as do stone monuments erected in 1897 to mark what was then the international boundary.

Franklin Mountains State Park

When developers started carving roads into the Franklin Mountains in the late 1970s, local preservationists cried foul – and took their cause to the Texas State Legislature. The state inaugurated Franklin Mountains State Park (☎ 915-566-6441) in 1979, creating the second-largest state park in Texas and preserving El Paso's scenic backdrop. At 23,863 acres, this is the largest urban park in the US, capped by 7192-foot North Franklin Mountain.

The park, still mostly undeveloped, is crossed by just one road: the Woodrow Bean/ Trans Mountain Rd (Loop 375), accessed from the west side via I-10 exit 6 (Canutillo) or from the east via US 54, the Patriot Freeway. En route are trailheads accessing 125 miles of trails, including 51 miles of mountain bike trails, 22 miles of equestrian trails and 52 miles of hiking trails. The most popular trek, the Ron Coleman Trail, takes off from Smuggler's Pass at about the mid-point on Trans Mountain Rd and winds 3½ miles to McKelligon Canyon on El Paso's east side.

Primitive tent camping is now allowed at Franklin Mountains State Park, and a few RV sites may be added in the future. Check with park officials at the telephone number above for updated information and restrictions. There's no charge to drive through, but cyclists, day hikers and other recreationists over age 12 are asked to pay the $2 park entrance fee. The following two museums are at the eastern gateway to Trans Mountain Rd.

Border Patrol Museum

One of the most interesting specialty museums in Texas, the Border Patrol Museum (☎ 915-759-6060), at 4315 Trans Mountain Rd (bus Nos 2 and 46 come close), describes the work of the 7000 men and women – nearly 3000 of them in Texas – who patrol the 8000-plus miles of border the US shares with Canada and Mexico, and the ingenuity of the criminals for whom the Border Patrol is but a minor nuisance. Interspersed among displays of Border Patrol heroics are exhibits of nasty-looking confiscated weapons, everything from ice picks to Chinese stars; narcotic 'bricks' wrapped in Christmas paper; and a makeshift boat made by welding two discarded pick-up truck hoods. There's also a film on Border Patrol recruitment and training, along with a tribute to women in the Border Patrol. A gift shop sells Border Patrol gear, everything from polo shirts to teddy bears. Open Tuesday to Sunday 9 am to 5 pm. Admission is by donation.

Wilderness Park Museum

If you have been wondering about the strange plants of the Chihuahuan Desert, this indoor-outdoor complex (☎ 915-755-4332), 4301 Trans Mountain Rd, is a good place to identify them. Self-guided nature trails offer a look at all kinds of cacti and other flora – ocotillo, sotol, Southwest barrel cactus, lechuguilla, prickly pear cactus, catclaw mimosa, Western honey mesquite and more. Inside, anthropological exhibits explain the pueblo-dwelling people who lived in the El Paso area until about 1400 and the Tarahumara Indians of Chihuahua. The museum is wildly popular for school field trips. Open Tuesday to Sunday 9 am to 4:45 pm, except major holidays. Admission is by donation. A footpath leads between the Wilderness Park Museum and the Border Patrol Museum.

Fort Bliss

Fort Bliss is named for Lieutenant Colonel William Wallace Smith Bliss (1815-1853), a veteran of the Mexican War who later served as private secretary to President Zachary Taylor. The fort has had six locations in its 150-year history. It currently consumes much of the desert northeast of El Paso and well into New Mexico as the largest air defense training center in the Western world. Troops from all the NATO allied nations regularly train here, and the base pumps an annual $1 billion into the local economy.

Located on-base along Pleasanton Rd, the **Fort Bliss Museum** (☎ 915-568-4518) (bus No 31) is housed in a reconstruction of the fort's 1854-68 location. It depicts life at the post in 1857 right down to the 31-star flag hanging outside. The museum was a gift to the base on its 100th anniversary in El Paso. One block south, near the junction of Pleasanton and Robert E Lee Rds, the **US Army Air Defense Artillery Museum** (☎ 915-568-5412) is the only one of its kind in the US. Its exhibits focus on the history of air defense artillery since 1917, including outdoor displays of various missiles and remote-control-guided drones. Both museums are open daily except major holidays 9 am to 4:30 pm, and admission is free.

El Paso Zoo

The El Paso Zoo (☎ 915-544-1928 for recorded information, 915-521-1850 business line), 4001 E Paisano Drive (bus Nos 58 and 65), is in Washington Park. It is home to a large number of endangered animals, including the Asian elephant, Mexican wolf, golden lion tamarin, Bali mynah, Malayan sun bear and Indo-Chinese tiger. A 'paraje' section, named after the Spanish word given to rest stops along the Camino Real, displays and interprets domesticated animals of the Southwest. All told, 700 animals represent 175 species. Open daily except Thanksgiving, Christmas and New Year's Day 9 am to 4 pm; $4 for everyone ages 13 to 61, $2 for seniors, $1.50 for children ages three to 12. The Grasslands Café and Ice Cream Oasis serve snacks and the Elephant's Trunk Gift Shop sells T-shirts, toys and gifts.

Ascarate Park

Located on El Paso's near east side between Delta Drive and Border Hwy, Ascarate Park (☎ 915-772-3941) (bus Nos 61, 62, 65 and 66) includes a public 21-hole golf course, lots of ball diamonds, a 50-meter swimming pool and a 44-acre lake stocked with bass, catfish and trout for year-round angling.

Western Playland This small amusement park (☎ 915-772-3914) within Ascarate Park has 16 major rides, 12 kiddie rides, game arcades, picnic areas and volleyball courts. From March through October, it's open on the weekends; from June through August, it's open daily.

El Paso Museum of History

We're not sure how this scruffy little museum (☎ 915-859-1928), 12901 Gateway Blvd W, wound up way out on the city's eastern outskirts, but now that the art museum has snagged prime downtown real estate, perhaps the historians will follow. For now, you'll find a Victorian dollhouse, a plaster copy of Pancho Villa's death mask and some neat pointillism-style murals, one showing the US-Mexican border from the Pacific Ocean to the Gulf of Mexico.

Despite the remote location and well-worn displays, the museum makes a good stop en route to the Mission Trail. Open Tuesday to Saturday 9 am to 4:50 pm; suggested donation is $1 for adults and 50¢ for children.

The Mission Trail

The Lower Valley area of El Paso was the first permanently settled part of Texas, and the Mission Trail preserves and interprets these early communities. Most visitors begin at Ysleta and travel down valley to Socorro and San Elizario. To find Ysleta and the Mission Trail from El Paso, take I-10 east to the Zaragoza exit, then turn right (south) and follow Zaragoza Rd to Old Pueblo Rd. The Mission Trail is served by bus Nos 3, 7, 61, 63, 64, 68 and 69. Bus Nos 3 and 63 go as far as Socorro, but no public transportation reaches San Elizario. For more information on the missions, contact the El Paso Mission

Trail Association (☎ 915-534-0677), One Civic Center Plaza, El Paso, TX 79901.

Ysleta del Sur Pueblo Nominally part of El Paso but officially sovereign home to the Tigua (pronounced TEE-wa) Tribe of Texas, Ysleta del Sur Pueblo – or Ysleta for short – is a fascinating community where a booming casino complex sits within sight of the oldest mission in Texas. Built with mud-chinked logs and willow reeds in 1682, the Mission San Antonio de Los Tiguas later was upgraded with logs and finally adobe construction. The beautiful silver-domed bell tower was added in the 1880s. Inside, a **Santo Entierro** (Christ in the Coffin) used in annual dramatizations of the Easter story dates from 1722. It was brought from Mexico and ferried across the Rio Grande. The Feast of St Anthony, June 13, is a major day of celebration at the mission.

Tigua Cultural Center Despite the Spanish influences, the Tigua have strived mightily to retain their identity as the oldest identifiable ethnic group in Texas. A visit to the tribe's cultural center (☎ 915-859-5287), 305 Yaya Lane, proves the struggles have not been in vain. Every Saturday and Sunday year round, social dancers fill the center's plaza with performances at 11 am, 1 pm and 3 pm. Bread-baking demonstrations are common on weekends, too. On weekdays, visitors can see exhibits documenting Tigua history, browse in several gift shops and dine in the Cacique Cafe. Open Tuesday to Sunday 8:30 am to 5 pm.

Socorro Mission Two miles east of Ysleta on Hwy 20 (Socorro Rd; bus Nos 3 and 63), the Socorro Mission is the oldest continually active parish in the US. Originally built in 1681 by the Piro Indians, who later assimilated into the Tiguas, the church has repeatedly been rebuilt after Rio Grande flooding. It still includes some hand-carved roof beams *(vigas)* sculpted by the Piro and a hand-carved wooden statue of St Michael, the parish patron saint. According to legend, the statue was being transported by oxcart from Mexico City to New Mexico when the

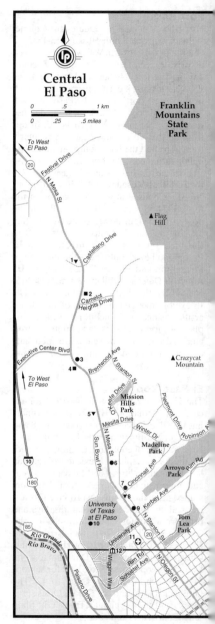

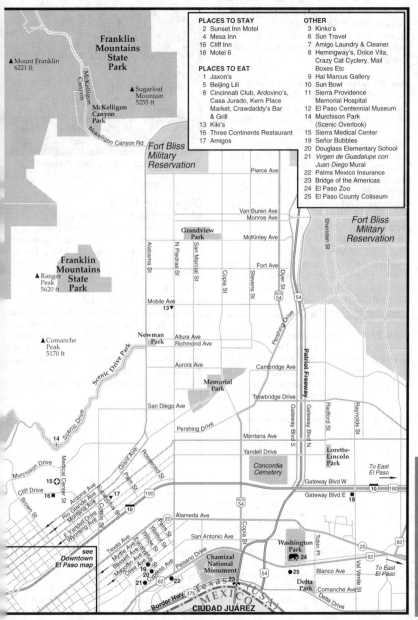

PLACES TO STAY
2 Sunset Inn Motel
4 Mesa Inn
16 Cliff Inn
18 Motel 6

PLACES TO EAT
1 Jaxon's
5 Beijing Lili
8 Cincinnati Club, Ardovino's,
Casa Jurado, Kern Place
Market, Crawdaddy's Bar
& Grill
13 Kiki's
16 Three Continents Restaurant
17 Amigos

OTHER
3 Kinko's
6 Sun Travel
7 Amigo Laundry & Cleaner
8 Hemingway's, Dolce Vita,
Crazy Cat Cyclery, Mail
Boxes Etc
9 Hal Marcus Gallery
10 Sun Bowl
11 Sierra Providence
Memorial Hospital
12 El Paso Centennial Museum
14 Murchison Park
(Scenic Overlook)
15 Sierra Medical Center
19 Señor Bubbles
20 Douglass Elementary School
21 *Virgen de Guadalupe con
Juan Diego* Mural
22 Palms Mexico Insurance
23 Bridge of the Americas
24 El Paso Zoo
25 El Paso County Coliseum

WEST TEXAS

cart became mired in the mud. The local parishioners took this as a sign that St Michael wanted to stop traveling and make Socorro his home. The church burial grounds lie east of the mission.

San Elizario Presidio Another 5 miles east on Hwy 20, San Elizario is the site of a presidio established for the Spanish government in 1789. Troops here defended Spanish interests for more than half a century, until 1849, when the area became part of the US and San Elizario was named seat of El Paso County. Today, peaceful San Elizario is notable for its 1877 church and the adjacent town plaza where de Oñate issued his 1598 proclamation claiming the region for Spain.

Activities

Bicycling Crazy Cat Cyclery (☎ 915-577-9666), 2625 N Mesa St, is the best source of local biking information and equipment. Some of the city's best mountain biking is five minutes away, and they'll point you in the right direction. Bikes rent for $15 for a full day or $10 for a half day.

Bird-Watching Feather Lake Wildlife Sanctuary, 9500 N Loop Drive between Ave of the Americas and Zaragoza Rd, is a 40-acre wetlands preserve overseen by the El Paso/Trans-Pecos Audubon Society. Its self-guided trail winds past Rio Grande cottonwood and saltcedar trees, and you might catch a glimpse of burrowing owl, black-crowned night heron or a variety of ducks. The sanctuary is open October to April, Saturdays 8 am to noon, Sundays 2 pm until dusk.

Golf El Paso is a golf-crazy town; just look at all the east side streets named after pro golfers. (Homeboy Lee Trevino gets the biggest tribute, but dozens of other PGA stars are on the map, too.) The marquee course is **Painted Dunes** (☎ 915-821-2122), 12000 McCombs St north of town. These public links are open to all. Weekday mornings, it costs $16.25 to play 18 holes, with discounts after 1:30 pm. Weekend fees are $21.10. Carts are about $10 extra.

The church at San Elizario Presidio

Organized Tours

Walking Tours Diane Roque (☎ 915-598-9661) and Joann Shaw (☎ 915-877-3002, 800-877-9040, fax 915-877-1953) lead customized walking tours of El Paso. They have no set schedule but will design a tour to your interests, so call and tell them what you have in mind. The basic tour ($10) includes a stop for a continental breakfast. They offer a walking tour of Juárez every third Saturday and conduct the El Paso Haunted History tour on Fridays from September through April ($15.95, includes a light supper). The visitors' center offers a self-guided pamphlet, *El Paso Downtown Walking Tour*, but the guided tours mentioned on the back no longer occur.

Trolley Tours In addition to its treks across the border, the El Paso-Juárez Trolley Co (☎ 915-544-0061, 800-259-6284), One Civic Center Plaza, runs summertime Trolley on a Mission tours along the Mission Trail. Cost is $19 a seat for all ages. In December, the company's Christmas Light Tour travels past many of the biggest houses and best holiday lights in El Paso. Cost is $12 a seat for all ages.

Shuttle Tours The following companies operate by appointment only. **Fiesta Tours** (☎ 915-772-9181, 800-688-4844) charges $15 per person for its four-hour Best of El Paso city tour. They need a minimum of six people. **Golden Tours** (☎ 915-779-0555) offers daily 3½-hour tours priced at $15 per person and $20 per person for a full day, not including

WEST TEXAS

JOHN ELK III

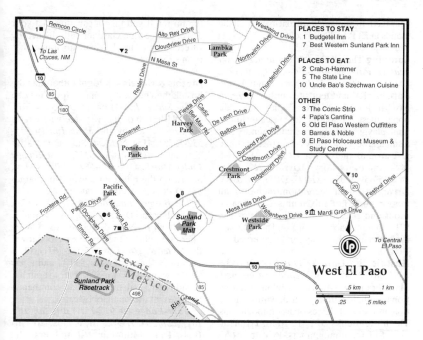

PLACES TO STAY
1 Budgetel Inn
7 Best Western Sunland Park Inn

PLACES TO EAT
2 Crab-n-Hammer
5 The State Line
10 Uncle Bao's Szechwan Cuisine

OTHER
3 The Comic Strip
4 Papa's Cantina
6 Old El Paso Western Outfitters
8 Barnes & Noble
9 El Paso Holocaust Museum &
   Study Center

West El Paso

lunch (though they do drop you at a restaurant and pick you up later). They pick up at most motels and hotels. **Johnny's Transportation** (☎ 915-549-7025 or 915-755-3475 evenings) offers a scenic drive that lasts about an hour and costs $38 for one to three people. If you like, you can interrupt the trip for a stroll to Juárez. **Rancho Grande Tours & Shuttle** (☎ 915-771-6661, 800-605-1257) offers daily El Paso tours priced at $18 per hour for one to four people with a 3½-hour minimum. Additional people are $3 per person per hour. All these companies also run tours to Juárez. In addition, Rancho Grande has trips to Carlsbad Caverns, White Sands National Monument and Old Mesilla in New Mexico and to Mexico's Copper Canyon.

Special Events

The Southwestern International Livestock Show & Rodeo takes over the El Paso County Coliseum the first two weeks each February. Don Juan de Oñate's First Thanks-

giving reenactment is staged on the last weekend of April, with festivities at Chamizal National Monument and San Elizario. Memorial Day weekend in late May brings the International Balloon Festival to nearby Anthony, Texas. In June, El Paso and Juárez team up for the International Mariachi Festival. Fort Biggs is the site for October's Amigo Airsho, and the Sun Bowl college football classic takes place on New Year's Eve Day, with many pre-game events held throughout the holiday season. For information on these and other special events, call the El Paso Civic, Convention & Tourism Department.

Places to Stay

El Paso has the highest lodging tax in the state – 15% – yet rooms are cheap here compared with other major Texas cities. Motels are concentrated mainly along Gateway Blvd E and Gateway Blvd W. On the east side, near the airport, they are on Montana Ave. On the west side, they are on Mesa St and near the I-10 Sunland Park exit. Nearly all the motels in El Paso have pools.

Camping The *El Paso Roadrunner Travel Trailer Park* (☎ 915-598-4469), at 1212 Lafayette Drive (I-10 Yarbrough Drive exit), has RV and tent sites; either way, you pay $18 for one or two people, with additional guests $1 apiece. Amenities include a pool, playground, showers, coin laundry and a small grocery store. A bit farther east and just around the corner from the El Paso Museum of History, *Mission RV Park* (☎ 915-859-1133, 800-447-3795), 1420 RV Drive, has great recreation, including an indoor pool, hot tub, tennis court, game room and playground. Full hook-ups run $21 and tent spaces go for $14. The latter are in short supply, but they can be reserved.

Hostels The *Gardner Hotel* (☎ 915-532-3661, fax 915-532-0302, epihostl@whc.net), 311 E Franklin Ave, is a Hostelling International affiliate with a great downtown location and several classes of accommodations. The hostel bunks cost $12.10 for HI members, $17 for nonmembers. Private rooms with two beds, either twins or bunks, linens and color TV cost $15 single and $30 double. Bathrooms are down the hall. European-style private rooms with a full-size bed and wash basin in the room and bathroom down the hall run $20 for one person, $40 for two. Finally, the Gardner's standard hotel rooms – all with telephone and TV, many with private bath and at least a wash basin – average $35 for either one or two people. Outlaw John Dillinger stayed in Room 104 shortly before his capture in Tucson, Arizona.

The Gardner is an accommodating place; there are no curfews, the office is open 24 hours and best of all, manager and longtime El Pasoan Joe Nebhan is a fount of information on what to see and do in the borderlands. The Gardner is a seven-block walk northeast of the Greyhound Bus Terminal and about 11 blocks from Union Depot and Amtrak. From the airport, take bus No 33 to San Jacinto Plaza, then walk one block north to Franklin then a block-and-a-half east to

the hostel. If you take a cab, don't let your driver confuse the Gardner with the nearby International Hotel, which no longer has rooms for rent.

Motels & Hotels – Budget Other than the hostel, the cheapest rooms in town may be at the *Sunset Inn Motel* (☎ 915-533-8201), 4532 N Mesa St on the west side, where rates are $20/22. Nearby, the *Mesa Inn* (☎ 915-532-7911), 4151 N Mesa St, seemed a bit cheerier with rooms for $27/29. The *Budget Lodge Motel* (☎ 915-533-6821), 1301 N Mesa St just up the hill from downtown, charges $23/27 double. All three have pools.

The *Budget Inn Motel* (☎ 915-772-8875), 5634 E Paisano Drive at I-10, has acceptable rooms with TV and phone for $28/34. There's a pool on the premises. Downtown, the *Gateway Hotel* (☎ 915-532-2611), 104 S Stanton St, has rooms for $30/35 and a few singles without TV for $23. Every room has a bathroom, and rates include continental breakfast at the small lobby cafe.

Valu-Lodge (☎ 915-751-1201, fax 915-751-5221), 9487 Dyer St, is close to Fort Bliss, Trans Mountain Rd and Franklin Mountains State Park. Rooms run $33 for one bed, $37 for two.

Motel 6 has three El Paso locations including 4800 Gateway Blvd E (☎ 915-533-7521). Rates are about $34/40 in summer, about $4 less the rest of the year.

The following three motels are all within a few blocks of one another west of the airport on Montana Ave. *Coral Motel* (☎ 915-772-3263, fax 915-779-6053), 6420 Montana Ave, is the cheapest AAA-rated motel in town, with rates of $34/38. *Knight's Inn* (☎ 915-778-6661, fax 915-778-7926), 6308 Montana Ave, has rooms for $39/44. *La Hacienda Inn* (☎ 915-772-4231, 800-772-4231, fax 915-779-2918), 6400 Montana Ave, has rates of $40/47 along with a pool, picnic area and restaurant/lounge.

Budgetel (☎ 915-585-2999, fax 915-585-1667), 7620 N Mesa St on the west side, has summer rates of $40/49. In winter, rooms dip to about $30/37. The high-rise *Travelodge* (☎ 915-544-3333, fax 915-533-4109), 409 E Missouri Ave, has rooms with balconies for

$42 and a convenient downtown location. There's a small outdoor pool plus a restaurant and lounge.

Motels & Hotels – Mid-Range At the bottom of this category and near the airport, *Econolodge* (☎ 915-778-3311, fax 915-778-1097), 6363 Montana Ave, has rooms starting at $45/50. *Comfort Inn-Airport East* (☎ 915-594-9111), in reality quite a ways from the airport at 900 Yarbrough Drive, has rooms starting at $59 single or double. The big *Quality Inn-Airport* (☎ 915-778-6611, fax 915-779-2270), 6201 Gateway Blvd W, is a good deal with about 300 rooms priced at $49/54. The *Ramada Inn* (☎ 915-772-3300, fax 915-775-0808), 6099 Montana Ave, has rooms for $64/59. On the west side, *Best Western Sunland Park Inn* (☎ 915-587-4900, fax 915-587-4950), 1045 Sunland Park Drive, has rooms for $59/69, all with microwaves and refrigerators.

With rooms starting at $59 for one or two people, the *Cliff Inn* (☎ 915-533-6700, 800-333-2543, fax 915-544-2127), 1600 Cliff Drive north of downtown in the Franklin Mountain foothills, is a good value and one of the classiest places in town. Guest rooms are well equipped (if a bit worn), with mini refrigerators and microwaves, but we were most taken with the delightful European-influenced public areas, full of trompe l'oeil artworks and lots of comfortable seating. There's an outdoor hot tub overlooking the city.

The *Hampton Inn* (☎ 915-771-6644), 6635 Gateway Blvd W, has rooms starting at $88/112 . Next door, *Holiday Inn-Airport* (☎ 915-778-6411, fax 915-778-6517), 6655 Gateway Blvd W, charges $99 for single or double occupancy.

Motels & Hotels – Top End *Sumner Suites* (☎ 915-771-0022, fax 915-771-0599), 6030 Gateway Blvd E, charges $95/105 for its large, comfortable rooms. The *Residence Inn* (☎ 915-772-8000), 6791 Montana Ave, is an apartment motel suited for long stays, with kitchens in each room. Rates run $109/119.

The three big airport hotels are all great buys if you happen to hit town on a weekend.

Rates at the *El Paso Airport Hilton* (☎ 915-778-4241, fax 915-772-6871), 2027 Airway Blvd; the *El Paso Marriott* (☎ 915-779-3300, fax 915-772-0915), 1600 Airway Blvd; and the *Concourse Clarion Hotel* (☎ 915-778-6789, fax 915-778-2288), 6789 Boeing Drive, are all in the $110 to $125 range for doubles during the week but fall to about half that on the weekend. The Hilton's pool comes complete with the Texas Twister water slide.

Weekend deals are also possible at the plush *Camino Real Hotel* (☎ 915-534-3000, 800-769-4300, fax 915-534-3024), 101 S El Paso St. Rates run $125/140 weekdays and start at $70 Friday through Sunday. The bright, sun-filled guest rooms are comfortable and inviting, and the public areas – including the rooftop pool and the lounge's Tiffany stained glass dome – are first class. Service is occasionally sullen, but we predict the bad apples don't last long enough to spoil the bunch. And you can't beat the Camino's location: downtown within a few blocks of everything.

B&Bs Last time we checked, El Paso had exactly one choice in this category, but it's a good one, convenient to downtown in one of the city's most stylish neighborhoods. The 1905 Victorian-styled *Sunset Heights Bed & Breakfast* (☎ 915-544-1743, fax 915-544-5119), 717 W Yandell Drive, has four welcoming rooms priced from $75 (with a queen bed and shower) to $150 (for the master suite complete with king bed and a jetted tub). There's a pool and outdoor fireplace, and the Martinez family serves up hearty Tex-Mex breakfasts each morning.

Places to Eat
El Paso has long proclaimed itself the Mexican food capital of the US, and there certainly are dozens of good restaurants in that category. But the area is also known for its steak houses, several of which are just far enough out of town to make dinner feel like an adventure. The influences of Fort Bliss and the maquiladoras have added other international tastes to El Paso's tables. Like its motels, El Paso's restaurants are generally inexpensive to moderate in price.

WEST TEXAS

Mexican, Tex-Mex & Southwestern

Where to begin? Possibly where El Paso did, at *La Hacienda Restaurant* (☎ 915-533-1919), 1720 W Paisano Drive under the Yandell Drive overpass. This is the former home of early settler Simeon Hart, who founded a mill on the site in 1849. The menu reels off 20 specialties of the house, all priced at $5.49; there's also a good selection of salads and sandwiches including the sincronizadas ($5), a grilled cheese tortilla sandwich with mushrooms and roasted peppers.

La Malinche is a popular family-owned chain around El Paso, with most meals in the $5 to $8 range and breakfasts for a few dollars less. There are several locations, including 910 Yarbrough Drive (☎ 915-598-3811), just off I-10 with appropriately speedy service, and downtown at 301 Texas Ave (☎ 915-544-8785), where the tiled tables and neat decor make for a more leisurely Mexican-courtyard atmosphere.

Kiki's (☎ 915-565-6713), 2719 N Piedras St, is packed at lunch with a mixed crowd of laborers, office workers and Fort Bliss personnel. Try the house specialty machaca ($7.65) packed with your choice of meat, chicken or crab plus onions, tomato, cheese, eggs and chili peppers. Other combination plates run $5 to $9. Arrive early for a table on Sunday evenings, when jazzman Art Lewis plays.

The Best Block in El Paso

If you're looking for variety – perhaps an area where you can restaurant-hop from one place to another for appetizers, entrées, dessert and drinks – look no farther than the Old Kern Place section of Cincinnati Ave between Stanton St and Mesa St near UTEP. Always lively with students, Old Kern Place offers a smorgasbord of good food and conviviality. The choices include:

Casa Jurado (☎ 915-532-6429), 226 Cincinnati Ave, serving fresh Mexican food such as meatball soup ($4), combination plates ($6 to $8) and chicken mole ($9) amid a relaxed yet refined decor.

Hemingway's (☎ 915-532-7333), 214 Cincinnati Ave, a popular pub specializing in microbrews and imported beers.

Crawdaddy's Bar & Grill (☎ 915-546-9104), 212 Cincinnati Ave, with arguably the best jukebox in town. There's good food, too, including pasta jambalaya ($7) and blackened mahimahi ($8).

Ardovino's (☎ 915-532-9483), 206 Cincinnati Ave, which is more of a postgrad place than a student hangout. This favorite has the best pizza in town and an extensive wine cellar. Gourmet pies start at $6 for a small and run about $13 to $14 for a large.

Cincinnati Club (☎ 915-532-5592), 207 Cincinnati Ave, a friendly bar with a basic menu specializing in chili. You can get either Doc's Terlingua variety or – Ohio expats rejoice – the real Cincinnati style complete with cinnamon.

Dolce Vita (☎ 915-533-8482), 205 Cincinnati Ave, which describes itself as a dependable oasis in the desert of El Paso. The mixed straight-gay clientele and cosmopolitan atmosphere make this coffeehouse and purveyor of creative pastries and sandwiches a good alternative to the bar scene.

Kern Place Market (☎ 915-533-4576), 2609 N Mesa St, just across Mesa St from the Cincinnati Ave enclave. This sun-drenched cafe serves wonderful scones at breakfast. For lunch or dinner, try the open-face panini sandwiches ($5.25 to $6.25) or the house soup, a tomato basil raviolini (with fresh bread for a mere $2.35).

Get a good Tex-Mex breakfast and a car wash at the same time at the **H&H Coffee Shop** (☎ 915-533-1144), at 701 E Yandell Drive. It's a hole in the wall, but H&H has had all kinds of great press, including articles in *Gourmet* and *Saveur* and visits from Julia Child. Despite all the attention, it remains authentic and friendly, a favorite morning hangout for El Paso power brokers. **Amigos** (☎ 915-533-0155), 2000 Montana Ave, is another reliable Mexican food favorite with low-to-moderate prices ($5 to $9).

For something different, try the shrimp fajitas or red chili stew at **Wyngs** (☎ 915-859-3916), 122 S Old Pueblo Rd next to the Speaking Rock Casino. The fare here (mostly in the $8 to $12 range) is Mexican with a Tigua influence.

American *Jaxon's Restaurant & Brewery* (☎ 915-778-9696), 1135 Airway Blvd, ranks among the most popular American eateries in town. The brewery's Chihuahua Brown Ale took a gold medal at the 1997 Great American Beer Festival in Denver, Colorado. Food choices range from a $6 bacon cheeseburger served with seasoned curly fries to a $10 half-rack of baby back ribs. Jaxon's is also on the west side at 4799 N Mesa St (☎ 915-544-1188).

Downtown near the Camino Real Hotel and the new art museum, **San Francisco Grill** (☎ 915-545-1386), 127 Pioneer Plaza, is a favorite upscale watering hole and restaurant, but not quite as chichi or expensive as the nearby Cafe Central or Dome Restaurant (see the Continental section). Dinner choices include prime rib and seafood fettuccine, either for $14. For dessert, there's a Ghirardelli chocolate mousse ($4) or key lime pie ($4.25). Ask for a copy of the martini menu.

Azulejos (☎ 915-534-3000) is one of several informal but still rather pricey choices in the Camino Real Hotel, 1 S El Paso St. Sunday brunch here runs $15 and the daily breakfast buffet costs $9, but most lunch items are in the $7 range.

For a funkier and cheaper downtown choice, try the **Back Door Grill & Bar** (☎ 915-546-9190), 916 N Mesa St. It comes highly recommended by the folks at the Gardner Hotel, who swear it has the best Philly cheese steak sandwich in town.

In the same vein but near the airport, **Elmer's Family Restaurant** (☎ 915-778-5485), at 6305 Montana Ave next to the Econolodge, is a nothing-fancy diner beloved by El Pasoans for its reliable food and homey atmosphere. It's a good place to catch a meal before or after your flight, as is the **Mountain View Grill** (☎ 915-779-3300) in the El Paso Marriott, 1600 Airway Blvd. Its name is somewhat misleading – the mountain vista is limited to one table in the corner – and service could be a bit speedier given the airport clientele, but food-wise, this is an above-average hotel restaurant. Even better is the **Three Continents Restaurant** (☎ 915-533-6700) in the Cliff Inn, 1600 Cliff Drive, serving breakfast ($4 to $8), lunch ($5 to $12.50) and dinner ($8.75 to $19) in casually elegant surroundings.

Continental The **Dome Restaurant** (☎ 915-534-3010) is the signature restaurant at the Camino Real Hotel, 101 S El Paso St, and it's an appropriately classy affair. For an appetizer, try pheasant ravioli with fennel artichokes ($7). Entrées ($15 to $21 at lunch, $26 to $30 at dinner) include New Zealand rack of lamb with Thai barbecue stir-fry vegetables ($21) or rattlesnake cakes with red pepper beurre rouge ($29).

Cafe Central (☎ 915-545-2233), 109 N Oregon St (but really on an alley just south of Pioneer Plaza), has a wide menu of unusual à la carte fare that changes daily. Starters include roast-duck quesadilla with Hatch green chili (a renowned variety of pepper from nearby New Mexico; $7), or a grilled portabella mushroom topped with goat cheese, garlic and herbs ($12). Entrées might include grilled Hawaiian moonfish with grapefruit beurre blanc ($16), European quail marinated in port, thyme and black pepper ($16) or broiled lobster tail with chipotle lime cream ($30). There's live jazz on Friday and Saturday evenings.

Fast Food El Paso has all the usual fast-food restaurants, plus a few local favorites. **Chicos Tacos**, with several locations, including 5305 Montana Ave (☎ 915-772-7777), sells its namesake fare – with lots of garlic – three for $1. Expect a crowd from about 10 pm to midnight, when El Pasoans citywide experience a collective Chic Attack (it's open till 2 am weekdays and 3 am on weekends). 'Once you've eaten a Chicos Taco, it's like you've become a member of a cult,' one fan told us.

Families flock to *Peter Piper Pizza*, which has several locations, including 1840 Lee Trevino Drive in the Vista Hills Shopping Center (☎ 915-591-3344), where the whole gang can munch out while the young 'uns play the arcade games. Large pies go for about $9.

Steak Houses & Barbecue Ask most El Pasoans where to get a great steak and they will suggest you leave town. The *Cattleman's Steakhouse* (☎ 915-544-3200), at Indian Cliffs Ranch, is 20 miles east of the city, then north via the I-10 Fabens exit, but local folks would probably drive 200 miles to eat here. The food ($9 to $23) is fine, but the scenery is even better. Come early, wander around the grounds (see Around El Paso for a more detailed description), then catch the sunset either before or after your meal.

A newer entry on the out-of-town steak house scene, the *Edge of Texas Steakhouse and Saloon* (☎ 915-822-3343) is on the Bowen Ranch north of El Paso via US 54, nearly on the New Mexico border. Its signature dishes include buffalo fajitas ($7 at lunch, $10 at dinner), a 10-ounce top sirloin ($11) and center-cut pork chops marinated in maple syrup, honey, brown sugar and Dijon mustard ($11).

If you'd rather not leave the city the *Great American Land & Cattle Co* (☎ 915-595-1772), 2200 Yarbrough Drive, is a good in-town option. For barbecue, El Pasoans typically take their out-of-town guests to the roadhouse-style *State Line* (☎ 915-581-3371), 1222 Sunland Park Drive.

Asian *Beijing Lili* offers an extensive all-you-can-eat buffet that's a good value ($6 lunch, $8 dinner) at two handy locations:

4017 N Mesa St (☎ 915-577-0888) and 10501 Gateway Blvd W at Yarbrough Drive (☎ 915-592-8808). *Uncle Bao's Szechwan Cuisine* (☎ 915-585-1818), 5668 N Mesa St, is a friendly eatery where you can't go wrong with General Tso's chicken ($5.25 at lunch, $11 at dinner). *Crab-n-Hammer* (☎ 915-833-7676), way out west at 7200 N Mesa St, specializes in seafood prepared Korean style.

Miscellaneous Located on the north side of the vast strip mall on Lee Trevino Drive at Montwood Drive, the *Puerto Rico Restaurant* (☎ 915-590-2002), 11040 Montwood Drive, has built a devoted following with its island dishes, especially the chicken combo plates. A quarter chicken with rice, beans and tostones (plantains) goes for $5. There's more unusual fare, too, including ostrich ($13). On Friday and Saturday, look for Spanish dishes including several paellas ($9 to $10.75 per person). The live keyboard music Saturday and Sunday nights may appeal to some diners, but it drove us out the door.

When German military trainees at Fort Bliss get hungrily homesick, they head for *Gunther's Edelweiss* (☎ 915-592-1084), 11055 Gateway Blvd W. The Bavarian decor, veal schnitzel and pork Jagerschnitzel are all warmly authentic. Dinners are in the $8 to $14 range. Indian food aficionados will like *Delhi Palace* (☎ 915-772-9334), 1160 E Airway Blvd, where there's a weekday lunch buffet for about $6.

Entertainment

El Paso has a lively fine arts scene and plenty going on in the bars and nightclubs, too, though there's little in the way of local original music. (A few exceptions include jazzman Art Lewis, who plays regularly in restaurants all over town, and the eclectic band Fronteras No Mas.) To learn what's on in town, try the *Tiempo* Friday supplement to the *El Paso Times*.

Classical Music & Dance Most of El Paso's major performing organizations and many touring concerts and plays hold court at the Abraham Chávez Theatre in the Civic Center downtown. These include the

El Paso Symphony Orchestra (☎ *915-534-3776, 915-532-3776*) and *El Paso Community Concert Association* (☎ *915-544-2022*). *El Paso Pro Musica* (☎ *915-532-9139, 915-833-9400*) presents a chamber music season at locations around town. *Ballet El Paso* (☎ *915-533-2200*) performs in various venues, including outdoors at the McKelligon Canyon Amphitheater.

Coffeehouses We found several very good java joints, including Dolce Vita and Kern Place Market (see the Best Block in El Paso boxed text). Our other favorites are downtown. *Sojourns Coffeehouse* (☎ *915-532-2817*), 127 Pioneer Plaza, looks down Mills Ave and El Paso St from a second-floor perch – or you can get away from the windows, grab a magazine and pretend you're in your very hip cousin's art- and plant-filled living room. Down Mills past San Jacinto Plaza, *Pike Street Market* (☎ *915-545-1010*), 207 E Mills Ave, is smaller, but its counter is a great place for people watching. Both places serve sandwiches and salads.

Theater *Viva El Paso!* (☎ *915-565-6900*), an outdoor drama, is presented mid-June through Labor Day Weekend in McKelligon Canyon Amphitheater. Performances run Thursday to Saturday evenings.

McKelligon Canyon is also the setting for *Shakespeare on the Rocks* (☎ *915-565-6900*), a September series that typically includes four of the Bard's plays in repertory. Each March, the *Siglo de Oro Drama Festival* (☎ *915-532-7273*) takes place at Chamizal National Memorial. This 10-day event celebrates Spain's golden age of drama from the mid-1500s to the mid-1600s, roughly the same time Shakespeare and his contemporaries were wowing British theatergoers. Chamizal hosts many other live performances year-round.

Bars, Discos & Nightclubs The five-clubs-in-one *Graham Central Station* (☎ *915-599-2553*), in the Vista Hills Shopping Center at 1840 Lee Trevino Drive, is El Paso's biggest party place. For one cover, guests can wander from a country/Tejano club to a karaoke

lounge to a pool hall, a Top-40 dance hall and a '70s disco.

Rock & Alternative Downtown, *The Edge* (☎ *915-532-6644*), 201 N Stanton St, is a newer upscale dance club, with hot dance, alternative, retro and modern rock on its ground floor and 1970s disco downstairs. *Club 101* (☎ *915-544-2101*), 500 San Francisco Ave, is more alternative with a warehouse feel and occasional live shows. On the west side, *Papa's Cantina* (☎ *915-585-8965*), 6315 Mesa St, packs in a mostly single crowd with live dance bands, but it also has good Spanish, Mexican and American food.

Country & Western The *Stampede Nightclub* (☎ *915-833-6397*), at 5500 Doniphan Drive, is a west side favorite, billing itself as 'all country with just a hint of rock 'n' roll.' *Margarita's* (☎ *915-592-9950*), 8750 Gateway Blvd E between Lee Trevino Drive and Zaragoza Rd, is a big club featuring Top 40, Tejano and country music.

Gay & Lesbian The *New Old Plantation* (☎ *915-533-6055*), 301 S Ochoa St, has been around forever. It's definitely the main gay bar and one of the best dance clubs in town. Nearby, the *Whatever Lounge* (☎ *915-533-0215*), 701 E Paisano Drive, has a predominantly Spanish-speaking gay clientele. *U-Got-It* (☎ *915-533-9510*), 216 S Ochoa St, is a lesbian bar open Friday nights. Juárez has a big gay scene, but nighttime revelers should travel across the border in groups.

Latin Rio Night Club (☎ *915-774-0406*), 1201 Airway Blvd, is the city's major Latin club, with frequent live music. *View at the Top* (☎ *915-544-3300*) atop the old International Hotel, 113 W Missouri Ave, has the city's best view and a mostly Hispanic clientele, with mariachis on Tuesday and Thursday nights.

Other The *Dome Bar* (☎ *915-534-3000 ext 5012*) at the Camino Real Hotel, 101 S El Paso St, is the perfect spot for a martini and intimate conversation. For a little comic relief, try the *Comic Strip* (☎ *915-581-8877*),

WEST TEXAS

6633 N Mesa St, where touring and local acts perform nightly Tuesday through Saturday. There's a nonsmoking show each Saturday at 8:30 pm. See the Best Block in El Paso boxed text for several good pubs on Cincinnati Ave near UTEP.

Casino Owned by the Tigua Tribe of Texas, *Speaking Rock (☎ 915-860-7777)*, 122 S Old Pueblo Rd via I-10's Zaragoza Rd exit, offers a variety of gaming options, including Tigua 21 (players vie against each other, not the dealer), bingo, poker, a low-stakes baccarat and pull-tabs. The casino is open 24 hours.

Cinema *Tinseltown at Las Palmas (☎ 915-590-6464)*, I-10 at Zaragoza, is El Paso's major movie palace. There are 20 screens with stereo surround sound. The big malls all have movie theaters, too.

Spectator Sports
UTEP's teams are part of the Western Athletic Conference, which is the largest collegiate conference in the US. Basketball is especially popular, but the football team has played well in recent years, too. Call ☎ 915-747-5330 for schedules.

The El Paso Diablos (☎ 915-755-2000) play Double A Texas League baseball April to August at Cohen Stadium, 97000 Gateway Blvd N (bus Nos 2, 7 or 46, or take the Diana Drive exit off of US 54). The El Paso Buzzards (☎ 915-534-7825) play professional hockey October to March at the El Paso County Coliseum (bus Nos 23, 24, 58 or 65). There's live and simulcast horse races just over the New Mexico border at Sunland Park Race Track (☎ 505-589-1131) (bus No 12 comes close).

Shopping
Western Gear More cowboy boots are made in El Paso than anywhere else on the planet, so the city is tops in both variety and bargains. Lucchese (☎ 915-778-8060), generally considered the best brand among mass-produced boots, has its only factory store at 6601 Montana Ave. Tony Lama has three El Paso outlet locations including 7156 Gateway Blvd E (☎ 915-772-4327). Justin

Retail Factory Outlet (☎ 915-779-5465) is practically next door at 7100 Gateway Blvd E. If you're looking for something custom made, check out Rocketbuster Boots (☎ 915-541-1300), 115 Anthony St. As boot-maker for the stars, Rocketbuster has shod such celebrities as Arnold Schwarzenegger, Tom Cruise, Sylvester Stallone, Emmylou Harris and dozens of others. Cost ranges from about $400 to several thousand dollars.

The El Paso Saddle Blanket Company (☎ 915-544-1000), 601 N Oregon St, is principally a wholesale operation shipping to 11,000 stores and dealers in all 50 states and a dozen foreign countries. But visitors to El Paso can go direct to the source, finding everything from $5 throws to $3840 Zapotec rugs hand-woven in Oaxaca, Mexico. You'll also see a wide range of other Western-theme items: stuffed rattlesnakes, mounted sets of longhorns, kachina dolls, pottery, piñatas, baskets and a lot more. If they don't have what you're looking for, try the esoteric Old El Paso Western Outfitters (☎ 915-587-0520), on the far west side at 1060

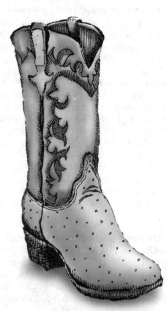

WEST TEXAS

Doniphan Park Circle Suite B, where the stock includes 19th century clothing, guns and other collectibles.

Food Fallen in love with Tex-Mex cuisine? The El Paso Chile Company (☎ 915-544-3434), 909 Texas Ave and in many other area gift stores, is the city's top source of Southwestern specialty foods, everything from their own Hellfire & Damnation picante sauce and Snakebite Salsa Bloody Mary Mix to hot stuff from other regional purveyors. They ship worldwide. Open Monday to Friday 10 am to 5 pm (Thursday till 6 pm), Saturday 10 am to 2 pm.

Hog Heaven Barnett Harley-Davidson (☎ 915-592-5804), 8272 Gateway Blvd E, is the world's largest Harley dealership, with hundreds of 'hogs' in stock along with a huge selection of Harley clothing and collectibles.

Fine Art Hal Marcus Gallery (☎ 915-533-9090), 2430 N Mesa St in the Old Kern Place neighborhood, showcases the work of a prominent El Paso artist in what once was his grandmother's home. Open Tuesday through Saturday 10 am to 5 pm. Galeria San Ysidro (☎ 915-544-4444), 801 Texas Ave, is a three-level former factory building full of imported furniture and accessories.

Duty Free US citizens can get tax- and duty-free deals on liquor, fragrances, jewelry, cigarettes and more at many shops along the Tex-Mex border. One of the largest such chains, UETA Duty Free Store, has three El Paso locations including 805 S Stanton St (☎ 915-532-5996). Examples: A liter of Absolut Vodka that typically retails for $23 goes for about $10 at UETA, while a carton of Marlboros that usually costs more than $20 sells for $10.50 here.

Shopping Malls Bassett Center (☎ 915-772-7479), 6101 Gateway Blvd W, and Cielo Vista Mall (☎ 915-779-7070), 8401 Gateway Blvd W, both are just off I-10 on the east side. Sunland Park Mall (☎ 915-833-5595), 750 Sunland Park Drive, is the major west side shopping center.

Getting There & Away

Air El Paso International Airport (☎ 915-772-4271) is 8 miles northeast of downtown El Paso. It's accessible by bus, taxi and shuttles; see the Getting Around section for more information.

Southwest Airlines (☎ 800-435-9792) is by far the biggest carrier at El Paso International, with about 60% of the domestic flights. AeroLitoral (☎ 915-778-7883) provides service to Chihuahua and Torreón, Mexico. Other airlines include:

American	☎ 800-433-7300
America West	☎ 800-235-9292
Continental	☎ 915-544-6223
Delta	☎ 800-221-1212
Frontier	☎ 800-932-1359

Bus Greyhound (☎ 915-532-2365) has its terminal at 200 W San Antonio Ave four blocks from the center of downtown. Some routes are handled by the Texas New Mexico & Oklahoma regional bus line. Greyhound/TNM&O services include:

to/from	frequency (per day)	trip duration	one way/ roundtrip
Las Cruces, NM	9	50 min.	$7/14
Albuquerque, NM	4	6 hours	$36/70
Alpine	2	4½ hours	$38/76
Dallas	6	13 hours	$62/124
San Antonio	4	10½ hours	$74/122

Train Amtrak's Sunset Limited serves Union Depot (☎ 915-545-2247), 700 San Francisco Ave. The train comes through westbound to Tucson, Arizona, and Los Angeles, California, on Monday, Thursday and Saturday about 4 pm and eastbound to San Antonio on Monday, Wednesday and Saturday about 3:10 pm. These are the scheduled times, but trains frequently run late; call ☎ 800-872-7245 for updates.

Car El Paso is on I-10 just 12 miles from the New Mexico line but a long day's drive or more from any other major city in Texas. Stay on I-10 eastbound for San Antonio or

Houston; I-20, the route to Fort Worth and Dallas, leaves I-10 about 150 miles east of El Paso. The only other major highways are US 54, which runs north to I-40, and US 62/180, the route to Guadalupe Mountains and Carlsbad Caverns national parks and eventually to Lubbock. I-25, the highway to Albuquerque and Denver, is 40 miles east at Las Cruces, New Mexico. Mexican Hwy 45 runs south from Juárez to Chihuahua.

Getting Around

To/From the Airport Sun Metro's bus No 33 ($1) makes hourly runs between the airport and downtown. Buses leave the airport at 54 minutes past the hour starting at 5:54 am and ending at 8:54 pm. Airport-bound buses leave San Jacinto Plaza roughly every hour from 5:10 am to 8:15 pm. Rancho Grande Shuttle (☎ 915-771-6661) runs citywide shuttles starting at $14 for one person ($2 for each additional person). Plan on a $14 base rate for downtown hotels. Many hotels and motels provide free shuttles from the airport; call to see if yours does. A taxi to downtown costs between $13 and $14.

Car rental agencies at the airport include:

Advantage	☎ 915-772-8570
Alamo	☎ 915-771-6022
Avis	☎ 915-779-2700
Budget	☎ 915-778-5287
Dollar	☎ 915-778-5445
Hertz	☎ 915-772-4255
National	☎ 915-778-9417

Bus Sun Metro (☎ 915-533-3333) at Union Depot, 700 San Francisco Ave, is El Paso's citywide bus service, operating 47 routes plus two downtown trolleys. Routes are extensive, but most stop running early in the evening. All routes originate at San Jacinto Plaza downtown; a kiosk just across Oregon St can provide information and maps. Exact change is required.

Bus fares are $1 for adults and 50¢ for children ages six to 13. Older students, seniors and disabled people can get reduced fares, too, but you have to ante up $2.50 for a Sun Metro Photo ID, so it may not be worth your while if you aren't staying long. Transfers cost 10¢ and should be requested when you board your original bus. Trolley fares are 25¢.

Car Downtown can be tricky, because there are one-way streets laid out at weird angles, but the outlying commercial areas and neighborhoods are easy to find via I-10 and the major surface streets. As in many larger US cities, drivers tend to run red lights, so beware. I-10 is frequently under construction, so watch for slowdowns. I-10 drivers should keep an eye peeled for the shadowy figures who occasionally dart across the freeway at night, almost certainly border jumpers from Juárez. Despite Border Patrol crackdowns, some hardy souls are still making it across.

Taxi Look for taxi stands at the airport and the Greyhound and Amtrak depots. Rates are $1.20 flagfall, $1.50 each additional mile and 50¢ per additional person. We've been warned about unscrupulous cabbies charging extortionate rates downtown (such as $5 for the seven-block ride from the bus station to the Gardner Hotel), so double-check rates before boarding and make sure the meter's on. Companies include:

Border Taxi	☎ 915-533-4282
Checker Taxi	☎ 915-532-2626
Diamond Cab	☎ 915-544-4464
El Paso Cab	☎ 915-598-9702
Sun City Cab	☎ 915-544-2211
Texas Cab	☎ 915-562-0022
United Independent Cab	☎ 915-590-8294
Yellow Cab	☎ 915-533-3433

AROUND EL PASO
Ciudad Juárez (Mexico)
Population 1.8 million
☎ 16 within Mexico, 011-52-16 from Texas

Although Juárez is a grimy, noisy, booming town, few visitors to El Paso can resist the urge to jump the border. The city, one of Mexico's largest, seems to radiate excitement. In recent years, however, Juárez has been a major battleground for drug lords, and murders are literally a daily occurrence. The city is reasonably safe for foreigners, especially during the day, but at night it's best to either take a reputable escorted tour or travel with a group.

History In the turbulent years of the Mexican Revolution, Juárez had a strategic importance beyond its then-small size. Pancho Villa stormed the town on May 10, 1911, enabling Francisco Madero's faction to force the resignation of the dictator Porfirio Díaz. After Victoriano Huerta's coup against Madero, Villa escaped to refuge in El Paso. In March 1913, he rode back across the Rio Grande with just eight followers to begin the reconquest of Mexico. Within months, he had recruited and equipped an army of thousands and conquered Juárez a second time – this time by loading his troops onto a train, deceiving the defenders into thinking it was one of their own, and steaming into the middle of town in a modern version of the Trojan horse tactic.

Today Juárez is a major center for maquiladoras (see the History section in the introductory Facts about Texas chapter for more information). These factories have added tens of thousands of new jobs each year, fueling Juárez's population boom. Many new arrivals live in makeshift homes that forever appear ready to topple, yet for most, the standard of living on the border far exceeds what they had in the heartland.

Orientation Four major bridges lead between El Paso and Juárez. From downtown El Paso, the Stanton Bridge is a one-way vehicular entrance (toll US$1.25) to Avenida Lerdo in Juárez, while the nearby Santa Fe Bridge (toll US$1.35) is used by vehicles returning to the US via Avenida Juárez. Pedestrians can walk either way on both bridges; the toll is US$0.25 into Juárez and US$0.30 coming back to El Paso. Avenida Juárez, lined with shops, bars, restaurants and seedy hotels, is the most important tourist street in Ciudad Juárez and the one to follow if you're heading for the center of town. Steer clear of Avenida Mariscal west of Avenida Juárez; it's the local red-light district.

Five miles east of downtown El Paso and near Chamizal National Monument, the Bridge of the Americas (also known as the Cordova Bridge or the Free Bridge, because there are no tolls) leads to a less congested part of Juárez and to a bypass road that in turn leads directly to the main highway south to Chihuahua. Eighteen miles east of downtown, the Zaragoza toll bridge entirely avoids both El Paso and Juárez. Tolls are US$1.25 into Mexico and US$1.35 coming back.

Information The Juárez tourist office (☎ 16-29-33-40) is located beside the southern end of the Bridge of the Americas. There is usually someone there who speaks English. The office is open weekdays 8 am to 8 pm, weekends until 3 pm.

There are plenty of currency exchange houses in the tourist areas, but dollars are as welcome as pesos at most businesses. Many shops and restaurants quote their prices in US dollars. For extensive explorations of Juárez, look for the *Index de México Ciudad Juárez*, a US$13 spiral-bound city atlas available in many Texas book and map stores.

Things to See 'Charm' and 'beauty' are not adjectives one often associates with Juárez, particularly near downtown. But the city is no cultural desert, and a couple of the old buildings near the Plaza Principal are of some interest.

The stone-sided **Misión Nuestra Señora de Guadalupe** was built in the mid-1600s, and its hand-carved roof beams and choir mezzanine are impressive. The mission is on the west side of the plaza, next to the cathedral, which also dates from the 17th century but is disappointing; its interior has not been preserved and bullet holes on its exterior from Pancho Villa days have yet to be patched.

East of the plaza, on the corner of Avenidas Juárez and 16 de Septiembre, is the **Museo Histórico**, in the old customs building. The museum gives a good overview of Mexican history and has some interesting artifacts, but all of the literature is in Spanish. Open Tuesday to Sunday 10 am to 6 pm; free.

Places to Stay The *Continental Hotel* (☎ 16-15-00-84), at the intersection of Lerdo and 16 de Septiembre, is biggish and a bit worn, but it's centrally located and offers secure parking – no small thing in crime-plagued Juárez. Rooms are about US$24 a night.

The middleweight champion of Juárez is the *María Bonita Suites Hotel* (☎ 16-27-03-03) on Avenida San Lorenzo just north of Hermanos Escobar. Starting at US$40 a night, every suite is cheerful and tastefully done and contains a large bedroom, private bathroom, a fully equipped kitchen and a sitting area with a large, comfy couch. For US$160 a master suite comes with a king bed and two doubles, a Jacuzzi tub and enough space to throw a party. A gym, pool, hot tub, bar and restaurant round out the facilities. Secure parking is provided.

Places to Eat Juárez is famous for its burritos, and some of the most authentic can be found at *El Burrito Crisostomo* burrito stand, which is named after the owner's donkey and is located at the corner of Guerrero and Huerta. Open 24 hours. Two burritos cost US$1.50. For tacos, try *Tacotote*, with several locations around town.

For marlin tacos and choice cuts of fish, *Los Arcos*, at the corner of Americas and Triunfo de la República, is a fine catch, with most meals in the US$7 range. For beef, look for *Restaurant Nuevo Martino* (☎ 16-12-33-70) at Avenida Juárez 643, a short walk from the border.

Entertainment The bars and discotheques on Avenida Juárez tend to be grimy and unspectacular – the *Kentucky Club* being the greatest exception – while those near the intersection of Ornelas and Triunfo de la República – *Chihuahua Charlie's*, *Ajuua!!* and *Amazonas* – are impressive. Juárez has lots of gay and lesbian bars, with many located near Calle Pena at Lerdo, including the *Ritz* and *Club Olímpico*.

The *Plaza de Toros Monumental* on the Pan American Highway is the fourth-largest bullring in the world (it can seat up to 17,000 people), with fights held April to September.

Shopping The best place to go for quality goods is Sanborn's on Paseo Triunfo de la República, adjacent to the Holiday Inn Express. There you will find beautifully carved figurines, colorful ceramics, exquisite gold and silver jewelry, and breathtaking pottery – all Mexican in style and reasonably priced.

The new Pueblito Mexicano Mall, a huge shopping center on Avenida Lincoln, was designed to recall a Mexican village. But many mall-weary visitors will instead want to check out the traditional mercados near the city center. The new city market on Avenida 16 de Septiembre gets the most visitor traffic, but the old market a few blocks away to the southwest is a lot more interesting.

Getting There & Away The El Paso-Juárez Trolley Co runs its Border Jumper from the El Paso Civic Center to Mexico every hour on the hour. Once in Juárez, the trolleys (actually buses) follow a route with about 10 stops; you're free to get on and off as you wish. Cost is $11 per adult and $8.50 apiece for children ages four to 12. April to October, the buses run Sunday to Tuesday from 9 am to 4 pm and Wednesday to Saturday from 9 am to 5 pm. November to March, there's daily service from 9 am to 4 pm.

Taxi rides between downtown El Paso and Juárez are about US$13. If you plan to drive into Juárez, plan on long delays at the bridges and make sure your vehicle is properly insured. Palms Mexico Insurance (☎ 915-533-0062), near the Bridge of the Americas at 2120 E Paisano Drive, sells supplemental policies, as does the AAA office in El Paso.

Sierra del Cristo Rey

Sierra del Cristo Rey – the Mountain of Christ the King – sits at 4675 feet where Texas, New Mexico and Mexico meet. Aside from being an area landmark, the mountain is held sacred by Christians on the borderlands, who make a pilgrimage to the summit on the last Sunday of each October. This is the best way to visit the mountain, because bandits have been known to prey on lone hikers.

Ranches

They're best known for their steak houses (see Places to Eat in the El Paso section), but Indian Cliffs Ranch and the Bowen Ranch make popular day-trip destinations, too.

Twenty miles east of El Paso via the I-10 Fabens exit, **Indian Cliffs Ranch** (☎ 915-544-3200) began as a horseback riding stable in the late 1960s. A restaurant was added in 1973, and the steak house has expanded several times since. Trail rides are no longer available, but there are many other amusements. A small zoo includes a rattlesnake pit, prairie dog town, deer, emus, buffalo and goats. Kids get a kick out of the Fort Apache playground, and people of all ages enjoy trying to make their way through the high-picket-fenced Indian Maze. Sundays, free hayrides are available to everyone who eats at the restaurant. Several movies have been made in the area including *Courage Under Fire*.

The **Bowen Ranch** (☎ 915-821-8000) is a working cattle and buffalo ranch that sprawls west of US 54 and straddles the Texas-New Mexico line. They've also added live entertainment, hayrides, a petting zoo and a Western art gallery. Activities are geared toward large groups and parties, but individual travelers and families are welcome to ride on in and see what's going on. You may well get to see some real live cowboys doing their thing.

Horseback Riding Neither Indian Cliffs nor the Bowen Ranch offers trail rides, but two stables just west of El Paso over the New Mexico border can get you in the saddle.

Cowboy Trading Post (☎ 915-581-1984), PO Box 952, Santa Teresa, New Mexico 88008 (the street address is 7155 McNutt Rd in Santa Teresa), charges $20 per person for an 80-minute ride. Greg Evans Quarter Horses (☎ 505-874-3092), 6864 McNutt Rd, Santa Teresa, New Mexico, charges $15 per person for up to two hours, $10 for each additional hour. Both outfits also run longer trips, including overnight pack trips. Call for details.

Wet 'n' Wild

This water-based amusement park (☎ 915-886-2222) is on the Texas-New Mexico line at I-10's Anthony exit. It features a volcanic garden theme, and there are plenty of slides and rides to keep everyone cool. The park is open May to September, weekends 10 am to 7 pm and weekdays 10 am to 6 pm. Admission is $17 for ages 13 and up and $14.50 for kids ages four to 12. Children age three and under are free. This is also the site of several major annual events including a Memorial Day hot air balloon festival and a mariachi festival in June.

Hueco Tanks State Historical Park

If you're a rock climber, you already know about Hueco Tanks (☎ 915-857-1135); it may well be the main reason you're headed to West Texas. This pockmarked high-desert playground is also an outstanding repository of Native American and prehistoric pictographs, as well as a fine site for camping, bird-watching and stargazing. Hueco Tanks is about 30 miles east of El Paso via US 62/180 (Montana Ave), then 6 miles north on Hueco Tanks Rd (FM 2775). From October through March it's open for day use from 8 am to 6 pm. From April through September it's open 7 am to 7 pm. There is a $4 per person entrance fee for visitors 13 and older; kids 12 and younger get in free. Camping is available only on a regulated basis.

Hueco Tanks recently introduced new access regulations aimed mainly at protecting the rock art. Generally, access to camping, climbing and other activities at Hueco Tanks is limited to people who are accompanied by a park-sanctioned volunteer or commercial guide. To arrange for a volunteer guide at no extra charge beyond park admission and camping fees, contact the park no earlier than six months and no later than three days before a planned visit. (Two weeks' lead time is recommended.) The park also maintains a list of commercial guides, who do charge fees for their services.

The park's North Mountain area is open to unguided day use, but access is limited to 50 people at a time and visitors must first complete a 20-minute orientation session. Reservations are accepted, but walk-ins may come too, until the 50-person limit has been reached. Visitors using North Mountain must check out before leaving the park. North Mountain isn't just for climbers; a flagged trail offers hikers access to rock art and bird-watching sites.

History The 860-acre park is named for the large natural rock basins, or 'huecos' (pronounced WAY-cos), that dot its landscape. For thousands of years, wildlife and people relied on the rain-trapping huecos as a water source in the desert. Park staff estimate there are about 2000 pictographs at the site, some dating back 5000 years. The artwork includes examples from the Desert Archaic people, the Jomada Branch of the Mogollon Culture (600 to 1400 AD) and the Apache, Comanche and Kiowa Indians of recent centuries. Hueco Tanks also served as a major watering stop on the Butterfield Overland Mail Route (see The Mail Coaches).

Rock Climbing From October through early April, Hueco Tanks ranks among the world's top rock climbing destinations. It's one of a very few high-quality sites available through the winter months, when other prime climbs become inaccessible (although in summer, the desert sun generally makes the rocks at Huecos too hot to handle). The challenges here even inspired a new term in the international climbing vocabulary – 'hueco pulling,' or using the huecos to ascend the rock. As noted previously, climbers either must be accompanied by a guide or, for

unguided areas on North Mountain, must complete the orientation session.

If you overhear climbers talking about their 'problems,' they're referring to a natural feature in search of a solution, or a route up the rock. Hueco Tanks has perhaps 2000 such problems. Many may be solved by scrambling; others require technical climbs. For a good overview of climbing opportunities, look for John Sherman's books *Classic Rock Climbs No 6: Hueco Tanks State Park* ($11) and the more comprehensive *Hueco Tanks: Climbing & Bouldering Guide* ($30), both published by Chockstone Press. Climbers must check in with the park office to get a backcountry permit and check route restrictions aimed at protecting the park pictographs.

Bird-Watching The El Paso/Trans-Pecos Audubon Society holds frequent birding events at Hueco Tanks. Look for a copy of their latest newsletter at the park, or write to PO Box 9655, El Paso, TX 79986.

Stargazing The Astronomy Club of El Paso holds viewings on the Saturday night closest to the new moon each month at a site near Hueco Tanks. Call the El Paso School District Planetarium's information line (☎ 915-779-4400) for current information and club activities, or look for the club's *Desert Skies* newsletter at many El Paso-area museums.

Camping There is no longer public camping per se at Hueco Tanks, but visitors accompanied by a park-sanctioned guide can reserve one of 20 available sites. The cost is $11 for hookups, $9 for water only. Park regulations state that campers must be accompanied by a guide at all times, but we're told that doesn't mean your guide must share your tent; he or she only needs to be at your site or, if one is available, at an adjacent site.

For years, rock climbers have congregated in the parking lot at Pete's Country Store, just south of the park on Hueco Tanks Road. Pete and Queta Zavala let people camp on their premises for a $2 donation per night. The store itself operates irregular hours;

when it's open, it sells a limited selection of snacks and climbing gear.

Organized Tours From October to March, guided tours to the pictographs are held Wednesday through Sunday at 10 am and 2 pm. From April to September, the tours take place Wednesday through Sunday at 9 am and 11 am. The cost is included in the park admission fee.

Special Events Hueco Tanks holds an annual interpretive fair in October. Activities have included free birding tours, a buffalo soldiers campfire talk, Native American speakers and drumming.

Getting There & Away Greyhound and TNM&O (Texas New Mexico & Oklahoma)

buses travel US 62/180 between El Paso and Carlsbad Caverns National Park. Drivers will drop you off or pick you up at Hueco Tanks Rd 6 miles from the park if you make arrangements at least one day in advance. Silver Stage Lines (☎ 915-778-0162, 800-522-0162) runs a shuttle from El Paso to Hueco Tanks for $15 one way per person.

VAN HORN
Population 2907

Van Horn is notable mainly as a travelers' oasis on the long desert that is I-10 in West Texas. Sitting at the crossroads of the interstate, Hwy 54 (which runs north to Guadalupe Mountains National Park) and US 90 (a major route to Big Bend country), Van Horn has about 600 motel rooms, 200 campsites and 20 restaurants. It's 120 miles west

---

Sierra Blanca

Sierra Blanca, a town of 700, sits 16 miles from the Rio Grande and Mexico. Most of its people are Hispanic, many speak little English and an estimated 40% live in poverty. It's no wonder they felt voiceless in a recent long-running debate whose outcome would profoundly affect their future: whether to build a low-level nuclear waste dump near their town.

Sierra Blanca was already infamous as the home of the nation's largest sewage dump. Each week, 250 tons of semitreated New York City sewage sludge is sprayed on fields outside town. According to the Sierra Blanca Legal Defense Fund, the sludge contains heavy metals, viruses and bacteria and may have a low radioactive content from New York's nuclear power plants. The proposed nuclear dump would have added waste not just from Texas but from Maine, Vermont and possibly other states as well, all placed in shallow graves atop the most active earthquake region in Texas.

The dump generated widespread opposition from environmental activists, the Mexican national legislature, an array of local governments and border dwellers up and down the Rio Grande. In one instance, 500 children from Ciudad Acuña, Coahuila, traveled with their parents, teachers, city council and mayor to Austin to protest to Governor George W Bush. Many opponents contended that with a dwindling stream of nuclear waste (no new nuclear plants have gone online in the US in 20 years), there simply was no need for another dump. At a protest in Mexico City, Alejandro Calvillo, coordinator of the Greenpeace Energy Program, said the dump proposal was 'a clear act of disrespect to Mexico and to the Mexican American citizens who live in that region. It's a clear act of environmental racism.'

In late 1998 the Texas Natural Resource Conservation Committee finally rejected the dump idea, ending years of legal and political wrangling. Despite the decision, bitterness lingers. Many Texans and Mexicans feel Sierra Blanca has been abused, and the wounds will take years to heal.

to El Paso from here, 200 miles southeast to Big Bend National Park and 165 miles northeast to Odessa.

Information

The Van Horn Visitors Bureau (☎ 915-283-2682), 1801 W Broadway St, has lots of literature and free tours of a Union Pacific caboose. Open Monday to Friday 8 am to 5 pm (closed noon to 1 pm).

Places to Stay

Camping *Mountain View RV Park* (☎ 915-283-2814, 800-209-4243), southwest of I-10 at exit 140B, charges $12.50 per site, and there's a laundry and showers. The campground is RV-oriented, but people with tents can ask about staking a claim outside the hookup area. The *Van Horn KOA* (☎ 915-283-2728), a half-mile south of exit 140A, has a pool, showers, laundry and rec room. Hookup sites are $18.50 and tent sites go for $15.50.

Motels Van Horn has plenty of motels in the $30 range, including the *Freeway Inn Motel* (☎ 915-283-2939), 505 Van Horn Drive, with $22 singles and $30 doubles and the *Motel 6* (☎ 915-283-2992, fax 915-283-2111), 1805 W Broadway St, where rooms run $28/32. For something a bit more deluxe, try the *Best Western American Inn* (☎ 915-283-2030, fax 915-283-2779), 1309 W Broadway St, with a pool, coin laundry and large rooms starting at $37. The *Holiday Inn Express* (☎ 915-283-7444, fax 915-283-7234), 1905 SW Frontage Rd, is the priciest place in town at $59/69 most of the year, a bit higher in December and January.

Places to Eat

Chuy's Spanish Inn (☎ 915-283-2066), 1200 W Broadway St, has earned a place in 'Madden's Haul of Fame,' so named by US football broadcaster John Madden. Because he won't fly, the well-traveled Madden spends a lot of time crossing the US by bus, and this is one of his favorite restaurants. The eatery's Mexican plates cost $5 to $8. The *Smokehouse Restaurant* (☎ 915-283-2453), 905 W Broadway St, is noted for its smoked meats (dinners run $5 to $12) and its Classic

Car Museum featuring restored vehicles from the early to mid-20th century.

GUADALUPE MOUNTAINS NATIONAL PARK

The vast salt flats of West Texas are a dry and inhospitable place, so it seems all the more dreamlike when the Guadalupe Mountains loom into view.

Guadalupe Mountains National Park is a Texas high spot, both figuratively and literally; at 8749 feet, Guadalupe Peak is the highest perch in the Lone Star State, and the fall foliage in McKittrick Canyon is the best in West Texas. More than half the park is a federally designated wilderness area.

Guadalupe Mountains National Park is on US 62/180, 110 miles east of El Paso and 55 miles southwest of Carlsbad, New Mexico. The National Park Service has deliberately curbed development at this park to keep it wild – there are no restaurants or indoor accommodations and only a smattering of services and programs. Consequently, relatively few people come here – only 223,000 in 1996, compared with nearly three times that number at nearby Carlsbad Caverns National Park. If you seek some of the best hiking and high-country splendor Texas can muster, put Guadalupe Mountains National Park on your itinerary.

History

Until the mid-19th century, the Guadalupe Mountains were used exclusively by Mescalero Apaches, who hunted and camped in the area. Members of this tribe, who called themselves Nde, themselves became prey starting in 1849 when the US Army began a three-decade campaign to drive them from the area. The mid-19th century also marked the brief tenure of the Butterfield Overland Mail Route (see The Mail Coaches). Guadalupe Mountains National Park was created in 1972, making it one of the newest in the national park system.

Geology

Guadalupe Mountains National Park sits amid the world's most extensive exposed fossil reef. The reef began to grow 250 million

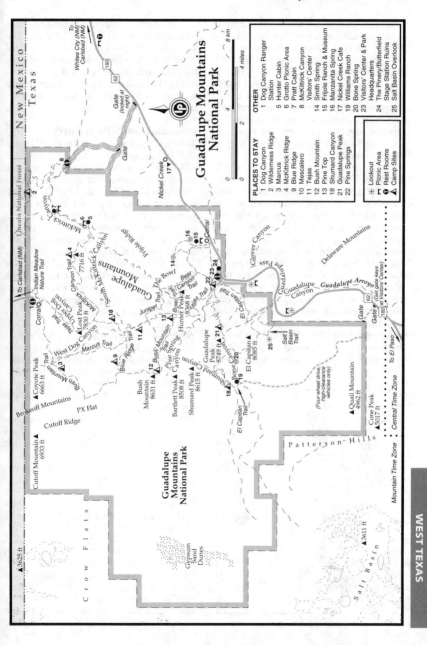

Guadalupe Mountains National Park

PLACES TO STAY
1 Dog Canyon
2 Wilderness Ridge
3 Marcus
4 McKittrick Ridge
9 Blue Ridge
10 Mescalero
11 Tejas
12 Bush Mountain
13 Pine Top
18 Shumard Canyon
21 Guadalupe Peak
22 Pine Springs

OTHER
1 Dog Canyon Ranger Station
5 Hunter Cabin
6 Grotto Picnic Area
7 Pratt Cabin
8 McKittrick Canyon Visitors Center
14 Smith Spring
15 Frijole Ranch & Museum
16 Manzanita Spring
17 Nickel Creek Cafe
19 Williams Ranch
20 Bone Spring
23 Visitors Center & Park Headquarters
24 The Pinery/Butterfield Stage Station Ruins
25 Salt Basin Overlook

☀ Lookout
⚑ Picnic Area
🚻 Rest Rooms
▲ Camp Sites

New Mexico
Texas
To Whites City (NM)/Carlsbad (NM)
Gate
Gate (locked at night)
Gate

Lincoln National Forest
To Carlsbad (NM)

Guadalupe Mountains

McKittrick Canyon
Indian Meadow Nature Trail
Coyote Peak 6663 ft
Cutoff Mountain 6933 ft
Brokeoff Mountains
Cutoff Ridge
PX Flat
Bush Mountain Trail
West Dog Canyon Trail
Lost Peak 7830 ft
South McKittrick Canyon
North McKittrick Canyon Trail
7716 ft
Frijole Ridge
Marcus Trail
Blue Ridge Trail
Bush Mountain 8631 ft
Bartlett Peak 8508 ft
Shumard Peak 8615 ft
Pine Spring Canyon
Juniper Trail
The Bowl
8368 ft
Bowl Trail
Hunter Trail
Bear Canyon Trail
Tejas Trail
Guadalupe Peak 8749 ft
Shumard Canyon
El Capitan Trail
Bone Spring
El Capitan Trail
El Capitan 8085 ft
Salt Basin Trail
Guadalupe Pass
Clover Canyon
Delaware Mountains
Guadalupe Canyon
Guadalupe Arroyo
Gate (Get gate keys at Visitors Center)
Gate

Quail Mountain 4962 ft
Cone Peak 5017 ft
(Four-wheel drive, high-clearance vehicles only)
To El Paso

Patterson Hills

Mountain Time Zone
Central Time Zone

Guadalupe Mountains National Park

Gypsum Sand Dunes

Crow Flats
3625 ft

Salt Basin
3611 ft

WEST TEXAS

years ago when an immense tropical ocean covered parts of Texas, New Mexico and Mexico. Over a period of 5 million years, lime-secreting marine organisms built the horseshoe-shaped reef to a length of 400 miles. After the sea evaporated, the reef was buried in sediment for millions more years, until a mountain-building geological uplift revealed part of it as the Guadalupe Mountains. The Apache Mountains east of Van Horn and the Glass Mountains east of Alpine are part of this same reef complex.

Flora & Fauna

Here in the Guadalupe Mountains and their valleys, Chihuahuan Desert plants such as sotol and prickly pear cactus mingle with big-tooth maples and gray oaks to create plant communities full of color and contrast. The woods are also full of Texas madrones, an adaptable tree more common in rain forests. This living fossil recalls the long-ago time when the mountains were under water. You'll know it by its smooth, reddish bark and oval evergreen leaves. A 2-mile-wide mountaintop area known as the Bowl offers a lush forest unlike anything else in West Texas, where animals roam amid ponderosa pine, southwestern white pine, Douglas fir and aspen.

Prickly pear cactus

Mule deer, jackrabbits, coyotes, gray foxes and porcupines all live in the park. The Guadalupe Mountains are home to a herd of 50 to 70 elk, which descend from animals brought from Wyoming and South Dakota in the 1920s, after the park's original herd was hunted to extinction, and to a similar number of mountain lions.

Information & Park Entry

The park headquarters and visitors' center at Pine Springs (☎ 915-828-3251, fax 915-828-2269, gumo_superintendent@nps.gov, www.nps.gov/gumo/) are open daily except Christmas Day. From late May till August, hours are 8 am to 6 pm; for the rest of the year, hours are 8 am to 4:30 pm. Park admission is free. Information, rest rooms and drinking water are also available at McKittrick Canyon and Dog Canyon.

The park's mailing address is HC 60 Box 400, Salt Flat, TX 79847. Like El Paso and Hudspeth counties (but nowhere else in Texas), Guadalupe Mountains National Park observes Mountain Standard Time.

When to Come Autumn is by far the best time to visit. McKittrick Canyon's fall colors are glorious from early October through mid-November and while nights can be chilly, daytime is warmly sublime. Spring and early summer bring high winds. Summer daytime temperatures are usually in the 80s, with overnight lows in the 60s. Winter daytime highs reach the low 50s, with overnight lows near freezing and occasional snow. But the weather can be unpredictable any time of year; park rangers warn against 'sudden and extreme weather changes.'

Services There are no restaurants, accommodations, gas or other supplies in the park. The little *Nickel Creek Cafe (☎ 915-828-3295)* on US 62/180 north of Pine Springs is open Monday to Saturday 7 am to 2 pm, with inexpensive sandwiches and Mexican fare. Other than that, the nearest visitor services are 35 miles northeast in Whites City, New Mexico. The closest gas stations are 30 miles west on US 62/180 and in Whites City. The nearest hospital is at Carlsbad, New Mexico,

WEST TEXAS

55 miles from Pine Springs, but there are first aid stations at Pine Springs, Dog Canyon and McKittrick Canyon. (The latter is not always open.) For emergencies, dial ☎ 911.

Maps & Literature The Park Service's free Guadalupe Mountains National Park map, available at the visitors' center, is fine for most park visitors. Backcountry travelers will want a topographic map, and these are sold at the visitors' center, too.

Pick up a copy of the *Capitan Reef* newspaper for information on both Guadalupe Mountains National Park and nearby Carlsbad Caverns National Park. All signs at Guadalupe Mountains are in both English and Spanish. Park information in French, German and Japanese is available on request at the visitors' center.

Carlsbad Caverns Guadalupe Mountains Association This educational group publishes the park newspaper and sponsors educational activities in the parks. For more information, call ☎ 505-785-2232 ext 480, fax 505-785-2318, write to PO Box 1417, Carlsbad, NM 88221 or visit the website at www.caverns.com\~ccgma.

Dangers & Annoyances Dehydration is the park's main danger. Carry and drink plenty of water – the park recommends one gallon per person per day. Five rattlesnake species live in the park, but rangers say no one has ever been bitten in the park's 27-year history. If you're camping, keep your tent flaps closed to keep out snakes, scorpions and desert centipedes. The latter are nasty stinging creatures, about 4 to 6 inches long and an inch across, with dark bodies and orange-reddish legs.

The Pinery

An easy and wheelchair-accessible 0.75-mile roundtrip trail leads from the Pine Springs visitors' center to the ruins of a Butterfield Overland Mail stagecoach stop known as the Pinery. En route, there are signs interpreting Chihuahuan Desert plant life. Despite its remote location, the Pinery is the only remaining Butterfield station ruin standing close to a major highway. The ruins are fragile and climbing on them is forbidden.

Williams Ranch

The 7-mile road to the historic Williams Ranch takes off from US 62/180 on the park's southern edge. This was a working ranch in the early 20th century, when James Adolphus Williams and an Indian buddy named Geronimo (not the Chiricahua Apache chief) ran several hundred longhorn cattle and later sheep on the spread. The ranch house, built in 1908, sits at the base of a 3000-foot cliff and at the entrance to Bone Canyon, site of the oldest rock in the Guadalupe Mountains.

The road is open only to high-clearance 4WD vehicles and mountain bikes. Keys to the road gate are available at the main park visitors' center. Allow about an hour each way to drive to and from the ranch. The site may also be reached via the El Capitan Trail from the Pine Springs trailhead.

Dog Canyon

Few visitors from Texas see this remote part of Guadalupe Mountains National Park. It takes two hours to drive here from Carlsbad, New Mexico, and facilities are even more limited than they are at Pine Springs. But those who make the effort will find a secluded forested canyon at 6300 feet with a small campground and trails that cut across the high Guadalupes.

Hiking & Backpacking

If ever there was a hiker's national park, this is it. The park has 80 miles of trails, ranging from short nature walks to strenuous climbs, most listed here. *Trails of the Guadalupes: A Hiker's Guide to the Trails of Guadalupe Mountains National Park*, by Don Kurtz and William D Goran ($4), is a concise trail guide. For more regional coverage, look for *Hiking Carlsbad Caverns & Guadalupe Mountains National Parks*, by Bill Schneider ($13).

Ten backcountry campsites dot the Guadalupe Mountain trails. Overnight hikers must get a free backcountry permit from the Pine Springs or Dog Canyon ranger stations. Wood fires are not allowed in the backcountry, and since water is generally unavailable,

WEST TEXAS

The Mail Coaches

Although it operated for only two years, five months and 17 days between 1858 and 1861, the Butterfield Overland Mail Company spurred a revolution in American communications and transportation. Before that time, a letter from the east bound for California was sent via steamship around Cape Horn. The Butterfield Overland Mail Company made it possible for a letter to move 2700 miles from St Louis to San Francisco via El Paso, Tucson and Los Angeles in a then-breathtaking 25 days. (The Butterfield Overland began operation shortly before the more fabled Pony Express, a horseback-based mail service that started in April 1860 along a more northerly route, between St Joseph, Missouri, and Sacramento, California.)

The Butterfield Overland's legacy is well known throughout West Texas, but it's especially well preserved here at Guadalupe Mountains National Park. At 5534 feet, the Pinery stage-coach station – one of 200 on the route – was the highest in the system. With plentiful water and good grazing nearby, it was also one of the best situated. When the stagecoach first called here on September 28, 1858, the Pinery consisted of a corral and a few tents. But within two months, the station had grown to include a wagon repair shop, a blacksmith shop, stables for the fresh horses and three mud-roofed rooms where stage drivers and the station staff could rest. Four times a week, a bugle call would herald the arrival of the stage-coach and its cargo of mail and passengers (as many as nine people could make the trip).

The Pinery station operated for 11 months, until the original Butterfield route was abandoned for a new road through Fort Stockton and Fort Davis – a thoroughfare better protected from Indian attacks. The Butterfield Overland Mail continued until 1861, when federal troops guarding the route were recalled to fight the Civil War. But the Pinery station lived on for decades after as a refuge for emigrants, trail drovers, outlaws and others.

it must be carried in. Pets are not allowed, nor are firearms. Don't forget to pack out your trash.

Guadalupe Peak If you seek to stand on the highest spot in Texas, this 8½ mile roundtrip trek is the one you'll want to make. No rock climbing is necessary, but there's a 3000-foot elevation gain, so go easy if you've just driven in from the lowlands. Thunderstorms are likely on summer afternoons, and winds frequently blow 40 to 50 mph in spring and early summer. The Guadalupe Peak backcountry campsite is in an open, level area 3 miles from the trailhead at the Pine Springs campground.

Tejas Trail The Tejas Trail runs between Pine Springs and Dog Canyon campgrounds for a total of nearly 12 miles, with many spur trails breaking off along the way. From Pine Springs to the Pine Top campground it's

3.8 miles, a good hike in itself. At Pine Top, the Tejas Trail continues straight ahead, Bush Mountain Trail takes off to the left (with the Pine Top campsite nearby) and the Bowl trail goes to the right. After another 2.6 miles on the Tejas Trail, hikers reach the Blue Ridge Trail junction; from that junction, it's 1½ miles to the McKittrick Canyon Trail junction, and from there, it's 4 miles to the Dog Canyon campground.

The Bowl Veteran Guadalupe hikers get misty-eyed over this strenuous loop through the high-country forest called the Bowl. The loop runs for 3.6 miles from Pine Top via 8368-foot Hunter Peak and the Bear Canyon and Juniper Trail junctions, making this a 7.4-mile roundtrip trek from the Pine Springs campground. Plan on either a good long day hike with a 2500-foot elevation gain or an excellent backpacking trip with an overnight at the Pine Top backcountry campsite in a wooded area 4 miles from the start of the Tejas Trail.

El Capitan Trail Leaving the Pine Springs campground via the Guadalupe Peak trail, this path soon takes off across the Chihuahuan Desert to the base of El Capitan, the hulking southern end of the Guadalupes. It's a 6.8-mile roundtrip hike to Guadalupe Canyon; it can be extended to 11.3 miles roundtrip via the Salt Basin Trail or a total of 16 miles with a trip to Williams Ranch and an overnight at the backcountry Shumard Canyon campsite.

McKittrick Canyon This is among the park's most popular trails, and deservedly so. It's level and scenic any time of year, though never so much as in the fall. The Pratt Cabin (4.8 miles roundtrip from the trailhead) is a highlight. The cabin was built in 1932 by petroleum geologist Wallace Pratt, whose family vacationed here for several decades, later donating their land to the Park Service. The cabin remains furnished as the family left it. Big Adirondack chairs beckon on the porch, and picnic tables and rest rooms make this a good lunch spot.

Beyond Pratt Cabin, the canyon trail climbs sharply to the Grotto picnic area and

Fall Frenzy

On peak foliage weekends, the McKittrick Canyon crowds can get intense. The parking lot holds only so many cars, so visitors may need to wait to get in. If you're coming on an autumn weekend, pack a picnic and a good book and be prepared to wait a while. Better yet, come on a weekday. The McKittrick Canyon gate opens at 8 am year-round. Late April to late October, it closes at 6 pm; the rest of the year, it closes at 4:30 pm. Also bear these hours in mind if you plan a backpacking trip that uses the McKittrick trailhead as a starting or ending point.

Hunter Cabin (6.8 miles roundtrip from the trailhead) and the McKittrick Ridge backcountry campsite (14.8 miles roundtrip from the trailhead).

Dog Canyon Trails The park's Dog Canyon area is the access point for three trails: The **Indian Meadow Nature Trail** is a 0.6-mile nature trail loop. The northern reach of the **Tejas Trail** climbs out of Dog Canyon to a conifer forest and 7830-foot Lost Peak; the hike is a strenuous 6.4-mile roundtrip trek, with 1500 feet of elevation gain. The **Marcus Trail** follows the Bush Mountain Trail to a ridge top with a view into West Dog Canyon; the area's only backcountry campsite sits nearby, and it's a 4½-mile roundtrip trail with 800 feet of elevation gain.

Horseback Riding

Although many park trails are open to horseback riding, no horses are available in or near the park, and no overnight pack trips are permitted. For people bringing their own horses, stock corrals and campsites are available at Dog Canyon and Frijole Ranch; they can be reserved by calling ☎ 915-828-3307 for Frijole or ☎ 505-981-2418 for Dog Canyon.

Other Activities

The Pine Springs visitors' center has extensive exhibits and a slide show on area natural history and geology. The **Frijole Ranch Museum**, a mile or so northeast of Pine Springs, has exhibits on area history, including an 1858 stagecoach similar to the kind used on the Butterfield Overland route.

Interpretive programs are held on summer evenings in the Pine Springs campground amphitheater, as well as several times a week during the spring. Topics depend on the rangers' interests, but they have included everything from stargazing to geology. Occasionally, a ranger will talk about the park's nightlife, then lead a short hike to illustrate points made.

A **Junior Ranger program** for children ages four to 10 invites young visitors to complete activities and earn a badge, patch and certificate. The park recommends that families allow four to six hours for the program, which includes your choice of hikes, historic sites and interpretive programs.

Bird-watchers flock to the park, especially McKittrick Canyon, for excellent viewing opportunities. No formal programs are held, but a checklist of the park's 260 species is available at the visitors' center.

Rock climbers shouldn't confuse El Capitan here with the more famous granite formation in California's Yosemite National Park. Guadalupe Mountains' limestone and sandstone formations are ill-suited for climbing.

Places to Stay

The park has campgrounds at Pine Springs (38 sites) and Dog Canyon (13 sites). The cost is $7 per site per night; Golden Age and Golden Access passport holders get a 50% discount. Pine Springs is the handiest campground, right along US 62/180 near the visitors' center, with one area for RVs (no hookups) and the other for tents. Campsite No 21 is wheelchair accessible. Neither campground has showers. Wood and charcoal fires are not allowed.

The first-come, first-served campgrounds fill up during spring break and several nights a week in the summer, although visitors arriving by early afternoon will usually find a site. If the Pine Springs campground is full, RVs are permitted to park overnight at the nearby state highway picnic areas.

Getting There & Away

Although there is no scheduled public transportation to the park, Greyhound or Texas New Mexico & Oklahoma bus drivers on the El Paso-Carlsbad route will drop you off or make a whistle-stop pickup if you make arrangements in advance. Silver Stage Lines (☎ 915-778-0162, 800-522-0162) also runs shuttles through the area. Call for prices and reservations.

CARLSBAD CAVERNS NATIONAL PARK (NEW MEXICO)

Carlsbad Caverns National Park, 40 miles over the New Mexico border from Guadalupe Mountains National Park, is an underground wonderland that contains more than 80 separate caves, including the nation's deepest limestone cave. Carlsbad is still under exploration. Spelunkers broke through to Lechuguilla Cave in 1986 and have since been surveying and mapping its depths, now totaling nearly 100 miles.

Information & Park Entry

Call the park at ☎ 505-785-2232, write 3225 National Parks Hwy, Carlsbad, NM 88220, or see the website at www.nps.gov/cave. There are no accommodations in the park, but all services are available just outside at Whites City.

From late May to mid-August, the park visitors' center is open 8 am to 7 pm; late August to mid-May, hours are 8 am to 5:30 pm. Cave entry fees are $6 for adults and $3 for children ages six to 15, with an extra $3 for an audio guide. Guided caving tours cost $4 to $12 extra for adults, half that price for children. Reservations are required for the guided caving tours, and minimum ages apply.

Things to See & Do

In addition to the self-guided tours of Big Room and Natural Entrance and the ranger-guided tours of Kings Palace and some of the undeveloped caves, activities at Carlsbad Caverns include bat viewing, the scenic Walnut Canyon Drive, bird-watching and picnicking at Rattlesnake Springs, and backcountry camping and hiking. Other area attractions include Living Desert State Park, Brantley Lake State Park, Carlsbad Museum and Arts Center and Lincoln National Forest. For more information on the Carlsbad Caverns region, see Lonely Planet's *Southwest*, which covers New Mexico, Arizona and Utah.

PECOS
Population 11,200

Throughout the 1990s, when most of Texas was the fastest-growing state in the US, Pecos lost 7% of its population. In many ways, it's a hardscrabble West Texas town, barely hanging on as I-20 blows on by. But the people are among the friendliest you'll meet anywhere in the state, there's a great little museum and the very name of the town (pronounced PAY-cuss) just seems to conjure up the free-spirited, frontier Texas that's still alive in these parts. Pecos is the birthplace of that most Texan of sports, rodeo, and of the legend of Pecos Bill – the roughest, toughest cowboy who ever rode.

If you come into Pecos from the Guadalupe Mountains and you have plenty of gas, take FM 652 from the Texas-New Mexico state line to the little town of Orla. We saw exactly two other vehicles on this gently rolling 41-mile two-lane road. From Orla, it's 38 miles south to Pecos on US 285. From Pecos, Odessa (76 miles) is a fast hour east on I-20, and Fort Stockton is 52 miles to the southeast via US 285. Or take Hwy 17 through the cotton fields 34 miles southwest to Balmorhea, gateway to the Davis Mountains and Big Bend country.

Orientation

Pecos is sandwiched between I-20 to the south and Business Loop 20 – the old highway, also called 3rd St or sometimes even Hwy 80 after some real old maps – to the north. US 285, connecting the two, is known as Cedar St in town. If you're looking for Palmer St, it's also called the I-20 W South Frontage Rd. Business Loop 20 divides addresses between south and north, and Cedar St divides streets east and west. But the truth is, no one in Pecos cares too much for addresses, since they know where they're going, anyway.

Information

The chamber of commerce (☎ 915-445-2406), 111 S Cedar St, has tons of brochures on attractions across Texas. Open Monday to Friday 9 am to 5 pm.

A drive-up ATM is available at the Security State Bank (☎ 915-445-9000), 115 W 3rd St. The post office (☎ 915-445-4415) is at 106 W 4th St. Address Poste Restante to General Delivery, Pecos, TX 79772.

The *Pecos Enterprise*, among the smallest daily newspapers in Texas, costs 35¢, or you can see it free on the web (pecos.net/news). Monday through Saturday at 9 am, check out the call-in show *Hotline* on KIUN (1400 AM). Tune in if you want to buy a camper shell for your pick-up, sell your bike or adopt a free kitten. KPTX (98.3 FM) plays country.

The Reeves County Library (☎ 915-445-5340), 505 S Park St, is open Monday to Friday 9 am to 6 pm, Saturday 9 am to noon.

Wash & Dry Gulch (☎ 915-445-4303), 1330 S Cedar St, is open Monday to Saturday 9 am to 7 pm.

Reeves County Hospital (☎ 915-447-3551) is at 2323 Texas St.

West of the Pecos Museum

On 1st St just around the corner from the chamber of commerce, this museum (☎ 915-445-5076) is often called one of the best small-town museums in Texas. The former saloon and hotel now house more than 50 rooms of exhibits plus a bookstore and gift shop with a good selection of books on Texas and Southwest history.

Each room has its own theme, so it's easy to find the ones that capture your interest and skip the rest. Clay Allison, the Gentleman Gunfighter who 'never killed a man who didn't need killing,' is buried out back near the replica of Judge Roy Bean's saloon. Open Monday to Saturday 9 am to 5 pm (until 6 pm weekdays in summer) and Sunday 1 to 4 pm; $3.50 for adults, $2.50 for seniors, $1 for teens and 50¢ for kids ages six to 12. Children under six get in free.

Maxey Park & Zoo

Pecos has the only zoo between Abilene and El Paso, with javelinas, zebras, a bear, buffalo, and mountain lions. Admission is free. It's in Maxey Park, which also has a playground (complete with a kid-size Alamo), picnic areas and miniature golf course. The park is south of I-20 along Palmer St.

Special Events

The West of the Pecos Rodeo, probably the oldest in the US, is held several days up to and including the Fourth of July, with preliminary festivities in late June. The rodeo, which is held at the West of the Pecos Rodeo Grounds, on the south side of town along Cedar St, dates to 1883, when dueling

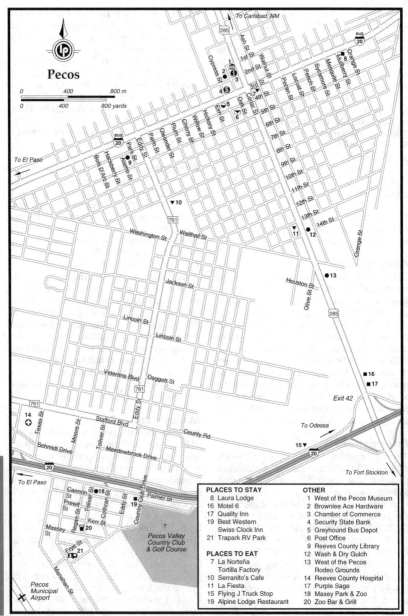

Pecos

To Carlsbad, NM

To El Paso

To El Paso

To Odessa

To Fort Stockton

Pecos Valley
Country Club
& Golf Course

Pecos Municipal
Airport

PLACES TO STAY
8 Laura Lodge
16 Motel 6
17 Quality Inn
19 Best Western
   Swiss Clock Inn
21 Trapark RV Park

PLACES TO EAT
7 La Norteña
   Tortilla Factory
10 Serranito's Cafe
11 La Fiesta
15 Flying J Truck Stop
19 Alpine Lodge Restaurant

OTHER
1 West of the Pecos Museum
2 Brownlee Ace Hardware
3 Chamber of Commerce
4 Security State Bank
5 Greyhound Bus Depot
6 Post Office
9 Reeves County Library
12 Wash & Dry Gulch
13 West of the Pecos
   Rodeo Grounds
14 Reeves County Hospital
17 Purple Sage
18 Maxey Park & Zoo
20 Zoo Bar & Grill

WEST TEXAS

cowboys decided to settle their scores with a riding-and-roping showdown. Although most of the events are for pro cowboys only, a few – including a wild horse race and wild cow milking contest – are open to all comers. Pecos celebrates its status as the cantaloupe capital of Texas with a festival the first weekend in August.

Places to Stay

Camping The *Trapark RV Park (915-447-2137)*, 3100 Moore St near Maxey Park, charges $15 for full hookups, $11 for water-and-electric sites and $8 for tent spaces. Extra people beyond two per site are $2 apiece.

Motels *Laura Lodge (☎ 915-445-4924)*, 1000 E 3rd St (Business Loop 20 East) on the city's northeast side, has singles for about $20 and doubles for less than $30. *Motel 6 (☎ 915-445-9034)*, 3002 S Cedar St, has rooms near I-20 for about $32 single and $36 double in summer, a bit lower the rest of the year.

The *Best Western Swiss Clock Inn (☎ 915-447-2215, fax 915-447-4463)*, 900 W Palmer St, has rates from $42/48. It's within walking distance of Maxey Park, and its small guest laundry has free washers and dryers. The *Quality Inn (☎ 915-445-5404)*, 4002 S Cedar St, is the priciest place in town, but it frequently discounts its basic room rate of $61,

so ask. Expect to pay a few bucks more all over town around rodeo time.

Places to Eat

With a population that's about 85% Hispanic, Pecos has plenty of tasty and cheap Mexican fare. We enjoyed a gordita plate ($6) at *Serranito's Cafe (☎ 915-445-2990)*, 802 S Eddy St, where American dishes are available, too. Other good bets for Mexican food include *La Fiesta (☎ 915-445-3323)*, 1313 S Cedar St, where the parking lot is always packed, and *La Norteña Tortilla Factory (☎ 915-445-3273)*, 212 E 3rd St, with to-die-for tamales priced at $2 to $5.

If you're looking for a wider menu, try the *Alpine Lodge Restaurant* at the Best Western Swiss Clock Inn, which serves breakfast and lunch daily and dinner Monday through Saturday. The restaurant at the *Flying J Truck Stop (☎ 915-445-9436)*, along I-20 at exit 42, is open 24 hours a day, 365 days a year.

Entertainment

Locally popular nightspots include the *Purple Sage* at the Quality Inn *(☎ 915-445-5404)*, where a DJ plays Tejano music some evenings, and the *Zoo Bar & Grill (☎ 915-447-3110)*, which features pool, shuffleboard and occasional live music. It's at 2905 Tolivar St near the real zoo.

Shopping

I-20 has taken its toll on Pecos, but a few locally owned shops are hanging on. Toone's Grocery (☎ 915-445-3662), 2136 Business Loop 80 W, and Brownlee Ace Hardware (☎ 915-445-2813), 131 S Oak St, are like living museums, well worth a browse.

Getting There & Away

Pecos has no scheduled air service. Greyhound (☎ 915-445-5016), 202 W 3rd St, offers these regularly scheduled trips:

to/from	trip duration	one way/ roundtrip
Odessa	1½ hours	$15/30
El Paso	4 hours	$36/72
San Antonio	9 hours	$55/110

AROUND PECOS
Mentone

Mentone, 23 miles north of Pecos via US 285 and FM 302, is the seat of Loving County, the most sparsely populated county in the lower 48 states: with about 100 residents, its population density is about 0.15 people per sq mile. Fewer than 20 people live in Mentone itself; the rest of the population lives on ranches. For an incisive look at the unique culture of Loving County, read *Miles from Nowhere: Tales from America's Contemporary Frontier*, by Dayton Duncan.

Balmorhea State Park

Swimming, scuba diving and snorkeling are the attractions at Balmorhea (pronounced BAL-mo-ray) State Park (☎ 915-375-2370, PO Box 15, Toyahvale, TX 79786), a true oasis in the West Texas desert. The swimming pool covers 1.75 acres, making it the largest spring-fed swimming facility in the US, 25 feet deep and about 75°F year-round. The park is at Toyahvale, 5 miles south of the town of Balmorhea, which itself is just off I-10 and midway between Pecos and Fort Davis on Hwy 17.

Things to See & Do Pool use is included in the $3 entrance fee. The pool is open for diving from 8 am to 10 pm and for swimming from 8 am until a half-hour before sunset. No lifeguards are on duty, and anyone under age 18 must have parental permission to swim.

Canals from the pool lead to a replicated desert wetland complete with an underwater viewing window, through which visitors can see the endangered Comanche Springs pupfish and Pecos mosquito fish. Other activities in the park include picnicking and birdwatching.

Toyahvale Desert Oasis (☎ 915-375-2572), just outside the state park, is a full-service scuba shop. Complete diving gear can be rented for $25 a day, and lessons are available if you call in advance.

Places to Stay & Eat The state park's 33-site campground has tent sites for $7 a day, water-and-electric hookups for $10 a day and premium hookups (water, electric and cable TV) for $12 a day. Camp fees do not include the per-person entrance fee, which must be paid. The park also has an 18-unit motel, *San Solomon Springs Courts* (☎ 512-389-8900). Rooms cost $35 for one adult, with extra fees of $5 per adult and $2 per child ages six to 12. Rooms with kitchenettes cost $5 more. Each room has a television but no telephone. A concession stand sells sandwiches, snacks and soft drinks during the summer.

FORT STOCKTON
Population 9072

Fort Stockton snags a spot on many Texas travelers' itineraries by virtue of geography. Despite having fewer than 10,000 people, Fort Stockton is by far the biggest town on I-10 between El Paso, which is 238 miles west, and San Antonio, which is 310 miles east. It's also a major gateway to Big Bend National Park, which is 100 miles south via US 385. So it's little surprise that Fort Stockton has more than 800 motel rooms, about 320 campsites and several dozen restaurants.

Orientation

Fort Stockton lies mostly south of I-10, with Dickinson Blvd being the main drag through town. Most of the town's many motels, campgrounds and restaurants are clustered around the I-10 exits, but Fort Stockton's real charm lies in its historic area along and near S Main St. First St marks the north-south dividing line, and Main St divides the town east and west.

Information

The Caboose Visitor Information Center (☎ 915-336-8052), south of I-10 exit 257 (US 285) is open daily 10 am to 8 pm between Memorial Day and Labor Day and 11 am to 6 pm the rest of the year. The chamber of commerce (☎ 915-336-2264) also has lots of brochures at its office in the old railroad depot at 1000 Railroad Ave.

Near the chamber, an oversize statue of roadrunner Paisano Pete is a popular photo stop for visitors to Fort Stockton. The city's tourism bureau has a toll-free number

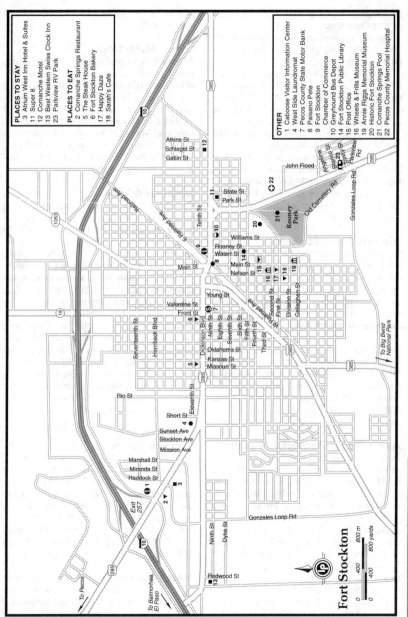

PLACES TO STAY
3 Atrium West Inn Hotel & Suites
11 Super 8
12 Comanche Motel
13 Best Western Swiss Clock Inn
23 Parkview RV Park

PLACES TO EAT
2 Comanche Springs Restaurant
5 The Steak House
6 Fort Stockton Bakery
17 Happy Daze
18 Sarah's Cafe

OTHER
1 Caboose Visitor Information Center
4 West Side Laundromat
7 Pecos County State Motor Bank
8 Paisano Pete
9 Fort Stockton
10 Greyhound Bus Depot
14 Chamber of Commerce
15 Fort Stockton Public Library
16 Post Office
17 Wheels & Frills Museum
19 Annie Riggs Memorial Museum
20 Historic Fort Stockton
21 Comanche Springs Pool
22 Pecos County Memorial Hospital

Fort Stockton

WEST TEXAS

(☎ 800-334-8525) in operation during weekday business hours.

An ATM is available at the Pecos County State Motor Bank (☎ 915-336-3331), 501 W Dickinson Blvd.

The post office (☎ 915-336-2313) is at 106 E Fourth St. Address Poste Restante to General Delivery, Fort Stockton, TX 79735.

The *Fort Stockton Pioneer* is published every Thursday and costs 50¢ a copy.

The Fort Stockton Public Library (☎ 915-336-3374) is at 500 N Water St.

Tote your dirty clothes to the West Side Laundromat, between Wal-Mart and the Pantry Food Store on W Dickinson Blvd.

Pecos County Memorial Hospital (☎ 915-336-2241) is on US 285 in the southeast part of town.

Historic Fort Stockton

Historic Fort Stockton (☎ 915-336-2400), 300 E 3rd St, includes several original and reconstructed buildings of a 19th-century fort on the Texas frontier. Barracks No 1, a reconstructed building, houses the Fort Museum where exhibits and a short video describe the post's history. Living History Days are held the first weekend of each November, with demonstrations, encampments and entertainment. Fall to spring, Historic Fort Stockton is open Monday to Saturday 10 am to 5 pm. During the summer, hours are Monday to Saturday 10 am to 5 pm and Sunday 1 to 5 pm. Admission is $2 for adults and 50¢ for children ages six to 12.

Annie Riggs Memorial Museum

Housed in a former hotel/boarding house at 301 S Main St, the Annie Riggs Memorial Museum (☎ 915-336-2167) is named for the frontier woman who bought the hotel and ran it for many years. Historic photographs and Texas memorabilia line the walls, and the gracious grounds are often used for special events including a summer concert series (see Entertainment). In summer, the museum stays open Monday to Saturday 10 am to 8 pm and Sunday 1:30 to 8 pm. September to May, the museum is open Monday to Saturday 10 am to noon and 1 to 5 pm, Sunday 1:30 to 5 pm. Admis-

sion is $1 for adults and 50¢ for children ages six to 12.

Other Attractions

Rooney Park is the site of Comanche Springs Pool, a popular summer swimming hole. The **Wheels & Frills Museum** (☎ 915-336-8421), 221 N Main St, includes a classic car collection and an art gallery. The reconstructed **Tunis Creek stage stop** from the Butterfield Overland Mail Company's San Antonio-San Francisco route can be seen at a rest area that's 20 miles east on I-10, about 1½ miles north of its original site.

Organized Tours

For such a small city, Fort Stockton goes all out to help visitors see the sights. In addition to self-guiding cassette tape tours available at the chamber of commerce, the city offers daily Roadrunner Bus Tours. Ninety-minute historical tours featuring Historic Fort Stockton and the Annie Riggs Memorial Museum cost $7 per person ($4.25 for children ages three to 12), with departures on weekday mornings and afternoons and weekend afternoons. A tour of nearby Ste Genevieve Winery is offered Saturday and Wednesday mornings. This tour lasts 2½ to three hours and costs $8 per person ($6.50 for children). Tours leave from the Caboose Visitor Information Center, the chamber of commerce and local motels. For reservations, call ☎ 915-336-8052 or 915-336-2264.

Places to Stay

Camping *Parkview RV Park* (☎ 915-336-7733, 800-344-0103) is at the intersection of Parkview Rd and US 285 on the southeast edge of town. Rates are $14 for full hookups and $10 for tent sites. Both rates cover up to two people; additional people are $1 extra per person. *KOA* (☎ 915-395-2494, 800-562-8607) is 3½ miles east of town on the north side of I-10 exit 264 (Warnock Rd). It charges $19.50 for hookups and $15.50 for tent sites.

Motels The *Comanche Motel* (☎ 915-336-5824), 1301 E Dickinson Blvd, has 14 hostel-type bunks priced at $12 for one person, $10 each for two to four people and $8 each for parties of five or more. Each of the three hostel rooms has a TV, bathroom and phone, but no kitchen facilities are available. Regular motel rooms at the Comanche go for $25 to $29. Although this is the only motel with hostel beds, there are at least a half-dozen other budget motels along Dickinson Blvd with regular rooms in the $25 to $30 range.

The *Best Western Swiss Clock Inn* (☎ 915-336-8521, fax 915-336-6513), 3201 W Dickinson St, has rooms starting at $38/44. The *Super 8* (☎ 915-336-9711, fax 915-336-5815), 800 E Dickinson Blvd, charges $44/52. The poshest place in town is the business-oriented *Atrium West Inn Hotel & Suites* (☎ 915-336-6666), 1305 US 285 N, with an indoor pool and exercise facilities. Rooms here run $70 and up.

B&Bs Twenty-six miles south of Fort Stockton on US 385, the road to Big Bend National Park, *Glass Mountain Manor* (☎ 915-395-2435, 800-695-8249) is a full house that will accommodate up to 12 people, with kitchen facilities and a continental breakfast included. Rates start at $75 for the first two people; additional people are $10 per adult or $5 per child. The inn is on a working ranch, and there's good mountain biking nearby.

Places to Eat
Sarah's Cafe (☎ 915-336-7700), 106 S Nelson St, may well be the main reason to visit Fort Stockton. The food is better-than-average Mexican, prices are reasonable (most items in the $3 to $7 range) and the service is outstanding: no one is a stranger to Cleo Castelo, who now runs the restaurant her family founded in 1929. Tell 'em it's your first time, and you'll receive a free quesadilla.

Comanche Springs Restaurant (☎ 915-336-9713), 2501 W I-10 at exit 257, is a truck-stop eatery with a gimmick similar to that offered by the Big Texan Steak Ranch up in Amarillo. Comanche Springs' version is a whopping 5lb cheeseburger served on a 10-inch bun with a whole plate of french fries on the side. Anyone who can eat all this alone in one hour gets it free; otherwise, it's $17 and will usually feed a party of four or five.

Happy Daze (☎ 915-336-3233), 101 N Main St, is a 1950s style diner and soda fountain open for breakfast ($2 to $4) and lunch ($3 to $5). *The Steak House* (☎ 915-336-5909), 1100 W Dickinson Blvd, draws big local crowds for breakfast and lunch as well as dinner. *Fort Stockton Bakery* (☎ 915-336-7232), 600 W Dickinson Blvd, sells a variety of doughnuts, cookies and breads, with day-old goods half off the already low prices.

Entertainment
Fort Stockton rolls up its sidewalks most nights. If you want a good time, try to arrange your visit on one of the summer Thursdays when 'An Evening Under the West Texas Stars' is planned. These events on the lawn of the Annie Riggs Memorial Museum feature live music, wine and hors d'oeuvres. Tickets are free, but seating is limited. Call the museum (☎ 915-336-2167) or the Fort Stockton tourism bureau (☎ 800-334-8525) for dates and tickets.

Getting There & Away
Air There's no scheduled air service to Fort Stockton. The nearest major airport, Midland International, is about 110 miles away.

Bus The Greyhound bus depot (☎ 915-336-5151) is at 800 N Williams St, where Williams intersects with Dickinson Blvd. Schedules include:

to/from	frequency (per day)	trip duration	one way/ roundtrip
El Paso	4	4 hours	$44/87
San Antonio	4	6 hours	$49/98

The Permian Basin

The Permian Basin is a flat, physically charmless region of Texas with a lack of vegetation so pronounced that early settlers named one small town Notrees. Instead, you'll see (and smell) forests of oil rigs, pump jacks and petroleum tanks, which have ruled the boom-and-bust economy here since the 1920s.

Unless you're in the oil business, the Permian Basin is no destination, but because

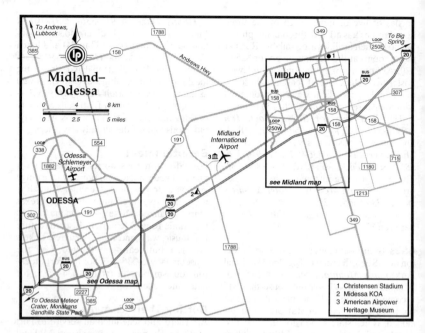

To Andrews, Lubbock

Midland–Odessa

ODESSA

MIDLAND

Midland International Airport

see Midland map

see Odessa map

To Odessa Meteor Crater, Monahans Sandhills State Park

To Big Spring

1 Christensen Stadium
2 Midessa KOA
3 American Airpower Heritage Museum

Texas is so dang big and Midland and Odessa sit strategically astride I-20, you may well end up spending the night here en route to somewhere else. (It's 617 miles from El Paso to Dallas, and Midland-Odessa are roughly halfway.) Don't despair; the sun will come up tomorrow, and you can be on your way. Meanwhile, because the two neighboring towns have close to 200,000 people and – sporadically, at least – a lot of money, you'll find some interesting museums and pockets of panache.

MIDLAND
Population 98,251
Despite being just 20 miles apart and far from everywhere else, Midland and Odessa have distinct personalities. Midland is a wanna-be Dallas, with its own little cluster of tall buildings, lots of white-collar workers and a martinis-and-cigars yuppie vibe.

Orientation
US 349 heads north from I-20 exit 136 into downtown Midland, becoming Big Spring St once it gets downtown. Main St divides the city east and west, and Wall St is the north-south dividing line. Business Rte 20 parallels I-20 about a mile to the interstate's north, providing access to Midland International Airport. Midland's major commercial areas are along Andrews Hwy (Business Loop 158) northwest of downtown and on the city's north side along Loop 250.

Information
Tourist Office The Midland Convention and Visitors Bureau (☎ 915-683-3381, 800-624-6435) is at 109 N Main St next to the Midland Center.

Money NationsBank (☎ 915-685-2000) is downtown at 303 W Wall St.

Post & Communications The downtown post office (☎ 915-682-3381) is at 100 E Wall St. Midland's main post office (☎ 915-560-5105), 10000 Sloan Field Blvd, is just west of Midland International Airport. The Ground

Floor Coffeehouse (☎ 915-498-8111), 111 W Wall St, lets customers use its high-speed Internet connection free.

Media The *Midland Reporter-Telegram* is published each morning and costs 50¢ daily, $1.50 Sunday. On the radio, NPR is on KOCV (91.3 FM). For Tejano, tune to KMRK (96.1 FM), while KBAT (93 FM) is a good adult rock station. KMND (1510 AM) has news and talk.

Bookstores Mrs Olsen's Coffee & Bookstore (☎ 915-570-5282) is in the Oak Ridge Square at 2200 W Wadley Ave. Stop by anytime after 7 am weekdays. Barnes & Noble (☎ 915-570-5827) is at 2617 W Loop 250 North.

Libraries The Midland County Library (☎ 915-688-8991) is on the south side of downtown at 301 W Missouri Ave. The Haley Memorial Library & History Center (☎ 915-682-5785), 1805 W Indiana Ave, focuses on cowboys and the range cattle industry. It's open Monday to Friday 9 am to 5 pm.

Laundry Nice & Clean Laundry Center (☎ 915-694-7486) is at 4309 W Illinois Ave.

Medical Services Primary Medical Clinic (☎ 915-697-0291), 3400 Andrews Hwy, has walk-in care for minor illnesses and injuries. Complete medical services are available at Memorial Hospital (☎ 915-685-1111), 2200 W Illinois Ave.

Emergency Midland Rape Crisis is at ☎ 915-682-7273. The local suicide prevention line is ☎ 915-570-3300.

Permian Basin Petroleum Museum

This museum (☎ 915-683-4403), 1500 I-20 W, is worth a stop even if you're not utterly fascinated with the oil business, for it's as much a history, art and geology museum as a shrine to the prominent local industry. Outside, there's a big collection of antique oil-drilling equipment. Inside, Tom Lovell's sensitive paintings depict the region's history before

and just after the oil boom. Interactive exhibits include one in which players can drill their own wells and another that simulates the roar of a blowout, an oil well gone wild. If there's a drawback to the museum, it's that conservation and reduction of oil use are barely mentioned. The overriding theme is that we need all the oil we can get and we must do whatever is necessary to find and drill it. One of the last exhibits notes that US residents consume petroleum-based products at the rate of 3½ gallons per person per day. Whether you're American or not, it's a sobering thought to ponder as you walk out to the parking lot and turn over that engine one more time.

Open Monday to Saturday 9 am to 5 pm, Sunday 2 to 5 pm; $4 for adults, $3 for seniors, $2 for children ages six to 11 (younger children are admitted free).

Museum of the Southwest

Housed in the 1934 Turner Mansion, itself a work of art, the Museum of the Southwest (☎ 915-683-2882), 1705 W Missouri Ave, has an art gallery, planetarium and children's

---

Praying for Oil

Seeking financing for his venture, early Permian Basin oilman Frank Pickrell managed to interest a group of Catholic women in the project. Uncertain they should participate, the women sought the advice of their priest. The minister advised them to seek the help of St Rita, patron saint of the impossible and advocate of desperate causes. Two of the women gave Pickrell a sealed envelope holding a red rose. They instructed him to climb to the top of the derrick, take the rose from the envelope, crush its petals and sprinkle them over the rig. As the petals fell, Pickrell christened the derrick Santa Rita. Soon after, the Santa Rita 'blew in' with one of the region's first big oil strikes. Guess somebody up there was listening.

museum. Some major touring art exhibits come here; in the fall of 1997, the museum had a show of works by Picasso, Chagall and Matisse. The museum is open Tuesday to Saturday 10 am to 5 pm and Sunday 2 to 5 pm. There's no admission charge. Planetarium shows take place Friday at 8 pm, with an admission fee of $3 for adults, $2 for children 12 and under.

American Airpower Heritage Museum

The airplanes of World War II are the stars at this museum, also known as the Confederate Air Force Museum (☎ 915-563-1000), 9600 Wright Drive near Midland International Airport. The CAF was formed in the 1950s as a rebel group determined to save the planes flown in WWII, which were then being scrapped. After outgrowing headquarters in Mercedes and Harlingen, Texas, the group was lured to Midland, where it now houses its 120-aircraft Ghost Squadron, the world's largest collection of WWII aircraft in flying condition. About 20 of the planes can be seen at a time; the rest are stored in the massive hangar nearby, and the collection rotates regularly. Open Monday to Saturday 9 am to 5 pm, Sunday and holidays noon to 5 pm (closed Christmas and Thanksgiving); $6 for adults, $5 for teens and seniors, $4 for kids ages six to 12, free for children five and under.

Special Events

Early each October, the Confederate Air Force puts on its AirSho extravaganza, featuring re-creations of World War II air battles, complete with explosions and fireballs but minus the gore. Other major annual events include Summer in the City gatherings each Thursday in June and July outside the Midland Center at Wall and Loraine Sts downtown and Septemberfest, an arts festival at Museum of the Southwest.

Places to Stay

Camping *Midland RV Campground* (☎ 915-697-0801), 2134 S Midland Drive, charges $10 for tent sites and $14 and up for RV sites. There's a laundry on the premises, but not much else.

Motels *West Wind Motel* (☎ 915-694-2576), 3808 W Wall St, charges $29 for singles and $33 for doubles. *Metro Inn* (☎ 915-697-3236, fax 915-697-0447), 3708 W Wall St, has rooms for $35/45.

Comfort Inn (☎ 915-683-1111), 902 I-20 W, is just east of the Permian Basin Petroleum Museum with rates starting at $69. The *Plaza Inn* (☎ 915-686-8733, 800-365-3222), 4108 N Big Spring St, is business oriented, with free van service to downtown and the airport and rooms starting at $59. *Lexington Hotel Suites* (☎ 915-697-3155, fax 915-699-2017), 1003 S Midkiff Rd, also caters to a business crowd with rates starting at $48/$54.

The *Midland Hilton & Towers* (☎ 915-683-6131, fax 915-683-0958), 117 W Wall St, charges $95 to $105. It has exercise facilities and a pool.

B&Bs We told you Midland has big-city aspirations. The town's only B&B, *Top o' the Mark* (☎ 915-682-4560, fax 915-570-7250), is in a downtown penthouse at 110 Loraine St. The mood is very New York City: walls of deep navy blue, mystical red and ether gray, with large windows overlooking the city lights. Rates for the guest rooms run $71 to $105, higher during special events.

Places to Eat

Wall Street Bar & Grill (☎ 915-684-8686), an American restaurant at 115 E Wall St, is especially popular for its Sunday brunch, served 10:30 am to 2:30 pm. Entrées are priced $6 to $13; prices also include a trip to the salad bar, locally famous for its bite-sized cinnamon rolls and tiny sweet strawberries. At dinner, entrées range from $6 to $16.

Jazz: A Louisiana Kitchen (☎ 915-689-7777), 2215 N Midland Drive in the Mesa Verde Center, is a regional Cajun chain with a strong local following. Specialties include the garlic seafood platter ($11) and Cajun stir-fry of beef, chicken and shrimp ($10 for a full order, $5 for a half).

Hunan Garden (☎ 915-697-9818), 4410 N Midkiff Rd, specializes in Asian fare that's just a bit spicier than the usual. Entrées range from $5 to $13, and there are daily specials. For Italian, Midlanders say *Luigi's*

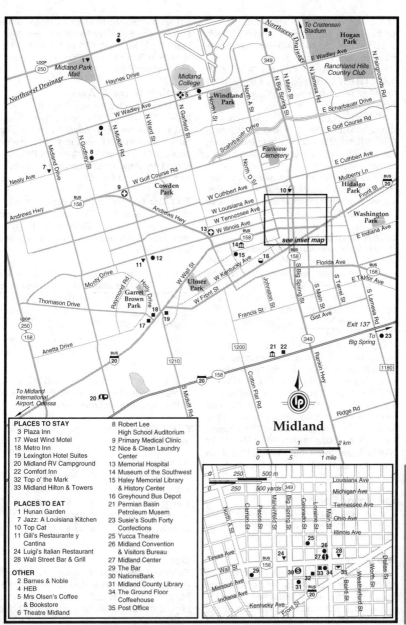

Midland

PLACES TO STAY
3 Plaza Inn
17 West Wind Motel
18 Metro Inn
19 Lexington Hotel Suites
20 Midland RV Campground
22 Comfort Inn
32 Top o' the Mark
33 Midland Hilton & Towers

PLACES TO EAT
1 Hunan Garden
7 Jazz: A Louisiana Kitchen
10 Top Cat
11 Gili's Restaurante y Cantina
24 Luigi's Italian Restaurant
28 Wall Street Bar & Grill

OTHER
2 Barnes & Noble
4 HEB
5 Mrs Olsen's Coffee & Bookstore
6 Theatre Midland

8 Robert Lee High School Auditorium
9 Primary Medical Clinic
12 Nice & Clean Laundry Center
13 Memorial Hospital
14 Museum of the Southwest
15 Haley Memorial Library & History Center
16 Greyhound Bus Depot
21 Permian Basin Petroleum Musem
23 Susie's South Forty Confections
25 Yucca Theatre
26 Midland Convention & Visitors Bureau
27 Midland Center
29 The Bar
30 NationsBank
31 Midland County Library
34 The Ground Floor Coffeehouse
35 Post Office

WEST TEXAS

(☎ 915-683-6363), 111 N Big Spring St, has the best pizza and lasagna in town. Lunch and dinner run $5 to $14. The restaurant is open for dinner only on Sunday.

Gili's Restaurant y Cantina *(☎ 915-699-7636)*, 4411 W Illinois Ave, is a Mexican and Tex-Mex restaurant serving good shrimp tostadas (a platter of three costs $10).

Midland has all the usual fast-food choices, plus a local favorite: ***Top Cat*** *(☎ 915-682-4166)*, 801 N Big Spring St, where the specialties include fried catfish and a shrimp poor boy sandwich.

If you're looking for a supermarket, the ***HEB*** *(☎ 915-697-1471)*, 3325 W Wadley Ave, is open until midnight and has an extensive deli and salad bar.

Entertainment

The ***Midland Symphony Orchestra*** *(☎ 915-563-0921)* performs at Robert Lee High School Auditorium, 3500 Neely Ave. ***Theatre Midland*** *(☎ 915-682-4111)*, 2000 W Wadley Ave, presents local talent in musicals, comedies and dramas. The ***Yucca Theatre*** *(☎ 915-682-4111)*, 208 N Colorado Ave, hosts touring theatrical groups.

Outdoor concerts in a variety of musical genres are held each Sunday evening June through August at the Museum of the Southwest, 1705 W Missouri Ave. Call ☎ 915-563-2882 for details. ***The Bar*** *(☎ 915-685-1757)*, 606 W Missouri Ave, is an Austin-flavored spot where upper-crust Midland parties to live R&B and occasional country. The ***Ground Floor Coffeehouse*** *(☎ 915-498-8111)*, 111 W Wall St, is the closest thing Midland has to an alternative scene, with frequent live entertainment and a friendly atmosphere.

Spectator Sports

The Midland Angels (☎ 915-683-4251) play Double-A professional baseball at Christensen Stadium, 4300 N Lamesa Rd.

Shopping

After oil, the Permian Basin's most famous product may well be pecan toffee from Susie's South Forty Confections (☎ 915-570-4040), a half-mile south of I-20 exit 137 at 2801 S County Rd 1180. The kitchen and

gift shop are open Monday to Friday 9 am to 5 pm and Saturday 10 am to 1 pm. Midland Park Mall (☎ 915-694-1663), 4511 N Midkiff Rd at Loop 250, is the city's largest shopping center.

Getting There & Away

Air Midland International Airport (☎ 915-560-2200) sits midway between Midland and Odessa off of Business Loop 20. The only major airport on the I-20 corridor between Dallas-Fort Worth and El Paso, it's served by American, Continental, Southwest and United Express.

Bus The Greyhound bus depot (☎ 915-682-2761) is at 1308 W Front St. Sample fares (one way/roundtrip) and approximate minimum one-way travel times are listed below:

to/from	frequency (per day)	trip duration	one way/ roundtrip
El Paso	4	4 hours	$44/87
San Antonio	4	6 hours	$49/98
Alpine	2	4½ hours	$23/44
El Paso	7	6 hours	$50/99
Dallas	5	7 hours	$55/110

Concho Coaches (☎ 915-658-7644) offers van shuttle service ($6) from the Midland Airport to the Midland Greyhound bus depot.

Car Major car rental companies with offices in Midland include:

Advantage	☎ 915-563-0065
Avis	☎ 915-563-0910
Budget	☎ 915-563-1640
Enterprise	☎ 915-689-9500
Hertz	☎ 915-563-0110
National	☎ 915-563-0378

Getting Around

To/From the Airport Figure on a $14 taxi ride from the airport to downtown Midland. Many hotels in Midland-Odessa offer free airport shuttles, so inquire when you book your room.

Bus Neither Midland nor Odessa has a public bus system.

Taxi Taxi rates in Midland are $1.55 flag-fall and $1.20 for each additional mile. Cab companies include City-Yellow Checker Cab (☎ 915-682-1661) and A-1 Taxi Service (☎ 915-697-2521). Cabs are plentiful at Midland International Airport; elsewhere in the area, you'll have to call for service.

ODESSA
Population 93,495
In contrast to Midland, Odessa has a scruffy, even downbeat feel, although it can boast a University of Texas branch campus and a replica of Shakespeare's Globe Theatre. Odessa is also the spot where former US president George Bush got his start in the oil business.

Orientation
Take I-20 exit 116 for US 385 north into downtown Odessa. US 385 becomes Grant Ave in downtown; at 18th St, it turns into Andrews Hwy, a major commercial area especially near its intersections with University Blvd and 42nd St. Business Rte 20 (E 2nd St in town) leads east to Midland International Airport.

Information
The Odessa Convention & Visitors Bureau (☎ 915-333-7871, 800-780-4678, fax 915-333-7858) is in the NationsBank building, at 700 N Grant Ave.

NationsBank (☎ 915-335-7200) is at 700 N Grant Ave.

The daily *Odessa American* costs 50¢ Monday to Saturday and $1.50 on Sunday. It's also online at www.oaoa.com.

The main post office (☎ 915-332-6436) is at 200 N Texas Ave.

Bookworm (☎ 915-333-9913, 800-239-2908), downtown at 517 N Grant Ave, handles mostly used and hard-to-find books.

The Ector County Library (☎ 915-333-9633) is at 321 W 5th St.

Odessa's Nice & Clean Laundry Center (☎ 915-333-5157) is at 801 S Grant Ave on the south edge of downtown.

The Primary Medical Clinic (☎ 915-362-4376), 3051 E University Blvd, has a no-appointments clinic for minor illnesses and injuries. Medical Center Hospital (☎ 915-640-4000), 500 W 4th St, is the major hospital in Odessa.

Presidential Museum
This place is worth a brief stop if you are into history. Its best exhibit, Every Four Years, details every US presidential election to date. The museum (☎ 915-332-7123), 622 N Lee Ave, is open Tuesday to Saturday 10 am to 5 pm. Admission is $2 for adults and $1 for seniors. Everyone under 18 gets in free. A historical marker out front tells how future President George Bush moved to Odessa in 1948 to start his career in the oil business.

Globe of the Great Southwest
Whether 'tis nobler to attend performances of Shakespearean classics or opt for the country-and-western revues also staged at this replica of the Bard's venue, we'll leave up to you. The grounds also include a copy of the cottage Shakespeare built for his paramour, Anne Hathaway, complete with a Shakespearean library. The Globe (☎ 915-332-1586) is on the Odessa College campus at 2308 Shakespeare Rd off the Kermit Hwy. In addition to performances, it's open to browsers Monday to Friday 9 am to 5 pm.

World's Largest Jackrabbit Statue
Not to be outdone by Fort Stockton's road-runner, Odessa has the world's largest jackrabbit statue. The 10-foot-tall photo op is on the grounds at 802 N Sam Houston Ave.

White-Pool House
Built in 1887 at 112 E Murphy St, this is the oldest existing house in Ector County (☎ 915-333-4072). It had just two owners for nearly a century before the Pool family deeded it to the county for preservation in 1973. Changing exhibits highlight different periods in Odessa history. Open Tuesday noon to 3 pm, Wednesday to Saturday 10 am to 3 pm, Sunday by appointment only.

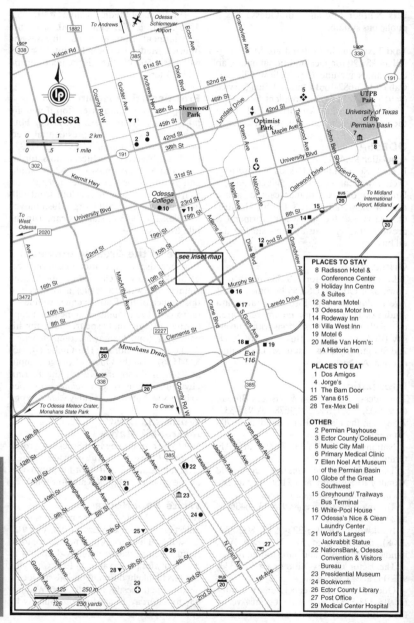

PLACES TO STAY
8 Radisson Hotel &
Conference Center
9 Holiday Inn Centre
& Suites
12 Sahara Motel
13 Odessa Motor Inn
14 Rodeway Inn
18 Villa West Inn
19 Motel 6
20 Mellie Van Horn's:
A Historic Inn

PLACES TO EAT
1 Dos Amigos
4 Jorge's
11 The Barn Door
25 Yana 615
28 Tex-Mex Deli

OTHER
2 Permian Playhouse
3 Ector County Coliseum
5 Music City Mall
6 Primary Medical Clinic
7 Ellen Noel Art Museum
of the Permian Basin
10 Globe of the Great
Southwest
15 Greyhound/ Trailways
Bus Terminal
16 White-Pool House
17 Odessa's Nice & Clean
Laundry Center
21 World's Largest
Jackrabbit Statue
22 NationsBank, Odessa
Convention & Visitors
Bureau
23 Presidential Museum
24 Bookworm
26 Ector County Library
27 Post Office
29 Medical Center Hospital

WEST TEXAS

Ellen Noel Art Museum of the Permian Basin

A sculpture garden and frequently changing exhibits make this museum (☎ 915-368-7222), 4909 E University Blvd on the UTPB campus, another feather in Odessa's cultural cap. Open Tuesday to Saturday 10 am to 5 pm, Sunday 2 to 5 pm; free.

Special Events

The Tejano Super Car Show is a celebration of the low rider, held the fourth weekend of November.

Places to Stay

Camping You could get a seedy motel room for what it costs to camp at the *Midessa KOA* (☎ 915-563-2368), 4220 S County Rd, where they charge $24 for full hookups and $19 for tents. Ah, but here you get that fresh Permian Basin air, a pool, a playground, a rec room, a coin laundry and no roaches. To get to the KOA, take Exit 126 off of I-20 and drive west on the service road. For cheaper public campgrounds, see the listings for Big Spring and Monahans Sandhills state parks.

Motels Among the cheapest places in town, the *Sahara Motel* (☎ 915-332-2201), 1423 E 2nd St (Business Rte 20), has singles for $20 and doubles for $22.60. Rooms appeared OK for the price, but we did set one roach a-scurryin' when we pulled back the drapes. The *Villa West Inn* (☎ 915-335-5055), 300 I-20 W, seemed better kept with rooms for $26/33. Nearby at 200 I-20 E is *Motel 6* (☎ 915-333-4025), with a pool, coin laundry and rooms for about $30/34 in summer, a bit lower in winter. *Odessa Motor Inn* (☎ 915-332-7341), 2021 E 2nd St, has two older rooms for $27, but most go for $35. *Rodeway Inn* (☎ 915-333-1528), 2505 E 2nd St, is a cut above the other places in this category, with in-room coffee, hairdryers and a free continental breakfast. Rooms here run $34/38.

Radisson Hotel & Conference Center (☎ 915-368-5885, fax 915-362-8958), 5200 E University Blvd, charges $62 single or double occupancy. Amenities include a pool and passes to a local racquetball club. *Holiday Inn Centre & Suites* (☎ 915-362-2311), 6201 E Business 20, has an indoor-outdoor pool, miniature golf and rooms starting at $66/76.

B&Bs *Mellie Van Horn's: A Historic Inn* (☎ 915-337-3000), 903 N Sam Houston Ave, began in 1938 as a boarding house for teachers, built during a time when Odessa had a hard time getting instructors because there was nowhere for them to live. Now restored, it has 16 rooms, each with a private bathroom. Rates range from $69 to $99.

Places to Eat

The *Barn Door* (☎ 915-337-4142), 2140 N Grant Ave, has been serving Odessa's best steaks ($10 to $22) for more than 30 years. The restaurant incorporates the old railroad depot from Pecos, moved to this site in 1972. Closed Sunday.

Dos Amigos (☎ 915-368-7556), at 2820 County Rd W (it's actually located along Golder Ave north of 42nd St), isn't just a restaurant – it's an entertainment emporium, with bull-riding and live music. Beef fajitas ($5.50) are the most popular item on the menu; inexpensive nachos, burritos, tacos, enchiladas and burgers round out your choices.

Jorge's (☎ 915-550-7101), 2151 E 42nd St, has good carne guisada ($8). The name of the *Tex-Mex Deli* (☎ 915-337-3354), 503 N Alleghaney Ave across from Medical Center Hospital, doesn't tell the whole story. It serves Indian food too, with a price range of $3 to $6.

Odessa isn't the sort of spot where you'd expect to find a restaurant like *Yana 615* (☎ 915-332-4305), 615 N Sam Houston Ave. Elegant lunches are served Sunday through Friday. The rosemary-seasoned orange roughy in a lemon-caper sauce is $9; other entrées run $6 to $9. Leave room for dessert; there are usually close to a dozen delectable choices.

Entertainment

The aforementioned *Dos Amigos* (☎ 915-368-7556) has long been the happening place in Odessa, with big-name country, Tejano or alternative concerts several times monthly and bull-riding every other Sunday afternoon nearly year-round. *Music City Mall* (☎ *915-550-2483*), 4101 E 42nd St, also doubles as an entertainment venue with some sort of live entertainment every day. In addition to the Great Globe of the Southwest, the *Permian Playhouse* (☎ *915-362-2329*), 310 W 42nd St, presents live community theater.

Spectator Sports
The Odessa Jackalopes (☎ 915-552-7825) play professional hockey at the Ector County Coliseum, 3800 E 42nd St.

Getting There & Away
Odessa is about 12 miles west of Midland International Airport (see above). The Greyhound/Trailways bus terminal (☎ 915-332-5711) is at 2624 E 8th St, with fares and schedules similar to those in Midland. Odessa has different cab companies than Midland, and rates are a bit higher. City Cab (☎ 915-337-5501) charges $1.85 flagfall and $1.50 per mile. A cab from the Midland airport to a hotel on Odessa's east side would run about $14.

AROUND MIDLAND-ODESSA
Odessa Meteor Crater
With a diameter of about 550 feet, this is the second-largest landmark of its kind in the US (though it's laughably small compared to the biggest crater, at Winslow, Arizona, which measures 4150 feet across). This crater, created 20,000 to 30,000 years ago, is 10 miles west of Odessa via Business Rte 20. There's a self-guided tour and a picnic area.

Monahans Sandhills State Park
These sand dunes offer 3840 acres of surfing and sledding fun, with toboggan and disk rentals available onsite. A nature center includes exhibits on the area's flora and fauna, complete with a large viewing window where visitors can watch birds and animals eat, drink and play. A 24-site campground has tent and RV spots starting at $7 and rest rooms with showers. The park (☎ 915-943-2092) is about a half-hour west of Odessa via I-20 and Park Rd 41.

Big Spring
The relentlessly flat Permian Basin landscape starts to show signs of a change 40 miles east of Midland. Big Spring is on the edge of the Caprock Escarpment, the defining topographical feature of the Texas Panhandle. The spring for which the town took its name sits in Comanche Trail Park, and nearby Big Spring State Park (☎ 915-263-4931) has a new campground, hiking trails, a prairie-dog town and scenic drive. It's open daily 8 am to 8 pm; $2 entrance fee, $6 per person to camp.

Panhandle Plains

The Panhandle Plains region of Texas may be the one that most typifies the state to outsiders. This is a land of sprawling cattle ranches and a place where people can still make a living

Highlights

- Driving the wide-open spaces (except during an ice and wind storm)
- Discovering an unexpected jazz scene in San Angelo
- Savoring chicken-fried steak at the Sutton County Steakhouse in Sonora
- Viewing the world-class collection at Albany's Old Jail Art Center
- Visiting Buddy Holly's grave in Lubbock
- Kicking back in Quitaque and Turkey, the Panhandle antitheses of Dallas-Fort Worth
- Watching the sunset at Caprock Canyons State Park
- Strolling through time at the Panhandle-Plains Historical Museum in Canyon
- Making a pilgrimage to the Cadillac Ranch in Amarillo
- Picking up an ancient stone tool at the federally protected Alibates Flint Quarries

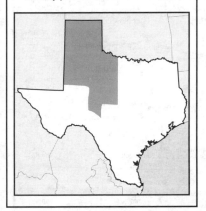

on the back of a horse. Its landscape seems endlessly flat, punctuated only by utility poles and windmills, until a vast canyon materializes almost miragelike to play tricks on the horizon.

When Spanish conquistador Francisco Vázquez de Coronado traversed the region back in 1541, he reportedly drove stakes into the earth to help him retrace his route (since natural landmarks were few). This is one explanation for how the Texas Panhandle became known as the Llano Estacado, or staked plain.

The Panhandle Plains' attractions are primarily outdoors, and principally in the canyon lands formed by eroding caprock – the layer of caliche, marl, chalk and gravel that lies beneath the plains. At such places as Palo Duro Canyon and Caprock Canyons state parks, travelers enjoy hiking, horseback riding, mountain biking, camping and sightseeing amid classic Western scenery. There's also good boating near San Angelo and at Lake Meredith National Recreation Area, north of Amarillo. And whereas none of the region's cities and towns qualify as major destinations, several (notably Lubbock and the small towns of Canyon and Quitaque and Turkey) are worth a visit of a weekend or more.

The scope and scale of the region make the Panhandle Plains a place where people tend to think big, but some of the area's purest pleasures are in its small details: the scent of sage after a rainfall, the presence of a flint quarry plied by Texas' first inhabitants thousands of years ago or the wistful love songs written by young troubadours whose legacies ultimately reached far beyond the Texas Plains.

SAN ANGELO
Population 93,314
Situated on the fringes of the Hill Country, serving as home to a well-endowed state university and blessed with an in-town river (the Concho), San Angelo feels just a

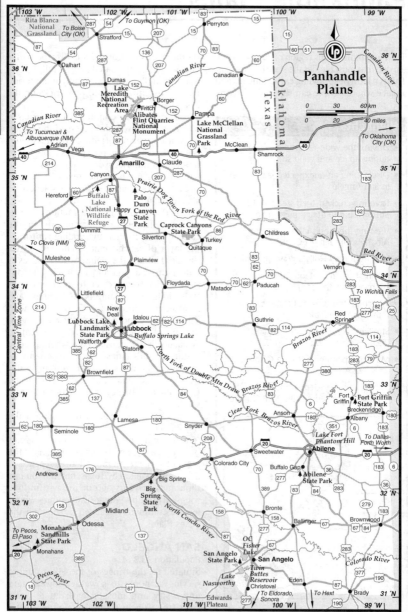

little bit like Austin or San Antonio. But because it has neither the name recognition nor the population heft of its big cousins, San Angelo makes relatively few travelers' itineraries. Those who do come here will find a city that is large enough to be interesting yet small enough to be easily digested, along with genuinely friendly people who will go out of their way to make you welcome.

The city sits between two sizable lakes, OC Fisher and Nasworthy, which make it a favorite with folks who enjoy boating, fishing and other fun on the water.

Orientation
Located just a bit west of Texas' geographical center, San Angelo is at the intersection of US 67 (which runs west to the Big Bend gateways of Fort Stockton and Alpine and east to Dallas), US 87 (which streaks north through Big Spring, Lubbock and Amarillo and southeast to San Antonio) and US 277 (with Del Rio to the south and Abilene to the north).

Within San Angelo, US 87 becomes Bryant Blvd, which – along with Chadbourne St – is the city's main north-south road, dividing nearby addresses east and west. Harris Ave, an east-west street that runs through downtown, divides addresses north and south. The downtown area is mainly east of Bryant Blvd along Beauregard, Twohig and Concho Aves. Sherwood Way and Knickerbocker Rd are main arteries in the southwest part of town, which is where both Angelo State University and the city's principal shopping areas are located. Knickerbocker Rd continues out southwest to Mathis Field, the local airport, which is also called San Angelo Regional Airport.

Information
Tourist Offices San Angelo's Convention and Visitors' Bureau (☎ 915-653-1206, fax 915-658-1110, 800-375-1206, www.sanangelo-tx .com), is at 500 Rio Concho Drive (Concho Ave turns into Rio Concho Drive east of downtown). With two weeks' notice, the visitors' center can offer personal guides to help you see the sights in San Angelo. Cost is $7 per hour if you provide the vehicle and $13 per hour if the guide provides transportation or drives a lead car.

Money NationsBank (☎ 915-653-2265) is downtown at 337 W Twohig Ave.

Post & Communications The central post office (☎ 915-659-7700), 1 N Abe St, is open Monday to Friday 8 am to 5:30 pm, Saturday 9 am to 4:30 pm. Address poste restante to General Delivery, San Angelo, TX 76902. Private mailboxes are available at Shipping Point (☎ 915-942-7082), at 1300 W Beauregard Ave.

Media The *San Angelo Standard-Times*, the local daily, sells on newsstands for 50¢ and $1.50 Sunday. Its print edition is supplemented online at www.texaswest.com/standard-times/news/daily.htm.

Austin's NPR affiliate, KUTX, is heard at 90.1 FM. For news, talk and sports, tune to KKSA at 1260 AM. Other stations include KYZZ 100.1 FM, which plays Tejano with a country twist, and classic rock on KWFR at 101.9 FM.

Bookstores The Cactus Book Shop (☎ 915-659-3788), 208 S Oakes St, carries mostly used books, but it does have a good selection of new Texana titles. The biggest bookstores in town are the usual suspects: a Hastings Books (☎ 915-949-9401) in the Southwest Shopping Plaza, 3552 Knickerbocker Rd, and a Waldenbooks (☎ 915-949-7040) in the Sunset Mall.

Libraries The main branch of the Tom Green County Public Library (☎ 915-655-7321), 113 W Beauregard Ave, is open Monday to Thursday 9 am to 9 pm, Friday 9 am to 6 pm and Saturday from 9 am to 5 pm. Angelo State University's Porter Henderson Library (☎ 915-942-2222) is open when school is in session Monday through Thursday 7:45 am to midnight, Friday 7:45 am to 6 pm, Saturday 9 am to 6 pm and Sunday 1 to 10 pm.

Campuses About 6200 students work toward getting their degrees at Angelo State

University (☎ 915-942-2041), which maintains its 286-acre campus on the southwest side of San Angelo, south of W Ave N and north of Knickerbocker Rd. ASU isn't as much of a presence in San Angelo as, say, Texas Tech is in Lubbock, but it still enriches the city with educational and cultural opportunities.

Laundry Have a beer and shoot some pool while doing laundry at the Scrub Pub (☎ 915-942-7093), in the University Plaza, corner of W Ave N and Johnson St. (The official address is 2408 Vanderventer Ave.) This place is open late most nights, with live rock bands on many Fridays and Saturdays. If bars aren't your scene, you can still do two things at once at Wash Pot Cleaning Center & Car Wash (☎ 915-949-7777), 2105 W Ave N.

Medical Services Shannon Medical Center has a minor emergency center (☎ 915-657-5161) on its Memorial Campus, at 120 E Harris Ave, and a full-scale ER (☎ 915-659-7111) on its St John's Campus, 2018 Pulliam St. The other big hospital in town is Columbia Medical Center (☎ 915-949-9511, 800-265-8624), 3501 Knickerbocker Rd.

Emergency The suicide prevention line is ☎ 915-653-5933, and the rape crisis hot line is ☎ 915-658-8888.

Fort Concho National Historic Landmark

No matter how many forts you've seen in your Texas travels, Fort Concho National Historic Landmark (☎ 915-657-4441) at 630 S Oakes St is worth a stop. Many folks claim it's the best-preserved western frontier fort in the US, and while that's a hard claim to authenticate, a Fort Concho visit will have you feeling like you've gone back in time.

Designed to protect settlers and people moving west on the overland trails, the fort went up in 1867 on the fringes of the Texas frontier and saw service until 1889. By the time it closed, a town was growing up around the fort, and the military buildings were quickly reclaimed for civilian use. By 1930, local preservationists had begun buying back the structures.

The city now owns nearly all the buildings on the fort grounds. Among the most interesting are the Headquarters Building, which includes the **Fort Concho Museum**, and the **Post Hospital** – a reconstructed building that is home to the Robert Wood Johnson Museum of Frontier Medicine.

Fort Concho is open Tuesday to Saturday 10 am to 5 pm and Sunday 1 to 5 pm. Admission is $2 for adults and $1.25 for students. If you can, stop in between September and May on a weekday morning, when you might catch a session of 'Frontier School,' in which San Angelo-area schoolchildren pretend they are 19th-century pupils, learning their lessons from McGuffey Readers and working out math problems on the chalkboard. Visitors are welcome to watch if classes are in session.

On the other hand, weekend visitors may be more likely to run into a corps of reenactments that involve sleeping in the barracks and drilling on the parade grounds. There are plenty of special events here, too, such as Black History Month exhibits during February, Frontier Day the third weekend in June and Christmas at Old Fort Concho on the first weekend in December.

The Fort Concho grounds also include the **EH Danner Museum of Telephony**, with displays of more than a hundred antique phones, telephone directories dating back to the 19th century and a 1910 switchboard. Hours are the same as for the fort.

El Paseo de Santa Angela

Santa Angela was San Angelo's original name, and El Paseo de Santa Angela marks the route that soldiers stationed at Fort Concho once used to visit the wanton town in its heyday. In 1870, the post surgeon at the fort wrote that 'the village across the Concho… is attaining an unenviable distinction from the numerous murders committed there… Over 100 murders have taken place in the radius of 10 miles.' And then there were the 35 bordellos and saloons that lined Santa Angela's sidewalks.

Today's El Paseo opened in 1995 as a heritage trail and recreational pathway; it crosses paths downtown with the River

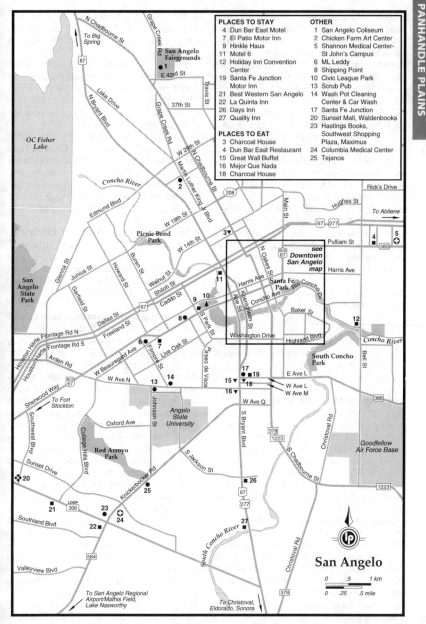

PLACES TO STAY
4 Dun Bar East Motel
7 El Patio Motor Inn
9 Hinkle Haus
11 Motel 6
12 Holiday Inn Convention Center
19 Santa Fe Junction Motor Inn
21 Best Western San Angelo
22 La Quinta Inn
26 Days Inn
27 Quality Inn

PLACES TO EAT
3 Charcoal House
4 Dun Bar East Restaurant
15 Great Wall Buffet
16 Mejor Que Nada
18 Charcoal House

OTHER
1 San Angelo Coliseum
2 Chicken Farm Art Center
5 Shannon Medical Center-St John's Campus
6 ML Leddy
8 Shipping Point
10 Civic League Park
13 Scrub Pub
14 Wash Pot Cleaning Center & Car Wash
17 Santa Fe Junction
20 Sunset Mall, Waldenbooks
23 Hastings Books, Southwest Shopping Plaza, Maximus
24 Columbia Medical Center
25 Tejanos

San Angelo

0   .5   1 km
0   .25   .5 mile

Walk development, which now winds more than 5 miles along the Concho River from just west of downtown east to Bell St. Note that a copy of the visitors' center's 'Guide to Accommodations' map picked up in late 1997 placed El Paseo de Santa Angela on the east side of S Oakes St; it's really on the west side.

El Paseo is still in its formative stage, but it's showing promise. The area's centerpiece is the winding Celebration Bridge, placed in the same spot as the wooden footbridge used by the soldiers of yore. Nearby, the *Pearl of the Conchos* statue by Jayne Charless Beck depicts a mermaid with an oversized 'pearl in her outstretched hand – see the boxed text later for more on the elusive Concho pearls, perhaps San Angelo's principal claim to fame. The bridge links the other attractions of El Paseo. The highlights are listed here, and there will probably be more by the time you read this.

RiverStage This is the site of some of San Angelo's biggest community bashes, including the San Angelo Symphony's July 4 pops concert and part of the **Cactus Jazz and Blues Festival** held early in the fall, a festival that has in the past featured performers such as trumpeter Arturo Sandoval and Marcia Ball.

San Angelo Museum of Fine Arts This museum (SAMFA; ☎ 915-658-4084, samfa@ airmail.net) is best known for its annual National Ceramic Competition, a juried event that *Ceramics Monthly* magazine once called the best of its kind in the US. It typically takes place from mid-April through May. Other recent exhibits have focused on everything from contemporary clocks to the 'Hero in World Art.'

Since its founding in 1981, SAMFA has occupied the Quartermaster Storehouse at Fort Concho. But by autumn of 1999, it should be in its new home on El Paseo de Santa Angela at 1 Love St. The new 22,000-sq-foot, $5.5 million facility was built in a partnership with Angelo State University. The design, which looks something like an outsize Conestoga wagon, is the work of Malcolm

Holzman of New York City, who previously had a hand in facilities for the Los Angeles County Museum of Art and the Virginia Museum.

Hours at the old site were Tuesday to Saturday from 10 am to 4 pm and Sunday from 1 to 4 pm. Admission was $2 for adults and $1 for students, with children younger than six admitted free. All that may change in the new quarters, so call ahead to ask.

For another look at San Angelo's visual arts scene, roll on over to the **Chicken Farm Art Center** (☎ 915-653-4936) at 2505 Martin Luther King Jr Blvd. This artists' compound, as it calls itself, is a good place to get a glimpse of some area artists at work. It's open to the public Tuesday to Saturday 10 am to 5 pm.

Concho Avenue Historic District

At the heart of downtown, the Concho Avenue Historic District is a good place to dine or shop. The most interesting section, known as Historic Block One, is between Chadbourne and Oakes Sts.

Miss Hattie's Bordello Museum One of the few museums of its kind in the US, Miss Hattie's (☎ 915-653-0989) operated as a house of pleasure at 18 E Concho Ave from its, um, erection in 1896 until the Texas Rangers shut it down 50 years later. It supposedly was the first place in San Angelo with indoor plumbing, and word has it there was an underground tunnel running between here and the old San Angelo National Bank (now the Spaghetti Western Italian Grill restaurant) a few doors down.

A guided tour takes visitors through a dozen rooms, many with original furnishings. But the stories, not the scenery, are what make the museum memorable. A baby basket in one room leads to a tale about how brothel employees had only unreliable folk remedies for birth control. The gentleman's waiting room was the scene of a wake for one regular who was run over by a wagon out front. And so on.

Tours are available continuously Thursday to Saturday noon to 5 pm. Admission is $3. The museum underwent renovations in 1998, and the hours may have changed, so call

Uncommon Pearls

San Angelo is a rootin', tootin' Texas town, but its greatest fame comes from a commodity that signifies elegance and beauty: Concho pearls.

Pearls have always been one of nature's greatest mysteries. A foreign object – say a piece of sand – gets into the shell of a mussel. The mussel can't shake the invader loose, so as protection, the animal coats the pest with layers of a fine, crystalline substance called nacre. A pearl is born. But because pearls are formed relatively rarely in nature, they are commonly cultured by humans.

The Concho River is one of the few remaining places where pearls occur naturally – and these are not just any pearls. They come in shades of pink and purple and sometimes even peach, usually in pastel but occasionally vivid shades.

The Concho pearls were discovered centuries ago by the Jumano people native to the Concho River area, who later shared their findings with Spanish explorers. But it wasn't until the late 1960s and early 1970s that Concho pearls became an industry. That's when local entrepreneurs Bart Mann and Jack Morgan heard about the pearls, started collecting Tampico pearly mussels by the bucketful and began fashioning the pearls into jewelry. Today, after decades of heavy harvesting, the Concho pearls are more rare than ever, and they can only be collected under license from the state. Even then, it's a tough racket; only one in 25 mussels contains a pearl, and maybe only one out of every 100 has a pearl considered gem quality.

Of course, the pearls can also be had for a price. Although most San Angelo jewelers carry Concho pearls, the best selection is at Legend Jewelers (☎ 915-653-0112), 16 E Concho Ave. Legend is owned by Mark Priest, who worked for Bart Mann Jewelers for 19 years. The pearls here start at $95 for a small charm and work their way up to $30,000 for a hand-strung necklace of 75 pearls. Priest says it took 17 years to collect the pearls for this particular necklace, all in shades of lavender and perfectly graduated in size. Just call it the mother of all pearl necklaces.

ahead. Just for laughs, ask for a copy of Miss Hattie's employment application when you visit. A sample question: 'Do you have any previous experience that you feel qualifies you for this position? Explain fully.'

Cactus Hotel

At 36 E Twohig Ave, the 14-story Cactus Hotel was among Conrad Hilton's first inns – probably the fourth in his empire. It was built in 1929 at a cost of $90,000, and although it no longer accepts guests, it is still something to see. The hotel's intimate lobby serves as the setting for the **Cactus Jazz Series**, which presents top performers in an environment that, aesthetically and acoustically, is simply superb. We couldn't believe our luck when

our visit to San Angelo coincided with a show by inventive guitarist Stanley Jordan. To check on upcoming shows, call ☎ 915-653-6793.

Children's Art Museum Lots of towns have children's museums, but not many have museums dedicated to introducing kids to the world of art. This one (☎ 915-659-4391), located on the first floor of the Cactus Hotel, has lots of hands-on exhibits that encourage creative problem solving and others that are just plain fun to look at (such as the recent animal alphabet sculptures by Leroy Archuleta). There's also a picture-book library and a better-than-average museum shop that specializes in toys. Museum hours are

Tuesday to Friday 1 to 5 pm, Saturday 10 am to 5 pm and Sunday 1 to 5 pm. Admission is free on Tuesday; otherwise, it's $2 for everyone older than two.

Civic League Park

Located at W Beauregard Ave and N Park St west of downtown, this park is worth a visit for its big rose gardens and the International Water Lily Collection. Among the water lilies is the largest variety in the world, the *Victoria*, with pads that can span 8 feet in diameter. Although the park has blooms day and night year-round, the lilies are best viewed March through September at midday.

San Angelo State Park

San Angelo State Park (☎ 915-949-4757) is on the western outskirts of town, accessible via FM 2288 (Loop 2288) off of W Ave N (which becomes Arden Rd west of downtown), US 87 or US 67. The 7563-acre park sprawls across four ecological zones: the High Plains to the north, the Texas Hill Country to the south, the Rolling Plains to the east and the Trans-Pecos to the west. It has more than 50 miles of trails with about half-again more under development, plus abundant water-based recreation on OC Fisher Lake.

The park is also notable for its archaeological and paleontological history. Recent findings show this area was occupied more than 10,000 years ago, first by the Paleo-American hunters of the Ice Age and then by the Comanches, who suffered their final military defeat in 1874. Before humans happened along, dinosaurs wandered the earth here (although the San Angelo tracks aren't nearly as cool as those at Dinosaur Valley State Park at Glen Rose southwest of Fort Worth – see the Dallas-Fort Worth chapter).

San Angelo State Park has a $2-per-person entrance fee. The park offers a wide variety of guided hikes to view Indian rock art, the dino tracks, an early pioneer grave site and other park features. The schedule varies, but staff will usually guide a hike on request for any group of 10 visitors or more. So if nothing is scheduled when you visit, round up some campground neighbors (camping is available here – see Places to Stay later) and ask.

Bird & Wildlife Watching Because the park is largely undeveloped (with plans to keep it that way), it's a real find for bird-watchers and other wildlife enthusiasts. The varied habitat means an abundance of bird species, about 350 at last count. Ask at the park office for a birding list. Horned lizards, armadillos and deer are among the 50 animal species.

OC Fisher Lake OC Fisher Reservoir was built by the US Army Corps of Engineers to stem frequent flooding on the North Concho River. The 5440-acre lake has four high- and low-water boat ramps, and it's a good place to fish for catfish, walleye, crappie and bass. Swimming is allowed.

Lake Nasworthy

Another big oasis, Lake Nasworthy is just south of where Knickerbocker Rd intersects with Loop 306, out near San Angelo Regional Airport/Mathis Field. Spring Creek Marina & RV Park (☎ 915-944-3850) is the area's outfitter, renting everything from cabins (see Camping in Places to Stay) to all kinds of boats and water toys. Canoes go for $10 an hour, while fishing boats with an outboard motor rent for $20 for two hours or $145 for eight hours. Other amenities include a waterfront café, grocery store, laundry, showers and game room. Anglers report good success fishing for bass and catfish in Lake Nasworthy and adjacent Twin Buttes Reservoir. Together, the two lakes cover about 11,000 acres.

San Angelo Nature Center This multisite complex (☎ 915-942-0121), with its headquarters at 7409 Knickerbocker Rd on Lake Nasworthy, features a nature trail, 260-acre wetlands and – on the opposite climactic extreme – a Xeriscape garden that shows how West Texans landscape their lawns in this semiarid environment. In June and July, it's open Wednesday to Sunday 10 am to 4 pm; the rest of the year, it's open Tuesday to Saturday noon to 5 pm; other hours vary by site. Admission is $2. Call for information and directions to satellite centers.

Jordan Llamas

Outfitter Ruth Jordan (☎ 915-651-7346), 1734 Calle Senderra, San Angelo, TX 76904, runs llama treks out of San Angelo and from her ranch near Hext, which is 80 miles southeast of town – take US 87 southeast to US 83 south to Hwy 29 east. She'll customize trips to your interest, or she can suggest sites, including San Angelo and Lost Maples state parks (see Around Kerrville in the South Central Texas chapter for information on

Lost Maples). A day trip including one meal costs $69 per person for a minimum of four people, and the cost goes down with more people.

Special Events

The International Armadillo Races are a highlight of Fiesta del Concho, San Angelo's biggest annual wingding, held the third weekend on June. Other big annual events include the Stock Show & Professional Rodeo Cowboys Association Rodeo the second week in March; the Texas Wine Festival the second week in April; the Bull Riding Fiesta in May;

PLACES TO EAT
10 Miss Hattie's Café and Saloon
18 Concho Valley Farmers Market
20 Enrique's

OTHER
1   Shannon Medical
    Center-Memorial Campus
2   Tom Green County Public Library
3   Cactus Hotel, Top of the Cactus,
    San Angelo Cultural Affairs
4   Cactus Book Shop
5   Concho Coaches
6   Post Office
7   JL Mercer & Son (bootmaker)
8   Legend Jewelers
9   Miss Hattie's Bordello Museum
11 J Wilde's
12 Eggemeyer's General Store
13 San Angelo Convention
    & Visitors' Bureau
14 NationsBank
15 Kerrville Bus Co
16 RiverStage
17 San Angelo Museum of Fine Arts
19 Santa Fe Depot
21 Fort Concho National
    Historic Landmark

**Downtown
San Angelo**

and the Fiestas Patrias, a Mexican heritage festival that takes place each September. At Christmas time, more than a million lights, give or take a thousand, line El Paseo de Santa Angela and nearby areas.

Places to Stay

Camping Seventy-two sites with water and electricity are available at **San Angelo State Park** for $9 per night, along with $4 primitive tent sites. Several cabins with one double bed and two sets of bunk beds are also available for $35 per night. Campsite and cabin reservations must be made by calling Texas Parks and Wildlife in Austin (☎ 512-389-8900).

In addition to San Angelo State Park, the **Concho Valley KOA** (☎ 915-949-3242) at 6699 Knickerbocker Rd has full hookups for $17.50 and tent sites for $12.50. **Spring Creek Marina & RV Park** (☎ 915-944-3850) on Lake Nasworthy south of town has campsites costing $11 to $13, along with $40 cabins complete with air-conditioning, cable TV and refrigerators.

Motels & Hotels Hands down, San Angelo's best budget lodging is at **Santa Fe Junction Motor Inn** (☎ 915-655-8101, 800-634-2599), 410 W Ave L , where rates are $30 for a single, $35 for a double. The nicely decorated rooms have refrigerators and large-screen TVs, and a courtyard, pool and picnic area provide pleasant surroundings outdoors, too. The only possible drawback to this place – or plus, depending on your perspective – is its location next door to the Santa Fe Junction country-and-western dance nightclub, which means things might get a bit noisy.

Another safe bet, though not as nice, is the **Dun Bar East Motel** (☎ 915-653-3366), 1728 Pulliam St. Rooms here run $25/34 for singles/doubles. It's a no-frills place, but it's clean and quiet. The on-premises Dun Bar East Restaurant (☎ 915-655-8780) is popular with area ranchers and farmers for its down-home grub and bottomless pitchers of iced tea; it's open Tuesday to Sunday 6 am to 9 pm. **Motel 6** (☎ 915-658-8061, fax 915-653-3102), 311 N Bryant Blvd, has rates of about $28/32. The **El Patio Motor Inn** (☎ 915-655-5711, fax 915-653-2717, 800-677-7735), at

1901 W Beauregard Ave, has rooms for $36/41; amenities include an outdoor pool and free local phone calls.

Quality Inn (☎ 915-653-6966), at 4205 S Bryant Blvd, sits along the Concho River, with an outdoor pool and rooms that run $44/50. The **Days Inn** (☎ 915-658-6594), at 4613 S Jackson St, has rooms for $45/55. The new **Best Western San Angelo** (☎ 915-223-1273, fax 915-942-1312), 3017 Loop 306, has a smart, Texas-inspired decor and a service-oriented staff that did everything from recommend a good nearby haircut to help us scrape the ice from our windshield after an overnight storm. Rates here are $56/61, and there's a free breakfast bar each morning. **La Quinta Inn** (☎ 915-949-0515, fax 915-944-1187), 2307 Loop 306, has rooms for $60/67. The high-rise **Holiday Inn Convention Center** (☎ 915-658-2828, fax 915-658-8741), 441 Rio Concho Drive, has the priciest rooms in town at $79/87 and a good range of amenities including an indoor pool and exercise room, all within walking distance of downtown.

B&Bs **Hinkle Haus** (☎ 915-653-1931), at 19 S Park St, has three rooms with private baths. Each rents for $65 per night with a full breakfast for two, or $55 if you prefer just coffee and juice in the morning. The Hinkle Haus is located across the street from Civic League Park, which has noted collections of roses and water lilies (see Civic League Park earlier).

Places to Eat

American At most places, 'scraps' are what end up in the dog's dish after dinner. But in San Angelo, scraps are the big draw at the **Twin Mountain Steakhouse** (☎ 915-949-4239), 6534 Hwy 67 S, a wildly popular eatery just past the western city limits, where scraps are the tender and tasty ends of beef tenderloin filets. At one time, scraps weren't even listed on the steak-house menu and diners had to be in the know to place an order. But now the secret is out. A 12oz helping big enough for sharing costs $17. The menu also includes catfish, chicken-fried steak and pasta with entrées in the $8 to $13 range. Expect a 10- to 15-minute wait on weekend nights.

Downtown at 26 E Concho Ave, *Miss Hattie's Café and Saloon* (☎ 915-653-0570) tips its hat to the bordello museum up the block, with early-20th-century decor featuring tapestries and gilt-edged picture frames. Lunch (served daily except Sunday) includes such dishes as fresh chicken salad on mixed greens with fruit ($5) and meat loaf ($6). At dinner, the still moderately priced menu moves a bit more upscale, with such fare as pork loin with an apricot-chardonnay glaze ($11) and salmon grilled in lemon-dill butter ($16).

For good, reasonably priced seafood, try *Catfish Corner*, with two locations in San Angelo: one at 3415 S Chadbourne St (☎ 915-651-4817) and the other at 1313 W Beauregard Ave (☎ 915-482-9085). Both feature all-day, all-you-can-eat down-home specials.

Chinese The *Great Wall Buffet* (☎ 915-653-1888) at 1601 S Bryant Blvd offers all-you-can-eat Chinese, salad and dessert bars for lunch ($5 per person) and dinner ($8) daily.

Fast Food All the national chains are well represented in San Angelo. Look for 'em on Southwest Blvd near Sunset Mall, on N Bryant Blvd, Knickerbocker Rd and Sherwood Way. Locals say the *Charcoal House* has some of the best burgers in town at its two locations, 1616 S Bryant Blvd (☎ 915-653-6666) and 1205 N Chadbourne St (☎ 915-657-2931).

Mexican *Mejor Que Nada* (☎ 915-655-3553), 1911 S Bryant Blvd, is one of the best-known Mexican eateries in the region. The name means 'better than nothing,' but locals say it's a lot better than that. Try the fajitas for $7 ($8 with jalapeños). The restaurant has lunch and dinner Tuesday through Saturday, with live entertainment each night.

A newer restaurant that is taking advantage of its location at 34 E Ave D in the El Paseo de Santa Angela area, *Enrique's* (☎ 915-653-8222) has year-round enclosed patio dining. Specialties include a Mexican combo platter with enchilada, taco, tamale, rice and beans for $5.50 and fajitas (beef, chicken or mixed) for $7.25; the steaks are reportedly a good bet, too. Mariachi bands perform Friday and Saturday evenings.

Markets The *Concho Valley Farmers Market* (☎ 915-651-7348, 659-1377) takes place late May through the fall every Tuesday, Thursday and Saturday morning in the marketplace on El Paseo de Santa Angela. The stalls open at 7:30 am and stay open until the goods are gone.

Entertainment
Fine Arts Local arts organizations include the *San Angelo Symphony* (☎ 915-658-5877), the *San Angelo Civic Ballet* (☎ 915-653-8877), *Angelo Civic Theatre* (☎ 915-949-4400) and the *Angelo State University Theatre* (☎ 915-942-2000). The San Angelo Cultural Affairs Council (☎ 915-653-6793) is a clearinghouse for all the arts in San Angelo. Call and ask what'll be on when you visit.

Bars & Nightclubs *Maximus* (☎ 915-949-6766), 3520 Knickerbocker Rd, is a mega club featuring several dance floors playing different types of raucous music. *Tejanos* (☎ 915-223-0686) draws Tex-Mex music fanciers to 3035 Knickerbocker Rd, while *Santa Fe Junction* (☎ 915-658-5068) packs in a lively country-and-western crowd at 1524 S Bryant Blvd. Santa Fe Junction is closed on Tuesdays.

Catch a Texas sunset and some live jazz or rhythm and blues at the *Top of the Cactus* (☎ 915-655-2582), in the Cactus Hotel at 36 E Twohig Ave, open Wednesday to Friday 5 pm to 2 am and Friday and Saturday 7 pm to 2 am. Thursday is swing night.

Star Shows The *Angelo State University Planetarium* (☎ 915-942-2136) on the university campus (see Campuses earlier) offers public programs Thursday at 8 pm and Saturday at 2 pm when ASU is in session. Cost is $3 for adults and $1.50 for students.

Spectator Sports
October through March, the San Angelo Outlaws (☎ 915-949-7825) play Western Professional Hockey League games at the San Angelo Coliseum, 50 E 43rd St. Tickets cost $6 to $15.

Shopping

The most unusual souvenir San Angelo has to offer is its multicolored Concho pearl jewelry – see the Uncommon Pearls boxed text earlier. San Angelo also is noted for its small custom boot shops, including JL Mercer & Son (☎ 915-658-7634), 224 S Chadbourne St, and ML Leddy (☎ 915-942-7655), 2200 W Beauregard Ave. Expect to pay $100 for a pair of off-the-shelf ropers and $800 or more for custom-made boots.

Concho Ave downtown has the city's most lively shopping, including women's clothing at J Wilde's (☎ 915-655-0878) at 15 E Concho Ave and everything from Texas gourmet food specialties to country-style collectibles at Eggemeyer's General Store (☎ 915-655-1166), 35 E Concho Ave. The Sunset Mall is San Angelo's largest mall, with about 85 stores including Dillard's, JC Penney, Sears, Beall's and Service Merchandise. It's at Southwest Blvd and Loop 306 in the southwest part of town.

Getting There & Away

Air San Angelo Regional Airport/Mathis Field (☎ 915-659-6409) is located south of town off of Knickerbocker Rd (Hwy 584). It's served by American Eagle, which has service to Dallas. Many people drive or catch the Concho Coaches shuttle (see Getting There & Away) to Midland-Odessa International Airport about 120 miles away – it offers more airlines and more destinations.

Bus Kerrville Bus Co (☎ 915-655-4159), at 31 W Concho Ave, provides long-distance bus service out of San Angelo. Sample fares (one way/roundtrip) and approximate one-way travel times are listed below:

to/from	trip duration	one way/ roundtrip
Dallas	5¹/₂ hours	$47/93
San Antonio	5 hours	$36/72

Austin is just about the same distance from San Angelo as it is from San Antonio, but Kerrville has no direct service to the state capital; riders must travel through San Antonio. So if Austin is your goal from San Angelo,

your best bet is probably renting a car or finding a ride share.

Car Rental cars are available at the airport from Avis (☎ 915-949-8681), Budget (☎ 915-944-4718), Hertz (☎ 915-944-1221), National (☎ 915-944-9505), and Sears (☎ 915-944-4458). Enterprise (☎ 915-658-1911) is near downtown at 815 S Koenigheim St.

Getting Around

To/From the Airport Concho Coaches (☎ 915-658-7644), 113 E Twohig Ave, offers van shuttle service to Midland-Odessa Airport Monday to Friday three times daily. Saturday and Sunday, the shuttles go once daily. Fares are $26 one way and $43 roundtrip, with courtesy pickup from area hotels. It typically costs $14 to take a cab from Mathis Field to downtown San Angelo.

Bus City Transit (☎ 915-655-9952) offers local bus service Monday to Friday from 6:30 am to 5:30 pm and Saturday from 9:30 am to 5:30 pm. Roundtrip fares are $1 for adults and 50¢ for students, senior citizens and people with handicaps. Buses leave from the Santa Fe Depot, 703 S Chadbourne St. Bus no 5 serves the southwest part of the city via Sherwood Way. Bus no 3 travels to Angelo State University before proceeding on to the southwest part of town. The San Angelo Street Railroad Co, part of the city bus operation, offers trolley service from the Santa Fe Depot. The same fares apply.

Taxi Cabs are easy to hail at the airport; elsewhere in San Angelo, call for service. All American (☎ 915-658-1982) charges $1.10 at flagfall, $1 for each additional mile plus an extra $1 fee if you're going to or from the airport. Fare into downtown from the airport is about $14 total. Checker Cab (☎ 915-655-3105) and Yellow Cab (☎ 915-655-5555) charge $1 at flagfall, $1.25 per mile and $5 per additional passenger from the airport.

AROUND SAN ANGELO
Hummer House

Christoval ('Chris-TOE-vil'), about 20 miles south of San Angelo, is one of the best birding areas in central Texas. Two miles south of Christoval, the Dan and Joann Brown Ranch (☎ 915-255-2254, fax 915-255-2463), PO Box 556, Christoval, TX 76935, has been recognized by the Texas Parks and Wildlife Dept as the state's largest hummingbird feeding area. The Browns have been nurturing the hummers for 35 years; in 1997, they went through 685lb of sugar – that's three gallons of sugar water – each day during the peak season.

A few years back, the Browns built Hummer House, a two-bedroom, two-bath native rock cottage to rent to visiting bird fanciers. Weekends between April 1 and September 30 (the peak birding season), the home rents for $150 for two the first weekend night, $125 for the second night. Two couples can share the facility for $250 per night the first weekend night, $225 the second night. Rates include a kitchen stocked with food for all meals. The cost goes down $25 per night on weekdays, and off-season rates are discounted, too. No smoking, no pets, no credit cards.

X Bar Ranch

Near Eldorado ('el-doe-RAY-do'), a town best known for its wool mills, the 7100-acre X Bar Ranch (☎ 915-853-2688, 888-853-2688, fax 915-853-3131,www.xbarranch.com) may be just what you seek if you're hankering for a real Western vacation. There's horseback riding, of course, plus stargazing, hikes to view Indian mounds, bird-watching and ranch activities. When it gets really hot, guests sometimes take a dip in the cleaned-out stock tanks.

The X Bar has a variety of accommodations that range from a rock bunkhouse that can sleep 18 people to more plush ranch-house quarters. Many guest ranches require a weeklong stay, but the X Bar welcomes travelers for as little as one night or even a day visit. The per-person rate for two is $60 to $80 per night or $455 to $525 per week, which includes daily continental breakfast, a barbecue dinner for folks staying at least a weekend, horseback riding and most other ranch activities. Various outings are available for extra charges, including day trips to

Hummingbird

the Mexican city of Acuña, Alamo Village at Brackettville, the Caverns of Sonora (see Sonora later) or the Paint Rock cliff paintings site. The ranch has well-traveled staffers who speak Spanish and Dutch.

The X Bar has about 10 miles of trails that are available to hikers and bird-watchers for a day-use fee of $4 for teens and adults and $3 for kids between three and 12 years old. Mountain bikers must pay an additional $3.50 per person for trail maintenance. Two-hour guided horseback rides cost $14, or $8 if you bring your own horse. The ranch requests a day's advance notice for horseback rides, and they're based on availability, with preference given to overnight guests.

Tent campsites are offered at $6 per adult and $4.50 for kids between three and 12 years old, including basic day-use fees. Water is available to campers, but there are no shower facilities. Call or stop at the ranch office at 5 N Divide St in Eldorado for directions and more information.

Fort McKavett State Historical Park

General William Tecumseh Sherman once called this fort along the San Saba River 'the prettiest post in Texas.' Today, Fort McKavett State Historical Park (☎ 915-396-2358) preserves the renovated and ruined remains of a Texas outpost that was not only scenic but of key strategic importance.

Fort McKavett was established by the Eighth Infantry of the US Army in 1852 as a bulwark against Comanche and Apache raids and to offer protection to travelers on the Upper El Paso Rd, a principal passage to California during the gold rush. The fort was built from limestone and of oak and pecan wood native to the area, as well as from lumber sent from San Antonio. At first, the site was known simply as Camp San Saba, but it was later renamed for Captain Henry McKavett, an Eighth Infantry officer killed in the Mexican War of 1846-48. Fort Mc-Kavett was abandoned in 1859 as both Indian and emigrant activity slowed, but it was reestablished in 1868 by units of the US Army's Fourth Calvary. The fort saw its peak in the mid-1870s, when it housed more than 400 troops and many civilians.

Troops from Fort McKavett took part in most of the major campaigns against Native Americans on the Texas frontier. But by the late 1870s, the outpost's importance had declined again, and it was closed in 1883. Like Fort Concho in San Angelo, its buildings were quickly put to use by settlers in the area, so Fort McKavett has remained well preserved. It was designated a Texas state historic site in 1968.

Begin your visit to the fort with a stop in the old post hospital, which now serves as an interpretive center. Pick up a copy of the $1 'Walking Guide to Fort McKavett State Historical Park' and make your way around the grounds. There are 25 buildings, many of them fully restored, others in ruins. You can also have a picnic (bring your own food; none is for sale here) and take a stroll on the half-mile interpretive trail to the military lime kiln and Government Springs.

Fort fanciers should visit Fort McKavett, of course, but so will photographers. The ruins here are among the most striking in Texas, and the rolling topography of the surrounding hills adds another dimension to photos. Late afternoon is probably the best time to capture good images.

Fort McKavett has minimal staffing most of the year, but the self-guiding tour booklet is excellent. An annual Living History Day typically takes place on the third weekend in March, but call ahead because this is subject to change. Late March through early May, the park is usually carpeted in bluebonnets, the Texas state flower, and many other wild spring blossoms. After-hours, Fort McKavett is considered excellent for stargazing; park staff say the Johnson Space Center Astronomical Society from Houston, which includes many NASA employees, makes twice-yearly treks to the site for star parties. These are open to the public, so call ahead for dates if you'd like to rub elbows with some star fanciers who really know their stuff.

Fort McKavett is located on FM 864 about 75 miles southeast of San Angelo. Park hours are 8 am to 5 pm daily except December 25, when it's closed. Admission is $2 for adults and $1 for kids six and older, with children younger than that admitted free.

Sonora
Population 3300

Situated on the western slope of the Edwards Plateau (just southwest of Christoval), Sonora is best known for its nearby namesake caverns. Only about 3000 people live here, but because Sonora is at the junction of I-10 and US 277, it makes a logical stopping point for travelers on either route.

Texas bluebonnet

Caverns of Sonora Unlike many other cavern complexes in North America, the Caverns of Sonora (☎ 915-387-3105) remain a work in progress. So while, for example, Carlsbad Caverns in New Mexico are only about 2% active, the Caverns of Sonora are still about 95% active. About 7 miles of the underground network have been explored; of these, about 2 miles are now accessible to the public.

Visitors to the caverns have a choice of three tours. The Crystal Palace tour ($9 for adults, $7 for children four to 11) takes about 45 minutes and covers three-quarters of a mile, with 232 steps, to a depth of 130 feet. The Horseshoe Lake tour ($12 for adults, $9.25 for kids) is 1¼ miles long and runs for about 75 minutes, reaching a depth of 155 feet underground, with 362 steps. A combination of both tours is offered, too; it takes 2½ hours (including a break) and has 594 steps. It costs $17 for adults and $13 for children. Kids younger than four are admitted to tours, but the longer treks may not be suitable for preschoolers.

Early in each tour, guides explain how the caverns' original 17-inch natural entrance was discovered (by a ranch hand's dog) and how early explorers inched their way along dark passageways; one such route, now seen from a parallel path, dead-ended at what came to be known as Devil's Pit for its seemingly endless drop. But of course, the formations are the real attractions at Caverns of Sonora, everything from cave popcorn that resembles dirty cauliflower and the hollow 'soda straw' tubular stalactites to a delicate butterfly formation showcased at the end of every tour. Cave experts have no explanation for some of the phenomena found here, such as the cave sponge, which absorbs sound like acoustical tile. And the caverns are especially noted for their helectites, which grow horizontally (unlike stalactites, which grow down from the ceiling, or stalagmites, which grow upward).

The caverns are located 7 miles south of I-10 exit 392, which is 8 miles west of Sonora. April through September, tours are offered continuously between 8 am and 6 pm. The rest of the year, tours run between 9 am and 5 pm. The temperature inside the caverns is always about 70°F with 98% humidity. Rubber-soled shoes are recommended. The gift shop here sells some interesting stuff, including socks, sweaters and blankets made of locally produced wool and mohair.

Sonora Walking Tour Stop by the Sonora Chamber of Commerce (☎ 915-387-2880) at 707 NE Crockett Ave for a free walking tour brochure written by longtime local historian Patricia Johnson. Highlights include the handsome Sutton County Courthouse and the site where Will Carver, a member of Butch Cassidy's Hole in the Wall Gang, was shot to death in 1901.

Places to Stay & Eat The Caverns of Sonora have an RV park with $13 full hook-ups and $9 tent sites. The campground has showers, which feel great after a tour through the humid depths. The ***Holiday Host Motel*** (☎ *915-387-2531*), at 127 Loop 467, has rates of $31/34 for singles/doubles and an outdoor swimming pool. The ***Days Inn Devil's River*** (☎ *915-387-3516, fax 915-387-2854*), at 1312 N Service Rd northwest of I-10 at exit 400, has singles for $39 and doubles for $54. The motel has a pool and laundry facilities, and it's adjacent to the ***Sutton County Steakhouse*** (☎ *915-387-3833*), at 1306 N Service Rd, which serves breakfast, lunch and dinner daily. Try the superbly seasoned chicken-fried steak ($5 for a good-size small portion, $7 for the large one).

ABILENE
Population 108,476
Abilene got its start as a railroad town, springing up within weeks after the Texas & Pacific Railway tracks were laid in 1881. By 1883, Abilene was thriving, able to survive even a fire that burned about a quarter of the city during that summer. Abilene has shown its mettle in other ways, too: After the US Army closed Camp Barkeley, a WWII-era training base, in 1945, Abilenians began a drive to get a new military facility. Abilene Air Force Base – later renamed Dyess Air Force Base – was dedicated in 1956 and remains the city's largest employer.

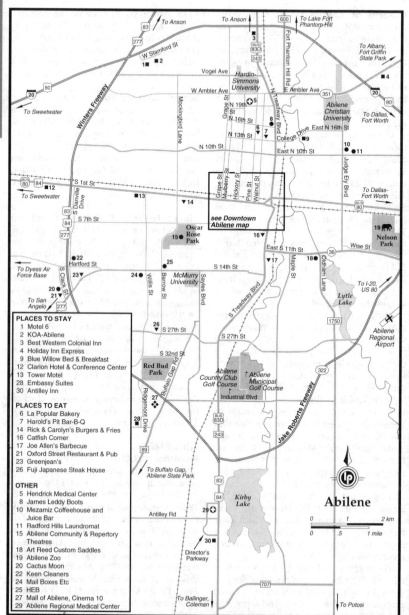

PLACES TO STAY
1 Motel 6
2 KOA-Abilene
3 Best Western Colonial Inn
4 Holiday Inn Express
5 Blue Willow Bed & Breakfast
12 Clarion Hotel & Conference Center
13 Tower Motel
28 Embassy Suites
30 Antilley Inn

PLACES TO EAT
6 La Popular Bakery
7 Harold's Pit Bar-B-Q
14 Rick & Carolyn's Burgers & Fries
16 Catfish Corner
17 Joe Allen's Barbecue
21 Oxford Street Restaurant & Pub
23 Greenjean's
26 Fuji Japanese Steak House

OTHER
5 Hendrick Medical Center
8 James Leddy Boots
10 Mezamiz Coffeehouse and Juice Bar
11 Radford Hills Laundromat
15 Abilene Community & Repertory Theatres
18 Art Reed Custom Saddles
19 Abilene Zoo
20 Cactus Moon
22 Keen Cleaners
24 Mail Boxes Etc
25 HEB
27 Mall of Abilene, Cinema 10
29 Abilene Regional Medical Center

Abilene

Abilene is also a college town, but with a twist. The three universities here all have strong Christian ties, and the majority of the 8000 students on the three campuses here are serious about religion. In fact, Abilene is frequently called the 'buckle of the Bible Belt,' and not without reason. This is a buttoned-down town where nonconformists can feel seriously out of place. Yet Abilene is able to poke fun at its image; while other Texas cities tout their wineries, the Abilene visitors bureau treats VIP guests to a bottle of Abilene Fire Water, otherwise known as spring water.

Abilene sits just south of I-20 roughly midway between Midland-Odessa to the west and Fort Worth to the east and about 150 miles from each. This part of Texas is known to locals as the 'Big Country' for the sweep of plains all around.

Orientation

Abilene is circled by US 83 on the west side of town, by Loop 322 on the southeast side and I-20 on the northeast. Treadway Blvd (Business Route 83D) is the main north-south street running through the central part of the city. Downtown falls between N 5th St and N 1st St and between Beech and Mesquite Sts west to east.

Maps The free map dispensed at the CVB is adequate for casual visits to Abilene and includes an inset of the downtown area.

Information

Tourist Offices The Abilene Convention and Visitors Bureau (☎ 915-676-2556, 800-727-7704, fax 915-676-1630, www.abilene.com/visitors) has its offices in the restored Texas & Pacific Railway Depot at 1101 N 1st St. It's open Monday to Friday 8:30 am to 5 pm, Saturday 10 am to 2 pm, Sunday 1 to 5 pm.

Money NationsBank (☎ 915-675-7500) has its main Abilene branch at 500 Chestnut St.

Post The main post office (☎ 915-738-2101), 341 Pine St downtown, is open Monday to Friday 8 am to 5 pm. Address any poste restante to General Delivery, Abilene, TX 79604. Mail Boxes Etc (☎ 915-692-9643) is at 3301 S 14th St.

Media The daily *Abilene Reporter-News* is available on area newsstands for 50¢ Monday through Saturday, for $1.50 on Sunday. The newspaper is also online at www.texnews.com. On radio, NPR is represented at 89.7 FM by KACU, a schizophrenic station that plays everything from solid jazz (Sunday nights) to lame light pop (weekday mornings). For insight into the local Christian community, tune into KGNZ at 88.1 FM. You'll hear everything from religiously inspired personal finance programs, to some good gospel music, to the occasional dose of intolerant haranguing. When it's time to change the dial, options include country on KEAN 105 FM, talk at 106.3 FM and classic rock on KROM at 92.5 FM.

Bookstores Abilene Bookstore (☎ 915-672-6657), the local independent bookseller since the 1960s, must be thriving because it recently opened a second, more convenient location at 174 Cypress St downtown. Its stock includes a good selection of books on Texas and travel; other strengths are cookbooks and children's fare. It's open Monday to Wednesday 10 am to 6 pm, Thursday to Saturday until 9 pm.

Libraries Abilene Public Library (☎ 915-677-2474) has its main branch at 202 Cedar St downtown. It's open Monday to Thursday 10 am to 9 pm (Friday and Saturday until 6 pm) and Sunday from 1 to 5 pm.

Campuses Abilene Christian University, affiliated with the Church of Christ, has about 4400 students attending classes on its campus in northeast Abilene. ACU has programs leading to 117 different bachelor's degrees, 39 master's degrees and one doctorate. Hardins-Simmons University was founded in 1891 as Simmons College, making it the oldest of Abilene's three universities. It's associated with the Baptist General Convention of Texas and has about 2300 students in 40 different academic programs on its campus in north-central Abilene. McMurry University, associated with the United Methodist Church, has 1660 students in its 40 programs, with a campus located in south-central Abilene. Cisco Junior College, Texas State Technical College and Texas A&M University's Engineering Extension Service all have a presence in Abilene, too.

Laundry These two spots come recommended: Keen Cleaners (☎ 915-695-9955) at 1301 S Danville Drive, in the city's southwest commercial area, and the Radford Hills Laundromat (☎ 915-672-6955), 1158 East N 10th St, near ACU.

Medical Services The two big hospitals in town are Hendrick Medical Center (☎ 915-670-2000), 1242 N 19th St, and Abilene Regional Medical Center (emergency department ☎ 915-691-2400 or 800-782-8428) at 6250 Hwy 83/84 at Antilley Rd.

Emergency The Crime Victim Crisis Center has a 24-hour, toll-free hot line at ☎ 915-677-7895.

Downtown Walking Tour

Abilene has a clean, compact downtown that has enjoyed a real renaissance over the past few years. For more information on the area, head for the CVB and pick up the 'Guide to Downtown Abilene,' which includes shopping and dining information as well as historic attractions, and 'Historical Walking Tour,' a pamphlet that points out 20 buildings of interest in the central city.

The Grace Museum

This fine museum complex (☎ 915-673-4587, www.abilene.com/grace), located at 102 Cypress St downtown and served by the downtown trolley (see Getting Around), includes three distinct museums housed in the former Grace Hotel, once the grandest in Abilene. The hotel, later known as the Drake, closed in the 1970s and appeared headed for demolition until local preservationists set about saving it a decade later.

The art museum features such interesting fare as *Treasures of Abilene*, a recent exhibition that showcased works from local private collections, with Henri Matisse, Joan Miró and Peter Hurd among the artists represented. The historical museum focuses on Abilene's history from 1900 through 1945. It's heavy on railroad and military memorabilia, but it doesn't shy away from touchy topics such as Abilene-area Ku Klux Klan activity. The children's museum has cool activities for the youngsters, who can do everything from experimenting with magnets to making their own television newscast on KIDD-TV.

The Grace Museum is open Tuesday to Saturday from 10 am to 5 pm (Thursday until 8:30 pm), Sunday and Monday 1 pm to 5 pm. Admission is $3 for adults, $2 for seniors and students and $1 for children younger than 12. Everyone gets in free Thursday after 5 pm.

Center for Contemporary Arts

Located in the **Grissom Building** at 220 Cypress St, this gallery (☎ 915-677-8389) features exhibits by national and regional talent in contemporary art and photography. The center also houses 13 artists' studios and the Wet Paint Shop, where their works can be purchased. The center is open Tuesday to Saturday 11 am to 5 pm, and admission is free.

Paramount Theatre

Stars twinkle and clouds drift across the velvet blue ceiling of this magical movie and performing-arts palace at 352 Cypress St. The Paramount (☎ 915-676-9620) also features such grand details as turreted Moorish towers flanking the stage and hand-blown glass chandeliers. If you can't visit the Paramount for an event (see Entertainment later), stop in weekdays from 1 to 5 pm for a self-guided tour.

Abilene Zoo

Jaguars, ocelots, elephants and giraffes are among the more than 800 animals from several hundred species making their home at the Abilene Zoo (☎ 915-676-6085), 2070 Zoo Lane, located in Nelson Park in southeast Abilene near the junction of Loop 322 and Highway 36. The zoo is most noted for the 'habi-trek' exhibits in its Discovery Center, which compare plants and animals of the

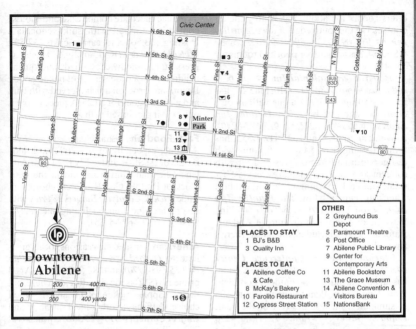

Civic Center

N 6th St

N 5th St

N 4th St

N 3rd St

N 2nd St

N 1st St

Minter Park

S 1st St

S 2nd St

S 3rd St

S 4th St

S 5th St

S 6th St

S 7th St

Downtown Abilene

0   200   400 m
0   200   400 yards

PLACES TO STAY
1 BJ's B&B
3 Quality Inn

PLACES TO EAT
4 Abilene Coffee Co & Cafe
8 McKay's Bakery
10 Farolito Restaurant
12 Cypress Street Station

OTHER
2 Greyhound Bus Depot
5 Paramount Theatre
6 Post Office
7 Abilene Public Library
9 Center for Contemporary Arts
11 Abilene Bookstore
13 The Grace Museum
14 Abilene Convention & Visitors Bureau
15 NationsBank

Southwest US and Central America to similar areas in Africa and Madagascar. Other exhibits feature aquatic animals, tropical birds and the lemurs and ring-tailed cats of the zoo's Terrestrial Trail. Late May through early September, the zoo is open Monday to Friday 9 am to 5 pm and weekends and holidays from 9 am to 7 pm. The rest of the year, hours are daily 9 am to 5 pm, except Thanksgiving, December 25 and January 1. Admission is $3 for teens and adults and $2 for children between three and 12 years old and seniors 60 and older. Strollers can be rented for $1. There's no bus service to the zoo.

Special Events
The Western Heritage Classic, held the second weekend of May, is a big rodeo featuring working cowboys from ranches across the US, along with campfire cookoffs, a Western art show, dances and more. Other big annual events include Celebrate Abilene, a downtown arts and model train festival

held the first weekend of April, and the West Texas Fair and Rodeo starting the first Friday after Labor Day.

Places to Stay
Camping Abilene State Park south of the city in Buffalo Gap (see Around Abilene) is the best choice for camping near town. If you need to stay closer to town, the *Abilene RV Park* (☎ 915-672-0657), 6195 I-20 E on the southeast side of exit 292B, has tent spaces for $10 and full hookup sites for $16. The *KOA-Abilene*, (☎ 915-672-3681), at 4851 W Stamford St, is pricier: $19 for tents or vans and $24 for full hookups.

Motels & Hotels The highest concentration of budget motels is along S 1st St west of downtown. *Tower Motel* (☎ 915-672-7849, fax 915-672-6597), at 3417 S 1st St, has rooms starting at $30; some with kitchenettes are available. *Motel 6* (☎ 915-672-8462, fax 915-672-3118), 4951 W Stamford St, offers rooms for about $30/35 for singles/ doubles. On the south edge of town, *Antilley Inn* (☎ *915-695-3330, 800-959-1001)*, 6550 US 83/84, has an outdoor pool and rooms for $32/41.

Best Western Colonial Inn (☎ *915-677-2683, fax 915-677-8211)*, 3210 Pine St, has rooms starting at $40/50, along with an outdoor pool and free breakfast. *Holiday Inn Express* (☎ *915-673-5271, fax 915-673-8240)*, convenient to I-20 at 1625 Hwy 351, has rooms ranging from $48 to $70, some with refrigerators and microwaves and all with coffeemakers. A complimentary breakfast bar is laid out each morning in the large lobby. Checkout can be slow. The *Quality Inn* (☎ *915-676-0222, fax 915-676-0513)*, 505 Pine St, is the only motel in downtown Abilene. Rates are $53/63, including breakfast. There's an outdoor pool.

Clarion Hotel & Conference Center (☎ *915-695-2150, 800-592-4466)*, 5403 S 1st St, has an atrium, indoor and outdoor pools and Ping-Pong tables. Plan to spend $65 to $85 in summer, a bit less the rest of the year. *Embassy Suites* (☎ *915-698-1234)*, at 4250 Ridgemont Drive, has rooms starting at about $85. Amenities include an indoor pool, whirlpool and sauna, and there are refrigerators, microwaves and coffeemakers in all rooms.

B&Bs Travelers seeking love, joy, peace or patience may want to check into the rooms bearing those names at *BJ's B&B* (☎ *915-675-5855, 800-675-5855)*, 508 Mulberry St, in downtown Abilene. Rates are $65 to $75. The *Blue Willow Bed & Breakfast* (☎ *915-677-8420)*, 435 College Drive near ACU, has a two-story studio apartment with fireplace for $85.

Places to Eat

Bakeries Downtown Abilene has two good bakery-coffeehouses in the European tradition. *Abilene Coffee Co & Cafe* (☎ *915-677-1188)*, at 421 Pine St, is open for breakfast, lunch and dinner Monday through Saturday. At breakfast, try the early bird sandwich – ham, eggs and cheese on a grilled bagel for $2.25. Desserts include the multilayered

incredible chocolate bombe cake-and-mousse confection topped with spiky chocolate frosting ($3.50) and carrot cake ($2.55). *McKay's Bakery* (☎ *915-672-9737)*, 266 Cypress St, has sandwiches, salads and quiche in addition to a wide variety of baked goods. Bacon-and-broccoli quiche served with fruit and a muffin goes for $4.25. A piece of pie is only 75¢ if purchased with a meal.

Fast Food The usual chains are all over Abilene, especially in the 3000 and 4000 blocks of 1st St, on Judge Ely Blvd near Abilene Christian University and in the 4000 block of Buffalo Gap Rd. Local choices include *Rick & Carolyn's Burgers & Fries*, with several area locations, including one at 2801 S 1st St (☎ *915-677-5335)*.

American For special occasions, locals gravitate to *Oxford Street Restaurant & Pub* (☎ *915-695-1770)* at 1882 S Clack St. Aged prime rib ($12) is the signature dish here, but the pineapple chicken ($9) is another good choice. Catfish is another local specialty, and *Catfish Corner* (☎ *915-672-3620)*, which is at 780 S Treadway Blvd, serves some of the best, with an all-day, all-you-can-eat special for $6.50. Catfish Corner originated here but now has two outlets in San Angelo, too. *Greenjean's* (☎ *915-692-1772)*, 4646 S 14th St, has dinner buffets for $8.

Barbecue *Harold's Pit Bar-B-Q* (☎ *915-672-4451)*, 1305 Walnut St, has been serving hungry Abilenians for more than 40 years. Try the beef and sausage plate for $5.50. Harold's is open Monday, Tuesday, Thursday and Friday 11 am to 6:30 pm, Wednesday 11 am to 2 pm and Saturday 11 am to 5 pm. It's closed Sunday. *Joe Allen's Barbecue* (☎ *915-672-6082)*, 1233 S Treadway Blvd, is another local favorite featuring mesquitegrilled rib-eye steaks cut to order.

Mexican North of downtown, *La Popular Bakery* (☎ *915-672-1570)*, 1465 Pine St, sells heaps of its breakfast burritos, especially the carne guisada – beef tips cooked in a spicy sauce. La Popular also makes its own tortillas and pan dulce. *Farolito Restaurant*

(☎ 915-672-0002), 209 Cottonwood St, has been in business since 1939 and serves lunch and dinner daily. It has $4.25 lunch specials and platters (the usual taco, enchilada and tamale combos) that cost $5 to $7. People rave about the hot sauce.

Eclectic *Cypress Street Station* (☎ 915-676-3463) at 158 Cypress St is considered by many locals the best restaurant in Abilene. It's certainly among the classiest, outfitted in dark woods and white linen in a spacious, no-smoking environment. Lunch selections include pasta carbonara, grilled chicken fajita salad or Thai chicken salad (each $7). At dinner, mesquite-smoked tenderloin medallions go for $20.50, and three-cheese chicken runs $20. Desserts include a wide array of cheesecakes, bourbon-pecan delight ($5) and bananas Foster prepared tableside ($7). Cypress Street Station is open for lunch and dinner Monday through Saturday, with a piano player setting the mood on Friday and Saturday evenings.

Japanese *Fuji Japanese Steak House* (☎ 915-695-9233), at 3110 S 27th St in the Brookhollow Center, has sushi on weekends. Locals love the $28 dinner for two, which includes steak, shrimp, chicken, fried rice, soup and salad.

Markets The *HEB* supermarket (☎ 915-690-5000), at 1345 Barrow St in southwest Abilene, has everything from a bakery to Chinese and Italian specialty shops.

Entertainment

Artwalk On the second Thursday of each month, downtown Abilene stages an Artwalk from 5 to 8:30 pm. It's an evening for folks to stroll around the museums and galleries, view new exhibits at about a dozen participating establishments, hear some live music and maybe take in the art film series at the Paramount Theatre. Admission is free, except for the Paramount films. For more information, call ☎ 915-677-8389.

Bars & Nightclubs If you're looking for a fun night out in Abilene, your best bet is

probably *Cactus Moon* (☎ 915-695-0781), 1850 S Clack St, which has several clubs under one roof.

Fine Arts The *Abilene Philharmonic* (☎ 915-677-6710, 800-460-0610) plays a nine-concert series at the Civic Center, at 1100 N 6th St. Two local theater companies – the *Abilene Community Theatre* (☎ 915-673-6271) and *Abilene Repertory Theatre* (☎ 915-672-9991) – share a stage in Oscar Rose Park at 801 S Mockingbird Blvd. The *Abilene Cultural Affairs Council* (☎ 915-677-1161) presents two annual performing arts series featuring touring acts.

Cinema *Cinema 10* (☎ 915-695-2122) at the Mall of Abilene has the most screens in town, all showing first-run films. Shows before 6 pm cost $4. The *Paramount Theatre* (☎ 915-676-9620), 352 Cypress St, screens classic films on weekends, with show times at 8 pm on Friday and 2 and 8 pm on Saturday, plus a monthly art film on the second Thursday of the month at 7 pm.

Coffeehouses *Mezamiz Coffeehouse and Juice Bar* (☎ 915-676-8150), a block away from ACU at 1059 Judge Ely Blvd, has eclectic live music most Saturdays and some Fridays starting about 8:30 pm. Abilene Coffee Co & Cafe (see Places to Eat earlier) also has performers most Friday and Saturdays from 9 to 11 pm.

Spectator Sports

The Abilene Prairie Dogs (☎ 915-673-7364) play Texas-Louisiana League professional baseball from late May through August at Abilene Christian University's Crutcher Scott Field.

Shopping

Abilene has several noted small manufacturers of custom-made Western gear. James Leddy Boots (☎ 915-677-7811), 1602 N Treadway Blvd, has prices ranging from $450 to $3500 and is open Monday to Friday 8:30 am to 5 pm. Art Reed Custom Saddles (☎ 915-677-4572), 361 East S 11th St, has a month-long waiting list for saddles that start at about $1500. Stop in Monday to Friday from 9 am to 5 pm.

Hickory St between 5th and 8th Sts near downtown Abilene has a good selection of antique and gift shops selling everything from fudge to stained glass to children's clothing. The Mall of Abilene (☎ 915-698-4351) is located in the southwest part of town at 4310 Buffalo Gap Rd, served by bus Nos 9 and 10.

Getting There & Away
Air Abilene Regional Airport (☎ 915-676-6367) is southeast of town along Hwy 36. It is served by American Eagle.

Bus Greyhound (☎ 915-677-8127) runs out of a terminal at 535 Cedar St downtown. Sample fares and approximate one-way travel times are listed below.

to/from	trip duration	one way/ roundtrip
Austin	8 hours	$32/64
Dallas	3 to 4 hours	$38/76
Houston	11 hours	$70/138

Car Car rentals are available at the airport from Budget (☎ 915-677-7777), Enterprise (☎ 915-690-9338), Hertz (☎ 915-673-6774) and National (☎ 915-673-2553).

Getting Around
To/From the Airport Abilene Regional Airport is southeast of the city center and accessible from downtown via East S 11th St, which becomes Hwy 36. Public buses do not service the airport, so if your'e traveling sans auto, you'll have to take a taxi (fare is around $10 one-way). Some of the larger hotels offer shuttle service to the airport – be sure to ask when checking in or making reservations.

Bus CityLink (☎ 915-676-6287) offers local public transportation. Bus fares are 75¢ for adults, 55¢ for students and 35¢ for senior citizens and people with disabilities. CityLink also runs a free trolley that courses the downtown area, with stops including the east side of the Civic Center along Pine St and

CityLink's transfer station at 1189 S 2nd St (at Sycamore), among others. The trolley runs area weekdays 7:15 am to 5:45 pm.

Taxi Cab rates in Abilene are $3 at flagfall and $1.15 per mile. Companies include A-1 Yellow Checker Cab (☎ 915-677-2446), Abilene Yellow Cab (☎ 915-677-4334) and Classic Cab (☎ 915-677-8294).

AROUND ABILENE
Buffalo Gap
Population fewer than 500
Bison used this natural pass in the Callahan Divide for many centuries; later on, it became an outpost on the Dodge Cattle Trail. Today's Buffalo Gap, a village of not quite 500 people, is an easy and enjoyable day trip 14 miles southwest of Abilene via FM 89.

Buffalo Gap Historic Village Nineteen buildings, many of them more than a century old, make up this attraction at the corner of William and Elm Sts. The main office and entrance are at 133 William St (☎ 915-572-3365). Buffalo Gap was named the Taylor County seat in 1878, an honor that has since moved to Abilene. But the old courthouse still stands, along with a log cabin that's the oldest structure in the area, a train station, church, doctor's office, cabinet mill, blacksmith shop, filling station and more. The village is open March 15 through September 15; hours are Monday to Saturday 10 am to 6 pm and Sunday noon to 6 pm. The rest of the year, the village is open Friday and Saturday 10 am to 5 pm and Sunday noon to 5 pm. Admission is $4 for adults, $3 for seniors 65 and older, $1.75 for children between six and 18 years old and free for kids five and younger.

Places to Eat Lots of Abilenians make the drive to Buffalo Gap to eat. The *Perini Ranch Steak House* (☎ 915-572-3339) on FM 89 W is frequently named among Texas' best steak houses. Try the rib-eye steak at $15 or the ranch-roast prime rib, only served Friday and Saturday nights ($12 for the small cut, $17 for the Texas cut). The restaurant is open Friday to Sunday for lunch and Wednesday to Sunday for dinner.

Franklin Mountains landscape

Sunset from Indian Cliffs Ranch, near El Paso

The view of downtown El Paso from Scenic Drive

Giant dagger yucca

Strawberry hedgehog cactus

Indian blanket

Whooping cranes in Aransas National Wildlife Refuge

White-tailed deer, Brazos Bend State Park

Prickly pear cactus

Alligator, Brazos Bend State Park

Ocotillo

Palo Duro Canyon State Park, in the Panhandle Plains

Cattle pens at the Amarillo Livestock Auction

Amarillo's Cadillac Ranch

The Butterfly, a delicate helectite in the Caverns of Sonora

Abilene State Park

Four miles southwest of Buffalo Gap, the 621-acre Abilene State Park (☎ 915-572-3204) sits along Elm Creek amid 4000 native pecan trees. Comanches often stayed here in centuries past, and the park remains a popular campground and recreation area. Attractions include hiking, birding and wildlife viewing (armadillos, white-tailed deer, Mississippi kite, hummingbirds and more), fishing, a swimming pool, playground and game area with room for sand volleyball, baseball, horseshoes and basketball.

The campground has 104 campsites priced from $6 to $11 per night, plus eight screened shelters available at $16 per night. All must be reserved through the state park reservation number, ☎ 512-389-8900. Camping fees don't include the $3-per-person day-use charge.

Fort Phantom Hill

Built in 1851 along the Clear Fork of the Brazos River, Fort Phantom Hill was among the outposts constructed to protect settlers on the Texas frontier. It was abandoned just three years later due to lack of action and was burned shortly after – no one knows by whom. Starting in 1858, the remaining portions of the fort were used as a stop on the Southern Overland Mail-Butterfield Trail route, and it later also saw service in the Civil War and as a subpost of Fort Griffin near Albany. A town near the fort had a similar fate – by 1880, 546 people had moved to the settlement, but a letter written to the *San Antonio Daily Express* in 1892 indicated the town had dwindled to 'one hotel, one saloon, one general store, one blacksmith shop and 10,000 prairie dogs.' Today, visitors find only a handful of buildings and about a dozen chimneys among the ruins.

Fort Phantom Hill was never officially named. At a distance, the hill on which it stands appears to rise sharply from the plains, yet once you're at the ruins, the hill seems to have vanished.

Fort Phantom Hill is on private land but it's open daily and free to the public. The grounds are 11 miles north of I-20 on FM 600. Nearby Lake Fort Phantom is popular for fishing, boating, picnicking and camping.

Albany

Population 2000

Albany ranks among the most interesting small towns in Texas. Sitting 35 miles northeast of Abilene, the Shackleford County seat of about 2000 people is a bit off the beaten path on Hwy 180 east of Hwy 351, but well worth a detour if you're traveling through this part of Texas.

Old Jail Art Center A remarkable facility, the Old Jail Art Center (☎ 915-762-2269), 201 S 2nd St, houses a collection that ranks among the Southwest's finest; included in it are ancient terra-cotta Chinese tomb figures and more recent art by such masters as Pablo Picasso, Amedeo Modigliani, Henry Moore and Grant Wood. The museum is open Tuesday to Saturday 10 am to 5 pm and Sunday 2 to 5 pm; admission is free.

Fort Griffin Fandangle Several hundred Albany townspeople get together and put on this outdoor musical Thursday through Saturday during the last two weeks of June. The *Fort Griffin Fandangle (Fandangle* for short) tells the story of the area's pioneer days, complete with a cattle drive, stagecoach chase and plenty of Old West tomfoolery. Tom Perini of the Perini Ranch in Buffalo Gap (see that section earlier in Around Abilene) comes up with his chuck wagon to serve supper before the show.

Performances take place at 8:30 pm at the Prairie Theatre a half-mile northwest of town. Tickets, priced at $5 to $15, should be purchased in advance. For tickets or more information, call ☎ 915-762-3838 or write to *Fandangle*, PO Box 155, Albany, TX 76430.

Places to Eat The *Fort Griffin General Merchandise Restaurant (☎ 915-762-3034)*, at the intersection of Hwy 283 and Hwy 180, is a top-notch steak house with tender rib-eye steaks.

Fort Griffin State Park

Fifteen miles north of Albany, this park (☎ 915-762-3592) showcases three restored buildings and the ruins of a fort that served the frontier from 1867 through 1881. Today, the park is probably best known as a principal home of the official Texas longhorn herd, portions of which have been sent to other state parks. Recreational attractions include a campground with sites priced at $7 to $12, hiking trails and fishing. You can guarantee a campsite through the state reservation line at ☎ 512-389-8900.

LUBBOCK
Population 193,565
Lubbock is a lot of things. It's the major retail and trade center for Texas' South Plains, hometown of the late, great rocker Buddy Holley and a star on the emerging Texas wine scene. But more than anything else, it is the home of Texas Tech University, the biggest college in West Texas and by far the largest employer in Lubbock. The presence of Tech, as it's known, gives Lubbock an ever-changing, always interesting scene for dining, arts and entertainment.

Francisco Vázquez de Coronado traipsed through the South Plains on his 1540 exploration of what would become the US Southwest, and archaeologists believe he probably camped at the present-day Lubbock Lake Landmark State Park and in Yellowhouse Canyon. The Comanches found the Lubbock area a good hunting ground, with abundant bison and other wildlife, yet by the late 19th century the US Army had driven the Indians from the area. The first white settlers were Quakers, and they quickly began cultivating the land. Cotton emerged as the major crop, and it still is today. The Texas Plains produce about 60% of the state's cotton crop, and Lubbock County harvests 3 million bales per year.

Orientation
Lubbock is known within Texas as the capital of the South Plains, or the southern part of the Texas Panhandle. It's also known as 'Hub City' because so many major highways meet here: I-27 from the north, US 82 from the east, US 84 from the southeast and northwest, US 87 from the south and US 62 from the southwest.

Loop 289 circles the city, making it easy to get anywhere in town within 10 or 15 minutes. The Texas Tech campus sprawls all over the city's near-northwest side but is mainly centered between 4th and 19th Sts north and south and University and Quaker Aves east and west. Motels are concentrated along Ave Q between downtown and the Tech campus and along the south side of Loop 289. The latter is also the largest shopping district. The Depot District, one of Lubbock's liveliest dining and nightlife areas, is centered on Buddy Holly Ave (formerly known as Ave H) and 19th St.

Information
Lubbock's tourism bureau (☎ 806-747-5232, 800-692-4035, www.lubbocklegends.com) sits in new digs at 1301 Broadway St.

Gay & Lesbian The best sources of information on local gay, lesbian and bisexual events are the *Texas Triangle*, a weekly gay newspaper, and the *Hub Triangle*, a newsletter online at www.geocities.com/WestHollywood/Heights/7439/. The Metropolitan Community Church (☎ 806-792-5562) at 4501 University Ave is probably the major gathering spot for gays and lesbians in Lubbock not just for its spiritual services, but also for its library and Pride Store. It's open Tuesday to Friday 9:30 am to 5:30 pm.

Money Find NationsBank locations throughout town: 1901 University Ave (☎ 806-766-2600), 916 Main St (☎ 806-766-2500) and 5144 82nd St (☎ 806-798-4900). There are ATMs all over town, and City Bank (☎ 806-785-2265), 6501 University Ave in Kmart, has Sunday banking from 1 to 5 pm. Foreign currency exchange is available at the main branch of Plains National Bank (☎ 806-795-7131) at 50th St and University Ave, but there is a $10 fee regardless of the transaction size. Many of the bigger banks, including local NationsBank branches, have no currency exchange available except to account holders.

Post & Communications The central post office (☎ 806-763-6461), 411 Ave L, is open Monday to Friday from 8:30 am to 5 pm and closed on Saturday and Sunday. This is the only post office in town that will hold mail

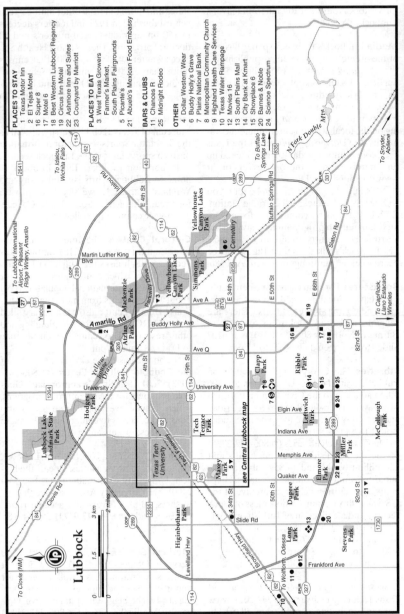

PLACES TO STAY
1 Texas Motor Inn
2 El Tejas Motel
16 Super 8
17 Motel 6
18 Best Western Lubbock Regency
19 Circus Inn Motel
22 Ashmore Inn and Suites
23 Courtyard by Marriott

PLACES TO EAT
3 West Texas Growers
Farmer's Market,
South Plains Fairgrounds
5 Picante's
21 Abuelo's Mexican Food Embassy

BARS & CLUBS
11 Chances R
25 Midnight Rodeo

OTHER
4 Dollar Western Wear
6 Buddy Holly's Grave
7 Plains National Bank
8 Metropolitan Community Church
9 Highland Health Care Services
10 Texas Water Rampage
12 Movies 16
13 South Plains Mall
14 City Bank at Kmart
15 Showplace 6
20 Barnes & Noble
24 Science Spectrum

Lubbock

To Clovis (NM)
To Wolfforth, Odessa
To Clovis, Wichita Falls
To Lubbock International Airport, Pleasant Ridge Winery, Amarillo
To Snyder, Abilene
To Buffalo Springs Lake
To CapRock, Llano Estacado Wineries

see Central Lubbock map

for visitors. Address it to General Delivery, Lubbock, TX 79408.

Media Lubbock's daily newspaper has one of the greatest names in Texas publishing – the *Avalanche-Journal* (50¢ daily, $1.50 Sunday; www.lubbockonline.com). The newspaper's Friday edition includes a guide to weekend events in town. Get a copy of the free monthly *Caprock Sun* for more reporting on the local arts and entertainment community. The *University Daily* serves the Texas Tech community. The daily can be picked up on campus, or read the online version at www.ttu.edu/~TheUD/.

NPR and classical music can be found on KOHM 89.1. The Texas Tech radio station, KTXT 88.1, can be counted on for engagingly amateurish programming heavy on the alt-rock. For country, tune into KLLL 96.3 FM. Lubbock's talk-show titan, Big Ed, can be heard weekday mornings on KRFE AM 580.

Bookstores For all its academic bent, Lubbock has no locally owned stores specializing in new general-interest books. There are religious and used bookstores galore, and Barnes & Noble (☎ 806-798-8990) is at 6707 Slide Rd. It's open daily 9 am to 11 pm.

Libraries The George and Helen Mahon Public Library (☎ 806-775-2834) is at 1306 8th St adjacent to the Civic Center. It's open Monday to Thursday 9 am to 9 pm, Friday and Saturday from 9 am to 6 pm and Sunday from 1 to 5 pm.

The Texas Tech libraries (☎ 806-742-2236) on the southeast side of campus hold about 1.3 million books and 14,859 subscriptions and offer numerous online resources. Highlights and oddities include an archive of the US war with Vietnam, a whole mess of ranch records and a collection of Turkish oral narratives. The Tech libraries are generally open Monday to Thursday 7:30 am to 1 am, Friday 7:30 am to 10 pm, Saturday 9 am to 10 pm and Sunday 11 am to 1:30 am.

Campuses About 24,000 students attend Texas Tech University (☎ 806-742-2011, www .ttu.edu), including people from all 50 US states and more than 100 other nations. Tech was established in 1925 and it offers degrees in 150 undergraduate, 100 master's and 50 doctoral programs. There's also a Health Sciences Center (☎ 806-743-1000) that enrolls more than 1300 students in its schools of medicine, nursing, allied health and biomedical sciences. The Tech campus is home to several major Lubbock attractions, too – see the Ranching Heritage Center and the Museum of Texas Tech University, as well as the Spectator Sports section for information on Tech sports, later in the Lubbock section.

In addition to Texas Tech, Lubbock is home to Lubbock Christian University and Wayland Baptist University, both private four-year schools, and South Plains College, a two-year community college.

Cultural Centers The International Cultural Center (☎ 806-742-2218), on the Texas Tech campus, houses the Office on International Affairs, which coordinates services for the university's international population (now about 1200 students from more than 100 nations). But the center also has a library filled with CD-ROMs great for trip planning and other research. The center is open Monday to Friday 8 am to 5 pm.

'Lubbock has more sky' is the motto of the **Godbold Cultural Center** (☎ 806-741-1953), 2601 19th St. It's appropriate: Godbold is known for its adventurous programs, which include everything from art exhibitions and concerts to conferences. There are also two restaurants and a gift shop.

Laundry As befits a college town, Lubbock has lots of laundry facilities. One of the biggest, University Coin Laundry (☎ 806-744-7400), 711 University Ave, has more than 60 washers, 40-plus dryers and a game room. Grubs N Suds (☎ 806-747-9274), 2918 4th St, is convenient to Tech.

Medical Services Highland Health Care Services (☎ 806-788-4180), 2412 50th St (north side entrance), is a walk-in clinic for minor illnesses and injuries, with fees starting at $49. The biggest hospital in town, University Medical Center (☎ 806-743-3111) offers complete emergency services at 602 Indiana Ave.

Emergency The poison center is at ☎ 800-764-7661; the rape crisis line is ☎ 806-763-7273. Women's Protective Service, a domestic violence hot line, is ☎ 806-747-6491.

Historic Homes & Buildings Tour

The Lubbock Heritage Society has prepared a map and brochure outlining 45 sites of architectural interest around town. Most of the notable structures are too spread out to see on foot, although the mansions along the south side of 19th St (facing the Tech campus) provide the elegant backdrop for one easy stroll of about six blocks. Ask at the Lubbock tourism bureau (☎ 806-747-5232, 800-692-4035, www.lubbocklegends.com), 1301 Broadway St, for a copy of the brochure. The bureau also has copies of 'A Guide to Lubbock's Architectural Heritage,' a booklet compiled by the city in 1993.

Buddy Holly's Hometown

Lubbock native Charles Hardin 'Buddy' Holley was just five years old when he won a local talent contest playing a toy violin. By the time he was a teen, Buddy became a regular performer on local radio in a band that blended country-and-western with rhythm and blues. But Holly (who dropped the 'e' from his name as his musical career revved up) soon became a leading pioneer of a new kind of music – rock and roll. Together with his backup band the Crickets, Holly drove to Clovis, New Mexico, in early 1957 to record a demo of a song called *That'll Be the Day*. Within months, Holly had a Top-10 record to his credit, with many more hits to follow, including *Peggy Sue*, *Not Fade Away*, *Maybe Baby*, *It's So Easy*, *Rave On*, *Fool's Paradise* and *Oh, Boy!*

Buddy Holly was among the first rock performers to write his own material, and he was also among the first to experiment with multitrack overdubbing and echo in the studio. An accomplished guitarist and pianist, he also used his voice as an instrument, with a hiccup here and falsetto there. He and the Crickets were the real deal. In Texas, they often served as warm-up act to visiting stars (including a young Elvis Presley), and when they hit it big, they were among the first white performers ever to perform at the legendary Apollo Theater in New York City's Harlem.

Sadly, Holly's career and life came to a premature end when the chartered airplane in which he was traveling on February 3, 1959, crashed near Clear Lake, Iowa. (Fellow rockers JP 'The Big Bopper' Richardson and Ritchie 'La Bamba' Valens also were onboard.) But Holly's music endured. His songs have been covered endlessly, and his style is still emulated by rockers worldwide. Holly's life was chronicled in a 1978 US film, the *Buddy Holly Story*, and he was the posthumous recipient of a 1997 Grammy Award for Lifetime Achievement.

Holly's roots in Lubbock are a major visitor attraction for the city, and a 'Buddy Holly Historical Tour' brochure is available to guide travelers to 14 city sites with some

Buddy Holly

TONY WHEELER

connection to the musician. There are some errors in the text – Holly's birth year, for example – but these are outweighed by the fun photos of 1950s Lubbock. Pick up a copy at the tourism bureau or stop by the Broadway Festivals office at 2313 Broadway St. The two most important sites are described in the following paragraphs. A Buddy Holly Center is being built in Lubbock's Depot District, with a tentative opening date of autumn 1999. The museum honors Holly and other West Texas musicians.

Statue & Walk of Fame In front of the Civic Center, 1501 6th St, between the Holiday Inn and La Quinta hotels, a larger-than-life-size statue of Holly is surrounded by plaques honoring him and other West Texans who made it big in arts and entertainment. Honorees include musicians Joe Ely, Roy Orbison, Bob Wills and Tanya Tucker and actor Barry Corbin, a Tech grad best known for his work as 'Maurice' in the quirky 1990s US television show *Northern Exposure*.

Buddy Holly's Grave The headstone in the Lubbock City Cemetery reads 'In Loving Memory of Our Own Buddy Holley. September 7, 1936 to February 3, 1959.' Musical notes and an electric guitar are engraved on the marker, too. The grave hasn't become a shrine in the way some other late rockers' have (think of Jim Morrison in Paris' Père Lachaise), but visitors do leave guitar picks, coins and other tokens at the site. We contributed a leftover token from the McKinney Ave Trolley in Dallas, just in case Buddy ever comes back for a gig in the Big D. The cemetery is located on the eastern edge of town at E 34th St and Martin Luther King Jr Blvd (bus No 1). Once inside the gate, turn down the lane to your right, then look for the grave just past the first large tree on your left-hand side.

Museum of Texas Tech University

Art, natural history and science are showcased at this fine museum (☎ 806-742-2490), which has more than 1.5 million items in its collections. There are frequent special exhibits

on such varied themes as American railroad history, a Tech professor's research of the Chernobyl nuclear disaster, Mexican masks and the African American buffalo soldiers who patrolled the frontier in the late 19th century. The museum is open Tuesday through Saturday 10 am to 5 pm (Thursday until 8:30 pm) and on Sunday 1 to 5 pm. It's near the intersection of 4th St and Indiana Ave (bus No 12); admission is free.

The Moody Planetarium is also part of the museum. It presents public shows Thursday at 7:30 pm, Friday at 3:30 pm, Saturday and Sunday at 2 and 3:30 pm. Admission is $1 for adults, 50¢ for students and free for kids ages five and younger and seniors at least 60 years old.

Ranching Heritage Center This impressive indoor-outdoor facility (☎ 806-742-2482), part of the Texas Tech museum complex, tells a detailed story of what life was like on the Texas High Plains from the late 1700s to about 1920. Patrick Murfee, administrator of the association that runs the center, calls it a 'Williamsburg of the West,' and the description is apt. Like its US colonial counterpart in Virginia, the Ranching Heritage Center deals in authenticity, not a glamorized version of history.

Inside, exhibits include an old-time general store, lots of historical photos and a truly huge collection of spurs. But the center's real heart is outdoors, where visitors can stroll through more than 30 buildings, most preserved from the late 19th and early 20th centuries, plus a collection of windmills, cattle pens, and a 1923 steam locomotive. Interpretive displays explain such topics as how barbed wire changed the cattle industry (by promoting better breeding and management practices) and how early settlers made do with what they had. In some ways, this ethic lives on – the hills along the center's paths were created with land-filled rubble left over from a tornado that hit Lubbock in the 1970s.

The Ranching Heritage Center is open Tuesday through Saturday 10 am to 5 pm and Sunday 1 to 5 pm. Admission is free, though donations are accepted. The center is easily toured on your own, but guided tours can sometimes be arranged by calling ☎ 806-742-2498 or 806-742-0498 a few days in advance. In mid-December, the center is transformed by holiday decorations and luminaria for 'A Candlelight Christmas.' Warm cider and hot Texas swing music make this an event worth attending if you're in the neighborhood 'round that time of year. Another annual event, Ranch Days, features living history in late September.

Lubbock Lake Landmark State Park

This site (☎ 806-765-0737) has proven a sort of time capsule for all the cultures that have inhabited the South Plains for 12,000 years. The archaeological evidence first was unearthed when agricultural irrigation caused Lubbock Lake's water table to decline in the 1930s, and excavations have gone on here since 1939.

An interpretive center and three hiking trails explain activity what became known as 'the Lubbock Lake Site,' now a National Historic Archaeological Landmark. Guided hikes into the main excavation area are available on request (just ask in the interpretive center), and a three-quarter-mile self-guiding tour leads around the site, with interpretive panels posted en route. There's also a 4-mile nature trail winding through Yellowhouse Draw, which is an excellent birding and wildlife-viewing area. Picnic areas are available, too.

Lubbock Lake Landmark State Park is open Tuesday through Saturday 9 am to 5 pm and Sunday 1 to 5 pm, closed Monday. To get there, follow Loop 289 to Clovis Rd west of I-27 on the northwest side of town. Admission is $2 for adults and $1 for students. Children five years old and younger are admitted free, as are Texas Conservation Passport holders.

American Wind Power Center

The American Wind Power Center (☎ 806-747-8734) located on a 28-acre site at E Broadway St south of MacKenzie in Canyon, showcases a collection of 170 windmills ranging from one of the earliest ever made back

in the 1860s to more modern models. The contraptions were mostly gathered by late windmill enthusiast Billie Wolfe, who managed to outbid the Smithsonian Institute for some of them. The center is open Tuesday to Friday 3 to 5 pm, Saturday 10 am to 5 pm and Sunday 1 to 5 pm.

Science Spectrum

More than 100 hands-on science and technology displays, an aquarium and an Omnimax movie theater are among the attractions at this museum (☎ 806-745-2525), at 2579 S Loop 289. The center is open Monday to Friday 10 am to 5:30 pm, Saturday 10 am to 7 pm and Sunday 1 to 5:30 pm. Admission is $5.50 for adults, $4.50 for kids between three and 16 years old and seniors older than 60. Omnimax shows cost $5.75 for adults, $4.75 for kids and seniors, or you can get a combo museum-Omnimax ticket costing $9 for adults and $7 for children or seniors. Recent Omnimax shows have included *Whales*, *Ring of Fire* (on volcanoes) and *Grand Canyon*.

Texas Water Rampage

Cool off at this outdoor water park (☎ 806-796-0701), 6600 Brownfield Hwy. Attractions include a large wave pool, several slides, a splash pool for toddlers, sand volleyball courts and picnic areas. Hours (daily June through mid-August; weekends only in May and late August; closed September through April) are Monday to Friday noon to 7 pm, Saturday 11 am to 7 pm and Sunday noon to 6 pm. Admission is $12.75 for adults and kids 4 feet tall or taller, $6.75 for the small fry and seniors 62 and up.

Mackenzie Park

Located off I-27 at Broadway St and Ave A, 248-acre Mackenzie Park is among the largest in Lubbock. Amenities include picnic areas, Meadowbrook Golf Course and a playground, plus two unusual attractions, Prairie Dog Town and Joyland.

Prairie Dog Town These little critters used to have the run of all of Mackenzie Park and beyond until folks got fed up with their excavation efforts on the nearby golf course.

Now confined by chicken wire and cement to 7 acres, the 'dogs' – actually rodents – keep busy building and repairing their dirt villages and warning each other of visiting grounds-keepers. It's good, free entertainment for kids of all ages.

Joyland Lubbock's amusement park (☎ 806-763-2719) has three roller coasters and about 20 other rides plus the usual array of arcades and games. From March to October, the park is open Saturday and Sunday 2 to 10 pm. June to August, it's also open Monday to Friday in the evenings. Admission is

$11 per person on weekends and $10 on weeknights. Discounts are in effect on some slower weeknight evenings, so ask.

Organized Tours

Old West aficionados will get a bang out of Bob Terry's Gunfighters Tours (☎ 915-776-2727). Terry, a descendant of legendary gunman 'Pink' Higgins, takes visitors to a bunch of sites where bad feelings turned worse during the open-range era on the Texas plains. Tour participants travel by minibus through a region few visitors ever see, and they dine and sleep at the Wagon Wheel

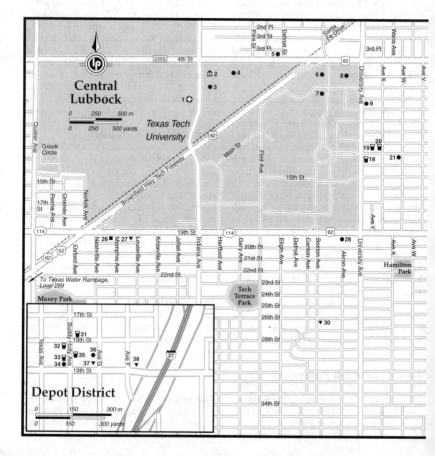

Ranch, a working cattle spread near Snyder. The tours typically begin and end in Lubbock, where travelers get a chance to visit the Ranching Heritage Center (see earlier in the Lubbock section), and they usually last two to three days at $160 to $180 per person per day, depending on extra activities (such as horseback riding or wagon treks) you may select. Fees also include food, lodging and the tour itself. You must have a group of folks already assembled to take Terry's tour, or you can call to see if you can join a group already booked; for more information, call Terry or write him at PO Box 457, Roby, TX 79543.

Special Events

Early September is a big time in Lubbock, with returning Tech students and two major parties happening in town – the National Cowboy Symposium and the Buddy Holly Music Festival. The cowboy symposium, held in mid-September, includes a parade of horses, trail rides, rodeo events, dances, Western-gear exhibits and sales and the national chuck wagon cookoff championship. More information may be had by calling ☎ 806-795-2455. The Holly bash, usually set to coincide with the musician's September 5 birthdate, is a street festival in the Depot

PLACES TO STAY
11 Four Points by ITT Sheraton
12 Travelers Inn
14 Holiday Inn Civic Center
15 EconoLodge
22 Broadway Manor Bed & Breakfast
26 Lubbock Inn

PLACES TO EAT
10 The Pancake House
14 The Greenery
27 Jazz: A Louisiana Kitchen
30 Alternative Food Co
37 Einstein's
38 Stubb's Bar-B-Q

BARS & CLUBS
18 J Patrick O'Malley's
19 Bash Riprock's
20 Captain Hollywood's
29 The Library
31 Bleachers
32 Clousseau's
33 Tom's Daquiri Place
35 Hub City Brewery
36 Liquid 2000

OTHER
1 University Medical Center
2 Museum of Texas Tech
   University, Moody Planetarium
3 International Cultural Center
4 Ranching Heritage Center
5 Grubs N Suds
6 Municipal Auditorium
7 Dan Law Field
8 Jones Stadium
9 University Coin Laundry
13 Buddy Holly Statue-Walk of Fame
16 Post Office
17 George & Helen Mahon
   Public Library
21 Broadway Festivals
23 Lubbock Tourism Bureau
24 New Mexico & Oklahoma Coaches
25 Downtown Plaza (Citibus Station)
28 Godbold Cultural Center
34 Cactus Theater

District. Music is the focus, of course; performers and guests for the past events have included musicians such as Joe Ely, the Mavericks, Carl Perkins and Holly's widow, Maria Elena Holly. For more information, call ☎ 806-749-2929 or 800-687-7393. September also brings the Panhandle South Plains Fair. Other major annual events include a Cork and Fork-Taste of Lubbock in February, the Lubbock Arts Festival in April, Cinco de Mayo in May and the Texas Tech Intercollegiate Rodeo each October.

Places to Stay

Camping The *Lubbock RV Park* (☎ 806-747-2366), which is north of town at exit 9 off of I-27, has shady sites, showers and a laundry, with tent sites for $10 and hookups going for $17. *Buffalo Springs Lake* (☎ 806-747-3353), located in Yellowhouse Canyon 5 miles southeast of Lubbock, charges $10 for tent campers, $12 for electric and water hookup sites and $15 for full hookups. (See the Around Lubbock section later for information on recreational activities at Buffalo Springs Lake.)

Motels & Hotels – Budget The *Texas Motor Inn* (☎ 806-744-0444), at 2121 Amarillo Rd, and *El Tejas Motel* (☎ 806-763-9343), at 1000 N Ave Q, are among the cheapest sleeps in Lubbock. Both are in the same general area north of downtown along I-27, and each looks to be pretty popular with truckers. Rates are $20/30 for singles/doubles at the Texas Motor Inn and $25/40 at El Tejas.

On the south side of town, the *Circus Inn Motel* (☎ 806-745-2515), 150 Slaton Rd, has rooms for $34/42, with a pool and restaurant on the premises; the locks on the doors were ridiculously hard to open. We had to go back and request another room when the key to the first one didn't work. The second one was nearly as intractable. The nearby *Motel 6* (☎ 806-745-5541, fax 806-748-0889), at 909 66th St, has rates of $32. In central Lubbock, the *Travelers Inn* (☎ 806-765-8847), 714 Ave Q, has rooms for $30 to $40 for singles and $40 to $55 for doubles. *EconoLodge* (☎ 806-765-6307), 910 Ave Q, has rates of $49/59.

Motels & Hotels – Mid-Range & Top End Many moderately priced motels can be found south of the junction of I-27 and Loop 289. The *Super 8* (☎ 806-762-8400), at 5410 I-27, has an indoor pool and rooms starting at $50 for singles and $56 for doubles. The *Best Western Lubbock Regency* (☎ 806-745-2208, fax 806-745-1265), 6624 I-27, has an indoor pool and full breakfast included in its $65 rates. Be sure to ask if the room rate is based on the size and bed-count or based on the number of people staying per room.

Another concentration of motels is along the south side of Loop 289 in southwest Lubbock. These include the *Ashmore Inn and Suites* (☎ 806-785-0060, 800-785-0061, fax 806-785-6001), at 4019 S Loop 289, with rooms at $62/72 and *Courtyard by Marriott* (☎ 806-795-1633), 4011 S Loop 289, with rates of $84/118.

Near the west side of Texas Tech, the *Lubbock Inn* (☎ 806-792-5181, 800-545-8226, fax 806-792-1319), 3901 19th St, has singles/doubles for about $55/63 and a restaurant and unusual double outdoor pool.

On the east side of campus, the full-service *Holiday Inn Civic Center* (☎ 806-763-1200, fax 806-763-2656), 801 Ave Q, has very comfortable rooms starting at $76/90. The *Four Points by ITT Sheraton* (☎ 806-747-0171, fax 806-747-9243), 505 Ave Q, has widely varying rates that run $79 to $89 depending on when you check. These highrise hotels cater to the convention and business trade, and both have atrium lobbies, indoor pools and restaurants.

B&Bs Right in town, *Broadway Manor Bed & Breakfast* (☎ 806-749-4707) at 1811 Broadway St, has five rooms going for $65 to $95 per night. The largest one, called the Mountain Lodge, has a private entrance and its own fireplace and sitting area amid knotty-pine decor.

Six miles southwest of Lubbock near Wolfforth, the *Country Place B&B* (☎ 806-863-2030) offers a pool and hot tub. It's a good spot for sky watching by night and country walks by day. Four large guest rooms share two baths, and rates are $70 per room, which are double occupancy.

Places to Eat

Fast Food All the chains are amply represented throughout Lubbock. For something local, try *Picante's* (☎ 806-793-8304), 3814 34th St, which gets raves for its freshly made Tex-Mex. Just about everything on the menu is less than $5.

On Campus Travelers are welcome to eat in Texas Tech residence-hall dining rooms, but they'll first need to buy an individual meal ticket at the appropriate residence-hall office. The all-you-can-eat meals cost $4 for breakfast, $5 for lunch and $5.75 for dinner. Dining rooms can be found in these dorm complexes: Bledsoe-Gordon-Sneed, Horn-Knapp, Hulen-Clement, Stange, Murdough, Wall-Gates and Wiggins. The Tech University Center has its own food court featuring fast fare (*Pizza Hut*, *Chick-fil-A* and *Blimpie's*), an espresso bar and a sit-down restaurant, *Raider Rock Grill*.

American There isn't much atmosphere at the *Greenery* in the Holiday Inn Civic Center (☎ 806-763-1200), 801 Ave Q, but chef Tyrone Willis was named Lubbock's 1997 chef of the year by his peers. Willis' signature dish is chicken St Charles ($13), a boneless breast of chicken topped with a crabmeat and shrimp sauce. Other dinner entrées range from $7 to $18. Dinner is from 6 to 10 pm.

The *Hub City Brewery* (☎ 806-747-1535), 1807 Buddy Holly Ave in the Depot District, is known for its brick-oven-baked pizzas ($6 to $12) and calzones ($6 to $7). Other choices include a chicken 'potted' pie served in a terra-cotta flower pot ($6) and a Southwest Philly steak sandwich ($6). The brewpub's selections include a golden ale, Raider Red Ale, Wild Bill's Yellowhouse Wheat and a stout.

The *Pancake House* (☎ 806-765-8506), 510 Ave Q, is open until 5 pm, but breakfast is the meal of choice here. Try the sweet-potato pancakes for $3.75 (you can buy a bag of mix to go on your way out). Monday through Friday between 2 and 10 pm, the restaurant offers an $8 special including bacon-wrapped chopped beef steak with salad, tater tots and toast.

Barbecue Follow your nose to *Stubb's Bar-B-Q* (☎ 806-747-4777), 620 19th St. Sandwiches run from $3.75 to $4.50, and plates piled with chicken, pork, ribs or beef cost $6 to $7 with rolls, potato salad and beans. It all washes down real well with a big ol' mug of iced tea or Shiner Bock.

Mexican People from the Panhandle's small towns regularly drive an hour or more and then spend another hour – sometimes longer – waiting for a table at *Abuelo's Mexican Food Embassy* (☎ 806-794-1762), 4401 82nd St at Quaker Ave. By that time, it's no wonder so many people order the Abuelo's Grande ($9), which includes three enchiladas, a cheese chile relleno, a taco, a tamale and side of guacamole salad. The restaurant is open for lunch and dinner daily, with patio seating in nice weather.

Vegetarian The West Texas Growers hold a farmer's market summer to fall on Tuesday, Thursday and Saturday from 7 am to mid-afternoon in the South Plains Fairgrounds at the intersection of I-27 and US 82 in northeast Lubbock. Stop by for locally grown produce, much of it organic.

The *Alternative Food Co* (☎ 806-747-8740), 2611 Boston Ave at 27th St, is both a health food store and a restaurant with a lunch bar featuring vegetarian sandwiches and power drinks. It's open daily 9 am to 5:30 pm except Sunday.

Einstein's (☎ 806-762-5320), 1824 Ave G in the Depot District, serves breakfast and lunch weekdays and brunchy stuff on weekends. Choice is the watchword here; diners can create their own breakfast tacos (two for $3.50), omelets ($3.75 to $5.25) or sandwiches ($3.50 to $4.50) from a nice array of ingredients heavy on the veggies. (But there's plenty for meat-eaters, too.)

Entertainment

Fine Arts The *Lubbock Symphony Orchestra* (☎ 806-762-1688) performs six to eight concerts each year, and *Ballet Lubbock* (☎ 806-785-3090) presents two programs annually, including a holiday run of the *Nutcracker*.

Blues & Barbecue

If the walls at **Stubb's Bar-B-Q** could talk, they'd be singing the blues. Since the 1960s, Stubb's has been a Lubbock legend, not just for its food – which is great – but for its role in nurturing Texas musicians. The current restaurant and nightclub on 19th St in the Depot District isn't the original, but just as the aroma of barbecue has already permeated the walls here, so have the spirits of the up-and-coming musicians who looked to Stubb's for a place to jam, a plate of ribs and a kind word from ol' Stubb himself. BB King, Joe Ely, Stevie Ray Vaughan, George Thorogood, Lucinda Williams, Jimmie Dale Gilmore, Butch Hancock, John Lee Hooker, Tom T Hall, Linda Ronstadt and dozens of others all performed at Stubb's out on 108 E Broadway St, where it was located until 1993. More often than not, they could coax owner CB 'Stubb' Stubblefield out of the kitchen and onto the stage to sing a few bars.

Before his death in 1995, Stubblefield had become a minor celebrity himself, with an appearance on *Late Night with David Letterman* and write-ups in *Bon Appétit* and the *Christian Science Monitor*. His barbecue sauce was served at the US Open tennis tournament and marketed worldwide via a ☎ 800-BAR-B-CUE (800-227-2283) toll-free number, and he opened another restaurant in Austin. But despite all the success, Stubb remained the salt-of-the-earth preacher's son he'd always been. 'I'm just a cook,' he always told reporters, adding that 'love and happiness' were his specialties. There are plans to put a monument to Stubb at the location of his original restaurant by 2001.

After Stubb passed away, his friend, Lubbock artist-musician Terry Allen, told the *Lubbock Avalanche-Journal*: 'His café was about good food, good music and the common dignity of human beings enjoying being human in the company of one another. A whole lot of black people and white people ate food and listened to music side by side for the first time at Stubb's.'

Theater The *Cactus Theater* (☎ 806-747-7047), 1812 Buddy Holly Ave in the Depot District, is a handsome building that opened as a movie house in 1938. These days, it mostly presents variety shows, including the *Buddy Holly Story*, *Always...Patsy Cline* and theme-nostalgia nights, each focusing on a different decade from the 1940s through the 1970s. Performances take place on weekends, nightly during holiday periods. Area muralist John Russell Thomasson has done some of his best work in the theater's interior, where the walls now recall the canyon country near Lubbock.

The *Texas Tech University Theatre* (☎ 806-742-3061) has main stage and lab theater productions each year. In addition, touring Broadway musicals sometimes appear at *Municipal Auditorium* at 2720 6th St on the Tech campus (where 6th St temporarily becomes Drive of Champions). Tickets for these and other big touring events can be obtained by calling Select-A-Seat at ☎ 806-770-2000 or 800-735-1288.

Bars & Clubs The Depot District is definitely Lubbock's party headquarters. The *Library* (☎ 806-762-3688), 2216 I-27 at Ave G, is a humongous dance club featuring mainstream rock. *Liquid 2000* (☎ 806-747-6156), 1812 Ave G, caters to a late-night crowd with occasional live music by the likes of Seven Mary Three or the Lords of Acid. *Stubb's Bar-B-Q* (☎ 806-747-4777), 620 19th St, is a legendary spot on the West Texas music scene (see the Blues & Barbecue boxed text), with live blues almost every night and an open jam every Sunday night starting about 10. Other Depot District nightclubs include *Tom's Daiquiri Place* (☎ 806-749-5442) at 1808 Buddy Holly Ave, with a huge indoor graffiti wall; *Bleachers* (☎ 806-744-7767), a new two-story sports café at 1719 Buddy Holly Ave; and *Clousseau's* (☎ 806-749-5282), featuring eclectic music in a cigar-smoke-filled space at 1802 Buddy Holly Ave.

Outside the Depot District, popular nightspots include *Jazz: A Louisiana Kitchen* (☎ 806-799-2124) at 3703C 19th St, which serves up Cajun food and live music; *Midnight Rodeo* (☎ 806-745-2813) at 7301 University Ave, with two dance floors – one country, one rock; and *Bash Riprock's* (☎ 806-762-2274) at 2491 Main St near the Tech campus, a sports-minded bar with a wide variety of brews in bottles or on tap. Plenty of Tech students start their weekends at Riprock's or *J Patrick O'Malley's* (☎ 806-762-0393), at 1211 University Ave, while an older crowd winds down from work at *Chances R* (☎ 806-799-3993), at 5610 Frankford Ave. The most-established gay and lesbian bar in Lubbock is *Captain Hollywood's* (☎ 806-744-4222) at 2401 Main St at Ave X.

Cinema *Movies 16* (☎ 806-792-0357), 5721 58th St, has, you guessed it, 16 screens. *Showplace 6* (☎ 806-745-3636), 6707 University Ave, shows films released a few months back for $1.50 per seat at all times.

Spectator Sports

Lubbock is gaga over **Texas Tech sports** and with much justification. The school is a member of the powerhouse Big 12 Conference (which also includes Texas, Texas A&M and Baylor). The football team almost always gets a bowl invitation, the baseball team took the Big 12 title in 1997 and the women's basketball team won the NCAA crown in 1993 with future Olympic gold medalist Sheryl Swoopes on the squad. In early 1999, Tech's basketball and volleyball teams began play in the new United Spirit Arena on campus. For Tech sports schedules and ticket prices, call ☎ 806-742-4412 or 888-462-4412, or check out the university's athletics website at www.texastech.com.

As on most US college campuses, fall football weekends provide Tech an all-out license to party. The tailgating action starts about three hours before kickoff at 'Raider Alley' just west of Jones Stadium. If Tech

Take That, A&M!

Texas Tech University and Texas A&M are fierce athletic rivals, and they have been for some time. In 1948, Fort Worth newspaper publisher Amon Carter donated to Tech one of four copies of the Electra Waggoner Biggs statue *Riding into the Sunset*, which depicts the legendary humorist Will Rogers – a big Tech fan – astride his horse Soapsuds. When the statue came to campus, it was positioned so the animal's rear would face in the direction of College Station, home of Texas A&M. The statue still stands east of Memorial Circle on the Tech campus.

wins, not just in football but in any sport, fans ring the campus Victory Bells for 30 minutes. Lubbock residents pleaded for the half-hour limit 60-some years ago after students rang the bells all night following a football victory over Texas Christian University.

The Lubbock Crickets (☎ 806-749-2255) play Texas-Louisiana League **baseball** at Dan Law Field on the Tech campus. Tickets cost $5 for general admission, $6 to $7 reserved.

Shopping

For a good selection of Buddy Holly memorabilia, visit Broadway Festivals (☎ 806-749-2929) at 2313 Broadway St. Lubbock also has lots of Western-gear shops. Dollar Western Wear (☎ 806-793-2818) at 5007 Brownfield Hwy is among the biggest.

The South Plains Mall (☎ 806-792-4653), 6002 Slide Rd, is the largest single-story mall in Texas with about 160 shops and restaurants and more than 200,000 weekly visitors. Bus No 6 or No 3 will get you there and to its surrounding temples of commerce.

It's not the usual souvenir, but classy custom-made furniture made by Ronny and Rita Peek (☎ 806-828-5024) will forever remind you of a visit to the Texas plains. The Peeks live and work on the rim of Yellowhouse Canyon near Slaton southeast of

Lubbock. Calling their business A Hare Raising Experience, the couple designs and crafts furniture that incorporates such indigenous plains motifs as prickly-pear cactus and chili peppers.

Getting There & Away

Air Lubbock International Airport (☎ 806-775-3126) is located north of town via the Regis exit off of I-27. Airlines include American Eagle, Continental, Delta ASA and Southwest. Travelers' services include a restaurant and a bar.

Bus Texas New Mexico and Oklahoma Coaches (☎ 806-765-6641) provides long-distance bus service out of Lubbock from its terminal at 1313 13th St. Sample fares are listed below.

to/from	trip duration	one way/ roundtrip
Amarillo	2 to 3 hours	$21/40
Dallas	8 to 9 hours	$52/104
San Antonio	9½ hours	$55/105

Car Major car rental companies with offices in Lubbock's airport include Advantage (☎ 806-744-8566), Avis (☎ 806-763-5433), Hertz (☎ 806-762-0222) and National (☎ 806-762-2161). In town, there are offices for Budget (☎ 806-763-6471), 1606 E Regis St, and Enterprise (☎ 806-765-0622), 1911 Ave Q.

Getting Around

To/From the Airport Yellow Cab (☎ 806-765-7777) charges about $9 from the airport to downtown locations and another $1 or so to the Tech campus. Citibus has no airport route. A few of the nicer hotels in town offer free airport shuttle service, so ask when you book your room.

Bus Citibus (☎ 806-762-0111) provides public transportation in Lubbock, with most routes running from about 6 am to 6:30 pm. Fares are $1 for adults, 75¢ for children between six and 12 years old and 50¢ for senior citizens and people with disabilities. Transfers are free, and kids younger than six ride free. Most routes originate from the Downtown Plaza at Broadway St and Buddy Holly Ave downtown.

Taxi Taxi rates in Lubbock are $1.70 at flag-fall and $1.30 each additional mile. Extra passengers cost 50¢ each, or $2 each to or from the airport. Cab companies include Yellow Cab (☎ 806-765-7777), City Cab (☎ 806-765-7474) and White Knight's Luxury Towncar Service (☎ 806-799-3366).

AROUND LUBBOCK
Wineries

Down in the Texas Hill Country, wine seems to make sense. Up here on the boot-scootin', teetotalin' High Plains, it sounds like a joke. Indeed, *Los Angeles Times* writer J Michael Kennedy opened a mid-1980s article on the region's wines thus: 'Napa Valley, take note: Chateau de Bubba, vin du Lone Star, has arrived.'

But as Kennedy went on to write, the Texas South Plains is 'a place where hailstones come the size of golf balls and sandstorms can peel the paint off a car.' It also has near-ideal wine grape-growing conditions: sandy soil, hot days and cool nights. The Texas High Plains appellation is now the largest wine-grape growing region in the state, and its reputation is growing mightily. Curiously, local laws make it impossible to buy wine at grocery stores in Lubbock, but travelers can enjoy local wine at many area restaurants or by visiting the wineries.

Llano Estacado Llano (pronounced 'YAH-no') Estacado Winery (☎ 806-863-2704) was founded in 1976, making it the oldest of the modern Texas wineries. It's among the largest, too; the winery is now in the midst of a five-year expansion that will boost wine-making capacity (now at 90,000 cases annually) to 215,000 cases each year. Although it has about 16 varieties that together have won more than 575 awards, Llano is probably best known for its cabernets and chardonnays.

Llano offers free tours and tastings Monday to Saturday 10 am to 5 pm and Sunday noon to 5 pm. Tours can be as brief or as comprehensive as you wish, but you're likely to hear all about how corks are made, how oak barrels influence a wine's taste and whether the Texas Tech scuba diving team really practices in the winery's 12,000-gallon tanks. Llano also has a good little gift shop featuring its wines (priced from $7.25 to $250 a bottle) and such gourmet goodies as chardonnay-garlic mayonnaise, jalapeño-blush jelly and chardonnay-raspberry fudge sauce. The winery is located on the south side of FM 1585 east of US 87.

CapRock Winery Although not as prominent nor as honored as Llano Estacado, CapRock Winery (☎ 806-863-2704) is near Llano Estacado and worth a visit for its beautiful mission-style headquarters, a showplace both inside and out. CapRock makes about a dozen wines. Tours and tastings are free and offered Monday to Saturday 10 am to 5 pm and Sunday noon to 5 pm. CapRock is on Woodrow Rd (south of FM 1585), a half-mile east of Hwy 87.

Pheasant Ridge Winery Located north of Lubbock near the town of New Deal, Pheasant Ridge (☎ 806-746-6033) dates back to 1979. Tours and tastings are offered by appointment only, and since the winery is located in a 'dry' area, you can taste – but not buy – the wares.

Apple Country Hi-Plains Orchards
Located east of Lubbock on US 62/82, and 4 miles east of Idalou, Apple Country Hi-Plains Orchards (☎ 806-892-2961) has pick-your-own apple orchards, a popular lunch buffet that costs $4 and a gift shop featuring apple products.

Buffalo Springs Lake
Since it's just 5 miles southeast of town via FM 835, Buffalo Springs Lake (office at ☎ 806-747-3353) provides a ready escape from cement-laden Lubbock on hot summer days. Set in Yellowhouse Canyon, Buffalo Springs Lake is popular for swimming, boating, fishing and camping. It's also the site of a 1.7-mile nature trail developed by the Llano Estacado Audubon Society. Admission fees

for Buffalo Springs Lake are $2 per person, $1 for seniors and kids between six and 12 years old and $3 per boat.

QUITAQUE & TURKEY
Population 1000
East of Lubbock and Amarillo and about a 100-minute drive from either of those metro areas, the two neighboring small towns of Quitaque (pronounced 'Kitty-quay') and Turkey on Hwy 86 have a total population of maybe 1000 folks. But if you're outdoors-minded, a small-town-o-phile or just in need of some serious relaxation, consider planning your vacation around these little burgs and their surrounding plains-and-canyon countryside.

Caprock Canyons State Park
Although it is not as well known as Palo Duro Canyon State Park, Caprock Canyons (☎ 806-455-1492) shares the same kind of stunning topography and abundant wildlife. Even the casual visitor is likely to see mule deer, roadrunners and aoudad, the North African barbary sheep transplanted to the Panhandle in the 1950s. The sunsets are stupendous, especially from the scenic point across from the Wild Horse Camping Area or the banks of little Lake Theo. But the trail system here is

Roadrunner: 'Beep beep'

what makes Caprock Canyons one of Texas' best state parks: 90 miles of outstanding and diverse hiking, mountain biking and horseback riding, including 26 miles in the park proper and another 64 miles on the Caprock Canyons State Park Trailways System.

In 1998, the park became home to a donated bison herd from the JA Ranch – the very herd started by pioneer rancher Charles Goodnight in 1876. Take well-marked FM 1065 from Quitaque to the park headquarters. There's a $2 per-person park entrance fee for each visitor age 12 or older, which also covers use of the Caprock Canyons Trailways.

The Trailways Running through three counties from Estelline to the northeast to South Plains to the southwest, the 64-mile abandoned railroad bed Caprock Canyons Trailways opened in 1993. Highlights include riding over about 50 bridges and through Clarity Tunnel, a historic railroad passage. It's all multiple use, meaning people on foot, horseback and bicycle are welcome. The surface is mostly packed gravel with a few large rocks, and although there are some high railroad trestles, they are well fenced.

Trail access points and parking lots can be found along Hwy 86 at Estelline, Parnell, Tampico Siding, Turkey and Quitaque. On this section, the trail runs parallel to but a good distance from the highway. At Quitaque, the trail swings south then west for the final 23 miles to South Plains, the portion that includes the 1000-foot Clarity Tunnel. Campsites are available along the route for $7, but people staying overnight on the Trailways need to get a permit from Caprock Canyons State Park before setting out. Day users can pay their $2 at the self-pay station at each trailhead. Trail users should carry drinking water or be prepared to treat any water collected along the trail. Garbage must be packed out. James Cathey (☎ 806-455-1221) rents bicycles for $10 a day and also runs a $20 shuttle service down to the end of the Trailways at South Plains. He'll run shuttles to other portions of the trail, too; call and tell him what you have in mind, or just stop by his base at the trading post by Lake Theo in the park proper.

Although most vehicles cannot access the trail, Queen of the Valley Inc (☎ 806-983-3639), PO Box 57, Quitaque, TX 79255, has a permit to offer motorized tours along part of the route. A two-hour tour to Clarity Tunnel and back runs Saturday at 9:30 am for $7.50, and the full four-hour tour is offered Saturday and Sunday at 2 pm for $15 per person. Weekday tours are possible by reservation.

Park Trails The state park proper has outstanding trail opportunities, too. Stop at the visitors' center for a park map showing trailheads and distances. For an easy trail of about 2½ miles roundtrip, follow the hikers-only Upper Canyon Trail from the South Prong tent camping area trailhead to the South Prong primitive camping area and back. Beyond the primitive camping area, the Upper Canyon Trail becomes increasingly steep and rugged; caution is essential along the cliffs and bluffs. Horseback riders and mountain bikers can join hikers along the Canyon Loop and Lower Canyon Trails; hikers and cyclists share the Old Ranch Rd Trail; and a bridle path east from the equestrian primitive camping area gives riders some solitude.

Horseback Riding The Quitaque Riding Stables (☎ 806-455-1208) is open daily from 8 am to 5 pm. Horses rent for $10.50 an hour, with a one-hour minimum if you just ride around the grounds and a two-hour minimum if they haul the horses to the state park for you. If possible, call a day ahead of time to schedule your ride.

Lake Theo It ain't big, but it sure is purty. No-wake Lake Theo has good fishing for bass, catfish, bluegill and crappie. April 1 to September 30, you can rent a paddleboat or canoe for $5 an hour from the lakeside trading post, which also sells snacks and limited camping equipment.

Camping Caprock Canyons gets busy around April and stays that way until early September, so campsite reservations are essential during that time. Call ☎ 512-389-8900 weekdays to reserve. The Honea Flat *camping area* is the park's most developed, with

25 water and electric sites that cost $12 and 10 water-only sites for $10. This campground has everything from rest rooms with showers to a playground, and it's an easy walk to Lake Theo. Other camping areas, all without water, include **Wild Horse** ($9) and the **Equestrian Primitive** camping area ($7), which cater to campers with horses; **Little Red Tent** ($9); and **South Prong** ($8). Backpackers are welcome to select any site at least a mile from the pavement for $7, but a permit is required.

If you have a good-size group and like a roof over your head, consider the **bunkhouse** overlooking Lake Theo. It sleeps 10 and has a stove, refrigerator, heating, air-conditioning and a flush toilet. Outside, there's a grill and picnic table. It's a deal for $48, although bed linens and cooking utensils are not provided. Some overflow RV camping is available for $14 at the **Big C Trading Post** (☎ 806-455-1221) north of Quitaque.

Circle Dot Ranch
The same people who run the Queen of the Valley tours (see the Trailways earlier) run the Circle Dot Ranch in these parts. May through October, they offer Comanchero Breakfast Tours (cost is $15 for adults and $9 for kids six to 12 years old) and Chuck Wagon Supper Tours (which run $18.50 and $10.50). Times vary by season. Call ☎ 806-983-3639 or write Circle Dot Ranch, HCR 3, Box 43, Lockney, TX 79241 for more information.

Bob Wills Museum
Many small-town museums are silent, gloomy places. Not the Bob Wills Museum (☎ 806-423-1253 or 806-423-1490) in Turkey, where visitors will likely be greeted by a recorded serenade from the Turkey homeboy himself. Wills was a major creator of a genre of music known as Western Swing, described by David Vinopal in the *All-Music Guide* like this:

Take fiddle-based old-time string-band music from the '20s and '30s, move it to a city such as Tulsa or Fort Worth, add jazz and blues and pop and sacred music, back it with strings and horns played by a dozen or so musicians, add an electric steel guitar along the way, and you have Western swing; and when you talk Western swing, you start with Bob Wills.

Wills reached his greatest fame in the 1940s with his band the Texas Playboys, with whom he recorded such hits as *San Antonio Rose* and *Faded Love*.

The museum includes lots of artifacts from the musician's life, including his fiddles, scrapbooks, a gazillion photos and a certificate naming him an admiral of the fleet of the Great Navy of the State of Oklahoma. The Bob Wills Museum is located in the Turkey City Hall, or it might be more accurate to say Turkey City Hall can be found in the Bob Wills Center, which also houses the town's library, senior citizens' center and justice of the peace.

Hours are Monday to Friday 9 to 11:30 am and 1 to 5 pm. The museum is closed weekends and holidays, but anyone calling in advance for an appointment can get in.

Turkey celebrates Wills' legacy with a festival the last Saturday of each April, when 10,000 or more people stuff themselves into Turkey for a weekend of pickin' and grinnin', with jam sessions galore. There's also a monument to Wills on the western edge of town.

Places to Stay & Eat
See under Caprock Canyons State Park for information on *camping* wihin the park. The **Hotel Turkey** (☎ 806-423-1151) is a welcome sight to travelers weary of chain motels. From the rocking chairs lined up on the front porch to the friendly hospitality of Gary and Suzie Johnson, the Hotel Turkey just begs visitors to forget their cares. Built in 1927, the inn has 15 rooms, including two ground-floor quarters reserved specifically for disabled visitors. Most rooms have their own bath, although a shower is shared. Rates are $49 to $89, including breakfast, and RV hookups are available for $15. There's a tennis court out in the back.

Although the Hotel Turkey serves occasional dinners (including a Thanksgiving feast, of course), guests often take their lunches or suppers at the **Peanut Patch** (☎ 806-423-1051), two blocks away on Turkey's main drag – and people just passing through town should consider stopping, too. Silvia Boeshart, originally from Switzerland, is known all over the region for her gourmet pizza ($10.50 for a large one-topping pie) and leisurely multicourse meals featuring such goodies as chicken breasts in a savory peanut sauce, pesto lasagna and a delightful sweet-potato cheesecake. The prix-fixe lunch is about $6 and dinner costs $13. Yes, you read those prices right.

In Quitaque, the ***Sportsman*** (☎ *806-455-1200*), 204 Main St, is the place to eat and meet; it seems half the town is here on Fridays for fajitas night. (A full order costs $7.50, a half $4.25.) The recently redecorated restaurant has high ceilings and gorgeously rustic light fixtures originally designed for a café in Amarillo. The regular menu features rib-eye steak ($10), burgers ($2.50) and chicken-fried steak ($5.50). The Sportsman is open for lunch and dinner every day but December 25. The back-room bar has karaoke every Friday and a disc jockey every Saturday, but live bands sometimes bump the poseurs.

AMARILLO
Population 169,588

For people in a hurry to get across the United States, Texas is represented wholly by a flat, 177-mile stretch on I-40 – the route across the state's Panhandle. Amarillo looms large on that stretch simply because it is the lone metropolitan area on the 543-mile route between Oklahoma City, Oklahoma, and Albuquerque, New Mexico.

Amarillo (it's Spanish for 'yellow') has an interesting past but, sadly, a rather dull present. In its heyday, the city was roughly the midpoint of Route 66, the fabled Chicago-to-Los Angeles highway. But when I-40 replaced Route 66, it sucked most of the city's life into its vortex, making this a remarkably soulless town.

Amarillo is synonymous with ranching, the quintessentially Western way of life – the city still has one of the state's largest cattle auctions, and this is also the headquarters of the American Quarter Horse Association. A few local artists and entrepreneurs have tried to give the city a personality beyond a cow town, so Amarillo has its quirks, the world-famous Cadillac Ranch (see later in

this chapter) chief among them. There are other signs of life, but if you visit Amarillo, you will need to look well beyond the I-40 facade to find them.

It's best to visit on Tuesday, to catch the Amarillo Livestock Auction and the Big Texan Opry, two of the town's most down-home Western experiences. Avoid Sundays and Mondays, when much of Amarillo shuts down.

Orientation

US 87 is the main north-south route through town, and Loop 335 makes a wide swing around the city's perimeter. Within the city, I-40 and its frontage roads are the primary east-west thoroughfares. Amarillo's mostly dead downtown is north of the interstate. A mile or so north of I-40, Amarillo Blvd (Business Route 40) is the other east-west passage.

The eastern reaches of Amarillo Blvd overlay what used to be Route 66, but the more interesting stretch of the historic highway is on what is now known as W 6th Ave, or Loop 279, west of downtown. This is the San Jacinto District, where Amarillo occasionally shows signs of having a pulse.

Loop 279 proceeds west on W 6th Ave and Bushland Blvd until it rejoins Business Route 40 just north of the Harrington Regional Medical Center's collection of hospitals, where you'll find the Don Harrington Discovery Center and the oddball Helium Monument. Amarillo lies in two counties: everything north of 29th Ave is in Potter County, everything south of it is in Randall County.

Addressing can be a bit confusing in Amarillo. Polk St divides the city east and west and 1st St divides it north and south. Businesses south of 1st St don't universally use the designation in practice, but we've added the south designation to our listings to help you find your way around town.

Maps The visitor council's free *City & Area Map* is unwieldy, but at least it's easier to read than most. The little map in the separate CVB brochure is actually pretty good, but it lacks much detail.

No Sacred Cows Here

Her fist in the air, Oprah Winfrey shouted 'Yes! Free speech not only lives, it rocks!' And that was the end of one of the most publicized courtroom battles Texas has seen in recent history: *Oprah v Big Beef*.

It all started when former Montana rancher and vegetarian activist Howard Lyman was a guest on Winfrey's popular television talk show for a 1996 segment called 'Dangerous Foods.' Discussing the British outbreak of bovine spongiform encephalopathy, or BSE, the so-called mad-cow disease that claimed human lives and ravaged the beef industry in the UK, Lyman contended it was only a matter of time before the disease surfaced in the US. Shocked, Winfrey said she'd never eat another hamburger.

In the US, many people take Oprah Winfrey's word as gospel. A mere mention of a film on her program is enough to make it a hit; a positive mention of a book sends it to the top of the *New York Times* best-seller list. The day after Oprah dissed burgers, the price of beef on commodities exchanges around the country plunged by more than 10%.

Several Amarillo cattlemen decided to sue Winfrey under the state's 'veggie libel law,' which prohibits people from publicly slamming perishable food products. The case went to trial in early 1998.

The jury didn't buy it. Not only did the jurors find that the plaintiffs' or Texas' beef had not been singled out by Winfrey, they also said they needed to send a message in defense of people's right to say what they want. 'We were a bunch of people who believe in free speech,' juror Pat Gowdy told reporters. 'Our rights have suffered enough in this country. Our freedom of speech may be the only one we have left to regain what we've lost.'

Winfrey gained immeasurable publicity and good will among Texans from the incident. She moved her entire show from its Chicago studio to Amarillo for the trial's five-week duration. She rented out the Amarillo Little Theatre as a studio and hired dozens of local workers. She featured Texas celebrities – everyone from Charles Barkley of the Houston Rockets to Molly Ivins of the *Fort Worth Star-Telegram* – as guests, and did fun shows on such topics as 'Why is everything in Texas so big?'

'I will continue to use my voice,' Winfrey, an African American woman, told shouting supporters once the verdict was announced. 'I believed from the beginning this was an attempt to muzzle that voice. I come from a people who have struggled and died in order to have a voice in this country, and I refuse to be muzzled.'

Information

Tourist Offices The Amarillo Convention and Visitor Council (☎ 806-374-1497, 800-692-1338, fax 806-373-3909, www.amarillo-cvb .org), 1000 S Polk St downtown, is on the second floor of the beautiful Lee and Mary E Bivins Home; it's open Monday to Friday 8 am to 5 pm. The council's slim visitors' guide is less of a draw than is the Georgian-Revival house, which really is a charmer (you'll also find several of the city's arts organizations and the chamber of commerce here).

The AAA has an office (☎ 806-354-8288) in the Wolflin Village Shopping Center, southeast of I-40 at Georgia St (exit 68). It doesn't have much in the way of travel accessories or guidebooks, but the staff is helpful.

Money The downtown branches of NationsBank (☎ 806-378-1400), 701 S Taylor St, and Amarillo National Bank (☎ 806-378-8000), 410 S Taylor St, offer currency exchange services. Amarillo National Bank has about 40 ATMs around town, including a convenient branch at 3401 Soncy Rd, and NationsBank has about three dozen ATMs.

Post & Communications The central post office (☎ 806-468-2148), 505 E 9th Ave at Buchanan St, is open Monday to Friday from 7:30 am to 5 pm. Address poste restante to General Delivery, Amarillo, TX 79105. Mail Boxes Etc (☎ 806-358-4060) is at 3300 Coulter St.

Media Amarillo has two daily newspapers: the *Amarillo Daily News* in the morning and the *Amarillo Globe-Times* in the evening. Each costs 50¢ on the newsstand. The papers combine on Sunday as the *Amarillo Globe News*, which costs $1.25. A monthly magazine, *Accent West*, targets Amarillo's upscale professional audience. The down-home *Prairie Dog Gazette*, published occasionally out of nearby Clarendon, includes articles about Panhandle history and upcoming events. KACV, Amarillo College's eclectic station at 90 FM, plays everything from Nirvana to Enya to Texas singer-songwriter Robert O'Keene.

Bookstores We couldn't find any truly independent bookstores specializing in new books, but since the book-music-video chain Hastings (☎ 806-352-4151), 2001 S Georgia St, has its corporate offices in Amarillo, most local folks think of it as a home-grown enterprise. Both Hastings and Barnes & Noble (☎ 806-352-2300), 2415 Soncy Rd, have good travel-book sections. B&N also has a packed special-events calendar, including a free-wheeling open poetry reading the first Saturday evening of each month and children's story times Tuesday at 10:30 am.

Libraries Amarillo Public Library (☎ 806-378-3054), 413 E 4th Ave at Buchanan St in downtown Amarillo, is open Monday to Thursday 9 am to 9 pm, Friday and Saturday 9 am to 6 pm, and Sunday 2 to 6 pm. For research purposes, don't overlook the library at the Panhandle-Plains Historical Museum in Canyon – see Around Amarillo.

Campuses Amarillo College is a public two-year junior college with about 6700 students. Its main campus is on Washington St south of I-40 between 22nd and 26th Aves SW. The college is mainly notable for its art museum (see the Amarillo Museum of Art later) and its radio station.

Laundry Try the new and nice Washbrite Coin Laundry (☎ 806-352-7344), 2506 Patterson Drive (I-40 to the Paramount exit). Other good choices are Mayco Laundry (☎ 806-352-9732), 3454 S Western St, and Village Homestyle Laundry (☎ 806-359-6974), 441 S Western St.

Medical Services Amarillo has two walk-in, doc-in-a-box clinics: Baptist St Anthony's Urgent Care Center (☎ 806-358-4835), 4510 S Bell St, and Immediate Care Clinic (☎ 806-356-7880), 3501 Soncy Rd. Harrington Regional Medical Center is the collective name given to the health-care facilities located north of I-40 on Amarillo's west side. Of these, the largest are Baptist St Anthony's (emergency room ☎ 806-358-5750), at 1600 Wallace Blvd, and Northwest Texas Hospital (☎ 806-354-1000), 1501 S Coulter St.

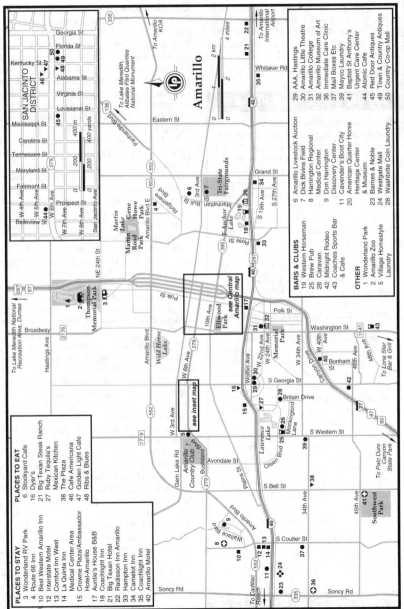

Emergency The number for poison control is ☎ 800-764-7661; the suicide and crisis center line is ☎ 806-359-6699, or 800-692-4039 within the 806 area code; and the rape crisis-domestic violence hot line is also ☎ 806-359-6699.

The Big Texan Steak Ranch

Like Wall Drug in South Dakota, South of the Border in South Carolina and the Little America truck stop in Wyoming, the Big Texan Steak Ranch, a restaurant, entertainment complex and motel in Amarillo, makes its presence known to travelers hundreds of miles before they get near the place. 'Free 72oz steak!' blare the billboards. And at the bottom of the billboard, in tiny print, they continue, 'if eaten in one hour.'

Let's review: 72oz is 4½lb, or a little more than 2kg, or 9oz more than the New York City telephone directory. No matter how you look at it, that's a whole mess o' meat, and you only get it free if you eat the steak plus the shrimp cocktail, baked potato, salad and dinner roll that come with it – all in no more than an hour.

Because the odds against your completing the task are so high (six to one), the restaurant makes you put up $50 – the cost of the meal if you fail the challenge – in advance. Wait staff attempt to discourage you with horrific descriptions of the condition your bowels will be in should you succeed.

Surely such Cool Hand Luke-style gluttony is rare, you say? Well, when last we checked, 27,560 people had tried. More disturbing are the stats on the ones who have grabbed the glory and gotten their name on the Steak Eater's Wall of Fame: the official record (9 minutes 45 seconds) is held by Frank Pastore. OK, he was a baseball player for the Cincinnati Reds franchise, but it takes all kinds: the oldest gourmand was a 69-year-old grandmother, and the youngest an 11-year-old boy. His folks must be so proud.

Cadillac Ranch

To millions of people whizzing across the Texas Panhandle each year, the Cadillac Ranch is the ultimate symbol of the US love affair with wheels. A salute to Route 66 and the spirit of the American road, it was created by burying, hood first, 10 west-facing Cadillacs in a wheat field outside town. Since its installation, millions of tourists have made the trip to see the ranch, making it one of Texas' best-known attractions.

In 1974 Amarillo businessman and arts patron Stanley Marsh 3 invited the San Francisco-based Ant Farm designers' collective to a field he owned to see what would transpire. Inspired by the wind-whipped, waving wheat (and who knows what else), the group saw fins – first, those of dolphins, which soon morphed into the fins of vintage Cadillacs – and the rest, as they say...

Former Ant Farmer Doug Michaels, who along with Chip Lord and Hudson Marquez conceived the Cadillac Ranch, says they intended the artwork to be 'a monument to the rise and fall of the Cadillac tail fin.' The trio spent three weeks scouting Amarillo for El Dorados and Coupe de Villes dating from 1948 to 1959 – a period in which tail fins just kept getting bigger and bigger – on to 1963, when the fin vanished. 'It was a bad year for America,' Michaels says. 'President Kennedy got shot and the Caddie tail fin disappeared.' Once found, the cars were planted at a 52° angle, the same as the Great Pyramid at Cheops in Egypt.

Marsh loved the results. Interviewed by *Texas Monthly* on the ranch's 20th anniversary in 1994, he said, 'What makes America the best country in the world is the car. In Germany, Africa, China or Russia, kids grow up thinking they'll have a house someday. But American kids dream that they'll have a car. A car represents freedom, romance, money. You can head west to Las Vegas, where you can break the bank, then go out to the beach in California and become a movie star.'

Pushed from their original location by creeping urban sprawl, the cars were relocated in 1997 to a field 4 miles west. To visit (it's free and open 24 hours a day), take

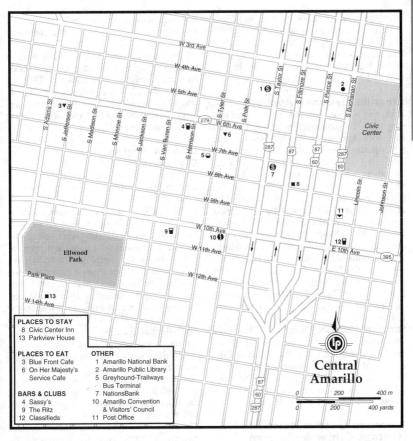

W 3rd Ave
W 4th Ave
W 5th Ave
W 6th Ave
W 7th Ave
W 8th Ave
W 9th Ave
W 10th Ave
W 11th Ave
E 10th Ave
W 12th Ave
W 14th Ave

S Adams St
S Jefferson St
S Madison St
S Monroe St
S Jackson St
S Van Buren St
S Harrison St
S Tyler St
S Polk St
S Taylor St
S Fillmore St
S Pierce St
S Buchanan St
Lincoln St
Johnson St

Ellwood Park
Park Place

Civic Center

Central Amarillo

279
287
87
87
87
60
287
60
87
60
287
395

1
2
3
4
5
6
7
8
9
10
11
12
13

0   200   400 m
0   200   400 yards

PLACES TO STAY
8 Civic Center Inn
13 Parkview House

PLACES TO EAT
3 Blue Front Cafe
6 On Her Majesty's
   Service Cafe

BARS & CLUBS
4 Sassy's
9 The Ritz
12 Classifieds

OTHER
1 Amarillo National Bank
2 Amarillo Public Library
5 Greyhound-Trailways
   Bus Terminal
7 NationsBank
10 Amarillo Convention
   & Visitors' Council
11 Post Office

I-40 west to exit 60 (Arnot Rd). The frontage road on the south side of the freeway leads right to a small parking lot on the shoulder and then to a well-worn footpath to the cars. Although the ranch is on private property, it remains very much a public treasure (or eyesore, if you're the wet-blanket type), since anyone who cares to may add his or her own personal touch to the scene via a can of spray paint. Ah, democracy at its finest.

West 6th Ave

Route 66 is gone, but it's not forgotten along West 6th Ave in Amarillo, easily the most interesting neighborhood in Amarillo. Locally dubbed the San Jacinto District, the strip between Georgia St and Western St is Amarillo's best dining district, and there's some good shopping, too. Bus No 8-Medical Center serves the area.

Antiques fans should set aside at least a few hours to peruse the 30 or so shops that feature antiques, collectibles and plenty of Route 66 souvenirs; several are antique malls that provide spaces to multiple dealers. There's a wide range of quality and price, but some of the best stuff can be found in the Country Co-op Mall (☎ 806-372-4472), at

2805 W 6th Ave, with 60 dealers; and Town & Country Antiques (☎ 806-373-3607), 2811 W 6th Ave. Nearby and in a class by itself is Red Door Antiques (☎ 806-373-0316), 3211 W 6th Ave, with fine furniture from the late 19th and early 20th centuries.

Amarillo Livestock Auction

A slice of real Western Americana is on display every Tuesday morning at the Amarillo Livestock Auction (☎ 806-373-7464), at 100 S Manhattan St, just north of 3rd Ave near the Tri-State Fairgrounds on the city's east side. The auction is still one of the state's largest, moving 120,000 to 150,000 animals annually (down from its 1970s peak of 715,000). The auction starts at 10 am and things happen fast: Cattle are herded in through one pneumatic gate and out through another, and most animals sell within about 30 seconds. The auctions draw few tourists, but all are welcome. The No 4-Sunrise bus gets within about eight blocks of the auction; get off at E 10th Ave and Browning St and walk north on Browning. If you can, plan a late breakfast or an early lunch and hit the popular Stockyard Cafe (see Places to Eat later) on your way in or out of the auction. The Western Horseman lounge in the Ramada Inn-East, 2501 I-40 E, is a major gathering spot for cattlemen during and after the Tuesday sales – go for a drink, and you may well rub elbows with a top Texas cattle baron.

American Quarter Horse Heritage Center & Museum

With 3.5 million animals recorded worldwide (and about 450,000 of those in Texas), the American Quarter Horse Association is the world's largest equine-breed registry. (Quarter horses, favored on the Texas range, were originally named for their prowess at galloping down early American racetracks, which were a quarter-mile long.) The American Quarter Horse Heritage Center and Museum (☎ 806-376-5181) is sure to please horse-happy youngsters who dream of having their own animal, but others will find a few interesting exhibits, too: one allows participants to get a jockey's-eye view from atop several life-size horse models poised in the

historic racing gates for the All-American Futurity. There's a gift shop and play area for the kids.

The museum, exit 72A at 2601 I-40 E, is open to Saturday 9 am to 5 pm, Sunday noon to 5 pm. Admission is $4 for adults, $3.50 for seniors and $2.50 for children between six and 17 years old. The No 4-Sunrise bus runs as far as Ross St and I-40. Get off there and walk four blocks east.

Don Harrington Discovery Center

A hands-on science museum, the Don Harrington Discovery Center (☎ 806-355-9547), 1200 Streit Drive (bus No 8-Medical Center), is fun for explorers of all ages, but especially children. There are special exhibits for babies, toddlers and preschoolers, and cool weather exhibits on such phenomena as hot-air balloons, clouds and tornadoes for older kids. The Discovery Center also has several aquariums and a planetarium. Hours are Tuesday to Saturday 10 am to 5 pm, Sunday 1 to 5 pm. Admission is free unless there's a special traveling exhibit on (if that's the case, plan on $3 to $7), and planetarium shows are typically $3.

The 8½-ton stainless steel Helium Monument in front of the Discovery Center, placed there by an army Chinook helicopter, was built to commemorate the centennial of the discovery of helium, the processing of which was once a major Amarillo industry. The monument contains four time capsules. Nearby, at 1400 Streit Drive, is the Amarillo Garden Center, which has a scent garden for the blind.

Amarillo Museum of Art

The Amarillo Museum of Art (☎ 806-371-5050), 2200 S Van Buren St on the Amarillo College campus (bus No 5), is housed in a fine arts complex designed by Edward Stone, the same architect responsible for the Kennedy Center in Washington, DC. Six galleries feature changing exhibitions and works from the museum's own collection, which include four watercolors by Georgia O'Keeffe. Other notable artists represented include Edward Weston, Dorothea Lange,

Amarillo Street Art

Many cities have murals. Amarillo has unofficial road signs, some 3000 of them, planted prominently in every part of town. Shaped and sized like the diamond-shape signs used as traffic cautions all over the US, Amarillo's signs are instead festooned with everything from paintings to platitudes to just plain gibberish. One sign on Monroe St features an artist's rendering of Marilyn Monroe. Another outside the Atomic Lounge declares 'Victory.' Still others are inexplicable: one shows a drawing of a bat, with the word 'Rabid' stenciled beneath.

Whose idea was this? Though he won't claim personal responsibility, all signs point to Stanley Marsh 3, the same man who commissioned the creation of the Cadillac Ranch. With businesses ranging from broadcasting to real estate, Marsh is really more of an entrepreneur than an artist, but between these signs and the Caddies, he is as responsible as anyone for giving Amarillo some semblance of a unique art scene.

Marsh says the signs, a work in progress, are a guerrilla art project collectively known as the Dynamite Museum. As the project's unofficial spokesman, he doesn't know how many people are involved with the project, nor is he certain how many signs there are. ('I have a rough idea, but on purpose I've forgotten,' he says.) He will tell you the signs aren't supposed to make sense to anyone from outside Amarillo. 'We hope you like them,' he adds. 'But we wouldn't tell you what the references are any more than James Joyce would tell you where he got his puns or Jerry Seinfeld gets his jokes.' Sometimes homeowners or business proprietors request a sign; other times, Dynamite Museum provocateurs ask permission to post one, but signs never go where they're unwanted.

There is no map nor directory to the Amarillo street art, mainly because they're always changing. But Marsh invites you to keep a watch for some of his personal favorites: 'Hey, Good Lookin, Whatcha Got Cookin,' 'Memories & Loneliness,' 'Good Time Girls,' 'More Tears Are Shed over Answered Prayers Than Those Left Unanswered' and 'Remember, You Promised Yourself Today Would Be a Good Day.'

JULIE FANSELOW

Francesco Guardi and Franz Kline. The museum is open Tuesday to Friday 10 am to 5 pm and Saturday and Sunday 1 to 5 pm (except college holidays), and admission is free.

Thompson Memorial Park

At 610 acres, Thompson Memorial Park (north of downtown off Hwy 287) is the one most likely to appeal to visitors. In addition to a swimming pool and a good selection of playground and picnic areas, Thompson Park is home to the local zoo and amusement park.

The Amarillo Zoo The Amarillo Zoo (☎ 806-381-7911) features animals indigenous to the Texas Panhandle, plus a few (such as spider monkeys and a black leopard) from afar. Squirrels, peacocks and other birds roam the grounds, too. Hours are Tuesday to Saturday 9:30 am to 5:30 pm, and admission is free (although donations are accepted).

Wonderland Park Wonderland Park (☎ 806-383-4712) is best known for the Texas Tornado, a double-loop steel roller coaster. There are about two dozen rides in all, plus the usual food, game and entertainment offerings. Admission is $15 on weekends and $9 on weekdays for all ages, which includes all rides except the Texas Tornado (an extra $2.50) and Fantastic Journey, a ride-through haunted house (an additional $1.50). From April to Labor Day, the park is open Saturday and Sunday 1 to 10 pm. Weekdays from June to August, it's also open Monday to Friday 7 pm to 10:30 pm.

Special Events

Western-style events are the big draw in Amarillo. In June, the Tri-State Fairgrounds plays host to the Cowboy Roundup-Coors Ranch Rodeo. The Working Ranch Cowboys Association (☎ 806-467-9722) holds its annual World Championship Ranch Rodeo at the Civic Center each November. As its name implies, this event attracts real working cowpokes for such events as bronco riding, wild-cow milking, team branding and even a wild horse race. Other major happenings on the local calendar include FunFest, a community party held Memorial Day Weekend at Thompson Memorial Park, the Tri-State Fair held each September and an Oktoberfest-Route 66 celebration on W 6th Ave the first weekend of October. For specific dates or more information, call the Amarillo Convention and Visitor Council (listed under Information earlier).

Places to Stay

Camping The best Amarillo-area camping is 22 miles south in Palo Duro Canyon State Park. But if you need to be closer to town, try the *Amarillo KOA* (☎ 806-335-1792), about 5 miles east of town off of US 60. Sites without hookups for tenters or self-contained RVs cost $17, while sites with electricity and

water are $20 and full hookups cost $22. *Wonderland RV Park* (☎ 806-383-1700), in Thompson Memorial Park, has full hookup RV sites for $20.

Motels & Hotels – Budget Amarillo's lowest motel rates are found along Amarillo Blvd, and while most are pretty seedy a few are good budget alternatives. Try the *Interstate Motel* (☎ 806-355-9987) at 7401 Amarillo Blvd W, where rates are $20 for singles and $28 for doubles; the *Civic Center Inn* (☎ 806-376-4603) at 715 S Fillmore St, where you can stay right downtown for $24/35 for singles/doubles; the *Route 66 Inn* (☎ 806-383-3318), 2806 Amarillo Blvd E, with rooms for $25/30; or the *Amarillo Motel* (☎ 806-353-9193), at 4051 Canyon Drive, with rooms for $28/30.

Cheap rooms are harder to find right along I-40; few places have rates less than $50 in summertime. One fairly nice exception is the *Camelot Inn* (☎ 806-373-3600), on the south side at exit 72A at 2508 I-40 E, where singles/doubles go for about $23/29 in winter and $30/36 in summer. The rooms are fine, and rates include continental breakfast. There's an outdoor swimming pool, hot tub and sauna, too. Elsewhere along I-40, the no-frills *Coachlight Inns* have locations at 6810 I-40 E at Whitaker Rd (☎ 806-373-6871) and 2115 I-40E at Ross-Osage Drive (☎ 806-376-5911). Rates at both run $27/35. The *Big Texan Motel* (☎ 806-372-5000, 800-657-7177) at the famous steak house runs $40/55 for singles/doubles including continental breakfast and use of the Texas-shaped pool.

Motels & Hotels – Mid-Range & Top End All the major chains are represented here, mostly along I-40. In the mid-range price category, look for the *Comfort Inn West* (☎ 806-358-6141), 2100 S Coulter St, with rates from $45 to $70; the *La Quinta Inn Medical Center Area* (☎ 806-352-6311), 2108 S Coulter St, with rooms in the $50 to $80 range; the *Hampton Inn* (☎ 806-372-1425), 1700 I-40 E, where rooms run $55 to $75; and the *Best Western Amarillo Inn* (☎ 806-358-7861), 1610 Coulter Drive, with rates about $70 in summertime and $60 the rest of the year.

The **Radisson Inn Amarillo** (☎ 806-373-3303), at 7909 I-40 E, has a handsome indoor atrium with a heated pool. Rates here usually run about $80/90 a night in summertime and about $30 lower in low seasons. The choicest upscale place in town is the **Crowne Plaza** (☎ 806-358-6161, 800-817-0521), 3100 I-40 W. Singles/doubles at this high-rise start at about $90/100.

B&Bs Amarillo's B&Bs are concentrated in a neighborhood of older homes on the fringe of downtown, making them ideal alternatives to the sameness of the I-40 motels. Among the nicest, **Parkview House** (☎ 806-373-9464), 1311 S Jefferson St, has, in addition to five guest rooms, music and world-travel theme common rooms. Rates are $65 to $85. At **Auntie's House Bed & Breakfast** (☎ 806-371-8054), 1712 S Polk St, the big attraction is the Enchanted Cottage, an 800-square-foot home that rents for $150 on weekday nights, $185 on Fridays and $210 on Saturdays, with breakfast delivered to the door. The main house has two rooms priced at $85 each and a suite for $110.

Places to Eat

Fast Food Amarillo is awash in chain eateries of both the regional and national variety. The highest concentrations are along the I-40 frontage roads, Amarillo Blvd, Western St and Coulter St. Among the local offerings, **Catfish Shack** sells seafood at two locations, at 3301 Olsen Blvd and at a drive-through at 2201 S Western St.

American The **Big Texan Steak Ranch** (☎ 806-372-6001), 7700 I-40 E, near the east edge of town, looms large on the Amarillo dining scene, both for its reputation and its mammoth meals. This is the home of the 'free' 72oz steak dinner (see the boxed text earlier in the Amarillo section), but most people choose a slightly less huge dinner, with options ranging from the 10oz prime rib ($14) to an 18oz top sirloin for two people ($27).

It's hard to imagine having room for either an appetizer or dessert at this place, but if you do, try the Texas hors d'oeuvres platter, with diamondback rattlesnake chunks, fried jackrabbit, buffalo meatballs and more for $13. The ridiculously outsize dish of strawberry shortcake ('so big we give non-Texans three forks') is $3.25. Special menus are available for seniors older than 55 and kids younger than 10 (who even get a free cowboy hat with every meal). Hardcore vegetarians won't want to get anywhere near this place, what with all the meat-worshiping and mounted game trophies on display.

Older locals have been eating at the **Blue Front Cafe** (☎ 806-372-0659), 801 W 6th Ave, for decades; it's open for breakfast and lunch daily except Sunday. It's nothing to plan a trip around, but the service is friendly and the food is good and cheap: the $4.65 lunch special includes your choice of chicken-fried steak, hamburger, roast beef or fried cod plus salad, potatoes, veggies, hot rolls and even dessert.

The **Golden Light Cafe** (☎ 806-374-9237), 2908 W 6th Ave in the San Jacinto District, has been open at the same location since 1946, which makes it one of the oldest continuously operating restaurants anywhere on Historic Route 66. It's best known for its burgers ($2.25 to $5) and Route 66 Chili ($3.75). It's closed Sunday. Next door, the Golden Light Cantina offers live music nightly. Don't miss the beer garden out back.

The **Stockyard Cafe** (☎ 806-374-6024), 100 S Manhattan St in the Amarillo Livestock Auction building (see the Armarillo Livestock Auction earlier), is a local favorite for steaks (an 8oz sirloin is $9, and good burgers are $3.25); it's jam-packed for breakfast during the Tuesday livestock auctions (scrambled eggs, diced ham, hash browns, biscuits and gravy run $3.50).

Locals say that the steaks and burgers at the **Lone Star Bar & Grill** (☎ 806-622-9827) are among the best in the area. It's southeast of Amarillo on FM 1151 (a mile east of Washington St-Route 1541) in a modest little building – look for the parking lot paved with long-neck beer-bottle caps. For barbecue, check out **Dyer's** (☎ 806-358-7104), in the Wellington Square shopping center at I-40 and Georgia St, or *Ribs & Blues* (☎ *806-372-7427*), 2917 W 6th Ave.

Mexican *Ruby Tequila's Mexican Kitchen* (☎ *806-358-7829*), 2108 Paramount Blvd south of I-40, has such a strong reputation all over the Panhandle Plains region that it seems hard to believe there's just one. But this is the lone location, and it's a fun spot with giant papier mâché chili peppers and piñatas hanging from the rafters. Open Sunday through Thursday 11 am to 10 pm and Friday and Saturday from 11 am to 11 pm, Ruby's is also a favorite with late-night diners. The wide menu includes dozens of entrées and combo plates priced from about $6 for a pechuga (chargrilled chicken breast) to $13 for heart-healthy ostrich fajitas. For dessert, try the margarita pie ($3) served straight-up in a cocktail glass with a twist of lime.

The *Plaza* (☎ *806-358-4897*), 3415 Bell St on the southeast corner of 34th Ave, has $4.69 lunch specials that range from two enchiladas to the queso papa asada – a big baked potato stuffed with chili and cheese, sour cream, guacamole and black olives. For dinner, plates run about $8 to $9 for such fare as stuff-your-own tortillas or el relleno presidente, a chile relleno filled with tomato sauce, sour cream, raisins and pecans. A half-dozen American dishes fill out the menu.

Eclectic *Cafe Americana* (☎ *806-373-1122*), 507 S Alabama St just off W 6th Ave in San Jacinto, specializes in pizza. The big kahoona, priced at $12 and ample enough for two or three people, is smothered in tomato-basil sauce and piled high with prosciutto, sausage, hamburger, pepperoni, veggies and mozzarella. The menu also includes steaks, salads, pastas and a good selection of microbrews. It's open for lunch and dinner Wednesday through Saturday, and there's live music most nights.

Hearty fare for both vegetarians and carnivores can be found at *On Her Majesty's Service Cafe* (☎ *806-373-3233*), 619 S Tyler St downtown, open only for lunch on weekdays and dinner on Friday and Saturday. Ah, but the food: for $6 at lunch and $7.50 to $10.50 at dinner, there's a choice of a half-dozen

creative, seasonally inspired dishes like mango-chutney chicken, red-chili linguine with cilantro pesto or even some of the best down-home macaroni and cheese you'll ever eat. There's live acoustic music on the weekends and a changing array of art exhibits, too.

Entertainment

Classical Music & Theater The *Amarillo Symphony* (☎ *806-376-8782*) and the *Lone Star Ballet* (☎ *806-372-2463*) perform in the Amarillo Civic Center auditorium, at 401 S Buchanan St. The *Amarillo Little Theatre* (☎ *806-355-9991*) presents plays at 2019 Civic Circle south of I-40 off of Wolflin Ave.

Western Every Tuesday night, the Big Texan Steak Ranch (☎ *806-372-6000*) – see Places to Eat earlier – puts on an old-time Opry show. Admission is free with a dinner purchase. The Big Texan also houses a playhouse where an old-style Western melodrama (staged summer weekends) and dinner go for about $25.

Bars & Clubs Amarillo isn't a big nightclubbing town, but a few of the local hot spots include the *Caravan* (☎ *806-359-5436*), at 3601 Olsen Blvd, a cavernous country-and-western club with frequent live music; *Midnight Rodeo* (☎ *806-358-7083*), 4400 S Georgia St, another country club; and *Coaches Sports Bar & Cafe* (☎ *806-376-1925*), at 4901 Washington St.

Amarillo has no bars that are strictly gay or lesbian, but several that do draw a mixed crowd of gays and straights. *Classifieds* (☎ *806-374-2435*), a dance club at 519 E 10th Ave, gets a straight crowd most of the week but goes heavily gay on Friday. The *Ritz* (☎ *806-372-9382*), 323 W 10th Ave, is mostly for men, while *Sassy's* (☎ *806-374-3029*), 309 W 6th Ave, draws more women.

Microbrewery The *Brew Pub* (☎ *806-353-2622*) at 3705 Olsen Blvd didn't use much imagination coming up with its name, but locals say it makes a good raspberry ale.

Coffeehouses On the west end of the San Jacinto District, look for the *Atomic Lounge*

(☎ 806-351-0084), 3808 W 6th Ave, which blends glam and rec-room comfort with its animal-print tablecloths, movie-star artwork, pool table and TV video games.

Spectator Sports
The Amarillo Rattlers (☎ 806-374-7825), part of the Western Professional Hockey League, play professional minor-league hockey at the Amarillo Civic Center, 401 S Buchanan St. The season runs October through March. Ticket prices range from $8.50 to $13.

The Amarillo Dillas are among the Texas-Louisiana League's top-drawing teams, with 160,000 baseball fans attending the season, which runs late May through August. Games take place at Dick Bivins Field at the Tri-State Fairgrounds, 3301 E 10th Ave. Tickets cost $4 to $7. For more information on games and tickets, call ☎ 806-342-3455.

Shopping
If you're looking for Western wear, you will love Cavender's Boot City (☎ 806-358-1400), 7920 I-40 W. This warehouse-size emporium is the second-biggest among Cavender's 30-odd locations around Texas. It has about 12,000 pairs of boots in stock at all times, ranging in price from $40 for a basic pair to $1,300 for Lucchese's prized hornback alligator style. What's more, you can get a shave, a haircut and a cup of coffee before you leave the place.

The big shopping center in Amarillo, Westgate Mall (☎ 806-358-7221), is located at 7701 I-40 W. It has about 100 stores including JC Penney, Sears, Mervyn's, Dillard and Beall's. Bus No 7-Western Plaza will get you there.

Getting There & Away
Air Amarillo International Airport (☎ 806-335-1671) is located on the east edge of town north of I-40 via exit 76. It's currently served by American, Continental, Delta ASA and Southwest.

Bus Greyhound and Trailways both operate out of the bus terminal at 700 S Tyler downtown (☎ 806-374-5371). Sample fares are listed here.

to/from	trip duration	one way/ roundtrip
Albuquerque, NM	5 hours	$52/104
Dallas	8 hours	$50/95
El Paso	10 hours	$57/117
Oklahoma City, OK	5 1/2 hours	$48/85

Car Most major car rental companies have offices at the airport including Advantage (☎ 806-335-1500), Avis (☎ 806-335-2313), Budget (☎ 806-335-2812), Enterprise (☎ 806-372-5549), Hertz (☎ 806-335-2331), National (☎ 806-335-2311) and Thrifty (☎ 806-335-3300).

Getting Around
To/From the Airport Taxi fares from the Amarillo airport run about $8 to $9 to east-side hotels, $12 to central Amarillo and $14 to $16 to the west side. No city bus line reaches the airport, but some local hotels and motels offer free shuttle service to the terminal.

Bus Amarillo City Transit (☎ 806-378-3094) runs the city buses. Fare is 75¢ for adults, 60¢ for kids between six and 12 years old and 35¢ for senior citizens and people with disabilities. All fares require exact change and include a transfer.

Taxi Taxi rates are $1.30 at flagfall and $1 per additional mile. Royal Cab (☎ 806-376-4276, fax 806-376-1211) provides standard cab service as well as custom-designed tours. For example, an excursion to Palo Duro Canyon for up to five people runs $38, while a tour of local sites including 6th Ave and the Cadillac Ranch costs $26 for up to five folks. Other cab companies include Amtex (☎ 806-371-8294), Bob's Taxi Service (☎ 806-373-1171) and Yellow Checker (☎ 806-765-7777).

AROUND AMARILLO
Canyon
Population 12,601
Just 16 miles south of Amarillo, the little college town of Canyon is in many ways more interesting than its neighbor to the north. Georgia O'Keeffe once taught art at what is now West Texas A&M University, and today's campus is home to what many people

figure is the best history museum in Texas – the Panhandle-Plains Historical Museum. Moreover, this is the main supply depot for Palo Duro Canyon State Park, among the state's natural showpieces.

Panhandle-Plains Historical Museum

First-class all the way, the Panhandle-Plains Historical Museum (☎ 806-651-2244), 2401 4th Ave, is the largest of its kind in Texas. It would be easy to spend an entire day wandering its halls, but it's worth a stop for even an hour.

The museum's entrance offers a microcosm of Texas life, from the cattle brands surrounding the exterior doors to the native animals engraved on the facade, all in magnificent art-deco style. Inside the entrance hall, murals by noted Lone Star artists Ben Carlton Mead and HD Bugbee depict Texas history.

The five main sections of the museum include the Don D Harrington Petroleum Wing, where the Panhandle's oil heyday is seen through the prism of the boomtown of Borger and the old-time Cal's Filling Station; Paleontology and Geology, which includes life-size casts of several prehistoric beasts plus a model of Palo Duro Canyon; Transportation, featuring a 1903 Ford Model A with the earliest-known serial number (28) of any surviving cars of that type, making it possibly the oldest assembly-line auto in the world; an outstanding art collection with everything from Texas painters and photographers to a Ming Dynasty vase and 15th-century European furniture; and Western Heritage, with a walk-through Pioneer Town and exhibits on ranching and Native American heritage. Interactive exhibits show visitors everything from how windmills work to how a range of mountains lies buried beneath the North Texas Plains today. Of course there's a neat gift shop and a fabulous library too.

June through August, the museum is open Monday to Saturday 9 am to 6 pm and Sunday 1 to 6 pm. Hours are the same the rest of the year except it closes at 5 pm Monday through Saturday and is closed altogether on Thanksgiving Day, December 24 and 25 and January 1. The suggested donation is $5 for adults and $1 for children ages 12 and under.

Palo Duro Canyon State Park At 120 miles long and about 5 miles wide, Palo Duro Canyon is the second-largest canyon in the US (next to the Grand Canyon in Arizona). Moreover, unlike the Grand Canyon, you can drive into Palo Duro. Whether that accessibility is a good or bad thing might be debatable, but the park isn't entirely paved over, and there are plenty of ways for visitors to get off the beaten path and deep into some of Texas' most splendid scenery.

Palo Duro Canyon was created by the Prairie Dog Town Fork of the Red River, a long name for a little river. The great gorge has sheltered and inspired people for a long time. Prehistoric Indians lived in the canyon 12,000 years ago, and Coronado may have stopped by in 1541. Palo Duro was the site of an 1874 battle between Comanche and Kiowa warriors and the US Army, and in 1876, ranching pioneer Charles Goodnight began raising cattle here. The 16,042 acres that make up the park were deeded to the state by private owners in 1933 and opened to the public a year later. Today, the park attracts hikers, horseback riders and mountain bikers eager for recreation and artists and photographers drawn by the magnificent blend of color and desert light.

Palo Duro Canyon State Park (☎ 806-488-2227) is at the end of Hwy 217, 12 miles east of Canyon and 24 miles southeast of Amarillo. The best time to visit is in the fall or winter because it gets dang hot here in the summertime. Pay the $3-per-person entry fee at the park gate, where they'll give you a map and help get you on your way. A visitors' center just down the road overlooks the canyon and has interpretive exhibits on the area's geology and history (inquire about plans for guided tours), and the Goodnight Trading Post serves meals and sells souvenirs and supplies.

Hiking Palo Duro's most popular trail leads to the Lighthouse, a hoodoo-style formation that's nearly 300 feet tall. Almost all of the 4½-mile roundtrip Lighthouse Trail is flat and easily traversed, though there is a 100-foot climb to the formation itself. The floodplain to the southwest of the Lighthouse Trail has perhaps the park's greatest concentration of wildlife including aoudad sheep, white-tailed mule deer and wild turkeys. Find the Lighthouse trailhead off Park Road 5 just past the second crossing of the Prairie Dog Town Fork.

Although it's much more rugged and twice as long, the so-called Running Trail earns praise from Palo Duro-area denizens as the best in the park. It, too, leads to the Lighthouse but takes its time on a winding, up-and-down 9-mile path. The trailhead is located at the Hackberry Camp Area, which is by the first river crossing. Carry and drink plenty of water on this or any other Palo Duro trail.

Horseback Riding The Goodnight Riding Stables (☎ 806-488-2786) offer a variety of trips in Palo Duro Canyon. The Lighthouse Trail Ride costs $75 per person including lunch, while a sunrise-to-sunset sojourn costs $100 including breakfast, lunch and dinner. An overnight ride runs $125 including meals. You'll need to bring a sleeping bag for this one; none are available to rent. There's a six-person minimum for these trips, but smaller parties can usually be accommodated by joining with another group. Reservations are necessary.

For shorter rides (no reservations necessary), the stables charge $10 per person per hour, with kids younger than six years old riding double with an adult for an additional $2. Pay up front for the first hour, and it's prorated after that. Goodnight's friendly staff can get you on the trail even if you've never been on a horse.

Mountain Biking A mountain-bikes-only trail makes a loop off of the Lighthouse Trail, and other trails in the park are open to bikes, too. The Goodnight Trading Post (☎ 806-488-2760) rents out mountain bikes for $5 per hour, with a $100 cash or credit-card deposit.

Texas About 3 million people have seen this musical drama, a pageant of Panhandle history. Mid-June through late August, it plays nightly at 8:30 except Sunday in the Pioneer Amphitheater.

Monday to Thursday, adult ticket prices range from $8 to $15. Friday and Saturday,

they're $10 to $19. Children younger than 12 are admitted for half price in all but the best seats (in the center back section, where they pay full price). There's no charge for kids younger than three years old who sit on someone's lap. Advanced reservations are suggested; call ☎ 806-655-2181 or write for a brochure to *Texas*, PO Box 268, Canyon, TX 79015. Many people make an evening of *Texas* by arriving early for a barbecue dinner served on performance days from 6 to 8 pm. Admiral Bus Service (☎ 806-354-8533) offers shuttle service to the musical from Amarillo and Canyon motels. Roundtrip cost is $10 for adults, $9 for seniors 62 and older and $6 for children 11 and younger. Call its office before 6 pm on the day of the performance to arrange for a ride.

Places to Stay There are several options for places to stay in Canyon or in the park. Palo Duro Canyon State Park has seven formal *camping* areas with nearly 150 sites, plus many primitive sites for backpackers and horseback riders. Campsites range from $9 to $12 depending on the type. Reservations are a must in spring, summer and fall and may be made by calling the Texas State Parks Central Reservations Center at ☎ 512-389-8900.

Palo Duro RV Park (☎ *806-488-2548*) has 60 sites, showers and laundry facilities at the junction of I-27 and Hwy 217. Full hookup rates run $14 to $16, and tents cost $10. The two rental *cabins* within Palo Duro Canyon State Park cost $69 a night for up to four people. (Park entrance fees are extra.) No kitchen facilities are included, and visitors must bring their own bed linens. Any cabin reservation for either Friday or Saturday must include both nights. Call ☎ 512-389-8900 for reservations.

The *Buffalo Inn* (☎ *806-655-2124, 800-526-9968*), 300 23rd St (US 87), is centrally located by the West Texas A&M campus, with summer rates of $42 singles and $46 doubles. At the south end of town on US 87, the *Goodnight Inn* (☎ *806-655-1132, 800-654-7350*) has an outdoor swimming pool. Rooms run $50 for a king-size bed and $55 for two double beds.

The *Country Home (☎ 806-655-7636, 800-664-7636)* is located south of town via 8th St on 200 acres. It has a hot tub, and a refreshments, continental breakfast and a late-night cheesecake snack are delivered to your room. Rates are $95.

Places to Eat Canyon has a good selection of both fast-food chain eateries and locally owned spots. If you're in town around noon on a Sunday, consider the buffet at *Teresa's Diner (☎ 806-655-0778)*, 601 23rd St. For $4.50 (a dollar more for a big plate), you can feed on chicken-fried steak, catfish or roast beef with all the trimmings. The deal even includes dessert; try the banana cream pudding. *Stomping Grounds Espresso (☎ 806-655-7711)*, 2320 4th Ave, serves soup and sandwiches daily except Sundays, when it's closed. It's also open late for coffee and an array of cheesecakes and other sweets.

Cowboy Morning and Evening

If you've a thirst to taste the cowboy way of life, head on out to Figure 3 Ranch (☎ 806-944-5562, 800-658-2613), a working spread that offers hearty meals overlooking Palo Duro Canyon. Breakfast visitors leave the ranch house at 8:30 am for a horse-drawn wagon ride to the canyon rim, where the repast includes biscuits and gravy, eggs, sausage, orange juice and cowboy coffee. Dinner departure times vary depending on the time of year, but the meal always includes rib-eye steak, salad, beans, biscuits and campfire cobbler. After chow, dudes can try their hands at roping and cow chip tossing.

June to August, Cowboy Morning and Evening is offered each day. The meals also take place at times in April, May, September and October, but you'll need to call ahead to check on availability. Breakfast costs $19 for adults and teens and $14.50 for children between four and 12 years old. Dinner goes for $22.50 for adults and $14.50 for kids. Advance reservations are necessary. Figure 3 Ranch is located on Ranch Road 1258 an hour's drive southeast of Amarillo (via I-40 exit 77). From Canyon or Palo Duro State Park, figure a 75-minute drive via ranch roads 1541 north, 1151 east then 1258 southeast.

Highway 207 Scenic Drive

Many Panhandle locals say the best views of Palo Duro Canyon aren't in the park but along Hwy 207 between Claude and Silverton. This 48-mile stretch enters the canyon lands about 13 miles south of Claude, with some of the most dramatic scenery at the crossings of the Prairie Dog Town Fork of the Red River and Tule Creek. Near the latter ford, MacKenzie Reservoir has camping, fishing and boating.

Lake Meredith National Recreation Area

Like the Palo Duro and Caprock canyon lands south of Amarillo, Lake Meredith National Recreation Area (☎ 806-857-3151) to the city's north comes as a major surprise. The lake, a result of the Sanford Dam on the Canadian River, was created mainly to get water to the otherwise-arid cities of Amarillo, Lubbock and nine other Panhandle towns. But the byproduct is a recreation area popular for boating and fishing.

Boating Boat launch ramps are available at Bates Canyon, Harbor Bay, Fritch Fortress, Cedar Canyon, and Sanford-Yake on the lake's east side and Blue West and Plum Creek on the west side. Fluctuating water levels occasionally leave Bates Canyon and Plum Creek high and dry. Sanford-Yake, on the other hand, is always accessible and always busy since it's the site of the lake marina.

Boat rentals are available at the lake through Forever Resorts (☎ 806-865-3391, 800-255-5561), which runs the marina. Rates run $135 a day (eight hours) plus a $135 deposit for a 26-foot deck cruiser and $100 a day plus a $100 deposit for a 20-foot power boat.

Houseboats are available, too. A 56-foot model that sleeps up to 10 people is outfitted with kitchen appliances, a TV, VCR, stereo, grill, a 500-square-foot sun deck and even a water slide. In June, July and August, the rigs rent for $1,995 a week; the late spring and early fall shoulder season rates are $1,650 per week; and the off-season cost is $1,100 a week. Shorter rentals are available year-round, too; June to August, the cost is $1,395 for three or four nights. No special licenses are needed, and inexperienced captains are taught basic boating on the spot before the rental begins.

Fishing Lake Meredith is home to large-mouth, small-mouth and white bass, catfish, white crappie, sunfish, carp and walleye. A Texas fishing license is required (see the Activities chapter for information on getting a state license). Hank McWilliams (☎ 806-857-2796) comes locally recommended for chartered fishing trips.

Camping Three kinds of campsites are available around Lake Meredith: caprock campgrounds on the bluffs overlooking the lake at Sanford-Yake, Fritch Fortress and Blue West; canyon campgrounds situated away from the lake at McBride Canyon, Rosita, Plum Creek and Blue Creek Bridge; and shoreline campgrounds at Cedar Canyon, Harbor Bay, Chimney Hollow, Bugbee and Spring Canyon. In addition, two sites – Sandy Point and Blue East – are accessible only by boat.

Camping at Lake Meredith is free, mainly because amenities are limited: There are no hookups or showers, but there are generally picnic tables, grills and toilets. All sites are first-come, first-served, and no one can camp in the NRA more than 14 days per year.

Alibates Flint Quarries National Monument

It's not every day you can pick up a hammer stone used to make tools 10,000 years ago or hold discarded shards of beautifully colored flint left behind by ancient peoples. But at Alibates Flint Quarries, visitors can touch the past and learn what it was like to live off the land when mammoths roamed the Plains.

History Back before the US Great Lakes were even formed, people of the Ice Age Clovis Culture came to what is now known as the Canadian River basin to mine flint for spear points, knives and scrapers. The flint has always been found in dolomite limestone outcrops atop the Canadian River breaks. The Stone-Age nomads would find it by digging just a few inches down. The flint was notable not just for its excellent quality, but for its varied hues: pink, purple, red, white and dark blue.

Most of the ancient visitors collected their flint and left for their homes in what is now New Mexico, but the area also saw some other, local farming-based civilization between 1150 and 1500. Although the name 'alibates' sounds faintly geological, it's actually the moniker of an early-20th-century settler for whom the monument was named: Ali Bates.

Visiting Unlike most National Park Service areas, visitors cannot simply stroll into Alibates Flint Quarries. The site may only be visited on a tour led by rangers or experienced volunteer guides. Tours involve about a 1½ miles of walking with plenty of rest stops along the way, where guides talk about the quarry and the people who worked it. Memorial Day through Labor Day, tours are given daily at 10 am and 2 pm; the rest of the year, tours are by advance reservation only. The tours leave from the small ranger contact station, reached by driving 5 miles west of State Hwy 136 on Alibates Rd. Allow about an hour for travel from Amarillo. Call ☎ 806-857-3151 for more information or to request an off-season tour. There are no services at or near the quarries, but camping is available at adjacent Lake Meredith National Recreation Area. The nearest gas and food are in Fritch, 6 miles north of the Alibates Rd turnoff.

Language

Visitors can get away with English only, but to do that is to write off experiencing a huge chunk of Texas culture and life. Spanish can prove indispensable here. It's the main language in many shops, cafés, coin laundries and restaurants along the border and in a surprising number of businesses elsewhere in the state, especially San Antonio.

See Food in the Facts for the Visitor chapter for Mexican and Tex-Mex menu information.

Books When you go, take along Lonely Planet's *Latin American Spanish phrasebook* by Anna Cody, which is comprehensive and compact. If you're planning on romancing some Latin types, the absolute finest resources for you are *Hot Spanish for Guys and Girls* and *Hot Spanish for Guys and Guys*; both contain an amazing number of useful phrases, from 'I'd like to hold your hand' to 'lick around the edges.'

Jonathan Maeder's brilliant *Wordless Travel Book* is great if you consider yourself clueless about language; it's full of pictures of pretty much anything you'll need on a vacation – just point at what you want in the book.

Pronunciation Spanish has five vowels: **a**, **e**, **i**, **o** and **u**. They are pronounced something like the highlighted letters of the following English words: f**a**ther, **e**nd, mar**i**ne, **o**r and tr**u**th. The stress is placed on the syllable with an accent over it (México=MEH-hiko) or the second to last syllable (hasta luego= AH-sta loo-EH-go).

Useful Words & Phrases

yes	*sí*
no	*no*
good/OK	*bueno*
bad	*malo*
best	*mejor*
more	*más*
less	*menos*
very little	*poco* or *poquito*
help!	*¡socorro!*

Greetings & Civilities

hello/hi	*hola*
good morning/day	*buenos días*
good afternoon	*buenas tardes*
good evening/night	*buenas noches*
see you later	*hasta luego*
goodbye	*adiós*
pleased to meet you	*mucho gusto*
please	*por favor*
thank you	*gracias*
you're welcome	*de nada*

excuse me (when someone is in the way or for getting attention)
   con permiso
excuse me (when apologizing)
   perdóneme

Buying

I would like…	*Quisiera…*
I want…	*Quiero…*
What do you want?	*¿Qué quiere?*
Do you have…?	*¿Tiene…?*
Is/are there…?	*¿Hay…?*
I understand.	*Entiendo.*
I do not understand.	*No entiendo.*
Do you understand?	*¿Entiende usted?*

How much does it cost?
   ¿Cuánto cuesta?
Please speak slowly.
   Por favor hable despacio.

Getting Around

street	*calle*
avenue	*avenida*
corner (of)	*esquina (de)*
block	*cuadra*
to the left	*a la izquierda*
to the right	*a la derecha*
straight ahead	*derecho*
Where is…?	*¿Dónde está…?*
the bus station	*el terminal de autobús, central camionera*
the train station	*la estación del ferrocarril*
bus	*autobús, camión*

train	*tren*
taxi	*taxi*
toilet	*servicio* or *baño*

Crossing the Border

border	*la frontera*
car-owner's title	*título de propiedad*
car registration	*registración*
customs	*aduana*
driver's license	*licencia de manejar*
identification	*identificación*
immigration	*inmigración*
insurance	*seguro*
passport	*pasaporte*
tourist card	*tarjeta de turista*
visa	*visado*

birth certificate
  certificado de nacimiento
temporary vehicle import permit
  permiso de importación temporal
  de vehículo

Numbers

0	*cero*
1	*un, uno* (m), *una* (f)
2	*dos*
3	*tres*
4	*cuatro*
5	*cinco*
6	*seis*
7	*siete*
8	*ocho*
9	*nueve*
10	*diez*
11	*once*
12	*doce*
13	*trece*
14	*catorce*
15	*quince*
16	*dieciséis*
17	*diecisiete*
18	*dieciocho*
19	*diecinueve*
20	*veinte*
30	*treinta*
40	*cuarenta*
50	*cincuenta*
100	*cien*
200	*doscientos*
500	*quinientos*
1000	*mil*
1,000,000	*millón*

Toll-Free Numbers

Toll-free number information
☎ 800-555-1212

Accommodations

Best Western	☎ 800-528-1234
Budgetel	☎ 800-428-3438
Choice	☎ 800-424-6423
Clarion	☎ 800-252-7466
Comfort Inn	☎ 800-221-2222
Courtyard by Marriott	☎ 800-321-2211
Days Inn	☎ 800-329-7466
EconoLodge	☎ 800-424-4777
Embassy Suites Hotels	☎ 800-362-2779
Fairfield Inns	☎ 800-228-2800
Fairmont	☎ 800-527-4727
Four Seasons	☎ 800-332-3442
Hampton Inns	☎ 800-426-7866
HI-AYH	☎ 800-909-4776
Hilton	☎ 800-445-8667
Holiday Inn	☎ 800-465-4329
Howard Johnson	☎ 800-446-4656
Hyatt	☎ 800-233-1234
Inter-Continental Hotels	☎ 800-327-0200
ITT Sheraton	☎ 800-325-3535
La Quinta Motor Inns	☎ 800-531-5900
Loews	☎ 800-235-6397
Marriott	☎ 800-228-9290
Meridien	☎ 800-543-5300
Motel 6	☎ 800-466-8356
Omni	☎ 800-843-6664
Radisson	☎ 800-333-3333
Ramada	☎ 800-272-6232
Red Lion Inns	☎ 800-547-8010
Red Roof Inns	☎ 800-843 7663
Rodeway Inn	☎ 800-424-4777
Sheraton	☎ 800-325-3535
Sleep Inns	☎ 800-424-4777
Super 8	☎ 800-800-8000
Susse Chalet	☎ 800-524-2538
Travelodge	☎ 800-578-7878
Vagabond Hotels	☎ 800-522-1555
Westin	☎ 800-228-3000
Wyndham	☎ 800-822-4200

Airlines (Domestic)

Airtran	☎ 800-825-8538
Alaska	☎ 800-426-0333
American	☎ 800-433-7300
America West	☎ 800-235-9292
Aspen Mountain Air-Lone Star	☎ 800-877-3932
Big Sky	☎ 800-237-7788
Continental	☎ 800-525-0280
Delta	
(Domestic)	☎ 800-221-1212
(International)	☎ 800-241-4141
Hawaiian	☎ 800-367-5320
Northwest	
(Domestic)	☎ 800-225-2525
(International)	☎ 800-447-4747
Skywest-Delta Connection	☎ 800-453-9417
Southwest	☎ 800-435-9792
Tower	☎ 800-348-6937
TWA	
(Domestic)	☎ 800-221-2000
(International)	☎ 800-892-4141
United	
(Domestic)	☎ 800-241-6522
(International)	☎ 800-631-1500
US Airways	☎ 800-428-4322

Airlines (International)

AeroLitoral	☎ 800-237-6639
AeroMexico	☎ 800-237-6639
Air Canada	☎ 800-776-3000
Air France	☎ 800-237-2747
Air New Zealand	☎ 800-262-1234
Aviateca	☎ 800-327-9832
British Airways	☎ 800-247-9297
Canadian	☎ 800-231-0856
Grupo TACA	☎ 800-535-8780
Japan Air	☎ 800-525-3663
KLM	☎ 800-374-7747
Lufthansa	☎ 800-645-3880
Mexicana	☎ 800-531-7921
Qantas	☎ 800-227-4500
Virgin Atlantic	☎ 800-862-8621

Car-Rental Agencies

Advantage	☎ 800-777-5500
Alamo	☎ 800-327-9633
Avis	☎ 800-831-2847
	800-331-1212
Budget	☎ 800-527-0700
	800-472-3325
CruiseAmerica	
(RV rental)	☎ 800-327-7799
Dollar	☎ 800-800-4000
Enterprise	☎ 800-325-8007
	800-736-8222
Hertz	☎ 800-654-3131
	800-227-7368
National	☎ 800-328-4567
	800-227-3876
National (TDD)	☎ 800-328-6323
Rent-a-Wreck	☎ 800-535-1391
Thrifty	☎ 800-367-2277

Money

Western Union	☎ 800-325-6000

State & Federal Agencies

Texas Department of Transportation	☎ 800-452-9292
Texas Information Center	☎ 800-452-9292
Texas Parks and Wildlife Department	☎ 800-792-1112
National Park Service	☎ 800-365-2267
US Forest Service	☎ 800-280-2267
US Postal Service	☎ 800-275-8777

Transportation

AAA	☎ 800-477-1222
Amtrak	☎ 800-872-7245
Green Tortoise	☎ 800-227-4766
Greyhound	☎ 800-231-2222
Greyhound International	☎ 800-246-8572
SuperShuttle	☎ 800-258-3826

Travel Agencies

Carlson-Wagonlit Travel	☎ 800-510-4703
Council Travel	☎ 800-226-8624
STA	☎ 800-777-0112

Phrasebooks

L onely Planet phrasebooks are packed with essential words and phrases to help travellers communicate with the locals. With color tabs for quick reference, an extensive vocabulary and use of script, these handy pocket-sized language guides cover day-to-day travel situations.

- handy pocket-sized books
- easy to understand Pronunciation chapter
- clear & comprehensive Grammar chapter
- romanization alongside script to allow ease of pronunciation
- script throughout so users can point to phrases for every situation
- full of cultural information and tips for the traveller

'...vital for a real DIY spirit and attitude in language learning'
– Backpacker

'the phrasebooks have good cultural backgrounders and offer solid advice for challenging situations in remote locations'
– San Francisco Examiner

Arabic (Egyptian) • Arabic (Moroccan) • Australian *(Australian English, Aboriginal and Torres Strait languages)* • Baltic States *(Estonian, Latvian, Lithuanian)* • Bengali • Brazilian • Burmese • Cantonese • Central Asia • Central Europe *(Czech, French, German, Hungarian, Italian, Slovak)* • Eastern Europe *(Bulgarian, Czech, Hungarian, Polish, Romanian, Slovak)* • Ethiopian (Amharic) • Fijian • French • German • Greek • Hill Tribes • Hindi/Urdu • Indonesian • Italian • Japanese • Korean • Lao • Latin American Spanish • Malay • Mandarin • Mediterranean Europe *(Albanian, Croatian, Greek, Italian, Macedonian, Maltese, Serbian, Slovene)* • Mongolian • Nepali • Papua New Guinea • Pilipino (Tagalog) • Quechua • Russian • Scandinavian Europe *(Danish, Finnish, Icelandic, Norwegian, Swedish)* • South-East Asia *(Burmese, Indonesian, Khmer, Lao, Malay, Tagalog Pilipino, Thai, Vietnamese)* • Spanish (Castilian) *(also includes Catalan, Galician and Basque)* • Sri Lanka • Swahili • Thai • Tibetan • Turkish • Ukrainian • USA *(US English, Vernacular, Native American languages, Hawaiian)* • Vietnamese • Western Europe *(Basque, Catalan, Dutch, French, German, Greek, Irish)*

LONELY PLANET

Guides by Region

onely Planet is known worldwide for publishing practical, reliable and no-nonsense travel information in our guides and on our Web site. The Lonely Planet list covers just about every accessible part of the world. Currently there are 16 series: Travel guides, Shoestring guides, Condensed guides, Phrasebooks, Read This First, Healthy Travel, Walking guides, Cycling guides, Watching Wildlife guides, Pisces Diving & Snorkeling guides, City Maps, Road Atlases, Out to Eat, World Food, Journeys travel literature and Pictorials.

AFRICA Africa on a shoestring • Cairo • Cape Town • Cape Town City Map • East Africa • Egypt • Egyptian Arabic phrasebook • Ethiopia, Eritrea & Djibouti • Ethiopian (Amharic) phrasebook • The Gambia & Senegal • Healthy Travel Africa • Kenya • Malawi • Morocco • Moroccan Arabic phrasebook • Mozambique • Read This First: Africa • South Africa, Lesotho & Swaziland • Southern Africa • Southern Africa Road Atlas • Swahili phrasebook • Tanzania, Zanzibar & Pemba • Trekking in East Africa • Tunisia • Watching Wildlife East Africa • Watching Wildlife Southern Africa • West Africa • World Food Morocco • Zimbabwe, Botswana & Namibia
Travel Literature: Mali Blues: Traveling to an African Beat • The Rainbird: A Central African Journey • Songs to an African Sunset: A Zimbabwean Story

AUSTRALIA & THE PACIFIC Auckland • Australia • Australian phrasebook • Australia Road Atlas • Bushwalking in Australia •Cycling New Zealand • Fiji • Fijian phrasebook • Healthy Travel Australia, NZ and the Pacific • Islands of Australia's Great Barrier Reef • Melbourne • Melbourne City Map • Micronesia • New Caledonia • New South Wales & the ACT • New Zealand • Northern Territory • Outback Australia • Out to Eat – Melbourne • Out to Eat – Sydney • Papua New Guinea • Pidgin phrasebook • Queensland • Rarotonga & the Cook Islands • Samoa • Solomon Islands • South Australia • South Pacific • South Pacific phrasebook • Sydney • Sydney City Map • Sydney Condensed • Tahiti & French Polynesia • Tasmania • Tonga • Tramping in New Zealand • Vanuatu • Victoria • Watching Wildlife Australia • Western Australia
Travel Literature: Islands in the Clouds: Travels in the Highlands of New Guinea • Kiwi Tracks: A New Zealand Journey • Sean & David's Long Drive

CENTRAL AMERICA & THE CARIBBEAN Bahamas, Turks & Caicos • Baja California • Bermuda • Central America on a shoestring • Costa Rica • Costa Rica Spanish phrasebook • Cuba • Dominican Republic & Haiti • Eastern Caribbean • Guatemala • Guatemala, Belize & Yucatán: La Ruta Maya • Healthy Travel Central & South America • Jamaica • Mexico • Mexico City • Panama • Puerto Rico • Read This First: Central & South America • World Food Mexico • Yucatán
Travel Literature: Green Dreams: Travels in Central America

EUROPE Amsterdam • Amsterdam City Map • Amsterdam Condensed • Andalucía • Austria • Baltic States phrasebook • Barcelona • Barcelona City Map • Berlin • Berlin City Map • Britain • British phrasebook • Brussels, Bruges & Antwerp • Budapest • Budapest City Map • Canary Islands • Central Europe • Central Europe phrasebook • Corfu & the Ionians • Corsica • Crete • Crete Condensed • Croatia • Cycling Britain • Cycling France • Cyprus • Czech & Slovak Republics • Denmark • Dublin • Dublin City Map • Eastern Europe • Eastern Europe phrasebook • Edinburgh • Estonia, Latvia & Lithuania • Europe on a shoestring • Finland • Florence • France • Frankfurt Condensed • French phrasebook • Georgia, Armenia & Azerbaijan • Germany • German phrasebook • Greece • Greek Islands • Greek phrasebook • Hungary • Iceland, Greenland & the Faroe Islands • Ireland • Istanbul • Italian phrasebook • Italy • Krakow • Lisbon • The Loire • London • London City Map • London Condensed • Madrid • Malta • Mediterranean Europe • Mediterranean Europe phrasebook • Moscow • Mozambique • Munich • Norway • Out to Eat – London • Paris • Paris City Map • Paris Condensed • Poland • Portugal • Portuguese phrasebook • Prague • Prague City Map • Provence & the Côte d'Azur • Read This First: Europe • Romania & Moldova • Rome • Russia, Ukraine & Belarus • Russian phrasebook • Scandinavian & Baltic Europe • Scandinavian Europe phrasebook • Scotland • Sicily • Slovenia • South-West France • Spain • Spanish phrasebook • St Petersburg • St Petersburg City Map • Sweden • Switzerland • Trekking in Spain • Tuscany • Ukrainian phrasebook • Venice • Vienna • Walking in Britain • Walking in France • Walking in Ireland • Walking in Italy • Walking in Spain • Walking in Switzerland • Western Europe • Western Europe phrasebook • World Food France • World Food Ireland • World Food Italy • World Food Spain
Travel Literature: Love and War in the Apennines • The Olive Grove: Travels in Greece • On the Shores of the Mediterranean • Round Ireland in Low Gear • A Small Place in Italy

INDIAN SUBCONTINENT Bangladesh • Bengali phrasebook • Bhutan • Delhi • Goa • Healthy Travel Asia & India • Hindi & Urdu phrasebook • India • Indian Himalaya • Karakoram Highway • Kerala • Mumbai

LONELY PLANET

Mail Order

Lonely Planet products are distributed worldwide. They are also available by mail order from Lonely Planet, so if you have difficulty finding a title please write to us. North and South American residents should write to 150 Linden St, Oakland, CA 94607, USA; European and African residents should write to 10a Spring Place, London NW5 3BH, UK; and residents of other countries to Locked Bag 1, Footscray, Victoria 3011, Australia.

(Bombay) • Nepal • Nepali phrasebook • Pakistan • Rajasthan • Read This First: Asia & India • South India • Sri Lanka • Sri Lanka phrasebook • Tibet • Tibetan phrasebook • Trekking in the Indian Himalaya • Trekking in the Karakoram & Hindukush • Trekking in the Nepal Himalaya
Travel Literature: The Age of Kali: Indian Travels and Encounters • Hello Goodnight: A Life of Goa • In Rajasthan • A Season in Heaven: True Tales from the Road to Kathmandu • Shopping for Buddhas • A Short Walk in the Hindu Kush • Slowly Down the Ganges

ISLANDS OF THE INDIAN OCEAN Madagascar & Comoros • Maldives • Mauritius, Réunion & Seychelles

MIDDLE EAST & CENTRAL ASIA Bahrain, Kuwait & Qatar • Central Asia • Central Asia phrasebook • Dubai • Hebrew phrasebook • Iran • Israel & the Palestinian Territories • Istanbul • Istanbul City Map • Istanbul to Cairo on a shoestring • Jerusalem • Jerusalem City Map • Jordan • Lebanon • Middle East • Oman & the United Arab Emirates • Syria • Turkey • Turkish phrasebook • World Food Turkey • Yemen
Travel Literature: Black on Black: Iran Revisited • The Gates of Damascus • Kingdom of the Film Stars: Journey into Jordan

NORTH AMERICA Alaska • Boston • Boston City Map • California & Nevada • California Condensed • Canada • Chicago • Chicago City Map • Deep South • Florida • Hawaii • Hiking in Alaska • Hiking in the USA • Honolulu • Las Vegas • Los Angeles • Miami • Miami City Map • New England • New Orleans • New York City • New York City City Map • New York Condensed • New York, New Jersey & Pennsylvania • Oahu • Out to Eat – San Francisco • Pacific Northwest • Puerto Rico • Rocky Mountains • San Francisco • San Francisco City Map • Seattle • Southwest • Texas • USA • USA phrasebook • Vancouver • Virginia & the Capital Region • Washington, DC City Map • World Food Deep South, USA
Travel Literature: Caught Inside: A Surfer's Year on the California Coast • Drive Thru America

NORTH-EAST ASIA Beijing • Cantonese phrasebook • China • Hiking in Japan • Hong Kong • Hong Kong City Map • Hong Kong Condensed • Hong Kong, Macau & Guangzhou • Japan • Japanese phrasebook • Korea • Korean phrasebook • Kyoto • Mandarin phrasebook • Mongolia • Mongolian phrasebook • Seoul • South-West China • Taiwan • Tokyo
Travel Literature: In Xanadu: A Quest • Lost Japan

SOUTH AMERICA Argentina, Uruguay & Paraguay • Bolivia • Brazil • Brazilian phrasebook • Buenos Aires • Chile & Easter Island • Colombia • Ecuador & the Galapagos Islands • Healthy Travel Central & South America • Latin American Spanish phrasebook • Peru • Quechua phrasebook • Read This First: Central & South America • Rio de Janeiro • Rio de Janeiro City Map • Santiago • South America on a shoestring • Santiago • Trekking in the Patagonian Andes • Venezuela
Travel Literature: Full Circle: A South American Journey

SOUTH-EAST ASIA Bali & Lombok • Bangkok • Bangkok City Map • Burmese phrasebook • Cambodia • Hanoi • Healthy Travel Asia & India • Hill Tribes phrasebook • Ho Chi Minh City • Indonesia • Indonesian phrasebook • Indonesia's Eastern Islands • Jakarta • Java • Lao phrasebook • Laos • Malay phrasebook • Malaysia, Singapore & Brunei • Myanmar (Burma) • Philippines • Pilipino (Tagalog) phrasebook • Read This First: Asia & India • Singapore • Singapore City Map • South-East Asia on a shoestring • South-East Asia phrasebook • Thailand • Thailand's Islands & Beaches • Thailand, Vietnam, Laos & Cambodia Road Atlas • Thai phrasebook • Vietnam • Vietnamese phrasebook • World Food Thailand • World Food Vietnam

ALSO AVAILABLE: Antarctica • The Arctic • The Blue Man: Tales of Travel, Love and Coffee • Brief Encounters: Stories of Love, Sex & Travel • Chasing Rickshaws • The Last Grain Race • Lonely Planet Unpacked • Not the Only Planet: Science Fiction Travel Stories • Lonely Planet On the Edge • Sacred India • Travel with Children • Travel Photography: A Guide to Taking Better Pictures

Lonely Planet Journeys

J OURNEYS is a unique collection of travel writing – published by the company that understands travel better than anyone else. It is a series for anyone who has ever experienced – or dreamed of – the magical moment when they encountered a strange culture or saw a place for the first time. They are tales to read while you're planning a trip, while you're on the road or while you're in an armchair in front of a fire.

These outstanding titles explore our planet through the eyes of a diverse group of international writers. JOURNEYS books catch the spirit of a place, illuminate a culture, recount a crazy adventure or introduce a fascinating way of life. They always entertain, and always enrich the experience of travel.

FULL CIRCLE
A South American Journey
Luis Sepúlveda (translated by Chris Andrews)

'A journey without a fixed itinerary' with Chilean writer Luis Sepúlveda. Extravagant characters and extraordinary situations are memorably evoked: gauchos organising a tournament of lies, a scheming heiress on the lookout for a husband, a pilot with a corpse on board his plane ... *Full Circle* brings us the distinctive voice of one of South America's most compelling writers.

WINNER 1996 Astrolabe – Etonnants Voyageurs award for the best work of travel literature published in France.

GREEN DREAMS
Travels in Central America
Stephen Benz

On the Amazon, in Costa Rica, Honduras and on the Mayan trail from Guatemala to Mexico, Stephen Benz describes his encounters with water, mud, insects and other wildlife – and not least with the ecotourists themselves. With witty insights into modern travel, *Green Dreams* discusses the paradox of cultural and 'green' tourism.

DRIVE THRU AMERICA
Sean Condon

If you've ever wanted to drive across the USA but couldn't find the time (or afford the gas), *Drive Thru America* is perfect for you. In his search for American myths and realities – along with comfort, cable TV and good, reasonably priced coffee – Sean Condon paints a hilarious road-portrait of the USA.

'entertaining and laugh-out-loud funny'– *Alex Wilber, Travel editor, Amazon.com*

SEAN & DAVID'S LONG DRIVE
Sean Condon

Sean and David are young townies who have rarely strayed beyond city limits. One day, for no good reason, they set out to discover their homeland, and what follows is a wildly entertaining adventure that covers half of Australia.

'a hilariously detailed log of two burned out friends' – *Rolling Stone*

Lonely Planet Travel Atlases

L onely Planet has long been famous for the number and quality of its guidebook maps. Now we've gone one step further and produced a handy companion series: Lonely Planet travel atlases – maps of a country produced in book form.

Unlike other maps, which look good but lead travellers astray, our travel atlases have been researched on the road by Lonely Planet's experienced team of writers. All details are carefully checked to ensure the atlas corresponds with the equivalent Lonely Planet guidebook.

- full-colour throughout
- maps researched and checked by Lonely Planet authors
- place names correspond with Lonely Planet guidebooks
- no confusing spelling differences
- legend and travelling information in English, French, German, Japanese and Spanish
- size: 230 x 160 mm

Available now: Chile & Easter Island • Egypt • India & Bangladesh • Israel & the Palestinian Territories • Jordan, Syria & Lebanon • Kenya • Laos • Portugal • South Africa, Lesotho & Swaziland • Thailand • Turkey • Vietnam • Zimbabwe, Botswana & Namibia

Lonely Planet TV Series & Videos

L onely Planet travel guides have been brought to life on television screens around the world. Like our guides, the programs are based on the joy of independent travel, and look honestly at some of the most exciting, picturesque and frustrating places in the world. Each show is presented by one of three travellers from Australia, England or the USA and combines an innovative mixture of video, Super-8 film, atmospheric soundscapes and original music.

Videos of each episode – containing additional footage not shown on television – are available from good book and video shops, but the availability of individual videos varies with regional screening schedules.

Video destinations include: Alaska • American Rockies • Australia – The South-East • Baja California & the Copper Canyon • Brazil • Central Asia • Chile & Easter Island • Corsica, Sicily & Sardinia – The Mediterranean Islands • East Africa (Tanzania & Zanzibar) • Ecuador & the Galapagos Islands • Greenland & Iceland • Indonesia • Israel & the Sinai Desert • Jamaica • Japan • La Ruta Maya • Morocco • New York • North India • Pacific Islands (Fiji, Solomon Islands & Vanuatu) • South India • South West China • Turkey • Vietnam • West Africa • Zimbabwe, Botswana • Namibia

The Lonely Planet TV series is produced by: Pilot Productions
The Old Studio
18 Middle Row
London W10 5AT, UK

Lonely Planet On-line
www.lonelyplanet.com *or* AOL keyword: lp

W hether you've just begun planning your next trip, or you're chasing down specific info on currency regulations or visa requirements, check out Lonely Planet On-line for up-to-the minute travel information.

As well as mini guides to more than 250 destinations, you'll find maps, photos, travel news, health and visa updates, travel advisories, and discussion of the ecological and political issues you need to be aware of as you travel. You'll also find timely upgrades to popular guidebooks which you can print out and stick in the back of your book.

There's also an on-line travellers' forum where you can share your experience of life on the road, meet travel companions and ask other travellers for their recommendations and advice.

And of course we have a complete and up-to-date list of all Lonely Planet travel products including travel guides, diving and snorkeling guides, phrasebooks, atlases, travel literature and videos, and a simple on-line ordering facility if you can't find the book you want elsewhere.

Lonely Planet Diving & Snorkeling Guides

K nown for indispensible guidebooks to destinations all over the world, Lonely Planet's Pisces Books are the most popular series of diving and snorkeling titles available.

There are three series: **Diving & Snorkeling Guides**, **Shipwreck Diving** series and **Dive Into History**. Full colour throughout, the **Diving & Snorkeling Guides** combine quality photographs with detailed descriptions of the best dive sites for each location, giving divers a glimpse of what they can expect both on land and in water. The **Dive Into History** series is perfect for the adventure diver or armchair traveller. The **Shipwreck Diving** series provides all the details for exploring the most interesting wrecks in the Atlantic and Pacific oceans. The list also includes underwater nature and technical guides.

FREE Lonely Planet Newsletters

We love hearing from you and think you'd like to hear from us.

Planet Talk

Our FREE quarterly printed newsletter is full of tips from travellers and anecdotes from Lonely Planet guidebook authors. Every issue is packed with up-to-date travel news and advice, and includes:

- a postcard from Lonely Planet co-founder Tony Wheeler
- a swag of mail from travellers
- a look at life on the road through the eyes of a Lonely Planet author
- topical health advice
- prizes for the best travel yarn
- news about forthcoming Lonely Planet events
- a complete list of Lonely Planet books and other titles

To join our mailing list, residents of the UK, Europe and Africa can email us at go@lonelyplanet.co.uk; residents of North and South America can email us at info@lonelyplanet.com; the rest of the world can email us at talk2us@lonelyplanet.com.au, or contact any Lonely Planet office.

Comet

Our FREE monthly email newsletter brings you all the latest travel news, features, interviews, competitions, destination ideas, travellers' tips & tales, Q&As, raging debates and related links. Find out what's new on the Lonely Planet Web site and which books are about to hit the shelves.

Subscribe from your desktop: www.lonelyplanet.com/comet

Index

Text

Bold indicates maps.

Bold indicates maps.

Bold indicates maps.

Boxed Text

MAP LEGEND

BOUNDARIES

- International
- State
- County

HYDROGRAPHY

- Water
- Reef
- Coastline
- Beach
- River, Waterfall
- Swamp, Spring

ROUTES & TRANSPORT

- Freeway
- Toll Freeway
- Primary Road
- Secondary Road
- Tertiary Road
- Unpaved Road
- Pedestrian Mall
- Trail
- Ferry Route
- Railway, Train Station
- Mass Transit Line & Station

ROUTE SHIELDS

- 10 Interstate Freeway
- 59 US Highway
- 6 State Highway
- 421 County Highway
- MEX 2 Mexican Highway

AREA FEATURES

- Park, Garden
- Forest, Grassland
- Cemetery
- Golf Course
- Reservation
- Plaza

⊗ NATIONAL CAPITAL

◉ State, Provincial Capital

● LARGE CITY

● Medium City

● Small City

● Town, Village

○ Point of Interest

■ Place to Stay

▲ Campground

⊕ RV Park

▼ Place to Eat

🍴 Bar (Place to Drink)

☕ Cafe

MAP SYMBOLS

- ✈ Airfield
- ✈ Airport
- ∴ Archaeological Site, Ruins
- 🏦 Bank
- ⚾ Baseball Diamond
- ✕ Battlefield, Historic Site
- ☂ Beach
- ✦ Border Crossing
- ☺ Bus Depot, Bus Stop
- ⛪ Cathedral
- ⌒ Cave
- ✝ Church
- ◎ Embassy
- ⊶ Foot Bridge
- ⛽ Gas Station
- ⛳ Golf Course
- ✚ Hospital, Clinic
- ❶ Information
- ☀ Lookout
- ▲ Monument
- ☪ Mosque

- ▲ Mountain
- 🏛 Museum
- 🔭 Observatory
- ← One-Way Street
- ▲ Park
- Ⓟ Parking
-)(Pass
- 🅿 Picnic Area
- ★ Police Station
- 🏊 Pool
- ✉ Post Office
- 🚻 Public Restroom
- ◆ Shopping Mall
- ⛷ Skiing (Alpine)
- ⛷ Skiing (Nordic)
- 🏛 Stately Home
- 🏄 Surfing
- 🥾 Trailhead
- ⛵ Windsurfing
- 🍷 Winery
- 🐘 Zoo

Note: Not all symbols displayed above appear in this book.

LONELY PLANET OFFICES

Australia
PO Box 617, Hawthorn, Victoria 3122
☎ 03 9819 1877 fax 03 9819 6459
email: talk2us@lonelyplanet.com.au

USA
150 Linden St, Oakland, CA 94607
☎ 510 893 8555 TOLL FREE: 800 275 5555
fax 510 893 8572
email: info@lonelyplanet.com

UK
10a Spring Place, London NW5 3BH
☎ 020 7428 4800 fax 020 7428 4828
email: go@lonelyplanet.co.uk

France
1 rue du Dahomey, 75011 Paris
☎ 01 55 25 33 00 fax 01 55 25 33 01
email: bip@lonelyplanet.fr

World Wide Web: www.lonelyplanet.com *or* AOL keyword: lp
Lonely Planet Images: lpi@lonelyplanet.com.au